PLACES

RATED

ALMANAC

W9-BSV-452

PLACES
RATED
ALMANAC

Millennium Edition

DAVID SAVAGEAU

with Ralph D'Agostino

IDG Books Worldwide, Inc.
An International Data Group Company
Foster City, CA • Chicago, IL • Indianapolis, IN • New York, NY • Southlake, TX

Acknowledgments

This revision of *Places Rated Almanac* could not have begun without criticisms from readers. Nor would the book have been finished minus the generous advice from experts.

Thanks to the most patient and insightful Kathy Iwasaki and the most patient and insightful Richard Kassel at IDG Books Worldwide, Inc. Thanks also to Alan Borne, *American Automobile Association*; Bob Fulton, *Open Cellular Systems*; Jim Kass, *National Golf Foundation*; Tom McCormack, *Strategic Projections*; George Pierson, *Travelscan*; Carole Seaward, *CMG Direct*; and Dale Tibbitts, *Elections Data Services*. Special thanks are due Martin Holdrich at *Woods & Poole Economics, Inc.*, of Washington, DC, for population, income and job forecasts. The use of this data and the conclusions drawn from it are solely the responsibility of the authors.

Publisher's Note

This book is a creative work protected by applicable copyright laws. The authors have added value to facts and statistics by original selection, coordination, expression, arrangement, and classification of the information. It is published for general reference and not as a substitute for independent verification by users when circumstances warrant. Although care and diligence have been used in its preparation, the interpretation of the data and the views expressed are the authors' and not necessarily those of IDG Books Worldwide, Inc.

IDG Books Worldwide, Inc.

An International Data Group Company
919 E. Hillsdale Blvd., Suite 400
Foster City, CA 94404
Find us online at www.frommers.com

Copyright © 2000 by Macmillan General Reference USA, Inc.,
a wholly owned subsidiary of IDG Books Worldwide, Inc.
Maps copyright by Places Rated Partnership
MACMILLAN is a registered trademark of Macmillan General Reference USA, Inc.
All rights reserved. No part of this book may be reproduced or transmitted in any form or by any means, electronic or mechanical, including photocopying, recording, or by any information storage and retrieval system, without permission in writing from the Publisher.

Editors: Kathy Iwasaki and Richard Kassel
Production Editors: Tammy Ahrens and Kristi Hart
Page Layout: Heather Pope
Photo Editor: Richard Fox
Design by Madhouse Studios
Digital Cartography: Jeff Amero and Ken Eulie, Cape Ann Mapping

ISBN 0-02-863447-0
ISSN 1526-517X

Special Sales

For general information on IDG Books Worldwide's books in the U.S., please call our Consumer Customer Service department at 1-800-762-2974. For reseller information, including discounts, bulk sales, customized editions, and premium sales, please call our Reseller Customer Service department at 1-800-434-3422.

Manufactured in the United States of America
10 9 8 7 6 5 4 3 2 1

CONTENTS

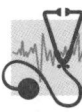

Health Care

Recreation

Putting It All Together

Appendixes

LIST OF TABLES, MAPS, AND DIAGRAMS

ABOUT THE AUTHORS

David Savageau has lived in Denver, South Bend, St. Louis, Indianapolis, Boston, and Washington, DC, and is contributing editor for *Expansion Management*. He is also the author of the best-selling *Retirement Places Rated*.

Ralph D'Agostino is professor of mathematics and head of the Statistics Consulting Unit at Boston University.

Contributors include John Crane, Heather Ferguson, Judith Kinney, Tom McCarty, Byung-Ho Nam, and Karyl Savageau.

The authors welcome comments, criticisms, and recommendations for the next edition of *Places Rated Almanac*. Please write to:

Places Rated Partnership
P.O. Box 1327
Gloucester, MA 01931
or
authors@placesrated.com

POSTAL ABBREVIATIONS

Here is a guide to the standard abbreviations for U.S. states and Canadian provinces used by the U.S. Post Office and the Canadian Postal Service. State and provincial abbreviations are used after metro-area names.

AB	Alberta	NB	New Brunswick
AK	Alaska	NC	North Carolina
AL	Alabama	ND	North Dakota
AR	Arkansas	NE	Nebraska
AZ	Arizona	NF	Newfoundland
BC	British Columbia	NH	New Hampshire
CA	California	NJ	New Jersey
CO	Colorado	NM	New Mexico
CT	Connecticut	NS	Nova Scotia
DC	District of Columbia	NV	Nevada
DE	Delaware	NY	New York
FL	Florida	OH	Ohio
GA	Georgia	OK	Oklahoma
HI	Hawaii	ON	Ontario
IA	Iowa	OR	Oregon
ID	Idaho	PA	Pennsylvania
IL	Illinois	PQ	Quebec
IN	Indiana	RI	Rhode Island
KS	Kansas	SC	South Carolina
KY	Kentucky	SD	South Dakota
LA	Louisiana	SK	Saskatchewan
MA	Massachusetts	TN	Tennessee
MB	Manitoba	TX	Texas
MD	Maryland	UT	Utah
ME	Maine	VA	Virginia
MI	Michigan	VT	Vermont
MN	Minnesota	WA	Washington
MO	Missouri	WI	Wisconsin
MS	Mississippi	WV	West Virginia
MT	Montana	WY	Wyoming

PREFACE

With so many lists of "best places" in magazines, and with so many places on the lists improbably plummeting or soaring every twelve months, readers may wonder whether it's the magazines or the places they rate that are unstable.

Places Rated, we believe, is consistent. Not only are most of the top thirty-five in this edition listed among the previous edition's top thirty-five, but thirteen super-solid locations are included in that select group each time they've been profiled since *Places Rated Almanac* first appeared in 1981.

Super-Solid Metro Areas

METRO AREA (2000 RANK)	HIGHEST RANK (EDITION)	LOWEST RANK (EDITION)
Atlanta, GA (#33)	1 (1981)	33 (2000)
Cincinnati, OH-KY-IN (#11)	1 (1993)	19 (1997)
Cleveland, OH (#28)	12 (1989)	28 (2000)
Philadelphia, PA-NJ (#29)	6 (1981)	29 (2000)
Pittsburgh, PA (#12)	1 (1985)	14 (1997)
Portland-Vancouver, OR-WA (#26)	8 (1981)	26 (2000)
Raleigh-Durham-Chapel Hill, NC (#6)	3 (1985)	32 (1997)
San Diego, CA (#19)	5 (1989)	28 (1985)
San Francisco, CA (#15)	2 (1989)	20 (1997)
Seattle-Bellevue-Everett, WA (#3)	1 (1989)	12 (1985)
Toronto, ON (#7)	4 (1993)	15 (1997)
Vancouver, BC (#18)	11 (1993)	30 (1997)
Washington, DC-MD-VA (#2)	2 (1981, 2000)	17 (1985)

Moreover, eight others are ranked among the top thirty-five in five out of six of *Places Rated*'s editions.

Solid Metro Areas

METRO AREA (2000 RANK)	HIGHEST RANK (EDITION)	LOWEST RANK (EDITION)
Baltimore, MD (#34)	17 (1989)	80 (1997)
Denver, CO (#5)	5 (2000)	39 (1989)
Indianapolis, IN (#23)	8 (1993)	36 (1997)
Louisville, KY-IN (#14)	11 (1981)	60 (1997)
Miami, FL (#17)	17 (2000)	52 (1985)
Nashville, TN (#30)	12 (1981)	37 (1997)
Orange County, CA (#16)	1 (1997)	48 (1985)
San Jose, CA (#27)	11 (1997)	33 (1981)

Still, readers may wonder about differences in the final rankings in *Places Rated*'s 1997 edition and this one. There are five reasons:

New scoring methods. Scores in each chapter are expressed in percents where 50.00 marks the point where half of the areas are better and the other half worse. Using this scheme, a score of 30.00 means seven out of ten metro areas do better. A score of 75.00 means three out of four metro areas lag. In addition, the methods used to rate each area in Climate, Crime, Transportation, Education, The Arts, Health Care, and Recreation have been fine tuned.

New scoring elements. The scoring has been further refined by new data elements. For example, the number of international nonstop flights originating from the local airport has been added to the Transportation chapter.

The interval effect. A minor change in just a handful of the 354 metro areas has resulted in shifting ranks throughout. Most metro areas have nearly the same Crime figures as they had in the previous edition, yet their rankings in this category slipped. They aren't necessarily getting more dangerous; it's just that other places are getting safer faster and have moved them to a lower ranking.

Time series data. Local population figures (for deriving per capita access to public golf courses, for example), prices (for measuring living costs), and household income have increased at varying rates since the 1997 edition was published.

New geography. Each July the federal government decides whether any locations, because of enough growth, can become metropolitan areas. Since *Places Rated*'s 1997 edition, three areas—Jonesboro, AR; Missoula, MT; and Pocatello, ID—have been added to the list and are profiled here for the first time. (Two others—Auburn-Opelika, AL, and Corvallis, OR—were created in July of 1999, too late for this edition.)

Finally, *Places Rated* introduces a new Appendix called "People." Containing current figures on age, racial diversity, politics, and income, this section plays no part in the scoring but supplements the differing pictures in each of the preceding chapters.

Places Rated, it is said later in this book, is like a snapshot of a moving target. Metro areas are dynamic and won't sit still for their numerical portraits. With so much in life that's changeable, you'd be wise to supplement this book with your own verification. For now, what follows are fresh facts and figures on nine factors most of us would agree influence livability in metropolitan North America.

Overall Ranking of the Metropolitan Areas

RANK	METROPOLITAN AREA MEAN SCORE
1. Salt Lake City-Ogden, UT	75.57
2. Washington, DC-MD-VA-WV	74.82
3. Seattle-Bellevue-Everett, WA	74.57
4. Tampa-St. Petersburg-Clearwater, FL	74.50
5. Denver, CO	74.09
6. Raleigh-Durham-Chapel Hill, NC	74.03
7. Toronto, ON	74.00
8. Houston, TX	73.94
9. Minneapolis-St. Paul, MN-WI	73.72
10. Phoenix-Mesa, AZ	73.37
11. Cincinnati, OH-KY-IN	73.34
12. Pittsburgh, PA	72.99
13. Knoxville, TN	72.74
14. Louisville, KY-IN	72.68
15. San Francisco, CA	72.61
16. Orange County, CA	72.43
17. Miami, FL	72.30
18. Vancouver, BC	72.05
19. San Diego, CA	71.61
20. Austin-San Marcos, TX	71.48
21. New Orleans, LA	71.36
22. Orlando, FL	71.04
23. Indianapolis, IN	71.01
24. Honolulu, HI	70.98
25. Greensboro–Winston-Salem–High Point, NC	70.95
26. Portland-Vancouver, OR-WA	70.88
27. San Jose, CA	70.69
28. Cleveland-Lorain-Elyria, OH	70.63
29. Philadelphia, PA-NJ	70.54
30. Nashville, TN	70.19
30. Rochester, NY	70.19
32. Syracuse, NY	70.16
33. Atlanta, GA	69.97
34. Baltimore, MD	69.75
35. Birmingham, AL	69.59
36. Long Island, NY	69.56
37. Edmonton, AB	69.37
38. St. Louis, MO-IL	69.18
39. San Antonio, TX	69.12
40. Jacksonville, FL	69.02
41. Boston, MA-NH	68.99
42. Milwaukee-Waukesha, WI	68.93
42. Omaha, NE-IA	68.93
44. Dallas, TX	68.59
45. Norfolk-Virginia Beach-Newport News, VA-NC	68.40
46. Boise City, ID	68.36
47. Columbus, OH	68.14
48. West Palm Beach-Boca Raton, FL	67.04
49. Memphis, TN-AR-MS	67.01
50. Lexington, KY	66.95
51. Richmond-Petersburg, VA	66.79
52. Spokane, WA	66.76
53. Kansas City, MO-KS	66.73
54. Charleston-North Charleston, SC	66.54
55. Charlotte-Gastonia-Rock Hill, NC-SC	66.41
55. Sarasota-Bradenton, FL	66.41
57. Albuquerque, NM	66.16
57. Oakland, CA	66.16

RANK	METROPOLITAN AREA MEAN SCORE
59. Buffalo-Niagara Falls, NY	66.10
60. Columbia, SC	66.07
60. Harrisburg-Lebanon-Carlisle, PA	66.07
62. Calgary, AB	66.04
63. Oklahoma City, OK	65.94
64. Dayton-Springfield, OH	65.82
65. New York, NY	65.72
65. Riverside-San Bernardino, CA	65.72
67. Chicago, IL	65.69
68. Tucson, AZ	65.66
69. Fort Lauderdale, FL	65.59
70. Montreal, PQ	65.53
71. Fort Worth-Arlington, TX	65.34
72. Portland, ME	65.31
73. Johnson City-Kingsport-Bristol, TN-VA	65.09
74. Los Angeles-Long Beach, CA	64.97
75. Greenville-Spartanburg-Anderson, SC	64.53
76. Sacramento, CA	64.52
77. Toledo, OH	64.30
78. Albany-Schenectady-Troy, NY	64.18
79. Madison, WI	64.08
80. Scranton–Wilkes-Barre–Hazleton, PA	63.83
81. Fargo-Moorhead, ND-MN	63.45
81. Fort Wayne, IN	63.45
83. Jackson, MS	63.36
84. Roanoke, VA	63.30
85. Grand Rapids-Muskegon-Holland, MI	63.01
86. Newark, NJ	62.89
87. Chattanooga, TN-GA	62.64
88. Ottawa-Hull, ON-PQ	62.51
89. Hartford, CT	62.35
90. Santa Barbara-Santa Maria-Lompoc, CA	62.01
91. Fayetteville-Springdale-Rogers, AR	61.88
92. Fort Myers-Cape Coral, FL	61.69
93. Halifax, NS	61.50
94. Detroit, MI	61.41
95. Little Rock-North Little Rock, AR	61.38
96. Reno, NV	60.75
97. Duluth-Superior, MN-WI	60.65
98. Appleton-Oshkosh-Neenah, WI	60.56
99. Gainesville, FL	60.37
100. Huntsville, AL	60.34
101. Providence-Fall River-Warwick, RI-MA	60.09
102. Tulsa, OK	59.99
103. Springfield, MO	59.90
104. Sioux Falls, SD	59.71
105. Akron, OH	59.42
106. Colorado Springs, CO	59.30
107. Des Moines, IA	59.17
108. Ann Arbor, MI	59.11
108. South Bend, IN	59.11
110. Lincoln, NE	59.05
111. Augusta-Aiken, GA-SC	58.86
112. Tacoma, WA	58.70
113. Asheville, NC	58.58
114. Mobile, AL	58.55
115. Daytona Beach, FL	58.26
116. Columbia, MO	58.07

continues

RANK	METROPOLITAN AREA MEAN SCORE
116. Tallahassee, FL	58.07
118. Winnipeg, MB	58.01
119. Melbourne-Titusville-Palm Bay, FL	57.76
120. Middlesex-Somerset-Hunterdon, NJ	57.57
121. Las Vegas, NV-AZ	57.38
122. Evansville-Henderson, IN-KY	57.25
123. Charlottesville, VA	57.00
124. Charleston, WV	56.97
125. Monmouth-Ocean, NJ	56.88
126. Huntington-Ashland, WV-KY-OH	56.47
127. Eugene-Springfield, OR	56.28
128. Davenport-Moline-Rock Island, IA-IL	56.18
129. Burlington, VT	55.99
130. Kalamazoo-Battle Creek, MI	55.68
131. Allentown-Bethlehem-Easton, PA	55.52
132. Quebec City, PQ	55.46
133. Wichita, KS	55.18
134. Trenton, NJ	55.02
135. Santa Rosa, CA	54.92
136. La Crosse, WI-MN	54.89
137. El Paso, TX	54.80
138. Peoria-Pekin, IL	54.74
139. Montgomery, AL	54.48
140. Baton Rouge, LA	53.89
141. Erie, PA	53.76
142. Bangor, ME	53.70
143. Savannah, GA	53.63
144. Victoria, BC	53.44
145. St. Cloud, MN	53.32
146. Saskatoon, SK	53.16
147. Biloxi-Gulfport-Pascagoula, MS	53.00
147. Pensacola, FL	53.00
149. Lynchburg, VA	52.97
150. Shreveport-Bossier City, LA	52.94
151. Lafayette, LA	52.72
152. Salinas, CA	52.60
153. Eau Claire, WI	52.50
153. Regina, SK	52.50
155. Wilmington, NC	52.28
156. Champaign-Urbana, IL	52.25
156. Ventura, CA	52.25
158. Bergen-Passaic, NJ	52.12
159. Worcester, MA-CT	51.97
160. Columbus, GA-AL	51.71
161. Provo-Orem, UT	51.49
162. New Haven-Meriden, CT	51.46
163. London, ON	51.37
164. Boulder-Longmont, CO	51.31
165. Bismarck, ND	51.18
165. Hamilton, ON	51.18
167. Wilmington-Newark, DE-MD	51.15
168. Bellingham, WA	51.12
169. Hattiesburg, MS	51.08
170. Olympia, WA	51.02
171. Lancaster, PA	50.90
172. Grand Forks, ND-MN	50.80
173. Lubbock, TX	50.55
174. Bloomington-Normal, IL	50.49
175. Santa Fe, NM	50.45

RANK	METROPOLITAN AREA MEAN SCORE
176. Macon, GA	50.39
177. Saginaw-Bay City-Midland, MI	50.24
178. Lansing-East Lansing, MI	49.57
179. Corpus Christi, TX	49.32
180. Hickory-Morganton-Lenoir, NC	48.94
181. Springfield, MA	48.85
182. Fresno, CA	48.79
183. Iowa City, IA	48.69
184. Amarillo, TX	48.66
185. Bryan-College Station, TX	48.06
185. Missoula, MT	48.06
187. Youngstown-Warren, OH	48.00
188. Bridgeport, CT	47.94
189. St. John's, NF	47.78
190. Green Bay, WI	47.46
190. Springfield, IL	47.46
192. Kitchener-Waterloo, ON	47.40
193. Parkersburg-Marietta, WV-OH	47.34
194. Wheeling, WV-OH	46.90
195. Canton-Massillon, OH	46.87
196. San Luis Obispo-Atascadero-Paso Robles, CA	46.77
197. Cedar Rapids, IA	46.55
198. Brownsville-Harlingen-San Benito, TX	46.43
199. Lafayette, IN	46.24
200. Utica-Rome, NY	45.77
201. Fort Smith, AR-OK	45.73
202. Vallejo-Fairfield-Napa, CA	45.70
203. Fort Walton Beach, FL	45.67
204. Bloomington, IN	45.54
205. Waterloo-Cedar Falls, IA	45.35
206. Medford-Ashland, OR	45.32
207. Richland-Kennewick-Pasco, WA	45.20
208. Fort Collins-Loveland, CO	45.07
209. Dutchess County, NY	45.04
210. Grand Junction, CO	44.95
211. Galveston-Texas City, TX	44.88
212. Atlantic-Cape May, NJ	44.76
213. Beaumont-Port Arthur, TX	44.57
214. Killeen-Temple, TX	44.35
214. Punta Gorda, FL	44.35
216. Tyler, TX	44.19
217. Binghamton, NY	44.00
218. Dubuque, IA	43.69
219. Fort Pierce-Port St. Lucie, FL	43.66
220. Salem, OR	43.62
221. Lakeland-Winter Haven, FL	43.47
221. Portsmouth-Rochester, NH-ME	43.47
223. Athens, GA	43.44
224. Rochester, MN	43.28
225. Billings, MT	43.06
226. Florence, AL	42.74
226. McAllen-Edinburg-Mission, TX	42.74
228. Jackson, TN	42.46
229. Dothan, AL	42.37
230. Windsor, ON	42.33
231. Abilene, TX	42.18
232. Johnstown, PA	42.05
233. Jamestown, NY	41.99
234. State College, PA	41.86

RANK	METROPOLITAN AREA MEAN SCORE	RANK	METROPOLITAN AREA MEAN SCORE
235. Saint John, NB	41.77	295. Lake Charles, LA	35.47
236. Monroe, LA	41.73	296. San Angelo, TX	35.32
237. Barnstable-Yarmouth, MA	41.55	297. Cumberland, MD-WV	35.19
238. Naples, FL	41.51	298. Greeley, CO	34.84
239. Manchester, NH	41.26	299. Trois-Rivieres, PQ	34.62
240. Myrtle Beach, SC	41.23	300. Clarksville-Hopkinsville, TN-KY	34.56
241. Redding, CA	41.17	300. Odessa-Midland, TX	34.56
242. Bakersfield, CA	41.11	302. Chicoutimi-Jonquiere, PQ	34.46
243. Fayetteville, NC	41.08	303. Decatur, AL	34.34
244. New London-Norwich, CT-RI	41.01	304. Kokomo, IN	34.28
245. Chico-Paradise, CA	40.95	305. Stockton-Lodi, CA	34.05
246. Sheboygan, WI	40.89	306. Casper, WY	33.93
247. Panama City, FL	40.85	307. Pittsfield, MA	33.87
248. Longview-Marshall, TX	40.82	308. Sudbury, ON	33.61
249. Greenville, NC	40.79	309. Gary, IN	33.43
250. Rapid City, SD	40.63	310. Pueblo, CO	33.05
250. Reading, PA	40.63	311. Benton Harbor, MI	32.86
252. Brazoria, TX	40.51	312. Elmira, NY	32.76
253. Alexandria, LA	40.48	313. Lowell, MA-NH	32.67
254. Sherbrooke, PQ	40.23	314. Flint, MI	32.61
255. St. Catharines-Niagara, ON	40.19	315. Danville, VA	32.36
256. Thunder Bay, ON	40.16	316. St. Joseph, MO	32.14
257. Houma, LA	40.10	317. Lewiston-Auburn, ME	31.76
258. Waco, TX	39.82	318. Jersey City, NJ	31.38
259. Bremerton, WA	39.75	319. Sharon, PA	31.25
260. Florence, SC	39.72	320. Oshawa, ON	31.19
261. Santa Cruz-Watsonville, CA	39.60	321. Steubenville-Weirton, OH-WV	31.16
262. Anchorage, AK	39.44	322. Elkhart-Goshen, IN	30.84
262. Terre Haute, IN	39.44	323. Lima, OH	30.75
264. Yakima, WA	39.15	324. Great Falls, MT	30.65
265. Joplin, MO	39.03	325. Modesto, CA	30.37
266. Wausau, WI	39.00	326. Ocala, FL	30.15
267. Laredo, TX	38.90	327. York, PA	29.78
268. Stamford-Norwalk, CT	38.34	328. Yuma, AZ	29.74
269. Flagstaff, AZ-UT	38.15	329. Rocky Mount, NC	29.52
269. Las Cruces, NM	38.15	330. Visalia-Tulare-Porterville, CA	29.43
271. Pocatello, ID	38.05	331. Decatur, IL	29.27
272. Rockford, IL	37.61	332. Anniston, AL	29.24
273. Tuscaloosa, AL	37.58	333. Glens Falls, NY	29.05
274. Sioux City, IA-NE	37.55	333. Mansfield, OH	29.05
275. Janesville-Beloit, WI	37.46	335. Lawrence, MA-NH	28.77
276. Hamilton-Middletown, OH	37.42	336. Brockton, MA	28.61
277. Altoona, PA	37.30	337. Merced, CA	28.33
278. Owensboro, KY	37.23	338. Gadsden, AL	27.41
279. Williamsport, PA	37.20	339. Nashua, NH	27.07
280. Hagerstown, MD	36.98	340. Sumter, SC	27.04
281. Victoria, TX	36.73	341. New Bedford, MA	26.94
282. Muncie, IN	36.67	342. Danbury, CT	26.85
282. Newburgh, NY-PA	36.67	343. Dover, DE	26.44
282. Topeka, KS	36.67	344. Jackson, MI	26.19
285. Kenosha, WI	36.57	345. Fitchburg-Leominster, MA	26.00
286. Yolo, CA	36.45	346. Lawton, OK	25.84
287. Wichita Falls, TX	36.38	347. Waterbury, CT	25.72
288. Cheyenne, WY	36.32	348. Enid, OK	25.24
289. Jacksonville, NC	36.10	349. Racine, WI	24.83
290. Texarkana, TX-Texarkana, AR	36.07	350. Pine Bluff, AR	23.92
291. Albany, GA	36.01	351. Goldsboro, NC	22.94
291. Jonesboro, AR	36.01	352. Yuba City, CA	22.72
293. Lawrence, KS	35.98	353. Vineland-Millville-Bridgeton, NJ	20.87
294. Sherman-Denison, TX	35.66	354. Kankakee, IL	20.36

INTRODUCTION

Oh, for San Francisco's ambience, the job market in Las Vegas, for Miami's winters and the safe streets of St. Cloud. Ah, for Salt Lake City skiing and Topeka's affordable homes, for Pittsburgh's Carnegie Museums, for Montreal's quiet subway. If you could snap your fingers and suddenly find yourself living somewhere else, would you?

Forget the usual constraints: Family ties, friendships, a good job, lack of cash, and a sentimental attachment to familiar turf can certainly snap you out of such a fantasy. Let's pose the question in another way: What if there was a place somewhere in North America that suited you better than the one you're living in now, and you knew nothing about it?

Every so often people tell pollsters they would rather be somewhere else when asked whether they are satisfied with where they currently live. Most of us change our address eleven times throughout our lives, but we do it by simply moving from one house to another within the same city. However, there are 7 million North Americans who move to another state or province each year. They may have 7 million different reasons for relocating beyond their old city's limits, but they do have one thing in common—the need for information.

Like its five predecessors, this edition of *Places Rated Almanac* is meant for people who are mulling over the idea of relocation as well as for anyone who enjoys learning about cities and towns and what they have to offer. As an almanac, it provides thousands of facts—found neither in standard guidebooks nor in chamber of commerce blandishments—about all of the 354 officially defined metropolitan areas in which four out of five of us live.

Places Rated Almanac is more than a collection of interesting, odd, and useful information about metropolitan areas. It also rates and ranks the metro areas on nine factors that greatly influence the quality of a place: costs of living, job outlook, transportation, education, health care, crime, the arts, recreation, and climate. *Places Rated Almanac* could be considered a self-help book with one caveat: Instead of pointing the way toward inner peace or upward mobility as most self-help books do, it helps you decide whether geographical mobility could lead to a more satisfying life.

Where you live affects your happiness and personal success. It just may be that your present location doesn't fit your needs and preferences. After all, given the amazing variety that North American cities offer, what are the odds that the place you happen to live is the right one for you?

POPULATION GROWTH, 1995–2000

The Sun Belt rules and the Rust Belt loses when it comes to growth rates, a story that began in the early 1970s. For the latest 5 years, 4.3 percent is the typical metro area rate of growth.

Fastest Growing	Percent Growth
Las Vegas, NV-AZ	21.6%
Laredo, TX	16.1
Provo-Orem, UT	15.6
Myrtle Beach, SC	15.1
Wilmington, NC	15.1
Austin-San Marcos, TX	14.5
Phoenix-Mesa, AZ	14.0
McAllen-Edinburg-Mission, TX	13.9
Naples, FL	13.3
Orlando, FL	13.1
Boise City, ID	13.1
Fayetteville-Springdale-Rogers, AR	12.6
Raleigh-Durham-Chapel Hill, NC	12.1
Yuma, AZ	12.0
Punta Gorda, FL	11.9
Fort Collins-Loveland, CO	11.6

No Growth	Percent Loss
Utica-Rome, NY	–3.3%
Steubenville-Weirton, OH-WV	–3.1
Wheeling, WV-OH	–2.5
Binghamton, NY	–2.4
Cumberland, MD-WV	–2.4
Decatur, IL	–2.1
Scranton–Wilkes-Barre–Hazelton, PA	–2.0
Johnstown, PA	–1.8
Great Falls, MT	–1.5
Elmira, NY	–1.4
Pittsfield, MA	–1.3
Buffalo-Niagra Falls, NY	–1.2
Chicoutimi-Jonquiere, PQ	–1.2
Lawton, OK	–1.2
Pittsburgh, PA	–1.0

Source: Strategic Projections, Inc., and Woods & Poole Economics, Inc.

After using *Places Rated Almanac*, you may very well confirm your hunch that you've never had it so good. But if you're part of the discontented majority identified by pollsters, you may find yourself asking: What am I waiting for?

RATING PLACES: A CONTINENTAL PASTIME

"The tradition of hating New York started long before it began asking the rest of us to pay its bills while condescendingly viewing us as amusing rustics," the late Mike Royko once wrote in his *Chicago Sun-Times* column. "Actually, I like New York," he continued. "There are better reasons to hate cities like Cleveland or Indianapolis or Detroit or Dallas. But I do dislike New Yorkers."

It may seem the utmost of brass, this business of judging places. Yet everyone does it, privately. Some suspect that culture in Omaha or Des Moines or Saskatoon is a contradiction. Others surmise that daily life in Miami consists of surviving drug-trade shoot-outs, that cold and windy Winnipeg is no place for the seasonally depressed, that Waco has more than a few berserk evangelists walking about, and that people in Los Angeles spend most of their waking hours behind a steering wheel waiting for the Big One.

Judging places from best to worst with numbers may seem the highest effrontery of all. Ultimately, how can intangible things like friendliness and optimism be measured with statistics? Yet numeracy is almost as strong a North American character trait as literacy. When it comes to choosing where to live, people have been digesting statistics for a long, long time. To sell newcomers on settling in colonial Maryland instead of neighboring Virginia, 17th-century promoters put together figures showing heavier livestock, more plentiful game, and lower mortality from foul air and Indian attacks.

California for Health, Wealth, and Residence, just one volume in a library of post–Civil War guides touting the West's superior quality of life, compiled data to show the climate along the southern Pacific coast to be the world's best. Not so, countered the Union Pacific Railroad's land office in 1871; settlers will find the most "genial and healthy" seasons in western Kansas.

In this century, the statistical nets were flung even wider. "There are plenty of Americans who regard Kansas as almost barbaric," noted H. L. Mencken in 1931, "just as there are other Americans who shudder whenever they think of Arkansas, Ohio, Indiana, Oklahoma, Texas, or California." Mencken wrote these words in his *American Mercury* magazine to introduce his formula for statistically measuring the progress of civilization in each of the states. He mixed the numbers of Boy Scouts and *Atlantic Monthly* subscribers with lynchings and pellagra cases, added a dash of Who's Who listing along with rates for divorce and murder, threw in figures for rainfall and gasoline consumption, and found that, hands down, Mississippi was the worst American state.

METROPOLITAN AREAS

Places Rated Almanac, we believe, is more useful than any system that considers only states or provinces because broad-brush averages hide local realities. Instead, *Places Rated Almanac* focuses on metropolitan areas, the smallest unit of urban geography for which there is the largest amount of comparable data. From Abilene to Yuma; from huge Los Angeles-Long Beach (pop. 9,230,312) to tiny Enid (pop. 56,720); from foggy St. John's to sunny San Diego, these 354 metro areas cover a lot of ground, indeed.

There is at least one in every state. Texas has 27, California 25 and Florida 20. There are 25 in Canada. They fill up less than 1 percent of North America's land mass yet hold nearly 80 percent of its population. Among them, you'll find agricultural centers and fashion markets, college towns and mill towns and cow towns, bedroom communities, financial centers, resorts and retirement colonies, and cultural havens right next to international gateways and industrial giants.

Ever since the late 1940s, metro areas have been defined by detailed standards. Essentially, an area qualifies as "metropolitan" by the following rules:

United States—any city with a population of at least 50,000, or an urbanized area (embracing one or more towns) of at least 50,000, located in a county or counties with a total population of at least 100,000 (75,000 in New England).

Canada—an urban area of at least 100,000 people located in the midst of surrounding urban and rural areas that have strong economic and social ties with the urban area as determined by the number of people commuting there to work.

In either case, the metro area's boundaries coincide with those of the surrounding county or counties (in Canada and in New England, metro areas are defined by groups of towns and cities). For a view of metro geography, see the regional maps on the following pages.

The metropolitan areas are primarily within single states and provinces. However, forty cross state lines. Washington includes not just the District of Columbia, but counties in suburban Maryland, counties and independent cities in northern Virginia, and counties in West Virginia's eastern panhandle. Memphis takes in counties in Tennessee, another across the river in Arkansas, and another in Mississippi. Ottawa-Hull, the only Canadian metro area in more than one province, embraces cities in Ontario and *villes* across the river in Quebec.

There are ample reasons for focusing on metro areas rather than on individual cities, counties, or states. Thanks to the four-lane highway, cities, counties, and states are less relevant to our daily personal geography.

POPULATION SIZE

The metro area nearest the population midpoint is Fayetteville, NC, with 290,000 people. Sixty-five metro areas have more than 1 million people. The 40 largest have more people than the other 314 metro areas combined.

Largest	2000 Population
Los Angeles-Long Beach, CA	9,220,312
New York, NY	8,603,992
Chicago, IL	7,864,846
Philadelphia, PA-NJ	4,966,257
Washington, DC-MD-VA-WV	4,745,302
Toronto, ON	4,605,000
Detroit, MI	4,505,455
Houston, TX	4,008,119
Atlanta, GA	3,807,451
Montreal, PQ	3,441,000
Boston, MA-NH	3,296,878
Dallas, TX	3,277,816
Riverside-San Bernardino, CA	3,234,161
Phoenix-Mesa, AZ	3,034,464
Minneapolis-St. Paul, MN-WI	2,909,888

Smallest	2000 Population
Enid, OK	56,720
Casper, WY	64,821
Pocatello, ID	77,353
Jonesboro, AR	77,979
Great Falls, MT	79,681
Cheyenne, WY	80,079
Pine Bluff, AR	82,727
Pittsfield, MA	84,477
Victoria, TX	84,739
Dubuque, IA	88,553
Rapid City, SD	90,805
Lewiston-Auburn, ME	91,155
Elmira, NY	92,846
Missoula, MT	93,055
Owensboro, KY	93,087

Source: Strategic Projections, Inc., and Woods & Poole Economics, Inc.

Commonly, we live in one community; commute to work in another; and eat at the restaurants, shop at the stores, and take advantage of the recreational assets of all the towns around us. We pay taxes or fees for water, sewer, parks, and school districts that often cross city lines. And every so often we keep or throw out of office our local representative whose district seems to encompass everything in sight.

The perimeters of metro areas supersede the anachronistic political boundaries of incorporated areas and include not just the troubled and depressed older city cores, but also the newer parts of suburbia with their sleek new malls, mirror-windowed office parks, low-rise factories, and choice neighborhoods. Greater Newark,

for example, includes affluent Morris County. Buffalo-Niagara Falls includes quaint and tony Lewiston. Cleveland embraces Shaker Heights, and Boston, with its 129 cities and towns, takes in a wealthy fringe of high-tech industries. In the Appendix at the end of this book, a "Metropolitan Place Finder" lists not only the cities after which metro areas are named, but suburban and rural towns within the area's boundaries as well.

The list "354 Metropolitan Areas" on the following pages shows the county definitions of the metropolitan areas in this edition of *Places Rated Almanac*. The chances are good that you live in one of the official metropolitan areas profiled here.

354 Metropolitan Areas

METRO AREAS AND COMPONENT COUNTIES	POPULATION 2000	POPULATION 1995	PERCENT GROWTH
Abilene, TX	123,711	122,422	1.1
Taylor County			
Akron, OH	689,538	676,135	2.0
Portage and Summit counties			
Albany, GA	120,838	116,383	3.8
Dougherty and Lee counties			
Albany-Schenectady-Troy, NY	885,782	880,902	0.6
Albany, Montgomery, Rensselaer, Saratoga, Schenectady, and Schoharie counties			
Albuquerque, NM	734,255	685,109	7.2
Bernalillo, Sandoval, and Valencia counties			
Alexandria, LA	127,635	126,683	0.8
Rapides Parish			
Allentown-Bethlehem-Easton, PA	616,924	611,278	0.9
Carbon, Lehigh, and Northampton counties			
Altoona, PA	131,388	131,987	−0.5
Blair County			
Amarillo, TX	212,395	204,321	4.0
Potter and Randall counties			
Anchorage, AK	263,727	250,864	5.1
Anchorage Borough			
Ann Arbor, MI	554,998	521,462	6.4
Lenawee, Livingston, and Washtenaw counties			
Anniston, AL	118,556	116,653	1.6
Calhoun County			
Appleton-Oshkosh-Neenah, WI	352,708	335,712	5.1
Calumet, Outagamie, and Winnebago counties			
Asheville, NC	218,552	206,973	5.6
Buncombe and Madison counties			
Athens, GA	144,889	134,580	7.7
Clarke, Madison, and Oconee counties			
Atlanta, GA	3,807,451	3,432,090	10.9
Barrow, Bartow, Carroll, Cherokee, Clayton, Cobb, Coweta, DeKalb, Douglas, Fayette, Forsyth, Fulton, Gwinnett, Henry, Newton, Paulding, Pickens, Rockdale, Spalding, and Walton counties			
Atlantic City-Cape May, NJ	341,541	331,145	3.1
Atlantic and Cape May counties			
Augusta-Aiken, GA-SC	474,398	452,359	4.9
Columbia, McDuffie, and Richmond counties, GA; Aiken and Edgefield counties, SC			
Austin-San Marcos, TX	1,149,201	1,003,926	14.5
Bastrop, Caldwell, Hays, Travis, and Williamson counties			
Bakersfield, CA	654,208	615,591	6.3
Kern County			
Baltimore, MD	2,528,739	2,463,148	2.7
Anne Arundel, Baltimore, Carroll, Harford, Howard, Queen Anne's counties, and Baltimore city			
Bangor, ME	93,703	93,431	0.3
3 cities and 11 towns in Penobscot and Waldo counties			
Barnstable-Yarmouth, MA	152,930	143,531	6.5
10 towns in Barnstable County			
Baton Rouge, LA	604,025	562,101	7.5
Ascension, East Baton Rouge, Livingston, and West Baton Rouge parishes			
Beaumont-Port Arthur, TX	380,075	374,831	1.4
Hardin, Jefferson, and Orange counties			
Bellingham, WA	164,563	149,085	10.4
Whatcom County			
Benton Harbor, MI	161,605	161,647	0.0
Berrien County			

Sources: Woods & Poole Economics Inc. population estimates (U.S.) and Strategic Projections population estimates (Canada).

METRO AREAS AND COMPONENT COUNTIES	POPULATION 2000	POPULATION 1995	PERCENT GROWTH
Bergen-Passaic, NJ	1,337,377	1,320,087	1.3
Bergen and Passaic counties			
Billings, MT	130,916	124,462	5.2
Yellowstone County			
Biloxi-Gulfport-Pascagoula, MS	356,565	340,997	4.6
Hancock, Harrison, and Jackson counties			
Binghamton, NY	251,438	257,556	−2.4
Broome and Tioga counties			
Birmingham, AL	921,945	888,326	3.8
Blount, Jefferson, St. Clair, and Shelby counties			
Bismarck, ND	95,004	89,066	6.7
Burleigh and Morton counties			
Bloomington, IN	121,679	115,239	5.6
Monroe County			
Bloomington-Normal, IL	144,879	138,637	4.5
McLean County			
Boise City, ID	408,256	361,107	13.1
Ada and Canyon counties			
Boston, MA-NH	3,296,878	3,247,742	1.5
Suffolk County and 18 cities and 108 towns in Bristol, Essex, Middlesex, Norfolk, Plymouth, and Worcester counties, MA; and Rockingham County, NH			
Boulder-Longmont, CO	271,464	253,679	7.0
Boulder County			
Brazoria, TX	235,492	215,739	9.2
Brazoria County			
Bremerton, WA	246,036	225,844	8.9
Kitsap County			
Bridgeport, CT	445,239	442,842	0.5
5 cities and 10 towns in Fairfield and New Haven counties			
Brockton, MA	254,014	243,816	4.2
1 city and 13 towns in Bristol, Norfolk, and Plymouth counties			
Brownsville-Harlingen-San Benito, TX	332,385	306,260	8.5
Cameron County			
Bryan-College Station, TX	137,543	131,320	4.7
Brazos County			
Buffalo-Niagara Falls, NY	1,166,581	1,180,505	−1.2
Erie and Niagara counties			
Burlington, VT	169,145	161,226	4.9
4 cities and 15 towns in Chittenden, Franklin, and Grand Isle counties			
Calgary, AB	875,000	831,800	5.2
2 cities, 3 towns, and 5 minor civil divisions			
Canton-Massillon, OH	404,836	402,217	0.7
Carroll and Stark counties			
Casper, WY	64,821	63,818	1.6
Natrona County			
Cedar Rapids, IA	186,710	179,007	4.3
Linn County			
Champaign-Urbana, IL	169,573	166,894	1.6
Champaign County			
Charleston-North Charleston, SC	535,689	509,612	5.1
Berkeley, Charleston, and Dorchester counties			
Charleston, WV	256,038	254,324	0.7
Kanawha and Putnam counties			

METRO AREAS AND COMPONENT COUNTIES	POPULATION 2000	POPULATION 1995	PERCENT GROWTH
Charlotte-Gastonia-Rock Hill, NC-SC	1,413,215	1,287,472	9.8
Cabarrus, Gaston, Lincoln, Mecklenburg, Rowan, and Union counties, NC; York County, SC			
Charlottesville, VA	152,105	142,342	6.9
Albemarle, Fluvanna, and Greene counties, and Charlottesville city			
Chattanooga, TN-GA	459,565	442,182	3.9
Hamilton and Marion counties, TN; Catoosa, Dade, and Walker counties, GA			
Cheyenne, WY	80,079	78,305	2.3
Laramie County			
Chicago, IL	7,864,846	7,682,478	2.4
Cook, DeKalb, DuPage, Grundy, Kane, Kendall, Lake, McHenry, and Will counties			
Chico-Paradise, CA	202,151	192,988	4.7
Butte County			
Chicoutimi-Jonquiere, PQ	165,000	167,000	−1.2
4 villes and 6 minor civil divisions			
Cincinnati, OH-KY-IN	1,641,098	1,587,370	3.4
Brown, Clermont, Hamilton, and Warren counties, OH; Boone, Campbell, Gallatin, Grant, Kenton, and Pendleton counties, KY; Dearborn and Ohio counties, IN			
Clarksville-Hopkinsville, TN-KY	205,913	187,746	9.7
Montgomery County, TN; Christian County, KY			
Cleveland-Lorain-Elyria, OH	2,228,317	2,230,526	−0.1
Ashtabula, Cuyahoga, Geauga, Lake, Lorain, and Medina counties			
Colorado Springs, CO	509,836	464,763	9.7
El Paso County			
Columbia, MO	134,314	123,434	8.8
Boone County			
Columbia, SC	533,121	490,678	8.6
Lexington and Richland counties			
Columbus, GA-AL	279,453	271,536	2.9
Chattahoochee, Harris, and Muscogee counties, GA; Russell County, AL			
Columbus, OH	1,502,584	1,434,236	4.8
Delaware, Fairfield, Franklin, Licking, Madison, and Pickaway counties			
Corpus Christi, TX	398,896	378,773	5.3
Nueces and San Patricio counties			
Cumberland, MD-WV	98,418	100,822	−2.4
Allegany County, MD; Mineral County, WV			
Dallas, TX	3,277,816	2,965,502	10.5
Collin, Dallas, Denton, Ellis, Henderson, Hunt, Kaufman, and Rockwall counties			
Danbury, CT	200,544	198,621	1.0
1 city and 11 towns in Fairfield and Litchfield counties			
Danville, VA	108,666	109,326	−0.6
Pittsylvania County and Danville city			

continues

Sources: Woods & Poole Economics Inc. population estimates (U.S.) and Strategic Projections population estimates (Canada).

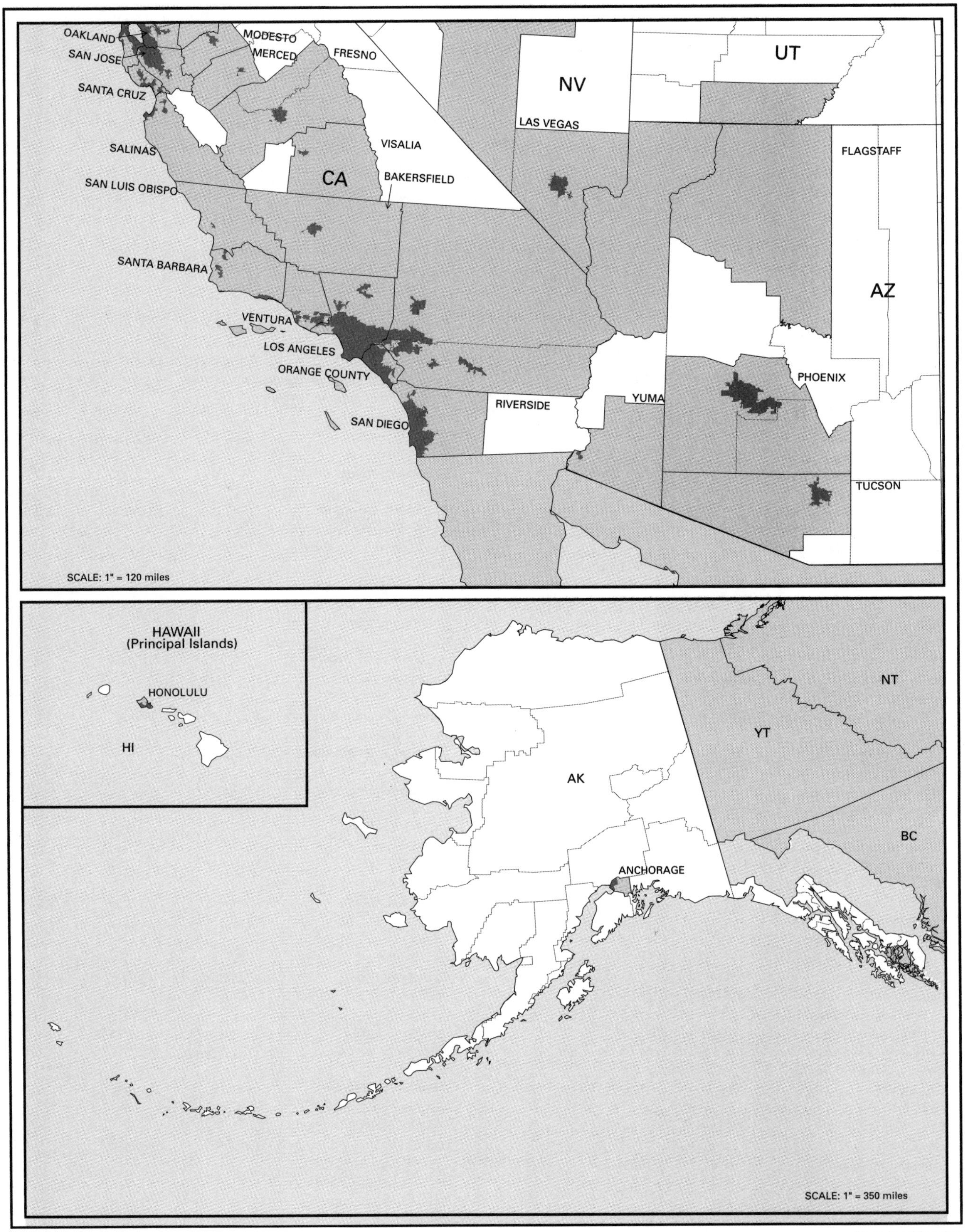

SCALE: 1" = 120 miles

OAKLAND
SAN JOSE
SANTA CRUZ
SALINAS
SAN LUIS OBISPO
SANTA BARBARA
VENTURA
LOS ANGELES
ORANGE COUNTY
SAN DIEGO

MODESTO
MERCED
FRESNO
VISALIA
BAKERSFIELD
CA

NV
LAS VEGAS

UT

FLAGSTAFF

AZ

PHOENIX

YUMA
RIVERSIDE

TUCSON

HAWAII
(Principal Islands)

HONOLULU

HI

AK

ANCHORAGE

NT

YT

BC

SCALE: 1" = 350 miles

Copyright © 2000 by Places Rated Partnership

Cape Ann Mapping

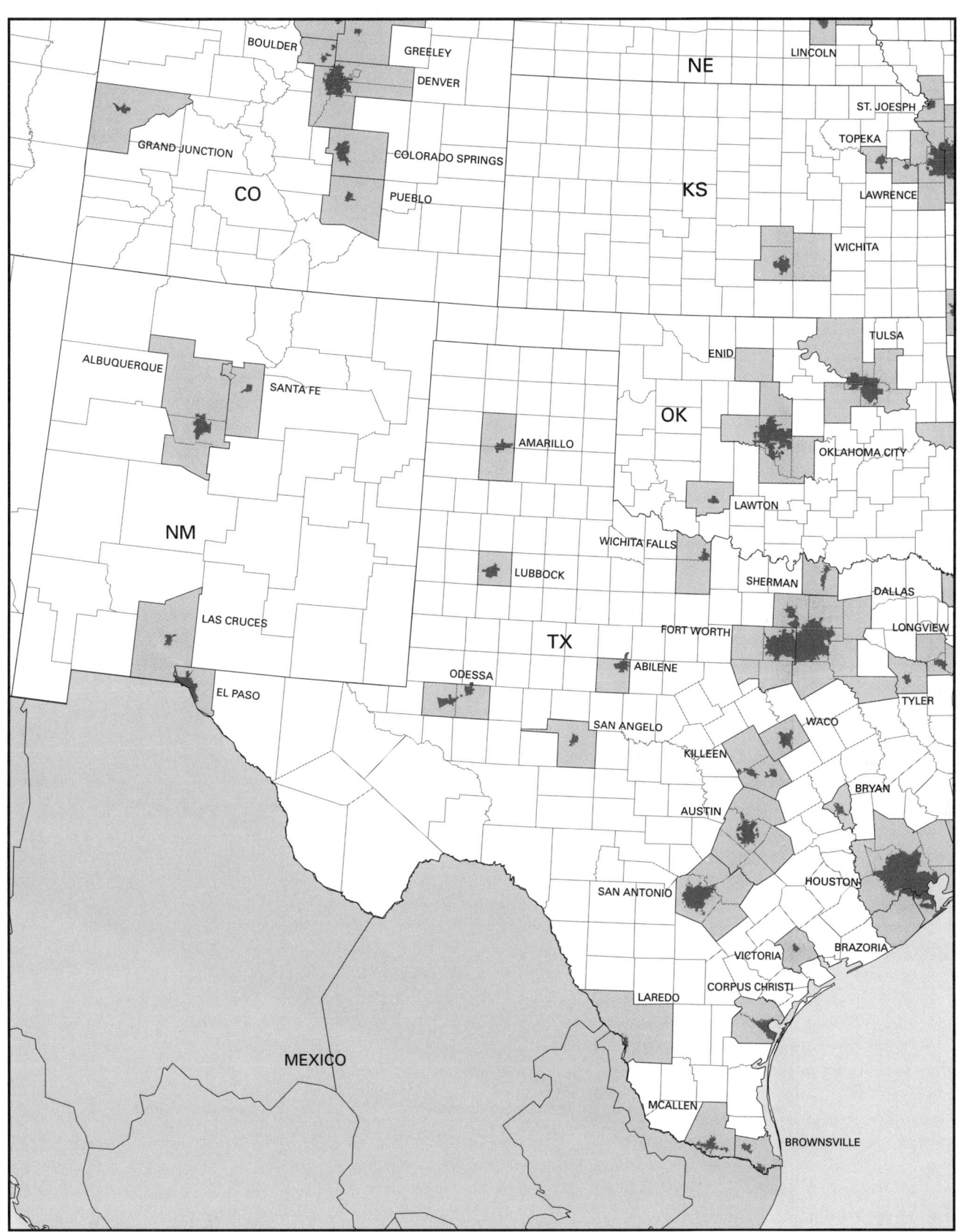

Copyright © 2000 by Places Rated Partnership

Cape Ann Mapping

Introduction

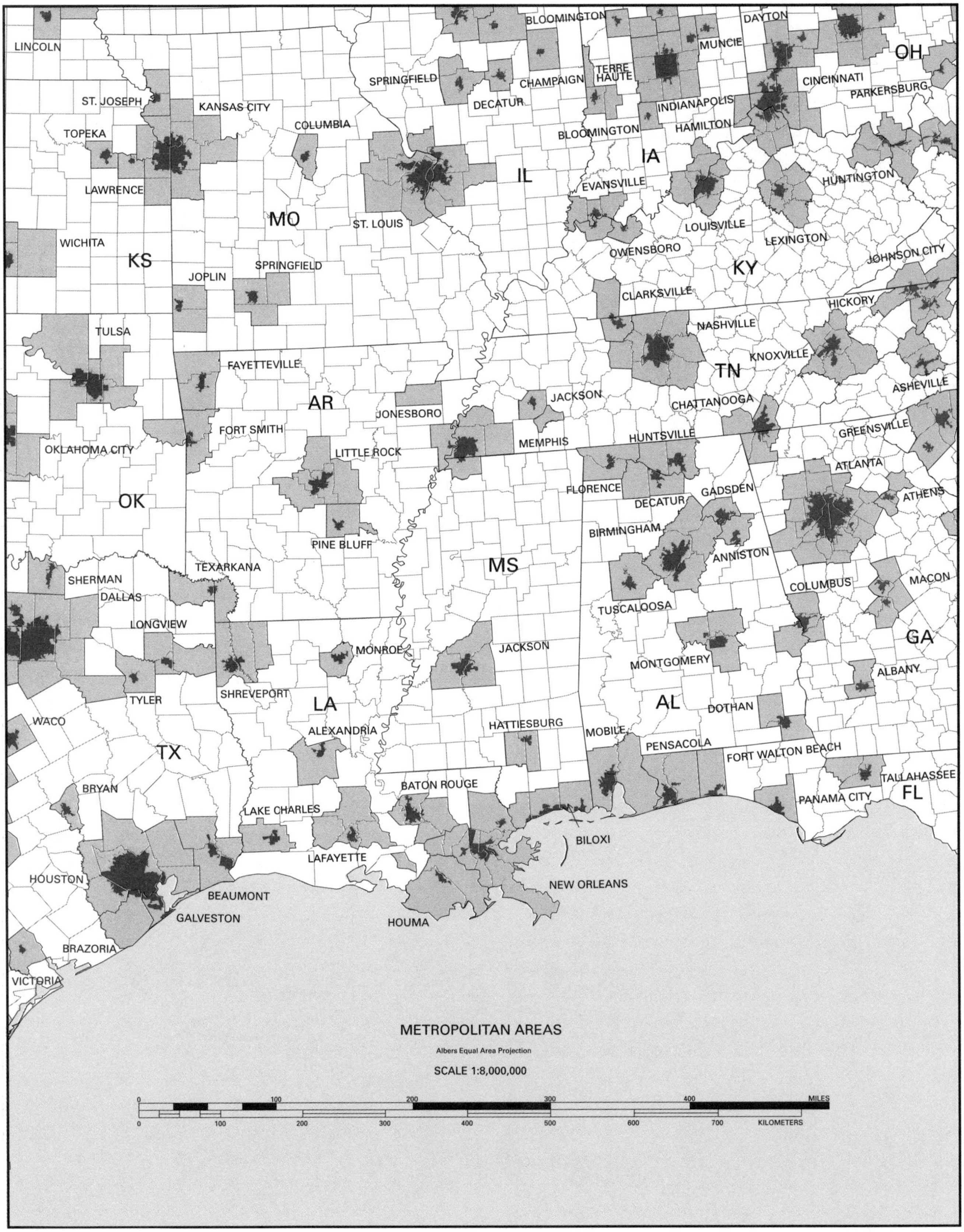

LINCOLN

ST. JOSEPH   KANSAS CITY

TOPEKA   COLUMBIA

LAWRENCE

MO

WICHITA   KS

JOPLIN   SPRINGFIELD

TULSA

FAYETTEVILLE

AR

OKLAHOMA CITY   FORT SMITH   JONESBORO

OK   LITTLE ROCK

PINE BLUFF

TEXARKANA

SHERMAN
DALLAS

LONGVIEW

TYLER   MONROE   JACKSON

WACO   SHREVEPORT   LA

TX   ALEXANDRIA   MS

BRYAN

LAKE CHARLES   HATTIESBURG

HOUSTON   LAFAYETTE   BATON ROUGE

BEAUMONT

GALVESTON   HOUMA

BRAZORIA

VICTORIA

BLOOMINGTON   DAYTON

SPRINGFIELD   CHAMPAIGN   TERRE   MUNCIE   OH
DECATUR   HAUTE   INDIANAPOLIS   CINCINNATI   PARKERSBURG
BLOOMINGTON   HAMILTON

IL   IA
EVANSVILLE   HUNTINGTON

LOUISVILLE   LEXINGTON   JOHNSON CITY
OWENSBORO   KY

CLARKSVILLE   HICKORY

NASHVILLE

KNOXVILLE   ASHEVILLE
JACKSON   TN

CHATTANOOGA   GREENSVILLE
MEMPHIS   HUNTSVILLE
ATLANTA   ATHENS
FLORENCE   GADSDEN
DECATUR
BIRMINGHAM   ANNISTON
COLUMBUS   MACON

TUSCALOOSA
GA
JACKSON   ALBANY
MONTGOMERY

AL   DOTHAN

MOBILE   PENSACOLA   FORT WALTON BEACH   TALLAHASSEE
PANAMA CITY   FL

BILOXI

NEW ORLEANS

METROPOLITAN AREAS

Albers Equal Area Projection

SCALE 1:8,000,000

| 0 | 100 | 200 | 300 | 400 | MILES |

| 0 | 100 | 200 | 300 | 400 | 500 | 600 | 700 | KILOMETERS |

Copyright © 2000 by Places Rated Partnership

Cape Ann Mapping

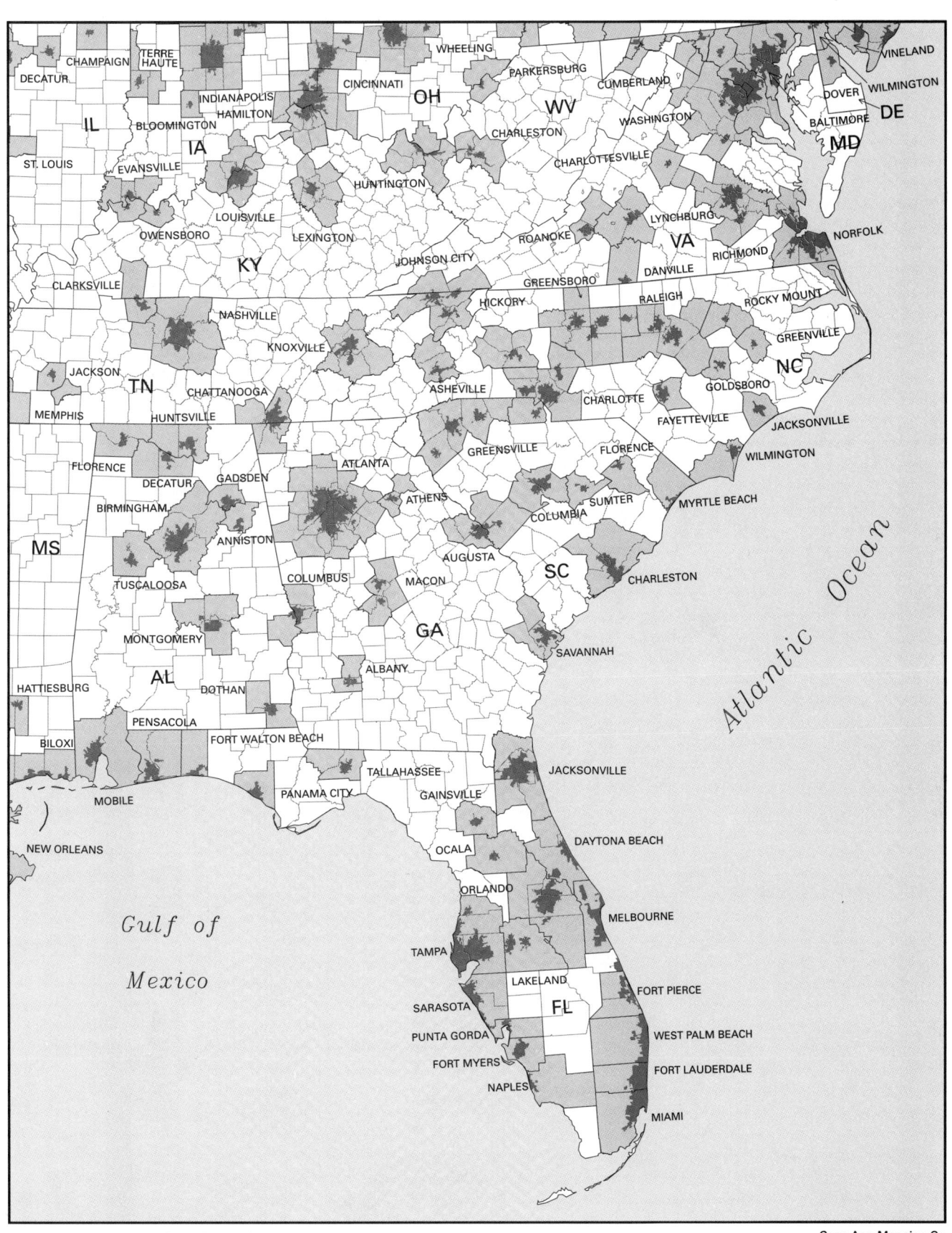

CHAMPAIGN
DECATUR
TERRE HAUTE
IL
IA
ST. LOUIS
BLOOMINGTON
INDIANAPOLIS
HAMILTON
EVANSVILLE
CINCINNATI
OH
WHEELING
PARKERSBURG
CUMBERLAND
WV
CHARLESTON
WASHINGTON
CHARLOTTESVILLE
VINELAND
WILMINGTON
DOVER
BALTIMORE
MD
DE

OWENSBORO
LOUISVILLE
LEXINGTON
HUNTINGTON
KY
JOHNSON CITY
ROANOKE
LYNCHBURG
VA
RICHMOND
DANVILLE
NORFOLK

CLARKSVILLE
NASHVILLE
GREENSBORO
RALEIGH
ROCKY MOUNT
GREENVILLE

JACKSON
KNOXVILLE
HICKORY
NC
GOLDSBORO

TN
CHATTANOOGA
ASHEVILLE
CHARLOTTE
FAYETTEVILLE
JACKSONVILLE

MEMPHIS
HUNTSVILLE
GREENSVILLE
FLORENCE
WILMINGTON

FLORENCE
DECATUR
GADSDEN
ATLANTA
SUMTER
MYRTLE BEACH

BIRMINGHAM
ATHENS
COLUMBIA

MS
ANNISTON
AUGUSTA
SC
CHARLESTON

TUSCALOOSA
COLUMBUS
MACON

MONTGOMERY
GA
SAVANNAH

AL
ALBANY

HATTIESBURG
DOTHAN

PENSACOLA
FORT WALTON BEACH

BILOXI
TALLAHASSEE
JACKSONVILLE

MOBILE
PANAMA CITY
GAINSVILLE

NEW ORLEANS
OCALA
DAYTONA BEACH

Gulf of
Mexico
ORLANDO
MELBOURNE

TAMPA
LAKELAND
FORT PIERCE

SARASOTA
FL

PUNTA GORDA
WEST PALM BEACH

FORT MYERS
FORT LAUDERDALE

NAPLES
MIAMI

Atlantic Ocean

Copyright © 2000 by Places Rated Partnership

Cape Ann Mapping Co.

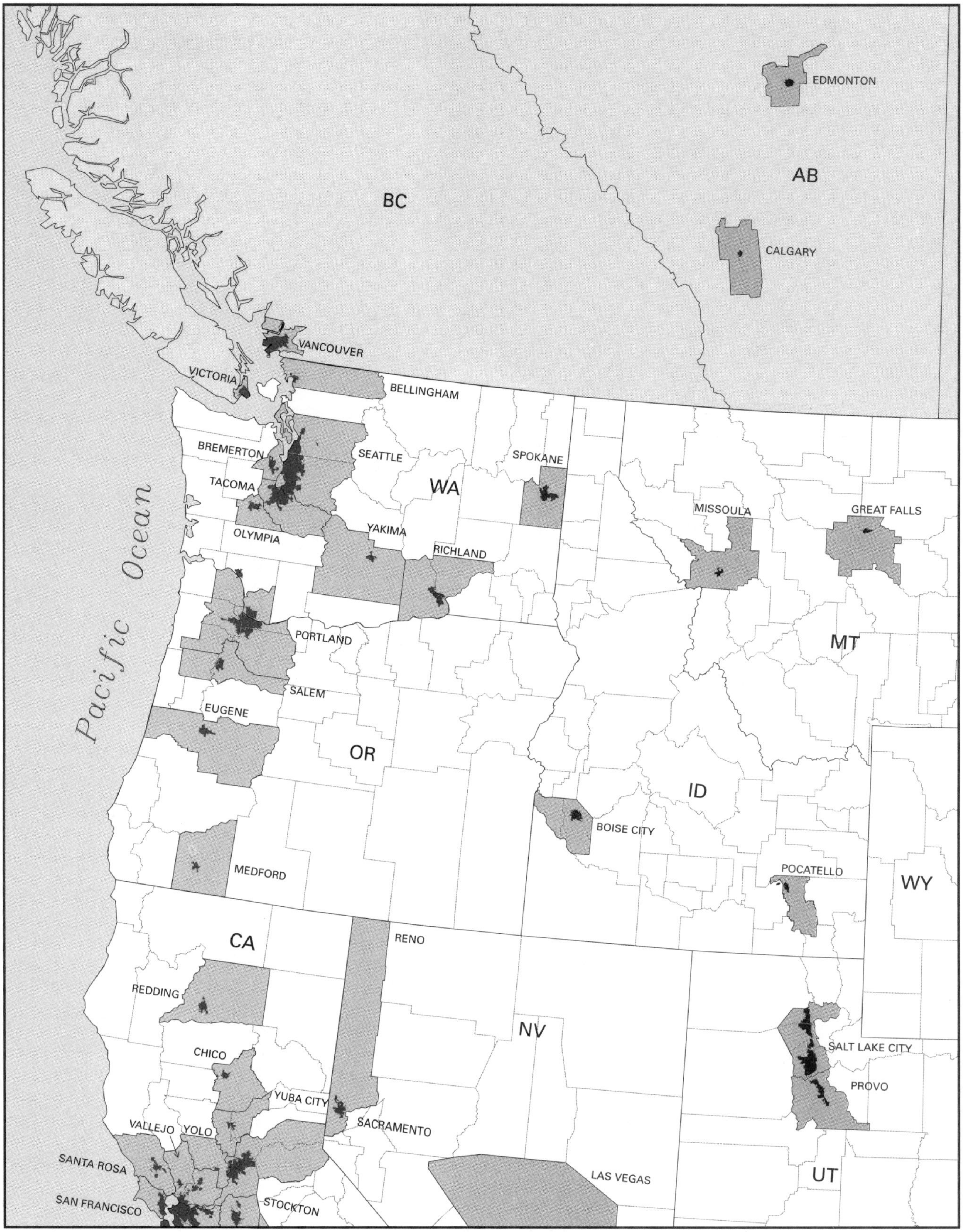

BC

EDMONTON

AB

CALGARY

VANCOUVER

VICTORIA

BELLINGHAM

BREMERTON

SEATTLE

SPOKANE

TACOMA

WA

OLYMPIA

YAKIMA

MISSOULA

GREAT FALLS

RICHLAND

Pacific Ocean

PORTLAND

SALEM

MT

EUGENE

OR

ID

BOISE CITY

POCATELLO

MEDFORD

WY

CA

RENO

REDDING

NV

SALT LAKE CITY

CHICO

YUBA CITY

PROVO

VALLEJO YOLO

SACRAMENTO

SANTA ROSA

LAS VEGAS

UT

SAN FRANCISCO

STOCKTON

Copyright © 2000 by Places Rated Partnership

Cape Ann Mapping

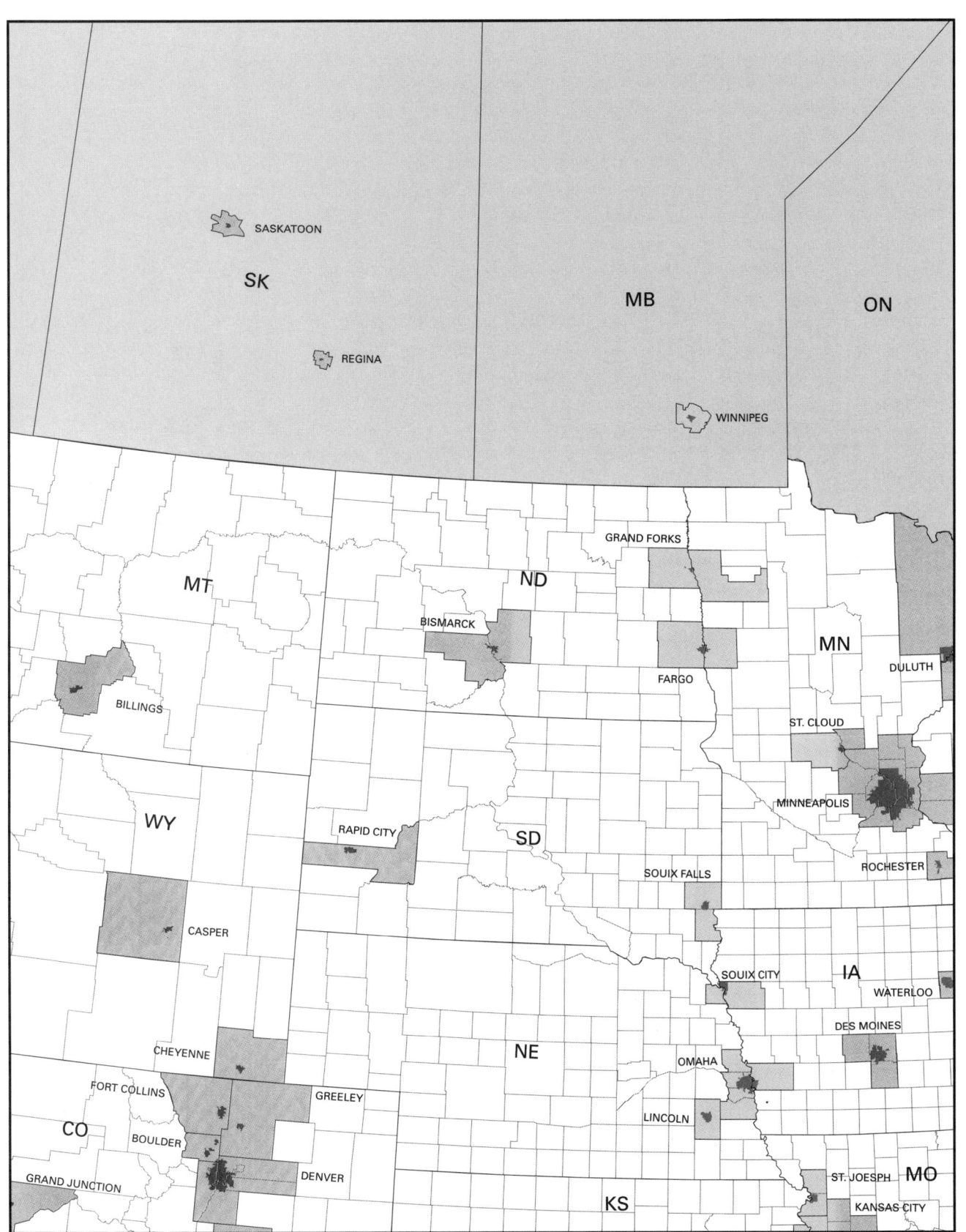

Copyright © 2000 by Places Rated Partnership

Cape Ann Mapping

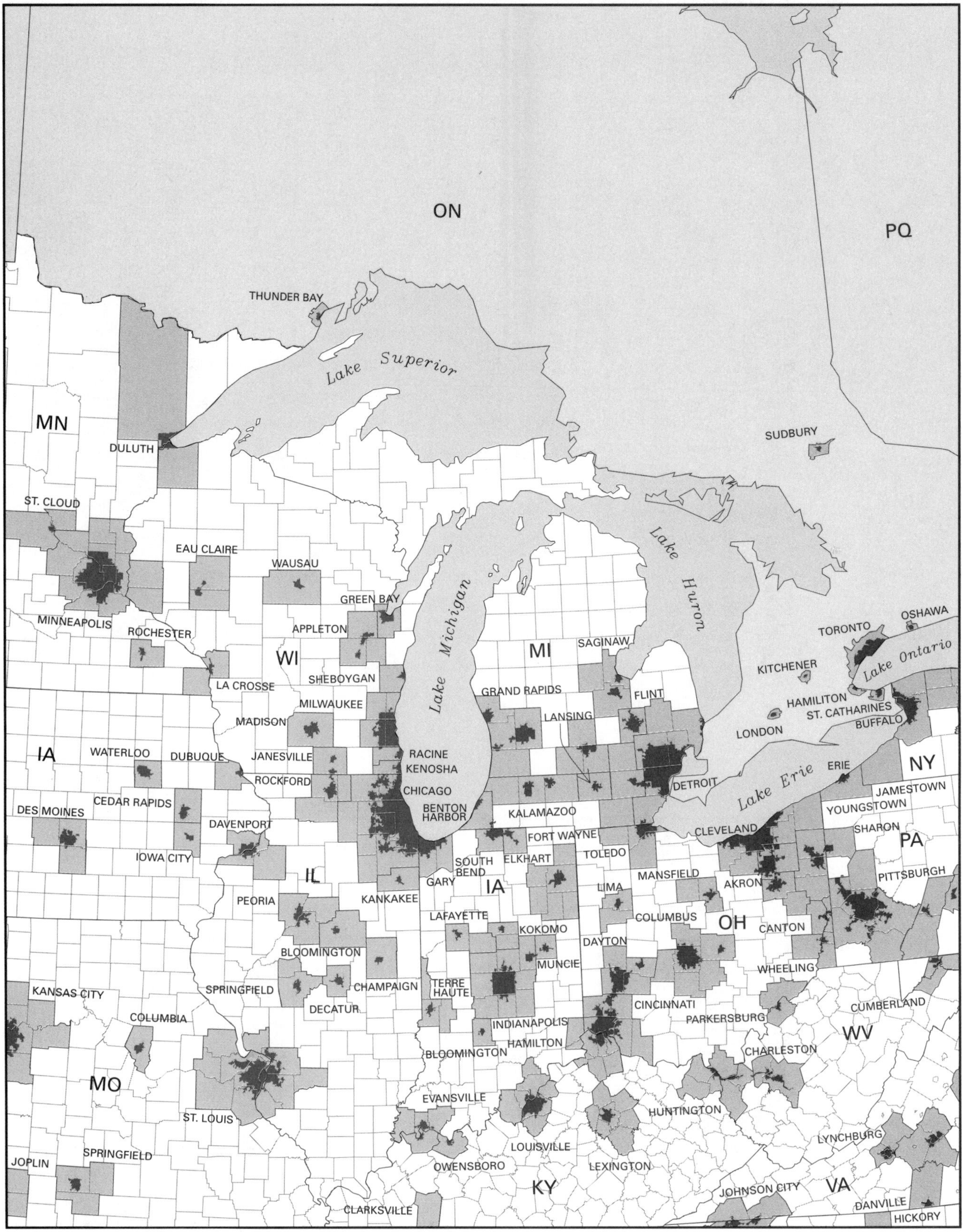

ON

PQ

THUNDER BAY

Lake Superior

SUDBURY

MN

DULUTH

ST. CLOUD

EAU CLAIRE

WAUSAU

Lake Huron

TORONTO   OSHAWA

GREEN BAY

MINNEAPOLIS

APPLETON

WI

Lake Michigan

MI

SAGINAW

KITCHENER

Lake Ontario

ROCHESTER

SHEBOYGAN

GRAND RAPIDS

LANSING

FLINT

HAMILITON
ST. CATHARINES

LA CROSSE

LONDON

BUFFALO

MILWAUKEE

MADISON

IA

WATERLOO

DUBUQUE

JANESVILLE

ROCKFORD

RACINE
KENOSHA

CHICAGO

KALAMAZOO

DETROIT

Lake Erie

ERIE

NY

JAMESTOWN

DES MOINES

CEDAR RAPIDS

DAVENPORT

BENTON
HARBOR

FORT WAYNE

CLEVELAND

YOUNGSTOWN

SHARON

PA

PITTSBURGH

IOWA CITY

IL

SOUTH
BEND

ELKHART

TOLEDO

MANSFIELD

AKRON

CANTON

PEORIA

GARY

IA

LIMA

KANSAS CITY

LAFAYETTE

KOKOMO

COLUMBUS

OH

WHEELING

KANKAKEE

DAYTON

BLOOMINGTON

SPRINGFIELD

CHAMPAIGN

MUNCIE

CINCINNATI

PARKERSBURG

CUMBERLAND

COLUMBIA

DECATUR

TERRE
HAUTE

INDIANAPOLIS

WV

MO

BLOOMINGTON

HAMILTON

CHARLESTON

LYNCHBURG

EVANSVILLE

HUNTINGTON

ST. LOUIS

LOUISVILLE

VA

JOPLIN

SPRINGFIELD

OWENSBORO

LEXINGTON

DANVILLE

CLARKSVILLE

KY

JOHNSON CITY

HICKORY

Copyright © 2000 by Places Rated Partnership

Cape Ann Mapping

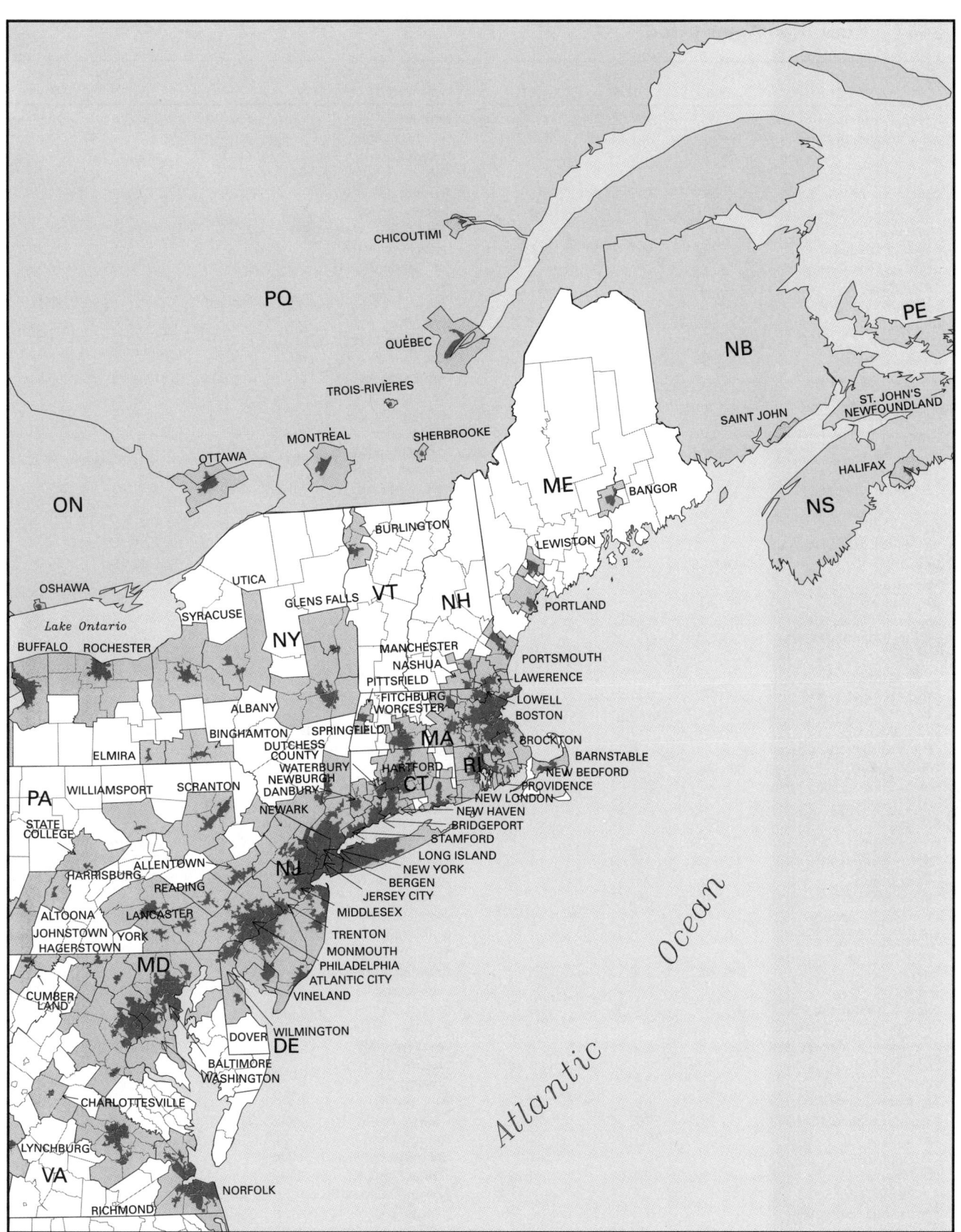

Copyright © 2000 by Places Rated Partnership

Cape Ann Mapping

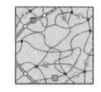

METRO AREAS AND COMPONENT COUNTIES	POPULATION 2000	POPULATION 1995	PERCENT GROWTH
Davenport-Moline-Rock Island, IA-IL	359,260	357,244	0.6
Scott County, IA; Henry and Rock Island counties, IL			
Dayton-Springfield, OH	947,067	952,421	–0.6
Clark, Greene, Miami, and Montgomery counties			
Daytona Beach, FL	488,292	450,434	8.4
Flagler and Volusia counties			
Decatur, AL	145,728	139,519	4.5
Lawrence and Morgan counties			
Decatur, IL	113,808	116,232	–2.1
Macon County			
Denver, CO	1,993,142	1,827,232	9.1
Adams, Arapahoe, Denver, Douglas, and Jefferson counties			
Des Moines, IA	447,613	422,604	5.9
Dallas, Polk, and Warren counties			
Detroit, MI	4,505,455	4,423,787	1.8
Lapeer, Macomb, Monroe, Oakland, St. Clair, and Wayne counties			
Dothan, AL	137,822	134,058	2.8
Dale and Houston counties			
Dover, DE	126,932	121,017	4.9
Kent County			
Dubuque, IA	88,553	88,262	0.3
Dubuque County			
Duluth-Superior, MN-WI	239,774	237,945	0.8
St. Louis County, MN; Douglas County, WI			
Dutchess County, NY	266,779	261,365	2.1
Dutchess County			
Eau Claire, WI	147,776	142,175	3.9
Chippewa and Eau Claire counties			
Edmonton, AB	890,000	884,700	0.6
5 cities, 9 towns, and 22 minor civil divisions			
El Paso, TX	733,504	676,711	8.4
El Paso County			
Elkhart-Goshen, IN	173,753	166,599	4.3
Elkhart County			
Elmira, NY	92,846	94,131	–1.4
Chemung County			
Enid, OK	56,720	57,183	–0.8
Garfield County			
Erie, PA	280,282	280,188	0.0
Erie County			
Eugene-Springfield, OR	321,288	302,958	6.1
Lane County			
Evansville-Henderson, IN-KY	293,236	286,961	2.2
Posey, Vanderburgh, and Warrick counties, IN; Henderson County, KY			
Fargo-Moorhead, ND-MN	173,852	163,561	6.3
Cass County, ND; Clay County, MN			
Fayetteville, NC	291,439	284,313	2.5
Cumberland County			
Fayetteville-Springdale-Rogers, AR	285,475	253,457	12.6
Benton and Washington counties			
Fitchburg-Leominster, MA	142,191	138,779	2.5
3 cities and 6 towns in Middlesex, and Worcester counties			
Flagstaff, AZ-UT	124,306	116,373	6.8
Coconino and Kane counties			

METRO AREAS AND COMPONENT COUNTIES	POPULATION 2000	POPULATION 1995	PERCENT GROWTH
Flint, MI	436,446	434,070	0.5
Genesee County			
Florence, AL	140,291	135,923	3.2
Colbert and Lauderdale counties			
Florence, SC	127,602	122,479	4.2
Florence County			
Fort Collins-Loveland, CO	242,111	216,942	11.6
Larimer County			
Fort Lauderdale, FL	1,533,988	1,413,649	8.5
Broward County			
Fort Myers-Cape Coral, FL	409,546	375,112	9.2
Lee County			
Fort Pierce-Port St. Lucie, FL	314,593	282,871	11.2
Martin and St. Lucie counties			
Fort Smith, AR-OK	198,623	188,372	5.4
Crawford and Sebastian counties, AR; Sequoyah County, OK			
Fort Walton Beach, FL	173,763	163,294	6.4
Okaloosa County			
Fort Wayne, IN	486,939	470,803	3.4
Adams, Allen, DeKalb, Huntington, Wells, and Whitley counties			
Fort Worth-Arlington, TX	1,637,606	1,489,044	10.0
Hood, Johnson, Parker, and Tarrant counties			
Fresno, CA	903,664	845,741	6.8
Fresno and Madera counties			
Gadsden, AL	106,167	102,002	4.1
Etowah County			
Gainesville, FL	205,110	195,511	4.9
Alachua County			
Galveston-Texas City, TX	255,296	237,401	7.5
Galveston County			
Gary, IN	634,616	619,798	2.4
Lake and Porter counties			
Glens Falls, NY	123,794	122,350	1.2
Warren and Washington counties			
Goldsboro, NC	114,186	110,616	3.2
Wayne County			
Grand Forks, ND-MN	103,531	103,976	–0.4
Grand Forks County, ND; Polk County, MN			
Grand Junction, CO	115,327	106,123	8.7
Mesa County			
Grand Rapids-Muskegon-Holland, MI	1,059,044	1,002,334	5.7
Allegan, Kent, Muskegon, and Ottawa counties			
Great Falls, MT	79,681	80,881	–1.5
Cascade County			
Greeley, CO	161,563	148,262	9.0
Weld County			
Green Bay, WI	221,728	210,237	5.5
Brown County			
Greensboro–Winston-Salem–High Point, NC	1,187,143	1,123,429	5.7
Alamance, Davidson, Davie, Forsyth, Guilford, Randolph, Stokes, and Yadkin counties			
Greenville, NC	128,121	117,828	8.7
Pitt County			
Greenville-Spartanburg-Anderson, SC	933,016	882,392	5.7
Anderson, Cherokee, Greenville, Pickens, and Spartanburg counties			

Sources: Woods & Poole Economics Inc. population estimates (U.S.) and Strategic Projections population estimates (Canada).

METRO AREAS AND COMPONENT COUNTIES	POPULATION 2000	POPULATION 1995	PERCENT GROWTH
Hagerstown, MD Washington County	129,890	126,946	2.3
Halifax, NS 2 cities, 1 town, 2 minor civil divisions, and 5 county subdivisions	346,000	342,500	1.0
Hamilton, ON 3 cities, 4 towns, and 1 minor civil division	655,000	643,100	1.9
Hamilton-Middletown, OH Butler County	344,292	319,464	7.8
Harrisburg-Lebanon-Carlisle, PA Cumberland, Dauphin, Lebanon, and Perry counties	636,375	610,943	4.2
Hartford, CT 4 cities and 55 towns in Hartford, Litchfield, Middlesex, New London, Tolland, and Windham counties	1,149,141	1,154,113	–0.4
Hattiesburg, MS Forrest and Lamar counties	112,810	105,917	6.5
Hickory-Morganton-Lenoir, NC Alexander, Burke, Caldwell, and Catawba counties	325,102	310,215	4.8
Honolulu, HI Honolulu County	884,956	869,141	1.8
Houma, LA Lafourche and Terrebonne parishes	193,996	188,011	3.2
Houston, TX Chambers, Fort Bend, Harris, Liberty, Montgomery, and Waller counties	4,008,119	3,709,751	8.0
Huntington-Ashland, WV-KY-OH Cabell and Wayne counties, WV; Boyd, Carter, and Greenup counties, KY; Lawrence County, OH	314,783	316,339	–0.5
Huntsville, AL Limestone and Madison counties	343,802	327,735	4.9
Indianapolis, IN Boone, Hamilton, Hancock, Hendricks, Johnson, Madison, Marion, Morgan, and Shelby counties	1,545,986	1,473,470	4.9
Iowa City, IA Johnson County	107,168	101,248	5.8
Jackson, MI Jackson County	157,144	153,444	2.4
Jackson, MS Hinds, Madison, and Rankin counties	439,450	415,478	5.8
Jackson, TN Chester and Madison counties	102,566	97,208	5.5
Jacksonville, FL Clay, Duval, Nassau, and St. Johns counties	1,086,690	984,989	10.3
Jacksonville, NC Onslow County	144,512	142,373	1.5
Jamestown, NY Chautauqua County	140,084	141,292	–0.9
Janesville-Beloit, WI Rock County	153,306	148,207	3.4
Jersey City, NJ Hudson County	547,753	548,849	–0.2
Johnson City–Kingsport-Bristol, TN-VA Carter, Hawkins, Sullivan, Unicoi, and Washington counties, TN; Scott and Washington counties and Bristol city, VA	467,061	453,480	3.0
Johnstown, PA Cambria and Somerset counties	236,001	240,249	–1.8
Jonesboro, AR Craighead County	77,979	74,738	4.3
Joplin, MO Jasper and Newton counties	151,975	143,590	5.8
Kalamazoo-Battle Creek, MI Calhoun, Kalamazoo, and Van Buren counties	454,942	442,573	2.8
Kankakee, IL Kankakee County	102,904	101,298	1.6
Kansas City, MO-KS Cass, Clay, Clinton, Jackson, Lafayette, Platte, and Ray counties, MO; Johnson, Leavenworth, Miami, and Wyandotte counties, KS	1,759,224	1,671,645	5.2
Kenosha, WI Kenosha County	148,199	139,349	6.4
Killeen-Temple, TX Bell and Coryell counties	311,803	291,167	7.1
Kitchener-Waterloo, ON 3 cities and 2 minor civil divisions	398,000	395,400	0.7
Knoxville, TN Anderson, Blount, Knox, Loudon, Sevier, and Union counties	681,865	639,662	6.6
Kokomo, IN Howard and Tipton counties	100,812	99,679	1.1
La Crosse, WI-MN La Crosse County, WI; Houston County, MN	124,563	120,611	3.3
Lafayette, LA Acadia, Lafayette, St. Landry, and St. Martin parishes	379,456	364,516	4.1
Lafayette, IN Clinton and Tippecanoe counties	176,733	169,762	4.1
Lake Charles, LA Calcasieu Parish	183,364	175,754	4.3
Lakeland-Winter Haven, FL Polk County	460,634	436,213	5.6
Lancaster, PA Lancaster County	466,773	447,306	4.4
Lansing-East Lansing, MI Clinton, Eaton, and Ingham counties	453,992	445,128	2.0
Laredo, TX Webb County	199,698	171,935	16.1
Las Cruces, NM Dona Ana County	176,926	159,577	10.9
Las Vegas, NV-AZ Clark and Nye counties, NV; Mohave County, AZ	1,384,481	1,138,764	21.6
Lawrence, KS Douglas County	95,114	88,259	7.8

continues

Sources: Woods & Poole Economics Inc. population estimates (U.S.) and Strategic Projections population estimates (Canada).

Introduction

METRO AREAS AND COMPONENT COUNTIES	POPULATION 2000	POPULATION 1995	PERCENT GROWTH
Lawrence, MA-NH	384,762	368,510	4.4
2 cities and 21 towns in Essex County, MA; Rockingham County, NH			
Lawton, OK	113,903	115,235	–1.2
Comanche County			
Lewiston-Auburn, ME	91,156	90,780	0.4
2 cities and 7 towns in Androscoggin County			
Lexington, KY	459,021	434,256	5.7
Bourbon, Clark, Fayette, Jessamine, Madison, Scott, and Woodford counties			
Lima, OH	155,899	155,546	0.2
Allen and Auglaize counties			
Lincoln, NE	243,417	229,143	6.2
Lancaster County			
Little Rock-North Little Rock, AR	567,511	541,667	4.8
Faulkner, Lonoke, Pulaski, and Saline counties			
London, ON	415,000	413,200	0.4
2 cities and 9 minor civil divisions			
Long Island, NY	2,671,294	2,651,362	0.8
Nassau and Suffolk counties			
Longview-Marshall, TX	213,782	203,610	5.0
Gregg, Harrison, and Upshur counties			
Los Angeles-Long Beach, CA	9,220,312	9,054,394	1.8
Los Angeles County			
Louisville, KY-IN	1,010,464	984,469	2.6
Bullitt, Jefferson, and Oldham counties, KY; Clark, Floyd, Harrison, and Scott counties, IN			
Lowell, MA-NH	293,801	289,160	1.6
1 city and 10 towns in Middlesex County, MA; Hillsborough County, NH			
Lubbock, TX	233,678	231,329	1.0
Lubbock County			
Lynchburg, VA	210,578	204,006	3.2
Amherst, Bedford, Campbell, counties; Bedford and Lynchburg cities			
Macon, GA	322,398	308,630	4.5
Bibb, Houston, Jones, Peach, and Twiggs counties			
Madison, WI	413,350	392,203	5.4
Dane County			
Manchester, NH	188,757	179,876	4.9
1 city and 8 towns in Hillsborough, Merrimack, and Rockingham counties			
Mansfield, OH	175,478	175,287	0.1
Crawford and Richland counties			
McAllen-Edinburg-Mission, TX	547,433	480,694	13.9
Hidalgo County			
Medford-Ashland, OR	181,704	165,448	9.8
Jackson County			
Melbourne-Titusville-Palm Bay, FL	477,944	449,835	6.2
Brevard County			

METRO AREAS AND COMPONENT COUNTIES	POPULATION 2000	POPULATION 1995	PERCENT GROWTH
Memphis, TN-AR-MS	1,116,341	1,064,633	4.9
Fayette, Shelby, and Tipton counties, TN; Crittenden County, AR; DeSoto County, MS			
Merced, CA	204,463	193,437	5.7
Merced County			
Miami, FL	2,089,376	2,028,508	3.0
Dade County			
Middlesex-Somerset-Hunterdon, NJ	1,128,973	1,076,859	4.8
Hunterdon, Middlesex, and Somerset counties			
Milwaukee-Waukesha, WI	1,467,865	1,452,179	1.1
Milwaukee, Ozaukee, Washington, and Waukesha counties			
Minneapolis-St. Paul, MN-WI	2,909,888	2,726,337	6.7
Anoka, Carver, Chisago, Dakota, Hennepin, Isanti, Ramsey, Scott, Sherburne, Washington, and Wright counties, MN; Pierce and St. Croix counties, WI			
Missoula, MT	93,055	87,360	6.5
Missoula County			
Mobile, AL	549,628	515,763	6.6
Baldwin and Mobile counties			
Modesto, CA	444,155	410,491	8.2
Stanislaus County			
Monmouth-Ocean, NJ	1,105,377	1,049,346	5.3
Monmouth and Ocean counties			
Monroe, LA	149,390	146,521	2.0
Ouachita Parish			
Montgomery, AL	330,269	313,911	5.2
Autauga, Elmore, and Montgomery counties			
Montreal, PQ	3,441,000	3,335,600	3.2
2 cities, 80 villes, and 31 minor civil divisions			
Muncie, IN	117,849	118,739	–0.7
Delaware County			
Myrtle Beach, SC	181,343	157,533	15.1
Horry County			
Naples, FL	207,115	182,876	13.3
Collier County			
Nashua, NH	183,795	176,351	4.2
1 city and 12 towns in Hillsborough County			
Nashville, TN	1,186,108	1,091,934	8.6
Cheatham, Davidson, Dickson, Robertson, Rutherford, Sumner, Williamson, and Wilson counties			
New Bedford, MA	178,612	174,560	2.3
1 city and 7 towns in Bristol and Plymouth counties			
New Haven-Meriden, CT	524,855	524,440	0.1
3 cities and 14 towns in Middlesex and New Haven counties			
New London-Norwich, CT-RI	290,139	286,588	1.2
3 cities and 19 towns in Middlesex, New London, Windham counties, CT; Washington County, RI			
New Orleans, LA	1,325,345	1,310,421	1.1
Jefferson, Orleans, Plaquemines, St. Bernard, St. Charles, St. James, St. John the Baptist, and St. Tammany parishes			

Sources: Woods & Poole Economics Inc. population estimates (U.S.) and Strategic Projections population estimates (Canada).

METRO AREAS AND COMPONENT COUNTIES	POPULATION 2000	POPULATION 1995	PERCENT GROWTH
New York, NY	8,603,992	8,593,929	0.1
Bronx, Kings, New York, Putnam, Queens, Richmond, Rockland, and Westchester counties			
Newark, NJ	1,944,061	1,933,126	0.6
Essex, Morris, Sussex, Union, and Warren counties			
Newburgh, NY-PA	374,504	358,563	4.4
Orange County, NY; Pike County, PA			
Norfolk-Virginia Beach- Newport News, VA-NC	1,585,776	1,531,027	3.6
Gloucester, Isle of Wight, James City, Mathews, and York counties, VA; Currituck County, NC; Chesapeake, Hampton, Newport News, Norfolk, Poquoson, Portsmouth, Suffolk, Virginia Beach, and Williamsburg cities, VA			
Oakland, CA	2,347,638	2,213,438	6.1
Alameda and Contra Costa counties			
Ocala, FL	248,325	225,821	10.0
Marion County			
Odessa-Midland, TX	246,361	237,032	3.9
Ector and Midland counties			
Oklahoma City, OK	1,050,216	1,013,353	3.6
Canadian, Cleveland, Logan, McClain, Oklahoma, and Pottawatomie counties			
Olympia, WA	212,044	192,327	10.3
Thurston County			
Omaha, NE-IA	712,460	669,998	6.3
Pottawattamie, Cass, Douglas, Sarpy, and Washington counties			
Orange County, CA	2,778,415	2,586,431	7.4
Orange County			
Orlando, FL	1,574,284	1,391,620	13.1
Lake, Orange, Osceola, and Seminole counties			
Oshawa, ON	284,000	275,600	3.0
1 city and 2 towns			
Ottawa-Hull, ON-PQ	1,065,000	1,023,200	4.1
5 cities, 5 villes, 1 town, and 16 minor civil divisions			
Owensboro, KY	93,087	90,507	2.9
Daviess County			
Panama City, FL	154,135	141,886	8.6
Bay County			
Parkersburg-Marietta, WV-OH	150,830	151,545	–0.5
Wood County, WV; Washington County, OH			
Pensacola, FL	417,800	378,136	10.5
Escambia and Santa Rosa counties			
Peoria-Pekin, IL	350,446	345,807	1.3
Peoria, Tazewell, and Woodford counties			
Philadelphia, PA-NJ	4,966,257	4,952,905	0.3
Bucks, Chester, Delaware, Montgomery, and Philadelphia counties, PA; Burlington, Camden, Gloucester, and Salem counties, NJ			
Phoenix-Mesa, AZ	3,034,464	2,661,463	14.0
Maricopa and Pinal counties			

METRO AREAS AND COMPONENT COUNTIES	POPULATION 2000	POPULATION 1995	PERCENT GROWTH
Pine Bluff, AR	82,727	83,501	–0.9
Jefferson County			
Pittsburgh, PA	2,361,710	2,386,036	–1.0
Allegheny, Beaver, Butler, Fayette, Washington, and Westmoreland counties			
Pittsfield, MA	84,478	85,599	–1.3
1 city and 9 towns in Berkshire County			
Pocatello, ID	77,353	73,035	5.9
Bannock County			
Portland, ME	236,101	226,967	4.0
3 cities and 17 towns in Cumberland and York counties			
Portland-Vancouver, OR-WA	1,888,819	1,713,268	10.2
Clackamas, Columbia, Multnomah, Washington, and Yamhill counties, OR; Clark County, WA			
Portsmouth- Rochester, NH-ME	241,120	227,745	5.9
4 cities and 27 towns in Rockingham and Strafford counties, NH; York County, ME			
Providence-Fall River- Warwick, RI-MA	1,088,433	1,079,558	0.8
9 cities and 32 towns in Bristol, Kent, Newport, Providence, and Washington counties, RI; Bristol County, MA			
Provo-Orem, UT	359,164	310,826	15.6
Utah County			
Pueblo, CO	134,452	129,389	3.9
Pueblo County			
Punta Gorda, FL	144,605	129,201	11.9
Charlotte County			
Quebec City, PQ	689,000	693,400	–0.6
21 villes and 24 minor civil divisions			
Racine, WI	188,391	183,801	2.5
Racine County			
Raleigh-Durham– Chapel Hill, NC	1,114,141	993,632	12.1
Chatham, Durham, Franklin, Johnston, Orange, and Wake counties			
Rapid City, SD	90,805	87,088	4.3
Pennington County			
Reading, PA	359,189	350,325	2.5
Berks County			
Redding, CA	169,879	160,870	5.6
Shasta County			
Regina, SK	199,000	198,600	0.2
1 city, 4 towns, and 12 minor civil divisions			
Reno, NV	317,545	290,757	9.2
Washoe County			
Richland-Kennewick- Pasco, WA	192,843	179,267	7.6
Benton and Franklin counties			
Richmond-Petersburg, VA	969,641	925,967	4.7
Charles City, Chesterfield, Dinwiddie, Goochland, Hanover, Henrico, New Kent, Powhatan, and Prince George counties; Colonial Heights, Hopewell, Petersburg, and Richmond cities			

continues

Sources: Woods & Poole Economics Inc. population estimates (U.S.) and Strategic Projections population estimates (Canada).

METRO AREAS AND COMPONENT COUNTIES	POPULATION 2000	POPULATION 1995	PERCENT GROWTH
Riverside-San Bernardino, CA Riverside and San Bernardino counties	3,234,161	2,963,977	9.1
Roanoke, VA Botetourt and Roanoke counties; Roanoke and Salem cities	232,642	228,305	1.9
Rochester, MN Olmsted County	119,373	112,434	6.2
Rochester, NY Genesee, Livingston, Monroe, Ontario, Orleans, and Wayne counties	1,095,210	1,085,709	0.9
Rockford, IL Boone, Ogle, and Winnebago counties	361,633	348,805	3.7
Rocky Mount, NC Edgecombe and Nash counties	149,063	142,330	4.7
Sacramento, CA El Dorado, Placer, and Sacramento counties	1,584,266	1,458,304	8.6
Saginaw-Bay City-Midland, MI Bay, Midland, and Saginaw counties	404,499	402,504	0.5
St. Catharines-Niagara, ON 5 cities, 4 towns, and 1 minor civil division	384,000	386,500	−0.6
St. Cloud, MN Benton and Stearns counties	167,491	158,554	5.6
Saint John, NB 1 city, 3 towns, and 17 minor civil divisions	130,000	129,300	0.5
St. John's, NF 2 cities and 17 towns	179,000	178,500	0.3
St. Joseph, MO Andrew and Buchanan counties	96,917	97,402	−0.5
St. Louis, MO-IL Crawford, Franklin, Jefferson, Lincoln, St. Charles, St. Louis, and Warren counties, MO; St. Louis city, MO; Clinton, Jersey, Madison, Monroe, and St. Clair counties, IL	2,584,538	2,541,514	1.7
Salem, OR Marion and Polk counties	340,751	313,192	8.8
Salinas, CA Monterey County	370,650	344,886	7.5
Salt Lake City-Ogden, UT Davis, Salt Lake, and Weber counties	1,324,187	1,205,636	9.8
San Angelo, TX Tom Green County	103,645	101,437	2.2
San Antonio, TX Bexar, Comal, Guadalupe, and Wilson counties	1,597,810	1,457,979	9.6
San Diego, CA San Diego County	2,859,202	2,645,571	8.1
San Francisco, CA Marin, San Francisco, and San Mateo counties	1,675,039	1,639,457	2.2
San Jose, CA Santa Clara County	1,646,595	1,566,557	5.1
San Luis Obispo-Atascadero-Paso Robles, CA San Luis Obispo County	241,428	226,778	6.5
Santa Barbara-Santa Maria-Lompoc, CA Santa Barbara County	396,774	383,270	3.5

METRO AREAS AND COMPONENT COUNTIES	POPULATION 2000	POPULATION 1995	PERCENT GROWTH
Santa Cruz-Watsonville, CA Santa Cruz County	243,227	236,121	3.0
Santa Fe, NM Los Alamos and Santa Fe counties	150,734	135,464	11.3
Santa Rosa, CA Sonoma County	444,428	416,124	6.8
Sarasota-Bradenton, FL Manatee and Sarasota counties	568,065	524,898	8.2
Saskatoon, SK 1 city, 9 towns, and 11 minor civil divisions	226,000	220,500	2.5
Savannah, GA Bryan, Chatham, and Effingham counties	290,618	278,867	4.2
Scranton–Wilkes-Barre–Hazleton, PA Columbia, Lackawanna, Luzerne, and Wyoming counties	619,242	631,626	−2.0
Seattle-Bellevue-Everett, WA Island, King, and Snohomish countiess	2,356,143	2,197,036	7.2
Sharon, PA Mercer County	122,959	122,020	0.8
Sheboygan, WI Sheboygan County	111,706	108,607	2.9
Sherbrooke, PQ 4 villes and 10 minor civil divisions	152,000	148,200	2.6
Sherman-Denison, TX Grayson County	103,371	98,144	5.3
Shreveport-Bossier City, LA Bossier, Caddo, and Webster parishes	384,145	378,566	1.5
Sioux City, IA-NE Woodbury County, IA; Dakota County, NE	124,328	120,435	3.2
Sioux Falls, SD Lincoln and Minnehaha counties	170,629	156,740	8.9
South Bend, IN St. Joseph County	261,136	256,478	1.8
Spokane, WA Spokane County	418,288	401,315	4.2
Springfield, IL Menard and Sangamon counties	206,294	202,986	1.6
Springfield, MO Christian, Greene, and Webster counties	317,270	293,955	7.9
Springfield, MA 5 cities and 24 towns in Franklin, Hampden, and Hampshire counties	574,951	578,390	−0.6
Stamford-Norwalk, CT 2 cities and 6 towns in Fairfield County	333,180	330,812	0.7
State College, PA Centre County	137,580	130,412	.5
Steubenville-Weirton, OH-WV Jefferson County, OH; Brooke and Hancock counties, WV	135,054	139,346	−3.1
Stockton-Lodi, CA San Joaquin County	563,423	524,512	7.4
Sudbury, ON 1 city, 5 towns, and 1 minor civil division	166,000	166,400	−0.2
Sumter, SC Sumter County	108,108	106,654	1.4

Sources: Woods & Poole Economics Inc. population estimates (U.S.) and Strategic Projections population estimates (Canada).

METRO AREAS AND COMPONENT COUNTIES	POPULATION 2000	POPULATION 1995	PERCENT GROWTH
Syracuse, NY Cayuga, Madison, Onondaga, and Oswego counties	744,044	748,533	–0.6
Tacoma, WA Pierce County	706,508	647,192	9.2
Tallahassee, FL Gadsden and Leon counties	272,026	257,563	5.6
Tampa-St. Petersburg-Clearwater, FL Hernando, Hillsborough, Pasco, and Pinellas counties	2,308,247	2,176,919	6.0
Terre Haute, IN Clay, Vermillion, and Vigo counties	149,323	149,395	0.0
Texarkana, AR Bowie County, TX; Miller County, AR	125,226	122,685	2.1
Thunder Bay, ON 1 city and 7 minor civil divisions	131,000	131,000	0.0
Toledo, OH Fulton, Lucas, and Wood counties	615,385	611,044	0.7
Topeka, KS Shawnee County	166,972	164,747	1.4
Toronto, ON 8 cities, 16 towns, and 5 minor civil divisions	4,605,000	4,346,300	6.0
Trenton, NJ Mercer County	331,692	329,251	0.7
Trois-Rivieres, PQ 5 villes and 5 minor civil divisions	143,000	143,200	–0.1
Tucson, AZ Pima County	820,787	754,727	8.8
Tulsa, OK Creek, Osage, Rogers, Tulsa, and Wagoner counties	784,331	745,371	5.2
Tuscaloosa, AL Tuscaloosa County	166,631	158,469	5.2
Tyler, TX Smith County	171,087	161,698	5.8
Utica-Rome, NY Herkimer and Oneida counties	297,641	307,857	–3.3
Vallejo-Fairfield-Napa, CA Napa and Solano counties	524,088	480,515	9.1
Vancouver, BC 11 cities, 9 district municipalities, and 22 minor civil divisions	1,934,000	1,832,900	5.5
Ventura, CA Ventura County	752,053	706,971	6.4
Victoria, BC 2 cities, 2 towns, 4 district municipalities, and 11 minor civil divisions	314,000	311,400	0.8
Victoria, TX Victoria County	84,739	80,572	5.2
Vineland-Millville-Bridgeton, NJ Cumberland County	141,735	141,229	0.4
Visalia-Tulare-Porterville, CA Tulare County	365,607	347,314	5.3
Waco, TX McLennan County	207,628	198,603	4.5

METRO AREAS AND COMPONENT COUNTIES	POPULATION 2000	POPULATION 1995	PERCENT GROWTH
Washington, DC-MD-VA-WV District of Columbia; Calvert, Charles, Frederick, Montgomery, and Prince George's counties, MD; Arlington, Clarke, Culpeper, Fairfax, Fauquier, King George, Loudoun, Prince William, Spotsylvania, Stafford, and Warren counties, VA; Alexandria, Fairfax, Falls Church, Fredericksburg, Manassas, and Manassas Park cities, VA; Berkeley and Jefferson counties, WV	4,745,302	4,498,058	5.5
Waterbury, CT 1 city and 9 towns in Litchfield and New Haven counties	222,825	221,918	0.4
Waterloo-Cedar Falls, IA Black Hawk County	122,671	122,648	0.0
Wausau, WI Marathon County	126,153	120,756	4.5
West Palm Beach-Boca Raton, FL Palm Beach County	1,084,445	977,799	10.9
Wheeling, WV-OH Marshall and Ohio counties, WV; Belmont County, OH	152,472	156,373	–2.5
Wichita, KS Butler, Harvey, and Sedgwick counties	545,225	517,579	5.3
Wichita Falls, TX Archer and Wichita counties	137,732	135,227	1.9
Williamsport, PA Lycoming County	118,650	119,776	–0.9
Wilmington, NC Brunswick and New Hanover counties	230,460	200,273	15.1
Wilmington-Newark, DE-MD New Castle County, DE; Cecil County, MD	569,974	545,001	4.6
Windsor, ON 1 city, 4 towns, and 7 minor civil divisions	292,000	285,900	2.1
Winnipeg, MB 1 city and 7 minor civil divisions	681,000	677,300	0.5
Worcester, MA-CT 1 city and 34 towns in Hampden and Worcester counties, MA; Windham County, CT	494,787	482,988	2.4
Yakima, WA Yakima County	224,732	213,297	5.4
Yolo, CA Yolo County	160,028	148,274	7.9
York, PA York County	377,507	364,493	3.6
Youngstown-Warren, OH Columbiana, Mahoning, and Trumbull counties	594,673	599,820	–0.9
Yuba City, CA Sutter and Yuba counties	147,052	136,281	7.9
Yuma, AZ Yuma County	152,389	136,080	12.0

Sources: Woods & Poole Economics Inc. population estimates (U.S.) and Strategic Projections population estimates (Canada).

Decisions, Decisions

early 30 years ago a group of futurists, academics, and government scientists got together at a hotel outside Washington, DC, for a conference sponsored by the Environmental Protection Agency. Their job was to discover just how to define "quality of life."

The players quickly split into three groups over the issue. The first argued that defining what's good for all people at all times is not only unfair, it's impossible and shouldn't be tried at all. Livable for whom?, went their argument. The artist who wants mountain vistas? The entrepreneur who wants low taxes and no red tape? The new college graduate looking to start a career, retired workers in need of health care, or parents in search of alternatives to public schools?

The second group held that you *can* rate places but *should not* because measuring a touchy and hazy thing like livability makes places unwilling rivals of one another. When you claim your own turf is quite livable, you're implying others aren't. Look at the old jokes and occasional ill will between neighbors like Dallas and Ft. Worth, Minneapolis and St. Paul, or San Francisco and Oakland. Rating places is an unbecoming exercise, according to this view. Every place is habitable—that's why people live in them. Since we're all in this together, then together we'll make our cities and towns even more livable.

The third group said nonsense to the first two. Of course you can measure livability. As long as you know who your audience is, make clear what your statistical yardsticks are, and use them consistently, you'll be doing what's done all the time by chambers of commerce from Miami to Puget Sound and from West Quoddy Head, Maine, to San Diego.

Although viewpoints one and two may be valid, *Places Rated* sides with the third.

RATING PLACES: ONE WAY

This is a book of current statistics about North American metropolitan areas. Certainly it is a more objective source of information about urban livability than the hearsay that people share at a dinner party, a rest stop on the interstate, an airport bar, or a news group on the Internet. All of the 354 metro areas in this book are rated

27

by nine factors, each of which would be highly important to anyone considering a move.

- The **Costs of Living** chapter looks at household incomes and taxes, and it also measures the costs of such important items as housing, food, health care, and college tuition.

- **Transportation** is rated by local commuting time, public transit, and the diverse inter-city travel options by air, rail, and interstate highway.

- The **Jobs** chapter weighs prospects for employment growth to the year 2005 in nine basic industries, including manufacturing, trade, services, finance, and government.

- Each metro area's schools and its collection of colleges and universities produces an **Education** rating.

- **Climate** is rated on mildness, that is, how close temperatures remain to 65° Fahrenheit throughout the year. Brightness and stability also are part of the rating.

- A metro area's **Crime** rating is determined by the average annual number of violent and property crimes per 100,000 people over the past 5 years.

- The chapter on **the Arts** compares cultural assets, among them art museums, opera and ballet companies, and symphony orchestras.

- The supply of health-care facilities and practitioners, plus available special options, forms the basis for a metro area's **Health Care** rating.

- **Recreation** also rates assets, from good restaurants to public golf courses, zoos, professional sports, ocean coastlines, and national parks acreage.

Some readers may fault *Places Rated*'s choice of criteria. Admittedly, its yardsticks for health care, public transportation, options for higher education, and the performing arts all favor bigger places over smaller ones. On the other hand, the methods for scoring safety from crime, high living costs, and cleaner air favor smaller places over bigger ones. *Places Rated*'s standards for climate and outdoor recreation assets are certainly not everyone's, but they have nothing to do with population size.

Gathered here are the most up-to-date figures for all 354 metro areas. The sources, which are documented throughout this book, come from federal and state/provincial agencies and a growing number of private organizations.

This edition of *Places Rated Almanac* is as much a snapshot of a moving target as were its predecessors. Metro areas are dynamic and just don't sit still for statistical portraits. An economic rebound in many Great Lakes metro areas continues to draw native sons and daughters back from the Sun Belt. Likewise, the deepest slump in California in decades is over, and many of the thousands who emigrated to other, more promising areas may decide to return. With so much in life that is unpredictable, you'd be wise to supplement *Places Rated Almanac* with your own independent verification.

RATING PLACES: YOUR WAY

At the end of this book, in "Putting It All Together," costs of living, climate, housing, crime, health care, transportation, education, the arts, recreation, and jobs get equal weight when identifying metro areas with across-the-board strengths.

You may not agree with this equal-weight system. You may give more importance to forecasted job growth than to a relative lack of crime or an outstanding calendar of performing arts events. For you, a place where living costs are low may be much more important than an ocean coastline, an abundance of medical specialists, or an active higher education scene. To identify which factors are more important and which factors are less, you may want to take stock of your preferences.

Your Preference Inventory

The following Preference Inventory has seventy-two pairs of statements. For each pair, decide which statement is more important to you when judging whether a place is livable. Even if both statements are equally important or neither is important, select one anyway. If you can't decide quickly, pass up the item, but return to it after you complete the rest of the inventory.

Don't worry about being consistent. The paired statements aren't repeated. There aren't any right or wrong answers, only those that are best for you. Although the inventory takes about 10 minutes to finish, there is no time limit. Before you start, you might want to photocopy the inventory and ask your spouse or a friend to take it independently. Comparing your preference inventory with another person's can be an interesting exercise.

Directions

For each numbered item, decide which of the two statements is more important to you when choosing a place to live. Mark the box next to that statement. Be sure to make a choice for all items.

1. E. ❑ The number of days over 90 degrees.
   A. ❑ Average property taxes.

2. F. ❑ The number of murders.
   D. ❑ The size of public school districts.

3. H. ❑ Variety of medical specialists.
   B. ❑ Local public transit.

4. G. ❑ Classical music broadcasting.
   E. ❑ Local elevation, wind speed, and humidity.

5. A. ❑ The cost of food and clothing.
   B. ❑ How long it takes to commute to work.

6. G. ❑ Opera and professional theatre.
   I. ❑ Local college sports.

7. H. ❑ Good children's hospitals.
   E. ❑ Annual amount of rain and snow.

8. A. ❑ The price of houses.
   F. ❑ Local property crime rates.

9. C. ❑ Forecasted job growth.
   D. ❑ The pupil/teacher ratio in public schools.

10. G. ❑ Art museums and repertory theaters.
    F. ❑ The number of auto thefts in a year.

11. I. ❑ The number of public golf courses.
    B. ❑ Freeway traffic congestion.

12. H. ❑ Local emergency medical care.
    G. ❑ Fine-arts broadcasting.

13. G. ❑ Repertory theatre companies.
    A. ❑ The cost of living.

14. A. ❑ The cost of food and clothing.
    C. ❑ The outlook for job growth.

15. H. ❑ Family medical services.
    D. ❑ Books held in local libraries.

16. G. ❑ Performing arts facilities.
    C. ❑ Job opportunities in the service sector.

17. C. ❑ Local threat of unemployment.
    E. ❑ Annual number of clear and cloudy days.

18. I. ❑ Accessible ski areas.
    D. ❑ Variety of public and private colleges.

19. B. ❑ Public transportation.
    A. ❑ Median prices of homes.

20. A. ❑ State income tax and sales tax bite.
    H. ❑ Medical schools and teaching hospitals.

21. A. ❑ The cost of health care.
    I. ❑ Public golf courses.

22. G. ❑ Local art museums.
    B. ❑ Airlines and interstate highways.

23. H. ❑ Supply of family medical practitioners.
    I. ❑ Protected recreation land.

24. F. ❑ The violent crime rate.
    E. ❑ Annual amounts of rain and snow.

25. D. ❑ Pupil/teacher ratio in public schools.
    E. ❑ Annual number of clear and cloudy days.

26. I. ❑ Local professional sports teams.
    F. ❑ Number of robberies and assaults.

27. H. ❑ Hospitals affiliated with medical schools.
    F. ❑ Number of burglaries during the year.

28. D. ❑ Local support of public schools.
    G. ❑ Ballet companies and repertory theaters.

29. I. ❑ Accessible water recreation.
    C. ❑ Number of new manufacturing jobs by 2005.

30. I. ❑ Nearby national parks and forests.
    E. ❑ Number of stormy days during the year.

31. C. ❑ The mix of white- and blue-collar jobs.
    F. ❑ Number of robberies in a year.

32. B. ❑ Airlines serving the local airport.
    F. ❑ Number of auto thefts in a year.

33. B. ❑ Buses, subways, and commuter railroads.
    D. ❑ Local colleges and universities.

34. A. ❑ State income and sales tax bite.
    H. ❑ General hospitals and family doctors.

35. D. ❑ Dollars/student ratio in the public schools.
    A. ❑ Costs for utilities and property taxes.

36. B. ❑ Interstate highways and airline service.
    E. ❑ How cold the winters are.

37. H. ❑ Variety of medical specialists.
   E. ❑ Number of annual rainy and snowy days.

38. F. ❑ Local auto thefts and burglaries.
   A. ❑ Local household income and taxes.

39. G. ❑ Live theatres and concert halls.
   I. ❑ Zoos and family amusement parks.

40. F. ❑ Annual muggings per capita.
   D. ❑ Pupil/teacher ratio in public schools.

41. C. ❑ Outlook for job growth.
   B. ❑ Average daily commuting time.

42. E. ❑ Seasonal temperature variation.
   A. ❑ Typical property taxes.

43. H. ❑ Medical schools and teaching hospitals.
   G. ❑ Operas and symphony orchestras.

44. I. ❑ Opportunities for pari-mutuel wagering.
   B. ❑ Freeway traffic congestion.

45. C. ❑ Mix of white- and blue-collar jobs.
   D. ❑ Alternatives to public schools.

46. E. ❑ Seasonal temperature variation.
   C. ❑ Forecasted growth of jobs.

47. F. ❑ Auto thefts, muggings, and shootings.
   E. ❑ Annual number of freezing days.

48. A. ❑ Cost of heating a home.
   D. ❑ Variety of private K–12 schools.

49. C. ❑ Expected white-collar job growth.
   F. ❑ Annual property crime rate.

50. C. ❑ The number of new jobs created by 2005.
   A. ❑ Annual state income and sales tax bite.

51. G. ❑ Classical music broadcasting.
   B. ❑ Freeway traffic congestion.

52. H. ❑ Primary medical care.
   I. ❑ Nearby state parks and forests.

53. D. ❑ The quality of public libraries.
   E. ❑ Local wind speed and humidity.

54. I. ❑ Thoroughbred horse racing.
   C. ❑ Jobs in health and education services.

55. E. ❑ Number of days over 90 degrees.
   B. ❑ Supply of public transit.

56. I. ❑ Good places for dining out.
   D. ❑ Variety of public and private colleges.

57. G. ❑ Opera and professional theatre.
   C. ❑ The threat of unemployment.

58. I. ❑ Professional sports teams.
   E. ❑ Annual amounts of rain and snow.

59. G. ❑ Repertory theaters and symphony orchestras.
   E. ❑ How cold the winters are.

60. A. ❑ Median price of homes.
   G. ❑ Local performing arts bookings.

61. F. ❑ The violent crime rate.
   G. ❑ Local art museums.

62. F. ❑ Burglaries and auto thefts.
   H. ❑ Specialized medical care.

63. C. ❑ Job outlook from now to the year 2005.
   B. ❑ Freeway traffic congestion.

64. F. ❑ The property crime rate.
   I. ❑ Nearby national parks and forests.

65. H. ❑ Surgeons and medical specialists.
   C. ❑ Forecast for white-collar job growth.

66. D. ❑ Higher education opportunities.
   G. ❑ Opera and professional theatre.

67. B. ❑ Access to interstate highways.
   D. ❑ Private alternatives to public schools.

68. I. ❑ Movie theaters and good restaurants.
   A. ❑ The cost of food and clothing.

69. H. ❑ The number of doctors in family practice.
   D. ❑ Variety of public school districts.

70. B. ❑ Airlines serving the area.
   F. ❑ Local burglaries and auto thefts.

71. H. ❑ Family doctors and children's hospitals.
   B. ❑ Quality of public transit.

72. H. ❑ Local medical specialists who see patients.
   C. ❑ Prospects for white-collar job growth.

Plotting Your Preference Profile

It is important that you make a choice for each of the seventy-two items. Have you left any unchecked? If not, you're ready to draw your Preference Profile.

First Step. Count all the marks you've made in the boxes next to the letter A. Then enter the number of "A" statements on the line next to the words "Costs of Living" on your Preference Profile. In the same way, count the number of statements for each of the other letters. Enter their totals in their respective places on your Preference Profile.

Second Step. Now plot your totals on the blank chart. Place a dot on the appropriate line for each of the numbers and connect the dots to form a line graph of your results (see the Sample Preference Profile below).

Analyzing Your Preference Profile

Each of the factors in your Preference Profile—the costs of living, transportation, job outlook, higher education, climate, crime, the arts, health care, and recreation—is not only a big concern when choosing a place to live, but it also has a complete chapter in this book. The purpose of the Preference Inventory is to help you decide the relative importance of each of these nine factors to you.

If your scores are high for one or two of these factors, you may want to give extra attention to the chapters devoted to them. Likewise, if your scores are low for any of the nine factors, you may not need to give as much consideration to them as you would to those with high scores. Bear in mind that the inventory orders your preferences in a hierarchy, that each of the factors has some importance to you, and that none should be completely ignored.

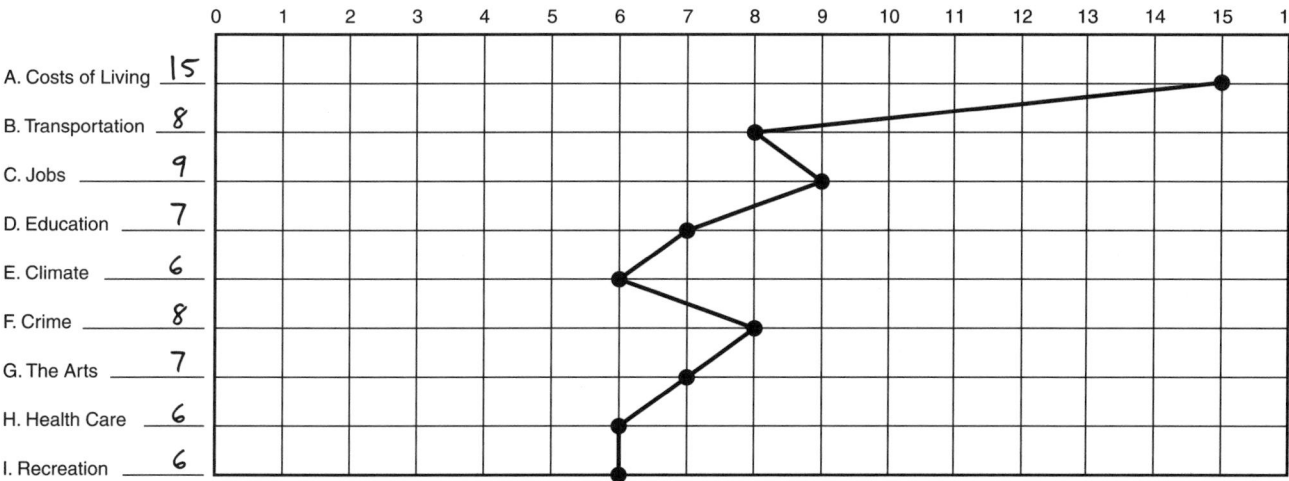

	0	1	2	3	4	5	6	7	8	9	10	11	12	13	14	15	16
A. Costs of Living 15
B. Transportation 8
C. Jobs 9
D. Education 7
E. Climate 6
F. Crime 8
G. The Arts 7
H. Health Care 6
I. Recreation 6

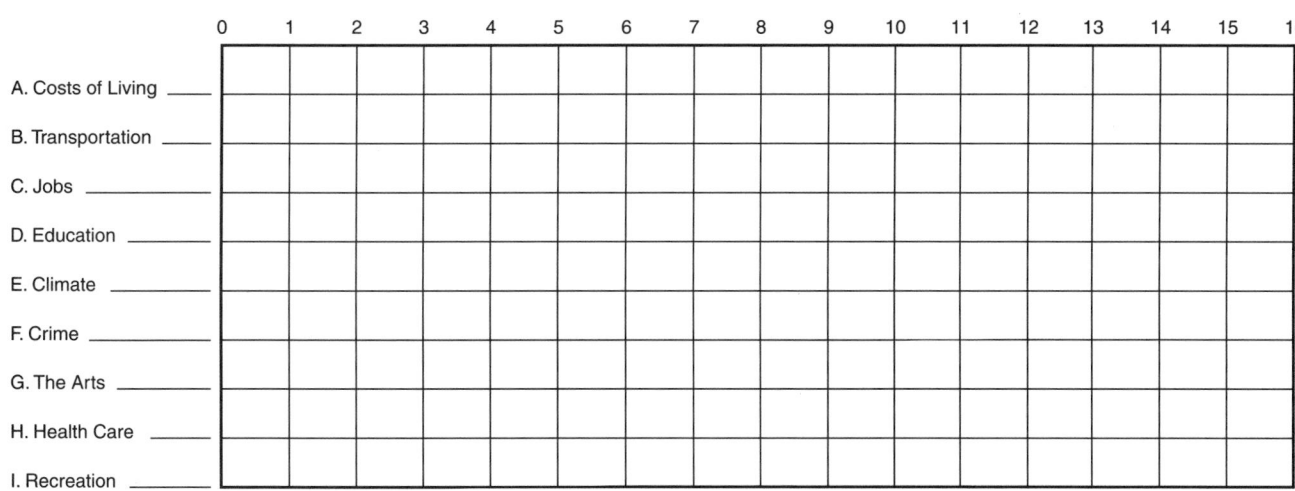

	0	1	2	3	4	5	6	7	8	9	10	11	12	13	14	15	16
A. Costs of Living
B. Transportation
C. Jobs
D. Education
E. Climate
F. Crime
G. The Arts
H. Health Care
I. Recreation

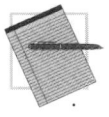

Rating Places: Your Way

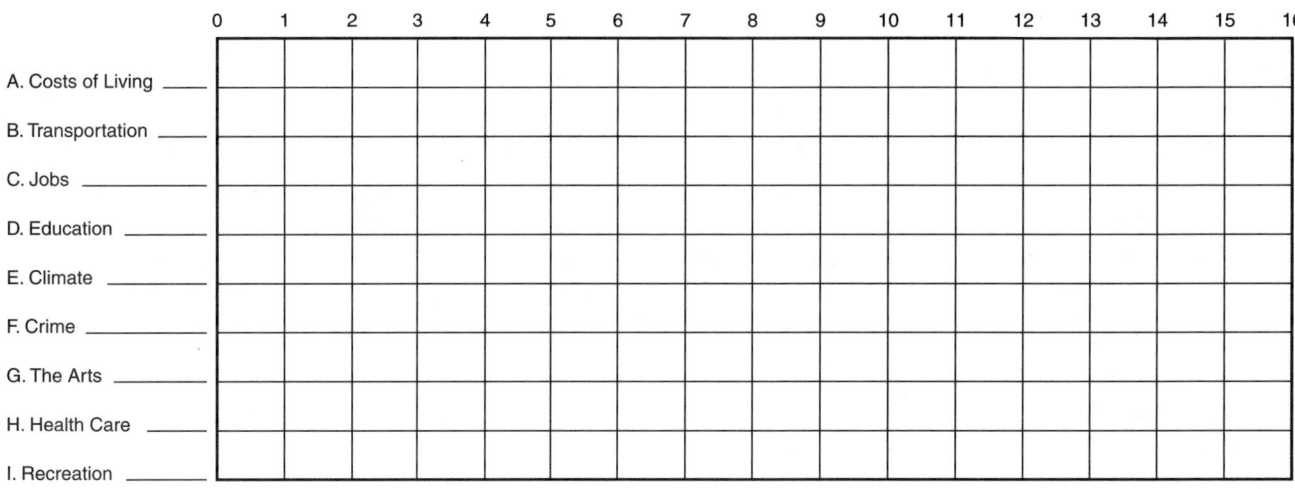

	0	1	2	3	4	5	6	7	8	9	10	11	12	13	14	15	16
A. Costs of Living _____																	
B. Transportation _____																	
C. Jobs _____																	
D. Education _____																	
E. Climate _____																	
F. Crime _____																	
G. The Arts _____																	
H. Health Care _____																	
I. Recreation _____																	

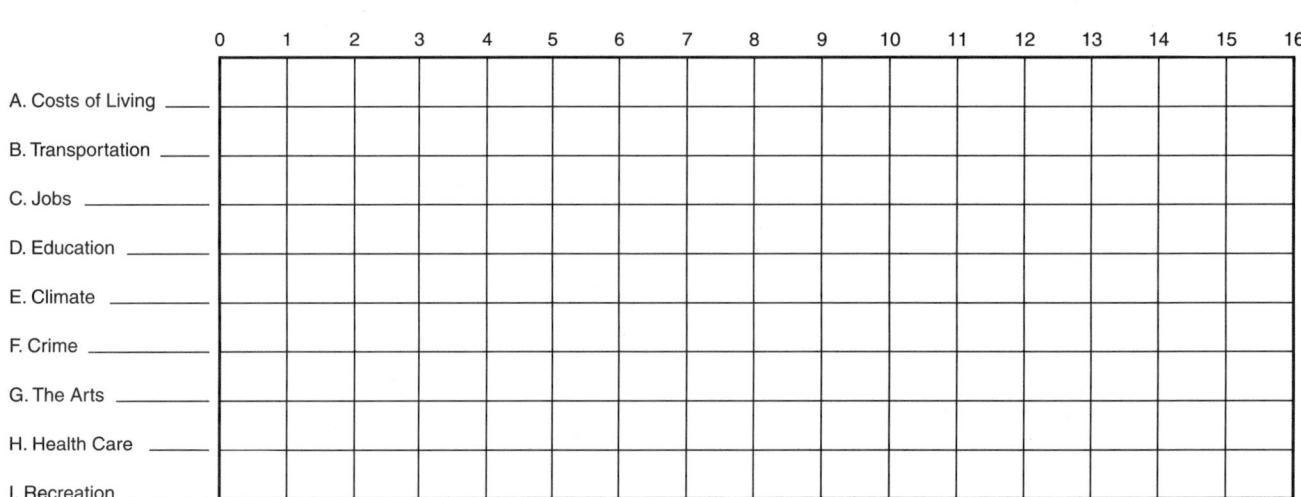

	0	1	2	3	4	5	6	7	8	9	10	11	12	13	14	15	16
A. Costs of Living _____																	
B. Transportation _____																	
C. Jobs _____																	
D. Education _____																	
E. Climate _____																	
F. Crime _____																	
G. The Arts _____																	
H. Health Care _____																	
I. Recreation _____																	

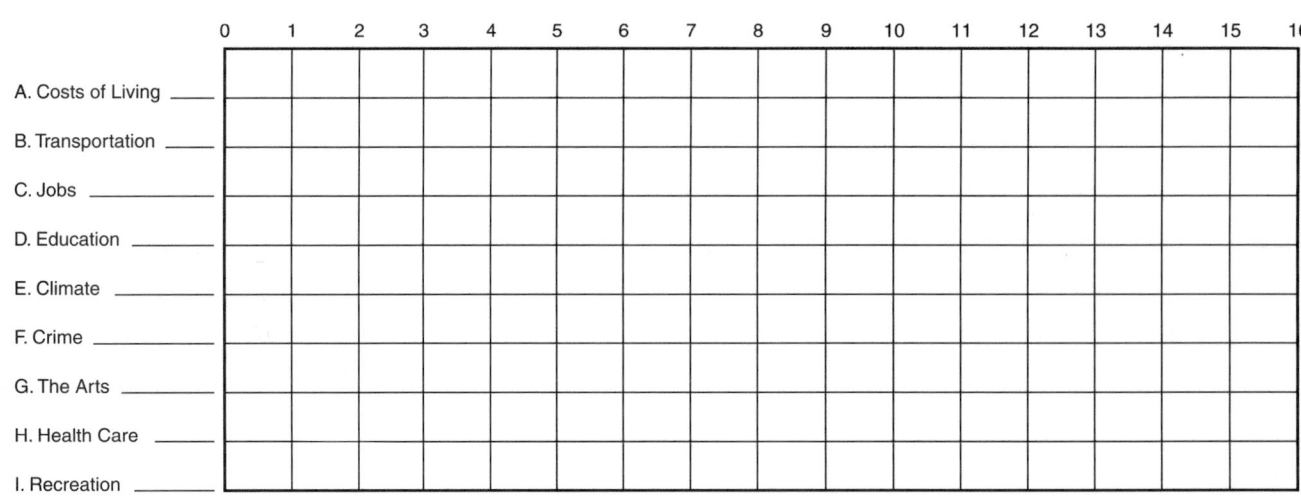

	0	1	2	3	4	5	6	7	8	9	10	11	12	13	14	15	16
A. Costs of Living _____																	
B. Transportation _____																	
C. Jobs _____																	
D. Education _____																	
E. Climate _____																	
F. Crime _____																	
G. The Arts _____																	
H. Health Care _____																	
I. Recreation _____																	

Costs of Living

In the dry viewpoint of economists, we're all living and breathing capital looking for our highest valued use. We readily switch jobs if the money is right. If the prospects are promising, we'll even change careers. And we'll risk these changes even if it means packing up and moving far away.

We also flee living costs that have gotten so high we can't afford them. Metro areas attract people because of expanding job opportunities, sure. But people also vote with their feet by heading for metro areas where cost-of-living factors like income taxes and house prices look like bargains.

This is nothing new. For centuries, Americans have moved from rich places where the benefits of good incomes are made empty by high costs of living to places where cheap land and no taxes more than make up for the drawback of paltry incomes.

"Money's no problem," an accountant will tell you. "Lack of money . . . now *that's* a problem." As is the case for most people, your own short-term economic worries may come down to the price of hamburger, jeans, gasoline, or haircuts. Over the long run, your concerns may focus on tax bites and boosting your household's income at least to the level where it can provide basic day-to-day necessities.

PULLING DOWN $75,000 A YEAR . . .

Do average household incomes in different parts of the continent indicate local living costs? For the most part, they do. According to economists at the Labor Department, two-thirds of the variation in personal incomes between Cincinnati and San Francisco, for example, reflect their different costs of living. The other third reflects their different employers, worker skills, and prevailing wages.

Households aren't always families. Three in ten are composed either of one person or of several people unrelated to one another (including millions of POSSLQs—Persons of Opposite Sex Sharing Living Quarters). There are 12 million single-parent households with at least one child present, 2 million of them headed by men. The rest are married couples, some with younger children, some childless, some whose older children have left home, and about 1 million whose older children have moved back in with Mom and Dad.

...And Scraping By on It

METRO AREA HOUSEHOLD INCOMES, 2000

The money coming into households isn't entirely from wages and salaries. It also includes interest from savings, dividends from stock holdings, government transfer payments, rents, and a multitude of other sources. If these typical incomes seem high, bear in mind that typical households now have two or more employed persons in them.

Highest

Long Island, NY	$117,600
Stamford-Norwalk, CT	$114,200
Bergen-Passaic, NJ	$112,200
San Francisco, CA	$111,800
San Jose, CA	$111,500
Newark, NJ	$107,400
Middlesex-Somerset-Hunterdon, NJ	$106,700
Trenton, NJ	$106,500
Naples, FL	$100,000
West Palm Beach-Boca Raton, FL	$100,000
Washington, DC-MD-VA-WV	$97,500
Orange County, CA	$97,300

Lowest

McAllen-Edinburg-Mission, TX	$47,900
Las Cruces, NM	$48,100
Bryan-College Station, TX	$48,500
Yuma, AZ	$48,900
Brownsville-Harlingen-San Benito, TX	$50,000
Hattiesburg, MS	$50,800
Gadsden, AL	$51,400
Cumberland, MD-WV	$52,400
Laredo, TX	$52,500
Anniston, AL	$52,600
Huntington-Ashland, WV-KY-OH	$52,700
El Paso, TX	$52,800

Source: Woods & Poole Economics, Inc., Washington, DC, 1998. This data is estimated. See introduction to the "Place Profiles" in this chapter for more information.

The average household income among 354 metro areas is $75,000 a year, according to estimates by the Washington, DC–based firm of Woods & Poole Economics, Inc., and *Places Rated Almanac*. These incomes range from $117,000 in suburban Long Island, New York, to less than $48,000 in the poorer parts of south Texas and the Rio Grande valley.

. . . AND SCRAPING BY ON IT

"It's a black hole," the *Wall Street Journal* commented on what is meant by costs of living. So what if the Consumer Price Index has gone up tenfold since World War II; what does all that have to do with the high price of getting by in San Francisco as opposed to Peoria?

Several years ago, a special committee appointed by the Department of Labor to look into better ways to measure cost-of-living variations among places threw in the towel. Given the infinite range of consumer tastes and household tactics for saving a dollar, the only way to pin down why life in one place was more expensive than in another was to focus on the weather's effect on clothing costs and household utility bills. Then look at taxes.

Taxes certainly do make a difference. But clothing and home energy bills? Not that much. According to one national retailer, the price difference between cotton and synthetic Sun Belt wardrobes and woolen and down-filled Frost Belt clothing amounts to about 1 percent of a household's budget. As for the comparative costs of keeping warm in Duluth and staying cool in Dallas, often the only difference is the season during which local residents pay the largest portion of their annual bill.

One firm that counsels transferred employees adopts an 80/20 rule. In its experience, 80 percent of the difference in living costs between where you've come from and where you're going comes down to two things: home ownership (mortgage, insurance, utilities, and property taxes) and state and local income and sales taxes. The other 20 percent comes from prices for everything from a splint for a broken thumb to frozen orange juice; laundry detergent; a shampoo, trim, and blow-dry at a salon; and a 3-hour computer course at the local community college.

Based on the latest surveys on how households spend their income, let's look at the biggest items for a two-paycheck couple with two children earning $75,000 U.S. dollars a year. From most to least, they are presented in the following sections.

Home Mortgage and Property Taxes— $12,480

Paying off a mortgage is the biggest single item in the household's budget. Based on average home prices among 354 metro markets, the typical annual payments on a 7 percent, 25-year loan add up to $10,500 and claim 14 percent of the budget. Small wonder most newcomers start out renting. While it contributes nothing to net worth, renting does permit a household to avoid much of the

Places Rated Market Basket

Percentage weight given to different items in a $75,000-a-year, two earner, two children household

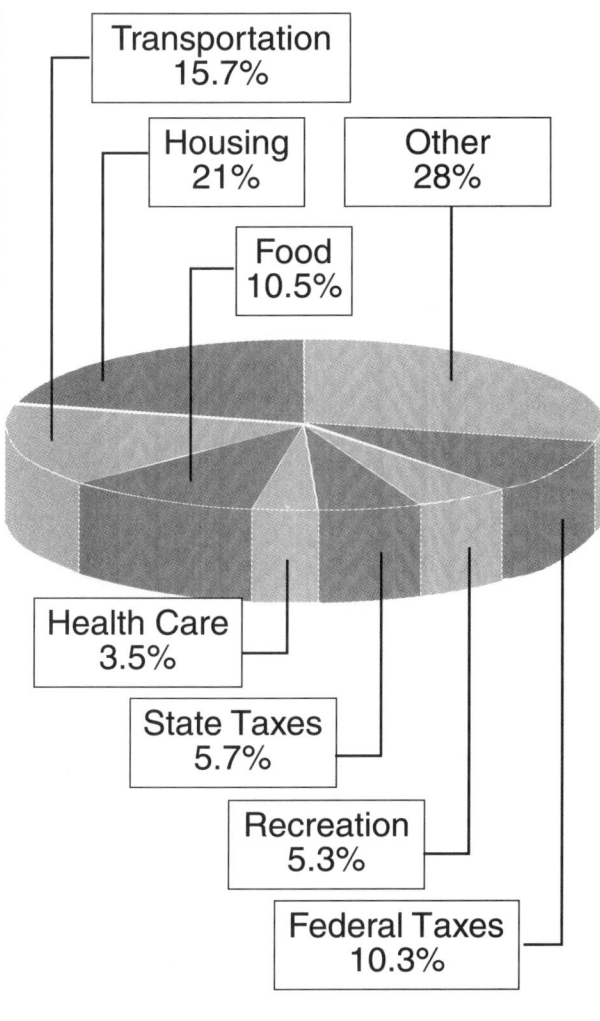

Transportation 15.7%

Housing 21%

Other 28%

Food 10.5%

Health Care 3.5%

State Taxes 5.7%

Recreation 5.3%

Federal Taxes 10.3%

Copyright © 2000 by Places Rated Partnership
Cape Ann Mapping

EXPENSIVE HOUSES

Prices in the northeast and in southern California have generally rebounded from nearly a decade of stagnation.

Metro Area	Average Home Price	Property Taxes
San Francisco, CA	$359,100	$2,770
Honolulu, HI	$322,000	$1,530
Orange County, CA	$296,800	$2,810
Santa Barbara-Santa Maria-Lompoc, CA	$287,200	$2,390
San Jose, CA	$278,400	$2,440
New York, NY	$278,000	$5,560
Stamford-Norwalk, CT	$267,000	$4,990
Santa Cruz-Watsonville, CA	$248,600	$2,170
Boston, MA-NH	$239,900	$4,750
Danbury, CT	$234,100	$4,380
San Diego, CA	$233,900	$2,240
Bergen-Passaic, NJ	$232,700	$4,600

CHEAP HOUSES

It's hard to imagine some areas of the continent experiencing the 30 to 40 percent home price inflation that other markets have seen since the mid-1990s. Here are twelve where typical resale prices look like bargains.

Metro Area	Average Home Price	Property Taxes
Chicoutimi-Jonquiere, PQ	$54,800	$1,140
Trois-Rivieres, PQ	$59,000	$1,270
Regina, SK	$61,700	$1,620
Winnipeg, MB	$62,900	$1,700
Quebec City, PQ	$66,800	$1,360
Saint John, NB	$70,600	$1,110
St. John's, NF	$74,400	$1,280
Waterloo-Cedar Falls, IA	$75,700	$960
Ocala, FL	$76,400	$1,660
Thunder Bay, ON	$77,800	$1,300
Albany, GA	$78,800	$960
Jacksonville, NC	$81,400	$1,420

cost-of-living differences among areas. This style of housing tenure also offers greater flexibility.

Property taxes on the typical home take 2.64 percent, or $1,980, of the household's budget. Critics during the late 1970s likened them to a ransom homeowners paid to keep the house off the tax assessor's auction block. Using this analogy, homeowners in parts of Long Island, NY, buy their homes back every 20 years, since the effective tax rate (a tax on the home's full value) approaches 5 percent. Down in Mobile, AL, on the other hand, the ransom period is 222 years because of an extremely low effective rate of 0.45 percent.

Property taxes can vary enormously and can be madly confusing to home owners. In California, two houses on the same block with identical prices and physical characteristics can have substantially different, yet legally

35

THE INFLATED 1990S

The years from 1990 and 2000 were low-inflation years, but some of the 400 items on the Consumer Price Index (CPI) increased at twice the rate of all the items combined. At the other extreme, a personal computer ended up costing 60 percent less at the end of the decade than it did at the beginning.

CPI Item	% Increase / % Decrease
College tuition and fees	83.7
Hospital services	72.2
Bank services	70.2
Cable TV	69.5
Hotel rooms	68.6
Dental services	59.0
Oranges and tangerines	57.0
Funerals	56.5
Airline tickets	54.9
Prescription medicine	52.3
Medical services	50.2
Legal services	48.0
Auto insurance	47.8
Movie tickets	41.4
Newspapers	40.1
Bus and tram fare	36.3
Wine	31.0
All CPI Items	**30.5**
Haircuts	28.8
Postage	28.1
Eyeglasses	26.6
Liquor	25.6
Dining out	24.8
Beer	22.9
New cars	16.6
Dogs and Cats	16.1
Bicycles	10.3
Men's suits	8.4
Electricity	8.3
Long-distance telephone	7.4
Toys	2.6
Gasoline	2.4
Tires	0.1
Audio equipment	−10.5
Women's dresses	−12.2
Televisions	−22.8
Personal computers	−60.5

Source: Bureau of Labor Statistics, Consumer Price Index, January 1990 through mid-1999.

impeccable, tax bills if one of them was sold before the approval of Proposition 13 and the other after. In Texas, a home's value can be assessed at different levels at different times of the year by different assessors.

Transportation—$11,760

Since the typical household has two cars, transportation is the largest item on the budget—after combined mortgage payments and property tax. This item claims 15.68 percent and covers everything from new-car lease payments to tires and gasoline, from auto body work to the fare you'd pay if you took the bus. Since there is a national market for cars, meaning you can buy one anywhere for a similar price, the cost of purchasing one doesn't vary much by location. What do vary are taxes, insurance, title and registration fees, and gasoline excise taxes.

Food—$7,900

Groceries and dining out claim another 10.53 percent. The cost of going out to a middling restaurant differs widely in North America, hence the need for *per diem* food allowances for business travelers that vary by the destination. Food at home doesn't vary widely except in New York where not a leaf of cabbage reaches the supermarket except by truck, or in Anchorage and Honolulu where a great many packaged goods arrive by container ship. While prices for prepared foods don't vary enough to hit budgets with differing effect, prices for fresh fruits, vegetables, and dairy products do.

State Income and Sales Taxes—$4,205

In a calendar year, mid-May marks the mythical Tax Freedom Day on which we stop handing over all of our earnings to federal, state, and local tax collectors and start pocketing that money for ourselves. Looking at it another way, we spend 2 hours and 47 minutes of every 8-hour working day earning enough money to pay taxes according to the Tax Foundation, the Washington-based lobby that created Tax Freedom Day.

No matter where you live, Social Security taxes hit you with the same impact. So can federal personal income taxes. But state and local taxes vary tremendously. To determine the relative tax bite among metro areas, *Places Rated Almanac* focuses on common levies: state personal income taxes and state and local sales taxes.

Places Rated Almanac estimates state or provincial **income taxes** for the $75,000-a-year couple with two

TAXING THE NECESSITIES

You'll pay sales tax on groceries in . . .

Alabama	Oklahoma
Arkansas	South Carolina
Hawaii	South Dakota
Idaho	Tennessee
Kansas	Utah
Louisiana	Virginia
Mississippi	West Virginia
New Mexico	Wyoming
North Carolina	

And sales taxes on prescriptions in . . .

Illinois	New Mexico

You'll pay no sales tax on clothing in . . .

Connecticut	Nova Scotia
Massachusetts	Pennsylvania
Minnesota	Prince Edward Island
New Brunswick	Rhode Island
New Jersey	Saskatchewan

And no sales tax at all in . . .

Alaska	Montana
Alberta	New Hampshire
Delaware	Oregon

Source: Commerce Clearing House.

children, filing either a joint or a combined separate return (whichever would result in the smaller amount of taxes owed in each state; there are no joint returns in Canada), after taking typical exemptions and deductions. All of their income consists of earnings from employment.

Among 354 metro areas, this tax averages $3,130, or 4.17 percent of a four-person household's budget. Canadian provincial income taxes take the biggest bites in North America. In the United States, income taxes are highest in the District of Columbia, Hawaii, Maryland, New York, Oregon, and Wisconsin. In seven states—Alaska, Florida, Nevada, South Dakota, Texas, Washington, and Wyoming—there is no income tax at all.

What these latter states pass up on April 15, however, they collect with a vengeance every time a purchase is made at the store. Without an income tax, there is an overdependence on *sales taxes*—especially in Florida, Texas, and Washington—to make up the difference. In Seattle, for example, the sales tax rate is 8.2 percent; in Pensacola, it's 7.5 percent. Around the continent, this levy averages a shade less than 1.5 percent of the household's budget. As with income taxes, the sales tax bite is greatest in Canada. When the national 7 percent Goods and Services Tax is tacked on to a province's sales tax, the bite can exceed 15 percent.

Recreation—$3,970

Places Rated Almanac uses the blanket term recreation to cover everything from a health club membership, weekday play at an 18-hole public golf course, overnight camping at a state park, and movie tickets. It claims 5.29 percent of the household's budget.

Utilities—$3,380

Covering everything from water and telephone to piped-in natural gas and electricity, utilities take about 4.5 percent of the $75,000-a-year, four-person household's expenses in metro areas. Utility bills around the continent vary widely for several reasons. Customer density, distance from oil and coal fuel sources, age of the power plant, and the type and size of equipment used in generating electricity all play a part in the charges to consumers.

Health Care—$2,590

At 3.45 percent, health care's importance on a household budget is almost on par with home heating and lighting, water, and telephone. It covers everything from an over-the-counter cold remedy to a semiprivate hospital room. To measure part of the cost in each metro area, *Places Rated Almanac* looks at the amounts five doctors charge their patients for specific services:

- Family practitioner—office outpatient visit

- Internist—routine EKG with interpretation and report

- Psychiatrist—individual psychotherapy, 75–80 minutes

- Surgeon—arthroscopic-aided treatment of tibial fracture

- Ophthalmologist—exam for glaucoma

While Canadian households do not budget for physician treatment or a hospital stay, they do pay for dental care and for some drugs. Indeed, about three out of every ten health-care dollars spent in that country come out of consumers' pockets.

It is impossible to put a dollar figure to every single item in a typical four-person household's budget. *Places Rated* makes a reasonable attempt to price nine major ones that vary the most by location. Together, these account for almost 60 percent of a household budget. Federal income taxes claim another 10.25 percent, on average. The remaining 30 percent covers everything from gifts, personal insurance and pensions, savings and investments, clothing, alcohol and tobacco, and personal care and services.

Let's admit here that pricing living costs for all people or for all the time can't be done with complete accuracy. The number of unique items that fill a market basket trundled by a household over a year is close to one thousand. Some of us trade at Wal-Mart, others at convenience stores, some by mail order and others at Price Club, BJs Wholesale, and Burlington Coat Factory—and increasingly, many of us buy on the Internet.

SCORING: COSTS OF LIVING

For the same money, can you live equally well in Topeka, Toronto, or Tuscaloosa? Do costs of living really vary all that much among North American metro areas, or can skillful budgeting keep your head above water anywhere you choose to live?

To help you answer that question, *Places Rated* prices the following nine items that, aside from federal income taxes, savings, investments, and miscellaneous goods and services, account for most of a typical four-person household's budget: (1) state income taxes, (2) state and local sales taxes, (3) property taxes, (4) home mortgage, (5) utilities, (6) food, (7) health care, (8) transportation, and (9) recreation.

The annual costs for these nine items in each of the 354 metro areas are totaled. Clarksville-Hopkinsville's total, for example, is $32,576; Des Moines's is $40,663; and New York's is $67,745. These totals are ranked from lowest to highest and then scored such that 100 represents the least expensive, 50 indicates the median (the point dividing the rankings into two equal parts), and 0 means the most expensive. In the examples given, Clarksville-Hopkinsville, Des Moines, and New York are respectively the least, the most typical, and the most expensive metro areas in North America.

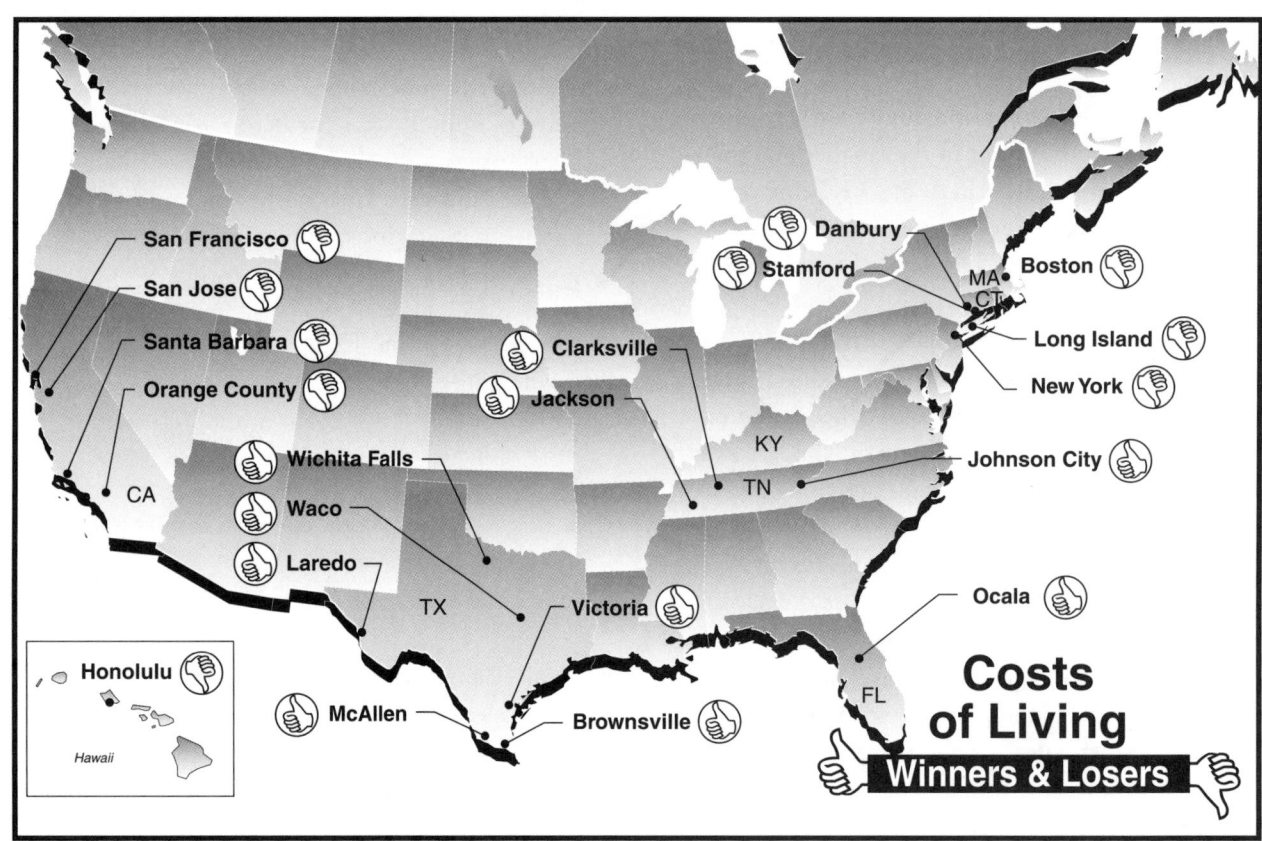

Scoring: Costs of Living

Copyright © 2000 by Places Rated Partnership

RANKINGS: Costs of Living

To rank metro areas for costs of living, the costs of nine items in a typical four-person household's annual expenses—(1) state income taxes, (2) state and local sales taxes, (3) property taxes, (4) home mortgage, (5) utilities, (6) food, (7) health care, (8) transportation, and (9) recreation—are added up. The totals are ranked from least to most and scored. Lower scores indicate more expensive metro areas. Higher scores indicate less expensive metro areas. Places that are tied get the same rank and are listed in alphabetical order.

Metro Areas from Least to Most Expensive

RANK	SCORE
1. Clarksville-Hopkinsville, TN-KY	100.00
2. Laredo, TX	99.72
3. Victoria, TX	99.44
4. Jackson, TN	99.16
5. Wichita Falls, TX	98.87
6. McAllen-Edinburg-Mission, TX	98.59
7. Brownsville-Harlingen-San Benito, TX	98.31
8. Waco, TX	98.02
9. Ocala, FL	97.74
10. Johnson City-Kingsport-Bristol, TN-VA	97.46
11. Sherman-Denison, TX	97.17
12. Amarillo, TX	96.89
13. Killeen-Temple, TX	96.61
14. Abilene, TX	96.32
15. Longview-Marshall, TX	96.04
16. Tyler, TX	95.76
17. El Paso, TX	95.47
18. Odessa-Midland, TX	95.19
19. Chattanooga, TN-GA	94.91
20. Corpus Christi, TX	94.62
21. Texarkana, TX-Texarkana, AR	94.34
22. Daytona Beach, FL	94.06
23. Sioux Falls, SD	93.77
24. Beaumont-Port Arthur, TX	93.49
25. Anniston, AL	93.21
26. San Angelo, TX	92.92
27. Topeka, KS	92.64
28. Alexandria, LA	92.36
29. Shreveport-Bossier City, LA	92.07
30. San Antonio, TX	91.79
31. Bryan-College Station, TX	91.51
32. Gadsden, AL	91.22
33. Decatur, AL	90.94
34. Casper, WY	90.66
35. Enid, OK	90.37
36. Lafayette, LA	90.09
37. Dothan, AL	89.81
38. Waterloo-Cedar Falls, IA	89.52
39. Lawton, OK	89.24
40. Lubbock, TX	88.96
41. Springfield, MO	88.67
42. Brazoria, TX	88.39
43. Knoxville, TN	88.11
44. Joplin, MO	87.82
45. Fargo-Moorhead, ND-MN	87.54
46. Monroe, LA	87.26
47. Fort Myers-Cape Coral, FL	86.97
48. Rapid City, SD	86.69
49. Jackson, MS	86.41
50. Albany, GA	86.12
51. Cheyenne, WY	85.84
52. Evansville-Henderson, IN-KY	85.56
53. South Bend, IN	85.27
54. Houma, LA	84.99
55. Elkhart-Goshen, IN	84.71
56. Florence, AL	84.42
57. Lake Charles, LA	84.14
58. Bismarck, ND	83.86
59. Fort Wayne, IN	83.57
60. Melbourne-Titusville-Palm Bay, FL	83.29
61. Danville, VA	83.01
62. Jacksonville, NC	82.72
63. Oklahoma City, OK	82.44
64. St. Joseph, MO	82.16
65. Hattiesburg, MS	81.87
66. Fort Smith, AR-OK	81.59
67. Parkersburg-Marietta, WV-OH	81.31
68. Pine Bluff, AR	81.02
69. Tulsa, OK	80.74
70. Pensacola, FL	80.46
71. Columbus, GA-AL	80.17
72. Tampa-St. Petersburg-Clearwater, FL	79.89
73. Sumter, SC	79.61
74. Springfield, IL	79.33
75. Owensboro, KY	79.04
76. Florence, SC	78.76
77. Lima, OH	78.48
78. Fayetteville, NC	78.19
79. Augusta-Aiken, GA-SC	77.91
80. Tuscaloosa, AL	77.63
81. Kokomo, IN	77.34
82. Memphis, TN-AR-MS	77.06
83. Hagerstown, MD	76.78
84. Great Falls, MT	76.49
85. Terre Haute, IN	76.21
86. Pueblo, CO	75.93
87. Goldsboro, NC	75.64
88. Lawrence, KS	75.36
89. Lynchburg, VA	75.08
90. Biloxi-Gulfport-Pascagoula, MS	74.79
91. Huntington-Ashland, WV-KY-OH	74.51
92. Fort Worth-Arlington, TX	74.23
93. Galveston-Texas City, TX	73.94
94. Jonesboro, AR	73.66
95. Yakima, WA	73.38

continues

Metro Areas from Least to Most Expensive (cont.)

RANK	SCORE		RANK	SCORE
96. Lakeland-Winter Haven, FL	73.09		156. Rockford, IL	56.10
97. Davenport-Moline-Rock Island, IA-IL	72.81		157. Sioux City, IA-NE	55.81
98. Fayetteville-Springdale-Rogers, AR	72.53		158. Indianapolis, IN	55.53
99. Richland-Kennewick-Pasco, WA	72.24		159. Sharon, PA	55.25
100. Peoria-Pekin, IL	71.96		160. Boise City, ID	54.96
101. Grand Forks, ND-MN	71.68		161. New Orleans, LA	54.68
102. Jacksonville, FL	71.39		162. Appleton-Oshkosh-Neenah, WI	54.40
103. Macon, GA	71.11		163. Asheville, NC	54.11
104. Billings, MT	70.83		164. Janesville-Beloit, WI	53.83
105. Orlando, FL	70.54		165. Tucson, AZ	53.55
106. Youngstown-Warren, OH	70.26		166. Fort Walton Beach, FL	53.26
107. Fort Pierce-Port St. Lucie, FL	69.98		167. Wausau, WI	52.98
108. Decatur, IL	69.69		168. Grand Rapids-Muskegon-Holland, MI	52.70
109. Lafayette, IN	69.41		169. Cedar Rapids, IA	52.41
110. Las Cruces, NM	69.13		170. Scranton–Wilkes-Barre–Hazleton, PA	52.13
111. Steubenville-Weirton, OH-WV	68.84		171. Missoula, MT	51.85
112. Columbia, MO	68.56		172. Omaha, NE-IA	51.56
113. Baton Rouge, LA	68.28		173. Birmingham, AL	51.28
114. Gainesville, FL	67.99		174. Louisville, KY-IN	51.00
115. Huntsville, AL	67.71		175. St. Louis, MO-IL	50.71
116. Wheeling, WV-OH	67.43		176. Austin-San Marcos, TX	50.43
117. Nashville, TN	67.14		177. Des Moines, IA	50.15
118. Wichita, KS	66.86		178. La Crosse, WI-MN	49.86
119. Saginaw-Bay City-Midland, MI	66.58		179. Sheboygan, WI	49.58
120. Champaign-Urbana, IL	66.29		180. Dallas, TX	49.30
121. Spokane, WA	66.01		181. Portland, ME	49.01
122. Rocky Mount, NC	65.73		182. Harrisburg-Lebanon-Carlisle, PA	48.73
123. Panama City, FL	65.44		183. Dayton-Springfield, OH	48.45
124. Pocatello, ID	65.16		184. Provo-Orem, UT	48.16
125. Mobile, AL	64.88		185. Regina, SK	47.88
126. Charleston, WV	64.59		186. Charleston-North Charleston, SC	47.60
127. Lincoln, NE	64.31		187. Akron, OH	47.31
128. Columbia, SC	64.03		188. Kansas City, MO-KS	47.03
129. Bloomington, IN	63.74		189. Redding, CA	46.75
130. Dubuque, IA	63.46		190. Toledo, OH	46.46
131. Little Rock-North Little Rock, AR	63.18		191. Gary, IN	46.18
132. Muncie, IN	62.89		192. Lansing-East Lansing, MI	45.90
133. Tallahassee, FL	62.61		193. Benton Harbor, MI	45.61
134. Roanoke, VA	62.33		194. Duluth-Superior, MN-WI	45.33
135. Athens, GA	62.04		195. Kankakee, IL	45.05
136. Altoona, PA	61.76		196. Norfolk-Virginia Beach-Newport News, VA	44.76
137. Williamsport, PA	61.48		197. Albuquerque, NM	44.48
138. Punta Gorda, FL	61.19		198. Eau Claire, WI	44.20
139. Sarasota-Bradenton, FL	60.91		199. Iowa City, IA	43.91
140. Hickory-Morganton-Lenoir, NC	60.63		200. Edmonton, AB	43.63
141. Montgomery, AL	60.34		201. Yuma, AZ	43.35
142. Cumberland, MD-WV	60.06		202. Winnipeg, MB	43.06
143. Mansfield, OH	59.78		203. Medford-Ashland, OR	42.78
144. Houston, TX	59.50		204. Myrtle Beach, SC	42.50
145. Lexington, KY	59.21		205. Eugene-Springfield, OR	42.21
146. Greenville, NC	58.93		206. Grand Junction, CO	41.93
147. Canton-Massillon, OH	58.65		207. Colorado Springs, CO	41.65
148. Greeley, CO	58.36		208. Buffalo-Niagara Falls, NY	41.36
149. Greenville-Spartanburg-Anderson, SC	58.08		209. Kenosha, WI	41.08
150. Bloomington-Normal, IL	57.80		210. St. Cloud, MN	40.80
151. Savannah, GA	57.51		211. Wilmington, NC	40.51
152. Jackson, MI	57.23		212. Fresno, CA	40.23
153. Johnstown, PA	56.95		213. Green Bay, WI	39.95
154. Erie, PA	56.66		214. West Palm Beach-Boca Raton, FL	39.67
155. Kalamazoo-Battle Creek, MI	56.38		215. Atlanta, GA	39.38

RANK	SCORE	RANK	SCORE
216. Hamilton-Middletown, OH	39.10	276. Denver, CO	22.10
217. Pittsburgh, PA	38.82	277. Windsor, ON	21.82
218. Las Vegas, NV-AZ	38.53	278. Minneapolis-St. Paul, MN-WI	21.53
219. Jamestown, NY	38.25	279. Cleveland-Lorain-Elyria, OH	21.25
220. Syracuse, NY	37.97	280. New Bedford, MA	20.97
221. Phoenix-Mesa, AZ	37.68	281. Naples, FL	20.68
222. Bremerton, WA	37.40	282. Charlottesville, VA	20.40
223. Visalia-Tulare-Porterville, CA	37.12	283. Burlington, VT	20.12
224. Lancaster, PA	36.83	284. London, ON	19.84
225. Chico-Paradise, CA	36.55	285. Sherbrooke, PQ	19.55
226. Olympia, WA	36.27	286. Waterbury, CT	19.27
227. Salem, OR	35.98	287. Vineland-Millville-Bridgeton, NJ	18.99
228. Rochester, MN	35.70	288. Providence-Fall River-Warwick, RI-MA	18.70
229. Saint John, NB	35.42	289. St. Catharines-Niagara, ON	18.42
230. Miami, FL	35.13	290. Madison, WI	18.14
231. Cincinnati, OH-KY-IN	34.85	291. Oshawa, ON	17.85
232. Bangor, ME	34.57	292. Halifax, NS	17.57
233. Tacoma, WA	34.28	293. Kitchener, ON	17.29
234. Springfield, MA	34.00	294. Utica-Rome, NY	17.00
235. Allentown-Bethlehem-Easton, PA	33.72	295. Milwaukee-Waukesha, WI	16.72
236. Fort Lauderdale, FL	33.43	296. Hamilton, ON	16.44
237. Yuba City, CA	33.15	297. Quebec City, PQ	16.15
238. Dover, DE	32.87	298. Anchorage, AK	15.87
239. Greensboro–Winston-Salem–High Point, NC	32.58	299. Portsmouth-Rochester, NH-ME	15.59
240. Fort Collins-Loveland, CO	32.30	300. Worcester, MA-CT	15.30
241. Richmond-Petersburg, VA	32.02	301. Boulder-Longmont, CO	15.02
242. Merced, CA	31.73	302. Detroit, MI	14.74
243. Elmira, NY	31.45	303. Lowell, MA-NH	14.45
244. York, PA	31.17	304. Fitchburg-Leominster, MA	14.17
245. Thunder Bay, ON	30.88	305. Bridgeport, CT	13.89
246. State College, PA	30.60	306. New Haven-Meriden, CT	13.60
247. Salt Lake City-Ogden, UT	30.32	307. Raleigh-Durham-Chapel Hill, NC	13.32
248. Atlantic City-Cape May, NJ	30.03	308. Nashua, NH	13.04
249. Flagstaff, AZ-UT	29.75	309. St. John's, NF	12.75
250. Modesto, CA	29.47	310. Ottawa-Hull, ON-PQ	12.47
251. Wilmington-Newark, DE-MD	29.18	311. Brockton, MA	12.19
252. Binghamton, NY	28.90	312. Hartford, CT	11.90
253. Columbus, OH	28.62	313. Monmouth-Ocean, NJ	11.62
254. Reno, NV	28.33	314. Lawrence, MA-NH	11.34
255. Rochester, NY	28.05	315. Montreal, PQ	11.05
256. Bellingham, WA	27.77	316. Portland-Vancouver, OR-WA	10.77
257. Reading, PA	27.48	317. Yolo, CA	10.49
258. Charlotte-Gastonia-Rock Hill, NC-SC	27.20	318. Philadelphia, PA-NJ	10.20
259. Trois-Rivieres, PQ	26.92	319. Santa Fe, NM	9.92
260. Lewiston-Auburn, ME	26.63	320. Trenton, NJ	9.64
261. Saskatoon, SK	26.35	321. Chicago, IL	9.35
262. Calgary, AB	26.07	322. Salinas, CA	9.07
263. Sudbury, ON	25.78	323. New London-Norwich, CT-RI	8.79
264. Sacramento, CA	25.50	324. Seattle-Bellevue-Everett, WA	8.50
265. Albany-Schenectady-Troy, NY	25.22	325. Ventura, CA	8.22
266. Flint, MI	24.93	326. Vallejo-Fairfield-Napa, CA	7.94
267. Bakersfield, CA	24.65	327. Victoria, BC	7.65
268. Racine, WI	24.37	328. Ann Arbor, MI	7.37
269. Chicoutimi-Jonquiere, PQ	24.08	329. San Luis Obispo-Atascadero-Paso Robles, CA	7.09
270. Stockton-Lodi, CA	23.80	330. Newburgh, NY-PA	6.80
271. Riverside-San Bernardino, CA	23.52	331. Santa Rosa, CA	6.52
272. Manchester, NH	23.23	332. Barnstable-Yarmouth, MA	6.24
273. Glens Falls, NY	22.95	333. Toronto, ON	5.95
274. Pittsfield, MA	22.67	334. Los Angeles-Long Beach, CA	5.67
275. Baltimore, MD	22.38		

Costs of Living

continues

RANK	SCORE		RANK	SCORE
335. Jersey City, NJ	5.39		345. Bergen-Passaic, NJ	2.55
336. Middlesex-Somerset-Hunterdon, NJ	5.10		346. Long Island, NY	2.27
337. Vancouver, BC	4.82		347. Santa Barbara-Santa Maria-Lompoc, CA	1.99
338. Washington, DC-MD-VA-WV	4.54		348. San Jose, CA	1.70
339. Dutchess County, NY	4.25		349. Stamford-Norwalk, CT	1.42
340. Newark, NJ	3.97		350. Boston, MA-NH	1.14
341. Oakland, CA	3.69		351. Orange County, CA	0.85
342. Santa Cruz-Watsonville, CA	3.40		352. Honolulu, HI	0.57
343. San Diego, CA	3.12		353. San Francisco, CA	0.29
344. Danbury, CT	2.84		354. New York, NY	0.00

PLACE PROFILES: COSTS OF LIVING

The following profiles detail cost-of-living factors used to rank the metro areas.

Typical Household Income is a figure that ranges from over $117,000 on Long Island, NY, to less than $48,000 in southernmost Texas. Canadian figures are derived from Statistics Canada data on per capita income multiplied by each metro area's average household size. American figures are estimates from Woods & Poole Economics, Inc., of Washington, DC, based on historical data, 1969–96, from the U.S. Dept. of Commerce. Typical household income is total personal income less estimated group quarters personal income divided by the number of households. Projections are uncertain and future data may differ substantially from Woods & Poole projections. *Note:* Woods & Poole does not guarantee the accuracy of these data and projections. The use of these data and projections, and the conclusions drawn therefrom, are solely the responsibility of the author.

State and Local Taxes detail the estimated income and sales taxes for a $75,000 a year, two-paycheck couple with two children.

Housing Costs give typical home prices, utilities costs, and property taxes. Monthly rent on a one-bedroom apartment is also given.

Other Costs show annual expenses for food, health care, transportation, and recreation for our $75,000 a year, two-paycheck, two-child household.

Figures to the right of dollar amounts are indexes against the North American average of 100. An index of 95 for health care, for example, means that the dollar amount is 5 percent less than the metro area average. An index of 110 for transportation, for another example, means the dollar amount is 10 percent greater than the metro area average.

Finally, the **Combined Cost Index** indicates how much higher or lower the total for all nine items is versus the North American average: $41,568. A combined cost index of 98, for example, means 2 percent less expensive than the metro area average, while an index of 120 means 20 percent more expensive. See the box, "Priced to Move: Using *Places Rated*'s Cost Indexes," on page 43.

The data comes mainly from Places Rated Partnership tax and consumer price surveys through the spring of 1999. In addition, a number of sources were used: American Association of Realtors, *Existing Home Sales* (median home sales prices), 1st quarter, 1999; American Automobile Association, *Digest of Motor* Laws (state motor vehicle license, registration fees, and gasoline excise taxes), 1999; American Gas Association, *Gas Facts* (natural gas heating bills) 1999; Canadian Real Estate Association, *MLS Resale Data* (home sales prices) spring 1999; Commerce Clearing House, *Canadian Master Tax Guide* and *State Tax Guide* (state and provincial income and sales taxes) 1999; Fodor's Travel Publications, *Mobil Travel Guides* (state park fees), 1999; National Golf Foundation, unpublished public golf course fees, 1999; Statistics Canada, *Consumer Prices and Price Indexes* and *Inter-City Indexes of Retail Price Differentials,* June 1999; U.S. Department of Defense, Office of Civilian Health and Medical Program of the Uniformed Services, *CMAC Pricing File* (health care costs), 1999; U.S. Department of Energy, *Electric Sales and Revenue* (electricity costs) 1999; U.S. Department of Labor, Bureau of Labor Statistics, *Consumer Expenditure Survey* and *CPI Detailed Report* and *Relative Importance of Components in the Consumer Price Index* (budget expense weights), 1999; U.S. General Services Administration, *Federal Travel Directory* (local *per diems* for food away from

PRICED TO MOVE: USING *PLACES RATED*'S COST INDEXES

The "Combined Costs" figure at the end of each metro area's profile is an index against a supposed North American average of 100. It is a useful starting point for figuring cost differences between any two metro areas.

From Lower to Higher. Suppose you are thinking of a job offer in a distant metro area with a higher costs-of-living index than the one where you live now. In the jargon of corporate recruiters, how much more income will you need in the new location to "stay whole"? In other words, how much of an income boost will you need to hang on to your current lifestyle?

A preliminary answer involves three steps: (1) determine the difference in *Places Rated* indexes between your present location and the alternate, (2) divide that amount by your present location's index, (3) then multiply by 100. The answer is the approximate percent increase in income you'll need.

For example, the difference between Miami's combined costs index of 112 and Ann Arbor's combined costs of 132 is 20. When that difference is divided by Miami's index and multiplied by 100, the result is 17.85. Moving from Miami to Ann Arbor, therefore, would require about an 18% increase in compensation.

From Higher to Lower. The same formula applies if your move is in the opposite direction. How much of a cut in after-tax income can you handle without crimping your lifestyle?

The difference between Miami's index of 112 and Ann Arbor's index of 132 is 20. When that figure is divided by Ann Arbor's figure and multiplied by 100, the result is 15.15. You can "stay whole" relocating to Miami from Ann Arbor as long as you're not facing a greater than 15 percent pay cut.

Several Cautions. (1) A big part of *Places Rated*'s combined cost indexes means you're paying off a mortgage on a typically priced home. If you rent, cost differences between any two metro areas shrink dramatically. (2) *Places Rated*'s combined cost index doesn't account for savings, investments, personal care, and education. (3) Budgeting with a sharp pencil permits many a moderate income to live anywhere. Often the costs-of-living differences between two areas come down to the individual household's shopping skills. (4) Finally, be aware that prices are the most rapidly changing of criteria in *Places Rated Almanac*.

home), May 1999; and Woods & Poole Economics, Inc., (U.S. metro area household income estimates), 1999.

A star (★) preceding a metro area's name highlights it as one of the lowest thirty-five places for costs of living.

★Abilene, TX
Typical Household Income: $60,500

State and Local Taxes		
Income	$0	0
Sales	$1,214	113
Housing Costs		
Price	$82,900	67
Utilities	$2,420	80
Property Taxes	$1,440	81
Rent	$490	86
Other Costs		
Food	$7,269	92
Health Care	$2,453	99
Transportation	$12,352	105
Recreation	$3,225	81

Combined Costs: 90
Score: 96.32   Rank: 14

Akron, OH
Typical Household Income: $74,100

State and Local Taxes		
Income	$2,648	85
Sales	$1,030	96
Housing Costs		
Price	$114,900	93
Utilities	$3,600	119
Property Taxes	$1,760	99
Rent	$560	98
Other Costs		
Food	$7,664	97
Health Care	$3,123	125
Transportation	$11,529	98
Recreation	$3,384	85

Combined Costs: 108
Score: 47.31   Rank: 187

Albany, GA
Typical Household Income: $60,900

State and Local Taxes		
Income	$3,100	99
Sales	$1,030	96
Housing Costs		
Price	$78,800	64
Utilities	$2,830	93
Property Taxes	$960	54
Rent	$440	77
Other Costs		
Food	$7,506	95
Health Care	$2,529	102
Transportation	$11,764	100
Recreation	$4,216	106

Combined Costs: 96
Score: 86.12   Rank: 50

Albany-Schenectady-Troy, NY
Typical Household Income: $71,500

State and Local Taxes		
Income	$4,088	131
Sales	$1,250	116
Housing Costs		
Price	$119,600	97
Utilities	$3,190	105
Property Taxes	$2,230	125
Rent	$610	107
Other Costs		
Food	$8,217	104
Health Care	$2,242	90

Transportation	$12,587	107
Recreation	$3,618	91

Combined Costs: 116
Score: 25.22　　　　**Rank: 265**

Albuquerque, NM
Typical Household Income: $66,800

State and Local Taxes		
Income	$2,439	78
Sales	$1,011	94
Housing Costs		
Price	$140,700	114
Utilities	$3,340	110
Property Taxes	$1,130	63
Rent	$590	104
Other Costs		
Food	$7,743	98
Health Care	$2,246	90
Transportation	$11,529	98
Recreation	$3,571	90

Combined Costs: 109
Score: 44.48　　　　**Rank: 197**

★Alexandria, LA
Typical Household Income: $60,800

State and Local Taxes		
Income	$1,625	52
Sales	$1,228	114
Housing Costs		
Price	$93,300	75
Utilities	$2,330	77
Property Taxes	$490	27
Rent	$450	79
Other Costs		
Food	$7,585	96
Health Care	$2,658	107
Transportation	$11,646	99
Recreation	$2,457	62

Combined Costs: 93
Score: 92.36　　　　**Rank: 28**

Allentown-Bethlehem-Easton, PA
Typical Household Income: $72,800

State and Local Taxes		
Income	$2,100	67
Sales	$883	82
Housing Costs		
Price	$127,000	103
Utilities	$3,460	114
Property Taxes	$2,220	124
Rent	$680	119
Other Costs		
Food	$8,454	107
Health Care	$2,969	119
Transportation	$11,882	101
Recreation	$3,786	95

Combined Costs: 112
Score: 33.72　　　　**Rank: 235**

Altoona, PA
Typical Household Income: $58,200

State and Local Taxes		
Income	$2,100	67
Sales	$883	82

Housing Costs		
Price	$97,900	79
Utilities	$3,400	112
Property Taxes	$2,050	115
Rent	$440	77
Other Costs		
Food	$7,901	100
Health Care	$2,697	108
Transportation	$11,646	99
Recreation	$3,113	78

Combined Costs: 103
Score: 61.76　　　　**Rank: 136**

★Amarillo, TX
Typical Household Income: $61,400

State and Local Taxes		
Income	$0	0
Sales	$1,214	113
Housing Costs		
Price	$84,600	68
Utilities	$2,360	78
Property Taxes	$1,350	76
Rent	$450	79
Other Costs		
Food	$7,506	95
Health Care	$2,383	96
Transportation	$12,117	103
Recreation	$3,906	98

Combined Costs: 90
Score: 96.89　　　　**Rank: 12**

Anchorage, AK
Typical Household Income: $86,400

State and Local Taxes		
Income	$0	0
Sales	$0	0
Housing Costs		
Price	$182,700	148
Utilities	$3,250	107
Property Taxes	$2,180	122
Rent	$780	137
Other Costs		
Food	$9,560	121
Health Care	$2,820	113
Transportation	$12,940	110
Recreation	$3,946	99

Combined Costs: 122
Score: 15.87　　　　**Rank: 298**

Ann Arbor, MI
Typical Household Income: $90,900

State and Local Taxes		
Income	$2,977	95
Sales	$883	82
Housing Costs		
Price	$187,400	151
Utilities	$3,540	117
Property Taxes	$3,170	177
Rent	$710	125
Other Costs		
Food	$8,454	107
Health Care	$2,946	118
Transportation	$12,117	103
Recreation	$4,003	101

Combined Costs: 132
Score: 07.37　　　　**Rank: 328**

★Anniston, AL

Typical Household Income: $52,500

State and Local Taxes		
Income	$2,455	79
Sales	$1,228	114
Housing Costs		
Price	$82,100	66
Utilities	$2,600	86
Property Taxes	$650	36
Rent	$390	68
Other Costs		
Food	$7,427	94
Health Care	$2,704	109
Transportation	$11,058	94
Recreation	$3,402	86

Combined Costs: 92
Score: 93.21   Rank: 25

Appleton-Oshkosh-Neenah, WI

Typical Household Income: $73,900

State and Local Taxes		
Income	$3,960	127
Sales	$846	79
Housing Costs		
Price	$102,900	83
Utilities	$3,100	102
Property Taxes	$2,110	118
Rent	$510	89
Other Costs		
Food	$7,585	96
Health Care	$2,157	87
Transportation	$11,646	99
Recreation	$4,020	101

Combined Costs: 106
Score: 54.40   Rank: 162

Asheville, NC

Typical Household Income: $62,500

State and Local Taxes		
Income	$3,638	117
Sales	$921	85
Housing Costs		
Price	$110,300	89
Utilities	$2,950	97
Property Taxes	$1,940	109
Rent	$550	96
Other Costs		
Food	$7,822	99
Health Care	$2,213	89
Transportation	$11,293	96
Recreation	$4,387	111

Combined Costs: 106
Score: 54.11   Rank: 163

Athens, GA

Typical Household Income: $58,800

State and Local Taxes		
Income	$3,100	99
Sales	$1,030	96
Housing Costs		
Price	$107,000	86
Utilities	$2,750	91
Property Taxes	$1,120	63
Rent	$530	93
Other Costs		
Food	$7,980	101
Health Care	$2,569	103

Transportation	$11,293	96
Recreation	$4,413	111

Combined Costs: 102
Score: 62.04   Rank: 135

Atlanta, GA

Typical Household Income: $82,400

State and Local Taxes		
Income	$3,100	99
Sales	$1,030	96
Housing Costs		
Price	$126,900	103
Utilities	$2,890	95
Property Taxes	$1,390	78
Rent	$700	123
Other Costs		
Food	$8,059	102
Health Care	$3,113	125
Transportation	$11,646	99
Recreation	$4,708	119

Combined Costs: 111
Score: 39.38   Rank: 215

Atlantic City-Cape May, NJ

Typical Household Income: $83,800

State and Local Taxes		
Income	$1,759	56
Sales	$883	82
Housing Costs		
Price	$121,400	98
Utilities	$3,750	124
Property Taxes	$2,200	123
Rent	$750	132
Other Costs		
Food	$8,138	103
Health Care	$3,166	127
Transportation	$12,823	109
Recreation	$5,665	143

Combined Costs: 113
Score: 30.03   Rank: 248

Augusta-Aiken, GA-SC

Typical Household Income: $62,000

State and Local Taxes		
Income	$3,100	99
Sales	$1,030	96
Housing Costs		
Price	$94,000	76
Utilities	$2,750	91
Property Taxes	$1,050	59
Rent	$510	89
Other Costs		
Food	$7,585	96
Health Care	$2,556	103
Transportation	$11,529	98
Recreation	$3,636	92

Combined Costs: 99
Score: 77.91   Rank: 79

Austin-San Marcos, TX

Typical Household Income: $67,700

State and Local Taxes		
Income	$0	0
Sales	$1,214	113
Housing Costs		
Price	$149,300	121
Utilities	$2,360	78

Property Taxes	$2,540	142
Rent	$710	125
Other Costs		
Food	$7,506	95
Health Care	$2,362	95
Transportation	$11,999	102
Recreation	$4,110	104

Combined Costs: 107
Score: 50.43   Rank: 176

Bakersfield, CA

Typical Household Income: $61,600

State and Local Taxes		
Income	$2,564	82
Sales	$1,066	99
Housing Costs		
Price	$139,800	113
Utilities	$2,750	91
Property Taxes	$1,740	97
Rent	$520	91
Other Costs		
Food	$8,612	109
Health Care	$3,026	122
Transportation	$12,470	106
Recreation	$3,405	86

Combined Costs: 116
Score: 24.65   Rank: 267

Baltimore, MD

Typical Household Income: $82,500

State and Local Taxes		
Income	$4,186	134
Sales	$735	68
Housing Costs		
Price	$133,900	108
Utilities	$2,830	93
Property Taxes	$1,770	99
Rent	$640	112
Other Costs		
Food	$8,217	104
Health Care	$3,368	135
Transportation	$11,999	102
Recreation	$4,364	110

Combined Costs: 117
Score: 22.38   Rank: 275

Bangor, ME

Typical Household Income: $56,200

State and Local Taxes		
Income	$3,527	113
Sales	$883	82
Housing Costs		
Price	$120,100	97
Utilities	$3,100	102
Property Taxes	$2,660	149
Rent	$550	96
Other Costs		
Food	$8,138	103
Health Care	$2,157	87
Transportation	$11,999	102
Recreation	$3,717	94

Combined Costs: 112
Score: 34.57   Rank: 232

Barnstable-Yarmouth, MA

Typical Household Income: $76,300

State and Local Taxes		
Income	$3,824	123
Sales	$735	68
Housing Costs		
Price	$190,100	154
Utilities	$3,900	129
Property Taxes	$2,630	147
Rent	$840	147
Other Costs		
Food	$8,533	108
Health Care	$2,861	115
Transportation	$12,705	108
Recreation	$4,584	116

Combined Costs: 135
Score: 06.24   Rank: 332

Baton Rouge, LA

Typical Household Income: $67,200

State and Local Taxes		
Income	$1,625	52
Sales	$1,228	114
Housing Costs		
Price	$107,200	87
Utilities	$2,420	80
Property Taxes	$560	31
Rent	$480	84
Other Costs		
Food	$7,980	101
Health Care	$3,336	134
Transportation	$12,117	103
Recreation	$3,300	83

Combined Costs: 101
Score: 68.28   Rank: 113

★Beaumont-Port Arthur, TX

Typical Household Income: $61,200

State and Local Taxes		
Income	$0	0
Sales	$1,214	113
Housing Costs		
Price	$83,000	67
Utilities	$2,570	85
Property Taxes	$1,300	73
Rent	$480	84
Other Costs		
Food	$7,348	93
Health Care	$3,497	141
Transportation	$12,117	103
Recreation	$3,278	83

Combined Costs: 92
Score: 93.49   Rank: 24

Bellingham, WA

Typical Household Income: $63,100

State and Local Taxes		
Income	$0	0
Sales	$2,162	201
Housing Costs		
Price	$172,600	139
Utilities	$2,480	82
Property Taxes	$2,220	124
Rent	$690	121
Other Costs		
Food	$8,217	104
Health Care	$2,157	87

Transportation	$11,646	99
Recreation	$3,951	100

Combined Costs: 115
Score: 27.77   Rank: 256

Benton Harbor, MI

Typical Household Income: $66,500

State and Local Taxes		
Income	$2,977	95
Sales	$883	82
Housing Costs		
Price	$115,600	93
Utilities	$3,400	112
Property Taxes	$1,740	97
Rent	$510	89
Other Costs		
Food	$7,901	100
Health Care	$2,487	100
Transportation	$11,999	102
Recreation	$3,789	95

Combined Costs: 108
Score: 45.61   Rank: 193

Bergen-Passaic, NJ

Typical Household Income: $112,200

State and Local Taxes		
Income	$1,759	56
Sales	$883	82
Housing Costs		
Price	$232,700	188
Utilities	$3,750	124
Property Taxes	$4,600	258
Rent	$890	156
Other Costs		
Food	$8,691	110
Health Care	$2,958	119
Transportation	$13,058	111
Recreation	$5,694	143

Combined Costs: 146
Score: 02.55   Rank: 345

Billings, MT

Typical Household Income: $62,900

State and Local Taxes		
Income	$2,893	93
Sales	$0	0
Housing Costs		
Price	$104,800	85
Utilities	$2,690	89
Property Taxes	$1,270	71
Rent	$510	89
Other Costs		
Food	$8,217	104
Health Care	$2,157	87
Transportation	$12,117	103
Recreation	$2,982	75

Combined Costs: 101
Score: 70.83   Rank: 104

Biloxi-Gulfport-Pascagoula, MS

Typical Household Income: $56,600

State and Local Taxes		
Income	$2,225	71
Sales	$1,119	104
Housing Costs		
Price	$98,400	79
Utilities	$2,300	76

Property Taxes	$1,450	81
Rent	$490	86
Other Costs		
Food	$7,980	101
Health Care	$3,394	136
Transportation	$11,176	95
Recreation	$5,011	126

Combined Costs: 100
Score: 74.79   Rank: 90

Binghamton, NY

Typical Household Income: $62,900

State and Local Taxes		
Income	$4,088	131
Sales	$1,250	116
Housing Costs		
Price	$115,600	93
Utilities	$3,490	115
Property Taxes	$2,270	127
Rent	$510	89
Other Costs		
Food	$8,217	104
Health Care	$2,157	87
Transportation	$12,117	103
Recreation	$3,450	87

Combined Costs: 114
Score: 28.90   Rank: 252

Birmingham, AL

Typical Household Income: $71,200

State and Local Taxes		
Income	$2,455	79
Sales	$1,081	100
Housing Costs		
Price	$130,900	106
Utilities	$2,570	85
Property Taxes	$860	48
Rent	$490	86
Other Costs		
Food	$7,585	96
Health Care	$3,163	127
Transportation	$11,646	99
Recreation	$4,000	101

Combined Costs: 106
Score: 51.28   Rank: 173

Bismarck, ND

Typical Household Income: $62,800

State and Local Taxes		
Income	$1,218	39
Sales	$1,030	96
Housing Costs		
Price	$92,800	75
Utilities	$3,190	105
Property Taxes	$1,210	68
Rent	$510	89
Other Costs		
Food	$8,217	104
Health Care	$2,193	88
Transportation	$11,764	100
Recreation	$3,934	99

Combined Costs: 97
Score: 83.86   Rank: 58

Bloomington, IN
Typical Household Income: $54,000

State and Local Taxes		
Income	$2,414	77
Sales	$735	68
Housing Costs		
Price	$109,300	88
Utilities	$3,340	110
Property Taxes	$1,210	68
Rent	$640	112
Other Costs		
Food	$7,980	101
Health Care	$2,221	89
Transportation	$11,529	98
Recreation	$3,826	96

Combined Costs: 102
Score: 63.74   **Rank: 129**

Bloomington-Normal, IL
Typical Household Income: $74,100

State and Local Taxes		
Income	$2,130	68
Sales	$1,079	100
Housing Costs		
Price	$107,100	87
Utilities	$4,020	133
Property Taxes	$1,490	83
Rent	$560	98
Other Costs		
Food	$7,980	101
Health Care	$2,157	87
Transportation	$11,529	98
Recreation	$3,087	78

Combined Costs: 104
Score: 57.80   **Rank: 150**

Boise City, ID
Typical Household Income: $73,600

State and Local Taxes		
Income	$3,805	122
Sales	$799	74
Housing Costs		
Price	$118,100	95
Utilities	$2,270	75
Property Taxes	$1,370	77
Rent	$550	96
Other Costs		
Food	$7,822	99
Health Care	$2,157	87
Transportation	$11,529	98
Recreation	$3,872	98

Combined Costs: 105
Score: 54.96   **Rank: 160**

Boston, MA-NH
Typical Household Income: $94,700

State and Local Taxes		
Income	$3,824	123
Sales	$735	68
Housing Costs		
Price	$239,900	194
Utilities	$4,020	133
Property Taxes	$4,750	266
Rent	$920	161
Other Costs		
Food	$9,086	115
Health Care	$3,358	135

| Transportation | $13,176 | 112 |
| Recreation | $4,032 | 102 |

Combined Costs: 156
Score: 01.14   **Rank: 350**

Boulder-Longmont, CO
Typical Household Income: $83,800

State and Local Taxes		
Income	$2,660	85
Sales	$921	85
Housing Costs		
Price	$187,700	152
Utilities	$2,780	92
Property Taxes	$1,320	74
Rent	$780	137
Other Costs		
Food	$8,375	106
Health Care	$2,533	102
Transportation	$12,117	103
Recreation	$3,648	92

Combined Costs: 123
Score: 15.02   **Rank: 301**

Brazoria, TX
Typical Household Income: $66,600

State and Local Taxes		
Income	$0	0
Sales	$1,214	113
Housing Costs		
Price	$91,800	74
Utilities	$2,540	84
Property Taxes	$1,510	85
Rent	$630	111
Other Costs		
Food	$7,664	97
Health Care	$3,069	123
Transportation	$12,235	104
Recreation	$4,066	102

Combined Costs: 95
Score: 88.39   **Rank: 42**

Bremerton, WA
Typical Household Income: $65,000

State and Local Taxes		
Income	$0	0
Sales	$2,162	201
Housing Costs		
Price	$158,100	128
Utilities	$2,420	80
Property Taxes	$1,960	110
Rent	$630	111
Other Costs		
Food	$8,296	105
Health Care	$2,264	91
Transportation	$11,764	100
Recreation	$3,686	93

Combined Costs: 111
Score: 37.40   **Rank: 222**

Bridgeport, CT
Typical Household Income: $127,700

State and Local Taxes		
Income	$3,036	97
Sales	$883	82
Housing Costs		
Price	$155,200	125
Utilities	$3,840	127

Property Taxes	$2,800	157
Rent	$710	125
Other Costs		
Food	$8,296	105
Health Care	$2,935	118
Transportation	$12,117	103
Recreation	$5,952	150

Combined Costs: 124
Score: 13.89   Rank: 305

Brockton, MA

Typical Household Income: $81,900

State and Local Taxes		
Income	$3,824	123
Sales	$735	68
Housing Costs		
Price	$144,200	116
Utilities	$4,020	133
Property Taxes	$2,130	119
Rent	$710	125
Other Costs		
Food	$8,691	110
Health Care	$3,064	123
Transportation	$12,823	109
Recreation	$3,954	100

Combined Costs: 125
Score: 12.19   Rank: 311

★Brownsville-Harlingen-San Benito, TX

Typical Household Income: $50,000

State and Local Taxes		
Income	$0	0
Sales	$1,214	113
Housing Costs		
Price	$82,500	67
Utilities	$2,300	76
Property Taxes	$1,420	80
Rent	$540	95
Other Costs		
Food	$7,111	90
Health Care	$2,321	93
Transportation	$11,999	102
Recreation	$3,720	94

Combined Costs: 88
Score: 98.31   Rank: 7

★Bryan-College Station, TX

Typical Household Income: $48,400

State and Local Taxes		
Income	$0	0
Sales	$1,214	113
Housing Costs		
Price	$103,400	84
Utilities	$2,690	89
Property Taxes	$1,760	99
Rent	$560	98
Other Costs		
Food	$7,269	92
Health Care	$2,242	90
Transportation	$11,646	99
Recreation	$3,126	79

Combined Costs: 94
Score: 91.51   Rank: 31

Buffalo-Niagara Falls, NY

Typical Household Income: $68,500

State and Local Taxes		
Income	$4,088	131
Sales	$1,250	116
Housing Costs		
Price	$90,400	73
Utilities	$3,190	105
Property Taxes	$2,040	114
Rent	$520	91
Other Costs		
Food	$8,612	109
Health Care	$2,368	95
Transportation	$12,587	107
Recreation	$3,126	79

Combined Costs: 110
Score: 41.36   Rank: 208

Burlington, VT

Typical Household Income: $72,800

State and Local Taxes		
Income	$2,176	70
Sales	$735	68
Housing Costs		
Price	$163,400	132
Utilities	$3,460	114
Property Taxes	$2,210	124
Rent	$700	123
Other Costs		
Food	$8,454	107
Health Care	$2,252	90
Transportation	$11,764	100
Recreation	$3,851	97

Combined Costs: 118
Score: 20.12   Rank: 283

Calgary, AB

Typical Household Income: $69,600

State and Local Taxes		
Income	$4,852	156
Sales	$1,030	96
Housing Costs		
Price	$121,600	98
Utilities	$2,830	93
Property Taxes	$1,490	83
Rent	$710	125
Other Costs		
Food	$8,849	112
Health Care	$1,130	45
Transportation	$13,293	113
Recreation	$3,717	94

Combined Costs: 115
Score: 26.07   Rank: 262

Canton-Massillon, OH

Typical Household Income: $66,800

State and Local Taxes		
Income	$2,648	85
Sales	$1,030	96
Housing Costs		
Price	$107,700	87
Utilities	$3,340	110
Property Taxes	$1,730	97
Rent	$480	84
Other Costs		
Food	$7,664	97
Health Care	$2,321	93

| Transportation | $11,529 | 98 |
| Recreation | $3,547 | 89 |

Combined Costs: 104

Score: 58.65   Rank: 147

★Casper, WY

Typical Household Income: $72,700

State and Local Taxes		
Income	$0	0
Sales	$934	87
Housing Costs		
Price	$108,100	87
Utilities	$2,630	87
Property Taxes	$1,160	65
Rent	$480	84
Other Costs		
Food	$8,217	104
Health Care	$2,328	94
Transportation	$11,293	96
Recreation	$2,536	64

Combined Costs: 94

Score: 90.66   Rank: 34

Cedar Rapids, IA

Typical Household Income: $72,100

State and Local Taxes		
Income	$3,221	103
Sales	$959	89
Housing Costs		
Price	$115,000	93
Utilities	$3,630	120
Property Taxes	$1,340	75
Rent	$500	88
Other Costs		
Food	$7,506	95
Health Care	$2,157	87
Transportation	$11,646	99
Recreation	$3,387	85

Combined Costs: 106

Score: 52.41   Rank: 169

Champaign-Urbana, IL

Typical Household Income: $60,900

State and Local Taxes		
Income	$2,130	68
Sales	$1,079	100
Housing Costs		
Price	$99,300	80
Utilities	$3,990	132
Property Taxes	$1,400	78
Rent	$600	105
Other Costs		
Food	$7,901	100
Health Care	$2,157	87
Transportation	$11,411	97
Recreation	$3,176	80

Combined Costs: 101

Score: 66.29   Rank: 120

Charleston-North Charleston, SC

Typical Household Income: $60,400

State and Local Taxes		
Income	$3,254	104
Sales	$946	88
Housing Costs		
Price	$133,500	108
Utilities	$2,450	81

Property Taxes	$1,580	88
Rent	$540	95
Other Costs		
Food	$7,585	96
Health Care	$2,541	102
Transportation	$11,411	97
Recreation	$5,528	139

Combined Costs: 108

Score: 47.60   Rank: 186

Charleston, WV

Typical Household Income: $65,100

State and Local Taxes		
Income	$3,230	104
Sales	$959	89
Housing Costs		
Price	$95,600	77
Utilities	$2,810	93
Property Taxes	$820	46
Rent	$500	88
Other Costs		
Food	$7,901	100
Health Care	$2,654	107
Transportation	$12,117	103
Recreation	$3,480	88

Combined Costs: 102

Score: 64.59   Rank: 126

Charlotte-Gastonia-Rock Hill, NC-SC

Typical Household Income: $74,700

State and Local Taxes		
Income	$3,638	117
Sales	$921	85
Housing Costs		
Price	$148,500	120
Utilities	$2,810	93
Property Taxes	$2,420	135
Rent	$560	98
Other Costs		
Food	$7,743	98
Health Care	$2,288	92
Transportation	$11,176	95
Recreation	$4,189	106

Combined Costs: 115

Score: 27.20   Rank: 258

Charlottesville, VA

Typical Household Income: $76,000

State and Local Taxes		
Income	$2,922	94
Sales	$719	67
Housing Costs		
Price	$157,800	127
Utilities	$3,040	100
Property Taxes	$2,230	125
Rent	$660	116
Other Costs		
Food	$7,980	101
Health Care	$2,397	96
Transportation	$12,235	104
Recreation	$3,323	84

Combined Costs: 118

Score: 20.40   Rank: 282

★Chattanooga, TN-GA

Typical Household Income: $65,400

State and Local Taxes		
Income	$0	0
Sales	$1,364	127
Housing Costs		
Price	$108,100	87
Utilities	$2,300	76
Property Taxes	$760	43
Rent	$520	91
Other Costs		
Food	$7,427	94
Health Care	$2,968	119
Transportation	$10,705	91
Recreation	$3,295	83

Combined Costs: 91
Score: 94.91   Rank: 19

Cheyenne, WY

Typical Household Income: $62,500

State and Local Taxes		
Income	$0	0
Sales	$934	87
Housing Costs		
Price	$108,300	87
Utilities	$2,690	89
Property Taxes	$1,190	67
Rent	$610	107
Other Costs		
Food	$8,138	103
Health Care	$2,276	91
Transportation	$11,999	102
Recreation	$3,355	85

Combined Costs: 96
Score: 85.84   Rank: 51

Chicago, IL

Typical Household Income: $94,200

State and Local Taxes		
Income	$2,130	68
Sales	$1,300	121
Housing Costs		
Price	$183,800	148
Utilities	$3,900	129
Property Taxes	$2,600	146
Rent	$750	132
Other Costs		
Food	$8,059	102
Health Care	$3,199	129
Transportation	$12,117	103
Recreation	$4,319	109

Combined Costs: 129
Score: 09.35   Rank: 321

Chico-Paradise, CA

Typical Household Income: $55,000

State and Local Taxes		
Income	$2,564	82
Sales	$1,066	99
Housing Costs		
Price	$131,200	106
Utilities	$2,980	98
Property Taxes	$1,160	65
Rent	$570	100
Other Costs		
Food	$8,296	105
Health Care	$2,616	105

Transportation	$12,587	107
Recreation	$3,126	79

Combined Costs: 112
Score: 36.55   Rank: 225

Chicoutimi-Jonquiere, PQ

Typical Household Income: $51,200

State and Local Taxes		
Income	$5,942	190
Sales	$2,206	205
Housing Costs		
Price	$54,800	44
Utilities	$3,660	121
Property Taxes	$1,140	64
Rent	$420	74
Other Costs		
Food	$8,849	112
Health Care	$1,198	48
Transportation	$16,470	140
Recreation	$3,402	86

Combined Costs: 116
Score: 24.08   Rank: 269

Cincinnati, OH-KY-IN

Typical Household Income: $76,100

State and Local Taxes		
Income	$2,648	85
Sales	$1,030	96
Housing Costs		
Price	$128,100	103
Utilities	$3,310	109
Property Taxes	$2,050	115
Rent	$540	95
Other Costs		
Food	$8,138	103
Health Care	$2,731	110
Transportation	$11,764	100
Recreation	$3,496	88

Combined Costs: 112
Score: 34.85   Rank: 231

★Clarksville-Hopkinsville, TN-KY

Typical Household Income: $53,200

State and Local Taxes		
Income	$0	0
Sales	$1,364	127
Housing Costs		
Price	$89,600	72
Utilities	$2,210	73
Property Taxes	$600	34
Rent	$450	79
Other Costs		
Food	$7,506	95
Health Care	$2,357	95
Transportation	$10,941	93
Recreation	$3,194	80

Combined Costs: 86
Score: 100   Rank: 1

Cleveland-Lorain-Elyria, OH

Typical Household Income: $79,200

State and Local Taxes		
Income	$2,648	85
Sales	$1,030	96
Housing Costs		
Price	$135,800	110
Utilities	$3,990	132

Property Taxes	$2,150	120
Rent	$600	105
Other Costs		
Food	$8,217	104
Health Care	$3,080	124
Transportation	$11,999	102
Recreation	$3,520	89

Combined Costs: 117
Score: 21.25   Rank: 279

Colorado Springs, CO
Typical Household Income: $66,100

State and Local Taxes		
Income	$2,660	85
Sales	$750	70
Housing Costs		
Price	$153,100	124
Utilities	$2,540	84
Property Taxes	$890	50
Rent	$630	111
Other Costs		
Food	$7,822	99
Health Care	$2,502	101
Transportation	$11,646	99
Recreation	$3,459	87

Combined Costs: 110
Score: 41.65   Rank: 207

Columbia, MO
Typical Household Income: $63,800

State and Local Taxes		
Income	$2,616	84
Sales	$1,042	97
Housing Costs		
Price	$103,900	84
Utilities	$3,040	100
Property Taxes	$1,270	71
Rent	$490	86
Other Costs		
Food	$7,822	99
Health Care	$2,569	103
Transportation	$11,176	95
Recreation	$3,112	78

Combined Costs: 101
Score: 68.56   Rank: 112

Columbia, SC
Typical Household Income: $66,800

State and Local Taxes		
Income	$3,254	104
Sales	$946	88
Housing Costs		
Price	$116,700	94
Utilities	$2,540	84
Property Taxes	$1,220	68
Rent	$550	96
Other Costs		
Food	$7,585	96
Health Care	$2,183	88
Transportation	$11,058	94
Recreation	$3,841	97

Combined Costs: 102
Score: 64.03   Rank: 128

Columbus, GA-AL
Typical Household Income: $60,200

State and Local Taxes		
Income	$3,100	99
Sales	$1,030	96
Housing Costs		
Price	$93,000	75
Utilities	$2,720	90
Property Taxes	$1,150	64
Rent	$470	82
Other Costs		
Food	$7,664	97
Health Care	$2,285	92
Transportation	$11,411	97
Recreation	$4,543	114

Combined Costs: 98
Score: 80.17   Rank: 71

Columbus, OH
Typical Household Income: $71,900

State and Local Taxes		
Income	$2,648	85
Sales	$1,030	96
Housing Costs		
Price	$133,800	108
Utilities	$3,280	108
Property Taxes	$2,150	120
Rent	$560	98
Other Costs		
Food	$8,217	104
Health Care	$2,637	106
Transportation	$12,117	103
Recreation	$3,627	91

Combined Costs: 114
Score: 28.62   Rank: 253

★Corpus Christi, TX
Typical Household Income: $62,200

State and Local Taxes		
Income	$0	0
Sales	$1,158	108
Housing Costs		
Price	$94,600	76
Utilities	$2,330	77
Property Taxes	$1,610	90
Rent	$560	98
Other Costs		
Food	$7,190	91
Health Care	$2,853	115
Transportation	$11,529	98
Recreation	$3,776	95

Combined Costs: 91
Score: 94.62   Rank: 20

Cumberland, MD-WV
Typical Household Income: $52,300

State and Local Taxes		
Income	$4,186	134
Sales	$735	68
Housing Costs		
Price	$95,400	77
Utilities	$2,630	87
Property Taxes	$1,380	77
Rent	$510	89
Other Costs		
Food	$7,585	96
Health Care	$3,182	128

Transportation	$11,411	97
Recreation	$3,678	93

Combined Costs: 103
Score: 60.06   Rank: 142

Dallas, TX

Typical Household Income: $85,200

State and Local Taxes		
Income	$0	0
Sales	$1,214	113
Housing Costs		
Price	$133,200	108
Utilities	$2,630	87
Property Taxes	$2,600	146
Rent	$730	128
Other Costs		
Food	$7,822	99
Health Care	$2,992	120
Transportation	$12,235	104
Recreation	$4,235	107

Combined Costs: 107
Score: 49.30   Rank: 180

Danbury, CT

Typical Household Income: $132,300

State and Local Taxes		
Income	$3,036	97
Sales	$883	82
Housing Costs		
Price	$234,100	189
Utilities	$3,630	120
Property Taxes	$4,380	245
Rent	$920	161
Other Costs		
Food	$8,375	106
Health Care	$2,913	117
Transportation	$12,235	104
Recreation	$5,135	129

Combined Costs: 146
Score: 02.84   Rank: 344

Danville, VA

Typical Household Income: $52,900

State and Local Taxes		
Income	$2,922	94
Sales	$719	67
Housing Costs		
Price	$89,500	72
Utilities	$2,630	87
Property Taxes	$1,330	74
Rent	$440	77
Other Costs		
Food	$7,743	98
Health Care	$2,157	87
Transportation	$11,646	99
Recreation	$3,166	80

Combined Costs: 97
Score: 83.01   Rank: 61

Davenport-Moline-Rock Island, IA-IL

Typical Household Income: $66,500

State and Local Taxes		
Income	$3,221	103
Sales	$883	82
Housing Costs		
Price	$86,400	70
Utilities	$3,490	115

Property Taxes	$1,210	68
Rent	$490	86
Other Costs		
Food	$7,980	101
Health Care	$2,174	87
Transportation	$11,764	100
Recreation	$3,190	80

Combined Costs: 100
Score: 72.81   Rank: 97

Dayton-Springfield, OH

Typical Household Income: $70,500

State and Local Taxes		
Income	$2,648	85
Sales	$1,030	96
Housing Costs		
Price	$114,600	93
Utilities	$3,540	117
Property Taxes	$1,730	97
Rent	$550	96
Other Costs		
Food	$7,901	100
Health Care	$2,658	107
Transportation	$11,764	100
Recreation	$3,367	85

Combined Costs: 108
Score: 48.45   Rank: 183

★Daytona Beach, FL

Typical Household Income: $54,000

State and Local Taxes		
Income	$0	0
Sales	$1,103	102
Housing Costs		
Price	$86,500	70
Utilities	$2,510	83
Property Taxes	$1,870	105
Rent	$590	104
Other Costs		
Food	$7,743	98
Health Care	$2,545	102
Transportation	$11,882	101
Recreation	$4,766	120

Combined Costs: 92
Score: 94.06   Rank: 22

★Decatur, AL

Typical Household Income: $62,000

State and Local Taxes		
Income	$2,455	79
Sales	$1,081	100
Housing Costs		
Price	$82,500	67
Utilities	$2,360	78
Property Taxes	$580	32
Rent	$450	79
Other Costs		
Food	$7,664	97
Health Care	$2,698	108
Transportation	$11,882	101
Recreation	$3,292	83

Combined Costs: 94
Score: 90.94   Rank: 33

Decatur, IL

Typical Household Income: $67,500

State and Local Taxes		
Income	$2,130	68
Sales	$1,116	104
Housing Costs		
Price	$93,800	76
Utilities	$4,170	138
Property Taxes	$1,430	80
Rent	$460	81
Other Costs		
Food	$7,901	100
Health Care	$2,157	87
Transportation	$11,411	97
Recreation	$3,071	77

Combined Costs: 101
Score: 69.69   Rank: 108

Denver, CO

Typical Household Income: $82,600

State and Local Taxes		
Income	$2,660	85
Sales	$956	89
Housing Costs		
Price	$161,900	131
Utilities	$2,890	95
Property Taxes	$1,170	66
Rent	$670	118
Other Costs		
Food	$7,980	101
Health Care	$2,754	111
Transportation	$12,352	105
Recreation	$4,623	117

Combined Costs: 117
Score: 22.10   Rank: 276

Des Moines, IA

Typical Household Income: $74,200

State and Local Taxes		
Income	$3,221	103
Sales	$883	82
Housing Costs		
Price	$119,200	96
Utilities	$3,280	108
Property Taxes	$1,520	85
Rent	$560	98
Other Costs		
Food	$7,901	100
Health Care	$2,337	94
Transportation	$11,411	97
Recreation	$3,709	93

Combined Costs: 107
Score: 50.15   Rank: 177

Detroit, MI

Typical Household Income: $85,300

State and Local Taxes		
Income	$2,977	95
Sales	$883	82
Housing Costs		
Price	$145,000	117
Utilities	$3,540	117
Property Taxes	$2,040	114
Rent	$640	112
Other Costs		
Food	$8,533	108
Health Care	$3,634	146

Transportation	$12,823	109
Recreation	$3,943	99

Combined Costs: 123
Score: 14.74   Rank: 302

Dothan, AL

Typical Household Income: $57,500

State and Local Taxes		
Income	$2,455	79
Sales	$1,081	100
Housing Costs		
Price	$87,700	71
Utilities	$2,480	82
Property Taxes	$690	39
Rent	$400	70
Other Costs		
Food	$7,506	95
Health Care	$2,693	108
Transportation	$11,529	98
Recreation	$3,796	96

Combined Costs: 94
Score: 89.81   Rank: 37

Dover, DE

Typical Household Income: $61,100

State and Local Taxes		
Income	$3,220	103
Sales	$0	0
Housing Costs		
Price	$144,000	116
Utilities	$3,250	107
Property Taxes	$1,540	86
Rent	$620	109
Other Costs		
Food	$8,533	108
Health Care	$2,335	94
Transportation	$11,764	100
Recreation	$4,663	118

Combined Costs: 113
Score: 32.87   Rank: 238

Dubuque, IA

Typical Household Income: $68,500

State and Local Taxes		
Income	$3,221	103
Sales	$883	82
Housing Costs		
Price	$106,200	86
Utilities	$2,720	90
Property Taxes	$1,260	71
Rent	$470	82
Other Costs		
Food	$7,743	98
Health Care	$2,157	87
Transportation	$11,764	100
Recreation	$3,671	93

Combined Costs: 102
Score: 63.46   Rank: 130

Duluth-Superior, MN-WI

Typical Household Income: $59,200

State and Local Taxes		
Income	$3,815	122
Sales	$956	89
Housing Costs		
Price	$108,100	87
Utilities	$2,950	97

Property Taxes	$1,630	91
Rent	$470	82
Other Costs		
Food	$8,059	102
Health Care	$2,157	87
Transportation	$12,470	106
Recreation	$3,231	81

Combined Costs: 108
Score: 45.33   Rank: 194

Dutchess County, NY

Typical Household Income: $83,300

State and Local Taxes		
Income	$4,088	131
Sales	$1,250	116
Housing Costs		
Price	$201,600	163
Utilities	$3,690	122
Property Taxes	$4,130	231
Rent	$890	156
Other Costs		
Food	$8,691	110
Health Care	$2,539	102
Transportation	$11,882	101
Recreation	$3,729	94

Combined Costs: 140
Score: 04.25   Rank: 339

Eau Claire, WI

Typical Household Income: $61,300

State and Local Taxes		
Income	$3,960	127
Sales	$846	79
Housing Costs		
Price	$113,200	91
Utilities	$3,100	102
Property Taxes	$2,340	131
Rent	$500	88
Other Costs		
Food	$7,901	100
Health Care	$2,157	87
Transportation	$11,529	98
Recreation	$3,946	99

Combined Costs: 109
Score: 44.20   Rank: 198

Edmonton, AB

Typical Household Income: $60,800

State and Local Taxes		
Income	$4,852	156
Sales	$1,030	96
Housing Costs		
Price	$86,300	70
Utilities	$2,860	94
Property Taxes	$1,390	78
Rent	$610	107
Other Costs		
Food	$9,718	123
Health Care	$1,125	45
Transportation	$13,411	114
Recreation	$3,678	93

Combined Costs: 110
Score: 43.63   Rank: 200

★El Paso, TX

Typical Household Income: $52,700

State and Local Taxes		
Income	$0	0
Sales	$1,214	113
Housing Costs		
Price	$87,200	70
Utilities	$2,540	84
Property Taxes	$1,530	86
Rent	$540	95
Other Costs		
Food	$7,585	96
Health Care	$2,593	104
Transportation	$11,646	99
Recreation	$3,318	84

Combined Costs: 91
Score: 95.47   Rank: 17

Elkhart-Goshen, IN

Typical Household Income: $72,400

State and Local Taxes		
Income	$2,414	77
Sales	$735	68
Housing Costs		
Price	$101,500	82
Utilities	$3,070	101
Property Taxes	$980	55
Rent	$540	95
Other Costs		
Food	$7,506	95
Health Care	$2,157	87
Transportation	$11,176	95
Recreation	$3,140	79

Combined Costs: 96
Score: 84.71   Rank: 55

Elmira, NY

Typical Household Income: $61,100

State and Local Taxes		
Income	$4,088	131
Sales	$1,250	116
Housing Costs		
Price	$102,800	83
Utilities	$3,490	115
Property Taxes	$2,080	116
Rent	$500	88
Other Costs		
Food	$8,454	107
Health Care	$2,157	87
Transportation	$12,705	108
Recreation	$3,192	80

Combined Costs: 113
Score: 31.45   Rank: 243

★Enid, OK

Typical Household Income: $58,600

State and Local Taxes		
Income	$3,415	109
Sales	$1,161	108
Housing Costs		
Price	$87,500	71
Utilities	$2,720	90
Property Taxes	$870	49
Rent	$410	72
Other Costs		
Food	$7,348	93
Health Care	$2,218	89

Transportation	$10,588	90
Recreation	$2,693	68

Combined Costs: 94

Score: 90.37 Rank: 35

Erie, PA

Typical Household Income: $64,600

State and Local Taxes		
Income	$2,100	67
Sales	$883	82
Housing Costs		
Price	$100,500	81
Utilities	$3,370	111
Property Taxes	$2,390	134
Rent	$450	79
Other Costs		
Food	$7,901	100
Health Care	$2,475	99
Transportation	$11,882	101
Recreation	$3,497	88

Combined Costs: 104

Score: 56.66 Rank: 154

Eugene-Springfield, OR

Typical Household Income: $61,600

State and Local Taxes		
Income	$4,642	149
Sales	$0	0
Housing Costs		
Price	$135,200	109
Utilities	$2,300	76
Property Taxes	$1,560	87
Rent	$610	107
Other Costs		
Food	$7,664	97
Health Care	$2,157	87
Transportation	$11,999	102
Recreation	$4,534	114

Combined Costs: 110

Score: 42.21 Rank: 205

Evansville-Henderson, IN-KY

Typical Household Income: $66,700

State and Local Taxes		
Income	$2,414	77
Sales	$735	68
Housing Costs		
Price	$91,800	74
Utilities	$3,160	104
Property Taxes	$930	52
Rent	$500	88
Other Costs		
Food	$7,743	98
Health Care	$2,382	96
Transportation	$11,293	96
Recreation	$3,424	86

Combined Costs: 96

Score: 85.56 Rank: 52

Fargo-Moorhead, ND-MN

Typical Household Income: $62,800

State and Local Taxes		
Income	$1,218	39
Sales	$1,030	96
Housing Costs		
Price	$102,100	82
Utilities	$2,920	96

Property Taxes	$1,150	64
Rent	$560	98
Other Costs		
Food	$7,901	100
Health Care	$2,157	87
Transportation	$11,058	94
Recreation	$3,520	89

Combined Costs: 95

Score: 87.54 Rank: 45

Fayetteville, NC

Typical Household Income: $63,100

State and Local Taxes		
Income	$3,638	117
Sales	$921	85
Housing Costs		
Price	$88,200	71
Utilities	$2,810	93
Property Taxes	$1,390	78
Rent	$490	86
Other Costs		
Food	$7,822	99
Health Care	$2,199	88
Transportation	$11,293	96
Recreation	$3,906	98

Combined Costs: 99

Score: 78.19 Rank: 78

Fayetteville-Springdale-Rogers, AR

Typical Household Income: $61,600

State and Local Taxes		
Income	$3,058	98
Sales	$886	82
Housing Costs		
Price	$107,000	86
Utilities	$2,510	83
Property Taxes	$1,290	72
Rent	$520	91
Other Costs		
Food	$7,585	96
Health Care	$2,157	87
Transportation	$11,529	98
Recreation	$3,539	89

Combined Costs: 100

Score: 72.53 Rank: 98

Fitchburg-Leominster, MA

Typical Household Income: $74,300

State and Local Taxes		
Income	$3,824	123
Sales	$735	68
Housing Costs		
Price	$157,100	127
Utilities	$3,220	106
Property Taxes	$2,130	119
Rent	$620	109
Other Costs		
Food	$8,296	105
Health Care	$3,119	125
Transportation	$12,352	105
Recreation	$3,772	95

Combined Costs: 124

Score: 14.17 Rank: 304

Flagstaff, AZ-UT

Typical Household Income: $61,400

State and Local Taxes		
Income	$2,062	66
Sales	$853	79
Housing Costs		
Price	$136,800	111
Utilities	$3,430	113
Property Taxes	$1,680	94
Rent	$600	105
Other Costs		
Food	$8,138	103
Health Care	$2,186	88
Transportation	$13,176	112
Recreation	$4,237	107

Combined Costs: 113
Score: 29.75   Rank: 249

Flint, MI

Typical Household Income: $71,800

State and Local Taxes		
Income	$2,977	95
Sales	$883	82
Housing Costs		
Price	$125,900	102
Utilities	$3,430	113
Property Taxes	$1,910	107
Rent	$530	93
Other Costs		
Food	$8,296	105
Health Care	$3,644	146
Transportation	$12,235	104
Recreation	$3,473	88

Combined Costs: 116
Score: 24.93   Rank: 266

Florence, AL

Typical Household Income: $55,900

State and Local Taxes		
Income	$2,455	79
Sales	$1,154	107
Housing Costs		
Price	$98,300	79
Utilities	$2,390	79
Property Taxes	$750	42
Rent	$440	77
Other Costs		
Food	$7,585	96
Health Care	$2,594	104
Transportation	$11,411	97
Recreation	$2,845	72

Combined Costs: 97
Score: 84.42   Rank: 56

Florence, SC

Typical Household Income: $62,100

State and Local Taxes		
Income	$3,254	104
Sales	$946	88
Housing Costs		
Price	$100,400	81
Utilities	$2,570	85
Property Taxes	$1,320	74
Rent	$480	84
Other Costs		
Food	$7,506	95
Health Care	$2,521	101

Transportation	$10,823	92
Recreation	$3,717	94

Combined Costs: 99
Score: 78.76   Rank: 76

Fort Collins-Loveland, CO

Typical Household Income: $68,400

State and Local Taxes		
Income	$2,660	85
Sales	$883	82
Housing Costs		
Price	$147,100	119
Utilities	$2,510	83
Property Taxes	$1,740	97
Rent	$670	118
Other Costs		
Food	$8,059	102
Health Care	$2,343	94
Transportation	$12,235	104
Recreation	$3,775	95

Combined Costs: 113
Score: 32.30   Rank: 240

Fort Lauderdale, FL

Typical Household Income: $75,800

State and Local Taxes		
Income	$0	0
Sales	$1,103	102
Housing Costs		
Price	$145,300	117
Utilities	$2,450	81
Property Taxes	$3,140	176
Rent	$710	125
Other Costs		
Food	$7,901	100
Health Care	$3,843	154
Transportation	$11,999	102
Recreation	$5,079	128

Combined Costs: 113
Score: 33.43   Rank: 236

Fort Myers-Cape Coral, FL

Typical Household Income: $70,400

State and Local Taxes		
Income	$0	0
Sales	$1,103	102
Housing Costs		
Price	$97,000	78
Utilities	$2,450	81
Property Taxes	$2,100	118
Rent	$590	104
Other Costs		
Food	$7,743	98
Health Care	$2,818	113
Transportation	$11,764	100
Recreation	$5,952	150

Combined Costs: 95
Score: 86.97   Rank: 47

Fort Pierce-Port St. Lucie, FL

Typical Household Income: $72,900

State and Local Taxes		
Income	$0	0
Sales	$1,103	102
Housing Costs		
Price	$112,500	91
Utilities	$2,750	91

Property Taxes	$2,430	136
Rent	$670	118
Other Costs		
Food	$7,743	98
Health Care	$2,923	117
Transportation	$11,764	100
Recreation	$4,907	124

Combined Costs: 101

Score: 69.98   **Rank: 107**

Fort Smith, AR-OK
Typical Household Income: $56,700

State and Local Taxes		
Income	$3,058	98
Sales	$960	89
Housing Costs		
Price	$97,800	79
Utilities	$2,540	84
Property Taxes	$1,270	71
Rent	$410	72
Other Costs		
Food	$7,506	95
Health Care	$2,405	97
Transportation	$11,058	94
Recreation	$3,017	76

Combined Costs: 98

Score: 81.59   **Rank: 66**

Fort Walton Beach, FL
Typical Household Income: $65,300

State and Local Taxes		
Income	$0	0
Sales	$1,103	102
Housing Costs		
Price	$129,200	104
Utilities	$2,660	88
Property Taxes	$2,800	157
Rent	$510	89
Other Costs		
Food	$7,822	99
Health Care	$2,689	108
Transportation	$12,117	103
Recreation	$4,656	117

Combined Costs: 106

Score: 53.26   **Rank: 166**

Fort Wayne, IN
Typical Household Income: $73,000

State and Local Taxes		
Income	$2,414	77
Sales	$735	68
Housing Costs		
Price	$99,100	80
Utilities	$3,100	102
Property Taxes	$1,070	60
Rent	$510	89
Other Costs		
Food	$7,664	97
Health Care	$2,157	87
Transportation	$11,176	95
Recreation	$3,472	87

Combined Costs: 97

Score: 83.57   **Rank: 59**

Fort Worth-Arlington, TX
Typical Household Income: $72,000

State and Local Taxes		
Income	$0	0
Sales	$1,214	113
Housing Costs		
Price	$106,500	86
Utilities	$2,630	87
Property Taxes	$2,230	125
Rent	$600	105
Other Costs		
Food	$7,901	100
Health Care	$2,875	116
Transportation	$12,117	103
Recreation	$4,083	103

Combined Costs: 100

Score: 74.23   **Rank: 92**

Fresno, CA
Typical Household Income: $64,300

State and Local Taxes		
Income	$2,564	82
Sales	$1,140	106
Housing Costs		
Price	$124,200	100
Utilities	$2,950	97
Property Taxes	$1,240	69
Rent	$510	89
Other Costs		
Food	$8,533	108
Health Care	$2,243	90
Transportation	$12,705	108
Recreation	$3,949	100

Combined Costs: 110

Score: 40.23   **Rank: 212**

★Gadsden, AL
Typical Household Income: $51,400

State and Local Taxes		
Income	$2,455	79
Sales	$1,081	100
Housing Costs		
Price	$87,500	71
Utilities	$2,570	85
Property Taxes	$680	38
Rent	$370	65
Other Costs		
Food	$7,427	94
Health Care	$2,893	116
Transportation	$11,176	95
Recreation	$4,387	111

Combined Costs: 94

Score: 91.22   **Rank: 32**

Gainesville, FL
Typical Household Income: $60,500

State and Local Taxes		
Income	$0	0
Sales	$1,103	102
Housing Costs		
Price	$114,700	93
Utilities	$3,010	99
Property Taxes	$2,480	139
Rent	$550	96
Other Costs		
Food	$7,743	98
Health Care	$2,652	107

| Transportation | $11,646 | 99 |
| Recreation | $3,528 | 89 |

Combined Costs: 101
Score: 67.99　　Rank: 114

Galveston-Texas City, TX

Typical Household Income: $66,100

State and Local Taxes		
Income	$0	0
Sales	$1,214	113
Housing Costs		
Price	$103,600	84
Utilities	$2,450	81
Property Taxes	$2,150	120
Rent	$570	100
Other Costs		
Food	$7,743	98
Health Care	$3,431	138
Transportation	$12,235	104
Recreation	$2,785	70

Combined Costs: 100
Score: 73.94　　Rank: 93

Gary, IN

Typical Household Income: $71,400

State and Local Taxes		
Income	$2,414	77
Sales	$735	68
Housing Costs		
Price	$115,400	93
Utilities	$3,750	124
Property Taxes	$1,500	84
Rent	$630	111
Other Costs		
Food	$7,980	101
Health Care	$3,082	124
Transportation	$11,882	101
Recreation	$3,382	85

Combined Costs: 108
Score: 46.18　　Rank: 191

Glens Falls, NY

Typical Household Income: $60,600

State and Local Taxes		
Income	$4,088	131
Sales	$1,250	116
Housing Costs		
Price	$122,400	99
Utilities	$3,250	107
Property Taxes	$2,910	163
Rent	$580	102
Other Costs		
Food	$8,138	103
Health Care	$2,157	87
Transportation	$12,117	103
Recreation	$3,586	90

Combined Costs: 117
Score: 22.95　　Rank: 273

Goldsboro, NC

Typical Household Income: $53,600

State and Local Taxes		
Income	$3,638	117
Sales	$921	85
Housing Costs		
Price	$89,700	72
Utilities	$3,010	99

Property Taxes	$1,500	84
Rent	$440	77
Other Costs		
Food	$7,585	96
Health Care	$2,157	87
Transportation	$11,411	97
Recreation	$4,137	104

Combined Costs: 100
Score: 75.64　　Rank: 87

Grand Forks, ND-MN

Typical Household Income: $57,300

State and Local Taxes		
Income	$1,218	39
Sales	$1,030	96
Housing Costs		
Price	$114,600	93
Utilities	$2,950	97
Property Taxes	$1,410	79
Rent	$550	96
Other Costs		
Food	$8,059	102
Health Care	$2,157	87
Transportation	$11,646	99
Recreation	$3,112	78

Combined Costs: 101
Score: 71.68　　Rank: 101

Grand Junction, CO

Typical Household Income: $56,700

State and Local Taxes		
Income	$2,660	85
Sales	$846	79
Housing Costs		
Price	$131,000	106
Utilities	$2,780	92
Property Taxes	$1,550	87
Rent	$530	93
Other Costs		
Food	$8,217	104
Health Care	$2,157	87
Transportation	$12,470	106
Recreation	$4,210	106

Combined Costs: 110
Score: 41.93　　Rank: 206

Grand Rapids-Muskegon-Holland, MI

Typical Household Income: $77,900

State and Local Taxes		
Income	$2,977	95
Sales	$883	82
Housing Costs		
Price	$107,800	87
Utilities	$3,040	100
Property Taxes	$1,960	110
Rent	$570	100
Other Costs		
Food	$8,217	104
Health Care	$2,211	89
Transportation	$11,764	100
Recreation	$3,716	94

Combined Costs: 106
Score: 52.70　　Rank: 168

Great Falls, MT

Typical Household Income: $60,700

State and Local Taxes		
Income	$2,893	93
Sales	$0	0
Housing Costs		
Price	$97,800	79
Utilities	$2,660	88
Property Taxes	$1,180	66
Rent	$500	88
Other Costs		
Food	$8,296	105
Health Care	$2,308	93
Transportation	$11,999	102
Recreation	$3,796	96

Combined Costs: 99

Score: 76.49   Rank: 84

Greeley, CO

Typical Household Income: $58,400

State and Local Taxes		
Income	$2,660	85
Sales	$883	82
Housing Costs		
Price	$111,100	90
Utilities	$2,810	93
Property Taxes	$1,100	62
Rent	$590	104
Other Costs		
Food	$7,980	101
Health Care	$2,431	98
Transportation	$12,117	103
Recreation	$3,619	91

Combined Costs: 104

Score: 58.36   Rank: 148

Green Bay, WI

Typical Household Income: $74,200

State and Local Taxes		
Income	$3,960	127
Sales	$846	79
Housing Costs		
Price	$118,400	96
Utilities	$3,100	102
Property Taxes	$2,480	139
Rent	$540	95
Other Costs		
Food	$7,585	96
Health Care	$2,157	87
Transportation	$11,764	100
Recreation	$3,861	97

Combined Costs: 110

Score: 39.95   Rank: 213

Greensboro–Winston-Salem–High Point, NC

Typical Household Income: $69,900

State and Local Taxes		
Income	$3,638	117
Sales	$921	85
Housing Costs		
Price	$136,100	110
Utilities	$2,950	97
Property Taxes	$2,240	125
Rent	$560	98
Other Costs		
Food	$7,822	99
Health Care	$2,251	90

Transportation	$11,529	98
Recreation	$3,602	91

Combined Costs: 113

Score: 32.58   Rank: 239

Greenville, NC

Typical Household Income: $61,000

State and Local Taxes		
Income	$3,638	117
Sales	$921	85
Housing Costs		
Price	$107,000	86
Utilities	$2,950	97
Property Taxes	$1,760	99
Rent	$540	95
Other Costs		
Food	$7,664	97
Health Care	$2,467	99
Transportation	$10,823	92
Recreation	$3,599	91

Combined Costs: 103

Score: 58.93   Rank: 146

Greenville-Spartanburg-Anderson, SC

Typical Household Income: $61,900

State and Local Taxes		
Income	$3,254	104
Sales	$946	88
Housing Costs		
Price	$118,100	95
Utilities	$2,570	85
Property Taxes	$1,470	82
Rent	$490	86
Other Costs		
Food	$7,822	99
Health Care	$2,175	87
Transportation	$11,176	95
Recreation	$3,910	99

Combined Costs: 104

Score: 58.08   Rank: 149

Hagerstown, MD

Typical Household Income: $59,500

State and Local Taxes		
Income	$4,186	134
Sales	$735	68
Housing Costs		
Price	$86,400	70
Utilities	$2,510	83
Property Taxes	$1,150	64
Rent	$510	89
Other Costs		
Food	$7,901	100
Health Care	$2,253	91
Transportation	$11,529	98
Recreation	$3,599	91

Combined Costs: 99

Score: 76.78   Rank: 83

Halifax, NS

Typical Household Income: $59,100

State and Local Taxes		
Income	$5,132	164
Sales	$2,648	246
Housing Costs		
Price	$90,700	73
Utilities	$3,280	108

Property Taxes	$1,460	82
Rent	$560	98
Other Costs		
Food	$9,244	117
Health Care	$1,170	47
Transportation	$15,058	128
Recreation	$3,796	96

Combined Costs: 120
Score: 17.57   Rank: 292

Hamilton, ON
Typical Household Income: $63,900

State and Local Taxes		
Income	$4,969	159
Sales	$2,206	205
Housing Costs		
Price	$113,700	92
Utilities	$3,250	107
Property Taxes	$1,440	81
Rent	$660	116
Other Costs		
Food	$8,691	110
Health Care	$1,233	50
Transportation	$14,587	124
Recreation	$3,875	98

Combined Costs: 121
Score: 16.44   Rank: 296

Hamilton-Middletown, OH
Typical Household Income: $69,300

State and Local Taxes		
Income	$2,648	85
Sales	$1,030	96
Housing Costs		
Price	$125,900	102
Utilities	$3,630	120
Property Taxes	$1,890	106
Rent	$580	102
Other Costs		
Food	$7,901	100
Health Care	$2,582	104
Transportation	$11,646	99
Recreation	$3,757	95

Combined Costs: 111
Score: 39.10   Rank: 216

Harrisburg-Lebanon-Carlisle, PA
Typical Household Income: $72,400

State and Local Taxes		
Income	$2,100	67
Sales	$883	82
Housing Costs		
Price	$109,200	88
Utilities	$3,540	117
Property Taxes	$2,210	124
Rent	$570	100
Other Costs		
Food	$7,822	99
Health Care	$2,548	102
Transportation	$12,587	107
Recreation	$4,130	104

Combined Costs: 108
Score: 48.73   Rank: 182

Hartford, CT
Typical Household Income: $89,100

State and Local Taxes		
Income	$3,036	97
Sales	$883	82
Housing Costs		
Price	$162,100	131
Utilities	$3,990	132
Property Taxes	$3,040	170
Rent	$700	123
Other Costs		
Food	$8,217	104
Health Care	$2,812	113
Transportation	$11,999	102
Recreation	$4,489	113

Combined Costs: 126
Score: 11.90   Rank: 312

Hattiesburg, MS
Typical Household Income: $50,700

State and Local Taxes		
Income	$2,225	71
Sales	$1,119	104
Housing Costs		
Price	$98,400	79
Utilities	$2,690	89
Property Taxes	$1,130	63
Rent	$410	72
Other Costs		
Food	$7,743	98
Health Care	$2,731	110
Transportation	$10,941	93
Recreation	$3,686	93

Combined Costs: 97
Score: 81.87   Rank: 65

Hickory-Morganton-Lenoir, NC
Typical Household Income: $61,600

State and Local Taxes		
Income	$3,638	117
Sales	$921	85
Housing Costs		
Price	$100,900	82
Utilities	$3,010	99
Property Taxes	$1,640	92
Rent	$500	88
Other Costs		
Food	$7,743	98
Health Care	$2,231	90
Transportation	$11,411	97
Recreation	$3,576	90

Combined Costs: 103
Score: 60.63   Rank: 140

Honolulu, HI
Typical Household Income: $92,300

State and Local Taxes		
Income	$4,734	152
Sales	$639	59
Housing Costs		
Price	$322,000	260
Utilities	$2,860	94
Property Taxes	$1,530	86
Rent	$870	153
Other Costs		
Food	$11,140	141
Health Care	$2,259	91

| Transportation | $14,234 | 121 |
| Recreation | $5,952 | 150 |

Combined Costs: 170
Score: 0.57　　　**Rank:** 352

Houma, LA

Typical Household Income: $59,500

State and Local Taxes		
Income	$1,625	52
Sales	$1,228	114
Housing Costs		
Price	$97,300	79
Utilities	$2,510	83
Property Taxes	$490	27
Rent	$420	74
Other Costs		
Food	$7,506	95
Health Care	$3,219	129
Transportation	$11,764	100
Recreation	$3,330	84

Combined Costs: 96
Score: 84.99　　　**Rank:** 54

Houston, TX

Typical Household Income: $85,000

State and Local Taxes		
Income	$0	0
Sales	$1,214	113
Housing Costs		
Price	$109,400	88
Utilities	$2,750	91
Property Taxes	$2,250	126
Rent	$610	107
Other Costs		
Food	$7,743	98
Health Care	$3,530	142
Transportation	$12,470	106
Recreation	$4,331	109

Combined Costs: 103
Score: 59.50　　　**Rank:** 144

Huntington-Ashland, WV-KY-OH

Typical Household Income: $52,700

State and Local Taxes		
Income	$3,230	104
Sales	$959	89
Housing Costs		
Price	$96,100	78
Utilities	$3,040	100
Property Taxes	$650	36
Rent	$450	79
Other Costs		
Food	$7,901	100
Health Care	$2,415	97
Transportation	$11,646	99
Recreation	$3,095	78

Combined Costs: 100
Score: 74.51　　　**Rank:** 91

Huntsville, AL

Typical Household Income: $66,300

State and Local Taxes		
Income	$2,455	79
Sales	$1,154	107
Housing Costs		
Price	$114,100	92
Utilities	$2,420	80

| Property Taxes | $780 | 44 |
| Rent | $530 | 93 |
Other Costs		
Food	$7,664	97
Health Care	$2,453	99
Transportation	$11,764	100
Recreation	$3,582	90

Combined Costs: 101
Score: 67.71　　　**Rank:** 115

Indianapolis, IN

Typical Household Income: $75,000

State and Local Taxes		
Income	$2,414	77
Sales	$735	68
Housing Costs		
Price	$119,500	97
Utilities	$2,950	97
Property Taxes	$1,240	69
Rent	$560	98
Other Costs		
Food	$7,980	101
Health Care	$2,702	109
Transportation	$11,529	98
Recreation	$3,670	92

Combined Costs: 104
Score: 55.53　　　**Rank:** 158

Iowa City, IA

Typical Household Income: $66,600

State and Local Taxes		
Income	$3,221	103
Sales	$883	82
Housing Costs		
Price	$125,500	101
Utilities	$3,630	120
Property Taxes	$1,550	87
Rent	$580	102
Other Costs		
Food	$7,664	97
Health Care	$2,157	87
Transportation	$11,764	100
Recreation	$3,537	89

Combined Costs: 109
Score: 43.91　　　**Rank:** 199

Jackson, MI

Typical Household Income: $63,700

State and Local Taxes		
Income	$2,977	95
Sales	$883	82
Housing Costs		
Price	$96,100	78
Utilities	$3,570	118
Property Taxes	$1,540	86
Rent	$510	89
Other Costs		
Food	$7,980	101
Health Care	$2,535	102
Transportation	$11,882	101
Recreation	$3,216	81

Combined Costs: 104
Score: 57.23　　　**Rank:** 152

Jackson, MS
Typical Household Income: $67,000

State and Local Taxes		
Income	$2,225	71
Sales	$1,119	104
Housing Costs		
Price	$92,900	75
Utilities	$2,690	89
Property Taxes	$1,110	62
Rent	$510	89
Other Costs		
Food	$7,822	99
Health Care	$2,375	95
Transportation	$11,058	94
Recreation	$3,582	90

Combined Costs: 95
Score: 86.41   Rank: 49

★Jackson, TN
Typical Household Income: $62,700

State and Local Taxes		
Income	$0	0
Sales	$1,364	127
Housing Costs		
Price	$86,400	70
Utilities	$2,810	93
Property Taxes	$670	38
Rent	$470	82
Other Costs		
Food	$7,506	95
Health Care	$2,422	97
Transportation	$10,941	93
Recreation	$3,382	85

Combined Costs: 87
Score: 99.16   Rank: 4

Jacksonville, FL
Typical Household Income: $72,000

State and Local Taxes		
Income	$0	0
Sales	$1,103	102
Housing Costs		
Price	$107,400	87
Utilities	$2,750	91
Property Taxes	$2,320	130
Rent	$580	102
Other Costs		
Food	$7,980	101
Health Care	$3,052	123
Transportation	$11,882	101
Recreation	$4,823	122

Combined Costs: 101
Score: 71.39   Rank: 102

Jacksonville, NC
Typical Household Income: $54,000

State and Local Taxes		
Income	$3,638	117
Sales	$921	85
Housing Costs		
Price	$81,400	66
Utilities	$3,070	101
Property Taxes	$1,420	80
Rent	$470	82
Other Costs		
Food	$7,506	95
Health Care	$2,357	95

Transportation	$10,941	93
Recreation	$4,978	125

Combined Costs: 97
Score: 82.72   Rank: 62

Jamestown, NY
Typical Household Income: $55,300

State and Local Taxes		
Income	$4,088	131
Sales	$1,250	116
Housing Costs		
Price	$98,900	80
Utilities	$3,250	107
Property Taxes	$2,220	124
Rent	$490	86
Other Costs		
Food	$8,375	106
Health Care	$2,157	87
Transportation	$12,352	105
Recreation	$3,304	83

Combined Costs: 111
Score: 38.25   Rank: 219

Janesville-Beloit, WI
Typical Household Income: $68,300

State and Local Taxes		
Income	$3,960	127
Sales	$846	79
Housing Costs		
Price	$98,300	79
Utilities	$3,190	105
Property Taxes	$2,060	115
Rent	$560	98
Other Costs		
Food	$8,059	102
Health Care	$2,157	87
Transportation	$11,529	98
Recreation	$3,978	100

Combined Costs: 106
Score: 53.83   Rank: 164

Jersey City, NJ
Typical Household Income: $72,900

State and Local Taxes		
Income	$1,759	56
Sales	$883	82
Housing Costs		
Price	$183,400	148
Utilities	$3,750	124
Property Taxes	$5,150	288
Rent	$790	139
Other Costs		
Food	$8,691	110
Health Care	$3,125	126
Transportation	$12,940	110
Recreation	$4,032	102

Combined Costs: 136
Score: 05.39   Rank: 335

★Johnson City-Kingsport-Bristol, TN-VA
Typical Household Income: $55,600

State and Local Taxes		
Income	$0	0
Sales	$1,364	127
Housing Costs		
Price	$91,800	74
Utilities	$2,330	77

Property Taxes	$760	43
Rent	$460	81
Other Costs		
Food	$7,664	97
Health Care	$2,422	97
Transportation	$11,293	96
Recreation	$3,666	92

Combined Costs: 88
Score: 97.46   **Rank: 10**

Johnstown, PA

Typical Household Income: $55,900

State and Local Taxes		
Income	$2,100	67
Sales	$883	82
Housing Costs		
Price	$90,100	73
Utilities	$3,600	119
Property Taxes	$1,980	111
Rent	$450	79
Other Costs		
Food	$7,822	99
Health Care	$3,025	122
Transportation	$12,470	106
Recreation	$3,615	91

Combined Costs: 104
Score: 56.95   **Rank: 153**

Jonesboro, AR

Typical Household Income: $54,900

State and Local Taxes		
Income	$3,058	98
Sales	$886	82
Housing Costs		
Price	$98,300	79
Utilities	$2,510	83
Property Taxes	$1,430	80
Rent	$410	72
Other Costs		
Food	$7,743	98
Health Care	$2,281	92
Transportation	$11,764	100
Recreation	$3,428	86

Combined Costs: 100
Score: 73.66   **Rank: 94**

Joplin, MO

Typical Household Income: $57,900

State and Local Taxes		
Income	$2,616	84
Sales	$986	92
Housing Costs		
Price	$96,600	78
Utilities	$2,540	84
Property Taxes	$1,170	66
Rent	$400	70
Other Costs		
Food	$7,506	95
Health Care	$2,256	91
Transportation	$10,823	92
Recreation	$2,709	68

Combined Costs: 95
Score: 87.82   **Rank: 44**

Kalamazoo-Battle Creek, MI

Typical Household Income: $68,800

State and Local Taxes		
Income	$2,977	95
Sales	$883	82
Housing Costs		
Price	$113,300	92
Utilities	$3,370	111
Property Taxes	$170	10
Rent	$540	95
Other Costs		
Food	$8,217	104
Health Care	$2,459	99
Transportation	$11,882	101
Recreation	$3,610	91

Combined Costs: 104
Score: 56.38   **Rank: 155**

Kankakee, IL

Typical Household Income: $66,200

State and Local Taxes		
Income	$2,130	68
Sales	$932	87
Housing Costs		
Price	$116,100	94
Utilities	$4,110	136
Property Taxes	$1,740	97
Rent	$560	98
Other Costs		
Food	$7,980	101
Health Care	$2,849	114
Transportation	$11,646	99
Recreation	$3,658	92

Combined Costs: 109
Score: 45.05   **Rank: 195**

Kansas City, MO-KS

Typical Household Income: $77,000

State and Local Taxes		
Income	$2,616	84
Sales	$1,005	93
Housing Costs		
Price	$125,600	101
Utilities	$3,100	102
Property Taxes	$1,590	89
Rent	$540	95
Other Costs		
Food	$7,743	98
Health Care	$2,869	115
Transportation	$11,529	98
Recreation	$3,303	83

Combined Costs: 108
Score: 47.03   **Rank: 188**

Kenosha, WI

Typical Household Income: $66,100

State and Local Taxes		
Income	$3,960	127
Sales	$846	79
Housing Costs		
Price	$108,400	88
Utilities	$3,160	104
Property Taxes	$2,280	128
Rent	$590	104
Other Costs		
Food	$7,901	100
Health Care	$2,493	100

| Transportation | $11,999 | 102 |
| Recreation | $3,895 | 98 |

Combined Costs: 110

Score: 41.08   **Rank: 209**

★Killeen-Temple, TX

Typical Household Income: $52,900

State and Local Taxes		
Income	$0	0
Sales	$1,214	113
Housing Costs		
Price	$97,200	79
Utilities	$2,540	84
Property Taxes	$1,790	100
Rent	$530	93
Other Costs		
Food	$7,269	92
Health Care	$2,157	87
Transportation	$10,941	93
Recreation	$3,491	88

Combined Costs: 90

Score: 96.61   **Rank: 13**

Kitchener-Waterloo, ON

Typical Household Income: $63,400

State and Local Taxes		
Income	$4,969	159
Sales	$2,206	205
Housing Costs		
Price	$108,800	88
Utilities	$3,370	111
Property Taxes	$1,340	75
Rent	$610	107
Other Costs		
Food	$9,244	117
Health Care	$1,176	47
Transportation	$14,352	122
Recreation	$4,111	104

Combined Costs: 121

Score: 17.29   **Rank: 293**

Knoxville, TN

Typical Household Income: $62,900

State and Local Taxes		
Income	$0	0
Sales	$1,364	127
Housing Costs		
Price	$115,500	93
Utilities	$2,330	77
Property Taxes	$1,110	62
Rent	$480	84
Other Costs		
Food	$7,506	95
Health Care	$2,552	103
Transportation	$11,411	97
Recreation	$4,439	112

Combined Costs: 95

Score: 88.11   **Rank: 43**

Kokomo, IN

Typical Household Income: $71,600

State and Local Taxes		
Income	$2,414	77
Sales	$735	68
Housing Costs		
Price	$93,100	75
Utilities	$3,430	113

Property Taxes	$1,270	71
Rent	$540	95
Other Costs		
Food	$7,743	98
Health Care	$2,796	112
Transportation	$11,293	96
Recreation	$3,274	83

Combined Costs: 99

Score: 77.34   **Rank: 81**

La Crosse, WI-MN

Typical Household Income: $65,400

State and Local Taxes		
Income	$3,960	127
Sales	$846	79
Housing Costs		
Price	$104,100	84
Utilities	$3,160	104
Property Taxes	$2,290	128
Rent	$470	82
Other Costs		
Food	$7,743	98
Health Care	$2,157	87
Transportation	$11,764	100
Recreation	$4,117	104

Combined Costs: 107

Score: 49.86   **Rank: 178**

Lafayette, LA

Typical Household Income: $58,800

State and Local Taxes		
Income	$1,625	52
Sales	$1,154	107
Housing Costs		
Price	$90,700	73
Utilities	$2,630	87
Property Taxes	$460	26
Rent	$410	72
Other Costs		
Food	$7,585	96
Health Care	$2,739	110
Transportation	$11,882	101
Recreation	$2,788	70

Combined Costs: 94

Score: 90.09   **Rank: 36**

Lafayette, IN

Typical Household Income: $60,400

State and Local Taxes		
Income	$2,414	77
Sales	$735	68
Housing Costs		
Price	$104,100	84
Utilities	$3,430	113
Property Taxes	$1,350	76
Rent	$590	104
Other Costs		
Food	$7,822	99
Health Care	$2,163	87
Transportation	$11,529	98
Recreation	$3,138	79

Combined Costs: 101

Score: 69.41   **Rank: 109**

Lake Charles, LA

Typical Household Income: $61,700

State and Local Taxes		
Income	$1,625	52
Sales	$1,301	121
Housing Costs		
Price	$96,100	78
Utilities	$2,510	83
Property Taxes	$540	30
Rent	$560	98
Other Costs		
Food	$7,822	99
Health Care	$2,972	119
Transportation	$11,764	100
Recreation	$3,692	93

Combined Costs: 97
Score: 84.14   Rank: 57

Lakeland-Winter Haven, FL

Typical Household Income: $59,400

State and Local Taxes		
Income	$0	0
Sales	$1,103	102
Housing Costs		
Price	$116,000	94
Utilities	$2,690	89
Property Taxes	$2,510	141
Rent	$490	86
Other Costs		
Food	$7,743	98
Health Care	$2,260	91
Transportation	$11,882	101
Recreation	$4,548	115

Combined Costs: 100
Score: 73.09   Rank: 96

Lancaster, PA

Typical Household Income: $75,200

State and Local Taxes		
Income	$2,100	67
Sales	$883	82
Housing Costs		
Price	$125,900	102
Utilities	$3,540	117
Property Taxes	$2,500	140
Rent	$590	104
Other Costs		
Food	$7,822	99
Health Care	$2,157	87
Transportation	$12,705	108
Recreation	$4,253	107

Combined Costs: 112
Score: 36.83   Rank: 224

Lansing-East Lansing, MI

Typical Household Income: $69,900

State and Local Taxes		
Income	$2,977	95
Sales	$883	82
Housing Costs		
Price	$109,600	89
Utilities	$3,310	109
Property Taxes	$1,650	92
Rent	$610	107
Other Costs		
Food	$8,138	103
Health Care	$2,816	113

Transportation	$12,117	103
Recreation	$3,699	93

Combined Costs: 108
Score: 45.90   Rank: 192

★Laredo, TX

Typical Household Income: $52,500

State and Local Taxes		
Income	$0	0
Sales	$1,177	109
Housing Costs		
Price	$86,700	70
Utilities	$2,330	77
Property Taxes	$1,530	86
Rent	$500	88
Other Costs		
Food	$7,190	91
Health Care	$2,323	93
Transportation	$10,941	93
Recreation	$2,929	74

Combined Costs: 86
Score: 99.72   Rank: 2

Las Cruces, NM

Typical Household Income: $48,100

State and Local Taxes		
Income	$2,439	78
Sales	$1,011	94
Housing Costs		
Price	$111,100	90
Utilities	$3,070	101
Property Taxes	$910	51
Rent	$450	79
Other Costs		
Food	$7,585	96
Health Care	$2,190	88
Transportation	$11,646	99
Recreation	$3,136	79

Combined Costs: 101
Score: 69.13   Rank: 110

Las Vegas, NV-AZ

Typical Household Income: $73,100

State and Local Taxes		
Income	$0	0
Sales	$956	89
Housing Costs		
Price	$142,100	115
Utilities	$2,420	80
Property Taxes	$1,180	66
Rent	$700	123
Other Costs		
Food	$8,375	106
Health Care	$2,966	119
Transportation	$14,117	120
Recreation	$5,952	150

Combined Costs: 111
Score: 38.53   Rank: 218

Lawrence, KS

Typical Household Income: $53,800

State and Local Taxes		
Income	$2,613	84
Sales	$1,077	100
Housing Costs		
Price	$103,700	84
Utilities	$2,810	93

Property Taxes	$1,350	76
Rent	$550	96
Other Costs		
Food	$7,585	96
Health Care	$2,192	88
Transportation	$11,411	97
Recreation	$3,382	85

Combined Costs: 100

Score: 75.36   Rank: 88

Lawrence, MA-NH
Typical Household Income: $87,600

State and Local Taxes		
Income	$3,824	123
Sales	$735	68
Housing Costs		
Price	$158,400	128
Utilities	$3,720	123
Property Taxes	$2,090	117
Rent	$720	126
Other Costs		
Food	$8,849	112
Health Care	$2,842	114
Transportation	$12,352	105
Recreation	$3,583	90

Combined Costs: 126

Score: 11.34   Rank: 314

Lawton, OK
Typical Household Income: $55,300

State and Local Taxes		
Income	$3,415	109
Sales	$1,197	111
Housing Costs		
Price	$86,700	70
Utilities	$2,750	91
Property Taxes	$920	52
Rent	$480	84
Other Costs		
Food	$7,348	93
Health Care	$2,267	91
Transportation	$10,705	91
Recreation	$2,732	69

Combined Costs: 95

Score: 89.24   Rank: 39

Lewiston-Auburn, ME
Typical Household Income: $58,700

State and Local Taxes		
Income	$3,527	113
Sales	$883	82
Housing Costs		
Price	$136,800	111
Utilities	$2,860	94
Property Taxes	$2,380	133
Rent	$510	89
Other Costs		
Food	$8,138	103
Health Care	$2,231	90
Transportation	$12,117	103
Recreation	$3,993	101

Combined Costs: 115

Score: 26.63   Rank: 260

Lexington, KY
Typical Household Income: $67,200

State and Local Taxes		
Income	$3,294	106
Sales	$883	82
Housing Costs		
Price	$117,900	95
Utilities	$2,300	76
Property Taxes	$1,470	82
Rent	$530	93
Other Costs		
Food	$7,822	99
Health Care	$2,214	89
Transportation	$11,293	96
Recreation	$3,689	93

Combined Costs: 103

Score: 59.21   Rank: 145

Lima, OH
Typical Household Income: $63,400

State and Local Taxes		
Income	$2,648	85
Sales	$1,030	96
Housing Costs		
Price	$89,600	72
Utilities	$3,430	113
Property Taxes	$1,240	69
Rent	$460	81
Other Costs		
Food	$7,743	98
Health Care	$2,247	90
Transportation	$11,529	98
Recreation	$3,210	81

Combined Costs: 99

Score: 78.48   Rank: 77

Lincoln, NE
Typical Household Income: $66,500

State and Local Taxes		
Income	$2,790	89
Sales	$883	82
Housing Costs		
Price	$107,700	87
Utilities	$2,950	97
Property Taxes	$1,820	102
Rent	$540	95
Other Costs		
Food	$7,506	95
Health Care	$2,157	87
Transportation	$11,411	97
Recreation	$3,210	81

Combined Costs: 102

Score: 64.31   Rank: 127

Little Rock-North Little Rock, AR
Typical Household Income: $67,900

State and Local Taxes		
Income	$3,058	98
Sales	$813	75
Housing Costs		
Price	$101,700	82
Utilities	$3,100	102
Property Taxes	$1,170	66
Rent	$510	89
Other Costs		
Food	$7,585	96
Health Care	$2,707	109

Transportation	$11,764	100
Recreation	$3,364	85

Combined Costs: 102
Score: 63.18   Rank: 131

London, ON

Typical Household Income: $60,100

State and Local Taxes		
Income	$4,969	159
Sales	$2,206	205
Housing Costs		
Price	$99,800	81
Utilities	$3,400	112
Property Taxes	$1,620	91
Rent	$610	107
Other Costs		
Food	$8,928	113
Health Care	$1,130	45
Transportation	$14,234	121
Recreation	$4,032	102

Combined Costs: 118
Score: 19.84   Rank: 284

Long Island, NY

Typical Household Income: $117,600

State and Local Taxes		
Income	$4,088	131
Sales	$1,250	116
Housing Costs		
Price	$192,000	155
Utilities	$3,990	132
Property Taxes	$3,890	218
Rent	$1,110	195
Other Costs		
Food	$8,770	111
Health Care	$3,362	135
Transportation	$13,882	118
Recreation	$4,210	106

Combined Costs: 146
Score: 02.27   Rank: 346

★Longview-Marshall, TX

Typical Household Income: $60,300

State and Local Taxes		
Income	$0	0
Sales	$1,214	113
Housing Costs		
Price	$86,700	70
Utilities	$2,570	85
Property Taxes	$1,510	85
Rent	$450	79
Other Costs		
Food	$7,427	94
Health Care	$2,383	96
Transportation	$11,764	100
Recreation	$3,019	76

Combined Costs: 90
Score: 96.04   Rank: 15

Los Angeles-Long Beach, CA

Typical Household Income: $83,400

State and Local Taxes		
Income	$2,564	82
Sales	$1,214	113
Housing Costs		
Price	$214,400	173
Utilities	$2,630	87

Property Taxes	$2,060	115
Rent	$760	133
Other Costs		
Food	$8,849	112
Health Care	$3,679	148
Transportation	$12,587	107
Recreation	$3,720	94

Combined Costs: 136
Score: 05.67   Rank: 334

Louisville, KY-IN

Typical Household Income: $72,600

State and Local Taxes		
Income	$3,294	106
Sales	$883	82
Housing Costs		
Price	$116,300	94
Utilities	$2,860	94
Property Taxes	$1,330	74
Rent	$510	89
Other Costs		
Food	$7,743	98
Health Care	$2,744	110
Transportation	$11,764	100
Recreation	$3,572	90

Combined Costs: 107
Score: 51.00   Rank: 174

Lowell, MA-NH

Typical Household Income: $102,200

State and Local Taxes		
Income	$3,824	123
Sales	$735	68
Housing Costs		
Price	$144,200	116
Utilities	$3,720	123
Property Taxes	$2,030	114
Rent	$750	132
Other Costs		
Food	$8,849	112
Health Care	$3,333	134
Transportation	$12,235	104
Recreation	$3,268	82

Combined Costs: 124
Score: 14.45   Rank: 303

Lubbock, TX

Typical Household Income: $63,300

State and Local Taxes		
Income	$0	0
Sales	$1,158	108
Housing Costs		
Price	$94,000	76
Utilities	$2,720	90
Property Taxes	$1,540	86
Rent	$510	89
Other Costs		
Food	$7,506	95
Health Care	$3,428	138
Transportation	$11,646	99
Recreation	$2,969	75

Combined Costs: 95
Score: 88.96   Rank: 40

Lynchburg, VA
Typical Household Income: $60,700

State and Local Taxes		
Income	$2,922	94
Sales	$719	67
Housing Costs		
Price	$103,700	84
Utilities	$2,690	89
Property Taxes	$1,400	78
Rent	$450	79
Other Costs		
Food	$7,743	98
Health Care	$2,157	87
Transportation	$11,529	98
Recreation	$3,498	88

Combined Costs: 100
Score: 75.08   Rank: 89

Macon, GA
Typical Household Income: $63,000

State and Local Taxes		
Income	$3,100	99
Sales	$1,030	96
Housing Costs		
Price	$96,300	78
Utilities	$2,830	93
Property Taxes	$1,220	68
Rent	$510	89
Other Costs		
Food	$7,822	99
Health Care	$2,886	116
Transportation	$11,176	95
Recreation	$3,965	100

Combined Costs: 101
Score: 71.11   Rank: 103

Madison, WI
Typical Household Income: $78,800

State and Local Taxes		
Income	$3,960	127
Sales	$846	79
Housing Costs		
Price	$145,200	117
Utilities	$3,460	114
Property Taxes	$2,620	147
Rent	$670	118
Other Costs		
Food	$7,980	101
Health Care	$2,193	88
Transportation	$12,117	103
Recreation	$4,208	106

Combined Costs: 120
Score: 18.14   Rank: 290

Manchester, NH
Typical Household Income: $83,700

State and Local Taxes		
Income	$0	0
Sales	$0	0
Housing Costs		
Price	$161,700	131
Utilities	$3,780	125
Property Taxes	$4,030	226
Rent	$690	121
Other Costs		
Food	$8,059	102
Health Care	$2,372	95

Transportation	$12,235	104
Recreation	$4,647	117

Combined Costs: 116
Score: 23.23   Rank: 272

Mansfield, OH
Typical Household Income: $60,700

State and Local Taxes		
Income	$2,648	85
Sales	$1,030	96
Housing Costs		
Price	$107,000	86
Utilities	$3,660	121
Property Taxes	$1,600	90
Rent	$440	77
Other Costs		
Food	$7,664	97
Health Care	$2,259	91
Transportation	$11,293	96
Recreation	$3,220	81

Combined Costs: 103
Score: 59.78   Rank: 143

★McAllen-Edinburg-Mission, TX
Typical Household Income: $47,900

State and Local Taxes		
Income	$0	0
Sales	$1,214	113
Housing Costs		
Price	$84,400	68
Utilities	$2,330	77
Property Taxes	$1,570	88
Rent	$430	75
Other Costs		
Food	$7,348	93
Health Care	$2,297	92
Transportation	$11,411	97
Recreation	$3,179	80

Combined Costs: 88
Score: 98.59   Rank: 6

Medford-Ashland, OR
Typical Household Income: $61,500

State and Local Taxes		
Income	$4,642	149
Sales	$0	0
Housing Costs		
Price	$129,900	105
Utilities	$2,570	85
Property Taxes	$1,570	88
Rent	$610	107
Other Costs		
Food	$7,585	96
Health Care	$2,157	87
Transportation	$12,235	104
Recreation	$3,816	96

Combined Costs: 110
Score: 42.78   Rank: 203

Melbourne-Titusville-Palm Bay, FL
Typical Household Income: $62,600

State and Local Taxes		
Income	$0	0
Sales	$1,103	102
Housing Costs		
Price	$99,500	80
Utilities	$2,630	87

Property Taxes	$2,150	120
Rent	$580	102
Other Costs		
Food	$7,743	98
Health Care	$2,905	117
Transportation	$11,764	100
Recreation	$4,320	109

Combined Costs: 97
Score: 83.29   Rank: 60

Memphis, TN-AR-MS

Typical Household Income: $78,000

State and Local Taxes		
Income	$0	0
Sales	$1,364	127
Housing Costs		
Price	$119,200	96
Utilities	$2,330	77
Property Taxes	$1,320	74
Rent	$540	95
Other Costs		
Food	$7,980	101
Health Care	$2,723	109
Transportation	$11,764	100
Recreation	$4,104	103

Combined Costs: 99
Score: 77.06   Rank: 82

Merced, CA

Typical Household Income: $60,700

State and Local Taxes		
Income	$2,564	82
Sales	$1,066	99
Housing Costs		
Price	$136,300	110
Utilities	$3,040	100
Property Taxes	$1,240	69
Rent	$550	96
Other Costs		
Food	$8,296	105
Health Care	$2,819	113
Transportation	$12,352	105
Recreation	$3,686	93

Combined Costs: 113
Score: 31.73   Rank: 242

Miami, FL

Typical Household Income: $71,900

State and Local Taxes		
Income	$0	0
Sales	$1,103	102
Housing Costs		
Price	$132,800	107
Utilities	$2,450	81
Property Taxes	$2,870	161
Rent	$710	125
Other Costs		
Food	$8,059	102
Health Care	$4,421	178
Transportation	$12,352	105
Recreation	$5,164	130

Combined Costs: 112
Score: 35.13   Rank: 230

Middlesex-Somerset-Hunterdon, NJ

Typical Household Income: $106,600

State and Local Taxes		
Income	$1,759	56
Sales	$883	82
Housing Costs		
Price	$210,500	170
Utilities	$3,750	124
Property Taxes	$3,390	190
Rent	$970	170
Other Costs		
Food	$8,691	110
Health Care	$2,956	119
Transportation	$12,705	108
Recreation	$5,299	134

Combined Costs: 137
Score: 05.10   Rank: 336

Milwaukee-Waukesha, WI

Typical Household Income: $82,200

State and Local Taxes		
Income	$3,960	127
Sales	$846	79
Housing Costs		
Price	$145,100	117
Utilities	$3,190	105
Property Taxes	$2,960	166
Rent	$620	109
Other Costs		
Food	$8,059	102
Health Care	$2,463	99
Transportation	$12,235	104
Recreation	$4,473	113

Combined Costs: 121
Score: 16.72   Rank: 295

Minneapolis-St. Paul, MN-WI

Typical Household Income: $88,100

State and Local Taxes		
Income	$3,815	122
Sales	$956	89
Housing Costs		
Price	$142,200	115
Utilities	$3,250	107
Property Taxes	$1,670	94
Rent	$680	119
Other Costs		
Food	$7,822	99
Health Care	$2,372	95
Transportation	$12,587	107
Recreation	$3,718	94

Combined Costs: 117
Score: 21.53   Rank: 278

Missoula, MT

Typical Household Income: $59,900

State and Local Taxes		
Income	$2,893	93
Sales	$0	0
Housing Costs		
Price	$126,500	102
Utilities	$2,690	89
Property Taxes	$1,520	85
Rent	$510	89
Other Costs		
Food	$8,217	104
Health Care	$2,172	87

| Transportation | $12,117 | 103 |
| Recreation | $3,205 | 81 |

Combined Costs: 106
Score: 51.85   Rank: **171**

Mobile, AL
Typical Household Income: $59,100

State and Local Taxes		
Income	$2,455	79
Sales	$1,228	114
Housing Costs		
Price	$103,500	84
Utilities	$2,600	86
Property Taxes	$680	38
Rent	$490	86
Other Costs		
Food	$7,822	99
Health Care	$2,993	120
Transportation	$11,999	102
Recreation	$4,478	113

Combined Costs: 101
Score: 64.88   Rank: **125**

Modesto, CA
Typical Household Income: $63,400

State and Local Taxes		
Income	$2,564	82
Sales	$1,085	101
Housing Costs		
Price	$148,500	120
Utilities	$2,330	77
Property Taxes	$1,460	82
Rent	$580	102
Other Costs		
Food	$8,217	104
Health Care	$2,719	109
Transportation	$12,352	105
Recreation	$4,100	103

Combined Costs: 114
Score: 29.47   Rank: **250**

Monmouth-Ocean, NJ
Typical Household Income: $88,200

State and Local Taxes		
Income	$1,759	56
Sales	$883	82
Housing Costs		
Price	$175,900	142
Utilities	$3,310	109
Property Taxes	$3,110	174
Rent	$890	156
Other Costs		
Food	$8,454	107
Health Care	$2,912	117
Transportation	$12,470	106
Recreation	$5,374	135

Combined Costs: 126
Score: 11.62   Rank: **313**

Monroe, LA
Typical Household Income: $61,000

State and Local Taxes		
Income	$1,625	52
Sales	$1,301	121
Housing Costs		
Price	$91,800	74
Utilities	$2,390	79

Property Taxes	$560	31
Rent	$460	81
Other Costs		
Food	$7,822	99
Health Care	$3,226	130
Transportation	$11,411	97
Recreation	$3,688	93

Combined Costs: 95
Score: 87.26   Rank: **46**

Montgomery, AL
Typical Household Income: $66,800

State and Local Taxes		
Income	$2,455	79
Sales	$1,007	94
Housing Costs		
Price	$116,900	94
Utilities	$2,600	86
Property Taxes	$780	44
Rent	$510	89
Other Costs		
Food	$7,664	97
Health Care	$2,650	106
Transportation	$12,117	103
Recreation	$4,038	102

Combined Costs: 103
Score: 60.34   Rank: **141**

Montreal, PQ
Typical Household Income: $53,000

State and Local Taxes		
Income	$5,942	190
Sales	$2,206	205
Housing Costs		
Price	$90,000	73
Utilities	$3,460	114
Property Taxes	$1,800	101
Rent	$610	107
Other Costs		
Food	$9,007	114
Health Care	$1,125	45
Transportation	$16,705	142
Recreation	$3,938	99

Combined Costs: 126
Score: 11.05   Rank: **315**

Muncie, IN
Typical Household Income: $60,900

State and Local Taxes		
Income	$2,414	77
Sales	$735	68
Housing Costs		
Price	$109,200	88
Utilities	$3,160	104
Property Taxes	$1,470	82
Rent	$440	77
Other Costs		
Food	$7,664	97
Health Care	$2,370	95
Transportation	$11,764	100
Recreation	$3,080	78

Combined Costs: 102
Score: 62.89   Rank: **132**

Myrtle Beach, SC

Typical Household Income: $57,700

State and Local Taxes		
Income	$3,254	104
Sales	$946	88
Housing Costs		
Price	$136,400	110
Utilities	$2,810	93
Property Taxes	$1,580	88
Rent	$560	98
Other Costs		
Food	$7,822	99
Health Care	$2,396	96
Transportation	$11,411	97
Recreation	$5,952	150

Combined Costs: 110
Score: 42.5   Rank: 204

Naples, FL

Typical Household Income: $100,000

State and Local Taxes		
Income	$0	0
Sales	$1,103	102
Housing Costs		
Price	$173,600	140
Utilities	$2,450	81
Property Taxes	$3,750	210
Rent	$740	130
Other Costs		
Food	$7,901	100
Health Care	$2,687	108
Transportation	$12,117	103
Recreation	$4,742	119

Combined Costs: 118
Score: 20.68   Rank: 281

Nashua, NH

Typical Household Income: $82,700

State and Local Taxes		
Income	$0	0
Sales	$0	0
Housing Costs		
Price	$188,400	152
Utilities	$3,780	125
Property Taxes	$4,710	264
Rent	$780	137
Other Costs		
Food	$8,059	102
Health Care	$2,357	95
Transportation	$12,235	104
Recreation	$5,301	134

Combined Costs: 124
Score: 13.04   Rank: 308

Nashville, TN

Typical Household Income: $77,300

State and Local Taxes		
Income	$0	0
Sales	$1,364	127
Housing Costs		
Price	$125,900	102
Utilities	$2,450	81
Property Taxes	$1,040	58
Rent	$640	112
Other Costs		
Food	$7,980	101
Health Care	$3,007	121

Transportation	$11,882	101
Recreation	$3,999	101

Combined Costs: 101
Score: 67.14   Rank: 117

New Bedford, MA

Typical Household Income: $69,800

State and Local Taxes		
Income	$3,824	123
Sales	$735	68
Housing Costs		
Price	$141,700	114
Utilities	$3,400	112
Property Taxes	$1,670	94
Rent	$640	112
Other Costs		
Food	$8,296	105
Health Care	$2,691	108
Transportation	$11,999	102
Recreation	$3,402	86

Combined Costs: 117
Score: 20.97   Rank: 280

New Haven-Meriden, CT

Typical Household Income: $87,000

State and Local Taxes		
Income	$3,036	97
Sales	$883	82
Housing Costs		
Price	$153,400	124
Utilities	$3,930	130
Property Taxes	$2,880	161
Rent	$800	140
Other Costs		
Food	$8,375	106
Health Care	$2,857	115
Transportation	$12,117	103
Recreation	$4,560	115

Combined Costs: 124
Score: 13.60   Rank: 306

New London-Norwich, CT-RI

Typical Household Income: $81,000

State and Local Taxes		
Income	$3,036	97
Sales	$883	82
Housing Costs		
Price	$185,200	150
Utilities	$3,870	128
Property Taxes	$3,230	181
Rent	$730	128
Other Costs		
Food	$8,059	102
Health Care	$2,565	103
Transportation	$11,764	100
Recreation	$4,166	105

Combined Costs: 129
Score: 08.79   Rank: 323

New Orleans, LA

Typical Household Income: $68,300

State and Local Taxes		
Income	$1,625	52
Sales	$1,375	128
Housing Costs		
Price	$113,700	92
Utilities	$2,920	96

Property Taxes	$760	43
Rent	$530	93
Other Costs		
Food	$8,059	102
Health Care	$3,700	149
Transportation	$11,999	102
Recreation	$4,272	108

Combined Costs: 105
Score: 54.68   Rank: 161

New York, NY
Typical Household Income: $94,800

State and Local Taxes		
Income	$4,088	131
Sales	$1,250	116
Housing Costs		
Price	$278,000	225
Utilities	$4,050	134
Property Taxes	$5,560	311
Rent	$900	158
Other Costs		
Food	$10,982	139
Health Care	$4,002	161
Transportation	$14,234	121
Recreation	$4,575	115

Combined Costs: 178
Score: 00.00   Rank: 354

Newark, NJ
Typical Household Income: $107,400

State and Local Taxes		
Income	$1,759	56
Sales	$883	82
Housing Costs		
Price	$227,600	184
Utilities	$3,750	124
Property Taxes	$3,320	186
Rent	$830	146
Other Costs		
Food	$8,691	110
Health Care	$3,028	122
Transportation	$12,940	110
Recreation	$4,377	110

Combined Costs: 141
Score: 03.97   Rank: 340

Newburgh, NY-PA
Typical Household Income: $74,300

State and Local Taxes		
Income	$4,088	131
Sales	$1,250	116
Housing Costs		
Price	$155,500	126
Utilities	$3,990	132
Property Taxes	$3,590	201
Rent	$720	126
Other Costs		
Food	$8,770	111
Health Care	$2,769	111
Transportation	$13,176	112
Recreation	$4,172	105

Combined Costs: 134
Score: 06.80   Rank: 330

Norfolk-Virginia Beach-Newport News, VA
Typical Household Income: $65,200

State and Local Taxes		
Income	$2,922	94
Sales	$719	67
Housing Costs		
Price	$120,000	97
Utilities	$3,070	101
Property Taxes	$1,630	91
Rent	$590	104
Other Costs		
Food	$8,138	103
Health Care	$2,468	99
Transportation	$12,117	103
Recreation	$5,435	137

Combined Costs: 109
Score: 44.76   Rank: 196

Oakland, CA
Typical Household Income: $92,000

State and Local Taxes		
Income	$2,564	82
Sales	$1,214	113
Housing Costs		
Price	$228,600	185
Utilities	$3,250	107
Property Taxes	$2,380	133
Rent	$870	153
Other Costs		
Food	$8,770	111
Health Care	$3,339	134
Transportation	$12,940	110
Recreation	$4,677	118

Combined Costs: 142
Score: 03.69   Rank: 341

★Ocala, FL
Typical Household Income: $54,800

State and Local Taxes		
Income	$0	0
Sales	$1,103	102
Housing Costs		
Price	$76,400	62
Utilities	$2,390	79
Property Taxes	$1,660	93
Rent	$510	89
Other Costs		
Food	$7,901	100
Health Care	$2,420	97
Transportation	$11,646	99
Recreation	$4,029	102

Combined Costs: 88
Score: 97.74   Rank: 9

★Odessa-Midland, TX
Typical Household Income: $68,900

State and Local Taxes		
Income	$0	0
Sales	$1,177	109
Housing Costs		
Price	$86,400	70
Utilities	$2,570	85
Property Taxes	$1,760	99
Rent	$480	84
Other Costs		
Food	$7,269	92
Health Care	$2,638	106

Transportation	$11,764	100
Recreation	$3,087	78

Combined Costs: 91
Score: 95.19   Rank: 18

Oklahoma City, OK

Typical Household Income: $61,700

State and Local Taxes		
Income	$3,415	109
Sales	$1,289	120
Housing Costs		
Price	$91,000	74
Utilities	$2,690	89
Property Taxes	$810	45
Rent	$480	84
Other Costs		
Food	$7,585	96
Health Care	$2,522	101
Transportation	$10,823	92
Recreation	$3,145	79

Combined Costs: 97
Score: 82.44   Rank: 63

Olympia, WA

Typical Household Income: $71,500

State and Local Taxes		
Income	$0	0
Sales	$2,162	201
Housing Costs		
Price	$158,100	128
Utilities	$2,540	84
Property Taxes	$1,880	105
Rent	$670	118
Other Costs		
Food	$8,296	105
Health Care	$2,279	92
Transportation	$11,882	101
Recreation	$3,816	96

Combined Costs: 112
Score: 36.27   Rank: 226

Omaha, NE-IA

Typical Household Income: $75,500

State and Local Taxes		
Income	$2,790	89
Sales	$883	82
Housing Costs		
Price	$113,000	91
Utilities	$2,920	96
Property Taxes	$2,240	125
Rent	$590	104
Other Costs		
Food	$7,585	96
Health Care	$2,485	100
Transportation	$11,882	101
Recreation	$3,358	85

Combined Costs: 106
Score: 51.56   Rank: 172

Orange County, CA

Typical Household Income: $97,300

State and Local Taxes		
Income	$2,564	82
Sales	$1,140	106
Housing Costs		
Price	$296,800	240
Utilities	$2,810	93

Property Taxes	$2,810	157
Rent	$880	154
Other Costs		
Food	$8,612	109
Health Care	$3,384	136
Transportation	$13,176	112
Recreation	$5,525	139

Combined Costs: 157
Score: 00.85   Rank: 351

Orlando, FL

Typical Household Income: $68,000

State and Local Taxes		
Income	$0	0
Sales	$1,103	102
Housing Costs		
Price	$109,400	88
Utilities	$2,860	94
Property Taxes	$2,370	133
Rent	$690	121
Other Costs		
Food	$7,901	100
Health Care	$2,958	119
Transportation	$11,764	100
Recreation	$5,362	135

Combined Costs: 101
Score: 70.54   Rank: 105

Oshawa, ON

Typical Household Income: $70,000

State and Local Taxes		
Income	$4,969	159
Sales	$2,206	205
Housing Costs		
Price	$102,700	83
Utilities	$3,310	109
Property Taxes	$1,930	108
Rent	$660	116
Other Costs		
Food	$8,691	110
Health Care	$1,227	49
Transportation	$14,470	123
Recreation	$3,796	96

Combined Costs: 120
Score: 17.85   Rank: 291

Ottawa-Hull, ON-PQ

Typical Household Income: $69,500

State and Local Taxes		
Income	$4,969	159
Sales	$2,206	205
Housing Costs		
Price	$112,000	90
Utilities	$3,340	110
Property Taxes	$1,980	111
Rent	$710	125
Other Costs		
Food	$9,165	116
Health Care	$1,284	52
Transportation	$14,940	127
Recreation	$4,190	106

Combined Costs: 125
Score: 12.47   Rank: 310

Owensboro, KY
Typical Household Income: $58,800

State and Local Taxes		
Income	$3,294	106
Sales	$883	82
Housing Costs		
Price	$92,800	75
Utilities	$2,330	77
Property Taxes	$1,140	64
Rent	$420	74
Other Costs		
Food	$7,743	98
Health Care	$2,237	90
Transportation	$11,882	101
Recreation	$3,737	94

Combined Costs: 98
Score: 79.04　　　**Rank: 75**

Panama City, FL
Typical Household Income: $57,100

State and Local Taxes		
Income	$0	0
Sales	$1,103	102
Housing Costs		
Price	$110,300	89
Utilities	$2,810	93
Property Taxes	$2,390	134
Rent	$510	89
Other Costs		
Food	$7,901	100
Health Care	$2,745	110
Transportation	$12,235	104
Recreation	$4,237	107

Combined Costs: 101
Score: 65.44　　　**Rank: 123**

Parkersburg-Marietta, WV-OH
Typical Household Income: $59,700

State and Local Taxes		
Income	$3,230	104
Sales	$959	89
Housing Costs		
Price	$84,200	68
Utilities	$2,980	98
Property Taxes	$590	33
Rent	$430	75
Other Costs		
Food	$7,901	100
Health Care	$2,533	102
Transportation	$11,764	100
Recreation	$3,323	84

Combined Costs: 98
Score: 81.31　　　**Rank: 67**

Pensacola, FL
Typical Household Income: $59,200

State and Local Taxes		
Income	$0	0
Sales	$1,103	102
Housing Costs		
Price	$102,700	83
Utilities	$2,570	85
Property Taxes	$2,220	124
Rent	$510	89
Other Costs		
Food	$7,822	99
Health Care	$2,746	110

| Transportation | $11,999 | 102 |
| Recreation | $3,993 | 101 |

Combined Costs: 98
Score: 80.46　　　**Rank: 70**

Peoria-Pekin, IL
Typical Household Income: $70,700

State and Local Taxes		
Income	$2,130	68
Sales	$1,116	104
Housing Costs		
Price	$94,400	76
Utilities	$3,660	121
Property Taxes	$1,330	74
Rent	$560	98
Other Costs		
Food	$8,059	102
Health Care	$2,197	88
Transportation	$11,646	99
Recreation	$3,366	85

Combined Costs: 100
Score: 71.96　　　**Rank: 100**

Philadelphia, PA-NJ
Typical Household Income: $87,000

State and Local Taxes		
Income	$2,100	67
Sales	$883	82
Housing Costs		
Price	$151,500	122
Utilities	$3,720	123
Property Taxes	$3,450	193
Rent	$730	128
Other Costs		
Food	$8,691	110
Health Care	$3,535	142
Transportation	$13,058	111
Recreation	$4,056	102

Combined Costs: 127
Score: 10.20　　　**Rank: 318**

Phoenix-Mesa, AZ
Typical Household Income: $68,300

State and Local Taxes		
Income	$2,062	66
Sales	$809	75
Housing Costs		
Price	$132,400	107
Utilities	$2,920	96
Property Taxes	$990	55
Rent	$640	112
Other Costs		
Food	$8,217	104
Health Care	$2,904	117
Transportation	$13,058	111
Recreation	$5,952	150

Combined Costs: 111
Score: 37.68　　　**Rank: 221**

Pine Bluff, AR
Typical Household Income: $54,700

State and Local Taxes		
Income	$3,058	98
Sales	$886	82
Housing Costs		
Price	$89,700	72
Utilities	$3,010	99

Property Taxes	$1,310	73
Rent	$460	81
Other Costs		
Food	$7,427	94
Health Care	$2,157	87
Transportation	$11,646	99
Recreation	$3,807	96

Combined Costs: 98
Score: 81.02   Rank: 68

Pittsburgh, PA

Typical Household Income: $72,500

State and Local Taxes		
Income	$2,100	67
Sales	$883	82
Housing Costs		
Price	$102,700	83
Utilities	$3,900	129
Property Taxes	$2,140	120
Rent	$510	89
Other Costs		
Food	$8,217	104
Health Care	$3,394	136
Transportation	$12,705	108
Recreation	$3,573	90

Combined Costs: 111
Score: 38.82   Rank: 217

Pittsfield, MA

Typical Household Income: $72,300

State and Local Taxes		
Income	$3,824	123
Sales	$735	68
Housing Costs		
Price	$136,400	110
Utilities	$3,570	118
Property Taxes	$1,970	110
Rent	$570	100
Other Costs		
Food	$7,980	101
Health Care	$2,794	112
Transportation	$11,999	102
Recreation	$3,528	89

Combined Costs: 117
Score: 22.67   Rank: 274

Pocatello, ID

Typical Household Income: $57,600

State and Local Taxes		
Income	$3,805	122
Sales	$799	74
Housing Costs		
Price	$103,700	84
Utilities	$2,270	75
Property Taxes	$1,210	68
Rent	$430	75
Other Costs		
Food	$7,980	101
Health Care	$2,157	87
Transportation	$11,529	98
Recreation	$3,993	101

Combined Costs: 101
Score: 65.16   Rank: 124

Portland, ME

Typical Household Income: $73,400

State and Local Taxes		
Income	$3,527	113
Sales	$883	82
Housing Costs		
Price	$107,100	87
Utilities	$2,920	96
Property Taxes	$1,620	91
Rent	$650	114
Other Costs		
Food	$8,296	105
Health Care	$2,258	91
Transportation	$12,235	104
Recreation	$3,969	100

Combined Costs: 107
Score: 49.01   Rank: 181

Portland-Vancouver, OR-WA

Typical Household Income: $77,300

State and Local Taxes		
Income	$4,642	149
Sales	$0	0
Housing Costs		
Price	$174,400	141
Utilities	$2,420	80
Property Taxes	$2,950	165
Rent	$660	116
Other Costs		
Food	$8,059	102
Health Care	$2,268	91
Transportation	$12,823	109
Recreation	$3,991	101

Combined Costs: 126
Score: 10.77   Rank: 316

Portsmouth-Rochester, NH-ME

Typical Household Income: $75,500

State and Local Taxes		
Income	$0	0
Sales	$0	0
Housing Costs		
Price	$181,900	147
Utilities	$3,660	121
Property Taxes	$4,540	254
Rent	$720	126
Other Costs		
Food	$8,138	103
Health Care	$2,345	94
Transportation	$12,352	105
Recreation	$4,072	103

Combined Costs: 122
Score: 15.59   Rank: 299

Providence-Fall River-Warwick, RI-MA

Typical Household Income: $69,500

State and Local Taxes		
Income	$2,393	77
Sales	$1,030	96
Housing Costs		
Price	$138,500	112
Utilities	$3,340	110
Property Taxes	$2,570	144
Rent	$670	118
Other Costs		
Food	$8,454	107
Health Care	$2,723	109

Transportation	$13,176	112
Recreation	$4,199	106

Combined Costs: 120
Score: 18.70   Rank: **288**

Provo-Orem, UT
Typical Household Income: $67,000

State and Local Taxes		
Income	$3,484	112
Sales	$934	87
Housing Costs		
Price	$125,600	101
Utilities	$2,540	84
Property Taxes	$1,510	85
Rent	$560	98
Other Costs		
Food	$7,585	96
Health Care	$2,175	87
Transportation	$12,117	103
Recreation	$3,830	97

Combined Costs: 108
Score: 48.16   Rank: **184**

Pueblo, CO
Typical Household Income: $55,600

State and Local Taxes		
Income	$2,660	85
Sales	$956	89
Housing Costs		
Price	$104,100	84
Utilities	$2,690	89
Property Taxes	$730	41
Rent	$550	96
Other Costs		
Food	$7,743	98
Health Care	$2,406	97
Transportation	$11,764	100
Recreation	$4,023	101

Combined Costs: 99
Score: 75.93   Rank: **86**

Punta Gorda, FL
Typical Household Income: $57,300

State and Local Taxes		
Income	$0	0
Sales	$1,103	102
Housing Costs		
Price	$120,000	97
Utilities	$2,570	85
Property Taxes	$2,600	146
Rent	$630	111
Other Costs		
Food	$7,743	98
Health Care	$3,096	124
Transportation	$11,764	100
Recreation	$4,925	124

Combined Costs: 103
Score: 61.19   Rank: **138**

Quebec City, PQ
Typical Household Income: $53,000

State and Local Taxes		
Income	$5,942	190
Sales	$2,206	205
Housing Costs		
Price	$66,800	54
Utilities	$3,520	116

Property Taxes	$1,360	76
Rent	$640	112
Other Costs		
Food	$9,402	119
Health Care	$1,102	44
Transportation	$16,823	143
Recreation	$4,269	108

Combined Costs: 121
Score: 16.15   Rank: **297**

Racine, WI
Typical Household Income: $75,700

State and Local Taxes		
Income	$3,960	127
Sales	$846	79
Housing Costs		
Price	$132,000	107
Utilities	$3,160	104
Property Taxes	$2,600	146
Rent	$550	96
Other Costs		
Food	$8,059	102
Health Care	$2,157	87
Transportation	$12,117	103
Recreation	$3,855	97

Combined Costs: 116
Score: 24.37   Rank: **268**

Raleigh-Durham-Chapel Hill, NC
Typical Household Income: $74,600

State and Local Taxes		
Income	$3,638	117
Sales	$921	85
Housing Costs		
Price	$177,700	144
Utilities	$2,920	96
Property Taxes	$2,640	148
Rent	$660	116
Other Costs		
Food	$7,901	100
Health Care	$2,474	99
Transportation	$11,529	98
Recreation	$3,801	96

Combined Costs: 124
Score: 13.32   Rank: **307**

Rapid City, SD
Typical Household Income: $62,000

State and Local Taxes		
Income	$0	0
Sales	$934	87
Housing Costs		
Price	$104,200	84
Utilities	$3,160	104
Property Taxes	$1,500	84
Rent	$560	98
Other Costs		
Food	$7,901	100
Health Care	$2,157	87
Transportation	$11,764	100
Recreation	$3,343	84

Combined Costs: 95
Score: 86.69   Rank: **48**

Reading, PA

Typical Household Income: $74,400

State and Local Taxes		
Income	$2,100	67
Sales	$883	82
Housing Costs		
Price	$128,700	104
Utilities	$3,570	118
Property Taxes	$2,550	143
Rent	$550	96
Other Costs		
Food	$8,296	105
Health Care	$2,413	97
Transportation	$12,823	109
Recreation	$3,344	84

Combined Costs: 115
Score: 27.48   Rank: 257

Redding, CA

Typical Household Income: $61,000

State and Local Taxes		
Income	$2,564	82
Sales	$1,066	99
Housing Costs		
Price	$125,600	101
Utilities	$2,270	75
Property Taxes	$880	49
Rent	$530	93
Other Costs		
Food	$8,296	105
Health Care	$2,788	112
Transportation	$12,587	107
Recreation	$4,000	101

Combined Costs: 108
Score: 46.75   Rank: 189

Regina, SK

Typical Household Income: $59,400

State and Local Taxes		
Income	$5,474	175
Sales	$2,354	219
Housing Costs		
Price	$61,700	50
Utilities	$2,390	79
Property Taxes	$1,620	91
Rent	$610	107
Other Costs		
Food	$8,691	110
Health Care	$1,085	44
Transportation	$14,234	121
Recreation	$3,796	96

Combined Costs: 108
Score: 47.88   Rank: 185

Reno, NV

Typical Household Income: $81,600

State and Local Taxes		
Income	$0	0
Sales	$956	89
Housing Costs		
Price	$162,300	131
Utilities	$3,040	100
Property Taxes	$1,310	73
Rent	$720	126
Other Costs		
Food	$8,059	102
Health Care	$2,572	103

Transportation	$13,764	117
Recreation	$5,952	150

Combined Costs: 114
Score: 28.33   Rank: 254

Richland-Kennewick-Pasco, WA

Typical Household Income: $65,400

State and Local Taxes		
Income	$0	0
Sales	$2,162	201
Housing Costs		
Price	$113,000	91
Utilities	$2,570	85
Property Taxes	$1,500	84
Rent	$690	121
Other Costs		
Food	$8,059	102
Health Care	$2,364	95
Transportation	$11,882	101
Recreation	$3,489	88

Combined Costs: 100
Score: 72.24   Rank: 99

Richmond-Petersburg, VA

Typical Household Income: $78,600

State and Local Taxes		
Income	$2,922	94
Sales	$719	67
Housing Costs		
Price	$134,500	109
Utilities	$3,100	102
Property Taxes	$1,930	108
Rent	$630	111
Other Costs		
Food	$7,901	100
Health Care	$2,576	104
Transportation	$12,352	105
Recreation	$4,884	123

Combined Costs: 113
Score: 32.02   Rank: 241

Riverside-San Bernardino, CA

Typical Household Income: $65,500

State and Local Taxes		
Income	$2,564	82
Sales	$1,140	106
Housing Costs		
Price	$134,700	109
Utilities	$3,070	101
Property Taxes	$1,660	93
Rent	$610	107
Other Costs		
Food	$8,296	105
Health Care	$3,094	124
Transportation	$12,940	110
Recreation	$5,952	150

Combined Costs: 116
Score: 23.52   Rank: 271

Roanoke, VA

Typical Household Income: $71,300

State and Local Taxes		
Income	$2,922	94
Sales	$719	67
Housing Costs		
Price	$107,000	86
Utilities	$2,690	89

Property Taxes	$1,390	78
Rent	$490	86
Other Costs		
Food	$7,822	99
Health Care	$2,265	91
Transportation	$11,999	102
Recreation	$3,757	95

Combined Costs: 102

Score: 62.33   Rank: 134

Rochester, MN

Typical Household Income: $77,900

State and Local Taxes		
Income	$3,815	122
Sales	$956	89
Housing Costs		
Price	$122,400	99
Utilities	$3,280	108
Property Taxes	$1,400	78
Rent	$580	102
Other Costs		
Food	$7,743	98
Health Care	$2,448	98
Transportation	$12,470	106
Recreation	$3,061	77

Combined Costs: 112

Score: 35.7   Rank: 228

Rochester, NY

Typical Household Income: $76,300

State and Local Taxes		
Income	$4,088	131
Sales	$1,250	116
Housing Costs		
Price	$101,200	82
Utilities	$3,630	120
Property Taxes	$2,410	135
Rent	$620	109
Other Costs		
Food	$8,691	110
Health Care	$2,358	95
Transportation	$12,470	106
Recreation	$3,519	89

Combined Costs: 114

Score: 28.05   Rank: 255

Rockford, IL

Typical Household Income: $69,700

State and Local Taxes		
Income	$2,130	68
Sales	$932	87
Housing Costs		
Price	$102,400	83
Utilities	$4,170	138
Property Taxes	$1,460	82
Rent	$570	100
Other Costs		
Food	$7,980	101
Health Care	$2,157	87
Transportation	$12,117	103
Recreation	$3,454	87

Combined Costs: 104

Score: 56.1   Rank: 156

Rocky Mount, NC

Typical Household Income: $58,300

State and Local Taxes		
Income	$3,638	117
Sales	$921	85
Housing Costs		
Price	$92,900	75
Utilities	$2,810	93
Property Taxes	$1,840	103
Rent	$440	77
Other Costs		
Food	$7,743	98
Health Care	$2,277	91
Transportation	$11,411	97
Recreation	$3,954	100

Combined Costs: 101

Score: 65.73   Rank: 122

Sacramento, CA

Typical Household Income: $74,300

State and Local Taxes		
Income	$2,564	82
Sales	$1,140	106
Housing Costs		
Price	$137,800	111
Utilities	$2,920	96
Property Taxes	$1,330	74
Rent	$620	109
Other Costs		
Food	$8,454	107
Health Care	$2,937	118
Transportation	$12,823	109
Recreation	$4,430	112

Combined Costs: 115

Score: 25.50   Rank: 264

Saginaw-Bay City-Midland, MI

Typical Household Income: $73,200

State and Local Taxes		
Income	$2,977	95
Sales	$883	82
Housing Costs		
Price	$83,500	67
Utilities	$3,460	114
Property Taxes	$1,310	73
Rent	$510	89
Other Costs		
Food	$8,138	103
Health Care	$2,605	105
Transportation	$11,999	102
Recreation	$3,887	98

Combined Costs: 101

Score: 66.58   Rank: 119

St. Catharines-Niagara, ON

Typical Household Income: $53,800

State and Local Taxes		
Income	$4,969	159
Sales	$2,206	205
Housing Costs		
Price	$102,400	83
Utilities	$3,220	106
Property Taxes	$1,820	102
Rent	$630	111
Other Costs		
Food	$8,849	112
Health Care	$1,147	46

| Transportation | $14,587 | 124 |
| Recreation | $4,190 | 106 |

Combined Costs: 120
Score: 18.42   Rank: 289

St. Cloud, MN

Typical Household Income: $62,400

State and Local Taxes		
Income	$3,815	122
Sales	$956	89
Housing Costs		
Price	$114,700	93
Utilities	$3,460	114
Property Taxes	$1,390	78
Rent	$500	88
Other Costs		
Food	$7,980	101
Health Care	$2,157	87
Transportation	$12,352	105
Recreation	$3,372	85

Combined Costs: 110
Score: 40.80   Rank: 210

St. John's, NF

Typical Household Income: $53,200

State and Local Taxes		
Income	$5,516	177
Sales	$3,015	280
Housing Costs		
Price	$74,400	60
Utilities	$3,520	116
Property Taxes	$1,280	72
Rent	$420	74
Other Costs		
Food	$9,481	120
Health Care	$1,267	51
Transportation	$16,940	144
Recreation	$3,954	100

Combined Costs: 125
Score: 12.75   Rank: 309

Saint John, NB

Typical Household Income: $45,300

State and Local Taxes		
Income	$5,274	169
Sales	$2,648	246
Housing Costs		
Price	$70,600	57
Utilities	$3,370	111
Property Taxes	$1,110	62
Rent	$510	89
Other Costs		
Food	$8,770	111
Health Care	$988	40
Transportation	$14,352	122
Recreation	$3,560	90

Combined Costs: 112
Score: 35.42   Rank: 229

St. Joseph, MO

Typical Household Income: $58,900

State and Local Taxes		
Income	$2,616	84
Sales	$1,042	97
Housing Costs		
Price	$99,400	80
Utilities	$2,830	93

Property Taxes	$1,340	75
Rent	$400	70
Other Costs		
Food	$7,348	93
Health Care	$2,195	88
Transportation	$11,058	94
Recreation	$3,028	76

Combined Costs: 97
Score: 82.16   Rank: 64

St. Louis, MO-IL

Typical Household Income: $80,000

State and Local Taxes		
Income	$2,616	84
Sales	$1,023	95
Housing Costs		
Price	$113,400	92
Utilities	$3,540	117
Property Taxes	$1,090	61
Rent	$510	89
Other Costs		
Food	$8,375	106
Health Care	$2,647	106
Transportation	$11,646	99
Recreation	$4,074	103

Combined Costs: 107
Score: 50.71   Rank: 175

Salem, OR

Typical Household Income: $61,600

State and Local Taxes		
Income	$4,642	149
Sales	$0	0
Housing Costs		
Price	$133,100	108
Utilities	$2,450	81
Property Taxes	$1,930	108
Rent	$580	102
Other Costs		
Food	$7,427	94
Health Care	$2,157	87
Transportation	$12,587	107
Recreation	$3,990	101

Combined Costs: 112
Score: 35.98   Rank: 227

Salinas, CA

Typical Household Income: $85,900

State and Local Taxes		
Income	$2,564	82
Sales	$1,066	99
Housing Costs		
Price	$195,000	158
Utilities	$3,160	104
Property Taxes	$1,640	92
Rent	$760	133
Other Costs		
Food	$8,375	106
Health Care	$2,803	113
Transportation	$12,940	110
Recreation	$5,952	150

Combined Costs: 129
Score: 09.07   Rank: 322

Salt Lake City-Ogden, UT
Typical Household Income: $74,200

State and Local Taxes		
Income	$3,484	112
Sales	$985	91
Housing Costs		
Price	$144,800	117
Utilities	$2,600	86
Property Taxes	$1,670	94
Rent	$650	114
Other Costs		
Food	$7,822	99
Health Care	$2,163	87
Transportation	$11,999	102
Recreation	$3,151	79

Combined Costs: 113
Score: 30.32   Rank: 247

★San Angelo, TX
Typical Household Income: $60,000

State and Local Taxes		
Income	$0	0
Sales	$1,140	106
Housing Costs		
Price	$100,500	81
Utilities	$2,600	86
Property Taxes	$1,840	103
Rent	$450	79
Other Costs		
Food	$7,585	96
Health Care	$2,157	87
Transportation	$11,293	96
Recreation	$2,732	69

Combined Costs: 92
Score: 92.92   Rank: 26

★San Antonio, TX
Typical Household Income: $68,400

State and Local Taxes		
Income	$0	0
Sales	$1,140	106
Housing Costs		
Price	$100,200	81
Utilities	$2,390	79
Property Taxes	$1,710	96
Rent	$560	98
Other Costs		
Food	$7,585	96
Health Care	$2,792	112
Transportation	$11,411	97
Recreation	$4,896	123

Combined Costs: 93
Score: 91.79   Rank: 30

San Diego, CA
Typical Household Income: $76,900

State and Local Taxes		
Income	$2,564	82
Sales	$1,140	106
Housing Costs		
Price	$233,900	189
Utilities	$3,630	120
Property Taxes	$2,240	125
Rent	$740	130
Other Costs		
Food	$8,691	110
Health Care	$3,056	123

| Transportation | $13,293 | 113 |
| Recreation | $5,471 | 138 |

Combined Costs: 143
Score: 03.12   Rank: 343

San Francisco, CA
Typical Household Income: $111,700

State and Local Taxes		
Income	$2,564	82
Sales	$1,250	116
Housing Costs		
Price	$359,100	290
Utilities	$3,250	107
Property Taxes	$2,770	155
Rent	$1,180	207
Other Costs		
Food	$8,849	112
Health Care	$2,914	117
Transportation	$13,529	115
Recreation	$4,658	117

Combined Costs: 173
Score: 00.29   Rank: 353

San Jose, CA
Typical Household Income: $111,500

State and Local Taxes		
Income	$2,564	82
Sales	$1,214	113
Housing Costs		
Price	$278,400	225
Utilities	$3,130	103
Property Taxes	$2,440	137
Rent	$1,150	202
Other Costs		
Food	$8,533	108
Health Care	$2,841	114
Transportation	$13,411	114
Recreation	$4,253	107

Combined Costs: 152
Score: 01.70   Rank: 348

San Luis Obispo-Atascadero-Paso Robles, CA
Typical Household Income: $63,400

State and Local Taxes		
Income	$2,564	82
Sales	$1,066	99
Housing Costs		
Price	$200,900	162
Utilities	$3,540	117
Property Taxes	$2,020	113
Rent	$740	130
Other Costs		
Food	$8,533	108
Health Care	$2,285	92
Transportation	$13,058	111
Recreation	$4,330	109

Combined Costs: 132
Score:0 7.09   Rank: 329

Santa Barbara-Santa Maria-Lompoc, CA
Typical Household Income: $86,200

State and Local Taxes		
Income	$2,564	82
Sales	$1,140	106
Housing Costs		
Price	$287,200	232
Utilities	$3,040	100

Property Taxes	$2,390	134
Rent	$880	154
Other Costs		
Food	$8,454	107
Health Care	$2,307	93
Transportation	$12,823	109
Recreation	$5,952	150

Combined Costs: 150
Score: 01.99 Rank: 347

Santa Cruz-Watsonville, CA

Typical Household Income: $86,000

State and Local Taxes		
Income	$2,564	82
Sales	$1,177	109
Housing Costs		
Price	$248,600	201
Utilities	$3,160	104
Property Taxes	$2,170	122
Rent	$960	168
Other Costs		
Food	$8,612	109
Health Care	$2,714	109
Transportation	$12,940	110
Recreation	$5,394	136

Combined Costs: 143
Score: 03.40 Rank: 342

Santa Fe, NM

Typical Household Income: $73,900

State and Local Taxes		
Income	$2,439	78
Sales	$1,011	94
Housing Costs		
Price	$198,200	160
Utilities	$3,370	111
Property Taxes	$1,600	90
Rent	$750	132
Other Costs		
Food	$8,217	104
Health Care	$2,157	87
Transportation	$12,823	109
Recreation	$5,175	130

Combined Costs: 127
Score: 09.20 Rank: 319

Santa Rosa, CA

Typical Household Income: $81,600

State and Local Taxes		
Income	$2,564	82
Sales	$1,103	102
Housing Costs		
Price	$210,500	170
Utilities	$3,100	102
Property Taxes	$1,860	104
Rent	$840	147
Other Costs		
Food	$8,533	108
Health Care	$2,781	112
Transportation	$13,176	112
Recreation	$5,052	127

Combined Costs: 134
Score: 06.52 Rank: 331

Sarasota-Bradenton, FL

Typical Household Income: $84,700

State and Local Taxes		
Income	$0	0
Sales	$1,103	102
Housing Costs		
Price	$122,200	99
Utilities	$2,390	79
Property Taxes	$2,640	148
Rent	$660	116
Other Costs		
Food	$7,980	101
Health Care	$2,637	106
Transportation	$11,999	102
Recreation	$4,751	120

Combined Costs: 103
Score: 60.91 Rank: 139

Saskatoon, SK

Typical Household Income: $55,800

State and Local Taxes		
Income	$5,474	175
Sales	$2,354	219
Housing Costs		
Price	$85,100	69
Utilities	$2,630	87
Property Taxes	$2,050	115
Rent	$650	114
Other Costs		
Food	$8,533	108
Health Care	$1,017	41
Transportation	$14,470	123
Recreation	$3,481	88

Combined Costs: 115
Score: 26.35 Rank: 261

Savannah, GA

Typical Household Income: $67,800

State and Local Taxes		
Income	$3,100	99
Sales	$1,030	96
Housing Costs		
Price	$108,100	87
Utilities	$3,040	100
Property Taxes	$1,190	67
Rent	$530	93
Other Costs		
Food	$7,901	100
Health Care	$2,999	121
Transportation	$11,058	94
Recreation	$4,040	102

Combined Costs: 104
Score: 57.51 Rank: 151

Scranton–Wilkes-Barre–Hazleton, PA

Typical Household Income: $61,900

State and Local Taxes		
Income	$2,100	67
Sales	$883	82
Housing Costs		
Price	$101,700	82
Utilities	$3,490	115
Property Taxes	$2,240	125
Rent	$490	86
Other Costs		
Food	$8,059	102
Health Care	$2,847	114

| Transportation | $11,999 | 102 |
| Recreation | $3,458 | 87 |

Combined Costs: 106
Score: **52.13**   Rank: **170**

Seattle-Bellevue-Everett, WA
Typical Household Income: $91,400

State and Local Taxes		
Income	$0	0
Sales	$2,162	201
Housing Costs		
Price	$217,900	176
Utilities	$2,270	75
Property Taxes	$2,600	146
Rent	$750	132
Other Costs		
Food	$8,533	108
Health Care	$2,486	100
Transportation	$12,705	108
Recreation	$3,822	96

Combined Costs: 130
Score: **08.50**   Rank: **324**

Sharon, PA
Typical Household Income: $57,800

State and Local Taxes		
Income	$2,100	67
Sales	$883	82
Housing Costs		
Price	$99,400	80
Utilities	$3,370	111
Property Taxes	$2,280	128
Rent	$450	79
Other Costs		
Food	$7,901	100
Health Care	$2,851	115
Transportation	$11,882	101
Recreation	$3,036	77

Combined Costs: 104
Score: **55.25**   Rank: **159**

Sheboygan, WI
Typical Household Income: $70,700

State and Local Taxes		
Income	$3,960	127
Sales	$846	79
Housing Costs		
Price	$103,200	83
Utilities	$3,190	105
Property Taxes	$1,980	111
Rent	$490	86
Other Costs		
Food	$8,138	103
Health Care	$2,157	87
Transportation	$11,764	100
Recreation	$5,952	150

Combined Costs: 107
Score: **49.58**   Rank: **179**

Sherbrooke, PQ
Typical Household Income: $58,200

State and Local Taxes		
Income	$5,942	190
Sales	$2,206	205
Housing Costs		
Price	$82,000	66
Utilities	$3,490	115

Property Taxes	$1,410	79
Rent	$440	77
Other Costs		
Food	$8,928	113
Health Care	$988	40
Transportation	$15,176	129
Recreation	$3,717	94

Combined Costs: 119
Score: **19.55**   Rank: **285**

★Sherman-Denison, TX
Typical Household Income: $57,800

State and Local Taxes		
Income	$0	0
Sales	$1,177	109
Housing Costs		
Price	$86,400	70
Utilities	$2,570	85
Property Taxes	$1,440	81
Rent	$480	84
Other Costs		
Food	$7,427	94
Health Care	$2,430	98
Transportation	$11,411	97
Recreation	$5,346	135

Combined Costs: 89
Score: **97.17**   Rank: **11**

★Shreveport-Bossier City, LA
Typical Household Income: $62,100

State and Local Taxes		
Income	$1,625	52
Sales	$1,264	117
Housing Costs		
Price	$93,200	75
Utilities	$2,330	77
Property Taxes	$470	26
Rent	$500	88
Other Costs		
Food	$7,743	98
Health Care	$2,646	106
Transportation	$11,529	98
Recreation	$3,374	85

Combined Costs: 93
Score: **92.07**   Rank: **29**

Sioux City, IA-NE
Typical Household Income: $67,000

State and Local Taxes		
Income	$3,221	103
Sales	$883	82
Housing Costs		
Price	$107,400	87
Utilities	$3,190	105
Property Taxes	$1,430	80
Rent	$520	91
Other Costs		
Food	$7,901	100
Health Care	$2,157	87
Transportation	$11,764	100
Recreation	$3,115	79

Combined Costs: 104
Score: **55.81**   Rank: **157**

★Sioux Falls, SD

Typical Household Income: $74,500

State and Local Taxes		
Income	$0	0
Sales	$934	87
Housing Costs		
Price	$97,800	79
Utilities	$3,010	99
Property Taxes	$1,430	80
Rent	$600	105
Other Costs		
Food	$7,822	99
Health Care	$2,157	87
Transportation	$11,411	97
Recreation	$3,380	85

Combined Costs: 92
Score: 93.77 Rank: 23

South Bend, IN

Typical Household Income: $67,200

State and Local Taxes		
Income	$2,414	77
Sales	$735	68
Housing Costs		
Price	$92,000	74
Utilities	$3,130	103
Property Taxes	$1,300	73
Rent	$570	100
Other Costs		
Food	$7,585	96
Health Care	$2,210	89
Transportation	$11,411	97
Recreation	$3,217	81

Combined Costs: 96
Score: 85.27 Rank: 53

Spokane, WA

Typical Household Income: $62,100

State and Local Taxes		
Income	$0	0
Sales	$2,162	201
Housing Costs		
Price	$115,600	93
Utilities	$2,390	79
Property Taxes	$1,580	88
Rent	$530	93
Other Costs		
Food	$8,375	106
Health Care	$2,422	97
Transportation	$11,764	100
Recreation	$3,494	88

Combined Costs: 101
Score: 66.01 Rank: 121

Springfield, IL

Typical Household Income: $66,700

State and Local Taxes		
Income	$2,130	68
Sales	$1,079	100
Housing Costs		
Price	$94,200	76
Utilities	$3,250	107
Property Taxes	$1,100	62
Rent	$520	91
Other Costs		
Food	$7,980	101
Health Care	$2,524	101

Transportation	$11,293	96
Recreation	$3,044	77

Combined Costs: 98
Score: 79.33 Rank: 74

Springfield, MO

Typical Household Income: $62,700

State and Local Taxes		
Income	$2,616	84
Sales	$968	90
Housing Costs		
Price	$91,700	74
Utilities	$2,630	87
Property Taxes	$1,000	56
Rent	$450	79
Other Costs		
Food	$7,506	95
Health Care	$2,192	88
Transportation	$11,293	96
Recreation	$3,518	89

Combined Costs: 95
Score: 88.67 Rank: 41

Springfield, MA

Typical Household Income: $69,700

State and Local Taxes		
Income	$3,824	123
Sales	$735	68
Housing Costs		
Price	$117,500	95
Utilities	$3,520	116
Property Taxes	$1,860	104
Rent	$660	116
Other Costs		
Food	$8,059	102
Health Care	$2,502	101
Transportation	$12,235	104
Recreation	$3,639	92

Combined Costs: 112
Score: 34.00 Rank: 234

Stamford-Norwalk, CT

Typical Household Income: $141,100

State and Local Taxes		
Income	$3,036	97
Sales	$883	82
Housing Costs		
Price	$267,000	216
Utilities	$3,870	128
Property Taxes	$4,990	279
Rent	$1,120	196
Other Costs		
Food	$8,296	105
Health Care	$2,959	119
Transportation	$12,235	104
Recreation	$5,952	150

Combined Costs: 155
Score: 01.42 Rank: 349

State College, PA

Typical Household Income: $60,300

State and Local Taxes		
Income	$2,100	67
Sales	$883	82
Housing Costs		
Price	$147,200	119
Utilities	$3,130	103

Property Taxes	$1,990	111
Rent	$630	111
Other Costs		
Food	$7,901	100
Health Care	$2,397	96
Transportation	$12,117	103
Recreation	$4,131	104

Combined Costs: 113
Score: 30.60   Rank: 246

Steubenville-Weirton, OH-WV
Typical Household Income: $53,700

State and Local Taxes		
Income	$2,648	85
Sales	$1,030	96
Housing Costs		
Price	$89,400	72
Utilities	$3,370	111
Property Taxes	$1,350	76
Rent	$430	75
Other Costs		
Food	$7,743	98
Health Care	$3,038	122
Transportation	$11,529	98
Recreation	$3,118	79

Combined Costs: 101
Score: 68.84   Rank: 111

Stockton-Lodi, CA
Typical Household Income: $64,600

State and Local Taxes		
Income	$2,564	82
Sales	$1,140	106
Housing Costs		
Price	$146,900	119
Utilities	$3,040	100
Property Taxes	$1,520	85
Rent	$600	105
Other Costs		
Food	$8,375	106
Health Care	$2,592	104
Transportation	$12,470	106
Recreation	$3,363	85

Combined Costs: 116
Score: 23.80   Rank: 270

Sudbury, ON
Typical Household Income: $62,800

State and Local Taxes		
Income	$4,969	159
Sales	$2,206	205
Housing Costs		
Price	$86,700	70
Utilities	$3,660	121
Property Taxes	$1,320	74
Rent	$500	88
Other Costs		
Food	$9,007	114
Health Care	$1,198	48
Transportation	$14,117	120
Recreation	$4,032	102

Combined Costs: 115
Score: 25.78   Rank: 263

Sumter, SC
Typical Household Income: $53,200

State and Local Taxes		
Income	$3,254	104
Sales	$946	88
Housing Costs		
Price	$92,300	75
Utilities	$3,160	104
Property Taxes	$1,250	70
Rent	$440	77
Other Costs		
Food	$7,743	98
Health Care	$2,157	87
Transportation	$10,941	93
Recreation	$3,579	90

Combined Costs: 98
Score: 79.61   Rank: 73

Syracuse, NY
Typical Household Income: $67,400

State and Local Taxes		
Income	$4,088	131
Sales	$1,250	116
Housing Costs		
Price	$90,800	73
Utilities	$3,220	106
Property Taxes	$2,590	145
Rent	$580	102
Other Costs		
Food	$8,691	110
Health Care	$2,177	87
Transportation	$12,470	106
Recreation	$3,403	86

Combined Costs: 111
Score: 37.97   Rank: 220

Tacoma, WA
Typical Household Income: $67,900

State and Local Taxes		
Income	$0	0
Sales	$2,162	201
Housing Costs		
Price	$152,100	123
Utilities	$2,270	75
Property Taxes	$1,970	110
Rent	$600	105
Other Costs		
Food	$8,533	108
Health Care	$2,350	94
Transportation	$12,470	106
Recreation	$3,668	92

Combined Costs: 112
Score: 34.28   Rank: 233

Tallahassee, FL
Typical Household Income: $62,200

State and Local Taxes		
Income	$0	0
Sales	$1,103	102
Housing Costs		
Price	$126,500	102
Utilities	$2,720	90
Property Taxes	$2,740	153
Rent	$610	107
Other Costs		
Food	$7,822	99
Health Care	$2,349	94

Transportation	$11,411	97
Recreation	$3,599	91

Combined Costs: 102

Score: 62.61　　　　Rank: 133

Tampa-St. Petersburg-Clearwater, FL
Typical Household Income: $65,900

State and Local Taxes		
Income	$0	0
Sales	$1,103	102
Housing Costs		
Price	$99,100	80
Utilities	$2,450	81
Property Taxes	$2,150	120
Rent	$590	104
Other Costs		
Food	$8,059	102
Health Care	$2,984	120
Transportation	$12,117	103
Recreation	$4,476	113

Combined Costs: 98

Score: 79.89　　　　Rank: 72

Terre Haute, IN
Typical Household Income: $54,600

State and Local Taxes		
Income	$2,414	77
Sales	$735	68
Housing Costs		
Price	$97,200	79
Utilities	$3,370	111
Property Taxes	$1,290	72
Rent	$440	77
Other Costs		
Food	$7,506	95
Health Care	$2,371	95
Transportation	$11,764	100
Recreation	$3,131	79

Combined Costs: 99

Score: 76.21　　　　Rank: 85

★Texarkana, TX-Texarkana, AR
Typical Household Income: $56,200

State and Local Taxes		
Income	$0	0
Sales	$1,214	113
Housing Costs		
Price	$92,900	75
Utilities	$2,450	81
Property Taxes	$1,540	86
Rent	$470	82
Other Costs		
Food	$7,427	94
Health Care	$2,915	117
Transportation	$11,411	97
Recreation	$3,402	86

Combined Costs: 92

Score: 94.34　　　　Rank: 21

Thunder Bay, ON
Typical Household Income: $60,100

State and Local Taxes		
Income	$4,969	159
Sales	$2,206	205
Housing Costs		
Price	$77,800	63
Utilities	$3,660	121

Property Taxes	$1,300	73
Rent	$510	89
Other Costs		
Food	$8,928	113
Health Care	$1,204	48
Transportation	$14,117	120
Recreation	$3,866	97

Combined Costs: 113

Score: 30.88　　　　Rank: 245

Toledo, OH
Typical Household Income: $71,200

State and Local Taxes		
Income	$2,648	85
Sales	$1,030	96
Housing Costs		
Price	$101,100	82
Utilities	$4,170	138
Property Taxes	$1,670	94
Rent	$540	95
Other Costs		
Food	$7,822	99
Health Care	$3,207	129
Transportation	$11,999	102
Recreation	$3,411	86

Combined Costs: 108

Score: 46.46　　　　Rank: 190

★Topeka, KS
Typical Household Income: $68,000

State and Local Taxes		
Income	$2,613	84
Sales	$967	90
Housing Costs		
Price	$85,700	69
Utilities	$2,630	87
Property Taxes	$1,150	64
Rent	$500	88
Other Costs		
Food	$7,743	98
Health Care	$2,228	90
Transportation	$10,823	92
Recreation	$2,966	75

Combined Costs: 93

Score: 92.64　　　　Rank: 27

Toronto, ON
Typical Household Income: $76,400

State and Local Taxes		
Income	$4,969	159
Sales	$2,206	205
Housing Costs		
Price	$163,500	132
Utilities	$3,250	107
Property Taxes	$2,030	114
Rent	$810	142
Other Costs		
Food	$9,165	116
Health Care	$1,363	55
Transportation	$14,823	126
Recreation	$4,269	108

Combined Costs: 136

Score: 05.95　　　　Rank: 333

Trenton, NJ
Typical Household Income: $106,400

State and Local Taxes		
Income	$1,759	56
Sales	$883	82

Housing Costs		
Price	$168,100	136
Utilities	$3,840	127
Property Taxes	$3,730	209
Rent	$820	144

Other Costs		
Food	$8,533	108
Health Care	$3,287	132
Transportation	$12,470	106
Recreation	$5,359	135

Combined Costs: 128
Score: 09.64   Rank: 320

Trois-Rivieres, PQ
Typical Household Income: $48,100

State and Local Taxes		
Income	$5,942	190
Sales	$2,206	205

Housing Costs		
Price	$59,000	48
Utilities	$3,540	117
Property Taxes	$1,270	71
Rent	$410	72

Other Costs		
Food	$8,928	113
Health Care	$1,028	41
Transportation	$15,764	134
Recreation	$3,717	94

Combined Costs: 115
Score: 26.92   Rank: 259

Tucson, AZ
Typical Household Income: $58,000

State and Local Taxes		
Income	$2,062	66
Sales	$735	68

Housing Costs		
Price	$125,000	101
Utilities	$2,600	86
Property Taxes	$1,030	58
Rent	$610	107

Other Costs		
Food	$8,138	103
Health Care	$2,743	110
Transportation	$12,235	104
Recreation	$5,952	150

Combined Costs: 106
Score: 53.55   Rank: 165

Tulsa, OK
Typical Household Income: $67,000

State and Local Taxes		
Income	$3,415	109
Sales	$1,161	108

Housing Costs		
Price	$98,000	79
Utilities	$2,720	90
Property Taxes	$1,010	57
Rent	$530	93

Other Costs		
Food	$7,348	93
Health Care	$2,573	103

Transportation	$10,588	90
Recreation	$3,437	87

Combined Costs: 98
Score: 80.74   Rank: 69

Tuscaloosa, AL
Typical Household Income: $57,700

State and Local Taxes		
Income	$2,455	79
Sales	$934	87

Housing Costs		
Price	$99,400	80
Utilities	$2,600	86
Property Taxes	$1,010	57
Rent	$490	86

Other Costs		
Food	$7,585	96
Health Care	$2,680	108
Transportation	$11,882	101
Recreation	$4,623	117

Combined Costs: 99
Score: 77.63   Rank: 80

★Tyler, TX
Typical Household Income: $67,100

State and Local Taxes		
Income	$0	0
Sales	$1,214	113

Housing Costs		
Price	$92,200	74
Utilities	$2,600	86
Property Taxes	$1,950	109
Rent	$490	86

Other Costs		
Food	$7,190	91
Health Care	$2,466	99
Transportation	$11,176	95
Recreation	$4,839	122

Combined Costs: 91
Score: 95.76   Rank: 16

Utica-Rome, NY
Typical Household Income: $60,500

State and Local Taxes		
Income	$4,088	131
Sales	$1,250	116

Housing Costs		
Price	$128,200	104
Utilities	$3,250	107
Property Taxes	$3,030	170
Rent	$500	88

Other Costs		
Food	$8,533	108
Health Care	$2,157	87
Transportation	$12,705	108
Recreation	$3,460	87

Combined Costs: 121
Score: 17.00   Rank: 294

Vallejo-Fairfield-Napa, CA
Typical Household Income: $76,100

State and Local Taxes		
Income	$2,564	82
Sales	$1,140	106

Housing Costs		
Price	$190,300	154
Utilities	$3,130	103

Property Taxes	$2,010	113
Rent	$760	133
Other Costs		
Food	$8,612	109
Health Care	$3,026	122
Transportation	$12,823	109
Recreation	$4,971	125

Combined Costs: 130

Score: 07.94 **Rank: 326**

Vancouver, BC
Typical Household Income: $61,700

State and Local Taxes		
Income	$5,045	162
Sales	$2,059	191
Housing Costs		
Price	$195,800	158
Utilities	$3,010	99
Property Taxes	$1,460	82
Rent	$840	147
Other Costs		
Food	$8,770	111
Health Care	$1,227	49
Transportation	$13,999	119
Recreation	$4,348	110

Combined Costs: 137

Score: 04.82 **Rank: 337**

Ventura, CA
Typical Household Income: $91,700

State and Local Taxes		
Income	$2,564	82
Sales	$1,066	99
Housing Costs		
Price	$196,000	158
Utilities	$3,010	99
Property Taxes	$1,880	105
Rent	$800	140
Other Costs		
Food	$8,612	109
Health Care	$2,945	118
Transportation	$12,705	108
Recreation	$4,894	123

Combined Costs: 130

Score: 08.22 **Rank: 325**

Victoria, BC
Typical Household Income: $56,500

State and Local Taxes		
Income	$5,045	162
Sales	$2,059	191
Housing Costs		
Price	$160,200	129
Utilities	$2,950	97
Property Taxes	$1,680	94
Rent	$710	125
Other Costs		
Food	$9,323	118
Health Care	$1,170	47
Transportation	$13,646	116
Recreation	$4,426	112

Combined Costs: 130

Score: 07.65 **Rank: 327**

★Victoria, TX
Typical Household Income: $71,100

State and Local Taxes		
Income	$0	0
Sales	$1,214	113
Housing Costs		
Price	$85,000	69
Utilities	$2,390	79
Property Taxes	$1,550	87
Rent	$460	81
Other Costs		
Food	$7,111	90
Health Care	$2,670	107
Transportation	$10,823	92
Recreation	$2,929	74

Combined Costs: 87

Score: 99.44 **Rank: 3**

Vineland-Millville-Bridgeton, NJ
Typical Household Income: $68,200

State and Local Taxes		
Income	$1,759	56
Sales	$883	82
Housing Costs		
Price	$147,300	119
Utilities	$3,900	129
Property Taxes	$2,770	155
Rent	$700	123
Other Costs		
Food	$8,138	103
Health Care	$2,968	119
Transportation	$12,352	105
Recreation	$3,271	82

Combined Costs: 119

Score: 18.99 **Rank: 287**

Visalia-Tulare-Porterville, CA
Typical Household Income: $59,800

State and Local Taxes		
Income	$2,564	82
Sales	$1,066	99
Housing Costs		
Price	$139,800	113
Utilities	$2,690	89
Property Taxes	$1,080	60
Rent	$520	91
Other Costs		
Food	$8,375	106
Health Care	$2,309	93
Transportation	$12,352	105
Recreation	$3,172	80

Combined Costs: 111

Score: 37.12 **Rank: 223**

★Waco, TX
Typical Household Income: $57,500

State and Local Taxes		
Income	$0	0
Sales	$1,214	113
Housing Costs		
Price	$85,400	69
Utilities	$2,570	85
Property Taxes	$1,430	80
Rent	$510	89
Other Costs		
Food	$7,269	92
Health Care	$2,157	87

| Transportation | $11,646 | 99 |
| Recreation | $2,788 | 70 |

Combined Costs: 88

Score: 98.02   **Rank: 8**

Washington, DC-MD-VA-WV
Typical Household Income: $97,400

State and Local Taxes		
Income	$4,463	143
Sales	$846	79
Housing Costs		
Price	$191,900	155
Utilities	$2,920	96
Property Taxes	$3,000	168
Rent	$830	146
Other Costs		
Food	$9,165	116
Health Care	$2,638	106
Transportation	$13,411	114
Recreation	$4,635	117

Combined Costs: 139

Score: 04.54   **Rank: 338**

Waterbury, CT
Typical Household Income: $87,400

State and Local Taxes		
Income	$3,036	97
Sales	$883	82
Housing Costs		
Price	$144,200	116
Utilities	$3,810	126
Property Taxes	$2,210	124
Rent	$750	132
Other Costs		
Food	$8,138	103
Health Care	$2,837	114
Transportation	$11,999	102
Recreation	$4,055	102

Combined Costs: 119

Score: 19.27   **Rank: 286**

Waterloo-Cedar Falls, IA
Typical Household Income: $60,800

State and Local Taxes		
Income	$3,221	103
Sales	$883	82
Housing Costs		
Price	$75,700	61
Utilities	$3,160	104
Property Taxes	$960	54
Rent	$440	77
Other Costs		
Food	$7,743	98
Health Care	$2,195	88
Transportation	$11,293	96
Recreation	$3,118	79

Combined Costs: 94

Score: 89.52   **Rank: 38**

Wausau, WI
Typical Household Income: $69,300

State and Local Taxes		
Income	$3,960	127
Sales	$846	79
Housing Costs		
Price	$103,000	83
Utilities	$3,070	101

Property Taxes	$2,060	115
Rent	$490	86
Other Costs		
Food	$8,059	102
Health Care	$2,157	87
Transportation	$11,293	96
Recreation	$4,200	106

Combined Costs: 106

Score: 52.98   **Rank: 167**

West Palm Beach-Boca Raton, FL
Typical Household Income: $100,000

State and Local Taxes		
Income	$0	0
Sales	$1,103	102
Housing Costs		
Price	$143,500	116
Utilities	$2,450	81
Property Taxes	$3,100	174
Rent	$730	128
Other Costs		
Food	$7,822	99
Health Care	$3,345	134
Transportation	$11,999	102
Recreation	$5,086	128

Combined Costs: 110

Score: 39.67   **Rank: 214**

Wheeling, WV-OH
Typical Household Income: $54,500

State and Local Taxes		
Income	$3,230	104
Sales	$959	89
Housing Costs		
Price	$95,100	77
Utilities	$3,070	101
Property Taxes	$750	42
Rent	$430	75
Other Costs		
Food	$7,822	99
Health Care	$2,600	104
Transportation	$11,882	101
Recreation	$3,570	90

Combined Costs: 101

Score: 67.43   **Rank: 116**

Wichita, KS
Typical Household Income: $69,500

State and Local Taxes		
Income	$2,613	84
Sales	$930	86
Housing Costs		
Price	$103,100	83
Utilities	$3,310	109
Property Taxes	$1,490	83
Rent	$530	93
Other Costs		
Food	$7,585	96
Health Care	$2,573	103
Transportation	$11,176	95
Recreation	$2,911	73

Combined Costs: 101

Score: 66.86   **Rank: 118**

★Wichita Falls, TX
Typical Household Income: $62,100

State and Local Taxes		
Income	$0	0
Sales	$1,214	113
Housing Costs		
Price	$84,500	68
Utilities	$2,630	87
Property Taxes	$1,520	85
Rent	$470	82
Other Costs		
Food	$7,506	95
Health Care	$2,240	90
Transportation	$10,823	92
Recreation	$3,099	78

Combined Costs: 87
Score: 98.87   Rank: 5

Williamsport, PA
Typical Household Income: $58,200

State and Local Taxes		
Income	$2,100	67
Sales	$883	82
Housing Costs		
Price	$100,800	81
Utilities	$3,570	118
Property Taxes	$2,030	114
Rent	$450	79
Other Costs		
Food	$7,901	100
Health Care	$2,357	95
Transportation	$11,646	99
Recreation	$3,481	88

Combined Costs: 103
Score: 61.48   Rank: 137

Wilmington-Newark, DE-MD
Typical Household Income: $85,300

State and Local Taxes		
Income	$3,220	103
Sales	$0	0
Housing Costs		
Price	$136,800	111
Utilities	$3,250	107
Property Taxes	$1,480	83
Rent	$680	119
Other Costs		
Food	$8,849	112
Health Care	$3,044	122
Transportation	$11,882	101
Recreation	$4,357	110

Combined Costs: 114
Score: 29.18   Rank: 251

Wilmington, NC
Typical Household Income: $60,000

State and Local Taxes		
Income	$3,638	117
Sales	$921	85
Housing Costs		
Price	$125,800	102
Utilities	$3,040	100
Property Taxes	$2,240	125
Rent	$610	107
Other Costs		
Food	$7,743	98
Health Care	$2,442	98

Transportation	$11,176	95
Recreation	$5,952	150

Combined Costs: 110
Score: 40.51   Rank: 211

Windsor, ON
Typical Household Income: $62,200

State and Local Taxes		
Income	$4,969	159
Sales	$2,206	205
Housing Costs		
Price	$101,800	82
Utilities	$3,280	108
Property Taxes	$1,340	75
Rent	$560	98
Other Costs		
Food	$8,533	108
Health Care	$1,193	48
Transportation	$14,352	122
Recreation	$3,875	98

Combined Costs: 117
Score: 21.82   Rank: 277

Winnipeg, MB
Typical Household Income: $54,400

State and Local Taxes		
Income	$5,397	173
Sales	$2,059	191
Housing Costs		
Price	$62,900	51
Utilities	$3,720	123
Property Taxes	$1,700	95
Rent	$630	111
Other Costs		
Food	$8,612	109
Health Care	$1,062	43
Transportation	$13,882	118
Recreation	$3,954	100

Combined Costs: 110
Score: 43.06   Rank: 202

Worcester, MA-CT
Typical Household Income: $73,600

State and Local Taxes		
Income	$3,824	123
Sales	$735	68
Housing Costs		
Price	$150,900	122
Utilities	$3,220	106
Property Taxes	$2,370	133
Rent	$640	112
Other Costs		
Food	$8,296	105
Health Care	$3,103	125
Transportation	$12,235	104
Recreation	$3,995	101

Combined Costs: 123
Score: 15.30   Rank: 300

Yakima, WA
Typical Household Income: $60,700

State and Local Taxes		
Income	$0	0
Sales	$2,162	201
Housing Costs		
Price	$114,700	93
Utilities	$2,540	84

Property Taxes	$1,570	88
Rent	$550	96
Other Costs		
Food	$8,217	104
Health Care	$2,157	87
Transportation	$11,646	99
Recreation	$3,875	98

Combined Costs: 100

Score: 73.38 Rank: 95

Yolo, CA

Typical Household Income: $69,500

State and Local Taxes		
Income	$2,564	82
Sales	$1,066	99
Housing Costs		
Price	$188,900	153
Utilities	$2,890	95
Property Taxes	$1,740	97
Rent	$670	118
Other Costs		
Food	$8,454	107
Health Care	$2,554	103
Transportation	$12,940	110
Recreation	$3,835	97

Combined Costs: 127

Score: 10.49 Rank: 317

York, PA

Typical Household Income: $70,900

State and Local Taxes		
Income	$2,100	67
Sales	$883	82
Housing Costs		
Price	$136,000	110
Utilities	$3,630	120
Property Taxes	$2,550	143
Rent	$550	96
Other Costs		
Food	$7,822	99
Health Care	$2,216	89
Transportation	$12,235	104
Recreation	$4,826	122

Combined Costs: 113

Score: 31.17 Rank: 244

Youngstown-Warren, OH

Typical Household Income: $63,300

State and Local Taxes		
Income	$2,648	85
Sales	$1,030	96

Housing Costs		
Price	$86,900	70
Utilities	$3,750	124
Property Taxes	$1,170	66
Rent	$450	79
Other Costs		
Food	$7,743	98
Health Care	$2,894	116
Transportation	$11,646	99
Recreation	$3,146	79

Combined Costs: 101

Score: 70.26 Rank: 106

Yuba City, CA

Typical Household Income: $57,700

State and Local Taxes		
Income	$2,564	82
Sales	$1,066	99
Housing Costs		
Price	$135,700	110
Utilities	$3,040	100
Property Taxes	$1,190	67
Rent	$500	88
Other Costs		
Food	$8,296	105
Health Care	$2,694	108
Transportation	$12,470	106
Recreation	$3,528	89

Combined Costs: 113

Score: 33.15 Rank: 237

Yuma, AZ

Typical Household Income: $48,900

State and Local Taxes		
Income	$2,062	66
Sales	$883	82
Housing Costs		
Price	$126,300	102
Utilities	$3,070	101
Property Taxes	$1,580	88
Rent	$570	100
Other Costs		
Food	$7,901	100
Health Care	$2,715	109
Transportation	$12,823	109
Recreation	$3,168	80

Combined Costs: 110

Score: 43.35 Rank: 201

ET CETERA: COSTS OF LIVING

THE HIGH COST OF COLLEGE

Some say that in the future white-collar workplace, only those who have college degrees will get the nod for new slots in management training or even entry-level jobs behind the counter or in the mail room.

But coming up with 4 years of tuition and fees to help their children launch a career is breaking a lot of middle-income families. More than any other item on the Consumer Price Index, college tuition has inflated the most during the 1990s. Aside from parental largess, to go away

PUBLIC/PRIVATE COLLEGE TUITIONS

United States	Public	Private	United States	Public	Private
Alabama	$2,500	$8,100	New Mexico	$2,100	$10,000
Alaska	$2,700	$8,200	New York	$3,900	$14,600
Arizona	$2,100	$7,900	North Carolina	$1,900	$11,700
Arkansas	$2,500	$7,100	North Dakota	$2,600	$7,500
California	$2,800	$14,500	Ohio	$4,100	$13,000
Colorado	$2,700	$12,100	Oklahoma	$2,100	$7,700
Connecticut	$4,300	$17,500	Oregon	$3,500	$14,800
Delaware	$4,400	$7,500	Pennsylvania	$5,200	$15,000
District of Columbia	$2,000	$15,600	Rhode Island	$4,100	$15,700
Florida	$2,000	$11,200	South Carolina	$3,500	$10,300
Georgia	$2,400	$11,000	South Dakota	$2,900	$9,700
Hawaii	$2,800	$6,600	Tennessee	$2,300	$10,500
Idaho	$2,300	$12,300	Texas	$2,300	$9,400
Illinois	$3,800	$12,400	Utah	$2,200	$3,100
Indiana	$3,400	$13,300	Vermont	$6,500	$16,500
Iowa	$2,800	$12,500	Virginia	$4,100	$11,200
Kansas	$2,400	$9,200	Washington	$3,100	$13,700
Kentucky	$2,400	$8,200	West Virginia	$2,200	$10,800
Louisiana	$2,300	$12,900	Wisconsin	$3,000	$12,800
Maine	$3,900	$17,000	Wyoming	$2,400	$ N/A
Maryland	$4,200	$15,400			
Massachusetts	$4,000	$17,200	Canada	Public	
Michigan	$4,200	$9,600	Alberta	$2,100	
Minnesota	$3,800	$13,700	British Columbia	$1,650	
Mississippi	$2,600	$7,300	Manitoba	$1,800	
Missouri	$3,400	$10,000	New Brunswick	$2,695	
Montana	$2,700	$7,900	Newfoundland	$2,200	
Nebraska	$2,500	$9,800	Nova Scotia	$2,558	
Nevada	$1,900	$7,800	Ontario	$2,250	
New Hampshire	$5,200	$15,900	Quebec	$1,180	
New Jersey	$4,600	$14,400	Saskatchewan	$1,980	

Source: National Center for Education Statistics, Statistics Canada. Figures are in American dollars. United States figures are weighted averages; Canadian figures are for undergraduate study at the largest public university in the province.

to college and make it through in standard time most students need at least two out of three sources of money: a scholarship, a student loan, and a part-time job.

The best way to cut costs at the very start is to do some sharp thinking when choosing a college. If you are planning on college, consider your options. You can:

- Live at home, enroll in a low-cost 2-year college that offers courses good toward a bachelor's degree. Then transfer to a local four-year state college for your junior and senior years. This is the least expensive way to get a college education.

- Enroll in a public 4-year college or university in your home state. The tuition will definitely be higher than that of a 2-year college. If you decide to live on campus, it will cost you $5,500 more per year than attending college while living at home.

- Enroll in a public college or university outside your home state. This will mean paying stiff tuition charges. But establishing legal residency could save you a big amount. Tuition in California public colleges, for example, is one-fifth what you'd pay in several northeastern states.

- Register at a private college or university. This is the most expensive option, even if you live at home.

TAXES

Question: Where in North America can you find rock-bottom property taxes, no sales taxes, no taxes on any of your income, no niggling nickel-and-dime fees for registering a car or taking out a license to catch largemouth bass, and no inheritance taxes for your heirs to pay?

Answer: Dream on. This ideal tax haven would have to combine Louisiana's low property taxes with Alberta's absence of retail sales taxes and South Dakota's forgiveness of taxes on personal income. Unfortunately, you just can't find all these terrific tax breaks in one place. Although federal income taxes take nearly the same bite whether you live in New Bedford, New Orleans, or New York, states' taxes differ dramatically around the country. Sales taxes, excise taxes, license taxes, income taxes, property taxes, death taxes, gift taxes, and head taxes are just some of the forms that state taxes take. Depending on where you live, you many encounter all of them or only a few.

Property Taxes

Taxes on land and the buildings on it—whether they are homes, farms, industrial plants, or commercial buildings—are the biggest source of cash for local governments. They are imposed not by states but by the tens of thousands of cities, townships, counties, school districts, sanitary districts, hospital districts, and other assessing jurisdictions.

The state's role is to specify the maximum rate on the market value of the property, or a percentage of it, as the legal standard for local assessors to follow. The local assessor determines the value to be taxed. If you think the valuation is too high, you have a limited right of appeal. You can't escape property taxes in any state except Alaska, where you must be over 65 to take advantage of the exemption, but you can find significantly low rates in certain parts of the country. Nationally, the average bills on homes amount to 1.25 percent of their

market value, whereas the average bills in Alabama, Hawaii, Louisiana, New Mexico, and West Virginia are less than half that rate.

Sales Taxes

If people had a choice of raising income taxes or raising sales taxes, they would opt for the latter by a big margin according to recent polls. Sometimes called retail taxes or consumption taxes, sales taxes are collected at the store on the total amount of good purchased. After income taxes, they account for the largest source of revenue for state and provincial governments.

Among the states, the average base sales tax is edging up to 6 percent. Throughout Canada, the rate is much higher. If you're living in Mississippi or Rhode Island, you're paying America's highest state rate: 7 percent. If you're from Newfoundland, you're paying North America's highest rate: 12 percent. Canada also imposes a 7 percent value-added tax—the Goods and Services Tax, or GST—payable by consumers in addition to the provincial sales tax.

Alaska has no statewide sales tax but permits local governments to levy their own. Fifteen states levy a single tax, and thirty-one others permit cities and counties to add to the base rate. In Colorado, for example, the combined state and local sales tax can be more than double the state's 3 percent base rate. New Orleans International Airport adds 6 percent to Louisiana's 4 percent base rate. Hawaii has a general excise tax, New Mexico a gross receipts tax. Alberta, Delaware, Montana, New Hampshire, and Oregon collect no sales taxes at all. To a four-person family, this could mean a savings of a thousand dollars. But you can avoid paying almost that much in areas where food, medicine, and clothing are exempted.

Income Taxes

When the first federal income tax went into effect in 1913, two states—Mississippi and Wisconsin—were already collecting income taxes on their own. It was only during the 1920s and 1930s that the majority of states began to raise cash by tapping personal incomes. Today, forty-one states impose the tax. Two, New Hampshire and Tennessee, apply it only to income from interest and dividends. Seven states—Alaska, Florida, Nevada, South Dakota, Texas, Washington, and Wyoming—don't tax incomes at all.

North American Sales Tax Rates

UNITED STATES	RATE	HIGHEST LOCAL RATE
Alabama	4%	5%
Alaska	0	7
Arizona	5	4.25
Arkansas	4.625	
California	6	1.25
Colorado	3	4
Connecticut*	6	
District of Columbia	5.75	
Florida	6	1.5
Georgia	4	3
Hawaii*	4	
Idaho*	5	
Illinois	6.25	2.5
Indiana*	5	
Iowa	5	1
Kansas	4.9	2
Kentucky	6	
Louisiana	4	6.5
Maine*	5.5	
Maryland*	5	
Massachusetts*	5	
Michigan*	6	
Minnesota	6.5	1
Mississippi	7	3
Missouri	4.225	3.5
Nebraska	4.5	1.5
Nevada	6.5	
New Jersey*	6	
New Mexico	5	1.875

UNITED STATES	RATE	HIGHEST LOCAL RATE
New York	4	4.5
North Carolina	4	
North Dakota	5	2
Ohio	5	2
Oklahoma	4.5	5
Pennsylvania	6	1
Rhode Island*	7	
South Carolina	5	1
South Dakota	4	2
Tennessee	6	2.75
Texas	6.25	2
Utah	4.75	1.25
Vermont*	5	
Virginia*	3.5	
Washington	6.5	1.7
West Virginia*	6	
Wisconsin	5	.75
Wyoming	4	2

CANADA	RATE	HIGHEST LOCAL RATE
British Columbia*	7	
Manitoba*	7	
New Brunswick*	11	
Newfoundland*	12	
Nova Scotia*	11	
Ontario*	8	
Quebec*	8	
Saskatchewan*	9	

Source: Commerce Clearing House, Canadian Master Tax Guide and State Tax Guide.

Alaska, Alberta, Delaware, Montana, New Hampshire, and Oregon have no general sales tax.

*Indicates a single tax rate throughout the state or province. All other states allow local additions to their base tax rate.

Hawaii, Idaho, Kansas, South Dakota, Vermont, and Wyoming tax food, but allow an income tax credit to compensate poor households.

State Income Tax Rates

STATE	TAX RATE (%) LOW	HIGH	BRACKETS	INCOME BRACKETS ($) LOW	HIGH	PERSONAL EXEMPTION ($) SINGLE	MARRIED	CHILD
Alabama	2.0	5.0	3	500	3,000	1,500	3,000	300
Arizona	2.87	5.04	5	10,000	150,000	2,100	4,200	2,300
Arkansas	1.0	7.0	6	2,999	25,000	20 (c)	40 (c)	20
California	1.0	9.3	6	5,131	33,673	70 (c)	140 (c)	253
Colorado	5.0 flat rate							
Connecticut	3.0	4.5	2	6,250	6,250	12,000	24,000	0
Delaware	2.6	6.4	7	2,000	60,000	100 (c)	200 (c)	100
District of Columbia		6.0	9.5	310,000	20,000	1,370	2,740	1,370
Georgia	1.0	6.0	6	750	7,000	1,500	3,000	2,500
Hawaii	1.6	8.75	8	1,500	20,500	1,040	2,080	1,040
Idaho	2.0	8.2	8	1,000	20,000	2,750	5,500	2,750
Illinois	3.0 flat rate					1,650	3,300	1,650
Indiana	3.4 flat rate					1,000	2,000	1,000
Iowa	0.36	8.98	9	1,148	51,660	40 (c)	80 (c)	40

STATE	TAX RATE (%) LOW	HIGH	BRACKETS	INCOME BRACKETS ($) LOW	HIGH	PERSONAL EXEMPTION ($) SINGLE	MARRIED	CHILD
Kansas	4.1	6.45	315,000	30,000	2,250	4,500	2,250	
Kentucky	2.0	6.0	5	3,000	8,000	20 (c)	40 (c)	20
Louisiana	2.0	6.0	310,000	50,000	4,500	9,000	1,000	
Maine	2.0	8.5	4	4,150	16,500	2,750	5,500	2,750
Maryland	2.0	4.85	4	1,000	3,000	1,850	3,700	1,850
Massachusetts	5.95 flat rate					4,400	8,800	1,000
Michigan	4.4 flat rate					2,500	5,000	2,500
Minnesota	6.0	8.5	317,250	56,680	2,550	5,100	2,550	
Mississippi	3.0	5.0	3	5,000	10,000	6,000	9,500	1,500
Missouri	1.5	6.0	10	1,000	9,000	1,200	2,400	1,200
Montana	2.0	11.0	10	2,000	69,000	1,580	3,160	1,580
Nebraska	2.62	6.99	4	2,400	26,500	88 (c)	176 (c)	88
New Jersey	1.4	6.37	620,000	75,000	1,000	2,000	1,500	
New Mexico	1.7	8.2	7	5,500	65,000	2,750	5,500	2,750
New York	4.0	6.85	5	8,000	20,000	0	0	1,000
North Carolina	6.0	7.75	312,750	60,000	2,750	5,500	2,750	
North Dakota	2.67	12.0	8	3,000	50,000	2,750	5,500	2,750
Ohio	0.673	6.79	9	5,000	200,000	1,050	2,100	1,050
Oklahoma	0.5	6.75	8	1,000	10,000	1,000	2,000	1,000
Oregon	5.0	9.0	3	2,250	5,700	124 (c)	248 (c)	124
Pennsylvania	2.8 flat rate							
Rhode Island	26.5% Federal tax liability							
South Carolina	2.5	7.0	6	2,310	11,550	2,750	5,500	2,750
Utah	2.3	7.0	6	750	3,750	2,063	4,125	2,063
Vermont	25.0% Federal tax liability							
Virginia	2.0	5.75	4	3,000	17,000	800	1,600	800
West Virginia	3.0	6.5	510,000	60,000	2,000	4,000	2,000	
Wisconsin	4.77	6.77	3	7,500	15,001	0	0	50 (c)

Source: Federation of Tax Administrators.

Tax rates and brackets are for single individual returns. Alaska, Florida, Nevada, South Dakota, Texas, Washington, and Wyoming do not tax personal income. New Hampshire and Tennessee tax income from interest and dividends. (c) indicates a tax credit.

Transportation

If you travel often enough, you might take for granted expressway networks, airline routes, and passenger rails that lace up the continent's different points. But spreading out a map would show you that certain metro areas are transportation hubs with highway, rail, and air-route spokes, while others appear as lesser intersections, removed from the mainstream of inter-city travel.

Population size has something to do with an area's transportation assets, but so do the accidents of geography. There are twenty-six metro areas bigger than Denver, but because the Mile-High City is plunked down at the edge of the Rocky Mountains halfway between Chicago and Southern California, and midway from Houston to Seattle, only five other airports in North America are busier than Denver International.

Inter-city travel is only part of the picture. Some metro areas have efficient public transit fleets relied on by hundreds of thousands of commuters each working day. In other metro areas, aging diesel buses with optimistic schedules lurch along routes that rarely reach any neighborhoods except those close to downtown. Still other metro areas have no public transit at all.

GETTING AROUND TOWN

If you are moving to Atlanta, might your family get by without a second car if MARTA's routes reach your new neighborhood? If you are being transferred to company headquarters in downtown Cleveland, will it be more convenient to carpool or ride the RTA rails if you settle in Shaker Heights? How much time should you expect to spend each day getting to and from work? Becoming familiar with the local transportation features of a particular metro area will help you answer some of these questions.

The Commuting Life

Each weekday morning, in cities and towns all over, traffic trickles out of suburban streets, flows into arterial roads, and floods freeways to capacity with people bound for work. The morning rush hour lasts 118 minutes, between 7:01 and 8:59am, transportation experts say. Most workers travel by automobile, alone. One of five belongs to a car pool, and one of fifteen opts for public transit.

97

GETTING TO WORK AND BACK

For thousands of years, the longest any urban dweller had for a commute was 45 minutes. From ancient Athens and Rome to medieval Paris and London, that was the time it took to walk 3 miles from the edge of the city to its center.

Longest Commute (in minutes)

1. New York, NY	75.8
2. Long Island, NY	64.6
3. Washington, DC-MD-VA-WV	63.0
4. Chicago, IL	61.5
5. Riverside-San Bernardino, CA	59.3
6. Newburgh, NY	58.5
7. Monmouth-Ocean, NJ	57.5
8. Oakland, CA	57.5
9. Houston, TX	56.9
10. Vallejo-Fairfield-Napa, CA	56.8

Shortest Commute (in minutes)

1. Bismarck, ND	27.1
2. Grand Forks, ND-MN	27.4
3. Cheyenne, WY	29.5
4. Dubuque, IA	30.1
5. Fargo-Moorhead, ND-MN	30.7
6. Enid, OK	30.8
7. Great Falls, MT	30.9
8. Sheboygan, WI	31.5
9. Rochester, MN	31.6
10. Waterloo-Cedar Falls, IA	31.9

Source: Bureau of the Census. Figures are average journey-to-work minutes multiplied by 2.2 for a round-trip total.

The evening rush hour lasts longer: 150 minutes, from 4:30 to 7:00pm. There are more traffic delays at this time than in the morning when people so purposefully leave home and arrive at work in the shortest possible time. In the evening, many commuters stop for a drink, go shopping, run errands, or just dawdle. After all, you can't be fired for being late for supper. In fact, traffic experts say, even if you head straight home, the evening trip not only seems longer than the trip to work but actually is—20 percent longer.

How much time do metro-area workers spend going to and from the job each day? To allow for the longer trip home in the evening, *Places Rated* multiplies the average journey-to-work figure by 2.2 to estimate the round-trip time in each of the metro areas.

Daily commuting time increases with city size. Workers in Bismarck, ND, for instance, putting in 220 working days a year, spend about 100 hours commuting. Workers residing on Staten Island spend 325 hours taking the ferry to and from their Manhattan jobs. The contrast between Bismarck and Staten Island, then, is more than one between a prairie state capital and a section of the continent's largest city. Based on commuting time alone, Bismarckers have more free time than Staten Islanders, the equivalent of six 40-hour weeks each year.

Public Mass Transit

One reason for the long commute in big cities is the often exhausting job of making linked transit trips to get to work. The average duration of an *unlinked* transit trip—a direct route, with no transfers—is about 15 minutes. But many big-city commuters have to make linked trips: driving to a park-and-ride or kiss-and-ride lot; boarding a train, ferry, or bus; and sometimes switching again before finally getting to work.

Still, in larger cities where the tab for daily parking in a downtown garage nears $20, where rush-hour traffic approaches gridlock, and where distances are long and time always seems short, public transit really counts. In many a large city—Houston and Phoenix, for example—daily driving over long distances is a way of life unrelieved by rapid public transit; taking the bus is the only alternative. In other places, such as Atlanta, Toronto, Washington, and San Francisco, large local bus fleets are complemented by rapid transit rail systems.

Depending on where they want to go, New York City commuters can choose from bus, heavy rail, light rail, commuter railroad, ferryboat, and even aerial tramway service. New York straphangers may not always enjoy their subway ride to work, but few among the jostled riders aboard a rocking, grimy subway car would ever envy a Houston driver who has missed his or her exit on the Southwest Freeway at rush hour.

By Bus

In most cities, public transit and a roaring fleet of diesel-powered buses are synonymous. Unlike rapid rail and trolley networks, a bus system requires no expensive construction, cities can buy the service from private contractors, and routes can be easily changed to meet demand.

Each of the continent's 1,500 transit systems with fixed-route service puts motor buses on the street, but these systems vary in size and type of operation. Several large systems—Chicago's CTA, Toronto's TCC,

Getting Around Town

Washington's WMATA, and New York's NYCTA, for example—operate thousands of GMC, Orion, and Flyer buses around the clock with less than 2 minutes' wait between buses on the heaviest routes during morning and evening rush hours. At the other extreme are the one- and two-bus shoppers' specials that run loops in the central business district of smaller metro areas.

By Rail

Although buses can meet the demand for public transit nearly everywhere, rail lines are more efficient in carrying large numbers of rush-hour commuters in the major cities. Several kinds of rail service are available in the big metro areas, from rapid rail to trolley car to commuter train.

Rapid rail lines.   Owing to their exclusive rights-of-way, they are unaffected by traffic jams. Their trains and trams not only carry thousands of people, but carry them quickly. The average speed of buses during peak rush hour, nationwide, is 13 miles per hour. Rapid rail systems average more than 22 miles per hour.

There are two types of rapid rail lines in use today in twenty-four metro areas—heavy rail, which accounts for 2.5 billion passenger trips in a year, and light rail, which accounts for 150 million passenger trips. Both are electrically powered, and both may be found in the same city.

Heavy rail systems.   Known locally as subways, elevated rail, or Els, heavy rail systems have high-level platform stations. The cars are individually powered through the third rail, and are hitched together to form longer trains during rush hours. A typical passenger trip aboard a heavy rail train is over 5 miles and speeds along at 20 miles per hour. New York City's heavy rail system, composed of two separate networks, is the world's largest, with 6,248 cars traveling more than 450 miles of track. Philadelphia also has two systems. Sixteen other metro areas have heavy rail systems.

Light rail cars.   Powered by overhead electrical wires, light rail cars travel at half the speed of heavy rail cars. Because their tracks are laid aboveground, they are less expensive to build and therefore are the fastest-growing form of mass transit.

Trolley coaches.   Trolleys are streetcar-type railways that travel on city streets with semiprivate or exclusive rights-of-way. They are a less efficient form of travel than rapid rail—trams are at the mercy of automobile traffic and, in some cities, must stop for streetlights. Another disadvantage is that their routes cannot be altered. These systems have been largely replaced by buses; in fact, only nine metro areas in North America still have trolley coach operations.

Commuter railroads.   Since the 19th century, trains have been an important form of transportation in areas ranging from more distant suburbs to the central part of major cities. Using both locomotive-hauled and self-propelled passenger cars, this service is marked by multi-trip tickets, station-to-station fares, railroad employment practices, and usually only one or two stations in the central business district.

A typical passenger trip covers 23 miles at over 35 miles per hour. Twenty-four commuter railroads in fifteen metro areas ferry nearly 1.5 million commuters to and from work. The largest commuter railroad network, made up of seven firms, is found in New York and uses 1,650 cars to move 525,000 riders in a typical weekday. In Chicago, the next largest commuter railroad center, nine carriers operating 850 cars transport 300,000 workers in a typical day.

LIGHT RAIL: A DESIRE NAMED STREETCAR

North America's light rail revolution began in 1978 in Edmonton, AB. The San Diego Trolley, incorrectly credited as the first new system, opened 2 years later in 1980. Twenty-four cities now operate light rail systems . . .

City	Route Miles	City	Route Miles
Baltimore	44	New Orleans	16
Boston	56	Philadelphia	69
Buffalo	12	Pittsburgh	38
Calgary	79	Portland	30
Cleveland	31	Sacramento	36
Dallas	41	St. Louis	34
Denver	11	San Diego	48
Edmonton	48	San Francisco	50
Galveston	5	San Jose	39
Los Angeles	82	Seattle	4
Memphis	4	Toronto	4
Newark	8	Vancouver	18

. . . and in five other cities, new light rail lines are under construction or are about to be opened . . .

Cincinnati	Orlando	Victoria, BC
Minneapolis	Salt Lake City	

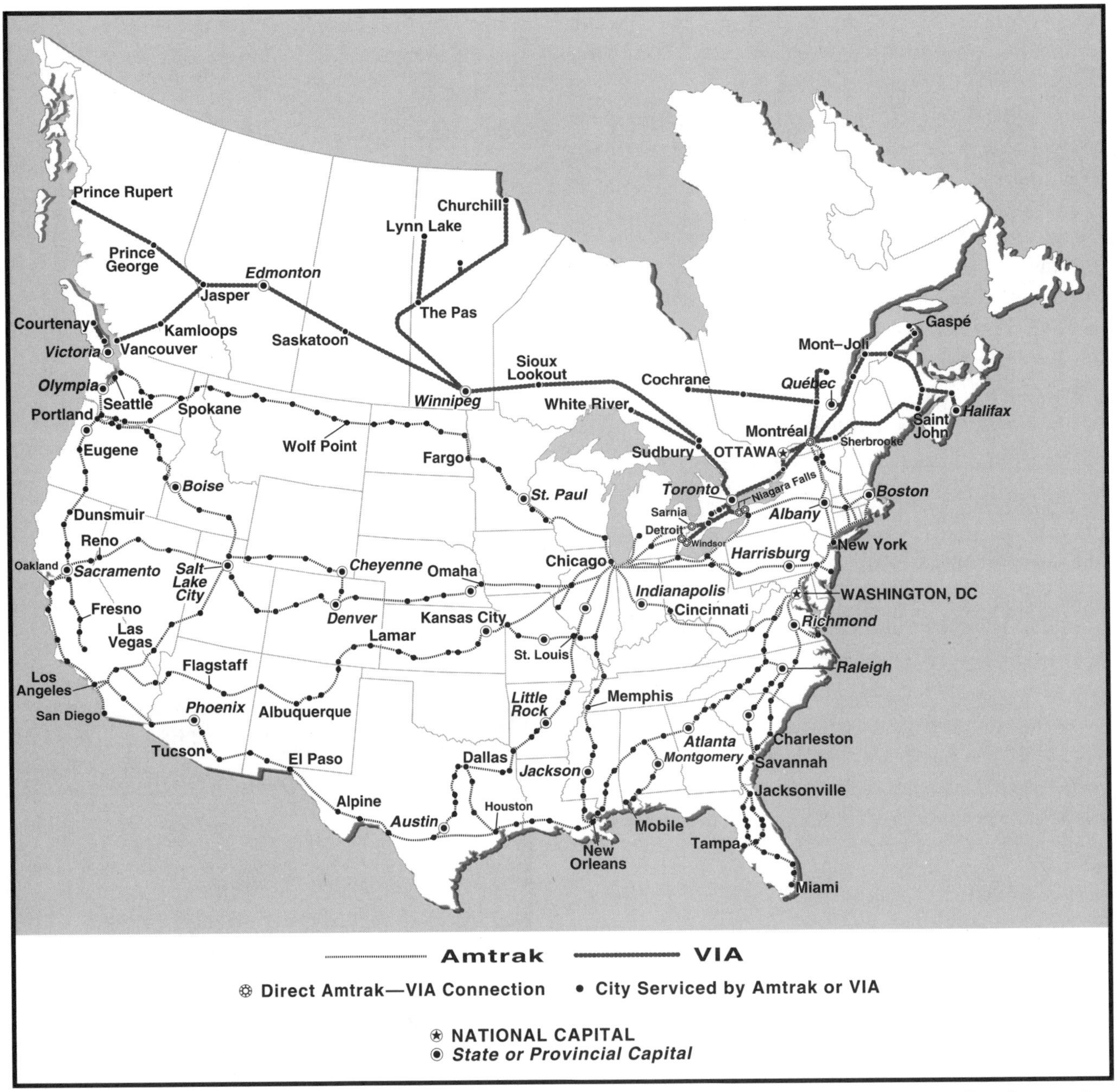

The map shows Amtrak and VIA rail routes across the United States and Canada, with cities including Prince Rupert, Prince George, Courtenay, Victoria, Olympia, Portland, Seattle, Spokane, Kamloops, Vancouver, Jasper, Edmonton, Saskatoon, Lynn Lake, Churchill, The Pas, Winnipeg, Sioux Lookout, White River, Cochrane, Mont-Joli, Gaspé, Québec, Halifax, Saint John, Sherbrooke, Montréal, OTTAWA, Sudbury, Boston, Toronto, Niagara Falls, Albany, Sarnia, Detroit, Windsor, New York, Harrisburg, Chicago, WASHINGTON, DC, Richmond, Indianapolis, Cincinnati, Raleigh, St. Louis, Memphis, Little Rock, Kansas City, Lamar, Denver, Cheyenne, Omaha, St. Paul, Fargo, Wolf Point, Boise, Dunsmuir, Reno, Oakland, Sacramento, Salt Lake City, Fresno, Las Vegas, Los Angeles, San Diego, Flagstaff, Phoenix, Albuquerque, Tucson, El Paso, Alpine, Austin, Dallas, Jackson, Houston, New Orleans, Mobile, Montgomery, Atlanta, Charleston, Savannah, Jacksonville, Tampa, Miami, Eugene.

Legend:

·········· Amtrak   ———— VIA

⊕ Direct Amtrak—VIA Connection   • City Serviced by Amtrak or VIA

✪ NATIONAL CAPITAL
◉ State or Provincial Capital

Copyright © 1997 by Places Rated Partnership

Thomas Nast, Cartographer

INTER-CITY TRAVEL

"You can't get there from here" is the punch line of the old joke about the lost city sharper who asked directions of a bemused farmer. The line has little meaning in today's metropolitan areas, given the networks of well-traveled highways, railroads, and airways that connect these places.

Or does it? Obviously, you can't ramp onto the interstate or board AMTRAK if your destination is Anchorage or Honolulu. For that matter, you can't get to Bloomington, Brazoria, or Bremerton by the same means. When it comes to inter-city travel options, some metro areas are better off than others.

National Highways

Back in 1938, when President Franklin Roosevelt idly penciled three east-west and five north-south lines on a U.S. map as part of a proposed national highway system, he probably had no idea that his drawing would become so important in determining whether many rural towns would grow and many others would decline. He was thinking originally of a 34,000-mile network of multilane toll roads.

Although the Bureau of Public Roads soon dropped the concept of collecting tolls, the basic routes on Roosevelt's map foresaw the Interstate Highway System,

The numbers in the middle of the red, white, and blue shield-shaped signs along the interstate system were developed in 1957 by American Association of State Highway Transportation officials. There are 35 odd-numbered routes running north and south and 27 even-numbered routes running east and west. The lowest-numbered routes are in the West and the South; I-5, for example, lies along the nation's West Coast and I-10 runs along the southern border.

In cities, these one- or two-digit numbers don't change as long as they are part of the major traffic stream. Beltways around the city, on the other hand, carry three numbers; the main route number with an even-numbered prefix. For example, I-495, an 88-mile long route around Boston, and I-287, a 94-mile long loop skirting New York City, are the two longest beltways in the interstate system. If a main route carries an odd-numbered prefix (such as I-195 in Miami or I-780 in San Francisco), the route is a spur that connects with the main route at only one end.

Three-digit route numbers are never used twice in the same state. In New York, I-90 runs through Schenectady, Syracuse, Rochester, and Buffalo, and the beltways off this main route in those cities are numbered, respectively, I-890, I-690, I-490, and I-290. This rule isn't carried across state lines, however. Two cities on I-10 but in different states, Houston and New Orleans, have the identical beltway number of I-610.

Empty and Congested Interstates

According to the U.S. Department of Transportation, the busiest stretches on the interstate carry 300,000 to 500,000 vehicles every 24 hours. The loneliest carry fewer than 2,500.

Busiest Stretches

I-5, I-20, I-405, I-605 in Los Angeles

I-5 in Seattle

I-10, I-45, I-59, I-610 in Houston

I-25 in Denver

I-35E, I-635 in Dallas

I-75 in Atlanta

I-80, I-580 in Oakland

I-80, I-380 in San Francisco

I-90, I-94, I-290 in Chicago

I-95 in New York

I-280 in San Jose

I-395 in Washington, DC

Loneliest Stretches

I-15 between Idaho Falls, ID, and Butte, MT

I-25 between Buffalo, WY, and Casper, WY

I-29 between Grand Forks, ND, and the Canadian border

I-29 between Sioux Falls, SD, and Fargo-Moorehead, ND

I-70 between Cove Fort, UT, and the Colorado border

I-90 between Buffalo, WY, and Gillette, WY

I-91 between Derby Line, VT, and St. Johnsbury, VT

I-94 between Billings, MT, and the North Dakota border

Transportation

a river of economic life to cities and towns along the way and possibly a cause of stagnation for those that were bypassed.

The interstate system is a complete 42,500-mile road network, at least four traffic lanes wide, linking nearly every American city with a population of more than 50,000. Even though interstate routes account for only 1 percent of all road and street mileage in the United States, they carry 25 percent of all the traffic. Yet one in six U.S. metro areas isn't on the interstate network. In Canada, half of the metro areas aren't on that country's counterpart, the 4,800-mile Trans-Canada Highway.

Boarding Pass, Please

It's getting to be an old saying in the South that when you die and are en route to heaven or hell, you'll have to make connections in Atlanta. Atlanta's airport, Hartsfield International, is now the world's busiest.

Like other airports reached by scheduled airlines, Hartsfield is a 20th-century urban landmark in the same way the railroad station was a sign of the times in the late 19th century. Most of the 296 airports served by major airlines in the United States and Canada are quiet, even desolate places.

But some, like Hartsfield, resemble self-contained cities and, of the nearly 600 million people who board domestic flights, one in ten travels between thirty of these airports in the continent's large hubs. Both Hartsfield and Chicago's O'Hare International Airport board more passengers than the 200 smallest airports combined.

SOME DAYS . . .

You stand the best chance of dodging airport jams if you fly on Thursday afternoon and Saturday night. The worst travel days used to be Friday and Sunday. Now they are Tuesday and Wednesday because more people take advantage of special fares requiring midweek travel.

. . . You're Better Off in Large Hubs

The Federal Aviation Administration (FAA) rates each metro area for its share of airline service.

A metro area is a . . .	if passengers departing its airports total . . .
large hub	1% or more
medium hub	0.25% to 0.99%
small hub	0.05% to 0.24%
nonhub	less than 0.05%
	. . . of all U.S. airline passengers in a year.

There's one big advantage to living in a large hub, besides having a wider choice of carriers with more frequent nonstop flights to more destinations. Flying between large hubs is cheaper.

The cost of an airline ticket into and out of Bismarck, ND (a nonhub) or Charleston, WV (a small hub) helps subsidize the same airline's small profit from a New York vacationer's air travel to Miami or a Los Angeles conventioneer's trip to Chicago. When airlines skirmish with bargain fares between large hubs, travelers in the smaller hubs end up paying part of the tab.

THE BUSIEST INTER-CITY RAIL ROUTES

Service aboard trains in VIA Rail Canada's St. Lawrence Corridor and AMTRAK's Northeast Corridor account for half of each country's passenger rail traffic.

AMTRAK Northeast Corridor	Annual Passengers
NortheastDirect (Boston-Washington)	5,510,000
Metroliners (New York-Washington)	2,025,000
New York-Philadelphia	1,711,000
New York-Albany-Niagara Falls	1,071,000
New York-Philadelphia-Harrisburg	550,000
AMTRAK Inter-City	
Chicago-Salt Lake City-Oakland	638,000
Chicago-Seattle/Portland	453,000
Chicago-Milwaukee	447,000
New York-Charleston-Miami/Tampa	421,000
Chicago-Detroit-Pontiac/Toledo	395,000
AMTRAK Western	
Santa Barbara-LAX-San Diego	1,629,000
Oakland-Bakersfield	554,000
Los Angeles-Seattle	452,000
San Jose-Roseville	367,000
Seattle-Portland-Eugene	127,000
VIA The Corridor	
Montreal-Toronto	924,000
Toronto-Windsor	656,000
Toronto-Ottawa	524,000

Source: AMTRAK, VIA Rail Canada.

Riding the Rails

Seventy years ago, eight of ten people who had to get from one North American city to another did so aboard a train. There were 20,000 different ones from which to choose, if you didn't care where you were going. The Twentieth Century Limited, El Capitan, Blue Streak—each had a unique, trademarked name. They still do—Bay State, Bonaventure, California Zephyr, Canadian, City of New Orleans, Hiawatha, Sunset Limited, Empire Builder, Texas Eagle, and Yankee Clipper—but today there are just 292 of them. Over the years, their share of the commercial inter-city passenger traffic has dwindled to less than 5 percent.

If passenger trains are ever to rise again, the renaissance will be caused not by high gasoline prices and spot fuel shortages, but by intolerable congestion on inter-city highways. Railroads have two priceless assets:

existing tracks and rights-of-way into the continent's population centers.

The National Railroad Passenger Corporation, a profit-making body, was created by Congress to subsidize the passenger business of its member railroads. Better known as AMTRAK, it started operation in 1971. Today it carries virtually all of the 25 million passengers who board U.S. inter-city trains each year. VIA, Canada's inter-city passenger rail counterpart, also carries nearly all of that country's train passengers.

The passenger rails don't reach everywhere, however. Although AMTRAK's and VIA's timetables boast of stops at hundreds of cities and towns from Halifax, NS, to San Diego, CA, 157 of the 354 metro areas aren't on the route system. The metro areas bypassed include

BUSIEST INTERNATIONAL ROUTES

Half of the 70 million passengers aboard nonstop international flights fly between just nineteen city pairs. Los Angeles's LAX is now North America's dominant international gateway.

From/To	From/To	Passengers (in Millions)
New York (JFK)	London (LHR)	5.1
Honolulu	Tokyo	4.3
Los Angeles	Tokyo	3.6
Los Angeles	London (LHR)	2.7
Chicago (ORD)	London (LHR)	2.1
Chicago (ORD)	Toronto	2.1
Honolulu	Osaka	2.1
Los Angeles	Taipei	1.9
Miami	Caracas	1.9
San Francisco	London (LHR)	1.9
New York (LGA)	Toronto	1.8
Washington (IAD)	London (LHR)	1.8
San Francisco	Tokyo	1.7
Los Angeles	Osaka	1.6
Los Angeles	Mexico City	1.5
Los Angeles	Seoul	1.5
Los Angeles	Sydney	1.5
Los Angeles	Vancouver	1.5
New York (JFK)	Tokyo	1.5

Source: Derived from most recent FAA origin and destination surveys. The heaviest domestic jet traffic between a Canadian city pair is that of Montreal and Toronto at 1.1 million passengers. The busiest Canadian international route is Chicago and Toronto with 2 million passengers.

BUSIEST COMMUTER ROUTES

One in ten passengers who fly aboard commuter airlines travel between just thirteen airports. Commuter aircraft are officially defined as all non-jet commercial aircraft with fewer than sixty seats.

From/To	From/To	Passengers (in Thousands)
Miami	Orlando	296
Miami	Tampa	229
Fresno	Los Angeles	217
Bangor	Boston	209
Los Angeles	Monterey	209
Anchorage	Kenai	207
Grand Canyon	Las Vegas	197
Fresno	San Francisco	186
Sacramento	San Francisco	185
Charlotte	Hilton Head	178
Boston	Portland	166
Hyannis	Nantucket	159
Key West	Miami	153

Busiest Domestic Jet Routes

City pairs in the Pacific and Southwestern states now dominate the top nineteen jet airline routes.

From/To	From/To	Passengers (in Millions)
Honolulu	Kahului	3.5
Las Vegas	Los Angeles	3.2
Honolulu	Los Angeles	2.8
Atlanta	Dallas	2.6
Chicago	Los Angeles	2.5
Chicago	Denver	2.4
Los Angeles	Phoenix	2.4
Atlanta	Chicago	2.3
Honolulu	Lihue	2.3
Las Vegas	Phoenix	2.3
Los Angeles	New York	2.3
Chicago	San Francisco	2.1
Chicago	New York	1.9
Dallas	Houston	1.9
Denver	Los Angeles	1.9
New York	Atlanta	1.9
Tampa	Atlanta	1.9
Chicago	Dallas	1.8
Honolulu	Kailua/Kona	1.8

such large places as Calgary, Tulsa, Louisville, and Des Moines.

By far the biggest markets for train service are in the U.S. northeast corridor and the St. Lawrence corridor in Canada. But the fastest-growing markets are on the West Coast, particularly for the 2-hour-and-40-minute run between Los Angeles and San Diego and for the 6-hour San Francisco–Bakersfield route.

JUDGING TRANSPORTATION

Would a shopper in Syracuse or San Angelo have a better chance of finding a seat on a bus? Which airport—Calgary's or Denver's—has departures to more nonstop destinations? Which metro area at opposite ends of the

continent, Seattle or New York, is nearer the greatest number of other metro areas?

Transportation, let's admit, means differing things to the first 100 people walking out of Grand Central Terminal or passengers finding their seats between rows 25 and 15 on a 737 at Los Angeles International. For some, it takes in the waiting time for a subway, the sanitation of seats and floors, and the price of a ticket. Fine, others might say, but it also includes the ease of getting around town and getting around the rest of the country. Do you have to make a connection every time you want to fly somewhere?

To reconcile these disparate views, *Places Rated* groups each metro area's transportation features into three factors: Commute, Connectivity, and Centrality.

Commute   considers the time it takes to get to work and back plus the miles the local public transit fleet racks up each year carrying passengers. The shorter the commuting time and the more transit revenue miles, the better. Both get equal weight. Winners include small and mid-size Canadian metro areas. Losers are small southern metro areas without public transit.

Connectivity   combines national (Interstate System and Trans-Canada) highways, passenger rail departures, and nonstop airline destinations. Passenger rail departures get the least weight. Except in dense urban corridors, riding the rails plays a minor part in inter-city travel. National highways get more weight, but are counted only if a metro area is a junction of one or more. A metro area's nonstop commuter, domestic jet, and international airline destinations are weighted equally. Connectivity winners are New York, Chicago, Toronto, and Los Angeles.

Centrality   measures how near a metro area is to all other metro areas. Quick: In North America, which two airports ship the most freight each year? Answer: Louisville's Standiford Field and Memphis International. Not for nothing is one the hub for United Parcel Service and the other for FedEx. Both airports are near a geographic point where every other metro area airport is nearest. Centrality winners include Louisville and Memphis, and Cincinnati and Indianapolis as well. Losers are Anchorage, Edmonton, Honolulu, Seattle, and Vancouver.

SCORING: TRANSPORTATION

Each factor is weighted differently—connectivity is 60 percent of the final score, commute is 30 percent, and centrality, 10 percent. A metro area's final score is its percentile on a scale of 0 to 100 corresponding to its rank. Chicago's final score is 100.00, Lafayette, IN's is 49.85; and Houma, LA's is 0.00. They are, respectively, the best, average, and worst North American metro areas for transportation.

RANKINGS: TRANSPORTATION

Three broad factors are used to rate each metro area for transportation: (1) its supply of public transit and the typical time it takes to get to work and back; (2) its connectivity with other metro areas via national highways, scheduled air service, and passenger rail service; and (3) its relative nearness to all other metro areas.

Metro Areas from Best to Worst

RANK	SCORE
1. Chicago, IL	100.00
2. Pittsburgh, PA	99.71
3. New York, NY	99.43
4. Cincinnati, OH-KY-IN	99.15
5. Detroit, MI	98.86
6. Denver, CO	98.58
7. Atlanta, GA	98.30
8. Toronto, ON	98.01
9. St. Louis, MO-IL	97.73
10. Minneapolis-St. Paul, MN-WI	97.45

RANK	SCORE
11. Washington, DC-MD-VA-WV	97.16
12. Salt Lake City-Ogden, UT	96.88
13. Milwaukee-Waukesha, WI	96.60
14. Cleveland-Lorain-Elyria, OH	96.31
15. Newark, NJ	96.03
16. Philadelphia, PA-NJ	95.75
17. Dallas, TX	95.46
18. Montreal, PQ	95.18
19. Baltimore, MD	94.90
20. Boston, MA-NH	94.61

RANK	SCORE
21. Houston, TX	94.33
22. Charlotte-Gastonia-Rock Hill, NC-SC	94.05
23. Kansas City, MO-KS	93.76
24. Los Angeles-Long Beach, CA	93.48
25. Indianapolis, IN	93.20
26. Memphis, TN-AR-MS	92.91
27. Fort Worth-Arlington, TX	92.63
28. Springfield, MA	92.35
29. Raleigh-Durham-Chapel Hill, NC	92.06
30. Edmonton, AB	91.78
31. Tampa-St. Petersburg-Clearwater, FL	91.50
32. Columbus, OH	91.21
33. Regina, SK	90.93
34. Miami, FL	90.65
35. Calgary, AB	90.36
36. Louisville, KY-IN	90.08
37. Ottawa-Hull, ON-PQ	89.80
38. Phoenix-Mesa, AZ	89.51
39. San Diego, CA	89.23
40. Nashville, TN	88.95
41. Syracuse, NY	88.66
42. Dayton-Springfield, OH	88.38
43. Portland-Vancouver, OR-WA	88.10
44. Hartford, CT	87.81
45. Las Vegas, NV-AZ	87.53
46. Orlando, FL	87.25
47. Seattle-Bellevue-Everett, WA	86.96
48. San Francisco, CA	86.68
49. Reno, NV	86.40
50. Buffalo-Niagara Falls, NY	86.11
51. Greensboro–Winston-Salem–High Point, NC	85.83
52. Omaha, NE-IA	85.55
53. Halifax, NS	85.26
54. New Orleans, LA	84.98
55. Vancouver, BC	84.70
56. Anchorage, AK	84.41
57. Albuquerque, NM	84.13
58. Victoria, BC	83.85
59. Winnipeg, MB	83.56
60. Saskatoon, SK	83.28
61. Providence-Fall River-Warwick, RI-MA	83.00
62. Albany-Schenectady-Troy, NY	82.71
63. Tacoma, WA	82.43
64. Rochester, NY	82.15
65. Jacksonville, FL	81.86
66. Fort Lauderdale, FL	81.58
67. Norfolk-Virginia Beach-Newport News, VA-NC	81.30
68. Quebec City, PQ	81.01
69. San Antonio, TX	80.73
70. Richmond-Petersburg, VA	80.45
71. Davenport-Moline-Rock Island, IA-IL	80.16
72. Birmingham, AL	79.88
73. Riverside-San Bernardino, CA	79.60
74. San Jose, CA	79.32
75. Sacramento, CA	79.03
76. Austin-San Marcos, TX	78.75
77. Honolulu, HI	78.47
78. Des Moines, IA	78.18
79. West Palm Beach-Boca Raton, FL	77.90
80. Harrisburg-Lebanon-Carlisle, PA	77.62
81. Grand Rapids-Muskegon-Holland, MI	77.33
82. Spokane, WA	77.05

RANK	SCORE
83. Colorado Springs, CO	76.77
84. Saint John, NB	76.48
85. Little Rock-North Little Rock, AR	76.20
86. Greenville-Spartanburg-Anderson, SC	75.92
87. Windsor, ON	75.63
88. Fort Myers-Cape Coral, FL	75.35
89. Toledo, OH	75.07
90. Oklahoma City, OK	74.78
91. Wichita, KS	74.50
92. Billings, MT	74.22
93. Champaign-Urbana, IL	73.93
94. Madison, WI	73.65
95. Charleston, WV	73.37
96. Lexington, KY	73.08
97. Oakland, CA	72.80
98. Orange County, CA	72.52
99. Bloomington-Normal, IL	72.23
100. Portland, ME	71.95
101. South Bend, IN	71.67
102. Tulsa, OK	71.38
103. Tucson, AZ	71.10
104. Appleton-Oshkosh-Neenah, WI	70.82
105. Lansing-East Lansing, MI	70.53
106. El Paso, TX	70.25
107. Knoxville, TN	69.97
108. Akron, OH	69.68
109. Sarasota-Bradenton, FL	69.40
110. Fresno, CA	69.12
111. Thunder Bay, ON	68.83
112. Kitchener, ON	68.55
113. Lincoln, NE	68.27
114. Jackson, MS	67.98
115. Roanoke, VA	67.70
116. Boise City, ID	67.42
117. Binghamton, NY	67.13
118. Atlantic City-Cape May, NJ	66.85
119. Allentown-Bethlehem-Easton, PA	66.57
120. Bangor, ME	66.28
121. Burlington, VT	66.00
122. Fort Wayne, IN	65.72
123. Canton-Massillon, OH	65.43
124. Evansville-Henderson, IN-KY	65.15
125. Santa Barbara-Santa Maria-Lompoc, CA	64.87
126. Shreveport-Bossier City, LA	64.58
127. Pensacola, FL	64.30
128. Cedar Rapids, IA	64.02
129. Columbia, SC	63.73
130. Elmira, NY	63.45
131. Long Island, NY	63.17
132. Lubbock, TX	62.88
133. Springfield, IL	62.60
134. Scranton–Wilkes-Barre–Hazleton, PA	62.32
135. Tallahassee, FL	62.03
136. Sioux Falls, SD	61.75
137. Kalamazoo-Battle Creek, MI	61.47
138. Richland-Kennewick-Pasco, WA	61.18
139. Erie, PA	60.90
140. Myrtle Beach, SC	60.62
141. Green Bay, WI	60.33
142. Amarillo, TX	60.05
143. Eugene-Springfield, OR	59.77

Transportation

continues

Metro Areas from Best to Worst (cont.)

RANK	SCORE		RANK	SCORE
144. St. John's, NF	59.49		204. Alexandria, LA	42.49
145. London, ON	59.20		205. New Haven-Meriden, CT	42.20
146. Flint, MI	58.92		206. Beaumont-Port Arthur, TX	41.92
147. Charleston-North Charleston, SC	58.64		207. Fargo-Moorhead, ND-MN	41.64
148. Great Falls, MT	58.35		208. Daytona Beach, FL	41.35
149. Wausau, WI	58.07		209. Huntington-Ashland, WV-KY-OH	41.07
150. Peoria-Pekin, IL	57.79		210. Pocatello, ID	40.79
151. Missoula, MT	57.50		211. Lancaster, PA	40.50
152. Baton Rouge, LA	57.22		212. Fort Smith, AR-OK	40.22
153. Chattanooga, TN-GA	56.94		213. Worcester, MA-CT	39.94
154. Sudbury, ON	56.65		214. San Luis Obispo-Atascadero-Paso Robles, CA	39.66
155. Monroe, LA	56.37		215. Hamilton, ON	39.37
156. Salinas, CA	56.09		216. Utica-Rome, NY	39.09
157. Springfield, MO	55.80		217. Casper, WY	38.81
158. Gainesville, FL	55.52		218. Williamsport, PA	38.52
159. Savannah, GA	55.24		219. Barnstable-Yarmouth, MA	38.24
160. Rapid City, SD	54.95		220. Cheyenne, WY	37.96
161. Asheville, NC	54.67		221. Grand Forks, ND-MN	37.67
162. Dubuque, IA	54.39		222. Johnstown, PA	37.39
163. Saginaw-Bay City-Midland, MI	54.10		223. Yuma, AZ	37.11
164. Odessa-Midland, TX	53.82		224. Biloxi-Gulfport-Pascagoula, MS	36.82
165. State College, PA	53.54		225. Abilene, TX	36.54
166. Charlottesville, VA	53.25		226. Decatur, IL	36.26
167. La Crosse, WI-MN	52.97		227. Wichita Falls, TX	35.97
168. Waterloo-Cedar Falls, IA	52.69		228. Naples, FL	35.69
169. Duluth-Superior, MN-WI	52.40		229. Augusta-Aiken, GA-SC	35.41
170. Rockford, IL	52.12		230. Lake Charles, LA	35.12
171. Huntsville, AL	51.84		231. Bridgeport, CT	34.84
172. Grand Junction, CO	51.55		232. Parkersburg-Marietta, WV-OH	34.56
173. Mobile, AL	51.27		233. Columbia, MO	34.27
174. St. Cloud, MN	50.99		234. Waco, TX	33.99
175. Bakersfield, CA	50.70		235. Santa Fe, NM	33.71
176. Montgomery, AL	50.42		236. Bismarck, ND	33.42
177. Fayetteville-Springdale-Rogers, AR	50.14		237. Florence, SC	33.14
178. Lafayette, IN	49.85		238. Joplin, MO	32.86
179. Johnson City-Kingsport-Bristol, TN-VA	49.57		239. New Bedford, MA	32.57
180. Corpus Christi, TX	49.29		240. McAllen-Edinburg-Mission, TX	32.29
181. Youngstown-Warren, OH	49.00		241. Las Cruces, NM	32.01
182. Newburgh, NY-PA	48.72		242. Bryan-College Station, TX	31.72
183. Reading, PA	48.44		243. Hagerstown, MD	31.44
184. Bellingham, WA	48.15		244. Killeen-Temple, TX	31.16
185. Medford-Ashland, OR	47.87		245. Jacksonville, NC	30.87
186. Manchester, NH	47.59		246. Jackson, TN	30.59
187. Rochester, MN	47.30		247. Chico-Paradise, CA	30.31
188. Yakima, WA	47.02		248. Owensboro, KY	30.02
189. Laredo, TX	46.74		249. Dothan, AL	29.74
190. Chicoutimi-Jonquiere, PQ	46.45		250. Athens, GA	29.46
191. Sioux City, IA-NE	46.17		251. Macon, GA	29.17
192. Wilmington, NC	45.89		252. Pueblo, CO	28.89
193. Benton Harbor, MI	45.60		253. Cumberland, MD-WV	28.61
194. Eau Claire, WI	45.32		254. Tyler, TX	28.32
195. Columbus, GA-AL	45.04		255. Albany, GA	28.04
196. Topeka, KS	44.75		256. Terre Haute, IN	27.76
197. Lafayette, LA	44.47		257. Brownsville-Harlingen-San Benito, TX	27.47
198. Trenton, NJ	44.19		258. Jamestown, NY	27.19
199. Lynchburg, VA	43.90		259. Altoona, PA	26.91
200. Redding, CA	43.62		260. Greenville, NC	26.62
201. Panama City, FL	43.34		261. San Angelo, TX	26.34
202. Fort Walton Beach, FL	43.05		262. Enid, OK	26.06
203. Fayetteville, NC	42.77		263. Sherbrooke, PQ	25.77

RANK	SCORE
264. Jonesboro, AR	25.49
265. Flagstaff, AZ-UT	25.21
266. Lawton, OK	24.92
267. Hickory-Morganton-Lenoir, NC	24.64
268. Visalia-Tulare-Porterville, CA	24.36
269. Texarkana, TX-Texarkana, AR	24.07
270. Melbourne-Titusville-Palm Bay, FL	23.79
271. Longview-Marshall, TX	23.51
272. Dutchess County, NY	23.22
273. Merced, CA	22.94
274. Iowa City, IA	22.66
275. Santa Rosa, CA	22.37
276. Rocky Mount, NC	22.09
277. Sheboygan, WI	21.81
278. Oshawa, ON	21.52
279. Modesto, CA	21.24
280. St. Catharines-Niagara, ON	20.96
281. New London-Norwich, CT-RI	20.67
282. Hattiesburg, MS	20.39
283. Bremerton, WA	20.11
284. Yolo, CA	19.83
285. Pittsfield, MA	19.54
286. Gary, IN	19.26
287. Middlesex-Somerset-Hunterdon, NJ	18.98
288. Muncie, IN	18.69
289. Wilmington-Newark, DE-MD	18.41
290. Lima, OH	18.13
291. Bloomington, IN	17.84
292. Florence, AL	17.56
293. Janesville-Beloit, WI	17.28
294. Victoria, TX	16.99
295. Mansfield, OH	16.71
296. St. Joseph, MO	16.43
297. Elkhart-Goshen, IN	16.14
298. Ann Arbor, MI	15.86
299. Tuscaloosa, AL	15.58
300. Vineland-Millville-Bridgeton, NJ	15.29
301. Lewiston-Auburn, ME	15.01
302. Salem, OR	14.73
303. Bergen-Passaic, NJ	14.44
304. Wheeling, WV-OH	14.16
305. Olympia, WA	13.88
306. Sumter, SC	13.59
307. Fort Collins-Loveland, CO	13.31
308. Clarksville-Hopkinsville, TN-KY	13.03
309. Boulder-Longmont, CO	12.74

RANK	SCORE
310. Sharon, PA	12.46
311. Monmouth-Ocean, NJ	12.18
312. Kokomo, IN	11.89
313. Greeley, CO	11.61
314. Lawrence, KS	11.33
315. Provo-Orem, UT	11.04
316. York, PA	10.76
317. Trois-Rivieres, PQ	10.48
318. Dover, DE	10.19
319. Jersey City, NJ	9.91
320. Kenosha, WI	9.63
321. Stamford-Norwalk, CT	9.34
322. Racine, WI	9.06
323. Jackson, MI	8.78
324. Lakeland-Winter Haven, FL	8.49
325. Pine Bluff, AR	8.21
326. Danville, VA	7.93
327. Santa Cruz-Watsonville, CA	7.64
328. Steubenville-Weirton, OH-WV	7.36
329. Anniston, AL	7.08
330. Hamilton-Middletown, OH	6.79
331. Goldsboro, NC	6.51
332. Glens Falls, NY	6.23
333. Kankakee, IL	5.94
334. Vallejo-Fairfield-Napa, CA	5.66
335. Lawrence, MA-NH	5.38
336. Ventura, CA	5.09
337. Yuba City, CA	4.81
338. Fitchburg-Leominster, MA	4.53
339. Gadsden, AL	4.24
340. Waterbury, CT	3.96
341. Brockton, MA	3.68
342. Danbury, CT	3.39
343. Punta Gorda, FL	3.11
344. Lowell, MA-NH	2.83
345. Portsmouth-Rochester, NH-ME	2.54
346. Decatur, AL	2.26
347. Galveston-Texas City, TX	1.98
348. Ocala, FL	1.69
349. Stockton-Lodi, CA	1.41
350. Nashua, NH	1.13
351. Fort Pierce-Port St. Lucie, FL	0.84
352. Sherman-Denison, TX	0.56
353. Brazoria, TX	0.28
354. Houma, LA	0.00

PLACE PROFILES: TRANSPORTATION

The following pages detail local commuting time, mass transit, and inter-city travel assets in each metro area.

Information sources include American Public Transit Association, *Transit Fact Book*, 1999; Canadian Urban Transit Association, *Canadian Transit Fact Book*, 1999; Jane's Information Group, *Jane's Urban Transport Systems*, 1999; National Railroad Passenger Corporation, *AMTRAK's America*, 1999, and AMTRAK *Timetable*, Spring 1999; Official Airline Guides, Inc., *Travel Planner*, Spring 1999; Pentrex Publishing Company, *Passenger Train Journal*; Statistics Canada, Aviation Statistics Center, *Aviation Bulletins*, 1999; U.S. Department of

Transportation, Federal Aviation Administration, unpublished Form 298-C nonstop destination data for commuter carriers and Form 41 T-100 nonstop destination data for domestic and international carriers; Federal Transit Administration, *National Transit Database for 1997,* 1999; and VIA Rail Canada *Timetable,* Spring 1999.

The first entry, **Daily Commute,** is the minutes workers spend getting to and from the job, regardless of the mode of transportation. These minutes are journey-to-work figures multiplied by 2.2 to represent a round-trip whose return half takes slightly longer than the first half.

Next to the heading **Public Transit** is the name of the local transit agency (or the name of the largest agency if there is more than one). Under the heading is the VOMS, or "vehicles operated in maximum service" in industry jargon, from all local agencies on the street at rush hour.

A major part of a metro area's freeways is the heavily traveled routes of the country's **Interstate Highways.** These highways are inter-city travel assets, too. Accordingly, each main route in the system that reaches the metro area is listed. The source is U.S. Department of Transportation, Federal Highway Administration, unpublished "Interstate System Log and Finder List," 1999.

Canadian metro areas easily reached by northbound U.S. Interstate Highway termini show those routes in parentheses. For example, Vancouver, BC, can be reached from Seattle by I-5. Accordingly, Vancouver's place profile includes the entry (I-5).

Under **AMTRAK (or VIA) Weekly Departures** are the number of trains pulling out each week, listed by their outbound direction and the city of final destination.

Next to the heading **Air Service** is the FAA's hub classification for the metro area: large hub, medium hub,

small hub, or nonhub. Hub classifications for Canadian airports are derived by *Places Rated* from their share in total North American passenger enplanements.

The airport's name comes underneath. Thanks to local boosterism, airports like the ones in Great Falls, Montana and Midland, Texas have the word *international* in their names, but offer no customs and immigration services for aircraft arriving from abroad—the practical definition of an international airport.

Next to the airport's name is its three-letter identifier enclosed in parentheses. Every scheduled-service airport in the world has a unique identifier. When Baltimore's Friendship Airport (BAL) changed its name to Baltimore-Washington International, it could not get the identifier BWI until Bewani, a small airfield in the Papua New Guinea bush, agreed to take another identifier (BWP).

After the airport's identifier comes its distance and direction from the central business district. For instance, "3 miles N" means the airport is 3 miles north of downtown. Such distances range from 1 mile, between Cheyenne and Cheyenne Municipal Airport, to 34 miles between Montreal and Mirabel International Airport.

Below the airport's name are the number of nonstop jet destinations with more than 1,000 outbound passengers per year and the top three destinations listed in order of passengers enplaned. A similar listing is given for commuter airline (aircraft with fewer than sixty seats) destinations and for international airline destinations.

For areas that neither have airports nor share them, the location of the nearest airport is given along with its distance and direction.

A star (★) preceding a metro area's name highlights it as one of North America's top thirty-five areas for transportation assets.

Abilene, TX
Daily Commute: 32.3 minutes
Public Transit: *CityLink*
  9 city buses, 82 route miles
Interstate Highway: I-20
Airline Service: Nonhub
  Abilene Regional (ABI) 3 miles SE

Nonstop Destinations
	Total	Top Cities
Commuter	1	Dallas
Domestic Jet	1	Dallas

Score: 36.54   Rank: **225**

Akron, OH
Daily Commute: 44.6 minutes
Public Transit: *METRO*
  145 city buses, 1,028 route miles
Interstate Highways: I-76, I-77

Airline Service: Nonhub
  Akron-Canton Regional (CAK) 12 miles SE

Nonstop Destinations
	Total	Top Cities
Commuter	4	Cincinatti, Pittsburgh, Charlotte
Domestic Jet	7	Chicago, Pittsburgh, Atlanta

Score: **69.68**   Rank: **108**

Albany, GA
Daily Commute: 36.5 minutes
Public Transit: *ATS*
  9 city buses, 88 route miles
Airline Service: Nonhub
  Dougherty County (ABY) 4 miles SW

Nonstop Destination
	Total	Top Cities
Domestic Jet	1	Atlanta

Score: **28.04**   Rank: **255**

Albany-Schenectady-Troy, NY
Daily Commute: 43.9 minutes
Public Transit: *CDTA*
   183 city buses, 1,046 route miles
Interstate Highways: I-87, I-88, I-90
AMTRAK Weekly Departures

7 Northbound	14 Southbound
Montreal	New York
7 Eastbound	7 Westbound
Boston	Chicago
	Toronto

Airline Service: Small hub
   Albany County (ALB) 8 miles NW

Nonstop Destinations		
	Total	Top Cities
Commuter	13	Boston, Baltimore, Buffalo
Domestic Jet	13	Philadelphia, Chicago, Pittsburgh

Score: 82.71   Rank: 62

Albuquerque, NM
Daily Commute: 43.2 minutes
Public Transit: *Sun Tran*
   104 city buses, 557 route miles
Interstate Highways: I-25, I-40
AMTRAK Weekly Departures

7 Eastbound	7 Westbound
Chicago	Los Angeles

Airline Service: Medium hub
   Albuquerque International Sunport (ABQ) 5 miles SE

Nonstop Destinations		
	Total	Top Cities
Commuter	11	Farmington, Roswell, Salt Lake City
Domestic Jet	27	Dallas, Phoenix, Denver

Score: 84.13   Rank: 57

Alexandria, LA
Daily Commute: 43.6 minutes
Public Transit: *ATRANS*
   8 city buses, 127 route miles
Interstate Highway: I-49
Airline Service: Nonhub
   Alexandria Esler Regional (ESF) 15 miles NE

Nonstop Destinations		
	Total	Top Cities
Commuter	2	Memphis, Dallas
Domestic Jet	3	Dallas, Columbus, Houston

Score: 42.49   Rank: 204

Allentown-Bethlehem-Easton, PA
Daily Commute: 44.8 minutes
Public Transit: *LANTA*
   50 city buses, 554 route miles
Interstate Highway: I-78
Airline Service: Small hub
   Lehigh Valley International (ABE) 4 miles NE

Nonstop Destinations		
	Total	Top Cities
Commuter	6	Philadelphia, Cincinnati, Boston
Domestic Jet	10	Atlanta, Chicago, Pittsburgh

Score: 66.57   Rank: 119

Altoona, PA
Daily Commute: 35.0 minutes
Interstate Highway: I-99
Public Transit: *AMTRAN*
   24 city buses, 148 route miles
AMTRAK Weekly Departures

14 Eastbound	14 Westbound
New York	Chicago

Airline Service: Nonhub
   Altoona/Blair County (AOO) 12 miles S

Nonstop Destination		
	Total	Top Cities
Commuter	1	Pittsburgh

Score: 26.91   Rank: 259

Amarillo, TX
Daily Commute: 37.1 minutes
Public Transit: *ACT*
   13 city buses, 106 route miles
Interstate Highways: I-27, I-40
Airline Service: Small hub
   Amarillo International (AMA) 9 miles E

Nonstop Destinations		
	Total	Top Cities
Domestic Jet	7	Dallas (DAL), Albuquerque, Dallas (DFW)
Commuter	1	Denver

Score: 60.05   Rank: 142

Anchorage, AK
Daily Commute: 39.2 minutes
Public Transit: *APT People Mover*
   42 city buses, 358 route miles
Airline Service: Medium hub
   Anchorage International (ANC) 5 miles SW

Nonstop Destinations		
	Total	Top Cities
Commuter	19	Kenai, Kodiak, Homer
Domestic Jet	24	Fairbanks, Salt Lake City, Seattle
International	16	Tokyo, Seoul, Taipei

Score: 84.41   Rank: 56

Ann Arbor, MI
Daily Commute: 46.8 minutes
Public Transit: *AATA*
   58 city buses, 393 route miles
Interstate Highway: I-94
AMTRAK Weekly Departures

21 Eastbound	21 Westbound
Pontiac	Chicago

Airline Service:
   Nearest is Detroit (DTW) 25 miles E
Score: 15.86   Rank: 298

Anniston, AL
Daily Commute: 40.0 minutes
Interstate Highway: I-20
AMTRAK Weekly Departures

7 Northbound	7 Southbound
New York	New Orleans

Airline Service:
   Nearest is Birmingham (BHM) 45 miles SW
Score: 7.08   Rank: 329

Appleton-Oshkosh-Neenah, WI
Daily Commute: 33.8 minutes
Public Transit: *Valley Transit/OTS*
  32 city buses, 143 route miles
Airline Service: Nonhub
  Outagamie County (ATW) 5 miles W

Nonstop Destinations

	Total	Top Cities
Commuter	3	Cincinnati, Milwaukee, Charlotte
Domestic Jet	7	Minneapolis, Milwaukee, Chicago

Score: 70.82   Rank: **104**

Asheville, NC
Daily Commute: 41.1 minutes
Public Transit: *City Coach*
  12 city buses, 119 route miles
Interstate Highways: I-26, I-40
Airline Service: Small hub
  Asheville Regional (AVL) 12 miles S

Nonstop Destinations

	Total	Top Cities
Commuter	4	Charlotte, Cincinnati, Raleigh
Domestic Jet	2	Charlotte, Atlanta

Score: 54.67   Rank: **161**

Athens, GA
Daily Commute: 37.8 minutes
Public Transit: *ATS*
  17 city buses, 142 route miles
Airline Service: Nonhub
  Athens/Ben Epps (AHN) 3 miles E

Nonstop Destinations

	Total	Top Cities
Commuter	1	Charlotte

Score: 29.46   Rank: **250**

★Atlanta, GA
Daily Commute: 55.8 minutes
Public Transit: *MARTA*
  569 city buses, 2,010 route miles
  182 heavy rail cars, 92 route miles
Interstate Highways: I-20, I-75, I-85
AMTRAK Weekly Departures

7 Northbound	7 Southbound
New York	New Orleans

Airline Service: Large hub
  Hartsfield Atlanta International (ATL) 9 miles S

Nonstop Destinations

	Total	Top Cities
Commuter	4	Washington, Nashville, Hilton Head
Domestic Jet	131	Chicago, New York, Dallas
International	34	Frankfurt, Toronto, London

Score: 98.30   Rank: **7**

Atlantic City-Cape May, NJ
Daily Commute: 42.8 minutes
Public Transit: *NJTC*
  152 city buses, 613 route miles
  NJTC commuter rail to Philadelphia

Airline Service: Small hub
  Atlantic City International (ACY) 9 miles NW

Nonstop Destinations

	Total	Top Cities
Commuter	2	Philadelphia, Baltimore
Domestic Jet	10	Fort Myers, Fort Lauderdale, Orlando

Score: 66.85   Rank: **118**

Augusta-Aiken, GA-SC
Daily Commute: 47.1 minutes
Public Transit: *APT*
  22 city buses, 130 route miles
Interstate Highway: I-20
Airline Service: Nonhub
  Augusta Bush Field (AGS) 8 miles S

Nonstop Destinations

	Total	Top Cities
Commuter	1	Charlotte
Domestic Jet	2	Savannah, Atlanta

Score: 35.41   Rank: **229**

Austin-San Marcos, TX
Daily Commute: 46.3 minutes
Public Transit: *CAPITAL METRO*
  192 city buses, 192 route miles
Interstate Highway: I-35
AMTRAK Weekly Departures

4 Northbound	4 Southbound
Chicago	San Antonio

Airline Service: Medium hub
  Austin-Bergstrom International (AUS) 4 miles NE

Nonstop Destinations

	Total	Top Cities
Commuter	5	Fort Worth, Tyler, Corpus Christi
Domestic Jet	28	Dallas (DFW), Dallas (DAL), Houston

Score: 78.75   Rank: **76**

Bakersfield, CA
Daily Commute: 42.2 minutes
Public Transit: *GET*
  56 city buses, 301 route miles
AMTRAK Weekly Departures

35 Northbound
Oakland

Airline Service: Nonhub
  Meadows Field (BFL) 4 miles NW

Nonstop Destinations

	Total	Top Cities
Commuter	4	Los Angeles, San Francisco, Sacramento
Domestic Jet	2	Dallas, Los Angeles

Score: 50.70   Rank: **175**

★Baltimore, MD
Daily Commute: 55.9 minutes
Public Transit: *MTA*
  700 city buses, 1507 route miles
  54 heavy rail cars, 29 route miles
  30 light rail cars, 44 route miles
  MARC commuter rail to Washington
Interstate Highways: I-70, I-83, I-95, I-97

AMTRAK Weekly Departures

224 Northbound	237 Southbound
Boston	Charlotte
New York	Miami
Springfield	New Orleans
St. Albans	Newport News
	Richmond
	Washington

Airline Service: Large hub

Baltimore-Washington International (BWI) 10 miles S

Nonstop Destinations

	Total	Top Cities
Commuter	24	Philadelphia, Norfolk, Albany
Domestic Jet	47	Providence, Chicago, St. Louis
International	7	London, Montego Bay, Reykjavik

Score: 94.90　　　Rank: 19

Bangor, ME

Daily Commute: 32.0 minutes
Public Transit: *The Bus*
　10 city buses, 100 route miles
Interstate Highway: I-95
Airline Service: Nonhub
　Bangor International (BGR) 2 miles NW

Nonstop Destinations

	Total	Top Cities
Commuter	4	Boston, New York, Washington
Domestic Jet	5	Newark, Providence, Portland

Score: 66.28　　　Rank: 120

Barnstable-Yarmouth, MA

Daily Commute: 41.4 minutes
Public Transit: *Cape Cod RTA*
　12 city buses, 47 route miles
Airline Service: Nonhub
　Barnstable Municipal (HYA)

Nonstop Destination

	Total	Top Cities
Commuter	4	Nantucket, New York, Boston

Score: 38.24　　　Rank: 219

Baton Rouge, LA

Daily Commute: 48.9 minutes
Public Transit: *CTC*
　39 city buses, 287 route miles
Interstate Highways: I-10, I-12
Airline Service: Small hub
　Baton Rouge Metropolitan (BTR) 8 miles N

Nonstop Destinations

	Total	Top Cities
Commuter	2	Dallas, New Orleans
Domestic Jet	8	Houston, Dallas, Atlanta

Score: 57.22　　　Rank: 152

Beaumont-Port Arthur, TX

Daily Commute: 42.5 minutes
Public Transit: *BMT/PAT*
　17 city buses, 162 route miles
Interstate Highway: I-10

AMTRAK Weekly Departures

3 Eastbound	3 Westbound
Orlando	Los Angeles

Airline Service: Nonhub

Beaumont Jefferson County (BPT) 10 miles SE

Nonstop Destinations

	Total	Top Cities
Commuter	2	New Orleans, Austin
Domestic Jet	2	Houston, Dallas

Score: 41.92　　　Rank: 206

Bellingham, WA

Daily Commute: 36.1 minutes
Public Transit: *WTA*
　29 city buses, 300 route miles
Interstate Highway: I-5

AMTRAK Weekly Departures

7 Northbound	7 Southbound
Vancouver	Seattle

Airline Service: Nonhub

Bellingham International (BLI) 4 miles NW

Nonstop Destinations

	Total	Top Cities
Commuter	2	Seattle, Firday Harbor
Domestic Jet	2	Seattle, Elko

Score: 48.15　　　Rank: 184

Benton Harbor, MI

Daily Commute: 37.0 minutes
Public Transit: *Twin Cities TA*
　2 city buses, 14 route miles
Interstate Highways: I-94, I-96

AMTRAK Weekly Departures

28 Eastbound	28 Westbound
Pontiac	Chicago
	Toronto

Airline Service:

Ross Field (BEH) 2 miles NE

Nonstop Destination

	Total	Top Cities
Domestic Jet	3	Detroit, Lafayette, Muskegon

Score: 45.6　　　Rank: 193

Bergen-Passaic, NJ

Daily Commute: 53.2 minutes
Public Transit: *NJTC*
　423 city buses, 1,664 route miles
　METRO NORTH commuter rail to New York
Interstate Highways: I-80, I-95
Airline Service:
　Nearest is Newark (EWR) 14 miles S
Score: 14.44　　　Rank: 303

Billings, MT

Daily Commute: 34.1 minutes
Public Transit: *MET*
　20 city buses, 176 route miles
Interstate Highways: I-90, I-94
Airline Service: Small hub
　Billings Logan International (BIL) 2 miles NW

Nonstop Destinations

	Total	Top Cities
Commuter	11	Salt Lake City, Missoula, Helena
Domestic Jet	5	Salt Lake City, Minneapolis, Denver

Score: 74.22　　　Rank: 92

Biloxi-Gulfport-Pascagoula, MS
Daily Commute: 44.5 minutes
Public Transit: *Mississippi Coast*
18 city buses, 182 route miles
Interstate Highway: I-10
AMTRAK Weekly Departures

3 Eastbound	3 Westbound
Orlando	Los Angeles

Airline Service: Nonhub
Gulfport-Biloxi Regional (GPT) 3 miles N

Nonstop Destinations

	Total	Top Cities
Commuter	1	Memphis
Domestic Jet	4	Atlanta, Houston, Memphis

Score: 36.82   Rank: 224

Binghamton, NY
Daily Commute: 37.2 minutes
Public Transit: *Broome County*
36 city buses, 210 route miles
Interstate Highways: I-81, I-88
Airline Service: Nonhub
Binghamton Regional/Edwin Link (BGM) 7 miles N

Nonstop Destinations

	Total	Top Cities
Commuter	6	Philadelphia, Pittsburgh, Washington
Domestic Jet	3	Pittsburgh, Elmira/ Corning, Detroit

Score: 67.13   Rank: 117

Birmingham, AL
Daily Commute: 49.4 minutes
Public Transit: *MAX*
67 city buses, 264 route miles
Interstate Highways: I-20, I-59, I-65
AMTRAK Weekly Departures

7 Northbound	7 Southbound
New York	New Orleans

Airline Service: Small hub
Birmingham Municipal (BHM) 5 miles NE

Nonstop Destinations

	Total	Top Cities
Commuter	7	Orlando, Cincinnati, Philadelphia
Domestic Jet	20	New Orleans, Charlotte, Atlanta

Score: 79.88   Rank: 72

Bismarck, ND
Daily Commute: 27.1 minutes
Interstate Highway: I-94
Airline Service: Nonhub
Bismarck Municipal (BIS) 3 miles SE

Nonstop Destinations

	Total	Top Cities
Commuter	1	Denver
Domestic Jet	1	Minneapolis

Score: 33.42   Rank: 236

Bloomington, IN
Daily Commute: 37.8 minutes
Public Transit: *BPT*
17 city buses, 144 route miles

Airline Service:
Nearest is Indianapolis (IND) 40 miles NE
Score: 17.84   Rank: 291

Bloomington-Normal, IL
Daily Commute: 33.9 minutes
Public Transit: *B-N PTS*
14 city buses, 122 route miles
Interstate Highways: I-39, I-55, I-74
AMTRAK Weekly Departures

25 Northbound	7 Southbound
Chicago	Kansas City
	San Antonio
	St. Louis

Airline Service: Nonhub
Bloomington/Normal (BMI) 3 miles E

Nonstop Destination

	Total	Top Cities
Domestic Jet	8	Atlanta, Chicago, St. Louis

Score: 72.23   Rank: 99

Boise City, ID
Daily Commute: 36.6 minutes
Public Transit: *Boise Urban Stages*
30 city buses, 130 route miles
Interstate Highway: I-84
Airline Service: Small hub
Boise Air Terminal (BOI) 4 miles SW

Nonstop Destinations

	Total	Top Cities
Commuter	1	Salt Lake City
Domestic Jet	15	Salt Lake City, Seattle, Portland

Score: 67.42   Rank: 116

★Boston, MA-NH
Daily Commute: 51.8 minutes
Public Transit: *MBTA*
765 city buses, 1,415 route miles
325 heavy rail cars, 76 route miles
177 light rail cars, 56 route miles
23 trolley coaches, 22 route miles
MBTA commuter rail hub and ferry system
Interstate Highways: I-90, I-93, I-95
AMTRAK Weekly Departures

69 Southbound	7 Westbound
Washington	Albany
Newport News	
Philadelphia	
Richmond	

Airline Service: Large hub
Boston Logan International (BOS) 3 miles NE

Nonstop Destinations

	Total	Top Cities
Commuter	36	Bangor, Portland, Burlington
Domestic Jet	51	Atlanta, Chicago, New York
International	20	London, Frankfurt, Toronto

Score: 94.61   Rank: 20

Boulder-Longmont, CO
  Daily Commute: 43.1 minutes
  Public Transit: *RTD-The Ride*
    32 city buses, 126 route miles
  Interstate Highway: I-25
  Airline Service:
    Nearest is Denver (DEN) 47 miles E
  Score: 12.74   Rank: 309

Brazoria, TX
  Daily Commute: 51.5 minutes
  Airline Service:
    Nearest is Houston (HOU) 50 miles NE
  Score: 0.28   Rank: 353

Bremerton, WA
  Daily Commute: 51.5 minutes
  Public Transit: *Kitsap Transit*
    88 city buses, 1,219 route miles
    5 ferries
  Airline Service:
    Bremerton National (BEH) 7 miles SW

Nonstop Destinations		
	Total	Top Cities
Commuter	1	Seattle

  Score: 20.11   Rank: 283

Bridgeport, CT
  Daily Commute: 44.7 minutes
  Public Transit: *GBTD*
    39 city buses, 234 route miles
    METRO NORTH commuter rail to New York
  Interstate Highway: I-95
  AMTRAK Weekly Departures

49 Northbound	49 Southbound
Boston	Washington
Springfield	Philadelphia
St. Albans	

  Airline Service: Nonhub
    Igor Sikorsky Memorial (BDR) 4 miles S

Nonstop Destination		
	Total	Top Cities
Commuter	2	Baltimore, Philadelphia

  Score: 34.84   Rank: 231

Brockton, MA
  Daily Commute: 57.6 minutes
  Public Transit: *BAT*
    45 city buses, 177 route miles
  Airline Service:
    Nearest is Boston (BOS) 25 miles N
  Score: 3.68   Rank: 341

Brownsville-Harlingen-San Benito, TX
  Daily Commute: 36.5 minutes
  Public Transit: *BUS*
    12 city buses, 131 route miles
  Airline Service: Nonhub
    South Padre Island International (BRO) 4 miles E

Nonstop Destination		
	Total	Top Cities
Domestic Jet	1	Houston

  Score: 27.47   Rank: 257

Bryan-College Station, TX
  Daily Commute: 32.3 minutes
  Public Transit: *Brazos Transit*
    8 city buses, 161 route miles
  Airline Service: Nonhub
    Easterwood Field (CLL) 3 miles S

Nonstop Destination		
	Total	Top Cities
Domestic Jet	2	Houston, Dallas

  Score: 31.72   Rank: 242

Buffalo-Niagara Falls, NY
  Daily Commute: 41.9 minutes
  Public Transit: *NFTA*
    299 city buses, 1.231 route miles
    23 light rail cars, 12 route miles
  Interstate Highway: I-90
  AMTRAK Weekly Departures

14 Northbound	28 Eastbound	7 Westbound
Niagara Falls	New York	Chicago
	Toronto	

  Airline Service: Medium hub
    Greater Buffalo International (BUF) 9 miles E

Nonstop Destinations		
	Total	Top Cities
Commuter	12	Albany, Baltimore, Newark
Domestic Jet	17	Atlanta, Chicago, Newark

  Score: 86.11   Rank: 50

Burlington, VT
  Daily Commute: 37.0 minutes
  Public Transit: *Chittenden TA*
    24 city buses, 103 route miles
  Interstate Highway: I-89
  AMTRAK Weekly Departures

7 Northbound	7 Southbound
St. Albans	Washington

  Airline Service: Small hub
    Burlington International (BTV) 3 miles E

Nonstop Destinations		
	Total	Top Cities
Commuter	8	Boston, New York, Washington
Domestic Jet	4	Philadelphia, Chicago, Pittsburgh

  Score: 66   Rank: 121

★Calgary, AB
  Daily Commute: 42.0 minutes
  Public Transit: *Calgary Transit*
    698 city buses, 2,746 route miles
    85 light rail coaches, 79 route miles
  National Highways: AB-2, TC-1
  Airline Service: Large hub
    Calgary International (YYC) 9 miles NE

Nonstop Destination		
	Total	Top Cities
Domestic Jet	40	Vancouver, Toronto, Edmonton
International	13	Dallas, Chicago, Minneapolis

  Score: 90.36   Rank: 35

Canton-Massillon, OH
Daily Commute: 41.3 minutes
Public Transit: *RTA Proline*
 40 city buses, 143 route miles
Interstate Highway: I-77
AMTRAK Weekly Departures

14 Eastbound	14 Westbound
New York	Chicago
Washington	

Airline Service: Nonhub
 Akron-Canton Regional (CAK) 12 miles N

Nonstop Destinations	Total	Top Cities
Commuter	4	Cincinnati, Pittsburgh, Charlotte
Domestic Jet	7	Atlanta, Pittsburgh, Chicago

Score: 65.43   Rank: 123

Casper, WY
Daily Commute: 32.6 minutes
Interstate Highway: I-25
Airline Service: Nonhub
 Natrona County International (CPR) 8 miles NW

Nonstop Destinations	Total	Top Cities
Commuter	2	Salt Lake City, Denver
Domestic Jet	1	Denver

Score: 38.81   Rank: 217

Cedar Rapids, IA
Daily Commute: 34.1 minutes
Public Transit: *Five Seasons Transit*
 31 city buses, 84 route miles
Interstate Highway: I-80
Airline Service: Small hub
 Cedar Rapids Municipal (CID) 8 miles SW

Nonstop Destinations	Total	Top Cities
Commuter	3	Cincinnati, Kansas City, Greenville
Domestic Jet	4	St. Louis, Minneapolis, Chicago

Score: 64.02   Rank: 128

Champaign-Urbana, IL
Daily Commute: 31.9 minutes
Public Transit: *MTD*
 68 city buses, 186 route miles
Interstate Highways: I-57, I-72, I-74
AMTRAK Weekly Departures

14 Northbound	7 Southbound
Chicago	Carbondale
	New Orleans

Airline Service: Nonhub
 University of Illinois/Willard (CMI) 6 miles SW

Nonstop Destinations	Total	Top Cities
Commuter	2	Pittsburgh, Indianapolis
Domestic Jet	4	St. Louis, Chicago, Detroit

Score: 73.93   Rank: 93

Charleston, WV
Daily Commute: 42.9 minutes
Public Transit: *KRT*
 44 city buses, 306 route miles
Interstate Highways: I-64, I-77, I-79
AMTRAK Weekly Departures

3 Eastbound	3 Westbound
Washington	Chicago

Airline Service: Nonhub
 Charleston/Yeager Field (CRW) 4 miles NE

Nonstop Destinations	Total	Top Cities
Commuter	7	Charlotte, Cincinnati, Washington
Domestic Jet	5	Pittsburgh, Atlanta, Detroit

Score: 73.37   Rank: 95

Charleston-North Charleston, SC
Daily Commute: 48.5 minutes
Public Transit: *Charleston DASH*
 35 city buses, 138 route miles
Interstate Highway: I-26
AMTRAK Weekly Departures

14 Northbound	14 Southbound
New York	Miami

Airline Service: Small hub
 Charleston International (CHS) 13 miles NW

Nonstop Destinations	Total	Top Cities
Commuter	7	Pittsburgh, Washington (IAD), Washington (DCA)
Domestic Jet	6	Charlotte, Newark, Atlanta

Score: 58.64   Rank: 147

★Charlotte-Gastonia-Rock Hill, NC-SC
Daily Commute: 46.7 minutes
Public Transit: *CTS*
 128 city buses, 478 route miles
Interstate Highways: I-77, I-85
AMTRAK Weekly Departures

21 Northbound	7 Southbound
New York	New Orleans
Raleigh	

Airline Service: Large hub
 Charlotte-Douglas International (CLT) 6 miles W

Nonstop Destinations	Total	Top Cities
Commuter	43	Hilton Head, New Bern, Cincinnati
Domestic Jet	6	Philadelphia, New York, Atlanta
International	8	London, Nassau, Grand Cayman

Score: 94.05   Rank: 22

Charlottesville, VA
Daily Commute: 40.9 minutes
Public Transit: *Charlottesville Transit*
 11 city buses, 80 route miles
Interstate Highway: I-64

AMTRAK Weekly Departures

7 Northbound	7 Southbound
New York	New Orleans
3 Eastbound	3 Westbound
Washington	Chicago

Airline Service: Nonhub

Charlottesville-Albemarle (CHO) 8 miles N

Nonstop Destination

	Total	Top Cities
Commuter	7	Pittsburgh, Charlotte, Philadelphia

Score: 53.25   Rank: 166

Chattanooga, TN-GA
Daily Commute: 46.6 minutes
Public Transit: *CARTA*

52 city buses, 261 route miles
2 cable inclines, 2 route miles

Interstate Highways: I-24, I-75
Airline Service: Nonhub

Chattanooga Lovell Field (CHA) 8 miles E

Nonstop Destinations

	Total	Top Cities
Commuter	4	Cincinnati, Memphis, Charlotte
Domestic Jet	3	Chicago, Atlanta, Charlotte

Score: 56.94   Rank: 153

Cheyenne, WY
Daily Commute: 29.5 minutes
Public Transit: *Cheyenne Transit*

11 city buses, 98 route miles

Interstate Highways
I-25, I-80

Airline Service: Nonhub

Cheyenne Municipal (CYS) 1 mile N

Nonstop Destinations

	Total	Top Cities
Commuter	1	Denver
Domestic Jet	1	Denver

Score: 37.96   Rank: 220

★Chicago, IL
Daily Commute: 61.5 minutes
Public Transit: *RTA-CTA*

1,973 city buses, 4,250 route miles
938 heavy rail cars, 206 route miles
METRA commuter rail hub

Interstate Highways: I-55, I-57, I-80, I-88, I-90, I-94
AMTRAK Weekly Departures

41 Northbound	35 Southbound
Milwaukee	Carbondale
	Indianapolis
	Kansas City
	New Orleans
	San Antonio
	St. Louis
66 Eastbound	35 Westbound
New York	Chicago
Washington	Los Angeles
Toronto	Oakland
Grand Rapids	Quincy
Pontiac	Seattle

Airline Service: Large hub
O'Hare International (ORD) 18 miles NW
Midway (MDW) 11 miles SW

Nonstop Destinations

	Total	Top Cities
Commuter	29	Lansing, Sioux Falls, Springfield
Domestic Jet	172	Los Angeles, Denver, Atlanta
International	54	London, Toronto, Frankfurt

Score: 100   Rank: 1

Chico-Paradise, CA
Daily Commute: 36.5 minutes
Public Transit: *CAT*

12 city buses, 47 route miles

AMTRAK Weekly Departures

7 Northbound	7 Southbound
Seattle	Los Angeles

Airline Service: Nonhub
Chico Municipal (CIC) 4 miles N

Nonstop Destination

	Total	Top Cities
Commuter	1	San Francisco

Score: 30.31   Rank: 247

Chicoutimi-Jonquiere, PQ
Daily Commute: 36.5 minutes
Public Transit: *CITS*

30 city buses, 118 route miles

Airline Service: Nonhub
Bagotville (YBG) 11 miles SE

Nonstop Destination

	Total	Top Cities
Domestic Jet	4	Quebec, Montreal

Score: 46.45   Rank: 190

★Cincinnati, OH-KY-IN
Daily Commute: 48.9 minutes
Public Transit: *SORTA/TANK*

419 city buses, 1,243 route miles

Interstate Highways: I-71, I-74, I-75
AMTRAK Weekly Departures

3 Eastbound	3 Westbound
Washington	Chicago

Airline Service: Large hub
Cincinnati International (CVG) 13 miles SW

Nonstop Destinations

	Total	Top Cities
Commuter	68	Charlotte, Detroit, Dayton
Domestic Jet	72	Salt Lake City, Chicago, Atlanta
International	10	Brussels, London, Frankfurt

Score: 99.15   Rank: 4

Clarksville-Hopkinsville, TN-KY
Daily Commute: 40.6 minutes
Public Transit: *CTS*

6 city buses, 93 route miles

Interstate Highway: I-24
Airline Service:

Nearest is Nashville (BNA) 45 miles SSE

Score: 13.03   Rank: 308

★Cleveland-Lorain-Elyria, OH

Daily Commute: 48.1 minutes
Public Transit: *RTA*
  612 city buses, 1,962 route miles
  30 heavy rail cars, 38 route miles
  26 light rail cars, 31 route miles
Interstate Highways: I-71, I-77, I-80, I-90
AMTRAK Weekly Departures

21 Eastbound	21 Westbound
New York	Chicago
Washington	

Airline Service: Medium hub
  Cleveland-Hopkins International (CLE) 10 miles SW

Nonstop Destinations

	Total	Top Cities
Commuter	8	Cincinnati, Washington, Indianapolis
Domestic Jet	71	Chicago (ORD), Chicago (MDW), Baltimore
International	2	Toronto, Freeport

Score: 96.31   Rank: 14

Colorado Springs, CO

Daily Commute: 39.8 minutes
Public Transit: *CST*
  43 city buses, 358 route miles
Interstate Highway: I-25
Airline Service: Small hub
  Colorado Springs Municipal (COS) 6 miles SE

Nonstop Destinations

	Total	Top Cities
Commuter	5	Denver, Salt Lake City Albuquerque,
Domestic Jet	14	Denver, Dallas Las Vegas,

Score: 76.77   Rank: 83

Columbia, MO

Daily Commute: 35.6 minutes
Public Transit: *CATS*
  9 city buses, 94 route miles
Interstate Highway: I-70
Airline Service: Nonhub
  Columbia Regional (COU) 12 miles S

Nonstop Destination

	Total	Top Cities
Domestic Jet	1	St. Louis

Score: 34.27   Rank: 233

Columbia, SC

Daily Commute: 44.4 minutes
Public Transit: *SCE&G*
  35 city buses, 177 route miles
Interstate Highways: I-20, I-26, I-77
AMTRAK Weekly Departures

7 Northbound	7 Southbound
New York	Miami

Airline Service: Small hub
  Columbia Metropolitan (CAE) 7 miles S

Nonstop Destinations

	Total	Top Cities
Commuter	5	Cincinnati, Charlotte, Pittsburgh
Domestic Jet	4	Newark, Charlotte, Atlanta

Score: 63.73   Rank: 129

Columbus, GA-AL

Daily Commute: 38.6 minutes
Public Transit: *METRA*
  17 city buses, 170 route miles
Interstate Highway: I-185
Airline Service: Nonhub
  Columbus Metropolitan (CSG) 7 miles NE

Nonstop Destinations

	Total	Top Cities
Commuter	2	Charlotte, Memphis
Domestic Jet	1	Atlanta

Score: 45.04   Rank: 195

★Columbus, OH

Daily Commute: 45.6 minutes
Public Transit: *COTA*
  252 city buses, 1,002 route miles
Interstate Highways: I-70, I-71
Airline Service: Medium hub
  Port Columbus International (CMH) 7 miles NE

Nonstop Destinations

	Total	Top Cities
Commuter	7	Cincinnati, Washington, Indianapolis
Domestic Jet	33	Chicago (ORD), St. Louis, Chicago (MDW)

Score: 91.21   Rank: 32

Corpus Christi, TX

Daily Commute: 41.4 minutes
Public Transit: *The B*
  49 city buses, 321 route miles
Interstate Highway: I-37
Airline Service: Small hub
  Corpus Christi International (CRP) 10 miles NW

Nonstop Destinations

	Total	Top Cities
Commuter	1	Austin
Domestic Jet	4	Houston (HOU), Houston (IAH), Dallas

Score: 49.29   Rank: 180

Cumberland, MD-WV

Daily Commute: 40.5 minutes
Public Transit: *ACTA*
  11 city buses, 43 route miles
Interstate Highway: I-68
AMTRAK Weekly Departures

7 Eastbound	7 Westbound
Washington	Chicago

Airline Service: Nonhub
  Wiley Ford (CBE) 3 miles S

Nonstop Destination

	Total	Top Cities
Commuter	2	Pittsburgh, Latrobe

Score: 28.61   Rank: 253

★Dallas, TX

Daily Commute: 52.9 minutes
Public Transit: *DART/ATE*
  704 city buses, 2,633 route miles
  36 light rail cars, 41 route miles
  DART commuter rail hub
Interstate Highways: I-20, I-30, I-35E, I-45

AMTRAK Weekly Departures

4 Northbound	4 Southbound
Chicago	San Antonio

Airline Service: Large hub

Dallas/Fort Worth International (DFW) 12 miles NW
Dallas Love Field (DAL) 6 miles NW

Nonstop Destinations

	Total	Top Cities
Commuter	28	Shreveport, Fort Smith, Lafayette
Domestic Jet	113	Denver, Chicago, Atlanta
International	25	London, Mexico City, Toronto

Score: 95.46   Rank: 17

Danbury, CT

Daily Commute: 55.0 minutes
Public Transit: *HART*

16 city buses, 132 route miles
METRO NORTH commuter rail to New York

Interstate Highway: I-84
Airline Service:

Nearest is Bridgeport (BDR) 25 miles SE

Score: 3.39   Rank: 342

Danville, VA

Daily Commute: 41.1 minutes
Public Transit: *DTS*

8 city buses, 109 route miles

AMTRAK Weekly Departures

7 Northbound	7 Southbound
New York	New Orleans

Airline Service:

Nearest is Greensboro (GSO) 45 miles SW

Score: 7.93   Rank: 326

Davenport-Moline-Rock Island, IA-IL

Daily Commute: 37.2 minutes
Public Transit: *Metro Link/CitiBus*

68 city buses, 281 route miles

Interstate Highways: I-74, I-80, I-88

AMTRAK Weekly Departures

7 Eastbound	7 Westbound
Chicago	Quincy

Airline Service: Small hub

Quad-City (MLI) 4 miles S

Nonstop Destinations

	Total	Top Cities
Commuter	1	Tallahassee
Domestic Jet	9	St. Louis, Chicago, Denver

Score: 80.16   Rank: 71

Dayton-Springfield, OH

Daily Commute: 42.1 minutes
Public Transit: *RTA/SCAT*

176 city buses, 1,084 route miles
33 trolly coaches, 108 route miles

Interstate Highways: I-70, I-75

Airline Service: Medium hub

James M. Cox International (DAY) 13 miles N

Nonstop Destinations

	Total	Top Cities
Commuter	11	Cincinnati, Pittsburgh, Washington
Domestic Jet	14	Atlanta, Chicago, St. Louis

Score: 88.38   Rank: 42

Daytona Beach, FL

Daily Commute: 45.0 minutes
Public Transit: *VOTRAN*

42 city buses, 442 route miles

Interstate Highways: I-4, I-95
Airline Service: Small hub

Daytona Beach Regional (DAB) 3 miles SW

Nonstop Destinations

	Total	Top Cities
Domestic Jet	2	Newark, Atlanta
International	1	Duesseldorf

Score: 41.35   Rank: 208

Decatur, AL

Daily Commute: 47.0 minutes
Interstate Highway: I-65
Airline Service:

Nearest is Huntsville (HSV) 15 miles ENE

Score: 2.26   Rank: 346

Decatur, IL

Daily Commute: 35.4 minutes
Public Transit: *DPTS*

19 city buses, 152 route miles

Interstate Highway: I-72
Airline Service: Nonhub

Decatur Regional (DEC) 4 miles E

Nonstop Destination

	Total	Top Cities
Domestic Jet	1	St. Louis

Score: 36.26   Rank: 226

★Denver, CO

Daily Commute: 48.1 minutes
Public Transit: *RTD The Ride*

534 city buses, 2,744 route miles
16 light rail cars, 11 route miles

Interstate Highways: I-25, I-70, I-76

AMTRAK Weekly Departures

7 Eastbound	7 Westbound
Chicago	Oakland

Airline Service: Large hub

Denver International (DEN) 16 miles NE

Nonstop Destinations

	Total	Top Cities
Commuter	54	Grand Junction, Rapid City, Durango
Domestic Jet	82	Chicago, Los Angeles, San Francisco
International	13	Vancouver, Calgary, Toronto

Score: 98.58   Rank: 6

Des Moines, IA

Daily Commute: 38.0 minutes
Public Transit: *METRO*
  78 city buses, 433 route miles
Interstate Highways: I-35, I-80
Airline Service: Small hub
  Des Moines Municipal (DSM) 3 miles SW

Nonstop Destinations	Total	Top Cities
Commuter	5	Phoenix, Cincinnati, Kansas City
Domestic Jet	9	St. Louis, Chicago, Denver

Score: 78.18   **Rank:** 78

★Detroit, MI

Daily Commute: 50.9 minutes
Public Transit: *DOT/SMART*
  614 city buses, 3,131 route miles
Interstate Highways: I-75, I-94, I-96
AMTRAK Weekly Departures

21 Eastbound	21 Westbound
Pontiac	Chicago

Airline Service: Large hub
  Detroit Metropolitan (DTW) 20 miles SW

Nonstop Destinations	Total	Top Cities
Commuter	4	Cincinnati, Washington, Birmingham
Domestic Jet	114	Chicago, Newark, Minneapolis
International	22	Toronto, Amsterdam, Tokyo

Score: 98.86   **Rank:** 5

Dothan, AL

Daily Commute: 37.0 minutes
Airline Service: Nonhub
  Dothan Municipal (DHN) 9 miles NW

Nonstop Destinations	Total	Top Cities
Commuter	1	Memphis
Domestic Jet	1	Atlanta

Score: 29.74   **Rank:** 249

Dover, DE

Daily Commute: 42.2 minutes
Public Transit: *DTC*
  133 city buses, 898 route miles
Airline Service:
  Nearest is Philadelphia (PHL) 60 miles NE
Score: 10.19   **Rank:** 318

Dubuque, IA

Daily Commute: 30.1 minutes
Public Transit: *KeyLine*
  9 city buses, 123 route miles
Airline Service: Nonhub
  Dubuque Municipal (DBQ) 9 miles S

Nonstop Destinations	Total	Top Cities
Commuter	1	Chicago
Domestic Jet	4	Minneapolis, Rockford, Chicago

Score: 54.39   **Rank:** 162

Duluth-Superior, MN-WI

Daily Commute: 37.0 minutes
Public Transit: *DTA*
  71 city buses, 209 route miles
Interstate Highway: I-35
Airline Service: Nonhub
  Duluth International (DLH) 7 miles NW

Nonstop Destination	Total	Top Cities
Domestic Jet	4	Chicago, Minneapolis, Detroit

Score: 52.40   **Rank:** 169

Dutchess County, NY

Daily Commute: 52.8 minutes
Public Transit: *LOOP*
  26 city buses, 732 route miles
METRO NORTH commuter rail to New York
Interstate Highways: I-87, I-97
AMTRAK Weekly Departures

35 Northbound	14 Southbound
Montreal	New York
New York	
Niagara Falls	

28 Eastbound	7 Westbound
New York	Toronto

Airline Service: Nonhub
  Dutchess County (POU) 4 miles S

Nonstop Destination	Total	Top Cities
Commuter	1	Burlington

Score: 23.22   **Rank:** 272

Eau Claire, WI

Daily Commute: 33.5 minutes
Public Transit: *ECT*
  13 city buses, 97 route miles
Interstate Highway: I-94
Airline Service: Nonhub
  Eau Claire County (EAU) 5 miles NE

Nonstop Destination	Total	Top Cities
Domestic Jet	3	Minneapolis, Escanaba, Rhinelander

Score: 45.32   **Rank:** 194

★Edmonton, AB

Daily Commute: 45.6 minutes
Public Transit: *ETS*
  788 city buses, 2,964 route miles
  48 trolley coaches
  27 light rail coaches
National Highways: AB-2, TC-16
VIA Weekly Departures

3 Eastbound	3 Westbound
Toronto	Vancouver

Airline Service: Large hub
  Edmonton International (YEG) 19 miles S

Nonstop Destination	Total	Top Cities
Domestic Jet	30	Vancouver, Calgary, Toronto
International	8	Dallas, Chicago, Los Angeles

Score: 91.78   **Rank:** 30

El Paso, TX
Daily Commute: 43.1 minutes
Public Transit: *Sun Metro*
  111 city buses, 521 route miles
Interstate Highway: I-10
AMTRAK Weekly Departures

7 Eastbound	7 Westbound
Orlando	Los Angeles
San Antonio	

Airline Service: Medium hub
  El Paso International (ELP) 8 miles E

Nonstop Destination		
	Total	Top Cities
Domestic Jet	18	Dallas (DFW), Phoenix, Dallas (DAL)

Score: 70.25   Rank: 106

Elkhart-Goshen, IN
Daily Commute: 35.4 minutes
Interstate Highway: I-80
AMTRAK Weekly Departures

21 Eastbound	21 Westbound
New York	Chicago
Washington	

Airline Service:
  Nearest is South Bend (SBN) 22 miles W
Score: 16.14   Rank: 297

Elmira, NY
Daily Commute: 36.3 minutes
Public Transit: *CCTS*
  25 city buses, 98 route miles
Airline Service: Nonhub
  Elmira/Corning Regional (ELM) 11 miles NW

Nonstop Destinations		
	Total	Top Cities
Commuter	4	Philadelphia, New York, Pittsburgh
Domestic Jet	4	Detroit, Pittsburgh, Ithaca

Score: 63.45   Rank: 130

Enid, OK
Daily Commute: 30.8 minutes
Airline Service:
  Enid Woodring Municipal (WDG) 4 miles SE

Nonstop Destination		
	Total	Top Cities
Commuter	1	Dallas

Score: 26.06   Rank: 262

Erie, PA
Daily Commute: 35.6 minutes
Public Transit: *EMTA*
  44 city buses, 259 route miles
Interstate Highways: I-79, I-90
AMTRAK Weekly Departures

7 Eastbound	7 Westbound
New York	Chicago

Airline Service: Nonhub
  Erie International (ERI) 6 miles SW

Nonstop Destinations		
	Total	Top Cities
Commuter	1	Pittsburgh
Domestic Jet	4	Cleveland, Detroit, Pittsburgh

Score: 60.9   Rank: 139

Eugene-Springfield, OR
Daily Commute: 38.1 minutes
Public Transit: *LTD*
  85 city buses, 547 route miles
Interstate Highway: I-5
AMTRAK Weekly Departures

7 Northbound	7 Southbound
Seattle	Los Angeles

Airline Service: Small hub
  Mahlon Sweet Field (EUG) 8 miles NW

Nonstop Destinations		
	Total	Top Cities
Commuter	3	Portland, Salt Lake City, Seattle
Domestic Jet	4	Denver, Seattle, San Francisco

Score: 59.77   Rank: 143

Evansville-Henderson, IN-KY
Daily Commute: 39.1 minutes
Public Transit: *METS*
  26 city buses, 199 route miles
Interstate Highway: I-64
Airline Service: Nonhub
  Evansville-Dress Regional (EVV) 6 miles NE

Nonstop Destination		
	Total	Top Cities
Domestic Jet	4	Chicago, St. Louis, Atlanta

Score: 65.15   Rank: 124

Fargo-Moorhead, ND-MN
Daily Commute: 30.7 minutes
Public Transit: *MAT*
  18 city buses, 71 route miles
Interstate Highway: I-29
AMTRAK Weekly Departures

7 Eastbound	7 Westbound
Chicago	Seattle

Airline Service: Nonhub
  Hector International (FAR) 3 miles NW

Nonstop Destinations		
	Total	Top Cities
Commuter	1	Chicago
Domestic Jet	1	Minneapolis

Score: 41.64   Rank: 207

Fayetteville, NC
Daily Commute: 38.3 minutes
Public Transit: *FAST*
  15 city buses, 116 route miles
Interstate Highway: I-95
AMTRAK Weekly Departures

14 Northbound	14 Southbound
New York	Miami

Airline Service: Nonhub
  Fayetteville Municipal (FAY) 3 miles S

Nonstop Destinations		
	Total	Top Cities
Commuter	1	Charlotte
Domestic Jet	2	Charlotte, Atlanta

Score: 42.77   Rank: 203

Transportation

Fayetteville-Springdale-Rogers, AR

Daily Commute: 36.5 minutes
Public Transit: *ATA*
  12 city buses, 33 route miles
Airline Service: Nonhub
  Drake Field (FYV) 3 miles S

Nonstop Destinations		
	Total	Top Cities
Commuter	4	Memphis, Dallas, Kansas City
Domestic Jet	2	St. Louis, Dallas
Score: 50.14	Rank: 177	

Fitchburg-Leominster, MA

Daily Commute: 46.2 minutes
Public Transit: *MART*
  21 city buses, 83 route miles
MBTA commuter rail to Boston
Airline Service:
  Nearest is Worcester (ORH) 29 miles S
Score: 4.53   Rank: 338

Flagstaff, AZ-UT

Daily Commute: 32.3 minutes
Interstate Highway: I-17
AMTRAK Weekly Departures

7 Eastbound	7 Westbound
Chicago	Los Angeles

Airline Service: Nonhub
  Pulliam Field (FLG) 5 miles S

Nonstop Destination		
	Total	Top Cities
Commuter	1	Phoenix
Score: 25.21	Rank: 265	

Flint, MI

Daily Commute: 44.9 minutes
Public Transit: *MTA*
  141 city buses, 187 route miles
Interstate Highways: I-69, I-75
AMTRAK Weekly Departures

7 Eastbound	7 Westbound
Toronto	Chicago

Airline Service: Nonhub
  Bishop International (FNT) 5 miles SW

Nonstop Destinations		
	Total	Top Cities
Commuter	2	Pittsburgh, Milwaukee
Domestic Jet	5	Detroit, Cleveland, Atlanta
Score: 58.92	Rank: 146	

Florence, AL

Daily Commute: 44.5 minutes
Airline Service:
  Nearest is Huntsville (HSV) 46 miles E
Score: 17.56   Rank: 292

Florence, SC

Daily Commute: 40.9 minutes
Public Transit: *PeeDeeRTA*
  3 city buses, 57 route miles
Interstate Highways: I-20, I-95

AMTRAK Weekly Departures

14 Northbound	14 Southbound
New York	Miami

Airline Service: Nonhub
  Florence Regional (FLO) 2 miles E

Nonstop Destinations		
	Total	Top Cities
Commuter	1	Charlotte
Domestic Jet	1	Atlanta
Score: 33.14	Rank: 237	

Fort Collins-Loveland, CO

Daily Commute: 39.6 minutes
Public Transit: *TRANSFORT*
  16 city buses, 128 route miles
Interstate Highway: I-25
Airline Service:
  Nearest is Denver (DEN) 50 miles SE
Score: 13.31   Rank: 307

Fort Lauderdale, FL

Daily Commute: 49.5 minutes
Public Transit: *BCT*
  155 city buses, 617 route miles
Tri-Rail commuter rail to Miami
Interstate Highway: I-95
AMTRAK Weekly Departures

21 Northbound	21 Southbound
New York	Miami
Jacksonville	

Airline Service: Medium hub
  Ft. Lauderdale/Hollywood (FLL) 3 miles SW

Nonstop Destinations		
	Total	Top Cities
Commuter	9	Tampa, Orlando, Key West
Domestic Jet	36	New York, Tampa, Atlanta
International	12	Toronto, Nassau, Freeport
Score: 81.58	Rank: 66	

Fort Myers-Cape Coral, FL

Daily Commute: 45.3 minutes
Public Transit: *LeeTran*
  37 city buses, 397 route miles
Interstate Highway: I-75
Airline Service: Medium hub
  Southwest Florida Regional (RSW) 10 miles SE

Nonstop Destinations		
	Total	Top Cities
Commuter	7	Orlando, Miami, Washington
Domestic Jet	28	Atlanta, Detroit, Charlotte
International	6	Duesseldorf, Puerto Vallarta, Toronto
Score: 75.35	Rank: 88	

Fort Pierce-Port St. Lucie, FL

Daily Commute: 44.8 minutes
Interstate Highway: I-95
Airline Service:
  Nearest is Melbourne (MLB) 57 miles NW
Score: 0.84   Rank: 351

Fort Smith, AR-OK
Daily Commute: 41.3 minutes
Interstate Highway: I-40
Airline Service: Nonhub
Fort Smith Regional (FSM) 4 miles SE

Nonstop Destinations		
	Total	Top Cities
Commuter	2	Dallas, Memphis
Domestic Jet	3	St. Louis, Fayetteville, Dallas

Score: 40.22   Rank: 212

Fort Walton Beach, FL
Daily Commute: 38.7 minutes
AMTRAK Weekly Departures

3 Eastbound	3 Westbound
Orlando	Los Angeles

Airline Service: Nonhub
Eglin AFB (VPS) 2 miles NE

Nonstop Destinations		
	Total	Top Cities
Commuter	3	Orlando, Tampa, Panama City
Domestic Jet	2	Memphis, Atlanta

Score: 43.05   Rank: 202

Fort Wayne, IN
Daily Commute: 40.9 minutes
Public Transit: *PTC*
20 city buses, 235 route miles
Interstate Highway: I-69
AMTRAK Weekly Departures

21 Eastbound	21 Westbound
New York	Chicago
Washington	

Airline Service: Nonhub
Fort Wayne/Baer Field (FWA) 9 miles SW

Nonstop Destinations		
	Total	Top Cities
Commuter	3	Pittsburgh, Cincinnati, Indianapolis
Domestic Jet	8	Atlanta, Detroit, Chicago

Score: 65.72   Rank: 122

★Fort Worth-Arlington, TX
Daily Commute: 49.7 minutes
Public Transit: *The T*
109 city buses, 391 route miles
Interstate Highways: I-20, I-35W
AMTRAK Weekly Departures

4 Northbound	4 Southbound
Chicago	San Antonio

Airline Service: Large hub
Dallas/Fort Worth International (DFW) 20 miles NE

Nonstop Destinations		
	Total	Top Cities
Commuter	28	Shreveport, Fort Smith, Lafayette
Domestic Jet	113	Atlanta, Denver, Chicago
International	25	Mexico City, Toronto, London

Score: 92.63   Rank: 27

Fresno, CA
Daily Commute: 41.2 minutes
Public Transit: *FAX*
76 city buses, 340 route miles
AMTRAK Weekly Departures

35 Northbound	35 Southbound
Oakland	Bakersfield

Airline Service: Small hub
Fresno Air Terminal (FAT) 5 miles NE

Nonstop Destinations		
	Total	Top Cities
Commuter	10	Los Angeles, San Francisco, Phoenix
Domestic Jet	6	Dallas, Reno, Los Angeles

Score: 69.12   Rank: 110

Gadsden, AL
Daily Commute: 42.5 minutes
Interstate Highway: I-59
Airline Service:
Nearest is Birmingham (BHM) 50 miles SW
Score: 4.24   Rank: 339

Gainesville, FL
Daily Commute: 39.8 minutes
Public Transit: *RTS*
37 city buses, 149 route miles
Interstate Highway: I-75
AMTRAK Weekly Departures

7 Northbound	7 Southbound
New York	Miami

Airline Service: Nonhub
J.R. Alison Municipal (GNV) 3 miles NE

Nonstop Destinations		
	Total	Top Cities
Commuter	5	Charlotte, Miami, Fort Lauderdale
Domestic Jet	1	Atlanta

Score: 55.52   Rank: 158

Galveston-Texas City, TX
Daily Commute: 51.3 minutes
Public Transit: *Island Transit*
12 city buses, 72 route miles
4 light rail cars, 5 route miles
Interstate Highway: I-45
Airline Service:
Nearest is Houston (HOU) 35 miles NW
Score: 1.98   Rank: 347

Gary, IN
Daily Commute: 51.2 minutes
Public Transit: *GPTC/East Chicago*
31 city buses, 243 route miles
METRA commuter rail to Chicago
Interstate Highways: I-65, I-80, I-90, I-94
AMTRAK Weekly Departures

63 Eastbound	63 Westbound
Grand Rapids	Chicago
New York	
Pontiac	
Toronto	
Washington	

Airline Service:
Nearest is Chicago (MDW) 38 miles NW
Score: 19.26   Rank: 286

Glens Falls, NY
Daily Commute: 41.3 minutes
Public Transit: *GGFT*
 6 city buses, 97 route miles
Interstate Highway: I-87
AMTRAK Weekly Departures

7 Northbound	14 Southbound
Montreal	New York

Airline Service:
 Nearest is Albany (ALB) 50 miles SW
Score: 6.23   Rank: 332

Goldsboro, NC
Daily Commute: 37.4 minutes
Airline Service:
 Nearest is Raleigh-Durham (RDU) 60 miles NW
Score: 6.51   Rank: 331

Grand Forks, ND-MN
Daily Commute: 27.4 minutes
Public Transit: *City Bus*
 12 city buses, 81 route miles
Interstate Highway: I-29
AMTRAK Weekly Departures

7 Eastbound	7 Westbound
Chicago	Seattle

Airline Service: Nonhub
 Grand Forks International (GFK) 10 miles NW

Nonstop Destination	Total	Top Cities
Domestic Jet	2	Minneapolis, Thief River Falls

Score: 37.67   Rank: 221

Grand Junction, CO
Daily Commute: 33.0 minutes
Interstate Highway: I-70
AMTRAK Weekly Departures

7 Eastbound	7 Westbound
Chicago	Oakland

Airline Service: Nonhub
 Walker Field (GJT) 3 miles NE

Nonstop Destinations	Total	Top Cities
Commuter	4	Denver, Salt Lake City, Phoenix
Domestic Jet	2	Denver, Elko

Score: 51.55   Rank: 172

Grand Rapids-Muskegon-Holland, MI
Daily Commute: 39.2 minutes
Public Transit: *GRATA*
 71 city buses, 388 route miles
Interstate Highway: I-96
Airline Service: Small hub
 Kent County International (GRR) 6 miles SE

Nonstop Destinations	Total	Top Cities
Commuter	7	Cincinnati, Indianapolis, Milwaukee
Domestic Jet	9	Detroit, Cincinnati, Chicago

Score: 77.33   Rank: 81

Great Falls, MT
Daily Commute: 30.8 minutes
Public Transit: *GFT*
 14 city buses, 88 route miles
Interstate Highway: I-15
Airline Service: Small hub
 Great Falls International (GTF) 4 miles SW

Nonstop Destinations	Total	Top Cities
Commuter	1	Billings
Domestic Jet	7	Helena, Salt Lake City, Minneapolis

Score: 58.35   Rank: 148

Greeley, CO
Daily Commute: 39.2 minutes
Public Transit: *The Bus*
 10 city buses, 145 route miles
Interstate Highway: I-25
Airline Service:
 Nearest is Denver (DEN) 33 miles SE
Score: 11.61   Rank: 313

Green Bay, WI
Daily Commute: 34.1 minutes
Public Transit: *GBT*
 36 city buses, 194 route miles
Interstate Highway: I-43
Airline Service: Nonhub
 Austin Straubel International (GRB) 8 miles SW

Nonstop Destinations	Total	Top Cities
Commuter	2	Milwaukee, Cincinnati
Domestic Jet	4	Minneapolis, Chicago, Detroit

Score: 60.33   Rank: 141

Greensboro–Winston-Salem–High Point, NC
Daily Commute: 40.6 minutes
Public Transit: *WSTA/Hitran*
 53 city buses, 290 route miles
Interstate Highways: I-40, I-85
AMTRAK Weekly Departures

21 Northbound	21 Southbound
New York	Charlotte
Raleigh	New Orleans

Airline Service: Nonhub
 Piedmont Triad International (GSO) 8 miles W
 Smith Reynolds (INT) 25 miles NE

Nonstop Destinations	Total	Top Cities
Commuter	6	Baltimore, Washington (DCA), Washington (IAD)
Domestic Jet	20	Atlanta, Charlotte, Philadelphia

Score: 85.83   Rank: 51

Greenville, NC
Daily Commute: 38.1 minutes
Public Transit: *GATD*
 7 city buses, 28 route miles

Airline Service: Nonhub

Pitt/Greenville (PGV) 2 miles N

Nonstop Destination	Total	Top Cities
Commuter	2	Charlotte, Cincinnati

Score: 26.62   Rank: 260

Greenville-Spartanburg-Anderson, SC

Daily Commute: 40.2 minutes

Public Transit: *SPARTA*

7 city buses, 44 route miles

Interstate Highways: I-26, I-85

AMTRAK Weekly Departures

7 Northbound	7 Southbound
New York	New Orleans

Airline Service: Small hub

Greenville-Spartanburg (GSP) 3 miles S

Nonstop Destinations	Total	Top Cities
Commuter	10	Cincinnati, Pittsburgh, Charlotte
Domestic Jet	9	Atlanta, Charlotte, Detroit

Score: 75.92   Rank: 86

Hagerstown, MD

Daily Commute: 47.1 minutes

Public Transit: *Hagerstown Commuter*

10 city buses, 90 route miles

Interstate Highways: I-70, I-81

Airline Service: Nonhub

Washington County Regional (HGR) 5 miles N

Nonstop Destination	Total	Top Cities
Commuter	2	Pittsburgh, Baltimore

Score: 31.44   Rank: 243

Halifax, NS

Daily Commute: 35.0 minutes

Public Transit: *METRO*

175 city buses, 689 route miles

VIA Weekly Departures

6 Westbound
Montreal

Airline Service: Small hub

Halifax International (YHZ) 26 miles NE

Nonstop Destination	Total	Top Cities
Domestic Jet	20	Toronto, Ottawa, Montreal
International	5	Boston, New York, London

Score: 85.26   Rank: 53

Hamilton, ON

Daily Commute: 41.7 minutes

Public Transit: *Hamilton Street Railway*

185 city buses, 728 route miles

GO Transit commuter rail to Toronto

National Highway: QEW

VIA Weekly Departures

6 Westbound
Montreal

Airline Service:

Nearest is Toronto (YYZ) 35 miles NE

Score: 39.37   Rank: 215

Hamilton-Middletown, OH

Daily Commute: 44.9 minutes

Public Transit: *MTS*

4 city buses, 59 route miles

Interstate Highway: I-75

AMTRAK Weekly Departures

3 Eastbound	3 Westbound
Washington	Chicago

Airline Service:

Nearest is Cincinnati (CVG) 34 miles SW

Score: 6.79   Rank: 330

Harrisburg-Lebanon-Carlisle, PA

Daily Commute: 41.7 minutes

Public Transit: *CAT*

49 city buses, 120 route miles

Interstate Highways: I-76, I-81, I-93

AMTRAK Weekly Departures

62 Eastbound	14 Westbound
New York	Chicago
Philadelphia	

Airline Service: Small hub

Harrisburg International (MDT) 8 miles SE

Nonstop Destinations	Total	Top Cities
Commuter	7	Philadelphia, Cincinnati, Boston
Domestic Jet	11	Detroit, Pittsburgh, Chicago

Score: 77.62   Rank: 80

Hartford, CT

Daily Commute: 44.4 minutes

Public Transit: *CT Transit*

203 city buses, 3,205 route miles

Interstate Highways: I-84, I-91

AMTRAK Weekly Departures

49 Northbound	41 Southbound
Boston	New Haven
Springfield	Washington
St. Albans	

Airline Service: Medium hub

Bradley International (BDL) 14 miles W

Nonstop Destinations	Total	Top Cities
Commuter	8	Washington, Baltimore, New York
Domestic Jet	29	Chicago, Orlando, Atlanta
International	1	Freeport

Score: 87.81   Rank: 44

Hattiesburg, MS

Daily Commute: 40.4 minutes

Interstate Highway: I-59

AMTRAK Weekly Departures

7 Northbound	7 Southbound
New York	New Orleans

Airline Service: Nonhub

Hattiesburg-Laurel Regional (PIB) 8 miles NW

Nonstop Destination	Total	Top Cities
Commuter	1	Memphis

Score: 20.39   Rank: 282

Hickory-Morganton-Lenoir, NC
Daily Commute: 38.9 minutes
Public Transit: *Piedmont Wagon*
  3 city buses, 12 route miles
Interstate Highway: I-40
Airline Service:
  Nearest is Charlotte (CLT) 50 miles SE

Nonstop Destination		
	Total	Top Cities
Commuter	1	Charlotte

Score: 24.64   Rank: 267

Honolulu, HI
Daily Commute: 52.8 minutes
Public Transit: *DTS*
  439 city buses, 867 route miles
Airline Service: Large hub
  Honolulu International (HNL) 3 miles N

Nonstop Destinations		
	Total	Top Cities
Commuter	6	Kapalua, Hoolehua, Lanai
Domestic Jet	23	Lihue, Kahului, Los Angeles
International	27	Nagoya, Tokyo, Osaka

Score: 78.47   Rank: 77

Houma, LA
Daily Commute: 51.0 minutes
Public Transit: *Parish Bus*
  5 city buses, 35 route miles
Airline Service:
  Nearest is New Orleans (MSY) 40 miles NE
Score: 0   Rank: 354

★Houston, TX
Daily Commute: 56.8 minutes
Public Transit: *METRO*
  931 city buses, 2,584 route miles
Interstate Highways: I-10, I-45
AMTRAK Weekly Departures

3 Eastbound	3 Westbound
Orlando	Los Angeles

Airline Service: Large hub
  George Bush/Houston Intercontinental (IAH) 20 miles N
  William P. Hobby (HOU) 10 miles SE

Nonstop Destinations		
	Total	Top Cities
Commuter	2	Fort Worth, Cincinnati
International	38	Mexico City, London, Cancun

Score: 94.33   Rank: 21

Huntington-Ashland, WV-KY-OH
Daily Commute: 41.7 minutes
Public Transit: *TTA*
  21 city buses, 171 route miles
Interstate Highway: I-64
AMTRAK Weekly Departures

3 Eastbound	3 Westbound
Washington	Chicago

Airline Service: Nonhub
  Tri-State/Furgeson Field (HTS) 7 miles SW

Nonstop Destination		
	Total	Top Cities
Commuter	3	Pittsburgh, Charlotte, Cincinnati

Score: 41.07   Rank: 209

Huntsville, AL
Daily Commute: 43.4 minutes
Public Transit: *HTA*
  10 city buses, 121 route miles
Interstate Highway: I-65
Airline Service: Small hub
  Huntsville International (HSV) 9 miles SW

Nonstop Destination		
	Total	Top Cities
Commuter	1	Memphis
Domestic Jet	5	Atlanta, Dallas, Charlotte

Score: 51.84   Rank: 171

★Indianapolis, IN
Daily Commute: 46.8 minutes
Public Transit: *METRO/CATS*
  94 city buses, 705 route miles
Interstate Highways: I-65, I-69, I-70, I-74
AMTRAK Weekly Departures

3 Northbound	3 Eastbound
Chicago	Washington

Airline Service: Medium hub
  Indianapolis International (IND) 7 miles SW

Nonstop Destinations		
	Total	Top Cities
Commuter	14	Cincinnati, Milwaukee, Washington
Domestic Jet	34	Detroit, St. Louis, Chicago
International	3	Montego Bay, Nassau, Cancun

Score: 93.2   Rank: 25

Iowa City, IA
Daily Commute: 34.5 minutes
Public Transit: *ICT/CAMBUS*
  35 city buses, 131 route miles
Interstate Highway: I-80
Airline Service:
  Nearest is Cedar Rapids (CVG) 16 miles NW
Score: 22.66   Rank: 274

Jackson, MI
Daily Commute: 43.8 minutes
Public Transit: *JTA*
  8 city buses, 67 route miles
Interstate Highway: I-94
AMTRAK Weekly Departures

21 Eastbound	21 Westbound
Pontiac	Chicago

Airline Service:
  Nearest is Lansing (LAN) 38 miles N
Score: 8.78   Rank: 323

Jackson, MS
Daily Commute: 43.8 minutes
Public Transit: *JATRAN*
27 city buses, 263 route miles
Interstate Highways: I-20, I-55
AMTRAK Weekly Departures

7 Northbound	7 Southbound
Chicago	New Orleans

Airline Service: Small hub
Jackson International (JAN) 10 miles E

Nonstop Destinations	Total	Top Cities
Commuter	5	Dallas, Cincinnati, Memphis
Domestic Jet	13	Houston, Dallas, Atlanta

Score: 67.98   Rank: 114

Jackson, TN
Daily Commute: 37.8 minutes
Public Transit: *JTA*
9 city buses, 95 route miles
Interstate Highway: I-40
Airline Service: Nonhub
McKellor Field (MKL) 7 miles W

Nonstop Destinations	Total	Top Cities
Commuter	1	Memphis

Score: 30.59   Rank: 246

Jacksonville, FL
Daily Commute: 48.4 minutes
Public Transit: *JTA*
136 city buses, 1,163 route miles
Interstate Highways: I-10, I-95
AMTRAK Weekly Departures

21 Northbound	14 Southbound
New York	Miami
3 Eastbound	3 Westbound
Orlando	Los Angeles

Airline Service: Medium hub
Jacksonville International (JAX) 9 miles N

Nonstop Destinations	Total	Top Cities
Commuter	11	Tampa, Washington, Miami
Domestic Jet	24	Charlotte, Atlanta, Dallas

Score: 81.86   Rank: 65

Jacksonville, NC
Daily Commute: 40.9 minutes
Airline Service: Nonhub
Albert J. Ellis (OAJ) 10 miles NE

Nonstop Destinations	Total	Top Cities
Commuter	2	Charlotte, Raleigh
Domestic Jet	1	Atlanta

Score: 30.87   Rank: 245

Jamestown, NY
Daily Commute: 32.3 minutes
Airline Service: Nonhub
Chautauqua County/Jamestown (JHW) 5 miles N

Nonstop Destination	Total	Top Cities
Commuter	1	Pittsburgh

Score: 27.19   Rank: 258

Janesville-Beloit, WI
Daily Commute: 38.3 minutes
Public Transit: *JTS*
25 city buses, 210 route miles
Interstate Highway: I-90
Airline Service:
Nearest is Madison (MSN) 35 miles NW
Score: 17.28   Rank: 293

Jersey City, NJ
Daily Commute: 59.4 minutes
Public Transit: *NJTC/Hudson Transit*
112 city buses, 441 route miles
METRO NORTH commuter rail to New York
Interstate Highways: I-78, I-95
Airline Service:
Nearest is Newark (EWR) 7 miles SW
Score: 9.91   Rank: 319

Johnson City-Kingsport-Bristol, TN-VA
Daily Commute: 41.9 minutes
Public Transit: *JCT*
9 city buses, 89 route miles
Interstate Highway: I-81
Airline Service: Nonhub
Tri-City Regional (TRI) 12 miles SW

Nonstop Destinations	Total	Top Cities
Commuter	4	Cincinnati, Pittsburgh, Nashville
Domestic Jet	3	Charlotte, Chicago, Atlanta

Score: 49.57   Rank: 179

Johnstown, PA
Daily Commute: 39.2 minutes
Public Transit: *CCTA*
25 city buses, 379 route miles
AMTRAK Weekly Departures

14 Eastbound	14 Westbound
New York	Chicago

Airline Service: Nonhub
Johnstown/Cambria County (JST) 5 miles E

Nonstop Destination	Total	Top Cities
Commuter	2	Pittsburgh, Lancaster

Score: 37.39   Rank: 222

Jonesboro, AK
Daily Commute: 34.7 minutes
Airline Service: Nonhub
Jonesboro Municipal (JBR) 3 miles E

Nonstop Destination	Total	Top Cities
Commuter	1	Dallas

Score: 25.49   Rank: 264

Joplin, MO
Daily Commute: 36.6 minutes
Interstate Highway: I-44
Airline Service: Nonhub
Joplin Municipal (JLN) 5 miles E

Nonstop Destinations	Total	Top Cities
Commuter	1	Memphis
Domestic Jet	1	St. Louis

Score: 32.86   Rank: 238

Kalamazoo-Battle Creek, MI

Daily Commute: 38.4 minutes
Public Transit: *BCT/METRO*
  2 city buses, 258 route miles
Interstate Highway: I-94
AMTRAK Weekly Departures

28 Eastbound	28 Westbound
Pontiac	Chicago
Toronto	

Airline Service: Nonhub
  Kalamazoo/Battle Creek International (AZO) 4 miles SE

Nonstop Destinations		
	Total	Top Cities
Commuter	2	Pittsburgh, Cincinnati
Domestic Jet	5	Chicago, Detroit, Minneapolis

Score: 61.47   Rank: 137

Kankakee, IL

Daily Commute: 42.7 minutes
Interstate Highway: I-57
AMTRAK Weekly Departures

14 Northbound	14 Southbound
Chicago	Carbondale
	New Orleans

Airline Service:
  Nearest is Chicago (MDW) 46 miles NE
Score: 5.94   Rank: 333

★Kansas City, MO-KS

Daily Commute: 46.0 minutes
Public Transit: *KCATA*
  92 city buses, 882 route miles
Interstate Highways: I-29, I-35, I-70
AMTRAK Weekly Departures

21 Eastbound	7 Westbound
Chicago	Los Angeles
St. Louis	

Airline Service: Medium hub
  Kansas City International (MCI) 15 miles NW

Nonstop Destinations		
	Total	Top Cities
Commuter	17	Wichita, Omaha, Des Moines
Domestic Jet	40	Dallas, Chicago, St. Louis

Score: 93.76   Rank: 23

Kenosha, WI

Daily Commute: 46.6 minutes
Public Transit: *KTC*
  34 city buses, 153 route miles
  METRA commuter rail to Chicago
Interstate Highway: I-94
Airline Service:
  Nearest is Chicago (ORD) 35 miles SW
Score: 9.63   Rank: 320

Killeen-Temple, TX

Daily Commute: 35.1 minutes
Interstate Highway: I-35
AMTRAK Weekly Departures

4 Northbound	4 Southbound
Chicago	San Antonio

Airline Service: Nonhub
  Killeen Municipal (ILE) 3 miles E

Nonstop Destination		
	Total	Top Cities
Domestic Jet	2	Houston, Dallas

Score: 31.16   Rank: 244

Kitchener-Waterloo, ON

Daily Commute: 39.0 minutes
Public Transit: *K Transit*
  99 city buses, 390 route miles
National Highway: ON-40
VIA Weekly Departures

20 Eastbound	14 Westbound
Toronto	Chicago
	Sarnia

Airline Service:
  Nearest is Toronto (YYZ) 40 miles E
Score: 68.55   Rank: 112

Knoxville, TN

Daily Commute: 45.8 minutes
Public Transit: *K-TRANS*
  49 city buses, 356 route miles
Interstate Highways: I-40, I-75
Airline Service: Small hub
  McGhee Tyson (TYS) 13 miles S

Nonstop Destinations		
	Total	Top Cities
Commuter	9	Cincinnati, Pittsburgh, Washington
Domestic Jet	8	Charlotte, Chicago, Atlanta
International	1	Freeport

Score: 69.97   Rank: 107

Kokomo, IN

Daily Commute: 36.3 minutes
Airline Service:
  Nearest is Indianapolis (IND) 47 miles S
Score: 11.89   Rank: 312

La Crosse, WI-MN

Daily Commute: 32.8 minutes
Public Transit: *LC Municipal*
  13 city buses, 78 route miles
Interstate Highway: I-90
AMTRAK Weekly Departures

7 Eastbound	7 Westbound
Chicago	Seattle

Airline Service: Nonhub
  La Crosse Municipal (LSE) 4 miles NW

Nonstop Destinations		
	Total	Top Cities
Commuter	1	Milwaukee
Domestic Jet	3	Minneapolis, Chicago, Rochester

Score: 52.97   Rank: 167

Lafayette, IN

Daily Commute: 35.1 minutes
Public Transit: *GLPTC*
  32 city buses, 97 route miles
Interstate Highway: I-65
AMTRAK Weekly Departures

3 Southbound	3 Eastbound	3 Westbound
Indianapolis	Washington	Chicago

Airline Service: Nonhub

Purdue University (LAF) 2 miles SW

Nonstop Destinations

	Total	Top Cities
Commuter	1	Chicago
Domestic Jet	2	Benton Harbor, Detroit

Score: 49.85   Rank: 178

Lafayette, LA

Daily Commute: 44.7 minutes

Public Transit: *COLT*

12 city buses, 85 route miles

Interstate Highways: I-10, I-49

AMTRAK Weekly Departures

3 Eastbound	3 Westbound
Orlando	Los Angeles

Airline Service: Nonhub

Lafayette Municipal (LFT) 2 miles SE

Nonstop Destinations

	Total	Top Cities
Commuter	2	Dallas, Memphis
Domestic Jet	3	Houston, Dallas, Meridian

Score: 44.47   Rank: 197

Lake Charles, LA

Daily Commute: 40.9 minutes

Public Transit: *LCTA*

8 city buses, 31 route miles

Interstate Highway: I-10

AMTRAK Weekly Departures

3 Eastbound	3 Westbound
Orlando	Los Angeles

Airline Service: Nonhub

Lake Charles Regional (LCH) 5 miles S

Nonstop Destinations

	Total	Top Cities
Commuter	1	Dallas
Domestic Jet	2	Houston, Dallas

Score: 35.12   Rank: 230

Lakeland-Winter Haven, FL

Daily Commute: 44.4 minutes

Public Transit: *Citrus Connect*

22 city buses, 165 route miles

Interstate Highway: I-4

AMTRAK Weekly Departures

7 Northbound	7 Southbound	7 Westbound
New York	Miami	Jacksonville

Airline Service:

Nearest is Tampa (TPA) 35 miles SW

Score: 8.49   Rank: 324

Lancaster, PA

Daily Commute: 38.5 minutes

Public Transit: *RRTA*

31 city buses, 345 route miles

AMTRAK Weekly Departures

62 Eastbound	62 Westbound
New York	Chicago
Philadelphia	Harrisburg

Airline Service: Nonhub

Lancaster Muncipal (LNS) 4 miles N

Nonstop Destination

	Total	Top Cities
Commuter	2	Pittsburgh, Philadelphia

Score: 40.50   Rank: 211

Lansing-East Lansing, MI

Daily Commute: 40.6 minutes

Public Transit: *CATA*

44 city buses, 310 route miles

Interstate Highways: I-69, I-96

AMTRAK Weekly Departures

7 Eastbound	7 Westbound
Toronto	Chicago

Airline Service: Nonhub

Capital City (LAN) 4 miles NW

Nonstop Destinations

	Total	Top Cities
Commuter	5	Pittsburgh, Chicago, Cincinnati
Domestic Jet	5	Detroit, Cleveland, Chicago

Score: 70.53   Rank: 105

Laredo, TX

Daily Commute: 37.6 minutes

Public Transit: *El Metro*

30 city buses, 313 route miles

Interstate Highway: I-35

Airline Service: Nonhub

Laredo International (LRD) 5 miles NE

Nonstop Destinations

	Total	Top Cities
Commuter	1	Dallas
Domestic Jet	2	Houston, Dallas
International	1	Mexico City

Score: 46.74   Rank: 189

Las Cruces, NM

Daily Commute: 40.7 minutes

Public Transit: *RoadRUNNER*

10 city buses, 53 route miles

Interstate Highways: I-10, I-25

Airline Service:

Las Cruces International (LRU) 8 miles W

Nonstop Destination

	Total	Top Cities
Commuter	2	Albuquerque, Alamogordo

Score: 32.01   Rank: 241

Las Vegas, NV-AZ

Daily Commute: 44.1 minutes

Public Transit: *ATC*

186 city buses, 992 route miles

Interstate Highway: I-15

Airline Service: Large hub

McCarran International (LAS) 7 miles S

Nonstop Destinations

	Total	Top Cities
Commuter	4	Grand Canyon, Fresno Los Angeles,
Domestic Jet	60	Chicago, Phoenix, Los Angeles
International	14	Mexico City, Toronto, Vancouver

Score: 87.53   Rank: 45

Lawrence, KS
Daily Commute: 37.0 minutes
Interstate Highway: I-70
AMTRAK Weekly Departures

7 Eastbound	7 Westbound
Chicago	Los Angeles

Airline Service:
Nearest is Topeka (FOE) 31 miles W
Score: 11.33   Rank: 314

Lawrence, MA-NH
Daily Commute: 49.1 minutes
Public Transit: *MVRTA*
36 city buses, 142 route miles
MBTA commuter rail to Boston
Interstate Highway: I-95
Airline Service:
Nearest is Boston (BOS) 35 miles S
Score: 5.38   Rank: 335

Lawton, OK
Daily Commute: 32.8 minutes
Interstate Highway: I-44
Airline Service: Nonhub
Lawton Municipal (LAW) 2 miles S

Nonstop Destination		
	Total	Top Cities
Domestic Jet	1	Dallas

Score: 24.92   Rank: 266

Lewiston-Auburn, ME
Daily Commute: 33.9 minutes
Public Transit: *Lewiston-Hudson Bus*
10 city buses, 40 route miles
Interstate Highway: I-95
Airline Service:
Auburn-Lewiston Municipal (LWS) 4 miles SW

Nonstop Destinations		
	Total	Top Cities
Commuter	1	Portland
Domestic Jet	3	Boise, Seattle, Elko

Score: 15.01   Rank: 301

Lexington, KY
Daily Commute: 39.8 minutes
Public Transit: *LexTran*
33 city buses, 132 route miles
Interstate Highways: I-64, I-75
Airline Service: Small hub
Blue Grass Field (LEX) 4 miles W

Nonstop Destinations		
	Total	Top Cities
Commuter	6	Cincinnati, Charlotte, Memphis
Domestic Jet	8	Chicago, Cincinnati, Atlanta

Score: 73.08   Rank: 96

Lima, OH
Daily Commute: 35.5 minutes
Public Transit: *ACRTA*
6 city buses, 24 route miles
Interstate Highway: I-75

AMTRAK Weekly Departures

4 Northbound	4 Southbound
Chicago	San Antonio

Airline Service:
Nearest is Dayton (DAY) 60 miles S
Score: 18.13   Rank: 290

Lincoln, NE
Daily Commute: 34.5 minutes
Public Transit: *StarTRAN*
49 city buses, 399 route miles
Interstate Highway: I-80
AMTRAK Weekly Departures

7 Southbound	7 Eastbound	7 Westbound
St. Louis	Chicago	Oakland

Airline Service: Nonhub
Lincoln Municipal (LNK) 4 miles NW

Nonstop Destinations		
	Total	Top Cities
Commuter	1	Kansas City
Domestic Jet	8	Denver, Chicago, St. Louis

Score: 68.27   Rank: 113

Little Rock-North Little Rock, AR
Daily Commute: 42.7 minutes
Public Transit: *CAT*
50 city buses, 310 route miles
Interstate Highways: I-30, I-40
AMTRAK Weekly Departures

4 Northbound	4 Southbound
Chicago	San Antonio

Airline Service: Small hub
Adams Field (LIT) 2 miles E

Nonstop Destinations		
	Total	Top Cities
Commuter	8	Charlotte, New Orleans, Fayetteville
Domestic Jet	11	St. Louis, Dallas (DFW), Dallas (DAL)

Score: 76.20   Rank: 85

London, ON
Daily Commute: 38.0 minutes
Public Transit: *Transit*
128 city buses, 504 route miles
National Highway: ON-40
VIA Weekly Departures

64 Eastbound	51 Westbound
Toronto	Chicago
	Sarnia
	Windsor

Airline Service: Nonhub
London Municipal (YXU) 7 miles NE

Nonstop Destination		
	Total	Top Cities
Domestic Jet	4	Toronto, Ottawa, Montreal

Score: 59.20   Rank: 145

Long Island, NY
Daily Commute: 64.6 minutes
Public Transit: *Suffolk Transit*
152 city buses, 598 route miles
LIRR commuter rail to New York

Airline Service: Large hub
Long Island MacArthur (ISP)

Nonstop Destinations

	Total	Top Cities
Commuter	9	Philadelphia, Boston, Washington
Domestic Jet	6	Chicago, Fort Lauderdale, Orlando

Score: 63.17   Rank: 131

Longview-Marshall, TX
Daily Commute: 40.8 minutes
Interstate Highway: I-20
AMTRAK Weekly Departures

4 Northbound	4 Southbound
Chicago	Los Angeles

Airline Service: Nonhub
Gregg County (GGG) 3 miles S

Nonstop Destinations

	Total	Top Cities
Commuter	1	Dallas
Domestic Jet	1	Dallas

Score: 23.51   Rank: 271

★Los Angeles-Long Beach, CA
Daily Commute: 56.8 minutes
Public Transit: *LACMTA/SCRTD*
2,401 city buses, 7,470 route miles
24 heavy rail cars, 10 route miles
48 light rail cars, 82 route miles
METRO LINK commuter rail hub
Interstate Highways: I-10, I-5
AMTRAK Weekly Departures

7 Northbound	77 Southbound	7 Eastbound
San Luis Obispo	San Diego	Chicago
Santa Barbara		Orlando
Seattle		San Antonio

Airline Service: Large hub
Los Angeles International (LAX) 10 miles SW
Daugherty Field (LGB) 22 miles SE
Burbank (BUR) 16 miles NW

Nonstop Destinations

	Total	Top Cities
Commuter	22	Fresno, Monterey, San Diego
Domestic Jet	78	Oakland, Phoenix, Las Vegas
International	64	Taipei, Tokyo, London

Score: 93.48   Rank: 24

Louisville, KY-IN
Daily Commute: 46.0 minutes
Public Transit: *TARC*
206 city buses, 1,113 route miles
Interstate Highways: I-64, I-65, I-71
Airline Service: Small hub
Standiford Field (SDF) 4 miles S

Nonstop Destinations

	Total	Top Cities
Commuter	3	Cincinnati, Memphis, Milwaukee
Domestic Jet	25	Atlanta, Chicago, St. Louis

Score: 90.08   Rank: 36

Lowell, MA-NH
Daily Commute: 49.5 minutes
Public Transit: *LRTA*
28 city buses, 166 route miles
MBTA commuter rail to Boston
Interstate Highway: I-95
Airline Service:
Nearest is Boston (BOS) 36 miles SE

Score: 2.83   Rank: 344

Lubbock, TX
Daily Commute: 35.0 minutes
Public Transit: *Citibus*
34 city buses, 155 route miles
Interstate Highway: I-27
Airline Service: Small hub
Lubbock International (LBB) 4 miles N

Nonstop Destinations

	Total	Top Cities
Commuter	1	Denver
Domestic Jet	7	Dallas (DAL), Dallas (DFW), Austin

Score: 62.88   Rank: 132

Lynchburg, VA
Daily Commute: 41.6 minutes
Public Transit: *GLTC*
17 city buses, 134 route miles
AMTRAK Weekly Departures

7 Northbound	7 Southbound
New York	New Orleans

Airline Service: Nonhub
Lynchburg/ Preston Glenn Field (LYH) 5 miles SW

Nonstop Destinations

	Total	Top Cities
Commuter	3	Charlotte, Pittsburgh, Washington
Domestic Jet	1	Atlanta

Score: 43.90   Rank: 199

Macon, GA
Daily Commute: 40.6 minutes
Public Transit: *BCTA*
26 city buses, 102 route miles
Interstate Highways: I-16, I-75
Airline Service: Nonhub
Middle Georgia Regional (MCN) 9 miles S

Nonstop Destination

	Total	Top Cities
Domestic Jet	2	Atlanta, Valdosta

Score: 29.17   Rank: 251

Madison, WI
Daily Commute: 38.5 minutes
Public Transit: *MMT*
141 city buses, 306 route miles
Interstate Highways: I-90, I-94
Airline Service: Small hub
Dane County/Truax Field (MSN) 5 miles NE

Nonstop Destinations

	Total	Top Cities
Commuter	2	Cincinnati, Milwaukee
Domestic Jet	7	Detroit, Chicago, Minneapolis

Score: 73.65   Rank: 94

Manchester, NH

Daily Commute: 48.8 minutes
Public Transit: *MTA*
    13 city buses, 133 route miles
Interstate Highway: I-93
Airline Service: Small hub
    Manchester Municipal (MHT) 3 miles S

Nonstop Destinations

	Total	Top Cities
Commuter	3	New York, Cincinnati, Washington
Domestic Jet	10	Philadelphia, Chicago, Baltimore

Score: 47.59   Rank: 186

Mansfield, OH

Daily Commute: 36.8 minutes
Public Transit: *RCT*
    8 city buses, 31 route miles
Interstate Highway: I-70
Airline Service:
    Nearest is Columbus (CMH) 67 miles SW
Score: 16.71   Rank: 295

McAllen-Edinburg-Mission, TX

Daily Commute: 38.5 minutes
Airline Service: Small hub
    McAllen International (MFE) 2 miles S

Nonstop Destinations

	Total	Top Cities
Domestic Jet	2	Dallas, Houston
International	1	Mexico City

Score: 32.29   Rank: 240

Medford-Ashland, OR

Daily Commute: 34.8 minutes
Public Transit: *RVTD*
    7 city buses, 113 route miles
Interstate Highway: I-5
Airline Service: Large hub
    Medford/Jackson County (MFR) 3 miles N

Nonstop Destinations

	Total	Top Cities
Commuter	1	Portland
Domestic Jet	3	San Francisco

Score: 47.87   Rank: 185

Melbourne-Titusville-Palm Bay, FL

Daily Commute: 44.4 minutes
Public Transit: *SCAT*
    18 city buses, 465 route miles
Interstate Highway: I-95
Airline Service: Nonhub
    Melbourne Regional (MLB) 2 miles NW

Nonstop Destination

	Total	Top Cities
Domestic Jet	2	Atlanta, New York

Score: 23.79   Rank: 270

★Memphis, TN-AR-MS

Daily Commute: 47.2 minutes
Public Transit: *MATA*
    160 city buses, 785 route miles
    9 light rail cars, 4 route miles
Interstate Highways: I-40, I-55

AMTRAK Weekly Departures

7 Northbound	7 Southbound
Chicago	New Orleans

Airline Service: Medium hub
    Memphis International (MEM) 10 miles SE

Nonstop Destinations

	Total	Top Cities
Commuter	41	Huntsville, Fayetteville, Pensacola
Domestic Jet	48	Detroit, Atlanta, Minneapolis
International	3	Amsterdam, Cancun, Freeport

Score: 92.91   Rank: 26

Merced, CA

Daily Commute: 35.9 minutes
Public Transit: *MTS*
    3 city buses, 12 route miles

AMTRAK Weekly Departures

35 Northbound	35 Southbound
Oakland	Bakersfield

Airline Service: Nonhub
    Merced Municipal (MCE) 3 miles SW

Nonstop Destination

	Total	Top Cities
Commuter	1	San Francisco

Score: 22.94   Rank: 273

★Miami, FL

Daily Commute: 53.5 minutes
Public Transit: *MDTA*
    502 city buses, 1,554 route miles
    86 heavy rail cars, 42 route miles
    Tri-Rail commuter rail hub
Interstate Highway: I-95

AMTRAK Weekly Departures

21 Northbound
Jacksonville
New York

Airline Service: Large hub
    Miami International (MIA) 8 miles NW

Nonstop Destinations

	Total	Top Cities
Commuter	14	Orlando, Tampa, Key West
Domestic Jet	48	New York, Atlanta, Chicago
International	88	Caracas, Sao Paulo, Buenos Aires

Score: 90.65   Rank: 34

Middlesex-Somerset-Hunterdon, NJ

Daily Commute: 56.6 minutes
Public Transit: *NJTC*
    559 city buses, 2,199 route miles
Interstate Highways: I-78, I-80

AMTRAK Weekly Departures

23 Northbound	5 Eastbound	7 Westbound
New York	New York	Harrisburg
Springfield		

Airline Service:
    Nearest is Newark (EWR) 23 miles NE
Score: 18.98   Rank: 287

★Milwaukee-Waukesha, WI
Daily Commute: 43.3 minutes
Public Transit: *County/Metro*
  460 city buses, 1,576 route miles
Interstate Highways: I-43, I-94
AMTRAK Weekly Departures

41 Southbound	7 Eastbound	7 Westbound
Chicago	Chicago	Seattle

Airline Service: Medium hub
  General Mitchell International (MKE) 5 miles S

Nonstop Destinations

	Total	Top Cities
Commuter	24	Cincinnati, Indianapolis, Grand Rapids
Domestic Jet	37	Minneapolis, Detroit, Chicago
International	1	Toronto

Score: 96.6   Rank: 13

★Minneapolis-St. Paul, MN-WI
Daily Commute: 45.0 minutes
Public Transit: *MCTO*
  751 city buses, 2,487 route miles
Interstate Highways: I-35, I-94
AMTRAK Weekly Departures

7 Eastbound	7 Westbound
Chicago	Seattle

Airline Service: Large hub
  Minneapolis-St. Paul International (MSP) 6 miles SW

Nonstop Destinations

	Total	Top Cities
Commuter	10	Cincinnati, Grand Island, Jamestown
Domestic Jet	116	Chicago, Detroit, Denver
International	24	Amsterdam, Tokyo, Winnipeg

Score: 97.45   Rank: 10

Missoula, MT
Daily Commute: 34.7 minutes
Public Transit: *Mountain Line*
  15 city buses, 152 route miles
Interstate Highway: I-90
Airline Service: Nonhub
  Missoula Municipal (MSO) 4 miles SE

Nonstop Destinations

	Total	Top Cities
Commuter	2	Salt Lake City, Billings
Domestic Jet	6	Salt Lake City, Seattle, Great Falls

Score: 57.5   Rank: 151

Mobile, AL
Daily Commute: 47.3 minutes
Public Transit: *MTA*
  25 city buses, 230 route miles
Interstate Highways: I-10, I-65
AMTRAK Weekly Departures

3 Eastbound	3 Westbound
Orlando	Los Angeles

Airline Service: Small hub
  Mobile Regional (MOB) 11 miles W

Nonstop Destinations

	Total	Top Cities
Commuter	1	Memphis
Domestic Jet	5	Baton Rouge, Dallas, Atlanta

Score: 51.27   Rank: 173

Modesto, CA
Daily Commute: 47.7 minutes
Public Transit: *MAX*
  28 city buses, 110 route miles
AMTRAK Weekly Departures

35 Northbound	35 Southbound
Oakland	Bakersfield

Airline Service: Nonhub
  Modesto Municipal (MOD) 3 miles E

Nonstop Destination

	Total	Top Cities
Commuter	1	San Francisco

Score: 21.24   Rank: 279

Monmouth-Ocean, NJ
Daily Commute: 58.3 minutes
Public Transit: *NJTC*
  342 city buses, 1,346 route miles
Airline Service:
  Nearest is Newark (EWR) 47 miles NW
Score: 12.18   Rank: 311

Monroe, LA
Daily Commute: 39.8 minutes
Public Transit: *MTS*
  16 city buses, 145 route miles
Interstate Highway: I-20
Airline Service: Nonhub
  Monroe Regional (MLU) 3 miles E

Nonstop Destinations

	Total	Top Cities
Commuter	2	Memphis, Baton Rouge
Domestic Jet	6	Dallas, Shreveport, Atlanta

Score: 56.37   Rank: 155

Montgomery, AL
Daily Commute: 42.1 minutes
Public Transit: *MAT*
  23 city buses, 297 route miles
Interstate Highways: I-65, I-85
Airline Service: Nonhub
  Dannelly Field (MGM) 6 miles SW

Nonstop Destinations

	Total	Top Cities
Commuter	1	Memphis
Domestic Jet	4	Chicago, Monroe, Atlanta

Score: 50.42   Rank: 176

★Montreal, PQ
Daily Commute: 48.7 minutes
Public Transit: *STCUM*
  2,292 city buses, 9,018 route miles
  594 heavy rail coaches
  STCUM commuter rail hub
National Highways: (I-87), (I-89), PQ-20, TC-1

VIA Weekly Departures

31 Northbound	9 Eastbound	63 Westbound
Jonquiere	Gaspe	Ottawa
Quebec	Halifax	Toronto
Senneterre		

Airline Service: Large hub

Dorval International (YUL) 14 miles W
Mirabel International (YMX) 34 miles NW

Nonstop Destination		
	Total	Top Cities
Domestic Jet	47	Toronto, Vancouver, Calgary
International	20	New York, Chicago, Paris

Score: 95.18   Rank: 18

Muncie, IN

Daily Commute: 38.3 minutes
Public Transit: *MITS*
  21 city buses, 129 route miles
Interstate Highway: I-69
Airline Service:
  Nearest is Indianapolis (IND) 69 miles SW
Score: 18.69   Rank: 288

Myrtle Beach, SC

Daily Commute: 40.3 minutes
Public Transit: *CRPTA*
  9 city buses, 264 route miles
Airline Service: Small hub
  Myrtle Beach Jetport (MYR) 2 miles S

Nonstop Destinations		
	Total	Top Cities
Commuter	3	Cincinnati, Raleigh, Charlotte
Domestic Jet	13	Atlanta, Detroit, Charlotte

Score: 60.62   Rank: 140

Naples, FL

Daily Commute: 40.0 minutes
Interstate Highway: I-75
Airline Service: Nonhub
  Naples Municipal (APF) 2 miles NE

Nonstop Destinations		
	Total	Top Cities
Commuter	3	Tampa, Miami, Key West
Domestic Jet	1	Miami

Score: 35.69   Rank: 228

Nashua, NH

Daily Commute: 48.8 minutes
Public Transit: *City Bus*
  4 city buses, 16 route miles
Interstate Highway: I-93
Airline Service:
  Nearest is Manchester (MHT) 12 miles N
Score: 1.13   Rank: 350

Nashville, TN

Daily Commute: 48.6 minutes
Public Transit: *MTA*
  105 city buses, 837 route miles
Interstate Highways: I-24, I-40, I-65

Airline Service: Medium hub

Nashville International (BNA) 5 miles SE

Nonstop Destinations		
	Total	Top Cities
Commuter	13	Cincinnati, Washington, Atlanta
Domestic Jet	39	Atlanta, Baltimore, Dallas

Score: 88.95   Rank: 40

New Bedford, MA

Daily Commute: 45.1 minutes
Public Transit: *SERTA*
  64 city buses, 252 route miles
Interstate Highway: I-195
Airline Service: Nonhub
  New Bedford Municipal (EWB) 3 miles NW

Nonstop Destination		
	Total	Top Cities
Commuter	2	Nantucket, Martha's Vineyard

Score: 32.57   Rank: 239

New Haven-Meriden, CT

Daily Commute: 42.9 minutes
Public Transit: *CT Transit/NET*
  123 city buses, 753 route miles
  METRO NORTH commuter rail to New York
Interstate Highways: I-91, I-95

AMTRAK Weekly Departures

105 Northbound	83 Southbound
Boston	Newport News
Springfield	Philadelphia
St. Albans	Richmond
	Washington

Airline Service: Nonhub
  Tweed-New Haven (HVN) 3 miles SE

Nonstop Destination		
	Total	Top Cities
Commuter	2	Philadelphia, Washington

Score: 42.2   Rank: 205

New London-Norwich, CT-RI

Daily Commute: 40.3 minutes
Interstate Highway: I-95

AMTRAK Weekly Departures

56 Northbound	58 Southbound
Boston	Newport News
	Philadelphia
	Washington

Airline Service: Nonhub
  Groton/New London (GON) 4 miles SE

Nonstop Destination		
	Total	Top Cities
Commuter	1	Philadelphia

Score: 20.67   Rank: 281

New Orleans, LA

Daily Commute: 52.5 minutes
Public Transit: *RTA/LA Transit*
  391 city buses, 819 route miles
  22 light rail cars, 16 route miles
  5 ferries
Interstate Highways: I-10, I-59

AMTRAK Weekly Departures

14 Northbound	3 Eastbound	3 Westbound
Chicago	Orlando	Los Angeles
New York		

Airline Service: Medium hub

New Orleans International (MSY) 10 miles W

		Nonstop Destinations	
	Total	Top Cities
Commuter	10	Orlando, Shreveport, Little Rock
Domestic Jet	35	Houston, Atlanta, Houston
International	4	Cancun, Belize City, Roatan

Score: 84.98   Rank: 54

★New York, NY

Daily Commute: 75.8 minutes

Public Transit: *NYCTA*

3,483 city buses, 2,535 route miles

4,873 heavy rail cars, 520 route miles

LIRR commuter rail hub

METRO NORTH commuter rail hub

NJTC commuter rail hub

8 ferries

Interstate Highways: I-78, I-87, I-95

AMTRAK Weekly Departures

263 Northbound	247 Southbound	7 Westbound
Boston	Charlotte	Chicago
Montreal	Miami	Harrisburg
Niagara Falls	New Orleans	Toronto
Springfield	Newport News	
St. Albans	Philadelphia	
	Richmond	
	Washington	

Airline Service: Large hub

Kennedy International (JFK) 15 miles SE

La Guardia (LGA) 8 miles NE

Westchester County (HPN) 25 miles NE

		Nonstop Destinations	
	Total	Top Cities
Commuter	53	Boston, Washington, Philadelphia
Domestic Jet	104	Atlanta, Boston, Chicago
International	105	Tokyo, Toronto, London

Score: 99.43   Rank: 3

★Newark, NJ

Daily Commute: 56.2 minutes

Public Transit: *NJTC*

492 city buses, 1,935 route miles

16 light rail cars, 8 route miles

METRO NORTH commuter rail to New York

Interstate Highways: I-78, I-80, I-95

AMTRAK Weekly Departures

242 Northbound	231 Southbound
Boston	Charlotte
New York	Miami
Springfield	New Orleans
St. Albans	Newport News
	Philadelphia
	Richmond
	Washington

44 Eastbound	38 Westbound
New York	Harrisburg

Airline Service: Large hub

Newark International (EWR) 3 miles S

		Nonstop Destinations	
	Total	Top Cities
Commuter	14	Washington, Baltimore, Boston
Domestic Jet	80	Chicago, Atlanta, Orlando
International	57	London (LGW), London (LHR), Paris

Score: 96.03   Rank: 15

Newburgh, NY-PA

Daily Commute: 58.5 minutes

Public Transit:

METRO NORTH commuter rail to New York

Interstate Highways: I-84, I-87

Airline Service: Small hub

Stewart International (SWF) 4 miles NW

		Nonstop Destinations	
	Total	Top Cities
Commuter	6	Philadelphia, Cincinnati, Washington
Domestic Jet	6	Raleigh, Atlanta, Chicago

Score: 48.72   Rank: 182

Norfolk-Virginia Beach-Newport News, VA-NC

Daily Commute: 45.6 minutes

Public Transit: *TRT/PenTran*

248 city buses, 1,198 route miles

2 ferries

Interstate Highway: I-64

AMTRAK Weekly Departures

16 Northbound
Boston
New York
Richmond

Airline Service: Nonhub

Norfolk International (ORF) 0.5 miles NE

Newport News-Patrick Henry International (PHF) 10 miles NW

		Nonstop Destinations	
	Total	Top Cities
Commuter	13	Charlotte, Washington, Philadelphia
Domestic Jet	19	Atlanta, Charlotte, Philadelphia

Score: 81.30   Rank: 67

Oakland, CA

Daily Commute: 57.5 minutes

Public Transit: *AC Transit*

670 city buses, 1,848 route miles

4 ferries

Interstate Highway: I-80

AMTRAK Weekly Departures

35 Northbound	28 Southbound
Sacramento	Bakersfield
Seattle	Los Angeles
	San Jose

Airline Service: Medium hub

Metropolitan Oakland International (OAK) 4 miles SE

Nonstop Destinations		
	Total	Top Cities
Commuter	1	Salt Lake City
Domestic Jet	21	Los Angeles, Burbank, Seattle
International	4	Zacatecas, Leon, Guadalajara

Score: 72.80   Rank: 97

Ocala, FL

Daily Commute: 44.7 minutes

Interstate Highway: I-75

AMTRAK Weekly Departures

7 Northbound	7 Southbound
New York	Miami

Airline Service:

Nearest is Gainesville (GNV) 40 miles N

Score: 1.69   Rank: 348

Odessa-Midland, TX

Daily Commute: 36.5 minutes

Interstate Highway: I-20

Airline Service: Small hub

Midland International (MAF) 15 miles NE

Nonstop Destinations		
	Total	Top Cities
Commuter	1	Lubbock
Domestic Jet	8	Dallas (DFW), Dallas (DAL), Houston

Score: 53.82   Rank: 164

Oklahoma City, OK

Daily Commute: 43.4 minutes

Public Transit: *COTPA*

46 city buses, 601 route miles

Interstate Highways: I-35, I-40, I-44

Airline Service: Medium hub

Will Rogers World (OKC) 10 miles SW

Nonstop Destinations		
	Total	Top Cities
Commuter	2	Denver, Memphis
Domestic Jet	16	St. Louis, Dallas (DAL), Dallas (DFW)

Score: 74.78   Rank: 90

Olympia, WA

Daily Commute: 44.0 minutes

Public Transit: *IT*

68 city buses, 544 route miles

Interstate Highway: I-5

AMTRAK Weekly Departures

14 Northbound	7 Southbound
Seattle	Eugene-Springfield
	Los Angeles
	Portland

Airline Service:

Nearest is Seattle (SEA) 45 miles NE

Score: 13.88   Rank: 305

Omaha, NE-IA

Daily Commute: 38.8 minutes

Public Transit: *OTA*

106 city buses, 610 route miles

Interstate Highway: I-80

AMTRAK Weekly Departures

7 Eastbound	7 Westbound
Chicago	Oakland

Airline Service: Small hub

Omaha Eppley (OMA) 4 miles NE

Nonstop Destinations		
	Total	Top Cities
Commuter	4	Kansas City, Cincinnati, Salt Lake City
Domestic Jet	22	Chicago, St. Louis, Denver

Score: 85.55   Rank: 52

Orange County, CA

Daily Commute: 54.6 minutes

Public Transit: *OCTA*

382 city buses, 1,503 route miles

Interstate Highway: I-5

AMTRAK Weekly Departures

77 Northbound	77 Southbound
Los Angeles	San Diego
San Luis Obispo	
Santa Barbara	

Airline Service: Large hub

John Wayne International (SNA) 0.3 miles

Nonstop Destinations		
	Total	Top Cities
Commuter	4	Los Angeles, Salt Lake City, Fresno
Domestic Jet	24	San Jose, Dallas, Oakland

Score: 72.52   Rank: 98

Orlando, FL

Daily Commute: 49.2 minutes

Public Transit: *LYNX*

156 city buses, 729 route miles

Interstate Highway: I-4

AMTRAK Weekly Departures

7 Northbound	14 Southbound	3 Westbound
New York	Miami	Los Angeles

Airline Service: Large hub

Orlando International (MCO) 6 miles SE

Nonstop Destinations		
	Total	Top Cities
Commuter	17	Miami, Tallahassee, Key West
Domestic Jet	74	Detroit, Dallas, Newark
International	24	Manchester, London, Toronto

Score: 87.25   Rank: 46

Oshawa, ON

Daily Commute: 35.1 minutes

Public Transit: *OT*

39 city buses, 153 route miles

GO Transit commuter rail to Toronto

National Highway: ON-40

VIA Weekly Departures

72 Eastbound	75 Westbound
Montreal	Toronto
Ottawa	

Airline Service:

Nearest is Toronto (YYZ) 50 miles W

Score: 21.52   Rank: 278

Ottawa-Hull, ON-PQ

Daily Commute: 44.3 minutes
Public Transit: *OC Transpo*
   792 city buses, 2,116 route miles
Interstate Highways: ON-41, TC-17
VIA Weekly Departures

26 Eastbound	30 Westbound
Montreal	Toronto

Airline Service: Medium hub
   MacDonald-Cartier International (YOW) 11 miles S

Nonstop Destination

	Total	Top Cities
Domestic Jet	17	Toronto, Vancouver, Halifax
International	6	New York, Chicago, Washington, DC

Score: 89.80   Rank: 37

Owensboro, KY

Daily Commute: 37.0 minutes
Public Transit: *OTS*
   6 city buses, 24 route miles
Airline Service: Nonhub
   Owensboro/Daviess County (OWB) 3 miles S

Nonstop Destination

	Total	Top Cities
Commuter	1	Memphis

Score: 30.02   Rank: 248

Panama City, FL

Daily Commute: 37.8 minutes
Public Transit: *Bay Council*
   3 city buses, 106 route miles
Airline Service: Nonhub
   Panama City/Bay County (PFN) 5 miles NW

Nonstop Destinations

	Total	Top Cities
Commuter	4	Memphis, Tampa, Orlando
Domestic Jet	1	Atlanta

Score: 43.34   Rank: 201

Parkersburg-Marietta, WV-OH

Daily Commute: 38.8 minutes
Public Transit: *Easy Rider*
   8 city buses, 32 route miles
Interstate Highway: I-77
Airline Service: Nonhub
   Wood County/Wilson Field (PKB) 6 miles NE

Nonstop Destination

	Total	Top Cities
Commuter	2	Pittsburgh, Clarksburg

Score: 34.56   Rank: 232

Pensacola, FL

Daily Commute: 42.8 minutes
Public Transit: *ECTS*
   31 city buses, 247 route miles
Interstate Highway: I-10
AMTRAK Weekly Departures

3 Eastbound	3 Westbound
Orlando	Los Angeles

Airline Service: Small hub
   Pensacola Regional (PNS) 3 miles NE

Nonstop Destinations

	Total	Top Cities
Commuter	8	Tampa, Memphis, Orlando
Domestic Jet	7	Atlanta, Charlotte, Houston

Score: 64.30   Rank: 127

Peoria-Pekin, IL

Daily Commute: 38.9 minutes
Public Transit: *GP Transit*
   39 city buses, 132 route miles
Interstate Highway: I-74
Airline Service: Small hub
   Greater Peoria Regional (PIA) 4 miles W

Nonstop Destination

	Total	Top Cities
Domestic Jet	6	Chicago, St. Louis, Moline

Score: 57.79   Rank: 150

★Philadelphia, PA-NJ

Daily Commute: 53.2 minutes
Public Transit: *SEPTA*
   1,074 city buses, 2,576 route miles
   375 heavy rail cars, 108 route miles
   111 light rail cars, 69 route miles
   49 trolley coaches, 43 route miles
NJTC commuter rail hub
SEPTA commuter rail hub
Interstate Highways: I-76, I-95
AMTRAK Weekly Departures

285 Northbound	243 Southbound	43 Westbound
Boston	Charlotte	Harrisburg
Montreal	Miami	Chicago
New York	New Orleans	
Springfield	Newport News	
	Richmond	
	Tampa	
	Washington	

Airline Service: Large hub
   Philadelphia International (PHL) 7 miles SW

Nonstop Destinations

	Total	Top Cities
Commuter	44	Middletown, Islip, Boston
Domestic Jet	62	Chicago, Atlanta, Boston
International	20	London, Toronto, Paris

Score: 95.75   Rank: 16

Phoenix-Mesa, AZ

Daily Commute: 49.0 minutes
Public Transit: *PTD*
   274 city buses, 1,325 route miles
Interstate Highways: I-10, I-17
AMTRAK Weekly Departures

7 Eastbound	7 Westbound
Orlando	Los Angeles
San Antonio	

Airline Service: Large hub

Sky Harbor International (PHX) 3 miles SE

Nonstop Destinations

	Total	Top Cities
Commuter	18	Des Moines, Flagstaff, Yuma
Domestic Jet	61	San Diego, Los Angeles, Las Vegas
International	19	Los Cabos, Vancouver, London

Score: **89.51** Rank: **38**

Pine Bluff, AR

Daily Commute: 40.0 minutes
Public Transit: *PBT*
  8 city buses, 32 route miles
Airline Service:
  Nearest is Little Rock (LIT) 45 miles N
Score: **8.21** Rank: **325**

★Pittsburgh, PA

Daily Commute: 48.4 minutes
Public Transit: *PAT/ GG&C Bus*
  760 city buses, 2,616 route miles
  38 light rail cars, 38 route miles
Interstate Highways: I-70, I-76, I-79
AMTRAK Weekly Departures

21 Eastbound	21 Westbound
New York	Chicago
Washington	

Airline Service: Large hub

Greater Pittsburgh International (PIT) 12 miles NW

Nonstop Destinations

	Total	Top Cities
Commuter	57	State College, Cincinnati, Fort Wayne
Domestic Jet	74	Charlotte, Chicago, Philadelphia
International	5	Toronto, Montreal, Frankfurt

Score: **99.71** Rank: **2**

Pittsfield, MA

Daily Commute: 33.2 minutes
Public Transit: *BRTA*
  14 city buses, 55 route miles
AMTRAK Weekly Departures

7 Eastbound	7 Westbound
Boston	Albany

Airline Service:
  Nearest is Albany (ALB) 45 miles NW
Score: **19.54** Rank: **285**

Pocatello, ID

Daily Commute: 35.9 minutes
Public Transit: *Urban Transit*
  8 city buses, 74 route miles
Interstate Highway: I-15
Airline Service: Nonhub
  Pocatello Municipal (PIH) 7 miles SE

Nonstop Destinations

	Total	Top Cities
Commuter	1	Salt Lake City
Domestic Jet	2	Idaho Falls, Boise

Score: **40.79** Rank: **210**

Portland, ME

Daily Commute: 37.6 minutes
Public Transit: *METRO*
  22 city buses, 119 route miles
  3 ferries
Interstate Highway: I-95
Airline Service: Small hub
  Portland International Jetport (PWM) 2 miles W

Nonstop Destinations

	Total	Top Cities
Commuter	9	Boston, New York, Washington
Domestic Jet	10	Newark, Cincinnati, Pittsburgh

Score: **71.95** Rank: **100**

Portland-Vancouver, OR-WA

Daily Commute: 46.3 minutes
Public Transit: *Tri-Met*
  599 city buses, 1,837 route miles
  25 light rail cars, 30 route miles
Interstate Highways: I-5, I-80
AMTRAK Weekly Departures

21 Northbound	14 Southbound	7 Eastbound
Seattle	Eugene	Chicago
Spokane	Los Angeles	

Airline Service: Medium hub
  Portland International (PDX) 9 miles NE

Nonstop Destinations

	Total	Top Cities
Commuter	9	Seattle, Redmond, Medford
Domestic Jet	43	Seattle, San Francisco, Los Angeles
International	4	Nagoya, Seoul, Tokyo

Score: **88.10** Rank: **43**

Portsmouth-Rochester, NH-ME

Daily Commute: 51.7 minutes
Public Transit: *COAST*
  10 city buses, 39 route miles
Interstate Highway: I-95
Airline Service:
  Nearest is Boston (BOS) 52 miles SW
Score: **2.54** Rank: **345**

Providence-Fall River-Warwick, RI-MA

Daily Commute: 41.9 minutes
Public Transit: *RIPTA*
  176 city buses, 458 route miles
Interstate Highway: I-95
AMTRAK Weekly Departures

56 Northbound	62 Southbound
Boston	Newport News
	Philadelphia
	Richmond
	Washington

Airline Service: Small hub
  Green State (PVD) 6 miles S

Nonstop Destinations

	Total	Top Cities
Commuter	9	New York, Washington, Newark
Domestic Jet	19	Chicago, Atlanta, Baltimore

Score: **83** Rank: **61**

Provo-Orem, UT
Daily Commute: 35.9 minutes
Interstate Highway: I-15
AMTRAK Weekly Departures

7 Eastbound	7 Westbound
Chicago	Oakland

Airline Service:
Nearest is Salt Lake City (SLC) 50 miles N
Score: 11.04   Rank: 315

Pueblo, CO
Daily Commute: 36.7 minutes
Public Transit: *CityBus*
10 city buses, 77 route miles
Interstate Highway: I-25
Airline Service: Nonhub
Pueblo Memorial (PUB) 5 miles E

Nonstop Destination		
	Total	Top Cities
Commuter	1	Denver

Score: 28.89   Rank: 252

Punta Gorda, FL
Daily Commute: 41.4 minutes
Interstate Highway: I-75
Airline Service:
Nearest is Fort Myers (RSW) 29 miles SE
Score: 3.11   Rank: 343

Quebec City, PQ
Daily Commute: 37.2 minutes
Public Transit: *CTCUQ*
398 city buses, 1,565 route miles
National Highway: PQ-20
Airline Service: Small hub
Jean Lesage International (YQB) 12 miles NW

Nonstop Destination		
	Total	Top Cities
Domestic Jet	22	Toronto, Montreal, Ottawa

Score: 81.01   Rank: 68

Racine, WI
Daily Commute: 39.8 minutes
Public Transit: *Belle Urban*
30 city buses, 160 route miles
Interstate Highway: I-94
AMTRAK Weekly Departures

14 Southbound
Chicago

Airline Service:
Nearest is Milwaukee (MKE) 30 miles N
Score: 9.06   Rank: 322

★Raleigh-Durham-Chapel Hill, NC
Daily Commute: 43.3 minutes
Public Transit: *CAT/DATA*
130 city buses, 955 route miles
Interstate Highways: I-40, I-85
AMTRAK Weekly Departures

14 Northbound	21 Southbound
New York	Charlotte
	Miami

Airline Service: Large hub
Raleigh-Durham International (RDU) 9 miles NW

Nonstop Destinations		
	Total	Top Cities
Commuter	20	Washington, Cincinnati, Baltimore
Domestic Jet	34	Chicago, Dallas, Atlanta
International	4	Cancun, Toronto, London

Score: 92.06   Rank: 29

Rapid City, SD
Daily Commute: 35.0 minutes
Public Transit: *RCTS*
5 city buses, 48 route miles
Interstate Highway: I-90
Airline Service: Nonhub
Rapid City Regional (RAP) 9 miles SE

Nonstop Destinations		
	Total	Top Cities
3 Commuter	3	Salt Lake City, Denver, Sioux Falls
4 Domestic Jet	4	Elko, Minneapolis, Denver

Score: 54.95   Rank: 160

Reading, PA
Daily Commute: 40.0 minutes
Public Transit: *BARTA*
38 city buses, 440 route miles
Interstate Highway: I-76
Airline Service: Nonhub
Reading Regional/Spaatz Field (RDG) 3 miles NW

Nonstop Destination		
	Total	Top Cities
Commuter	4	Pittsburgh, Philadelphia, Lancaster

Score: 48.44   Rank: 183

Redding, CA
Daily Commute: 36.5 minutes
Public Transit: *RABA*
11 city buses, 43 route miles
Interstate Highway: I-5
AMTRAK Weekly Departures

7 Northbound	7 Southbound
Seattle	Los Angeles

Airline Service: Nonhub
Redding Municipal (RDD) 6 miles SE

Nonstop Destinations		
	Total	Top Cities
Commuter	1	San Francisco
Domestic Jet	2	Arcata/Eureka, Portland

Score: 43.62   Rank: 200

★Regina, SK
Daily Commute: 34.8 minutes
Public Transit: *RTA*
85 city buses, 334 route miles
National Highways: SK-11, TC-1
Airline Service: Small hub
Regina Municipal (YQR) 4 miles SW

Nonstop Destination		
	Total	Top Cities
Domestic Jet	14	Calgary, Toronto, Vancouver

Score: 90.93   Rank: 33

Reno, NV
Daily Commute: 37.0 minutes
Public Transit: *CITIFARE*
49 city buses, 285 route miles
Interstate Highway: I-80
AMTRAK Weekly Departures

7 Eastbound	7 Westbound
Chicago	Oakland

Airline Service: Medium hub
Reno Cannon International (RNO) 3 miles SE

Nonstop Destinations	Total	Top Cities
Commuter	2	Elko, Salt Lake City
Domestic Jet	23	Seattle, Portland, Las Vegas
International	1	Vancouver

Score: 86.40   Rank: 49

Richland-Kennewick-Pasco, WA
Daily Commute: 41.0 minutes
Public Transit: *Ben Franklin Transit*
49 city buses, 264 route miles
Interstate Highway: I-82
AMTRAK Weekly Departures

7 Northbound	7 Eastbound	14 Westbound
Spokane	Chicago	Portland Seattle

Airline Service: Small hub
Tri-Cities (PSC) 12 miles E

Nonstop Destination	Total	Top Cities
Commuter	3	Seattle, Portland, Salt Lake City

Score: 61.18   Rank: 138

Richmond-Petersburg, VA
Daily Commute: 46.9 minutes
Public Transit: *GRTC*
128 city buses, 400 route miles
Interstate Highways: I-64, I-85, I-95
AMTRAK Weekly Departures

56 Northbound	43 Southbound
Boston	Charlotte
New York	Miami
	Newport News

Airline Service: Small hub
Richmond International (RIC) 6 miles E

Nonstop Destinations	Total	Top Cities
Commuter	6	Washington, Cincinnati, Baltimore
Domestic Jet	16	Atlanta, Philadelphia, Charlotte
International	1	Freeport

Score: 80.45   Rank: 70

Riverside-San Bernardino, CA
Daily Commute: 59.3 minutes
Public Transit: *OMNITRANS*
185 city buses, 1,555 route miles
METRO LINK commuter rail to Los Angeles
Interstate Highways: I-10, I-15
AMTRAK Weekly Departures

7 Eastbound	7 Westbound
Chicago	Los Angeles

Airline Service: Medium hub
Ontario International (ONT)
Palm Springs Regional (PSP) 2 miles E

Nonstop Destinations	Total	Top Cities
Commuter	8	Los Angeles, Phoenix, Salt Lake City
Domestic Jet	31	Oakland, Dallas, Phoenix
International	1	Winnipeg

Score: 79.60   Rank: 73

Roanoke, VA
Daily Commute: 39.3 minutes
Public Transit: *Valley Metro*
30 city buses, 190 route miles
Interstate Highway: I-81
Airline Service: Nonhub
Roanoke/Woodrum Regional (ROA) 3 miles NW

Nonstop Destinations	Total	Top Cities
Commuter	8	Cincinnati, Philadelphia, Washington
Domestic Jet	6	Atlanta, Pittsburgh, Charlotte

Score: 67.70   Rank: 115

Rochester, MN
Daily Commute: 31.5 minutes
Public Transit: *RTS*
19 city buses, 75 route miles
Interstate Highway: I-90
Airline Service: Small hub
Rochester Municipal (RST) 7 miles SW

Nonstop Destination	Total	Top Cities
Domestic Jet	3	Chicago, La Crosse, Minneapolis

Score: 47.30   Rank: 187

Rochester, NY
Daily Commute: 42.5 minutes
Public Transit: *RTS*
191 city buses, 978 route miles
Interstate Highway: I-90
AMTRAK Weekly Departures

14 Northbound	35 Eastbound	14 Westbound
Niagara Falls	New York	Chicago Toronto

Airline Service: Small hub
Greater Rochester International (ROC) 3 miles SW

Nonstop Destination	Total	Top Cities
Commuter	13	Boston, New York, Cincinnati

Score: 82.15   Rank: 64

Rockford, IL
Daily Commute: 39.4 minutes
Public Transit: *RMTD*
29 city buses, 292 route miles
Interstate Highways: I-39, I-90

Airline Service: Nonhub

Greater Rockford (RFD) 4 miles S

Nonstop Destination	Total	Top Cities
Domestic Jet	4	Minneapolis, Detroit, Chicago

Score: 52.12   Rank: 170

Rocky Mount, NC

Daily Commute: 38.7 minutes

Public Transit: *RMT*

5 city buses, 20 route miles

Interstate Highway: I-95

AMTRAK Weekly Departures

28 Northbound	28 Southbound
New York	Charlotte
	Miami

Airline Service: Nonhub

Rocky Mount/Wilson (RWI) 7 miles SW

Nonstop Destination	Total	Top Cities
Commuter	1	Charlotte

Score: 22.09   Rank: 276

Sacramento, CA

Daily Commute: 47.3 minutes

Public Transit: *SACRT*

173 city buses, 1,422 route miles

32 light rail cars, 36 route miles

Interstate Highways: I-5, I-80

AMTRAK Weekly Departures

7 Northbound	49 Southbound
Seattle	Bakersfield
	Los Angeles
	Oakland
	San Jose
7 Eastbound	**7 Westbound**
Chicago	Oakland

Airline Service: Medium hub

Sacramento Metropolitan (SMF) 10 miles NW

Nonstop Destinations	Total	Top Cities
Commuter	7	San Francisco, Santa Barbara, Arcata/ Eureka
Domestic Jet	19	San Diego, Ontario, Los Angeles

Score: 79.03   Rank: 75

Saginaw-Bay City-Midland, MI

Daily Commute: 40.7 minutes

Public Transit: *STS/Metro*

55 city buses, 571 route miles

Interstate Highway: I-75

Airline Service: Small hub

Tri-City International (MBS) 9 miles NW

Nonstop Destinations	Total	Top Cities
Commuter	1	Pittsburgh
Domestic Jet	4	Detroit, Chicago, Minneapolis

Score: 54.10   Rank: 163

St. Catharines-Niagara, ON

Daily Commute: 37.0 minutes

Public Transit: *SCT*

44 city buses, 173 route miles

National Highway: QEW

VIA Weekly Departures

11 Eastbound
New York
Toronto

Airline Service:

Nearest is Buffalo (BUF) 50 miles S

Score: 20.96   Rank: 280

St. Cloud, MN

Daily Commute: 33.4 minutes

Public Transit: *Metro Bus*

19 city buses, 126 route miles

Interstate Highway: I-94

AMTRAK Weekly Departures

7 Eastbound	7 Westbound
Chicago	Seattle

Airline Service:

St. Cloud Regional (STC) 4 miles E

Nonstop Destination	Total	Top Cities
Domestic Jet	4	Watertown, Minneapolis, Aberdeen

Score: 50.99   Rank: 174

Saint John, NB

Daily Commute: 32.0 minutes

Public Transit: *SJT*

37 city buses, 146 route miles

Airline Service: Small hub

Saint John Municipal (YSJ) 10 miles NE

Nonstop Destination	Total	Top Cities
Domestic Jet	7	Toronto, Halifax, Montreal

Score: 59.49   Rank: 144

St. John's, NF

Daily Commute: 36.0 minutes

Public Transit: *SJTC*

60 city buses, 236 route miles

Airline Service: Small hub

St. John's Municipal (YYT) 5 miles NW

Nonstop Destination	Total	Top Cities
Domestic Jet	12	Toronto, Halifax, Ottawa

Score: 76.48   Rank: 84

St. Joseph, MO

Daily Commute: 38.1 minutes

Public Transit: *Express*

6 city buses, 125 route miles

Interstate Highway: I-29

Airline Service:

Nearest is Kansas City (MCI) 30 miles SE

Score: 16.43   Rank: 296

★St. Louis, MO-IL
Daily Commute: 49.9 minutes
Public Transit: *Bi-State*
  528 city buses, 2,158 route miles
  26 light rail cars, 34 route miles
Interstate Highways: I-44, I-55, I-64, I-70
AMTRAK Weekly Departures

25 Northbound	4 Southbound	14 Westbound
Chicago	San Antonio	Kansas City

Airline Service: Large hub
  Lambert-St. Louis International (STL) 10 miles NW

Nonstop Destinations

	Total	Top Cities
Commuter	6	Cincinnati, Philadelphia, Mountain Home
Domestic Jet	100	Chicago, Kansas City, Phoenix
International	7	Paris, Toronto, London

Score: 97.73   Rank: 9

Salem, OR
Daily Commute: 41.4 minutes
Public Transit: *Cherriots*
  43 city buses, 127 route miles
Interstate Highway: I-5
AMTRAK Weekly Departures

7 Northbound	14 Southbound
Seattle	Eugene
	Los Angeles

Airline Service:
  Nearest is Portland (PDX) 55 miles N
Score: 14.73   Rank: 302

Salinas, CA
Daily Commute: 38.3 minutes
Public Transit: *MST*
  55 city buses, 431 route miles
AMTRAK Weekly Departures

7 Northbound	7 Southbound
Seattle	Los Angeles

Airline Service: Nonhub
  Monterey Peninsula (MRY) 21 miles SW

Nonstop Destinations

	Total	Top Cities
Commuter	4	Los Angeles, San Francisco, Santa Ana
Domestic Jet	2	San Francisco, Los Angeles

Score: 56.09   Rank: 156

★Salt Lake City-Ogden, UT
Daily Commute: 42.2 minutes
Public Transit: *UTA*
  553 city buses, 1,612 route miles
Interstate Highways: I-15, I-80, I-84
AMTRAK Weekly Departures

7 Eastbound	7 Westbound
Chicago	Oakland

Airline Service: Large hub
  Salt Lake City International (SLC) 3 miles W

Nonstop Destinations

	Total	Top Cities
Commuter	34	Boise, Sun Valley, Grand Junction
Domestic Jet	54	Las Vegas, Atlanta, Los Angeles
International	3	Calgary, Vancouver, Edmonton

Score: 96.88   Rank: 12

San Angelo, TX
Daily Commute: 33.9 minutes
Public Transit: *ANTRAN*
  5 city buses, 77 route miles
Airline Service: Nonhub
  Mathis Field (SJT) 7 miles SW

Nonstop Destination

	Total	Top Cities
Domestic Jet	1	Dallas

Score: 26.34   Rank: 261

San Antonio, TX
Daily Commute: 47.2 minutes
Public Transit: *VIA*
  400 city buses, 1,627 route miles
Interstate Highways: I-10, I-35, I-37
AMTRAK Weekly Departures

4 Northbound	3 Eastbound	7 Westbound
Chicago	Orlando	Los Angeles

Airline Service: Medium hub
  San Antonio International (SAT) 7 miles N

Nonstop Destinations

	Total	Top Cities
Commuter	2	Fort Worth, Colorado Springs
Domestic Jet	23	Houston, Dallas (DFW), Dallas (DAL)
International	2	Puerto Vallarta, Mexico City

Score: 80.73   Rank: 69

San Diego, CA
Daily Commute: 46.4 minutes
Public Transit: *SDT*
  363 city buses, 2,103 route miles
  64 light rail cars, 48 route miles
  San Diego COASTER commuter rail hub
Interstate Highways: I-15, I-5, I-8
AMTRAK Weekly Departures

77 Northbound
Los Angeles
San Luis Obispo
Santa Barbara

Airline Service: Large hub
  San Diego/Lindbergh International (SAN) 2 miles W

Nonstop Destinations

	Total	Top Cities
Commuter	6	Los Angeles, Burbank, Santa Barbara
Domestic Jet	35	Las Vegas, San Francisco, Phoenix
International	5	Vancouver, Puerto Vallarta, Los Cabos

Score: 89.23   Rank: 39

San Francisco, CA

Daily Commute: 54.9 minutes
Public Transit: *Muni/BART*
  800 city buses, 2,674 route miles
  480 heavy rail cars, 190 route miles
  100 light rail cars, 50 route miles
  258 trolley coaches, 132 route miles
  CALTRAIN commuter rail hub
  4 ferries
Interstate Highway: I-80
Airline Service: Large hub
  San Francisco International (SFO) 8 miles SE

Nonstop Destinations		
	Total	Top Cities
Commuter	16	Fresno, Sacramento, Arcata/Eureka
Domestic Jet	54	Seattle, Denver, Chicago
International	35	Tokyo, London, Hong Kong

Score: 86.68   Rank: 48

San Jose, CA

Daily Commute: 49.9 minutes
Public Transit: *SCCTD*
  386 city buses, 1,415 route miles
  33 light rail cars, 39 route miles
  ACE commuter rail to Stockton-Lodi
  CALTRAIN commuter rail to San Francisco
Interstate Highway: I-80
AMTRAK Weekly Departures

28 Northbound	7 Southbound
Sacramento	Los Angeles
Seattle	

Airline Service: Medium hub
  San Jose International (SJC) 2 miles NW

Nonstop Destinations		
	Total	Top Cities
Commuter	2	Los Angeles, Santa Barbara
Domestic Jet	28	San Diego, Santa Ana, Los Angeles
International	6	Los Cabos, Puerto Vallarta

Score: 79.32   Rank: 74

San Luis Obispo-Atascadero-Paso Robles, CA

Daily Commute: 38.7 minutes
Public Transit: *SLO*
  9 city buses, 35 route miles
AMTRAK Weekly Departures

7 Northbound	14 Southbound
Seattle	Los Angeles
	San Diego

Airline Service: Nonhub
  San Luis Obispo (SBP) 3 miles S

Nonstop Destinations		
	Total	Top Cities
Commuter	3	Los Angeles, San Francisco, Sacramento
Domestic Jet	1	Los Angeles

Score: 39.66   Rank: 214

Santa Barbara-Santa Maria-Lompoc, CA

Daily Commute: 37.4 minutes
Public Transit: *MTD*
  59 city buses, 208 route miles

AMTRAK Weekly Departures

14 Northbound	30 Southbound
San Luis Obispo	Los Angeles
Seattle	San Diego

Airline Service: Nonhub
  Santa Barbara Municipal (SBA) 7 miles W

Nonstop Destinations		
	Total	Top Cities
Commuter	6	Phoenix, Los Angeles, San Francisco
Domestic Jet	3	Denver, San Francisco, Los Angeles

Score: 64.87   Rank: 125

Santa Cruz-Watsonville, CA

Daily Commute: 51.0 minutes
Public Transit: *METRO*
  64 city buses, 395 route miles
Airline Service:
  Nearest is San Jose (SJC) 23 miles NE
Score: 7.64   Rank: 327

Santa Fe, NM

Daily Commute: 38.2 minutes
Public Transit: *Santa Fe Trails*
  17 city buses, 141 route miles
Interstate Highway: I-25
Airline Service: Nonhub
  Santa Fe Municipal (SAF) 10 miles SW

Nonstop Destination		
	Total	Top Cities
Commuter	2	Denver, Dallas

Score: 33.71   Rank: 235

Santa Rosa, CA

Daily Commute: 50.4 minutes
Public Transit: *SCTA*
  17 city buses, 110 route miles
Airline Service: Nonhub
  Sonoma County (STS) 6 miles NW

Nonstop Destination		
	Total	Top Cities
Commuter	1	San Francisco

Score: 22.37   Rank: 275

Sarasota-Bradenton, FL

Daily Commute: 40.0 minutes
Public Transit: *SCTA*
  34 city buses, 515 route miles
Interstate Highway: I-75
Airline Service: Small hub
  Sarasota-Bradenton (SRQ) 3 miles N

Nonstop Destinations		
	Total	Top Cities
Commuter	3	Orlando, Miami, Fort Lauderdale
Domestic Jet	13	Charlotte, Atlanta, Newark

Score: 69.40   Rank: 109

Saskatoon, SK

Daily Commute: 34.0 minutes
Public Transit: *STS*
  102 city buses, 401 route miles
National Highways: SK-11, TC-16

VIA Weekly Departures

3 Eastbound	3 Westbound
Toronto	Vancouver

Airline Service: Small hub
Diefenbaker (YXE) 5 miles NW

Nonstop Destination	Total	Top Cities
Domestic Jet	12	Toronto, Vancouver, Calgary

Score: 83.28   Rank: 60

Savannah, GA

Daily Commute: 45.1 minutes
Public Transit: *CAT*
  49 city buses, 225 route miles
Interstate Highways: I-16, I-95
AMTRAK Weekly Departures

21 Northbound	21 Southbound
New York	Miami

Airline Service: Small hub
  Savannah International (SAV) 7 miles NW

Nonstop Destinations	Total	Top Cities
Commuter	3	Washington, Raleigh, Charlotte
Domestic Jet	3	Charlotte, Atlanta, Newark

Score: 55.24   Rank: 159

Scranton–Wilkes-Barre–Hazleton, PA

Daily Commute: 38.3 minutes
Public Transit: *SCTA*
  56 city buses, 650 route miles
Interstate Highways: I-81, I-84
Airline Service: Nonhub
  Wilkes-Barre/Scranton International (AVP) 5 miles SW

Nonstop Destinations	Total	Top Cities
Commuter	3	Cincinnati, Philadelphia, Boston
Domestic Jet	3	Cleveland, Pittsburgh, Philadelphia

Score: 62.32   Rank: 134

Seattle-Bellevue-Everett, WA

Daily Commute: 51.6 minutes
Public Transit: *METRO*
  1,040 city buses, 3,693 route miles
  3 light rail cars, 4 route miles
  139 trolley coaches, 116 route miles
  25 ferries
Interstate Highways: I-5, I-90
AMTRAK Weekly Departures

7 Northbound	28 Southbound	7 Eastbound
Vancouver	Eugene	Chicago
	Los Angeles	
	Portland	

Airline Service: Large hub
  Seattle-Tacoma International (SEA) 10 miles S

Nonstop Destinations	Total	Top Cities
Commuter	12	Portland, Yakima, Bellingham
Domestic Jet	67	San Francisco, Los Angeles, Anchorage
International	18	Tokyo, Vancouver, London

Score: 86.96   Rank: 47

Sharon, PA

Daily Commute: 36.1 minutes
Public Transit: *SVT*
  5 city buses, 20 route miles
Interstate Highway: I-80
Airline Service:
  Nearest is Youngstown (YNG) 10 miles E
Score: 12.46   Rank: 310

Sheboygan, WI

Daily Commute: 31.5 minutes
Public Transit: *STA*
  25 city buses, 72 route miles
Interstate Highway: I-43
Airline Service:
  Nearest is Milwaukee (MKE) 63 miles S
Score: 21.81   Rank: 277

Sherbrooke, PQ

Daily Commute: 31.7 minutes
Public Transit: *CMTS*
  42 city buses, 165 route miles
National Highways: (I-91), PQ-10
Airline Service:
  Nearest is Montreal (YUL) 100 miles W
Score: 25.77   Rank: 263

Sherman-Denison, TX

Daily Commute: 44.0 minutes
Airline Service:
  Nearest is Dallas (DFW) 65 miles SW
Score: 0.56   Rank: 352

Shreveport-Bossier City, LA

Daily Commute: 42.1 minutes
Public Transit: *SparTran*
  37 city buses, 278 route miles
Interstate Highways: I-20, I-49
Airline Service: Small hub
  Shreveport Regional (SHV) 4 miles SW

Nonstop Destinations	Total	Top Cities
Commuter	3	Dallas, Memphis, New Orleans
Domestic Jet	7	Dallas, Atlanta, Houston

Score: 64.58   Rank: 126

Sioux City, IA-NE

Daily Commute: 32.3 minutes
Public Transit: *STC*
  21 city buses, 196 route miles
Interstate Highway: I-29
Airline Service: Nonhub
  Sioux Gateway (SUX) 6 miles S

Nonstop Destinations	Total	Top Cities
Commuter	1	Denver
Domestic Jet	2	Minneapolis, St. Louis

Score: 46.17   Rank: 191

Sioux Falls, SD

Daily Commute: 32.5 minutes
Public Transit: *The Bus*
  23 city buses, 172 route miles
Interstate Highways: I-29, I-90

Airline Service: Small hub
Joe Foss Field (FSD) 3 miles NW

Nonstop Destinations

	Total	Top Cities
Commuter	3	Chicago, Denver, Rapid City
Domestic Jet	4	Minneapolis, Denver, St. Louis

Score: 61.75   Rank: 136

South Bend, IN

Daily Commute: 38.9 minutes
Public Transit: *Transpo*
43 city buses, 177 route miles
Chicago South Shore commuter rail to Chicago
Interstate Highway: I-80
AMTRAK Weekly Departures

21 Eastbound	21 Westbound
New York Washington	Chicago

Airline Service: Small hub
Michiana Regional (SBN) 3 miles NW

Nonstop Destinations

	Total	Top Cities
Commuter	5	Cincinnati, Pittsburgh, Milwaukee
Domestic Jet	6	Chicago, Cincinnati, Pittsburgh

Score: 71.67   Rank: 101

Spokane, WA

Daily Commute: 39.6 minutes
Public Transit: *STA*
120 city buses, 577 route miles
Interstate Highway: I-90
AMTRAK Weekly Departures

7 Eastbound	14 Westbound
Chicago	Portland Seattle

Airline Service: Small hub
Spokane International (GEG) 5 miles SW

Nonstop Destinations

	Total	Top Cities
Commuter	1	Billings
Domestic Jet	18	Portland, Seattle, Salt Lake City

Score: 77.05   Rank: 82

Springfield, IL

Daily Commute: 38.2 minutes
Public Transit: *SMTD*
37 city buses, 242 route miles
Interstate Highways: I-55, I-72
AMTRAK Weekly Departures

25 Northbound	18 Southbound
Chicago	Kansas City San Antonio St. Louis

Airline Service: Nonhub
Springfield Capital (SPI) 3 miles NW

Nonstop Destinations

	Total	Top Cities
Commuter	1	Chicago
Domestic Jet	3	Chicago, St. Louis, Springfield

Score: 62.60   Rank: 133

★Springfield, MA

Daily Commute: 39.8 minutes
Public Transit: *PVTA*
116 city buses, 462 route miles
Interstate Highways: I-90, I-91
AMTRAK Weekly Departures

21 Northbound	41 Southbound
St. Albans	New Haven Washington
7 Eastbound	7 Westbound
Boston	Albany

Airline Service: Medium hub
Bradley International (BDL) 24 miles S

Nonstop Destinations

	Total	Top Cities
Commuter	8	Washington, Baltimore, New York
Domestic Jet	29	Chicago, Orlando, Atlanta
International	1	Freeport

Score: 92.35   Rank: 28

Springfield, MO

Daily Commute: 41.4 minutes
Public Transit: *City Utility*
16 city buses, 139 route miles
Interstate Highway: I-44
Airline Service: Small hub
Springfield Regional (SGF) 5 miles NW

Nonstop Destinations

	Total	Top Cities
Commuter	3	Memphis, Kansas City, Chicago
Domestic Jet	4	St. Louis, Denver, Dallas

Score: 55.80   Rank: 157

Stamford-Norwalk, CT

Daily Commute: 53.2 minutes
Public Transit: *CT Transit*
59 city buses, 312 route miles
METRO NORTH commuter rail to New York
Interstate Highway: I-95
AMTRAK Weekly Departures

84 Northbound	68 Southbound
Boston Springfield St. Albans	Newport News Philadelphia Richmond Washington

Airline Service:
Nearest is White Plains (HPM) 10 miles W
Score: 9.34   Rank: 321

State College, PA

Daily Commute: 36.3 minutes
Public Transit: *Centre Line*
27 city buses, 70 route miles
Airline Service: Nonhub
University Park (SCE) 4 miles N

Nonstop Destinations

	Total	Top Cities
Commuter	3	Pittsburgh, Philadelphia, Dallas
Domestic Jet	2	Detroit, Youngstown

Score: 53.54   Rank: 165

Transportation

143

Steubenville-Weirton, OH-WV
Daily Commute: 41.5 minutes
Public Transit: *SVTC*
  4 city buses, 16 route miles
Airline Service:
  Nearest is Pittsburgh (PIT) 33 miles NE
Score: 7.36   Rank: 328

Stockton-Lodi, CA
Daily Commute: 46.6 minutes
Public Transit: *SMART*
  68 city buses, 1,127 route miles
  ACE commuter rail to San Jose
Interstate Highway: I-5
AMTRAK Weekly Departures

35 Northbound	35 Southbound
Oakland	Bakersfield

Airline Service:
  Nearest is Modesto (MOD) 30 miles SE
Score: 1.41   Rank: 349

Sudbury, ON
Daily Commute: 30.7 minutes
Public Transit: *Sudbury Transit*
  37 city buses, 146 route miles
National Highway: TC-17
VIA Weekly Departures

3 Eastbound	6 Westbound
Toronto	Vancouver
	White River

Airline Service: Nonhub
  Sudbury Municipal (YSB) 16 miles NE

Nonstop Destinations		
	Total	Top Cities
Commuter	4	Toronto, Montreal, Ottawa

Score: 56.65   Rank: 154

Sumter, SC
Daily Commute: 37.4 minutes
Public Transit: *Santee Wateree*
  25 city buses, 108 route miles
Airline Service:
  Nearest is Columbia (CAE) 40 miles W
Score: 13.59   Rank: 306

Syracuse, NY
Daily Commute: 41.0 minutes
Public Transit: *RTA-Centro*
  149 city buses, 730 route miles
  ON TRACK commuter rail
Interstate Highways: I-81, I-90
AMTRAK Weekly Departures

14 Northbound	35 Eastbound	14 Westbound
Niagara Falls	New York	Chicago
	Toronto	

Airline Service: Small hub
  Syracuse-Hancock International (SYR) 4 miles NE

Nonstop Destinations		
	Total	Top Cities
Commuter	16	Boston, New York, Baltimore
Domestic Jet	14	Philadelphia, Chicago, Pittsburgh

Score: 88.66   Rank: 41

Tacoma, WA
Daily Commute: 51.0 minutes
Public Transit: *Pierce Transit*
  151 city buses, 991 route miles
  1 ferry
Interstate Highway: I-5
AMTRAK Weekly Departures

14 Northbound	28 Southbound
Seattle	Eugene
	Los Angeles
	Portland

Airline Service:
  Nearest is Seattle (SEA) 18 miles NE
Score: 82.43   Rank: 63

Tallahassee, FL
Daily Commute: 41.1 minutes
Public Transit: *TALTRAN*
  42 city buses, 200 route miles
Interstate Highway: I-10
AMTRAK Weekly Departures

3 Eastbound	3 Westbound
Orlando	Los Angeles

Airline Service: Small hub
  Tallahassee Regional (TLH) 4 miles SW

Nonstop Destinations		
	Total	Top Cities
Commuter	9	Miami, Tampa, Orlando
Domestic Jet	1	Atlanta

Score: 62.03   Rank: 135

★Tampa-St. Petersburg-Clearwater, FL
Daily Commute: 46.8 minutes
Public Transit: *Hartline/PSTA*
  257 city buses, 3,181 route miles
Interstate Highways: I-4, I-75
AMTRAK Weekly Departures

7 Northbound	7 Southbound
New York	Miami

Airline Service: Large hub
  Tampa International (TPA) 4 miles W
  St. Petersburg/Clearwater International (PIE) 17 miles SW

Nonstop Destinations		
	Total	Top Cities
Commuter	15	Miami, Tallahassee, West Palm Beach
Domestic Jet	50	Dallas, Fort Lauderdale, Atlanta
International	17	London, Montego Bay, Toronto

Score: 91.50   Rank: 31

Terre Haute, IN
Daily Commute: 40.5 minutes
Public Transit: *Transit Utility*
  8 city buses, 93 route miles
Interstate Highway: I-70
Airline Service: Nonhub
  Hulman Regional (HUF) 5 miles E

Nonstop Destination		
	Total	Top Cities
Commuter	1	Chicago

Score: 27.76   Rank: 256

Texarkana, TX-Texarkana, AR

Daily Commute: 40.8 minutes
Interstate Highway: I-30
AMTRAK Weekly Departures

4 Northbound	4 Southbound
Chicago	San Antonio

Airline Service: Nonhub
Texarkana Municipal (TXK) 4 miles NE

Nonstop Destinations		
	Total	Top Cities
Commuter	1	Dallas
Domestic Jet	1	Dallas

Score: 24.07   Rank: 269

Thunder Bay, ON

Daily Commute: 31.5 minutes
Public Transit: *TB Transit*
 39 city buses, 153 route miles
National Highway: TC-17
Airline Service: Nonhub
 Thunder Bay (YQT) 5 miles W

Nonstop Destination		
	Total	Top Destination
Domestic Jet	8	Toronto, Winnipeg, Ottawa

Score: 68.83   Rank: 111

Toledo, OH

Daily Commute: 40.0 minutes
Public Transit: *TARTA*
 122 city buses, 741 route miles
Interstate Highways: I-75, I-80
AMTRAK Weekly Departures

21 Eastbound	21 Westbound
New York	Chicago
Washington	

Airline Service: Nonhub
 Toledo Express (TOL) 10 miles W

Nonstop Destinations		
	Total	Top Cities
Commuter	3	Cincinnati, Pittsburgh, St. Louis
Domestic Jet	7	Atlanta, Pittsburgh, Chicago

Score: 75.07   Rank: 89

Topeka, KS

Daily Commute: 36.5 minutes
Public Transit: *TMTA*
 23 city buses, 164 route miles
Interstate Highways: I-35, I-70
AMTRAK Weekly Departures

7 Eastbound	7 Westbound
Chicago	Los Angeles

Airline Service: Nonhub
 Forbes Field (FOE) 6 miles S

Nonstop Destination		
	Total	Top Cities
Commuter	1	Kansas City

Score: 44.75   Rank: 196

★Toronto, ON

Daily Commute: 50.0 minutes
Public Transit: *TTC/GO Transit*
 1,804 city buses, 7,097 route miles
 953 heavy rail coaches
 295 light rail coaches, 4 route miles
 GO Transit commuter rail hub
National Highways: ON-2, ON-40, ON-40
VIA Weekly Departures

6 Northbound	79 Eastbound	59 Westbound
Cochrane	Montreal	Chicago
	New York	Sarnia
	Ottawa	Vancouver
		Windsor

Airline Service: Large hub
 Pearson International (YYZ) 18 miles NW

Nonstop Destination		
	Total	Top Cities
Domestic Jet	60	Montreal, Vancouver, Ottawa
International	38	Chicago, New York, Boston

Score: 98.01   Rank: 8

Trenton, NJ

Daily Commute: 47.3 minutes
Public Transit: *NJTC*
 247 city buses, 972 route miles
Interstate Highway: I-95
AMTRAK Weekly Departures

152 Northbound	180 Southbound
Boston	Charlotte
New York	Miami
Springfield	New Orleans
St. Albans	Newport News
	Philadelphia
	Richmond
	Washington

44 Eastbound	36 Westbound
New York	Harrisburg

Airline Service: Small hub
 Mercer County (TTN) 4 miles NW

Nonstop Destination		
	Total	Top Cities
Domestic Jet	3	Greensboro, Boston, Washington

Score: 44.19   Rank: 198

Trois-Rivieres, PQ

Daily Commute: 32.3 minutes
National Highway: PQ-40
Airline Service:
 Nearest is Quebec (YQB) 80 miles NE
Score: 10.48   Rank: 317

Tucson, AZ

Daily Commute: 45.3 minutes
Public Transit: *Sun Tran*
 156 city buses, 614 route miles
Interstate Highways: I-10, I-19
AMTRAK Weekly Departures

7 Eastbound	7 Westbound
Orlando	Los Angeles
San Antonio	

Airline Service: Medium hub

Tucson International (TUS) 6 miles S

Nonstop Destinations

	Total	Top Cities
Commuter	1	Salt Lake City
Domestic Jet	14	Phoenix, Los Angeles, Dallas
International	2	Culiacan, Hermosillo

Score: 71.10   Rank: 103

Tulsa, OK

Daily Commute: 42.3 minutes

Public Transit: *MTA*

55 city buses, 478 route miles

Interstate Highway: I-44

Airline Service: Medium hub

Tulsa International (TUL) 5 miles NE

Nonstop Destinations

	Total	Top Cities
Commuter	3	Memphis, Cincinnati, Denver
Domestic Jet	14	Dallas (DFW), Dallas (DAL), St. Louis

Score: 71.38   Rank: 102

Tuscaloosa, AL

Daily Commute: 39.8 minutes

Public Transit: *CP&TA*

5 city buses, 86 route miles

Interstate Highways: I-20, I-59

AMTRAK Weekly Departures

7 Northbound	7 Southbound
New York	New Orleans

Airline Service: Nonhub

Van De Graaf (TCL) 5 miles S

Nonstop Destination

	Total	Top Cities
Commuter	1	Nashville

Score: 15.58   Rank: 299

Tyler, TX

Daily Commute: 42.2 minutes

Public Transit: *Tyler Transit*

6 city buses, 24 route miles

Interstate Highway: I-20

Airline Service: Nonhub

Tyler/Pounds Field (TYR) 3 miles W

Nonstop Destinations

	Total	Top Cities
Commuter	1	Austin
Domestic Jet	2	Dallas, Houston

Score: 28.32   Rank: 254

Utica-Rome, NY

Daily Commute: 37.4 minutes

Public Transit: *UTA*

32 city buses, 191 route miles

Interstate Highway: I-90

AMTRAK Weekly Departures

14 Northbound	28 Eastbound	7 Westbound
Niagara Falls	New York	Toronto

Airline Service: Nonhub

Oneida County (UCA) 7 miles NW

Nonstop Destination

	Total	Top Cities
Commuter	2	Philadelphia, New York

Score: 39.09   Rank: 216

Vallejo-Fairfield-Napa, CA

Daily Commute: 56.8 minutes

Public Transit: *The VINE*

46 city buses, 181 route miles

Interstate Highway: I-80

Airline Service:

Nearest is Santa Rosa (STS)

Score: 5.66   Rank: 334

Vancouver, BC

Daily Commute: 55.0 minutes

Public Transit: *BC Transit*

675 city buses, 2,656 route miles

120 light rail coaches

212 trolley coaches

West Coast Express commuter rail hub

National Highways: (I-5), TC-1

VIA Weekly Departures

3 Eastbound
Toronto

Airline Service: Large hub

Vancouver International (YVR) 11 miles SW

Nonstop Destination

	Total	Top Cities
Domestic Jet	38	Toronto, Calgary, Edmonton
International	38	Los Angeles, Chicago, Hong Kong

Score: 84.70   Rank: 55

Ventura, CA

Daily Commute: 52.8 minutes

Public Transit: *SCAT*

30 city buses, 211 route miles

METRO LINK commuter rail to Los Angeles

AMTRAK Weekly Departures

35 Northbound	30 Southbound
San Luis Obispo	Los Angeles
Santa Barbara	San Diego
Seattle	

Airline Service: Nonhub

Oxnard Municipal (OXR) 1 miles W

Nonstop Destination

	Total	Top Cities
Commuter	1	Los Angeles

Score: 5.09   Rank: 336

Victoria, BC

Daily Commute: 35.0 minutes

Public Transit: *BC Transit*

154 city buses, 606 route miles

VIA Weekly Departures

7 Northbound
Courtenay

Airline Service: Large hub

Victoria International (YYJ) 19 miles N

Nonstop Destination

	Total	Top Cities
Domestic Jet	20	Vancouver, Calgary, Toronto

Score: 83.85   Rank: 58

Victoria, TX

Daily Commute: 41.4 minutes
Airline Service: Large hub
Victoria Regional (VCT) 6 miles NE

Nonstop Destination

	Total	Top Cities
Domestic Jet	1	Houston

Score: 16.99   Rank: 294

Vineland-Millville-Bridgeton, NJ

Daily Commute: 42.2 minutes
Public Transit: *NJTC*
12 city buses, 47 route miles
Airline Service:
Nearest is Atlantic City (ACY) 35 miles E
Score: 15.29   Rank: 300

Visalia-Tulare-Porterville, CA

Daily Commute: 37.8 minutes
Public Transit: *City Coach*
10 city buses, 39 route miles
Airline Service: Nonhub
Visalia Municipal (VIS) 6 miles W

Nonstop Destination

	Total	Top Cities
Commuter	1	Los Angeles

Score: 24.36   Rank: 268

Waco, TX

Daily Commute: 37.2 minutes
Public Transit: *WTS*
12 city buses, 144 route miles
Interstate Highway: I-35
Airline Service: Nonhub
Waco Regional (ACT) 5 miles NW

Nonstop Destination

	Total	Top Cities
Domestic Jet	2	Houston, Dallas

Score: 33.99   Rank: 234

★Washington, DC-MD-VA-WV

Daily Commute: 63.0 minutes
Public Transit: *WMATA*
1,155 city buses, 2,578 route miles
618 heavy rail cars, 185 route miles
MARC commuter rail to Baltimore
VRE commuter rail
Interstate Highways: I-66, I-95
AMTRAK Weekly Departures

63 Northbound	7 Southbound	10 Westbound
Boston	Charlotte	Chicago
New York	Miami	
Springfield	New Orleans	
St. Albans	Richmond	

Airline Service: Large hub
Dulles International (IAD) 26 miles W
Reagan/Washington National (DCA) 3 miles S

Nonstop Destinations

	Total	Top Cities
Commuter	76	Philadelphia, Norfolk, New York
Domestic Jet	86	New York, Atlanta, Chicago
International	20	London, Frankfurt, Paris

Score: 97.16   Rank: 11

Waterbury, CT

Daily Commute: 41.3 minutes
Public Transit: *NETC*
12 city buses, 47 route miles
METRO NORTH commuter rail to New York
Interstate Highway: I-84
Airline Service:
Nearest is New Haven (HVN) 30 miles SE
Score: 3.96   Rank: 340

Waterloo-Cedar Falls, IA

Daily Commute: 31.5 minutes
Public Transit: *MET*
13 city buses, 84 route miles
Interstate Highway: I-380
Airline Service: Nonhub
Waterloo Municipal (ALO) 4 miles NW

Nonstop Destinations

	Total	Top Cities
Commuter	1	Chicago
Domestic Jet	3	Dubuque, St. Louis, Minneapolis

Score: 52.69   Rank: 168

Wausau, WI

Daily Commute: 33.4 minutes
Public Transit: *WATS*
21 city buses, 107 route miles
Airline Service: Nonhub
Central Wisconsin Regional (CWA) 11 miles S

Nonstop Destinations

	Total	Top Cities
Commuter	1	Milwaukee
Domestic Jet	6	Chicago, Minneapolis, Detroit

Score: 58.07   Rank: 149

West Palm Beach-Boca Raton, FL

Daily Commute: 44.7 minutes
Public Transit: *CoTran*
122 city buses, 1,488 route miles
Tri-Rail commuter rail to Miami
Interstate Highway: I-95
AMTRAK Weekly Departures

21 Northbound	21 Southbound
New York	Miami
Jacksonville	

Airline Service: Medium hub
Palm Beach International (PBI) 3 miles W

Nonstop Destinations

	Total	Top Cities
Commuter	7	Tampa, Orlando, Tallahassee
Domestic Jet	27	Atlanta, New York, Newark
International	2	Freeport, Toronto

Score: 77.9   Rank: 79

Wheeling, WV-OH

Daily Commute: 42.4 minutes
Public Transit: *OVRTA*
16 city buses, 132 route miles
Interstate Highway: I-70
Airline Service:
Nearest is Pittsburgh (PIT) 50 miles NE
Score: 14.16   Rank: 304

Wichita, KS
Daily Commute: 38.7 minutes
Public Transit: *MTA*
  37 city buses, 258 route miles
Interstate Highway: I-35
AMTRAK Weekly Departures

7 Eastbound	7 Westbound
Chicago	Los Angeles

Airline Service: Small hub
  Wichita Mid-Continent (ICT) 5 miles SW

Nonstop Destinations	Total	Top Cities
Commuter	5	Kansas City, Cincinnati, Memphis
Domestic Jet	10	Dallas, Denver, St. Louis

Score: 74.5   Rank: 91

Wichita Falls, TX
Daily Commute: 33.2 minutes
Public Transit: *WFTS*
  10 city buses, 39 route miles
Interstate Highway: I-44
Airline Service: Nonhub
  Wichita Falls Municipal (SPS) 6 miles N

Nonstop Destination	Total	Top Cities
Domestic Jet	2	Elko, Dallas

Score: 35.97   Rank: 227

Williamsport, PA
Daily Commute: 35.6 minutes
Public Transit: *City Bus*
  14 city buses, 154 route miles
Airline Service: Nonhub
  Williamsport/Lycoming County (IPT) 4 miles E

Nonstop Destination	Total	Top Cities
Commuter	2	Pittsburgh, Philadelphia

Score: 38.52   Rank: 218

Wilmington, NC
Daily Commute: 39.2 minutes
Public Transit: *WTA*
  9 city buses, 81 route miles
Interstate Highway: I-40
Airline Service: Nonhub
  New Hanover International (ILM) 3 miles NE

Nonstop Destinations	Total	Top Cities
Commuter	3	Washington, Charlotte, Raleigh
Domestic Jet	2	Charlotte, Atlanta

Score: 45.89   Rank: 192

Wilmington-Newark, DE-MD
Daily Commute: 44.8 minutes
Public Transit: *DART*
  133 city buses, 898 route miles
Interstate Highway: I-95

AMTRAK Weekly Departures

224 Northbound	237 Southbound
Boston	Charlotte
New York	Miami
Springfield	New Orleans
St. Albans	Newport News
	Richmond
	Washington

Airline Service:
  Nearest is Philadelphia (PHL) 20 miles NE
Score: 18.41   Rank: 289

Windsor, ON
Daily Commute: 36.5 minutes
Public Transit: *Transit Windsor*
  73 city buses, 287 route miles
National Highways: (I-75), (I-94), ON-40
VIA Weekly Departures

44 Eastbound
Toronto

Airline Service: Large hub
  Windsor International (YQG) 6 miles SE

Nonstop Destinations	Total	Top Cities
Commuter	4	Ottawa, Toronto

Score: 75.63   Rank: 87

Winnipeg, MB
Daily Commute: 41.2 minutes
Public Transit: *WTS*
  478 city buses, 1,880 route miles
National Highways: (I-29), TC-1
VIA Weekly Departures

3 Northbound	3 Eastbound	3 Westbound
Gillam	Toronto	Vancouver

Airline Service: Medium hub
  Winnipeg International (YWG) 4 miles W

Nonstop Destination	Total	Top Cities
Domestic Jet	60	Toronto, Vancouver, Calgary
International	13	Dallas, Chicago, Minneapolis

Score: 83.56   Rank: 59

Worcester, MA-CT
Daily Commute: 46.2 minutes
Public Transit: *WRTA*
  43 city buses, 406 route miles
  MBTA commuter rail to Boston
Interstate Highway: I-90
AMTRAK Weekly Departures

7 Northbound	7 Southbound
Boston	Washington
7 Eastbound	7 Westbound
Boston	Albany

Airline Service: Nonhub
  Worcester Municipal (ORH) 3 miles W

Nonstop Destination	Total	Top Destination
Commuter	3	Philadelphia, New York, Washington

Score: 39.94   Rank: 213

Yakima, WA
Daily Commute: 34.8 minutes
Public Transit: *YTS*
  14 city buses, 117 route miles
Interstate Highway: I-82
Airline Service: Nonhub
  Yakima Air Terminal (YKM) 3 miles S

Nonstop Destinations		
	Total	Top Cities
Commuter	2	Seattle, Portland
Domestic Jet	2	Elko, Seattle

Score: 47.02   Rank: 188

Yolo, CA
Daily Commute: 38.1 minutes
Public Transit: *UNITRANS/YoloBus*
  27 city buses, 62 route miles
Interstate Highways: I-5, I-80
AMTRAK Weekly Departures

42 Northbound	42 Southbound
Sacramento	Los Angeles
Seattle	Oakland
	San Jose

7 Eastbound	7 Westbound
Chicago	Oakland

Airline Service:
  Nearest is Sacramento (SMF) 12 miles NE
Score: 19.83   Rank: 284

York, PA
Daily Commute: 43.3 minutes
Public Transit: *YCTA*
  18 city buses, 119 route miles
Interstate Highway: I-83
Airline Service:
  Nearest is Harrisburg (MDT) 20 miles NW
Score: 10.76   Rank: 316

Youngstown-Warren, OH
Daily Commute: 41.2 minutes
Public Transit: *WRTA*
  31 city buses, 222 route miles
Interstate Highways: I-76, I-80
Airline Service: Nonhub
  Youngstown-Warren Regional (YNG) 10 miles N

Nonstop Destinations		
	Total	Top Cities
Commuter	1	Pittsburgh
Domestic Jet	3	State College, Detroit, Akron

Score: 49   Rank: 181

Yuba City, CA
Daily Commute: 43.4 minutes
Public Transit: *Sutter Transit*
  7 city buses, 28 route miles
AMTRAK Weekly Departures

7 Northbound	7 Southbound
Seattle	Los Angeles

Airline Service:
  Nearest is Sacramento (SMF) 40 miles S
Score: 4.81   Rank: 337

Yuma, AZ
Daily Commute: 34.5 minutes
Interstate Highway: I-8
AMTRAK Weekly Departures

7 Eastbound	7 Westbound
San Antonio	Los Angeles
Orlando	

Airline Service: Nonhub
  Yuma International (YUM) 3 miles SE

Nonstop Destination		
	Total	Top Cities
Commuter	3	Phoenix, Los Angeles, El Centro

Score: 37.11   Rank: 223

ET CETERA: TRANSPORTATION

FERRYBOATS, CABLE CARS, MONORAILS, AERIAL TRAMS, AND INCLINES

Besides the ubiquitous bus and the different rail systems in larger cities, North American transit systems operate other types of vehicles. Although these modes have little impact on total mass transit, they are by far the most fun to watch and ride, undeniably adding to a city's flavor.

San Francisco has the continent's only **cable car** system. In operation since the 19th century, the MUNI's forty-one cars and the 75-year-old Perley Thomas Company cars in New Orleans's Charles Street **streetcar** system are the only transit properties in the National Register of Historic Places.

Aerial trams are passenger gondolas suspended from a system of aerial cables and propelled by separate cables attached to the vehicle suspension system. The cable system is powered by engines or motors at a central location, not on board the vehicle. New York operates the only public aerial tram, between Roosevelt Island and Manhattan.

Automated guideways, the newest public transit mode, includes personal rapid transit, group rapid transit, and people-mover systems. Electric vehicles running over fixed guideways, they are without operators or other crewpersons. Service may be on a fixed schedule or in response to a passenger-activated call button. You can catch one in six locations:

Detroit, MI   Detroit Transportation Corporation

Jacksonville, FL   Jacksonville Transportation Authority

TRAINS TO PLANES: COMMUTING TO THE AIRPORT

Most airports are miles from the central business district but are easily reached by freeways. Still, congestion and airport parking problems make any airport stop on a rapid rail route a frequent-flyer blessing.

Atlanta International	Heavy Rail
Baltimore-Washington International	Light Rail
Chicago Midway	Heavy Rail
Chicago O'Hare International	Heavy Rail
Cleveland-Hopkins International	Heavy Rail
Montreal Dorval International	Heavy Rail
Philadelphia International	Commuter Rail
Lambert-St. Louis International	Light Rail
South Bend Michiana Regional	Commuter Rail
Washington Reagan National	Heavy Rail

Source: American Public Transit Association. List excludes airports that require a bus ride between the train station and terminal and airports that have only rail circulation systems.

Las Colinas, TX	Las Colinas Area Rapid Transit
Miami, FL	Metro-Dade Transit Agency
Morgantown, WV	West Virginia University
Tampa, FL	Hillsborough Area RTA

The largest transit vehicles are **ferryboats,** which range in size up to 380 feet and can carry as many as 2,500 commuters per trip. Public ferryboat systems, which provide frequent "bridge" service over a fixed route and on a published schedule between two or more points, are part of the mass-transit mix in thirteen metro areas:

Boston, MA	Massachusetts Bay Transit Authority
Erie, PA	Erie Metropolitan Transit Authority
Galveston, TX	Texas Department of Transportation
Halifax, NS	METRO
New Orleans, LA	Mississippi River Bridge Authority
New York, NY	City of New York-Staten Island Ferry
Norfolk, VA	Tidewater Transportation District
Portland, ME	Casco Bay Transit District
San Francisco, CA	Golden Gate Bridge Transportation
Seattle, WA	Washington State Ferries
Tacoma, WA	Pierce County Ferry
Vallejo, CA	Vallejo TS
Vancouver, BC	BC Transit

Six metro areas still operate late 19th-century cog or cable **incline cars,** called "funiculars," that operate up and down steep slopes on rails via a cable mechanism so that passenger seats remain horizontal while the undercarriage (truck) is angled parallel to the slope:

Chattanooga, TN-GA	Lookout Mountain
Dubuque, IA	Fourth Street Elevator
Johnstown, PA	Johnstown-Westmont Incline
Los Angeles, CA	Angels Flight Railway
Pittsburgh, PA	Monongahela & Duquesne Heights
St. Catharines-Niagara, ON	Fallsview Park Incline

CONTRADICTORY RULES OF THE ROAD

Driving across political boundaries can mean a brush with contradictory traffic codes. Here are examples, with one caveat: The information comes from the American Automobile Association's latest *Digest of Motor Laws,* but it may not reflect recent changes in the law.

Speed Limits. There are two kinds of speed limits—absolute and prima facie, a legal phrase meaning "at first view." If the speed limit of 55 is absolute, going 56 means breaking the law. If the speed limit of 55 is prima facie, however, going 56 or even 60 is merely apparent evidence of unreasonable and imprudent speed. Drivers may escape a fine if they can convince the traffic court that their speed was reasonable and safe in light of the highway's condition, traffic, and visibility. In all Canadian provinces but Newfoundland and Nova Scotia, speed limits are absolute. States where all or some speed limits are prima facie are:

Arizona	Montana
Connecticut	New Hampshire
District of Columbia	New Jersey
Hawaii	New York
Idaho	Oregon

Cellular phone use while driving is permitted in all states and provinces. Dialing 1-800-525-5555 routes your emergency call directly to the state police/patrol of the state from which you are calling.

State/Province	Phone Number	State/Province	Phone Number
Alabama	*47	Nebraska	*55
Alaska	911	Nevada	*NHP
Alberta	911	New Brunswick	911
Arizona	911	Newfoundland	N/A
Arkansas	911	New Hampshire	*77
British Columbia	911	New Jersey	911
California	911	New Mexico	911
Colorado	911	New York	911
Connecticut	911	North Carolina	*47
Delaware	911	North Dakota	*2121
District of Columbia	727-6161	Nova Scotia	N/A
Florida	*FHP or *DUI	Ohio	911 or *DUI
Georgia	*GSP	Oklahoma	*55
Hawaii	911	Ontario	911
Idaho	*ISP	Oregon	911
Illinois	911 or *999	Pennsylvania	911
Indiana	911	Quebec	N/A
Iowa	911 or *55	Rhode Island	911
Kansas	*47	Saskatchewan	911
Kentucky	911	South Carolina	N/A
Louisiana	911	South Dakota	911
Maine	*77	Tennessee	*THP
Manitoba	911	Texas	911
Maryland	911	Utah	911
Massachusetts	*77 or *SP	Vermont	911
Michigan	911	Virginia	911
Minnesota	911	Washington	911
Mississippi	*47	West Virginia	*SP
Missouri	55	Wisconsin	911
Montana	1-800-525-5555	Wyoming	*HELP

Source: American Automobile Association.

Indiana
Louisiana
Maryland
Massachusetts

Rhode Island
Utah
West Virginia
Wisconsin

Right and Left Turn on Red. In 1947, California became the first state to permit drivers to turn right on a red signal after a complete stop. The most recent was Massachusetts, in 1980. Quebec and New York City now are the only major jurisdictions that prohibit the turn. According to the Federal Highway Administration, fewer accidents occur when drivers turn right on a red light than when they turn right on a green light. Furthermore, the rule saves an average of 14 seconds at each turn, cuts gasoline consumption and exhaust emissions, and allows intersections to handle more traffic.

In the past 15 years, most states have also enacted statutes permitting left turns on a red signal, but only after a complete stop and only from a one-way street into another one-way street. The practice remains prohibited everywhere in Canada except Alberta, British Columbia, and Ontario. In the U.S., the District of Columbia and eight states listed below continue to ban turning left on red:

Connecticut	New Jersey
District of Columbia	North Carolina
Maine	Rhode Island
Missouri	Vermont
New Hampshire	

The state of New York permits a left turn on red everywhere except New York City. Tennessee permits the turn when so marked by each city.

Studded Tires. Most states and provinces allow drivers to mount studded snow tires on their automobiles for better traction during an icy winter. Because the carbide-tipped studs damage road surfaces, some jurisdictions prohibit their use:

Alabama	Minnesota
Georgia (except in ice and snow)	Mississippi
Hawaii	Ontario
Illinois	Texas
Louisiana	Utah
Maryland (except western counties)	Wisconsin
Michigan	

Glass Tinting. Tinted automobile window glass is a frequently chosen factory option. Over the past 10 years, however, aftermarket application of black and gunmetal-gray plastic sheeting to the inside of the windshield has become extremely popular. Because it interferes with night vision, it is restricted in varying degrees everywhere.

Audio Headsets. The issue here is whether the ears are as necessary for safe driving as the eyes. When you don't hear an ambulance siren, a ticket for failing to yield the right-of-way to an emergency vehicle is the likely consequence. But when you can't hear a train whistle or the air horn of an oncoming 18-wheeler, the result could be far more serious. Accordingly, several jurisdictions prohibit the driver from wearing an audio headset:

Alaska	Massachusetts
California	Minnesota
Colorado	Ohio
Florida	Pennsylvania
Georgia	Quebec
Illinois	Rhode Island
Louisiana	Virginia
Manitoba	Washington
Maryland	

Motorcycle Helmets. The mileage fatality rate (deaths per 100 million miles) for motorcycle travel is five times that for auto travel, and the major cause is head injuries. Consequently, many states and all Canadian provinces require motorcycle riders to wear helmets. Motorcyclists have challenged the law, but state courts have generally upheld it because it affects the biker's right to receive insurance compensation for injuries. Only Colorado, Illinois, and Iowa do not require protective headgear of any kind for motorcyclists and passengers.

Mandatory Annual Safety Inspections. Many states and provinces require regular safety inspection and/or emissions testing of automobiles to rid the highways of dangerous vehicles with bald tires, wobbly suspensions, smoky exhausts, and defective brakes and lights. In many of those states where inspections are not mandatory, state troopers are authorized to stop and inspect vehicles they believe are a danger to other motorists or lack required equipment. The following jurisdictions require annual safety inspections:

Alberta	New York
British Columbia	Newfoundland
Connecticut	North Carolina
Delaware	Nova Scotia
District of Columbia	Oklahoma
Hawaii	Ontario
Louisiana	Pennsylvania
Maine	Rhode Island
Manitoba	Saskatchewan
Maryland	Texas
Massachusetts	Utah
Mississippi	Vermont
Missouri	Virginia
New Brunswick	Washington
New Hampshire	West Virginia
New Jersey	

Some states require emissions tests only in certain "high traffic" cities and counties. The following jurisdictions have a required emission inspection of some sort, either statewide or in extended counties or metro areas:

Alaska	Minnesota
Alberta	Missouri
Arizona	Nevada
British Columbia	New Brunswick
California	New Jersey
Colorado	New York
Connecticut	North Carolina
Delaware	Ohio
District of Columbia	Oklahoma
Florida	Ontario
Georgia	Oregon
Idaho	Pennsylvania
Illinois	Rhode Island
Indiana	Texas
Kentucky	Utah
Louisiana	Virginia
Manitoba	Washington
Maryland	Wisconsin
Massachusetts	

Mandatory Seat Belt Use. Because automobile accidents are the leading cause of death among young children, all states and provinces now require the use of special vehicle restraints for children who are less than preschool age. Most jurisdictions also require the use of seat belts by the driver and all front-seat passengers. Only New Hampshire does not.

Radar Detectors. All states and provinces use radar in their speed enforcement programs, and all but seven—Manitoba, Newfoundland, Ontario, Quebec, Virginia, and the District of Columbia—permit drivers to install radar detectors for advance warning.

DRIVER LICENSING

When you settle in a new state or province, you have to surrender your old driver's license and get a new one. The time permitted to do this ranges from "immediately" in twelve states and New Brunswick, to 30 days in twenty-one jurisdictions, and up to 6 months in British Columbia and Vermont. Hawaii and Wyoming let you keep your license until it expires.

Required Tests

For a new resident with a valid driver's license from a former state, the requirements for getting a license from the new jurisdiction vary considerably. All states now require a vision test, but all other tests may be waived in Nevada, New Brunswick, New Hampshire, Newfoundland, and Vermont. The written or road sign test is required in nineteen states and waived in twenty-one others. Hawaii and Saskatchewan require you to get behind the wheel with a license examiner for a road test; in twenty-seven other states or provinces, a road test may be waived or required at the discretion of the examiner.

Problem Drivers

If your license has been revoked, you won't get a new one simply by moving to another state. Every license application is checked with the National Driver Registry, a federal data file of persons whose license to drive has been denied or withdrawn. Moreover, forty-five states belong to the National Driver License Compact, an agreement among states to share information on drivers who accumulate tickets in one jurisdiction and try to escape control in another. All provinces are members of the Canadian Driver License Compact; traffic offense information covering eight categories is exchanged among the jurisdictions.

FINDING YOUR WAY ON THE INTERSTATE

By staying with a combination of interstate routes, it is possible for you to drive from one metro area in the United States to almost any other without stopping for a traffic light.

Five of the routes are more than 2,000 miles long. The longest, I-90, stretches 3,082 miles between downtown Boston and Seattle's waterfront. The next longest routes are I-80 (2,907 miles, from San Francisco to Hackensack, New Jersey), I-10 (2,460 miles along the nation's southern border, from Los Angeles to Jacksonville, Florida), I-40 (2,461 miles, from Barstow, California to Smithfield, North Carolina), and I-70 (2,175 miles from Cove Fort, Utah, to Baltimore). Three of these routes, I-10, I-80, and I-90, cross the country from coast to coast, and I-40 nearly makes it.

Seven interstate routes span the nation in a north-south direction: I-5 (1,382 miles, from San Diego to Bellingham, Washington), I-15 (1,437 miles, from San Diego to the Montana-Canada border), I-35 (1,568 miles, from suburban New Orleans to Chicago), I-65 (888 miles, from Mobile, Alabama, to Gary-Hammond, Indiana), I-75 (1,787 miles, from Naples, Florida, to the Michigan-Canada border), and 1-95 (1,894 miles, from the city of Miami to the Maine-Canada border).

Getting a Driver's License and Registering Your Car After Relocating:
A Guide for People with Current Paperwork from a Former Jurisdiction

Finding Your Way on the Interstate

STATE	DRIVER'S LICENSING TIME LIMIT	WRITTEN TEST	VISION TEST	ROAD TEST	NDL OR CDL COMPACT	VEHICLE REGISTRATION TIME LIMIT	INSPECTION REQUIRED
Alabama	30 days		●		✓	30 days	
Alaska	90 days		●			10 days	E
Alberta	90 days	●	●	●	✓	90 days	S
Arizona	Immediately	▲	●	▲	✓	Immediately	E
Arkansas	30 days		●		✓	10 days	
British Columbia	6 months	▲	●	▲	✓	30 days	E
California	10 days	●	●	▲		20 days	E
Colorado	30 days		●		✓	30 days	E
Connecticut	30 days	▲	●	▲	✓	60 days	S/E
Delaware	60 days	▲	●	▲	✓	60 days	S/E
District of Columbia	30 days	●	●	▲	✓	★	S/E
Florida	30 days	▲	●	▲	✓	10 days	E
Georgia	30 days	▲	●	▲	✓	30 days	E
Hawaii	★	●	●	●	✓	10 days	S
Idaho	Immediately	●	●	▲	✓	90 days	E
Illinois	90 days	●	●	▲	✓	30 days	E
Indiana	60 days	▲	●	▲	✓	60 days	E
Iowa	Immediately	▲	●	▲	✓	90 days	
Kansas	90 days	●	●		✓	★	
Kentucky	Immediately	●	●		✓	15 days	E
Louisiana	30 days		●		✓	Immediately	S/E
Maine	30 days	▲	●	▲	✓	30 days	S
Manitoba	90 days		●		✓	90 days	S
Maryland	30 days	▲	●	▲	✓	30 days	S/E
Massachusetts	Immediately		●		✓	Immediately	S/E
Michigan	Immediately	●	●			Immediately	
Minnesota	60 days	▲	●	▲	✓	60 days	
Mississippi	60 days	▲	●	▲	✓	30 days	S
Missouri	Immediately	●	●		✓	30 days	S/E
Montana	90 days	▲	●			Immediately	
Nebraska	30 days	●	●	▲	✓	★	
Nevada	30 days	▲	●	▲	✓	30 days	E
New Brunswick	Immediately	▲	▲	▲	✓	6 months	S
New Hampshire	60 days	▲	●	▲	✓	60 days	S
New Jersey	60 days	●	●		✓	60 days	S/E
New Mexico	30 days		●		✓	30 days	
New York	30 days	●	●		✓	30 days	S/E
Newfoundland	90 days	▲	▲	▲	✓	90 days	S
North Carolina	30 days	▲	●		✓	Immediately	S/E
North Dakota	60 days	▲	●	▲	✓	Immediately	
Nova Scotia	90 days	●	●	▲	✓	30 days	S
Ohio	Immediately	●	●		✓	Immediately	E
Oklahoma	Immediately		●		✓	30 days	S/E
Ontario	60 days		●		✓	★	S/E
Oregon	Immediately		●			Immediately	E
Pennsylvania	60 days	▲	●	▲	✓	60 days	S/E
Quebec	90 days		●		✓	90 days	
Rhode Island	30 days		●		✓	30 days	S/E
Saskatchewan	90 days				✓	90 days	
South Carolina	90 days	●	●		✓	45 days	
South Dakota	90 days		●		✓	90 days	
Tennessee	30 days		●		✓	Immediately	
Texas	30 days		●		✓	30 days	S/E
Utah	Immediately	●	●		✓	60 days	S/E
Vermont	6 months	▲	●	▲	✓	6 months	S
Virginia	30 days		●		✓	30 days	S/E
Washington	30 days	●	●	▲	✓	30 days	E
West Virginia	30 days		●		✓	30 days	S
Wisconsin	Immediately	●	●			Immediately	E
Wyoming	★	▲	●	▲	✓	Immediately	

● *Required,* ▲ *May be waived.*

★ *Home state license or registration valid until expiration.*

S Safety inspection, E Emissions test, S/E Both.

The Interstate System: A Route Log and Finder List

ROUTE	TOTAL MILEAGE	MILEAGE BY STATE		SELECTED CITIES SERVED
4	132	Florida	132	Daytona Beach, Lakeland, Orlando, Tampa, Winter Haven
5	1,382	California	797	Anaheim, Los Angeles, Redding, Sacramento, San Diego, Santa Ana, Stockton
		Oregon	308	Eugene, Medford, Portland, Salem
		Washington	277	Bellingham, Olympia, Seattle, Tacoma, Vancouver
8	348	California	170	El Centro, San Diego
		Arizona	178	Casa Grande, Yuma
10	2,460	California	243	Los Angeles, Riverside, San Bernardino
		Arizona	392	Phoenix, Tucson
		New Mexico	164	Deming, Las Cruces
		Texas	881	Beaumont, El Paso, Houston, San Antonio
		Louisiana	274	Baton Rouge, Lafayette, Lake Charles, New Orleans
		Mississippi	77	Biloxi, Gulfport, Pascagoula
		Alabama	66	Mobile
		Florida	363	Jacksonville, Pensacola, Tallahassee
12	86	Louisiana	86	Baton Rouge
15	1,436	California	287	Riverside, San Bernardino, San Diego
		Nevada	124	Las Vegas
		Arizona	29	—
		Utah	405	Brigham City, Ogden, Orem, Provo, Salt Lake City, St. George
		Idaho	196	Blackfoot, Idaho Falls, Pocatello
		Montana	395	Butte, Great Falls, Helena, Sweetgrass
16	165	Georgia	165	Macon, Savannah
17	145	Arizona	145	Flagstaff, Phoenix
19	63	Arizona	63	Nogales, Tucson
20	1,540	Texas	636	Abilene, Arlington, Dallas, Fort Worth, Longview, Marshall, Midland, Odessa, Tyler
		Louisiana	190	Monroe, Shreveport
		Mississippi	155	Jackson, Meridian, Vicksburg
		Alabama	215	Anniston, Birmingham, Tuscaloosa
		Georgia	202	Atlanta, Augusta
		South Carolina	142	Columbia, Florence
24	316	Illinois	39	Metropolis
		Kentucky	93	Hopkinsville, Paducah
		Tennessee	180	Chattanooga, Clarksville, Nashville
		Georgia	4	—

continues

Map

16 — Jasper

Edmonton

2

16 — *Calgary* — Saskatoon

2

4

11

15

1 — *Regina*

1 — *Winnipeg*

16

17

71

11

75

1 — Victoria

5

Vancouver

Seattle

90

82

Portland

84

5

84

90

15

29

94

35

90

94

35

St. Paul

90

35

380

80

80

Cheyenne

29

80

Des Moines

Salt Lake City

25

San Francisco

70

76

5

15

70

70

Denver

135

335

35

Kansas City

44

Las Vegas

35

40

Oklahoma City

70

Los Angeles

15

10

17

25

44

40

27

35

40

8

10

Phoenix

Albuquerque

40

30

19

25

20

Ft. Worth

20

10

45

49

10

Houston

35

37

OAHU — HI

2

1

Pearl City

3

1 — *Honolulu*

Copyright © 1997 by Places Rated Partnership

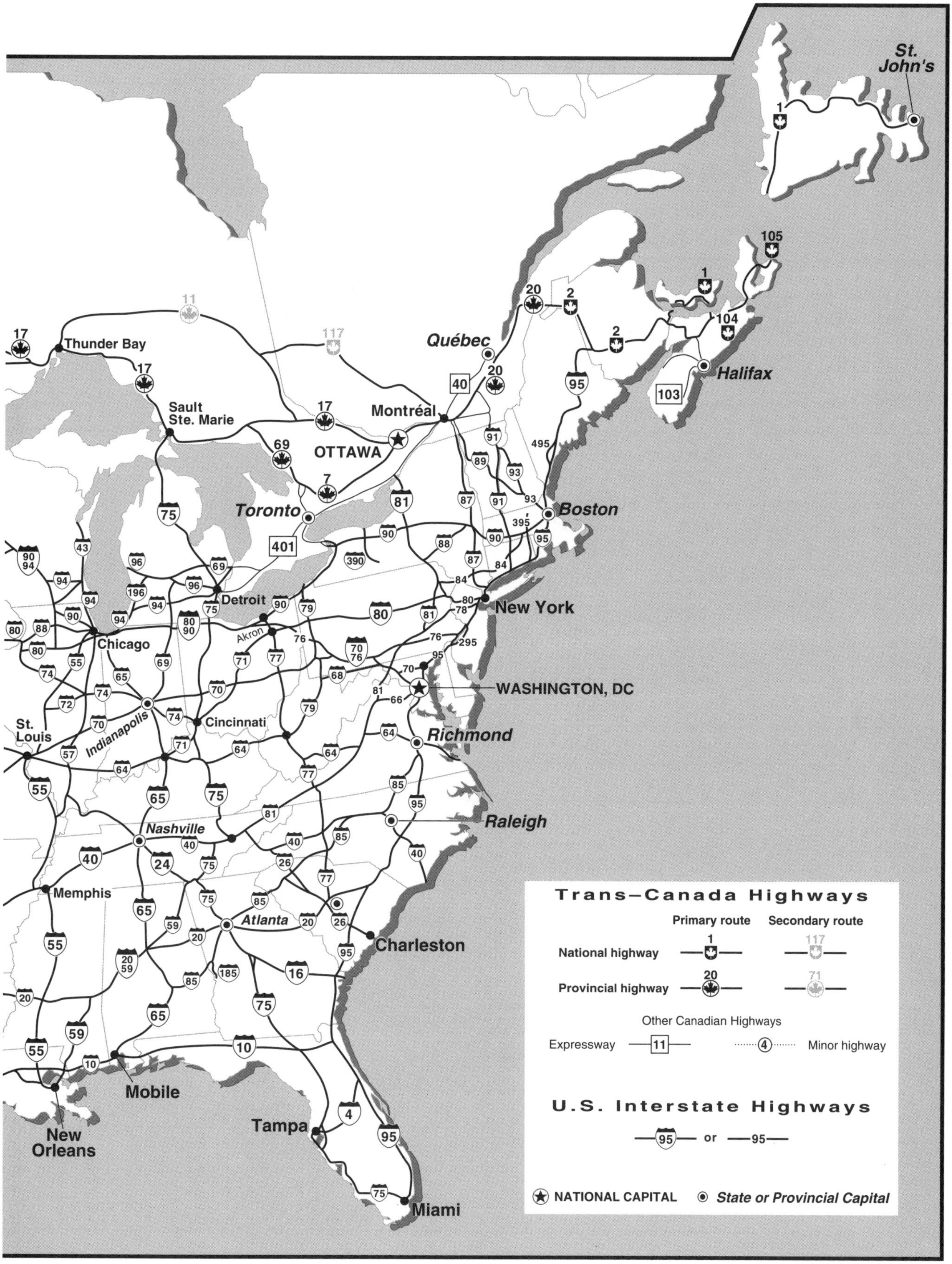

St. John's

105

1

104

20

2

2

103

95

Halifax

17   Thunder Bay

11

117

17

Québec

Sault
Ste. Marie

17

40

20

69

Montréal

OTTAWA

91

7

89

93

495

75

Toronto

81

87

91

93

Boston

401

390

90

88

87

395

95

96

84

84

43

196

96

69

Detroit

90

79

80

81

New York

94

94

75

80
90

78

295

80

88

94

Chicago

80
90

Akron

76

70
76

76

95

80

74

55

65

69

71

77

68

70

WASHINGTON, DC

72

70

74

79

81

66

St.
Louis

57

Indianapolis

74

Cincinnati

64

64

64

Richmond

55

64

64

77

65

75

85

81

95

Nashville

40

40

85

Raleigh

24

75

26

40

Memphis

65

75

77

40

59

Atlanta

20

26

85

Charleston

20
59

85

185

16

95

20

65

75

New
Orleans

59

55

10

10

Mobile

Tampa

4

95

75

Miami

Trans−Canada Highways

	Primary route	Secondary route
National highway	1	117
Provincial highway	20	71

Other Canadian Highways

Expressway   11   4   Minor highway

U.S. Interstate Highways

95   or   95

★ NATIONAL CAPITAL   ⊙ State or Provincial Capital

Thomas Nast, Cartographer

157

ROUTE	TOTAL MILEAGE	MILEAGE BY STATE		SELECTED CITIES SERVED
25	1,063	New Mexico	463	Albuquerque, Las Cruces, Santa Fe
		Colorado	299	Colorado Springs, Denver, Fort Collins, Longmont, Pueblo
		Wyoming	301	Casper, Cheyenne
26	261	North Carolina	40	Asheville, Hendersonville
		South Carolina	221	Charleston, Columbia, Spartanburg
27	124	Texas	124	Amarillo, Lubbock
29	753	Missouri	130	Kansas City, St. Joseph
		Iowa	152	Council Bluffs, Sioux City
		South Dakota	253	Sioux Falls
		North Dakota	218	Fargo, Grand Forks
30	367	Texas	224	Dallas, Fort Worth, Texarkana
		Arkansas	143	Little Rock, Texarkana
35	1,569	Texas	504	Arlington, Austin, Dallas, Fort Worth, Laredo, San Antonio, Temple, Waco
		Oklahoma	236	Norman, Oklahoma City
		Kansas	236	Kansas City, Lawrence, Topeka, Wichita
		Missouri	115	Kansas City
		Iowa	218	Ames, Des Moines
		Minnesota	260	Albert Lea, Duluth, Minneapolis, St. Paul
37	143	Texas	143	Corpus Christi, San Antonio
39	131	Illinois	131	Bloomington, Rockford
40	2,460	California	155	Barstow, Needles
		Arizona	359	Flagstaff, Kingman
		New Mexico	371	Albuquerque, Gallup, Tucumcari
		Texas	177	Amarillo
		Oklahoma	331	Clinton, Oklahoma City
		Arkansas	285	Fort Smith, Little Rock
		Tennessee	455	Jackson, Knoxville, Memphis, Nashville
		North Carolina	327	Asheville, Burlington, Durham, Greensboro, Hickory, Raleigh, Winston-Salem
43	183	Wisconsin	183	Green Bay, Milwaukee, Sheboygan
44	635	Texas	15	Wichita Falls
		Oklahoma	329	Oklahoma City, Tulsa
		Missouri	291	Joplin, Springfield, St. Louis
45	285	Texas	285	Dallas, Galveston, Houston, Texas City
49	207	Louisiana	207	Alexandria, Lafayette, Nachitoches, Opelousas, Shreveport

ROUTE	TOTAL MILEAGE	MILEAGE BY STATE		SELECTED CITIES SERVED
55	943	Louisiana	66	Hammond, LaPlace
		Mississippi	290	Grenada, Jackson, McComb
		Tennessee	12	Memphis
		Arkansas	72	Blytheville, West Memphis
		Missouri	209	Cape Girardeau, St. Louis
		Illinois	294	Bloomington, Chicago, East St. Louis, Joliet, Springfield
57	381	Missouri	22	Charleston, Sikeston
		Illinois	359	Champaign, Chicago, Kankakee, Rantoul, Urbana
59	443	Louisiana	11	New Orleans, Slidell
		Mississippi	171	Hattiesburg, Laurel, Meridian
		Alabama	241	Birmingham, Gadsden, Tuscaloosa
		Georgia	20	—
64	945	Missouri	15	St. Louis
		Illinois	128	Belleville, East St. Louis
		Indiana	124	Evansville, New Albany
		Kentucky	192	Frankfort, Lexington, Louisville
		West Virginia	187	Charleston, Huntington, White Sulphur Springs
		Virginia	299	Charlottesville, Newport News, Norfolk, Richmond
65	888	Alabama	367	Birmingham, Decatur, Mobile, Montgomery
		Tennessee	121	Nashville
		Kentucky	138	Bowling Green, Elizabethtown, Louisville
		Indiana	262	Gary, Indianapolis, Lafayette
66	76	Virginia	75	Arlington, Fairfax, Falls Church, Front Royal, Vienna
		District of Columbia	1	Washington, DC
68	72	West Virginia	72	Morgantown
69	356	Indiana	158	Anderson, Fort Wayne, Indianapolis, Muncie
		Michigan	198	Battle Creek, Flint, Lansing
70	2,175	Utah	231	Cove Fort, Green River, Richfield
		Colorado	450	Denver, Grand Junction
		Kansas	424	Kansas City, Lawrence, Topeka
		Missouri	252	Columbia, Kansas City, St. Louis
		Illinois	160	East St. Louis, Effingham, Vandalia
		Indiana	156	Indianapolis, Richmond, Terre Haute
		Ohio	226	Columbus, Dayton, Springfield, Zanesville
		West Virginia	14	Wheeling
		Pennsylvania	169	Pittsburgh
		Maryland	93	Baltimore, Hagerstown

continues

Finding Your Way on the Interstate

ROUTE	TOTAL MILEAGE	MILEAGE BY STATE		SELECTED CITIES SERVED
71	346	Kentucky	98	Covington, Louisville
		Ohio	248	Cincinnati, Cleveland, Columbus, Mansfield
72	79	Illinois	79	Champaign, Decatur, Springfield
74	416	Iowa	5	Davenport
		Illinois	220	Bloomington, Champaign, Moline, Peoria, Rock Island, Urbana
		Indiana	172	Crawfordsville, Indianapolis, Shelbyville
		Ohio	19	Cincinnati
75	1,788	Florida	472	Bradenton, Fort Myers, Gainesville, Lakeland, Naples, Ocala, Sarasota, St. Petersburg, Tampa
		Georgia	355	Atlanta, Macon, Valdosta
		Tennessee	162	Chattanooga, Knoxville
		Kentucky	192	Covington, Lexington, Richmond
		Ohio	212	Cincinnati, Dayton, Lima, Middletown, Toledo
		Michigan	395	Bay City, Detroit, Flint, Saginaw
76	618	Colorado	184	Denver, Fort Morgan, Sterling
		Nebraska	2	—
		Ohio	78	Akron, Youngstown
		Pennsylvania	351	Harrisburg, Lancaster, Philadelphia, Pittsburgh, Reading
		New Jersey	3	Camden
77	597	South Carolina	75	Columbia, Rock Hill
		North Carolina	105	Charlotte, Mooresville, Statesville
		Virginia	67	Bluefield, Wytheville
		West Virginia	187	Beckley, Bluefield, Charleston, Parkersburg
		Ohio	163	Akron, Canton, Cleveland, Marietta
78	146	Pennsylvania	77	Allentown, Bethlehem, Easton
		New Jersey	68	Irvington, Jersey City, Newark, Plainfield
		New York	1	New York City
79	345	West Virginia	161	Charleston, Fairmont, Morgantown
		Pennsylvania	184	Erie, Meadville, Pittsburgh, Washington
80	2,908	California	202	Davis, Fairfield, Oakland, Sacramento, San Francisco, Vallejo
		Nevada	411	Elko, Reno, Sparks, Winnemucca
		Utah	198	Salt Lake City
		Wyoming	403	Cheyenne, Evanston, Laramie, Rawlings, Rock Springs
		Nebraska	455	Grand Island, Kearney, Lincoln, Omaha
		Iowa	307	Davenport, Des Moines, Iowa City

ROUTE	TOTAL MILEAGE	MILEAGE BY STATE		SELECTED CITIES SERVED
		Illinois	164	Chicago, Joliet, Moline, Rock Island
		Indiana	152	Elkhart, Gary, Hammond, Mishawaka, South Bend
		Ohio	237	Cleveland, Elyria, Toledo, Warren, Youngstown
		Pennsylvania	311	Du Bois, Milton, Sharon, Stroudsburg
		New Jersey	68	Bergen–Passaic
81	855	Tennessee	75	Bristol, Johnson City, Kingsport, Knoxville
		Virginia	324	Bristol, Roanoke
		West Virginia	26	Martinsburg
		Maryland	12	Hagerstown
		New York	184	Binghamton, Syracuse
		Pennsylvania	234	Harrisburg, Scranton, Wilkes-Barre
82	143	Washington	132	Kennewick, Pasco, Richland, Yakima
		Oregon	11	Hermiston
83	84	Maryland	34	Baltimore
		Pennsylvania	50	Harrisburg, York
84	996	Oregon	375	Baker, Pendleton, Portland
		Idaho	275	Boise, Twin Falls
		Utah	117	Ogden
		Pennsylvania	50	Scranton
		New York	72	Newburgh
		Connecticut	99	Bristol, Danbury, Hartford, New Britain, Waterbury
		Massachusetts	8	—
85	667	Alabama	80	Auburn, Montgomery, Opelika
		Georgia	179	Atlanta
		South Carolina	106	Anderson, Greenville, Spartanburg
		North Carolina	233	Burlington, Charlotte, Durham, Gastonia, Greensboro, High Point
		Virginia	69	Petersburg
86	63	Idaho	63	American Falls, Pocatello
87	333	New York	333	Albany, Glens Falls, New York City, Newburgh, Poughkeepsie, Troy
88	173	Illinois	173	Chicago, Moline
89	191	New Hampshire	61	Concord, Lebanon
		Vermont	130	Burlington, Montpelier

Finding Your Way on the Interstate

ROUTE	TOTAL MILEAGE	MILEAGE BY STATE		SELECTED CITIES SERVED
90	2,983	Washington	297	Seattle, Spokane
		Idaho	74	Coeur d'Alene, Kellogg
		Montana	550	Billings, Bozeman, Butte, Missoula
		Wyoming	209	Buffalo, Sheridan
		South Dakota	413	Rapid City, Sioux Falls
		Minnesota	276	Albert Lea, Austin, Rochester
		Wisconsin	187	Beloit, Janesville, La Crosse, Madison
		Illinois	108	Chicago, Elgin, Rockford
		Indiana	157	Elkhart, Gary, Hammond, Mishawaka, South Bend
		Ohio	244	Cleveland, Elyria, Lorain, Toledo
		Pennsylvania	47	Erie
		New York	287	Albany, Buffalo, Rochester, Rome, Schenectady, Syracuse, Troy, Utica
		Massachusetts	134	Boston, Pittsfield, Springfield, Worcester
91	291	Connecticut	58	Hartford, New Haven, Meriden
		Massachusetts	55	Springfield
		Vermont	178	Brattleboro, St. Johnsbury
93	189	Massachusetts	46	Boston, Lawrence, Lowell
		New Hampshire	132	Concord, Manchester
		Vermont	11	St. Johnsbury
94	1,608	Montana	248	Billings, Glendive, Miles City
		North Dakota	353	Bismarck, Fargo
		Minnesota	260	Minneapolis, Moorehead, St. Cloud, St. Paul
		Wisconsin	348	Eau Claire, Kenosha, Madison, Milwaukee, Racine
		Illinois	77	Chicago
		Indiana	46	Gary, Hammond, Michigan City, Portage
		Michigan	276	Ann Arbor, Battle Creek, Benton, Harbor, Detroit, Jackson, Kalamazoo
95	1,894	Florida	382	Boca Raton, Daytona Beach, Fort Lauderdale, Fort Pierce, Hialeah, Hollywood, Jacksonville, Melbourne, Miami, Palm Beach, Pompano Beach
		Georgia	112	Brunswick, Savannah
		South Carolina	199	Florence
		North Carolina	181	Fayetteville
		Virginia	175	Arlington, Petersburg, Richmond
		District of Columbia	.5	Washington, DC
		Maryland	109	Baltimore
		Delaware	23	Wilmington
		Pennsylvania	52	Philadelphia

ROUTE	TOTAL MILEAGE	MILEAGE BY STATE		SELECTED CITIES SERVED
		New Jersey	79	Elizabeth, Newark, Trenton
		New York	23	New York City
		Connecticut	112	Bridgeport, Milford, New Haven, New London, Norwalk, Stamford
		Rhode Island	43	Cranston, Pawtucket, Providence, Warwick
		Massachusetts	90	Attleboro, Boston
		New Hampshire	16	Portsmouth
		Maine	298	Augusta, Bangor, Portland
96	193	Michigan	193	Detroit, Grand Rapids, Lansing, Muskegon
97	18	Maryland	18	Annapolis, Baltimore
99	58	Pennsylvania	58	Altoona

Transportation

Jobs

In early 1996, the *New York Times* began a seven-part *Downsizing of America* series. "On the Battlefields of Business, Millions of Casualties" said the opening article's headline. Just as the massive series reached its fifth installment, the federal government announced that 700,000 new jobs were created in February, the largest one-month increase in 12 years. Months and months later, the expansion continues.

Still the economy—meaning jobs—remains a pervasive issue. Among the mobility factors in *Places Rated,* it is the most important. For some, it is the *only* factor. While we don't see overheated metro areas, we see many such as Charlottesville, VA, Bryan-College Station, TX, and Portland-Vancouver, OR, where unemployment rates are under 2 percent. In fact, most metro areas have recovered jobs lost during the recessions of the early 1990s and gained a good many more besides.

FORECASTING WHERE THE JOBS WILL BE

Economists who follow employment trends have an old joke: If you take each local planner's numbers for job growth in his or her area and add them all together, the total jobs forecasted would require that every man, woman, and child hold down one day job and moonlight two others.

Fortunately, economists with a macro view have a better perspective. Although no one can predict the future with certainty, forecasting where jobs will be plentiful over the next few years isn't merely a matter of gazing into a crystal ball.

Let's ask the perennial question: Do people move to where the jobs are, or do jobs come to where the people are? Economists argue about this quite a bit, but most believe that jobs come to where the people are. In other words, any growing place that has a concentration of people with a variety of worker skills is by definition a job mecca.

But there's more to it than that. Some metro areas are saddled with sunset industries—shipbuilding, textiles, sawmills, and steel, for example—while others have sunrise industries—health care, higher education, and software. Most metro areas have varying mixes of both. Forecasting which ones will gain the jobs is as much a matter of determining the prospects for certain industries as it is predicting population shifts.

The great American job machine has churned out record numbers of jobs for decades and, depending on which expert is talking, the machine is either showing

wear and tear or has shifted into a new and different gear. Still, by the year 2005, millions of new jobs could be added to the U.S. economy. Although projected employment increases are expected to occur at half the pace compared with the past, the growth in certain occupations will be quite healthy.

The biggest continuing trend is massive growth in service-oriented sectors and marked decline in goods-producing industries. In other words, opportunities for highly trained white-collar workers are growing rapidly, with the blue-collar shade of many metro areas fading to white.

BLUE-COLLAR BLUES . . .

Shortly after World War II, white-collar jobs passed blue-collar jobs in number for the first time in the history of North America. White-collar workers as a group earn

ONE MILLION FADING OCCUPATIONS

Jobs on the decline are typically hit by technological advances and organizational change. Bank tellers are losing out to ATM machines, and typists and word processors are disappearing because technology now lets everyone, even bosses, do their own typing and word processing.

Occupation	Jobs Gone
Sewing machine operators	118,000
Farmers	112,000
Bookkeeping and accounting clerks	102,000
Typists and word processors	100,000
Secretaries, except legal and medical	87,000
Private household servants	84,000
Computer operators	77,000
Farm workers	75,000
Office machine operators	47,000
Welfare eligibility interviewers	34,000
Textile machine operators	28,000
Telephone installers and repairers	27,000
Private household child-care workers	25,000
Precision inspectors and testers	24,000
Telephone operators	23,000
Machine tool operators	22,000
Film strippers, printing	20,000

Source: U.S. Department of Labor, Monthly Labor Review. Listed are occupations that as a group are expected to shrink by 1 million positions between now and 2006.

somewhat less than blue-collar workers because so many white-collar jobs are low-pay clerical and retail positions and so many blue-collar jobs are skilled occupations protected by union contracts. But white-collar jobs, although paying less, provide a ladder of opportunity that blue-collar jobs don't. And the work is steadier. One of the biggest union issues now is security against layoffs and plant closings rather than higher wages. Blue-collar workers are beginning to want what's best in the white-collar world, and they are willing to sacrifice higher wage demands.

The shrinking world of blue-collar work is divided into five basic industries. For the most part, job opportunities in four are expected to drop or merely hold steady past the year 2005.

Farming, Forestry, and Fishing

From Mississippi to Saskatchewan, the family farm is disappearing as mechanized agribusiness rounds up more acreage and concentrates on fewer crops. Despite some modest recovery from the agricultural production slump in the mid-1980s, exports will probably not regain the world dominance they once enjoyed. Still, some metro areas—those in California's Central Valley (Stockton, Merced, Bakersfield, Fresno) and in Canada's prairie provinces (Regina, Saskatoon, Winnipeg)—have large numbers of farming jobs.

One portion of the agricultural sector—agricultural services, such as landscaping and lawn services—has been growing rapidly, and the growth is expected to continue. Here is yet another indication of the shift toward a service economy.

Mining—A Hard Place

Jobs in mining, once a stable employer in the West, are in a deep hole and likely to remain there. Half of these jobs are in hard-hatted oil and natural gas production and high-tech oil field services, disaster industries for the Southwest and Rockies. The simple reason is that foreign oil is cheaper.

Coal mining isn't as dangerous now, but it's still as dirty as depicted in *October Sky,* a film about growing up in a West Virginia company town. Output should increase to fuel the demand for more electricity. But companies aren't hiring, thanks to productivity boosts.

Metal mining isn't expected to recover any of the deep cuts experienced over the past decade, either. Exports of raw ores are expected to rise, but slow growth in basic steel, as well as iron and steel, foundries will limit increases in demand. And while coal is getting more important as alternative energy, the number of jobs in coal mines won't grow. Instead, new production methods will mean continued shrinking of employment.

Construction—Rebuilding Rather Than Building

Here's a footloose industry if there ever was one. Building contracts run out? Move on to another location. Why else do you think many itinerant general contractors have southwestern drawls? This industry, which thinks that half of North America's bridges, highways, and public buildings must be rebuilt within the next decade, is expected to provide most of the blue-collar jobs to 2005 and beyond. Whenever you see a place forecast to gain a large number of blue-collar jobs, you'll be seeing hammers, bulldozers, bricks, and lumber.

Slow population growth and household formation, however, will slow residential building. Although some growth is likely for new single-family homes or house alterations and additions, this trend will be offset by declines in new apartment and condo construction. Nonresidential construction may recover from the oversupply of office and commercial space, but getting rid of the excess stock could take years in certain parts of the continent.

Manufacturing—Anything but Durable

Here is another job sector that's predicted to grow glacially or not at all. Smokestacks, low-rise buildings near rail tracks, even high-tech assembly work—we can tell it good-bye over time. Much of it is moving offshore or to third-world countries.

Although manufacturing will lose hundreds of thousands of jobs by the year 2005, output is expected to almost keep pace with total GNP growth. At the same time, the occupational composition of the remaining manufacturing jobs will change. In general, following the trend of the disappearing blue-collar job, manufacturing employment will shift from production and assembly-line jobs toward professional, managerial, and technical occupations. The shift is more pronounced in industries where imports play a significant role. In some of those cases, design and engineering are done domestically, but much of the actual assembly is performed overseas.

The computer manufacturing industry, as we all might have guessed, has been one of the fastest-growing industries during the past 30 years. The nature of work in this industry, however, is uncharacteristic of manufacturing industries. It employs a high concentration of

FADING INDUSTRIES

Occupation	Jobs Gone
Clothing and footwear	183,700
Private households	152,800
State and local government	108,000
Oil and natural gas production	57,400
Coal and metal mining	53,200
Search and navigation equipment	51,200
Blast furnaces and basic steel	43,600
Tobacco and alcohol	40,300
Electrical industrial apparatus	33,600
Household appliances	24,600
Tires and inner tubes	20,200
Photographic equipment and supplies	19,800
Electrical distribution equipment	14,200
Metal cans and shipping containers	10,400

Source: U.S. Department of Labor, Monthly Labor Review. Listed are industries expected as a group to shed more than a quarter million jobs projected by 2006.

scientific personnel and a relatively low concentration of production workers. Employment in computer manufacturing is expected to expand beyond the year 2005, with even more of a shift at that time from production to research and development occupations.

The printing and publishing business is one of the manufacturing sectors to have registered consistent job gains in the past few years. Even during the recession, both output and employment increased steadily. And the introduction of electronic composition systems and other new technologies has not put a damper on this trend. As elsewhere, however, occupational shifts are occurring within the printing trades, from fewer typesetters and other craftspeople to more front-office personnel such as writers, editors, managers, and salesworkers.

Transportation, Communications, and Public Utilities

This catchall industry classification embraces electric power generation, 18-wheel trucking, airline food and baggage handlers, cable television, and much more. In recent years, deregulation has boosted employment in the air transportation industry, as many smaller firms entered the market and price competition stimulated demand. But, in the long run, consolidation and takeovers are expected to dampen the rate of job growth.

EIGHTEEN OCCUPATIONS: ONE-THIRD THE GROWTH

Occupations that will see the most new openings tend to (1) be large in size rather than fast growing; and, with exceptions in health care and in education, (2) require the least education and training, and (3) offer the lowest pay.

Occupation	New Openings
Cashiers	530,000
Systems analysts	520,000
General managers and top executives	467,000
Registered nurses	411,000
Retail salespersons	408,000
Truck drivers	404,000
Home health aides	378,000
Teacher aides	370,000
Nursing aides and orderlies	333,000
Receptionists and information clerks	318,000
High school teachers	312,000
Child-care workers	299,000
Clerical supervisors	262,000
Database administrators	249,000
Marketing and sales managers	246,000
General maintenance workers	246,000
Food counter and fountain workers	243,000
Special education teachers	241,000

Source: U.S. Department of Labor, Monthly Labor Review. Listed are occupations where one out of three of the 18 million new openings projected by 2006 will be found.

Overall, employment in this group is expected to decrease over the rest of the decade due to declining industry employment and technological changes. The railroad industry, for example, is expected to lose tens of thousands of jobs; likewise, the number of water transportation workers is expected to decline. Greater efficiency in scheduling, marketing, and cost control in the trucking industry is expected to produce greater gains in output than in employment.

. . . AND A WHITE-COLLAR CHORUS

White-collar work, which corresponds roughly with service-oriented occupations, is divided into four basic industry categories. With some variations within categories, this is where the real action is expected to occur through the early years of the 21st century.

Trade

Retail jobs outnumber wholesale positions by five to one and are expected to gain by nearly 1 million by the end of the decade. Unfortunately, retail trade jobs (hamburger flipping, counter help, damage estimating, aisle sweeping, cashiering) aren't worth having if your cash needs are immediate and above average. These jobs do, however, provide rapid advancement to managerial slots, which are still lower paid despite the title. BJ's Wholesale Club, Home Depot, Toys R Us, and Best Buy are the most ubiquitous establishments in North America, and heavy opportunity in this sector goes hand in hand with a local area that is swelling with people.

Finance, Insurance, and Real Estate

Referred to in regional developers' shorthand as *FIRE*, this is the purest of the white-collar industrial classifications. Here the compensation is greater than in the retail trade, and potentially greater by far than in any other industry. It is a briefcase and tie industry—an office-with-a-capital-O environment. It has both heavier government regulation than other industries and more unreported crime.

Banking, credit agencies, and investment offices—a big part of the FIRE industries—should enjoy substantial rates of business growth in the next decade, but not necessarily such growth in numbers of jobs. Consolidation and technological advances in automatic banking and other financial transactions will actually slow rates of employment gain. This doesn't mean no new jobs in these fields; there will be some growth—for example, thousands more in credit agencies and investment offices by the year 2000. But the rate of employment growth will be slower than in the past and will not match the growth in business output.

Similarly, greater efficiency in the insurance industry—computerized underwriting, for example—means that job gains will be limited for insurance carriers and for independent agents and brokers. Not zero growth, but slower growth. Rapid projected growth in the real estate industry is expected to have a favorable impact on employment for brokers (increasing by 44 percent) and appraisers (increasing by 41 percent).

Services

Think of high-rise marble and glass office buildings and medical centers with piped-in music. Think of white smocks and clipboards and shaded college campuses. These are the most desirable kinds of developments—

the kinds city fathers and mothers dream of. If the landscape is full of these buildings, you've got a well-educated work force, higher incomes, and a stable, service-oriented economy.

The service division includes careers in business, health, recreation, the professions, and education—an increasing proportion of which will require formal education and certification. Health and education, typically underwritten by government or third-party payers, lead the way in this division. It makes sense if you think about it; the numbers of educational staff are rising with the numbers of children of the baby-boom generation, and the health-care industry is growing as the population ages and needs more medical attention. Overall, this category has been and is projected to be the fastest-growing for new jobs well into the next century.

The big story in services is, as expected, computer and data processing, systems design, programming, and software development. Another big story in business services, with a very large projected increase in unemployment, is the personnel supply business, especially the temporary help industry. No longer limited to placing office workers, temporary personnel service businesses are beginning to place workers from industrial, medical, managerial, engineering, and technical occupations as well. The employers like the lower fringe benefits and the access to added help during peak times, and the temporary workers like the flexibility, variety, and experience.

With the trend toward development of new service businesses, the demand is growing for research, management, and consulting services. Independent laboratories for research and development, market researchers, personnel training or management consultants, economic researchers, efficiency experts, lobbyists, and other business consultants will be in increasing demand.

In the professions, the legal services industry has been growing, taking a place among the top ten fastest growing employment industries. If you thought the legal profession was filled to capacity, think again. Increasing liability litigation, corporate mergers and acquisitions, high divorce levels, geographic expansion of law firms, a greater degree of legal specialization within firms, and an increase in litigation in general keep things moving.

In health care, too, important shifts are taking place. Cost-containment policies have halted the expansion of hospitals and hospital employment, with health-care delivery moving from the hospital to outpatient-care centers. Look for employment growth in the emergency care clinics, surgicenters, and walk-in treatment centers that are popping up all around us.

Government

If you're considering a job in government, especially the federal government, you might reconsider. The federal government will definitely be shrinking because of military base closings and budgetary reductions. Total public employment is, however, projected to rise over the next decade, with most of the increase occurring among municipal workers such as teachers, firefighters, and police. On the other hand, count on a decline of jobs among clerical and administrative support workers.

For government jobs, though, some places—Austin, TX; Columbus, OH; Madison, WI; Toronto, ON; and Atlanta, GA—are in enviable positions. They are state or provincial capitals with large bureaucracies that face little unemployment threat. That they are all higher-education centers doesn't hurt, either.

JOB WINNERS, 2000–2005

No metro area will have a net job loss over the next 5 years. Of the ones forecasted to gain more than 100,000 jobs, three are in the former Rust Belt, a region analysts saw withering into the next century.

Metro Area	New Jobs
Chicago, IL	216,592
Atlanta, GA	215,407
Phoenix-Mesa, AZ	201,805
Washington, DC-MD-VA-WV	185,360
Houston, TX	160,044
Dallas, TX	152,844
San Diego, CA	150,491
Minneapolis-St. Paul, MN-WI	143,315
Las Vegas, NV-AZ	141,590
Seattle-Bellevue-Everett, WA	140,397
Orange County, CA	137,801
Riverside-San Bernardino, CA	126,259
Portland-Vancouver, OR-WA	122,841
Los Angeles-Long Beach, CA	120,102
Detroit, MI	111,573
Denver, CO	111,511
Orlando, FL	105,588
Fort Worth-Arlington, TX	103,001
Tampa-St. Petersburg-Clearwater, FL	102,014
Salt Lake City-Ogden, UT	100,685

Source: Woods & Poole Economics, Inc., Washington, DC, © 1999. This data is estimated; see notes to "Place Profiles" in this chapter for information on this data.

JUDGING JOBS

If you're out of work or looking for better employment, would the raw odds of tracking down a job be better in Dallas, Denver, or Duluth? What about Honolulu, Houston, or Huntsville? To help you answer these questions, *Places Rated* compares each metro area's percent rate of job growth forecast between now and the year 2005, its number of new jobs that will be created during this period, and its number of new jobs with higher-than-average pay.

Growth Rate

Some twenty metro areas have 5-year job growth forecasts greater than 10%. Certainly a rosy forecast—such as Punta Gorda, FL's 13.9 percent, Las Vegas's 16.5 percent, or the 14.1 percent seen for Oshawa, ON, where Canada makes automobiles—always looks good at first view. For small areas, however, a high rate translates to just 1,000 new jobs a year.

Number of New Jobs

In contrast, Chicago's modest 4.4 percent forecast results in over 50,000 new jobs a year and Washington, DC's expected 5.6 percent means nearly 40,000 new jobs a year. Because it is more likely that good executive, professional, and managerial jobs in growth industries will be found in larger numbers of newly created jobs, this factor may be the single most important of all.

Number of Higher-Paying Jobs

Most new jobs will be in the low-paying retail trade and modestly paying service industries. High-paying jobs are found there, too, but in fewer numbers. The industries with the biggest paychecks per worker are manufacturing, government, transportation, communications, and public utilities. Winners with the most number of jobs in these industries include Washington, Denver, and Anchorage.

SCORING: JOBS

To derive a score for jobs, each area's forecasted number of new jobs gets twice the weight as the percent rate of growth and how many of the expected jobs are higher paying ones. A metro area's final score is a percentile on a scale of 0 to 100 corresponding to its rank. Phoenix-Mesa's score is 100; Wichita's is 50.19; and Steubenville-Weirton, on the Ohio River separating West Virginia from Ohio, gets 0.00. They are respectively the best, average, and worst North American metro areas for jobs between now and into the new millennium.

RANKINGS: JOBS

In ranking the 354 metro areas for near-term employment growth, *Places Rated Almanac* factors three criteria: (1) the percent increase in new jobs by the year 2005, (2) the number of new jobs created between now and that date, and (3) the number of new jobs with above-average pay. Scores are given as percentiles where 0 is worst, 50 average, and 100 best. The higher the score, the more promising the metro area's job outlook. Places that are tied get the same rank and are listed in alphabetical order.

Metro Areas from Best to Worst

RANK	SCORE	RANK	SCORE
1. Phoenix-Mesa, AZ	100.00	12. Raleigh-Durham-Chapel Hill, NC	96.88
2. Las Vegas, NV-AZ	99.71	13. Toronto, ON	96.60
3. Riverside-San Bernardino, CA	99.43	14. San Antonio, TX	96.31
4. Atlanta, GA	99.15	15. Sacramento, CA	96.03
5. Portland-Vancouver, OR-WA	98.86	16. Orange County, CA	95.75
6. Fort Worth-Arlington, TX	98.58	17. Denver, CO	95.46
7. Salt Lake City-Ogden, UT	98.30	18. Dallas, TX	95.18
8. Austin-San Marcos, TX	98.01	19. Houston, TX	94.90
9. San Diego, CA	97.73	20. Minneapolis-St. Paul, MN-WI	94.61
10. Orlando, FL	97.45	21. Tampa-St. Petersburg-Clearwater, FL	94.33
11. Seattle-Bellevue-Everett, WA	97.16	22. Charlotte-Gastonia-Rock Hill, NC-SC	94.05

RANK	SCORE
23. Nashville, TN	93.76
24. Fort Lauderdale, FL	93.48
25. Vancouver, BC	93.20
26. Washington, DC-MD-VA-WV	92.91
27. Tucson, AZ	92.63
28. Memphis, TN-AR-MS	92.35
29. Sarasota-Bradenton, FL	92.06
30. Boise City, ID	91.78
31. Jacksonville, FL	91.50
32. Fayetteville-Springdale-Rogers, AR	91.21
33. West Palm Beach-Boca Raton, FL	90.93
34. Albuquerque, NM	90.65
35. Grand Rapids-Muskegon-Holland, MI	90.36
36. Colorado Springs, CO	90.08
37. Tacoma, WA	89.80
38. Provo-Orem, UT	89.51
39. Vallejo-Fairfield-Napa, CA	89.23
40. Columbia, SC	88.95
41. Ventura, CA	88.66
42. Knoxville, TN	88.38
43. McAllen-Edinburg-Mission, TX	88.10
44. Kansas City, MO-KS	87.81
45. Oakland, CA	87.53
46. Fresno, CA	87.25
47. Chicago, IL	86.96
48. El Paso, TX	86.68
49. Columbus, OH	86.40
50. Akron, OH	86.11
51. Greenville-Spartanburg-Anderson, SC	85.83
52. Bakersfield, CA	85.55
53. Fort Myers-Cape Coral, FL	85.26
54. Richmond-Petersburg, VA	84.98
55. Indianapolis, IN	84.70
56. Greensboro–Winston-Salem–High Point, NC	84.41
57. Omaha, NE-IA	84.13
58. Miami, FL	83.85
59. Calgary, AB	83.56
60. Ottawa-Hull, ON-PQ	83.28
61. Norfolk-Virginia Beach-Newport News, VA-NC	83.00
62. Cincinnati, OH-KY-IN	82.71
63. Baton Rouge, LA	82.43
64. Lexington, KY	82.15
65. Charleston-North Charleston, SC	81.86
66. San Jose, CA	81.58
67. Harrisburg-Lebanon-Carlisle, PA	81.30
68. Tallahassee, FL	81.01
69. Detroit, MI	80.73
70. Santa Rosa, CA	80.45
71. Louisville, KY-IN	80.16
72. Fort Collins-Loveland, CO	79.88
73. Madison, WI	79.60
74. Appleton-Oshkosh-Neenah, WI	79.32
75. Little Rock-North Little Rock, AR	79.03
76. Wilmington, NC	78.75
77. Montreal, PQ	78.47
78. Philadelphia, PA-NJ	78.18
79. Biloxi-Gulfport-Pascagoula, MS	77.90
80. Ann Arbor, MI	77.33
80. Birmingham, AL	77.33
82. Jackson, MS	77.05
83. Myrtle Beach, SC	76.77
84. Anchorage, AK	76.48

RANK	SCORE
85. Naples, FL	76.20
86. Baltimore, MD	75.92
87. Santa Fe, NM	75.63
88. Boulder-Longmont, CO	75.35
89. Cleveland-Lorain-Elyria, OH	75.07
90. New Orleans, LA	74.78
91. Pensacola, FL	74.50
92. Mobile, AL	74.22
93. Olympia, WA	73.93
94. Salem, OR	73.65
95. Spokane, WA	73.37
96. Columbia, MO	73.08
97. Laredo, TX	72.80
98. Tulsa, OK	72.52
99. Oklahoma City, OK	72.23
100. Bellingham, WA	71.95
101. Springfield, MO	71.67
102. St. Louis, MO-IL	71.38
103. Yolo, CA	71.10
104. Sioux Falls, SD	70.82
105. Lincoln, NE	70.53
106. Greenville, NC	70.25
107. Brownsville-Harlingen-San Benito, TX	69.97
108. Gainesville, FL	69.68
109. Daytona Beach, FL	69.40
110. Des Moines, IA	68.83
110. Lafayette, LA	68.83
112. Green Bay, WI	68.55
113. Hamilton-Middletown, OH	68.27
114. Huntsville, AL	67.98
115. Edmonton, AB	67.70
116. Fargo-Moorhead, ND-MN	67.42
117. Long Island, NY	67.13
118. San Francisco, CA	66.85
119. Eau Claire, WI	66.57
120. Honolulu, HI	66.28
121. Santa Barbara-Santa Maria-Lompoc, CA	66.00
122. Milwaukee-Waukesha, WI	65.72
123. Youngstown-Warren, OH	65.43
124. Chattanooga, TN-GA	65.15
125. Stockton-Lodi, CA	64.87
126. Middlesex-Somerset-Hunterdon, NJ	64.58
127. Fort Smith, AR-OK	64.30
128. Wilmington-Newark, DE-MD	64.02
129. Dayton-Springfield, OH	63.73
130. Augusta-Aiken, GA-SC	63.45
131. Flagstaff, AZ-UT	63.17
132. Pittsburgh, PA	62.88
133. Medford-Ashland, OR	62.60
134. Rochester, NY	62.32
135. Atlantic-Cape May, NJ	62.03
136. Reno, NV	61.75
137. South Bend, IN	61.47
138. Lansing-East Lansing, MI	61.18
139. Fort Pierce-Port St. Lucie, FL	60.90
140. Fayetteville, NC	60.62
141. Joplin, MO	60.33
142. Kalamazoo-Battle Creek, MI	60.05
143. Hamilton, ON	59.77
144. Galveston-Texas City, TX	59.49
145. Corpus Christi, TX	58.92

continues

Metro Areas from Best to Worst (cont.)

RANK	SCORE
145. Melbourne-Titusville-Palm Bay, FL	58.92
147. Toledo, OH	58.64
148. San Luis Obispo-Atascadero-Paso Robles, CA	58.35
149. Punta Gorda, FL	58.07
150. Eugene-Springfield, OR	57.79
151. Lancaster, PA	57.50
152. Clarksville-Hopkinsville, TN-KY	57.22
153. Longview-Marshall, TX	56.94
154. Canton-Massillon, OH	56.37
154. Hickory-Morganton-Lenoir, NC	56.37
156. Fort Wayne, IN	56.09
157. Richland-Kennewick-Pasco, WA	55.80
158. Fort Walton Beach, FL	55.52
159. Peoria-Pekin, IL	55.24
160. Monmouth-Ocean, NJ	54.95
161. Yuma, AZ	54.67
162. Syracuse, NY	54.39
163. Asheville, NC	54.10
164. Salinas, CA	53.82
165. Lakeland-Winter Haven, FL	53.54
166. Kitchener-Waterloo, ON	53.25
167. Albany-Schenectady-Troy, NY	52.97
168. St. Cloud, MN	52.40
168. State College, PA	52.40
170. Santa Cruz-Watsonville, CA	52.12
171. Winnipeg, MB	51.84
172. Sioux City, IA-NE	51.55
173. Chico-Paradise, CA	51.27
174. Buffalo-Niagara Falls, NY	50.99
175. Bremerton, WA	50.70
176. Bryan-College Station, TX	50.42
177. Wichita, KS	50.14
178. Jackson, TN	49.85
179. Johnson City-Kingsport-Bristol, TN-VA	49.57
180. Redding, CA	49.29
181. Boston, MA-NH	49.00
182. Savannah, GA	48.72
183. Portsmouth-Rochester, NH-ME	48.44
184. Los Angeles-Long Beach, CA	48.15
185. Florence, SC	47.87
186. Brazoria, TX	47.59
187. Athens, GA	47.30
188. Iowa City, IA	47.02
189. Newburgh, NY-PA	46.74
190. Quebec City, PQ	46.45
191. Oshawa, ON	45.89
191. York, PA	45.89
193. Monroe, LA	45.60
194. Lafayette, IN	45.32
195. Las Cruces, NM	45.04
196. Panama City, FL	44.75
197. Killeen-Temple, TX	44.47
198. Montgomery, AL	44.19
199. Modesto, CA	43.90
200. Ocala, FL	43.62
201. Roanoke, VA	43.34
202. Elkhart-Goshen, IN	43.05
203. Waco, TX	42.77
204. Tyler, TX	42.49
205. Missoula, MT	42.20

RANK	SCORE
206. New York, NY	41.92
207. London, ON	41.64
208. Trenton, NJ	41.35
209. Visalia-Tulare-Porterville, CA	41.07
210. Bloomington-Normal, IL	40.79
211. Charlottesville, VA	40.50
212. Wausau, WI	40.22
213. Shreveport-Bossier City, LA	39.94
214. Halifax, NS	39.66
215. Columbus, GA-AL	39.37
216. Lawrence, MA-NH	39.09
217. Tuscaloosa, AL	38.81
218. Lubbock, TX	38.52
219. Mansfield, OH	38.24
220. Saginaw-Bay City-Midland, MI	37.96
221. Yakima, WA	37.67
222. Yuba City, CA	37.39
223. Gary, IN	37.11
224. Portland, ME	36.82
225. Beaumont-Port Arthur, TX	36.26
225. Greeley, CO	36.26
227. Champaign-Urbana, IL	35.97
228. Macon, GA	35.69
229. Hartford, CT	35.41
230. Bismarck, ND	35.12
231. Davenport-Moline-Rock Island, IA-IL	34.84
232. Lake Charles, LA	34.56
233. Cedar Rapids, IA	34.27
234. Rockford, IL	33.99
235. Pocatello, ID	33.71
236. Kankakee, IL	33.42
237. Charleston, WV	33.14
238. Dothan, AL	32.86
239. Newark, NJ	32.57
240. Grand Junction, CO	32.29
241. Albany, GA	32.01
242. La Crosse, WI-MN	31.72
243. Merced, CA	31.16
243. Windsor, ON	31.16
245. Burlington, VT	30.87
246. Dutchess County, NY	30.59
247. Huntington-Ashland, WV-KY-OH	30.31
248. Reading, PA	30.02
249. Rapid City, SD	29.74
250. Allentown-Bethlehem-Easton, PA	29.46
251. Janesville-Beloit, WI	29.17
252. Billings, MT	28.89
253. Victoria, BC	28.61
254. Amarillo, TX	28.32
255. Bloomington, IN	28.04
256. Dover, DE	27.76
257. Evansville-Henderson, IN-KY	27.47
258. Kenosha, WI	27.19
259. Manchester, NH	26.91
260. Pueblo, CO	26.62
261. Barnstable-Yarmouth, MA	26.34
262. Bergen-Passaic, NJ	26.06
263. Lynchburg, VA	25.77
264. St. Catharines-Niagara, ON	25.49
265. Wichita Falls, TX	25.21

RANK	SCORE		RANK	SCORE
266. Jonesboro, AR	24.92		311. Altoona, PA	12.18
267. Springfield, IL	24.64		312. Waterloo-Cedar Falls, IA	11.89
268. Utica-Rome, NY	24.36		313. New Haven-Meriden, CT	11.61
269. Rocky Mount, NC	24.07		314. Cheyenne, WY	11.33
270. Providence-Fall River-Warwick, RI-MA	23.51		315. Goldsboro, NC	11.04
271. Rochester, MN	23.51		316. Springfield, MA	10.76
272. Hattiesburg, MS	22.94		317. San Angelo, TX	10.48
272. Houma, LA	22.94		318. Decatur, AL	10.19
274. Lawrence, KS	22.66		319. Sudbury, ON	9.91
275. Jacksonville, NC	22.37		320. St. John's, NF	9.63
276. Sharon, PA	22.09		321. Bridgeport, CT	9.34
277. Florence, AL	21.81		322. New Bedford, MA	9.06
278. Johnstown, PA	21.52		323. Dubuque, IA	8.78
279. Grand Forks, ND-MN	21.24		324. Lewiston-Auburn, ME	8.49
280. Scranton–Wilkes-Barre–Hazleton, PA	20.96		325. Vineland-Millville-Bridgeton, NJ	8.21
281. Sumter, SC	20.67		326. Lima, OH	7.93
282. Victoria, TX	20.39		327. Anniston, AL	7.64
283. Erie, PA	20.11		328. Pine Bluff, AR	7.36
284. Duluth-Superior, MN-WI	19.83		329. Benton Harbor, MI	7.08
285. Flint, MI	19.54		330. Terre Haute, IN	6.79
286. Alexandria, LA	19.26		331. Thunder Bay, ON	6.51
287. Brockton, MA	18.98		332. Sherbrooke, PQ	6.23
288. Odessa-Midland, TX	18.69		333. Stamford-Norwalk, CT	5.94
289. Muncie, IN	18.41		334. Trois-Rivieres, PQ	5.66
290. New London-Norwich, CT-RI	18.13		335. Cumberland, MD-WV	5.38
291. Hagerstown, MD	17.56		336. Waterbury, CT	5.09
291. Lawton, OK	17.56		337. Saint John, NB	4.81
293. Abilene, TX	17.28		338. Chicoutimi-Jonquiere, PQ	4.53
294. Sheboygan, WI	16.99		339. Danville, VA	4.24
295. Texarkana, TX-Texarkana, AR	16.71		340. Danbury, CT	3.96
296. Jersey City, NJ	16.43		341. Bangor, ME	3.11
297. Jackson, MI	16.14		341. Gadsden, AL	3.11
298. Sherman-Denison, TX	15.86		341. Kokomo, IN	3.11
299. Owensboro, KY	15.58		344. Fitchburg-Leominster, MA	2.83
300. Nashua, NH	15.29		345. Great Falls, MT	2.54
301. Topeka, KS	15.01		346. Enid, OK	2.26
302. Binghamton, NY	14.73		347. Glens Falls, NY	1.98
303. Saskatoon, SK	14.44		348. St. Joseph, MO	1.69
304. Worcester, MA-CT	14.16		349. Elmira, NY	1.41
305. Parkersburg-Marietta, WV-OH	13.88		350. Williamsport, PA	1.13
306. Wheeling, WV-OH	13.59		351. Jamestown, NY	0.84
307. Lowell, MA-NH	13.31		352. Pittsfield, MA	0.56
308. Racine, WI	13.03		353. Decatur, IL	0.28
309. Casper, WY	12.74		354. Steubenville-Weirton, OH-WV	0.00
310. Regina, SK	12.46			

PLACE PROFILES: JOBS

The following chart details jobs statistics for each metro area. Under **Growth Rate** is the forecasted percent increase in jobs between the years 2000 and 2005.

Next are the forecasted number of new jobs in predominantly blue-collar industries (farming, forestry, fishing, mining, construction, manufacturing, transportation, and public utilities) and in predominantly white-collar industries (trade, finance, insurance, real estate, services, and government other than military).

In addition, the number of new jobs in industries where a worker's pay is above average (government, manufacturing, transportation, and public utilities) is categorized under *High Earnings*. Those in industries where pay is typical (construction, services, finance, insurance, and

real estate) are under *Average Earnings*. Jobs in poorly paid industries (retail trade, wholesale trade, farming, and mining) are categorized under *Low Earnings*. Minus figures indicate forecasted losses in any of these categories.

Included in the charts under **Unemployment Threat** is an arrow symbol indicating the metro area's vulnerability to cyclical recession based on too many blue-collar jobs. Seventy-nine metro areas show an arrow pointing downward (↓) indicating that the threat of unemployment is lower than average. Eighty-four metro areas show an upward-pointing arrow (↑) indicating that the threat is higher. No arrow symbol at all indicates an average unemployment threat.

Growth forecasts for U.S. metro areas are from July 1, 2000, to July 1, 2005; those for Canadian metro areas are from December 31, 2000, to December 31, 2005. U.S. figures are derived from employment fore-

casts from Woods & Poole Economics, Inc., of Washington, DC. The projections are based on historical data, 1969–96, from the U.S. Department of Commerce; all data, 1997–2020, is projected by Woods & Poole, and employment in number of jobs includes proprietors and part-time jobs. Projections are uncertain, and future data may differ substantially from Woods & Poole projections. Woods & Poole does not guarantee the accuracy of these data and projections. The use of these data and projections, and the conclusions drawn from them, are solely the responsibility of the author. Canadian figures are derived from employment forecasts from Strategic Projections, Inc., of Oakville, Ontario, and similar caveats apply.

A star (★) in front of a metro area's name highlights it as one of the top thirty-five places for job growth between now and the year 2005.

New Jobs, 2000–2005

	GROWTH RATE	BLUE COLLAR	WHITE COLLAR	HIGH EARNINGS	AVERAGE EARNINGS	LOW EARNINGS	UNEMPLOYMENT THREAT	SCORE	RANK
Metro Area Average	**5.9**	**2,566**	**20,115**	**3,510**	**14,744**	**4,428**			
Abilene, TX	4.5	345	3,385	641	2,234	855		17.28	293
Akron, OH	7.5	6,363	24,773	6,728	18,638	5,770		86.11	50
Albany, GA	7.0	460	4,852	473	4,603	236		32.01	241
Albany-Schenectady-Troy, NY	3.7	88	20,043	1,325	15,233	3,573	↓	52.97	167
★ Albuquerque, NM	8.1	5,846	30,750	8,134	20,712	7,750	↓	90.65	34
Alexandria, LA	4.8	627	2,687	768	1,879	667	↓	19.26	286
Allentown-Bethlehem-Easton, PA	3.2	−2,473	13,096	−551	9,706	1,468		29.46	250
Altoona, PA	4.4	−171	3,449	−74	2,182	1,170		12.18	311
Amarillo, TX	4.4	502	5,141	1,169	3,531	943		28.32	254
Anchorage, AK	8.0	2,780	11,621	2,473	8,666	3,262	↓	76.48	84
Ann Arbor, MI	6.1	3,717	17,070	3,657	11,902	5,228		77.33	80
Anniston, AL	3.4	97	2,087	120	1,135	929		7.64	327
Appleton-Oshkosh-Neenah, WI	7.1	5,036	12,096	5,248	9,298	2,586	↑	79.32	74
Asheville, NC	6.8	667	9,009	1,366	5,471	2,839		54.10	163
Athens, GA	7.3	924	5,864	1,430	3,814	1,544		47.30	187
★ Atlanta, GA	8.5	39,133	176,274	51,718	114,414	49,275	↓	99.15	4
Atlantic-Cape May, NJ	5.6	867	11,817	1,835	10,267	582	↓	62.03	135
Augusta-Aiken, GA-SC	5.6	640	13,824	1,648	8,473	4,343		63.45	130
★ Austin-San Marcos, TX	12.3	11,355	83,887	18,070	61,768	15,404		98.01	8
Bakersfield, CA	7.9	7,862	17,307	6,013	8,736	10,420	↑	85.55	52
Baltimore, MD	5.4	2,758	79,138	1,497	66,018	14,381	↓	75.92	86
Bangor, ME	3.1	7	1,445	34	1,184	234		3.11	341
Barnstable-Yarmouth, MA	6.5	333	4,715	21	3,715	1,312	↓	26.34	261
Baton Rouge, LA	8.7	2,703	28,631	2,091	24,563	4,680		82.43	63
Beaumont-Port Arthur, TX	4.4	911	7,767	1,391	5,582	1,705	↑	36.26	225
Bellingham, WA	11.1	1,386	9,538	2,183	6,171	2,570		71.95	100
Benton Harbor, MI	3.1	−218	3,038	−191	2,418	593	↑	7.08	329
Bergen-Passaic, NJ	1.5	−7,601	19,166	−2,890	13,603	852		26.06	262
Billings, MT	6.2	655	4,766	319	3,766	1,336	↓	28.89	252
Biloxi-Gulfport-Pascagoula, MS	8.1	1,950	14,571	2,287	12,400	1,834		77.90	79
Binghamton, NY	2.8	90	3,860	1,023	2,749	178		14.73	302
Birmingham, AL	5.8	1,251	31,545	2,734	23,990	6,072		77.33	80
Bismarck, ND	7.5	337	4,628	954	3,358	653	↓	35.12	230
Bloomington, IN	5.9	437	4,187	845	2,715	1,064		28.04	255
Bloomington-Normal, IL	6.3	658	5,588	1,499	4,149	598		40.79	210

	GROWTH RATE	BLUE COLLAR	WHITE COLLAR	HIGH EARNINGS	AVERAGE EARNINGS	LOW EARNINGS	UNEMPLOYMENT THREAT	SCORE	RANK
Metro Area Average	**5.9**	**2,566**	**20,115**	**3,510**	**14,744**	**4,428**			
★ Boise City, ID	10.6	9,087	19,864	7,563	15,831	5,557	↑	91.78	30
Boston, MA-NH	3.3	−3,924	75,558	−7,205	66,100	12,739	↓	49.00	181
Boulder-Longmont, CO	7.0	3,885	11,644	3,139	8,187	4,203		75.35	88
Brazoria, TX	6.4	1,504	4,874	2,362	3,035	981	↑	47.59	186
Bremerton, WA	7.4	783	8,415	934	6,557	1,707	↓	50.70	175
Bridgeport, CT	2.0	−2,752	7,366	−2,691	6,641	664		9.34	321
Brockton, MA	4.6	435	4,622	21	3,448	1,587		18.98	287
Brownsville-Harlingen-San Benito, TX	7.9	775	9,449	3,672	4,206	2,346		69.97	107
Bryan-College Station, TX	7.1	491	5,648	2,611	2,561	967	↓	50.42	176
Buffalo-Niagara Falls, NY	2.4	1,122	14,918	2,077	10,945	3,018		50.99	174
Burlington, VT	5.6	579	6,138	164	5,343	1,210		30.87	245
Calgary, AB	10.0	6,467	10,331	4,944	9,347	2,507		83.56	59
Canton-Massillon, OH	4.8	2,670	8,469	2,595	5,729	2,815	↑	56.37	154
Casper, WY	5.2	100	2,147	163	1,713	371		12.74	309
Cedar Rapids, IA	5.6	885	6,770	550	5,999	1,106		34.27	233
Champaign-Urbana, IL	5.4	1,680	4,691	1,597	3,795	979		35.97	227
Charleston, WV	5.3	220	8,212	196	7,172	1,064	↓	33.14	237
Charleston-North Charleston, SC	8.7	1,878	24,516	2,405	18,528	5,461	↓	81.86	65
★ Charlotte-Gastonia-Rock Hill, NC-SC	7.7	8,415	64,174	15,370	41,001	16,218		94.05	22
Charlottesville, VA	5.9	465	5,665	1,776	3,780	574		40.50	211
Chattanooga, TN-GA	5.9	190	16,582	1,367	12,601	2,804		65.15	124
Cheyenne, WY	4.0	19	2,088	513	1,062	532	↓	11.33	314
Chicago, IL	4.4	21,442	195,150	21,334	170,426	24,832		86.96	47
Chico-Paradise, CA	8.4	395	8,214	856	7,158	595		51.27	173
Chicoutimi-Jonquiere, PQ	1.1	655	1,280	390	1,292	252		4.53	338
Cincinnati, OH-KY-IN	5.5	5,383	53,040	7,590	37,845	12,988		82.71	62
Clarksville-Hopkinsville, TN-KY	6.8	1,421	6,225	2,898	2,853	1,895		57.22	152
Cleveland-Lorain-Elyria, OH	3.4	8,307	39,609	9,681	29,002	9,233		75.07	89
Colorado Springs, CO	9.6	6,765	24,482	5,034	19,213	7,000		90.08	36
Columbia, MO	10.0	1,388	8,660	4,075	4,271	1,702	↓	73.08	96
Columbia, SC	8.0	2,238	27,070	7,251	17,291	4,766	↓	88.95	40
Columbus, GA-AL	5.4	630	8,038	939	5,852	1,877		39.37	215
Columbus, OH	5.9	3,219	57,358	7,024	36,337	17,216	↓	86.40	49
Corpus Christi, TX	5.7	1,227	10,732	1,609	8,417	1,933		58.92	145
Cumberland, MD-WV	3.3	20	1,551	76	1,073	422		5.38	335
★ Dallas, TX	6.8	21,661	131,183	29,407	95,754	27,683		95.18	18
Danbury, CT	2.3	−1,115	3,685	−1,138	3,393	314		3.96	340
Danville, VA	2.3	377	942	417	721	181	↑	4.24	339
Davenport-Moline-Rock Island, IA-IL	4.4	1,032	8,846	730	7,278	1,870		34.84	231
Dayton-Springfield, OH	3.7	294	21,509	2,415	14,674	4,714		63.73	129
Daytona Beach, FL	6.5	1,603	10,725	2,947	5,631	3,750		69.40	109
Decatur, AL	3.8	63	2,732	82	1,960	753	↑	10.19	318
Decatur, IL	1.3	−366	1,315	−465	1,287	127	↑	0.28	353
★ Denver, CO	7.9	20,492	91,019	14,457	77,931	19,123	↓	95.46	17
Des Moines, IA	6.3	68	21,506	1,390	14,265	5,919	↓	68.83	110
Detroit, MI	4.4	12,850	98,723	6,796	85,057	19,720		80.73	69
Dothan, AL	6.0	726	4,468	1,109	3,246	839		32.86	238
Dover, DE	6.1	126	4,172	817	2,137	1,344		27.76	256
Dubuque, IA	3.7	85	2,257	122	1,756	464	↑	8.78	323
Duluth-Superior, MN-WI	3.9	227	5,227	375	4,239	840		19.83	284
Dutchess County, NY	5.4	−699	8,370	−19	6,754	936		30.59	246
Eau Claire, WI	9.4	1,230	8,001	1,862	5,020	2,349		66.57	119
Edmonton, AB	4.8	5,233	9,828	4,272	8,549	2,239		67.70	115
El Paso, TX	7.7	1,694	22,927	7,689	13,642	3,290		86.68	48
Elkhart-Goshen, IN	4.7	3,562	3,086	3,892	1,739	1,017	↑	43.05	202
Elmira, NY	1.0	62	462	196	169	159	↑	1.41	349
Enid, OK	3.1	142	958	−43	921	222		2.26	346
Erie, PA	3.4	421	5,032	615	3,886	952	↑	20.11	283
Eugene-Springfield, OR	6.1	967	10,542	1,370	8,666	1,473		57.79	150
Evansville-Henderson, IN-KY	4.1	630	7,101	432	6,304	995	↑	27.47	257
Fargo-Moorhead, ND-MN	8.8	559	10,603	1,458	6,937	2,767	↓	67.42	116
Fayetteville, NC	5.8	792	9,650	2,381	5,834	2,227	↓	60.62	140

continues

Place Profiles: Jobs

	GROWTH RATE	BLUE COLLAR	WHITE COLLAR	HIGH EARNINGS	AVERAGE EARNINGS	LOW EARNINGS	UNEMPLOYMENT THREAT	SCORE	RANK
Metro Area Average	**5.9**	**2,566**	**20,115**	**3,510**	**14,744**	**4,428**			
★ Fayetteville-Springdale-Rogers, AR	12.5	6,878	17,568	6,955	10,655	6,836	↑	91.21	32
Fitchburg-Leominster, MA	2.9	–219	1,883	–324	1,539	450		2.83	344
Flagstaff, AZ-UT	11.4	452	7,680	1,462	4,616	2,054	↓	63.17	131
Flint, MI	3.0	–397	7,328	–713	6,736	908	↑	19.54	285
Florence, AL	5.0	406	3,429	670	1,801	1,364	↑	21.81	277
Florence, SC	7.7	–86	6,277	1,596	2,587	2,008		47.87	185
Fort Collins-Loveland, CO	9.7	3,958	10,940	2,815	7,765	4,318	↑	79.88	72
★ Fort Lauderdale, FL	7.7	8,331	54,554	13,179	36,226	13,480	↓	93.48	24
Fort Myers-Cape Coral, FL	9.5	2,336	17,672	4,529	10,789	4,690	↓	85.26	53
Fort Pierce-Port St. Lucie, FL	7.8	1,524	8,708	1,365	4,951	3,916		60.90	139
Fort Smith, AR-OK	6.9	2,774	5,962	3,521	3,895	1,320	↑	64.30	127
Fort Walton Beach, FL	9.0	591	9,263	647	6,216	2,991	↓	55.52	158
Fort Wayne, IN	4.1	1,055	12,752	2,075	9,700	2,032	↑	56.09	156
★ Fort Worth-Arlington, TX	10.8	20,403	82,598	26,660	57,843	18,498		98.58	6
Fresno, CA	7.4	9,665	24,871	6,866	17,311	10,359	↑	87.25	46
Gadsden, AL	3.2	–528	2,126	–480	1,813	265	↑	3.11	341
Gainesville, FL	8.2	439	11,289	2,003	8,576	1,149	↓	69.68	108
Galveston-Texas City, TX	6.5	–76	7,852	3,338	2,105	2,333	↓	59.49	144
Gary, IN	4.4	629	13,578	–169	11,499	2,877		37.11	223
Glens Falls, NY	2.3	–101	1,620	68	1,238	213		1.98	347
Goldsboro, NC	4.1	18	2,433	345	1,528	578		11.04	315
Grand Forks, ND-MN	5.3	344	3,453	485	2,388	924	↓	21.24	279
Grand Junction, CO	7.4	1,048	3,834	547	3,205	1,130		32.29	240
★ Grand Rapids-Muskegon-Holland, MI	7.2	11,088	38,666	12,642	23,848	13,264	↑	90.36	35
Great Falls, MT	3.0	–101	1,594	–47	1,200	340	↓	2.54	345
Greeley, CO	6.6	1,551	4,169	1,199	3,269	1,252	↑	36.26	225
Green Bay, WI	7.3	1,950	10,081	2,058	8,880	1,093	↑	68.55	112
Greensboro–Winston-Salem–High Point, NC	6.1	5,972	43,644	7,112	33,393	9,111	↑	84.41	56
Greenville, NC	10.8	1,090	7,531	4,071	3,053	1,497		70.25	106
Greenville-Spartanburg-Anderson, SC	6.5	5,942	32,468	7,679	19,555	11,176	↑	85.83	51
Hagerstown, MD	4.9	317	3,375	394	2,412	886		17.56	291
Halifax, NS	6.3	1,371	4,241	1,601	3,243	768		39.66	214
Hamilton, ON	5.8	4,043	6,311	2,334	6,639	1,380		59.77	143
Hamilton-Middletown, OH	7.6	1,173	10,369	1,960	5,561	4,021		68.27	113
Harrisburg-Lebanon-Carlisle, PA	6.7	3,154	26,868	5,238	19,990	4,794		81.30	67
Hartford, CT	3.2	–6,601	24,361	–6,310	19,431	4,640		35.41	229
Hattiesburg, MS	5.4	121	3,145	1,108	1,470	688		22.94	272
Hickory-Morganton-Lenoir, NC	4.9	1,646	9,031	2,434	4,480	3,763	↑	56.37	154
Honolulu, HI	4.2	1,837	22,624	2,473	17,692	4,296	↓	66.28	120
Houma, LA	4.5	1,279	2,803	1,234	1,599	1,249		22.94	272
★ Houston, TX	6.7	29,007	131,037	38,249	86,208	35,587	↑	94.90	19
Huntington-Ashland, WV-KY-OH	4.6	218	6,908	639	4,848	1,639		30.31	247
Huntsville, AL	6.0	1,688	11,245	2,724	7,434	2,775	↑	67.98	114
Indianapolis, IN	5.9	2,614	57,661	6,913	39,824	13,538		84.70	55
Iowa City, IA	6.9	872	4,778	2,210	2,364	1,076	↓	47.02	188
Jackson, MI	4.4	287	3,082	770	2,006	593	↑	16.14	297
Jackson, MS	6.3	2,465	15,454	3,892	10,941	3,086	↓	77.05	82
Jackson, TN	7.9	1,369	4,201	2,208	2,841	521	↑	49.85	178
★ Jacksonville, FL	8.2	3,426	52,152	4,976	42,083	8,519	↓	91.50	31
Jacksonville, NC	4.7	467	3,722	761	1,764	1,664	↓	22.37	275
Jamestown, NY	1.5	–215	1,344	–129	1,022	236	↑	0.84	351
Janesville-Beloit, WI	4.9	1,319	2,952	1,663	2,277	331	↑	29.17	251
Jersey City, NJ	2.4	–4,532	11,376	–2,620	6,713	2,751	↓	16.43	296
Johnson City-Kingsport-Bristol, TN-VA	4.7	1,624	10,945	1,317	8,778	2,474	↑	49.57	179
Johnstown, PA	4.7	–63	5,515	47	3,781	1,624		21.52	278

	GROWTH RATE	BLUE COLLAR	WHITE COLLAR	HIGH EARNINGS	AVERAGE EARNINGS	LOW EARNINGS	UNEMPLOYMENT THREAT	SCORE	RANK
Metro Area Average	**5.9**	**2,566**	**20,115**	**3,510**	**14,744**	**4,428**			
Jonesboro, AR	6.4	606	2,609	646	1,551	1,018	↑	24.92	266
Joplin, MO	7.4	2,537	4,910	2,839	3,105	1,503	↑	60.33	141
Kalamazoo-Battle Creek, MI	5.1	883	12,924	1,696	8,996	3,115	↑	60.05	142
Kankakee, IL	7.3	1,244	2,932	1,283	2,220	673	↑	33.42	236
Kansas City, MO-KS	5.7	8,587	56,794	11,610	43,575	10,196		87.81	44
Kenosha, WI	6.9	53	4,413	322	3,288	856		27.19	258
Killeen-Temple, TX	5.1	642	8,061	1,799	4,460	2,444	↓	44.47	197
Kitchener-Waterloo, ON	9.3	3,065	4,040	1,278	4,980	847		53.25	166
Knoxville, TN	8.2	5,758	29,789	3,635	23,886	8,026		88.38	42
Kokomo, IN	2.5	−351	1,970	75	1,331	213	↑	3.11	341
La Crosse, WI-MN	5.9	408	4,854	1,029	3,551	682		31.72	242
Lafayette, IN	5.8	1,479	5,121	2,368	3,461	771	↑	45.32	194
Lafayette, LA	6.0	3,126	9,041	3,846	5,498	2,823	↑	68.83	110
Lake Charles, LA	6.0	643	5,518	875	3,872	1,414	↑	34.56	232
Lakeland-Winter Haven, FL	4.7	362	10,190	2,605	6,069	1,878		53.54	165
Lancaster, PA	4.3	1,978	10,011	3,327	5,738	2,924	↑	57.50	151
Lansing-East Lansing, MI	4.7	2,492	11,010	2,389	8,476	2,637		61.18	138
Laredo, TX	12.1	2,721	6,683	3,720	3,432	2,252	↓	72.80	97
Las Cruces, NM	8.5	507	5,605	1,224	3,462	1,426		45.04	195
★ Las Vegas, NV-AZ	16.5	24,288	117,302	21,766	90,858	28,966	↓	99.71	2
Lawrence, KS	5.6	201	3,024	927	1,297	1,001		22.66	274
Lawrence, MA-NH	4.8	1,443	8,225	916	5,579	3,174		39.09	216
Lawton, OK	4.5	224	2,704	1,133	1,585	210	↓	17.56	291
Lewiston-Auburn, ME	4.2	−113	2,038	−177	1,917	185		8.49	324
Lexington, KY	7.3	5,825	17,937	6,649	12,808	4,305	↑	82.15	64
Lima, OH	2.9	−332	3,057	114	2,288	323	↑	7.93	326
Lincoln, NE	7.0	1,925	10,752	3,112	7,836	1,729		70.53	105
Little Rock-North Little Rock, AR	6.0	3,388	19,698	5,234	14,429	3,423		79.03	75
London, ON	6.4	2,202	4,450	1,325	4,399	929		41.64	207
Long Island, NY	3.5	−5,312	55,942	1,930	34,837	13,863	↓	67.13	117
Longview-Marshall, TX	6.7	2,253	6,078	2,402	3,903	2,026	↑	56.94	153
Los Angeles-Long Beach, CA	2.3	−24,895	144,997	−9,930	124,329	5,703		48.15	184
Louisville, KY-IN	5.7	5,503	32,166	6,523	22,870	8,276		80.16	71
Lowell, MA-NH	2.8	−927	6,519	−1,213	6,214	591		13.31	307
Lubbock, TX	5.2	370	7,445	1,343	5,146	1,326	↓	38.52	218
Lynchburg, VA	4.4	742	4,787	938	3,093	1,498	↑	25.77	263
Macon, GA	5.5	−119	10,440	−554	9,596	1,279		35.69	228
Madison, WI	6.1	3,378	17,044	6,948	10,438	3,036		79.60	73
Manchester, NH	5.1	609	5,145	439	3,728	1,588		26.91	259
Mansfield, OH	5.4	1,915	3,647	2,407	2,124	1,031	↑	38.24	219
McAllen-Edinburg-Mission, TX	10.4	1,629	17,560	6,431	7,355	5,403		88.10	43
Medford-Ashland, OR	9.1	1,496	7,658	1,395	5,833	1,926		62.60	133
Melbourne-Titusville-Palm Bay, FL	5.4	1,729	10,844	1,633	7,407	3,533		58.92	145
★ Memphis, TN-AR-MS	7.4	11,312	42,708	13,463	33,929	6,628	↓	92.35	28
Merced, CA	5.6	803	3,783	1,523	1,723	1,340	↑	31.16	243
Miami, FL	5.3	4,593	58,342	14,167	47,501	1,267	↓	83.85	58
Middlesex-Somerset-Hunterdon, NJ	5.9	−1,427	43,668	181	35,252	6,808		64.58	126
Milwaukee-Waukesha, WI	4.7	2,438	44,565	1,276	37,812	7,915		65.72	122
★ Minneapolis-St. Paul, MN-WI	6.9	17,876	125,439	27,535	98,568	17,212		94.61	20
Missoula, MT	8.4	644	4,997	1,005	3,281	1,355	↓	42.20	205
Mobile, AL	7.0	3,295	16,475	1,971	14,504	3,295		74.22	92
Modesto, CA	4.7	1,290	7,815	1,927	5,408	1,770	↑	43.90	199
Monmouth-Ocean, NJ	3.8	−707	19,004	1,487	11,172	5,638	↓	54.95	160
Monroe, LA	7.4	552	5,823	1,449	4,129	797		45.60	193
Montgomery, AL	5.7	538	10,740	521	8,933	1,824		44.19	198
Montreal, PQ	4.1	19,321	32,881	11,600	34,802	5,800		78.47	77
Muncie, IN	4.8	86	3,423	610	2,585	314	↓	18.41	289
Myrtle Beach, SC	11.2	2,298	11,140	1,854	7,294	4,290	↓	76.77	83
Naples, FL	10.9	2,388	11,240	1,726	7,467	4,435		76.20	85

continues

Place Profiles: Jobs

	GROWTH RATE	BLUE COLLAR	WHITE COLLAR	HIGH EARNINGS	AVERAGE EARNINGS	LOW EARNINGS	UNEMPLOYMENT THREAT	SCORE	RANK
Metro Area Average	**5.9**	**2,566**	**20,115**	**3,510**	**14,744**	**4,428**			
Nashua, NH	4.1	200	4,456	92	3,492	1,071		15.29	300
★ Nashville, TN	7.8	9,558	56,792	12,152	38,350	15,848		93.76	23
New Bedford, MA	3.6	−320	3,287	−439	1,777	1,629	↑	9.06	322
New Haven-Meriden, CT	2.2	−2,780	7,862	−2,512	6,464	1,130		11.61	313
New London- Norwich, CT-RI	4.0	−991	7,117	−1,175	6,162	1,139		18.13	290
New Orleans, LA	4.6	1,907	33,519	5,518	22,928	6,980	↓	74.78	90
New York, NY	1.3	−40,678	102,886	−20,001	72,912	9,297	↓	41.92	206
Newark, NJ	1.5	−12,596	30,098	−7,383	19,210	5,675	↓	32.57	239
Newburgh, NY-PA	5.4	−389	9,485	1,656	4,486	2,954	↓	46.74	189
Norfolk-Virginia Beach- Newport News, VA-NC	5.5	6,289	46,316	8,257	32,688	11,660	↓	83.00	61
Oakland, CA	5.6	7,224	65,723	8,822	48,241	15,884	↓	87.53	45
Ocala, FL	6.2	764	5,762	1,747	2,590	2,189		43.62	200
Odessa-Midland, TX	3.2	884	3,519	1,087	1,583	1,733	↑	18.69	288
Oklahoma City, OK	4.5	4,282	25,572	6,631	18,732	4,491		72.23	99
Olympia, WA	9.3	1,116	9,970	3,255	5,718	2,113	↓	73.93	93
Omaha, NE-IA	7.2	3,763	33,198	4,316	24,181	8,464	↓	84.13	57
★ Orange County, CA	7.8	15,744	122,057	18,604	82,595	36,602		95.75	16
★ Orlando, FL	10.8	11,396	94,192	16,539	64,643	24,406	↓	97.45	10
Oshawa, ON	14.1	2,154	2,947	1,285	3,255	560		45.89	191
Ottawa-Hull, ON-PQ	8.4	4,180	14,081	6,596	9,890	1,775		83.28	60
Owensboro, KY	4.8	347	2,286	742	1,585	306	↑	15.58	299
Panama City, FL	8.4	238	6,962	632	4,131	2,437	↓	44.75	196
Parkersburg- Marietta, WV-OH	4.3	275	3,514	359	2,805	625	↑	13.88	305
Pensacola, FL	8.3	1,834	15,334	1,525	11,035	4,608	↓	74.50	91
Peoria-Pekin, IL	5.5	729	11,282	1,464	7,577	2,970		55.24	159
Philadelphia, PA-NJ	3.0	7,435	75,942	9,780	63,507	10,090		78.18	78
★ Phoenix-Mesa, AZ	11.2	28,849	172,956	42,088	100,662	59,055		100.00	1
Pine Bluff, AR	3.7	118	1,539	328	1,250	79	↑	7.36	328
Pittsburgh, PA	3.9	1,746	50,496	1,103	41,479	9,660		62.88	132
Pittsfield, MA	2.0	−504	1,066	−509	990	81		0.56	352
Pocatello, ID	8.8	627	3,041	983	2,111	574		33.71	235
Portland, ME	5.6	717	8,666	394	7,931	1,058	↓	36.82	224
★ Portland- Vancouver, OR-WA	10.0	26,838	96,003	24,730	71,946	26,165		98.86	5
Portsmouth- Rochester, NH-ME	7.2	1,566	6,977	1,086	4,557	2,900		48.44	183
Providence-Fall River- Warwick, RI-MA	1.9	−2,886	12,949	−3,417	12,560	920		23.51	270
Provo-Orem, UT	13.0	6,144	18,441	3,623	15,250	5,712		89.51	38
Pueblo, CO	6.7	538	4,023	267	2,843	1,451		26.62	260
Punta Gorda, FL	13.9	883	6,550	1,250	3,781	2,402	↓	58.07	149
Quebec City, PQ	3.1	2,580	7,912	2,950	6,273	1,269		46.45	190
Racine, WI	4.1	−19	4,156	−78	3,814	401	↑	13.03	308
★ Raleigh-Durham- Chapel Hill, NC	10.1	10,185	68,585	17,156	41,176	20,438		96.88	12
Rapid City, SD	7.1	408	4,253	404	2,961	1,296	↓	29.74	249
Reading, PA	3.2	1,318	5,333	1,499	3,714	1,438	↑	30.02	248
Redding, CA	8.0	809	6,132	1,255	4,288	1,398		49.29	180
Regina, SK	1.3	972	2,339	1,039	1,861	411		12.46	310
Reno, NV	5.5	2,642	9,507	2,044	7,364	2,741	↓	61.75	136
Richland-Kennewick- Pasco, WA	8.6	1,851	7,278	963	5,492	2,674		55.80	157
Richmond-Petersburg, VA	6.4	4,512	37,434	8,131	26,758	7,057		84.98	54
★ Riverside- San Bernardino, CA	10.0	19,920	106,339	29,812	59,137	37,310		99.43	3
Roanoke, VA	5.2	788	8,377	1,428	5,967	1,770		43.34	201
Rochester, MN	5.2	298	4,515	445	3,578	790		23.51	270
Rochester, NY	2.9	1,708	17,733	3,313	13,361	2,767	↑	62.32	134
Rockford, IL	4.1	1,352	7,694	1,047	7,299	700	↑	33.99	234
Rocky Mount, NC	4.5	373	3,420	1,438	1,469	886	↑	24.07	269
★ Sacramento, CA	8.8	9,403	70,338	18,141	48,007	13,593	↓	96.03	15
Saginaw-Bay City- Midland, MI	4.6	749	9,667	748	7,302	2,366	↑	37.96	220

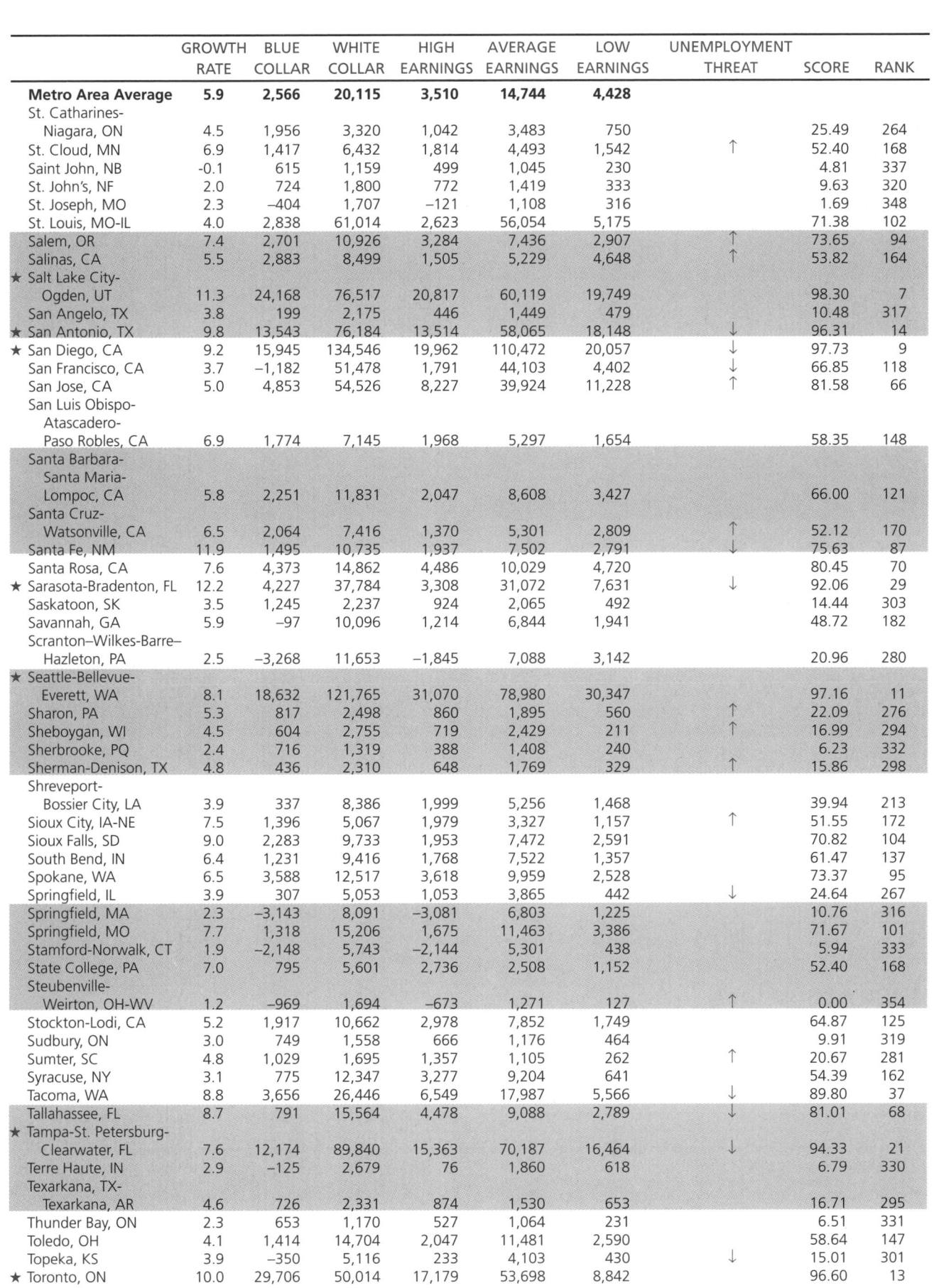

	GROWTH RATE	BLUE COLLAR	WHITE COLLAR	HIGH EARNINGS	AVERAGE EARNINGS	LOW EARNINGS	UNEMPLOYMENT THREAT	SCORE	RANK
Metro Area Average	**5.9**	**2,566**	**20,115**	**3,510**	**14,744**	**4,428**			
St. Catharines-Niagara, ON	4.5	1,956	3,320	1,042	3,483	750		25.49	264
St. Cloud, MN	6.9	1,417	6,432	1,814	4,493	1,542	↑	52.40	168
Saint John, NB	-0.1	615	1,159	499	1,045	230		4.81	337
St. John's, NF	2.0	724	1,800	772	1,419	333		9.63	320
St. Joseph, MO	2.3	−404	1,707	−121	1,108	316		1.69	348
St. Louis, MO-IL	4.0	2,838	61,014	2,623	56,054	5,175		71.38	102
Salem, OR	7.4	2,701	10,926	3,284	7,436	2,907	↑	73.65	94
Salinas, CA	5.5	2,883	8,499	1,505	5,229	4,648	↑	53.82	164
★ Salt Lake City-Ogden, UT	11.3	24,168	76,517	20,817	60,119	19,749		98.30	7
San Angelo, TX	3.8	199	2,175	446	1,449	479		10.48	317
★ San Antonio, TX	9.8	13,543	76,184	13,514	58,065	18,148	↓	96.31	14
★ San Diego, CA	9.2	15,945	134,546	19,962	110,472	20,057	↓	97.73	9
San Francisco, CA	3.7	−1,182	51,478	1,791	44,103	4,402	↓	66.85	118
San Jose, CA	5.0	4,853	54,526	8,227	39,924	11,228	↑	81.58	66
San Luis Obispo-Atascadero-Paso Robles, CA	6.9	1,774	7,145	1,968	5,297	1,654		58.35	148
Santa Barbara-Santa Maria-Lompoc, CA	5.8	2,251	11,831	2,047	8,608	3,427		66.00	121
Santa Cruz-Watsonville, CA	6.5	2,064	7,416	1,370	5,301	2,809	↑	52.12	170
Santa Fe, NM	11.9	1,495	10,735	1,937	7,502	2,791	↓	75.63	87
Santa Rosa, CA	7.6	4,373	14,862	4,486	10,029	4,720		80.45	70
★ Sarasota-Bradenton, FL	12.2	4,227	37,784	3,308	31,072	7,631	↓	92.06	29
Saskatoon, SK	3.5	1,245	2,237	924	2,065	492		14.44	303
Savannah, GA	5.9	−97	10,096	1,214	6,844	1,941		48.72	182
Scranton−Wilkes-Barre−Hazleton, PA	2.5	−3,268	11,653	−1,845	7,088	3,142		20.96	280
★ Seattle-Bellevue-Everett, WA	8.1	18,632	121,765	31,070	78,980	30,347		97.16	11
Sharon, PA	5.3	817	2,498	860	1,895	560	↑	22.09	276
Sheboygan, WI	4.5	604	2,755	719	2,429	211	↑	16.99	294
Sherbrooke, PQ	2.4	716	1,319	388	1,408	240		6.23	332
Sherman-Denison, TX	4.8	436	2,310	648	1,769	329	↑	15.86	298
Shreveport-Bossier City, LA	3.9	337	8,386	1,999	5,256	1,468		39.94	213
Sioux City, IA-NE	7.5	1,396	5,067	1,979	3,327	1,157	↑	51.55	172
Sioux Falls, SD	9.0	2,283	9,733	1,953	7,472	2,591		70.82	104
South Bend, IN	6.4	1,231	9,416	1,768	7,522	1,357		61.47	137
Spokane, WA	6.5	3,588	12,517	3,618	9,959	2,528		73.37	95
Springfield, IL	3.9	307	5,053	1,053	3,865	442	↓	24.64	267
Springfield, MA	2.3	−3,143	8,091	−3,081	6,803	1,225		10.76	316
Springfield, MO	7.7	1,318	15,206	1,675	11,463	3,386		71.67	101
Stamford-Norwalk, CT	1.9	−2,148	5,743	−2,144	5,301	438		5.94	333
State College, PA	7.0	795	5,601	2,736	2,508	1,152		52.40	168
Steubenville-Weirton, OH-WV	1.2	−969	1,694	−673	1,271	127	↑	0.00	354
Stockton-Lodi, CA	5.2	1,917	10,662	2,978	7,852	1,749		64.87	125
Sudbury, ON	3.0	749	1,558	666	1,176	464		9.91	319
Sumter, SC	4.8	1,029	1,695	1,357	1,105	262	↑	20.67	281
Syracuse, NY	3.1	775	12,347	3,277	9,204	641		54.39	162
Tacoma, WA	8.8	3,656	26,446	6,549	17,987	5,566	↓	89.80	37
Tallahassee, FL	8.7	791	15,564	4,478	9,088	2,789	↓	81.01	68
★ Tampa-St. Petersburg-Clearwater, FL	7.6	12,174	89,840	15,363	70,187	16,464	↓	94.33	21
Terre Haute, IN	2.9	−125	2,679	76	1,860	618		6.79	330
Texarkana, TX-Texarkana, AR	4.6	726	2,331	874	1,530	653		16.71	295
Thunder Bay, ON	2.3	653	1,170	527	1,064	231		6.51	331
Toledo, OH	4.1	1,414	14,704	2,047	11,481	2,590		58.64	147
Topeka, KS	3.9	−350	5,116	233	4,103	430	↓	15.01	301
★ Toronto, ON	10.0	29,706	50,014	17,179	53,698	8,842		96.60	13

continues

	GROWTH RATE	BLUE COLLAR	WHITE COLLAR	HIGH EARNINGS	AVERAGE EARNINGS	LOW EARNINGS	UNEMPLOYMENT THREAT	SCORE	RANK
Metro Area Average	**5.9**	**2,566**	**20,115**	**3,510**	**14,744**	**4,428**			
Trenton, NJ	3.5	−1,778	9,882	3,540	4,236	328	↓	41.35	208
Trois-Rivieres, PQ	1.6	724	1,140	496	1,120	248		5.66	334
★ Tucson, AZ	9.1	3,312	35,001	7,139	25,393	5,781	↓	92.63	27
Tulsa, OK	5.1	3,459	21,553	3,741	16,450	4,821		72.52	98
Tuscaloosa, AL	6.8	1,004	5,308	1,034	3,336	1,942	↑	38.81	217
Tyler, TX	6.0	1,027	5,411	1,730	3,368	1,340		42.49	204
Utica-Rome, NY	3.1	649	4,277	1,594	2,256	1,076		24.36	268
Vallejo-Fairfield-Napa, CA	10.0	3,785	19,300	5,711	10,931	6,443		89.23	39
★ Vancouver, BC	10.1	11,657	21,982	9,613	19,627	4,397		93.20	25
Ventura, CA	8.0	4,340	27,346	5,306	21,014	5,366		88.66	41
Victoria, BC	4.7	1,246	3,626	1,573	2,755	544		28.61	253
Victoria, TX	5.7	382	2,365	667	1,492	588		20.39	282
Vineland-Millville-Bridgeton, NJ	2.5	163	1,543	666	1,001	39	↑	8.21	325
Visalia-Tulare-Porterville, CA	4.9	1,015	7,310	1,577	4,921	1,827	↑	41.07	209
Waco, TX	5.7	967	5,839	1,840	3,427	1,539		42.77	203
★ Washington, DC-MD-VA-WV	5.6	28,785	156,575	31,698	116,100	37,562	↓	92.91	26
Waterbury, CT	2.6	−1,019	3,603	−953	3,051	487		5.09	336
Waterloo-Cedar Falls, IA	3.8	−352	3,566	188	1,892	1,134		11.89	312
Wausau, WI	6.4	1,857	3,364	2,128	2,381	712	↑	40.22	212
★ West Palm Beach-Boca Raton, FL	8.0	3,871	41,987	7,352	27,488	11,018	↓	90.93	33
Wheeling, WV-OH	4.4	−271	3,816	361	2,549	635	↓	13.59	306
Wichita, KS	4.7	−19	16,393	809	9,407	6,158	↑	50.14	177
Wichita Falls, TX	4.4	1,009	2,985	1,479	2,025	490		25.21	265
Williamsport, PA	2.3	−833	2,334	−584	1,402	683	↑	1.13	350
Wilmington, NC	11.1	1,142	13,698	2,015	7,844	4,981		78.75	76
Wilmington-Newark, DE-MD	4.5	624	15,289	2,830	11,426	1,657		64.02	128
Windsor, ON	7.3	1,918	2,534	714	3,289	449		31.16	243
Winnipeg, MB	3.9	4,098	7,304	2,947	7,056	1,398		51.84	171
Worcester, MA-CT	2.9	−798	6,518	−1,153	5,294	1,579		14.16	304
Yakima, WA	5.8	1,033	5,801	1,211	3,650	1,973	↑	37.67	221
Yolo, CA	9.8	1,377	9,175	2,757	5,506	2,289		71.10	103
York, PA	4.9	1,659	8,943	1,357	7,297	1,948	↑	45.89	191
Youngstown-Warren, OH	4.8	2,617	12,517	2,964	9,231	2,939	↑	65.43	123
Yuba City, CA	8.4	627	5,002	582	3,661	1,386	↑	37.39	222
Yuma, AZ	9.3	2,223	4,842	1,381	1,785	3,899	↑	54.67	161

ET CETERA: JOBS

LIFE IN A BOOM TOWN

If you could live anywhere you choose, would you choose a boom town? Their advantages include rising personal incomes; real estate appreciation; expanding personal employment opportunities; improved infrastructures; somewhat lower violent crime; increasing amenities; and high-quality health care and education.

The disadvantages of living in a boom town include rising costs of living, increased property crime rates, environmental pollution, and noticeable loss of personal discretionary time. But if you stay in a no-growth area, you face possible job loss, depreciating value of real estate, boarded-up businesses, and backwater schools and health care. Any advantages? Try declining living costs, increased personal time, and lower crime rates.

Employment opportunities are the single most important factor behind geographic mobility. Joblessness or underemployment can push a settled person to become a mobile one. Consider, for example, that in 1980 you moved from withering Chicago or Detroit to booming Los Angeles. It's 1990 and you're thinking about your next move. Who would have guessed during the 1980 job boom that California would later be grabbing the ropes or that the Great Lakes states would make a comeback?

The past decade has seen some surprising shifts in regional economic growth. So the big question remains: Will a move to Anaheim or San Jose or Raleigh really solve your jobless or underemployment problem? If there is any trend to be spotted from the past, it is that boom times and slumps aren't permanent in any metro area.

A JOBS MENU

Using "white collar" or "blue collar" to distinguish between jobs that deal with information or things, are physical or mental, clean or messy, salaried or non-salaried, high-paying or low-paying, seasonal or year-round, skilled or unskilled, or unionized or professional, isn't always precise.

According to Standard Occupational Classification definitions, white-collar jobs take in professional and technical workers, managers and administrators, sales workers, and clerical workers. Blue-collar occupations include craftsworkers, mechanics and installers, production operatives, drivers, and nonfarm laborers.

But a quick look at some white-collar clerical job titles in the following chart shows that many can be as unskilled, non-salaried, and seasonal as jobs in the laboring category, while many blue-collar craftsworker jobs can be as skilled, salaried, and highly paid as those in the professional and technical category.

Job Prospects

The numbers next to each job title are thousands of new job openings forecasted for 1994–2006 due to expansion and replacing workers who've left the labor force. An up arrow (↑) indicates a rate of growth higher than 25 percent, while a down arrow (↓) indicates that jobs in this area will be found only by taking the place of workers who've changed careers, retired, died, or otherwise moved on.

Education

Jobs requiring a high school diploma are indicated by (**HS**). Jobs needing post-secondary training (**PS**) mean beyond high school but short of a bachelor's degree, including on-the-job training, vocational school, or community college. College and above (**C**) demands at least a bachelor's degree. If no education level is indicated, as in the case for actors and musicians, the job can be entered with less than a high school education.

For some jobs, a range of education levels is shown. For example, some high school graduates become administrative services managers by advancing through the ranks of an organization. Even though a higher degree is not always required for administrative services managers, a college degree boosts their chance of advancing to top-level management. Education requirements also vary within an occupation. For instance, nursing can be entered by earning a diploma, associate degree, or bachelor's degree.

Working Conditions

Economically sensitive means these occupations have historically prospered or suffered along with the economy.

Geographically concentrated means the job is localized in a particular region. Most textile jobs are concentrated in a handful of states. Advertising and public relations jobs are found mainly in large cities. Most petroleum and mining engineers are found along the Gulf of Mexico and in the Southwest.

Mobile means different work settings for workers who don't stay in a single office, factory, or laboratory. For example, in addition to working in an office, property and real estate managers frequently visit properties they oversee; manufacturing sales representatives travel to different cities to visit customers; and messengers deliver packages to various locations.

Job stress or pressure means occupations that involve either tremendous pressure to complete work on deadlines or concerns over safety or other work-related issues.

Physical stamina means physically demanding. Workers must endure physical stress and strain, including lifting heavy objects. Construction work is often strenuous, and workers spend most of the day on their feet—bending, kneeling, lifting, and maneuvering heavy objects. On the other hand, teachers spend much of their day on their feet, which is physically tiring. However, the table does not indicate physical stamina as a key characteristic of teachers because they can teach while sitting at a desk.

Irregular hours means working under a schedule that's not the standard 8-hour day. This can include night or weekend shifts, rotating schedules, or working for several days and then having several days off. Many nurses and security guards work nights or weekends. Other occupations that work on shifts include firefighters, pilots, real estate agents, and flight attendants.

Part-time indicates opportunities for part-time work are high (**H**) or very high (**VH**). Most waiters and waitresses work part-time, as do retail salesworkers and security guards. Many medical assistants, cooks, librarians, and teacher assistants also work part-time.

Job Outlook 1994–2006

OCCUPATIONS	NEW JOBS IN THOUSANDS	GROWTH RATE %	EDUCATION	JOB PROSPECTS / JOB CHARACTERISTICS						
				ECONOMICALLY SENSITIVE	GEOGRAPHICALLY CONCENTRATED	MOBILE	JOB STRESS OR PRESSURE	PHYSICAL STAMINA	IRREGULAR HOURS	PART-TIME
EXECUTIVE, ADMINISTRATIVE, AND MANAGERIAL										
Accountants and auditors	330		C							
Administrative services managers	95		HS, PS, C							
Budget analysts	20		C							
Construction and building inspectors	29		HS, PS			•		•		
Construction contractors and managers	98		PS, C	•		•	•	•	•	
Cost estimators	45		PS, C							
Education administrators	146		C							
Employment interviewers	39		PS							
Engineering, science, and data processing managers	228	↑	C							
Financial managers	297		C							
Food services and lodging managers, restaurant and hotel	293	↑	C	•		•	•		•	
General managers and top executives	1,149		C			•	•			
Government chief executives and legislators	22		C			•	•			
Health services managers			C							
Industrial production managers	44	↓	C				•			
Inspectors and compliance officers, except construction	36		C			•				
Management analysts and consultants	79		C			•				
Marketing, advertising, and public relations managers	226	↑	C			•	•			
Personnel, training, and labor relations specialists and managers	97		C				•			
Property and real estate managers	87		C			•	•			H
Purchasing agents and managers	71		PS, C							
Underwriters	29		PS, C							
Wholesale and retail buyers and merchandise managers	48		PS, C							
PROFESSIONAL SPECIALTY										
Engineers										
Aerospace engineers	10		C		•					
Chemical engineers	22		C							
Civil engineers	82		C	•						
Electrical and electronics engineers	197	↑	C							
Industrial engineers	39		C			•				
Mechanical engineers	81		C							
Metallurgical, ceramic, and materials engineers	6		C							
Mining engineers	1	↓	C	•						
Nuclear engineers	4		C							
Petroleum engineers	4	↓	C	•	•	•				
Architects and surveyors										
Architects	39		C	•						
Landscape architects	7		C	•	•					
Surveyors	20	↓	PS, C	•		•				
Computer, mathematical, and operations research occupations										
Actuaries	3		C							
Computer systems analysts	1,072	↑	C							
Mathematicians	4		C							
Operations research analysts	18		C							
Statisticians	2		C							
Lawyers and judicial workers										
Judges and magistrates	14		C					•		
Lawyers	209		C							
Life scientists										
Agricultural scientists	10		C							
Biological scientists	26	↑	C							
Foresters and conservation scientists	14		C			•		•	•	
Physical scientists										
Chemists	36		C							
Geologists and geophysicists	17		C	•		•				

OCCUPATIONS	JOB PROSPECTS			JOB CHARACTERISTICS						
	NEW JOBS IN THOUSANDS	GROWTH RATE %	EDUCATION	ECONOMICALLY SENSITIVE	GEOGRAPHICALLY CONCENTRATED	MOBILE	JOB STRESS OR PRESSURE	PHYSICAL STAMINA	IRREGULAR HOURS	PART-TIME
Meteorologists	2		C							
Physicists and astronomers	4	↓	C	●	●					
Social scientists and urban planners										
Economists and marketing research analysts	23		C							
Psychologists	25		C							H
Sociologists			C							
Urban and regional planners	6		C	●						
Social and recreation workers										
Human services workers	131	↑	PS, C			●			●	VH
Recreation Workers	155		HS, PS, C			●		●	●	H
Social workers	277	↑	C			●				
Religious Workers	68									
Protestant ministers			PS, C			●	●		●	
Rabbis			PS, C			●	●		●	
Roman Catholic priests			PS, C			●	●		●	
Teachers, librarians, and counselors										
Adult education teachers	74		C						●	VH
Archivists and curators	8		C		●	●			●	H
College and university faculty	412		C				●			VH
Counselors	73		C							
Kindergarten and elementary school teachers	628		C							
Librarians	45		C						●	H
Secondary school teachers	731		C							
Special education teachers	299	↑	C							
Health diagnosing occupations										
Chiropractors	20	↑	C							
Dentists	47		C							H
Optometrists	13		C							
Physicians	197		C			●	●		●	
Podiatrists	3		C							
Veterinarians	25		C			●				
Health assessment and treating occupations										
Dietitians and nutritionists	22		C							H
Occupational therapists	44	↑	C							H
Pharmacists	64		C						●	
Physical therapists	94	↑	C					●	●	H
Physician assistants	39	↑	C						●	H
Recreational therapists	12		C			●		●		H
Registered nurses	683		PS, C				●	●	●	H
Respiratory therapists	46	↑	PS, C							H
Speech-language pathologists and audiologists	54	↑	C							H
Communications occupations										
Public relations specialists	69	↑	C		●	●				
Radio and television announcers and newscasters	21	↓	HS, PS, C						●	VH
Reporters and correspondents	17	↓	C	●		●			●	
Writers and editors	124		PS, C			●			●	
Visual arts occupations										
Designers	149	↑	HS, PS, C	●						H
Photographers and camera operators	48	↑	PS			●				H
Visual artists	135		HS, PS, C							H
Performing arts occupations										
Actors, directors, and producers						●		●	●	H
Dancers, and choreographers	12	↑				●		●	●	H
Musicians, and conductors	130	↑				●		●		VH

continues

A Jobs Menu

OCCUPATIONS	NEW JOBS IN THOUSANDS	GROWTH RATE %	EDUCATION	ECONOMICALLY SENSITIVE	GEOGRAPHICALLY CONCENTRATED	MOBILE	JOB STRESS OR PRESSURE	PHYSICAL STAMINA	IRREGULAR HOURS	PART-TIME
TECHNICIANS AND RELATED SUPPORT										
Health technologists and technicians										
Clinical laboratory technologists	70	↑	PS, C							H
Dental hygienists	104	↑	PS							VH
Dispensing opticians	24		HS, PS							
EEG technologists	3		PS							H
EKG technicians	3	↓	HS							H
Emergency medical technicians	96	↑	PS			•	•	•	•	H
Licensed practical nurses	296		PS					•	•	H
Medical record technicians	61	↑	PS							H
Nuclear medicine technologists	4		PS							H
Radiologic technologists	77	↑	PS							H
Surgical technologists	25	↑	PS							
Veterinary technicians	13	↑								H
Technicians, except health										
Air traffic controllers	8	↓	HS, PS, C				•		•	
Aircraft pilots	38		C			•	•		•	
Broadcast technicians	20		PS						•	
Computer programmers	306		C							
Drafters	68		PS							
Engineering technicians	378		PS							
Library technicians	44	↑	HS						•	
Paralegals	86	↑	PS							H
Science and mathematics technicians	82		PS			•			•	
Tool programmers, numerical control	2		PS, C							
MARKETING AND SALES										
Cashiers	1,902			•					•	VH
Counter and rental clerks	217			•					•	VH
Insurance agents and brokers	95		PS, C	•						
Manufacturers' and wholesale sales representatives				•		•				
Real estate agents, brokers, and appraisers	98		HS, PS	•		•			•	H
Retail sales workers	1,701			•		•			•	VH
Securities and financial services sales representatives	124	↑	C	•		•				
Services sales representatives			HS							
Travel agents	66		HS, PS	•		•			•	
ADMINISTRATIVE SUPPORT INCLUDING CLERICAL										
Adjusters, investigators, and collectors	523	↑	HS, PS, C							
Bank tellers	232	↓	HS, PS							VH
Clerical supervisors and managers	579		HS, PS, C							
Computer and peripheral equipment operators	45	↓	PS						•	
Credit clerks and authorizers	42	↓	HS							
General office clerks	923		HS							VH
Information clerks										
Hotel and motel desk clerks	94		HS						•	H
Interviewing and new accounts clerks	83		HS							VH
Mail clerks and messengers	89		HS			•		•		H
Receptionists and information clerks	518	↑	HS							VH
Reservation and transportation ticket agents and travel clerks	38	↓	HS						•	H
Material recording, scheduling, dispatching, and distributing										
Dispatchers	58		HS						•	
Postal clerks and mail carriers	134		HS			•		•		
Stock clerks	326		HS					•		
Traffic, shipping, and receiving clerks	235		HS					•		

OCCUPATIONS	NEW JOBS IN THOUSANDS	GROWTH RATE %	EDUCATION	ECONOMICALLY SENSITIVE	GEOGRAPHICALLY CONCENTRATED	MOBILE	JOB STRESS OR PRESSURE	PHYSICAL STAMINA	IRREGULAR HOURS	PART-TIME
Record clerks										
Billing clerks	115		HS							
Bookkeeping, accounting, and auditing clerks	379	↓	HS							VH
Brokerage clerks and statement clerks	22		HS		•					
File clerks	132		HS							VH
Order clerks	75		HS							
Payroll and timekeeping clerks	26	↓	HS							
Personnel clerks	27		HS							
Secretaries	70	↓	HS							H
Stenographers and court reporters	21		PS							
Teacher aides	500		HS, PS							VH
Telephone operators	68		HS				•		•	H
Typists, word processors, and data entry keyers	166	↓	HS							
SERVICE										
Food and beverage preparation and service occupations										
Bakers, bread and pastry	92	↑								
Chefs, cooks, and other kitchen workers	1,734		HS, PS						•	VH
Food and beverage service workers	2,904		HS						•	VH
Health service occupations										
Dental assistants	126	↑	HS							VH
Medical assistants	210	↑	HS							H
Nursing aids and psychiatric aides	533	↑	HS, PS						•	H
Personal service and cleaning occupations										
Animal caretakers, except farm	62		HS			•		•	•	
Barbers and cosmetologists	268	↓	PS						•	VH
Flight attendants	78	↑	HS, PS			•		•	•	VH
Gardeners and groundskeepers	398					•		•	•	H
Homemaker-home health aides	653	↑				•		•	•	H
Janitors and cleaners	743							•	•	H
Private child care workers	136	↓	HS, PS, C						•	VH
Private household workers	252	↓				•		•	•	VH
Protective service occupations										
Correction officers	152	↑	HS						•	
Firefighting occupations	128		HS			•		•	•	
Guards	420		HS						•	H
Police, detectives, and special agents	312		HS			•		•	•	
AGRICULTURE, FORESTRY, FISHING										
Farm operators and managers	247	↓			•	•		•	•	
Fishers, hunters, and trappers	10	↓			•	•		•	•	H
Timber cutting and logging workers	25	↓			•	•		•	•	
MECHANICS, INSTALLERS, AND REPAIRERS										
Aircraft mechanics and engine specialists	50									
Automotive body repairers	98		PS					•		
Automotive mechanics	298		PS					•		
Diesel mechanics			PS					•		
Electronic equipment repairers										
Commercial and industrial electronic equipment repairers	19		PS			•		•		
Communications equipment mechanics	29		PS			•		•		
Computer and office machine repairers	28		PS			•		•		
Electronic home entertainment equipment repairers	7	↓	PS			•		•		
Elevator installers and repairers	8		HS			•		•		

continues

A Jobs Menu

OCCUPATIONS	NEW JOBS IN THOUSANDS	GROWTH RATE %	EDUCATION	ECONOMICALLY SENSITIVE	GEOGRAPHICALLY CONCENTRATED	MOBILE	JOB STRESS OR PRESSURE	PHYSICAL STAMINA	IRREGULAR HOURS	PART-TIME
JOB PROSPECTS				**JOB CHARACTERISTICS**						
Farm equipment mechanics	10	↓	PS					●		
General maintenance mechanics	522		PS					●		
Heating, air-conditioning, and refrigeration technicians	104		HS, PS			●		●		
Home appliance and power tool repairers	20					●		●		
Industrial machinery repairers	131		PS			●		●	●	
Millwrights	18	↓		●						
Mobile heavy equipment mechanics	30		PS					●		
Motorcycle, boat, and small engine mechanics	15		PS	●				●		
Musical instrument repairers and tuners	3					●		●		
Telephone and cable line installers and repairers	82	↓	PS			●		●		
Vending machine servicers and repairers	4	↓	HS			●		●		
CONSTRUCTION TRADES										
Bricklayers and stonemasons	41		HS, PS	●		●		●		
Carpenters	232		HS, PS			●		●		
Carpet installers	28		HS, PS			●		●		
Concrete masons and terrazzo finishers	45		HS, PS	●		●		●		
Drywall workers and lathers	47		HS, PS	●		●		●		
Electricians	173		HS, PS			●		●		
Glaziers	10		HS, PS	●		●		●		
Insulation workers	28		HS, PS	●		●		●		
Numerical-control machine-tool operators	42		HS						●	
Painters and paperhangers	164		HS, PS			●		●		
Plasterers	11		HS, PS	●		●		●		
Plumbers and pipefitters	102		PS			●		●		
Roofers	47		HS, PS			●		●		
Roustabouts					●	●		●	●	
Sheet-metal workers	50		PS	●		●		●		
Structural and reinforcing ironworkers	3		HS, PS	●	●	●		●		
Tile setters	7		HS, PS	●		●		●		
PRODUCTION										
Assemblers										
Blue-collar worker supervisors	467		HS						●	
Precision assemblers	93		HS							
Food processing occupations										
Butchers and meat, poultry, and fish cutters	57	↓	HS							
Inspectors, testers, and graders	115	↓	HS						●	
Metalworking and plastics-working occupations										
Boilermakers	4	↓	HS			●		●		
Jewelers	6	↓	PS	●						
Machinists	85	↓								
Metalworking and plastics-working machine operators			HS						●	
Tool and die makers	21	↓	PS						●	
Welders, cutters, and welding machine operators	26	↓	PS					●	●	
Plant and systems operators										
Electric power generating plant operators and power distributors	14		HS						●	
Stationary engineers	5	↓	HS						●	
Water and wastewater treatment plant operators	38		HS						●	
Printing Occupations										
Bindery workers	14		HS							
Prepress workers	41	↓	HS						●	
Printing press operators	45		HS						●	
Textile, apparel, and furnishing occupations										
Apparel workers	34	↓								
Shoe and leather workers and repairers	2								●	
Textile machinery operators	164	↓	HS		●				●	

OCCUPATIONS	NEW JOBS IN THOUSANDS	GROWTH RATE %	EDUCATION	ECONOMICALLY SENSITIVE	GEOGRAPHICALLY CONCENTRATED	MOBILE	JOB STRESS OR PRESSURE	PHYSICAL STAMINA	IRREGULAR HOURS	PART-TIME
				JOB PROSPECTS			JOB CHARACTERISTICS			
Upholsterers	8	↓	HS							
Woodworking occupations	48	↓	HS	•						
Miscellaneous production occupations										
Dental laboratory technicians	12		PS, C							
Ophthalmic laboratory technicians	4		PS, C							H
Photographic process workers	5		HS						•	
TRANSPORTATION AND MATERIAL MOVING										
Bus drivers	197		HS			•			•	H
Material moving equipment operators	338		HS, PS	•		•				
Taxi drivers and chauffeurs	24					•			•	H
Truck drivers	903		HS	•		•		•	•	
Water transportation occupations	19	↓	HS, C	•		•		•	•	

HEADQUARTER METROS

For each of the past 45 years, *Fortune* magazine has produced a list of the 500 largest U.S. corporations ranked by annual revenue. A quick comparison of the 1959 list with the one for 1999 reveals the dramatic shift the American economy has taken from a muscle-bound, goods-producing machine to a light-on-its feet, service- and information-producing one. It also shows the remarkable westward and southward march of corporate headquarters away from major cities in the Northeast and Great Lakes.

The Fortune 500

Here are the Fortune 500 companies (with their 1999 ranking) that are located in the various metropolitan areas.

Akron, OH
130 Goodyear (Rubber and Plastic)
280 FirstEnergy (Utilities)
388 B.F. Goodrich (Aerospace)

Albuquerque, NM
463 Sun Healthcare (Health Care)

Allentown-Bethlehem-Easton, PA
323 Air Products (Chemicals)
346 Bethlehem Steel (Metals)
401 PP&L Resources (Utilities)

Appleton-Oshkosh-Neenah, WI
461 Aid Association for Lutherans (Life and Health Insurance)

Atlanta, GA
32 Home Depot (Specialty Retailers)
46 UPS (Freight Delivery)
52 BellSouth (Telecommunications)
73 Coca-Cola (Beverages)
111 Delta (Airline)
119 Coca-Cola Enterprises (Beverages)
122 Georgia-Pacific (Forest and Paper Products)
148 Southern (Utilities)
227 SunTrust Banks (Commercial Banking)
252 Genuine Parts (Wholesalers)
316 First Data (Computer and Data Services)

Austin-San Marcos, TX
78 Dell Computer (Computers and Office Equipment)

Baltimore, MD
298 US Food Service (Wholesalers)
342 Black & Decker (Industrial and Farm Equipment)
439 Baltimore Gas & Electric (Utilities)
492 Integrated Health Services (Health Care)

Benton Harbor, MI
155 Whirlpool (Electronics)

Bergen-Passaic, NJ
151 Toys R Us (Specialty Retailers)
194 Bestfoods (Food)
199 Ingersoll-Rand (Industrial and Farm Equipment)
344 Union Camp (Forest and Paper Products)
468 Becton Dickinson (Medical Products)

Birmingham, AL
241 Medpartners (Health Care)
267 Saks (General Merchandisers)
383 HealthSouth (Health Care)
409 Sonat (Pipelines)
476 Regions Financial (Commercial Banking)
493 Southtrust (Commercial Banking)

Bloomington-Normal, IL
12 State Farm (Property and Casualty Insurance)

Boise City, ID
92 Albertson's (Food and Drug Stores)
268 Boise Cascade (Forest and Paper Products)
487 Micron Technology (Electronics)

Boston, MA-NH
69 Ratheon (Electronics)
124 Liberty Mutual (Property and Casualty Insurance)
159 Gillette (Metal Products)
161 Fleet Financial (Commercial Banking)
179 John Hancock (Life and Health Insurance)
208 TJX (Specialty Retailers)
218 BankBoston (Commercial Banking)
365 Harcourt General (General Merchandisers)
366 State Street (Commercial Banking)
386 EMC (Computer Peripherals)
394 Thermo Electron (Medical Products)
421 BJ's Wholesale Club (Food and Drug Stores)
458 Reebok (Apparel)

Boulder-Longmont, CO
348 Corporate Express (Specialty Retailers)
500 Ball (Metal Products)

Bridgeport, CT
5 General Electric (Electronics)

Charlotte-Gastonia-Rock Hill, NC-SC
11 BankAmerica (Commercial Banking)
56 First Union (Commercial Banking)
81 Duke Energy (Utilities)
374 Nucor (Metals)

Chattanooga, TN-GA
393 Provident Companies (Life and Health Insurance)

Chicago, IL
15 Sears Roebuck (General Merchandisers)
34 Motorola (Electronics)
42 Allstate (Property and Casualty Insurance)
44 Bank One (Commercial Banking)
64 Sara Lee (Food)
82 UAL (Airline)
87 Ameritech (Tele-communications)
98 Walgreen (Food and Drug Stores)

133 Abbott Laboratories (Drugs)
134 McDonald's (Food Services)
185 Household International (Diversified Financial)
211 Navistar International (Motor Vehicles)
233 Unicom (Utilities)
254 Baxter International (Medical Products)
259 AON (Diversified Financial)
277 R.R. Donnelley & Sons (Printing and Publishing)
290 Illinois Tool Works (Metal Products)
325 Quaker Oats (Food)
333 ServiceMaster (Diversified Outsourcing Services)
341 Allegiance (Health Care)
355 FMC (Chemicals)
357 W.W. Grainger (Wholesalers)
360 Truserv (Specialty Retailers)
376 Ryerson Tull (Metals)
389 Brunswick (Transportation Equipment)
400 Smurfit-Stone Container (Forest and Paper Products)
429 IMC Global (Chemicals)
449 Dean Foods (Food)
455 Comdisco (Computer and Data Services)
466 USG (Building Materials)
467 ACE Hardware (Wholesalers)
473 Anixter International (Wholesalers)
480 United Stationers (Wholesalers)
491 Tribune (Printing and Publishing)

Cincinnati, OH-KY-IN
17 Proctor & Gamble (Soaps and Cosmetics)
36 Kroger (Food and Drug Stores)
95 Federated Department Stores (General Merchandisers)
242 Ashland (Oil Refining)
279 Cinergy (Utilities)
381 American Financial (Property and Casualty Insurance)

Cleveland-Lorain-Elyria, OH
142 TRW (Motor Vehicles)
201 National City (Commercial Banking)
238 Keycorp (Commercial Banking)
250 Eaton (Electronics)
305 Progressive (Property and Casualty Insurance)
322 Sherwin-Williams (Chemicals)
336 Parker Hannifin (Industrial and Farm Equipment)
358 OfficeMax (Specialty Retailers)
362 KTV (Metals)

Columbus, GA-AL
237 AFLAC (Life and Health Insurance)

Columbus, OH
93 Cardinal Health (Wholesalers)
125 Nationwide (Property and Casualty Insurance)
169 Limited (Specialty Retailers)
264 American Electric Power (Utilities)
369 Consolidated Stores (Specialty Retailers)

Dallas, TX
4 Exxon (Oil Refining)
31 JCPenney (General Merchandisers)
45 GTE (Telecommunications)
85 Halliburton (Engineering and Construction)
90 Electronic Data Systems (Computer and Data Services)
105 Texas Utilities (Utilities)
136 Kimberly-Clark (Forest and Paper Products)
154 Union Pacific (Railroads)
191 Texas Instruments (Semi-conductors)
300 Central & South West (Utilities)
307 CompUSA (Specialty Retailers)
371 Southwest (Airline)
385 Centex (Engineering and Construction)
443 Suiza (Food)

Danbury, CT
288 Union Carbide (Chemicals)
326 Praxair (Chemicals)

Davenport-Moline-Rock Island, IA-IL
113 Deere (Industrial and Farm Equipment)

Dayton-Springfield, OH
258 NCR (Computers and Office Equipment)
340 Mead (Forest and Paper Products)

Decatur, IL
91 Archer Daniels Midland (Food)

Denver, CO
135 US West (Telecommunications)
228 Tele-Communications (Telecommunications)
354 KN Energy (Pipelines)
418 New Century Energies (Utilities)

Des Moines, IA
213 Principal Financial (Life and Health Insurance)

Detroit, MI
- 1 General Motors (Motor Vehicles)
- 2 Ford Motor (Motor Vehicles)
- 21 Kmart (General Merchandisers)
- 173 Lear (Motor Vehicles)
- 314 CMS Energy (Utilities)
- 349 Federal-Mogul (Motor Vehicles)
- 356 Masco (Metal Products)
- 368 DTE Energy (Utilities)
- 377 Kelly Services (Temp Help)
- 397 Meritor Automotive (Wholesalers)
- 460 Comerica (Commercial Banking)

Duluth-Superior, MN-WI
- 494 AGCO (Industrial and Farm Equipment)

Fayetteville-Springdale-Rogers, AR
- 3 Wal-Mart (General Merchandisers)
- 226 Tyson Foods (Food)

Fort Lauderdale, FL
- 83 Republic Industries (Automotive Retailing and Services)

Fort Wayne, IN
- 270 Lincoln National (Life and Health Insurance)

Fort Worth-Arlington, TX
- 71 American (Airline)
- 178 Burlington Northern Santa Fe (Railroads)
- 330 Tandy (Specialty Retailers)

Gary, IN
- 497 Nipsco Industries (Utilities)

Green Bay, WI
- 490 Shopko Stores (General Merchandisers)

Greensboro–Winston-Salem– High Point, NC
- 276 Wachovia (Commercial Banking)
- 301 VF (Apparel)
- 488 BB&T (Commercial Banking)

Harrisburg-Lebanon-Carlisle, PA
- 149 Rite Aid (Food and Drug Stores)
- 299 AMP (Electronics)
- 350 Hershey Foods (Food)

Hartford, CT
- 43 United Technologies (Aerospace)
- 61 Aetna (Health Care)
- 102 Hartford (Property and Casualty Insurance)
- 402 Northeast Utilities (Utilities)
- 432 Phoenix Home Life (Life and Health Insurance)

Houston, TX
- 27 Enron (Pipelines)
- 28 Compaq (Computers and Office Equipment)
- 97 Sysco (Wholesalers)
- 110 Dynegy (Pipelines)
- 129 Waste Management (Waste Management)
- 147 Houston Industries (Utilities)
- 156 American General (Life and Health Insurance)
- 207 Continental (Airline)
- 235 Coastal (Oil Refining)
- 265 Baker Hughes (Industrial and Farm Equipment)
- 286 El Paso Energy (Pipelines)
- 317 Cooper Industries (Electronics)
- 332 Browning-Ferris Industries (Waste Management)

Huntsville, AL
- 245 SCI Systems (Electronics)

Indianapolis, IN
- 160 Eli Lilly (Drugs)
- 212 Conseco (Life and Health Insurance)
- 217 Bindley Western (Wholesalers)
- 278 Anthem (Health Care)

Jackson, MS
- 80 MCI Worldcom (Telecommunications)

Jacksonville, FL
- 115 Winn-Dixie (Food and Drug Stores)

Johnson City-Kingsport-Bristol, TN-VA
- 345 Eastman Chemical (Chemicals)

Joplin, MO
- 436 Legett & Platt (Furniture)

Kalamazoo-Battle Creek, MI
- 246 Kellogg (Food)

Kansas City, MO-KS
- 88 Sprint (Telecommunications)
- 132 Utilicorp United (Utilities)
- 184 Farmland Industries (Food)
- 451 Interstate Bakeries (Food)
- 469 Yellow (Trucking)

Lakeland-Winter Haven, FL
- 139 Publix (Food and Drug Stores)

Lexington, KY
- 486 Lexmark (Computer Peripherals)

Little Rock-North Little Rock, AR
- 203 Dillard's (General Merchandisers)
- 311 Alltel (Telecommunications)

Long Island, NY
- 197 Arrow Electronics (Wholesalers)
- 335 Computer Associates (Software)
- 338 Olsten (Temp Help)
- 452 Cablevision Systems (Telecommunications)

Los Angeles-Long Beach, CA
- 53 Walt Disney (Entertainment)
- 123 Atlantic Richfield (Oil Refining)
- 158 Edison International (Utilities)
- 180 Northrop Grumman (Aerospace)
- 181 Foundation Health Systems (Health Care)
- 253 Computer Sciences (Computer and Data Services)
- 255 Occidental Petroleum (Mining and Crude Oil Production)
- 304 Unocal (Mining and Crude Oil Production)
- 331 Mattel (Toys and Sporting Goods)
- 343 Merisel (Wholesalers)
- 352 Dole Food (Food)
- 353 Litton Industries (Electronics)
- 380 Hilton Hotels (Hotels and Resorts)
- 430 Avery Dennison (Chemicals)
- 446 Times Mirror (Printing and Publishing)

Louisville, KY-IN
- 165 Humana (Health Care)
- 190 Tricon Global Restaurants (Food)
- 295 LG&E Energy (Utilities)
- 464 Vencor (Health Care)

Madison, WI
- 384 American Family (Property and Casualty Insurance)

Melbourne-Titusville-Palm Bay, FL
- 390 Harris (Electronics)

Memphis, TN-AR-MS
- 94 FedEx (Freight Delivery)
- 456 Autozone (Specialty Retailers)

Miami, FL
- 189 CHS Electronics (Wholesalers)
- 312 Ryder System (Automotive Retailing and Services)

Middlesex-Somerset-Hunterdon, NJ
- 37 Merck (Drugs)
- 51 Johnson & Johnson (Drugs)
- 243 Pharmacia & Upjohn (Drugs)
- 249 American Standard (Industrial and Farm Equipment)
- 263 Chubb (Property and Casualty Insurance)
- 339 Foster Wheeler (Engineering and Construction)

370 Engelhard (Chemicals)
415 Supermarkets General (Food and Drug Stores)
438 US Industries (Metal Products)

Milwaukee-Waukesha, WI
107 Northwestern Mutual (Life and Health Insurance)
131 Johnson Controls (Motor Vehicles)
183 Manpower (Temp Help)
413 Kohl's (General Merchandisers)
427 Firstar (Commercial Banking)

Minneapolis-St. Paul, MN-WI
30 Dayton Hudson (General Merchandisers)
84 United Healthcare (Health Care)
86 Supervalu (Wholesalers)
103 3M (Scientific Equipment)
171 St. Paul Companies (Property and Casualty Insurance)
175 Northwest (Airline)
193 Honeywell (Electronics)
195 Best Buy (Specialty Retailers)
215 US Bancorp (Commercial Banking)
272 General Mills (Food)
372 Nash Finch (Wholesalers)
483 Lutheran Brotherhood (Life and Health Insurance)

Nashville, TN
74 Columbia/HCA Healthcare (Health Care)
441 Service Merchandise (Specialty Retailers)
459 Dollar General (General Merchandisers)

New Orleans, LA
146 Entergy (Utilities)

New York, NY
6 IBM (Computers and Office Equipment)
7 Citigroup (Diversified Financial)
8 Philip Morris (Tobacco)
10 AT&T (Telecommunications)
18 TIAA-CREF (Securities)
19 Merrill Lynch (Securities)
22 American International (Property and Casualty Insurance)
23 Chase Manhattan (Commercial Banking)
24 Texaco (Oil Refining)
25 Bell Atlantic (Tele-communications)
29 Morgan Stanley Dean Witter (Securities)
39 Metropolitan Life (Life and Health Insurance)
54 Pepsico (Beverages)
60 Loews (Property and Casualty Insurance)
66 Lehman Brothers (Securities)
68 New York Life (Life and Health Insurance)
70 International Paper (Forest and Paper Products)
72 American Express (Diversified Financial)
76 J.P. Morgan (Commercial Banking)
77 Bristol-Myers Squibb (Drugs)
89 RJR Nabisco (Food)
106 Pfizer (Drugs)
108 Time Warner (Entertainment)
138 Viacom (Entertainment)
140 Bankers Trust (Commercial Banking)
172 CBS (Entertainment)
177 Colgate-Palmolive (Soaps and Cosmetics)
204 Bear Sterns (Securities)
205 Guardian (Life and Health Insurance)
220 ITT Industries (Industrial and Farm Equipment)
230 Paine Webber (Securities)
232 Marsh & McLennan (Diversified Financial)
239 Consolidated Edison (Utilities)
251 Amerada Hess (Oil Refining)
282 Cendant (Miscellaneous)
285 Bank of New York (Commercial Banking)
287 Venator (Specialty Retailers)
308 Avon Products (Soaps and Cosmetics)
324 Dover (Industrial and Farm Equipment)
327 Starwood Hotels & Resorts (Hotels and Resorts)
375 Turner (Engineering and Construction)
378 Omnicom (Advertising and Marketing)
387 Interpublic (Advertising and Marketing)
396 Marketspan (Utilities)
406 McGraw-Hill (Printing and Publishing)
417 Estee Lauder (Soaps and Cosmetics)
424 Republic New York (Commercial Banking)
437 Reliance (Property and Casualty Insurance)
482 United Auto (Automotive Retailing and Services)
489 Barnes & Noble (Specialty Retailers)
495 New York Times (Printing and Publishing)
499 Westvaco (Forest and Paper Products)

Newark, NJ
20 Prudential (Life and Health Insurance)
33 Lucent Technologies (Electronics)
100 AlliedSignal (Aerospace)
117 American Home Products (Drugs)
157 Warner-Lambert (Drugs)
200 Schering-Plough (Drugs)
274 Public Service Enterprise (Utilities)
328 ADP (Computer and Data)
364 GPU (General Merchandisers)

Norfolk-Virginia Beach-Newport News, VA-NC
351 Norfolk Southern (Railroads)
395 Smithfield Foods (Food)

Oakland, CA
48 Safeway (Food and Drug Stores)
450 Longs Drug Stores (Food and Drug Stores)
471 Golden West Financial (Savings Banks)

Oklahoma City, OK
101 Fleming (Wholesalers)

Omaha, NE-IA
50 Conagra (Food)
112 Berkshire Hathaway (Property and Casualty Insurance)
363 Inacom (Wholesalers)
399 Mutual of Omaha (Life and Health Insurance)
434 Peter Kiewit Sons (Engineering and Construction)

Orange County, CA
55 Ingram Micro (Wholesalers)
114 Bergen Brunswig (Wholesalers)
116 Fluor (Engineering and Construction)
167 Pacificare Health Systems (Health Care)
202 Rockwell International (Electronics)
373 Pacific Life (Life and Health Insurance)
423 Western Digital (Computer Peripherals)

Orlando, FL
448 Darden Restaurants (Food Services)

Peoria-Pekin, IL
58 Caterpillar (Industrial and Farm Equipment)

Philadelphia, PA-NJ
- 57 Cigna (Health Care)
- 188 Amerisource Health (Wholesalers)
- 198 Crown Cork & Seal (Metal Products)
- 222 Campbell Soup (Food)
- 225 Unisource (Wholesalers)
- 231 UNISYS (Computer and Data Services)
- 240 Sunoco (Oil Refining)
- 262 Aramark (Diversified Outsourcing Services)
- 291 Ikon Office Solutions (Wholesalers)
- 292 Comcast (Specialty Retailers)
- 309 PECO Energy (Utilities)
- 408 Rohm & Haas (Chemicals)

Phoenix-Mesa, AZ
- 275 Avnet (Wholesalers)
- 297 Microage (Wholesalers)
- 479 Phelps Dodge (Metals)

Pittsburgh, PA
- 47 USX (Oil Refining)
- 96 Alcoa (Metals)
- 170 H.J. Heinz (Food)
- 209 PNC Bank (Commercial Banking)
- 221 PPG Industries (Chemicals)
- 283 Mellon Bank (Commercial Banking)
- 391 Allegheny Teledyne (Metals)
- 420 Consolidated Natural Gas (Utilities)
- 485 Wesco International (Wholesalers)

Portland, ME
- 337 UNUM (Life and Health Insurance)
- 442 Hannaford Brothers (Food and Drug Stores)

Portland-Vancouver, OR-WA
- 104 Fred Meyer (Food and Drug Stores)
- 166 Nike (Apparel)
- 168 Pacificorp (Utilities)
- 410 Willamette Industries (Forest and Paper Products)

Providence-Fall River-Warwick, RI-MA
- 99 CVS (Food and Drug Stores)
- 144 Textron (Aerospace)
- 445 Hasbro (Toys and Sporting Goods)

Racine, WI
- 269 Case (Industrial and Farm Equipment)

Raleigh-Durham-Chapel Hill, NC
- 465 Carolina P&L (Utilities)

Richmond-Petersburg, VA
- 162 CSX (Railroads)
- 182 Circuit City (Specialty Retailers)
- 271 Dominion Resources (Utilities)
- 281 Reynolds Metals (Metals)
- 361 Universal (Tobacco)
- 403 Pittston (Freight Delivery)
- 462 Richfood (Wholesalers)
- 474 Owens & Minor (Wholesalers)

Riverside-San Bernardino, CA
- 457 United States Filter (Industrial and Farm Equipment)
- 481 Fleetwood Enterprises (Engineering and Construction)

Rochester, NY
- 121 Eastman Kodak (Scientific Equipment)

Saginaw-Bay City-Midland, MI
- 75 Dow Chemical (Chemicals)

Salt Lake City-Ogden, UT
- 67 American Stores (Food and Drug Stores)
- 428 Autoliv (Motor Vehicles)

San Antonio, TX
- 35 SBC Communications (Telecommunications)
- 196 Ultramar Diamond Shamrock (Oil Refining)
- 214 United Services (Property and Casualty Insurance)
- 294 Valero Energy (Oil Refining)

San Diego, CA
- 223 Gateway 2000 (Computers and Office Equipment)
- 296 Sempra Energy (Utilities)
- 347 Science Applications (Wholesalers)
- 440 Qualcomm (Electronics)

San Francisco, CA
- 38 Chevron (Oil Refining)
- 59 McKesson (Wholesalers)
- 62 Wells Fargo (Commercial Banking)
- 65 PG&E (Utilities)
- 174 Gap (Specialty Retailers)
- 234 Oracle (Software)
- 261 Transamerica (Life and Health Insurance)
- 313 Airtouch Communications (Telecommunications)
- 435 Charles Schwab (Securities)
- 484 Golden State Bancorp (Savings Banks)

San Jose, CA
- 14 Hewlett-Packard (Computers and Office Equipment)
- 40 Intel (Semiconductors)

- 53 Walt Disney (Entertainment)
- 164 Sun Microsystems (Computers and Office Equipment)
- 192 Cisco Systems (Network Communications)
- 273 Apple Computer (Computers and Office Equipment)
- 284 Quantum (Computer Peripherals)
- 303 3Com (Network Communications)
- 306 Solectron (Electronics)
- 321 CNF Transportation (Trucking)
- 382 Applied Materials (Scientific Equipment)
- 470 Silicon Graphics (Computers and Office Equipment)
- 472 Knight-Ridder (Printing and Publishing)

Santa Barbara-Santa Maria-Lompoc, CA
- 163 Tenet Healthcare Systems (Health Care)

Santa Cruz-Watsonville, CA
- 244 Seagate Technology (Computer Peripherals)

Seattle-Bellevue-Everett, WA
- 9 Boeing (Aerospace)
- 49 Costco (Specialty Retailers)
- 128 Washington Mutual (Savings Banks)
- 152 Weyerhaeuser (Forest and Paper Products)
- 210 PACCAR (Motor Vehicles)
- 260 Safeco (Property and Casualty Insurance)
- 318 Nordstrom (General Merchandisers)
- 475 Airborne Freight (Freight Delivery)

Sioux City, IA-NE
- 126 IBP (Food)

Spokane, WA
- 412 Avista (Utilities)

Springfield, MA
- 153 Massachusetts Mutual (Life and Health Insurance)

St. Louis, MO-IL
- 118 Emerson Electric (Electronics)
- 120 May Department Stores (General Merchandisers)
- 150 Anheuser-Busch (Beverages)
- 187 Monsanto (Chemicals)
- 293 Ralston Purina (Food)
- 392 Genamerica (Life and Health Insurance)
- 404 Graybar Electric (Wholesalers)

Jobs

191

414 Clark USA (Oil Refining)
444 Ameren (Utilities)
454 Trans World Airlines (Airline)
496 Mercantile Bancorp (Commercial Banking)

Stamford-Norwalk, CT
63 Xerox (Computers and Office Equipment)
141 Tosco (Oil Refining)
219 Tenneco (Wholesalers)
224 Nebco Evans (Food Services)
289 Champion International (Forest and Paper Products)
329 Fortune Brands (Metal Products)
334 Oxford Health Plans (Health Care)
359 Pitney Bowes (Computers, Office Equipment)

Syracuse, NY
398 Niagara Mohawk Power (Utilities)

Tampa-St. Petersburg-Clearwater, FL
145 Tech Data (Wholesalers)
416 Florida Progress (Utilities)

Toledo, OH
127 Dana (Motor Vehicles)
302 Owens-Illinois (Building Materials)
319 Owens Corning (Building Materials)

Tulsa, OK
216 Williams (Pipelines)

Ventura, CA
256 Wellpoint Health Networks (Health Care)

Washington, DC-MD-VA-WV
13 Mobil (Oil Refining)
26 Fannie Mae (Diversified Financial)
41 Lockheed Martin (Aerospace)
79 Freddie Mac (Diversified Financial)
186 US Airways (Airline)
206 Marriott (Hotels and Resorts)
247 Sodexho Marriott Services (Diversified Outsourcing)
257 Columbia Energy (Utilities)
315 Gannett (Printing and Publishing)

320 General Dynamics (Aerospace)
367 Giant Food (Food and Drug Stores)
419 US Office Products (Wholesalers)
425 Host Marriott (Hotels and Resorts)
431 Hechinger (Specialty Retailers)
478 SLM Holdings (Diversified Financial)
498 Danaher (Metal Products)

West Palm Beach-Boca Raton, FL
176 Office Depot (Specialty Retailers)
248 FPL (Utilities)

Wilmington-Newark, DE-MD
16 Du Pont (Chemicals)
310 MBNA (Commercial Banking)
477 Conectiv (Utilities)

Worcester, MA-CT
236 Staples (Specialty Retailers)
433 AllAmerica Financial (Property and Casualty Insurance)

York, PA
447 York International (Industrial and Farm Equipment)

Source: Fortune © 1999.

LEGAL HOLIDAYS

The United States has no national holidays. A day off on Independence Day, Thanksgiving, or Christmas comes by the grace of local state legislatures rather than by presidential proclamations or acts of Congress.

The only thing *national* about the U.S. holiday calendar are the 10 days off given to everyone who works for the federal government: five fixed dates—Christmas, Independence Day, Labor Day, New Year's Day, and Thanksgiving—and five Mondays—Columbus Day, Memorial Day, Veterans Day, Washington's Birthday, and Martin Luther King Day.

The first four holiday Mondays were approved in 1968 to create predictable long weekends. The fifth, approved in 1986, honors Martin Luther King, Jr., on the third Monday of January.

If any of the fixed dates fall on Saturday, the Friday before is the holiday; if any fall on Sunday, the next day, Monday, is the holiday.

Most states observe federal legal holidays, and, depending on where you are, they commemorate 72 local ones as well. The Civil War era produced more events and heroes to honor with days off than any other period in American history. However, they aren't all celebrated nationwide. Just as no former secessionist state takes notice of Lincoln's birthday, so none of the Union states honor Robert E. Lee's birthday.

In contrast, the Canadian provinces celebrate ten national holidays in harmony with the terms of Canada's Holidays Act. Four days—Christmas, Labour Day, New Year's Day, and Remembrance Day (formerly Armistice Day, as was the U.S.'s Veterans Day)—may be said to be North American holidays since they are celebrated on the same date for the same reason throughout the United States. Again, depending on where you are in Canada, some fifteen local holidays are observed as well.

JANUARY

Fixed Dates

January 1, *New Year's Day:* All states and Canadian provinces

Movable Feasts

Third Monday, *Civil Rights Day:* New Hampshire

Third Monday, *Confederate Heroes Day/Martin Luther King Day:* Texas

Third Monday, *Lee-Jackson-King Day:* Virginia

Third Monday, *Martin Luther King Day:* 45 states

Third Monday, *Robert E. Lee's Birthday/Martin Luther King Day:* Alabama, Arkansas, and Mississippi

Third Monday, *Wyoming Equality Day:* Wyoming

FEBRUARY

Fixed Dates

February 2, *Groundhog Day:* Non-holiday observance

February 12, *Lincoln's Birthday:* California, Colorado, Connecticut, Florida, Illinois, Iowa, Maryland, Michigan, Missouri, New Jersey, New York, Pennsylvania, Vermont, Washington, and West Virginia

February 14, *Valentine's Day:* Non-holiday observance

Movable Feasts

First Monday, Lincoln's Birthday: Oregon

Third Monday, President's Day/Washington's Birthday: All states except Alabama, Indiana, and Louisiana

Third Monday, Alberta Family Day: Alberta

Tuesday before Ash Wednesday, Mardi Gras: Alabama, Florida (some counties), and Louisiana (some parishes)

MARCH

Fixed Dates

March 2, Texas Independence Day: Texas

March 17, Evacuation Day: Massachusetts (Suffolk County only)

March 17, St. Patrick's Day: Non-holiday observance

March 25, Maryland Day: Maryland

March 26, Prince Jonah Kuhio Kalanianaole Day: Hawaii

March 31, Cesar Chavez Day: California

Movable Feasts

First Monday, Casimir Pulaski's Birthday: Illinois

First Tuesday, Town Meeting Day: Vermont

Second Monday, Commonwealth Day: Newfoundland

Nearest Monday to March 17, St. Patrick's Day: Newfoundland

Last Monday, Seward's Day: Alaska

APRIL

Fixed Dates

April 1, *April Fool's Day:* Non-holiday observance

April 21, *San Jacinto Day:* Texas

Movable Feasts

Two days before Easter, *Good Friday:* California, Connecticut, Delaware, Hawaii, Illinois, Indiana, Kentucky, Louisiana, Maryland, New Jersey, North Carolina, North Dakota, Pennsylvania, and all Canadian provinces

One day after Easter, *Easter Monday:* All Canadian provinces except British Columbia

Third Monday, *Patriots' Day:* Maine and Massachusetts

Nearest Monday to April 23, *St. George's Day:* Newfoundland

Fourth Monday, *Confederate Memorial Day:* Alabama, Georgia, and Mississippi

Last Friday, *Arbor Day:* Nebraska

MAY

Fixed Dates

May 4, Rhode Island Independence Day: Rhode Island

May 8, Truman Day: Missouri

May 11, Minnesota Day: Minnesota

May 20, Mecklenburg Independence Day: North Carolina

Movable Feasts

First Monday before May 25, Victoria Day and the Sovereign's Birthday: All Canadian provinces

Second Sunday, Mother's Day: Non-holiday observance

Last Monday, Memorial Day: All states

JUNE

Fixed Dates

June 9, *Senior Citizens Day:* Non-holiday observance, Oklahoma

June 11, *King Kamehameha I Day:* Hawaii

June 14, *Flag Day:* Pennsylvania

June 15, *Separation Day:* Non-holiday observance, Delaware

June 17, *Bunker Hill Day:* Massachusetts (Suffolk County only)

June 19, *Emancipation Day:* Texas

June 20, *West Virginia Day:* West Virginia

June 24, *Discovery Day:* Newfoundland; *Quebec Day:* Quebec

continues

Jobs

Movable Feasts

Nearest Monday to June 24, *Discovery Day:* Newfoundland

Third Sunday, *Father's Day:* Non-holiday observance

JULY

Fixed Dates

July 1, *Canada Day:* All Canadian provinces

July 4, *Independence Day:* All states

July 24, *Pioneer Day:* Utah

Movable Feasts

Nearest Monday to July 12, *Orangemen's Day:* Newfoundland

AUGUST

Fixed Dates

August 5, Colorado Day: Colorado

August 16, Bennington Battle Day: Vermont

August 27, Lyndon Johnson's Birthday: Texas

August 30, Huey Long Day: Louisiana

Movable Feasts

First Monday, *British Columbia Day:* British Columbia

First Monday, *Civic Holiday:* Manitoba, Ontario, and Saskatchewan

First Monday, *Halifax and Dartmouth Natal Day:* Nova Scotia

First Monday, *Heritage Day:* Alberta

First Monday, *New Brunswick Day:* New Brunswick

Second Monday, *Victory Day:* Rhode Island

Third Friday, *Admission Day:* Hawaii

SEPTEMBER

Fixed Dates

September 9, *Admission Day:* California

September 12, *Defenders' Day:* Maryland

September 16, *Cherokee Strip Day:* Oklahoma

Movable Feasts

First Monday, *Labor Day:* All states and Canadian provinces

First Saturday after full moon, *Indian Day:* Oklahoma

OCTOBER

Fixed Dates

October 12, *Columbus Day:* Maryland

October 18, *Alaska Day:* Alaska

October 31, *Halloween:* Non-holiday observance

October 31, *Nevada Day:* Nevada

Movable Feasts

Second Monday, *Columbus Day:* All states except Arkansas, Iowa, Louisiana, Mississippi, and Nevada

Second Monday, *Native American Day:* South Dakota and Wyoming

Second Monday, *Thanksgiving Day:* All Canadian provinces

NOVEMBER

Fixed Dates

November 1, *All Saints' Day:* Louisiana

November 4, *Will Rogers Day:* Oklahoma

November 11, *Veterans Day:* All states

November 11, *Remembrance Day:* All Canadian provinces

Movable Feasts

First Tuesday after first Monday, *Election Day:* District of Columbia, Delaware, Hawaii, Illinois, Louisiana, Maryland, Montana, New Hampshire, New Jersey, New York, Pennsylvania, Rhode Island, South Carolina, and Wyoming

Fourth Thursday: *Thanksgiving:* All states

Friday after Thanksgiving: California, Georgia, Delaware, Maryland, and Nevada

DECEMBER

Fixed Dates

December 7, *Delaware Day:* Non-holiday observance, Delaware

December 10, *Wyoming Day:* Wyoming

December 24, *Christmas Eve:* Arkansas, Delaware, Georgia, Indiana, Kentucky, Michigan, North Carolina, Nova Scotia, Texas, and West Virginia

December 25, *Christmas Day:* All states and Canadian provinces

December 26, *Boxing Day:* North Carolina, South Carolina, Texas, and all Canadian provinces

December 31, *New Years Eve:* West Virginia

Legal Holidays

Education

Nine months of the year, three of every ten of us either work in an educational institution or learn in one. Keeping the enterprise going is the biggest item on city budgets. Whether the results are worth it is an excuse for teachers, administrators, parents, politicians, and taxpayers to raise their voices with one another occasionally.

Education isn't the sacred cow it once was. The scores of high school students on most standardized tests aren't much better today than they were in 1960. Among high school seniors, a surprising portion can't draw inferences from written material, write a persuasive essay, or solve a math problem requiring several steps.

Parents and teachers blame each other. Although the public trusts teachers more than they do politicians, journalists, or business people, teachers don't get high marks. For their part, teachers are even stingier graders: Most parents, they say, are too tired and uninterested to get involved in their child's schooling.

PUBLIC SCHOOLS

Economists comparing homes among neighborhoods know price differences have less to do with a well-designed, well-built house and a lot to do with how good the schools are. The quality of the schools usually tips the balance when a relocating family weighs a neighborhood's good and bad points. Often their choice is influenced by a real estate agent's hearsay that the schools are great or ought to be because the local tax rate is high. Are there ways to compare districts and schools more objectively?

Shopping for a District

A sign of the times: In some of Long Island's school districts, local cops check the addresses of children and discover imposters who live in New York City taking up seats in suburban schools. To meet residency requirements, parents register their kids under the addresses of relatives or friends.

Elsewhere, a new Illinois law makes fudging school registration to get children into a better district a misdemeanor punishable by 30 days in jail, a fine, and tuition restitution. In eastern Pennsylvania, districts routinely require parents to re-enroll their children to weed out interlopers from over the border in New Jersey.

In the 1930s, North America was fragmented into 130,000 school districts. After decades of consolidation, there are fewer than 15,000 in the United States and 1,000 in Canada. They range in size from hundreds that don't actually operate schools—but bus children to other districts—to the giants.

Moving into an unfamiliar area means stepping into a thicket of school districts, each with its own politics, funding, philosophy, standards, curricula, and results. Since your taxes support the district, you'll want to find out their differences with a consumer's eye. Visit the district principal or superintendent's office and consider several factors:

- A good district can give you a written philosophy or a statement of educational objectives approved within the past 5 years by the state board of education. If educational philosophy and objectives are explicit and under constant examination and review, then a district takes its mission seriously.

- The classroom teachers in the district should have not only a standard certificate but also (in 50 percent of the cases or better) at least a master's degree or equivalent in the subject they teach.

- A district's holding power—that is, the percentage of its ninth-grade pupils who stay in school and finish—should be at least 90 percent. If 95 percent of a district's enrollment is in average daily attendance, that's a good indication of how closely parents and schools keep tabs on children.

- Beware of the professional revolving door. A high number of eligible teachers not getting tenure might mean that the district has tough standards, but it could also be a sign that the district cuts costs by hiring beginners and then refusing them tenure at the end of their probationary period. Under this scheme, it is possible for a child to progress from kindergarten through high school and have inexperienced, unfamiliar teachers each year.

Shopping for a School

Outside Washington, DC, in late summer, days before the Prince Georges County school district throws open a single window, parents bring lawn chairs, paperbacks, and blankets to register children in choice magnet schools on a first-come, first-served basis.

Moving into a good school district doesn't necessarily mean you'll find quality education in all its schools.

Get a district map of neighborhood boundaries for the schools as well as a list of Parent-Teacher Association (PTA) contacts. Talking with a local parent will save you time. Don't listen to administrators and guidance counselors who claim it's the curriculum that counts, not the teacher. Find out who the best teachers are and where they teach. Then make an appointment with their school's principal or the head guidance counselor to get specific information. Note the following:

- A good high school should have one guidance counselor for every 200 students, and it should have at least one full-time career counselor.

- Classroom size in high school should average no more than 30 students. The size of the senior class shouldn't be smaller than 300 students. If the enrollment is much less than that, many worthwhile specialized courses won't be offered.

- A quality high school should offer 4 years of English, 3 years of mathematics, 3 years of science, 3 years of social studies, and 2 years of foreign languages; second-year courses in biology, astronomy, chemistry, and physics; college-preparatory courses in the humanities; at least 1 year of computer literacy; and Advanced Placement (AP) courses for college credit.

- Because one of five 4-year public colleges must accept every high school graduate within the state, regardless of program followed or grades earned, it is no longer noteworthy that most of a high school's graduating seniors go on to college. The question to ask is: Which colleges are accepting them—top schools with tough admissions standards, or open-admission institutions with no requirements but that the check be good and the diploma in hand?

Don't cross a high school off your list if it doesn't measure up on all these points. A school can have all but one or two and still be a good one. Relocation experts advise clients that the stability of a town is reflected best in its schools. If the high school is good, chances are that the schools at the lower levels will also be good.

In choosing an elementary school or a junior high, again ask questions of principals and other parents.

- Class size in elementary schools should average no more than 20 pupils. Reading should be emphasized over all other subjects, but writing,

NORTH AMERICA'S 50 LARGEST SCHOOL DISTRICTS

Representing less than 1 percent of all school districts, these systems educate one of every six public school students. While they are large enough to offer specialized courses and activities, two other items stand out: They operate larger schools (700 students compared to 500 in the average district) and they have a higher pupil/teacher ratio (19 to 1 compared to 16.5 to 1).

School System	Enrollment	School System	Enrollment
New York City Public Schools	1,071,853	Peel Board of Education (Mississauga, ON)	98,987
Los Angeles Unified District	680,430	Charlotte/Mecklenburg County Schools	95,795
City of Chicago Schools	477,610	Gwinnett County (GA) Schools	93,509
Dade County (Miami)	345,958	De Kalb County (GA) Schools	91,864
Broward County (Fort Lauderdale)	224,799	Wake County (Raleigh, NC) Schools	89,772
Philadelphia City Schools	221,865	Commission des Ecoles Catholiques (Montreal)	88,654
Houston Independent School District	210,988	Cobb County (Marietta, GA) Schools	88,266
Clark County (Las Vegas)	190,822	Jefferson County (CO) Schools	88,006
Hawaii Department of Education	188,887	Albuquerque Public Schools	87,274
Detroit Public Schools	174,730	Long Beach (CA) Unified District	85,908
Dallas Independent School District	157,622	Orleans Parish (New Orleans)	83,175
Hillsborough County (Tampa)	152,781	Scarborough (ON) Board of Education	79,813
Fairfax County (VA) Schools	145,722	Fresno Unified District	78,166
Palm Beach County (FL) Schools	142,724	Virginia Beach City Schools	77,521
San Diego Unified District	136,283	District of Columbia Schools	77,111
Orange County (Orlando) Schools	133,826	Fort Worth Independent School District	76,901
Prince Georges County (MD) Schools	128,347	Austin Independent School District	76,606
Duval County (Jacksonville) Schools	126,979	Cleveland City Schools	76,504
Montgomery County (MD) Schools	125,023	Polk County (FL) Schools	76,497
Memphis City School District	111,227	Granite (Salt Lake City) District	74,956
Metropolitan (Toronto) Separate Board	109,581	Ann Arundel County (MD) Schools	73,363
Pinellas County (St. Petersburg)	109,309	Jordan (Sandy, UT) District	73,181
Baltimore City Schools	107,416	Mesa (AZ) Unified School District	69,764
Baltimore County Public Schools	104,708	Brevard County (FL) Schools	67,879
Jefferson County (Louisville)	104,338	Denver County (CO) Schools	67,858
Milwaukee School District	101,253		

Source: U.S. Department of Education, Places Rated Partnership survey.

problem solving in math, hands-on work in science, and the social studies curriculum should get their due.

- In elementary schools, there should be a full-time librarian and a classroom-size library. There should also be one large room or auditorium for school meetings, arts performances, and special guest presentations.

- In junior high or middle schools—grades 7, 8, and 9—there should be special provisions for both bright students and slow learners.

PRIVATE SCHOOLS

One statistic about elementary and secondary education in the United States since 1930 is the nearly 100 percent growth in the number of private schools, in contrast to the 75 percent decline in the number of public schools. This isn't to say that the public schools are collapsing; most of the schools that have closed were rural, one-room buildings. But it does show that private schools are a thriving alternative.

Today, one of nine school-age children attends a private or parochial school. In spite of the decline in school

CATHOLIC PRIVATE SCHOOLS

Whatever the reason—religious content, cultural tradition, dress codes, discipline, more rigorous education—at least one of eight children attends a Catholic private school in these metro areas.

Dubuque, IA	33%
Philadelphia, PA-NJ	21
New Orleans, LA	18
Erie, PA	18
Owensboro, KY	17
Cincinnati, OH-KY-IN	16
Toledo, OH	15
Cleveland-Lorain-Elyria, OH	14
Johnstown, PA	14
Springfield, IL	14
Buffalo-Niagara Falls, NY	13
Green Bay, WI	13
Louisville, KY-IN	13
San Francisco, CA	13
Waterloo-Cedar Falls, IA	13
Wausau, WI	13
Wilmington-Newark, DE-MD	13

Source: CMG Information Services.

The percentage of children attending Catholic schools in several Canadian metro areas is much higher than the list above. These are *public* schools, however, operating under separate Catholic school boards.

enrollments during the 1980s, private schools held on to more of their enrollment than did public schools. Today, enrollment is on the rise in both sectors.

Recent research from the Department of Education shows that students in private high schools take more courses in smaller classes than do their public school counterparts. Critics of public education point out that because private institutions forego the smorgasbord of electives that public schools offer their students, graduates of private high schools have tougher basic courses on their transcripts and are better prepared for college study.

In most Canadian provinces, Catholic schools are publicly funded and run by separate school boards. In the United States, Catholic schools are the private school alternative with the biggest enrollment (2.4 million pupils).

Although half of all private school pupils sit in Catholic school classrooms, two of every three private schools are non-Catholic. Some 1.7 million pupils attend schools run by groups such as the Evangelical Lutheran Church, the Seventh-Day Adventist Board of Education, and the National Society for Hebrew Day Schools. Non-sectarian schools enroll another 800,000 pupils, most of whom pay tuition to institutions belonging to the National Association of Independent Schools (NAIS).

THE PUBLIC LIBRARY

At a bank of Internet terminals at a public library's main branch, you may see a cab driver researching family genealogy on your left. On your right, a high school senior is investigating jobs with the airlines. Behind you, a stack of Mexico City newspapers wait on a reshelving cart. And in front, an acre of tables is piled with briefcases and bookbags where people sit reading.

Every metro area, no matter how small, poor, or isolated, has a network of public libraries. More than any of the different education institutions mentioned in this chapter, the library is a vital center and ultimate education resource for everyone.

Within greater New York's five boroughs and suburban Putnam, Rockland, and Westchester counties, there are 66 library systems acquiring 2 million books each year to add to the 37 million already housed in 275 libraries. Immense as this sounds, that's one book for every five people. Other metro areas do better; small ones in the inner South and in Texas do a lot worse.

COLLEGES AND UNIVERSITIES

Educators like to say that schooling leads to just three outcomes: more schooling, employment, or unemployment. When high school graduates go on to college or find jobs, the public education system is considered successful; if they do neither, the system is judged a flop.

In fact, nearly half of metro-area high school graduates eventually go to college, and seven of ten of these begin their freshman year at an institution within 50 miles of home.

More Than an Education

Everywhere from Abilene to Yuma, chamber of commerce promotional brochures tout local colleges and universities more frequently than other urban assets—and with good reason. Among the 20 million students taking college courses, 15 million are studying in metro areas. For 21 million other people, the typical location

NORTH AMERICA'S 20 LARGEST COMMUNITY COLLEGES

About one in four people going on to college after high school attends a community college. Almost all institutions are publicly supported. Many of the largest ones below have several campuses.

College	Students
Miami-Dade Community College	47,060
Houston Community College System	39,541
Northern Virginia Community College	37,144
College of Du Page (Glen Ellyn, IL)	29,888
Pima Community College (Tucson)	27,866
Portland (OR) Community College	26,540
City College of San Francisco	26,019
Tarrant County Junior College (Ft. Worth)	25,953
Oakland Community College (Bloomfield, MI)	25,913
Broward Community College (Ft. Lauderdale)	25,738
Austin Community College	25,620
Macomb Community College (Warren, MI)	25,176
Valencia Community College (Orlando)	23,569
Cuyahoga Community College (Cleveland)	22,785
De Anza College (Cupertino, CA)	22,545
Mount San Antonio College (Walnut, CA)	22,202
Milwaukee Area Technical College	21,903
El Paso Community College	21,856
Nassau Community College (Garden City, NY)	21,737
El Camino College (Torrance, CA)	21,540

Source: Statistics Canada, Universities: Enrollment and Degrees; U.S. Department of Education, Directory of Postsecondary Institutions.

NORTH AMERICA'S 20 LARGEST UNIVERSITIES

Some 15 million people attend baccalaureate and graduate-level institutions in the United States and Canada. In a shift from the past in both countries, slightly more women than men enroll and a good many more women than men graduate. Below are the continent's largest universities.

University	Students
University of Minnesota, Minneapolis	51,445
University of Toronto, Toronto	50,381
Ohio State University, Columbus	48,676
University of Texas, Austin	47,905
Arizona State University, Tempe	42,040
Texas A&M University, College Station	41,790
Michigan State University, East Lansing	40,647
Université de Québec, Montreal	39,964
Pennsylvania State University, State College	39,646
University of Florida, Gainesville	39,412
Université de Montréal, Montreal	39,236
University of Wisconsin, Madison	39,005
York University, North York	38,865
University of Illinois, Champaign-Urbana	38,420
Université Laval, Quebec City	38,115
University of Michigan, Ann Arbor	36,687
Purdue University, West Lafayette	36,427
University of South Florida, Tampa	36,142
New York University, New York	35,835
Indiana University, Bloomington	35,063

Source: Statistics Canada, Universities: Enrollment and Degrees; U.S. Department of Education, Directory of Postsecondary Institutions.

Education

for their evening or weekend continuing education course is a local college classroom.

Colleges and universities contribute other things besides education. In smaller metro areas, a worthy theater where a touring group of professional players can stage *Playboy of the Western World* or an auditorium where an orchestra and choral group can perform Handel's *Messiah* can only be found at the local college campus.

Colleges and universities are stable white-collar employers, too. In Iowa City, IA, Lawrence, KS, and Tuscaloosa, AL, they are *the* major employers.

Finally, there is the connection between research-oriented universities and healthy economies. Two historic examples are Stanford University's impetus to the growth

of Silicon Valley high-tech enterprises in the San Jose and Bay Area environs, and MIT's faculty and alumni who started electronics firms along Route 128 outside Boston.

Half of the nearly 4,000 higher education institutions in North America are Associate of Arts colleges. Otherwise known as community or junior colleges, these institutions offer associate of arts certificates or degree programs (but no baccalaureate degrees) to 10 million full- and part-time students. Several of the larger institutions take in more students than all but the largest state universities.

Eight hundred forty-five *baccalaureate* institutions enroll 937,000 full- and part-time students. These

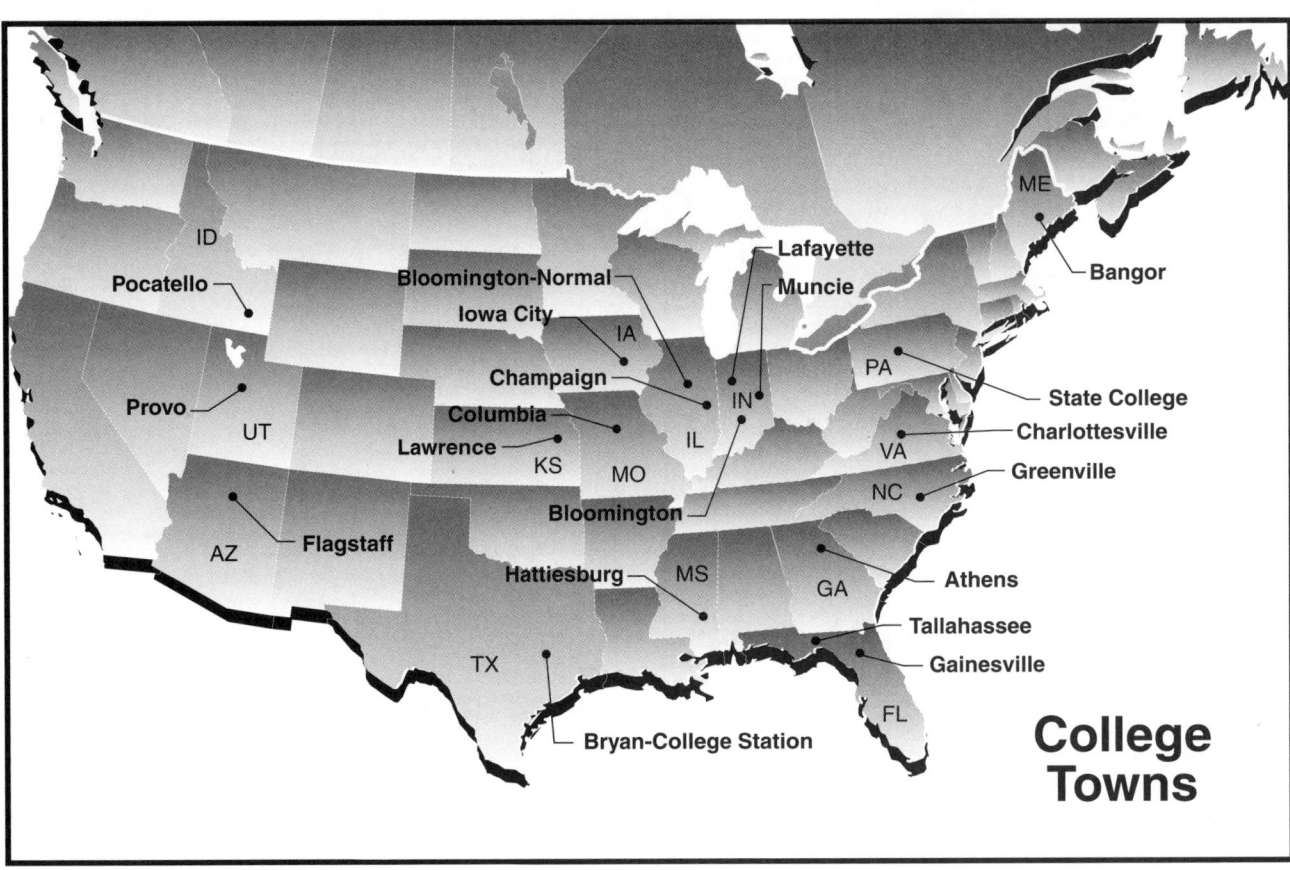

ME

Lafayette

Bloomington-Normal
Muncie

Iowa City
IA
Bangor

ID

Pocatello

Champaign
PA

Provo
Columbia
State College

UT
Lawrence
IN
Charlottesville

KS
IL
VA

MO
Greenville

NC

Bloomington

Flagstaff

AZ
Hattiesburg
MS
Athens

GA

Tallahassee

Gainesville

TX
FL

Bryan-College Station

**College
Towns**

Copyright © 2000 by Places Rated Partnership

Cape Ann Mapping

colleges are undergraduate-level institutions exclusively; their highest offering is the bachelor's degree. They are typically private, although the largest baccalaureate college is public: Provo-Orem's Utah Valley State College with 26,000 students

Comprehensive institutions enroll another 3 million full- and part-time students. Of 1,017 in North America, the largest by far are branches of the California State University system. Comprehensive universities and colleges are mainly undergraduate institutions, although their highest offering is the master's degree.

Doctoral universities award the Ph.D. as their highest degree. These institutions tend to be public and large. With 686 campuses, they enroll well over 5 million full- and part-time students.

SCORING: EDUCATION

In profiling metro-area education features, *Places Rated* details the local mix of public and private schools, libraries, and public and private colleges and universities. To rate each area, four criteria are considered:

School Support combines metro-area averages for the number of pupils per classroom teacher (the fewer the better) and the percent of funding the schools receive from local—as opposed to state and federal—sources (the more the better).

Library Popularity winners include Canadian metro areas and smaller American areas around the Great Lakes. Losers include the inner south and interior California. The number of books on library shelves tells half the

story of a place's reading habits. How much use those volumes get, or the metro area's circulation rate, is the other half. When the circulation figure is added to the number of volumes, and that sum divided by the population served, the result is Library Popularity.

College Town is enrollment weighted by number of years of typical attendance to get the highest degree offered (that is, associate of arts enrollment is weighted by 2, baccalaureate enrollment by 4, comprehensive enrollment by 6, and doctoral enrollment by 9). This large number is then divided by the metro area's population. As the map shows, places like Byran-College Station, Iowa City, Lawrence, and Columbia (MO) come out very high on this criterion. But there's only one game in town in Bryan-College Station (Texas A&M), in Lawrence (University of Kansas), and in Columbia (University of Missouri). Something else is needed to reward higher education variety.

College Options, the fourth criterion, is the variety of higher education institutions that meet the needs of residents: low-cost night and weekend continuing education courses for people who work, full-time graduate courses in the professions, courses leading to occupational certification in 2-year colleges, and the traditional bachelor's degree curriculum offered in a college or university. Here, the top-ranking places are New York, Chicago, Toronto, and Los Angeles.

Combining these factors by weighing College Options four times as heavily as College Town, and College Town twice as much as either School Support or Library Popularity, produces the score.

RANKINGS: EDUCATION

The following criteria are used to rate a metro area for education opportunities available to residents: (1) School Support, (2) Library Popularity, (3) College Town, and (4) College Options. Places with tie scores get the same rank and are listed alphabetically.

Metro Areas from Best to Worst

RANK	SCORE
1. Raleigh-Durham-Chapel Hill, NC	100.00
2. Boston, MA-NH	99.71
3. Albany-Schenectady-Troy, NY	99.43
4. St. Louis, MO-IL	99.15
5. Chicago, IL	98.86
6. Rochester, NY	98.58
7. Austin-San Marcos, TX	98.30
8. San Francisco, CA	98.01
9. Washington, DC-MD-VA-WV	97.73
10. Saskatoon, SK	97.45
11. Dayton-Springfield, OH	96.88
12. Portland-Vancouver, OR-WA	96.88
13. Cincinnati, OH-KY-IN	96.60
14. Des Moines, IA	96.31
15. Kansas City, MO-KS	96.03
16. Milwaukee-Waukesha, WI	95.75
17. Minneapolis-St. Paul, MN-WI	95.46
18. Columbus, OH	95.18
19. Trenton, NJ	94.90
20. New York, NY	94.61
21. Syracuse, NY	94.33
22. Baltimore, MD	94.05
23. Newark, NJ	93.76
24. Lexington, KY	93.48
25. Oklahoma City, OK	93.20
26. Madison, WI	92.91
27. Buffalo-Niagara Falls, NY	92.63
28. Columbia, SC	92.35
29. Denver, CO	92.06
30. Springfield, MO	91.78
31. Springfield, MA	91.50
32. Hartford, CT	91.21
33. Halifax, NS	90.93
34. New Haven-Meriden, CT	90.65
35. Bangor, ME	90.36
36. Dallas, TX	90.08
37. Philadelphia, PA-NJ	89.80
38. Huntsville, AL	89.51

RANK	SCORE
39. Portland, ME	89.23
40. Cleveland-Lorain-Elyria, OH	88.95
41. Providence-Fall River-Warwick, RI-MA	88.66
42. Lincoln, NE	88.38
43. Greensboro-Winston-Salem-High Point, NC	88.10
44. Omaha, NE-IA	87.81
45. South Bend, IN	87.53
46. San Jose, CA	87.25
47. Honolulu, HI	86.96
48. Norfolk-Virginia Beach-Newport News, VA-NC	86.68
49. Vancouver, BC	86.40
50. Seattle-Bellevue-Everett, WA	86.11
51. Duluth-Superior, MN-WI	85.83
52. Louisville, KY-IN	85.55
53. Toledo, OH	85.26
54. Phoenix-Mesa, AZ	84.98
55. Regina, SK	84.70
56. Oakland, CA	84.41
57. Nashville, TN	84.13
58. Indianapolis, IN	83.85
59. Charlotte-Gastonia-Rock Hill, NC-SC	83.56
60. Montreal, PQ	83.28
61. Ann Arbor, MI	83.00
62. Atlanta, GA	82.71
63. Worcester, MA-CT	82.43
64. La Crosse, WI-MN	82.15
65. Scranton-Wilkes-Barre-Hazleton, PA	81.86
66. Knoxville, TN	81.58
67. Salt Lake City-Ogden, UT	81.30
68. Santa Fe, NM	81.01
69. Birmingham, AL	80.73
70. Colorado Springs, CO	80.45
71. Dubuque, IA	80.16
72. Fort Wayne, IN	79.88
73. San Diego, CA	79.60
74. Grand Rapids-Muskegon-Holland, MI	79.32
75. Manchester, NH	79.03

continues

Metro Areas from Best to Worst (cont.)

RANK	SCORE	RANK	SCORE
76. London, ON	78.75	137. Melbourne-Titusville-Palm Bay, FL	61.47
77. Davenport-Moline-Rock Island, IA-IL	78.47	138. Eugene-Springfield, OR	61.18
78. Utica-Rome, NY	78.18	139. Hamilton-Middletown, OH	60.90
79. Burlington, VT	77.90	140. Mobile, AL	60.62
80. Orange County, CA	77.62	141. Champaign-Urbana, IL	60.33
81. Little Rock-North Little Rock, AR	77.33	142. Pittsburgh, PA	60.05
82. Los Angeles-Long Beach, CA	77.05	143. Asheville, NC	59.77
83. Winnipeg, MB	76.77	144. Monmouth-Ocean, NJ	59.49
84. Macon, GA	76.48	145. Fargo-Moorhead, ND-MN	59.20
85. Lynchburg, VA	76.20	146. Peoria-Pekin, IL	58.92
86. Spokane, WA	75.92	147. Youngstown-Warren, OH	58.64
87. Ottawa-Hull, ON-PQ	75.63	148. Trois-Rivieres, PQ	58.35
88. Kalamazoo-Battle Creek, MI	75.35	149. Richmond-Petersburg, VA	58.07
89. New Orleans, LA	75.07	150. Bridgeport, CT	57.79
90. Quebec City, PQ	74.78	151. Evansville-Henderson, IN-KY	57.50
91. Greenville-Spartanburg-Anderson, SC	74.50	152. Calgary, AB	57.22
92. Montgomery, AL	74.22	153. Chattanooga, TN-GA	56.94
93. Harrisburg-Lebanon-Carlisle, PA	73.93	154. Riverside-San Bernardino, CA	56.65
94. Miami, FL	73.65	155. Grand Forks, ND-MN	56.37
95. Middlesex-Somerset-Hunterdon, NJ	73.37	156. Cedar Rapids, IA	56.09
96. Toronto, ON	73.08	157. Orlando, FL	55.80
97. Wichita, KS	72.80	158. Sacramento, CA	55.52
98. Edmonton, AB	72.52	159. Kenosha, WI	55.24
99. Charlottesville, VA	72.23	160. Lubbock, TX	54.95
100. Akron, OH	71.95	161. Tucson, AZ	54.67
101. Albuquerque, NM	71.67	162. Muncie, IN	54.39
102. Lawrence, KS	71.38	163. Amarillo, TX	54.10
103. Houston, TX	71.10	164. New London-Norwich, CT-RI	53.82
104. Portsmouth-Rochester, NH-ME	70.82	165. Jamestown, NY	53.54
105. Detroit, MI	70.53	166. Lakeland-Winter Haven, FL	53.25
106. Erie, PA	70.25	167. Long Island, NY	52.97
107. Bergen-Passaic, NJ	69.97	168. Jackson, TN	52.69
108. Jackson, MS	69.68	169. Hattiesburg, MS	52.40
109. Terre Haute, IN	69.40	170. Sioux Falls, SD	52.12
110. Santa Barbara-Santa Maria-Lompoc, CA	69.12	171. Fresno, CA	51.84
111. Charleston-North Charleston, SC	68.83	172. Cumberland, MD-WV	51.55
112. Sherbrooke, PQ	68.55	173. Salinas, CA	51.27
113. Roanoke, VA	68.27	174. Provo-Orem, UT	50.99
114. Tampa-St. Petersburg-Clearwater, FL	67.98	175. Waco, TX	50.70
115. Memphis, TN-AR-MS	67.70	176. Tulsa, OK	50.42
116. Johnson City-Kingsport-Bristol, TN-VA	67.42	177. Gainesville, FL	50.14
117. Huntington-Ashland, WV-KY-OH	67.13	178. Lafayette, IN	49.85
118. Daytona Beach, FL	66.85	179. Parkersburg-Marietta, WV-OH	49.57
119. Fort Worth-Arlington, TX	66.57	180. Abilene, TX	49.29
120. Wilmington-Newark, DE-MD	66.28	181. Eau Claire, WI	49.00
121. San Antonio, TX	66.00	182. Reno, NV	48.72
122. Saginaw-Bay City-Midland, MI	65.72	183. Fort Lauderdale, FL	48.44
123. Dutchess County, NY	65.43	184. West Palm Beach-Boca Raton, FL	48.15
124. Tuscaloosa, AL	65.15	185. Canton-Massillon, OH	47.87
125. Bloomington-Normal, IL	64.87	186. Nashua, NH	47.59
126. Columbia, MO	64.58	187. Appleton-Oshkosh-Neenah, WI	47.30
127. Lansing-East Lansing, MI	64.30	188. Victoria, BC	47.02
128. Springfield, IL	64.02	189. Kitchener-Waterloo, ON	46.74
129. Tallahassee, FL	63.73	190. Augusta-Aiken, GA-SC	46.45
130. Allentown-Bethlehem-Easton, PA	63.45	191. Reading, PA	46.17
131. Gary, IN	63.17	192. Tyler, TX	45.89
132. Green Bay, WI	62.88	193. Longview-Marshall, TX	45.60
133. Charleston, WV	62.60	194. Athens, GA	45.32
134. Wheeling, WV-OH	62.32	195. Boulder-Longmont, CO	45.04
135. Salem, OR	62.03	196. Jacksonville, FL	44.75
136. Boise City, ID	61.75	197. Tacoma, WA	44.47

RANK	SCORE		RANK	SCORE
198. Lewiston-Auburn, ME	44.19		259. San Luis Obispo-Atascadero-Paso Robles, CA	26.91
199. Sioux City, IA-NE	43.90		260. Albany, GA	26.62
200. Galveston-Texas City, TX	43.62		261. Kankakee, IL	26.34
201. Flint, MI	43.34		262. Owensboro, KY	26.06
202. State College, PA	43.05		263. Dothan, AL	25.77
203. Waterloo-Cedar Falls, IA	42.77		264. Benton Harbor, MI	25.49
204. Savannah, GA	42.49		265. Sarasota-Bradenton, FL	25.21
205. Iowa City, IA	42.20		266. Florence, SC	24.92
206. Greenville, NC	41.92		267. Stockton-Lodi, CA	24.64
207. Killeen-Temple, TX	41.64		268. San Angelo, TX	24.36
208. Anchorage, AK	41.35		269. Monroe, LA	24.07
209. St. Cloud, MN	41.07		270. Vallejo-Fairfield-Napa, CA	23.79
210. Wilmington, NC	40.79		271. Elkhart-Goshen, IN	23.51
211. Kokomo, IN	40.50		272. Topeka, KS	23.22
212. Jersey City, NJ	40.22		273. Jonesboro, AR	22.94
213. Lancaster, PA	39.94		274. Danville, VA	22.66
214. Hamilton, ON	39.66		275. Rapid City, SD	22.37
215. Fayetteville-Springdale-Rogers, AR	39.37		276. Rocky Mount, NC	22.09
216. Baton Rouge, LA	39.09		277. Anniston, AL	21.81
217. St. Joseph, MO	38.81		278. Williamsport, PA	21.52
218. Bellingham, WA	38.52		279. Chico-Paradise, CA	21.24
219. Columbus, GA-AL	38.24		280. Decatur, AL	20.96
220. Florence, AL	37.96		281. Sherman-Denison, TX	20.67
221. Janesville-Beloit, WI	37.67		282. Atlantic-Cape May, NJ	20.39
222. Bismarck, ND	37.39		283. Victoria, TX	20.11
223. Binghamton, NY	37.11		284. Odessa-Midland, TX	19.83
224. Rochester, MN	36.82		285. Wausau, WI	19.54
225. Ventura, CA	36.54		286. Sudbury, ON	19.26
226. Santa Cruz-Watsonville, CA	36.26		287. Brownsville-Harlingen-San Benito, TX	18.98
227. Bloomington, IN	35.97		288. Bakersfield, CA	18.69
228. Brockton, MA	35.69		289. Redding, CA	18.41
229. Joplin, MO	35.41		290. Grand Junction, CO	18.13
230. Lima, OH	35.12		291. Pueblo, CO	17.84
231. Greeley, CO	34.84		292. Elmira, NY	17.56
232. Fort Collins-Loveland, CO	34.56		293. Danbury, CT	17.28
233. Fitchburg-Leominster, MA	34.27		294. Decatur, IL	16.99
234. Johnstown, PA	33.99		295. Corpus Christi, TX	16.71
235. Lawrence, MA-NH	33.71		296. Las Vegas, NV-AZ	16.43
236. Chicoutimi-Jonquiere, PQ	33.42		297. Mansfield, OH	16.14
237. Missoula, MT	33.14		298. Sharon, PA	15.86
238. Thunder Bay, ON	32.86		299. Waterbury, CT	15.58
239. Hickory-Morganton-Lenoir, NC	32.57		300. Rockford, IL	15.29
240. Bryan-College Station, TX	32.29		301. Glens Falls, NY	15.01
241. Sumter, SC	32.01		302. St. John's, NF	14.73
242. Lafayette, LA	31.72		303. St. Catharines-Niagara, ON	14.44
243. Dover, DE	31.44		304. Sheboygan, WI	14.16
244. Las Cruces, NM	31.16		305. Naples, FL	13.88
245. Pocatello, ID	30.87		306. Wichita Falls, TX	13.59
246. El Paso, TX	30.59		307. Lawton, OK	13.31
247. Texarkana, TX-Texarkana, AR	30.31		308. Stamford-Norwalk, CT	13.03
248. Beaumont-Port Arthur, TX	30.02		309. Myrtle Beach, SC	12.74
249. Fayetteville, NC	29.74		310. Cheyenne, WY	12.46
250. Newburgh, NY-PA	29.46		311. Lowell, MA-NH	12.18
251. Olympia, WA	29.17		312. Billings, MT	11.89
252. Flagstaff, AZ-UT	28.89		313. Alexandria, LA	11.61
253. Steubenville-Weirton, OH-WV	28.61		314. Panama City, FL	11.33
254. Yolo, CA	28.32		315. Hagerstown, MD	11.04
255. Windsor, ON	28.04		316. Lake Charles, LA	10.76
256. Clarksville-Hopkinsville, TN-KY	27.76		317. Jackson, MI	10.48
257. Santa Rosa, CA	27.47		318. Barnstable-Yarmouth, MA	10.19
258. Shreveport-Bossier City, LA	27.19			

Education

continues

Metro Areas from Best to Worst (cont.)

RANK	SCORE		RANK	SCORE
319. York, PA	9.91		337. Fort Walton Beach, FL	5.09
320. Pensacola, FL	9.63		338. Pittsfield, MA	4.81
321. Brazoria, TX	9.34		339. Modesto, CA	4.53
321. Fort Myers-Cape Coral, FL	9.34		340. Yakima, WA	4.24
323. Casper, WY	9.06		341. Enid, OK	3.96
324. Laredo, TX	8.78		342. McAllen-Edinburg-Mission, TX	3.68
325. Gadsden, AL	8.49		343. Yuba City, CA	3.39
326. Goldsboro, NC	8.21		344. Saint John, NB	3.11
327. Pine Bluff, AR	7.93		345. Great Falls, MT	2.54
328. Medford-Ashland, OR	7.64		346. Yuma, AZ	2.26
329. Fort Smith, AR-OK	7.36		347. Richland-Kennewick-Pasco, WA	1.98
330. Fort Pierce-Port St. Lucie, FL	7.08		348. Altoona, PA	1.69
331. Bremerton, WA	6.79		349. Visalia-Tulare-Porterville, CA	1.41
332. New Bedford, MA	6.51		350. Biloxi-Gulfport-Pascagoula, MS	1.13
333. Oshawa, ON	6.23		351. Jacksonville, NC	0.84
334. Houma, LA	5.94		352. Ocala, FL	0.56
335. Vineland-Millville-Bridgeton, NJ	5.66		353. Punta Gorda, FL	0.28
336. Racine, WI	5.38		354. Merced, CA	0.00

PLACE PROFILES: Education

The following pages detail seven kinds of education in metropolitan areas: (1) public schools, (2) private schools, (3) public libraries, (4) 2-year colleges, (5) baccalaureate colleges, (6) comprehensive colleges and universities, and (7) doctoral universities.

Finding a good public school district isn't easy. Metropolitan Chicago has 353. A typical metro area has 30 or more, each with varying indicators of school quality. Still, information on how much local public education is fragmented into different systems can be useful to newcomers.

The percent of **Children in Public Schools** is shown in parentheses to the right of that heading. A style box, *School Support*, follows and is an indicator combining metro-area averages for the number of pupils per classroom teacher and the percent of funding the schools receive from local sources. Each shaded cell represents a quintile (20 percent) of the total support, with the leftmost box indicating less support (0–20 percent) and the rightmost box indicating more support (81–100 percent). Typical support (see sample below) is indicated when the first three boxes are shaded (41–60 percent). Below School Support are the number of districts, the number of schools, and the total enrollment throughout the metro area.

School Support	■■■□□

The percent of **Children in Private Schools** (in Canada, nonfunded schools) is shown to the right of that

heading. Below this percentage are the number of local Catholic schools and students, the number of local schools that belong to the National Association of Independent Schools (NAIS) and their total enrollment, and the number of other private schools and students.

Under the **Public Libraries** heading is another style box indicating *Library Popularity,* derived by adding circulation to the number of volumes held, and dividing the result by the population served. Shaded cells up to the center column indicate typical popularity. Cells shaded to the right indicate higher popularity, and cells shaded to the left indicate less.

Under the **Colleges and Universities** heading are two style boxes. *College Options* indicate the variety of local higher education alternatives available. Shaded cells up to the center indicate typical choices. Cells shaded to the left mean fewer alternatives, and cells shaded to the right mean more. *College Town* points to the portion of local people in colleges and universities, weighted heavier the higher the degree. Cells shaded up to the center mean a typical portion of the population attends college. Cells shaded to the right mean higher portions, and cells shaded to the left mean lower.

Under "Associate of Arts" below **Colleges and Universities** is the number of community, junior, or 2-year colleges. Under the "Baccalaureate" subheading are the names of colleges where the highest degree granted is the bachelor's. Under the "Comprehensive" subheading are institutions where the master's is the highest degree granted. Under the "Doctoral" subheading are universities where the highest degree granted is the doctorate.

Enrollment figures (in parentheses) are the sum of full and part-time students. For Comprehensive and Doctoral institutions the first enrollment figure is undergraduate students, the second is graduate students; if there is only one figure, the institution's entire enrollment is graduate students. Publicly controlled institutions in the United States are *italicized*. In Canada, degree-granting institutions get their charters from the province or are affiliated with institutions that do. They are essentially publicly supported.

Figures for American public schools come from the U.S. Department of Education's unpublished "Common Core of Data" file. Figures for Canadian public and private schools come from the Places Rated Partnership survey. Figures for American private schools come from CMG Direct. The classifications used for grouping higher education institutions come from the Carnegie

Foundation, *A Classification of Institutions of Higher Education*, 1994.

Data for American public libraries comes from the U.S. Department of Education's Office of Education Research and Improvement. Data for Canadian public libraries comes from the Council of Administrators of Public Libraries and from the Places Rated Partnership survey.

Figures for American colleges and universities again come from the U.S. Department of Education's Office of Education Research and Improvement. Similar data for Canadian higher education institutions comes from the Association of Canadian Community Colleges, *ACCC Directory of Canadian Colleges and Institutes*, 1999; the Association of Universities and Colleges of Canada, *Directory of Canadian Universities*, 1999; and Statistics Canada's *Universities: Enrollment and Degrees*, 1999, and *Community Colleges and Related Institutions*, 1999.

A star (★) preceding the metro area's name identifies it as one of *Places Rated*'s top thirty-five places for education.

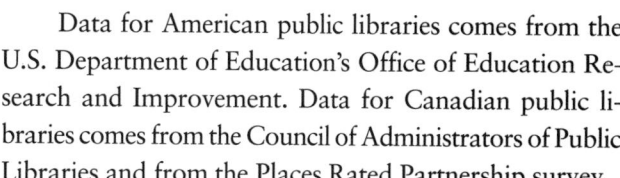

Abilene, TX
Children in Public Schools (99%)
School Support ■■■■■

5 districts, 59 schools, 24,648 students
Children in Private Schools (1%)
2 Other, 281 students
Public Libraries
Library Popularity ■■□□□

1 system, 1 branch
240,077 books; circulation: 483,385
Colleges and Universities
College Options ■■■□□
College Town ■■■■□

Baccalaureate
McMurry University (1,826)
Comprehensive
Hardin-Simmons University (2,200/478)
Doctoral
Abilene Christian University (4,199/1,217)
Score: **49.29**   Rank: **180**

Akron, OH
Children in Public Schools (89%)
School Support ■■□□□

34 districts, 212 schools, 109,763 students
Children in Private Schools (11%)
29 Catholic, 10,391 students
2 NAIS, 885 students
24 Other, 2,915 students
Public Libraries
Library Popularity ■■■■■

10 systems, 21 branches
1,949,532 books; circulation: 6,538,139
Colleges and Universities
College Options ■■■■□
College Town ■■■■■

Associate of Arts
3 campuses (4,640)
Baccalaureate
Hiram College (1,250)
Doctoral
Kent State University (19,355/7,803)
University of Akron (23,962/5,981)
Score: **71.95**   Rank: **100**

Albany, GA
Children in Public Schools (92%)
School Support ■■□□□

2 districts, 31 schools, 22,116 students
Children in Private Schools (8%)
1 Catholic, 429 students
7 Other, 1,676 students
Public Libraries
Library Popularity ■■■□□

1 system, 4 branches
287,728 books; circulation: 547,969
Colleges and Universities
College Options ■■■□□
College Town ■■■□□

Associate of Arts
2 campuses (6,988)
Comprehensive
Albany State College (2,812/339)
Score: **26.62**   Rank: **260**

★Albany-Schenectady-Troy, NY
Children in Public Schools (90%)
School Support ■■■■■

55 districts, 236 schools, 133,367 students
Children in Private Schools (10%)
47 Catholic, 12,795 students
7 NAIS, 2,842 students
5 Other, 578 students

Public Libraries

Library Popularity ▪▪▪▪☐

49 systems, 15 branches
2,481,063 books; circulation: 5,294,707

Colleges and Universities

College Options ▪▪▪▪▪

College Town ▪▪▪▪☐

Associate of Arts
6 campuses (22,854)
Baccalaureate
Albany College of Pharmacy (686/26)
SUNY College at Cobleskill (2,718)
Comprehensive
College of Saint Rose (3,069/1,944)
Russell Sage College (4,471/1,708)
Siena College (3,395/18)
Skidmore College (2,747/57)
SUNY Empire State College (9,616/478)
Doctoral
Albany Medical College (698)
Rensselaer Polytechnic Institute (4,368/2,875)
SUNY at Albany (12,993/6,425)
Union College (2,288/576)
Score: 99.43   Rank: 3

Albuquerque, NM

Children in Public Schools (93%)

School Support ▪▪▪☐☐

8 districts, 171 schools, 108,819 students

Children in Private Schools (7%)
13 Catholic, 4,393 students
3 NAIS, 1,888 students
11 Other, 1,344 students

Public Libraries

Library Popularity ▪▪▪☐☐

14 systems, 14 branches
1,710,871 books; circulation: 3,168,277

Colleges and Universities

College Options ▪▪▪▪☐

College Town ▪▪▪▪☐

Associate of Arts
3 campuses (25,769)
Doctoral
University of New Mexico (19,489/11,447)
Score: 71.67   Rank: 101

Alexandria, LA

Children in Public Schools (92%)

School Support ▪▪▪▪☐

2 districts, 55 schools, 24,856 students

Children in Private Schools (8%)
4 Catholic, 1,431 students
4 Other, 779 students

Public Libraries

Library Popularity ▪▪☐☐☐

1 system, 9 branches
342,042 books; circulation: 551,908

Colleges and Universities

College Options ▪▪☐☐☐

College Town ▪☐☐☐☐

Associate of Arts
2 campuses (3,845)
Baccalaureate
Louisiana College (1,210)
Score: 11.61   Rank: 313

Allentown-Bethlehem-Easton, PA

Children in Public Schools (84%)

School Support ▪▪☐☐☐

23 districts, 147 schools, 89,349 students

Children in Private Schools (16%)
43 Catholic, 13,031 students
6 NAIS, 2,526 students
11 Other, 1,616 students

Public Libraries

Library Popularity ▪▪☐☐☐

18 systems, 6 branches
1,079,282 books; circulation: 3,042,113

Colleges and Universities

College Options ▪▪▪▪▪

College Town ▪▪☐☐☐

Associate of Arts
3 campuses (14,039)
Baccalaureate
Lafayette College (2,297)
Muhlenberg College (2,733)
Pennsylvania State University (705/74)
Comprehensive
College of Saint Francis De Sales (2,619/806)
Cedar Crest College (2,347)
Moravian College (2,067/277)
Doctoral
Lehigh University (4,439/2,031)
Score: 63.45   Rank: 130

Altoona, PA

Children in Public Schools (90%)

School Support ▪▪☐☐☐

7 districts, 36 schools, 20,575 students

Children in Private Schools (10%)
11 Catholic, 1,924 students
2 Other, 284 students

Public Libraries

Library Popularity ▪▪▪☐☐

8 systems
399,513 books; circulation: 638,308

Colleges and Universities

College Options ▪☐☐☐☐

College Town ▪☐☐☐☐

Baccalaureate
Pennsylvania State University (3,245/50)
Score: 1.69   Rank: 348

Amarillo, TX

Children in Public Schools (97%)

School Support ▪▪▪▪☐

5 districts, 71 schools, 38,634 students

Children in Private Schools (3%)
6 Catholic, 673 students
2 Other, 590 students

Public Libraries

Library Popularity ▪▪▪▪▪

3 systems, 3 branches
598,340 books; circulation: 1,743,611

Colleges and Universities
College Options ▰▰▰▱▱
College Town ▰▰▰▱▱

Associate of Arts
1 campus (9,908)
Comprehensive
West Texas State University (6,525/1,771)
Score: 54.1   Rank: **163**

Anchorage, AK
Children in Public Schools (97%)
School Support ▰▰▱▱▱

1 district, 84 schools, 46,711 students
Children in Private Schools (3%)
1 Catholic, 174 students
9 Other, 1,134 students
Public Libraries
Library Popularity ▰▰▱▱▱

1 system, 5 branches
431,353 books; circulation: 1,262,797
Colleges and Universities
College Options ▰▰▰▱▱
College Town ▰▰▰▰▰

Comprehensive
Alaska Pacific University (379/201)
University of Alaska (23,867/816)
Score: 41.35   Rank: **208**

Ann Arbor, MI
Children in Public Schools (95%)
School Support ▰▱▱▱▱

27 districts, 159 schools, 81,503 students
Children in Private Schools (5%)
11 Catholic, 2,712 students
1 NAIS, 442 students
7 Other, 1,435 students
Public Libraries
Library Popularity ▰▰▰▱▱

21 system, 12 branches
1,263,565 books; circulation: 3,011,761
Colleges and Universities
College Options ▰▰▰▰▱
College Town ▰▰▰▰▰

Associate of Arts
1 campus (15,743)
Baccalaureate
Adrian College (1,081)
Cleary College (734)
Concordia College (726)
Comprehensive
Siena Heights College (2,141/341)
Doctoral
Eastern Michigan University (22,032/8,894)
University of Michigan (25,962/14,521)
Score: 83   Rank: **61**

Anniston, AL
Children in Public Schools (95%)
School Support ▰▰▱▱▱

5 districts, 37 schools, 19,665 students
Children in Private Schools (5%)
1 Catholic, 181 students
2 Other, 756 students

Public Libraries
Library Popularity ▰▱▱▱▱

4 systems, 1 branch
273,006 books; circulation: 328,388
Colleges and Universities
College Options ▰▰▱▱▱
College Town ▰▰▰▰▱

Associate of Arts
1 campus (1,196)
Comprehensive
Jacksonville State University (7,292/1,655)
Score: 21.81   Rank: **277**

Appleton-Oshkosh-Neenah, WI
Children in Public Schools (85%)
School Support ▰▰▰▰▰

18 districts, 118 schools, 54,111 students
Children in Private Schools (15%)
35 Catholic, 7,538 students
18 Other, 2,908 students
Public Libraries
Library Popularity ▰▰▰▰▰

14 systems, 3 branches
1,089,695 books; circulation: 3,700,809
Colleges and Universities
College Options ▰▰▱▱▱
College Town ▰▰▰▱▱

Associate of Arts
1 campus (12,955)
Baccalaureate
Lawrence University (1,238)
Comprehensive
University of Wisconsin (9,687/2,464)
Score: 47.3   Rank: **187**

Asheville, NC
Children in Public Schools (88%)
School Support ▰▰▰▰▰

3 districts, 53 schools, 29,674 students
Children in Private Schools (12%)
3 Catholic, 714 students
5 NAIS, 1,541 students
21 Other, 2,413 students
Public Libraries
Library Popularity ▰▰▰▱▱

2 systems, 11 branches
444,781 books; circulation: 1,285,458
Colleges and Universities
College Options ▰▰▰▰▱
College Town ▰▰▱▱▱

Associate of Arts
1 campus (6,361)
Baccalaureate
Mars Hill College (1,522)
Comprehensive
Montreat-Anderson College (491)
University of North Carolina (3,865/69)
Warren Wilson College (657/113)
Score: 59.77   Rank: **143**

Athens, GA
Children in Public Schools (90%)
School Support ▪▪▪▪□

4 districts, 43 schools, 22,562 students
Children in Private Schools (10%)
1 Catholic, 361 students
1 NAIS, 784 students
6 Other, 1,034 students
Public Libraries
Library Popularity ▪▪□□□

1 system, 10 branches
270,782 books; circulation: 916,189
Colleges and Universities
College Options ▪▪□□□

College Town ▪▪▪▪▪

Associate of Arts
  1 campus (2,554)
Doctoral
  University of Georgia (27,403/8,309)
Score: 45.32   Rank: 194

Atlanta, GA
Children in Public Schools (95%)
School Support ▪▪▪▪□

27 districts, 754 schools, 630,939 students
Children in Private Schools (5%)
12 Catholic, 5,015 students
11 NAIS, 8,901 students
170 Other, 20,093 students
Public Libraries
Library Popularity ▪▪□□□

12 systems, 114 branches
5,856,897 books; circulation: 17,179,797
Colleges and Universities
College Options ▪▪▪▪▪

College Town ▪▪□□□

Associate of Arts
  13 campuses (51,948)
Baccalaureate
  Atlanta College of Art (446)
  Beulah Heights Bible College (540)
  Clayton State College (7,156)
  Georgia Baptist College of Nursing (417)
  Morehouse College (3,016)
  Morris Brown College (2,410)
  Reinhardt College (1,281)
  Spelman College (2,036)
Comprehensive
  Agnes Scott College (607/32)
  Kennesaw State College (15,236/1,653)
  Life College (1,276/3,492)
  Oglethorpe University (1,704/191)
  Southern College of Technology (4,315/646)
  West Georgia College (7,786/4,059)
Doctoral
  Clark Atlanta University (4,828/2,234)
  Columbia Theological Seminary (623)
  Emory University (6,593/5,903)
  Georgia Institute of Technology (11,044/4,176)
  Georgia State University (20,920/9,139)
  Interdenominational Theological Center (483)
  Luther Rice Seminary (450/903)
Score: 82.71   Rank: 62

Atlantic-Cape May, NJ
Children in Public Schools (86%)
School Support ▪▪▪▪▪

41 districts, 117 schools, 54,307 students
Children in Private Schools (14%)
17 Catholic, 5,514 students
1 Other, 13 students
Public Libraries
Library Popularity ▪▪▪▪□

9 systems, 15 branches
1,187,767 books; circulation: 1,844,873
Colleges and Universities
College Options ▪▪□□□

College Town ▪□□□□

Associate of Arts
  1 campus (6,003)
Comprehensive
  Stockton State College of New Jersey (7,204)
Score: 20.39   Rank: 282

Augusta-Aiken, GA-SC
Children in Public Schools (94%)
School Support ▪▪▪□□

5 districts, 136 schools, 86,917 students
Children in Private Schools (6%)
5 Catholic, 1,966 students
2 NAIS, 480 students
33 Other, 3,371 students
Public Libraries
Library Popularity ▪□□□□

2 systems, 26 branches
678,599 books; circulation: 1,520,802
Colleges and Universities
College Options ▪▪▪▪□

College Town ▪▪□□□

Associate of Arts
  3 campuses (11,294)
Baccalaureate
  Paine College (1,045)
Comprehensive
  Augusta College (6,617/1,419)
  University of South Carolina (4,004/68)
Doctoral
  Medical College of Georgia (1,034/1,640)
Score: 46.45   Rank: 190

★Austin-San Marcos, TX
Children in Public Schools (97%)
School Support ▪▪▪▪▪

29 districts, 299 schools, 177,729 students
Children in Private Schools (3%)
9 Catholic, 2,129 students
2 NAIS, 690 students
16 Other, 3,039 students
Public Libraries
Library Popularity ▪▪▪□□

21 systems, 18 branches
1,591,201 books; circulation: 3,856,550
Colleges and Universities
College Options ▪▪▪▪▪

College Town ▪▪▪▪▪

Associate of Arts
  1 campus (45,668)

Baccalaureate
　　Concordia Lutheran College (858)
　　Huston-Tillotson College (733)
　　Southwestern University (1,305)
Comprehensive
　　St. Edward's University (3,063/684)
Doctoral
　　Presbyterian Theological Seminary (350)
　　Southwest Texas State University (20,225/4,355)
　　University of Texas (35,086/12,819)

Score: 98.3　　　　**Rank: 7**

Bakersfield, CA
Children in Public Schools (94%)
School Support ■□□□□

48 districts, 226 schools, 137,471 students
Children in Private Schools (6%)
13 Catholic, 5,039 students
49 Other, 4,283 students
Public Libraries
Library Popularity ■□□□□

1 system, 25 branches
998,346 books; circulation: 1,799,820
Colleges and Universities
College Options ■■■□□

College Town ■□□□□

Associate of Arts
　　3 campuses (25,590)
Comprehensive
　　California State University (4,860/1,739)

Score: 18.69　　　　**Rank: 288**

★Baltimore, MD
Children in Public Schools (90%)
School Support ■■■□□

7 districts, 615 schools, 386,122 students
Children in Private Schools (10%)
77 Catholic, 29,082 students
22 NAIS, 9,531 students
28 Other, 3,632 students
Public Libraries
Library Popularity ■■■■■

3 systems, 80 branches
6,836,648 books; circulation: 25,936,259
Colleges and Universities
College Options ■■■■■

College Town ■■■□□

Associate of Arts
　　10 campuses (82,569)
Baccalaureate
　　Sojourner-Douglas College (697)
　　United States Naval Academy (4,082)
Comprehensive
　　College of Notre Dame Maryland (3,197/948)
　　Coppin State College (3,530/902)
　　Goucher College (1,111/297)
　　Maryland Institute College of Art (1,694/162)
　　St. John's College (466/149)
　　Towson State University (15,683/2,668)
　　University of Baltimore (2,820/3,264)
　　Villa Julie College (1,999)
　　Western Maryland College (1,370/2,489)

Doctoral
　　Baltimore Hebrew University (319/118)
　　Johns Hopkins University (4,870/14,854)
　　Loyola College (3,446/5,291)
　　Morgan State University (6,067/479)
　　Ner Israel Rabbinical College (462/188)
　　Peabody Institute of Johns Hopkins University (254/356)
　　University of Maryland (10,573/2,078)
　　University of Maryland Professional (722/5,331)

Score: 94.05　　　　**Rank: 22**

★Bangor, ME
Children in Public Schools (94%)
School Support ■■■■■

7 districts, 40 schools, 13,653 students
Children in Private Schools (6%)
1 Catholic, 111 students
7 Other, 889 students
Public Libraries
Library Popularity ■■■■■

9 systems
720,305 books; circulation: 739,072
Colleges and Universities
College Options ■■■■□

College Town ■■■■■

Associate of Arts
　　1 campus (3,842)
Comprehensive
　　Husson College (2,260/479)
Doctoral
　　University of Maine (9,599/3,045)

Score: 90.36　　　　**Rank: 35**

Barnstable-Yarmouth, MA
Children in Public Schools (99%)
School Support ■■□□□

12 districts, 38 schools, 21,684 students
Children in Private Schools (1%)
1 Catholic, 82 students
2 NAIS, 329 students
2 Other, 155 students
Public Libraries
Library Popularity ■■■■□

25 systems
718,950 books; circulation: 1,604,371
Colleges and Universities
College Options ■■□□□

College Town ■□□□□

Associate of Arts
　　1 campus (5,773)
Baccalaureate
　　Massachusetts Maritime Academy (822)

Score: 10.19　　　　**Rank: 318**

Baton Rouge, LA
Children in Public Schools (83%)
School Support ■■■■□

7 districts, 183 schools, 96,559 students
Children in Private Schools (17%)
22 Catholic, 12,247 students
1 NAIS, 762 students
28 Other, 6,682 students

Public Libraries

Library Popularity ▪▪▪□□

4 systems, 20 branches
1,416,308 books; circulation: 3,152,187

Colleges and Universities

College Options ▪▪□□□

College Town ▪▪▪▪▪

Associate of Arts
4 campuses (2,233)
Doctoral
Louisiana State University (23,695/7,411)
Southern University (10,495/1,840)

Score: 39.09   Rank: 216

Beaumont-Port Arthur, TX

Children in Public Schools (95%)

School Support ▪▪▪▪▪

16 districts, 136 schools, 71,581 students

Children in Private Schools (5%)
9 Catholic, 2,562 students
8 Other, 1,614 students

Public Libraries

Library Popularity ▪▪□□□

13 systems, 5 branches
799,152 books; circulation: 1,269,313

Colleges and Universities

College Options ▪▪▪□□

College Town ▪▪□□□

Associate of Arts
2 campuses (5,835)
Doctoral
Lamar University (11,908/661)

Score: 30.02   Rank: 248

Bellingham, WA

Children in Public Schools (91%)

School Support ▪□□□□

7 districts, 53 schools, 24,680 students

Children in Private Schools (9%)
1 Catholic, 262 students
12 Other, 2,130 students

Public Libraries

Library Popularity ▪▪▪▪▪

1 system, 11 branches
458,940 books; circulation: 1,773,240

Colleges and Universities

College Options ▪▪□□□

College Town ▪▪▪▪▪

Associate of Arts
3 campuses (18,358)
Comprehensive
Western Washington University (15,145/1,324)

Score: 38.52   Rank: 218

Benton Harbor, MI

Children in Public Schools (94%)

School Support ▪▪□□□

16 districts, 77 schools, 29,824 students

Children in Private Schools (6%)
3 Catholic, 540 students
11 Other, 1,644 students

Public Libraries

Library Popularity ▪▪▪▪▪

14 systems
698,954 books; circulation: 1,171,849

Colleges and Universities

College Options ▪▪□□□

College Town ▪▪▪□□

Associate of Arts
1 campus (4,868)
Doctoral
Andrews University (2,472/3,568)

Score: 25.49   Rank: 264

Bergen-Passaic, NJ

Children in Public Schools (84%)

School Support ▪▪▪▪▪

96 districts, 392 schools, 177,748 students

Children in Private Schools (16%)
94 Catholic, 30,647 students
3 NAIS, 1,381 students
8 Other, 2,383 students

Public Libraries

Library Popularity ▪▪▪▪▪

78 systems, 8 branches
5,351,135 books; circulation: 8,517,792

Colleges and Universities

College Options ▪▪▪▪□

College Town ▪□□□□

Associate of Arts
3 campuses (24,477)
Comprehensive
Felician College (1,391)
Paterson State College (7,977/1,405)
Ramapo College (6,263/97)
Doctoral
Fairleigh Dickinson University (7,005/4,356)

Score: 69.97   Rank: 107

Billings, MT

Children in Public Schools (95%)

School Support ▪▪▪□□

19 districts, 59 schools, 22,264 students

Children in Private Schools (5%)
3 Catholic, 846 students
1 Other, 229 students

Public Libraries

Library Popularity ▪▪□□□

2 systems
280,920 books; circulation: 518,150

Colleges and Universities

College Options ▪▪□□□

College Town ▪▪□□□

Associate of Arts
1 campus (288)
Baccalaureate
Rocky Mountain College (1,018)
Comprehensive
Eastern Montana College (4,148/702)

Score: 11.89   Rank: 312

Biloxi-Gulfport-Pascagoula, MS

Children in Public Schools (94%)

School Support ▪▪▪□□

11 districts, 111 schools, 58,687 students

Children in Private Schools (6%)
14 Catholic, 4,577 students
1 Other, 100 students
Public Libraries
Library Popularity
4 systems, 16 branches
594,047 books; circulation: 1,624,405
Colleges and Universities
College Options
College Town
Associate of Arts
1 campus (667)
Score: 1.13   Rank: 350

Binghamton, NY
Children in Public Schools (93%)
School Support
19 districts, 78 schools, 44,254 students
Children in Private Schools (7%)
15 Catholic, 3,900 students
4 Other, 261 students
Public Libraries
Library Popularity
16 systems, 4 branches
676,194 books; circulation: 1,595,773
Colleges and Universities
College Options
College Town
Associate of Arts
1 campus (7,434)
Doctoral
SUNY at Binghamton (10,194/3,128)
Score: 37.11   Rank: 223

Birmingham, AL
Children in Public Schools (97%)
School Support
15 districts, 279 schools, 146,200 students
Children in Private Schools (3%)
15 Catholic, 3,588 students
3 NAIS, 987 students
5 Other, 682 students
Public Libraries
Library Popularity
37 systems, 21 branches
2,023,871 books; circulation: 4,335,127
Colleges and Universities
College Options
College Town
Associate of Arts
4 campuses (27,298)
Baccalaureate
Miles College (1,325)
Comprehensive
Birmingham Southern College (1,662/159)
University of Montevallo (3,154/826)
Doctoral
Samford University (3,486/1,809)
University of Alabama (14,045/6,160)
Score: 80.73   Rank: 69

Bismarck, ND
Children in Public Schools (90%)
School Support
21 districts, 58 schools, 16,796 students
Children in Private Schools (10%)
6 Catholic, 1,487 students
6 Other, 360 students
Public Libraries
Library Popularity
5 systems
248,044 books; circulation: 661,489
Colleges and Universities
College Options
College Town
Associate of Arts
2 campuses (3,414)
Comprehensive
University of Mary (2,042/446)
Score: 37.39   Rank: 222

Bloomington, IN
Children in Public Schools (96%)
School Support
2 districts, 26 schools, 13,400 students
Children in Private Schools (4%)
1 Catholic, 443 students
2 Other, 152 students
Public Libraries
Library Popularity
1 system, 1 branch
244,386 books; circulation: 1,169,029
Colleges and Universities
College Options
College Town
Doctoral
Indiana University (34,276/10,689)
Score: 35.97   Rank: 227

Bloomington-Normal, IL
Children in Public Schools (92%)
School Support
12 districts, 57 schools, 22,186 students
Children in Private Schools (8%)
4 Catholic, 1,248 students
2 Other, 679 students
Public Libraries
Library Popularity
13 systems
403,551 books; circulation: 1,148,075
Colleges and Universities
College Options
College Town
Associate of Arts
1 campus (5,347)
Baccalaureate
Illinois Wesleyan University (1,892)
Doctoral
Illinois State University (18,584/5,150)
Score: 64.87   Rank: 125

Boise City, ID
Children in Public Schools (94%)
School Support ▪▪☐☐☐

11 districts, 121 schools, 64,625 students
Children in Private Schools (6%)
6 Catholic, 2,002 students
16 Other, 2,290 students
Public Libraries
Library Popularity ▪▪▪☐☐

12 systems, 6 branches
705,269 books; circulation: 2,167,756
Colleges and Universities
College Options ▪▪▪▪☐
College Town ▪▪▪▪☐

Comprehensive
Albertson College of Idaho (622/370)
Northwest Nazarene College (1,317/2,939)
Doctoral
Boise State University (18,163/6,485)
Score: 61.75   Rank: 136

★Boston, MA-NH
Children in Public Schools (87%)
School Support ▪▪☐☐☐

125 districts, 851 schools, 431,131 students
Children in Private Schools (13%)
136 Catholic, 44,116 students
52 NAIS, 14,625 students
80 Other, 12,217 students
Public Libraries
Library Popularity ▪▪▪▪▪

131 system, 72 branches
17,640,052 books; circulation: 24,650,308
Colleges and Universities
College Options ▪▪▪▪▪
College Town ▪▪▪▪▪

Associate of Arts
20 campuses (63,105)
Baccalaureate
Art Institute of Boston (565)
Berklee College of Music (3,214)
Boston Architectural Center (766)
Endicott College (1,013)
Gordon College (1,299)
Lasell College (729)
Montserrat College of Art (330)
Mount Ida College (2,230)
Newbury College Inc (6,820)
Wellesley College (2,463)
Wentworth Institute of Technology (2,699)
Wheaton College (1,325)
Comprehensive
Atlantic Union College (1,436/37)
Babson College (1,903/1,830)
Bentley College (4,595/2,553)
Boston Conservatory (355/147)
Cambridge College (369/2,437)
Curry College (2,309/58)
Eastern Nazarene College (1,618/193)
Emmanuel College (1,863/254)
Framingham State College (6,166/612)
Massachusetts College of Art (2,881/126)

MGH Institute of Health Professions (654)
Pine Manor College (395/10)
Regis College (1,504/184)
Salem State College (10,392/2,003)
School of the Museum of Fine Arts (1,010/94)
Wheelock College (890/916)
Doctoral
Andover Newton Theological School (461)
Boston College (11,069/5,359)
Boston University (22,728/14,445)
Brandeis University (3,139/1,263)
Emerson College (3,519/1,024)
Gordon-Conwell Theological Seminary (1,121)
Harvard University (13,979/17,634)
Lesley College (1,940/7,706)
Massachusetts College of Pharmacy (1,413/65)
Massachusetts Institute of Technology (5,135/6,350)
New England Conservatory of Music (356/428)
Northeastern University (25,762/6,147)
Simmons College (1,432/2,681)
Suffolk University (3,468/3,694)
Tufts University (5,628/4,783)
University of Massachusetts (14,592/4,371)
Score: 99.71   Rank: 2

Boulder-Longmont, CO
Children in Public Schools (93%)
School Support ▪▪☐☐☐

2 districts, 83 schools, 41,785 students
Children in Private Schools (7%)
4 Catholic, 1,145 students
26 Other, 2,111 students
Public Libraries
Library Popularity ▪▪▪▪▪

6 systems, 3 branches
686,265 books; circulation: 2,974,512
Colleges and Universities
College Options ▪▪☐☐☐
College Town ▪▪▪▪▪

Comprehensive
Naropa Institute (329/527)
Doctoral
University of Colorado (22,315/5,547)
Score: 45.04   Rank: 195

Brazoria, TX
Children in Public Schools (98%)
School Support ▪▪▪▪☐

8 districts, 71 schools, 43,671 students
Children in Private Schools (2%)
1 Catholic, 298 students
4 Other, 715 students
Public Libraries
Library Popularity ▪▪☐☐☐

1 system, 10 branches
469,956 books; circulation: 1,082,707
Colleges and Universities
College Options ▪▪☐☐☐
College Town ▪☐☐☐☐

Associate of Arts
2 campuses (11,785)
Score: 9.34   Rank: 321

Bremerton, WA
Children in Public Schools (96%)
School Support

5 districts, 68 schools, 40,863 students
Children in Private Schools (4%)
1 Catholic, 178 students
14 Other, 1,707 students
Public Libraries
Library Popularity

1 system, 8 branches
375,088 books; circulation: 1,878,856
Colleges and Universities
College Options

College Town

Associate of Arts
1 campus (9,903)
Score: 6.79   Rank: 331

Bridgeport, CT
Children in Public Schools (90%)
School Support

17 districts, 138 schools, 71,257 students
Children in Private Schools (10%)
19 Catholic, 7,024 students
2 NAIS, 421 students
10 Other, 495 students
Public Libraries
Library Popularity

15 systems, 7 branches
1,794,159 books; circulation: 2,690,508
Colleges and Universities
College Options

College Town

Associate of Arts
3 campuses (4,246)
Comprehensive
Fairfield University (4,860/1,032)
Sacred Heart University (4,700/2,267)
Doctoral
University of Bridgeport (1,168/1,945)
Score: 57.79   Rank: 150

Brockton, MA
Children in Public Schools (97%)
School Support

10 districts, 69 schools, 35,284 students
Children in Private Schools (3%)
4 Catholic, 1,146 students
6 Other, 547 students
Public Libraries
Library Popularity

14 systems, 5 branches
738,072 books; circulation: 906,293
Colleges and Universities
College Options

College Town

Associate of Arts
2 campuses (8,322)
Baccalaureate
Stonehill College (3,335)
Comprehensive
Bridgewater State College (9,705/1,128)
Score: 35.69   Rank: 228

Brownsville-Harlingen-San Benito, TX
Children in Public Schools (95%)
School Support

10 districts, 116 schools, 78,447 students
Children in Private Schools (5%)
5 Catholic, 2,008 students
1 NAIS, 340 students
9 Other, 1,614 students
Public Libraries
Library Popularity

8 systems
278,047 books; circulation: 431,570
Colleges and Universities
College Options

College Town

Associate of Arts
2 campuses (14,079)
Comprehensive
University of Texas (2,807/898)
Score: 18.98   Rank: 287

Bryan-College Station, TX
Children in Public Schools (96%)
School Support

2 districts, 31 schools, 18,760 students
Children in Private Schools (4%)
1 Catholic, 420 students
3 Other, 447 students
Public Libraries
Library Popularity

1 system, 1 branch
173,112 books; circulation: 333,258
Colleges and Universities
College Options

College Town

Doctoral
Texas A&M University (37,193/9,029)
Score: 32.29   Rank: 240

★Buffalo-Niagara Falls, NY
Children in Public Schools (86%)
School Support

41 districts, 286 schools, 178,432 students
Children in Private Schools (14%)
94 Catholic, 26,347 students
5 NAIS, 1,510 students
14 Other, 1,580 students
Public Libraries
Library Popularity

35 systems, 30 branches
3,540,876 books; circulation: 9,921,053
Colleges and Universities
College Options

College Town

Associate of Arts
8 campuses (27,050)
Baccalaureate
Hilbert College (941)
Medaille College (1,054)
Comprehensive
Canisius College (3,768/1,897)
D'Youville College (1,668/555)
Daemen College (2,350/55)

Niagara University (2,110/838)
SUNY College at Buffalo (11,388/2,598)
Doctoral
SUNY at Buffalo (18,233/9,310)
Score: 92.63   Rank: 27

Burlington, VT
Children in Public Schools (93%)
School Support
10 districts, 53 schools, 23,463 students
Children in Private Schools (7%)
5 Catholic, 1,635 students
1 NAIS, 91 students
10 Other, 523 students
Public Libraries
Library Popularity
18 systems, 1 branch
355,624 books; circulation: 700,342
Colleges and Universities
College Options
College Town
Baccalaureate
Champlain College (2,472)
Comprehensive
Saint Michael's College (2,134/1,954)
Trinity College (1,142/842)
Doctoral
University of Vermont (12,065/1,809)
Score: 77.9   Rank: 79

Calgary, AB
Children in Public Schools (97%)
300 schools, 141,385 students
Children in Private Schools (3%)
22 Other, 4,406 students
Public Libraries
Library Popularity
2 systems, 18 branches
1,903,916 books; circulation: 10,847,484
Colleges and Universities
College Options
College Town
Associate of Arts
3 campuses (28,000)
Doctoral
University of Calgary (18,634/3,336)
Score: 57.22   Rank: 152

Canton-Massillon, OH
Children in Public Schools (91%)
School Support
20 districts, 131 schools, 69,327 students
Children in Private Schools (9%)
16 Catholic, 5,487 students
14 Other, 1,808 students
Public Libraries
Library Popularity
8 systems, 15 branches
1,689,697 books; circulation: 5,186,452
Colleges and Universities
College Options
College Town
Associate of Arts
2 campuses (8,135)

Baccalaureate
Mount Union College (1,809)
Comprehensive
Malone College (2,273/304)
Walsh University (1,388/266)
Score: 47.87   Rank: 185

Casper, WY
Children in Public Schools (100%)
School Support
2 districts, 41 schools, 12,980 students
Public Libraries
Library Popularity
1 system, 1 branch
237,333 books; circulation: 404,754
Colleges and Universities
College Options
College Town
Associate of Arts
1 campus (5,185)
Score: 9.06   Rank: 323

Cedar Rapids, IA
Children in Public Schools (90%)
School Support
11 districts, 72 schools, 30,287 students
Children in Private Schools (10%)
8 Catholic, 2,643 students
4 Other, 749 students
Public Libraries
Library Popularity
10 systems, 2 branches
508,560 books; circulation: 1,828,875
Colleges and Universities
College Options
College Town
Associate of Arts
1 campus (14,657)
Baccalaureate
Cornell College (1,201)
Mount Mercy College (1,367)
Comprehensive
Coe College (1,312/47)
Score: 56.09   Rank: 156

Champaign-Urbana, IL
Children in Public Schools (92%)
School Support
16 districts, 60 schools, 23,906 students
Children in Private Schools (8%)
4 Catholic, 1,130 students
5 Other, 986 students
Public Libraries
Library Popularity
11 systems, 1 branch
606,031 books; circulation: 2,013,429
Colleges and Universities
College Options
College Town
Associate of Arts
1 campus (14,140)
Doctoral
University of Illinois (29,904/12,353)
Score: 60.33   Rank: 141

Charleston, WV

Children in Public Schools (94%)

School Support

2 districts, 112 schools, 40,651 students

Children in Private Schools (6%)

5 Catholic, 1,523 students

11 Other, 1,309 students

Public Libraries

Library Popularity

4 systems, 12 branches

748,685 books; circulation: 1,458,774

Colleges and Universities

College Options

College Town

Associate of Arts
1 campus (712)
Baccalaureate
West Virginia State College (5,839)
Comprehensive
University of Charleston (1,669/64)
West Virginia Graduate College (5,166)

Score: 62.6   Rank: 133

Charleston-North Charleston, SC

Children in Public Schools (91%)

School Support

4 districts, 132 schools, 85,122 students

Children in Private Schools (9%)

38 Catholic, 14,352 students

8 NAIS, 3,032 students

171 Other, 14,758 students

Public Libraries

Library Popularity

3 systems, 19 branches

968,738 books; circulation: 2,506,594

Colleges and Universities

College Options

College Town

Associate of Arts
1 campus (13,823)
Baccalaureate
Johnson & Wales University (1,428)
Comprehensive
Charleston Southern University (2,413/488)
Citadel Military College (2,434/6,144)
College of Charleston (10,928/3,070)
Doctoral
Medical University of South Carolina (1,091/1,843)

Score: 68.83   Rank: 111

Charlotte-Gastonia-Rock Hill, NC-SC

Children in Public Schools (92%)

School Support

11 districts, 324 schools, 208,371 students

Children in Private Schools (8%)

11 Catholic, 4,915 students

3 NAIS, 3,735 students

78 Other, 11,050 students

Public Libraries

Library Popularity

5 systems, 42 branches

2,576,425 books; circulation: 8,625,500

Colleges and Universities

College Options

College Town

Associate of Arts
9 campuses (73,134)
Baccalaureate
Barber-Scotia College (496)
Davidson College (1,700)
Johnson Smith University (1,560)
Comprehensive
Belmont Abbey College (928/49)
Catawba College (1,162/17)
Livingstone College (731/74)
Queens College (1,433/520)
Wingate College (1,346/136)
Winthrop University (4,730/2,692)
Doctoral
University of North Carolina (16,490/3,658)

Score: 83.56   Rank: 59

Charlottesville, VA

Children in Public Schools (91%)

School Support

4 districts, 43 schools, 20,459 students

Children in Private Schools (9%)

4 NAIS, 1,642 students

2 Other, 385 students

Public Libraries

Library Popularity

2 systems, 7 branches

416,339 books; circulation: 1,542,215

Colleges and Universities

College Options

College Town

Associate of Arts
1 campus (6,998)
Doctoral
University of Virginia (14,645/13,743)

Score: 72.23   Rank: 99

Chattanooga, TN-GA

Children in Public Schools (95%)

School Support

8 districts, 130 schools, 67,389 students

Children in Private Schools (5%)

3 Catholic, 1,353 students

3 NAIS, 1,694 students

11 Other, 682 students

Public Libraries

Library Popularity

7 systems, 7 branches

632,215 books; circulation: 1,301,916

Colleges and Universities

College Options

College Town

Associate of Arts
2 campuses (13,735)
Comprehensive
Covenant College (818/48)
Southern College of Seventh-day Adventists (2,123/35)
Tennessee Temple University (614/13)
University of Tennessee (8,508/1,854)

Score: 56.94   Rank: 153

Cheyenne, WY
Children in Public Schools (96%)
| School Support | ■■■■□ |

2 districts, 42 schools, 14,898 students
Children in Private Schools (4%)
1 Catholic, 308 students
1 Other, 355 students
Public Libraries
| Library Popularity | ■■■□□ |

1 system, 2 branches
154,800 books; circulation: 583,294
Colleges and Universities
| College Options | ■□□□□ |
| College Town | ■■□□□ |

Associate of Arts
   1 campus (8,482)
Score: 12.46   Rank: 310

★Chicago, IL
Children in Public Schools (87%)
| School Support | ■■■□□ |

353 districts, 2,043 schools, 1,263,614 students
Children in Private Schools (13%)
421 Catholic, 166,756 students
13 NAIS, 6,396 students
91 Other, 16,289 students
Public Libraries
| Library Popularity | ■■■■■ |

164 systems, 16 branches
14,229,321 books; circulation: 37,756,669
Colleges and Universities
| College Options | ■■■■■ |
| College Town | ■■■■□ |

Associate of Arts
   25 campuses (463,283)
Baccalaureate
   Barat College (898)
   East-West University (564)
   Elmhurst College (3,426)
   Illinois College of Optometry (595)
   Industrial Engineering College (381)
   Judson College (801)
   Kendall College (620)
   Robert Morris College (2,888)
   Trinity Christian College (666)
Comprehensive
   Aurora University (1,647/1,304)
   Chicago College of Osteopathic Medicine (415/789)
   Chicago State University (8,265/3,588)
   College of Saint Francis (3,783/1,323)
   Columbia College (7,530/605)
   Concordia University (1,642/1,735)
   Governors State University (4,326/5,116)
   John Marshall Law School (1,448)
   Lake Forest College (1,124/18)
   Lake Forest Graduate School of Management (875)
   Lewis University (4,856/1,017)
   Moody Bible Institute (1,468/75)
   North Central College (2,577/604)
   North Park College and Theological Seminary (1,754/607)
   Northeastern Illinois University (9,226/4,652)
   Rosary College (1,133/1,390)

   Saint Xavier University (2,690/3,853)
   School of Art Institute of Chicago (1,682/588)
Doctoral
   Adler School of Professional Psychology (517)
   Catholic Theological Union at Chicago (542)
   Depaul University (13,822/8,692)
   Garrett Evangelical Theological Seminary (533)
   Illinois Benedictine College (1,928/1,438)
   Illinois Institute of Technology (2,689/5,447)
   Loyola University of Chicago (9,483/7,461)
   Lutheran School of Theology at Chicago (384)
   McCormick Theological Seminary (609)
   National-Louis University (4,560/10,204)
   Northern Illinois University (17,793/9,926)
   Northwestern University (11,199/7,813)
   Roosevelt University (6,274/2,971)
   Rush University (320/1,411)
   Trinity College (1,052/2,125)
   University of Chicago (3,606/9,743)
   University of Health Sciences (100/1,334)
   University of Illinois at Chicago (18,249/11,609)
   Wheaton College (2,432/535)
Score: 98.86   Rank: 5

Chico-Paradise, CA
Children in Public Schools (96%)
| School Support | ■□□□□ |

16 districts, 69 schools, 34,926 students
Children in Private Schools (4%)
3 Catholic, 572 students
15 Other, 970 students
Public Libraries
| Library Popularity | ■□□□□ |

1 system, 3 branches
255,423 books; circulation: 498,008
Colleges and Universities
| College Options | ■■□□□ |
| College Town | ■■■■■ |

Associate of Arts
   1 campus (15,078)
Comprehensive
   California State University (13,504/1,849)
Score: 21.24   Rank: 279

Chicotimi-Jonquier, PQ
Children in Public Schools
3 districts, 64 schools, 7,874 students
Public Libraries
| Library Popularity | ■□□□□ |

2 systems, 6 branches
107,159 books; circulation: 436,694
Colleges and Universities
| College Options | ■■■□□ |
| College Town | ■■■■□ |

Associate of Arts
   2 campuses (7,213)
Doctoral
   Université du Quebec (7,157/604)
Score: 33.42   Rank: 236

★Cincinnati, OH-KY-IN
Children in Public Schools (81%)
| School Support | ■■□□□ |

68 districts, 426 schools, 246,649 students

Children in Private Schools (19%)
122 Catholic, 49,614 students
3 NAIS, 1,255 students
60 Other, 7,619 students
Public Libraries
Library Popularity   ■■■■■

17 systems, 57 branches
6,293,727 books; circulation: 16,694,628
Colleges and Universities
College Options   ■■■■■
College Town   ■■■□□

Associate of Arts
7 campuses (19,518)
Comprehensive
Cincinnati Bible College and Seminary (680/474)
College of Mount Saint Joseph (4,480/323)
Northern Kentucky University (12,388/1,700)
Thomas More College (1,797/24)
Xavier University (4,828/3,715)
Doctoral
The Union Institute (794/1,450)
University of Cincinnati (25,284/9,981)
Score: 96.6   **Rank: 13**

Clarksville-Hopkinsville, TN-KY
Children in Public Schools (87%)
School Support   ■■□□□

2 districts, 46 schools, 30,220 students
Children in Private Schools (13%)
2 Catholic, 362 students
12 Other, 4,170 students
Public Libraries
Library Popularity   ■□□□□

3 systems
191,830 books; circulation: 537,795
Colleges and Universities
College Options   ■■■□□
College Town   ■■■□□

Associate of Arts
1 campus (4,289)
Comprehensive
Austin Peay State University (8,470/750)
Score: 27.76   **Rank: 256**

Cleveland-Lorain-Elyria, OH
Children in Public Schools (83%)
School Support   ■■■□□

81 districts, 597 schools, 343,421 students
Children in Private Schools (17%)
151 Catholic, 57,152 students
7 NAIS, 2,477 students
76 Other, 11,739 students
Public Libraries
Library Popularity   ■■■■■

33 systems, 85 branches
9,748,036 books; circulation: 32,049,407
Colleges and Universities
College Options   ■■■■■
College Town   ■■□□□

Associate of Arts
8 campuses (63,976)

Baccalaureate
Cleveland Institute of Art (542)
Dyke College (1,648)
Comprehensive
Baldwin-Wallace College (4,682/960)
John Carroll University (3,900/1,839)
Lake Erie College (582/143)
Notre Dame College (825/61)
Oberlin College (2,997/20)
Ursuline College (1,222/243)
Doctoral
Case Western Reserve University (3,701/6,391)
Cleveland Institute of Music (313/154)
Cleveland State University (14,556/7,720)
Score: 88.95   **Rank: 40**

Colorado Springs, CO
Children in Public Schools (95%)
School Support   ■■□□□

15 districts, 158 schools, 82,092 students
Children in Private Schools (5%)
5 Catholic, 1,581 students
2 NAIS, 468 students
27 Other, 2,734 students
Public Libraries
Library Popularity   ■■■■■

3 systems, 12 branches
1,072,690 books; circulation: 4,842,335
Colleges and Universities
College Options   ■■■■□
College Town   ■■■□□

Associate of Arts
1 campus (10,800)
Baccalaureate
Nazarene Bible College (499)
US Air Force Academy (4,212)
Comprehensive
Beth El College of Nursing (393/163)
Colorado College (2,464/235)
Doctoral
University of Colorado (5,235/2,551)
Score: 80.45   **Rank: 70**

Columbia, MO
Children in Public Schools (96%)
School Support   ■■■■■

6 districts, 41 schools, 18,695 students
Children in Private Schools (4%)
1 Catholic, 462 students
3 Other, 361 students
Public Libraries
Library Popularity   ■■■□□

2 systems, 2 branches
324,791 books; circulation: 1,046,241
Colleges and Universities
College Options   ■■■□□
College Town   ■■■■■

Baccalaureate
Stephens College (991)
Comprehensive
Columbia College (12,157/35)
Doctoral
University of Missouri (18,843/8,677)
Score: 64.58   **Rank: 126**

★Columbia, SC

Children in Public Schools (94%)
School Support ■■■■■

9 districts, 142 schools, 84,282 students

Children in Private Schools (6%)
5 Catholic, 1,373 students
2 NAIS, 891 students
41 Other, 3,671 students

Public Libraries
Library Popularity ■■■■□

2 systems, 17 branches
1,015,488 books; circulation: 3,620,469

Colleges and Universities
College Options ■■■■□
College Town ■■■■■

Associate of Arts
　1 campus (14,133)
Baccalaureate
　Benedict College (2,208)
Comprehensive
　Columbia College (1,405/182)
Doctoral
　Columbia Bible College and Seminary (537/567)
　University of South Carolina (18,343/16,098)

Score: 92.35　　　　Rank: 28

Columbus, GA-AL

Children in Public Schools (95%)
School Support ■■■□□

5 districts, 82 schools, 44,534 students

Children in Private Schools (5%)
1 Catholic, 170 students
6 Other, 2,117 students

Public Libraries
Library Popularity ■□□□□

2 systems, 9 branches
554,322 books; circulation: 714,027

Colleges and Universities
College Options ■■■■□
College Town ■■□□□

Associate of Arts
　3 campuses (5,985)
Comprehensive
　Columbus College (6,485/1,261)

Score: 38.24　　　　Rank: 219

★Columbus, OH

Children in Public Schools (90%)
School Support ■■□□□

50 districts, 464 schools, 239,130 students

Children in Private Schools (10%)
41 Catholic, 15,472 students
4 NAIS, 2,065 students
61 Other, 9,457 students

Public Libraries
Library Popularity ■■■■■

21 system, 33 branches
5,084,333 books; circulation: 21,312,082

Colleges and Universities
College Options ■■■■■
College Town ■■■■□

Associate of Arts
　2 campuses (29,423)
Baccalaureate
　College of Art and Design (1,991)
　Denison University (2,008)
　Mount Carmel College of Nursing (364)
　Ohio Dominican College (2,176)
　Ohio Wesleyan University (1,750)
Comprehensive
　Capital University (3,634/1,553)
　Franklin University (5,238/503)
　Ohio State University (1,807/189)
　Ohio University (2,467/273)
　Otterbein College (2,678/221)
Doctoral
　Ohio State University (41,944/17,934)

Score: 95.18　　　　Rank: 18

Corpus Christi, TX

Children in Public Schools (96%)
School Support ■■■■■

19 districts, 150 schools, 78,449 students

Children in Private Schools (4%)
15 Catholic, 2,963 students
4 Other, 822 students

Public Libraries
Library Popularity ■□□□□

9 systems, 4 branches
497,107 books; circulation: 1,121,021

Colleges and Universities
College Options ■■□□□
College Town ■■□□□

Associate of Arts
　1 campus (15,448)
Doctoral
　Texas A&M University (5,702/1,849)

Score: 16.71　　　　Rank: 295

Cumberland, MD-WV

Children in Public Schools (86%)
School Support ■■■■□

2 districts, 38 schools, 16,075 students

Children in Private Schools (14%)
6 Catholic, 2,121 students
1 NAIS, 339 students
1 Other, 162 students

Public Libraries
Library Popularity ■■□□□

3 systems, 6 branches
221,487 books; circulation: 540,942

Colleges and Universities
College Options ■■■□□
College Town ■■■■□

Associate of Arts
　3 campuses (5,675)
Comprehensive
　Frostburg State University (5,050/1,300)

Score: 51.55　　　　Rank: 172

Dallas, TX

Children in Public Schools (93%)
School Support ■■■■□

77 districts, 906 schools, 535,943 students

Children in Private Schools (7%)
44 Catholic, 16,332 students
12 NAIS, 6,799 students
68 Other, 17,827 students
Public Libraries

| Library Popularity | ■■□□□ |

56 systems, 35 branches
5,397,948 books; circulation: 13,634,334
Colleges and Universities

| College Options | ■■■■■ |
| College Town | ■■■□□ |

Associate of Arts
  11 campuses (107,752)
Baccalaureate
  Northwood University (1,021)
  Parker College of Chiropractic (1,210)
  Paul Quinn College (828)
Comprehensive
  Amber University (817/1,533)
  Criswell College (427/142)
  Dallas Baptist University (3,265/974)
  SW Assemblies of God College (1,343/23)
Doctoral
  Dallas Theological Seminary (2,408)
  East Texas State University (6,103/4,456)
  Southern Methodist University (5,433/4,664)
  Texas Woman's University (6,161/3,717)
  University of Dallas (1,231/2,433)
  University of North Texas (22,322/9,054)
  University of Texas (6,230/5,668)
  University of Texas SW Medical Center (555/1,366)
Score: **90.08**   Rank: **36**

Danbury, CT
Children in Public Schools (92%)

| School Support | ■■■■■ |

8 districts, 50 schools, 30,206 students
Children in Private Schools (8%)
8 Catholic, 2,317 students
3 NAIS, 703 students
9 Other, 145 students
Public Libraries

| Library Popularity | ■■■■■ |

13 systems, 1 branch
931,639 books; circulation: 2,084,987
Colleges and Universities

| College Options | ■□□□□ |
| College Town | ■■□□□ |

Comprehensive
  Western Connecticut State University (4,634/973)
Score: **17.28**   Rank: **293**

Danville, VA
Children in Public Schools (95%)

| School Support | ■■■■■ |

2 districts, 33 schools, 15,597 students
Children in Private Schools (5%)
1 Catholic, 312 students
1 NAIS, 304 students
3 Other, 317 students
Public Libraries

| Library Popularity | ■□□□□ |

2 systems, 4 branches
205,332 books; circulation: 442,153

Colleges and Universities

| College Options | ■■□□□ |
| College Town | ■■□□□ |

Associate of Arts
  1 campus (6,588)
Comprehensive
  Averett College (2,091/1,371)
Score: **22.66**   Rank: **274**

Davenport-Moline-Rock Island, IA-IL
Children in Public Schools (90%)

| School Support | ■■■■□ |

25 districts, 143 schools, 63,345 students
Children in Private Schools (10%)
17 Catholic, 5,626 students
3 Other, 835 students
Public Libraries

| Library Popularity | ■■■■□ |

20 systems, 15 branches
1,142,283 books; circulation: 2,772,418
Colleges and Universities

| College Options | ■■■■□ |
| College Town | ■■□□□ |

Associate of Arts
  2 campuses (17,604)
Baccalaureate
  Augustana College (2,668)
Comprehensive
  Palmer College of Chiropractic (93/2,198)
  Saint Ambrose University (2,067/942)
  Teikyo Marycrest University (963/410)
Score: **78.47**   Rank: **77**

★Dayton-Springfield, OH
Children in Public Schools (88%)

| School Support | ■■□□□ |

43 districts, 280 schools, 158,365 students
Children in Private Schools (12%)
34 Catholic, 14,490 students
1 NAIS, 385 students
31 Other, 5,300 students
Public Libraries

| Library Popularity | ■■■■■ |

13 systems, 32 branches
3,604,176 books; circulation: 12,269,423
Colleges and Universities

| College Options | ■■■■■ |
| College Town | ■■■■□ |

Associate of Arts
  5 campuses (39,388)
Baccalaureate
  Antioch College (633/18)
  Cedarville College (2,615)
  Wilberforce University (920)
  Wittenberg University (2,069)
Comprehensive
  Central State University (2,562/22)
  McGregor School of Antioch University (535/638)
Doctoral
  Air Force Institute of Technology (1,077)
  United Theological Seminary (686)
  University of Dayton (6,859/8,635)
  Wright State University (14,505/6,650)
Score: **96.88**   Rank: **11**

Daytona Beach, FL
Children in Public Schools (98%)
School Support
2 districts, 77 schools, 63,007 students
Children in Private Schools (2%)
7 Catholic, 1,758 students
3 Other, 133 students
Public Libraries
Library Popularity
1 system, 14 branches
738,158 books; circulation: 2,582,006
Colleges and Universities
College Options
College Town
Associate of Arts
1 campus (37,863)
Baccalaureate
Bethune Cookman College (2,544)
Comprehensive
Embry-Riddle Aeronautical University (12,921/5,920)
Stetson University (2,380/1,455)
Score: 66.85   Rank: 118

Decatur, AL
Children in Public Schools (99%)
School Support
4 districts, 54 schools, 25,140 students
Children in Private Schools (1%)
1 Catholic, 243 students
Public Libraries
Library Popularity
7 systems
168,172 books; circulation: 387,875
Colleges and Universities
College Options
College Town
Associate of Arts
1 campus (13,204)
Score: 20.96   Rank: 280

Decatur, IL
Children in Public Schools (93%)
School Support
9 districts, 52 schools, 20,249 students
Children in Private Schools (7%)
5 Catholic, 1,269 students
1 Other, 182 students
Public Libraries
Library Popularity
7 systems, 1 branch
331,029 books; circulation: 978,642
Colleges and Universities
College Options
College Town
Associate of Arts
1 campus (6,917)
Baccalaureate
Millikin University (1,995)
Score: 16.99   Rank: 294

★**Denver, CO**
Children in Public Schools (92%)
School Support
17 districts, 533 schools, 305,382 students
Children in Private Schools (8%)
33 Catholic, 11,265 students
6 NAIS, 2,650 students
144 Other, 13,905 students
Public Libraries
Library Popularity
8 systems, 56 branches
4,355,033 books; circulation: 14,988,451
Colleges and Universities
College Options
College Town
Associate of Arts
9 campuses (75,829)
Baccalaureate
Metropolitan State College (21,378)
Comprehensive
Colorado Christian University (1,844/449)
Regis University (7,105/2,543)
Doctoral
Colorado School of Mines (2,666/3,837)
Denver Conservative Baptist Seminary (725)
Iliff School of Theology (385)
University of Colorado (7,633/6,727)
University of Colorado Health Sciences Center (765/1,810)
University of Denver (4,208/7,378)
Score: 92.06   Rank: 29

★**Des Moines, IA**
Children in Public Schools (93%)
School Support
21 districts, 162 schools, 73,780 students
Children in Private Schools (7%)
12 Catholic, 5,351 students
7 Other, 384 students
Public Libraries
Library Popularity
29 systems, 5 branches
1,255,572 books; circulation: 3,212,515
Colleges and Universities
College Options
College Town
Associate of Arts
3 campuses (20,403)
Baccalaureate
Grand View College (1,766/14)
Simpson College (1,973)
Comprehensive
Faith Baptist Bible College and Seminary (285/69)
University of Osteopathic Health Sciences (73/1,203)
Doctoral
Drake University (4,542/12,422)
Score: 96.31   Rank: 14

Detroit, MI
Children in Public Schools (91%)
School Support
104 districts, 1,252 schools, 711,510 students

220

Children in Private Schools (9%)
158 Catholic, 50,091 students
6 NAIS, 2,837 students
66 Other, 12,822 students

Public Libraries

Library Popularity	■■□□□

78 systems, 92 branches
10,871,493 books; circulation: 19,713,354

Colleges and Universities

College Options	■■■■■
College Town	■■□□□

Associate of Arts
9 campuses (150,447)
Baccalaureate
Baker College Auburn Hills (971)
Baker College Mount Clemens (1,057)
Center For Creative Studies (1,164)
Detroit College of Business (6,606)
Michigan Christian College (386)
William Tyndale College (745)
Comprehensive
Baker College of Port Huron (989/10)
Lawrence Institute of Technology (4,852/661)
Madonna University (4,703/790)
Marygrove College (1,346/1,129)
University of Michigan (6,925/1,906)
Walsh College of Accounting (2,358/2,467)
Doctoral
Oakland University (13,526/4,010)
University of Detroit Mercy (5,414/3,698)
Wayne State University (21,478/15,842)

Score: 70.53   Rank: 105

Dothan, AL
Children in Public Schools (98%)

School Support	■■■□□

5 districts, 47 schools, 22,989 students

Children in Private Schools (2%)
1 NAIS, 435 students
1 Other, 65 students

Public Libraries

Library Popularity	■□□□□

6 systems, 2 branches
313,423 books; circulation: 399,650

Colleges and Universities

College Options	■■■□□
College Town	■■■□□

Associate of Arts
2 campuses (6,654)
Comprehensive
Troy State University (2,639/1,046)

Score: 25.77   Rank: 263

Dover, DE
Children in Public Schools (96%)

School Support	■■■■□

6 districts, 46 schools, 23,850 students

Children in Private Schools (4%)
1 Catholic, 510 students
4 Other, 406 students

Public Libraries

Library Popularity	■□□□□

3 systems
120,709 books; circulation: 326,684

Colleges and Universities

College Options	■■■□□
College Town	■■■□□

Associate of Arts
1 campus (2,814)
Comprehensive
Delaware State University (3,471/578)
Wesley College (1,842/7)

Score: 31.44   Rank: 243

Dubuque, IA
Children in Public Schools (67%)

School Support	■■■■■

2 districts, 26 schools, 12,123 students

Children in Private Schools (33%)
20 Catholic, 6,005 students

Public Libraries

Library Popularity	■■■■□

4 systems, 1 branch
328,870 books; circulation: 582,065

Colleges and Universities

College Options	■■■■□
College Town	■■■□□

Comprehensive
Clarke College (1,074/95)
Loras College (2,059/171)
Doctoral
University of Dubuque (779/332)

Score: 80.16   Rank: 71

Duluth-Superior, MN-WI
Children in Public Schools (94%)

School Support	■■■□□

18 districts, 117 schools, 38,842 students

Children in Private Schools (6%)
9 Catholic, 1,589 students
1 NAIS, 408 students
9 Other, 537 students

Public Libraries

Library Popularity	■■■■□

16 systems, 3 branches
957,250 books; circulation: 2,286,665

Colleges and Universities

College Options	■■■■□
College Town	■■■■■

Associate of Arts
5 campuses (13,773)
Comprehensive
College of Saint Scholastica (1,680/3,328)
University of Wisconsin (2,643/1,101)
Doctoral
University of Minnesota (11,272/817)

Score: 85.83   Rank: 51

Dutchess County, NY
Children in Public Schools (91%)

School Support	■■■■■

15 districts, 73 schools, 42,808 students

Children in Private Schools (9%)
12 Catholic, 3,301 students
5 NAIS, 1,092 students
3 Other, 182 students

Public Libraries
Library Popularity ■■■□□

21 system, 2 branches
638,558 books; circulation: 1,242,682

Colleges and Universities
College Options ■■■□□
College Town ■■■□□

Associate of Arts
1 campus (9,028)
Baccalaureate
Culinary Institute of America (3,383)
Comprehensive
Bard College (1,162/187)
Marist College (4,888/727)
Vassar College (2,456/2)
Score: 65.43   Rank: 123

Eau Claire, WI
Children in Public Schools (89%)
School Support ■■■■□

11 districts, 56 schools, 22,624 students
Children in Private Schools (11%)
16 Catholic, 2,473 students
7 Other, 408 students
Public Libraries
Library Popularity ■■■■■

10 systems
433,171 books; circulation: 1,394,524
Colleges and Universities
College Options ■■□□□
College Town ■■■■■

Associate of Arts
1 campus (5,013)
Comprehensive
University of Wisconsin (10,957/1,250)
Score: 49   Rank: 181

Edmonton, AB
Children in Public Schools (96%)
355 schools, 146,788 students
Children in Private Schools (4%)
28 Catholic and Other, 6,824 students
Public Libraries
Library Popularity ■■■■■

5 systems, 17 branches
1,586,160 books; circulation: 11,907,626
Colleges and Universities
College Options ■■■■□
College Town ■■□□□
Score: 72.52   Rank: 98

El Paso, TX
Children in Public Schools (96%)
School Support ■■■■□

9 districts, 202 schools, 145,250 students
Children in Private Schools (4%)
15 Catholic, 4,869 students
9 Other, 2,211 students

Public Libraries
Library Popularity ■□□□□

1 system, 10 branches
838,743 books; circulation: 1,581,458
Colleges and Universities
College Options ■■■□□
College Town ■■■□□

Associate of Arts
1 campus (30,132)
Doctoral
University of Texas (16,396/3,272)
Score: 30.59   Rank: 246

Elkhart-Goshen, IN
Children in Public Schools (94%)
School Support ■■□□□

7 districts, 54 schools, 30,174 students
Children in Private Schools (6%)
4 Catholic, 773 students
8 Other, 1,134 students
Public Libraries
Library Popularity ■■■■■

6 systems, 3 branches
487,893 books; circulation: 1,615,349
Colleges and Universities
College Options ■■■□□
College Town ■□□□□

Baccalaureate
Goshen College (1,166)
Score: 23.51   Rank: 271

Elmira, NY
Children in Public Schools (92%)
School Support ■■■■■

4 districts, 23 schools, 15,338 students
Children in Private Schools (8%)
5 Catholic, 1,177 students
Public Libraries
Library Popularity ■■■□□

2 systems, 4 branches
381,584 books; circulation: 622,787
Colleges and Universities
College Options ■■□□□
College Town ■□□□□

Comprehensive
Elmira College (1,843/648)
Score: 17.56   Rank: 292

Enid, OK
Children in Public Schools (99%)
School Support ■■■■■

8 districts, 32 schools, 10,285 students
Children in Private Schools (1%)
1 Other, 119 students
Public Libraries
Library Popularity ■□□□□

1 system
86,130 books; circulation: 144,717
Colleges and Universities
College Options ■□□□□
College Town ■□□□□

Associate of Arts
1 campus (2,946)

Comprehensive
Phillips University (807/92)
Score: 3.96   Rank: 341

Erie, PA
Children in Public Schools (81%)
School Support
13 districts, 76 schools, 43,852 students
Children in Private Schools (19%)
28 Catholic, 9,464 students
1 NAIS, 165 students
6 Other, 608 students
Public Libraries
Library Popularity
8 systems, 6 branches
654,667 books; circulation: 1,891,571
Colleges and Universities
College Options
College Town
Associate of Arts
2 campuses (7,339)
Comprehensive
Edinboro University (7,701/1,110)
Gannon University (3,280/838)
Mercyhurst College (2,893/77)
Pennsylvania State University (3,384/189)
Score: 70.25   Rank: 106

Eugene-Springfield, OR
Children in Public Schools (96%)
School Support
16 districts, 125 schools, 48,424 students
Children in Private Schools (4%)
3 Catholic, 1,178 students
4 Other, 668 students
Public Libraries
Library Popularity
7 systems, 1 branch
509,481 books; circulation: 2,163,092
Colleges and Universities
College Options
College Town
Associate of Arts
1 campus (15,472)
Comprehensive
Northwest Christian College (388/62)
Doctoral
University of Oregon (13,918/3,742)
Score: 61.18   Rank: 138

Evansville-Henderson, IN-KY
Children in Public Schools (88%)
School Support
6 districts, 82 schools, 44,898 students
Children in Private Schools (12%)
19 Catholic, 5,677 students
1 NAIS, 139 students
6 Other, 1,110 students
Public Libraries
Library Popularity
8 systems, 11 branches
1,109,116 books; circulation: 2,976,545

Colleges and Universities
College Options
College Town
Associate of Arts
2 campuses (6,415)
Comprehensive
University of Evansville (3,602/116)
University of Southern Indiana (8,644/693)
Score: 57.5   Rank: 151

Fargo-Moorhead, ND-MN
Children in Public Schools (94%)
School Support
13 districts, 65 schools, 27,662 students
Children in Private Schools (6%)
5 Catholic, 1,228 students
5 Other, 676 students
Public Libraries
Library Popularity
5 systems, 12 branches
516,555 books; circulation: 1,354,081
Colleges and Universities
College Options
College Town
Associate of Arts
1 campus (1,762)
Baccalaureate
Concordia College Moorhead (3,075)
Comprehensive
Moorhead State University (7,188/785)
Doctoral
North Dakota State University (9,203/1,518)
Score: 59.2   Rank: 145

Fayetteville, NC
Children in Public Schools (96%)
School Support
1 district, 72 schools, 48,340 students
Children in Private Schools (4%)
2 Catholic, 459 students
19 Other, 1,872 students
Public Libraries
Library Popularity
1 system, 6 branches
509,062 books; circulation: 1,967,537
Colleges and Universities
College Options
College Town
Associate of Arts
1 campus (12,823)
Baccalaureate
Methodist College (2,395)
Doctoral
Fayetteville State University (3,950/1,266)
Score: 29.74   Rank: 249

Fayetteville-Springdale-Rogers, AR
Children in Public Schools (97%)
School Support
15 districts, 82 schools, 39,938 students
Children in Private Schools (3%)
1 Catholic, 281 students
4 Other, 1,325 students

Public Libraries

Library Popularity

2 systems, 14 branches
380,814 books; circulation: 1,067,477

Colleges and Universities

College Options

College Town

Associate of Arts
1 campus (4,610)
Comprehensive
John Brown University (1,452/130)
Doctoral
University of Arkansas (12,949/3,434)

Score: 39.37   Rank: 215

Fitchburg-Leominster, MA

Children in Public Schools (86%)

School Support

7 districts, 36 schools, 20,462 students

Children in Private Schools (14%)

6 Catholic, 1,801 students
3 NAIS, 776 students
7 Other, 1,267 students

Public Libraries

Library Popularity

9 systems
562,317 books; circulation: 929,085

Colleges and Universities

College Options

College Town

Associate of Arts
1 campus (4,284)
Comprehensive
Fitchburg State College (5,068/6,576)

Score: 34.27   Rank: 233

Flagstaff, AZ-UT

Children in Public Schools (96%)

School Support

7 districts, 41 schools, 21,032 students

Children in Private Schools (4%)

1 Catholic, 247 students
1 NAIS, 90 students
2 Other, 589 students

Public Libraries

Library Popularity

8 systems, 1 branch
282,534 books; circulation: 629,669

Colleges and Universities

College Options

College Town

Associate of Arts
1 campus (2,738)
Doctoral
Northern Arizona University (16,753/8,991)

Score: 28.89   Rank: 252

Flint, MI

Children in Public Schools (94%)

School Support

21 districts, 156 schools, 82,874 students

Children in Private Schools (6%)

12 Catholic, 4,155 students
1 NAIS, 120 students
7 Other, 1,177 students

Public Libraries

Library Popularity

2 systems, 19 branches
1,072,452 books; circulation: 1,540,064

Colleges and Universities

College Options

College Town

Associate of Arts
1 campus (14,468)
Baccalaureate
Baker College of Flint (4,871)
Detroit College of Business (1,240)
Comprehensive
Baker College Corporate Services (996/125)
GMI Institute (2,455/823)
University of Michigan (7,134/557)

Score: 43.34   Rank: 201

Florence, AL

Children in Public Schools (98%)

School Support

6 districts, 49 schools, 22,355 students

Children in Private Schools (2%)

1 Catholic, 253 students
1 NAIS, 262 students

Public Libraries

Library Popularity

9 systems
234,142 books; circulation: 466,971

Colleges and Universities

College Options

College Town

Associate of Arts
1 campus (7,066)
Comprehensive
University of North Alabama (5,748/908)

Score: 37.96   Rank: 220

Florence, SC

Children in Public Schools (88%)

School Support

5 districts, 38 schools, 22,987 students

Children in Private Schools (12%)

1 Catholic, 275 students
16 Other, 2,786 students

Public Libraries

Library Popularity

1 system, 5 branches
162,997 books; circulation: 304,145

Colleges and Universities

College Options

College Town

Associate of Arts
1 campus (13,234)
Comprehensive
Francis Marion University (4,235/1,128)

Score: 24.92   Rank: 266

Fort Collins-Loveland, CO

Children in Public Schools (94%)
School Support ▪▪▫▫▫

3 districts, 73 schools, 35,915 students

Children in Private Schools (6%)
2 Catholic, 510 students
12 Other, 1,671 students

Public Libraries
Library Popularity ▪▪▪▪▫

5 systems, 1 branch
428,864 books; circulation: 1,794,186

Colleges and Universities
College Options ▪▪▫▫▫
College Town ▪▪▪▪▪

Comprehensive
    National Technological University (1,571)
Doctoral
    Colorado State University (20,858/4,475)
Score: **34.56**   Rank: **232**

Fort Lauderdale, FL

Children in Public Schools (93%)
School Support ▪▫▫▫▫

1 district, 196 schools, 202,010 students

Children in Private Schools (7%)
16 Catholic, 8,622 students
4 NAIS, 4,558 students
18 Other, 2,961 students

Public Libraries
Library Popularity ▪▪▫▫▫

5 systems, 32 branches
2,019,618 books; circulation: 7,355,770

Colleges and Universities
College Options ▪▪▪▪▫
College Town ▪▪▫▫▫

Associate of Arts
    6 campuses (65,331)
Doctoral
    Nova University (5,384/15,996)
Score: **48.44**   Rank: **183**

Fort Myers, FL

Children in Public Schools (95%)
School Support ▪▪▫▫▫

1 district, 72 schools, 50,670 students

Children in Private Schools (5%)
3 Catholic, 1,800 students
3 Other, 704 students

Public Libraries
Library Popularity ▪▪▪▫▫

3 systems, 10 branches
810,952 books; circulation: 2,445,655

Colleges and Universities
College Options ▪▪▫▫▫
College Town ▪▫▫▫▫

Associate of Arts
    3 campuses (16,686)
Comprehensive
    Florida Gulf Coast University (1,966/363)
Score: **9.34**   Rank: **321**

Fort Pierce, FL

Children in Public Schools (95%)
School Support ▪▪▫▫▫

2 districts, 53 schools, 41,018 students

Children in Private Schools (5%)
4 Catholic, 1,623 students
1 NAIS, 243 students
4 Other, 438 students

Public Libraries
Library Popularity ▪▪▫▫▫

2 systems, 9 branches
474,196 books; circulation: 1,410,141

Colleges and Universities
College Options ▪▪▫▫▫
College Town ▪▪▫▫▫

Associate of Arts
    1 campus (27,783)
Score: **7.08**   Rank: **330**

Fort Smith, AR

Children in Public Schools (96%)
School Support ▪▪▪▪▫

24 districts, 87 schools, 35,501 students

Children in Private Schools (4%)
4 Catholic, 989 students
2 Other, 498 students

Public Libraries
Library Popularity ▪▪▪▪▫

2 systems, 6 branches
227,270 books; circulation: 1,015,184

Colleges and Universities
College Options ▪▫▫▫▫
College Town ▪▫▫▫▫

Associate of Arts
    1 campus (8,244)
Score: **7.36**   Rank: **329**

Fort Walton Beach, FL

Children in Public Schools (94%)
School Support ▪▪▫▫▫

1 district, 37 schools, 29,454 students

Children in Private Schools (6%)
1 Catholic, 422 students
4 Other, 1,505 students

Public Libraries
Library Popularity ▪▪▫▫▫

6 systems
185,147 books; circulation: 287,646

Colleges and Universities
College Options ▪▫▫▫▫
College Town ▪▪▫▫▫

Associate of Arts
    1 campus (16,297)
Score: **5.09**   Rank: **337**

Fort Wayne, IN

Children in Public Schools (88%)
School Support ▪▪▫▫▫

13 districts, 128 schools, 72,487 students

Children in Private Schools (12%)
18 Catholic, 7,298 students
1 NAIS, 581 students
15 Other, 3,470 students

Public Libraries

| Library Popularity | ■■■■□ |

17 systems, 15 branches
3,987,822 books; circulation: 5,524,195

Colleges and Universities

| College Options | ■■■■□ |
| College Town | ■■■□□ |

Associate of Arts
  2 campuses (6,037)
Baccalaureate
  Indiana Institute of Technology (1,616)
  Lutheran College of Health Professions (756)
  Taylor University, Fort Wayne (541)
Comprehensive
  Huntington College (753/63)
  Indiana University-Purdue University (12,992/1,357)
  Saint Francis College (875/283)
Doctoral
  Concordia Theological Seminary (464)
Score: 79.88   **Rank: 72**

Fort Worth-Arlington, TX

Children in Public Schools (95%)

| School Support | ■■■■□ |

37 districts, 463 schools, 271,998 students

Children in Private Schools (5%)
15 Catholic, 5,307 students
4 NAIS, 2,570 students
32 Other, 7,094 students

Public Libraries

| Library Popularity | ■■□□□ |

29 systems, 14 branches
2,434,251 books; circulation: 6,931,103

Colleges and Universities

| College Options | ■■■■■ |
| College Town | ■■□□□ |

Associate of Arts
  2 campuses (44,840)
Comprehensive
  Southwestern Adventist College (1,157/38)
  Texas Wesleyan University (2,099/1,271)
Doctoral
  Southwestern Baptist Theological Seminary (275/3,476)
  Texas Christian University (6,908/1,484)
  University of North Texas Health Science Center (549)
  University of Texas (28,780/5,513)
Score: 66.57   **Rank: 119**

Fresno, CA

Children in Public Schools (97%)

| School Support | ■□□□□ |

46 districts, 332 schools, 198,578 students

Children in Private Schools (3%)
9 Catholic, 2,839 students
42 Other, 4,150 students

Public Libraries

| Library Popularity | ■□□□□ |

3 systems, 36 branches
1,104,636 books; circulation: 1,921,742

Colleges and Universities

| College Options | ■■■■□ |
| College Town | ■■□□ |

Associate of Arts
  4 campuses (37,382)
Comprehensive
  California State University (16,095/3,659)
  Fresno Pacific College (894/1,784)
  San Joaquin College of Law (58/272)
Doctoral
  California School of Professional Psychology (411)
Score: 51.84   **Rank: 171**

Gadsden, AL

Children in Public Schools (99%)

| School Support | ■■■□□ |

3 districts, 41 schools, 16,522 students

Children in Private Schools (1%)
1 Catholic, 148 students

Public Libraries

| Library Popularity | ■■□□□ |

5 systems, 3 branches
262,997 books; circulation: 338,838

Colleges and Universities

| College Options | ■□□□□ |
| College Town | ■■□□□ |

Associate of Arts
  1 campus (9,653)
Score: 8.49   **Rank: 325**

Gainesville, FL

Children in Public Schools (95%)

| School Support | ■■■□□ |

1 district, 42 schools, 28,834 students

Children in Private Schools (5%)
2 Catholic, 850 students
1 NAIS, 275 students
3 Other, 406 students

Public Libraries

| Library Popularity | ■■■■■ |

1 system, 10 branches
626,360 books; circulation: 1,929,737

Colleges and Universities

| College Options | ■■□□□ |
| College Town | ■■■■■ |

Associate of Arts
  2 campuses (18,570)
Doctoral
  University of Florida (34,717/10,960)
Score: 50.14   **Rank: 177**

Galveston-Texas City, TX

Children in Public Schools (96%)

| School Support | ■■■■□ |

9 districts, 89 schools, 61,069 students

Children in Private Schools (4%)
6 Catholic, 1,424 students
3 Other, 1,111 students

Public Libraries

| Library Popularity | ■■■□□ |

8 systems
715,687 books; circulation: 1,234,384

Colleges and Universities

| College Options | ■■■□□ |
| College Town | ■■□□ |

Associate of Arts
2 campuses (8,703)
Baccalaureate
Texas A&M University (1,395)
Doctoral
University of Texas Medical Branch (1,079/1,463)
Score: **43.62**   Rank: **200**

Gary, IN
Children in Public Schools (93%)
School Support   ■■□□□
24 districts, 197 schools, 110,887 students
Children in Private Schools (7%)
25 Catholic, 7,846 students
5 Other, 1,079 students
Public Libraries
Library Popularity   ■■■■■
9 systems, 35 branches
2,566,791 books; circulation: 5,424,357
Colleges and Universities
College Options   ■■■■□
College Town   ■■□□□
Associate of Arts
3 campuses (5,887)
Baccalaureate
Calumet College of Saint Joseph (1,436)
Comprehensive
Indiana University Northwest (6,857/959)
Purdue University Calumet (10,639/1,421)
Valparaiso University (3,091/996)
Score: **63.17**   Rank: **131**

Glens Falls, NY
Children in Public Schools (99%)
School Support   ■■■■■
21 districts, 46 schools, 22,355 students
Children in Private Schools (1%)
1 Catholic, 318 students
Public Libraries
Library Popularity   ■■■■■
18 systems
434,004 books; circulation: 969,880
Colleges and Universities
College Options   ■□□□□
College Town   ■□□□□
Associate of Arts
2 campuses (5,628)
Score: **15.01**   Rank: **301**

Goldsboro, NC
Children in Public Schools (94%)
School Support   ■■■■□
1 district, 27 schools, 18,871 students
Children in Private Schools (6%)
1 Catholic, 317 students
6 Other, 903 students
Public Libraries
Library Popularity   ■□□□□
1 system, 6 branches
106,675 books; circulation: 409,308
Colleges and Universities
College Options   ■■□□□
College Town   ■□□□□

Associate of Arts
1 campus (3,870)
Baccalaureate
Mount Olive College (1,673)
Score: **8.21**   Rank: **326**

Grand Forks, ND-MN
Children in Public Schools (94%)
School Support   ■■□□□
16 districts, 52 schools, 18,539 students
Children in Private Schools (6%)
7 Catholic, 951 students
6 Other, 292 students
Public Libraries
Library Popularity   ■■■■■
3 systems
259,540 books; circulation: 717,747
Colleges and Universities
College Options   ■■□□□
College Town   ■■■■■
Associate of Arts
1 campus (1,673)
Baccalaureate
University of Minnesota (3,052)
Doctoral
University of North Dakota (10,247/2,650)
Score: **56.37**   Rank: **155**

Grand Junction, CO
Children in Public Schools (95%)
School Support   ■■■□□
3 districts, 43 schools, 19,390 students
Children in Private Schools (5%)
1 Catholic, 446 students
8 Other, 618 students
Public Libraries
Library Popularity   ■■■□□
1 system, 7 branches
212,536 books; circulation: 696,295
Colleges and Universities
College Options   ■■□□□
College Town   ■■□□□
Baccalaureate
Mesa State College (5,823)
Score: **18.13**   Rank: **290**

Grand Rapids-Muskegon-Holland, MI
Children in Public Schools (88%)
School Support   ■□□□□
50 districts, 386 schools, 182,514 students
Children in Private Schools (12%)
44 Catholic, 11,435 students
34 Other, 11,052 students
Public Libraries
Library Popularity   ■■■■□
24 systems, 36 branches
2,894,444 books; circulation: 6,605,530
Colleges and Universities
College Options   ■■■■■
College Town   ■■■□□
Associate of Arts
2 campuses (27,554)

Baccalaureate
 Baker College of Muskegon (2,153)
 Davenport College (3,177)
 Davenport College of Business (1,169)
 Grand Rapids Baptist College and Seminary (1,049)
 Hope College (3,347)
 Kendall College of Art and Design (577)
Comprehensive
 Aquinas College (2,493/1,114)
 Calvin College (4,287/76)
 Grand Valley State University (13,130/4,506)
Score: 79.32   Rank: 74

Great Falls, MT
 Children in Public Schools (96%)

School Support	■■■□□

 13 districts, 41 schools, 15,096 students
 Children in Private Schools (4%)
 2 Catholic, 592 students
 Public Libraries

Library Popularity	■■□□□

 3 systems
 140,300 books; circulation: 438,834
 Colleges and Universities

College Options	■□□□□
College Town	■□□□□

 Associate of Arts
  1 campus (1,528)
 Comprehensive
  College of Great Falls (1,552/263)
Score: 2.54   Rank: 345

Greeley, CO
 Children in Public Schools (91%)

School Support	■■■□□

 13 districts, 63 schools, 25,762 students
 Children in Private Schools (9%)
 2 Catholic, 575 students
 19 Other, 2,066 students
 Public Libraries

Library Popularity	■■□□□

 9 systems, 2 branches
 396,481 books; circulation: 923,533
 Colleges and Universities

College Options	■■□□□
College Town	■■■■■

 Associate of Arts
  1 campus (14,103)
 Doctoral
  University of Northern Colorado (11,911/4,654)
Score: 34.84   Rank: 231

Green Bay, WI
 Children in (85%)

School Support	■■■■□

 8 districts, 66 schools, 35,662 students
 Children in (15%)
 19 Catholic, 5,473 students
 7 Other, 1,075 students
 Public Libraries

Library Popularity	■■■■□

 2 systems, 9 branches
 403,460 books; circulation: 1,705,684

Colleges and Universities

College Options	■■■□□
College Town	■■■■□

 Associate of Arts
  1 campus (12,946)
 Comprehensive
  Saint Norbert College (2,263/274)
  University of Wisconsin (6,132/715)
Score: 62.88   Rank: 132

Greensboro–Winston-Salem–High Point, NC
 Children in Public Schools (95%)

School Support	■■■■■

 12 districts, 305 schools, 185,918 students
 Children in Private Schools (5%)
 5 Catholic, 1,487 students
 4 NAIS, 1,967 students
 46 Other, 5,890 students
 Public Libraries

Library Popularity	■■□□□

 6 systems, 37 branches
 2,173,170 books; circulation: 5,936,305
 Colleges and Universities

College Options	■■■■■
College Town	■■■□□

 Associate of Arts
  5 campuses (29,283)
 Baccalaureate
  Bennett College (662)
  Greensboro College (1,151)
  Guilford College (1,726)
  Winston-Salem State University (3,525)
 Comprehensive
  Elon College (3,486/199)
  High Point University (3,178/69)
  North Carolina School of the Arts (702/57)
  Salem College (922/154)
 Doctoral
  North Carolina A&T State University (8,035/1,340)
  University of North Carolina (12,697/3,652)
  Wake Forest University (3,853/2,032)
Score: 88.1   Rank: 43

Greenville, NC
 Children in Public Schools (94%)

School Support	■■■■□

 1 district, 30 schools, 19,298 students
 Children in Private Schools (6%)
 1 Catholic, 506 students
 7 Other, 746 students
 Public Libraries

Library Popularity	■■□□□

 2 systems, 4 branches
 240,460 books; circulation: 525,098
 Colleges and Universities

College Options	■■□□□
College Town	■■■■■

 Associate of Arts
  1 campus (7,000)
 Doctoral
  East Carolina University (16,345/4,964)
Score: 41.92   Rank: 206

Greenville-Spartanburg-Anderson, SC

Children in Public Schools (94%)

School Support ▪▪▪▪□

16 districts, 261 schools, 141,339 students

Children in Private Schools (6%)

5 Catholic, 1,057 students

1 NAIS, 700 students

76 Other, 6,926 students

Public Libraries

Library Popularity ▪▪□□□

5 systems, 31 branches

1,774,428 books; circulation: 3,876,173

Colleges and Universities

College Options ▪▪▪▪▪

College Town ▪▪□□□

Associate of Arts

4 campuses (21,990)

Baccalaureate

Anderson College (1,097)

Limestone College (2,410)

North Greenville College (933)

Wofford College (1,193)

Comprehensive

Central Wesleyan College (1,499/105)

Converse College (738/1,052)

Furman University (2,679/299)

University of South Carolina (4,123/571)

Doctoral

Bob Jones University (3,891/678)

Clemson University (13,907/5,898)

Score: **74.5**   Rank: **91**

Hagerstown, MD

Children in Public Schools (96%)

School Support ▪▪▪▪□

1 district, 44 schools, 18,724 students

Children in Private Schools (4%)

1 Catholic, 291 students

3 Other, 570 students

Public Libraries

Library Popularity ▪▪▪□□

1 system, 6 branches

241,232 books; circulation: 865,779

Colleges and Universities

College Options ▪▪□□□

College Town ▪□□□□

Associate of Arts

1 campus (3,412)

Score: **11.04**   Rank: **315**

★Halifax, NS

Public K-13 (98%)

3 school boards, 148 schools, 56,848 students

Private K-13 (2%)

4 Catholic and Other, 1,039 students

Public Libraries

Library Popularity ▪▪▪▪▪

5 systems, 11 branches

1,166,341 books; circulation: 3,725,166

Colleges and Universities

College Options ▪▪▪▪▪

College Town ▪▪▪▪□

Associate of Arts

4 campuses (6,756)

Baccalaureate

University of King's College (694)

Comprehensive

Mount St. Vincent University (3,359/243)

Nova Scotia College of Art and Design (556/20)

St. Mary's University (6,928/677)

Doctoral

Dalhousie University (8,697/2,193)

Technical University of Nova Scotia (1,070/379)

Score: **90.93**   Rank: **33**

Hamilton, ON

Children in Public K-13 (64%)

91 schools, 40,615 students

Children in Catholic Separate K-13 (32%)

40 Schools, 20,233 students

Children in Private K-13 (4%)

11 schools, 2,310 students

Public Libraries

Library Popularity ▪▪▪▪□

4 systems, 31 branches

1,296,426 books; circulation: 4,978,756

Colleges and Universities

College Options ▪▪▪□□

College Town ▪▪□□□

Associate of Arts

1 campus (14,000)

Baccalaureate

Redeemer College (472)

Doctoral

McMaster University (14,453/2,632)

Score: **39.66**   Rank: **214**

Hamilton-Middletown, OH

Children in Public Schools (93%)

School Support ▪▪▪□□

10 districts, 78 schools, 53,903 students

Children in Private Schools (7%)

10 Catholic, 3,818 students

5 Other, 570 students

Public Libraries

Library Popularity ▪▪▪▪□

2 systems, 5 branches

637,759 books; circulation: 2,704,006

Colleges and Universities

College Options ▪▪▪□□

College Town ▪▪▪▪□

Associate of Arts

2 campuses (7,049)

Doctoral

Miami University (15,102/3,708)

Score: **60.9**   Rank: **139**

Harrisburg-Lebanon-Carlisle, PA

Children in Public Schools (89%)

School Support ▪▪▪▪□

37 districts, 192 schools, 107,484 students

Children in Private Schools (11%)

30 Catholic, 9,649 students

2 NAIS, 1,553 students

14 Other, 1,897 students

Public Libraries

Library Popularity ■■□□□

20 systems, 11 branches
928,141 books; circulation: 3,432,649

Colleges and Universities

College Options ■■■■■

College Town ■■■□

Associate of Arts
4 campuses (15,083)
Baccalaureate
Dickinson College (2,183)
Messiah College (2,581)
Comprehensive
Dickinson School of Law (536)
Lebanon Valley College (2,138/302)
Shippensburg University (6,155/1,554)
Widener University (814)
Doctoral
Pennsylvania State University (2,720/2,108)
Pennsylvania State University, Hershey Medical Center (596)
Score: **73.93**   Rank: **93**

★**Hartford, CT**

Children in Public Schools (94%)

School Support ■■■■■

62 districts, 364 schools, 182,278 students

Children in Private Schools (6%)

32 Catholic, 9,234 students
7 NAIS, 2,089 students
2 Other, 335 students

Public Libraries

Library Popularity ■■■■■

69 systems, 23 branches
4,940,466 books; circulation: 9,710,356

Colleges and Universities

College Options ■■■■■

College Town ■■□□

Associate of Arts
8 campuses (17,088)
Baccalaureate
Charter Oak State College (1,249)
Comprehensive
Central Connecticut State University (11,328/3,516)
Eastern Connecticut State University (5,583/451)
Hartford Graduate Center (1,772)
Saint Joseph College (1,461/977)
Trinity College (2,160/229)
Doctoral
University of Connecticut (14,667/7,804)
University of Hartford (6,096/2,999)
Wesleyan University (2,885/738)
Score: **91.21**   Rank: **32**

Hattiesburg, MS

Children in Public Schools (99%)

School Support ■■■■□

6 districts, 27 schools, 19,040 students

Children in Private Schools (1%)

4 Catholic, 752 students

Public Libraries

Library Popularity ■□□□□

1 system, 1 branch
90,387 books; circulation: 199,547

Colleges and Universities

College Options ■■□□□

College Town ■■■■■

Comprehensive
William Carey College (2,331/731)
Doctoral
University of Southern Mississippi (13,658/4,760)
Score: **52.4**   Rank: **169**

Hickory-Morganton-Lenoir, NC

Children in Public Schools (98%)

School Support ■■■■□

6 districts, 94 schools, 50,548 students

Children in Private Schools (2%)

1 NAIS, 25 students
17 Other, 1,116 students

Public Libraries

Library Popularity ■■□□□

5 systems, 7 branches
525,117 books; circulation: 1,320,861

Colleges and Universities

College Options ■■■□□

College Town ■□□□□

Associate of Arts
3 campuses (15,017)
Comprehensive
Lenoir-Rhyne College (1,588/329)
Score: **32.57**   Rank: **239**

Honolulu, HI

Children in Public Schools (86%)

School Support ■■□□□

1 district, 247 schools, 187,377 students

Children in Private Schools (14%)

28 Catholic, 9,746 students
10 NAIS, 11,505 students
49 Other, 9,226 students

Public Libraries

Library Popularity ■■■□□

1 system, 48 branches
3,502,155 books; circulation: 7,499,485

Colleges and Universities

College Options ■■■■■

College Town ■■■■□

Associate of Arts
6 campuses (27,053)
Baccalaureate
Brigham Young University (2,780)
University of Hawaii (899)
Comprehensive
Chaminade University of Honolulu (3,562/733)
Hawaii Pacific University (8,973/1,441)
Doctoral
University of Hawaii (17,661/13,631)
Score: **86.96**   Rank: **47**

Houma, LA

Children in Public Schools (87%)

School Support ■■□□□

2 districts, 70 schools, 38,518 students

Children in Private Schools (13%)

11 Catholic, 5,325 students
1 Other, 241 students

Public Libraries
Library Popularity
2 systems, 14 branches
311,713 books; circulation: 537,221

Colleges and Universities
College Options
College Town

Associate of Arts
2 campuses (1,267)
Comprehensive
Nicholls State University (8,147/1,400)
Score: 5.94   Rank: 334

Houston, TX
Children in Public Schools (96%)
School Support
44 districts, 936 schools, 719,073 students
Children in Private Schools (4%)
51 Catholic, 15,130 students
4 NAIS, 3,751 students
51 Other, 13,382 students
Public Libraries
Library Popularity
13 systems, 75 branches
6,724,984 books; circulation: 15,169,985
Colleges and Universities
College Options
College Town

Associate of Arts
10 campuses (137,538)
Baccalaureate
University of Houston (10,067)
Comprehensive
Houston Baptist University (2,046/887)
Prairie View A&M University (5,597/1,149)
University of Houston (4,473/4,692)
Doctoral
Baylor College of Medicine (4/1,140)
Rice University (3,151/1,584)
Texas Southern University (7,835/1,675)
University of Texas Health Science Center (363/3,127)
University of Saint Thomas (1,823/1,315)
Score: 71.1   Rank: 103

Huntington-Ashland, WV-KY-OH
Children in Public Schools (96%)
School Support
17 districts, 143 schools, 55,386 students
Children in Private Schools (4%)
7 Catholic, 1,376 students
6 Other, 829 students
Public Libraries
Library Popularity
5 systems, 15 branches
734,970 books; circulation: 1,560,786
Colleges and Universities
College Options
College Town

Associate of Arts
5 campuses (5,057)
Baccalaureate
Ohio University (2,679/364)

Comprehensive
Kentucky Christian College (540/60)
Doctoral
Marshall University (11,844/3,404)
Score: 67.13   Rank: 117

Huntsville, AL
Children in Public Schools (94%)
School Support
4 districts, 92 schools, 51,281 students
Children in Private Schools (6%)
3 Catholic, 847 students
1 NAIS, 650 students
4 Other, 1,705 students
Public Libraries
Library Popularity
2 systems, 8 branches
463,399 books; circulation: 1,988,137
Colleges and Universities
College Options
College Town

Associate of Arts
1 campus (1,094)
Baccalaureate
Athens State College (3,708)
Oakwood College (1,860)
Doctoral
Alabama A&M University (4,441/2,250)
University of Alabama (9,657/2,871)
Score: 89.51   Rank: 38

Indianapolis, IN
Children in Public Schools (98%)
School Support
54 districts, 427 schools, 240,871 students
Children in Private Schools (2%)
14 Catholic, 4,336 students
5 Other, 740 students
Public Libraries
Library Popularity
29 systems, 39 branches
3,831,651 books; circulation: 14,069,516
Colleges and Universities
College Options
College Town

Associate of Arts
2 campuses (9,406)
Baccalaureate
Franklin College of Indiana (938)
Marian College (1,430)
Comprehensive
Butler University (3,181/1,517)
Martin University (626/63)
Doctoral
Anderson University (2,286/254)
Christian Theological Seminary (534)
Indiana University-Purdue University (27,494/10,067)
University of Indianapolis (3,547/1,317)
Score: 83.85   Rank: 58

Iowa City, IA
Children in Public Schools (93%)
School Support
4 districts, 29 schools, 12,338 students

231

Children in Private Schools (7%)
2 Catholic, 901 students
1 Other, 25 students
Public Libraries
Library Popularity   ■■■■■
5 systems
275,641 books; circulation: 1,387,832
Colleges and Universities
College Options   ■□□□□
College Town   ■■■■■
Doctoral
University of Iowa (24,009/13,233)
Score: **42.2**   Rank: **205**

Jackson, MI
Children in Public Schools (91%)
School Support   ■■□□□
12 districts, 58 schools, 24,297 students
Children in Private Schools (9%)
8 Catholic, 2,423 students
2 Other, 56 students
Public Libraries
Library Popularity   ■■□□□
1 system, 12 branches
342,338 books; circulation: 744,701
Colleges and Universities
College Options   ■■□□□
College Town   ■■□□□
Associate of Arts
2 campuses (11,206)
Comprehensive
Baker College of Jackson (691)
Spring Arbor College (2,458/223)
Score: **10.48**   Rank: **317**

Jackson, MS
Children in Public Schools (94%)
School Support   ■■□□□
8 districts, 124 schools, 72,308 students
Children in Private Schools (6%)
7 Catholic, 2,466 students
6 Other, 1,926 students
Public Libraries
Library Popularity   ■□□□□
3 systems, 36 branches
941,089 books; circulation: 1,385,849
Colleges and Universities
College Options   ■■■■■
College Town   ■■■□
Associate of Arts
1 campus (12,188)
Baccalaureate
Belhaven College (1,648)
Tougaloo College (1,019)
Comprehensive
Millsaps College (1,382/179)
Mississippi College (2,373/1,731)
Doctoral
Jackson State University (6,813/1,552)
Reformed Theological Seminary (398)
University of Mississippi Medical Center (674/1,143)
Score: **69.68**   Rank: **108**

Jackson, TN
Children in Public Schools (94%)
School Support   ■■■■□
2 districts, 28 schools, 15,913 students
Children in Private Schools (6%)
1 Catholic, 252 students
1 NAIS, 757 students
1 Other, 25 students
Public Libraries
Library Popularity   ■□□□□
3 systems, 3 branches
170,887 books; circulation: 295,218
Colleges and Universities
College Options   ■■■□
College Town   ■■■■■
Associate of Arts
1 campus (4,960)
Baccalaureate
Lambuth University (1,427)
Lane College (667)
Comprehensive
Freed-Hardeman University (1,707/424)
Union University (2,204/159)
Score: **52.69**   Rank: **168**

Jacksonville, FL
Children in Public Schools (99%)
School Support   ■■□□□
4 districts, 221 schools, 170,664 students
Children in Private Schools (1%)
6 Catholic, 1,625 students
1 NAIS, 550 students
4 Other, 416 students
Public Libraries
Library Popularity   ■■□□□
3 systems, 23 branches
2,735,408 books; circulation: 4,374,505
Colleges and Universities
College Options   ■■■■□
College Town   ■□□□□
Associate of Arts
1 campus (36,619)
Baccalaureate
Edward Waters College (524)
Flagler College (1,540)
Jones College Jacksonville (1,207)
Trinity Baptist College (360)
Comprehensive
Jacksonville University (2,417/530)
Doctoral
University of North Florida (11,803/2,696)
Score: **44.75**   Rank: **196**

Jacksonville, NC
Children in Public Schools (97%)
School Support   ■■■□
1 district, 28 schools, 20,258 students
Children in Private Schools (3%)
1 Catholic, 281 students
8 Other, 454 students
Public Libraries
Library Popularity   ■□□□□
1 system, 3 branches
114,823 books; circulation: 359,949

Colleges and Universities

| College Options | ■□□□□ |
| College Town | ■□□□□ |

Associate of Arts
1 campus (5,898)

Score: **0.84**   Rank: **351**

Jamestown, NY
Children in Public Schools (92%)

| School Support | ■■■■■ |

18 districts, 55 schools, 24,327 students

Children in Private Schools (8%)
6 Catholic, 1,903 students
4 Other, 215 students

Public Libraries

| Library Popularity | ■■■■■ |

22 systems, 1 branch
639,838 books; circulation: 1,497,552

Colleges and Universities

| College Options | ■■□□□ |
| College Town | ■■■□□ |

Associate of Arts
1 campus (3,551)
Comprehensive
SUNY College Fredonia (4,764/740)

Score: **53.54**   Rank: **165**

Janesville-Beloit, WI
Children in Public Schools (95%)

| School Support | ■■■■■ |

8 districts, 57 schools, 27,345 students

Children in Private Schools (5%)
7 Catholic, 1,239 students
2 Other, 286 students

Public Libraries

| Library Popularity | ■■■■■ |

7 systems
442,188 books; circulation: 1,630,897

Colleges and Universities

| College Options | ■■□□□ |
| College Town | ■■■□□ |

Associate of Arts
1 campus (3,615)
Comprehensive
Beloit College (1,468/14)

Score: **37.67**   Rank: **221**

Jersey City, NJ
Children in Public Schools (79%)

| School Support | ■■■■■ |

13 districts, 113 schools, 74,633 students

Children in Private Schools (21%)
53 Catholic, 16,879 students
1 NAIS, 111 students

Public Libraries

| Library Popularity | ■■□□□ |

10 systems, 15 branches
2,022,343 books; circulation: 993,113

Colleges and Universities

| College Options | ■■■□□ |
| College Town | ■■□□□ |

Associate of Arts
3 campuses (6,185)

Comprehensive
Jersey City State College (8,198/3,305)
Saint Peter's College (4,239/726)
Doctoral
Stevens Institute of Technology (1,436/2,226)

Score: **40.22**   Rank: **212**

Johnson City-Kingsport-Bristol, TN-VA
Children in Public Schools (99%)

| School Support | ■■■■□ |

13 districts, 154 schools, 69,658 students

Children in Private Schools (1%)
3 Catholic, 489 students
1 Other, 105 students

Public Libraries

| Library Popularity | ■□□□□ |

11 systems, 18 branches
780,409 books; circulation: 1,974,028

Colleges and Universities

| College Options | ■■■■□ |
| College Town | ■■□□□ |

Associate of Arts
3 campuses (7,748)
Baccalaureate
Emory and Henry College (930)
King College (666)
Virginia Intermont College (843)
Comprehensive
Milligan College (905/88)
Doctoral
East Tennessee State University (10,656/3,217)

Score: **67.42**   Rank: **116**

Johnstown, PA
Children in Public Schools (82%)

| School Support | ■■■□□ |

24 districts, 71 schools, 33,252 students

Children in Private Schools (18%)
27 Catholic, 5,841 students
2 NAIS, 813 students
4 Other, 701 students

Public Libraries

| Library Popularity | ■□□□□ |

19 systems
469,874 books; circulation: 702,045

Colleges and Universities

| College Options | ■■■□□ |
| College Town | ■■□□□ |

Associate of Arts
1 campus (1,478)
Baccalaureate
Mount Aloysius College (3,246)
University of Pittsburgh (3,516)
Comprehensive
Saint Francis College (1,580/374)

Score: **33.99**   Rank: **234**

Jonesboro, AR
Children in Public Schools (99%)

| School Support | ■■■□□ |

8 districts, 31 schools, 12,054 students

Children in Private Schools (1%)
1 Catholic, 155 students

Public Libraries

Library Popularity ▪☐☐☐☐

1 system, 7 branches
143,434 books; circulation: 267,447

Colleges and Universities

College Options ▪☐☐☐☐

College Town ▪▪▪▪▪

Doctoral
Arkansas State University (10,565/1,841)

Score: **22.94**   Rank: **273**

Joplin, MO

Children in Public Schools (96%)

School Support ▪▪▪▪☐

12 districts, 68 schools, 24,993 students

Children in Private Schools (4%)

4 Catholic, 605 students
2 Other, 615 students

Public Libraries

Library Popularity ▪▪☐☐☐

5 systems, 1 branch
231,154 books; circulation: 580,826

Colleges and Universities

College Options ▪▪☐☐☐

College Town ▪▪▪☐☐

Associate of Arts
1 campus (2,890)
Baccalaureate
Missouri Southern State College (6,116)
Ozark Christian College (690)

Score: **35.41**   Rank: **229**

Kalamazoo-Battle Creek, MI

Children in Public Schools (93%)

School Support ▪▪☐☐☐

32 districts, 186 schools, 76,391 students

Children in Private Schools (7%)

13 Catholic, 3,745 students
14 Other, 2,271 students

Public Libraries

Library Popularity ▪▪▪☐☐

22 systems, 10 branches
1,274,065 books; circulation: 2,405,208

Colleges and Universities

College Options ▪▪▪▪☐

College Town ▪▪▪▪▪

Associate of Arts
3 campuses (28,863)
Baccalaureate
Albion College (1,641)
Davenport College (1,595)
Kalamazoo College (1,287)
Doctoral
Western Michigan University (21,879/9,772)

Score: **75.35**   Rank: **88**

Kankakee, IL

Children in Public Schools (87%)

School Support ▪▪▪☐☐

14 districts, 47 schools, 18,000 students

Children in Private Schools (13%)

7 Catholic, 2,121 students
4 Other, 749 students

Public Libraries

Library Popularity ▪▪▪▪☐

6 systems
214,820 books; circulation: 387,492

Colleges and Universities

College Options ▪▪☐☐☐

College Town ▪▪▪▪☐

Associate of Arts
1 campus (10,348)
Comprehensive
Olivet Nazarene University (2,203/507)

Score: **26.34**   Rank: **261**

★Kansas City, MO-KS

Children in Public Schools (92%)

School Support ▪▪▪▪▪

66 districts, 628 schools, 280,326 students

Children in Private Schools (8%)

51 Catholic, 17,256 students
2 NAIS, 1,309 students
37 Other, 5,514 students

Public Libraries

Library Popularity ▪▪▪▪▪

18 systems, 57 branches
6,398,726 books; circulation: 14,819,691

Colleges and Universities

College Options ▪▪▪▪▪

College Town ▪▪▪☐☐

Associate of Arts
8 campuses (69,120)
Baccalaureate
Cleveland Chiropractic College (67/613)
Kansas City Art Institute (596)
William Jewell College (2,101)
Comprehensive
Avila College (1,150/262)
Baker University Professional Studies (791/966)
Mid-America Nazarene College (1,590/212)
Ottawa University, Kansas City (756/107)
Park College (14,618/224)
Rockhurst College (2,303/868)
Saint Mary College (670/328)
U.S. Army Command & General Staff College (1,111)
Doctoral
Midwestern Baptist Theological Seminary (64/636)
University of Kansas Medical Center (657/2,560)
University of Missouri (10,035/7,770)

Score: **96.03**   Rank: **15**

Kenosha, WI

Children in Public Schools (92%)

School Support ▪▪▪☐☐

13 districts, 46 schools, 25,036 students

Children in Private Schools (8%)

9 Catholic, 1,904 students
2 Other, 254 students

Public Libraries

Library Popularity ▪▪▪▪☐

1 system, 6 branches
318,751 books; circulation: 1,136,467

Colleges and Universities

College Options ▪▪☐☐☐

College Town ▪▪▪▪▪

Associate of Arts
   1 campus (8,944)
Comprehensive
   Carthage College (2,573/157)
   University of Wisconsin (5,721/360)
Score: **55.24**   Rank: **159**

Killeen-Temple, TX
Children in Public Schools (99%)
   School Support
14 districts, 122 schools, 54,542 students
Children in Private Schools (1%)
2 Catholic, 326 students
3 Other, 360 students
Public Libraries
   Library Popularity
9 systems
282,204 books; circulation: 764,595
Colleges and Universities
   College Options
   College Town
Associate of Arts
   2 campuses (53,223)
Comprehensive
   University of Central Texas (997/443)
   University of Mary Hardin Baylor (2,462/381)
Score: **41.64**   Rank: **207**

Kitchener-Waterloo, ON
Children in Public K-13 (64%)
113 schools, 56,690 students
Children in Catholic Separate (26%)
52 schools, 23,303 students
Children in Private K-13 (10%)
42 schools, 8,887 students
Public Libraries
   Library Popularity
4 systems, 19 branches
780,363 books; circulation: 2,708,443
Colleges and Universities
   College Options
   College Town
Associate of Arts
   1 campus (4,500)
Doctoral
   University of Waterloo (20,508/2,107)
   Wilfrid Laurier University (7,387/773)
Score: **46.74**   Rank: **189**

Knoxville, TN
Children in Public Schools (96%)
   School Support
11 districts, 174 schools, 100,102 students
Children in Private Schools (4%)
4 Catholic, 1,692 students
2 NAIS, 1,193 students
6 Other, 798 students
Public Libraries
   Library Popularity
10 systems, 29 branches
1,132,407 books; circulation: 3,097,021

Colleges and Universities
   College Options
   College Town
Associate of Arts
   3 campuses (12,250)
Baccalaureate
   Knoxville College (516)
   Maryville College (945)
Comprehensive
   Johnson Bible College (476/60)
Doctoral
   University of Tennessee (21,766/9,160)
Score: **81.58**   Rank: **66**

Kokomo, IN
Children in Public Schools (96%)
   School Support
7 districts, 34 schools, 17,374 students
Children in Private Schools (4%)
2 Catholic, 495 students
2 Other, 232 students
Public Libraries
   Library Popularity
3 systems, 4 branches
439,308 books; circulation: 1,075,376
Colleges and Universities
   College Options
   College Town
Associate of Arts
   1 campus (2,681)
Comprehensive
   Indiana University (4,479/546)
Score: **40.5**   Rank: **211**

La Crosse, WI-MN
Children in Public Schools (84%)
   School Support
9 districts, 41 schools, 19,093 students
Children in Private Schools (16%)
10 Catholic, 2,246 students
9 Other, 1,305 students
Public Libraries
   Library Popularity
4 systems, 7 branches
383,617 books; circulation: 1,194,301
Colleges and Universities
   College Options
   College Town
Associate of Arts
   1 campus (8,188)
Comprehensive
   University of Wisconsin (9,177/1,898)
   Viterbo College (1,990/4,607)
Score: **82.15**   Rank: **64**

Lafayette, IN
Children in Public Schools (94%)
   School Support
7 districts, 49 schools, 24,576 students
Children in Private Schools (6%)
4 Catholic, 919 students
3 Other, 570 students

Public Libraries

Library Popularity ▪▪▪▪▪

5 systems, 3 branches
474,937 books; circulation: 1,460,347

Colleges and Universities

College Options ▪▪☐☐☐

College Town ▪▪▪▪▪

Associate of Arts
2 campuses (3,955)
Doctoral
Purdue University (32,432/8,762)
Score: **49.85**　　　　Rank: **178**

Lafayette, LA

Children in Public Schools (87%)

School Support ▪▪▪☐☐

4 districts, 121 schools, 69,282 students

Children in Private Schools (13%)

22 Catholic, 9,345 students
7 Other, 760 students

Public Libraries

Library Popularity ▪☐☐☐☐

5 systems, 20 branches
662,657 books; circulation: 1,484,481

Colleges and Universities

College Options ▪▪☐☐☐

College Town ▪▪▪☐☐

Associate of Arts
6 campuses (7,814)
Doctoral
University of Southwestern Louisiana (17,730/1,918)
Score: **31.72**　　　　Rank: **242**

Lake Charles, LA

Children in Public Schools (91%)

School Support ▪▪▪☐☐

1 district, 60 schools, 33,742 students

Children in Private Schools (9%)

8 Catholic, 2,518 students
5 Other, 659 students

Public Libraries

Library Popularity ▪▪☐☐☐

1 system, 13 branches
328,088 books; circulation: 724,767

Colleges and Universities

College Options ▪☐☐☐☐

College Town ▪▪▪☐☐

Associate of Arts
1 campus (1,889)
Comprehensive
McNeese State University (8,601/1,741)
Score: **10.76**　　　　Rank: **316**

Lakeland-Winter Haven, FL

Children in Public Schools (96%)

School Support ▪▪▪☐☐

1 district, 109 schools, 68,982 students

Children in Private Schools (4%)

5 Catholic, 1,574 students
5 Other, 1,428 students

Public Libraries

Library Popularity ▪▪▪☐☐

11 systems, 1 branch
440,636 books; circulation: 952,560

Colleges and Universities

College Options ▪▪▪▪☐

College Town ▪☐☐☐☐

Associate of Arts
2 campuses (11,163)
Baccalaureate
Southeastern College Assemblies of God (1,166)
Warner Southern College (775)
Webber College (509)
Comprehensive
Florida Southern College (4,198/76)
Score: **53.25**　　　　Rank: **166**

Lancaster, PA

Children in Public Schools (89%)

School Support ▪▪☐☐☐

16 districts, 125 schools, 65,193 students

Children in Private Schools (11%)

15 Catholic, 4,674 students
4 NAIS, 1,398 students
17 Other, 2,600 students

Public Libraries

Library Popularity ▪☐☐☐☐

10 systems, 7 branches
456,576 books; circulation: 1,587,747

Colleges and Universities

College Options ▪▪▪▪☐

College Town ▪☐☐☐☐

Associate of Arts
3 campuses (995)
Baccalaureate
Elizabethtown College (1,847)
Franklin and Marshall College (1,943)
Comprehensive
Lancaster Bible College (792/65)
Millersville University of Pennsylvania (7,938/3,117)
Score: **39.94**　　　　Rank: **213**

Lansing-East Lansing, MI

Children in Public Schools (95%)

School Support ▪▪☐☐☐

27 districts, 171 schools, 73,988 students

Children in Private Schools (5%)

12 Catholic, 3,097 students
7 Other, 674 students

Public Libraries

Library Popularity ▪▪☐☐☐

17 systems, 13 branches
736,782 books; circulation: 2,199,610

Colleges and Universities

College Options ▪▪▪☐☐

College Town ▪▪▪▪▪

Associate of Arts
2 campuses (32,065)
Baccalaureate
Davenport College (1,481)
Olivet College (929)
Doctoral
Michigan State University (35,514/11,513)
Score: **64.3**　　　　Rank: **127**

Laredo, TX

Children in Public Schools (96%)
School Support ■■■□□
4 districts, 60 schools, 42,210 students

Children in Private Schools (4%)
6 Catholic, 1,946 students
1 Other, 15 students

Public Libraries
Library Popularity ■□□□□
1 system, 2 branches
99,624 books; circulation: 207,693

Colleges and Universities
College Options ■■□□□
College Town ■■□□□
Associate of Arts
   1 campus (9,756)
Comprehensive
   Texas A&M International University (2,050/1,374)

Score: 8.78   Rank: 324

Las Cruces, NM

Children in Public Schools (99%)
School Support ■■□□□
3 districts, 60 schools, 34,703 students

Children in Private Schools (1%)
2 Catholic, 318 students
1 Other, 63 students

Public Libraries
Library Popularity ■■□□□
3 systems
164,168 books; circulation: 333,941

Colleges and Universities
College Options ■■□□□
College Town ■■■■■
Associate of Arts
   1 campus (3,893)
Doctoral
   New Mexico State University (15,208/3,207)

Score: 31.16   Rank: 244

Las Vegas, NV-AZ

Children in Public Schools (96%)
School Support ■□□□□
16 districts, 260 schools, 196,094 students

Children in Private Schools (4%)
7 Catholic, 3,399 students
2 NAIS, 832 students
31 Other, 3,367 students

Public Libraries
Library Popularity ■■□□□
13 systems, 33 branches
2,175,044 books; circulation: 5,492,167

Colleges and Universities
College Options ■■□□□
College Town ■■□□□
Associate of Arts
   2 campuses (43,346)
Doctoral
   University of Nevada (22,012/7,911)

Score: 16.43   Rank: 296

Lawrence, KS

Children in Public Schools (98%)
School Support ■■■■■
3 districts, 34 schools, 11,688 students

Children in Private Schools (2%)
1 Catholic, 305 students

Public Libraries
Library Popularity ■■■■□
3 systems
231,678 books; circulation: 592,943

Colleges and Universities
College Options ■■□□□
College Town ■■■■■
Baccalaureate
   Baker University (817)
   Haskell Indian Junior College (809)
Doctoral
   University of Kansas (18,087/6,949)

Score: 71.38   Rank: 102

Lawrence, MA-NH

Children in Public Schools (89%)
School Support ■□□□□
14 districts, 103 schools, 60,780 students

Children in Private Schools (11%)
18 Catholic, 5,880 students
3 NAIS, 1,944 students
6 Other, 996 students

Public Libraries
Library Popularity ■■■■□
24 systems, 2 branches
1,424,077 books; circulation: 2,389,637

Colleges and Universities
College Options ■■■□□
College Town ■□□□□
Associate of Arts
   2 campuses (8,498)
Baccalaureate
   Bradford College (586)
   Merrimack College (3,469)

Score: 33.71   Rank: 235

Lawton, OK

Children in Public Schools (99%)
School Support ■■■□□
11 districts, 64 schools, 22,698 students

Children in Private Schools (1%)
1 Catholic, 190 students

Public Libraries
Library Popularity ■□□□□
2 systems, 1 branch
127,692 books; circulation: 251,170

Colleges and Universities
College Options ■□□□□
College Town ■■■■□
Associate of Arts
   1 campus (411)
Comprehensive
   Cameron University (7,606/626)

Score: 13.31   Rank: 307

Education

237

Lewiston-Auburn, ME
Children in Public Schools (91%)
School Support ■■■■■
6 districts, 33 schools, 13,634 students
Children in Private Schools (9%)
4 Catholic, 1,167 students
4 Other, 360 students
Public Libraries
Library Popularity ■■■■□
7 systems, 1 branch
251,560 books; circulation: 532,957
Colleges and Universities
College Options ■■■□□
College Town ■□□□□
Associate of Arts
1 campus (1,273)
Baccalaureate
Bates College (1,720)
Score: **44.19**   Rank: **198**

★Lexington, KY
Children in Public Schools (93%)
School Support ■■■■□
9 districts, 124 schools, 65,550 students
Children in Private Schools (7%)
10 Catholic, 3,017 students
4 NAIS, 827 students
16 Other, 933 students
Public Libraries
Library Popularity ■■■□□
7 systems, 5 branches
891,699 books; circulation: 2,808,376
Colleges and Universities
College Options ■■■■■
College Town ■■■■■
Associate of Arts
2 campuses (8,124)
Baccalaureate
Asbury College (1,309)
Berea College (1,676)
Midway College (1,267)
Transylvania University (962)
Comprehensive
Eastern Kentucky University (15,776/3,095)
Georgetown College (1,235/528)
Doctoral
Asbury Theological Seminary (1,171)
University of Kentucky (19,204/7,593)
Score: **93.48**   Rank: **24**

Lima, OH
Children in Public Schools (90%)
School Support ■■□□□
16 districts, 62 schools, 29,576 students
Children in Private Schools (10%)
8 Catholic, 3,089 students
1 Other, 16 students
Public Libraries
Library Popularity ■■■■■
5 systems, 10 branches
550,409 books; circulation: 1,927,163

Colleges and Universities
College Options ■■■□□
College Town ■□□□□
Associate of Arts
2 campuses (5,592)
Comprehensive
Bluffton College (1,021/25)
Ohio State University (1,519/338)
Score: **35.12**   Rank: **230**

Lincoln, NE
Children in Public Schools (89%)
School Support ■■■■■
11 districts, 72 schools, 32,702 students
Children in Private Schools (11%)
12 Catholic, 3,561 students
6 Other, 559 students
Public Libraries
Library Popularity ■■■■■
1 system, 6 branches
568,485 books; circulation: 2,000,012
Colleges and Universities
College Options ■■■□□
College Town ■■■■■
Associate of Arts
2 campuses (12,762)
Baccalaureate
Nebraska Wesleyan University (1,696/9)
Union College (729)
Doctoral
University of Nebraska (21,608/7,110)
Score: **88.38**   Rank: **42**

Little Rock-North Little Rock, AR
Children in Public Schools (90%)
School Support ■■■■□
22 districts, 181 schools, 82,229 students
Children in Private Schools (10%)
11 Catholic, 4,286 students
1 NAIS, 1,290 students
8 Other, 4,388 students
Public Libraries
Library Popularity ■□□□□
4 systems, 18 branches
1,062,346 books; circulation: 1,622,146
Colleges and Universities
College Options ■■■■□
College Town ■■■■□
Associate of Arts
3 campuses (3,727)
Baccalaureate
Central Baptist College (345)
Hendrix College (969)
Philander Smith College (1,195)
Comprehensive
University of Central Arkansas (9,339/1,927)
Doctoral
University of Arkansas (11,872/3,129)
University of Arkansas For Medical Sciences (560/1,332)
Score: **77.33**   Rank: **81**

London, ON
  Children in Public K-13 (75%)
    114 schools, 61,172 students
  Children in Catholic Separate (21%)
    41 schools, 16,879 students
  Children in Private K-13 (4%)
    17 schools, 4,439 students
  Public Libraries
    Library Popularity
    4 systems, 36 branches
    1,154,426 books; circulation: 3,127,566
  Colleges and Universities
    College Options
    College Town
    Associate of Arts
      2 campuses (23,000)
    Baccalaureate
      Brescia College (847)
      Huron College (842)
      King's College (2,278)
    Doctoral
      University of Western Ontario (21,355/3,171)
  Score: **78.75**   Rank: **76**

Long Island, NY
  Children in Public Schools (88%)
    School Support
    128 districts, 635 schools, 409,881 students
  Children in Private Schools (12%)
    72 Catholic, 34,058 students
    10 NAIS, 3,562 students
    107 Other, 18,034 students
  Public Libraries
    Library Popularity
    108 systems, 18 branches
    13,990,632 books; circulation: 28,241,008
  Colleges and Universities
    College Options
    College Town
    Associate of Arts
      5 campuses (65,946)
    Baccalaureate
      SUNY College at Old Westbury (5,138)
      SUNY College of Technology (8,808)
      U.S. Merchant Marine Academy (926)
    Comprehensive
      Dowling College (4,613/3,241)
      Long Island University (1,988/1,394)
      Molloy College (2,554/232)
      New York Institute of Technology (1,252/71)
      St. Joseph's College (2,889/27)
    Doctoral
      Adelphi University (3,504/4,597)
      Hofstra University (9,682/4,796)
      Long Island University (5,218/5,687)
      New York Institute of Technology (3,818/3,680)
      SUNY at Stony Brook (13,868/7,417)
  Score: **52.97**   Rank: **167**

Longview-Marshall, TX
  Children in Public Schools (98%)
    School Support
    20 districts, 109 schools, 42,557 students

Children in Private Schools (2%)
    2 Catholic, 373 students
    3 Other, 619 students
  Public Libraries
    Library Popularity
    5 systems
    311,513 books; circulation: 505,684
  Colleges and Universities
    College Options
    College Town
    Associate of Arts
      1 campus (13,254)
    Baccalaureate
      Ambassador University (863)
      Wiley College (674)
    Comprehensive
      East Texas Baptist University (1,617/44)
      Letourneau University (2,740/304)
  Score: **45.6**   Rank: **193**

Los Angeles-Long Beach, CA
  Children in Public Schools (89%)
    School Support
    82 districts, 1,765 schools, 1,627,040 students
  Children in Private Schools (11%)
    250 Catholic, 87,921 students
    28 NAIS, 12,619 students
    843 Other, 94,190 students
  Public Libraries
    Library Popularity
    33 systems, 196 branches
    18,176,209 books; circulation: 37,430,513
  Colleges and Universities
    College Options
    College Town
    Associate of Arts
      28 campuses (431,401)
    Baccalaureate
      Claremont McKenna College (1,011)
      Life Bible College (440)
      Pitzer College (837)
      Pomona College (1,566)
      Scripps College (712/9)
      University of West Los Angeles (285/735)
    Comprehensive
      Antioch University (319/515)
      Art Center College of Design (1,741/91)
      California Institute of the Arts (707/402)
      California State Polytechnic University (17,614/2,667)
      Cal State University (23,872/6,153)
      Cal State University Dominguez Hills (8,157/3,816)
      Cal State University Northridge (23,197/6,267)
      College of Osteopathic Medicine (127/858)
      Harvey Mudd College (647/8)
      Loyola Marymount University (5,458/3,037)
      Mount St. Mary's College (2,064/580)
      Occidental College (1,640/72)
      Otis College of Art and Design (732/20)
      Pacific Oaks College (293/532)
      Samra University of Oriental Medicine (313)
      Southern California Institute of Architecture (258/182)
      The Masters College (970/304)
      West Coast University (530/636)

239

Whittier College (1,436/887)
Woodbury University (1,116/276)
Doctoral
   Azusa Pacific University (2,763/3,240)
   Biola University (2,338/1,212)
   California Institute of Technology (939/1,149)
   California School of Professional Psychology (673)
   California State University (17,101/6,500)
   Claremont Graduate School (2,066)
   Fuller Theological Seminary (/)
   Pepperdine University (3,597/5,300)
   School of Theology at Claremont (441)
   University of California (25,132/10,944)
   University of Laverne (4,269/3,959)
   University of Southern California (16,833/14,784)
Score: 77.05   **Rank: 82**

Louisville, KY-IN
Children in Public Schools (82%)
| School Support | ▪▪▪□□ |

13 districts, 262 schools, 147,367 students
Children in Private Schools (18%)
62 Catholic, 22,597 students
6 NAIS, 1,361 students
60 Other, 9,401 students
Public Libraries
| Library Popularity | ▪▪□□ |

8 systems, 28 branches
1,636,558 books; circulation: 4,957,642
Colleges and Universities
| College Options | ▪▪▪▪▪ |
| College Town | ▪▪▪□□ |

Associate of Arts
   4 campuses (17,533)
Comprehensive
   Bellarmine College (2,663/641)
   Indiana University Southeast (6,648/787)
Doctoral
   Southern Baptist Theological Seminary (642/1,557)
   Spalding University (1,179/467)
   University of Louisville (17,874/6,737)
Score: 85.55   **Rank: 52**

Lowell, MA-NH
Children in Public Schools (91%)
| School Support | ▪▪□□ |

15 districts, 78 schools, 46,594 students
Children in Private Schools (9%)
14 Catholic, 3,949 students
2 NAIS, 642 students
2 Other, 225 students
Public Libraries
| Library Popularity | ▪▪▪□ |

11 systems, 1 branch
799,094 books; circulation: 1,621,009
Colleges and Universities
| College Options | ▪□□□ |
| College Town | ▪▪▪□ |

Doctoral
   University of Massachusetts (10,519/2,885)
Score: 12.18   **Rank: 311**

Lubbock, TX
Children in Public Schools (97%)
| School Support | ▪▪▪▪▪ |

8 districts, 95 schools, 42,547 students
Children in Private Schools (3%)
2 Catholic, 413 students
2 Other, 758 students
Public Libraries
| Library Popularity | ▪□□□□ |

4 systems, 1 branch
317,736 books; circulation: 628,839
Colleges and Universities
| College Options | ▪▪□□ |
| College Town | ▪▪▪▪▪ |

Associate of Arts
   1 campus (257)
Comprehensive
   Lubbock Christian University (1,506/27)
   Texas Tech University Health Sciences Center (746/718)
Doctoral
   Texas Tech University (22,435/5,831)
Score: 54.95   **Rank: 160**

Lynchburg, VA
Children in Public Schools (98%)
| School Support | ▪▪▪▪ |

4 districts, 65 schools, 32,528 students
Children in Private Schools (2%)
1 Catholic, 340 students
1 NAIS, 191 students
1 Other, 45 students
Public Libraries
| Library Popularity | ▪▪▪□ |

4 systems, 9 branches
399,201 books; circulation: 1,219,815
Colleges and Universities
| College Options | ▪▪▪□ |
| College Town | ▪▪▪▪▪ |

Associate of Arts
   2 campuses (6,105)
Baccalaureate
   Randolph-Macon Woman's College (760)
   Sweet Briar College (806)
Comprehensive
   Lynchburg College (1,753/761)
Doctoral
   Liberty University (9,452/3,151)
Score: 76.2   **Rank: 85**

Macon, GA
Children in Public Schools (89%)
| School Support | ▪▪▪▪ |

5 districts, 84 schools, 53,698 students
Children in Private Schools (11%)
4 Catholic, 1,525 students
27 Other, 5,603 students
Public Libraries
| Library Popularity | ▪▪▪□ |

3 systems, 16 branches
637,525 books; circulation: 2,654,266
Colleges and Universities
| College Options | ▪▪▪▪ |
| College Town | ▪▪▪▪ |

Associate of Arts
    4 campuses (11,893)
Comprehensive
    Fort Valley State College (2,944/369)
    Wesleyan College (471/4)
Doctoral
    Mercer University (5,478/3,410)
Score: 76.48   Rank: 84

★Madison, WI
Children in Public Schools (93%)
  School Support
16 districts, 129 schools, 56,616 students
Children in Private Schools (7%)
14 Catholic, 3,623 students
6 Other, 665 students
Public Libraries
  Library Popularity
17 systems, 7 branches
1,269,880 books; circulation: 4,677,948
Colleges and Universities
  College Options
  College Town
Associate of Arts
    3 campuses (31,014)
Comprehensive
    Edgewood College (1,790/799)
Doctoral
    University of Wisconsin (32,049/12,655)
Score: 92.91   Rank: 26

Manchester, NH
Children in Public Schools (91%)
  School Support
5 districts, 40 schools, 28,310 students
Children in Private Schools (9%)
14 Catholic, 2,757 students
1 NAIS, 295 students
8 Other, 627 students
Public Libraries
  Library Popularity
9 systems, 2 branches
557,040 books; circulation: 925,138
Colleges and Universities
  College Options
  College Town
Associate of Arts
    1 campus (2,377)
Baccalaureate
    Saint Anselm College (2,272)
Comprehensive
    New Hampshire College (6,159/2,689)
    Notre Dame College (1,089/692)
Score: 79.03   Rank: 75

Mansfield, OH
Children in Public Schools (88%)
  School Support
16 districts, 77 schools, 32,065 students
Children in Private Schools (12%)
13 Catholic, 3,033 students
6 Other, 1,029 students

Public Libraries
  Library Popularity
5 systems, 8 branches
528,396 books; circulation: 2,013,244
Colleges and Universities
  College Options
  College Town
Associate of Arts
    2 campuses (3,946)
Comprehensive
    Ohio State University (1,624/456)
Score: 16.14   Rank: 297

McAllen-Edinburg-Mission, TX
Children in Public Schools (99%)
  School Support
15 districts, 180 schools, 122,358 students
Children in Private Schools (1%)
3 Catholic, 1,144 students
4 Other, 442 students
Public Libraries
  Library Popularity
9 systems
561,298 books; circulation: 1,076,495
Colleges and Universities
  College Options
  College Town
Associate of Arts
    1 campus (6,923)
Doctoral
    University of Texas Pan American (15,698/1,528)
Score: 3.68   Rank: 342

Medford-Ashland, OR
Children in Public Schools (95%)
  School Support
9 districts, 54 schools, 27,931 students
Children in Private Schools (5%)
1 Catholic, 201 students
1 NAIS, 350 students
2 Other, 787 students
Public Libraries
  Library Popularity
1 system, 14 branches
383,280 books; circulation: 1,351,740
Colleges and Universities
  College Options
  College Town
Comprehensive
    Southern Oregon State College (5,492/1,852)
Score: 7.64   Rank: 328

Melbourne-Titusville-Palm Bay, FL
Children in Public Schools (93%)
  School Support
1 district, 84 schools, 62,935 students
Children in Private Schools (7%)
9 Catholic, 3,707 students
8 Other, 1,328 students
Public Libraries
  Library Popularity
1 system, 15 branches
1,012,229 books; circulation: 3,078,787

Colleges and Universities

College Options	■■■■□
College Town	■■□□□

Associate of Arts
    1 campus (22,655)
Doctoral
    Florida Institute of Technology (2,022/3,442)
Score: **61.47**   Rank: **137**

Memphis, TN-AR-MS
Children in Public Schools (94%)

School Support	■■□□□

11 districts, 275 schools, 195,325 students
Children in Private Schools (6%)
19 Catholic, 6,487 students
5 NAIS, 3,071 students
10 Other, 2,242 students
Public Libraries

Library Popularity	■■■□□

6 systems, 33 branches
2,017,119 books; circulation: 4,736,742
Colleges and Universities

College Options	■■■■■
College Town	■■□□□

Associate of Arts
    9 campuses (30,785)
Baccalaureate
    Crichton College (710)
Comprehensive
    Christian Brothers University (1,883/417)
    Le Moyne-Owen College (1,563/65)
    Rhodes College (1,778/6)
Doctoral
    Memphis State University (17,564/6,494)
    University of Tennessee (485/1,684)
Score: **67.7**   Rank: **115**

Merced, CA
Children in Public Schools (96%)

School Support	■□□□□

21 districts, 77 schools, 47,474 students
Children in Private Schools (4%)
4 Catholic, 1,076 students
11 Other, 725 students
Public Libraries

Library Popularity	■□□□□

1 system, 11 branches
372,920 books; circulation: 230,945
Colleges and Universities

College Options	■□□□□
College Town	■□□□□

Score: **0**   Rank: **354**

Miami, FL
Children in Public Schools (94%)

School Support	■■□□□

1 district, 320 schools, 326,045 students
Children in Private Schools (6%)
30 Catholic, 15,904 students
4 NAIS, 2,431 students
26 Other, 3,943 students

Public Libraries

Library Popularity	■■□□□

7 systems, 32 branches
3,872,287 books; circulation: 10,518,317
Colleges and Universities

College Options	■■■■■
College Town	■■■□□

Associate of Arts
    4 campuses (82,013)
Baccalaureate
    Florida Memorial College (1,780)
    Johnson & Wales University (888)
    Trinity College (452)
Comprehensive
    Saint Thomas University (1,853/1,390)
Doctoral
    Barry University (6,477/3,881)
    Florida International University (21,598/13,762)
    University of Miami (9,585/6,668)
Score: **73.65**   Rank: **94**

Middlesex-Somerset-Hunterdon, NJ
Children in Public Schools (86%)

School Support	■■■■■

73 districts, 300 schools, 145,662 students
Children in Private Schools (14%)
53 Catholic, 19,204 students
8 NAIS, 4,060 students
5 Other, 993 students
Public Libraries

Library Popularity	■■■■□

41 systems, 15 branches
4,104,956 books; circulation: 7,753,612
Colleges and Universities

College Options	■■■■□
College Town	■■□□□

Associate of Arts
    4 campuses (20,050)
Doctoral
    Rutgers University (26,106/8,731)
Score: **73.37**   Rank: **95**

★Milwaukee-Waukesha, WI
Children in Public Schools (86%)

School Support	■■■■□

47 districts, 399 schools, 224,846 students
Children in Private Schools (14%)
102 Catholic, 29,017 students
3 NAIS, 1,456 students
56 Other, 10,030 students
Public Libraries

Library Popularity	■■■■□

41 systems, 12 branches
5,312,755 books; circulation: 12,359,713
Colleges and Universities

College Options	■■■■■
College Town	■■■■□

Associate of Arts
    3 campuses (73,878)
Baccalaureate
    Milwaukee Institute of Art Design (573)
    Wisconsin Lutheran College (491)

Comprehensive
    Alverno College (2,624/120)
    Cardinal Stritch College (3,587/5,333)
    Carroll College (2,558/92)
    Concordia University (3,520/704)
    Milwaukee School of Engineering (2,974/565)
    Mount Mary College (1,677/217)
Doctoral
    Marquette University (8,291/3,505)
    Medical College of Wisconsin (1,302)
    University of Wisconsin (21,687/5,954)
Score: 95.75   Rank: 16

★Minneapolis-St. Paul, MN-WI
Children in Public Schools (92%)
School Support	■□□□□

88 districts, 697 schools, 446,251 students
Children in Private Schools (8%)
60 Catholic, 18,419 students
4 NAIS, 3,774 students
122 Other, 19,194 students
Public Libraries
Library Popularity	■■■■■

25 systems, 109 branches
7,481,218 books; circulation: 28,227,421
Colleges and Universities
College Options	■■■■■
College Town	■■■□□

Associate of Arts
    15 campuses (104,606)
Baccalaureate
    Macalester College (1,858/26)
    North Central Bible College (1,163)
    Northwestern College (1,712)
Comprehensive
    Augsburg College (3,184/296)
    Bethel College (2,456/267)
    College of Saint Catherine (2,929/1,592)
    Concordia College (1,714/19)
    Crown College (773/19)
    Hamline University (1,727/7,935)
    Metropolitan State University (7,834/433)
    Minneapolis College of Art and Design (549/24)
    University of Wisconsin (5,557/1,644)
    William Mitchell College of Law (1,109)
Doctoral
    Bethel Theological Seminary (565)
    Luther Northwestern Theological Seminary (779)
    University of Minnesota (43,799/17,622)
    University of St. Thomas (5,512/7,659)
Score: 95.46   Rank: 17

Missoula, MT
Children in Public Schools (93%)
School Support	■■■□□

14 districts, 43 schools, 13,900 students
Children in Private Schools (7%)
2 Catholic, 465 students
3 Other, 644 students
Public Libraries
Library Popularity	■■■■□

1 system, 2 branches
170,000 books; circulation: 685,172

Colleges and Universities
College Options	■□□□□
College Town	■■■■■

Doctoral
    University of Montana (12,046/2,198)
Score: 33.14   Rank: 237

Mobile, AL
Children in Public Schools (90%)
School Support	■■■□□

2 districts, 136 schools, 83,135 students
Children in Private Schools (10%)
13 Catholic, 5,146 students
2 NAIS, 1,644 students
7 Other, 3,188 students
Public Libraries
Library Popularity	■□□□□

16 systems, 7 branches
808,713 books; circulation: 2,127,893
Colleges and Universities
College Options	■■■■□
College Town	■■□□□

Associate of Arts
    2 campuses (12,360)
Comprehensive
    Spring Hill College (1,305/494)
    University of Mobile (2,226/320)
Doctoral
    U.S. Sports Academy (582)
    University of South Alabama (12,081/2,738)
Score: 60.62   Rank: 140

Modesto, CA
Children in Public Schools (94%)
School Support	■□□□□

30 districts, 132 schools, 90,095 students
Children in Private Schools (6%)
6 Catholic, 1,738 students
34 Other, 3,779 students
Public Libraries
Library Popularity	■□□□□

1 system, 12 branches
584,839 books; circulation: 1,268,696
Colleges and Universities
College Options	■□□□□
College Town	■■□□□

Associate of Arts
    1 campus (19,790)
Comprehensive
    California State University (5,517/1,437)
Score: 4.53   Rank: 339

Monmouth-Ocean, NJ
Children in Public Schools (87%)
School Support	■■■■■

81 districts, 280 schools, 160,217 students
Children in Private Schools (13%)
34 Catholic, 16,608 students
2 NAIS, 773 students
11 Other, 1,993 students
Public Libraries
Library Popularity	■■■■□

28 systems, 32 branches
3,282,891 books; circulation: 7,504,887

Colleges and Universities

| College Options | ■■■■☐ |
| College Town | ■☐☐☐☐ |

Associate of Arts
3 campuses (30,711)
Comprehensive
Beth Medrash Govoha (509/1,524)
Georgian Court College (2,168/1,038)
Monmouth College (4,157/1,473)

Score: **59.49**   Rank: **144**

Monroe, LA

Children in Public Schools (92%)

| School Support | ■■■☐☐ |

2 districts, 52 schools, 29,115 students

Children in Private Schools (8%)
5 Catholic, 1,056 students
5 Other, 1,555 students

Public Libraries

| Library Popularity | ■■☐☐☐ |

1 system, 4 branches
296,343 books; circulation: 791,852

Colleges and Universities

| College Options | ■☐☐☐☐ |
| College Town | ■■■■■ |

Associate of Arts
1 campus (853)
Doctoral
Northeast Louisiana University (12,479/2,048)

Score: **24.07**   Rank: **269**

Montgomery, AL

Children in Public Schools (95%)

| School Support | ■■■☐☐ |

5 districts, 89 schools, 53,775 students

Children in Private Schools (5%)
5 Catholic, 1,355 students
1 NAIS, 786 students
3 Other, 713 students

Public Libraries

| Library Popularity | ■☐☐☐☐ |

4 systems, 16 branches
545,288 books; circulation: 660,563

Colleges and Universities

| College Options | ■■■■☐ |
| College Town | ■■■■☐ |

Associate of Arts
4 campuses (74,652)
Baccalaureate
Faulkner University (2,969/503)
Huntingdon College (768)
Comprehensive
Alabama State University (5,415/1,324)
Auburn University (6,901/1,440)
Troy State University (4,860/930)

Score: **74.22**   Rank: **92**

Montreal, PQ

Children in Public Schools
27 districts, 903 schools, 324,874 students

Public Libraries

| Library Popularity | ■■☐☐☐ |

55 systems, 196 branches
6,481,409 books; circulation: 14,386,819

Colleges and Universities

| College Options | ■■■■■ |
| College Town | ■■■☐☐ |

Associate of Arts
15 campuses (75,338)
Comprehensive
Ecole de Technologie Superieure (2,478/63)
Doctoral
Concordia University (22,126/3,703)
Ecole des Hautes Etudes Commerciales (7,601/1,740)
Ecole Polytechnique (4,298/1,546)
McGill University (20,276/8,203)
Universite de Montreal (31,581/8,570)
Universite du Quebec (36,680/4,377)

Score: **83.28**   Rank: **60**

Muncie, IN

Children in Public Schools (97%)

| School Support | ■■■■☐ |

8 districts, 41 schools, 17,955 students

Children in Private Schools (3%)
2 Catholic, 451 students
1 Other, 20 students

Public Libraries

| Library Popularity | ■■■■■ |

1 system, 5 branches
310,186 books; circulation: 742,196

Colleges and Universities

| College Options | ■☐☐☐☐ |
| College Town | ■■■■■ |

Associate of Arts
1 campus (3,655)
Doctoral
Ball State University (24,761/4,579)

Score: **54.39**   Rank: **162**

Myrtle Beach, SC

Children in Public Schools (97%)

| School Support | ■■■■■ |

1 district, 39 schools, 25,411 students

Children in Private Schools (3%)
1 Catholic, 269 students
8 Other, 587 students

Public Libraries

| Library Popularity | ■☐☐☐☐ |

2 systems, 5 branches
261,925 books; circulation: 687,263

Colleges and Universities

| College Options | ■☐☐☐☐ |
| College Town | ■☐☐☐☐ |

Associate of Arts
1 campus (4,560)
Comprehensive
Coastal Carolina University (5,028/567)

Score: **12.74**   Rank: **309**

Naples, FL

Children in Public Schools (95%)

| School Support | ■■☐☐☐ |

1 district, 35 schools, 27,565 students

Children in Private Schools (5%)
3 Catholic, 868 students
1 NAIS, 550 students

Public Libraries
Library Popularity

1 system, 7 branches
254,775 books; circulation: 1,327,267
Colleges and Universities
College Options

College Town

Score: **13.88**   Rank: **305**

Nashua, NH
Children in Public Schools (92%)
School Support

7 districts, 49 schools, 30,681 students
Children in Private Schools (8%)
7 Catholic, 2,234 students
1 NAIS, 98 students
6 Other, 572 students
Public Libraries
Library Popularity

13 systems, 1 branch
573,636 books; circulation: 1,424,808
Colleges and Universities
College Options

College Town

Associate of Arts
   1 campus (1,901)
Baccalaureate
   Daniel Webster College (1,294)
Comprehensive
   Rivier College (2,315/1,509)
Score: **47.59**   Rank: **186**

Nashville, TN
Children in Public Schools (95%)
School Support

10 districts, 274 schools, 173,390 students
Children in Private Schools (5%)
10 Catholic, 3,675 students
8 NAIS, 3,739 students
7 Other, 1,532 students
Public Libraries
Library Popularity

16 systems, 26 branches
1,390,969 books; circulation: 4,537,512
Colleges and Universities
College Options

College Town

Associate of Arts
   6 campuses (23,165)
Baccalaureate
   Aquinas Junior College (655)
   Free Will Baptist Bible College (373)
Comprehensive
   Belmont University (3,260/551)
   Cumberland University (1,163/110)
   David Lipscomb University (3,011/189)
   Fisk University (860/41)
   Trevecca Nazarene College (1,355/579)
Doctoral
   Meharry Medical College (721)
   Middle Tennessee State University (18,664/3,325)
   Tennessee State University (8,038/2,286)
   Vanderbilt University (5,960/4,774)
Score: **84.13**   Rank: **57**

New Bedford, MA
Children in Public Schools (91%)
School Support

10 districts, 50 schools, 26,619 students
Children in Private Schools (9%)
8 Catholic, 1,932 students
2 NAIS, 742 students
2 Other, 81 students
Public Libraries
Library Popularity

8 systems, 7 branches
686,161 books; circulation: 967,361
Colleges and Universities
College Options

College Town

Doctoral
   University of Massachusetts (7,734/656)
Score: **6.51**   Rank: **332**

★New Haven-Meriden, CT
Children in Public Schools (90%)
School Support

17 districts, 154 schools, 76,132 students
Children in Private Schools (10%)
22 Catholic, 6,115 students
5 NAIS, 2,825 students
2 Other, 391 students
Public Libraries
Library Popularity

18 systems, 9 branches
2,137,265 books; circulation: 3,601,893
Colleges and Universities
College Options

College Town

Associate of Arts
   1 campus (6,792)
Comprehensive
   Albertus Magnus College (1,373/26)
   Quinnipiac College (4,053/1,575)
   Southern Connecticut State University (12,139/6,364)
Doctoral
   University of New Haven (3,406/2,518)
   Yale University (5,326/5,567)
Score: **90.65**   Rank: **34**

New London-Norwich, CT-RI
Children in Public Schools (92%)
School Support

15 districts, 68 schools, 27,143 students
Children in Private Schools (8%)
14 Catholic, 2,963 students
2 NAIS, 511 students
1 Other, 200 students
Public Libraries
Library Popularity

25 systems, 1 branch
1,202,467 books; circulation: 2,441,568
Colleges and Universities
College Options

College Town

Associate of Arts
   2 campuses (6,060)

Baccalaureate
U.S. Coast Guard Academy (862)
Comprehensive
Connecticut College (2,134/60)
Score: 53.82   Rank: 164

New Orleans, LA
Children in Public Schools (77%)
School Support
8 districts, 322 schools, 206,642 students
Children in Private Schools (23%)
98 Catholic, 49,630 students
8 NAIS, 3,948 students
40 Other, 8,276 students
Public Libraries
Library Popularity
8 systems, 48 branches
2,834,222 books; circulation: 4,415,418
Colleges and Universities
College Options
College Town
Associate of Arts
8 campuses (27,479)
Baccalaureate
Dillard University (1,679)
Comprehensive
Loyola University (3,853/2,003)
Our Lady of Holy Cross College (1,420/84)
Southern University (5,650/557)
Xavier University (3,333/738)
Doctoral
Louisiana State University Medical Center (1,318/2,100)
New Orleans Baptist Theological Seminary (844/1,396)
Tulane University (7,084/5,071)
University of New Orleans (14,768/5,451)
Score: 75.07   Rank: 89

★New York, NY
Children in Public Schools (88%)
School Support
65 districts, 1,451 schools, 1,178,328 students
Children in Private Schools (12%)
325 Catholic, 136,510 students
42 NAIS, 15,681 students
43 Other, 8,058 students
Public Libraries
Library Popularity
66 systems, 209 branches
37,714,591 books; circulation: 46,092,164
Colleges and Universities
College Options
College Town
Associate of Arts
31 campuses (122,133)
Baccalaureate
Barnard College (2,361)
College of Aeronautics (1,382)
Concordia College (822)
CUNY Medgar Evers College (6,857)
CUNY New York City Technical College (13,478)
CUNY York College (8,039)
Marymount College (1,289)

Marymount Manhattan College (2,335)
New York School of Interior Design (959)
Rabbinical College Bobover Yeshiva Bnei Zion (498/24)
St Francis College (2,353)
St. Joseph's College (1,736)
Comprehensive
Audrey Cohen College (1,339/144)
Bank Street College of Education (1,423)
Boricua College (2,355)
College of Mount Saint Vincent (1,417/271)
College of New Rochelle (6,506/3,373)
Cooper Union (937/80)
CUNY Bernard Baruch College (16,631/2,801)
CUNY Brooklyn College (14,342/7,293)
CUNY City College (13,120/4,674)
CUNY College of Staten Island (13,203/1,999)
CUNY Hunter College (17,503/5,343)
CUNY John Jay College Criminal Justice (11,541/1,053)
CUNY Lehman College (9,801/2,653)
Dominican College of Blauvelt (1,881/30)
Fashion Institute of Technology (16,660/63)
Iona College (4,710/2,187)
Long Island University (489)
Manhattan College (2,835/935)
Manhattanville College (1,196/1,129)
Mercy College (9,062/407)
Mount Sinai School of Medicine (508)
New York Institute of Technology (2,056/1,083)
Nyack College (942/337)
Pace University, Pleasantville (4,514/376)
Pace University, White Plains (2,738)
Pratt Institute (1,954/1,975)
Queens College (17,927/4,387)
Saint Thomas Aquinas College (2,000/162)
Sarah Lawrence College (1,125/256)
SUNY College at Purchase (4,975/82)
SUNY Maritime College (696/304)
The College of Insurance (609/175)
Touro College (10,628/1,521)
Wagner College (1,754/405)
Doctoral
Columbia University (8,147/13,870)
Cornell University Medical College (39/618)
CUNY Graduate School and University Center (4,407)
Fordham University (6,800/11,105)
Long Island University (8,047/2,368)
Manhattan School of Music (422/436)
New School for Social Research (6,323/3,350)
New York Medical College (1,615)
New York University (20,149/23,959)
Pace University (7,096/2,747)
Polytechnic University (1,684/2,755)
St. John's University (13,853/5,757)
SUNY Health Science Center (594/1,025)
Teachers College at Columbia University (5,872)
The Juilliard School (754/317)
Yeshiva University (2,632/3,629)
Score: 94.61   Rank: 20

★Newark, NJ
Children in Public Schools (85%)
School Support
135 districts, 607 schools, 292,823 students

Children in Private Schools (15%)
- 121 Catholic, 38,184 students
- 15 NAIS, 6,118 students
- 15 Other, 2,911 students

Public Libraries

Library Popularity

80 systems, 37 branches
8,675,300 books; circulation: 11,795,726

Colleges and Universities

College Options

College Town

Associate of Arts
- 9 campuses (45,244)

Baccalaureate
- Bloomfield College (2,583)

Comprehensive
- Caldwell College (2,012/119)
- Centenary College (1,187/24)
- College of Saint Elizabeth (1,737/349)
- *Kean College of New Jersey* (12,146/2,344)
- *Montclair State College* (9,855/4,746)

Doctoral
- Drew University (1,648/682)
- *New Jersey Institute of Technology* (7,094/3,421)
- *Rutgers University* (6,116/3,762)
- Seton Hall University (6,363/5,334)
- *University of Medicine and Dentistry* (1,057/3,592)

Score: 93.76   Rank: 23

Newburgh, NY-PA

Children in Public Schools (94%)

School Support

20 districts, 92 schools, 62,855 students

Children in Private Schools (6%)
- 14 Catholic, 3,591 students
- 6 Other, 558 students

Public Libraries

Library Popularity

20 systems, 7 branches
851,717 books; circulation: 1,705,633

Colleges and Universities

College Options

College Town

Associate of Arts
- 1 campus (7,898)

Baccalaureate
- *U.S. Military Academy* (4,091)

Comprehensive
- Mount Saint Mary College (1,717/440)

Score: 29.46   Rank: 250

Norfolk-Virginia Beach-Newport News,

Children in Public Schools (97%)

School Support

21 districts, 372 schools, 263,891 students

Children in Private Schools (3%)
- 13 Catholic, 4,721 students
- 5 NAIS, 3,204 students
- 8 Other, 1,172 students

Public Libraries

Library Popularity

11 systems, 43 branches
3,699,072 books; circulation: 9,467,840

Colleges and Universities

College Options

College Town

Associate of Arts
- 7 campuses (42,555)

Baccalaureate
- Virginia Wesleyan College (1,883)

Comprehensive
- *Christopher Newport University* (5,509/313)

Doctoral
- *College of William and Mary* (5,715/3,009)
- Eastern Virginia Medical School (715)
- Hampton University (7,508/556)
- *Norfolk State University* (8,229/1,479)
- *Old Dominion University* (14,111/8,301)
- Regent University (1,688)

Score: 86.68   Rank: 48

Oakland, CA

Children in Public Schools (90%)

School Support

38 districts, 562 schools, 343,879 students

Children in Private Schools (10%)
- 60 Catholic, 21,072 students
- 6 NAIS, 2,044 students
- 150 Other, 15,466 students

Public Libraries

Library Popularity

9 systems, 61 branches
4,275,044 books; circulation: 12,482,685

Colleges and Universities

College Options

College Town

Associate of Arts
- 17 campuses (138,433)

Baccalaureate
- Patten College (673)

Comprehensive
- California College of Arts and Crafts (1,199/77)
- *California State University* (12,435/3,933)
- Holy Names College (785/778)
- Mills College (871/298)
- Saint Mary's College of California (2,931/1,389)
- Samuel Merritt College (348/304)

Doctoral
- California School of Professional Psychology (692)
- Graduate Theological Union (391)
- John F. Kennedy University (426/2,080)
- *University of California* (23,110/8,717)

Score: 84.41   Rank: 56

Ocala, FL

Children in Public Schools (98%)

School Support

1 district, 44 schools, 34,065 students

Children in Private Schools (2%)
- 1 Catholic, 556 students
- 2 Other, 190 students

Public Libraries

Library Popularity

1 system, 10 branches
176,950 books; circulation: 692,664

Colleges and Universities

| College Options | ■□□□□ |
| College Town | ■□□□□ |

Associate of Arts
1 campus (10,751)
Score: **0.56**   Rank: **352**

Odessa-Midland, TX

Children in Public Schools (96%)

| School Support | ■■■□□ |

3 districts, 83 schools, 52,503 students

Children in Private Schools (4%)
2 Catholic, 590 students
1 NAIS, 490 students
3 Other, 1,255 students

Public Libraries

| Library Popularity | ■□□□□ |

2 systems, 1 branch
364,562 books; circulation: 825,436

Colleges and Universities

| College Options | ■■□□□ |
| College Town | ■■□□□ |

Associate of Arts
2 campuses (12,944)
Comprehensive
University of Texas Permian Basin (2,503/503)
Score: **19.83**   Rank: **284**

★Oklahoma City, OK

Children in Public Schools (97%)

| School Support | ■■■■□ |

55 districts, 365 schools, 173,087 students

Children in Private Schools (3%)
17 Catholic, 3,820 students
3 NAIS, 2,219 students

Public Libraries

| Library Popularity | ■■■□□ |

7 systems, 19 branches
1,322,121 books; circulation: 6,161,697

Colleges and Universities

| College Options | ■■■■■ |
| College Town | ■■■■□ |

Associate of Arts
8 campuses (53,671)
Baccalaureate
Mid America Bible College (493)
Comprehensive
Langston University (5,815/70)
Oklahoma Baptist University (2,732/36)
Oklahoma Christian University (1,397/33)
Oklahoma City University (2,798/3,342)
Southern Nazarene University (1,925/426)
University of Central Oklahoma (15,122/5,346)
Doctoral
University of Biblical Studies and Seminary (849/495)
University of Oklahoma (17,371/5,535)
University of Oklahoma Health Sciences Center (1,234/2,129)
Score: **93.2**   Rank: **25**

Olympia, WA

Children in Public Schools (96%)

| School Support | ■■□□□ |

8 districts, 70 schools, 37,121 students

Children in Private Schools (4%)
4 Catholic, 844 students
15 Other, 1,768 students

Public Libraries

| Library Popularity | ■■■■■ |

27 branches
834,383 books; circulation: 3,977,358

Colleges and Universities

| College Options | ■■□□□ |
| College Town | ■■□□□ |

Associate of Arts
1 campus (6,835)
Comprehensive
Evergreen State College (4,388/286)
Saint Martins College (1,930/444)
Score: **29.17**   Rank: **251**

Omaha, NE-IA

Children in Public Schools (86%)

| School Support | ■■■■□ |

35 districts, 260 schools, 113,033 students

Children in Private Schools (14%)
47 Catholic, 17,198 students
2 NAIS, 440 students
14 Other, 1,559 students

Public Libraries

| Library Popularity | ■■■□□ |

23 systems, 9 branches
1,373,536 books; circulation: 3,109,651

Colleges and Universities

| College Options | ■■■■■ |
| College Town | ■■■■□ |

Associate of Arts
2 campuses (30,358)
Baccalaureate
College of Saint Mary (1,289)
Dana College (747)
Nebraska Methodist College (387)
Comprehensive
Bellevue College (3,341/337)
Clarkson College (459/198)
Grace College of the Bible (428/47)
Doctoral
Creighton University (4,504/2,757)
University of Nebraska (13,916/3,451)
University of Nebraska Medical Center (1,172/1,884)
Score: **87.81**   Rank: **44**

Orange County, CA

Children in Public Schools (89%)

| School Support | ■□□□□ |

28 districts, 534 schools, 444,401 students

Children in Private Schools (11%)
49 Catholic, 20,823 students
5 NAIS, 2,807 students
231 Other, 29,270 students

Public Libraries

| Library Popularity | ■■□□□ |

9 systems, 44 branches
4,649,282 books; circulation: 12,928,824

Colleges and Universities

| College Options | ■■■■■ |
| College Town | ■■■□□ |

Associate of Arts
    10 campuses (195,616)
Comprehensive
    California State University (21,852/4,427)
    Chapman University (7,614/10,042)
    Christ College Irvine (1,215/328)
    Pacific Christian College (893/172)
    Southern California College (1,314/183)
Doctoral
    University of California (13,716/3,540)
Score: 77.62   Rank: 80

Orlando, FL
Children in Public Schools (95%)
School Support   ▪▪▫▫▫
4 districts, 290 schools, 225,963 students
Children in Private Schools (5%)
13 Catholic, 6,524 students
1 NAIS, 1,092 students
23 Other, 6,233 students
Public Libraries
Library Popularity   ▪▪▫▫▫
13 systems, 23 branches
2,502,932 books; circulation: 8,108,679
Colleges and Universities
College Options   ▪▪▪▪▫
College Town   ▪▪▫▫▫
Associate of Arts
    9 campuses (86,468)
Comprehensive
    Rollins College (3,156/841)
Doctoral
    University of Central Florida (23,655/6,882)
Score: 55.8   Rank: 157

Oshawa, ON
Children in Public K-13 (67%)
117 schools, 58,376 students
Children in Catholic Separate (27%)
46 schools, 4,830 students
Children in Private Schools (5%)
24 schools, 4,933 students
Public Libraries
Library Popularity   ▪▪▫▫▫
2 systems, 23 branches
466,205 books; circulation: 1,513,099
Colleges and Universities
College Options   ▪▫▫▫▫
College Town   ▪▪▫▫▫
Associate of Arts
    1 campus (25,000)
Score: 6.23   Rank: 333

Ottawa, ON
Children in Public K-13 (71%)
210 schools, 128,782 students
Children in Catholic Separate (23%)
87 schools, 34,688 students
Children in Private K-13 (6%)
38 schools, 7,980 students
Public Libraries
Library Popularity   ▪▪▫▫▫
15 systems, 84 branches
1,964,514 books; circulation: 6,110,024

Colleges and Universities
College Options   ▪▪▪▪▫
College Town   ▪▪▪▫▫
Associate of Arts
    4 campuses (22,000)
Doctoral
    Carleton University (19,121/2,642)
    College Dominicain de Philosophe (466/27)
    Saint Paul University (432/283)
    Universite du Quebec (5,485/326)
    University of Ottawa (20,162/4,110)
Score: 75.63   Rank: 87

Owensboro, KY
Children in Public Schools (82%)
School Support   ▪▪▫▫▫
2 districts, 35 schools, 14,809 students
Children in Private Schools (18%)
10 Catholic, 2,860 students
5 Other, 151 students
Public Libraries
Library Popularity   ▪▫▫▫▫
1 system
135,134 books; circulation: 321,075
Colleges and Universities
College Options   ▪▪▪▫▫
College Town   ▪▪▫▫▫
Associate of Arts
    3 campuses (4,326)
Baccalaureate
    Kentucky Wesleyan College (716)
Comprehensive
    Brescia College (914/9)
Score: 26.06   Rank: 262

Panama City, FL
Children in Public Schools (98%)
School Support   ▪▪▪▫▫
1 district, 34 schools, 24,369 students
Children in Private Schools (2%)
1 Catholic, 268 students
2 Other, 235 students
Public Libraries
Library Popularity   ▪▫▫▫▫
1 system, 6 branches
160,310 books; circulation: 419,465
Colleges and Universities
College Options   ▪▫▫▫▫
College Town   ▪▪▪▪▫
Associate of Arts
    2 campuses (24,205)
Score: 11.33   Rank: 314

Parkersburg-Marietta, WV-OH
Children in Public Schools (96%)
School Support   ▪▪▪▪▫
8 districts, 59 schools, 26,631 students
Children in Private Schools (4%)
4 Catholic, 856 students
2 Other, 166 students
Public Libraries
Library Popularity   ▪▪▪▫▫
3 systems, 5 branches
356,603 books; circulation: 983,135

Colleges and Universities

| College Options | ■■■□□ |
| College Town | ■■□□□ |

Associate of Arts
   1 campus (2,922)
Baccalaureate
   Ohio Valley College (341)
   West Virginia University (4,608)
Comprehensive
   Marietta College (1,410/79)
Score: **49.57**   Rank: **179**

Pensacola, FL
   Children in Public Schools (96%)

| School Support | ■■■□□ |

   2 districts, 100 schools, 61,340 students
   Children in Private Schools (4%)
   9 Catholic, 2,409 students
   4 Other, 605 students
   Public Libraries

| Library Popularity | ■□□□□ |

   1 system, 6 branches
   256,433 books; circulation: 900,504
   Colleges and Universities

| College Options | ■□□□□ |
| College Town | ■■□□□ |

   Associate of Arts
      3 campuses (21,169)
   Doctoral
      University of West Florida (9,095/1,782)
   Score: **9.63**   Rank: **320**

Peoria-Pekin, IL
   Children in Public Schools (92%)

| School Support | ■■■□□ |

   46 districts, 156 schools, 57,319 students
   Children in Private Schools (8%)
   14 Catholic, 4,676 students
   4 Other, 509 students
   Public Libraries

| Library Popularity | ■■■■■ |

   24 systems, 9 branches
   1,561,109 books; circulation: 2,378,677
   Colleges and Universities

| College Options | ■■■□□ |
| College Town | ■■□□□ |

   Associate of Arts
      2 campuses (20,145)
   Baccalaureate
      Eureka College (503)
   Comprehensive
      Bradley University (5,641/1,143)
   Score: **58.92**   Rank: **146**

Philadelphia, PA-NJ
   Children in Public Schools (76%)

| School Support | ■■■□□ |

   185 districts, 1,126 schools, 709,541 students
   Children in Private Schools (24%)
   349 Catholic, 141,239 students
   36 NAIS, 16,248 students
   44 Other, 7,080 students

Public Libraries

| Library Popularity | ■■□□□ |

   122 systems, 91 branches
   12,449,852 books; circulation: 24,202,337
Colleges and Universities

| College Options | ■■■■■ |
| College Town | ■■■□□ |

Associate of Arts
   26 campuses (111,708)
Baccalaureate
   Delaware Valley College (2,537)
   Haverford College (1,155)
   Moore College of Art and Design (399)
   Penn State University Delaware (1,883/29)
   Penn State University Ogontz (4,013/166)
   Ursinus College (2,664)
   Valley Forge Christian College (569)
Comprehensive
   American College (1,010)
   Beaver College (1,879/1,674)
   Cabrini College (1,976/706)
   Chestnut Hill College (940/790)
   Cheyney University (1,283/486)
   Eastern College (2,006/999)
   Gwynedd-Mercy College (1,932/281)
   Holy Family College (2,875/705)
   La Salle University (4,568/1,843)
   Lincoln University (1,299/254)
   Neumann College (1,344/137)
   Pennsylvania College of Optometry (650)
   Philadelphia College of Bible (972/417)
   Philadelphia College of Textiles (3,269/812)
   Rosemont College (961/100)
   Rutgers University (3,576/1,285)
   St. Charles Borromeo Seminary (272/257)
   St. Joseph's University (4,645/4,442)
   Swarthmore College (1,353)
   The University of the Arts (1,242/133)
   West Chester University of Pennsylvania (11,341/2,979)
Doctoral
   Bryn Mawr College (1,370/567)
   Drexel University (7,800/4,041)
   Eastern Baptist Theological Seminary (457)
   Hahnemann University (1,399/2,114)
   Immaculata College (1,876/873)
   Pennsylvania State University (2,138)
   Philadelphia College of Osteopathic Medicine (1,028)
   Philadelphia College of Pharmacy and Science (1,473/615)
   Rowan College of New Jersey (9,300/2,147)
   Temple University (22,657/12,079)
   Thomas Jefferson University (1,320/1,508)
   University of Pennsylvania (12,630/12,319)
   Villanova University (8,402/3,795)
   Westminster Theological Seminary (610)
   Widener University (4,436/3,029)
Score: **89.8**   Rank: **37**

Phoenix-Mesa, AZ
   Children in Public Schools (97%)

| School Support | ■■□□□ |

   77 districts, 589 schools, 438,624 students

Children in Private Schools (3%)

26 Catholic, 10,549 students
3 NAIS, 1,283 students
11 Other, 1,636 students

Public Libraries

Library Popularity

29 systems, 25 branches
4,896,379 books; circulation: 15,855,388

Colleges and Universities

College Options

College Town

Associate of Arts
14 campuses (174,682)
Comprehensive
American School of International Management (2,194)
Arizona State University (5,641/2,135)
Grand Canyon University (2,106/564)
Ottawa University (1,069/2,610)
Western International University (1,471/626)
Doctoral
Arizona State University (37,904/14,617)
Score: 84.98   Rank: 54

Pine Bluff, AR

Children in Public Schools (98%)

School Support

6 districts, 38 schools, 16,504 students

Children in Private Schools (2%)

2 Catholic, 259 students
1 Other, 52 students

Public Libraries

Library Popularity

1 system, 2 branches
120,281 books; circulation: 221,989

Colleges and Universities

College Options

College Town

Associate of Arts
2 campuses (2,423)
Comprehensive
University of Arkansas (3,710/219)
Score: 7.93   Rank: 327

Pittsburgh, PA

Children in Public Schools (86%)

School Support

103 districts, 620 schools, 327,549 students

Children in Private Schools (14%)

167 Catholic, 45,716 students
14 NAIS, 6,169 students
26 Other, 3,095 students

Public Libraries

Library Popularity

98 systems, 32 branches
5,684,304 books; circulation: 10,341,352

Colleges and Universities

College Options

College Town

Associate of Arts
15 campuses (46,818)
Baccalaureate
Penn State University Beaver (929/55)
Penn State University Fayette (1,183/1)

Penn State University McKeesport (996/2)
Penn State University New Kensington (1,158/9)
Saint Vincent College (1,376)
University of Pittsburgh Greensburg (1,564)
Comprehensive
California University (5,766/1,288)
Carlow College (2,607/223)
Chatham College (701/250)
Geneva College (1,881/153)
La Roche College (1,504/395)
Point Park College (2,577/86)
Robert Morris College (5,221/1,226)
Seton Hill College (1,232/20)
Washington and Jefferson College (1,341)
Doctoral
Carnegie Mellon University (5,216/3,107)
Duquesne University (5,997/5,638)
Pittsburgh Theological Seminary (309)
Slippery Rock University (7,783/1,040)
University of Pittsburgh (20,561/11,311)
Score: 60.05   Rank: 142

Pittsfield, MA

Children in Public Schools (89%)

School Support

6 districts, 36 schools, 14,733 students

Children in Private Schools (11%)

7 Catholic, 1,785 students
1 NAIS, 130 students
1 Other, 35 students

Public Libraries

Library Popularity

10 systems
383,191 books; circulation: 666,020

Colleges and Universities

College Options

College Town

Associate of Arts
1 campus (3,334)
Score: 4.81   Rank: 338

Pocatello, ID

Children in Public Schools (97%)

School Support

2 districts, 35 schools, 15,549 students

Children in Private Schools (3%)

1 Catholic, 175 students
3 Other, 303 students

Public Libraries

Library Popularity

3 systems, 1 branch
181,150 books; circulation: 626,679

Colleges and Universities

College Options

College Town

Doctoral
Idaho State University (18,759/6,380)
Score: 30.87   Rank: 245

Portland, ME

Children in Public Schools (93%)

School Support

13 districts, 76 schools, 30,977 students

Education

Children in Private Schools (7%)
6 Catholic, 1,328 students
2 NAIS, 764 students
14 Other, 493 students
Public Libraries

Library Popularity	▪▪▪▪☐

28 systems, 6 branches
896,606 books; circulation: 1,852,673
Colleges and Universities

College Options	▪▪▪☐☐
College Town	▪▪▪▪☐

Associate of Arts
  1 campus (3,747)
Baccalaureate
  Maine College of Art (312)
Comprehensive
  Saint Joseph's College (3,963/1,241)
  University of Southern Maine (10,769/2,746)
Score: 89.23   Rank: 39

★Portland-Vancouver, OR-WA
Children in Public Schools (95%)

School Support	▪☐☐☐☐

55 districts, 548 schools, 299,312 students
Children in Private Schools (5%)
35 Catholic, 10,716 students
2 NAIS, 1,394 students
30 Other, 4,517 students
Public Libraries

Library Popularity	▪▪▪▪▪

34 systems, 26 branches
3,478,827 books; circulation: 17,566,152
Colleges and Universities

College Options	▪▪▪▪▪
College Town	▪▪▪▪☐

Associate of Arts
  5 campuses (77,429)
Baccalaureate
  Western States Chiropractic College (520)
Comprehensive
  Concordia College (1,218)
  Lewis and Clark College (1,850/1,973)
  Linfield College (3,166/31)
  Reed College (1,276/14)
  University of Portland (3,538/1,161)
  Warner Pacific College (854/11)
Doctoral
  George Fox College (1,608/477)
  Oregon Institute of Science & Technology (635)
  Oregon Health Science University (737/1,311)
  Pacific University (1,215/1,036)
  Portland State University (17,021/16,511)
  Western Conservative Baptist Seminary (681)
Score: 96.88   Rank: 12

Portsmouth-Rochester, NH-ME
Children in Public Schools (90%)

School Support	▪▪▪▪☐

14 districts, 74 schools, 34,176 students
Children in Private Schools (10%)
5 Catholic, 1,974 students
2 NAIS, 1,394 students
8 Other, 713 students

Public Libraries

Library Popularity	▪▪▪▪☐

31 systems
856,416 books; circulation: 1,825,020
Colleges and Universities

College Options	▪▪▪☐☐
College Town	▪▪▪▪▪

Associate of Arts
  1 campus (1,531)
Baccalaureate
  College For Lifelong Learning (3,129/466)
Doctoral
  University of New Hampshire (14,103/4,234)
Score: 70.82   Rank: 104

Providence-Fall River-Warwick, RI-MA
Children in Public Schools (87%)

School Support	▪▪▪☐☐

32 districts, 312 schools, 142,472 students
Children in Private Schools (13%)
70 Catholic, 20,278 students
6 NAIS, 2,398 students
8 Other, 852 students
Public Libraries

Library Popularity	▪▪▪▪☐

52 systems, 27 branches
4,580,274 books; circulation: 6,923,442
Colleges and Universities

College Options	▪▪▪▪▪
College Town	▪▪▪▪☐

Associate of Arts
  3 campuses (30,893)
Baccalaureate
  New England Institute of Technology (3,211)
  Roger Williams University (4,284)
  Zion Bible Institute (380)
Comprehensive
  Bryant College (3,114/688)
  Rhode Island School of Design (1,815/184)
Doctoral
  Brown University (6,435/1,713)
  Johnson & Wales University (8,784/746)
  Providence College (4,656/901)
  Rhode Island College (8,615/3,081)
  University of Rhode Island (12,518/4,222)
Score: 88.66   Rank: 41

Provo-Orem, UT
Children in Public Schools (99%)

School Support	▪☐☐☐☐

3 districts, 107 schools, 76,260 students
Children in Private Schools (1%)
13 Other, 895 students
Public Libraries

Library Popularity	▪▪▪▪☐

9 systems
556,590 books; circulation: 2,657,647
Colleges and Universities

College Options	▪▪☐☐☐
College Town	▪▪▪▪▪

Baccalaureate
  Utah Valley State College (25,979)

Doctoral
Brigham Young University (33,868/3,540)
Score: 50.99   Rank: **174**

Pueblo, CO
Children in Public Schools (96%)
School Support
2 districts, 52 schools, 22,402 students
Children in Private Schools (4%)
2 Catholic, 408 students
6 Other, 455 students
Public Libraries
Library Popularity
1 system, 2 branches
294,973 books; circulation: 794,134
Colleges and Universities
College Options
College Town
Associate of Arts
1 campus (6,600)
Comprehensive
University of Southern Colorado (4,635/523)
Score: 17.84   Rank: **291**

Punta Gorda, FL
Children in Public Schools (96%)
School Support
1 district, 21 schools, 15,531 students
Children in Private Schools (4%)
1 Catholic, 276 students
7 Other, 633 students
Public Libraries
Library Popularity
1 system, 4 branches
138,448 books; circulation: 521,839
Colleges and Universities
College Options
College Town
Associate of Arts
1 campus (939)
Score: 0.28   Rank: **353**

Quebec City, PQ
Public Instruction
3 districts, 250 schools, 48,872 students
Public Libraries
Library Popularity
11 systems, 125 branches
1,061,416 books; circulation: 3,563,422
Colleges and Universities
College Options
College Town
Associate of Arts
5 campuses (19,500)
Comprehensive
Ecole Nationale d'Administration Publique (963)
Doctoral
Universite Laval (31,251/7,262)
Score: 74.78   Rank: **90**

Racine, WI
Children in Public Schools (84%)
School Support
12 districts, 58 schools, 29,982 students

Children in Private Schools (16%)
16 Catholic, 4,060 students
1 NAIS, 500 students
8 Other, 1,598 students
Public Libraries
Library Popularity
5 systems
334,271 books; circulation: 1,235,946
Score: 5.38   Rank: **336**

★Raleigh-Durham-Chapel Hill, NC
Children in Public Schools (94%)
School Support
9 districts, 232 schools, 149,908 students
Children in Private Schools (6%)
9 Catholic, 2,631 students
3 NAIS, 1,945 students
43 Other, 5,262 students
Public Libraries
Library Popularity
4 systems, 31 branches
1,877,479 books; circulation: 7,792,501
Colleges and Universities
College Options
College Town
Associate of Arts
6 campuses (25,046)
Baccalaureate
Peace College (440)
Saint Augustine's College (1,917)
Shaw University (2,866)
Comprehensive
Meredith College (2,666/273)
North Carolina Central University (4,872/1,841)
Doctoral
Duke University (6,804/6,719)
North Carolina State University (26,668/6,835)
SE Baptist Theological Seminary (153/1,235)
University of North Carolina (17,463/10,385)
Score: 100   Rank: **1**

Rapid City, SD
Children in Public Schools (93%)
School Support
5 districts, 47 schools, 18,714 students
Children in Private Schools (7%)
2 Catholic, 780 students
4 Other, 576 students
Public Libraries
Library Popularity
4 systems
133,249 books; circulation: 451,885
Colleges and Universities
College Options
College Town
Doctoral
South Dakota School of Mines (2,383/303)
Score: 22.37   Rank: **275**

Reading, PA
Children in Public Schools (92%)
School Support
19 districts, 102 schools, 58,441 students

Children in Private Schools (8%)
15 Catholic, 4,886 students
9 Other, 784 students
Public Libraries
Library Popularity
16 systems, 3 branches
475,282 books; circulation: 918,863
Colleges and Universities
College Options
College Town
Associate of Arts
1 campus (4,312)
Baccalaureate
Albright College (1,459)
Alvernia College (1,905)
Penn State University (1,957/200)
Comprehensive
Kutztown University of Pennsylvania (7,707/1,487)
Score: 46.17   Rank: 191

Redding, CA
Children in Public Schools (93%)
School Support
26 districts, 68 schools, 29,930 students
Children in Private Schools (7%)
4 Catholic, 679 students
16 Other, 1,494 students
Public Libraries
Library Popularity
1 system, 2 branches
222,288 books; circulation: 246,156
Colleges and Universities
College Options
College Town
Associate of Arts
1 campus (18,200)
Comprehensive
Simpson College (905/213)
Score: 18.41   Rank: 289

Regina, SK
Children in Public K-13 (70%)
3 divisions, 76 schools, 27,105 students
Children in Catholic Separate (27%)
29 schools, 10,724 students
Children in Private Schools (3%)
1 school, 1,216 students
Public Libraries
Library Popularity
2 systems, 10 branches
683,589 books; circulation: 2,740,860
Colleges and Universities
College Options
College Town
Associate of Arts
1 campus (9,000)
Baccalaureate
Campion College (1,265)
Canadian Bible College (333)
Luther College (902)
Saskatchewan Indian College (756)

Doctoral
University of Regina (7,502/904)
Score: 84.7   Rank: 55

Reno, NV
Children in Public Schools (96%)
School Support
1 district, 81 schools, 47,533 students
Children in Private Schools (4%)
5 Catholic, 1,370 students
20 Other, 987 students
Public Libraries
Library Popularity
1 system, 9 branches
602,023 books; circulation: 1,163,536
Colleges and Universities
College Options
College Town
Associate of Arts
1 campus (16,370)
Baccalaureate
Sierra Nevada College (367/273)
Doctoral
University of Nevada (9,845/3,842)
Score: 48.72   Rank: 182

Richland-Kennewick-Pasco, WA
Children in Public Schools (95%)
School Support
9 districts, 69 schools, 37,167 students
Children in Private Schools (5%)
3 Catholic, 1,070 students
11 Other, 1,388 students
Public Libraries
Library Popularity
2 systems, 10 branches
446,721 books; circulation: 1,068,149
Colleges and Universities
College Options
College Town
Associate of Arts
1 campus (9,094)
Score: 1.98   Rank: 347

Richmond-Petersburg, VA
Children in Public Schools (94%)
School Support
12 districts, 240 schools, 153,503 students
Children in Private Schools (6%)
13 Catholic, 4,739 students
8 NAIS, 4,095 students
5 Other, 953 students
Public Libraries
Library Popularity
7 systems, 40 branches
2,650,334 books; circulation: 6,587,309
Colleges and Universities
College Options
College Town
Associate of Arts
4 campuses (25,172)
Baccalaureate
Randolph-Macon College (1,114)

Comprehensive
   University of Richmond (3,955/1,051)
   Virginia State University (3,682/1,386)
Doctoral
   Virginia Commonwealth University (17,568/8,668)
   Virginia Union University (1,497/216)
Score: **58.07**   Rank: **149**

Riverside-San Bernardino, CA
Children in Public Schools (93%)
| School Support | ■□□□□ |

59 districts, 774 schools, 611,729 students
Children in Private Schools (7%)
42 Catholic, 12,880 students
3 NAIS, 376 students
265 Other, 30,852 students
Public Libraries
| Library Popularity | ■□□□□ |

13 systems, 60 branches
3,915,462 books; circulation: 11,291,096
Colleges and Universities
| College Options | ■■■■■ |
| College Town | ■□□□□ |

Associate of Arts
   9 campuses (120,820)
Comprehensive
   California Baptist College (1,350/189)
   California State University (10,556/3,864)
   University of Redlands (3,857/1,382)
Doctoral
   La Sierra University (1,995/675)
   Loma Linda University (1,872/2,392)
   University of California (7,988/1,586)
Score: **56.65**   Rank: **154**

Roanoke, VA
Children in Public Schools (97%)
| School Support | ■■■■■ |

4 districts, 74 schools, 34,896 students
Children in Private Schools (3%)
1 Catholic, 421 students
1 NAIS, 550 students
2 Other, 159 students
Public Libraries
| Library Popularity | ■■■□□ |

4 systems, 13 branches
711,511 books; circulation: 1,477,436
Colleges and Universities
| College Options | ■■■■□ |
| College Town | ■■□□□ |

Associate of Arts
   1 campus (11,238)
Baccalaureate
   Roanoke College (1,880)
   Roanoke Valley College of Health Sciences (682)
Comprehensive
   Hollins College (925/395)
Score: **68.27**   Rank: **113**

Rochester, MN
Children in Public Schools (88%)
| School Support | ■□□□□ |

7 districts, 44 schools, 20,800 students

Children in Private Schools (12%)
5 Catholic, 2,137 students
7 Other, 661 students
Public Libraries
| Library Popularity | ■■■■■ |

2 systems
322,127 books; circulation: 1,253,371
Colleges and Universities
| College Options | ■■■□□ |
| College Town | ■□□□□ |

Associate of Arts
   1 campus (6,759)
Score: **36.82**   Rank: **224**

★Rochester, NY
Children in Public Schools (91%)
| School Support | ■■■■■ |

64 districts, 301 schools, 188,649 students
Children in Private Schools (9%)
59 Catholic, 17,289 students
4 NAIS, 1,215 students
14 Other, 1,421 students
Public Libraries
| Library Popularity | ■■■■■ |

61 systems, 16 branches
3,440,245 books; circulation: 9,353,216
Colleges and Universities
| College Options | ■■■■■ |
| College Town | ■■■■□ |

Associate of Arts
   4 campuses (32,791)
Baccalaureate
   Hobart William Smith Colleges (1,834)
Comprehensive
   Nazareth College (2,085/1,580)
   Roberts Wesleyan College (1,589/179)
   Saint John Fisher College (2,366/378)
   SUNY College Brockport (8,278/2,922)
   SUNY College Geneseo (5,457/605)
Doctoral
   Rochester Institute of Technology (12,612/2,655)
   University of Rochester (6,185/5,500)
Score: **98.58**   Rank: **6**

Rockford, IL
Children in Public Schools (90%)
| School Support | ■■■□□ |

25 districts, 127 schools, 57,532 students
Children in Private Schools (10%)
12 Catholic, 5,055 students
1 NAIS, 320 students
5 Other, 1,383 students
Public Libraries
| Library Popularity | ■■■■□ |

17 systems, 6 branches
1,088,354 books; circulation: 2,168,074
Colleges and Universities
| College Options | ■□□□□ |
| College Town | ■□□□□ |

Associate of Arts
   1 campus (15,759)
Comprehensive
   Rockford College (1,355/523)
Score: **15.29**   Rank: **300**

Rocky Mount, NC
Children in Public Schools (94%)

School Support ▪▪▪▪□

2 districts, 42 schools, 25,900 students

Children in Private Schools (6%)

1 Catholic, 109 students

15 Other, 1,537 students

Public Libraries

Library Popularity ▪□□□□

2 systems, 1 branch

255,809 books; circulation: 528,728

Colleges and Universities

College Options ▪▪□□□

College Town ▪□□□□

Associate of Arts
2 campuses (6,267)

Baccalaureate
North Carolina Wesleyan College (2,622)

Score: 22.09   Rank: 276

Sacramento, CA
Children in Public Schools (93%)

School Support ▪□□□□

53 districts, 465 schools, 268,115 students

Children in Private Schools (7%)

33 Catholic, 11,558 students

1 NAIS, 485 students

141 Other, 11,080 students

Public Libraries

Library Popularity ▪□□□□

6 systems, 37 branches

2,237,972 books; circulation: 5,145,371

Colleges and Universities

College Options ▪▪▪▪▪

College Town ▪▪□□□

Associate of Arts
8 campuses (114,650)

Comprehensive
California State University (20,991/5,392)

Score: 55.52   Rank: 158

Saginaw-Bay City-Midland, MI
Children in Public Schools (91%)

School Support ▪□□□□

22 districts, 155 schools, 69,405 students

Children in Private Schools (9%)

20 Catholic, 4,496 students

15 Other, 2,260 students

Public Libraries

Library Popularity ▪▪▪▪□

13 systems, 10 branches

1,517,624 books; circulation: 2,855,731

Colleges and Universities

College Options ▪▪▪▪□

College Town ▪▪▪▪□

Associate of Arts
4 campuses (16,667)

Comprehensive
Northwood University (3,427/63)
Saginaw Valley State University (7,517/2,349)

Score: 65.72   Rank: 122

St. Catharines-Niagara, ON
Children in Public K-13 (65%)

68 schools, 30,259 students

Children in Catholic Separate (23%)

30 schools, 10,264 students

Children in Private K-13 (12%)

24 schools, 5,050 students

Public Libraries

Library Popularity ▪▪▪▪□

10 systems, 22 branches

1,085,510 books; circulation: 2,898,260

Colleges and Universities

College Options ▪□□□□

College Town ▪□□□□

Associate of Arts
1 campus (5,600)

Comprehensive
Brock University (10,443/617)

Score: 14.44   Rank: 303

St. Cloud, MN
Children in Public Schools (93%)

School Support ▪□□□□

13 districts, 53 schools, 30,142 students

Children in Private Schools (7%)

10 Catholic, 1,757 students

3 Other, 318 students

Public Libraries

Library Popularity ▪▪□□□

1 system, 29 branches

667,762 books; circulation: 1,794,370

Colleges and Universities

College Options ▪▪□□□

College Town ▪▪▪▪▪

Associate of Arts
1 campus (3,960)

Baccalaureate
College of Saint Benedict (2,106)

Comprehensive
Saint Cloud State University (16,361/3,023)
Saint John's University (1,847/418)

Score: 41.07   Rank: 209

Saint John, NB
Children in Public K-13 (99%)

2 districts, 67 schools, 24,732 students

Children in Private K-13 (1%)

2 Other, 222 students

Public Libraries

Library Popularity ▪▪▪□□

1 system, 9 branches

388,221 books; circulation: 618,925

Colleges and Universities

College Options ▪□□□□

College Town ▪□□□□

Comprehensive
Mount Allison University (2,361/3)

Score: 3.11   Rank: 344

St. John's, NF
Children in Public K-13 (45%)

2 integrated board, 42 schools, 15,427 students

Children in Catholic Separate (54%)

42 schools, 18,441 students

Children in Private K-13 (1%)
2 schools, 19,547 students
Public Libraries
Library Popularity ■□□□□
3 systems, 28 branches
361,986 books; circulation: 694,513
Colleges and Universities
College Options ■■□□□
College Town ■□□□□
Associate of Arts
2 campuses (9,000)
Doctoral
Memorial University (15,750/1,419)
Score: 14.73   Rank: 302

St. Joseph, MO
Children in Public Schools (93%)
School Support ■■■■■
7 districts, 48 schools, 16,864 students
Children in Private Schools (7%)
5 Catholic, 1,271 students
Public Libraries
Library Popularity ■■■■■
1 system, 4 branches
443,665 books; circulation: 744,846
Colleges and Universities
College Options ■□□□□
College Town ■■■□□
Baccalaureate
Missouri Western State College (6,377)
Score: 38.81   Rank: 217

★St. Louis, MO-IL
Children in Public Schools (91%)
School Support ■■■□□
117 districts, 779 schools, 390,553 students
Children in Private Schools (9%)
114 Catholic, 31,774 students
1 NAIS, 184 students
35 Other, 5,369 students
Public Libraries
Library Popularity ■■■■■
57 systems, 53 branches
10,336,609 books; circulation: 19,522,086
Colleges and Universities
College Options ■■■■■
College Town ■■■■□
Associate of Arts
13 campuses (105,112)
Baccalaureate
Deaconess College of Nursing (451)
Harris-Stowe State College (2,376)
McKendree College (2,327)
Missouri Baptist College (2,487)
Principia College (629)
Comprehensive
Fontbonne College (2,011/818)
Lindenwood College (3,216/2,820)
Maryville University (3,142/960)
Parks College of Saint Louis University (808/18)
St. Louis College of Pharmacy (776/83)

Doctoral
Concordia Seminary (696)
Covenant Theological Seminary (752)
Saint Louis University (6,189/5,361)
Southern Illinois University (10,266/4,109)
University of Missouri (16,956/4,538)
Washington University (6,357/6,047)
Webster University (5,675/15,382)
Score: 99.15   Rank: 4

Salem, OR
Children in Public Schools (96%)
School Support ■□□□□
29 districts, 124 schools, 55,466 students
Children in Private Schools (4%)
7 Catholic, 1,403 students
11 Other, 934 students
Public Libraries
Library Popularity ■■■□□
10 systems, 1 branch
593,041 books; circulation: 2,302,054
Colleges and Universities
College Options ■■■□□
College Town ■■■■□
Associate of Arts
1 campus (16,048)
Baccalaureate
Western Baptist College (768)
Comprehensive
Western Oregon State College (4,034/1,257)
Willamette University (1,895/739)
Score: 62.03   Rank: 135

Salinas, CA
Children in Public Schools (93%)
School Support ■□□□□
26 districts, 110 schools, 66,409 students
Children in Private Schools (7%)
8 Catholic, 2,826 students
3 NAIS, 869 students
12 Other, 1,040 students
Public Libraries
Library Popularity ■■■□□
4 systems, 18 branches
1,092,490 books; circulation: 2,182,189
Colleges and Universities
College Options ■■■□□
College Town ■■■□□
Associate of Arts
3 campuses (29,573)
Comprehensive
Monterey Institute of International Studies (405/647)
Doctoral
Naval Postgraduate School (3,717)
Score: 51.27   Rank: 173

Salt Lake City-Ogden, UT
Children in Public Schools (98%)
School Support ■□□□□
7 districts, 381 schools, 279,447 students
Children in Private Schools (2%)
11 Catholic, 3,878 students
3 NAIS, 1,260 students
12 Other, 1,524 students

Place Profiles: Education

Public Libraries

Library Popularity ▪▪▪▪☐

5 systems, 28 branches
2,712,338 books; circulation: 10,723,627

Colleges and Universities

College Options ▪▪▪▪☐

College Town ▪▪▪☐☐

Associate of Arts
2 campuses (32,403)
Comprehensive
Weber State University (19,707/239)
Westminster College (1,802/492)
Doctoral
University of Utah (28,633/5,773)
Score: 81.3   Rank: 67

San Angelo, TX

Children in Public Schools (97%)

School Support ▪▪▪▪☐

6 districts, 51 schools, 19,686 students

Children in Private Schools (3%)
1 Catholic, 200 students
2 Other, 376 students

Public Libraries

Library Popularity ▪▪▪☐☐

1 system, 2 branches
266,571 books; circulation: 571,616

Colleges and Universities

College Options ▪☐☐☐☐

College Town ▪▪▪▪☐

Comprehensive
Angelo State University (6,862/617)
Score: 24.36   Rank: 268

San Antonio, TX

Children in Public Schools (93%)

School Support ▪▪▪▪▪

26 districts, 450 schools, 280,513 students

Children in Private Schools (7%)
43 Catholic, 14,971 students
1 NAIS, 735 students
14 Other, 4,474 students

Public Libraries

Library Popularity ▪☐☐☐☐

11 systems, 21 branches
1,081,593 books; circulation: 3,914,727

Colleges and Universities

College Options ▪▪▪▪☐

College Town ▪▪☐☐☐

Associate of Arts
5 campuses (57,007)
Baccalaureate
Texas Lutheran College (1,539)
Comprehensive
Incarnate Word College (3,000/814)
Trinity University (2,244/262)
Doctoral
Our Lady of the Lake University (2,826/1,374)
St. Mary's University (2,803/1,947)
The University of Texas (19,111/3,272)
The University of Texas Health Science (1,221/1,828)
Score: 66   Rank: 121

San Diego, CA

Children in Public Schools (92%)

School Support ▪☐☐☐☐

44 districts, 549 schools, 432,521 students

Children in Private Schools (8%)
45 Catholic, 16,779 students
5 NAIS, 2,466 students
188 Other, 17,832 students

Public Libraries

Library Popularity ▪▪☐☐☐

7 systems, 69 branches
4,733,373 books; circulation: 13,523,118

Colleges and Universities

College Options ▪▪▪▪▪

College Town ▪▪▪☐☐

Associate of Arts
11 campuses (178,033)
Baccalaureate
California State University (3,628/756)
Christian Heritage College (586)
Comprehensive
Coleman College (1,525/17)
National University (5,348/6,252)
Point Loma Nazarene College (2,205/632)
Doctoral
California School of Professional Psychology (637)
San Diego State University (26,220/6,786)
U.S. International University (505/1,313)
University of California (15,212/3,481)
University of San Diego (4,307/2,375)
Score: 79.6   Rank: 73

★San Francisco, CA

Children in Public Schools (79%)

School Support ▪☐☐☐☐

46 districts, 352 schools, 188,562 students

Children in Private Schools (21%)
80 Catholic, 31,643 students
21 NAIS, 6,915 students
183 Other, 11,872 students

Public Libraries

Library Popularity ▪▪▪☐☐

14 systems, 59 branches
4,543,220 books; circulation: 10,219,316

Colleges and Universities

College Options ▪▪▪▪▪

College Town ▪▪▪▪☐

Associate of Arts
8 campuses (136,249)
Baccalaureate
Menlo College (557)
Comprehensive
California College of Podiatric Medicine (472)
College of Notre Dame (1,063/1,020)
Dominican College of San Rafael (1,166/398)
Lincoln University (239/221)
New College of California (521/109)
San Francisco Art Institute (716/236)
Doctoral
California Institute of Integral Studies (103/1,243)
Golden Gate Baptist Seminary (47/602)
Golden Gate University (2,524/6,403)
San Francisco State University (23,500/7,517)

258

San Francisco Theological Seminary (827)
Saybrook Institute (350)
University of California (35/8,353)
University of San Francisco (5,701/4,158)

Score: 98.01   Rank: **8**

San Jose, CA

Children in Public Schools (89%)

| School Support | ■□□□□ |

34 districts, 357 schools, 261,345 students

Children in Private Schools (11%)
40 Catholic, 17,681 students
3 NAIS, 746 students
107 Other, 13,500 students

Public Libraries

| Library Popularity | ■■■■□ |

6 systems, 33 branches
3,641,761 books; circulation: 13,747,805

Colleges and Universities

| College Options | ■■■■■ |
| College Town | ■■■■□ |

Associate of Arts
    9 campuses (132,209)
Baccalaureate
    Cogswell College (498)
    National Hispanic University (434)
Comprehensive
    San Jose State University (22,831/6,501)
Doctoral
    Institute of Transpersonal Psychology (318)
    Pacific Graduate School of Psychology (317)
    Santa Clara University (4,599/4,492)
    Stanford University (7,232/9,961)

Score: 87.25   Rank: **46**

San Luis Obispo-Atascadero-Paso Robles, CA

Children in Public Schools (91%)

| School Support | ■□□□□ |

13 districts, 76 schools, 35,496 students

Children in Private Schools (9%)
5 Catholic, 1,549 students
19 Other, 2,119 students

Public Libraries

| Library Popularity | ■■■□□ |

2 systems, 14 branches
403,619 books; circulation: 1,681,130

Colleges and Universities

| College Options | ■□□□□ |
| College Town | ■■■■□ |

Associate of Arts
    1 campus (11,123)
Comprehensive
    California Polytechnic State University (16,439/1,385)

Score: 26.91   Rank: **259**

Santa Barbara-Santa Maria-Lompoc, CA

Children in Public Schools (91%)

| School Support | ■□□□□ |

24 districts, 105 schools, 60,450 students

Children in Private Schools (9%)
10 Catholic, 2,933 students
5 NAIS, 1,039 students
26 Other, 2,425 students

Public Libraries

| Library Popularity | ■■□□□ |

3 systems, 12 branches
710,015 books; circulation: 2,368,391

Colleges and Universities

| College Options | ■■■■□ |
| College Town | ■■■■■ |

Associate of Arts
    2 campuses (40,021)
Baccalaureate
    Westmont College (1,308)
Doctoral
    The Fielding Institute (1,043)
    University of California (16,867/2,379)

Score: 69.12   Rank: **110**

Santa Cruz-Watsonville, CA

Children in Public Schools (91%)

| School Support | ■□□□□ |

12 districts, 64 schools, 39,156 students

Children in Private Schools (9%)
2 Catholic, 497 students
25 Other, 3,434 students

Public Libraries

| Library Popularity | ■■■□□ |

2 systems, 9 branches
479,309 books; circulation: 1,569,119

Colleges and Universities

| College Options | ■■□□□ |
| College Town | ■■■■□ |

Associate of Arts
    1 campus (18,165)
Comprehensive
    Bethany College Assemblies of God (713)
Doctoral
    University of California (9,320/1,064)

Score: 36.26   Rank: **226**

Santa Fe, NM

Children in Public Schools (92%)

| School Support | ■■■■□ |

4 districts, 39 schools, 18,826 students

Children in Private Schools (8%)
5 Catholic, 1,341 students
1 NAIS, 120 students
3 Other, 160 students

Public Libraries

| Library Popularity | ■■■■■ |

5 systems, 3 branches
398,174 books; circulation: 952,735

Colleges and Universities

| College Options | ■■■■□ |
| College Town | ■■■□□ |

Associate of Arts
    3 campuses (11,027)
Comprehensive
    College of Santa Fe (1,801/326)
    St. John's College (404/153)

Score: 81.01   Rank: **68**

Santa Rosa, CA
Children in Public Schools (92%)

| School Support | ■□□□ |

40 districts, 147 schools, 70,010 students

Children in Private Schools (8%)
8 Catholic, 2,751 students
3 NAIS, 819 students
59 Other, 3,418 students

Public Libraries

| Library Popularity | ■■□□ |

1 system, 12 branches
670,578 books; circulation: 2,583,487

Colleges and Universities

| College Options | ■■□□ |
| College Town | ■■■□ |

Associate of Arts
  2 campuses (38,371)
Comprehensive
  Sonoma State University (6,388/1,392)

Score: 27.47   Rank: 257

Sarasota-Bradenton, FL
Children in Public Schools (93%)

| School Support | ■■□□ |

2 districts, 85 schools, 61,321 students

Children in Private Schools (7%)
5 Catholic, 2,076 students
2 NAIS, 983 students
8 Other, 1,475 students

Public Libraries

| Library Popularity | ■■□□ |

2 systems, 12 branches
748,425 books; circulation: 3,206,573

Colleges and Universities

| College Options | ■■■□ |
| College Town | ■□□□ |

Associate of Arts
  2 campuses (15,168)
Baccalaureate
  Ringling School of Art (827)

Score: 25.21   Rank: 265

★Saskatoon, SK
Children in Public K-13 (67%)
4 divisions, 72 schools, 29,935 students

Children in Catholic Separate (30%)
36 schools, 14,094 students

Children in Private K-13 (3%)
8 Other, 1,444 students

Public Libraries

| Library Popularity | ■■■■■ |

2 systems, 7 branches
3,574,087 books; circulation: 742,990

Colleges and Universities

| College Options | ■■■■■ |
| College Town | ■■■■■ |

Associate of Arts
  5 campuses (18,450)
Baccalaureate
  St. Thomas More College (1,229)
Doctoral
  University of Saskatchewan (15,758/2,115)

Score: 97.45   Rank: 10

Savannah, GA
Children in Public Schools (87%)

| School Support | ■■■□ |

3 districts, 63 schools, 47,751 students

Children in Private Schools (13%)
6 Catholic, 2,148 students
2 NAIS, 1,275 students
26 Other, 3,657 students

Public Libraries

| Library Popularity | ■□□□ |

1 system, 18 branches
564,940 books; circulation: 1,051,031

Colleges and Universities

| College Options | ■■■□ |
| College Town | ■■□□ |

Associate of Arts
  1 campus (3,645)
Comprehensive
  Armstrong State College (6,472/327)
  Savannah College of Art (3,159/409)
  Savannah State College (3,802/40)

Score: 42.49   Rank: 204

Scranton–Wilkes-Barre–Hazleton, PA
Children in Public Schools (86%)

| School Support | ■■■□ |

32 districts, 151 schools, 85,245 students

Children in Private Schools (14%)
45 Catholic, 11,637 students
4 NAIS, 1,710 students
10 Other, 1,072 students

Public Libraries

| Library Popularity | ■□□□ |

25 systems, 11 branches
1,108,774 books; circulation: 1,986,065

Colleges and Universities

| College Options | ■■■■■ |
| College Town | ■■■■□ |

Associate of Arts
  4 campuses (12,970)
Baccalaureate
  Penn State University Hazleton (1,418/4)
  Penn State University Wilkes-Barre (889/113)
  Penn State University Worthington-Scranton (1,384/406)
Comprehensive
  Bloomsburg University of Pennsylvania (7,931/1,150)
  College Misericordia (1,624/162)
  King's College (2,600/204)
  University of Scranton (4,490/984)
  Wilkes University (2,754/1,843)
Doctoral
  Baptist Bible College and Seminary (633/259)
  Marywood College (1,950/1,660)

Score: 81.86   Rank: 65

Seattle-Bellevue-Everett, WA
Children in Public Schools (90%)

| School Support | ■□□□ |

35 districts, 603 schools, 334,177 students

Children in Private Schools (10%)
46 Catholic, 15,314 students
11 NAIS, 2,838 students
140 Other, 20,241 students

Public Libraries

Library Popularity ■■■■■

5 systems, 80 branches
6,379,148 books; circulation: 23,984,314

Colleges and Universities

College Options ■■■■■

College Town ■■■☐☐

Associate of Arts
11 campuses (121,652)
Baccalaureate
Cornish College of the Arts (652)
Northwest College Assemblies of God (899)
Comprehensive
Antioch University (209/789)
Bastyr College (318/862)
City University (4,111/7,250)
University of Washington (983/119)
Doctoral
Seattle Pacific University (2,620/817)
Seattle University (3,294/2,694)
University of Washington (30,426/10,202)
Score: 86.11   **Rank: 50**

Sharon, PA

Children in Public Schools (93%)

School Support ■■■☐☐

12 districts, 40 schools, 19,742 students

Children in Private Schools (7%)
5 Catholic, 1,398 students
1 Other, 28 students

Public Libraries

Library Popularity ■☐☐☐☐

5 systems
172,290 books; circulation: 264,081

Colleges and Universities

College Options ■■☐☐☐

College Town ■☐☐☐☐

Associate of Arts
1 campus (163)
Baccalaureate
Pennsylvania State University (1,276/63)
Thiel College (1,150)
Comprehensive
Grove City College (2,350/24)
Score: 15.86   **Rank: 298**

Sheboygan, WI

Children in Public Schools (87%)

School Support ■■■■☐

9 districts, 46 schools, 18,750 students

Children in Private Schools (13%)
7 Catholic, 1,426 students
10 Other, 1,469 students

Public Libraries

Library Popularity ■■■■■

8 systems
436,886 books; circulation: 1,170,492

Colleges and Universities

College Options ■☐☐☐☐

College Town ■☐☐☐☐

Comprehensive
Lakeland College (4,383/216)
Score: 14.16   **Rank: 304**

Sherbrooke, PQ

Children in Public Schools
2 districts, 62 schools, 15,396 students

Public Libraries

Library Popularity ■☐☐☐☐

3 systems, 46 branches
256,879 books; circulation: 633,020

Colleges and Universities

College Options ■■■☐☐

College Town ■■■■■

Associate of Arts
2 campuses (10,243)
Baccalaureate
Thomas More Institute (240)
Comprehensive
Bishop's University (2,554/24)
Doctoral
Universite de Sherbrooke (15,172/3,826)
Score: 68.55   **Rank: 112**

Sherman-Denison, TX

Children in Public Schools (99%)

School Support ■■■■■

13 districts, 55 schools, 18,927 students

Children in Private Schools (1%)
1 Catholic, 149 students
1 Other, 80 students

Public Libraries

Library Popularity ■■■☐☐

7 systems, 1 branch
274,741 books; circulation: 582,517

Colleges and Universities

College Options ■☐☐☐☐

College Town ■☐☐☐☐

Associate of Arts
1 campus (4,864)
Comprehensive
Austin College (1,076/33)
Score: 20.67   **Rank: 281**

Shreveport-Bossier City, LA

Children in Public Schools (94%)

School Support ■■■☐☐

3 districts, 129 schools, 78,002 students

Children in Private Schools (6%)
6 Catholic, 1,974 students
1 NAIS, 244 students
9 Other, 2,288 students

Public Libraries

Library Popularity ■■☐☐☐

3 systems, 33 branches
759,481 books; circulation: 1,673,337

Colleges and Universities

College Options ■■■☐☐

College Town ■☐☐☐☐

Associate of Arts
4 campuses (14,086)
Comprehensive
Centenary College of Louisiana (826/697)
Louisiana State University (4,818/1,063)
Score: 27.19   **Rank: 258**

Sioux City, IA-NE
Children in Public Schools (87%)

| School Support | ■■■■■ |

10 districts, 57 schools, 21,864 students
Children in Private Schools (13%)
11 Catholic, 3,006 students
1 Other, 107 students
Public Libraries

| Library Popularity | ■■■■□ |

7 systems, 5 branches
416,991 books; circulation: 860,794
Colleges and Universities

| College Options | ■■□□ |
| College Town | ■■□□ |

Associate of Arts
2 campuses (5,039)
Baccalaureate
Briar Cliff College (1,497)
Comprehensive
Morningside College (1,201/215)
Score: 43.9   **Rank: 199**

Sioux Falls, SD
Children in Public Schools (90%)

| School Support | ■■■□ |

11 districts, 74 schools, 27,323 students
Children in Private Schools (10%)
9 Catholic, 2,368 students
4 Other, 852 students
Public Libraries

| Library Popularity | ■■■■■ |

4 systems, 10 branches
411,537 books; circulation: 1,239,251
Colleges and Universities

| College Options | ■■■■□ |
| College Town | ■□□□ |

Associate of Arts
3 campuses (3,846)
Comprehensive
Augustana College (1,862/164)
Sioux Falls College (1,129/143)
Score: 52.12   **Rank: 170**

South Bend, IN
Children in Public Schools (88%)

| School Support | ■■■□ |

5 districts, 65 schools, 38,186 students
Children in Private Schools (12%)
18 Catholic, 6,508 students
1 NAIS, 408 students
1 Other, 45 students
Public Libraries

| Library Popularity | ■■■■■ |

4 systems, 8 branches
732,130 books; circulation: 3,187,971
Colleges and Universities

| College Options | ■■■■□ |
| College Town | ■■■■■ |

Associate of Arts
3 campuses (5,793)
Baccalaureate
Saint Mary's College (2,020)

Comprehensive
Bethel College (1,569/56)
Indiana University (8,770/2,675)
Doctoral
University of Notre Dame (8,186/3,044)
Score: 87.53   **Rank: 45**

Spokane, WA
Children in Public Schools (92%)

| School Support | ■□□□□ |

14 districts, 144 schools, 72,233 students
Children in Private Schools (8%)
13 Catholic, 2,909 students
1 NAIS, 290 students
23 Other, 3,155 students
Public Libraries

| Library Popularity | ■■■■□ |

1 system, 13 branches
940,738 books; circulation: 3,717,685
Colleges and Universities

| College Options | ■■■■□ |
| College Town | ■■■■□ |

Associate of Arts
2 campuses (26,165)
Comprehensive
Eastern Washington University (10,918/1,483)
Whitworth College (2,071/509)
Doctoral
Gonzaga University (3,526/2,192)
Score: 75.92   **Rank: 86**

Springfield, IL
Children in Public Schools (84%)

| School Support | ■■□□ |

18 districts, 118 schools, 42,956 students
Children in Private Schools (16%)
15 Catholic, 6,514 students
4 Other, 1,095 students
Public Libraries

| Library Popularity | ■■■■□ |

11 systems, 6 branches
566,835 books; circulation: 1,229,330
Colleges and Universities

| College Options | ■■■□ |
| College Town | ■■■■□ |

Associate of Arts
2 campuses (19,339)
Comprehensive
Sangamon State University (2,840/2,259)
Score: 64.02   **Rank: 128**

★Springfield, MA
Children in Public Schools (90%)

| School Support | ■■□□ |

24 districts, 175 schools, 86,262 students
Children in Private Schools (10%)
22 Catholic, 7,714 students
4 NAIS, 1,070 students
29 Other, 3,084 students
Public Libraries

| Library Popularity | ■■■■□ |

30 systems, 16 branches
2,266,799 books; circulation: 4,421,285

Colleges and Universities

College Options ■■■■■

College Town ■■■■■

Associate of Arts
  3 campuses (16,056)
Baccalaureate
  Amherst College (1,690)
  Bay Path College (662)
  Hampshire College (1,192)
Comprehensive
  College of Our Lady of the Elms (1,368/319)
  Mount Holyoke College (1,968/48)
  Western New England College (3,076/1,867)
  Westfield State College (4,792/1,329)
Doctoral
  American International College (1,638/591)
  Smith College (2,806/516)
  Springfield College (2,815/1,092)
  University of Massachusetts Amherst (23,022/7,683)

Score: 91.5   **Rank: 31**

★Springfield, MO

Children in Public Schools (97%)

School Support ■■■■□

18 districts, 114 schools, 44,928 students

Children in Private Schools (3%)
5 Catholic, 1,760 students
12 Other, 1,428 students

Public Libraries

Library Popularity ■■■■□

3 systems, 6 branches
515,537 books; circulation: 2,069,222

Colleges and Universities

College Options ■■■■□

College Town ■■■■■

Associate of Arts
  4 campuses (6,505)
Baccalaureate
  Central Bible College (1,076)
  Evangel College (1,621)
Comprehensive
  Baptist Bible College (1,795/161)
  Drury College (4,170/870)
  Southwest Missouri State University (16,733/2,939)

Score: 91.78   **Rank: 30**

Stamford-Norwalk, CT

Children in Public Schools (86%)

School Support ■■■■■

8 districts, 86 schools, 47,084 students

Children in Private Schools (14%)
13 Catholic, 3,807 students
9 NAIS, 3,717 students
4 Other, 355 students

Public Libraries

Library Popularity ■■■■■

11 systems, 6 branches
2,002,569 books; circulation: 4,673,233

Colleges and Universities

College Options ■□□□□

College Town ■□□□□

Associate of Arts
  2 campuses (8,382)

Score: 13.03   **Rank: 308**

State College, PA

Children in Public Schools (96%)

School Support ■■■□□

4 districts, 28 schools, 13,201 students

Children in Private Schools (4%)
2 Catholic, 519 students
1 Other, 90 students

Public Libraries

Library Popularity ■■■□□

4 systems
295,396 books; circulation: 697,855

Colleges and Universities

College Options ■□□□□

College Town ■■■■■

Doctoral
  Penn State University (35,934/8,352)

Score: 43.05   **Rank: 202**

Steubenville-Weirton, OH-WV

Children in Public Schools (86%)

School Support ■■■□□

8 districts, 59 schools, 21,582 students

Children in Private Schools (14%)
14 Catholic, 2,952 students
6 Other, 368 students

Public Libraries

Library Popularity ■■□□□

5 systems, 1 branch
233,040 books; circulation: 382,066

Colleges and Universities

College Options ■■■□□

College Town ■□□□□

Associate of Arts
  2 campuses (2,162)
Baccalaureate
  Bethany College (784)
Comprehensive
  Franciscan University (1,793/985)

Score: 28.61   **Rank: 253**

Stockton-Lodi, CA

Children in Public Schools (93%)

School Support ■□□□□

18 districts, 159 schools, 106,846 students

Children in Private Schools (7%)
10 Catholic, 3,519 students
32 Other, 4,880 students

Public Libraries

Library Popularity ■□□□□

2 systems, 9 branches
1,065,448 books; circulation: 2,073,201

Colleges and Universities

College Options ■■■□□

College Town ■■□□□

Associate of Arts
  2 campuses (25,458)
Baccalaureate
  Humphreys College (873/98)
Doctoral
  University of the Pacific (3,306/3,907)

Score: 24.64   **Rank: 267**

Sudbury, ON

Children in Public K-13 (52%)
55 schools, 21,615 students

Children in Catholic Separate (47%)
68 schools, 19,291 students

Children in Private K-13, (1%)
2 schools, 513 students

Public Libraries

Library Popularity	■■□□□

5 systems, 13 branches
331,572 books; circulation: 694,820

Colleges and Universities

College Options	■□□□□
College Town	■■■□□

Associate of Arts
  1 campus (6,000)
Comprehensive
  Laurentian University (7,472/285)

Score: 19.26   **Rank: 286**

Sumter, SC

Children in Public Schools (92%)

School Support	■■■□□

2 districts, 28 schools, 19,095 students

Children in Private Schools (8%)
1 Catholic, 230 students
6 Other, 1,479 students

Public Libraries

Library Popularity	■□□□□

1 system, 2 branches
125,668 books; circulation: 306,173

Colleges and Universities

College Options	■■□□□
College Town	■■■□□

Associate of Arts
  2 campuses (5,194)
Baccalaureate
  Morris College (1,026)

Score: 32.01   **Rank: 241**

★Syracuse, NY

Children in Public Schools (93%)

School Support	■■■■■

48 districts, 230 schools, 132,256 students

Children in Private Schools (7%)
33 Catholic, 8,573 students
1 NAIS, 500 students
6 Other, 449 students

Public Libraries

Library Popularity	■■■□□

48 systems, 9 branches
1,987,942 books; circulation: 5,468,580

Colleges and Universities

College Options	■■■■■
College Town	■■■■□

Associate of Arts
  5 campuses (18,753)
Baccalaureate
  Cazenovia College (1,416)
  Wells College (385)

Comprehensive
  Colgate University (3,025/12)
  Le Moyne College (2,858/958)
  SUNY College Oswego (8,457/1,927)
Doctoral
  *SUNY College of Environmental Science
    and Forestry* (1,179/657)
  SUNY Health Science Center (540/739)
  Syracuse University (12,130/7,981)

Score: 94.33   **Rank: 21**

Tacoma, WA

Children in Public Schools (93%)

School Support	■□□□□

15 districts, 210 schools, 116,345 students

Children in Private Schools (7%)
8 Catholic, 3,094 students
2 NAIS, 1,060 students
31 Other, 4,912 students

Public Libraries

Library Popularity	■■■■■

3 systems, 25 branches
2,054,355 books; circulation: 7,550,918

Colleges and Universities

College Options	■■■□□
College Town	■□□□□

Associate of Arts
  4 campuses (57,315)
Comprehensive
  Pacific Lutheran University (3,703/2,002)
  University of Puget Sound (2,813/341)
  University of Washington (1,029/91)

Score: 44.47   **Rank: 197**

Tallahassee, FL

Children in Public Schools (92%)

School Support	■■■□□

2 districts, 62 schools, 38,211 students

Children in Private Schools (8%)
2 Catholic, 952 students
1 NAIS, 941 students
7 Other, 1,865 students

Public Libraries

Library Popularity	■■□□□

2 systems, 6 branches
353,285 books; circulation: 1,522,279

Colleges and Universities

College Options	■■■□□
College Town	■■■■■

Associate of Arts
  1 campus (13,955)
Doctoral
  Florida A&M University (10,044/1,114)
  Florida State University (26,633/9,940)

Score: 63.73   **Rank: 129**

Tampa-St. Petersburg-Clearwater, FL

Children in Public Schools (94%)

School Support	■■■□□

4 districts, 395 schools, 314,413 students

Children in Private Schools (6%)
43 Catholic, 12,754 students
5 NAIS, 2,245 students
21 Other, 3,706 students

Public Libraries

Library Popularity ▮▮▯▯▯

20 systems, 38 branches
3,271,810 books; circulation: 10,650,829

Colleges and Universities

College Options ▮▮▮▮▮

College Town ▮▮▯▯▯

Associate of Arts
    6 campuses (124,781)
Baccalaureate
    Clearwater Christian College (590)
    Eckerd College (1,442)
    Florida College (390)
Comprehensive
    Saint Leo College (14,940/168)
    University of Tampa (2,442/698)
Doctoral
    University of South Florida (34,853/13,153)
Score: **67.98**   Rank: **114**

Terre Haute, IN

Children in Public Schools (96%)

School Support ▮▮▮▯▯

6 districts, 47 schools, 24,728 students

Children in Private Schools (4%)

5 Catholic, 634 students
4 Other, 773 students

Public Libraries

Library Popularity ▮▮▮▮▯

4 systems, 10 branches
406,094 books; circulation: 994,392

Colleges and Universities

College Options ▮▮▮▯▯

College Town ▮▮▮▮▮

Associate of Arts
    1 campus (4,179)
Comprehensive
    Rose-Hulman Institute of Technology (1,440/130)
    Saint Mary-of-the-Woods College (1,552/92)
Doctoral
    Indiana State University (12,956/2,664)
Score: **69.4**   Rank: **109**

Texarkana, TX-Texarkana, AR

Children in Public Schools (92%)

School Support ▮▮▮▮▮

16 districts, 48 schools, 18,535 students

Children in Private Schools (8%)

1 Catholic, 354 students
5 Other, 1,179 students

Public Libraries

Library Popularity ▮▮▮▮▯

5 systems
205,294 books; circulation: 436,763

Colleges and Universities

College Options ▮▯▯▯▯

College Town ▮▮▯▯▯

Associate of Arts
    1 campus (6,368)
Comprehensive
    East Texas State University (1,006/704)
Score: **30.31**   Rank: **247**

Thunder Bay, ON

Children in Public K-13 (65%)

6 districts, 43 schools, 15,264 students

Children in Catholic Separate (26%)

24 schools, 8,066 students

Children in Private K-13 (8%)

10 schools, 2,100 students

Public Libraries

Library Popularity ▮▮▮▮▯

2 systems, 5 branches
328,608 books; circulation: 1,014,698

Colleges and Universities

College Options ▮▯▯▯▯

College Town ▮▮▮▮▯

Associate of Arts
    1 campus (3,700)
Comprehensive
    Lakehead University (7,495/356)
Score: **32.86**   Rank: **238**

Toledo, OH

Children in Public Schools (83%)

School Support ▮▮▮▯▯

25 districts, 186 schools, 98,107 students

Children in Private Schools (17%)

49 Catholic, 17,789 students
1 NAIS, 465 students
20 Other, 2,334 students

Public Libraries

Library Popularity ▮▮▮▮▮

14 systems, 25 branches
3,413,620 books; circulation: 7,833,748

Colleges and Universities

College Options ▮▮▮▮▯

College Town ▮▮▮▮▮

Associate of Arts
    3 campuses (13,724)
Baccalaureate
    Lourdes College (2,072)
Doctoral
    Bowling Green State University (16,385/5,090)
    Medical College of Ohio (1,098)
    University of Toledo (24,368/6,057)
Score: **85.26**   Rank: **53**

Topeka, KS

Children in Public Schools (93%)

School Support ▮▮▮▮▮

5 districts, 68 schools, 24,847 students

Children in Private Schools (7%)

8 Catholic, 2,337 students
2 Other, 250 students

Public Libraries

Library Popularity ▮▮▮▮▮

3 systems
458,458 books; circulation: 1,610,056

Colleges and Universities

College Options ▮▯▯▯▯

College Town ▮▮▮▯▯

Comprehensive
    Washburn University (5,620/922)
Score: **23.22**   Rank: **272**

Toronto, ON
Children in Public K-13 (65%)
32 districts, 1,111 schools, 519,446 students
Children in Catholic Separate (28%)
301 schools, 149,321 students
Children in Private K-13 (7%)
179 Catholic, 38,331 students
Public Libraries
Library Popularity
23 systems, 152 branches
9,529,632 books; circulation: 29,785,512
Colleges and Universities
College Options
College Town
Associate of Arts
7 campuses (49,000)
Baccalaureate
Ontario Bible College (551)
Ryerson Polytechnical Institute (21,791)
Comprehensive
Ontario Theological Seminary (314/232)
Doctoral
Ontario Institute (37/2,518)
University of Toronto (40,639/9,511)
York University (35,481/3,305)
Score: 73.08   Rank: 96

★Trenton, NJ
Children in Public Schools (78%)
School Support
11 districts, 96 schools, 50,694 students
Children in Private Schools (22%)
23 Catholic, 6,457 students
7 NAIS, 2,908 students
4 Other, 745 students
Public Libraries
Library Popularity
7 systems, 12 branches
1,354,677 books; circulation: 2,253,555
Colleges and Universities
College Options
College Town
Associate of Arts
3 campuses (12,353)
Comprehensive
Rider College (6,752/2,923)
Thomas Edison State College (8,575)
Trenton State College (6,574/1,913)
Doctoral
Princeton Theological Seminary (858)
Princeton University (4,740/1,810)
Score: 94.9   Rank: 19

Trois Rivieres, PQ
Children in Public Schools
2 districts, 60 schools, 14,640 students
Public Libraries
Library Popularity
4 systems, 4 branches
616,915 books; circulation: 1,310,548
Colleges and Universities
College Options
College Town

Associate of Arts
2 campuses (5,003)
Doctoral
Universite du Quebec (11,030/957)
Score: 58.35   Rank: 148

Tucson, AZ
Children in Public Schools (95%)
School Support
15 districts, 207 schools, 118,515 students
Children in Private Schools (5%)
12 Catholic, 4,923 students
3 NAIS, 583 students
8 Other, 1,220 students
Public Libraries
Library Popularity
1 system, 17 branches
1,164,000 books; circulation: 5,248,200
Colleges and Universities
College Options
College Town
Associate of Arts
1 campus (38,852)
Doctoral
University of Arizona (27,738/9,519)
Score: 54.67   Rank: 161

Tulsa, OK
Children in Public Schools (96%)
School Support
57 districts, 284 schools, 139,050 students
Children in Private Schools (4%)
15 Catholic, 4,659 students
1 NAIS, 964 students
Public Libraries
Library Popularity
17 systems, 21 branches
1,325,268 books; circulation: 4,296,147
Colleges and Universities
College Options
College Town
Associate of Arts
3 campuses (34,565)
Doctoral
Oral Roberts University (3,664/872)
University of Tulsa (3,422/2,087)
Score: 50.42   Rank: 176

Tuscaloosa, AL
Children in Public Schools (97%)
School Support
2 districts, 49 schools, 24,624 students
Children in Private Schools (3%)
1 Catholic, 321 students
1 NAIS, 462 students
3 Other, 139 students
Public Libraries
Library Popularity
1 system, 3 branches
204,660 books; circulation: 441,457
Colleges and Universities
College Options
College Town

Associate of Arts
    1 campus (10,398)
Baccalaureate
    Stillman College (911)
Doctoral
    University of Alabama (16,474/5,584)
Score: **65.15**   Rank: **124**

Tyler, TX
Children in Public Schools (94%)
School Support ■■■■■

8 districts, 59 schools, 29,588 students
Children in Private Schools (6%)
2 Catholic, 615 students
4 Other, 1,410 students
Public Libraries
Library Popularity ■□□□□

4 systems
174,672 books; circulation: 258,763
Colleges and Universities
College Options ■■□□□
College Town ■■■■□

Associate of Arts
    1 campus (10,820)
Baccalaureate
    Texas College (392)
Comprehensive
    University of Texas at Tyler (2,657/2,517)
Score: **45.89**   Rank: **192**

Utica-Rome, NY
Children in Public Schools (94%)
School Support ■■■■■

28 districts, 99 schools, 50,705 students
Children in Private Schools (6%)
12 Catholic, 3,345 students
Public Libraries
Library Popularity ■■■■□

34 systems, 4 branches
854,561 books; circulation: 1,667,165
Colleges and Universities
College Options ■■■■□
College Town ■■□□□

Associate of Arts
    3 campuses (10,799)
Baccalaureate
    Hamilton College (1,760)
    Utica College of Syracuse University (2,410)
Comprehensive
    SUNY Institute of Technology (2,768/437)
Score: **78.18**   Rank: **78**

Vallejo-Fairfield-Napa, CA
Children in Public Schools (93%)
School Support ■□□□□

13 districts, 137 schools, 87,186 students
Children in Private Schools (7%)
12 Catholic, 4,108 students
31 Other, 2,387 students
Public Libraries
Library Popularity ■■□□□

5 systems, 7 branches
855,536 books; circulation: 2,654,541

Colleges and Universities
College Options ■■■□□
College Town ■□□□□

Associate of Arts
    2 campuses (26,432)
Baccalaureate
    California Maritime Academy (383)
Comprehensive
    Pacific Union College (1,773/33)
Score: **23.79**   Rank: **270**

Vancouver, BC
Children in Public K-13 (91%)
11 districts, 575 schools, 263,989 students
Children in Private K-13 (9%)
133 Catholic and Other, 28,138 students
Public Libraries
Library Popularity ■■■■■

10 systems, 35 branches
4,880,891 books; circulation: 19,523,564
Colleges and Universities
College Options ■■■■■
College Town ■■□□□

Associate of Arts
    11 campuses (71,716)
Comprehensive
    Northwest Baptist Theological College (252/30)
    Regent College (416/190)
    Trinity Western University (2,082/89)
Doctoral
    Simon Fraser University (15,890/2,321)
University of British Columbia (23,784/6,947)
Score: **86.4**   Rank: **49**

Ventura, CA
Children in Public Schools (90%)
School Support ■□□□□

21 districts, 184 schools, 131,766 students
Children in Private Schools (10%)
15 Catholic, 5,200 students
5 NAIS, 751 students
70 Other, 7,376 students
Public Libraries
Library Popularity ■■□□□

4 systems, 18 branches
1,596,018 books; circulation: 3,036,219
Colleges and Universities
College Options ■■■■□
College Town ■□□□□

Associate of Arts
    4 campuses (54,981)
Comprehensive
    California Lutheran University (2,281/1,563)
Score: **36.54**   Rank: **225**

Victoria, BC
Children in Public K-13 (90%)
3 districts, 116 schools, 43,830 students
Children in Private K-13 (10%)
27 Catholic and Other, 4,811 students
Public Libraries
Library Popularity ■■■■■

1 system, 6 branches
720,733 books; circulation: 2,945,692

Colleges and Universities

| College Options | ■■□□□ |
| College Town | ■■■□□ |

Associate of Arts
1 campus (4,842)
Doctoral
University of Victoria (13,602/1,973)
Score: 47.02   Rank: **188**

Victoria, TX
Children in Public Schools (89%)

| School Support | ■■■□ |

3 districts, 31 schools, 15,502 students
Children in Private Schools (11%)
3 Catholic, 1,588 students
2 Other, 281 students
Public Libraries

| Library Popularity | ■■□□□ |

1 system
144,805 books; circulation: 332,051
Colleges and Universities

| College Options | ■□□□□ |
| College Town | ■■■□□ |

Associate of Arts
1 campus (5,487)
Comprehensive
University of Houston (2,339/1,325)
Score: 20.11   Rank: **283**

Vineland-Millville-Bridgeton, NJ
Children in Public Schools (88%)

| School Support | ■■■■■ |

16 districts, 54 schools, 25,007 students
Children in Private Schools (12%)
6 Catholic, 1,613 students
1 NAIS, 193 students
1 Other, 180 students
Public Libraries

| Library Popularity | ■□□□□ |

5 systems
431,678 books; circulation: 383,764
Colleges and Universities

| College Options | ■□□□□ |
| College Town | ■□□□□ |

Associate of Arts
1 campus (3,821)
Score: 5.66   Rank: **335**

Visalia-Tulare-Porterville, CA
Children in Public Schools (96%)

| School Support | ■□□□□ |

50 districts, 145 schools, 83,084 students
Children in Private Schools (4%)
4 Catholic, 979 students
26 Other, 2,352 students
Public Libraries

| Library Popularity | ■□□□□ |

3 systems, 14 branches
508,898 books; circulation: 869,661
Colleges and Universities

| College Options | ■□□□□ |
| College Town | ■□□□□ |

Associate of Arts
2 campuses (16,108)
Score: **1.41**   Rank: **349**

Waco, TX
Children in Public Schools (96%)

| School Support | ■■■■■ |

18 districts, 97 schools, 37,512 students
Children in Private Schools (4%)
4 Catholic, 866 students
1 NAIS, 190 students
7 Other, 652 students
Public Libraries

| Library Popularity | ■□□□□ |

4 systems, 3 branches
298,222 books; circulation: 550,889
Colleges and Universities

| College Options | ■■□□□ |
| College Town | ■■■■■ |

Associate of Arts
2 campuses (14,322)
Doctoral
Baylor University (11,289/2,337)
Score: **50.7**   Rank: **175**

★Washington, DC-MD-VA-WV
Children in Public Schools (92%)

| School Support | ■■■■□ |

23 districts, 1,168 schools, 676,220 students
Children in Private Schools (8%)
112 Catholic, 40,411 students
35 NAIS, 13,125 students
49 Other, 7,978 students
Public Libraries

| Library Popularity | ■■■■□ |

16 systems, 139 branches
12,248,113 books; circulation: 36,203,170
Colleges and Universities

| College Options | ■■■■■ |
| College Town | ■■■■□ |

Associate of Arts
10 campuses (135,175)
Baccalaureate
Columbia Union College (1,910)
Corcoran School of Art (347)
Shepherd College (4,280)
Comprehensive
Bowie State University (4,058/2,502)
Capitol College (766/163)
Defense Intelligence College (46/389)
Hood College (1,330/1,708)
Mary Washington College (4,256/102)
Marymount University (2,372/2,589)
Mount Saint Mary's College (1,482/697)
Mount Vernon College (520/116)
Southeastern University (264/221)
Trinity College (1,266/683)
University of Maryland University College (16,065/5,139)
University of the District of Columbia (11,285/770)
Washington Bible College (388/190)
Doctoral
American University (6,525/6,998)
Catholic University of America (2,632/4,165)
Gallaudet University (1,625/490)

George Mason University (17,200/14,124)
George Washington University (8,765/15,121)
Georgetown University (7,874/6,981)
Howard University (7,640/3,869)
Uniformed Services University Health Sciences (821)
University of Maryland College Park (28,826/10,333)
Wesley Theological Seminary (670)
Score: **97.73**   Rank: **9**

Waterbury, CT
Children in Public Schools (85%)
School Support   ▪▪▪▪▪

7 districts, 67 schools, 34,194 students
Children in Private Schools (15%)
15 Catholic, 4,867 students
3 NAIS, 1,105 students
4 Other, 139 students
Public Libraries
Library Popularity   ▪▪▪

10 systems, 2 branches
630,308 books; circulation: 1,053,512
Colleges and Universities
College Options   ▪
College Town   ▪

Associate of Arts
1 campus (7,101)
Baccalaureate
Teikyo Post University (2,363)
Score: **15.58**   Rank: **299**

Waterloo-Cedar Falls, IA
Children in Public Schools (84%)
School Support   ▪▪▪▪

6 districts, 46 schools, 18,761 students
Children in Private Schools (16%)
8 Catholic, 2,864 students
3 Other, 621 students
Public Libraries
Library Popularity   ▪▪▪

6 systems
335,741 books; circulation: 828,715
Colleges and Universities
College Options   ▪
College Town   ▪▪▪▪▪

Associate of Arts
1 campus (4,995)
Doctoral
University of Northern Iowa (12,631/2,397)
Score: **42.77**   Rank: **203**

Wausau, WI
Children in Public Schools (83%)
School Support   ▪▪▪▪▪

8 districts, 44 schools, 19,567 students
Children in Private Schools (17%)
19 Catholic, 3,118 students
8 Other, 1,007 students
Public Libraries
Library Popularity   ▪▪▪

1 system, 8 branches
246,953 books; circulation: 765,056
Colleges and Universities
College Options   ▪
College Town   ▪▪▪

Associate of Arts
1 campus (5,483)
Score: **19.54**   Rank: **285**

West Palm Beach-Boca Raton, FL
Children in Public Schools (93%)
School Support   ▪▪▪

1 district, 156 schools, 124,955 students
Children in Private Schools (7%)
14 Catholic, 5,882 students
6 NAIS, 2,964 students
12 Other, 2,035 students
Public Libraries
Library Popularity   ▪▪▪

11 system, 12 branches
1,516,736 books; circulation: 5,598,831
Colleges and Universities
College Options   ▪▪▪▪
College Town   ▪

Associate of Arts
3 campuses (53,868)
Baccalaureate
Northwood University, Florida (863)
Comprehensive
Lynn University (1,765/190)
Palm Beach Atlantic College (2,203/196)
Doctoral
Florida Atlantic University (25,185/3,125)
Score: **48.15**   Rank: **184**

Wheeling, WV-OH
Children in Public Schools (86%)
School Support   ▪▪▪▪

10 districts, 62 schools, 22,838 students
Children in Private Schools (14%)
12 Catholic, 2,748 students
3 NAIS, 555 students
8 Other, 345 students
Public Libraries
Library Popularity   ▪▪▪

6 systems, 18 branches
661,330 books; circulation: 1,460,288
Colleges and Universities
College Options   ▪▪▪
College Town   ▪▪▪

Associate of Arts
2 campuses (6,441)
Baccalaureate
Ohio University Eastern Campus (1,460/386)
West Liberty State College (2,749)
Comprehensive
Wheeling Jesuit College (1,808/252)
Score: **62.32**   Rank: **134**

Wichita, KS
Children in Public Schools (91%)
School Support   ▪▪▪▪

24 districts, 213 schools, 87,420 students
Children in Private Schools (9%)
19 Catholic, 6,778 students
1 NAIS, 870 students
12 Other, 2,171 students

Public Libraries

Library Popularity ▪▪▪▪☐

25 systems, 11 branches
1,444,439 books; circulation: 2,709,015

Colleges and Universities

College Options ▪▪▪▪☐

College Town ▪▪▪▪☐

Associate of Arts
3 campuses (23,158)
Baccalaureate
Bethel College (766)
Comprehensive
Friends University (2,913/841)
Kansas Newman College (2,443/774)
Doctoral
Wichita State University (15,077/4,860)

Score: 72.8 Rank: 97

Wichita Falls, TX

Children in Public Schools (97%)

School Support ▪▪▪▪▪

8 districts, 55 schools, 24,720 students

Children in Private Schools (3%)

1 Catholic, 522 students
2 Other, 247 students

Public Libraries

Library Popularity ▪☐☐☐☐

5 systems
197,650 books; circulation: 426,253

Colleges and Universities

College Options ▪☐☐☐☐

College Town ▪▪▪☐

Comprehensive
Midwestern State University (6,289/985)

Score: 13.59 Rank: 306

Williamsport, PA

Children in Public Schools (97%)

School Support ▪▪▪☐

8 districts, 40 schools, 20,455 students

Children in Private Schools (3%)

4 Catholic, 731 students

Public Libraries

Library Popularity ▪▪☐☐

6 systems
209,904 books; circulation: 902,849

Colleges and Universities

College Options ▪☐☐☐☐

College Town ▪▪▪☐

Baccalaureate
Lycoming College (1,556)
Pennsylvania College of Technology (5,488)

Score: 21.52 Rank: 278

Wilmington, NC

Children in Public Schools (94%)

School Support ▪▪▪▪▪

2 districts, 44 schools, 30,474 students

Children in Private Schools (6%)

2 Catholic, 301 students
1 NAIS, 328 students
19 Other, 1,448 students

Public Libraries

Library Popularity ▪▪▪▪☐

1 system, 7 branches
361,661 books; circulation: 1,153,081

Colleges and Universities

College Options ▪▪☐☐☐

College Town ▪▪▪☐

Associate of Arts
2 campuses (6,806)
Comprehensive
University of North Carolina (11,908/887)

Score: 40.79 Rank: 210

Wilmington-Newark, DE-MD

Children in Public Schools (82%)

School Support ▪▪▪☐

7 districts, 135 schools, 76,730 students

Children in Private Schools (18%)

28 Catholic, 12,468 students
9 NAIS, 3,802 students
8 Other, 1,649 students

Public Libraries

Library Popularity ▪▪☐☐☐

12 systems, 8 branches
1,084,379 books; circulation: 2,343,183

Colleges and Universities

College Options ▪▪▪▪☐

College Town ▪▪▪▪▪

Associate of Arts
2 campuses (11,113)
Comprehensive
Goldey-Beacom College (1,661/104)
Widener University (556/1,359)
Doctoral
University of Delaware (21,287/3,942)
Wilmington College (5,028/1,716)

Score: 66.28 Rank: 120

Windsor, ON

Children in Public K-13 (52%)

41 schools, 20,057 students

Children in Catholic Separate (42%)

41 Catholic, 16,167 students

Children in Private K-13 (6%)

11 schools, 2,310 students

Public Libraries

Library Popularity ▪▪▪☐

4 systems, 26 branches
914,766 books; circulation: 1,888,288

Colleges and Universities

College Options ▪☐☐☐☐

College Town ▪▪▪☐

Associate of Arts
1 campus (4,800)
Doctoral
University of Windsor (14,678/910)

Score: 28.04 Rank: 255

Winnipeg, MB

Children in Public K-13 (92%)

10 divisions, 256 schools, 108,476 students

Children in Private K-13 (8%)

41 Catholic and Other, 9,230 students

Public Libraries

Library Popularity   ■■■■□

2 systems, 23 branches
1,444,235 books; circulation: 5,646,781

Colleges and Universities

College Options   ■■■■□
College Town   ■■■□□

Associate of Arts
  2 campuses (14,000)
Comprehensive
  University of Winnipeg (7,085/190)
Doctoral
  University of Manitoba (20,343/3,574)

Score: **76.77**   Rank: **83**

Worcester, MA-CT

Children in Public Schools (90%)

School Support   ■■□□□

24 districts, 151 schools, 74,226 students

Children in Private Schools (10%)

20 Catholic, 7,057 students
4 NAIS, 1,351 students
14 Other, 1,695 students

Public Libraries

Library Popularity   ■■■■□

35 systems, 5 branches
1,922,274 books; circulation: 3,216,244

Colleges and Universities

College Options   ■■■■□
College Town   ■■■■□

Associate of Arts
  2 campuses (7,417)
Baccalaureate
  Becker College (1,159)
  College of the Holy Cross (2,774)
Comprehensive
  Anna Maria College (1,073/2,891)
  Assumption College (2,787/531)
  Nichols College (1,357/362)
  Worcester State College (12,541/1,799)
Doctoral
  Clark University (2,721/1,679)
  University of Massachusetts Medical School (653)
  Worcester Polytechnic Institute (2,747/1,018)

Score: **82.43**   Rank: **63**

Yakima, WA

Children in Public Schools (95%)

School Support   ■□□□□

15 districts, 88 schools, 48,782 students

Children in Private Schools (5%)

3 Catholic, 1,010 students
10 Other, 1,328 students

Public Libraries

Library Popularity   ■■□□□

2 systems, 20 branches
649,033 books; circulation: 887,459

Colleges and Universities

College Options   ■□□□□
College Town   ■□□□□

Associate of Arts
  2 campuses (7,322)

Comprehensive
  Heritage College (1,011/897)

Score: **4.24**   Rank: **340**

Yolo, CA

Children in Public Schools (84%)

School Support   ■□□□□

5 districts, 34 schools, 16,109 students

Children in Private Schools (16%)

8 Catholic, 2,109 students
20 Other, 2,980 students

Public Libraries

Library Popularity   ■■□□□

1 system, 7 branches
324,618 books; circulation: 771,298

Colleges and Universities

College Options   ■□□□□
College Town   ■■■■■

Associate of Arts
  1 campus (597)
Doctoral
  University of California (18,092/5,465)

Score: **28.32**   Rank: **254**

York, PA

Children in Public Schools (93%)

School Support   ■■□□□

16 districts, 97 schools, 52,747 students

Children in Private Schools (7%)

14 Catholic, 3,242 students
1 NAIS, 264 students
4 Other, 472 students

Public Libraries

Library Popularity   ■□□□□

10 systems, 6 branches
328,889 books; circulation: 1,148,755

Colleges and Universities

College Options   ■■□□□
College Town   ■□□□□

Baccalaureate
  Penn State University (2,336/434)
Comprehensive
  York College Pennsylvania (5,504/159)

Score: **9.91**   Rank: **319**

Youngstown-Warren, OH

Children in Public Schools (88%)

School Support   ■■□□□

48 districts, 214 schools, 98,495 students

Children in Private Schools (12%)

37 Catholic, 9,939 students
17 Other, 3,170 students

Public Libraries

Library Popularity   ■■■■□

15 systems, 23 branches
1,512,174 books; circulation: 4,541,849

Colleges and Universities

College Options   ■■■■□
College Town   ■□□□□

Associate of Arts
  3 campuses (4,083)
Doctoral
  Youngstown State University (14,797/2,030)

Score: **58.64**   Rank: **147**

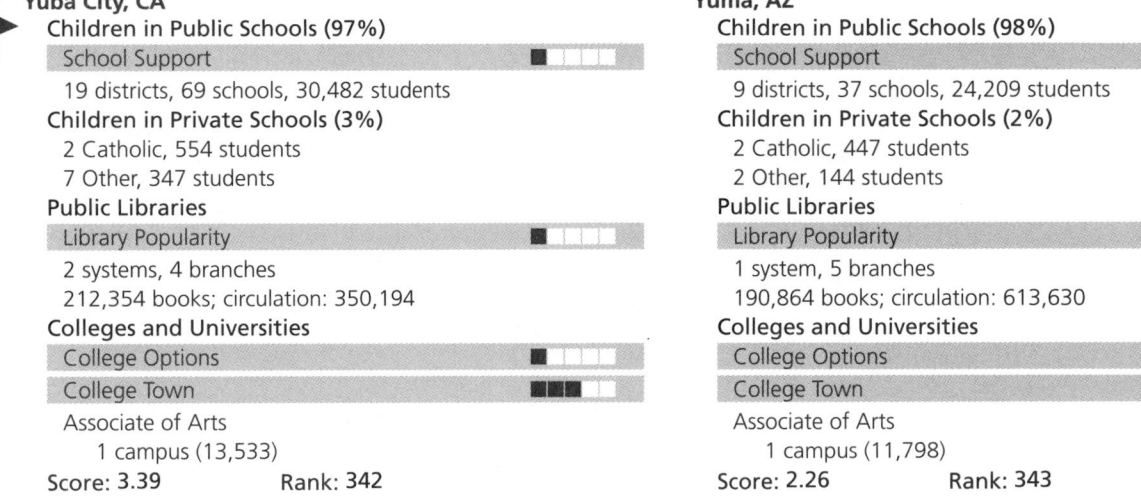

Yuba City, CA
 Children in Public Schools (97%)
  School Support ▮□□□□
   19 districts, 69 schools, 30,482 students
 Children in Private Schools (3%)
  2 Catholic, 554 students
  7 Other, 347 students
 Public Libraries
  Library Popularity ▮□□□□
   2 systems, 4 branches
   212,354 books; circulation: 350,194
 Colleges and Universities
  College Options ▮□□□□
  College Town ▮▮▮□
   Associate of Arts
    1 campus (13,533)
 Score: 3.39   Rank: 342

Yuma, AZ
 Children in Public Schools (98%)
  School Support ▮▮□□□
   9 districts, 37 schools, 24,209 students
 Children in Private Schools (2%)
  2 Catholic, 447 students
  2 Other, 144 students
 Public Libraries
  Library Popularity ▮▮□□□
   1 system, 5 branches
   190,864 books; circulation: 613,630
 Colleges and Universities
  College Options ▮□□□□
  College Town ▮□□□□
   Associate of Arts
    1 campus (11,798)
 Score: 2.26   Rank: 343

ET CETERA: Education

CONTINUING EDUCATION: A GROWING TREND

More and more, education is seen as a lifelong experience rather than one that ends abruptly upon graduation from high school or college. There are reasons for this: Workers in technical industries need retraining; professionals need state-of-the-art courses for recertification; and others pursue personal and vocational interests. Today, there are more than twice as many adults enrolled in part-time education as there are full-time college students.

One measure of the importance of continuing education is the way states have responded to demands that professionals such as dentists, doctors, lawyers, nurses, psychologists, and social workers be certified as competent. In most states, mandatory continuing education is a condition for renewing a license to practice in many of these professions; Connecticut, Colorado, Hawaii, New Jersey, and New York are exceptions.

SOLVING THE SAT PUZZLE . . . OR TRYING

After 17 years of unbroken decline, the average scores of students on the Scholastic Aptitude Tests (SAT), given by the College Entrance Examination Board, bottomed out in 1980 and started slowly upward in 1982. At the current rate of recovery, however, math scores will finally match their 1963 high in the year 2000, and verbal scores not until well into the 21st century. Even more troubling is the slow rate of improving test scores between 1990 and 1999, when the percentage of students taking the test who had "A" averages in high school rose from 28 percent to 38 percent.

Two researchers point out that SAT scores started declining 18 years after the 1945 atomic bomb tests and began rising 18 years after the United States suspended all but underground atomic testing in 1963. The steepest drops in scores occurred in states nearest the bomb detonations, especially Nevada and Utah; smaller declines occurred in the northeastern and southeastern states far from the proving grounds. According to these researchers, those who blame the drop in SAT scores on television viewing, the Vietnam War, the declining birth rate, changes in the number and mix of students taking the test, and poorer performance of schools are overlooking the effects of atomic fallout on the cognitive abilities of children.

Mandatory Continuing Education for Selected Professions

	DENTISTS	LAWYERS	NURSES	MENTAL HEALTH COUNSELORS	PHYSICIANS	THERAPISTS	PHYSICAL VETERINARIANS	SOCIAL WORKERS
Alabama	•	•	•	•	•		•	•
Alaska	•		•		•	•	•	•
Alberta	•				•			
Arizona	•	•		•	•		•	•
Arkansas	•	•		•	E	•	•	•
British Columbia	•							
California	•	•	•		•			•
Colorado		•					•	
Connecticut								
Delaware	•				•	•	•	•
District of Columbia	•		•		•	•	•	•
Florida	•		•		•		•	•
Georgia	•	•		•	•		•	
Hawaii					•			
Idaho	•	•		•			•	•
Illinois	•			•	•		•	
Indiana	•	•			•		•	E
Iowa	•	•	•	•	•	•	•	•
Kansas	•	•		•	•	•	•	•
Kentucky	•	•	•		•	•	•	
Louisiana	•	•	•	•		•	•	•
Maine	•			•			•	•
Manitoba	•			•				
Maryland	•				•	•	•	
Massachusetts	•		•		•			•
Michigan	•				•			
Minnesota	•	•	•		•	•	•	•
Mississippi	•	•			•	•	•	•
Missouri	•	•			•		•	•
Montana	•	•		•		•	•	•
Nebraska	•		•	•	E		•	•
Nevada	•	•	•		•	•	•	•
New Brunswick	•				•			
New Hampshire	•	•	•	•	•	•	•	
New Jersey	•							E
New Mexico	•	•	•		•		•	•
New York	•	•						
Newfoundland	•							
North Carolina	•	•	•	•		•	•	
North Dakota	•	•		•		•	•	
Nova Scotia								
Ohio	•	•	•	•	•	•	•	•
Oklahoma	•	•		•	•		•	
Ontario	•				•			
Oregon		•		•			•	
Pennsylvania	E	•					•	E
Quebec	•							
Rhode Island	•				•			•
Saskatchewan	•				•			
South Carolina	•	•		•			•	•
South Dakota	•			•			•	
Tennessee	•	•					•	
Texas	•	•	•		•	•	•	•
Utah	•	•	•	•	•		•	•
Vermont				•				
Virginia	•	•					•	
Washington		•			•	•	•	•
West Virginia	•	•	•	•	•	•	•	•
Wisconsin		•		•	•			•
Wyoming		•	•				•	

Source: Louis Phillips and Associates; Places Rated Partnership Survey 1999.
•: *Continuing education required;* E: *Enabling legislation passed but not implemented.*

SAT Scores by State

	VERBAL	MATH	% GRADUATES TAKING TEST
United States	505	511	42
Alabama	561	555	8
Alaska	520	517	48
Arizona	523	522	29
Arkansas	567	558	6
California	496	514	45
Colorado	536	539	30
Connecticut	509	507	79
Delaware	505	498	65
District of Columbia	490	475	60
Florida	499	499	50
Georgia	486	481	63
Hawaii	483	512	54
Idaho	544	539	15
Illinois	562	578	14
Indiana	494	497	57
Iowa	589	601	5
Kansas	578	575	9
Kentucky	548	546	12
Louisiana	560	553	10
Maine	507	504	67
Maryland	507	507	64
Massachusetts	508	508	80
Michigan	557	566	11
Minnesota	582	592	9
Mississippi	567	551	4
Missouri	567	568	9
Montana	545	548	22
Nebraska	562	564	9
Nevada	508	509	32
New Hampshire	521	518	70
New Jersey	497	508	69
New Mexico	554	545	12
New York	495	502	74
North Carolina	490	488	59
North Dakota	588	595	5
Ohio	535	536	25
Oklahoma	568	560	8
Oregon	525	524	50
Pennsylvania	498	495	72
Rhode Island	499	493	70
South Carolina	479	474	56
South Dakota	574	570	4
Tennessee	564	556	13
Texas	494	501	49
Utah	576	570	4
Vermont	508	502	69
Virginia	506	497	69
Washington	523	523	46
West Virginia	524	508	18
Wisconsin	579	590	7
Wyoming	543	543	12

Source: College Entrance Examination Board.

In Texas, two other scholars of SAT trends have a different theory, however. The states that have produced the highest scores, they claim, are not those that spend the most money for education, nor those with a long tradition of quality public education, but those with the coldest winters. Average scores from cold-weather states are consistently higher than scores from warm-weather states. They offer two explanations for this link: (1) Research on thermal conditions and human behavior suggests that cool room temperatures reduce mistakes on tests, and (2) long winters force children to remain inside after school and on weekends, thereby favoring the family interaction so critical to pupil achievement.

Nonsense, other researchers contend, for if one were to rank the states by average total SATs, one would be, in effect, ranking them by the percentage of college-bound seniors who actually took the test. When the percentage is low, students taking the test are among the highest achievers; the more students in the test-taking pool, the more students of average ability are included.

The highest possible score on the SAT is 800 for the verbal and 800 for the math sections, for a total of 1600.

OUTSTANDING SECONDARY SCHOOLS

Every other year, the U.S. Department of Education asks each state's superintendent of instruction and the Council for American Private Education for the names of the best secondary schools in the country.

Of the thousands nominated since 1990, just 1,151 have received official recognition for excellence in education. The judges who do the screening are specialists in school improvement and accreditation. None of them work for the federal government.

The schools must survive a tough screening that includes a careful look at curricula and academic achievement. Buildings and classrooms are inspected. Judges sit in on classes and assemblies and even sample lunch in the cafeteria. They interview everyone: students, parents, teachers, and administrators.

Of these outstanding schools, 1,059 are located in metro areas. The schools include 558 junior high schools (JHS), middle schools (MS), and intermediate schools (IS), as well as 501 high schools (HS). The names of 148 private schools are in italics.

Akron, OH
Archbishop Hoban HS, Akron
Aurora HS, Aurora
Revere HS, Richfield

Albany-Schenectady-Troy, NY
Academy of the Holy Names, Albany
Bouton HS, Voorheesville
La Salle Institute, Troy
O'Brien Academy, Albany
Shaker JHS, Latham

Albuquerque, NM
Cleveland MS, Albuquerque
Lyndon Johnson MS, Albuquerque
McKinley MS, Albuquerque
Roosevelt MS, Tijeras
Taylor MS, Albuquerque
Van Buren MS, Albuquerque

Allentown-Bethlehem-Easton, PA
Central Catholic HS, Allentown
Feaser MS, Middletown
Southern Lehigh MS, Center Valley

Amarillo, TX
Crockett MS, Amarillo

Anchorage, AK
East Anchorage HS, Anchorage
West Anchorage HS, Anchorage

Ann Arbor, MI
Hartland HS, Hartland
Pinckney MS, Pinckney

Appleton-Oshkosh-Neenah, WI
Hortonville MS, Hortonville
Seymour MS, Seymour

Athens, GA
Cedar Shoals HS, Athens

Atlanta, GA
Banneker HS, College Park
Chamblee HS, Chamblee
Duluth HS, Duluth
Edwards MS, Conyers
Flat Rock MS, Tyrone
Lost Mountain MS, Kennesaw
McCleskey MS, Marietta
Mundy's Mill MS, Jonesboro
Otwell MS, Cumming
Pinckneyville MS, Norcross
Ralph Bunche MS, Atlanta
Roswell HS, Roswell
St. John Neumann HS, Lilburn
St. John the Evangelist HS, Hapeville
Samuel Inman MS, Atlanta
South Cobb HS, Austell
Sprayberry HS, Marietta
Trickum MS, Lilburn

Atlantic-Cape May, NJ
Mainland Regional HS, Linwood
Our Lady Star of the Sea School, Cape May
Teitelman MS, Cape May

Augusta-Aiken, GA-SC
Thomson HS, Thomson

Austin-San Marcos, TX
Canyon Vista MS, Austin
Chisholm Trail MS, Round Rock
Georgetown HS, Georgetown
Grisham MS, Austin
Hill Country MS, Austin
James Bowie HS, Austin
Lanier HS, Austin
West Ridge MS, Austin
Westwood HS, Austin

Bakersfield, CA
Fruitvale JHS, Bakersfield
Highland HS, Bakersfield

Baltimore, MD
Archbishop Spalding HS, Severn
Atholton HS, Columbia
Baltimore School for the Arts, Baltimore
Dumbarton MS, Baltimore
Havre de Grace HS, Havre de Grace
Howard HS, Ellicott City
John Carroll HS, Bel Air
Kennedy Krieger MS, Baltimore
North Harford MS, Pylesville

Baton Rouge, LA
Catholic HS, Baton Rouge
Episcopal HS, Baton Rouge
St. Joseph's Academy, Baton Rouge

Beaumont-Port Arthur, TX
Monsignor Kelly HS, Beaumont

Benton Harbor, MI
McCord Renaissance Center, Benton Harbor

Bergen-Passaic, NJ
Benjamin Franklin MS, Ridgewood
Fair Lawn HS, Fair Lawn
Immaculate Heart Academy, Washington
Northern Valley Regional HS, Old Tappan
Queen of Peace HS, North Arlington
River Dell Regional HS, Oradell

Binghamton, NY
East MS, Binghamton

Birmingham, AL
Grantswood Community School, Irondale
Hewitt-Trussville HS, Trussville
Homewood MS, Homewood

Louis Pizitz MS, Birmingham
Mountain Brook HS, Mountain Brook
Vestavia Hills HS, Vestavia Hills

Bismarck, ND
Century HS, Bismarck

Boston, MA-NH
Broad Meadows MS, Quincy
Clarke MS, Lexington
Coyle and Cassidy HS, Taunton
Fay School, Southborough
Mansfield HS, Mansfield
Marblehead MS, Marblehead
Simonds MS, Burlington
Timilty MS, Roxbury

Bridgeport, CT
Stratfield School, Fairfield

Buffalo-Niagara Falls, NY
Ben Franklin MS, Kenmore
Kenmore East HS, Tonawanda

Canton-Massillon, OH
Canton Country Day School, Canton

Cedar Rapids, IA
Harding MS, Cedar Rapids
Metro HS, Cedar Rapids
Washington HS, Cedar Rapids

Champaign-Urbana, IL
Champaign Central HS, Champaign

Charleston, WV
Capital HS, Charleston
DuPont JHS, Belle
Jackson MS, Cross Lanes
Winfield HS, Winfield

Charleston-North Charleston, SC
Williams MS, Charleston

Charlotte-Gastonia-Rock Hill, NC-SC
Charlotte Latin School, Charlotte
Piedmont MS, Monroe
Piedmont Open MS, Charlotte
Providence Senior HS, Charlotte
West Rowan HS, Mount Ulla

Chattanooga, TN-GA
Fort Oglethorpe HS, Fort Oglethorpe
Girls Prep, Chattanooga
Red Bank HS, Chattanooga

Chicago, IL
Adlai Stevenson HS, Lincolnshire
Adlai Stevenson HS, Prairie View
Barrington HS, Barrington
Carmel HS, Mundelein
Community HS, West Chicago
Conant HS, Hoffman Estates
Crete-Monee MS, Crete
Deer Path JHS, Lake Forest
Deerfield HS, Deerfield

Elk Grove HS, Elk Grove Village
Flossmoor HS, Flossmoor
Frankfort JHS, Frankfort
Grayslake MS, Grayslake
Highland MS, Libertyville
Immaculate Heart of Mary HS,
  Westchester
James Hart MS, Homewood
Lake Bluff JHS, Lake Bluff
Lake Forest Country Day School,
  Lake Forest
Libertyville HS, Libertyville
Madonna HS, Chicago
Maine Township HS West, Des Plaines
Margaret Mead JHS, Elk Grove Village
Marian Catholic HS, Chicago Heights
Mother McAuley HS, Chicago
Mundelein HS, Mundelein
New Trier Township HS, Winnetka
Niles North HS, Skokie
Niles West HS, Skokie
Northbrook JHS, Northbrook
Northwood MS, Woodstock
Our Lady of the Wayside School,
  Arlington Heights
Palatine HS, Palatine
Plum Grove JHS, Rolling Meadows
Prospect HS, Mount Prospect
Regina Dominican HS, Wilmette
Rolling Meadows HS, Rolling
  Meadows
St. Charles HS, St. Charles
St. Damian School, Oak Forest
St. Luke School, River Forest
Schaumburg HS, Schaumburg
Stagg HS, Palos Hills
Trinity Lutheran School, Roselle
Walter R. Sundling JHS, Palatine
Wilmette JHS, Wilmette

Chico-Paradise, CA
Chico HS, Chico

Cincinnati, OH-KY-IN
Anderson HS, Cincinnati
Blessed Sacrament School,
  Fort Mitchell
Madeira HS, Cincinnati
Mason MS, Mason
Notre Dame Academy, Park Hills
Princeton HS, Cincinnati
Princeton JHS, Cincinnati
Reading Central Community School,
  Reading
St. James White Oak School,
  Cincinnati
St. Mary School, Cincinnati
St. Therese of the Little Flower School,
  Cincinnati
Sellman MS, Cincinnati
William Henry Harrison HS, Harrison

Clarkesville-Hopkinsville, TN-KY
Fort Campbell HS, Fort Campbell
  North
Mahaffey MS, Fort Campbell North

Cleveland-Lorain-Elyria, OH
Beachwood MS, Beachwood
Beaumont Catholic HS, Cleveland
  Heights
Elyria Catholic HS, Elyria
Gesu Catholic School, University
  Heights
Kenston HS, Bainbridge
Kirtland MS, Kirtland
Mentor Shore JHS, Mentor
Metro Catholic Parish School,
  Cleveland
Olmsted Falls HS, Olmsted Falls
Orange HS, Pepper Pike
Perry HS, Perry
Regina HS, South Euclid
Rocky River HS, Rocky River
Rocky River MS, Rocky River
St. Edward HS, Lakewood
St. John Bosco School, Parma Heights
St. Joseph Academy, Cleveland
St. Martin of Tours School, Maple
  Heights
St. Thomas More School, Brooklyn
Solon HS, Solon
Whitney Young MS, Cleveland
Willoughby South HS, Willoughby

Colorado Springs, CO
Rampart HS, Colorado Springs

Columbia, MO
Hickman HS, Columbia
Jefferson JHS, Columbia

Columbia, SC
Chapin HS, Chapin
Chapin MS, Chapin
Dent MS, Columbia
Dutch Fork HS, Irmo
Heathwood Hall Episcopal School,
  Columbia
Irmo HS, Columbia
Irmo MS, Columbia
Lexington MS, Lexington
Richland Northeast HS, Columbia
Spring Valley HS, Columbia
Summit Parkway MS, Columbia

Columbus, OH
Columbus School for Girls, Columbus
Granville HS, Granville
Immaculate Conception School,
  Columbus
Kilbourne HS, Worthington
Our Lady of Perpetual Help School,
  Grove City
St. Andrew School, Columbus

St. Francis DeSales HS, Columbus
St. Joseph Montessori School,
  Columbus

Corpus Christi, TX
St. James Episcopal School, Corpus
  Christi

Dallas, TX
Anna MS, Anna
Armstrong MS, Plano
Bishop Lynch HS, Dallas
Blalack JHS, Carrollton
BT Washington Performing Arts HS,
  Dallas
Carpenter MS, Plano
Christ the King Catholic School,
  Dallas
Clark HS, Plano
Coppell MS, Dallas
Forest Meadow JHS, Dallas
Good Shepherd Episcopal School,
  Dallas
Jesuit Prep, Dallas
Lyles MS, Garland
Marcus HS, Flower Mound
McCulloch MS, Dallas
Milliken MS, Lewisville
Newman Smith HS, Carrollton
Parkhill JHS, Dallas
Plano East HS, Plano
Plano HS, Plano
Renner MS, Plano
Richardson JHS, Richardson
St. Mark the Evangelist Catholic
  School, Plano
St. Thomas Aquinas School, Dallas
Strickland MS, Denton
Turner HS, Carrollton
Ursuline Academy, Dallas
Vivian Field JHS, Farmers Branch

Danbury, CT
Barlow HS, West Redding
Shepaug Valley HS, Washington

Dayton-Springfield, OH
Centerville HS, Centerville
Greene Academy, Dayton
Mad River MS, Dayton
Miamisburg HS, Miamisburg
Oakwood HS, Dayton
Tower Heights MS, Centerville
Yellow Springs HS, Yellow Springs

Daytona Beach, FL
Mainland HS, Daytona Beach
Spruce Creek HS, Port Orange

Denver, CO
Arapahoe HS, Littleton
Cherry Creek HS, Englewood
Cherry Creek West MS, Littleton

Flood MS, Englewood
Heritage HS, Littleton
Horizon HS, Thornton
Lutheran HS, Denver
Powell MS, Littleton
Regis Jesuit HS, Aurora
St. Mary's Academy, Englewood
Smoky Hill HS, Aurora

Detroit, MI
Cass Technical HS, Detroit
Covington MS, Birmingham
De La Salle Collegiate HS, Warren
East Hills MS, Bloomfield Hills
The Grosse Pointe Academy, Grosse Pointe Farms
L'Anse Creuse MS Central, Harrison Township
L'Anse Creuse MS North, Macomb
L'Anse Creuse MS South, Harrison Township
North Farmington HS, Farmington Hills
Orchard Lake MS, West Bloomfield
Rochester Adams HS, Rochester Hills
St. Clare of Montefalco Catholic School, Grosse
St. Joan of Arc School, St. Clair Shores
Southfield Christian School, Southfield
Southfield-Lathrup HS, Lathrup Village
Troy Athens HS, Troy
Troy HS, Troy
Van Hoosen MS, Rochester
West Bloomfield HS, West Bloomfield

Dutchess County, NY
Astor Learning Center, Rhinebeck

Eau Claire, WI
Seymour MS, Seymour

El Paso, TX
Montwood HS, El Paso
St. Clement's Episcopal Parish School, El Paso
Slider MS, El Paso
Socorro HS, El Paso

Erie, PA
Mercyhurst Prep, Erie

Evansville-Henderson, IN-KY
North HS, Evansville

Fayetteville-Springdale-Rogers, AR
Old High MS, Bentonville

Florence, AL
Mars Hill Bible School, Florence
Muscle Shoals HS, Muscle Shoals

Fort Lauderdale, FL
Chaminade-Madonna Prep, Hollywood
Cooper City HS, Cooper City
Coral Springs MS, Coral Springs
Forest Glen MS, Coral Springs
Pompano Beach MS, Pompano Beach
Ramblewood MS, Coral Springs
Rogers MS, Fort Lauderdale
St. David Catholic School, Davie
St. Thomas Aquinas HS, Fort Lauderdale
Tequestra Trace MS, Fort Lauderdale
University School of Nova, Fort Lauderdale

Fort Myers-Cape Coral, FL
Bonita Springs MS, Bonita Springs
Caloosa MS, Cape Coral
Fort Myers MS, Fort Myers
Saint Michael Lutheran School, Fort Myers

Fort Smith, AR-OK
Northside HS, Fort Smith

Fort Walton Beach, FL
Niceville HS, Niceville

Fort Worth-Arlington, TX
Carroll HS, Southlake
Carroll MS, Southlake
Fort Worth Country Day, Fort Worth
Grapevine MS, Grapevine
Heritage MS, Colleyville
Lawrence Bell HS, Hurst

Fresno, CA
Buchanan HS, Clovis
Clark IS, Clovis
Clovis HS, Clovis
Edison Computech MS, Fresno
Kastner IS, Fresno

Gary, IN
Munster HS, Munster
Wilbur Wright MS, Munster

Grand Rapids-Muskegon-Holland, MI
Caledonia HS, Caledonia
East Grand Rapids HS, Grand Rapids
East Grand Rapids MS, East Grand Rapids
Rockford HS, Rockford
Rockford MS, Rockford
Roguewood School, Rockford

Green Bay, WI
Bay View MS, Green Bay

Greensboro-Winston-Salem-High Point, NC
Williams HS, Burlington

Greenville-Spartanburg-Anderson, SC
Hill MS, Duncan
Spartanburg HS, Spartanburg

Hagerstown, MD
Hancock Middle Senior HS, Hancock

Hamilton-Middletown, OH
Lakota HS, West Chester

Harrisburg-Lebanon-Carlisle, PA
Feaser MS, Middletown
Harrisburg Academy, Wormleysburg
Hershey HS, Hershey
Trinity HS, Camp Hill

Hartford, CT
Edwin Smith HS, Storrs
Granby Memorial MS, Granby
John Wallace MS, Newington
Mansfield MS, Storrs
RHAM HS, Hebron
Silas Deane MS, Wethersfield
Southington HS, Southington
Union School, Unionville
West District School, Unionville
Wethersfield HS, Wethersfield

Hattiesburg, MS
Oak Grove School, Hattiesburg

Honolulu, HI
ASSETS School, Honolulu
Governor Dole IS, Honolulu
James Castle HS, Kaneohe
Kailua IS, Kailua
Kaimuki IS, Honolulu
Kalaheo HS, Kailua
Leilehua HS, Wahiawa

Houston, TX
Arnold JHS, Cypress
Bleyl JHS, Houston
BT Washington JHS, Conroe
Duchesne Academy, Houston
James Taylor HS, Katy
John Paul II Catholic School, Houston
Katy HS, Katy
Klein Oak HS, Spring
Labay JHS, Houston
Langham Creek HS, Houston
Mayde Creek HS, Houston
Michael DeBakey HS, Houston
Northbrook MS, Houston
Olle MS, Houston
River Oaks Baptist School, Houston
Rogers Education Center, Houston
St. Thomas More Parish School, Houston
Spring Branch MS, Houston
Spring Forest MS, Houston
Spring HS, Spring
Spring Oaks MS, Houston

Spring Woods HS, Houston
Strack IS, Klein
Thomas Stovall JHS, Houston
Woodlands HS, The Woodlands

Huntington-Ashland, WV-KY-OH
Our Lady of Fatima School, Huntington

Huntsville, AL
Bob Jones HS, Madison

Indianapolis, IN
Hebrew Academy, Indianapolis
Craig MS, Indianapolis
Lutheran HS, Indianapolis
Roncalli HS, Indianapolis
St. Jude Catholic School, Indianapolis
St. Lawrence Catholic School, Indianapolis

Jackson, MS
Pearl HS, Pearl

Jacksonville, FL
Landrum MS, Ponte Vedra Beach

Janesville-Beloit, WI
St. Paul's Lutheran School, Janesville

Johnson City-Kingsport-Bristol, TN-VA
Science Hill HS, Johnson City

Kansas City, MO-KS
Blue Valley North HS, Overland Park
Genesis School, Kansas City
Mission Valley MS, Shawnee Mission
Oak Grove MS, Oak Grove
Olathe East HS, Olathe
Olathe South HS, Olathe
Oregon Trail JHS, Olathe
Oxford MS, Overland Park
Rogers Academy, Kansas City
Shawnee Mission South HS, Overland Park
Truman HS, Independence
Volker Magnet School, Kansas City

Knoxville, TN
Farragut HS, Knoxville
Maryville MS, Maryville
Sacred Heart Cathedral School, Knoxville

La Crosse, WI-MN
Onalaska MS, Onalaska

Lafayette, IN
Jefferson HS, Lafayette

Lafayette, LA
St. Thomas More HS, Lafayette

Lansing-East Lansing, MI
Everett HS, Lansing
Holt HS, Holt

Las Vegas, NV-AZ
O'Callaghan MS, Las Vegas

Long Island, NY
Baldwin HS, Baldwin
Elmont Memorial HS, Elmont
Floral Park Memorial HS, Floral Park
Green Vale HS, Glen Head
Herricks MS, Albertson
Jericho HS, Jericho
Longwood MS, Middle Island
Lynbrook HS, Lynbrook
New Hyde Park Memorial HS, New Hyde Park
North Shore HS, Glen Head
Our Lady of the Hamptons Regional, Southampton
Sacred Heart Academy, Hempstead
St. Joseph's School, Long Island
Sewanhaka HS, Floral Park
South Side HS, Rockville Centre
Syosset HS, Syosset
Thompson MS, Syosset
Wantagh HS, Wantagh
Wantagh MS, Wantagh

Longview-Marshall, TX
Forest Park MS, Longview
Pine Tree HS, Longview
Pine Tree JHS, Longview
Pine Tree MS, Longview

Los Angeles-Long Beach, CA
Alvarado IS, Rowland Heights
Calle Mayor MS, Torrance
Carmenita JHS, Cerritos
Center for Enriched Studies, Los Angeles
Chaminade Prep, Chatsworth
Culver City HS, Culver City
Dana MS, Arcadia
El Monte HS, El Monte
Flintridge Sacred Heart Academy, La Canada
Harkham Hillel Hebrew Academy, Beverly Hills
Huntington MS, San Marino
La Canada HS, La Canada
Louisville HS, Woodland Hills
Manhattan Beach IS, Manhattan Beach
Mayfield JHS of the Holy Child, Pasadena
Medea Creek MS, Agoura
Mira Costa HS, Manhattan Beach
Notre Dame Academy, Los Angeles
Notre Dame HS, Sherman Oaks
Oak Park HS, Agoura
Pacific School, Manhattan Beach
Parras MS, Redondo Beach
Providence HS, Burbank
Ramona Convent HS, Alhambra
Rosemont MS, La Crescenta
Rowland HS, Rowland Heights

St. James' Episcopal School, Los Angeles
St. Thomas the Apostle School, Los Angeles
South Pasadena MS, South Pasadena
Walnut HS, Walnut
Whitney HS, Cerritos

Louisville, KY-IN
Assumption HS, Louisville
duPont Manual Magnet HS, Louisville
Floyd Central HS, Floyds Knobs
Louisville Male HS, Louisville
Sacred Heart Academy, Louisville
St. Xavier HS, Louisville
St. Raphael the Archangel, Louisville
South Oldham HS, Crestwood
Trinity HS, Louisville

Lowell, MA-NH
Lighthouse School, Chelmsford

Lubbock, TX
Lubbock HS, Lubbock
All Saints Episcopal School, Lubbock

Lynchburg, VA
Glass HS, Lynchburg
Heritage HS, Lynchburg

Macon, GA
Houston County HS, Warner Robins
Mount de Sales Academy, Macon
Warner Robins HS, Warner Robins

Madison, WI
James Madison HS, Madison

Mansfield, OH
St. Peter's HS, Mansfield

McAllen-Edinburg-Mission, TX
Travis MS, McAllen

Melbourne-Titusville-Palm Bay, FL
Melbourne Central Catholic HS, Melbourne
St. Joseph Catholic School, Palm Bay

Memphis, TN-AR-MS
Craigmont HS, Memphis
Germantown HS, Germantown
St. Mary's Episcopal School, Memphis

Miami, FL
Arvida MS, Miami
The Cushman School, Miami
Design and Architecture HS, Miami
George Washington Carver MS, Miami
Gulliver Academy, Coral Gables
Gulliver Prep, Miami
MAST Academy, Miami
New World School of the Arts, Miami
Our Lady of Lourdes Academy, Miami

St. Rose of Lima, Miami Shores
Thomas Jefferson MS, Miami

Middlesex-Somerset-Hunterdon, NJ
Churchill JHS, East Brunswick
Crossroads MS, Monmouth Junction
East Brunswick HS, East Brunswick
Hammarskjold MS, East Brunswick
Hillcrest Magnet School, Somerset
Hillsborough MS, Hillsborough
Hunterdon Central Regional HS,
  Flemington
Immaculata HS, Somerville
Montgomery HS, Skillman
Rutgers Prep, Somerset
South Brunswick HS, Monmouth
  Junction
Spotswood HS, Spotswood
The Midland School, North Branch
Watchung Hills Regional HS, Warren

Milwaukee-Waukesha, WI
Bayside MS, Milwaukee
Custer HS, Milwaukee
Fritsche MS, Milwaukee
Milwaukee Lutheran HS, Milwaukee
Milwaukee Trade HS, Milwaukee
Nicolet HS, Glendale
Oconomowoc HS, Oconomowoc
Pius XI HS, Milwaukee
Rufus King HS, Milwaukee
St. Alphonsus School, Greendale
Samuel Morse MS, Milwaukee
Thomas Jefferson MS, Port
  Washington
Thomas More HS, Milwaukee

Minneapolis-St. Paul, MN-WI
Academy of Holy Angels, Richfield
Apple Valley HS, Apple Valley
Benilde St. Margaret's HS, St. Louis
  Park
The Blake Lower School, Minneapolis
The Blake School, Minneapolis
Breck School, Minneapolis
Cedar Manor IS, St. Louis Park
Central HS, St. Paul
Cretin-Derham Hall School, St. Paul
Dassel-Cokato HS, Cokato
Eagan HS, Eagan
Eden Prairie HS, Eden Prairie
Farmington MS, Farmington
Groves Academy, St. Louis Park
Hastings MS, Hastings
Highland Park HS, St. Paul
Hosterman MS, New Hope
Irondale HS, New Brighton
Mounds Park Academy LS, St. Paul
Oak Grove IS, Bloomington
St. Anthony MS, St. Anthony Village
Shakopee JHS, Shakopee
Stillwater JHS, Stillwater
Trinity School, Bloomington

Valley MS, Apple Valley
Wayzata HS, Plymouth

Mobile, AL
Davidson HS, Mobile
Phillips Prep, Mobile
St. Ignatius School, Mobile

Monmouth-Ocean, NJ
High Tech HS, Lincroft
Marine Academy, Sandy Hook

Myrtle Beach, SC
Conway MS, Conway
Socastee HS, Myrtle Beach
St. James MS, Surfside Beach

Nashua, NH
Amherst MS, Amherst

Nashville, TN
Eagleville School, Eagleville
Glendale MS, Nashville
St. Cecilia Academy, Nashville
Wright MS, Nashville

New Bedford, MA
Bishop Stang HS, North Dartmouth

New Haven-Meriden, CT
Dodd MS, Cheshire
Sacred Heart Academy, Hamden
The Peck Place School, Orange

New London-Norwich, CT-RI
Plainfield Central MS, Plainfield
Old Saybrook MS, Old Saybrook

New Orleans, LA
Archbishop Blenk HS, Gretna
Archbishop Chapelle HS, Metairie
De La Salle HS, New Orleans
McDonogh HS, New Orleans
McMain Magnet HS, New Orleans
Mount Carmel Academy, New Orleans
Our Lady of Divine Providence,
  Metairie
St. Benilde, Metairie
St. Christopher, Metairie
St. Frances Xavier Cabrini, New
  Orleans
St. Mary's Dominican HS, New Orleans
St. Paul's Episcopal School, New
  Orleans
St. Scholastica Academy, Covington
Ursuline Academy, New Orleans
Warren Easton Fundamental HS, New
  Orleans
Xavier University Prep, New Orleans

New York, NY
Alexander Hamilton HS, Elmsford
Berkeley Carroll School, Brooklyn
Bowne HS, Flushing
Bronxville HS, Bronxville

Catherine McAuley HS, Brooklyn
Convent Sacred Heart HS, New York
Dominican Academy, New York
Eastchester HS, Eastchester
Forest Hills HS, Forest Hills
Fox Lane HS, Bedford
Irvington HS, Irvington
Isaac Young MS, New Rochelle
Louis Klein MS, Harrison
Midwood HS at Brooklyn College,
  Brooklyn
Mother Cabrini HS, New York
Mount St. Michael Academy, Bronx
New Rochelle HS, New Rochelle
Pelham Memorial HS, Pelham
Pelham MS, Pelham
Pleasantville HS, Pleasantville
Rice HS, New York
Rye Neck HS, Mamaroneck
Sacred Heart/Mt. Carmel, Mount
  Carmel
St. Catharine Academy, Bronx
St. Raymond HS for Boys, Bronx
Salanter Akiba Academy, Riverdale
Saunders Trades and Tech HS, Yonkers
Shenendehowa HS, Clifton Park
Shulamith HS for Girls, Brooklyn
Urban Academy, New York
The Ursuline School, New Rochelle
Webster Magnet School, New
  Rochelle
Xavier HS, New York
Yeshiva of Central Queens, Flushing

Newark, NJ
Columbia HS, Maplewood
High Point Regional HS, Sussex
Kimberley Academy, Montclair
Kittatinny Regional HS, Newton
Livingston HS, Livingston

Newburgh, NY-PA
Horizons Magnet School, Newburgh

**Norfolk-Virginia Beach-Newport
News, VA-NC**
Cape Henry Collegiate, Virginia Beach
Gildersleeve MS, Newport News
Hampton Roads Academy, Newport
  News
Hines MS, Newport News
Norfolk Academy LS, Norfolk
Northside MS, Norfolk
Syms MS, Hampton

Oakland, CA
Alameda HS, Alameda
Alvarado MS, Union City
Bishop O'Dowd HS, Oakland
Charlotte Wood MS, Danville
Holy Names HS, Oakland
Irvington HS, Fremont
Miramonte HS, Orinda
Mission San Jose HS, Fremont

St. Isidore, Danville
St. Joseph, Fremont
San Lorenzo HS, San Lorenzo
Stone Valley MS, Alamo

Oklahoma City, OK
Cimarron MS, Edmond
Sequoyah MS, Edmond
Summit MS, Edmond

Olympia, WA
Capital HS, Olympia
New Century HS, Lacey

Omaha, NE-IA
Duchesne Academy, Omaha
Gretna HS, Gretna
Marian HS, Omaha
Millard Central MS, Omaha
Ralston HS, Ralston
Valley Middle/HS, Valley
Westside HS, Omaha
Westside MS, Omaha

Orange County, CA
Brea Olinda HS, Brea
Corona del Mar HS, Newport Beach
Dana Hills HS, Dana Point
Fairmont JHS, Anaheim
Foothill HS, Santa Ana
Hebrew Academy, Westminster
Hewes MS, Santa Ana
La Habra HS, La Habra
La Paz IS, Mission Viejo
Laguna Beach HS, Laguna Beach
Laguna Hills HS, Laguna Hills
Lakeside MS, Irvine
Los Alamitos HS, Los Alamitos
Los Alisos IS, Mission Viejo
Mission Viejo HS, Mission Viejo
Newhart MS, Mission Viejo
Rancho San Joaquin MS, Irvine
Santa Margarita HS, Rancho Santa
  Margarita
Venado MS, Irvine
Westminster HS, Westminster

Orlando, FL
Apopka HS, Apopka
Neptune MS, Kissimmee
University HS, Orlando

Pensacola, FL
Pensacola Catholic HS, Pensacola

Philadelphia, PA-NJ
Abington HS, Abington
Ancillae-Assumpta Academy,
  Wyncote
Arcola IS, Norristown
East HS, West Chester
Franklin Learning Center,
  Philadelphia
Fugett MS, West Chester

General Wayne MS, Malvern
Gordon MS, Coatesville
Gwynedd Mercy Academy, Gwynedd
  Valley
Harriton HS, Rosemont
Hatboro-Horsham HS, Horsham
Holy Ghost Prep, Bensalem
Indian Valley MS, Harleysville
Keith Valley MS, Horsham
Lower Moreland HS, Huntingdon
  Valley
Masterman School, Philadelphia
Merion Mercy Academy, Merion
  Station
Mount St. Joseph Academy,
  Flourtown
North Penn HS, Lansdale
Radnor HS, Radnor
South Brandywine MS, Coatesville
Tamanend MS, Warrington
Upper Dublin HS, Fort Washington
Upper Moreland MS, Hatboro
Upper Perkiomen HS, Pennsburg
Upper Perkiomen MS, East Greenville
Villa Joseph Marie HS, Holland
West Philadelphia Catholic HS,
  Philadelphia

Phoenix-Mesa, AZ
Desert Sky MS, Glendale
Greenway HS, Phoenix
Mohave MS, Scottsdale
Red Mountain HS, Mesa
Rhodes JHS, Mesa
Saguaro HS, Scottsdale
St. Thomas the Apostle, Phoenix
Western Sky MS, Goodyear
Xavier Prep, Phoenix

Pittsburgh, PA
Boyce MS, Upper St. Clair
Carson MS, Pittsburgh
Dorseyville MS, Pittsburgh
Fort Couch MS, Upper St. Clair
Fox Chapel Area HS, Pittsburgh
Gateway HS, Monroeville
Hampton HS, Allison Park
Independence MS, Bethel Park
Ingomar MS, Pittsburgh
Mt. Lebanon HS, Pittsburgh
Mt. Lebanon JHS, Pittsburgh
North Allegheny HS, Wexford
Quaker Valley HS, Leetsdale
Sewickley Academy, Sewickley
Shaler Area MS, Glenshaw
Taylor Allderdice HS, Pittsburgh

Portland, ME
Old Orchard Beach HS, Old Orchard
  Beach

Portland-Vancouver, OR-WA
Jemtegaard MS, Washougal
Jesuit HS, Portland
St. Mary's Academy, Portland

Providence-Fall River-Warwick, RI-MA
Bishop Hendricken HS, Warwick
Davisville MS, North Kingstown
La Salle Academy, Providence
Mercymount Country Day School,
  Cumberland
Mt. St. Charles Academy, Woonsocket
St. Luke School, Barrington
St. Mary Academy, Riverside
St. Rocco School, Johnston

Punta Gorda, FL
Murdock MS, Port Charlotte

Reading, PA
Wyomissing Area HS, Wyomissing

Richmond-Petersburg, VA
Freeman HS, Henrico County
Liberty MS, Ashland
St. Gertrude HS, Richmond
Stonewall Jackson MS, Mechanicsville
Tuckahoe MS, Richmond

Riverside-San Bernardino, CA
Eisenhower HS, Rialto
University Heights MS, Riverside
Vineyard JHS, Alta Loma

Roanoke, VA
Highland Park Magnet School,
  Roanoke

Rochester, NY
Canandaigua Academy, Canandaigua

Rockford, IL
Boylan Central Catholic HS, Rockford

Sacramento, CA
Pliocene Ridge HS, North San Juan
Rio Americano HS, Sacramento

St. Louis, MO-IL
Cor Jesu Academy, St. Louis
Crestview MS, Ellisville
Green MS, Richmond Heights
Hoech MS, St. Ann
LaSalle Springs MS, Glencoe
Lutheran HS South, St. Louis
Nerinx Hall HS, Webster Groves
North Kirkwood MS, Kirkwood
Oak Grove MS, Oak Grove
Parkway South HS, Manchester
Pattonville HS, Maryland Heights
Rockwood Eureka HS, Eureka
St. John Vianney HS, St. Louis
St. Joseph's Academy, St. Louis
Ste. Genevieve du Bois, St. Louis
Villa Duchesne School, St. Louis
Westminster Christian Academy,
  St. Louis
Wydown MS, Clayton

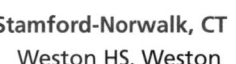

Salinas, CA
The York School, Monterey

Salt Lake City-Ogden, UT
Bryant IS, Salt Lake City
Granger HS, West Valley
Judge Memorial Catholic HS, Salt Lake City
Northwest MS, Salt Lake City

San Antonio, TX
Coke Stevenson MS, San Antonio
Health Careers HS, San Antonio
John Marshall HS, San Antonio
Lackland JHS, San Antonio
Robert Cole HS, San Antonio
William Howard Taft HS, San Antonio

San Diego, CA
Academy of Our Lady of Peace, San Diego
Black Mountain MS, San Diego
Cajon Park School, Santee
Coronado HS, Coronado
Diegueno JHS, Encinitas
Earl Warren JHS, Solana Beach
Hebrew Day School, San Diego
La Mesa MS, La Mesa
Oak Grove MS, Jamul
Olive Peirce MS, Ramona
Our Lady of Peace Academy, San Diego
Poway HS, Poway
Rancho Buena Vista HS, Vista
The Bishop's School, La Jolla
Torrey Pines HS, Encinitas
Torrey Pines HS, San Diego
Twin Peaks MS, Poway
University of San Diego HS, San Diego
Vista HS, Vista

San Francisco, CA
Convent Sacred Heart HS, San Francisco
Crocker School, Hillsborough
Davidson MS, San Rafael
Hall MS, Larkspur
Hillsdale HS, San Mateo
Lowell HS, San Francisco
Nathaniel Bowditch MS, Foster City
San Mateo HS, San Mateo
South Hillsborough School, Hillsborough
Taylor MS, Millbrae
West Hillsborough School, Hillsborough

San Jose, CA
Bullis Purissima School, Los Altos Hills
Cupertino HS, Cupertino
Davis IS, San Jose
Kennedy JHS, Cupertino
Lincoln Magnet School, San Jose
Los Gatos HS, Los Gatos
Monta Vista HS, Cupertino
Providence HS, Burbank
Rogers MS, San Jose
Rolling Hills MS, Los Gatos
St. Francis HS, Mountain View
St. Simon Catholic School, Los Altos
Westmont HS, Campbell

San Luis Obispo-Atascadero-Paso Robles, CA
Paulding MS, Arroyo Grande

Santa Barbara-Santa Maria-Lompoc, CA
Lakeview JHS, Santa Maria
Midland School, Los Olivos
Orcutt JHS, Orcutt
St. Joseph HS, Santa Maria

Santa Rosa, CA
Montgomery HS, Santa Rosa

Savannah, GA
Jenkins HS, Savannah
Myers MS, Savannah
Savannah Country Day School, Savannah

Seattle-Bellevue-Everett, WA
Blanchet HS, Seattle
Cedarcrest HS, Duvall
Chief Kanim MS, Fall City
Eton School, Bellevue
Holy Names Academy, Seattle
Holy Rosary, Seattle
Inglewood JHS, Redmond
Kent-Meridian HS, Kent
Liberty HS, Renton
The Northwest School, Seattle
St. Philomena, Des Moines
Shorewood HS, Shoreline

Sharon, PA
Hillview Intermediate Center, Grove City

Sheboygan, WI
Horace Mann MS, Sheboygan

Shreveport-Bossier City, LA
Byrd HS, Shreveport
Christ the King School, Bossier City
Cope MS, Bossier City

South Bend, IN
Trinity School, South Bend
John Young MS, Mishawaka
Penn HS, Mishawaka

Spokane, WA
Gonzaga Prep, Spokane

Springfield, MA
Williston Northampton HS, Easthampton

Springfield, MO
Kickapoo HS, Springfield

Stamford-Norwalk, CT
Weston HS, Weston

State College, PA
State College Area HS, State College

Steubenville-Weirton, OH-WV
Weir HS, Weirton
Weir MS, Weirton

Sumter, SC
Bates MS, Sumter
Sumter HS, Sumter

Syracuse, NY
Skaneateles HS, Skaneateles
Westhill HS, Syracuse

Tampa-St. Petersburg-Clearwater, FL
Academy of the Holy Names, Tampa
Berkeley Prep, Tampa
Plant HS, Tampa
Woodrow Wilson MS, Tampa

Toledo, OH
Central Catholic HS, Toledo
Notre Dame Academy, Park Hills
St. Ursula Academy, Toledo

Trenton, NJ
West Windsor-Plainsboro HS, Princeton Junction

Tucson, AZ
Flowing Wells HS, Tucson
Magnet MS, Tucson

Tulsa, OK
Saint Pius X School, Tulsa

Tyler, TX
Bishop Gorman HS, Tyler

Utica-Rome, NY
Mount Markham MS, West Winfield

Vallejo-Fairfield-Napa, CA
Benicia MS, Benicia

Ventura, CA
Adolfo Camarillo HS, Camarillo
Anacapa MS, Ventura
Charles Blackstock JHS, Oxnard
Green JHS, Oxnard
The Thacher School, Ojai

Washington, DC-MD-VA-WV
Academy of the Holy Cross, Kensington
Banneker Academic HS, Washington
Bishop O'Connell HS, Arlington
DeMatha Catholic HS, Hyattsville
Duke Ellington School of Arts, Washington

Dunbar HS, Washington
Eleanor Roosevelt HS, Greenbelt
Frederick HS, Frederick
George Mason MS, Falls Church
Good Counsel HS, Wheaton
Governor Johnson HS, Frederick
Hebrew Academy, Silver Spring
Herbert Hoover MS, Rockville
Johnson HS, Bethesda
Kettering MS, Upper Marlboro
The Lab School of Washington, Washington
Lemon Hine JHS, Washington
Linganore HS, Frederick
Martin Luther King MS, Beltsville
Middletown MS, Middletown
Montgomery HS, Rockville

Redland MS, Rockville
School for Contemporary Education, Annandale
St. Camillus, Silver Spring
Stone Ridge Country Day School, Bethesda
Stone Ridge-School of the Sacred Heart, Bethesda
Washington Episcopal School, Bethesda
Westland IS, Bethesda
Winston Churchill HS, Potomac

Waterbury, CT

Alcott MS, Wolcott
Rochambeau MS, Southbury

West Palm Beach-Boca Raton, FL

Boca Raton Christian School, Boca Raton
Loggers' Run Community MS, Boca Raton
Suncoast Community HS, Riviera Beach

Wilmington, NC

Hoggard HS, Wilmington

Wilmington-Newark, DE-MD

Padua Academy, Wilmington
Perryville MS, Perryville
St. Matthew School, Wilmington

HOMESCHOOLING

Call it what you will, home is the place where 1.23 million American children, most in grades K–9, go to school. Since the 1980s, in response to problems in the public schools, this style of education has enjoyed a small boom.

Parents have the legal right to homeschool their children in every state. Since education is governed by state law, there are as many requirements as there are states, and these are sometimes modified and interpreted by local school boards.

Forty states use the category Home Instruction by Parents in their legal language. The other states bring homeschooling under: Church School (Alabama); Private School (California, Kansas, Kentucky, Nebraska, Texas); Alternative School (Idaho); Home Education (Michigan, Pennsylvania, Wisconsin); or Home Study (Georgia).

Although twelve states require no formal notice from parents of their intent to homeschool a child, most school districts want to know when a child is being educated at home. Except in cases when the district requests an annual renewal, the notice to homeschool remains in force unless and until the parents decide to stop.

Seven states require a high school diploma or GED certificate of homeschool teachers, but the others have no specific requirements except that, in a few states, teachers should be "capable," "competent," or "qualified." Four states have "extensive requirements"; others have extensive explanations why there are no requirements.

Curricula for homeschools must match the public schools in thirty-six states. Ten states have more specific requirements in subjects ranging from reading to social studies, namely Arizona, Georgia, Hawaii, Kentucky, Missouri, Nebraska, New Mexico, South Dakota, Texas, and West Virginia. Alabama, Alaska, Arkansas, and Florida have no curriculum requirements. No standardized tests are used to evaluate the progress of homeschool students in twenty-three states.

State school attendance requirements are satisfied in most states by the submission of attendance records or by periodic reports on a child's progress. The most consistent record keeping required of homeschooling parents is the maintenance of a daily attendance register, but twenty-five states do not require any record keeping. States also vary on the amount of time a child must be in school.

Requirements to Homeschool

STATE	TEACHER QUALIFICATIONS	ATTENDANCE REQUIRED	TESTING REQUIRED
Alabama	No	No	No
Alaska	No	No	No
Arizona	No	No	No
Arkansas	No	No	Yes
California	Capable	No	No
Colorado	No	172 days	Yes
Connecticut	No	180 days	No
Delaware	No	180 days	Yes
District of Columbia	No	Match Public	No
Florida	No	No	Yes
Georgia	HS/GED	180 days	Yes
Hawaii	No	No	Yes
Idaho	No	Match Public	No
Illinois	No	176 days	No
Indiana	No	180 days	No
Iowa	No	148 days	Yes
Kansas	Competent	Match Public	No
Kentucky	No	185 days	No
Louisiana	No	180 days	Yes
Maine	No	175 days	Yes
Maryland	No	No	No
Massachusetts	No	No	Progress Report
Michigan	No	No	No
Minnesota	No	No	Yes
Mississippi	No	As needed	No
Missouri	No	1,000 hours	No
Montana	No	180 days	No
Nebraska	No	1,032 hours	No
Nevada	Extensive	180 days	No
New Hampshire	No	No	Yes
New Jersey	No	No	No
New Mexico	HS/GED	Match Public	Yes
New York	Competent	180 days	Yes
North Carolina	HS/GED	9 months	Yes
North Dakota	Extensive	175 days	Yes
Ohio	HS/GED	900 hours	Yes/ Portfolio
Oklahoma	No	No	No
Oregon	No	Match Public	Yes
Pennsylvania	HS/GED	180 days	Yes
Rhode Island	No	Match Public	Yes
South Carolina	HS/GED; BA	180 days	Yes
South Dakota	No	Match Public	Yes
Tennessee	K–8:HS; 9–12: BA	180 days	Yes
Texas	No	No	No
Utah	No	Match Public	No
Vermont	No	175 days	Yes
Virginia	Extensive	Match Public	Yes
Washington	Extensive	Match Public	Yes
West Virginia	Qualified	Match Public	Yes
Wisconsin	No	875 hours	No
Wyoming	No	175 days	No

Source: Homeschool Legal Defense Association.
HS/GED: High school or general equivalency diploma.
BA: Bachelor's degree.

Climate

"The fortunate people of the planet," John Kenneth Galbraith wrote years ago in *Harper's*, "are those who live by the seasons. There is far more difference between a Vermont farm in the summer and that farm in the winter than there is between San Diego and São Paulo. This means that people who live where the seasons are good and strong have no need to travel; they can stay at home and let change come to them. This simple truth will one day be recognized and then we will see a great reverse migration from Florida to Maine and on into Quebec."

Galbraith's forecast may be too optimistic. Pathways to seasonal sun are well worn. A quick count of Maine and Quebecois license plates in Florida and Texas Gulf parking lots in February proves that. Americans and Canadians say they prefer mild, sunny climates, and when asked where in the continent these climates are, they point to the fast-growing lower half of the Pacific Coast, Florida, and anywhere along the South Atlantic and Gulf Coast shore. Certainly this area, between 25 degrees and 135 degrees latitude, has been drawing migrants for decades.

But other places north of the Mason-Dixon line and hundreds of miles from ocean beaches benefit from population growth, and many of these enjoy mild climates, too. The names of some might surprise you.

What has always been surprising is the enormous variety of global climates found right here at home. Northern maritime, mild Mediterranean, southerly mountain, lowland desert, tropical "paradise," desert highland, rugged northern continental, windward slope, leeward slope, humid subtropical—you name it, and you'll meet up with it somewhere in North America.

Climate is a part of your circumstances that can't be bought, built, remodeled, or relocated. A place's climate is there for keeps, and the weather events that make up a place's climate—rain, snow, heat, cold, drought, wind—will have a profound effect on your life.

THE DIFFERENCE IS GEOPHYSICAL

If you can live anywhere you wish and are open to all the variety the continent offers, know that a combination of water, latitude, elevation, prevailing winds, mountain ranges, and urban development lies behind any metro area's climate.

285

Water

Oceans and other large bodies of water take the edge off temperature. Water warms up slowly, holds much more heat than land, and cools more slowly. Places near or surrounded by water tend to be cooler in summer and warmer in winter than others far from water.

The hottest it gets in July on the Santa Monica Pier in Los Angeles is 75°F; meanwhile, 15 miles north in the San Fernando Valley, it's 95. If Toronto were to be gathered up and then set down at the same latitude, but hundreds of miles west of its Lake Ontario shore, winter would arrive a month sooner and spring a month later.

NORTH AMERICAN GEOGRAPHICAL EXTREMES

Among all metro areas, Honolulu, Hawaii, is both the southernmost and westernmost. Among all metro areas on the North American continent, the westernmost and northernmost is Anchorage, Alaska.

Coterminous United States

Geographic center: near Lebanon, Smith County, Kansas

Northernmost point: Lake of the Woods Projection, Minnesota

Northernmost metro area: Bellingham, Washington

Southernmost point: Cape Sable, Florida

Southernmost metro area: Miami, Florida

Easternmost point: West Quoddy Head, Maine

Easternmost metro area: Bangor, Maine

Westernmost point: Cape Alava, Washington

Westernmost metro area: Eugene-Springfield, Oregon

Highest point: Mount Whitney, California: 14,494 feet

Highest metro area: Santa Fe, New Mexico: 7,360 feet

Canada

Geographic center: Arviat, Northwest Territories

Northernmost point: Cape Columbia, Ellesmere Island

Northernmost metro area: Edmonton, Alberta

Southernmost point: Middle Island, Lake Erie

Southernmost metro area: London, Ontario

Easternmost point: Cape Spear, Newfoundland

Easternmost metro area: St. John's Newfoundland

Westernmost point: Yukon-Alaska border

Westernmost metro area: Victoria, British Columbia

Highest point: Mount Logan, Yukon: 19,524 feet

Highest metro area: Calgary, Alberta: 3,501 feet

Source: U.S. Geological Survey; Canadian National Atlas Information Service.

While bodies of water soften hot and cold temperatures, they also influence a place's microclimate. Utah's ancient Great Salt Lake is the big reason there is much more snow in Salt Lake City than in other nearby areas. Face Lake Michigan in a Chicago winter and you may have to grab a rail, so strong is the easterly wind that comes in unobstructed from miles offshore.

Latitude

Places located in the continent's heartland away from the moderating effects of water experience wide swings of temperature. These continental climates tend to be even more rigorous in the higher latitudes. The closer to the poles you get, the more exaggerated the seasonal shifts because extreme northerly or southerly locations see the greatest seasonal variation in the amount and intensity of sunlight.

In Edmonton, AB (53.55 N), 800,000 residents see 8am sunrises and 3:30pm sunsets in late December with daylight saving time. In late June, building contractors schedule double shifts as the day lengthens to 17 hours and the city becomes an intensely sunlit spot.

Far to the southwest, the solar energy pouring over Honolulu (21.20 N) varies by just 50 percent from time of maximum in June to time of minimum in December, but in Anchorage (61.10 N) it is twenty times as great. Places in the far north experience not only Siberian winters but short, sunbaked summers.

Elevation

Greater height above sea level has the same effect as a higher latitude. Each 1,000 feet of elevation lowers the average temperature by 3.3°F. In New Mexico, for

INHERITING CLIMATES

Early in the next century, greenhouse warming will cause Canadian metro areas to experience the same seasonal temperatures and weather events that American metro areas farther south have now.

This area's weather	will seem like
Toronto, ON	Indianapolis, IN
Sudbury, ON	Cleveland-Lorain-Elyria, OH
Winnipeg, MB	Minneapolis-St. Paul, MN-WI
Edmonton, AB	Cheyenne, WY
Vancouver, BC	San Francisco, CA

Source: Environment Canada, Climates of Canada.

LIFE AT THE TOP

Metro areas in the Rockies are high indeed. East of the Mississippi, the highest is Asheville, NC, at 2,140 feet. In Canada, at 3,501 feet, it's Calgary, AB.

Metro Area	Elevation (feet)
Santa Fe, NM	7,360
Flagstaff, AZ-UT	7,000
Cheyenne, WY	6,120
Colorado Springs, CO	6,090
Boulder-Longmont, CO	5,480
Casper, WY	5,340
Albuquerque, NM	5,310
Denver, CO	5,290
Fort Collins-Loveland, CO	5,000
Grand Junction, CO	4,840
Greeley, CO	4,720
Provo-Orem, UT	4,720
Pueblo, CO	4,680
Pocatello, ID	4,462
Reno, NV	4,400
Las Cruces, NM	4,270
Salt Lake City-Ogden, UT	4,220

Source: U.S. Geological Survey, National Gazetteer of the United States.

WINDY METRO AREAS

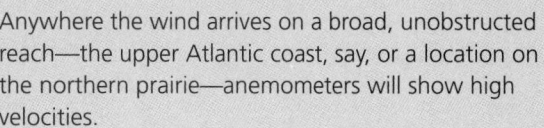

Anywhere the wind arrives on a broad, unobstructed reach—the upper Atlantic coast, say, or a location on the northern prairie—anemometers will show high velocities.

	Average Wind Speed
St. John's, NF	15.1 mph
Amarillo, TX	13.5
Rochester, MN	13.1
Casper, WY	12.9
Cheyenne, WY	12.9
Regina, SK	12.9
Great Falls, MT	12.7
Barnstable-Yarmouth, MA	12.5
Boston, MA-NH	12.5
Manchester, NH	12.5
Portsmouth-Rochester, NH-ME	12.5
Lubbock, TX	12.4
Fargo-Moorhead, ND-MN	12.3
Oklahoma City, OK	12.3
Wichita, KS	12.3
Corpus Christi, TX	12.0
New Haven-Meriden, CT	12.0

Listed above are metro areas described in the Place Profiles with average annual wind speeds of 12 miles per hour or more.

example, there are just 3° of difference in annual average temperature between Clayton and Lordsburg, two locations with similar elevations. But Clayton sits up near the Oklahoma panhandle while Lordsburg is 440 miles southwest near the Sonoran Desert in Mexico. At Albuquerque's airport and at the top of Sandia Peak, two weather stations just 15 miles apart but differing in elevation by 4,700 feet, the average annual temperatures differ by 16°F.

In the United States, places that combine high altitudes with southerly latitudes get the mild, short winters of the south and the cooler nights and crisp falls of the north. Asheville, NC, in the southern Appalachians, and Santa Fe, NM, in the southern Rockies have long been known for their mild, four-season climates.

Wind

Consider a pair of metro areas 3,200 miles apart: Bellingham, WA, and Portland, ME. Both sit high in

northern latitudes on their respective coasts. Both peek through some of the foggiest mornings on the continent. You'd naturally suppose the two have similar climates.

But Bellingham is much milder because of the winds that blow from west to east across the continent. The west coast is a landfall for air that has moved thousands of miles over water. Cities hundreds of miles inland still feel the beneficial effects of the Pacific winds. Interior cities in the east feel few consequences of the Atlantic except on those rare occasions when the prevailing wind direction doesn't prevail. Sad to say, this reversal of wind direction often means a storm.

Mountain Ranges

The only barriers big enough to deflect and channel winds, rain, and snow are mountains. Mountain people aren't telling tall tales when they tell visitors that the weather on one side of a mountain range is often radically different from that on the other.

CLEAR METRO AREAS

Clear days are recorded when clouds cover less than 30 percent of the sky.

	Clear Days
Yuma, AZ	242
Phoenix-Mesa, AZ	211
Las Vegas, NV-AZ	211
Fresno, CA	196
Tucson, AZ	194
El Paso, TX	193
Laredo, TX	193
Las Cruces, NM	193
Bakersfield, CA	192
Riverside-San Bernardino, CA	192
Sacramento, CA	189
Modesto, CA	185

Listed above are weather stations described in the Place Profiles where more than half the year are clear days.

WET METRO AREAS

Precipitation days detailed in the Place Profiles are days on which at least one-tenth of an inch of precipitation falls.

	Precipitation Days
St. John's, NF	144
Halifax, NS	138
Saint John, NB	138
Missoula, MT	123
Montreal, PQ	120
Quebec City, PQ	117
Vancouver, BC	114
Portland-Vancouver, OR-WA	100
Victoria, BC	100
Pocatello, ID	95
Seattle-Bellevue-Everett, WA	95
Bellingham, WA	93
Charleston, WV	93
Eugene-Springfield, OR	90
Binghamton, NY	87
Washington, DC-MD-VA-WV	87
Olympia, WA	84

Listed above are weather stations described in the Place Profiles with the equivalent of 12 or more weeks of precipitation throughout the year.

The windward side of British Columbia's Coast Mountains is a lush coastal rain forest; the leeward side, a dry grass and sagebrush steppe. In winter, the Great Divide shields Colorado Springs from much of the Arctic air that moves down the continent. In summer, the hidden, windward side of the city's mountain vista is a lush, evergreen parkland at lower elevations; the leeward side where the city sits is a semi-arid steppe descending to dry, short-grass prairie.

Urban Development

Finally, urban development makes heat islands within the surrounding countryside. Office buildings, factories, and cars produce enormous amounts of waste heat. Brick, concrete, and asphalt surfaces absorb and store heat during the day; at night the stored heat drifts up into the air, keeping the city from cooling off. At night in winter, Montreal's core can be 30° warmer than the environs. In general, wind speed, visibility, sunshine, and heating needs are less in the center of the city than in nearby country, but temperature, cloudiness, thunderstorm frequency, and air pollution levels are higher.

JUDGING CLIMATE

It is difficult to name many important aspects in life that aren't influenced in some way by climate. It decides what we'll wear, when we vacation, whether we'll work outside, how much we pay to keep the indoors comfortable. It affects travel safety and mobility. Certainly, it affects how we feel and behave.

Rating places by their climates isn't new. Canada has a "severity index" for hundreds of locations. There's one for New Zealand rating human comfort in various cities using rainfall, sunshine, temperature, humidity, and wind. In the United States, the "weather stress index" from the National Oceanic and Atmospheric Administration (NOAA) uses temperature, humidity, and wind speed to calculate discomfort based on deviation of those three elements from the normal.

To rate the climates in 354 metro areas, *Places Rated* considers thirteen data elements, including monthly high and low temperatures, wind speeds, humidity, darkness, clear days, partly cloudy days, cloudy days, thunderstorms, fog, and precipitation in the form of rain and snow.

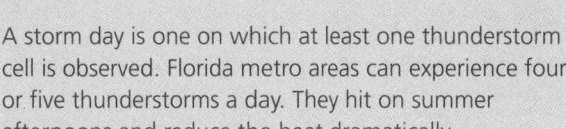

SNOWY METRO AREAS

Canada and the U.S. are among the few countries that keep meteorological records of snow depth. Most others measure snow in terms of water content.

St. John's, NF	141.4 inches
Quebec City, PQ	135.1
Saint John, NB	115.1
Syracuse, NY	114.0
Flagstaff, AZ-UT	100.8
Montreal, PQ	92.5
Buffalo-Niagara Falls, NY	91.1
Rochester, NY	89.9
Ottawa-Hull, ON-PQ	89.6
Bangor, ME	85.6
Thunder Bay, ON	84.0
Binghamton, NY	82.4
Casper, WY	78.8
Halifax, NS	78.2
Duluth-Superior, MN-WI	78.0
Burlington, VT	76.9

Listed above are weather stations described in the Place Profiles with average annual snowfalls of 75 inches or more.

STORMY METRO AREAS

A storm day is one on which at least one thunderstorm cell is observed. Florida metro areas can experience four or five thunderstorms a day. They hit on summer afternoons and reduce the heat dramatically.

	Storm Days
Fort Myers-Cape Coral, FL	89
Naples, FL	89
Punta Gorda, FL	89
Lakeland-Winter Haven, FL	87
Sarasota-Bradenton, FL	87
Tampa-St. Petersburg-Clearwater, FL	87
Ocala, FL	83
Tallahassee, FL	83
Gainesville, FL	81
Orlando, FL	80
Mobile, AL	79
West Palm Beach-Boca Raton, FL	79
Daytona Beach, FL	75
Melbourne-Titusville-Palm Bay, FL	75

Listed above are metro areas described in the Place Profiles with 75 or more thunderstorms a year.

Winter Mildness

To measure how mild the winters are, windchill, the number of months the temperature falls to 32°F or less, and the average 24-hour temperature of the coldest month are taken into account. Honolulu's winter mildness score is 100; Oklahoma City's is 50; and the metro areas in Canada's prairie provinces (Regina, Saskatoon, and Winnipeg) each get a score of 0. These areas are respectively the best, average, and worst for winter mildness.

Summer Mildness

To measure how mild the summers are, humidity, the average 24-hour temperature of the hottest month, and the number of months the temperature tops 90°F are each taken into account. San Francisco's summer mildness score is 100; Honolulu's is 50; and McAllen-Edinburg-Mission, in southernmost Texas, gets a 0. These metro areas are respectively the best, average, and worst for summer mildness.

Hazardousness

Bad weather isn't just inconvenient, it's downright dangerous. Aside from delaying and canceling social and business events, it contributes to injury and even death. The general hazardousness of an area is measured by normal winter snowfall and the frequencies of two other elements: strong winds and thunderstorms. To score for relative freedom from these hazards, *Places Rated* weights snow three times as heavily as thunderstorms, and thunderstorms three times as heavily as strong winds. The higher the score, the freer the metro area is from these hazards. Los Angeles and three other nearby areas on the southern California coast, each with 99 scores, do best here. Typical 50 scores—or average hazardousness—are found around New York City. Buffalo and several other areas near the Great Lakes score 0.

Seasonal Affect

If you need a single guilty party to blame for tiredness, depression, irritability, lack of sleep, lack of focus,

DAMP PLACES

In Florida, cars can be sponged clean using nothing more than the heavy morning dew. Mushrooms on the Pacific Northwest coast get enormous quickly.

	Humidity (%)
St. John's, NF	83
Halifax, NS	81
Vancouver, BC	81
Victoria, BC	80
Olympia, WA	79
Bellingham, WA	78
Galveston-Texas City, TX	78
Kitchener-Waterloo, ON	78
Saint John, NB	78
Barnstable-Yarmouth, MA	77
Corpus Christi, TX	76
Eugene-Springfield, OR	76
Gainesville, FL	76
Ocala, FL	76

Listed above are weather stations described in the Place Profiles with more than 75 percent annual relative humidity.

DRY PLACES

In some spots with low humidities, it's cheaper and more efficient to cool interiors with evaporative air conditioners—known locally as swamp coolers—rather than the more expensive refrigerated air conditioners.

	Humidity (%)
Grand Junction, CO	49
Albuquerque, NM	45
Santa Fe, NM	45
El Paso, TX	43
Laredo, TX	43
Las Cruces, NM	43
Tucson, AZ	39
Phoenix-Mesa, AZ	37
Yuma, AZ	36
Las Vegas, NV-AZ	30

Listed above are weather stations described in the Place Profiles with less than 50 percent annual relative humidity.

headache, chest and joint pains, hallucinations, and any other ailments, stick it to the weather.

To measure the local weather's seasonal affect, or psychological impact, the number of cloudy (more than 80 percent cloud cover) and wet (precipitation greater than 0.1 inch) days are weighted twice as heavily as the number of fog (visibility less than one-half mile) days, and fog days are weighted twice as heavily as latitude, an indicator of potential sunlight.

Arizona's major metro areas—Phoenix-Mesa and Tucson—each earn 100; Montgomery and Tuscaloosa in Alabama get 50; Bremerton and Olympia on Washington's Puget Sound each score a 0. They are respectively the best, average, and worst for seasonal affect.

SCORING: CLIMATE

Each metro area's score for climate comes from averaging four broad factors: winter mildness, summer mildness, seasonal affect, and hazardousness. A metro area's final score is its percentile on a scale of 0 to 100 corresponding to its rank. San Francisco's final score is 97.45; Charleston, WV's is 51.27; and Winnipeg's is 3.96. They are, respectively, among the best, average, and worst North American metro areas for climate.

Scoring Examples

A location near the center of California's Pacific coast, another in the western foothills of the Allegheny Mountains, and still another on the prairie illustrate the best, average, and worst metro areas by *Places Rated*'s scoring method for climate.

Among the Best: San Francisco, CA. Beware of chamber of commerce blandishments about a place's annual average temperature. San Francisco's is 57°F. So is St. Louis's. But San Francisco enjoys both a diurnal (24-hour) temperature range of 12° and an annual range (the difference between January's and July's average temperatures) of 12°. St. Louis has a diurnal range of 17° and an annual range of 47°.

The temperature swings in these two cities highlight the difference between a marine climate and a hot continental climate. San Francisco's somewhat cool climate is remarkably stable year-round; St. Louis's is neither.

In spite of sea fogs and the low stratus associated with them (which appeals to many San Franciscans), this metro area's percent of possible sunshine is greater than that of New York, Boston, and Washington, DC. Thunderstorms here are rare. On none of the year's 365 days do temperatures hit zero; on just a handful do they fall to freezing or exceed 90°F. More than any other factor, it is San Francisco's infrequent extremes of heat and cold, coupled with a temperature range ideal for human activity and comfort, that produces a top *Places Rated* climate rating.

Among the Average: Charleston, WV. This capital city sits in the midst of the largest North American climate zone, the hot continental. The climate here is marked by sharp temperature contrasts between the days and nights and between the seasons as well. For all that, winters are short and only moderately cold compared with those of cities in the northeast and around the Great Lakes. Thanks somewhat to its elevation and surrounding topography, summers are cooler than in locations farther south.

For mildness, Charleston earns a respectable 53 for winter and 52 for summer. Its seasonal affect score of 3, however, is among the worst on the Continent and the stormy months of June and July are the biggest reasons behind a hazardousness score of just 40. When all factors are weighted by their importance in *Places Rated*'s scoring method, they produce a final score of 51.27.

Among the Worst: Winnipeg, MB. Sometimes called Winterpeg, Manisnowba, this city—an hour and a half's drive over the North Dakota border—endures many humorous jabs about its infamous winters. When it comes to extremes of cold and snow, though, there are many other weather stations in the Canadian and American Arctic that regularly record worse winters than here.

COLD METRO AREAS

It gets so frigid for so long in some Canadian areas that radio weather reports commonly give out Celsius temperatures without bothering to say "minus."

	0°F Days	32°F Days
Anchorage, AK	34	194
Bismarck, ND	51	186
Calgary, AB	33	201
Duluth-Superior, MN-WI	51	186
Edmonton, AB	35	185
Fargo-Moorhead, ND-MN	54	180
Minneapolis-St. Paul, MN-WI	34	158
Regina, SK	55	204
Rochester, MN	35	165
Saskatoon, SK	59	202
Sioux Falls, SD	33	171
Thunder Bay, ON	49	204
Waterloo-Cedar Falls, IA	31	159
Winnipeg, MB	62	195

Listed above are weather stations described in the Place Profiles where more than 30 zero-degree days per year are combined with more than 150 freezing days.

HOT METRO AREAS

Areas in Florida and Texas are stricken by summer combinations of days over 90°F and high humidities. Three desert metro areas have more than 130 90-degree days per year—Phoenix (167), Tucson (140), and Las Vegas (134)—but all have an annual average relative humidity of less than 40 percent.

	90°F Days	Humidity (%)
Abilene, TX	102	63
Austin-San Marcos, TX	107	70
Brownsville-Harlingen-San Benito, TX	116	75
Bryan-College Station, TX	101	71
Corpus Christi, TX	106	76
Fort Myers-Cape Coral, FL	114	73
Lakeland-Winter Haven, FL	108	73
McAllen-Edinburg-Mission, TX	104	75
Naples, FL	101	73
Ocala, FL	120	77
Punta Gorda, FL	120	73
San Angelo, TX	109	64
San Antonio, TX	111	70
Victoria, TX	105	75
Waco, TX	111	71
Wichita Falls, TX	106	67

Listed above are weather stations described in the Place Profiles that combine 100 or more 90° days with an average annual relative humidity of 60 percent or higher.

Still, January at the corner of Portage and Main in the center of Manitoba's capital may be the coldest spot of any major city in North America. The Pacific is 1,200 miles west and the Atlantic 1,800 miles east; any moderating effect from either ocean has dissipated long before getting here. Moreover, cold arctic air moves unobstructed over the flat Manitoba prairie and isn't altered in the slightest when it hits Winnipeg.

Daily and seasonal temperatures swing wildly, producing a great variation in climate from month to month in a single winter or from year to year depending on the character and origin of air masses blustering through. In its favor, Winnipeg is relatively dry and bright, with a seasonal affect score of 61. But in the winter, its mildness and hazardousness factors are 0 and 14, respectively.

RANKINGS: CLIMATE

Four factors are used to determine a score for climate: (1) winter mildness, (2) summer mildness, (3) hazardousness, and (4) seasonal affect. Scores are rounded to two decimal places. Locations with tie scores get the same rank and are listed alphabetically. Metro areas described in the Place Profiles later on in this chapter are shown in boldface type in the list below.

Metro Areas from Best to Worst

RANK	SCORE	RANK	SCORE
1. **Santa Barbara-Santa Maria-Lompoc, CA**	100.00	38. Richland-Kennewick-Pasco, WA	89.51
2. **San Diego, CA**	99.71	39. **Medford-Ashland, OR**	89.23
3. Ventura, CA	99.43	40. **Yuma, AZ**	88.95
4. **Los Angeles-Long Beach, CA**	99.15	41. **Brownsville-Harlingen-San Benito, TX**	88.66
5. **San Luis Obispo-Atascadero-Paso Robles, CA**	98.86	42. **West Palm Beach-Boca Raton, FL**	88.38
6. **Honolulu, HI**	98.58	43. **Reno, NV**	88.10
7. Orange County, CA	98.30	44. **Las Vegas, NV-AZ**	87.81
8. **Salinas, CA**	98.01	45. **Orlando, FL**	87.53
9. **Riverside-San Bernardino, CA**	97.73	46. **Tucson, AZ**	87.25
10. **San Francisco, CA**	97.45	47. **Yakima, WA**	86.96
11. Oakland, CA	97.16	48. **Lakeland-Winter Haven, FL**	86.68
12. **Bakersfield, CA**	96.88	49. **Daytona Beach, FL**	86.40
13. Santa Cruz-Watsonville, CA	96.60	50. **Jacksonville, FL**	86.11
14. San Jose, CA	96.31	51. Dothan, AL	85.83
15. Visalia-Tulare-Porterville, CA	96.03	52. **Pensacola, FL**	85.55
16. **Modesto, CA**	95.75	53. **Boise City, ID**	85.26
17. Stockton-Lodi, CA	95.46	54. **Santa Fe, NM**	84.98
18. **Santa Rosa, CA**	95.18	55. **Panama City, FL**	84.70
19. Merced, CA	94.90	56. **Gainesville, FL**	84.41
20. **Chico-Paradise, CA**	94.61	57. **Corpus Christi, TX**	84.13
21. **Phoenix-Mesa, AZ**	94.33	58. **Ocala, FL**	83.85
22. **Sacramento, CA**	94.05	59. **Tallahassee, FL**	83.56
23. **Fresno, CA**	93.76	60. **Charleston-North Charleston, SC**	83.28
24. Yolo, CA	93.48	61. **Galveston-Texas City, TX**	83.00
25. Vallejo-Fairfield-Napa, CA	93.20	62. **Biloxi-Gulfport-Pascagoula, MS**	82.71
26. **Fort Myers-Cape Coral, FL**	92.91	63. **Victoria, BC**	82.43
27. **Redding, CA**	92.63	64. **El Paso, TX**	82.15
28. Melbourne-Titusville-Palm Bay, FL	92.35	65. **Long Island, NY**	81.86
29. **Naples, FL**	92.06	66. Florence, SC	81.58
30. **Laredo, TX**	91.78	67. Brazoria, TX	81.30
31. Fort Pierce-Port St. Lucie, FL	91.50	68. **Savannah, GA**	81.01
32. **Miami, FL**	91.21	69. **Greensboro–Winston-Salem– High Point, NC**	80.73
33. Fort Lauderdale, FL	90.93	70. **Houston, TX**	80.45
34. **Tampa-St. Petersburg-Clearwater, FL**	90.65	71. Salem, OR	80.16
35. Yuba City, CA	90.36	72. **Vancouver, BC**	79.88
36. Punta Gorda, FL	90.08	73. **Eugene-Springfield, OR**	79.60
37. **Sarasota-Bradenton, FL**	89.80		

RANK	SCORE
74. **Bellingham, WA**	79.32
75. Houma, LA	79.03
76. Bremerton, WA	78.75
77. **McAllen-Edinburg-Mission, TX**	78.47
78. **Albuquerque, NM**	78.18
79. **Olympia, WA**	77.90
80. **Seattle-Bellevue-Everett, WA**	77.62
81. Lynchburg, VA	77.33
82. Tacoma, WA	77.05
83. **Columbus, GA-AL**	76.77
84. Fort Walton Beach, FL	76.48
85. Jersey City, NJ	76.20
86. **New Orleans, LA**	75.92
87. Albany, GA	75.63
88. **Barnstable-Yarmouth, MA**	75.35
89. **Baton Rouge, LA**	75.07
90. **Greenville-Spartanburg-Anderson, SC**	74.78
91. **Flagstaff, AZ-UT**	74.50
92. **Grand Junction, CO**	74.22
93. Sumter, SC	73.93
94. **Bryan-College Station, TX**	73.65
95. **Roanoke, VA**	73.37
96. **Montgomery, AL**	73.08
97. **Charlotte-Gastonia-Rock Hill, NC-SC**	72.80
98. Augusta-Aiken, GA-SC	72.52
99. Lafayette, LA	72.23
100. Monmouth-Ocean, NJ	71.95
101. **Austin-San Marcos, TX**	71.67
102. **Charlottesville, VA**	71.38
103. **Anchorage, AK**	71.10
104. **Raleigh-Durham-Chapel Hill, NC**	70.82
105. **New York, NY**	70.53
106. Hickory-Morganton-Lenoir, NC	70.25
107. **Atlanta, GA**	69.97
108. **Baltimore, MD**	69.68
109. **Norfolk-Virginia Beach-Newport News, VA-NC**	69.40
110. **Athens, GA**	69.12
111. Lake Charles, LA	68.83
112. **Wilmington, NC**	68.55
113. **Columbia, SC**	68.27
114. **Victoria, TX**	67.98
115. **Spokane, WA**	67.70
116. **Mobile, AL**	67.42
117. **Portland-Vancouver, OR-WA**	67.13
118. **Birmingham, AL**	66.85
119. **Asheville, NC**	66.57
120. Jacksonville, NC	66.28
121. Alexandria, LA	66.00
122. New Bedford, MA	65.72
123. **Atlantic-Cape May, NJ**	65.43
124. **San Antonio, TX**	65.15
125. Beaumont-Port Arthur, TX	64.87
126. **Chattanooga, TN-GA**	64.58
127. **Johnson City-Kingsport-Bristol, TN-VA**	64.30
128. Fayetteville, NC	64.02
129. Texarkana, TX-Texarkana, AR	63.73
130. **Richmond-Petersburg, VA**	63.45
131. Rocky Mount, NC	63.17
132. Tuscaloosa, AL	62.88
133. **Myrtle Beach, SC**	62.60
134. Anniston, AL	62.32

RANK	SCORE
135. **Salt Lake City-Ogden, UT**	62.03
136. Vineland-Millville-Bridgeton, NJ	61.75
137. Boulder-Longmont, CO	61.47
138. Goldsboro, NC	61.18
139. Gadsden, AL	60.90
140. Bridgeport, CT	60.33
140. **New Haven-Meriden, CT**	60.33
142. Newark, NJ	60.05
143. **Wilmington-Newark, DE-MD**	59.77
144. **Dover, DE**	59.49
145. **Boston, MA-NH**	59.20
146. **Las Cruces, NM**	58.92
147. **Colorado Springs, CO**	58.64
148. **Greenville, NC**	58.35
149. Macon, GA	58.07
150. **Provo-Orem, UT**	57.79
151. **Knoxville, TN**	57.50
152. Huntington-Ashland, WV-KY-OH	57.22
153. **Philadelphia, PA-NJ**	56.94
154. Danville, VA	56.65
155. **Harrisburg-Lebanon-Carlisle, PA**	56.37
156. **Washington, DC-MD-VA-WV**	56.09
157. Parkersburg-Marietta, WV-OH	55.80
158. **Abilene, TX**	55.52
159. **Hattiesburg, MS**	55.24
160. Altoona, PA	54.95
161. **Providence-Fall River-Warwick, RI-MA**	54.67
162. **Shreveport-Bossier City, LA**	54.39
163. **Odessa-Midland, TX**	54.10
164. Trenton, NJ	53.82
165. Longview-Marshall, TX	53.54
166. **Huntsville, AL**	53.25
167. Pine Bluff, AR	52.97
168. **San Angelo, TX**	52.69
169. Killeen-Temple, TX	52.40
170. Oshawa, ON	52.12
171. Tyler, TX	51.84
172. **Missoula, MT**	51.55
173. **Charleston, WV**	51.27
174. Halifax, NS	50.99
175. **Lancaster, PA**	50.70
176. **Denver, CO**	50.42
177. **Middlesex-Somerset-Hunterdon, NJ**	50.14
178. **Jackson, MS**	49.85
179. Newburgh, NY-PA	49.57
180. **Fayetteville-Springdale-Rogers, AR**	49.29
181. **Little Rock-North Little Rock, AR**	49.00
182. Brockton, MA	48.72
183. **Calgary, AB**	48.44
184. **Pittsburgh, PA**	48.15
185. **Dallas, TX**	47.59
185. Fort Worth-Arlington, TX	47.59
187. **Allentown-Bethlehem-Easton, PA**	47.30
188. **Louisville, KY-IN**	47.02
189. **Fort Collins-Loveland, CO**	46.74
190. Sherman-Denison, TX	46.45
191. **St. John's, NF**	46.17
192. Decatur, AL	45.60
192. Florence, AL	45.60
194. **Lubbock, TX**	45.32

continues

RANK	SCORE
195. **Portland, ME**	45.04
196. **Columbus, OH**	44.75
197. **Lexington, KY**	44.47
198. Bergen-Passaic, NJ	44.19
199. Monroe, LA	43.90
200. **Waco, TX**	43.62
201. **Fort Smith, AR-OK**	43.34
202. Dutchess County, NY	43.05
203. Williamsport, PA	42.77
204. **Nashville, TN**	42.49
205. Worcester, MA-CT	42.20
206. Owensboro, KY	41.92
207. Hagerstown, MD	41.64
208. **Hartford, CT**	41.35
209. Fitchburg-Leominster, MA	41.07
210. **Memphis, TN-AR-MS**	40.79
211. Lawrence, MA-NH	40.50
212. **Cheyenne, WY**	40.22
213. **Scranton–Wilkes-Barre–Hazleton, PA**	39.94
214. **Amarillo, TX**	39.66
215. **Cincinnati, OH-KY-IN**	39.37
216. **Evansville-Henderson, IN-KY**	39.09
217. **New London-Norwich, CT-RI**	38.81
218. Pueblo, CO	38.52
219. **Wichita Falls, TX**	38.24
220. Lowell, MA-NH	37.96
221. Danbury, CT	37.67
222. Muncie, IN	37.39
223. Waterbury, CT	37.11
224. York, PA	36.82
225. **Tulsa, OK**	36.54
226. **Edmonton, AB**	36.26
227. Stamford-Norwalk, CT	35.97
228. **Kitchener-Waterloo, ON**	35.69
229. Sheboygan, WI	35.41
230. Jackson, TN	35.12
231. Lawton, OK	34.84
232. **Oklahoma City, OK**	34.56
233. **Rochester, NY**	34.27
234. **State College, PA**	33.99
235. Terre Haute, IN	33.71
236. Lewiston-Auburn, ME	33.42
237. Greeley, CO	33.14
238. **Pocatello, ID**	32.86
239. Ann Arbor, MI	32.57
240. Reading, PA	32.29
241. Sharon, PA	32.01
242. **Toronto, ON**	31.72
243. Joplin, MO	31.44
244. Clarksville-Hopkinsville, TN-KY	31.16
245. Enid, OK	30.87
246. **Saint John, NB**	30.59
247. Kenosha, WI	30.31
248. **Detroit, MI**	30.02
249. **Toledo, OH**	29.74
250. Hamilton-Middletown, OH	29.46
251. Elmira, NY	29.17
252. **Billings, MT**	28.89
253. **St. Louis, MO-IL**	28.61
254. **Topeka, KS**	28.32

RANK	SCORE
255. Champaign-Urbana, IL	28.04
256. Flint, MI	27.76
257. **Springfield, MO**	27.47
258. **Bangor, ME**	27.19
259. **Kansas City, MO-KS**	26.91
260. **Rapid City, SD**	26.62
261. Steubenville-Weirton, OH-WV	26.34
262. Lawrence, KS	26.06
263. **Columbia, MO**	25.77
264. Hamilton, ON	25.49
265. Sherbrooke, PQ	25.21
266. St. Catharines-Niagara, ON	24.92
267. Cumberland, MD-WV	24.64
268. **Binghamton, NY**	24.36
269. Erie, PA	24.07
270. **Wichita, KS**	23.79
271. **Indianapolis, IN**	23.51
272. Lafayette, IN	23.22
273. **Akron, OH**	22.66
274. Canton-Massillon, OH	22.66
275. Pittsfield, MA	22.37
276. **Youngstown-Warren, OH**	22.09
277. Jackson, MI	21.81
278. Bloomington-Normal, IL	21.52
279. **Wheeling, WV-OH**	21.24
280. **Dayton-Springfield, OH**	20.96
281. **La Crosse, WI-MN**	20.67
282. Johnstown, PA	20.39
283. **Davenport-Moline-Rock Island, IA-IL**	20.11
284. Lima, OH	19.83
285. Bloomington, IN	19.54
286. **Buffalo-Niagara Falls, NY**	19.26
287. Kankakee, IL	18.98
288. **Peoria-Pekin, IL**	18.69
289. Jonesboro, AR	18.41
290. St. Cloud, MN	18.13
291. **Syracuse, NY**	17.84
292. Saginaw-Bay City-Midland, MI	17.56
293. **Portsmouth-Rochester, NH-ME**	17.28
294. Windsor, ON	16.99
295. **Great Falls, MT**	16.71
296. **Cleveland-Lorain-Elyria, OH**	16.43
297. **Chicago, IL**	16.14
298. **Saskatoon, SK**	15.86
299. Kokomo, IN	15.58
300. **Milwaukee-Waukesha, WI**	15.29
301. Utica-Rome, NY	15.01
302. Kalamazoo-Battle Creek, MI	14.73
303. Jamestown, NY	14.44
304. **Lincoln, NE**	14.16
305. **Fort Wayne, IN**	13.88
306. St. Joseph, MO	13.59
307. Decatur, IL	13.31
308. **Bismarck, ND**	13.03
309. Rockford, IL	12.74
310. **Omaha, NE-IA**	12.46
311. Racine, WI	12.18
312. **Springfield, IL**	11.89
313. Grand Forks, ND-MN	11.61
314. **Sioux City, IA-NE**	11.33

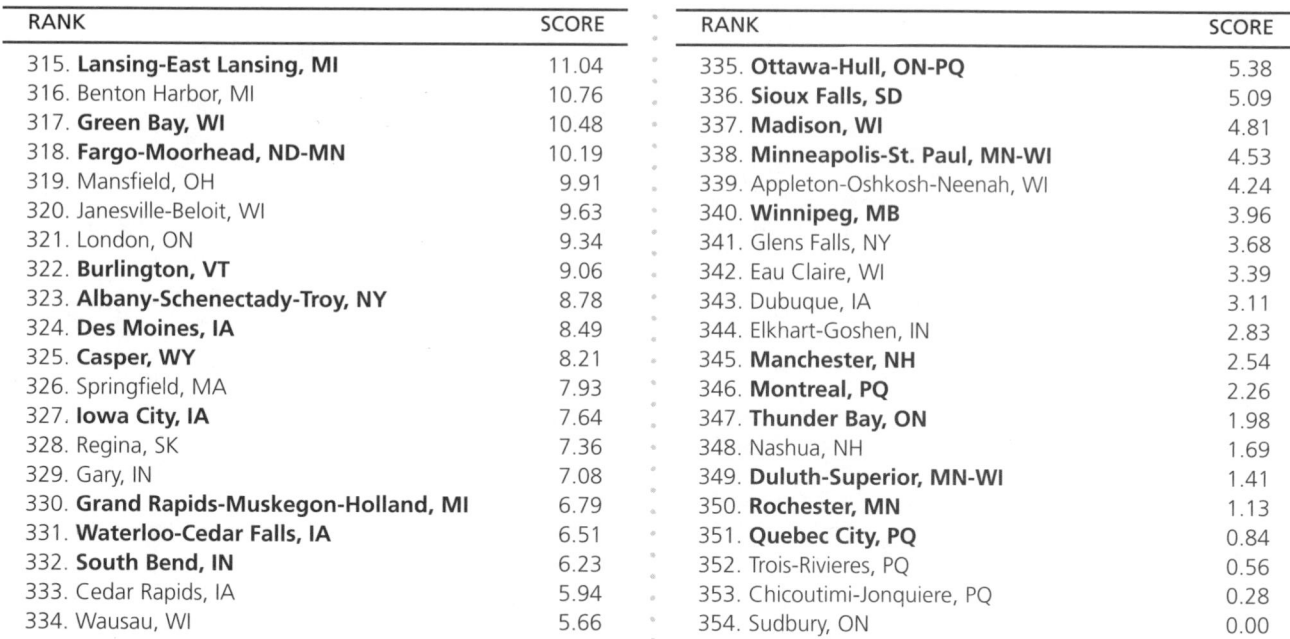

RANK	SCORE
315. **Lansing-East Lansing, MI**	11.04
316. Benton Harbor, MI	10.76
317. **Green Bay, WI**	10.48
318. **Fargo-Moorhead, ND-MN**	10.19
319. Mansfield, OH	9.91
320. Janesville-Beloit, WI	9.63
321. London, ON	9.34
322. **Burlington, VT**	9.06
323. **Albany-Schenectady-Troy, NY**	8.78
324. **Des Moines, IA**	8.49
325. **Casper, WY**	8.21
326. Springfield, MA	7.93
327. **Iowa City, IA**	7.64
328. Regina, SK	7.36
329. Gary, IN	7.08
330. **Grand Rapids-Muskegon-Holland, MI**	6.79
331. **Waterloo-Cedar Falls, IA**	6.51
332. **South Bend, IN**	6.23
333. Cedar Rapids, IA	5.94
334. Wausau, WI	5.66

RANK	SCORE
335. **Ottawa-Hull, ON-PQ**	5.38
336. **Sioux Falls, SD**	5.09
337. **Madison, WI**	4.81
338. **Minneapolis-St. Paul, MN-WI**	4.53
339. Appleton-Oshkosh-Neenah, WI	4.24
340. **Winnipeg, MB**	3.96
341. Glens Falls, NY	3.68
342. Eau Claire, WI	3.39
343. Dubuque, IA	3.11
344. Elkhart-Goshen, IN	2.83
345. **Manchester, NH**	2.54
346. **Montreal, PQ**	2.26
347. **Thunder Bay, ON**	1.98
348. Nashua, NH	1.69
349. **Duluth-Superior, MN-WI**	1.41
350. **Rochester, MN**	1.13
351. **Quebec City, PQ**	0.84
352. Trois-Rivieres, PQ	0.56
353. Chicoutimi-Jonquiere, PQ	0.28
354. Sudbury, ON	0.00

PLACE PROFILES: Climate

The following pages are brief profiles of 212 weather stations across the continent. The narrative summaries describing climate and landscape at United States and Canadian points are condensed from those that appear in the NOAA's *Local Climatological Data* and in Environment Canada's *Canadian Climate Programme* series, respectively. Canadian climate data have been converted from Celsius and metric measurements to Fahrenheit and English measurements.

These summaries describe each metro area's location and its distinctive climate and landscape features. *Location* details the place's elevation and its latitude north of the equator and longitude west of Greenwich, England. With these coordinates, you can roughly determine whether one place is farther north, south, east, or west from another.

When *landscape* is described, it is usually how the terrain influences a place's climate and what varieties of vegetation grow there naturally. Few people would deny that landscape is an important element on its own; for many, it is as important as climate. Some prefer mountains or seacoast, others rolling hills or flatwood forests, while still others favor stark desert vistas. Rather than rate landscapes, I have described them briefly here and left the decision up to you.

The descriptions for *climate* are capsule summaries of each location's type and general features. To help you visualize the annual temperature and precipitation patterns for each place, look at the graphic boxes to the right.

In the TEMPERATURE box, the white wave shows the normal high and low air temperatures as they rise and fall over the year. The darkened wave underneath shows the apparent temperature, which is air temperature reduced by winter windchill and heightened by summer humidity.

In each PRECIPITATION box is a graph showing the amount of rain and snow for each month of the year. The white lumps that occur in many places during the winter months indicate snow. Rainfall is shown by the dark wave. A vertical band shows thunderstorms in the months they occur most frequently.

Rounding out each place's climate picture are annual summaries for relative humidity, wind speed, snowfalls and rainfalls, clear and cloudy days, very hot and very cold days, thunderstorm days and precipitation days (days on which there is at least 0.1 inch of precipitation).

A star (★) preceding a metro area's name highlights it as one of the top thirty-five metro areas in the continent for a combination of climate mildness, brightness, and stability.

Abilene, TX

Location: 32.25 N, 99.41 W, at 1,780 feet, in west central Texas; 216 miles northwest of Austin.

Landscape: Rolling treeless plains are broken by low hills to the south and west. To the east, there is a continual gentle rise. Except for some cotton and feed production, cattle grazing dominates the surrounding terrain.

Cimate: Roughly midway between the humid climate of East Texas and the semiarid desert to the west and north. Most of the annual 24 inches of rainfall occurs in thunderstorms from April through June, and in September and October. Severe storms and tornadoes are rare. Summer brings hot days with clear skies, southwesterly winds, and dry air. Cool nights and low relative humidity make the climate comfortable. In winter, rapid temperature changes occur as polar air replaces warm, moist tropical air. The strongest winds come from the north and often bring cold and severe weather. Indeed, temperatures may fall 30° in an hour. Throughout the year, the region receives almost 70 percent of possible sunshine.

Winter mildness: 68   **Seasonal affect:** 91
Summer mildness: 7   **Hazardousness:** 54
Score: 55.52   **Rank:** 158

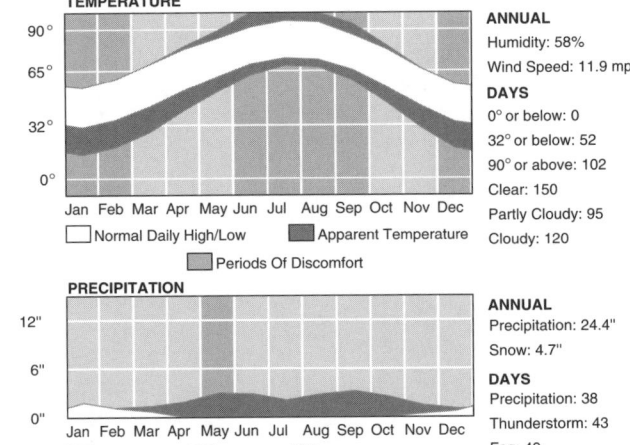

ANNUAL
Humidity: 58%
Wind Speed: 11.9 mph
DAYS
0° or below: 0
32° or below: 52
90° or above: 102
Clear: 150
Partly Cloudy: 95
Cloudy: 120

ANNUAL
Precipitation: 24.4"
Snow: 4.7"
DAYS
Precipitation: 38
Thunderstorm: 43
Fog: 49

Akron, OH

Location: 40.55 N, 81.26 W, at 1,210 feet, on the Little Cuyahoga River in the northeastern part of the state; 37 miles north of Cleveland.

Landscape: Rolling, with highest elevations almost 1,300 feet above sea level. The city spreads over the watershed dividing the drainage of northern Ohio into the St. Lawrence and Mississippi River systems. Many small lakes provide water for local industry as well as recreation for the densely populated region. The area is mainly industrial, the number of farms having fallen dramatically in recent years.

Climate: Lake Erie has a considerable effect on the weather, tempering cold air masses during the winter and contributing to brief but heavy snow squalls until the lake freezes over. Snowfall is much heavier north of the weather station near the lake. Spring comes late here, the last freeze arriving May 8. Summers are moderately warm and humid. September, October, and November are pleasant, but there is considerable morning fog. The first freeze usually comes around October 6.

Winter mildness: 34   **Seasonal affect:** 11
Summer mildness: 75   **Hazardousness:** 13
Score: 22.66   **Rank:** 273

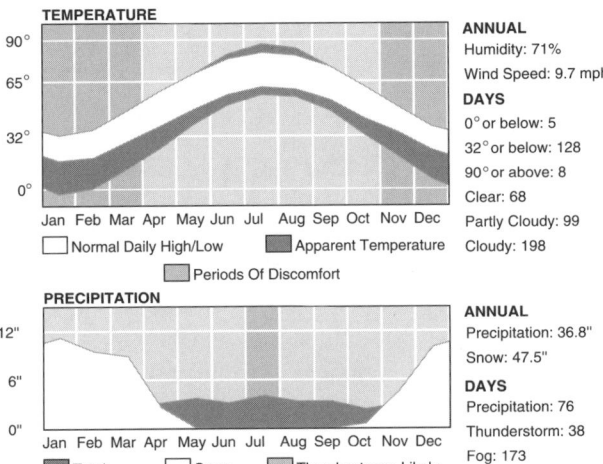

ANNUAL
Humidity: 71%
Wind Speed: 9.7 mph
DAYS
0° or below: 5
32° or below: 128
90° or above: 8
Clear: 68
Partly Cloudy: 99
Cloudy: 198

ANNUAL
Precipitation: 36.8"
Snow: 47.5"
DAYS
Precipitation: 76
Thunderstorm: 38
Fog: 173

Albany-Schenectady-Troy, NY

Location: 42.45 N, 73.48 W, at 270 feet, on the west bank of the Hudson River where the river meets the New York State Barge Canal system; 150 miles north of New York City.

Landscape: The city's riverfront is only a few feet above sea level. Eleven miles west, the Helderberg escarpment rises to between 1,400 and 1,800 feet. To the east is a rugged valley floor rising to hills 1,600 to 2,000 feet high. The city sits on a gently rolling valley floor.

Cimate: Harsh Continental subject to some moderating influences from the Atlantic Ocean to the south. The first frost arrives at the end of September. Winters are cold and occasionally severe with maximum temperatures not rising above 32°F over long stretches. The last frost occurs mid-May, and during the warmer months, temperatures rise quickly to moderate levels during the day, then plunge to cool at night. Occasional hot spells of a week or more occur during the summer.

Winter mildness: 13   **Seasonal affect:** 22
Summer mildness: 63   **Hazardousness:** 25
Score: 8.78   **Rank:** 323

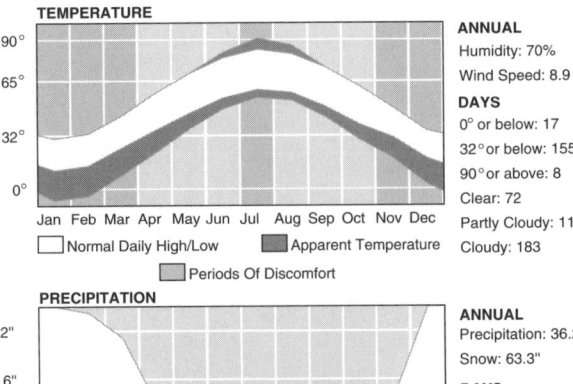

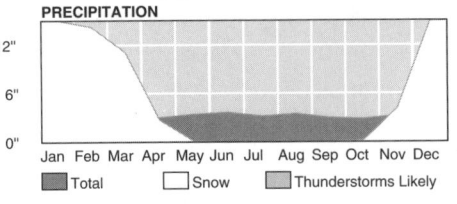

ANNUAL
Humidity: 70%
Wind Speed: 8.9 mph
DAYS
0° or below: 17
32° or below: 155
90° or above: 8
Clear: 72
Partly Cloudy: 110
Cloudy: 183

ANNUAL
Precipitation: 36.2"
Snow: 63.3"
DAYS
Precipitation: 71
Thunderstorm: 24
Fog: 151

Albuquerque, NM

Location: 35.03 N, 106.37 W, at 5,310 feet, on the upper Rio Grande River opposite a pass between the Sandia and Manzano mountains to the east; 55 miles southwest of Santa Fe.

Landscape: On a high plateau encircled by sections of the Cibola National Forest. The area—a center for mining, timber, and ranching operations—is a typical steppe or shortgrass prairie with a covering of scattered shrubs and low trees.

Cimate: Arid Continental, with low humidity making the heat feel much less intense; cool nights. There are no muggy days. Half the annual precipitation falls as brief but severe thunderstorms between July and September. These storms have a moderating effect on the heat and do not interfere much with outdoor activities. Long drizzles are unknown. The low rainfall and mild temperatures—91°F in July, 46° in January—make the city a health resort. The last freeze usually falls around May 5, the first freeze around October 11.

Winter mildness: 50	**Seasonal affect:** 98
Summer mildness: 14	**Hazardousness:** 63
Score: 78.18	**Rank: 78**

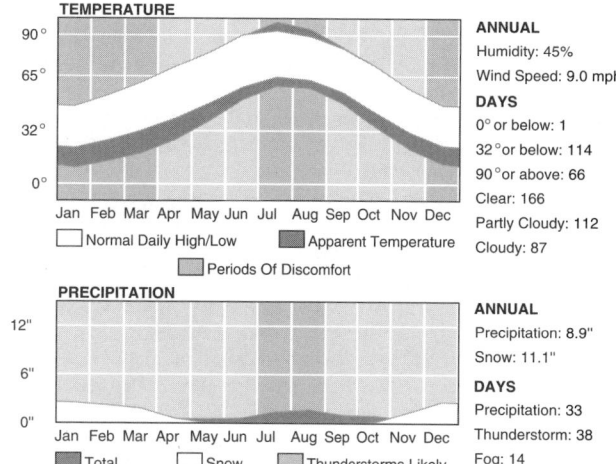

TEMPERATURE

□ Normal Daily High/Low ■ Apparent Temperature ▨ Periods Of Discomfort

PRECIPITATION

■ Total □ Snow ▨ Thunderstorms Likely

ANNUAL
Humidity: 45%
Wind Speed: 9.0 mph
DAYS
0° or below: 1
32° or below: 114
90° or above: 66
Clear: 166
Partly Cloudy: 112
Cloudy: 87

ANNUAL
Precipitation: 8.9"
Snow: 11.1"
DAYS
Precipitation: 33
Thunderstorm: 38
Fog: 14

Allentown-Bethlehem-Easton, PA

Location: 40.39 N, 75.26 W, at 390 feet, in the Lehigh River valley in east central Pennsylvania. Allentown is 82 miles northeast of Harrisburg, the state capital. Easton lies on the Delaware River, across from New Jersey. Bethlehem is along the Lehigh River between Allentown and Easton.

Landscape: The Blue Mountain is 12 miles north, the South Mountain fringes the southern edge. Other than these rises of up to 2,000 feet, the country is gently rolling with numerous small streams. Lots of eastern deciduous forest alternate with open hills or fields.

Cimate: Four-season Continental climate with long, pleasant autumns and a spring that starts in late April. Temperatures are modified by the mountains, and often there may be a 10 to 15 degree difference between Allentown and Philadelphia, which is just 50 miles south. Maximum summer temperatures aren't high, but humidity is often uncomfortable. Winters are comparatively mild, with temperatures rarely dropping below zero. Rain falls as spring showers. Stormy days occur from mid-June through August.

Winter mildness: 42	**Seasonal affect:** 34
Summer mildness: 59	**Hazardousness:** 46
Score: 47.30	**Rank: 187**

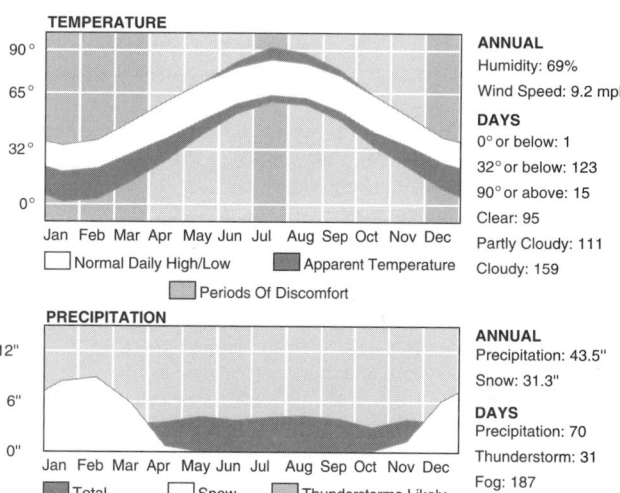

TEMPERATURE

□ Normal Daily High/Low ■ Apparent Temperature ▨ Periods Of Discomfort

PRECIPITATION

■ Total □ Snow ▨ Thunderstorms Likely

ANNUAL
Humidity: 69%
Wind Speed: 9.2 mph
DAYS
0° or below: 1
32° or below: 123
90° or above: 15
Clear: 95
Partly Cloudy: 111
Cloudy: 159

ANNUAL
Precipitation: 43.5"
Snow: 31.3"
DAYS
Precipitation: 70
Thunderstorm: 31
Fog: 187

Amarillo, TX

Location: 35.14 N, 101.42 W, at 3,600 feet, between the Canadian and Red rivers in the heart of the Texas Panhandle. Nearer the capitals of four other states than to Austin, which is 500 miles to the southwest.

Landscape: The city sits atop the cap rock, or High Plains, of the Southwest. The low prairie and scrubby vegetation offer a distant, flat horizon. Spanish for "yellow," amarillo refers to the color of the clay soil in the area. Cotton and sorghum are primary crops.

Cimate: Semiarid Continental. The area is generally dry, but thunderstorms occur between April and September. This varies from year to year, and droughts are somewhat frequent. In November, rapid and great temperature changes start when fast-moving cold air comes down from the Plains and the Rocky Mountains. The city's nearness to paths of moving pressure systems causes strong winds, especially in March and April. Though summer days are hot, the low humidity lessens the feeling of heat and makes for pleasant mornings and nights.

Winter mildness: 48	**Seasonal affect:** 90
Summer mildness: 19	**Hazardousness:** 35
Score: 39.66	**Rank: 214**

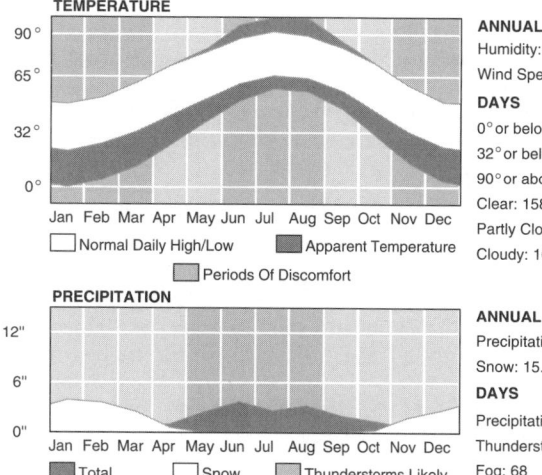

TEMPERATURE

□ Normal Daily High/Low ■ Apparent Temperature ▨ Periods Of Discomfort

PRECIPITATION

■ Total □ Snow ▨ Thunderstorms Likely

ANNUAL
Humidity: 60%
Wind Speed: 13.6 mph
DAYS
0° or below: 2
32° or below: 111
90° or above: 66
Clear: 158
Partly Cloudy: 102
Cloudy: 105

ANNUAL
Precipitation: 19.6"
Snow: 15.4"
DAYS
Precipitation: 38
Thunderstorm: 49
Fog: 68

Anchorage, AK

Location: 61.10 N, 150.01 W, at 110 feet, in a broad valley on Alaska's south coast. Surrounded by Cook Inlet and the Chugach Mountains.

Landscape: The land lifts gradually to the east with marshes interspersed with glacial moraines, depressions, streams, and knolls. Beyond, the Chugach Mountains rise sharply to between 4,000 feet and 5,000 feet, with some peaks reaching 8,000 feet to 10,000 feet.

Cimate: The four seasons are well marked in Anchorage, but their length differs considerably from the standards of the middle latitudes. The rivers and lakes thaw in mid-April to early May. The last freeze is May 29. The first freeze arrives September 4 with snow following in early October and departing in mid-April. The mountains block the warm air and moisture from the Gulf of Alaska. One hundred miles north, the Alaska Range blocks the cold air from the interior. When interior temperatures are minus 50°F to 60°F, they will be 15°F to 30°F in Anchorage.

Winter mildness: 9	**Seasonal affect:** 34
Summer mildness: 100	**Hazardousness:** 45
Score: 71.10	**Rank: 103**

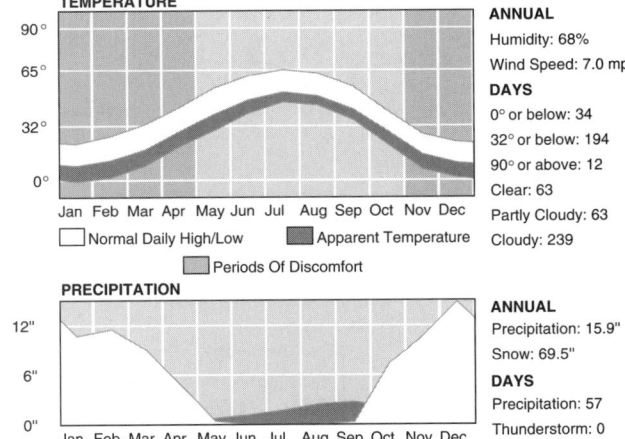

Asheville, NC

Location: 35.26 N, 82.33 W, at 2,140 feet, on the French Broad River in western North Carolina, the eastern gateway to the Great Smoky Mountains.

Landscape: The city sits on a plateau, flanked on the east and west by mountain ranges. Thirty miles south, the Blue Ridge Mountains form an escarpment, with an average elevation of 2,700 feet. Local forests include oak, hickory, walnut, maple, and basswood that make a dense canopy in summer, but shed their leaves completely in winter. There are lower layers of small trees and dogwood, blueberry, and haw.

Cimate: Temperate but invigorating, with considerable variation in temperature occurring from day to day throughout the year. Spring arrives early— around April 10—and is long, with warm, clear days. The French Broad Valley has a pronounced effect on wind direction, which is mostly from the northwest. Destructive weather events are rare. However, the valley is subject to flooding, with high water occurring in 12-year cycles. The first freeze is October 24.

Winter mildness: 57	**Seasonal affect:** 30
Summer mildness: 69	**Hazardousness:** 56
Score: 66.57	**Rank: 119**

Athens, GA

Location: 33.57 N, 83.19 W, at 800 feet, on the Oconee River in the Piedmont Plateau section of northeast Georgia; 60 miles east of Atlanta.

Landscape: Elevations range between 600 and 800 feet, and the topography is rolling and hilly. The streams drain southeast to the Savannah River. In the midst of stands of southern yellow pine are varieties of oak, elm, hickory, and walnut.

Cimate: Continental, moderated by the Atlantic Ocean 200 miles to the southeast, the Gulf of Mexico 275 miles to the south, and the southern Appalachians to the north and northwest. The last freeze occurs around April 3. Summers are hot and humid, but without long stretches of extreme heat. Precipitation is evenly distributed throughout the year, usually as rain, but snow is possible. The mountains to the north are a barrier to extremely cold airflow, and the first freeze arrives around November 6. Winters aren't severe. Cold spells are shortlived and broken up by periods of warm southerly airflow.

Winter mildness: 71	**Seasonal affect:** 46
Summer mildness: 33	**Hazardousness:** 72
Score: 69.12	**Rank: 110**

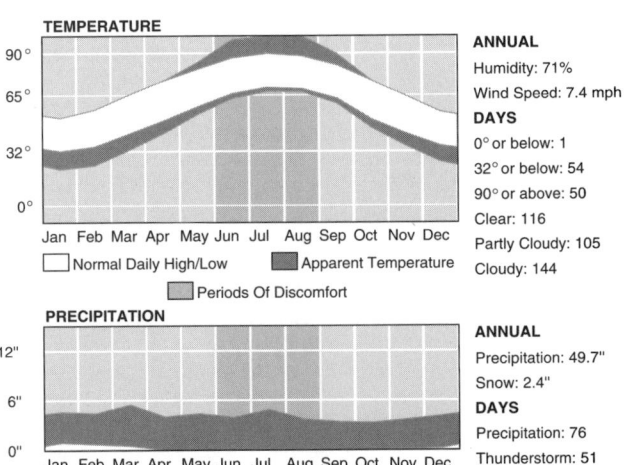

Atlanta, GA

Location: 33.39 N, 84.26 W, at 1,010 feet, in the foothills of the Blue Ridge Mountains in north central Georgia.

Landscape: The land is rolling to hilly, sloping downward toward the east, west, and south. Because Atlanta is located on a plateau with mountains to the north, its exposure to cold air from the north and moist hot air from the Gulf of Mexico is blocked.

Cimate: Moderate with four distinct seasons. Abundant rainfall fosters natural vegetation and growth of crops. In summer, afternoon high temperatures equal or exceed 90°F one day in five, but a temperature of 100°F is rare. Atlanta's winters are mild. Cold spells aren't unusual, but don't hinder outdoor activities. Snow is light and doesn't remain on the ground. Ice storms, however, occur about one year in ten and cause heavy damage. Atlanta averages 50 thunderstorms a year, which sometimes spin off destructive tornadoes. The typical date of the last freeze is April 3. The first freeze arrives around mid-November.

Winter mildness: 70	**Seasonal affect:** 54
Summer mildness: 42	**Hazardousness:** 66
Score: 69.97	**Rank: 107**

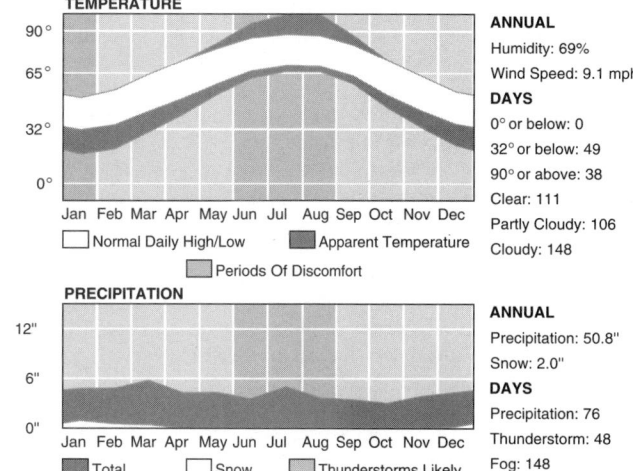

TEMPERATURE

□ Normal Daily High/Low ■ Apparent Temperature
□ Periods Of Discomfort

ANNUAL
Humidity: 69%
Wind Speed: 9.1 mph
DAYS
0° or below: 0
32° or below: 49
90° or above: 38
Clear: 111
Partly Cloudy: 106
Cloudy: 148

PRECIPITATION

■ Total □ Snow ■ Thunderstorms Likely

ANNUAL
Precipitation: 50.8"
Snow: 2.0"
DAYS
Precipitation: 76
Thunderstorm: 48
Fog: 148

Atlantic City-Cape May, NJ

Location: 39.27 N, 74.34 W, at 60 feet on a sand island south of Absecon Inlet on New Jersey's Atlantic shore; some 60 miles southeast of Philadelphia.

Landscape: The surrounding terrain is flat and sandy. Immense tidal marshes are crossed over by highways and rail track, which hide deep channels that cut the island from the mainland. The natural vegetation is scrubby evergreen and laurel. Stands of pine are common.

Cimate: Continental, with the moderating influence of the Atlantic Ocean apparent throughout the year. Summers are relatively cooler, winters warmer than those of other places at the same latitude. During the warm season, sea breezes in the late morning and the afternoon prevent excessive heat. Fall is long, lasting until the first freeze around November 10. Spring warming is somewhat delayed; the last freeze occurs around March 30. Average ocean temperatures range from near 37°F in winter to 72°F in August. Precipitation is moderate and well distributed throughout the year.

Winter mildness: 49	**Seasonal affect:** 54
Summer mildness: 59	**Hazardousness:** 66
Score: 65.43	**Rank: 123**

TEMPERATURE

□ Normal Daily High/Low ■ Apparent Temperature
□ Periods Of Discomfort

ANNUAL
Humidity: 69%
Wind Speed: 10.0 mph
DAYS
0° or below: 3
32° or below: 108
90° or above: 17
Clear: 96
Partly Cloudy: 111
Cloudy: 158

PRECIPITATION

■ Total □ Snow ■ Thunderstorms Likely

ANNUAL
Precipitation: 40.3"
Snow: 16.1"
DAYS
Precipitation: 64
Thunderstorm: 26
Fog: 174

Augusta, GA-Aiken, SC

Location: 33.22 N, 81.58 W, at 150 feet, on the Savannah River, the boundary between Georgia and South Carolina.

Landscape: Generally flat, with gentle slopes and local relief of less than 200 feet. The fall line dividing the upcountry Piedmont Plateau and the low country Coastal Plain is nearby. Low-rise sandhills are to the west. The trees are a mixed forest of southern yellow pine, oak, and hickory.

Cimate: Warm and mild, with occasional hot spells. Measurable snow is a rarity and it remains on the ground for only a short time. Frosts are typical in late spring or early fall, but in 100 years of weather records, a temperature of zero has never been reached. The growing season averages 241 days, from the last freeze on March 16 to the first freeze on November 16. However frosts have been reported as late as April 21 and as early as October 17. In some low-lying areas, Savannah River flooding is still a threat.

Winter mildness: 71	**Seasonal affect:** 60
Summer mildness: 19	**Hazardousness:** 77
Score: 72.52	**Rank: 98**

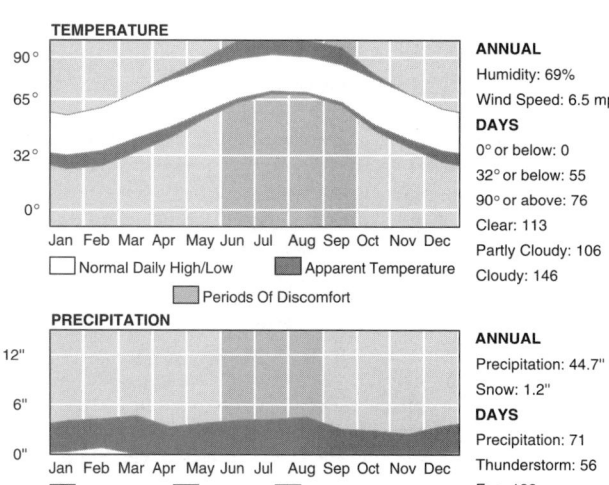

TEMPERATURE

□ Normal Daily High/Low ■ Apparent Temperature
□ Periods Of Discomfort

ANNUAL
Humidity: 69%
Wind Speed: 6.5 mph
DAYS
0° or below: 0
32° or below: 55
90° or above: 76
Clear: 113
Partly Cloudy: 106
Cloudy: 146

PRECIPITATION

■ Total □ Snow ■ Thunderstorms Likely

ANNUAL
Precipitation: 44.7"
Snow: 1.2"
DAYS
Precipitation: 71
Thunderstorm: 56
Fog: 188

Climate

Austin-San Marcos, TX

Location: 30.17 N, 97.42 W, at 590 feet, on the Colorado River where it crosses the Balcones Escarpment.

Landscape: Elevations within the city vary from 400 to 900 feet above sea level as neighborhoods spread over low hills and wide terraces. Native trees include cedar, oak, walnut, mesquite, and pecan. A series of dams on the Colorado River, which curves through the city and separates the Texas Hill Country from the Blackland Prairies of East Texas, have formed the nearby Highland Lakes.

Cimate: Humid Subtropical. Although summers are hot, night temperatures usually drop into the 70s. Winters are mild, with below-freezing temperatures on fewer than 25 days. The first freeze is in mid-November, the last in mid-March. Prevailing winds are southerly, but strong northers bring cold spells rarely lasting more than a few days. Precipitation is well distributed, though heaviest in late spring with a secondary peak in September. Summer can bring thunderstorms. Winter rains are slow and steady. Snowfall is inconsequential and destructive weather infrequent.

Winter mildness: 85　　　**Seasonal affect:** 82
Summer mildness: 7　　　**Hazardousness:** 80
Score: 71.67　　　　　　**Rank: 101**

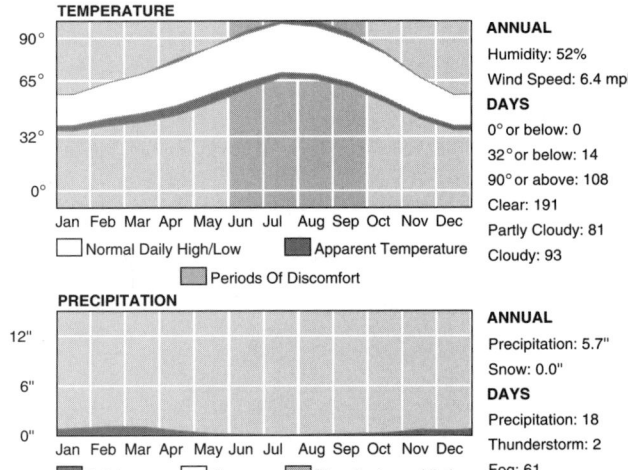

TEMPERATURE

Normal Daily High/Low　Apparent Temperature　Periods Of Discomfort

ANNUAL
Humidity: 67%
Wind Speed: 9.2 mph
DAYS
0° or below: 0
32° or below: 21
90° or above: 107
Clear: 119
Partly Cloudy: 114
Cloudy: 132

PRECIPITATION

Total　Snow　Thunderstorms Likely

ANNUAL
Precipitation: 31.9"
Snow: 0.9"
DAYS
Precipitation: 47
Thunderstorm: 41
Fog: 115

★Bakersfield, CA

Location: 35.25 N, 119.03 W, at 490 feet, in the extreme southern end of the great San Joaquin Valley in south central California. The city is partially surrounded by a horseshoe-shaped rim of mountains with an opening at the northwest.

Landscape: The surrounding land is relatively flat and dry and reminds many of the surface of the moon. An occasional oil derrick pocks the horizon. Distant to the northeast are the foothills of the Sierras. This snowy range catches and stores the water for crops in the valley below.

Cimate: Because of the surrounding topography, there are three different climates within short distances of each other: valley, mountain, and desert. The overall climate, however, is warm and semi-arid. Ninety percent of the precipitation falls between October and April, which is typical of the southern half of California. Thunderstorms and snow are rare in the valley. Summers are hot, cloudless, and dry, but occasionally relieved by ocean breezes from the west. Winters are mild. Average growing season: 265 days. The first freeze is around November 23; the last is an early February 18.

Winter mildness: 85　　　**Seasonal affect:** 98
Summer mildness: 2　　　**Hazardousness:** 98
Score: 96.88　　　　　　**Rank: 12**

TEMPERATURE

Normal Daily High/Low　Apparent Temperature　Periods Of Discomfort

ANNUAL
Humidity: 52%
Wind Speed: 6.4 mph
DAYS
0° or below: 0
32° or below: 14
90° or above: 108
Clear: 191
Partly Cloudy: 81
Cloudy: 93

PRECIPITATION

Total　Snow　Thunderstorms Likely

ANNUAL
Precipitation: 5.7"
Snow: 0.0"
DAYS
Precipitation: 18
Thunderstorm: 2
Fog: 61

Baltimore, MD

Location: 39.17 N, 76.37 W, at 10 feet, on the western shore of the Chesapeake Bay; about 40 miles northeast of Washington, D.C.

Landscape: The low, long rolling hills, forested with broadleaf deciduous and needleleaf evergreen trees, are drained by the wide Severn River into the upper Bay.

Cimate: Subtropical, midway between the rigorous climates of the North and the milder ones of the South, but with a definite Marine influence. The last freeze is at the beginning of April. Summers are hot and humid though often relieved by a bay breeze. The first freeze arrives at the end of October, followed by a chilly and rainy winter. Snow is minimal and doesn't last long. Rain falls throughout the year, but is greatest in late summer and early fall. This is also the time of hurricanes and severe thunderstorms. The Appalachian Mountains to the west and the Atlantic Ocean to the east produce an equable climate compared with other locations inland at the same latitude.

Winter mildness: 63　　　**Seasonal affect:** 61
Summer mildness: 39　　　**Hazardousness:** 64
Score: 69.68　　　　　　**Rank: 108**

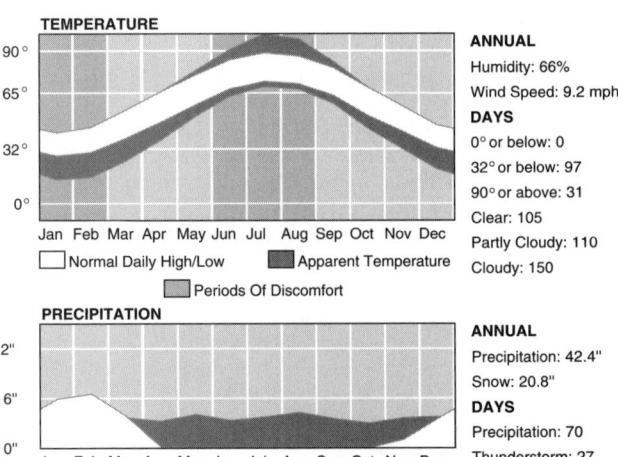

TEMPERATURE

Normal Daily High/Low　Apparent Temperature　Periods Of Discomfort

ANNUAL
Humidity: 66%
Wind Speed: 9.2 mph
DAYS
0° or below: 0
32° or below: 97
90° or above: 31
Clear: 105
Partly Cloudy: 110
Cloudy: 150

PRECIPITATION

Total　Snow　Thunderstorms Likely

ANNUAL
Precipitation: 42.4"
Snow: 20.8"
DAYS
Precipitation: 70
Thunderstorm: 27
Fog: 146

Bangor, ME

Location: 44.48 N, 68.49 W, at 190 feet, in east central Maine, where the Penobscot and Kenduskeag rivers meet; 18 miles from the Atlantic Ocean.

Landscape: Rolling hills, low mountains, and high relief predominate. Much of the topography is the result of glacial activity. The soil is generally acid, not highly productive for crop farming, but well suited to growing conifers. The city is surrounded by vast timber stands of spruce-fir, mixed hardwoods, and white pine that cover nearly 90 percent of Maine's total land area. Bangor is a port of entry and gateway to a large resort and lumber area.

Cimate: Alternating air masses create strong seasonal contrasts in temperature. Winters are moderately long and somewhat severe. Snow cover tends to stay on the ground all winter. Though daily highs top 50°F one-third of the year, typical springs and falls are short and aren't warm. Summer is mild. The frost-free growing season here is just 140 days, from around May 27 to September 18.

Winter mildness: 9	**Seasonal affect:** 3
Summer mildness: 92	**Hazardousness:** 22
Score: 27.19	**Rank: 258**

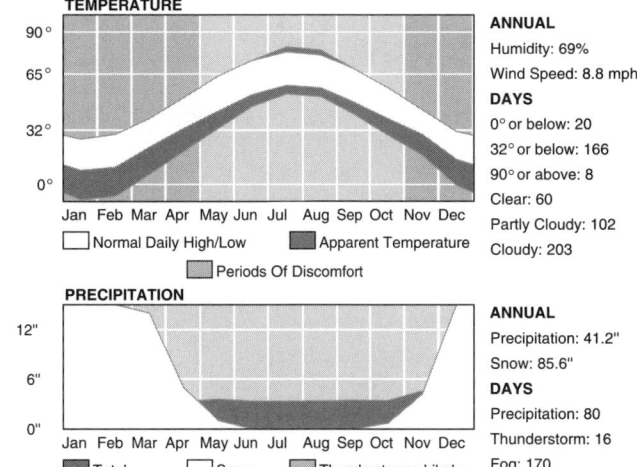

ANNUAL
Humidity: 69%
Wind Speed: 8.8 mph
DAYS
0° or below: 20
32° or below: 166
90° or above: 8
Clear: 60
Partly Cloudy: 102
Cloudy: 203

ANNUAL
Precipitation: 41.2"
Snow: 85.6"
DAYS
Precipitation: 80
Thunderstorm: 16
Fog: 170

Barnstable-Yarmouth, MA

Location: 41.40 N, 69.58 W, at 50 feet, on a hooked peninsula jutting out 65 miles into the Atlantic Ocean; 60 miles southeast of Boston.

Landscape: The western end of the cape is higher and hillier than the flat and treeless eastern end. Only 1 to 20 miles wide, the peninsula is bounded by Cape Cod Bay to the north and west, Buzzards Bay to the west, and Vineyard and Nantucket Sounds in the south. The sandy soil of glacial origin is arranged in rolling hills and dunes. The northern hook has been designated a National Seashore.

Cimate: Mild Maritime, with cool summers and cold, wet winters that are seldom severe. In summer, temperatures are ideal for outdoor recreation. Both subzero and air temperatures exceeding 90°F are rare. The first freeze arrives by October 20, and the last is at the end of April. Because the Cape extends into the warm Gulf Stream, its warmer winters and cooler summers contrast favorably with the rest of southern New England.

Winter mildness: 56	**Seasonal affect:** 49
Summer mildness: 97	**Hazardousness:** 46
Score: 75.35	**Rank: 88**

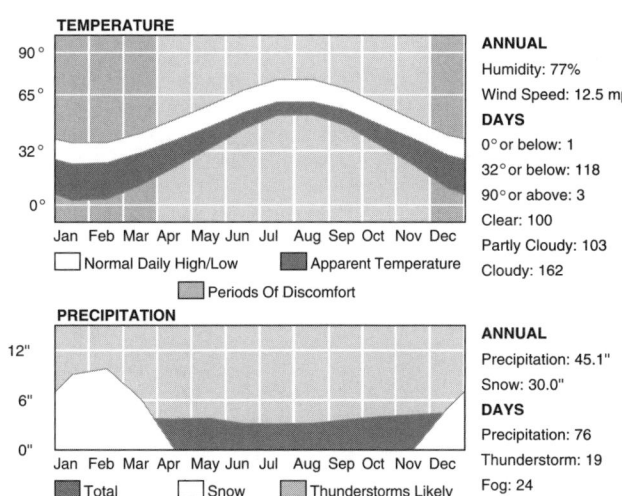

ANNUAL
Humidity: 77%
Wind Speed: 12.5 mph
DAYS
0° or below: 1
32° or below: 118
90° or above: 3
Clear: 100
Partly Cloudy: 103
Cloudy: 162

ANNUAL
Precipitation: 45.1"
Snow: 30.0"
DAYS
Precipitation: 76
Thunderstorm: 19
Fog: 24

Baton Rouge, LA

Location: 30.32 N, 91.08 W, at 60 feet, at the head of deepwater navigation on the Mississippi River, in the southeastern part of the state; 80 miles west of New Orleans.

Landscape: Terrain is related to the Mississippi River, flat, irregular, and gently sloping. The many streams are sluggish. Marshes, swamps, and lakes are numerous. Organic marsh soils are naturally fertile, but poorly drained and subject to flooding. The vegetation is a typical temperate rain forest of evergreen, live oak, laurel, and magnolia.

Cimate: Humid Subtropical, with an annual range of temperatures that is small to moderate. Rainfall is an abundant 40–60 inches and well distributed throughout the year, though February and March tend to be slightly wetter. The last freeze comes around March 5. Early summer mornings may be as much as twenty degrees cooler than the afternoons. There are tropical storms in summer and hurricanes in summer and fall, occasionally accompanied by tornadoes. Winter temperatures can fall below freezing. The first such occurrence is usually around November 17.

Winter mildness: 87	**Seasonal affect:** 57
Summer mildness: 21	**Hazardousness:** 78
Score: 75.07	**Rank: 89**

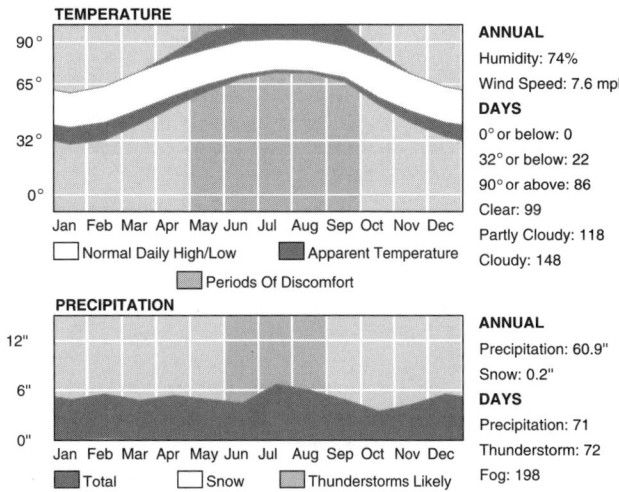

ANNUAL
Humidity: 74%
Wind Speed: 7.6 mph
DAYS
0° or below: 0
32° or below: 22
90° or above: 86
Clear: 99
Partly Cloudy: 118
Cloudy: 148

ANNUAL
Precipitation: 60.9"
Snow: 0.2"
DAYS
Precipitation: 71
Thunderstorm: 72
Fog: 198

Bellingham, WA

Location: 48.48 N, 122.32 W, at 150 feet, on Bellingham Bay at lower Whatcom Falls; 40 miles south of Vancouver, British Columbia.

Landscape: Dominated by the broad, glacier-carved Skagit River Valley with fjords and deep undersea troughs. The North Cascade Mountains and 10,775 foot Mt. Baker are east of the city. The San Juan Islands archipelago is in nearby Puget Sound. The humid needle-leaf forests are dominated by Douglas fir and hemlock, western red cedar, spruce, and other conifers. Deciduous trees include alder, birch, and maple.

Cimate: Distinctly Marine, with slight seasonal temperature variations. Winter days are mild, but the nights are chilly. The cooler air reduces evaporation, producing a damp, humid climate with heavy cloud cover. Summers are cool and drier. There are few clear days. Snow is likely from mid-November through March, occasionally even in April. The first freeze is around October 20, the last around April 21. Winter temperatures will fall to freezing, but there are no records of zero.

Winter mildness: 71 **Seasonal affect:** 1
Summer mildness: 99 **Hazardousness:** 87
Score: 79.32 **Rank: 74**

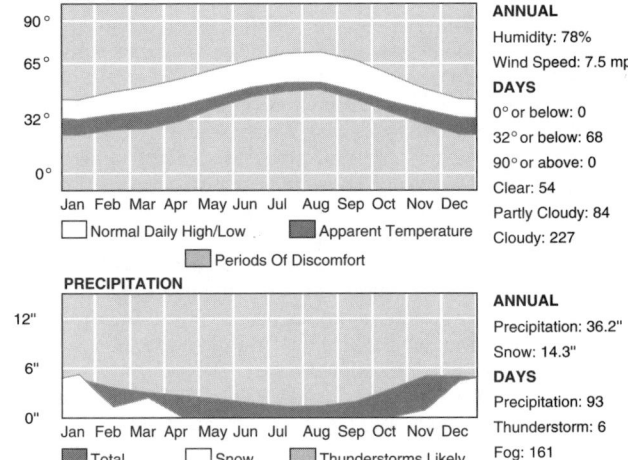

ANNUAL
Humidity: 78%
Wind Speed: 7.5 mph
DAYS
0° or below: 0
32° or below: 68
90° or above: 0
Clear: 54
Partly Cloudy: 84
Cloudy: 227

ANNUAL
Precipitation: 36.2"
Snow: 14.3"
DAYS
Precipitation: 93
Thunderstorm: 6
Fog: 161

Billings, MT

Location: 45.48 N, 108.32 W, at 3,570 feet, on the west bank of the Yellowstone River in south central Montana, near the border between the Great Plains and the Rocky Mountains.

Landscape: The natural vegetation is a northern floodplain forest of mixed hardwood and pine. The area is the center of a vast, rich agricultural belt; irrigation and sufficient rain during early spring and fall make it possible to raise a variety of crops here, including sugar beets.

Cimate: Semiarid Continental. About a third of the annual rain falls during May and June. Winters are usually dry and cold, but heavy snows can occur anytime, especially in spring or fall when the temperatures can drop unexpectedly. Blizzard conditions are expected. Freezes typically arrive September 28 and depart around May 9. Severe cold spells are sometimes relieved by the Chinook winds moving down the Yellowstone Valley bringing warm Pacific air. Springs are changeable, cloudy, and cool. Summers are mild, dry, and sunny, with cool to cold nights.

Winter mildness: 20 **Seasonal affect:** 76
Summer mildness: 48 **Hazardousness:** 10
Score: 28.89 **Rank: 252**

ANNUAL
Humidity: 55%
Wind Speed: 11.2 mph
DAYS
0° or below: 18
32° or below: 150
90° or above: 29
Clear: 90
Partly Cloudy: 113
Cloudy: 162

ANNUAL
Precipitation: 15.1"
Snow: 56.5"
DAYS
Precipitation: 29
Thunderstorm: 27
Fog: 48

Biloxi-Gulfport-Pascagoula, MS

Location: 30.23 N, 88.59 W, at 10 feet, along the thickly settled stretch of the Gulf of Mexico coast; 60 miles east of New Orleans.

Landscape: Flat, consisting of low-lying delta floodplains sloping down to sand beaches and shallow harbors and bays. Gulf Islands National Seashore lies offshore in the Mississippi Sound and the Intracoastal Waterway passes between New Orleans and Biloxi. Common trees here are evergreens, oaks, laurel, and magnolia. Tree ferns, small palms, and shrubs make up the lower growth.

Cimate: The Gulf modifies local climate, an effect not felt farther inland. Temperatures of 90° or higher occur only half as often here as they do in Hattiesburg, 60 miles north. However, there is no such reverse effect on cold air moving down from the north in winter. Rainfall is plentiful and is heaviest in July, March, and September. Hurricane and tropical storm damage can occur six to seven times a year. The first freeze arrives in late November, and the last leaves by February 20.

Winter mildness: 92 **Seasonal affect:** 60
Summer mildness: 30 **Hazardousness:** 68
Score: 82.71 **Rank: 62**

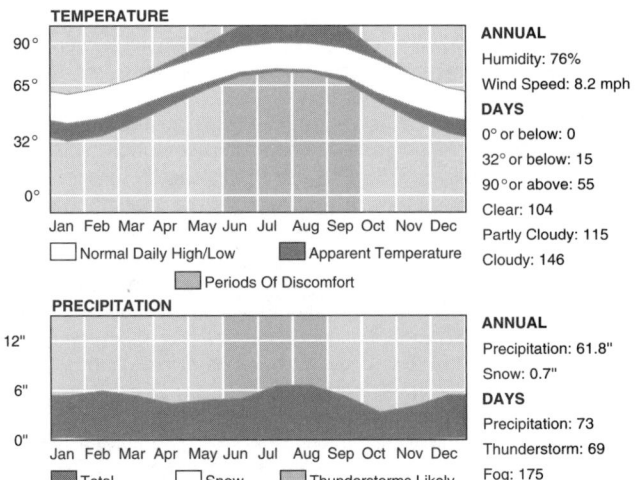

ANNUAL
Humidity: 76%
Wind Speed: 8.2 mph
DAYS
0° or below: 0
32° or below: 15
90° or above: 55
Clear: 104
Partly Cloudy: 115
Cloudy: 146

ANNUAL
Precipitation: 61.8"
Snow: 0.7"
DAYS
Precipitation: 73
Thunderstorm: 69
Fog: 175

Binghamton, NY

Location: 42.13 N, 75.59 W, at 1,600 feet, in a narrow valley where the Susquehanna and Chenango rivers meet in south central New York state.

Landscape: Hills rise to some 1,400 feet to 1,600 feet within a radius of approximately 5 miles around the city. In the spring, melting snow and rains sometimes cause flooding along the riverbanks. Remnants of an extensive northern hardwood forest, cleared in the last century, can still be seen on the tops of hills.

Cimate: Representative of the humid area of the northeastern United States and decidedly Continental in character. Since the area is next to the St. Lawrence Valley storm track and subject to intruding arctic air masses that approach from the west and north, the local weather undergoes frequent and rapid changes. Winters are cold, but usually not severe. However, moisture-laden winds from the Great Lakes bring much snow. Summers are pleasantly cool and invigorating. The first freeze is at the beginning of October; the last is in mid-May.

Winter mildness: 23	**Seasonal affect:** 1
Summer mildness: 91	**Hazardousness:** 4
Score: 24.36	**Rank: 268**

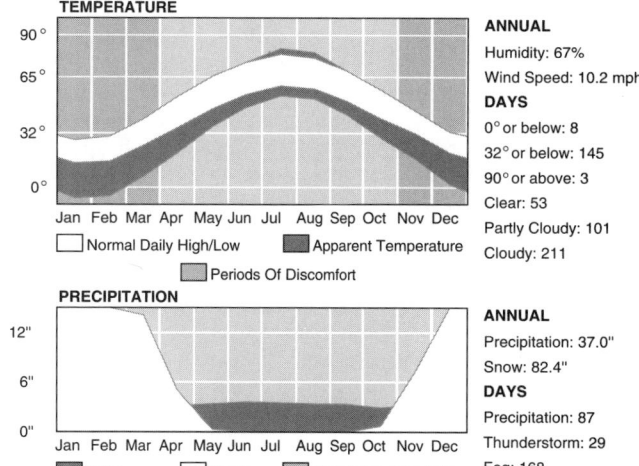

ANNUAL
Humidity: 67%
Wind Speed: 10.2 mph
DAYS
0° or below: 8
32° or below: 145
90° or above: 3
Clear: 53
Partly Cloudy: 101
Cloudy: 211

ANNUAL
Precipitation: 37.0"
Snow: 82.4"
DAYS
Precipitation: 87
Thunderstorm: 29
Fog: 168

Birmingham, AL

Location: 33.34 N, 86.45 W, at 620 feet, in north central Alabama in the Appalachian foothills; 300 miles inland from the Gulf of Mexico.

Landscape: The city sits in a valley between a ridge of hills extending from the northeast to the west, and the Red Mountain ridge covering the east to the southwest. The valley is 8 miles long and 2 to 4 miles wide. The Red Mountain ridge approaches a height of 600 feet above the valley floor. Rolling terrain extends to the southwest and west.

Cimate: Ideal solar radiation and cold air drainage produce extreme temperature inversions and low minimum temperatures. A location 300 miles from the Gulf of Mexico provides a safe distance from the direct effects of hurricanes, but the area does receive heavy rains from these storms. Temperatures occasionally drop to freezing. The average growing season is 239 days, from the first freeze at the beginning of November to the last at the end of March.

Winter mildness: 69	**Seasonal affect:** 46
Summer mildness: 32	**Hazardousness:** 70
Score: 66.85	**Rank: 118**

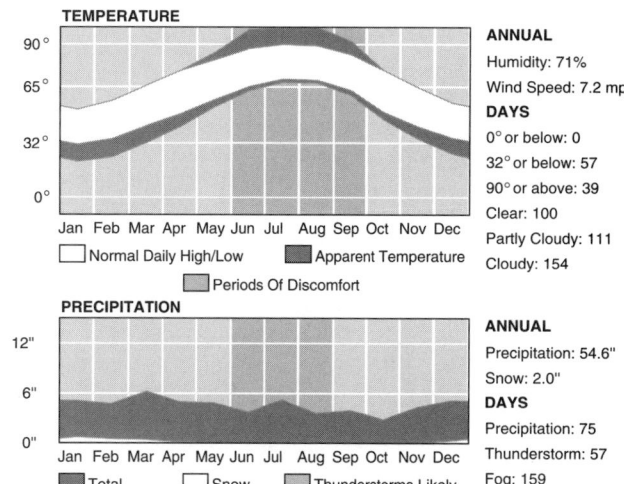

ANNUAL
Humidity: 71%
Wind Speed: 7.2 mph
DAYS
0° or below: 0
32° or below: 57
90° or above: 39
Clear: 100
Partly Cloudy: 111
Cloudy: 154

ANNUAL
Precipitation: 54.6"
Snow: 2.0"
DAYS
Precipitation: 75
Thunderstorm: 57
Fog: 159

Bismarck, ND

Location: 46.46 N, 100.45 W, at 1,650 feet, on the east bank of the Missouri River in south central North Dakota, near the center of the North American landmass.

Landscape: The capital city sits in a shallow basin 7 miles wide and 11 miles long. The closest hills, about 3 miles away, are 200 feet to 300 feet high. To the west, across the river, the land is hilly with higher altitudes.

Cimate: Semiarid Continental in character, and invigorating. The temperature range from summer's hottest to winter's coldest is 135 degrees, typical of the northern Great Plains. In summer, readings of 100°F or more may be expected 6 years out of 10. Readings of -30°F in winter are seen 7 years out of 10. January averages just 8°F, while July averages 71°F. The first freeze is around September 23, the last around May 13. Wind is often steady, and clothes dry quickly on the line.

Winter mildness: 3	**Seasonal affect:** 72
Summer mildness: 60	**Hazardousness:** 27
Score: 13.03	**Rank: 308**

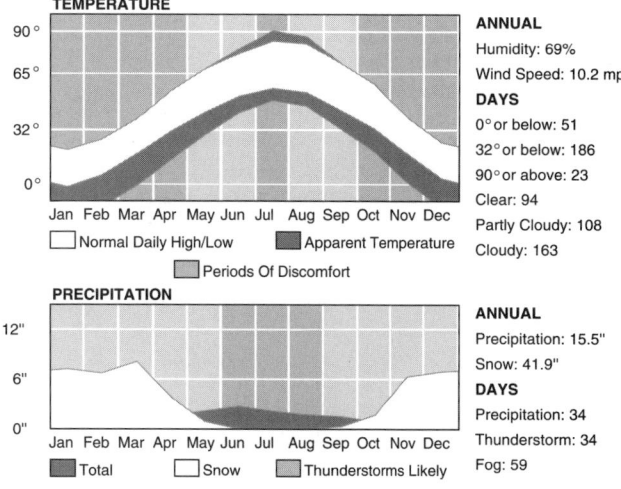

ANNUAL
Humidity: 69%
Wind Speed: 10.2 mph
DAYS
0° or below: 51
32° or below: 186
90° or above: 23
Clear: 94
Partly Cloudy: 108
Cloudy: 163

ANNUAL
Precipitation: 15.5"
Snow: 41.9"
DAYS
Precipitation: 34
Thunderstorm: 34
Fog: 59

Boise, ID

Location: 43.34 N, 116.13 W, at 2,840 feet, cradled in the valley of the Boise River about 8 miles below the mouth of a mountain canyon, where the valley widens.

Landscape: The Boise Mountains rise to a height of 5,000 feet to 6,000 feet within 8 miles. Their slopes are partially mantled with sagebrush and chaparral, changing to stands of fir, spruce, and pine trees higher up.

Cimate: Upland Continental climate in summer with periods of cloudy, stormy, and mild weather almost every winter. The cause of this modification in the winter months is the flow of warm, moist Pacific air—the Chinook winds. Summer hot spells rarely last longer than a few days, but temperatures may reach 100°F. However, due to the low humidity, the average July evening temperature of 62°F is comfortable. The last freeze arrives around Memorial Day, the first in mid-September. In general, the climate is dry and temperate, with enough variation to be stimulating.

Winter mildness: 49   **Seasonal affect:** 78
Summer mildness: 28   **Hazardousness:** 78
Score: 85.26   **Rank: 53**

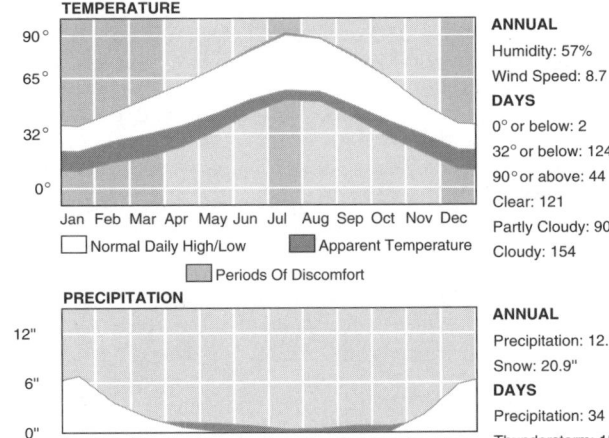

ANNUAL
Humidity: 57%
Wind Speed: 8.7 mph
DAYS
0° or below: 2
32° or below: 124
90° or above: 44
Clear: 121
Partly Cloudy: 90
Cloudy: 154

ANNUAL
Precipitation: 12.1"
Snow: 20.9"
DAYS
Precipitation: 34
Thunderstorm: 15
Fog: 51

Boston, MA-NH

Location: 42.22 N, 71.02 W, at 20 feet, at the mouths of the Mystic and Charles rivers, on Massachusetts Bay.

Landscape: The western section of Massachusetts Bay is called Boston Bay, and its innermost part is called Boston Harbor, a large, sheltered body of water studded with many small islands, known as the Harbor Islands. One of the finest natural harbors in the United States, the city is New England's most important seaport. Sections of Boston are rolling; two of the more famous hills are Beacon Hill in Boston and Bunker Hill in Charlestown.

Cimate: The Atlantic greatly influences the climate roughly described as damp, changeable, and relatively mild considering its northern location. Sea breezes moderate the temperature in both summer and winter. The first freeze is around mid-October; the last is in early May. Rain is plentiful and well distributed throughout the year. Greater Boston receives a great amount of snow, though in the city and south it often becomes sleet with little accumulation.

Winter mildness: 49   **Seasonal affect:** 53
Summer mildness: 78   **Hazardousness:** 37
Score: 59.20   **Rank: 145**

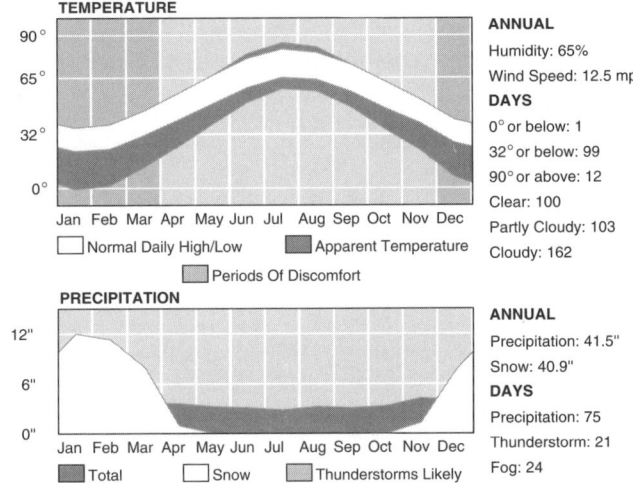

ANNUAL
Humidity: 65%
Wind Speed: 12.5 mph
DAYS
0° or below: 1
32° or below: 99
90° or above: 12
Clear: 100
Partly Cloudy: 103
Cloudy: 162

ANNUAL
Precipitation: 41.5"
Snow: 40.9"
DAYS
Precipitation: 75
Thunderstorm: 21
Fog: 24

Brownsville-Harlingen-San Benito, TX

Location: 25.54 N, 97.26 W, at 20 feet, at the extreme southern tip of Texas on the Mexican border. After Honolulu and Miami, this is the southernmost metro area in America.

Landscape: The Gulf of Mexico is 18 miles to the east. More than half the land toward the coast consists of tidal marshlands, which have the net effect of "moving" the coast 10 miles nearer to the city. The Rio Grande winds through the city, making Brownsville a port with a deepwater channel to the Gulf of Mexico. The fertile valley between the coastal prairie and the western desert flourishes with palm trees and bougainvillea as well as citrus groves.

Cimate: Humid Subtropical. Citrus fruits, cotton, and warm weather vegetables thrive. Man-made irrigation, used for all the crops, adds to the humidity. Summer temperatures are in the lower 90s in the day and middle 70s at night. Gulf breezes help temper the summer heat. The normal daily January minimum is 51°F, making this a popular tourist spot in the winter.

Winter mildness: 97   **Seasonal affect:** 82
Summer mildness: 10   **Hazardousness:** 92
Score: 88.66   **Rank: 41**

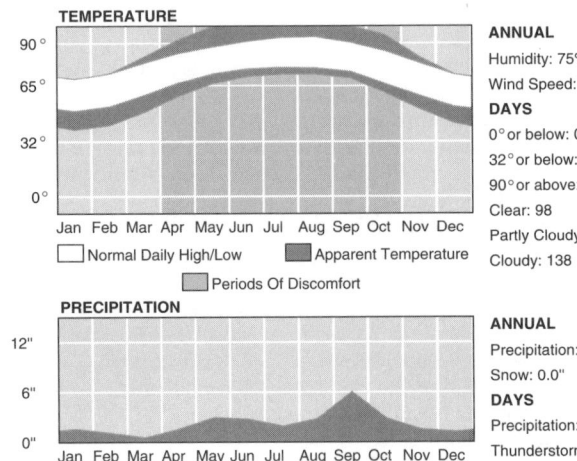

ANNUAL
Humidity: 75%
Wind Speed: 11.4 mph
DAYS
0° or below: 0
32° or below: 2
90° or above: 116
Clear: 98
Partly Cloudy: 129
Cloudy: 138

ANNUAL
Precipitation: 26.6"
Snow: 0.0"
DAYS
Precipitation: 40
Thunderstorm: 27
Fog: 112

Bryan-College Station, TX

Location: 30.35 N, 96.22 W, at 320 feet, on the Brazos River in east central Texas; 100 miles northeast of Austin, the state capital.

Landscape: Part of the Blacklands area of the Coastal Plains. Streams wind through oak and hickory woods. Elm, sycamore, and cottonwood are also common. Once a center of large plantations, the soil allows a broad range of agricultural efforts, including vineyards.

Cimate: Spring arrives early with daytime temperatures in March in the 70s. The last freeze is around March 7. Thunderstorms occur in every month, peaking in May and June. Summers are long and hot, unrelieved by moderate temperatures at night. Winters are comparatively mild, with an occasional freezing day and a rare trace of snow. The area can be frost-free up to 300 days in a mild year. The first real freeze is at the end of November. The annual precipitation of 30 to 40 inches falls mostly during the growing season.

Winter mildness: 86 **Seasonal affect:** 82
Summer mildness: 9 **Hazardousness:** 73
Score: 73.65 **Rank: 94**

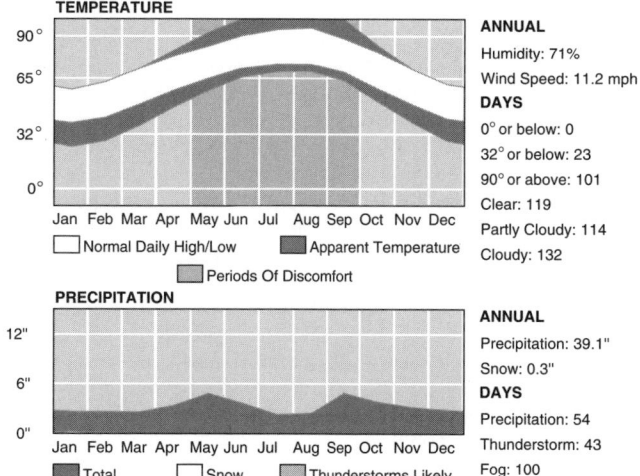

TEMPERATURE

Normal Daily High/Low — Apparent Temperature
Periods Of Discomfort

PRECIPITATION

Total — Snow — Thunderstorms Likely

ANNUAL
Humidity: 71%
Wind Speed: 11.2 mph
DAYS
0° or below: 0
32° or below: 23
90° or above: 101
Clear: 119
Partly Cloudy: 114
Cloudy: 132

ANNUAL
Precipitation: 39.1"
Snow: 0.3"
DAYS
Precipitation: 54
Thunderstorm: 43
Fog: 100

Buffalo-Niagara Falls, NY

Location: 42.56 N, 78.44 W, at 710 feet, at the eastern end of Lake Erie, which is 9 miles to the southwest; Lake Ontario is 25 miles north. The two lakes are connected by the Niagara River and the famous falls of the same name.

Landscape: The surrounding country is comparatively low and level to the west, and gently rolling east and south, rising to pronounced hills within 12 to 18 miles. At a point 35 miles south-southeast of the city, the elevation rises to 1,000 feet above Lake Erie.

Cimate: The weather here is varied and changeable. Wide seasonal swings of temperature are tempered somewhat by the surrounding lakes. Spring comes late primarily because of the ice buildup and cold water on Lake Erie. The last freeze is around May 19. Summers are mild, with more sun here than anywhere else in the state. Thunderstorms are infrequent. Autumn has long, dry periods and is frost-free until mid-October. Winters are famous for snow: 90 inches are expected each year.

Winter mildness: 35 **Seasonal affect:** 20
Summer mildness: 86 **Hazardousness:** 1
Score: 19.26 **Rank: 286**

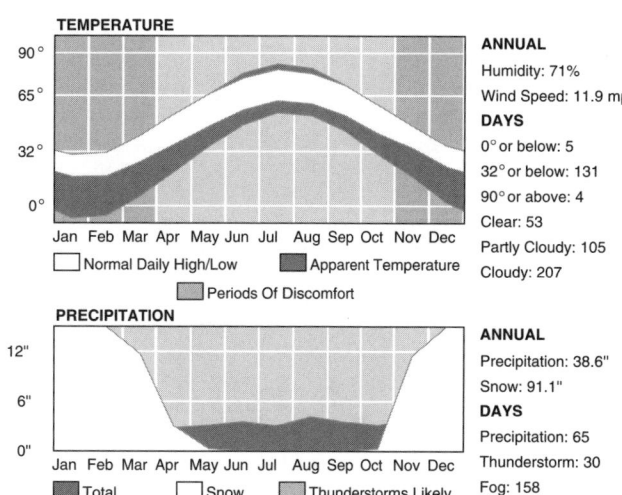

TEMPERATURE

Normal Daily High/Low — Apparent Temperature
Periods Of Discomfort

PRECIPITATION

Total — Snow — Thunderstorms Likely

ANNUAL
Humidity: 71%
Wind Speed: 11.9 mph
DAYS
0° or below: 5
32° or below: 131
90° or above: 4
Clear: 53
Partly Cloudy: 105
Cloudy: 207

ANNUAL
Precipitation: 38.6"
Snow: 91.1"
DAYS
Precipitation: 65
Thunderstorm: 30
Fog: 158

Burlington, VT

Location: 44.28 N, 73.09 W, at 330 feet, on the eastern shore of Lake Champlain; 75 miles south of Montreal, Quebec.

Landscape: The highest peaks of the Adirondacks in New York state are visible 35 miles west across the lake. Vermont's Green Mountain foothills begin 10 miles to the east and southeast. Northern white pine, eastern hemlock, maple, oak, and beech are common trees in the surrounding forest.

Cimate: The northerly latitude assures the variety and vigor of a true New England climate. The last freeze here is in late May. The summer, while not long, is pleasant. Fall is cool; the first freeze occurs in late September. Winters are cold, with brief, intense cold snaps formed by high-pressure systems moving down from central Canada and Hudson Bay. Lake Champlain's tempering effect produces temperatures along the lakeshore from 5 to 10 degrees warmer than those at the airport, 3.5 miles inland. This is one of the cloudiest cities in the United States.

Winter mildness: 8 **Seasonal affect:** 16
Summer mildness: 82 **Hazardousness:** 20
Score: 9.06 **Rank: 322**

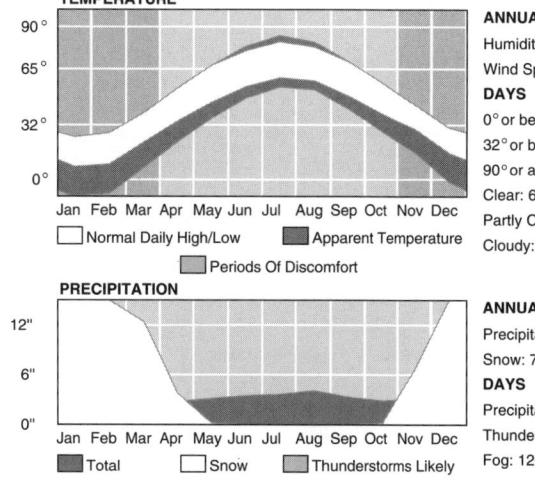

TEMPERATURE

Normal Daily High/Low — Apparent Temperature
Periods Of Discomfort

PRECIPITATION

Total — Snow — Thunderstorms Likely

ANNUAL
Humidity: 68%
Wind Speed: 9.0 mph
DAYS
0° or below: 28
32° or below: 157
90° or above: 6
Clear: 60
Partly Cloudy: 102
Cloudy: 203

ANNUAL
Precipitation: 34.5"
Snow: 76.9"
DAYS
Precipitation: 75
Thunderstorm: 22
Fog: 120

Calgary, AB

Location: 51.06 N, 114.01 W, at 3,501 feet; less than 50 miles east of the Continental Divide in southern Alberta.

Landscape: The Elbow and Bow rivers provide strong relief in an otherwise large, treeless tract of undulating prairie grassland. Rocky Mountain foothills begin rising west of the city. In the east, gently rolling ground meets flat prairie land.

Cimate: Continental, with strong temperature contrasts between day and night as well as summer and winter. Situated on the eastern side of the Rockies, the area rarely enjoys the moderating effects of the Pacific. Embedded in the zone of westerly winds, changing seasons are marked by northerly air circulation in winter and occasional instances of moist, tropical air from the Gulf of Mexico bringing heavy rainfall in the summer. The higher elevation of the city contributes to longer winters and shorter summers. Temperatures are influenced by the northerly latitude, as well as the location on a valley floor.

Winter mildness: 3	**Seasonal affect:** 65
Summer mildness: 97	**Hazardousness:** 13
Score: 36.26	**Rank:** 226

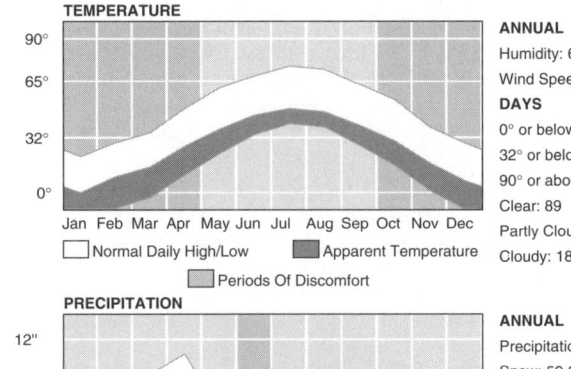

ANNUAL
Humidity: 64%
Wind Speed: 10.1 mph
DAYS
0° or below: 33
32° or below: 201
90° or above: 5
Clear: 89
Partly Cloudy: 88
Cloudy: 188

ANNUAL
Precipitation: 16.7"
Snow: 59.9"
DAYS
Precipitation: 36
Thunderstorm: 25
Fog: 22

Casper, WY

Location: 42.55 N, 106.28 W, at 5,340 feet, in east central Wyoming in the North Platte River valley; 170 miles north of Cheyenne.

Landscape: The surrounding countryside is rolling and hilly with considerable flat prairie land used mostly for grazing sheep and cattle. Chief vegetation is sagebrush or shadscale, with a mixture of short grasses. To the south, the Casper Range of the Laramie Mountains and Medicine Bow National Forest rise 3,500 feet above the valley floor.

Cimate: Rather dry due to the effective moisture barrier of the Cascades, the Sierra Nevada, and the Rocky Mountains, which block most of the moist Pacific winds. Summertime precipitation is almost all in the form of thunderstorms, which generally provide ample moisture for grasslands. Annual snowfall averages 79 inches, but the winter season is not severe. The dryness of the air prevents discomfort during both the warm summer months and winter cold snaps. Summer highs average 84°F, winter lows 15°F. The first freeze is in mid-September, the last in mid-May.

Winter mildness: 15	**Seasonal affect:** 80
Summer mildness: 43	**Hazardousness:** 0
Score: 8.21	**Rank:** 325

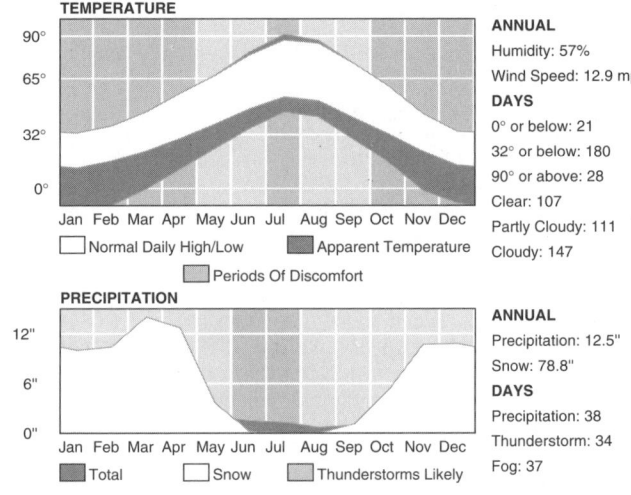

ANNUAL
Humidity: 57%
Wind Speed: 12.9 mph
DAYS
0° or below: 21
32° or below: 180
90° or above: 28
Clear: 107
Partly Cloudy: 111
Cloudy: 147

ANNUAL
Precipitation: 12.5"
Snow: 78.8"
DAYS
Precipitation: 38
Thunderstorm: 34
Fog: 37

Charleston-North Charleston, SC

Location: 32.47 N, 79.56 W, at 10 feet, on the south Atlantic coast; 113 miles from Columbia, the state capital.

Landscape: The traditional geography lesson of Charleston school children states that "Charleston is the place where the Ashley and Cooper Rivers meet to form the Atlantic Ocean." Its peninsula terrain is generally level and the soil is sandy to sandy loam. Because of the low elevation, a portion of the city and nearby coastal islands are vulnerable to tidal flooding.

Cimate: Generally temperate, modified considerably by the ocean. Summer is warm and humid, but temperatures over 100°F are infrequent. Forty percent of the annual rainfall occurs then. The fall passes from an Indian summer to the pre-winter cold spells that begin in November. The weather is pleasantly cool and sunny from late September to early November. Winters are mild; temperatures of 20°F or less are unusual. Spring is warm, windy, and changeable. Most storms occur then.

Winter mildness: 88	**Seasonal affect:** 49
Summer mildness: 41	**Hazardousness:** 68
Score: 83.28	**Rank:** 60

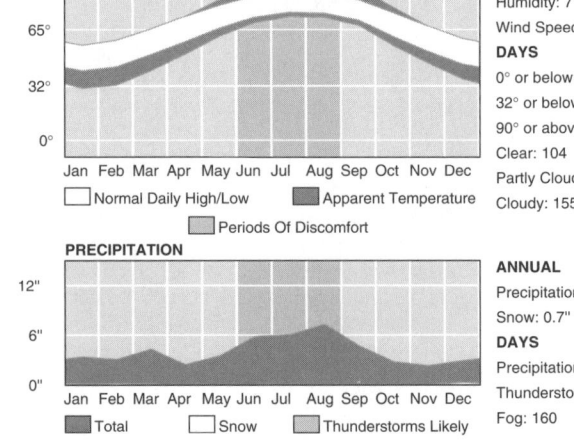

ANNUAL
Humidity: 71%
Wind Speed: 8.6 mph
DAYS
0° or below: 0
32° or below: 34
90° or above: 52
Clear: 104
Partly Cloudy: 106
Cloudy: 155

ANNUAL
Precipitation: 48.5"
Snow: 0.7"
DAYS
Precipitation: 74
Thunderstorm: 58
Fog: 160

Charleston, WV

Location: 38.22 N, 81.36 W, at 1,020 feet, in the western foothills of the Allegheny Mountains at the junction of the Kanawha and Elk rivers.

Landscape: Forested hills and valleys. The surrounding hilltops are around 1,100 feet above sea level, about 500 feet higher than the valleys. Forests are oak, beech, maple, sweet chestnut, and birch. In spite of extensive clear-cutting to make room for coal production and petrochemical plants, remnants of the ancient Appalachian oak forest can still be seen here.

Cimate: Hot Continental, characterized by sharp temperature contrasts, both seasonal and day-to-day. May through September is generally warm; November through March moderately cold. The last freeze is at the beginning of May, the first at the beginning of October. Cold spells in winter don't last long. Ample precipitation is well distributed throughout the year, with a maximum in July and a minimum in October. Charleston experiences 236 fog days per year, more than any other major city in North America.

Winter mildness: 53	**Seasonal affect:** 3
Summer mildness: 52	**Hazardousness:** 40
Score: 51.27	**Rank: 173**

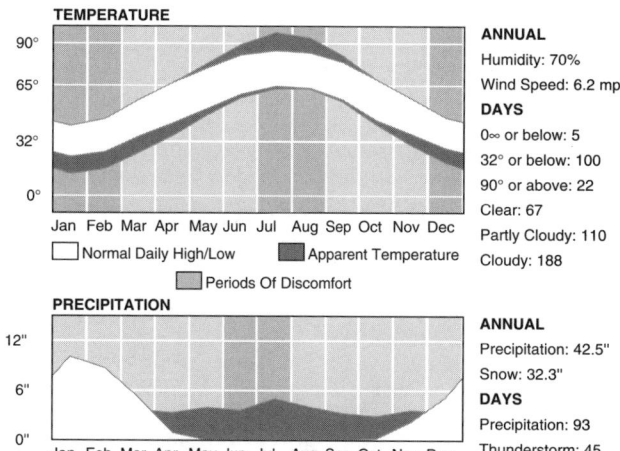

TEMPERATURE

□ Normal Daily High/Low ■ Apparent Temperature
▨ Periods Of Discomfort

PRECIPITATION

■ Total □ Snow ▨ Thunderstorms Likely

ANNUAL
Humidity: 70%
Wind Speed: 6.2 mph
DAYS
0∞ or below: 5
32° or below: 100
90° or above: 22
Clear: 67
Partly Cloudy: 110
Cloudy: 188

ANNUAL
Precipitation: 42.5"
Snow: 32.3"
DAYS
Precipitation: 93
Thunderstorm: 45
Fog: 236

Charlotte-Gastonia-Rock Hill, NC-SC

Location: 35.13 N, 80.56 W, at 720 feet, in the southern Piedmont; 137 miles southwest of Raleigh, NC, and 92 miles north of Columbia, SC.

Landscape: Sits amid rolling country between mountains 80 miles to the west and the Coastal Plain to the east. Once covered by the eastern hardwood forest, there are still wooded areas of oak, hickory, birch, beech, and maple.

Cimate: Moderate, with cool winters and summers that are quite warm. The mountains have a moderating effect on winter temperatures, causing appreciable warming of cold air coming from the west and northwest. The ocean is too distant to affect summer weather, but it moderates the winter, which is changeable, alternating between mild and cool spells, with occasional cold periods. Snow is infrequent, occurring an average of once a month from December through March. Summers are long and warm, with afternoon temperatures frequently in the 90s. Nights are cooler, with temperatures dropping into the low 70s. The first freeze occurs around November 1, the last in early April.

Winter mildness: 66	**Seasonal affect:** 40
Summer mildness: 38	**Hazardousness:** 78
Score: 72.80	**Rank: 97**

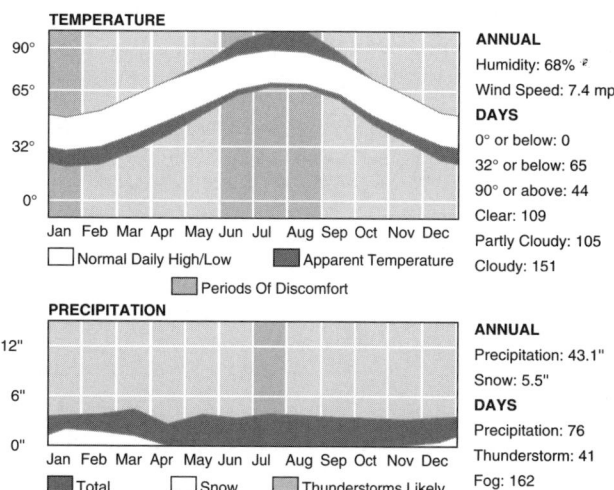

TEMPERATURE

□ Normal Daily High/Low ■ Apparent Temperature
▨ Periods Of Discomfort

PRECIPITATION

■ Total □ Snow ▨ Thunderstorms Likely

ANNUAL
Humidity: 68%
Wind Speed: 7.4 mph
DAYS
0° or below: 0
32° or below: 65
90° or above: 44
Clear: 109
Partly Cloudy: 105
Cloudy: 151

ANNUAL
Precipitation: 43.1"
Snow: 5.5"
DAYS
Precipitation: 76
Thunderstorm: 41
Fog: 162

Charlottesville, VA

Location: 38.02 N, 78.31 W, at 870 feet, in the center of Virginia's Albemarle County on the central Piedmont Plateau; 110 miles southwest of Washington, DC.

Landscape: Among the red clay foothills of the Blue Ridge Mountains to the west. Topography is rolling to quite steep. Elevations range from 300 to 800 feet, with some points in the Blue Ridge as high as 3,200 feet. The Rivana River marks the eastern border. Approaches to the natural bowl are through wooded hills, orchards, and fertile pastures.

Cimate: Modified Continental, with mild winters and warm, humid summers. The mountains produce various steering and blocking effects on storms and air masses. Chesapeake Bay to the east further modifies the climate, making it warmer in winter, cooler in summer. Precipitation is well distributed throughout the year, with the maximum in July, the minimum in January. First freeze is around November 4, the last around April 7. Tornadoes and violent storms are rare, but severe thunderstorms occur each year.

Winter mildness: 59	**Seasonal affect:** 68
Summer mildness: 48	**Hazardousness:** 53
Score: 71.38	**Rank: 102**

TEMPERATURE

□ Normal Daily High/Low ■ Apparent Temperature
▨ Periods Of Discomfort

PRECIPITATION

■ Total □ Snow ▨ Thunderstorms Likely

ANNUAL
Humidity: 67%
Wind Speed: 7.7 mph
DAYS
0° or below: 0
32° or below: 87
90° or above: 31
Clear: 112
Partly Cloudy: 107
Cloudy: 146

ANNUAL
Precipitation: 47.3"
Snow: 24.2"
DAYS
Precipitation: 72
Thunderstorm: 39
Fog: 122

Chattanooga, TN-GA

Location: 35.02 N, 85.12 W, at 690 feet, in the southern portion of the Great Valley of the Tennessee River, between the Cumberland Mountains to the west and the Appalachian Mountains to the east.

Landscape: Local topography is complex, with the difference in elevation between minor valleys and ridges being as much as 500 feet. Most of the city lies south of the river and is almost completely surrounded by steep mountains. Nearby Signal Mountain overlooks the "Grand Canyon of the Tennessee," where the Tennessee River cuts a gorge 1,000 feet deep.

Cimate: Moderate Continental, with cool winters and summers that are quite warm. In winter the Cumberlands have a moderating influence on the local climate. Winter weather is changeable and alternates between cool spells and an occasional cold period. Extreme or prolonged cold is rare. Summer temperatures average in the high 80s or low 90s. Most afternoon summer temperatures are modified by brief thundershowers, which cause the mercury to drop 10 degrees to 15 degrees.

Winter mildness: 63	**Seasonal affect:** 25
Summer mildness: 37	**Hazardousness:** 69
Score: 64.58	**Rank: 126**

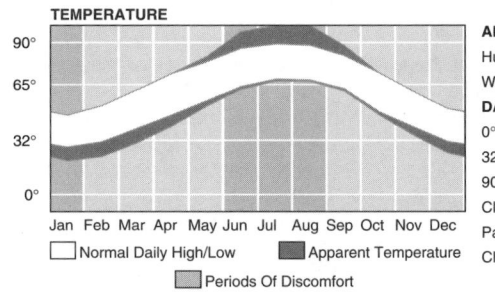

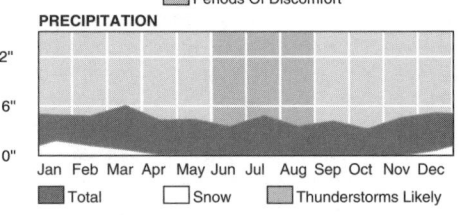

ANNUAL
Humidity: 71%
Wind Speed: 6.0 mph
DAYS
0° or below: 0
32° or below: 73
90° or above: 48
Clear: 105
Partly Cloudy: 108
Cloudy: 152

ANNUAL
Precipitation: 53.5"
Snow: 4.4"
DAYS
Precipitation: 83
Thunderstorm: 55
Fog: 160

Cheyenne, WY

Location: 41.09 N, 104.49 W, at 6,120 feet, on a broad plateau between the North and South Platte rivers in extreme southeastern Wyoming.

Landscape: The surrounding country is mostly rolling prairie, rising rapidly to the Laramie Mountains, 9,000 feet high and 30 miles west. Short prairie grasses, greasewood, and sagebrush grow in the highly alkaline soil.

Cimate: Continental, with characteristics of large daily and annual temperature ranges. Freezes arrive in early September and depart by June 1. Cheyenne lies in the wind shadow of the Laramie Mountain ridge, which spares it from some of the cold air masses blowing down from Canada. While strong winds are noticeable, they are from a westerly direction and tend to raise the temperature. Lying in the lee of the mountain also prevents moisture from reaching the area, producing a semiarid climate. Showers, thunderstorms, and hail are not infrequent. There may be heavy snows through early May and freezes occurring as late as mid-June.

Winter mildness: 26	**Seasonal affect:** 88
Summer mildness: 76	**Hazardousness:** 0
Score: 40.22	**Rank: 212**

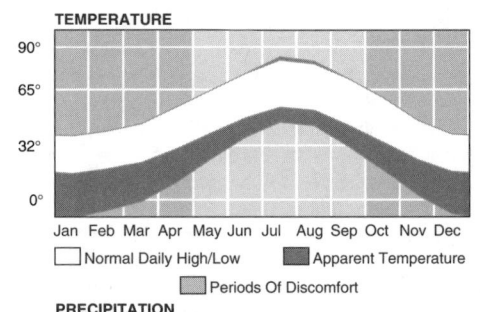

ANNUAL
Humidity: 55%
Wind Speed: 12.9 mph
DAYS
0° or below: 12
32° or below: 173
90° or above: 9
Clear: 109
Partly Cloudy: 126
Cloudy: 130

ANNUAL
Precipitation: 14.4"
Snow: 55.2"
DAYS
Precipitation: 28
Thunderstorm: 50
Fog: 58

Chicago, IL

Location: 41.44 N, 87.46 W, at 620 feet, on a plain along the southwest shore of Lake Michigan which, for the most part, is only some tens of feet above the lake.

Landscape: Because the surrounding land is flat, topography does not significantly affect airflow in or near the city, except that lower frictional drag over Lake Michigan permits winds to be frequently stronger along the lakeshore. Chicago has been appropriately nicknamed "The Windy City."

Cimate: Predominantly Continental, with warm to hot summers and cold winters. The first freeze occurs in mid-October, the last in the beginning of May. Lake Michigan exerts a strong influence on the city's climate. Summer temperatures near the shore are often 10 degrees cooler than the city proper. Hot spells bring an uncomfortable combination of high temperature and high humidity, which may last for several days, then end abruptly with a shift of winds to the north or northwest. They are often accompanied by thunderstorms.

Winter mildness: 25	**Seasonal affect:** 40
Summer mildness: 60	**Hazardousness:** 21
Score: 16.14	**Rank: 297**

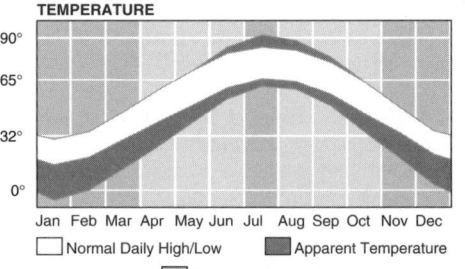

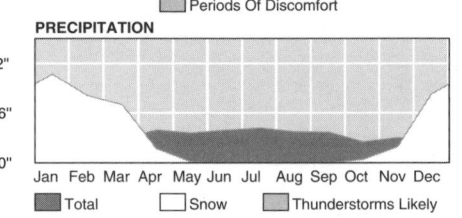

ANNUAL
Humidity: 70%
Wind Speed: 10.4 mph
DAYS
0° or below: 7
32° or below: 132
90° or above: 17
Clear: 85
Partly Cloudy: 106
Cloudy: 174

ANNUAL
Precipitation: 37.4"
Snow: 38.2"
DAYS
Precipitation: 67
Thunderstorm: 38
Fog: 124

★Chico-Paradise, CA

Location: 39.42 N, 121.49 W, at 190 feet, in the Sierra Nevada foothills along the eastern edge of the Sacramento Valley; 90 miles north of Sacramento, the state capital.

Landscape: Chaparral Province where steep slopes climb steadily to high mountains. Stream-cut canyons drain to the Sacramento River. Tall digger pine and blue oak dominate the forest. Between valley and mountain, there is a transitional mix of chaparral-covered rounded hills, pine forests, and open grassy fields. The area is noted for almond production. Paradise is 1,010 feet higher than Chico.

Cimate: Temperate Continental, high enough to feel the bite of four seasons. Protected from ocean influences, summers are longer, winters colder, and there is a greater range of daily and seasonal temperatures. The first freeze is late—around November 15; the last an early March 28. Winter winds tend to blow from the northwest bringing isotherms in a north-south parallel with the contours of the mountains. This is the rainy season. Summer is long and dry.

Winter mildness: 77	**Seasonal affect:** 86
Summer mildness: 9	**Hazardousness:** 95
Score: 94.61	**Rank: 20**

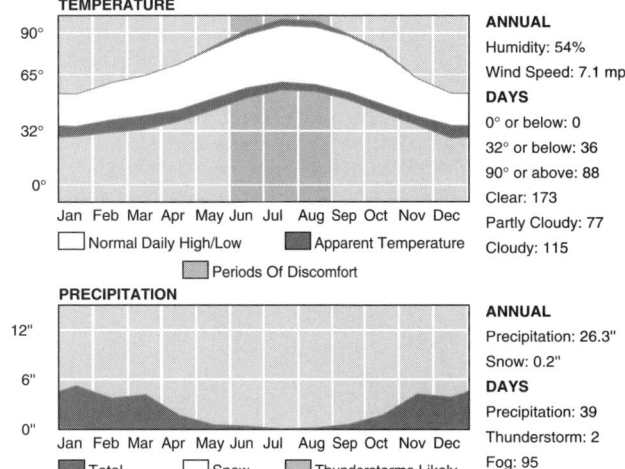

TEMPERATURE

☐ Normal Daily High/Low   ■ Apparent Temperature
▨ Periods Of Discomfort

PRECIPITATION

■ Total   ☐ Snow   ▨ Thunderstorms Likely

ANNUAL
Humidity: 54%
Wind Speed: 7.1 mph
DAYS
0° or below: 0
32° or below: 36
90° or above: 88
Clear: 173
Partly Cloudy: 77
Cloudy: 115

ANNUAL
Precipitation: 26.3"
Snow: 0.2"
DAYS
Precipitation: 39
Thunderstorm: 2
Fog: 95

Cincinnati, OH-KY-IN

Location: 39.06 N, 84.31 W, at 683 feet, on the north bank of the Ohio River; 103 miles southwest of Columbus, the state capital.

Landscape: The city extends over two ranges of hills bisected by the Mill Creek Valley, with hills extending some 400 feet above the valley floor. Metro Cincinnati incorporates the lower portion of the Little Miami Valley to the east and extends to within 5 or 6 miles of the Great Miami Valley to the west.

Cimate: Basically moderate Continental, with a twenty degree range in daily temperatures. December is the coldest month with the average high at 37°F. In July the average temperature is 85°F. Changes in regional weather are frequent due to the passage of numerous cyclonic storms in winter and spring, and thunderstorms during the summer. Fall is pleasant, with the least rainfall of any season, an abundance of sunshine, and comfortable temperatures. The first freeze is around October 12, the last is late April.

Winter mildness: 44	**Seasonal affect:** 21
Summer mildness: 54	**Hazardousness:** 49
Score: 39.37	**Rank: 215**

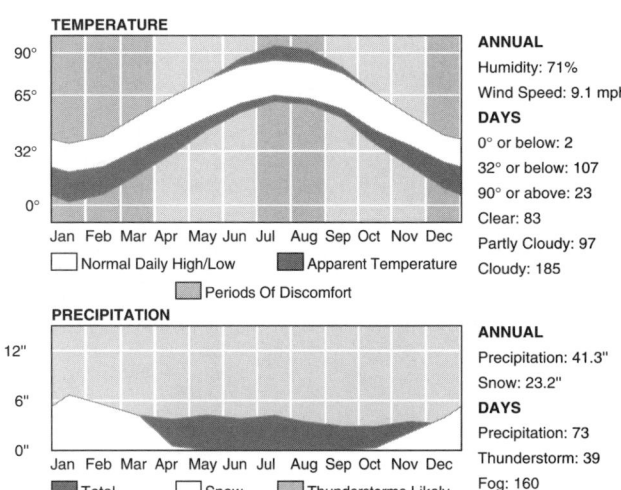

TEMPERATURE

☐ Normal Daily High/Low   ■ Apparent Temperature
▨ Periods Of Discomfort

PRECIPITATION

■ Total   ☐ Snow   ▨ Thunderstorms Likely

ANNUAL
Humidity: 71%
Wind Speed: 9.1 mph
DAYS
0° or below: 2
32° or below: 107
90° or above: 23
Clear: 83
Partly Cloudy: 97
Cloudy: 185

ANNUAL
Precipitation: 41.3"
Snow: 23.2"
DAYS
Precipitation: 73
Thunderstorm: 39
Fog: 160

Cleveland-Lorain-Elyria, OH

Location: 41.25 N, 81.52 W, at 770 feet, situated on the south shore of Lake Erie, with a lake frontage of 31 miles.

Landscape: The lake is a major feature of local topography. The surrounding terrain is mostly level. The Cuyahoga River flows in a north-south valley, which bisects the city. A ridge at the southeastern edge of the city rises some 500 feet above shore level.

Cimate: The city lies in the path of cold winter air masses, which advance south and east out of Canada. Extreme low temperatures are modified as the air passes over the comparatively warm water of the lake. But this also means considerable winter cloudiness and frequent snows. Throughout the year, one of three days is foggy. Spring is generally a brief transition period. The last freeze is around May 4. Summer heat is also moderated by the lake. Fall is the most pleasant season, with mild, sunny weather often extending into November or even early December. The first freeze is in mid-October.

Winter mildness: 39	**Seasonal affect:** 9
Summer mildness: 75	**Hazardousness:** 6
Score: 16.43	**Rank: 296**

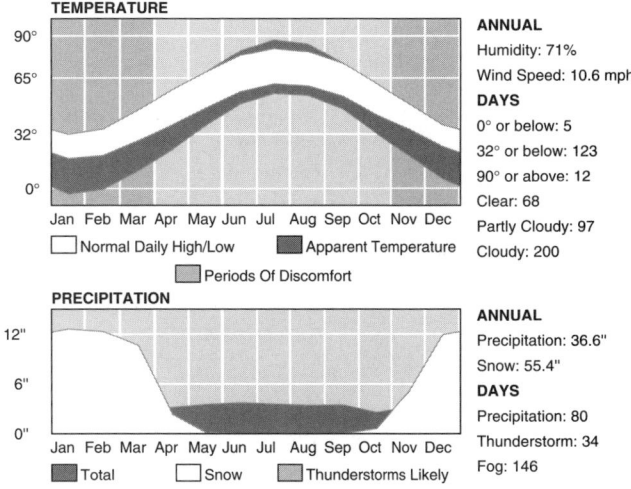

TEMPERATURE

☐ Normal Daily High/Low   ■ Apparent Temperature
▨ Periods Of Discomfort

PRECIPITATION

■ Total   ☐ Snow   ▨ Thunderstorms Likely

ANNUAL
Humidity: 71%
Wind Speed: 10.6 mph
DAYS
0° or below: 5
32° or below: 123
90° or above: 12
Clear: 68
Partly Cloudy: 97
Cloudy: 200

ANNUAL
Precipitation: 36.6"
Snow: 55.4"
DAYS
Precipitation: 80
Thunderstorm: 34
Fog: 146

Colorado Springs, CO

Location: 38.49 N, 104.43 W, at 6,090 feet, on the eastern slope of Colorado's Rocky Mountains; 75 miles south of Denver.

Landscape: Relatively flat and gently undulating semiarid prairie land of eastern Colorado. Here the high plains prairie with its typical short grasses and woody shrubs abruptly meets the Rocky Mountain foothills with their stands of mixed spruce-fir forests. Immediately to the west, the mountains rise abruptly to heights ranging from 10,000 feet to 14,000 feet. The land slopes upward to the north, reaching an average height of 8,000 feet within 20 miles at the top of Palmer Lake Divide.

Cimate: Continental, moderated by outlying elevations gives this area the pleasant plains-and-mountain mixture of climate that has established it as a resort. Precipitation is generally light, with 80 percent falling as rain from April to October. The last freeze is around May 3; the first is October 12. Temperatures are on the mild side for a city in this latitude and at this elevation.

Winter mildness: 30	**Seasonal affect:** 91
Summer mildness: 60	**Hazardousness:** 5
Score: 58.64	**Rank: 147**

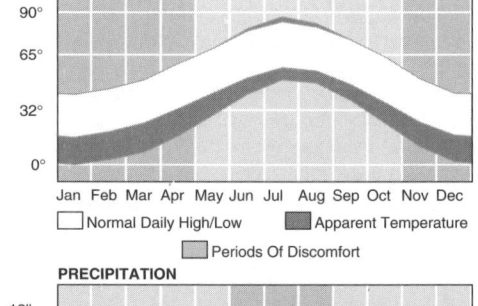

ANNUAL
Humidity: 52%
Wind Speed: 10.0 mph
DAYS
0° or below: 7
32° or below: 160
90° or above: 19
Clear: 128
Partly Cloudy: 120
Cloudy: 117

ANNUAL
Precipitation: 16.2"
Snow: 42.6"
DAYS
Precipitation: 27
Thunderstorm: 50
Fog: 55

Columbia, MO

Location: 38.49 N, 92.13 W, at 890 feet, in northern Missouri in the valley of the Missouri River; 120 miles east of Kansas City, 100 miles west of St. Louis.

Landscape: Gently rolling plains of the broad river valley. The area features ecologies of both prairie and eastern forest. Columbia's elevation is almost 900 feet as the land slopes gradually to the western high prairie.

Cimate: The interior location and wide temperature ranges indicate a Continental climate. The first freeze is around October 16, followed by a moderately cold winter. The latest frost occurs at the beginning of May, followed by a warm and often humid summer. Each summer brings some temperatures over 100°F, and winter lows reach zero two or three times annually. Summer hot spells are often relieved by thunderstorms, and winter cold snaps are often interrupted by days that are almost balmy. The late spring and early summer months are the rainiest, but the rain diminishes by late summer.

Winter mildness: 41	**Seasonal affect:** 61
Summer mildness: 39	**Hazardousness:** 32
Score: 25.77	**Rank: 263**

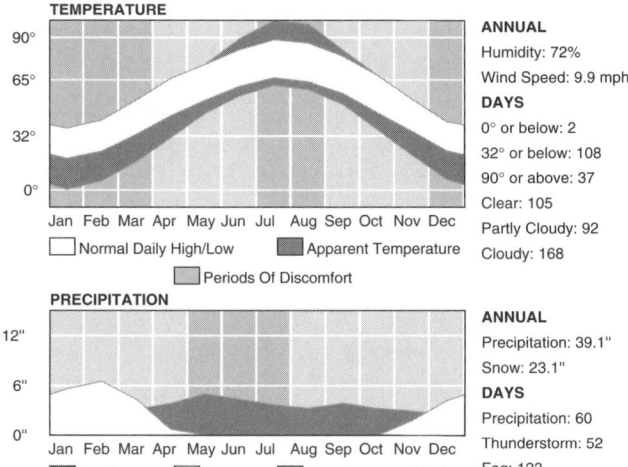

ANNUAL
Humidity: 72%
Wind Speed: 9.9 mph
DAYS
0° or below: 2
32° or below: 108
90° or above: 37
Clear: 105
Partly Cloudy: 92
Cloudy: 168

ANNUAL
Precipitation: 39.1"
Snow: 23.1"
DAYS
Precipitation: 60
Thunderstorm: 52
Fog: 123

Columbia, SC

Location: 33.57 N, 81.07 W, at 210 feet, on the Congaree River in the center of the state, near the confluence of the Broad and Saluda rivers.

Landscape: The fall line between the Piedmont and the Coastal Plain is near here. The soil ranges from sand to clay loam. Terrain is rolling, sloping from about 350 feet above sea level in the northern part of the city to about 200 feet at the city's southeastern edge

Cimate: Although the Appalachians to the north shield the city from northern cold fronts in the winter, the surrounding gently rolling terrain offers little moderating effect on summer heat. Summers are long and hot, with high temperatures from May to September. Temperatures will surpass 100°F an average of six times a year. Winters are mild, only about a third of the days have freezing temperatures. Snow accumulation is rare. Spring is changeable and may bring some violent weather. Fall is cool, pleasant, and sunny. Some grazing crops are grown year-round.

Winter mildness: 72	**Seasonal affect:** 56
Summer mildness: 20	**Hazardousness:** 76
Score: 68.27	**Rank: 113**

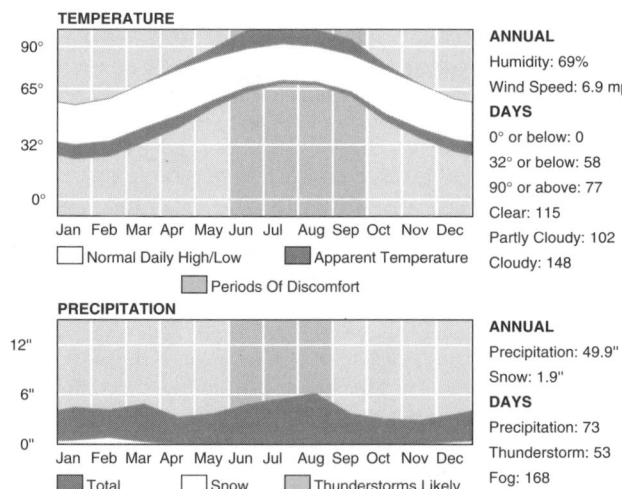

ANNUAL
Humidity: 69%
Wind Speed: 6.9 mph
DAYS
0° or below: 0
32° or below: 58
90° or above: 77
Clear: 115
Partly Cloudy: 102
Cloudy: 148

ANNUAL
Precipitation: 49.9"
Snow: 1.9"
DAYS
Precipitation: 73
Thunderstorm: 53
Fog: 168

Columbus, GA-AL

Location: 32.31 N, 84.57 W, at 450 feet, on the Chattahoochee River at Georgia's western border; about 225 miles west of the Atlantic Ocean, and 170 miles north of the Gulf of Mexico.

Landscape: This is an area between the Coastal Plain and the Piedmont. Elevations range from between 200 feet to 500 feet, though the terrain is basically level and effects of terrain on climate are negligible. The surrounding wooded areas include oak, hickory, and pine.

Cimate: Subtropical, with alternating periods of Maritime with Continental effects. Rainfall averages 50 inches a year. The stormiest and wettest month is July, the driest October. The last freeze is an early March 18. The first freeze is November 10. Snow is rare but by no means unknown, with each winter seeing a few flakes. From June through August most days will see temperatures of 90°F or higher, with uncomfortable humidity. The unpleasant effects of this heat are balanced by mild winters, during which temperatures seldom drop below 20°F.

Winter mildness: 79	**Seasonal affect:** 58
Summer mildness: 19	**Hazardousness:** 81
Score: 76.77	**Rank: 83**

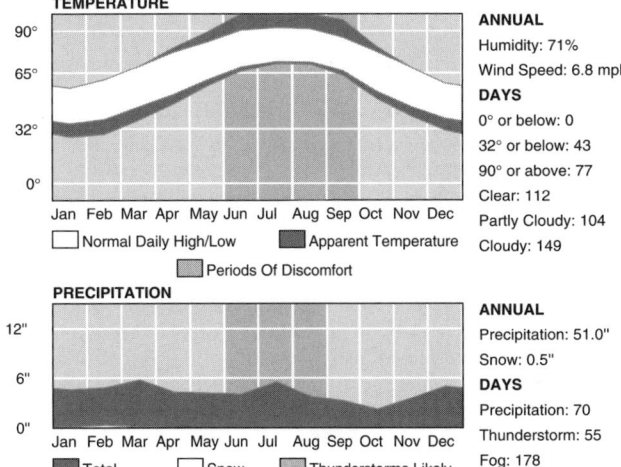

ANNUAL
Humidity: 71%
Wind Speed: 6.8 mph
DAYS
0° or below: 0
32° or below: 43
90° or above: 77
Clear: 112
Partly Cloudy: 104
Cloudy: 149

ANNUAL
Precipitation: 51.0"
Snow: 0.5"
DAYS
Precipitation: 70
Thunderstorm: 55
Fog: 178

Columbus, OH

Location: 0.40 N, 82.53 W, at 810 feet, in the center of Ohio in the drainage area of the Ohio River.

Landscape: Four small rivers—the Scioto, Alum, Big Walnut, and Olentangy—flow through and near the city. These are gorge-like in character with little flood plain. Tall, broad-leafed trees are in wooded areas. Ash, elm, hickory, oak, and maple are common.

Cimate: The city is located in an area of changeable weather. The first freeze is October 6. Cold air masses from central and northwest Canada frequently invade the region. The last frost departs May 3. Tropical Gulf masses often reach central Ohio during the summer but to a much lesser extent in fall and winter. Temperatures in July are in the mid- to high-eighties. Columbus's four rivers provide variations in the micro-climate of the area, contributing to the formation of shallow ground fog at daybreak in the summer and fall.

Winter mildness: 41	**Seasonal affect:** 10
Summer mildness: 66	**Hazardousness:** 43
Score: 44.75	**Rank: 196**

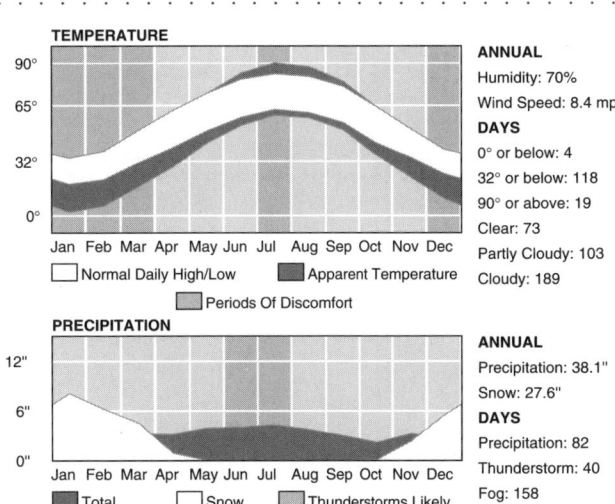

ANNUAL
Humidity: 70%
Wind Speed: 8.4 mph
DAYS
0° or below: 4
32° or below: 118
90° or above: 19
Clear: 73
Partly Cloudy: 103
Cloudy: 189

ANNUAL
Precipitation: 38.1"
Snow: 27.6"
DAYS
Precipitation: 82
Thunderstorm: 40
Fog: 158

Corpus Christi, TX

Location: 27.46 N, 97.30 W, at 40 feet, on Corpus Christi Bay in the southern part of the Texas Gulf coastline, halfway between Galveston to the north and Brownsville to the south.

Landscape: Coastal prairie. Padre and Mustang Islands shelter the harbor from the Gulf. Long sand beaches and occasional salt marshes are common along the bay. Inland to the west are level blacklands, important for agriculture. The Bay is a landlocked harbor connected by deepwater channel to the Gulf of Mexico.

Cimate: Midway between the humid Subtropical conditions of the northeast Gulf Coast and the semiarid Desert ones to the west and southwest. Tropical storms, usual from June through November, add to the total rainfall. Peak rainfall months are May and September. There is little variation in the summer temperature from day to day, averaging in the high 80s or low 90s. Sea breezes bring cooler nights, with temperatures dropping into the low 70s. The freeze-free growing season is long—from mid-February to mid-December.

Winter mildness: 94	**Seasonal affect:** 83
Summer mildness: 10	**Hazardousness:** 89
Score: 84.13	**Rank: 57**

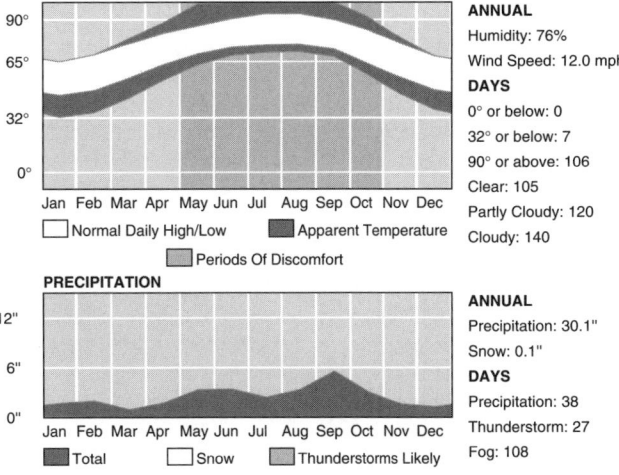

ANNUAL
Humidity: 76%
Wind Speed: 12.0 mph
DAYS
0° or below: 0
32° or below: 7
90° or above: 106
Clear: 105
Partly Cloudy: 120
Cloudy: 140

ANNUAL
Precipitation: 30.1"
Snow: 0.1"
DAYS
Precipitation: 38
Thunderstorm: 27
Fog: 108

Dallas, TX

Location: 32.51 N, 96.51 W, at 440 feet, in north central Texas, 190 miles northeast of Austin, near the headwaters of the Trinity River.

Landscape: Located on flat prairies of the Coastal Plain on both sides of the Trinity River. The area is a gently rolling river valley with ridge-and-bluff relief to the west. Forest-steppe vegetation is characterized by the intermingling of prairie, groves, and strips of deciduous trees. The upland forest is dominated by post oak, blackjack oak, and Texas hickory.

Cimate: Humid, Subtropical, with hot summers. It is also Continental, characterized by a wide range in annual temperature. The first freeze occurs around November 12, the last around March 25. Winters tend to be mild, but northers bring cold air masses down from the Great Plains and the Rocky Mountains. These cold snaps are not prolonged, however. Much of the rain falls at night. Downpours may accompany thunderstorms during April and May. July and August are relatively dry. Snowfall is slight and doesn't accumulate.

Winter mildness: 77	**Seasonal affect:** 84
Summer mildness: 5	**Hazardousness:** 55
Score: 47.59	**Rank: 185**

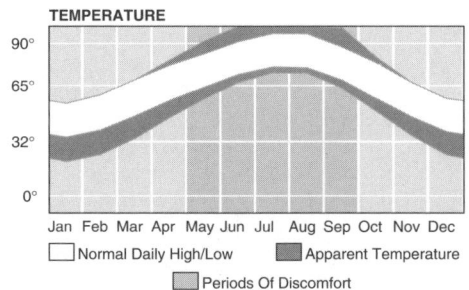

ANNUAL
Humidity: 69%
Wind Speed: 10.7 mph
DAYS
0° or below: 0
32° or below: 40
90° or above: 100
Clear: 138
Partly Cloudy: 95
Cloudy: 132

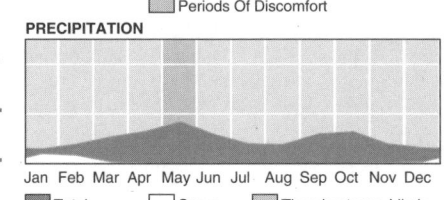

ANNUAL
Precipitation: 36.1"
Snow: 2.7"
DAYS
Precipitation: 49
Thunderstorm: 47
Fog: 79

Davenport-Moline-Rock Island, IA-IL

Location: 41.35 N, 90.25 W, at 580 feet, on the banks of the Mississippi River between Iowa and Illinois; 160 miles west of Chicago and 160 miles east of Des Moines.

Landscape: The topography is rolling prairie. Close to the river there is considerable truck gardening and dairying. Field production of grains and livestock is greater away from the large streams.

Cimate: Temperate Continental, with a wide temperature range throughout the year. There are some intensely hot, humid periods in summer and severely cold periods in winter. The first freeze is October 23 and the last is mid-April. Nearness to major storm tracks brings substantial weather changes, frequently occurring at three- or four-day intervals. Maximum of 90°F or higher have occurred as frequently as 55 days a year (1936), but in 1882 there were none. Readings of zero or below have been made during every winter, ranging from 37 times in 1874–75 to one time during four other winters. The city experienced heavy flooding in 1993.

Winter mildness: 14	**Seasonal affect:** 56
Summer mildness: 61	**Hazardousness:** 24
Score: 20.11	**Rank: 283**

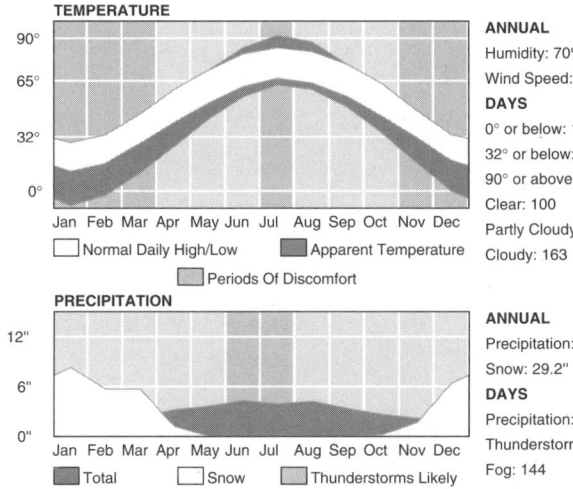

ANNUAL
Humidity: 70%
Wind Speed: 9.9 mph
DAYS
0° or below: 15
32° or below: 129
90° or above: 14
Clear: 100
Partly Cloudy: 102
Cloudy: 163

ANNUAL
Precipitation: 33.8"
Snow: 29.2"
DAYS
Precipitation: 61
Thunderstorm: 46
Fog: 144

Dayton-Springfield, OH

Location: 39.53 N, 84.53 W, at 1,020 feet, near the center of the Miami River Valley; 50 miles north of Cincinnati at the forks of the Great Miami River.

Landscape: Situated about 750 feet above sea level, Dayton is 50 to 200 feet below the adjacent rolling country and spreads over the flood plain and into the surrounding hills. Three rivers converge from the north and join within the city limits flowing south to the Ohio River. Natural vegetation is pitch pine, large-leaf magnolia, and sourwood, as well as a hardwood forest of oak, hickory, yellow poplar, ash, and maple.

Cimate: Continental. Cold, polar air flowing across the Great Lakes causes cloudiness during the winter, accompanied by frequent snow flurries that add little to the total snowfall. Extreme temperatures are usually of short duration in either the summer or winter. High relative humidity during much of the year causes some discomfort. The first freeze is usually October 8, the last at the beginning of May.

Winter mildness: 29	**Seasonal affect:** 16
Summer mildness: 59	**Hazardousness:** 39
Score: 20.96	**Rank: 280**

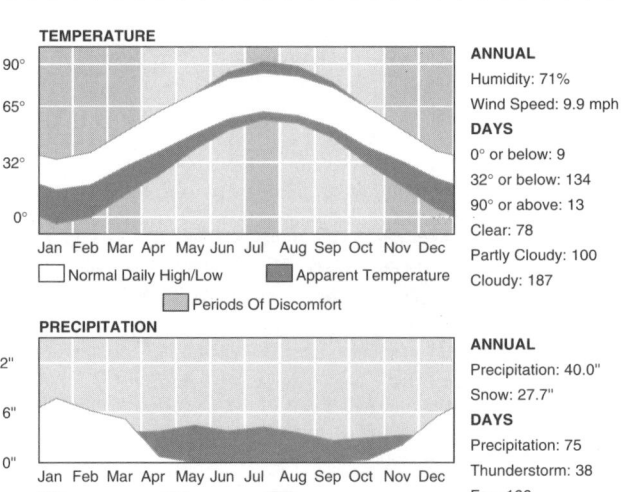

ANNUAL
Humidity: 71%
Wind Speed: 9.9 mph
DAYS
0° or below: 9
32° or below: 134
90° or above: 13
Clear: 78
Partly Cloudy: 100
Cloudy: 187

ANNUAL
Precipitation: 40.0"
Snow: 27.7"
DAYS
Precipitation: 75
Thunderstorm: 38
Fog: 166

Daytona Beach, FL

Location: 29.11 N, 81.03 W, at 30 feet, on the Halifax River and Intracoastal Waterway along the state's northeast Atlantic coast; 60 miles north of Cape Canaveral.

Landscape: A tidewater lagoon and part of the Intracoastal Waterway. The surrounding land is flat with mainly sandy soil; no elevations above 35 feet—very suitable for auto racing. Coastal Plain vegetation in this region is palm and sea grape. The dominant forest is evergreen, oak, and magnolia. The hard white-sand beach is 25 miles long and 500 feet wide at low tide.

Cimate: Nearness to the ocean results in a climate tempered by land and sea breezes. Days in June through September can be humid and hot. A sea breeze starts at midday and afternoon thundershowers lower temperatures to comfortable levels. Winters can have cold airflows from the north, but usually are mild because of the city's ocean setting and southerly latitude. The first freeze occurs around Christmas Day, the last a very early February 4.

Winter mildness: 95   **Seasonal affect:** 58
Summer mildness: 32   **Hazardousness:** 84
Score: **86.40**   **Rank:** **49**

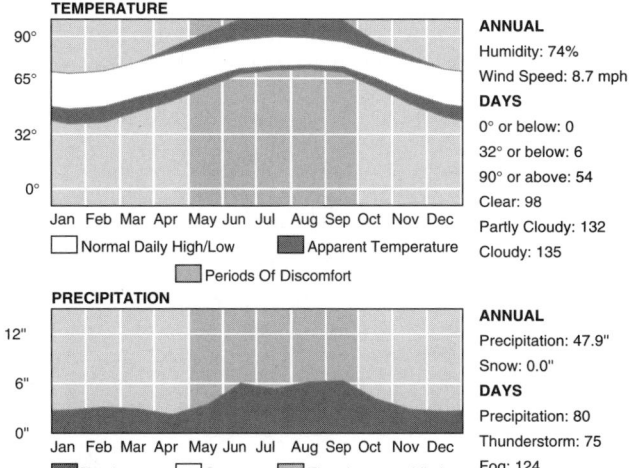

Denver, CO

Location: 39.46 N, 104.52 W, at 5,290 feet; the Mile High City rests on the eastern slope of the Rocky Mountains in north central Colorado.

Landscape: Denver is isolated from the Pacific Ocean by three mountain ranges: the Coastal Ranges, the Sierra Nevada, and the Rockies nearby. The topography of Denver proper is unimpressive prairie.

Cimate: Mild, sunny, semiarid, and lacking the extremely cold winter mornings of the high elevations and remote mountain valleys, as well as the hot summer afternoons of lower altitudes. There is little humidity or precipitation and lots of sunshine. During the cold months, cold air invasion from the north can be abrupt and severe. Yet many of these air masses are deflected off to the east by the mountains. Denver often has milder winters than cities of comparable latitude on the Great Plains. The last freeze is May 11; the first freeze arrives around September 30. Spring is wet, cloudy, and windy. Summers are cool. Fall is the most pleasant season.

Winter mildness: 30   **Seasonal affect:** 89
Summer mildness: 41   **Hazardousness:** 8
Score: **50.42**   **Rank:** **176**

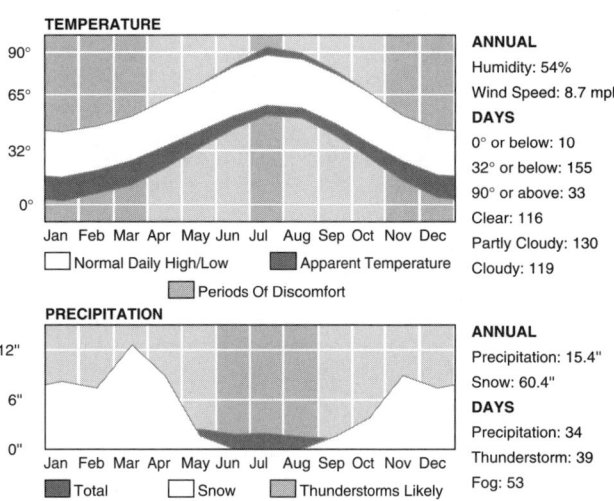

Des Moines, IA

Location: 41.32 N, 93.39 W, at 940 feet, close to the center of Iowa at the confluence of the Des Moines and Racoon rivers in the heart of the Corn Belt, the geographic center of the continental United States.

Landscape: The terrain is flat to gently rolling prairie, ideally suited to agriculture. Most of the soil in Iowa is dark, rich, sandy loam with good drainage.

Cimate: Situated in the center of the country far from any large body of water, Des Moines has a Continental climate, with long, cold winters, hot summers, and short springs and falls. The first freeze arrives by October 6. The last freeze departs by the beginning of May. Winter cold is often intensified by the winds that sweep over the flat land though bitterly cold days are rare. Prevailing winds are southerly and precipitation falls in showers or occasional thunderstorms from late April through October. Autumn is sunny with diminishing precipitation. The city suffered extensive damage from flooding in 1993.

Winter mildness: 12   **Seasonal affect:** 66
Summer mildness: 48   **Hazardousness:** 12
Score: **8.49**   **Rank:** **324**

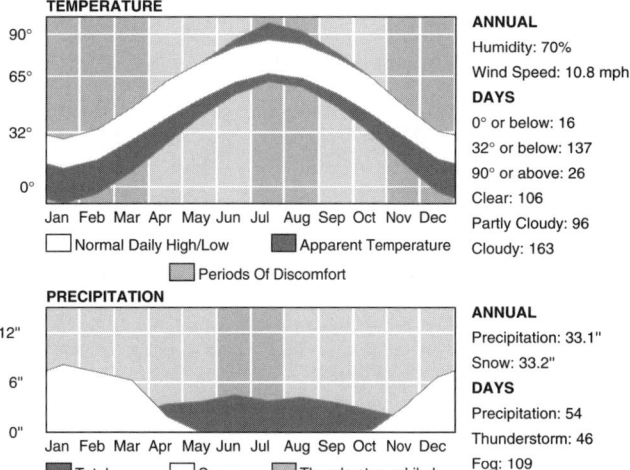

Detroit, MI

Location: 42.14 N, 83.20 W, at 630 feet, in the southeastern corner of the state, across the St. Clair River from Windsor, Ontario, Canada.

Landscape: Situated on an important waterway that connects Lake Huron to Lake Erie. Nearly flat land slopes up gently from the water's edge northwestward for about 10 miles, then gives way to increasingly rolling terrain.

Cimate: Detroit's nearness to the Great Lakes helps give it a milder climate than one would expect in a place so far north. The cold winters are modified by the Great Lakes, warming and moistening the arctic air that passes over the northern Plains. As a result the area is quite cloudy, especially in the winter. Summers in the city are warm and sunny. Brief showers can occur every few days but often fall on only part of the city. Winter storms may bring rain, snow, or both. Freezing rain and sleet are common. The first freeze is around October 22, and the last is late April.

Winter mildness: 28	**Seasonal affect:** 31
Summer mildness: 68	**Hazardousness:** 29
Score: 30.02	**Rank: 248**

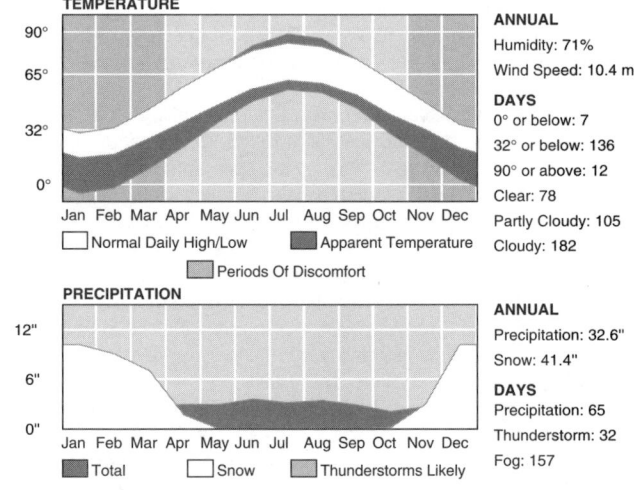

ANNUAL
Humidity: 71%
Wind Speed: 10.4 mph
DAYS
0° or below: 7
32° or below: 136
90° or above: 12
Clear: 78
Partly Cloudy: 105
Cloudy: 182

ANNUAL
Precipitation: 32.6"
Snow: 41.4"
DAYS
Precipitation: 65
Thunderstorm: 32
Fog: 157

Dover, DE

Location: 39.09 N, 75.31 W, at 30 feet, in the center of the state on the St. Jones River, a fertile farming and fruit-growing region.

Landscape: On the Atlantic Coastal Plain with flat, low, gently undulating land sloping down to the marshy shore of the Atlantic Ocean. Salt and freshwater marshlands are prevalent. Loblolly and Virginia pines are mixed with sweet and black gums, oaks, maples, yellow poplars, and hollies.

Cimate: Continental, with long, warm and humid summers and relatively mild winters. During the summer, maximum temperatures are usually in the 80s, with the humidity at 75 percent. During January, the coldest month of the year, the daily average temperature is 32 degrees. Snow is frequently mixed with rain and sleet, and seldom remains on the ground more than a few days. The first frost is October 29, and the last is April 13. The proximity of large water areas and the inflow of southerly winds cause the relative humidity to be quite high all year.

Winter mildness: 57	**Seasonal affect:** 37
Summer mildness: 43	**Hazardousness:** 66
Score: 59.49	**Rank: 144**

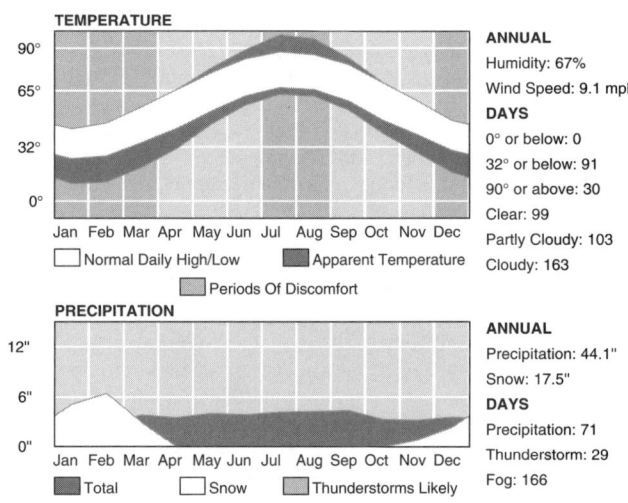

ANNUAL
Humidity: 67%
Wind Speed: 9.1 mph
DAYS
0° or below: 0
32° or below: 91
90° or above: 30
Clear: 99
Partly Cloudy: 103
Cloudy: 163

ANNUAL
Precipitation: 44.1"
Snow: 17.5"
DAYS
Precipitation: 71
Thunderstorm: 29
Fog: 166

Duluth-Superior, MN-WI

Location: 46.50 N, 92.11 W, at 1,430 feet, at Lake Superior's western tip. Directly opposite, on the flats occupying the east banks of St. Louis Bay, lies the city of Superior, Wisconsin.

Landscape: Situated at the base of a range of hills that rise abruptly to between 600 feet and 800 feet above the lake level. Two or three miles back from the waterfront the country assumes the character of a slightly rolling plateau. Duluth-Superior harbor, the second largest of the Great Lakes ports, is ice-bound four months of the year.

Cimate: Rugged Continental. Winters are long and quite cold. Snow comes early and remains on the ground until springtime. The first freeze is normally recorded on September 22, the last on May 26. While the airport area to the north receives more than 75 inches of snow a year, the city proper receives only about 55 inches. Summers are seldom hot due to the northerly latitude and proximity of Lake Superior.

Winter mildness: 3	**Seasonal affect:** 35
Summer mildness: 93	**Hazardousness:** 2
Score: 1.41	**Rank: 349**

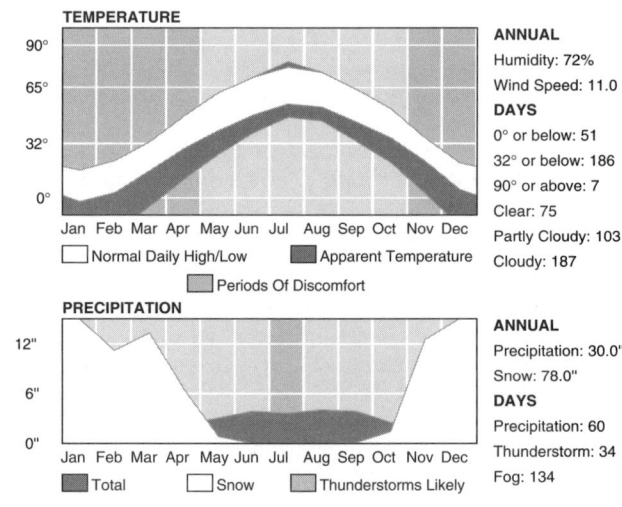

ANNUAL
Humidity: 72%
Wind Speed: 11.0 mph
DAYS
0° or below: 51
32° or below: 186
90° or above: 7
Clear: 75
Partly Cloudy: 103
Cloudy: 187

ANNUAL
Precipitation: 30.0"
Snow: 78.0"
DAYS
Precipitation: 60
Thunderstorm: 34
Fog: 134

Edmonton, AB

Location: 53.34 N, 113.31 W, at 2,201 feet, occupying a rolling plain on both banks of the North Saskatchewan River in central Alberta.

Landscape: Elevation ranges are only plus or minus 100 feet within a 10-mile radius. The land slopes off to the northeast and southeast, except for ridges 20 miles southeast and 20 miles west, which rise 350 feet above the airport elevation. The North Saskatchewan River flows northeast. The Sturgeon, a secondary river, is 7 miles to the northwest.

Cimate: Continental, characterized by two major seasons of summer and winter, with short, rarely orderly transitions of spring and autumn. The occurrence of snow divides the year. The warmer five months rarely have measurable snowfalls. The cooler five receive nearly all their precipitation as snow. The remaining two months, April and October, average half their totals as snow. Winter snow cover begins November 16 and stays through the season until around March 17. Average summer temperature is 61°F. Average winter temperature is 13°F.

Winter mildness: 2	**Seasonal affect:** 63
Summer mildness: 97	**Hazardousness:** 34
Score: 48.44	**Rank: 183**

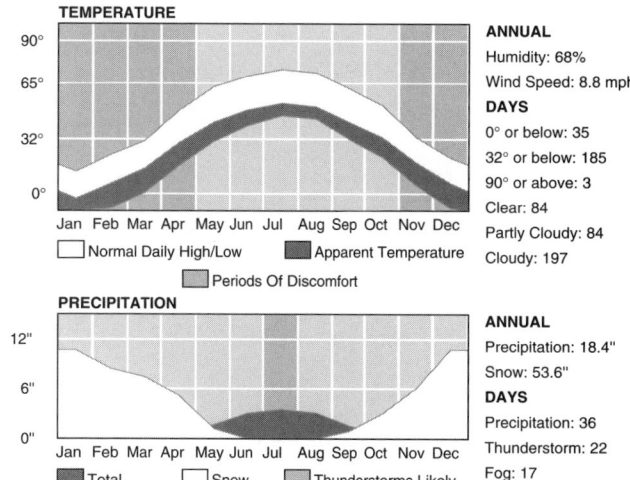

TEMPERATURE

Normal Daily High/Low — Apparent Temperature
Periods Of Discomfort

PRECIPITATION

Total — Snow — Thunderstorms Likely

ANNUAL
Humidity: 68%
Wind Speed: 8.8 mph
DAYS
0° or below: 35
32° or below: 185
90° or above: 3
Clear: 84
Partly Cloudy: 84
Cloudy: 197

ANNUAL
Precipitation: 18.4"
Snow: 53.6"
DAYS
Precipitation: 36
Thunderstorm: 22
Fog: 17

El Paso, TX

Location: 31.48 N, 106.24 W, at 3,920 feet, at the extreme western tip of Texas, across the Rio Grande from Ciudad Juarez, Mexico.

Landscape: High Desert with sparse vegetation. Shrubs and cacti predominate. An underground lake supplies abundant water. Mountains and mesas characterize the terrain. The Franklin Mountains begin within the city limits and extend northward some 16 miles. This is a region of cattle ranches and irrigated farms, producing cotton, fruits, and vegetables.

Cimate: Semiarid Desert; dry and sunny. Summer temperatures are high but not extreme. The low relative humidity lessens the felt heat. The winter is mild, typical of arid areas at low altitudes. The first freeze is November 1, the last is April 11. Rainfall is scarce year-round and fosters only scrub-like desert vegetation. Winter nights can be cold, but the days are warm, averaging in the 50s. Summer days are hot but the nights cool, averaging in the 60s. Days can be windy, with annoying dust and sandstorms.

Winter mildness: 65	**Seasonal affect:** 99
Summer mildness: 3	**Hazardousness:** 79
Score: 82.15	**Rank: 64**

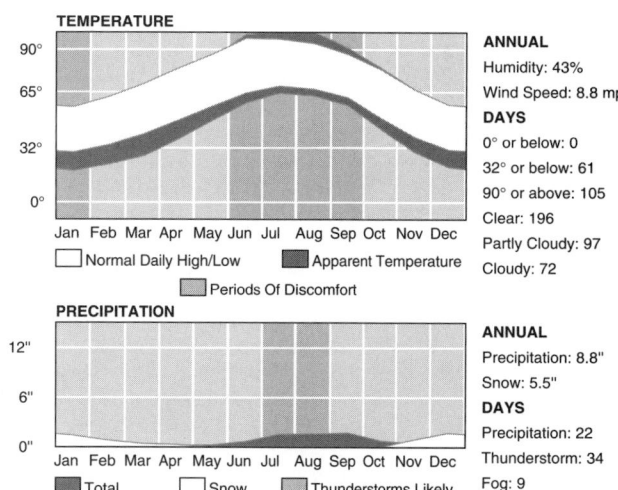

TEMPERATURE

Normal Daily High/Low — Apparent Temperature
Periods Of Discomfort

PRECIPITATION

Total — Snow — Thunderstorms Likely

ANNUAL
Humidity: 43%
Wind Speed: 8.8 mph
DAYS
0° or below: 0
32° or below: 61
90° or above: 105
Clear: 196
Partly Cloudy: 97
Cloudy: 72

ANNUAL
Precipitation: 8.8"
Snow: 5.5"
DAYS
Precipitation: 22
Thunderstorm: 34
Fog: 9

Eugene-Springfield, OR

Location: 44.07 N, 123.13 W, at 360 feet, at the southern end of the fertile Willamette Valley and bounded by mountain ranges. The Cascades lie to the east and the Coastal Ranges to the west.

Landscape: To the north, the valley widens and levels out. Hills of the rolling, wooded Coastal Ranges begin about 5 miles west of the airport and rise to between 1,500 feet and 2,000 feet midway between the city and the Pacific, 50 miles to the west. The Cascades, 75 miles east, reach heights of 10,000 feet. These sheltering ranges and the proximity of the ocean contribute to the extremely mild climate. This is one of the nation's most important agricultural and lumbering areas.

Cimate: Mild Maritime climate. Temperature minima below 20°F occur only five times a year. The temperature rarely reaches the mid 90s. Seasonal change is gradual, with intermediate seasons being as long as summer and winter. The first freeze usually occurs around the beginning of November, the last at the end of April.

Winter mildness: 79	**Seasonal affect:** 3
Summer mildness: 79	**Hazardousness:** 90
Score: 79.60	**Rank: 73**

TEMPERATURE

Normal Daily High/Low — Apparent Temperature
Periods Of Discomfort

PRECIPITATION

Total — Snow — Thunderstorms Likely

ANNUAL
Humidity: 76%
Wind Speed: 7.6 mph
DAYS
0° or below: 0
32° or below: 54
90° or above: 15
Clear: 76
Partly Cloudy: 81
Cloudy: 208

ANNUAL
Precipitation: 49.4"
Snow: 6.6"
DAYS
Precipitation: 90
Thunderstorm: 3
Fog: 137

Evansville-Henderson, IN-KY

Location: 38.03 N, 87.32 W, at 380 feet, on the Ohio River near the juncture of Indiana, Illinois, and Kentucky.

Landscape: The country around Evansville ranges from level to rolling. The city is in a shallow valley with low hills to the east and west that run parallel to the valley but slope downward to the south. The open end of this valley slopes down to the southwest toward Evansville and the Ohio River.

Cimate: Prevailing wind here is from the south, and, although Evansville is 550 miles from the Gulf of Mexico, its weather generally resembles that of its neighbors to the south. Strong cold winds sometimes blow from the north and northwest following cold fronts. As soon as the high-pressure ridge moves by, the wind backs around again from the south. Snowfall varies a great deal from year to year but accumulation is rare. Average growing season: 199 days. Average date of last freeze: April 7. First freeze: October 23.

Winter mildness: 48	**Seasonal affect:** 37
Summer mildness: 37	**Hazardousness:** 58
Score: 39.09	**Rank: 216**

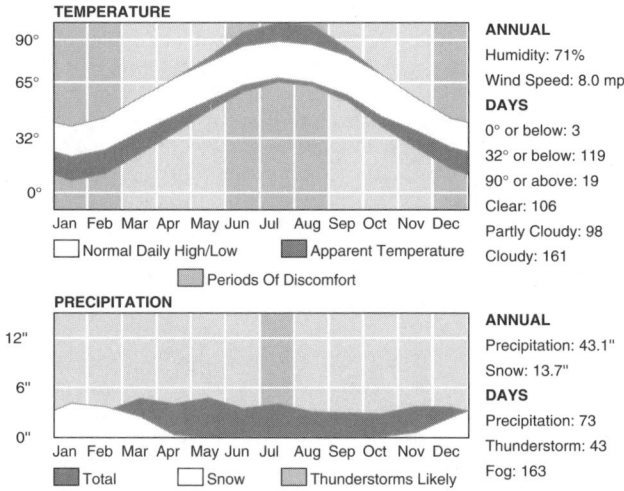

ANNUAL
Humidity: 71%
Wind Speed: 8.0 mph
DAYS
0° or below: 3
32° or below: 119
90° or above: 19
Clear: 106
Partly Cloudy: 98
Cloudy: 161

ANNUAL
Precipitation: 43.1"
Snow: 13.7"
DAYS
Precipitation: 73
Thunderstorm: 43
Fog: 163

Fargo-Moorhead, ND-MN

Location: 46.54 N, 96.48 W, at 900 feet, these twin cities lie in the valley of the Red River, the boundary between Minnesota and North Dakota.

Landscape: The Red River flows between the two cities, and is part of the Hudson Bay drainage area. The river has no effect on the climate but does cause occasional, severe spring flooding. The surrounding terrain is flat, open and fertile, suitable for crop and dairy farming.

Cimate: Summers are generally comfortable, with a few days of hot and humid weather; nights are cool. Winter months are cold and dry, with maximum temperatures rising above freezing only six times per month. At night, the temperature drops below zero half the time. The first freeze is mid-September; the last, mid-May. With the flat terrain, surface friction has little slowing effect on the wind, contributing to the legendary Dakota blizzards. Strong winds with even, light snowfall cause heavy snowdrifts. Surprisingly, the area averages only 38 inches of snow per year.

Winter mildness: 2	**Seasonal affect:** 67
Summer mildness: 67	**Hazardousness:** 28
Score: 10.19	**Rank: 318**

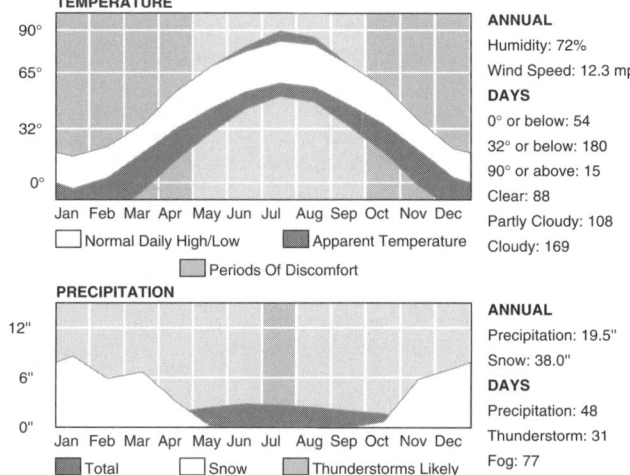

ANNUAL
Humidity: 72%
Wind Speed: 12.3 mph
DAYS
0° or below: 54
32° or below: 180
90° or above: 15
Clear: 88
Partly Cloudy: 108
Cloudy: 169

ANNUAL
Precipitation: 19.5"
Snow: 38.0"
DAYS
Precipitation: 48
Thunderstorm: 31
Fog: 77

Fayetteville-Springdale-Rogers, AR

Location: 36.06 N, 94.10 W, at 1,270 feet, in northwestern Arkansas; 180 miles northwest of the state capital at Little Rock.

Landscape: Situated on the White River in the Boston Mountains where elevations can reach over 2,000 feet. This is the highest part of the Ozark Plateau; it is rugged, wooded mountain country. Broadleaf deciduous oak and hickory predominate with lower layers of weakly developed small trees and shrubs, redbud, and dogwood.

Cimate: Modified Continental, with hot, humid summers and briefer winters than other locations at this latitude. Winters can vary from warm and humid Maritime to cold and dry Continental, but each winter is relatively free from climatic extremes. Snowfalls are minimal; precipitation in January and February falls as icy rain. Temperatures can be freezing or below from late November through February, but seldom are they zero or below. Spring is likely to be a wet transition period from late February through April. Freezes arrive by mid-October and depart by late April.

Winter mildness: 53	**Seasonal affect:** 79
Summer mildness: 36	**Hazardousness:** 42
Score: 49.29	**Rank: 180**

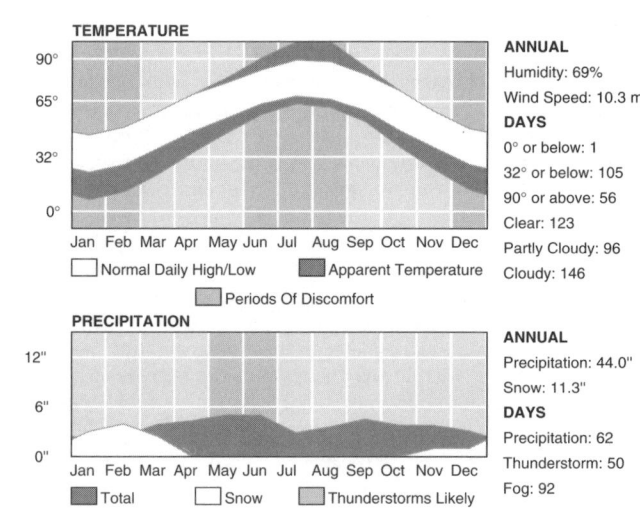

ANNUAL
Humidity: 69%
Wind Speed: 10.3 mph
DAYS
0° or below: 1
32° or below: 105
90° or above: 56
Clear: 123
Partly Cloudy: 96
Cloudy: 146

ANNUAL
Precipitation: 44.0"
Snow: 11.3"
DAYS
Precipitation: 62
Thunderstorm: 50
Fog: 92

Flagstaff, AZ-UT

Location: 35.08 N, 111.40 W, at 7,000 feet; 80 miles south of the Grand Canyon and 125 miles northeast of Phoenix.

Landscape: Part of a geographic region known as the Colorado Plateau, which is a series of generally level plateaus mostly separated by steep-sided chasms. There is little arable land. Near here, the highest point in Arizona is Humphreys Peak in the San Francisco Mountains. The city sits on the northern border of the Prescott National Forest. Lumbering is an important economic base for the area.

Cimate: Vigorous, cool to cold winters, warm summers. In Flagstaff the mean January temperature is 28°F, and the average July temperature is 66°F. The first freeze is October 21, and the last freeze is May 14. Flagstaff proper gets about 23 inches of precipitation yearly, though surrounding mountains and plateaus receive somewhat more moisture, 20 to 40 inches, with up to 5 feet of snow falling in peak areas. Accumulations vary from year to year.

Winter mildness: 26	**Seasonal affect:** 94
Summer mildness: 77	**Hazardousness:** 9
Score: 74.50	**Rank: 91**

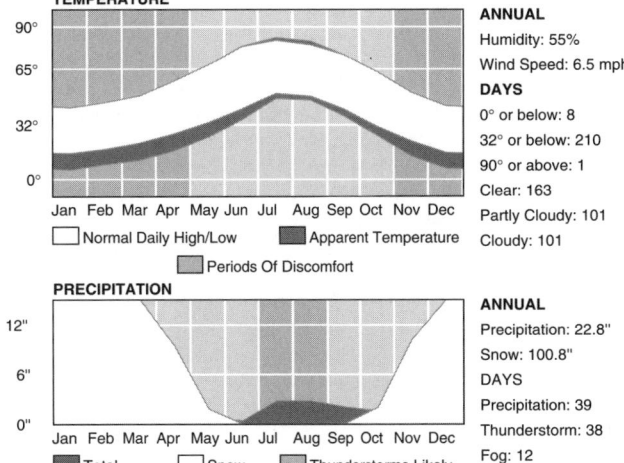

Fort Collins-Loveland, CO

Location: 40.35 N, 105.05 W, at 5,003 feet, on the Cache la Poudre River in the eastern foothills of the Rockies' Front Range; 55 miles north of Denver.

Landscape: On the western horizon is some of the most spectacular mountain terrain in the country with nearly vertical cliffs, high waterfalls, and forested mountain slopes cut by swift rivers. The immediate area is a semiarid steppe prairie with scattered shrubs, low trees, and numerous species of short grasses.

Cimate: Near the center of the continent, Fort Collins and Loveland are removed from any major source of airborne moisture and are shielded from rainfall by the Rockies to the west. The four seasons are well defined, with sunny days year-round. Cold air masses from Canada may bring winter temperatures well below zero at night. In summer, hot, dry air from the southwestern desert brings daytime temperatures of 90°F. However, felt heat is low because of dryness. The first freeze is early October; the last is the end of May.

Winter mildness: 22	**Seasonal affect:** 87
Summer mildness: 54	**Hazardousness:** 1
Score: 46.74	**Rank: 189**

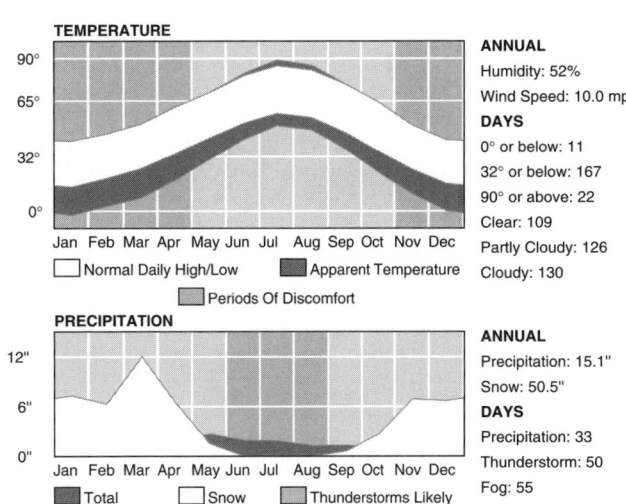

★ Fort Myers-Cape Coral, FL

Location: 26.35 N, 81.52 W, at 20 feet, on the broad Caloosahatchee River in southwestern Florida; 120 miles south of Tampa.

Landscape: The city is the western terminus of the cross-state Okeechobee Waterway, linking the Atlantic Ocean and the Gulf of Mexico about 15 miles away. The land is level and low. The climax growth of the coastal plain in this area north of the Everglades is evergreen-oak and magnolia. Spanish moss trails from live oak and bald cypress. Tree ferns, small palms and shrubs make up the lower layer. Significant petroleum deposits have been found near Fort Myers.

Cimate: Subtropical as summer and winter temperature extremes are checked by the influence of the Gulf. Mild winters have many bright, warm days. Nights are moderately cool. Rainfall averages more than 50 inches annually, with two-thirds of this total coming daily between June and September. Most rain falls as late afternoon or early evening thunderstorms, bringing welcome relief from the heat.

Winter mildness: 99	**Seasonal affect:** 80
Summer mildness: 24	**Hazardousness:** 84
Score: 92.91	**Rank: 26**

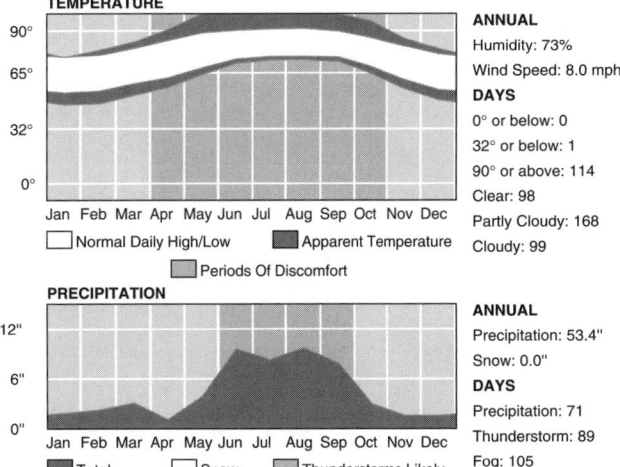

Fort Smith, AR-OK

Location: 35.20 N, 94.22 W, at 450 feet, at the confluence of the Poteau and Arkansas rivers in the western part of the state.

Landscape: About 20 miles to the northwest are the Cookson Hills, which have an elevation of 1,500 feet. To the northeast, the Boston Mountains of the Ozark region of Arkansas rise 2,700 feet. West, south, and east, the terrain is broken hills separated by creek and riverbottom land. The bottomlands are fertile and produce large yields of hay, beans, and spinach. Small wild game is plentiful; lakes and streams have an abundance of fish. The economy depends on the deposits of coal and natural gas, timber, and fertile farmlands of the surrounding region.

Cimate: Hot Continental, and well suited to raising fruits and berries. This is Arkansas wine country. The climate is generally mild, except during the summer, which can be hot. Precipitation is markedly greater in the summer months. The last freeze is mid-April; the first, mid-October.

Winter mildness: 59	**Seasonal affect:** 79
Summer mildness: 12	**Hazardousness:** 57
Score: 43.34	**Rank: 201**

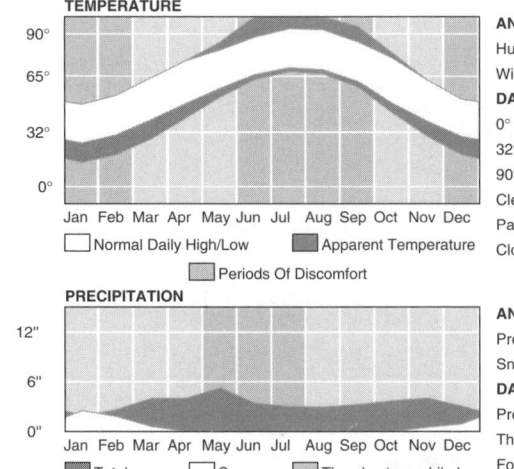

TEMPERATURE

Normal Daily High/Low — Apparent Temperature — Periods Of Discomfort

ANNUAL
Humidity: 71%
Wind Speed: 7.6 mph
DAYS
0° or below: 0
32° or below: 77
90° or above: 77
Clear: 123
Partly Cloudy: 96
Cloudy: 146

PRECIPITATION

Total — Snow — Thunderstorms Likely

ANNUAL
Precipitation: 40.9"
Snow: 6.3"
DAYS
Precipitation: 62
Thunderstorm: 57
Fog: 93

Fort Wayne, IN

Location: 41.00 N, 85.12 W, at 790 feet, at the junction of the St. Mary's, St. Joseph, and Maumee rivers in northeast Indiana. Indianapolis, the state capital, is 120 miles southwest.

Landscape: The topography is generally level south and east of the city. Southwest and west, the land is somewhat rolling, while to the northwest and north it becomes hilly. The highest point in the area is 40 miles north, near the town of Angola, where the elevation is 1,060 feet above sea level.

Cimate: Similar to that of other midwestern cities at the same latitude. Precipitation is well distributed throughout the year, varying from a monthly rate of 2 inches in February to 4 inches in May. Damaging hailstorms may be expected twice a year. Snow usually covers the ground for 30 days each winter, but heavy snowstorms are rare. The typical date of the last freeze is in late April, and the typical date of the first freeze is mid-October.

Winter mildness: 27	**Seasonal affect:** 24
Summer mildness: 58	**Hazardousness:** 31
Score: 13.88	**Rank: 305**

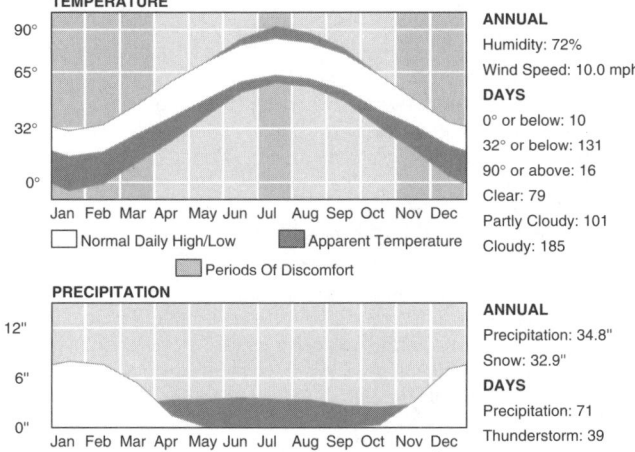

TEMPERATURE

Normal Daily High/Low — Apparent Temperature — Periods Of Discomfort

ANNUAL
Humidity: 72%
Wind Speed: 10.0 mph
DAYS
0° or below: 10
32° or below: 131
90° or above: 16
Clear: 79
Partly Cloudy: 101
Cloudy: 185

PRECIPITATION

Total — Snow — Thunderstorms Likely

ANNUAL
Precipitation: 34.8"
Snow: 32.9"
DAYS
Precipitation: 71
Thunderstorm: 39
Fog: 157

★ Fresno, CA

Location: 36.47 N, 119.43 W, at 340 feet, in the middle of the long, agriculturally rich San Joaquin Valley is near its eastern edge.

Landscape: The valley runs northwest to southeast and is about 225 miles long, with an average width of about 50 miles. The terrain around Fresno is generally level, with an abrupt upward slope 15 miles eastward to the foothills of the Sierra Nevada. This mountain range lies 50 miles to the east and has elevations from 12,000 feet to 14,000 feet. Forty-five miles to the west lie the foothills of the Coastal Ranges.

Cimate: Dry and sunny. Winters are mild with 90 percent of the city's precipitation falling between November and April. The first freeze is November 29, the last in mid-February. Summer months are hot, less humid, and virtually rainless. Because of the great amount of sunshine the valley receives, and the blockage of cooler moist air from the Pacific, daily maximum temperatures in July climb to the upper 90s.

Winter mildness: 83	**Seasonal affect:** 93
Summer mildness: 1	**Hazardousness:** 95
Score: 93.76	**Rank: 23**

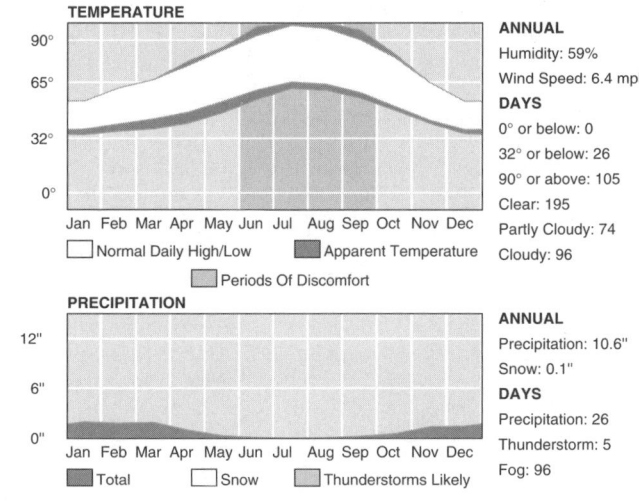

TEMPERATURE

Normal Daily High/Low — Apparent Temperature — Periods Of Discomfort

ANNUAL
Humidity: 59%
Wind Speed: 6.4 mph
DAYS
0° or below: 0
32° or below: 26
90° or above: 105
Clear: 195
Partly Cloudy: 74
Cloudy: 96

PRECIPITATION

Total — Snow — Thunderstorms Likely

ANNUAL
Precipitation: 10.6"
Snow: 0.1"
DAYS
Precipitation: 26
Thunderstorm: 5
Fog: 96

Gainesville, FL

Location: 29.41 N, 82.16 W, at 140 feet, in north central Florida; 66 miles southwest of Jacksonville and midway between the Atlantic Coast and the Gulf of Mexico.

Landscape: The terrain is rolling ranch and farm country with several lakes to the east and south. Geological relief includes sink holes and caverns in this area of Florida's underlying limestone. Nearby are swamps and flatwoods forests with long-leaf and slash pines. Gallberry, saw palmetto, and fetterbush are the undergrowth. Plants and animals normally found in the Appalachian Mountains are at home here.

Cimate: Subtropical in character, with a small annual range of temperature changes. Humid, hot summers are cooled by frequent, heavy afternoon thunderstorms. While winters are mild, there can be freezing temperatures a dozen times a year; October through mid-April, it is mostly dry and clear with warm days and cool nights. The usual first freeze is November 27; the last is at the beginning of March.

Winter mildness: 92	**Seasonal affect:** 47
Summer mildness: 25	**Hazardousness:** 88
Score: 84.41	**Rank:** 56

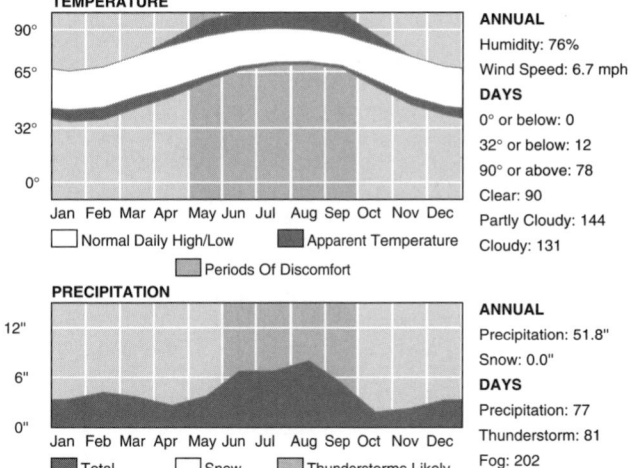

ANNUAL
Humidity: 76%
Wind Speed: 6.7 mph
DAYS
0° or below: 0
32° or below: 12
90° or above: 78
Clear: 90
Partly Cloudy: 144
Cloudy: 131

ANNUAL
Precipitation: 51.8"
Snow: 0.0"
DAYS
Precipitation: 77
Thunderstorm: 81
Fog: 202

Galveston-Texas City, TX

Location: 29.18 N, 94.48 W, at 10 feet, on Galveston Island off the southeast coast of Texas; 49 miles from Houston.

Landscape: A deepwater port of entry, the island is nearly 3 miles across at its widest point and 29 miles long. It is typical of Gulf barrier islands with wide, sandy beaches and salt marshes. Palms, oleander, bougainville and other subtropical plants flourish. The island's low-lying terrain makes it especially vulnerable to tidal surges.

Cimate: Predominantly mild Marine. Tourists are attracted to the mild climate and the resort facilities along the beaches. Though cold fronts from the northwest can sometimes reach the coast, winters tend to be mild. Temperatures go below freezing perhaps four times a year. Normal daily maximum temperatures range from 60°F in January to 88°F in August, while minimum temperatures range from 48°F in January to the upper 70s in the summer. Hurricanes are possible and tropical rains with high winds likely.

Winter mildness: 95	**Seasonal affect:** 50
Summer mildness: 44	**Hazardousness:** 58
Score: 83.00	**Rank:** 61

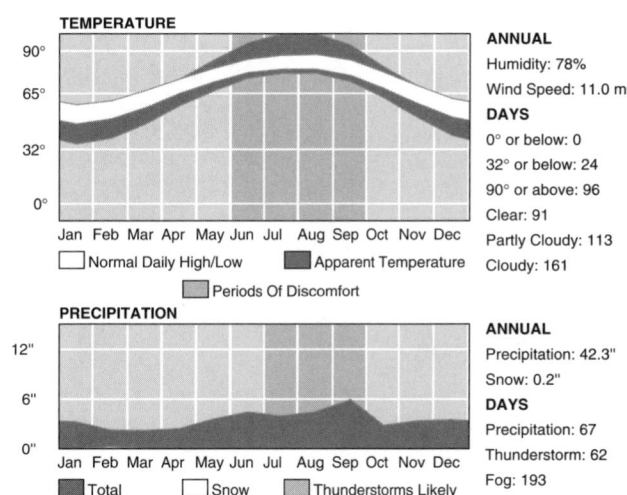

ANNUAL
Humidity: 78%
Wind Speed: 11.0 mph
DAYS
0° or below: 0
32° or below: 24
90° or above: 96
Clear: 91
Partly Cloudy: 113
Cloudy: 161

ANNUAL
Precipitation: 42.3"
Snow: 0.2"
DAYS
Precipitation: 67
Thunderstorm: 62
Fog: 193

Grand Junction, CO

Location: 39.06 N, 108.33 W, at 4,840 feet, in the Grand Valley of western Colorado, at the junction of the Colorado and Gunnison rivers; 20 miles east of the Utah border.

Landscape: Nearby is the lake-studded Grand Mesa, the Colorado National Monument, and the Grand Mesa and Uncompahgre National Forests. Sagebrush and cactus can be found in the canyons. Pine, spruce, and aspen forests cover the sub-alpine areas. Sparse shortgrass prairie, scattered trees and shrubs are the growth in the desert plateau.

Cimate: The interior location plus the ring of high mountains mean low rainfall. Winter snows are frequent but light and do not remain long. Summer humidity is low, making the region as dry as parts of Arizona. Sunny days predominate in all seasons. The city's climate is marked by wide seasonal temperature changes, but thanks to the protection of the surrounding mountains, sudden and severe weather changes are infrequent. The first freeze arrives at the end of September; the last comes at the end of May.

Winter mildness: 24	**Seasonal affect:** 92
Summer mildness: 9	**Hazardousness:** 52
Score: 74.22	**Rank:** 92

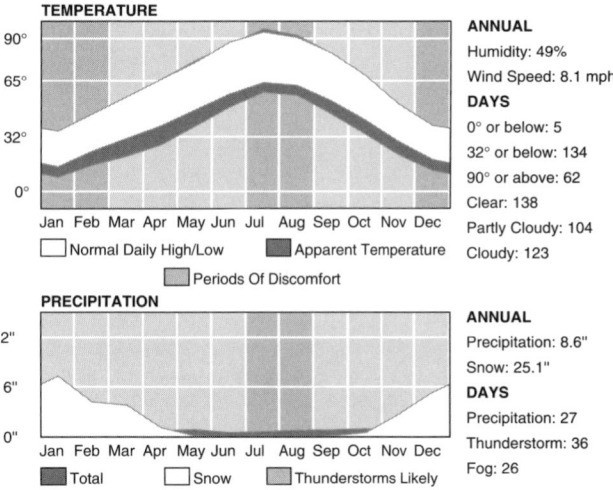

ANNUAL
Humidity: 49%
Wind Speed: 8.1 mph
DAYS
0° or below: 5
32° or below: 134
90° or above: 62
Clear: 138
Partly Cloudy: 104
Cloudy: 123

ANNUAL
Precipitation: 8.6"
Snow: 25.1"
DAYS
Precipitation: 27
Thunderstorm: 36
Fog: 26

Place Profiles: Climate

Grand Rapids-Muskegon-Holland, MI

Location: 42.53 N, 85.31 W, at 780 feet, in the river valley at the rapids (now largely dredged) of the Grand River in west central Michigan; 30 miles east of Lake Michigan.

Landscape: The Grand River, Michigan's largest stream, bisects the city. The valley has tall hills and bluffs rising on all sides, ranging in elevation from 600 feet to 1,000 feet. The area is known for fruit growing, especially peaches and cherries.

Cimate: Largely determined by the proximity of Lake Michigan. In spring, the cooling effect of the lake retards the growth of vegetation until the danger of frost is past. In the fall, the warming effect holds off frost until the crops have matured. Summer days are warm and pleasant, with cooler nights. Winters are snowy and cold, but extremely cold temperatures or prolonged cold spells are rare because of the warm lake breeze. The growing season averages 170 days. The date of the last freeze is usually May 10. The first freeze comes on October 17.

Winter mildness: 24	**Seasonal affect:** 15
Summer mildness: 70	**Hazardousness:** 5
Score: 6.79	**Rank:** 330

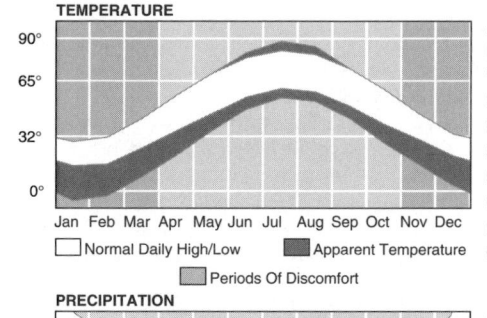

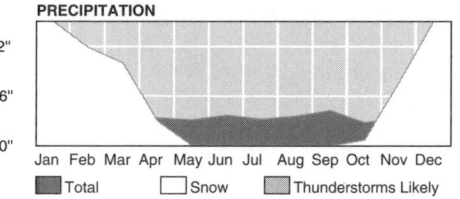

ANNUAL
Humidity: 73%
Wind Speed: 9.8 mph
DAYS
0° or below: 8
32° or below: 146
90° or above: 11
Clear: 66
Partly Cloudy: 94
Cloudy: 205

ANNUAL
Precipitation: 36.0"
Snow: 71.6"
DAYS
Precipitation: 75
Thunderstorm: 34
Fog: 137

Great Falls, MT

Location: 47.29 N, 111.22 W, at 3,660 feet, astride the main stem of the Missouri River at its confluence with the Sun River in west central Montana, near the 93-foot Great Falls.

Landscape: The valley is bordered by mountain ranges which lie about 30 miles away from east to south, 40 miles to the southwest, and 60 miles to 100 miles from west to northwest. Terrain plays an important part in the climate here; the Continental Divide to the west and the Big Belt and Little Belt mountains to the south are major factors in producing the frequent wintertime Chinook winds blowing through this part of the state.

Cimate: Semiarid Steppe. Summers are cool, sunny, and pleasant. Seventy percent of the annual rainfall occurs between April and September, the freeze-free growing season. The first frost arrives in mid-September. Winters are cold but continually modified by Chinook winds, which bear warm air from the Pacific, causing rapid warming and preventing accumulation of snow. By mid-May, the last frost has departed.

Winter mildness: 14	**Seasonal affect:** 69
Summer mildness: 68	**Hazardousness:** 7
Score: 16.71	**Rank:** 295

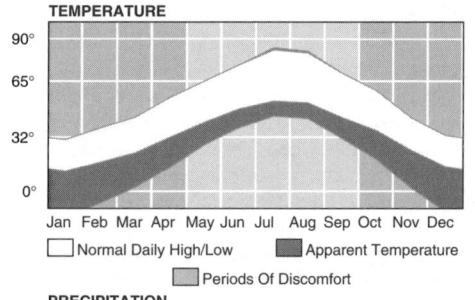

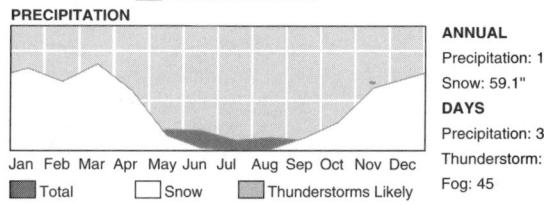

ANNUAL
Humidity: 56%
Wind Speed: 12.7 mph
DAYS
0° or below: 28
32° or below: 155
90° or above: 18
Clear: 79
Partly Cloudy: 107
Cloudy: 179

ANNUAL
Precipitation: 15.2"
Snow: 59.1"
DAYS
Precipitation: 32
Thunderstorm: 25
Fog: 45

Green Bay, WI

Location: 44.29 N, 88.08 W, at 700 feet, at the mouth of the Fox River which empties into the southmost end of Green Bay, a long and narrow bay off Lake Michigan in northeast Wisconsin.

Landscape: The comparatively small temperature variation and the fact that the majority of precipitation falls during the growing periods contribute to successful dairy farming, as well as large areas of vegetables grown mostly for canning. Apple and cherry orchards predominate locally, with potatoes grown widely farther west.

Cimate: Continental, modified somewhat by the proximity of Lake Superior to the northwest and Lake Michigan and Green Bay to the east. The first freeze is early October; the last is mid-May. Summers are pleasant, with cool evenings and nights. Thunderstorms and heavy rains can be expected in late summer and fall. Winters tend to be long and cold and seem to come early. Packer football fans are hardy souls. The area experiences a moderate amount of snow for a city in this region and latitude.

Winter mildness: 7	**Seasonal affect:** 42
Summer mildness: 85	**Hazardousness:** 21
Score: 10.48	**Rank:** 317

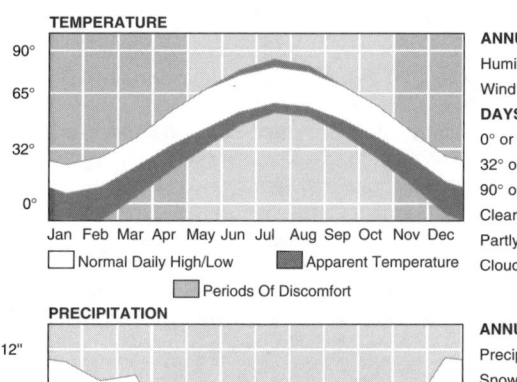

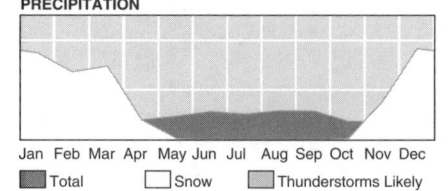

ANNUAL
Humidity: 73%
Wind Speed: 9.9 mph
DAYS
0° or below: 29
32° or below: 163
90° or above: 7
Clear: 86
Partly Cloudy: 103
Cloudy: 176

ANNUAL
Precipitation: 28.8"
Snow: 46.1"
DAYS
Precipitation: 63
Thunderstorm: 33
Fog: 124

Greensboro–Winston-Salem–High Point, NC

Location: 36.05 N, 79.57 W, at 900 feet, in the northern Piedmont section of north central North Carolina at the headwaters of the Haw and Deep rivers.

Landscape: Bounded to the west and north by ridges beyond which lie the Brushy and Blue Ridge mountains. Local gently rolling hills merge to higher elevations. Red clay soil dominates and heavy applications of lime and fertilizers are necessary for good crop yields. There are no major rivers, but a dense network of streams keeps the area well drained.

Cimate: Winter temperatures and rainfall are modified by the mountain barrier. Freezing temperatures occur on more than half the winter days, but zero weather is almost unknown. Light snow may fall, perhaps two snows of an inch or more per year; ice-glazing is more common here than in most of North Carolina—an average of four times a year—but it is seldom severe or longlasting. The first freeze comes in late October, the last at the beginning of April.

Winter mildness: 61	**Seasonal affect:** 71
Summer mildness: 46	**Hazardousness:** 69
Score: 80.73	**Rank: 69**

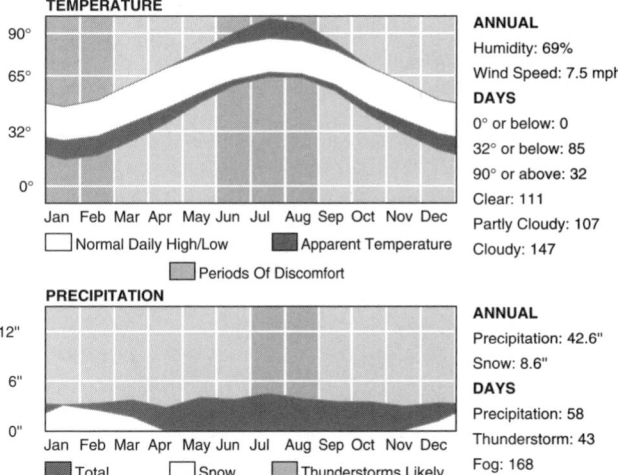

TEMPERATURE

□ Normal Daily High/Low ■ Apparent Temperature
■ Periods Of Discomfort

PRECIPITATION

■ Total □ Snow ■ Thunderstorms Likely

ANNUAL
Humidity: 69%
Wind Speed: 7.5 mph
DAYS
0° or below: 0
32° or below: 85
90° or above: 32
Clear: 111
Partly Cloudy: 107
Cloudy: 147

ANNUAL
Precipitation: 42.6"
Snow: 8.6"
DAYS
Precipitation: 58
Thunderstorm: 43
Fog: 168

Greenville, NC

Location: 35.37 N, 77.23 W, at 30 feet, in eastern North Carolina on the Tar River; 70 miles east of Raleigh, the state capital.

Landscape: Coastal Plain, divided into the Tidewater Area, which is quite flat, poorly drained, and often marshy, and the Inner Coastal Plain, which is higher, better drained, and better suited for agriculture. Fronted with pines, sandy soils dominate the plain. Red clay dominates in the Piedmont. Heavy applications of lime and fertilizers are necessary for good yields, and continued care must be taken to prevent erosion. The area is an overlapping ecological zone, and vegetation is both mid-latitude and subtropical.

Cimate: Subtropical, with humid hot summers and winters that are generally mild. The last freeze occurs at the beginning of April, the first at the beginning of November. There are no zero degree days. Mountains to the north and northwest protect the area from cold fronts. Rain falls throughout the year with thunderstorms peaking in July and August. Occasional tropical storms and hurricanes from the Atlantic Ocean, beyond the Outer Banks some 100 miles east, may strike this location.

Winter mildness: 66	**Seasonal affect:** 33
Summer mildness: 34	**Hazardousness:** 70
Score: 58.35	**Rank: 148**

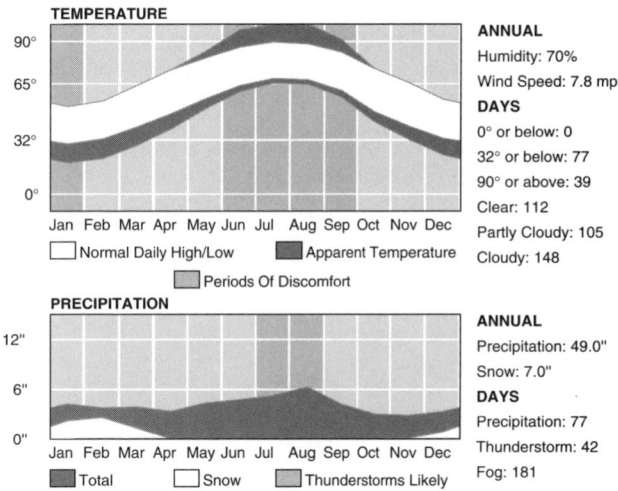

TEMPERATURE

□ Normal Daily High/Low ■ Apparent Temperature
■ Periods Of Discomfort

PRECIPITATION

■ Total □ Snow ■ Thunderstorms Likely

ANNUAL
Humidity: 70%
Wind Speed: 7.8 mph
DAYS
0° or below: 0
32° or below: 77
90° or above: 39
Clear: 112
Partly Cloudy: 105
Cloudy: 148

ANNUAL
Precipitation: 49.0"
Snow: 7.0"
DAYS
Precipitation: 77
Thunderstorm: 42
Fog: 181

Greenville-Spartanburg-Anderson, SC

Location: 34.54 N, 82.13 W, at 860 feet, on the Piedmont Plateau, on the eastern slope of the southern Appalachian Mountains.

Landscape: Rolling country with the first ridge of mountains about 20 miles to the northwest. These mountains protect the area from the full force of the cold air masses that move southeastward from central Canada during the winter.

Cimate: The area's elevation is conducive to cool nights, even during the summer months. Temperatures rise to 90°F or above on almost half of the days during the summer, then fall to 70°F or lower at night. Winters are mild and pleasant, with the temperature falling below freezing during daylight hours only several times annually, though the nights are colder. There are usually two freezing rainstorms and two or three small snowstorms each winter. Rainfall is abundant and well distributed throughout the year. The region is fairly stormy, but tornadoes are infrequent. Average growing season: 225 days.

Winter mildness: 67	**Seasonal affect:** 42
Summer mildness: 41	**Hazardousness:** 71
Score: 74.78	**Rank: 90**

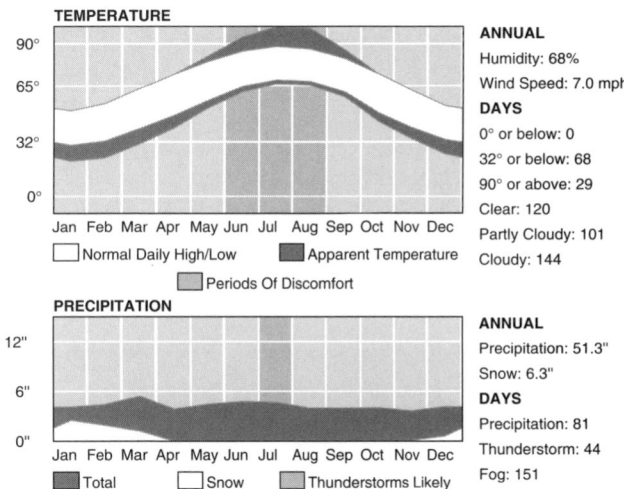

TEMPERATURE

□ Normal Daily High/Low ■ Apparent Temperature
■ Periods Of Discomfort

PRECIPITATION

■ Total □ Snow ■ Thunderstorms Likely

ANNUAL
Humidity: 68%
Wind Speed: 7.0 mph
DAYS
0° or below: 0
32° or below: 68
90° or above: 29
Clear: 120
Partly Cloudy: 101
Cloudy: 144

ANNUAL
Precipitation: 51.3"
Snow: 6.3"
DAYS
Precipitation: 81
Thunderstorm: 44
Fog: 151

Halifax, NS

Location: 44.38 N, 63.30 W, at 476 feet, on the west side of the harbor on a peninsula with the Gulf of St. Lawrence to the north, the Bay of Fundy to the west, and the Atlantic Ocean to the south and east.

Landscape: The area is flat to rolling with numerous small lakes. Elevations of 500 feet are reached in three areas: 11 miles to the north, 21 miles to the north-northwest in the Devon area, and in the Mt. Uniacke area, 25 miles to the northwest.

Cimate: At the International Airport, fog is observed 122 days every year. Atlantic and Fundy waters help to keep the air temperature cool in spring and summer and moderate the harshness of winter. The presence of the Gulf Stream is credited with prolonging fall, the season Nova Scotians consider to be the finest of the year. Precipitation is experienced as rain and is spread evenly throughout the year. Atlantic storms produce highly changeable weather; winter storms are especially devastating.

Winter mildness: 48
Summer mildness: 97
Score: 50.99

Seasonal affect: 4
Hazardousness: 12
Rank: 174

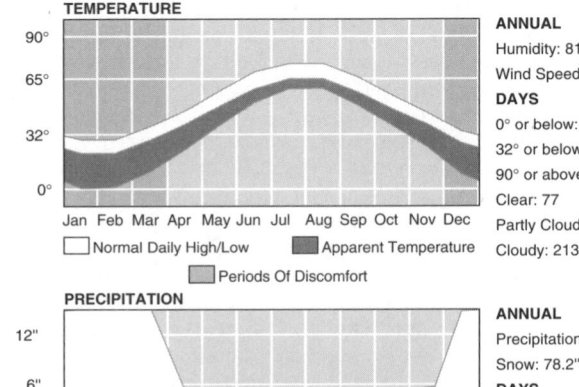

ANNUAL
Humidity: 81%
Wind Speed: 11.2 mph
DAYS
0° or below: 2
32° or below: 146
90° or above: 0
Clear: 77
Partly Cloudy: 75
Cloudy: 213

ANNUAL
Precipitation: 53.7"
Snow: 78.2"
DAYS
Precipitation: 138
Thunderstorm: 10
Fog: 101

Harrisburg-Lebanon-Carlisle, PA

Location: 40.13 N, 76.51 W, at 340 feet, on the east bank of the Susquehanna River in the Great Valley formed by the eastern foothills of the Appalachian chain and about 60 miles southeast of the state's geographic center.

Landscape: Area is nestled in a saucer-like depression 8 miles to 10 miles south of the Blue Mountains. This serves as a barrier to the severe winter weather experienced 50 miles to 100 miles to the north and west. Although Harrisburg is too far inland to derive full benefits of the coastal climate, it does receive precipitation produced when warm, Maritime air from the Atlantic is forced upslope to cross the Blue Ridge Mountains.

Cimate: Although the saucer-shaped valley protects the area from generally severe winter weather, it often traps cool air, which causes the accumulation of heavy fog and industrial smoke. Fortunately, the weather is changeable enough so that this trapped air does not remain for long. Average growing season: 201 days.

Winter mildness: 48
Summer mildness: 52
Score: 56.37

Seasonal affect: 21
Hazardousness: 51
Rank: 155

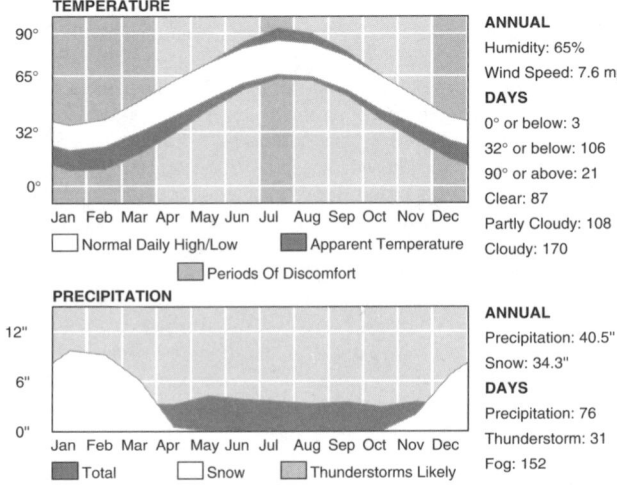

ANNUAL
Humidity: 65%
Wind Speed: 7.6 mph
DAYS
0° or below: 3
32° or below: 106
90° or above: 21
Clear: 87
Partly Cloudy: 108
Cloudy: 170

ANNUAL
Precipitation: 40.5"
Snow: 34.3"
DAYS
Precipitation: 76
Thunderstorm: 31
Fog: 152

Hartford, CT

Location: 41.56 N, 72.41 W, at 160 feet, on the Connecticut River about 40 miles due north of Long Island Sound; 110 miles northeast of New York.

Landscape: On a slight rise of ground between low north-south mountain ranges near the state's geographic center, in the region known as the Central Lowlands. Forests in the mountains are deciduous hardwood. Cleared land areas are fertile. The Connecticut River drains the surrounding land.

Cimate: Varies from cold Continental in winter to the warm Maritime air of summer. Hartford's latitude places it well within the northern temperate climate zone, with westerly winds bearing the majority of weather systems. Its nearness to the ocean is also significant, since many storms move upward along the Atlantic Coast frequently producing strong and persistent northeast winds. Hartford has a mean January temperature of 25°F and a mean July temperature of 78°F; it receives 44 inches of precipitation yearly. The first frost is October 12, the last, April 23.

Winter mildness: 29
Summer mildness: 56
Score: 41.35

Seasonal affect: 16
Hazardousness: 43
Rank: 208

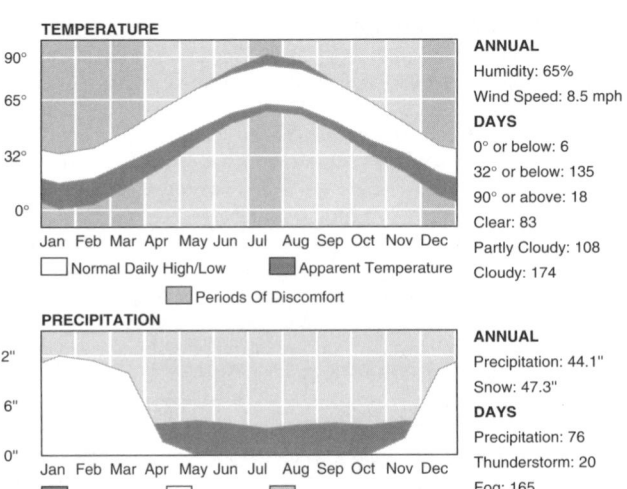

ANNUAL
Humidity: 65%
Wind Speed: 8.5 mph
DAYS
0° or below: 6
32° or below: 135
90° or above: 18
Clear: 83
Partly Cloudy: 108
Cloudy: 174

ANNUAL
Precipitation: 44.1"
Snow: 47.3"
DAYS
Precipitation: 76
Thunderstorm: 20
Fog: 165

Hattiesburg, MS

Location: 31.19 N, 89.18 W, at 160 feet, in the southern part of Mississippi some 70 miles north of Gulfport and the Gulf of Mexico.

Landscape: In the Piney Woods section of the Gulf Coastal Plain, a long-leaf pine belt that has slash and loblolly pine. Mississippi, as a whole, has large forest resources. Hattiesburg was founded by pioneer lumbermen in the 1880s. Topographical features include alluvial soils, gentle sloping plains, and extensive ground water resources. Most of the numerous streams are sluggish. There are many marshes, lakes, and swamps.

Cimate: Subtropical with local average precipitation of 60 to 70 inches each year falling as rain. The area is subject to thunderstorms in midsummer and hurricanes in the late summer and early autumn. The first freeze is typically November 8. Winter minimums average 44°F; consequently, snow and sleet are rare. The last frost usually occurs on March 17. With high relative humidity and high temperatures that can top 95°F, summers are uncomfortably hot.

Winter mildness: 76	**Seasonal affect:** 46
Summer mildness: 19	**Hazardousness:** 74
Score: 55.24	**Rank: 159**

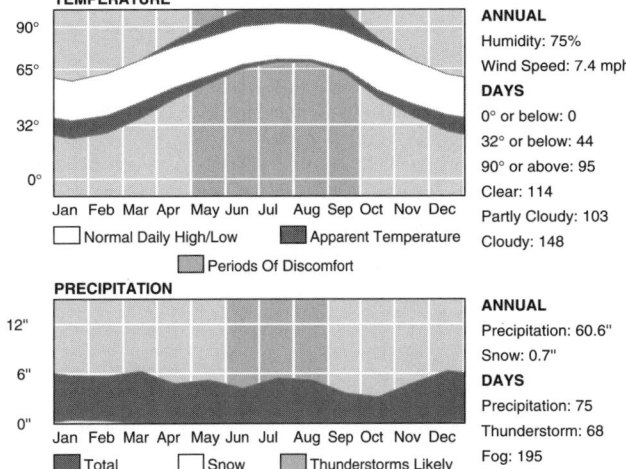

★Honolulu, HI

Location: 21.20 N, 157.55 W, at 10 feet, just south of the Tropic of Cancer in the Pacific.

Landscape: Oahu, the island on which Honolulu is located, is the third largest of the Hawaiian Islands. The Koolau Range, at an average height of 2,000 feet, parallels the northeast coast. The Waianae Mountains parallel the west coast. Much of the city lies along the Coastal Plain, leeward of the Koolaus. Honolulu's natural assets—Waikiki Beach, the Koolau Mountains rising dramatically beyond the hotels, and extinct volcanic craters, such as Diamond Head—attract up to 6.5 million visitors annually.

Cimate: Mild Marine Tropical, shows the least seasonal temperature change of any American city; the difference between the mean January minimum temperature and the August maximum mean temperature is only about 22°. There is no snow, fog, or freezing weather, and an average of twenty-three 90° days and fourteen thunderstorms a year. Although it is sometimes uncomfortably warm, persistent trade winds give relief. The annual average temperature is 77°F.

Winter mildness: 100	**Seasonal affect:** 97
Summer mildness: 44	**Hazardousness:** 93
Score: 98.58	**Rank: 6**

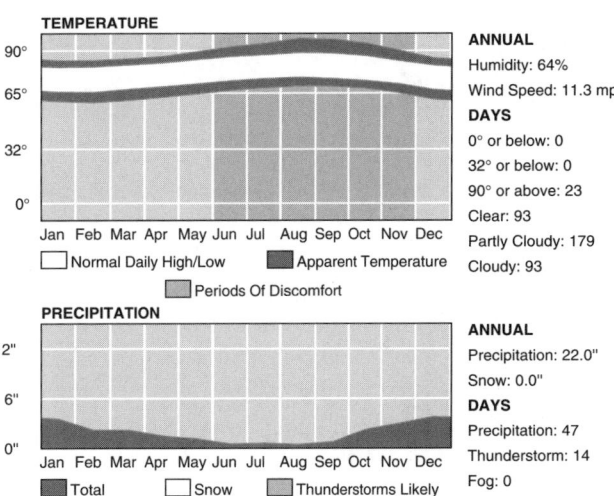

Houston, TX

Location: 29.39 N, 95.17 W, at 50 feet, in the flat Coastal Plain of Texas, about 50 miles inland from the Gulf of Mexico and 25 miles from Galveston Bay.

Landscape: Coastal Prairie includes low, flat lands suitable for agriculture; bayous bordered by magnolias; and wooded heights. The numerous small streams and bayous, together with the bay, favor the development of fog. Meandering Buffalo Bayou, the original city site, has become the famed Houston Ship Channel.

Cimate: Predominantly mild Marine. Temperatures are modified by winds from the Gulf, but these breezes also assure high humidity year-round. Summer days are hot and humid, though the evenings are relatively cool. The first freeze is December 6. Winters are mild. Polar air penetrates the area frequently enough to provide some stimulating variety. Although temperatures dip below freezing occasionally, they never remain there long, accounting for a year-round growing season. The latest frost is February 16. Destructive windstorms are infrequent, but thunderstorms and hurricanes do occur.

Winter mildness: 93	**Seasonal affect:** 55
Summer mildness: 16	**Hazardousness:** 74
Score: 80.45	**Rank: 70**

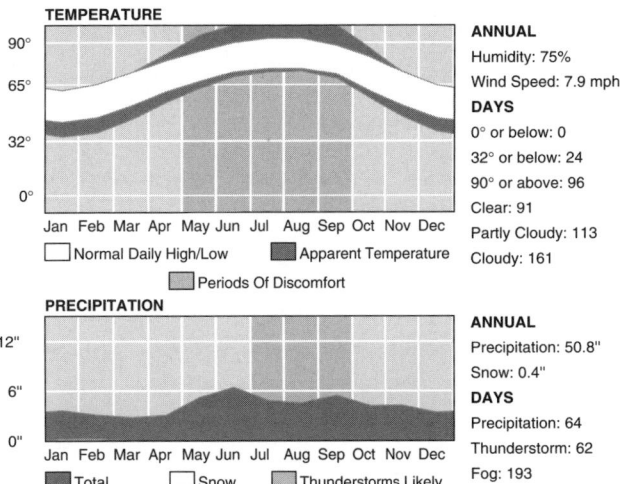

Climate

Huntsville, AL

Location: 34.39 N, 86.46 W, at 620 feet, just north of the Tennessee River; 20 miles from the border with Tennessee.

Landscape: The city is almost surrounded by the foothills of the Appalachian Mountains. The Tennessee River winds its way westward about 7 miles south of the city, and the broad and fertile Tennessee Valley, with flat to gently rolling terrain, extends to the west.

Cimate: Cold air masses from the north predominate during the winter, but at times mild air from the Gulf of Mexico may persist for several days. There are few severely cold days. Temperatures drop below zero perhaps once a year. Springs are variable and stormy as cold polar air and warm Gulf air meet. Summers are hot and humid, relieved only by showers that come about every three days. Falls are dry, cooler, and pleasant. The high rainfall and length of the growing season, 241 days—from the end of March to the beginning of November—make the area suitable for truck farming.

Winter mildness: 65	**Seasonal affect:** 25
Summer mildness: 37	**Hazardousness:** 64
Score: 53.25	**Rank: 166**

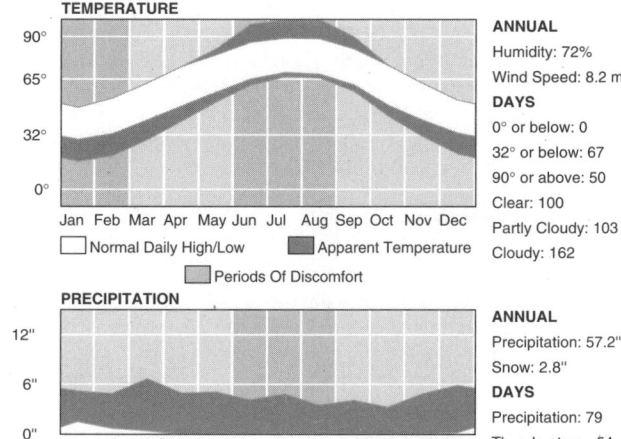

TEMPERATURE

☐ Normal Daily High/Low   ■ Apparent Temperature   ☐ Periods Of Discomfort

ANNUAL
Humidity: 72%
Wind Speed: 8.2 mph
DAYS
0° or below: 0
32° or below: 67
90° or above: 50
Clear: 100
Partly Cloudy: 103
Cloudy: 162

PRECIPITATION

■ Total   ☐ Snow   ☐ Thunderstorms Likely

ANNUAL
Precipitation: 57.2"
Snow: 2.8"
DAYS
Precipitation: 79
Thunderstorm: 54
Fog: 148

Indianapolis, IN

Location: 39.44 N, 86.16 W, at 790 feet, in the central part of Indiana; the greater part of the city lies east of the White River.

Landscape: Mostly level or slightly rolling terrain. The river flows north to south. From the airport, 7 miles southwest of the city, the terrain slopes gradually downward to the city, then upward again past the city to the east. Several flood control reservoirs protect most formerly flood-prone areas.

Cimate: Continental with rather warm summers, moderately cold winters, and occasional wide variations in temperatures, especially during the cold season. Snowfalls of 3 inches or more occur about three times annually. Periods of muggy weather can occur in summer, although these air masses from the Gulf of Mexico are soon replaced by cooler air from the northern Plains and Great Lakes. Occasionally, hot dry winds from the Southwest prevail. The last freeze is April 21. The first freeze is October 18. Precipitation, well distributed throughout the year, is normally adequate for good crops.

Winter mildness: 37	**Seasonal affect:** 27
Summer mildness: 54	**Hazardousness:** 43
Score: 23.51	**Rank: 271**

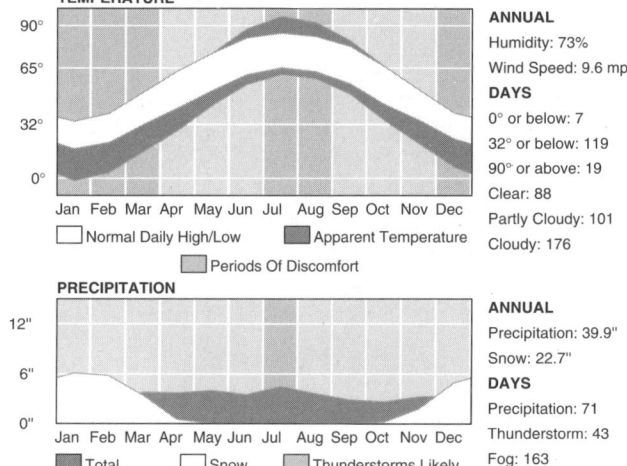

TEMPERATURE

☐ Normal Daily High/Low   ■ Apparent Temperature   ☐ Periods Of Discomfort

ANNUAL
Humidity: 73%
Wind Speed: 9.6 mph
DAYS
0° or below: 7
32° or below: 119
90° or above: 19
Clear: 88
Partly Cloudy: 101
Cloudy: 176

PRECIPITATION

■ Total   ☐ Snow   ☐ Thunderstorms Likely

ANNUAL
Precipitation: 39.9"
Snow: 22.7"
DAYS
Precipitation: 71
Thunderstorm: 43
Fog: 163

Iowa City, IA

Location: 41.39 N, 91.32 W, at 640 feet, along both banks of the Iowa River in eastern Iowa; 25 miles south of Cedar Rapids.

Landscape: Iowa has more prime agricultural soil than any other state. Iowa City is the center of a region dominated by cattle, grain, hogs, and poultry production. The area is characterized by rolling to fairly steep hills. Soil is prairie, high in organic content. The Iowa River provides an extensive drainage basin.

Cimate: Continental climate with extremes in both temperature and precipitation; potential for violent storms. Summer highs can reach 100°F accompanied by high humidity. Winter low temperatures range from 15°F to 25°F, but can get much colder. The typical frost-free season is 150 days, from April 22 to October 11. Precipitation can be highly variable, with large amounts falling all at once and then none at all for long periods. The area is typical of the state as a whole, susceptible to droughts, floods, blizzards, and tornadoes.

Winter mildness: 14	**Seasonal affect:** 52
Summer mildness: 44	**Hazardousness:** 28
Score: 7.64	**Rank: 327**

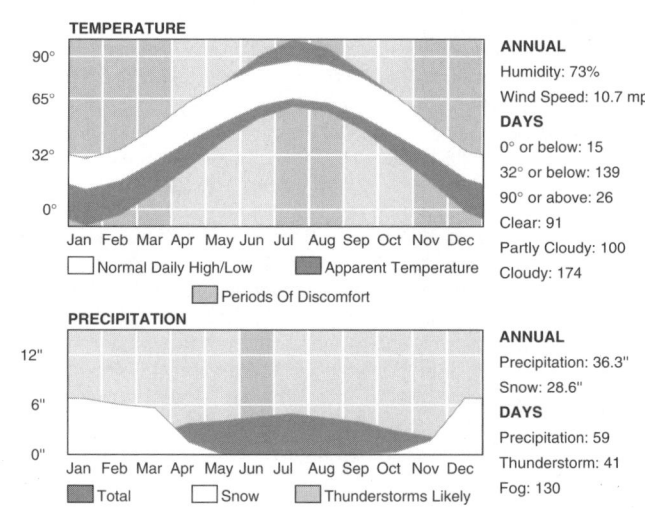

TEMPERATURE

☐ Normal Daily High/Low   ■ Apparent Temperature   ☐ Periods Of Discomfort

ANNUAL
Humidity: 73%
Wind Speed: 10.7 mph
DAYS
0° or below: 15
32° or below: 139
90° or above: 26
Clear: 91
Partly Cloudy: 100
Cloudy: 174

PRECIPITATION

■ Total   ☐ Snow   ☐ Thunderstorms Likely

ANNUAL
Precipitation: 36.3"
Snow: 28.6"
DAYS
Precipitation: 59
Thunderstorm: 41
Fog: 130

Jackson, MS

Location: 32.19 N, 90.05 W, at 310 feet, about 45 miles east of the Mississippi River on the west bank of the Pearl River and about 150 miles north of the Gulf of Mexico.

Landscape: Alluvial plains up to 3 miles wide extend along the river near Jackson, and some levees have been built on both sides of the river. Rolling hills of the Central Coastal Plain are predominant but there are bluffs along the river. Forests are mixed broadleafed deciduous and southern yellow pine.

Cimate: Significantly humid during most of the year, with one short cold season and one long warm one. In summer, the southerly winds and accompanying warm Gulf air masses predominate, resulting in a warm, humid Maritime climate. Summer days are hot and humid, and often so are the nights. In winter, colder northern air occasionally invades the area, causing rapid and sometimes dramatic temperature shifts. The average freeze-free period totals 235 days, from mid-March to mid-November.

Winter mildness: 74	**Seasonal affect:** 54
Summer mildness: 15	**Hazardousness:** 72
Score: 49.85	**Rank: 178**

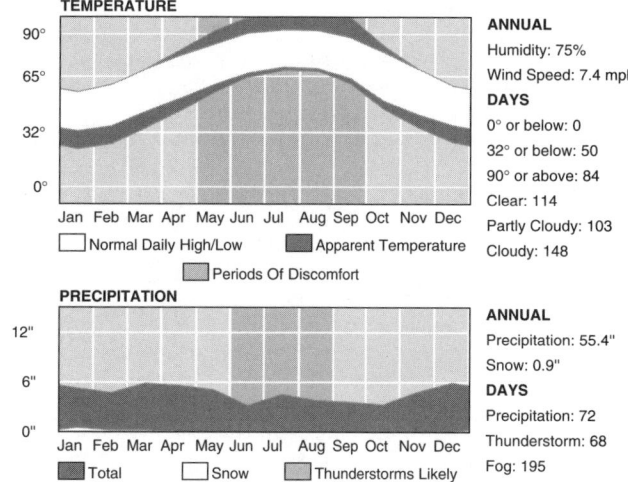

Jacksonville, FL

Location: 30.30 N, 81.42 W, at 30 feet, on the St. Johns River inland about 16 miles from the Atlantic Ocean in extreme northeast Florida.

Landscape: The surrounding terrain is irregular and level. Jacksonville is the leading deep-water port of entry on the southern United States Atlantic coast; a rail, air, and highway focal point; and a major East Coast center of U.S. Navy operations. The St. Johns River is Florida's longest. The surrounding vegetation is a typical southern mixed forest with pine predominating.

Cimate: Subtropical atmosphere is heavy with humidity. The average daily sunshine ranges from five and a half hours in December to nine hours in May. The greatest amount of rain, mostly in the form of local thundershowers, falls during July and August, when a measurable amount can be expected every other day. There is over 50 inches annually. Temperatures average 55°F in January and 82°F in July. The first freeze is mid-December; the last, mid-February.

Winter mildness: 88	**Seasonal affect:** 67
Summer mildness: 21	**Hazardousness:** 87
Score: 86.11	**Rank: 50**

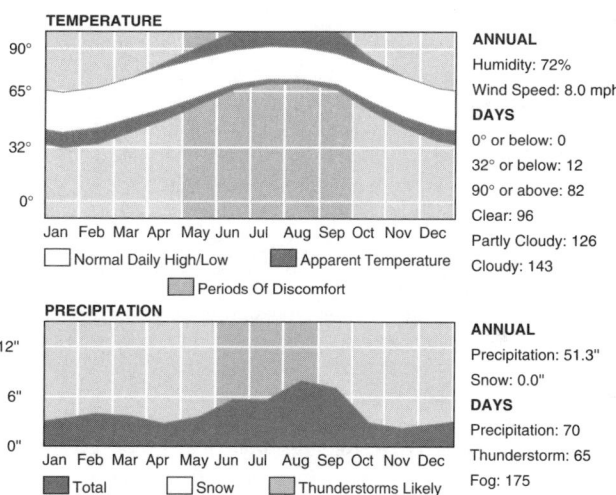

Johnson City-Kingsport-Bristol, TN-VA

Location: 36.31 N, 82.32 W, at 1,280 feet, the tri-city area is located in the extreme upper east Tennessee Valley.

Landscape: Gently rolling on the east and south, hilly on the west and north. Mountain ranges begin about 10 miles to the southeast and 15 miles to the west and north, with many peaks and ridges rising four to six thousand feet.

Cimate: The topography influences the weather changes. The moist, easterly airflow in the lower levels of the atmosphere affects the eastern slopes of the mountains, producing an abundance of precipitation in the higher ridges. The air masses reach the tri-city area drier and slightly warmer. Although average annual rainfall is 41 inches in the vicinity, annual amounts of 80 inches have been recorded in mountainous sections to the east and south. The first freeze is October 20; the last, April 16. Snowfall seldom begins before November and rarely remains on the ground more than a few days. Mountainous regions are often blanketed for long periods.

Winter mildness: 60	**Seasonal affect:** 17
Summer mildness: 45	**Hazardousness:** 64
Score: 64.30	**Rank: 127**

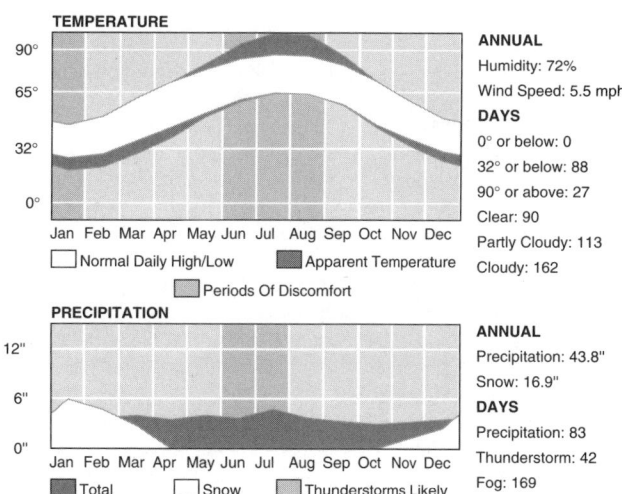

Climate

Kansas City, MO-KS

Location: 39.19 N, 94.43 W, at 970 feet, near the geographic center of the United States. Kansas City, Kansas, located in the northeastern part of its state, and Kansas City, Missouri, on the western side of its state are on opposite banks of the Kansas River where it meets the Missouri River. The two cities form one economic unit.

Landscape: The surrounding terrain is gently rolling. Its Continental climate is modified by a lack of natural obstructions to the free sweep of air currents from all directions. The metropolitan area did suffer extensive damage from flooding during the summer of 1993.

Cimate: Early spring brings a period of frequent and rapid fluctuations of weather, tapering off as spring progresses. Summer days are warm, sometimes hot, but nights are mild with moderate humidity. As with so many locations in America's heartland, fall is the most pleasant season, characterized by many mild sunny days and cool nights. The typical date of winter's last freeze is April 7. The first freeze occurs around October 26.

Winter mildness: 33	**Seasonal affect:** 74
Summer mildness: 39	**Hazardousness:** 30
Score: 26.91	**Rank: 259**

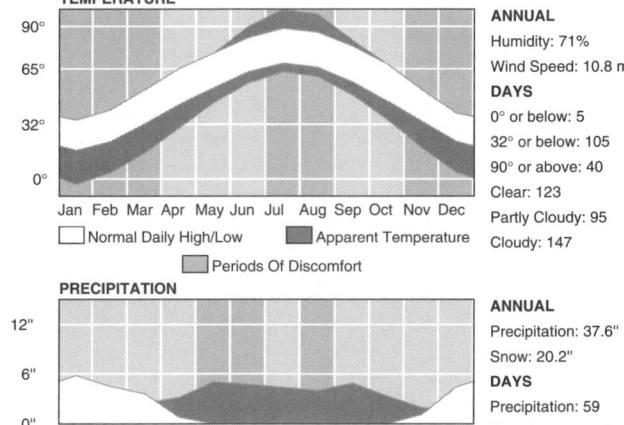

TEMPERATURE

Normal Daily High/Low — Apparent Temperature — Periods Of Discomfort

ANNUAL
Humidity: 71%
Wind Speed: 10.8 mph
DAYS
0° or below: 5
32° or below: 105
90° or above: 40
Clear: 123
Partly Cloudy: 95
Cloudy: 147

PRECIPITATION

Total — Snow — Thunderstorms Likely

ANNUAL
Precipitation: 37.6"
Snow: 20.2"
DAYS
Precipitation: 59
Thunderstorm: 51
Fog: 124

Kitchener-Waterloo, ON

Location: 43.27 N, 80.23 W, at 1,030 feet, in the heartland of southern Ontario in the Grand River Valley.

Landscape: Brown and gray-brown soils cover most of the flat low-lying plains of the Ontario Peninsula. Naturally fertile, these soils can support a wide range of crops and other agricultural activities when properly farmed. Waterloo is the center of a farming region known for its mushrooms. The metro area, with the cities of Cambridge and Guelph, make up what is known as Canada's Technology Triangle. Much of the landscape is urban and industrial.

Cimate: Humid Continental. The surrounding presence of the Great Lakes influences temperature, the number of frost-free days, and the ratio of sunshine to cloudy days. The winter months are long and cold and snowy with highs around 30°F. Summers are short and warm with average temperatures of 70°F. Frost-free periods average 170 to 180 days, from the beginning of May to mid-October. Average precipitation is 31 inches annually.

Winter mildness: 15	**Seasonal affect:** 18
Summer mildness: 87	**Hazardousness:** 21
Score: 35.69	**Rank: 228**

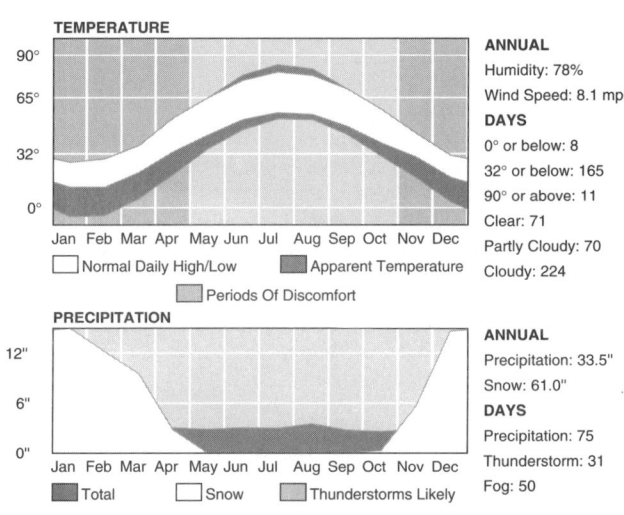

TEMPERATURE

Normal Daily High/Low — Apparent Temperature — Periods Of Discomfort

ANNUAL
Humidity: 78%
Wind Speed: 8.1 mph
DAYS
0° or below: 8
32° or below: 165
90° or above: 11
Clear: 71
Partly Cloudy: 70
Cloudy: 224

PRECIPITATION

Total — Snow — Thunderstorms Likely

ANNUAL
Precipitation: 33.5"
Snow: 61.0"
DAYS
Precipitation: 75
Thunderstorm: 31
Fog: 50

Knoxville, TN

Location: 35.49 N, 83.59 W, at 880 feet, on the Tennessee River in a broad valley between the Cumberland Mountains and the Great Smoky Mountains; 175 miles east of Nashville.

Landscape: The Cumberlands serve to retard and weaken the force of the cold winter air moving down from the northern Plains during the colder months. The Smokies shelter Knoxville from much of the hot, humid tropical air that moves northward during the summertime.

Cimate: Moderate Continental, thanks to the sheltering effects of the two mountain ranges. The latest freeze usually occurs April 15. Though summers are long, the nights are almost always cool, with the average diurnal variation being about 20 degreees. The mean daytime temperature for July is 81°F, but nighttime temperatures are in the mid-70s. The earliest frost arrives by the end of October. Freezing temperatures are common from December to March but seldom fall to zero or below.

Winter mildness: 60	**Seasonal affect:** 19
Summer mildness: 45	**Hazardousness:** 60
Score: 57.50	**Rank: 151**

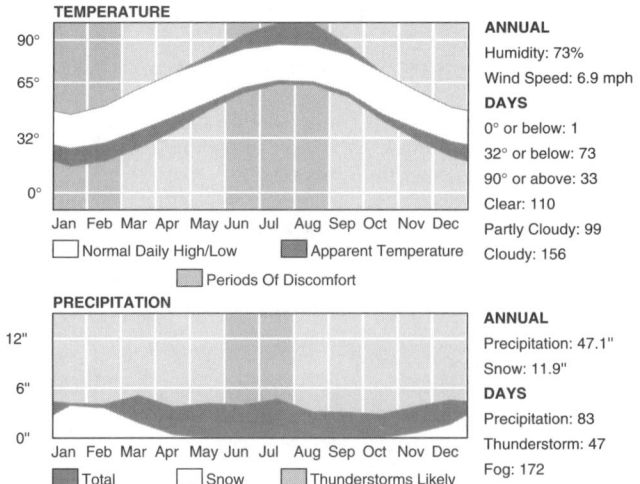

TEMPERATURE

Normal Daily High/Low — Apparent Temperature — Periods Of Discomfort

ANNUAL
Humidity: 73%
Wind Speed: 6.9 mph
DAYS
0° or below: 1
32° or below: 73
90° or above: 33
Clear: 110
Partly Cloudy: 99
Cloudy: 156

PRECIPITATION

Total — Snow — Thunderstorms Likely

ANNUAL
Precipitation: 47.1"
Snow: 11.9"
DAYS
Precipitation: 83
Thunderstorm: 47
Fog: 172

La Crosse, WI-MN

Location: 43.52 N, 91.15 W, at 650 feet, the city is at the foot of the high bluffs on the east bank of the Mississippi River, at the confluence with the Black and La Crosse rivers; 65 miles northeast of the Twin Cities—Minneapolis and St. Paul.

Landscape: Situated on a level, sandy plain, but steep-sided hills with narrow valleys are characteristic of most of the surrounding area. The leading field crops are corn, hay, and oats. Dairying is the principal farm activity.

Cimate: The location of the city in a natural bowl between the hills results in colder temperatures at night due to air drainage and in valley fogs that often persist through forenoon. The Continental climate means frequent variations in temperature. Winters are cold and humid; snows are frequent. Summers are warm and moderately humid. Most of the annual precipitation falls during the main growing season extending from May to September. The last freeze is May 3; the first is October 7.

Winter mildness: 6   **Seasonal affect:** 60
Summer mildness: 59   **Hazardousness:** 33
Score: 20.67   **Rank:** 281

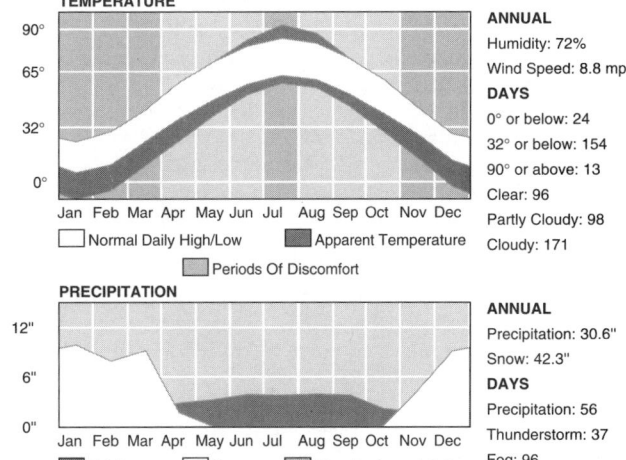

ANNUAL
Humidity: 72%
Wind Speed: 8.8 mph
DAYS
0° or below: 24
32° or below: 154
90° or above: 13
Clear: 96
Partly Cloudy: 98
Cloudy: 171

ANNUAL
Precipitation: 30.6"
Snow: 42.3"
DAYS
Precipitation: 56
Thunderstorm: 37
Fog: 96

Lakeland-Winter Haven, FL

Location: 28.01 N, 81.55 W, at 150 feet, in the highland region of central Florida; 32 miles east of Tampa, 50 miles from the Gulf of Mexico, and 70 miles from the Atlantic.

Landscape: This rolling lake-ridge section has the highest elevation in the Florida peninsula. Floodplain prairies and pine flatwoods mix with live oak hammocks. Forests are a mix of hardwood, longleaf and slash pine found in coastal areas. Aromatic and evergreen bayberry and sweet bay are scattered throughout. There are 97 lakes within a radius of 5 miles and a boat course of 17 connected lakes.

Cimate: The Subtropical latitude and proximity of the Gulf of Mexico and Atlantic make winters pleasant. Days are bright and warm; nights are cool. Rainfall is light to moderate. Occasionally, major cold waves spread over the area bringing below-freezing temperatures. The first freeze is mid-December; the last is at the beginning of February. High temperatures of the long summers are moderated by afternoon thundershowers.

Winter mildness: 97   **Seasonal affect:** 69
Summer mildness: 17   **Hazardousness:** 83
Score: 86.68   **Rank:** 48

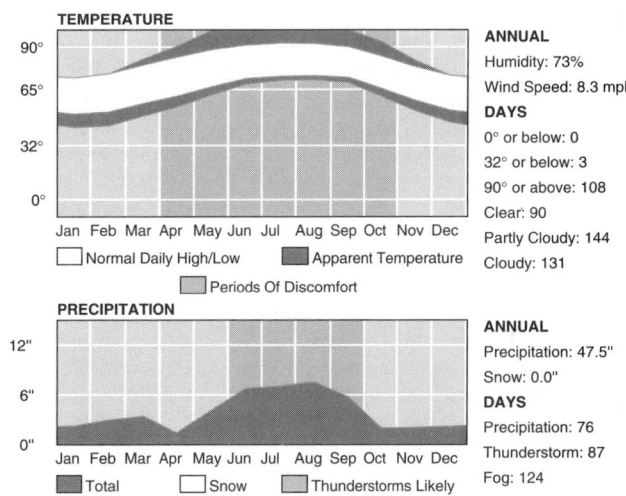

ANNUAL
Humidity: 73%
Wind Speed: 8.3 mph
DAYS
0° or below: 0
32° or below: 3
90° or above: 108
Clear: 90
Partly Cloudy: 144
Cloudy: 131

ANNUAL
Precipitation: 47.5"
Snow: 0.0"
DAYS
Precipitation: 76
Thunderstorm: 87
Fog: 124

Lancaster, PA

Location: 40.03 N, 76.17 W, at 270 feet, on the Conestoga River in the heart of southeastern Pennsylvania Dutch Country; 60 miles west of Philadelphia.

Landscape: In the center of the fertile Piedmont plateau, where grain, livestock, tobacco, and dairy products are produced. The relief is gently sloping upward as hill rises above valley. The soil is fine and fertile. The area is drained by the Susquehanna River system flowing 20 miles to the west. The forest is mixed deciduous hardwoods, with oak, maple, ash, and elm. The famous Conestoga wagon was developed here.

Cimate: Pennsylvania has a humid Continental climate, but topographic differences result in local eccentricities. Lancaster, in the southeast, has long, hot summers and comparatively mild winters. The growing season is 170 to 200 days, starting usually the first week in May and ending mid-October. Precipitation is more than adequate, averaging 35 to 50 inches. Average annual snowfall is 30 inches. The seasons are distinct but not harsh.

Winter mildness: 43   **Seasonal affect:** 24
Summer mildness: 57   **Hazardousness:** 62
Score: 50.70   **Rank:** 175

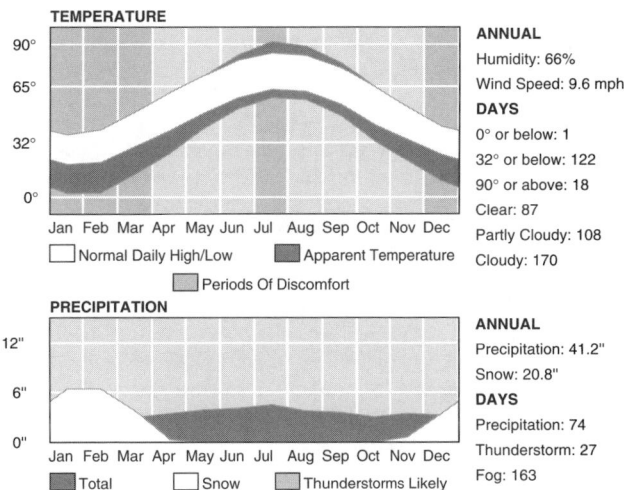

ANNUAL
Humidity: 66%
Wind Speed: 9.6 mph
DAYS
0° or below: 1
32° or below: 122
90° or above: 18
Clear: 87
Partly Cloudy: 108
Cloudy: 170

ANNUAL
Precipitation: 41.2"
Snow: 20.8"
DAYS
Precipitation: 74
Thunderstorm: 27
Fog: 163

Lansing-East Lansing, MI

Location: 42.46 N, 84.36 W, at 840 feet, at the junction of the Grand, Red Cedar, and Sycamore rivers in the southern part of the state; 84 miles west of Detroit.

Landscape: Large agricultural area. The topography is lowland punctuated with glacial uplands. The soil is productive, mixed organic bog, created when prehistoric inland lakes filled in with rich nutrients. Bog soils are well adapted for vegetable production. Throughout southern Michigan, hardwood tree species are regenerating in the original forests.

Cimate: Humid Continental; however, the presence of the Great Lakes influences temperature, the number of frost-free days, and the ratio of sunshine to cloudy days. Average annual temperature is 50°F. Frost-free periods average 170 to 180 days, from the beginning of May to mid-October. Average precipitation is 31 inches annually. Snow, sleet, hail, and ice storms are common, and tornadoes and blizzards sometimes occur. Snowfall averages 45 inches annually. Heavy cloud cover in the fall and early winter is common because the Great Lakes rarely freeze totally.

Winter mildness: 19	**Seasonal affect:** 27
Summer mildness: 73	**Hazardousness:** 18
Score: 11.04	**Rank: 315**

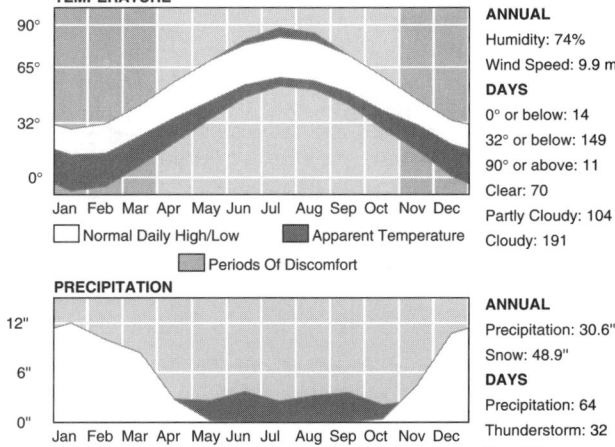

ANNUAL
Humidity: 74%
Wind Speed: 9.9 mph
DAYS
0° or below: 14
32° or below: 149
90° or above: 11
Clear: 70
Partly Cloudy: 104
Cloudy: 191

ANNUAL
Precipitation: 30.6"
Snow: 48.9"
DAYS
Precipitation: 64
Thunderstorm: 32
Fog: 153

★Laredo, TX

Location: 27.34 N, 99.30 W, at 430 feet, in south Texas on the Rio Grande River, opposite Nuevo Laredo, Mexico; 230 miles southwest of Austin, the state capital.

Landscape: Prairie; rolling hills and undulating plains, with western shrub vegetation. On the slopes leading down to the Rio Grande, the ceniza shrub dominates. The Rio Grande valley is covered by brush, mesquite, cedar, pot oak, and occasional dense growth of prickly pear. Extensive irrigation has brought once arid land into fertile agricultural farms. Level land toward the east is suitable for grazing.

Cimate: Semiarid Desert. The climate is distinctly dry. Rainfall, as showers, is less than 10 inches annually. Summers are long and hot; temperatures are in the mid-90s over 150 days. Typical to the desert, night temperatures fall about twenty degrees. Winters are short. December and January, the driest months, record minimum temperatures in the 40s. The average first freeze is mid-December; the last is the beginning of February. There are no temperatures of zero.

Winter mildness: 93	**Seasonal affect:** 93
Summer mildness: 1	**Hazardousness:** 90
Score: 91.78	**Rank: 30**

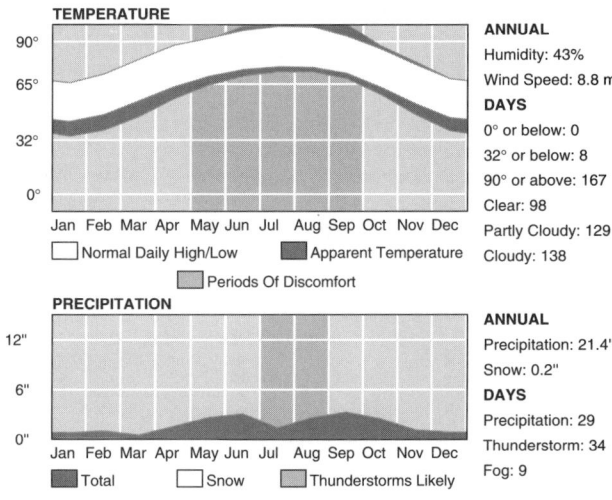

ANNUAL
Humidity: 43%
Wind Speed: 8.8 mph
DAYS
0° or below: 0
32° or below: 8
90° or above: 167
Clear: 98
Partly Cloudy: 129
Cloudy: 138

ANNUAL
Precipitation: 21.4"
Snow: 0.2"
DAYS
Precipitation: 29
Thunderstorm: 34
Fog: 9

Las Cruces, NM

Location: 32.37 N, 106.44 W, at 4,270 feet, on the Rio Grande River, near the southern edge of the state; 40 miles northwest of El Paso, TX.

Landscape: The wide, level Mesilla Valley, irrigated by Elephant Butte Dam, runs northwest to southeast. Rolling desert borders the southwest and west. About 12 miles to the east, the Organ Mountains, with peaks above 8,500 feet, form a rugged backdrop. The northwest portion of the valley narrows to low hills and buttes. Only plants adapted to the highly alkaline dry-desert conditions survive here. There are belts of oak and juniper woodland.

Cimate: Desert characterized by low rainfall, summers with hot days and cool nights, and pleasant winters. The rainfall—brief showers, drizzles are unknown—at 11 inches per year, is light. Since almost all of it falls during the summer growing months, considerable forage is available on nearby grazing lands. Winters tend to be mild and sunny. The average first freeze is mid-December; the last is mid-February.

Winter mildness: 44	**Seasonal affect:** 99
Summer mildness: 6	**Hazardousness:** 79
Score: 58.92	**Rank: 146**

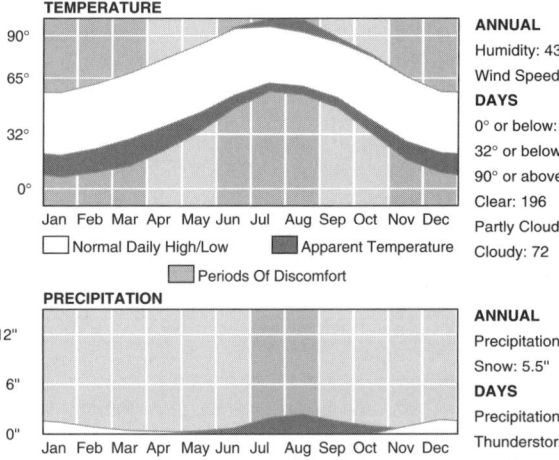

ANNUAL
Humidity: 43%
Wind Speed: 8.8 mph
DAYS
0° or below: 0
32° or below: 38
90° or above: 86
Clear: 196
Partly Cloudy: 97
Cloudy: 72

ANNUAL
Precipitation: 10.5"
Snow: 5.5"
DAYS
Precipitation: 22
Thunderstorm: 34
Fog: 9

Las Vegas, NV-AZ

Location: 36.05 N, 115.10 W, at 2,160 feet, at the tip of southern Nevada just west of the Colorado River valley; about 300 miles northeast of Los Angeles.

Landscape: Near the center of a broad desert valley surrounded by mountains from 2,000 to 10,000 feet higher than the valley's floor. These mountains act as effective barriers to moisture laden storms moving in from the Pacific Ocean. The thick-branched Joshua tree grows among creosote bushes and jumbled boulders in the Mojave Desert region. Las Vegas is the center of a large mining and ranching area.

Cimate: Summers are typical of a Desert climate. Humidity is low with maximum temperatures in the 100 degree levels. Nearby mountains contribute to relatively cool nights. Spring and fall are ideal, rarely interrupted by adverse weather conditions. Winters, too, are mild, with daytime averages of 60°F, clear skies, and warm sunshine. There are few overcast or rainy days. The average first freeze is mid-December. The last freeze is the beginning of February.

Winter mildness: 75	**Seasonal affect:** 99
Summer mildness: 1	**Hazardousness:** 90
Score: 87.81	**Rank: 44**

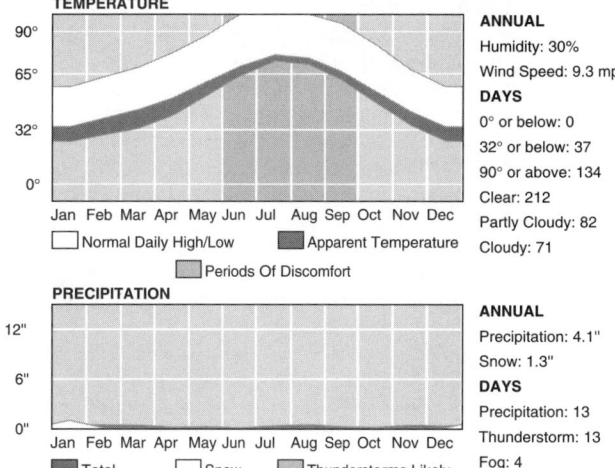

ANNUAL
Humidity: 30%
Wind Speed: 9.3 mph
DAYS
0° or below: 0
32° or below: 37
90° or above: 134
Clear: 212
Partly Cloudy: 82
Cloudy: 71

ANNUAL
Precipitation: 4.1"
Snow: 1.3"
DAYS
Precipitation: 13
Thunderstorm: 13
Fog: 4

Lexington, KY

Location: 38.02 N, 84.36 W, at 970 feet, in the heart of Kentucky Bluegrass country; 23 miles east of Frankfort, the capital.

Landscape: Gently rolling plateau with varying elevations of 900 feet to 1,050 feet. The surrounding country is noted for its beauty, fertile soil, excellent grass, stock farms, and burley tobacco. There are no bodies of water nearby that are large enough to have an effect on climate.

Cimate: Decidedly Continental; temperate, yet prone to sudden large, but brief changes in temperature. The first freeze arrives October 21, and the last occurs April 22. Precipitation is evenly distributed throughout the winter, spring, and summer, with an average of 12 inches falling in each of these seasons. Snowfall is variable, but the ground does not retain snow for more than a few days at a time. The months of September and October are the most pleasant of the year; they have the least precipitation, the most clear days, and generally comfortable temperatures.

Winter mildness: 51	**Seasonal affect:** 22
Summer mildness: 52	**Hazardousness:** 49
Score: 44.47	**Rank: 197**

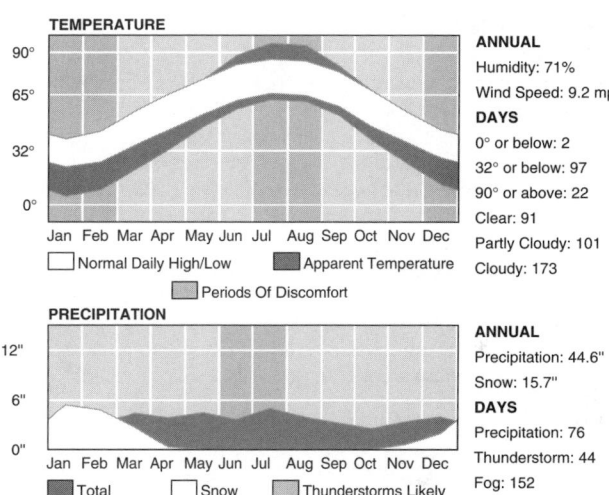

ANNUAL
Humidity: 71%
Wind Speed: 9.2 mph
DAYS
0° or below: 2
32° or below: 97
90° or above: 22
Clear: 91
Partly Cloudy: 101
Cloudy: 173

ANNUAL
Precipitation: 44.6"
Snow: 15.7"
DAYS
Precipitation: 76
Thunderstorm: 44
Fog: 152

Lincoln, NE

Location: 40.51 N, 96.45 W, at 1,190 feet, in southeastern Nebraska, about 50 miles west of the Missouri River.

Landscape: Lies on level, gently rolling prairie in the central lowlands of the state. Soil is deep, rich silt loam and sandy loam, noted for fertility in growing corn, grain, and wheat. The Missouri River provides drainage, except in times of heavy rainfall when severe flooding can occur.

Cimate: In winter, severely cold air from Canada can move over the Lincoln area. However, the centers of some cold air masses move so far to the east that their full effect is not felt. Chinooks often produce rapid rises in temperature during the winter, with a shift of the wind to the west. An average winter brings 26 inches of snow, which doesn't melt until spring. The frost-free growing season, April through September, receives three-fourths of the yearly precipitation. Humidity remains at a comfortable level, except for short periods during the summer.

Winter mildness: 12	**Seasonal affect:** 76
Summer mildness: 30	**Hazardousness:** 23
Score: 14.16	**Rank: 304**

ANNUAL
Humidity: 70%
Wind Speed: 10.3 mph
DAYS
0° or below: 17
32° or below: 146
90° or above: 43
Clear: 117
Partly Cloudy: 98
Cloudy: 150

ANNUAL
Precipitation: 28.3"
Snow: 27.1"
DAYS
Precipitation: 49
Thunderstorm: 46
Fog: 95

Little Rock-North Little Rock, AR

Location: 34.44 N, 92.14 W, at 260 feet, on the Arkansas River near the geographic center of the state.

Landscape: To the west lie the Ouachita Mountains and to the east the flat lowlands of the Mississippi River valley. Little Rock is surrounded by farmland. Poultry, cattle, and a variety of agricultural products are processed in the city. Bauxite and other minerals are mined nearby. Lumber also contributes to the economic base.

Cimate: Modified four-season Continental climate. The area is exposed to all North American air-mass types, but the Gulf of Mexico gives the summer season prolonged periods of warmer and more humid weather. Sixty-two percent of the normal annual precipitation occurs during the frost-free growing season of 233 days, from the beginning of November to mid-March. Winters are mild, but polar and arctic outbreaks are not uncommon. Glaze and ice storms, though infrequent, can be severe.

Winter mildness: 65	**Seasonal affect:** 67
Summer mildness: 15	**Hazardousness:** 59
Score: 49.00	**Rank: 181**

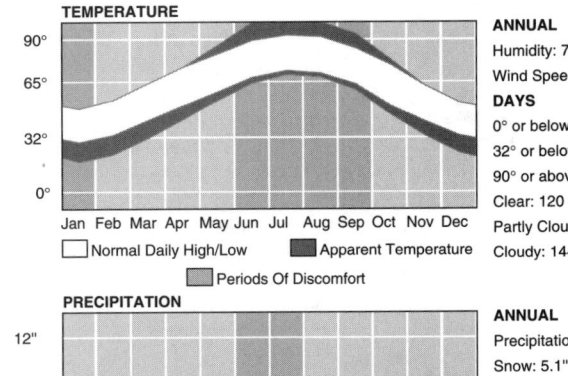

ANNUAL
Humidity: 71%
Wind Speed: 7.8 mph
DAYS
0° or below: 0
32° or below: 57
90° or above: 73
Clear: 120
Partly Cloudy: 101
Cloudy: 144

ANNUAL
Precipitation: 50.9"
Snow: 5.1"
DAYS
Precipitation: 72
Thunderstorm: 57
Fog: 142

Long Island, NY

Location: 40.44 N, 73.37 W, at 100 feet, station is at the extreme tip of Long Island; 120 miles east of New York City.

Landscape: This peninsula ranges from 12 to 23 miles wide, and is 118 miles long. Terrain is generally flat, with only a gradual rise in elevation. The eastern deciduous forest of oak, beech, birch, hickory, tulip tree, and sweet chestnut provides a dense canopy in summer and sheds its leaves entirely in winter.

Cimate: Summers tend to be hot and humid with afternoon showers. In coastal areas, there is an average of 7 days between June and September when afternoon temperatures exceed 90°F. Inland, there are 10 to 15 such days. Winters can be cold with icy rain. Snowfall is light, averaging about 29 inches, and doesn't last long. Occasionally tropical weather systems produce storms of strong winds and heavy rain in the late summer or fall, and coastal low pressure systems will produce a heavy snowfall in winter.

Winter mildness: 57	**Seasonal affect:** 63
Summer mildness: 73	**Hazardousness:** 59
Score: 81.86	**Rank: 65**

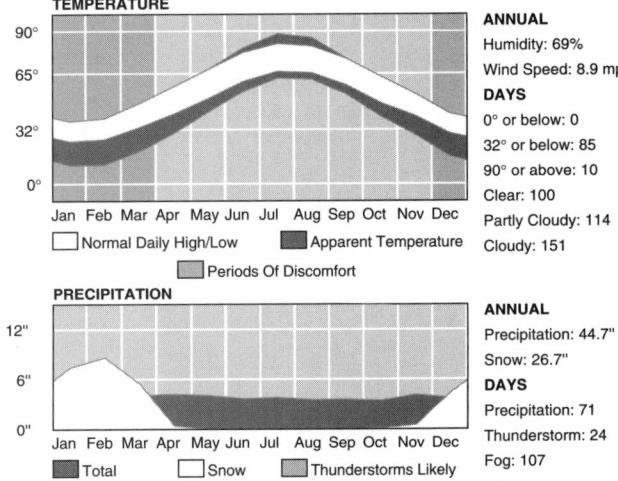

ANNUAL
Humidity: 69%
Wind Speed: 8.9 mph
DAYS
0° or below: 0
32° or below: 85
90° or above: 10
Clear: 100
Partly Cloudy: 114
Cloudy: 151

ANNUAL
Precipitation: 44.7"
Snow: 26.7"
DAYS
Precipitation: 71
Thunderstorm: 24
Fog: 107

★Los Angeles-Long Beach, CA

Location: 33.56 N, 118.24 W, at 100 feet, on the Pacific Coast of Southern California.

Landscape: Major features are the Pacific Ocean, 3 miles to the west, and the southern California coastal mountain ranges, a buffer on the inland side of the Coastal Plain to the more extreme conditions of the interior. Coastal Plain vegetation includes chaparral, oak, laurel, and Pacific bayberry. Geologic faults cause periodic tremors, and the strong dry Santa Ana winds pose the seasonal threat of fires spreading into the brush hills around the city.

Cimate: Semiarid Mediterranean, pleasant and mild throughout the year. Characteristics of the two-season climate are low clouds at night and morning, and sunny afternoons during spring and summer and often during the remainder of the year. Combined with a sea breeze, the coastal cloudiness causes mild temperatures throughout the year. There can be great differences in temperature, humidity, fog, sunshine, and rain over short distances. Temperature range differences are the least, and humidity is higher close to the coast; precipitation increases with elevation.

Winter mildness: 95	**Seasonal affect:** 95
Summer mildness: 95	**Hazardousness:** 99
Score: 99.15	**Rank: 4**

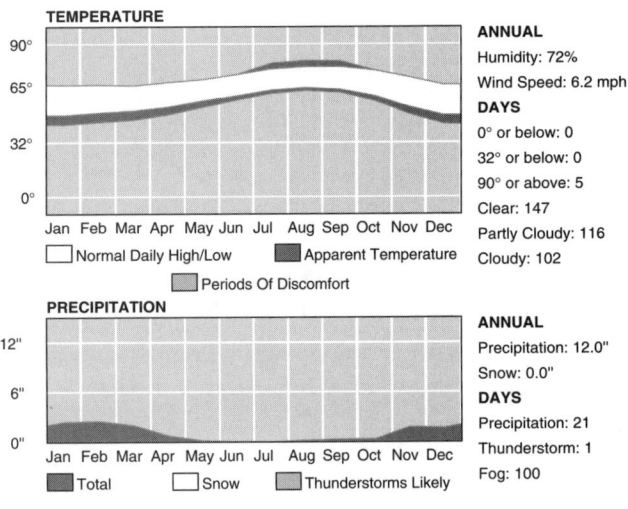

ANNUAL
Humidity: 72%
Wind Speed: 6.2 mph
DAYS
0° or below: 0
32° or below: 0
90° or above: 5
Clear: 147
Partly Cloudy: 116
Cloudy: 102

ANNUAL
Precipitation: 12.0"
Snow: 0.0"
DAYS
Precipitation: 21
Thunderstorm: 1
Fog: 100

Louisville, KY-IN

Location: 38.11 N, 85.44 W, at 480 feet, on the south bank of the Ohio River across from Indiana; 54 miles west of Frankfort, Kentucky's state capital.

Landscape: The eastern part of the city is residential and consists of rolling hills and plateaus. Kentucky bluegrass grows on rich limestone soil. The western, industrial part of the city lies on the river's floodplain. A low range of hills on the Indiana bank provides a partial barrier to icy blasts of winter.

Cimate: Continental, but more variable because of its position in mid-latitudes in the belt of westerly winds, and because it's not completely shut off from influences of the Gulf of Mexico. The first freeze is October 22. Winters are moderately cold. Snows, although seldom heavy, are a regular occurrence from November through March. Spring arrives in early April. The last freeze is April 20. Summers are quite warm, with notable temperatures in June. High relative humidity and high-intensity rainstorms are common in both spring and summer.

Winter mildness: 54	**Seasonal affect:** 23
Summer mildness: 45	**Hazardousness:** 54
Score: 47.02	**Rank: 188**

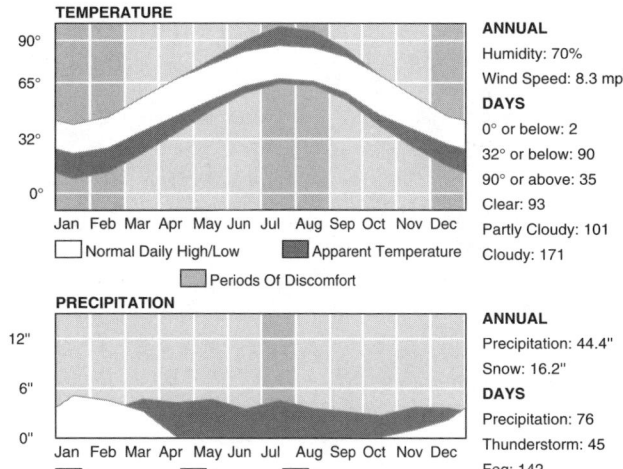

TEMPERATURE

Normal Daily High/Low — Apparent Temperature — Periods Of Discomfort

PRECIPITATION

Total — Snow — Thunderstorms Likely

ANNUAL
Humidity: 70%
Wind Speed: 8.3 mph
DAYS
0° or below: 2
32° or below: 90
90° or above: 35
Clear: 93
Partly Cloudy: 101
Cloudy: 171

ANNUAL
Precipitation: 44.4"
Snow: 16.2"
DAYS
Precipitation: 76
Thunderstorm: 45
Fog: 142

Lubbock, TX

Location: 33.39 N, 101.49 W, at 3,250 feet, in the Texas high plateau area called the South Plains region; over 380 miles northwest of Austin.

Landscape: The *LLano Estacado* or High Plains form a great tableland, essentially level with numerous small *playas,* small stream valleys, and low hummocks. Steppe vegetation is generally short grasses that are bunched and sparsely distributed. Gently sloping and generally treeless, there are no appreciable terrain features that affect wind flow across the plateau. Land is suitable for growing cotton, grains and, most recently, vineyard grapes.

Cimate: Semiarid Continental, a transition between western desert conditions and humid eastern climates. Normal precipitation is 18 inches per year, with most occurring May through September when warm tropical air is carried inland from the Gulf of Mexico. This air mass produces moderate to heavy afternoon and evening convective thunderstorms, sometimes with hail. The first freeze arrives October 29, and the latest is April 9. Dry westerly winds are gentle and help alleviate summer heat.

Winter mildness: 56	**Seasonal affect:** 95
Summer mildness: 18	**Hazardousness:** 39
Score: 45.32	**Rank: 194**

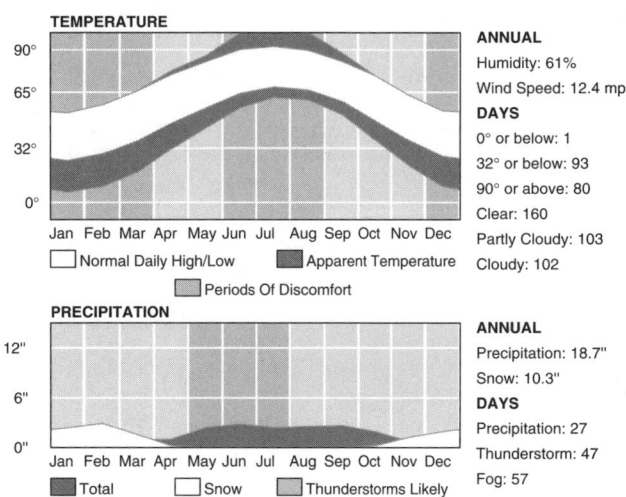

TEMPERATURE

Normal Daily High/Low — Apparent Temperature — Periods Of Discomfort

PRECIPITATION

Total — Snow — Thunderstorms Likely

ANNUAL
Humidity: 61%
Wind Speed: 12.4 mph
DAYS
0° or below: 1
32° or below: 93
90° or above: 80
Clear: 160
Partly Cloudy: 103
Cloudy: 102

ANNUAL
Precipitation: 18.7"
Snow: 10.3"
DAYS
Precipitation: 27
Thunderstorm: 47
Fog: 57

Madison, WI

Location: 43.08 N, 89.20 W, at 860 feet, on an eight-block-wide isthmus of land between Lakes Mendota and Monona in south central Wisconsin.

Landscape: There are 18,000 acres of lake surface within or just outside the city limits. However, lakes are frozen from December 17 to April 5. Madison is a commercial and manufacturing center in a rich agricultural region. Farming includes dairying, with field crops mainly of corn, oats, and alfalfa. The majority of fruits grown are apples, strawberries, and raspberries.

Cimate: Continental, typical of interior North America, with a large annual temperature range and frequent short periods of temperature changes. Winter temperatures average 20°F and summer ones 68°F. The most common air masses are of polar origin, with occasional outbreaks of arctic air during the winter. Much of the precipitation falls between May and September. Lighter winter precipitation falls over a longer period of time. The average growing season is 175 days, from the end of April to mid-October.

Winter mildness: 8	**Seasonal affect:** 35
Summer mildness: 75	**Hazardousness:** 16
Score: 4.81	**Rank: 337**

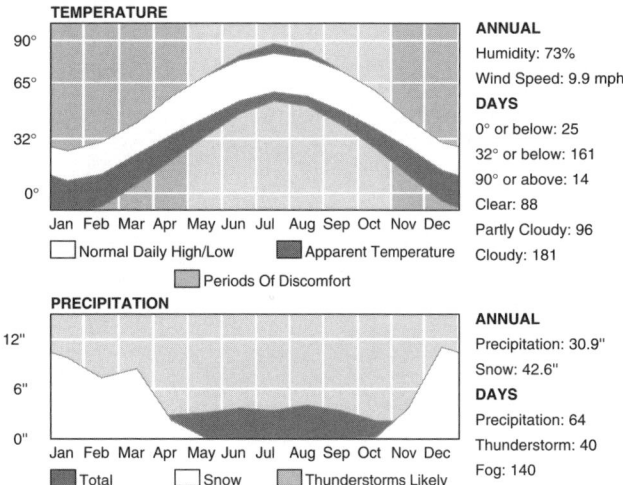

TEMPERATURE

Normal Daily High/Low — Apparent Temperature — Periods Of Discomfort

PRECIPITATION

Total — Snow — Thunderstorms Likely

ANNUAL
Humidity: 73%
Wind Speed: 9.9 mph
DAYS
0° or below: 25
32° or below: 161
90° or above: 14
Clear: 88
Partly Cloudy: 96
Cloudy: 181

ANNUAL
Precipitation: 30.9"
Snow: 42.6"
DAYS
Precipitation: 64
Thunderstorm: 40
Fog: 140

Manchester, NH

Location: 42.59 N, 71.24 W, at 250 feet, rises from both banks of the Merrimack River in southeast New Hampshire; 53 miles north of Boston.

Landscape: Loosely encircled by the New Hampshire hills, the area relief consists of low rolling hills and low mountains. Rural farmlands have fertile soils. Dairy and poultry farming and growing fruit, vegetables, corn, potatoes, and hay are the major agricultural pursuits. There are a few somewhat poorly drained lakes and basin areas. Evergreen forests alternate with deciduous wooded areas and marshy terrain.

Cimate: Four-season Continental climate; the air is cold and dry in winter, cool and dry in summer. Hot summer weather is infrequent. The winter wind-chill factor is low as the area is protected from strong winds by the hilly terrain. The annual precipitation is 37 inches with annual snowfall averaging 53 inches. The typical New England frost-free days number 150. The first freeze is around September 24, the last around May 17.

Winter mildness: 10	**Seasonal affect:** 14
Summer mildness: 80	**Hazardousness:** 19
Score: 2.54	**Rank: 345**

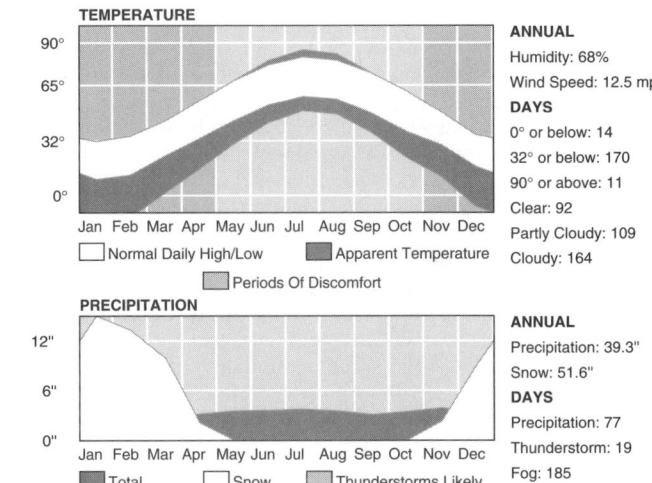

TEMPERATURE

☐ Normal Daily High/Low   ■ Apparent Temperature   ▨ Periods Of Discomfort

PRECIPITATION

■ Total   ☐ Snow   ▨ Thunderstorms Likely

ANNUAL
Humidity: 68%
Wind Speed: 12.5 mph
DAYS
0° or below: 14
32° or below: 170
90° or above: 11
Clear: 92
Partly Cloudy: 109
Cloudy: 164

ANNUAL
Precipitation: 39.3"
Snow: 51.6"
DAYS
Precipitation: 77
Thunderstorm: 19
Fog: 185

McAllen-Edinburg-Mission, TX

Location: 26.11 N, 98.14 W, at 100 feet, in the lower Rio Grande valley of south Texas; 75 miles west of the Gulf of Mexico.

Landscape: Flat topography of the Rio Grande Plain with little relief. Date palms, bougainvillea, and winter poinsettias color the valley towns, but the native upland sage and chaparral have lost out to development, both agricultural and urban. Citrus groves and winter gardens are the result of intensive irrigation.

Cimate: Subtropical, influenced by the Gulf of Mexico. Winters are mild, with average minimum temperatures in the mid-40s. Summers can be hot, humid, and stormy. There are more than 100 days over 90°F. High humidity is constant throughout the year; during the months of May through August it feels oppressive. While the Sierra Madre Oriental Mountains in Mexico block the Chihuahuan Desert, both affect the climate of this river plain. The year is frost-free, with the exception of the month of January.

Winter mildness: 96	**Seasonal affect:** 84
Summer mildness: 5	**Hazardousness:** 92
Score: 78.47	**Rank: 77**

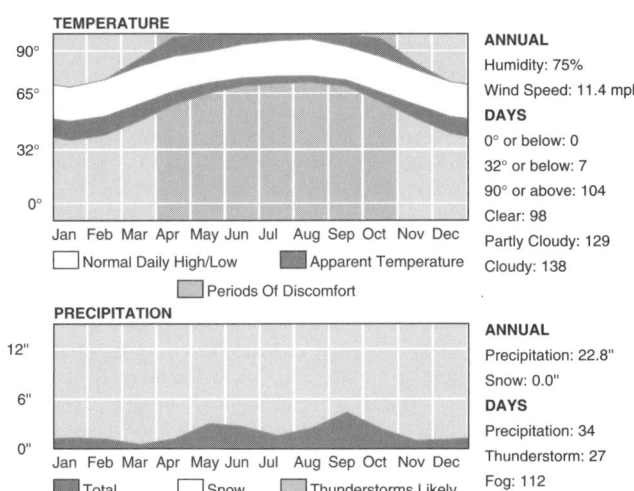

TEMPERATURE

☐ Normal Daily High/Low   ■ Apparent Temperature   ▨ Periods Of Discomfort

PRECIPITATION

■ Total   ☐ Snow   ▨ Thunderstorms Likely

ANNUAL
Humidity: 75%
Wind Speed: 11.4 mph
DAYS
0° or below: 0
32° or below: 7
90° or above: 104
Clear: 98
Partly Cloudy: 129
Cloudy: 138

ANNUAL
Precipitation: 22.8"
Snow: 0.0"
DAYS
Precipitation: 34
Thunderstorm: 27
Fog: 112

Medford-Ashland, OR

Location: 42.23 N, 122.53 W, at 1,300 feet, in extreme southwest Oregon, 25 miles north of the California border; Crater Lake National Park is nearby.

Landscape: In a mountain valley formed by the Rogue River and Bear Creek. The valley's outlet to the ocean 80 miles west is the narrow canyon of the Rogue. The dense Pacific conifer forest is filled with Douglas fir, western red cedar, western hemlock, silver fir, and Sitka spruce.

Cimate: Moderate, with marked seasonal characteristics. Late fall, winter, and early spring are cloudy, damp, and cool. First freeze: October 20. Last freeze: April 30. The rest of the year is sunny, warm, and dry. The rain shadow afforded by the Siskiyous and the Coastal Range results in relatively light rainfall, most of which falls in the wintertime. Snowfalls are light and seldom stay on the ground more than 24 hours. Winters are mild, with the temperatures just dipping below freezing during December and January. Summer days can reach 90°F, but nights are cool.

Winter mildness: 67	**Seasonal affect:** 66
Summer mildness: 26	**Hazardousness:** 91
Score: 89.23	**Rank: 39**

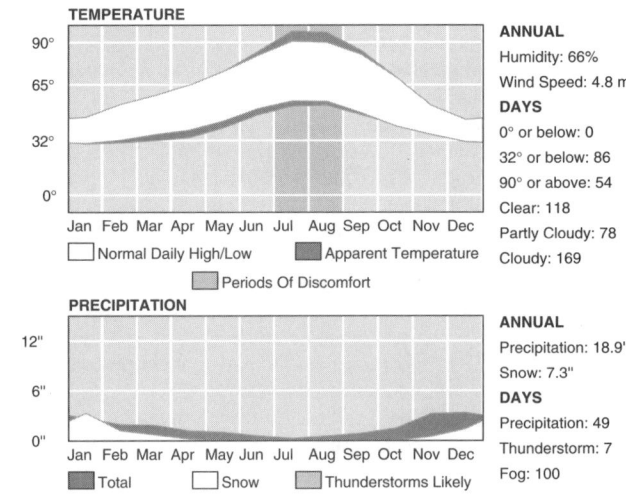

TEMPERATURE

☐ Normal Daily High/Low   ■ Apparent Temperature   ▨ Periods Of Discomfort

PRECIPITATION

■ Total   ☐ Snow   ▨ Thunderstorms Likely

ANNUAL
Humidity: 66%
Wind Speed: 4.8 mph
DAYS
0° or below: 0
32° or below: 86
90° or above: 54
Clear: 118
Partly Cloudy: 78
Cloudy: 169

ANNUAL
Precipitation: 18.9"
Snow: 7.3"
DAYS
Precipitation: 49
Thunderstorm: 7
Fog: 100

Memphis, TN-AR-MS

Location: 35.03 N, 0.90 W, at 270 feet, on the Mississippi River in the southwest corner of the state, covering the tri-state borders.

Landscape: Slightly rolling delta topography, across from the level alluvial area on the Arkansas side. Major crops are cotton, corn, and other vegetables, as well as orchards of peaches and apples. The favorable terrain supports dairying and the raising of cattle and hogs.

Cimate: Moderate climate blends features of Continental with Subtropical. Though not in the normal paths of storms coming either from the Gulf of Mexico or from Canada, Memphis is affected by both and has comparatively frequent changes in weather. Freezing days are not uncommon during winter. Hot steamy weather can be expected during summer. But extremes in highs and lows are rare; the average annual temperature is in the low 60s and varies from the low 40s in January to the low 80s in July. Average growing season is 230 days with annual rainfall of more than 40 inches.

Winter mildness: 69	**Seasonal affect:** 43
Summer mildness: 16	**Hazardousness:** 53
Score: 40.79	**Rank: 210**

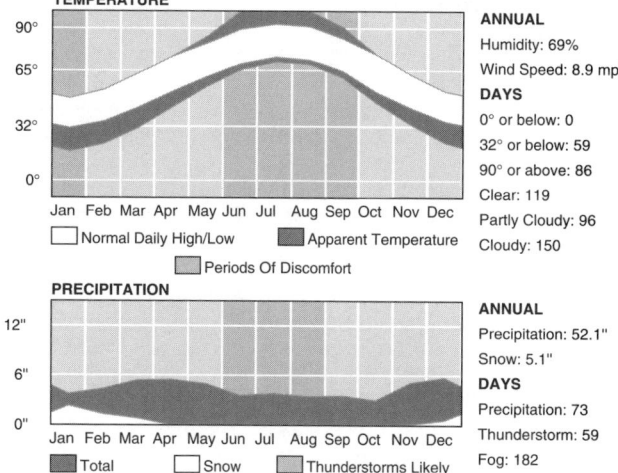

TEMPERATURE
- Normal Daily High/Low
- Apparent Temperature
- Periods Of Discomfort

PRECIPITATION
- Total
- Snow
- Thunderstorms Likely

ANNUAL
Humidity: 69%
Wind Speed: 8.9 mph
DAYS
0° or below: 0
32° or below: 59
90° or above: 86
Clear: 119
Partly Cloudy: 96
Cloudy: 150

ANNUAL
Precipitation: 52.1"
Snow: 5.1"
DAYS
Precipitation: 73
Thunderstorm: 59
Fog: 182

★Miami, FL

Location: 25.48 N, 80.18 W, at 10 feet, on the lower southeast coast of Florida; some 465 miles south of Tallahassee, the state capital.

Landscape: To the south lies Biscayne Bay, and to the east of it Miami Beach. The surrounding countryside is level and sparsely wooded, with obvious coastal lowlands and poorly drained soil.

Cimate: Subtropical Marine with a long, warm summer, abundant rainfall, and a mild, dry winter. The Atlantic Ocean is responsible for the city's small range of daily temperatures, and it aids the rapid warming of colder air masses passing east of the state. During the morning, more rainfall occurs at Miami Beach than at the airport 9 miles inland, while during the afternoon the reverse is true. More striking is the difference in the annual number of days over 90°F: 15 days at Miami Beach; 60 at the airport. Freezing temperatures occur occasionally in surrounding farming districts, but almost never near the ocean. Hurricanes affect the area and are most frequent in early fall.

Winter mildness: 100	**Seasonal affect:** 71
Summer mildness: 37	**Hazardousness:** 82
Score: 91.21	**Rank: 32**

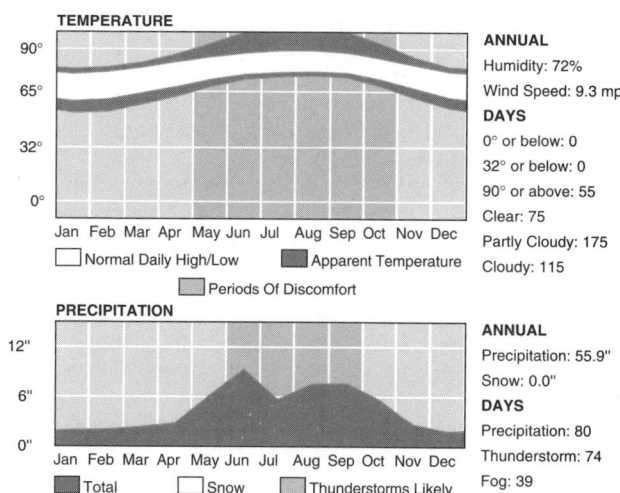

TEMPERATURE
- Normal Daily High/Low
- Apparent Temperature
- Periods Of Discomfort

PRECIPITATION
- Total
- Snow
- Thunderstorms Likely

ANNUAL
Humidity: 72%
Wind Speed: 9.3 mph
DAYS
0° or below: 0
32° or below: 0
90° or above: 55
Clear: 75
Partly Cloudy: 175
Cloudy: 115

ANNUAL
Precipitation: 55.9"
Snow: 0.0"
DAYS
Precipitation: 80
Thunderstorm: 74
Fog: 39

Middlesex-Somerset-Hunterdon, NJ

Location: 40.36 N, 74.38 W, at 160 feet, in eastern New Jersey at the head of navigation on the Raritan River, midway between New York City and Trenton, the state capital.

Landscape: Terrain near the weather station is flat and marshy, with low to moderate ridges to the northwest running in a south-southwest to north-northeast direction.

Cimate: The interaction of cold, dry air masses from the northwest with warm, moist air masses from the south produces varied weather patterns. Precipitation is evenly distributed annually, with a bit more in late summer. Storms producing 4 inches or more of snow occur from two to five times a winter. The drying effect of the downslope winds accounts for the relatively few local thunderstorms. The July average temperature range is 70° to 76°F, and the January range is 26° to 37°F. The average dates of the last occurrence of freezing temperatures in spring and their first occurrence in fall are May 2 and October 12.

Winter mildness: 36	**Seasonal affect:** 58
Summer mildness: 56	**Hazardousness:** 53
Score: 50.14	**Rank: 177**

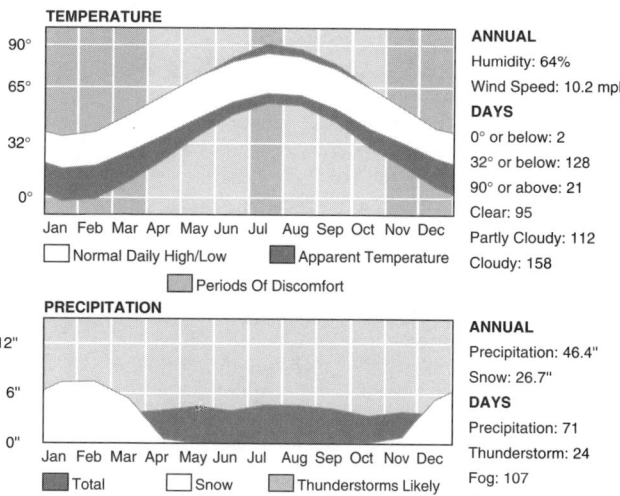

TEMPERATURE
- Normal Daily High/Low
- Apparent Temperature
- Periods Of Discomfort

PRECIPITATION
- Total
- Snow
- Thunderstorms Likely

ANNUAL
Humidity: 64%
Wind Speed: 10.2 mph
DAYS
0° or below: 2
32° or below: 128
90° or above: 21
Clear: 95
Partly Cloudy: 112
Cloudy: 158

ANNUAL
Precipitation: 46.4"
Snow: 26.7"
DAYS
Precipitation: 71
Thunderstorm: 24
Fog: 107

Place Profiles: Climate

Milwaukee-Waukesha, WI

Location: 42.57 N, 87.54 W, at 670 feet, on the west shore of Lake Michigan; 80 miles north of Chicago.

Landscape: Rolling prairie. The St. Lawrence Seaway and the Milwaukee, Menomonee, and Kinnickinnic rivers are integral parts of the landscape, forming a natural harbor as they enter Lake Michigan.

Cimate: Influenced by storms that move eastward across the upper Ohio River valley and the Great Lakes region. Large high pressure systems moving southeastward out of Canada also have an effect, and it is seldom that two or three days will pass without a distinct change in the weather. The major influence on the climate is Lake Michigan, cooling the shoreline in summer and warming it in winter. Winter days can be cold, and severe winter storms produce 10 or more inches of snow. Annual average snowfall is 50 inches. Winters are cloudy. Summers are clear, receiving an average of 70 percent of possible sunshine. The first freeze arrives October 12, and the last one departs May 2.

Winter mildness: 14	**Seasonal affect:** 37
Summer mildness: 88	**Hazardousness:** 10
Score: 15.29	**Rank: 300**

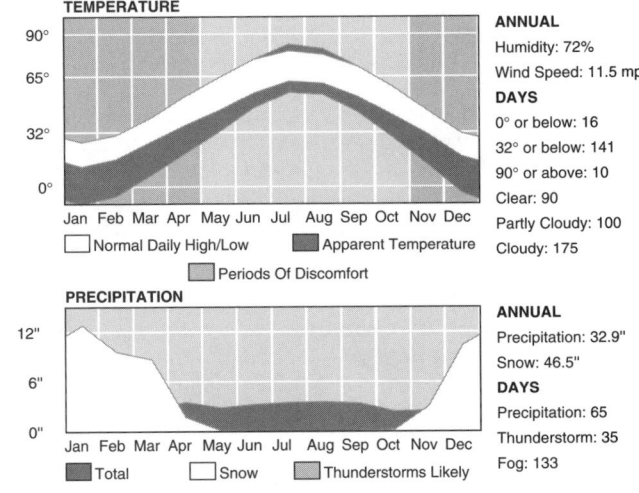

ANNUAL
Humidity: 72%
Wind Speed: 11.5 mph
DAYS
0° or below: 16
32° or below: 141
90° or above: 10
Clear: 90
Partly Cloudy: 100
Cloudy: 175

ANNUAL
Precipitation: 32.9"
Snow: 46.5"
DAYS
Precipitation: 65
Thunderstorm: 35
Fog: 133

Minneapolis-St. Paul, MN-WI

Location: 44.53 N, 93.13 W, at 830 feet; the Twin Cities are located where the Mississippi and Minnesota rivers meet over the heart of an artesian water basin in the southeast section of the state. Minneapolis is on the east bank of the Mississippi; St. Paul is on the west bank.

Landscape: The topography is flat or gently rolling grasslands with numerous lakes that are small, shallow, and ice-covered in winter. Gallery forests line the waterways. Structurally the area is part of the Canadian Shield, underlain with granite, gneiss, and schist.

Cimate: Predominantly Continental in climate, the two cities are near the geographic center of North America. There are wide variations in temperature, ample summer rainfall, and scanty winter precipitation. In general, there exists a tendency toward extremes in almost all climate features. Severe storms of all types—blizzards, freezing rain, tornadoes, wind, and hail—occur. The first freeze is an early October 1; the last is in mid-May.

Winter mildness: 5	**Seasonal affect:** 63
Summer mildness: 63	**Hazardousness:** 7
Score: 4.53	**Rank: 338**

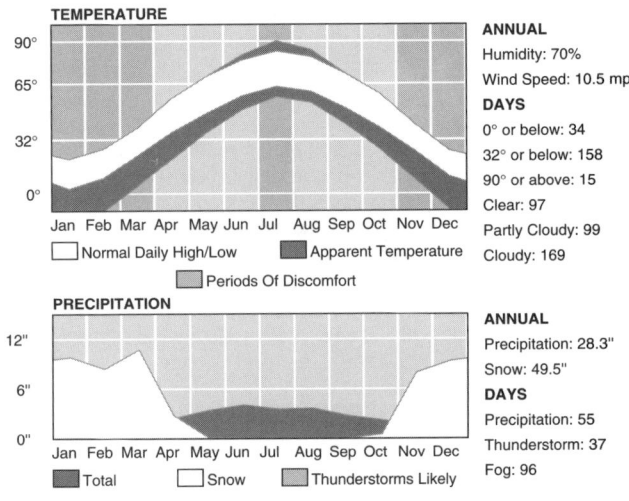

ANNUAL
Humidity: 70%
Wind Speed: 10.5 mph
DAYS
0° or below: 34
32° or below: 158
90° or above: 15
Clear: 97
Partly Cloudy: 99
Cloudy: 169

ANNUAL
Precipitation: 28.3"
Snow: 49.5"
DAYS
Precipitation: 55
Thunderstorm: 37
Fog: 96

Missoula, MT

Location: 46.52 N, 113.59 W, at 3,220 feet in the heart of the Montana Rocky Mountains, about 5 miles east of the confluence of the Bitterroot and Clark Fork rivers.

Landscape: The Clark Fork Valley begins at Missoula and extends about 20 miles west-northwest. The Bitterroot Valley extends about 70 miles due south. The Continental Divide is 60 to 80 miles east, and the Bitterroot Range is only about 20 miles to the southwest.

Cimate: The mountain ranges have a marked effect on the climate. The flow of air over western Montana loses much of its moisture over the Bitterroot Range. Missoula receives only 12 to 15 inches of precipitation annually, making for a semi-arid climate. There are about 137 growing days each year, from May 10 to September 20. The summer months are dry with moderate temperatures and cool nights. In winter, the Continental Divide shields the area from severely cold air. On occasion, however, there can be severe blizzard conditions, referred to locally as Hell Gate Blizzards.

Winter mildness: 21	**Seasonal affect:** 7
Summer mildness: 63	**Hazardousness:** 47
Score: 51.55	**Rank: 172**

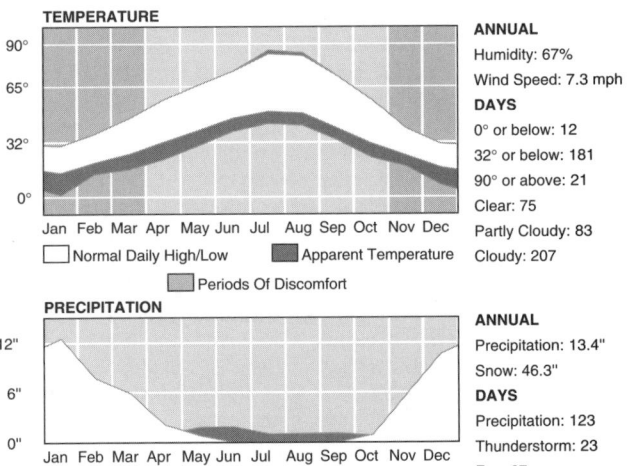

ANNUAL
Humidity: 67%
Wind Speed: 7.3 mph
DAYS
0° or below: 12
32° or below: 181
90° or above: 21
Clear: 75
Partly Cloudy: 83
Cloudy: 207

ANNUAL
Precipitation: 13.4"
Snow: 46.3"
DAYS
Precipitation: 123
Thunderstorm: 23
Fog: 67

Mobile, AL

Location: 30.41 N, 88.15 W, at 210 feet, station is 35 miles south of Mobile on the Gulf of Mexico near the entrance to Mobile Bay; 80 miles east of New Orleans.

Landscape: Gulf Coastal Plain where ecologies range from sea-level sandy beaches and saltmarshes to typical southern pine forests. From sea level inland the local relief doesn't exceed 250 feet.

Cimate: Subtropical in character, as the normal annual rainfall amount here is one of the highest in the continental United States. It is evenly distributed throughout the year, with a slight maximum at the height of the summer thunderstorm season. Although destructive hurricanes are extremely infrequent, this seems due more to chance than to location. The area is subject to hurricanes from the West Indies and the Gulf of Mexico. The growing season averages 274 days—from late February to the end of November. Summers are consistently warm; winters are mild.

Winter mildness: 87   **Seasonal affect:** 48
Summer mildness: 22   **Hazardousness:** 60
Score: 67.42   **Rank: 116**

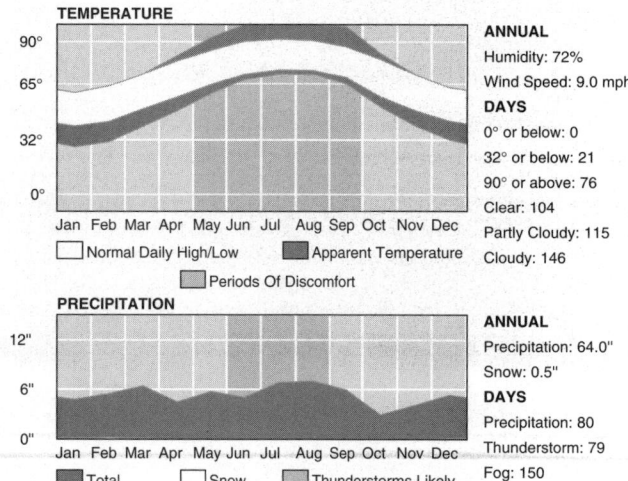

TEMPERATURE

Normal Daily High/Low   Apparent Temperature
Periods Of Discomfort

ANNUAL
Humidity: 72%
Wind Speed: 9.0 mph
DAYS
0° or below: 0
32° or below: 21
90° or above: 76
Clear: 104
Partly Cloudy: 115
Cloudy: 146

PRECIPITATION

Total   Snow   Thunderstorms Likely

ANNUAL
Precipitation: 64.0"
Snow: 0.5"
DAYS
Precipitation: 80
Thunderstorm: 79
Fog: 150

★Modesto, CA

Location: 37.39 N, 1.21 W, at 90 feet, south of Sacramento, east of San Francisco, at the northern end of the San Joaquin Valley.

Landscape: The rich farmlands and grasslands of the valley are drained and irrigated by snow-fed streams flowing from the slopes of the Sierra Nevada. These streams have been dammed to hold water supplies for irrigation and for industrial and domestic use. Modesto is the gateway to Yosemite National Park to the east and Gold Country to the north.

Cimate: The San Joaquin Valley lies between the Coastal Range and the Sierra Nevada. The area, well protected from the Pacific Ocean, displays Continental climate characteristics of warmer summers, colder winters, greater daily and seasonal temperature ranges, and generally lower relative humidities. Annual precipitation averages less than 15 inches. The valley has a freeze-free season of 225 to 300 days, from late February to the end of November. In winter the area is subject to northers, rather mild temperatures accompanied by dry, persistent winds that many people find unpleasant.

Winter mildness: 83   **Seasonal affect:** 93
Summer mildness: 9   **Hazardousness:** 95
Score: 95.75   **Rank: 16**

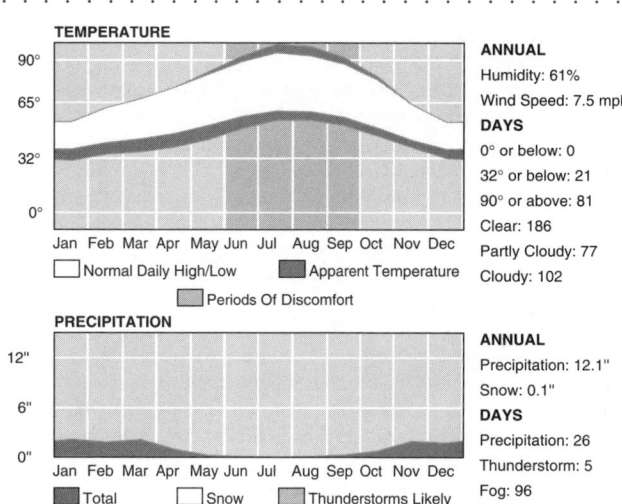

TEMPERATURE

Normal Daily High/Low   Apparent Temperature
Periods Of Discomfort

ANNUAL
Humidity: 61%
Wind Speed: 7.5 mph
DAYS
0° or below: 0
32° or below: 21
90° or above: 81
Clear: 186
Partly Cloudy: 77
Cloudy: 102

PRECIPITATION

Total   Snow   Thunderstorms Likely

ANNUAL
Precipitation: 12.1"
Snow: 0.1"
DAYS
Precipitation: 26
Thunderstorm: 5
Fog: 96

Montgomery, AL

Location: 32.18 N, 86.24 W, at 220 feet, the capital is on the Alabama River in the south central part of the state.

Landscape: Located in a fertile, gently rolling area of southern Alabama. About two-thirds of Alabama is covered by forests, largely made up of southern yellow pine, red cedar, and other conifers. No local topographic features appreciably influence climate.

Cimate: From June through September, humidity and temperature conditions show little daily change. During summer, 100-degree readings are infrequent. From April through September, all precipitation is from local heat thundershowers in the afternoon. Rain is abundant and includes all types and intensities from December through March. During the coldest months—from December through February—there are frequent shifts between mild, moist air from the Gulf of Mexico and dry, cool Continental air. Hard freezes are infrequent during winter, and snow is rare enough to be a curiosity. The first freeze arrives at the beginning of November; the last comes at the very end of March.

Winter mildness: 80   **Seasonal affect:** 50
Summer mildness: 24   **Hazardousness:** 79
Score: 73.08   **Rank: 96**

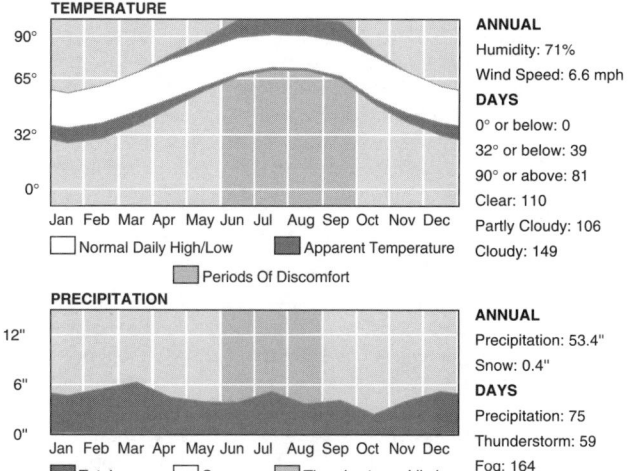

TEMPERATURE

Normal Daily High/Low   Apparent Temperature
Periods Of Discomfort

ANNUAL
Humidity: 71%
Wind Speed: 6.6 mph
DAYS
0° or below: 0
32° or below: 39
90° or above: 81
Clear: 110
Partly Cloudy: 106
Cloudy: 149

PRECIPITATION

Total   Snow   Thunderstorms Likely

ANNUAL
Precipitation: 53.4"
Snow: 0.4"
DAYS
Precipitation: 75
Thunderstorm: 59
Fog: 164

Climate

Montreal, PQ

Location: 45.28 N, 73.45 W, at 118 feet, in the St. Lawrence River plain at the confluence of the Ottawa and St. Lawrence rivers.

Landscape: The Laurentian Mountains lie to the north, the Appalachians to the south and southeast. Most of Montreal Island is situated between 100 feet and 150 feet above sea level with the exception of Mount Royal, which rises to 750 feet over the city.

Cimate: Roughly halfway between the equator and the North Pole, the city has climate influenced by aspects of Continental and Maritime regimes. There can be severe temperature differences between summer and winter, but because of the Maritime influence, it is wet more or less uniformly throughout the year. Every Montrealer is familiar with the cold waves of winter, the mild spells of spring, the sultry days of summer, and the gray periods of fall. On average, the first snowflakes appear in mid-November and the first winter broadside of 5 inches hits a month later.

Winter mildness: 7	**Seasonal affect:** 10
Summer mildness: 90	**Hazardousness:** 8
Score: 2.26	**Rank: 346**

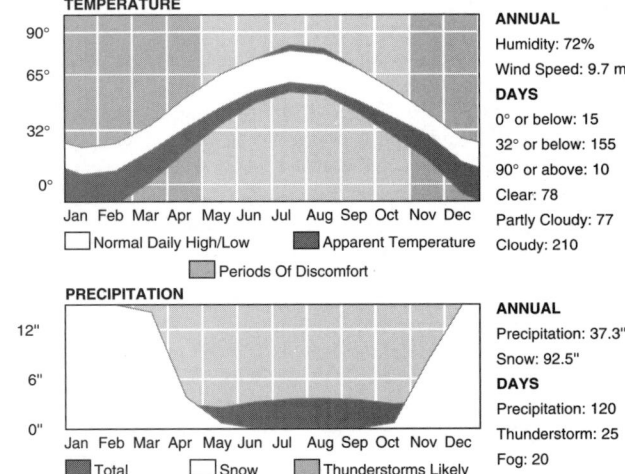

TEMPERATURE

ANNUAL
Humidity: 72%
Wind Speed: 9.7 mph
DAYS
0° or below: 15
32° or below: 155
90° or above: 10
Clear: 78
Partly Cloudy: 77
Cloudy: 210

PRECIPITATION

ANNUAL
Precipitation: 37.3"
Snow: 92.5"
DAYS
Precipitation: 120
Thunderstorm: 25
Fog: 20

Myrtle Beach, SC

Location: 34.03 N, 78.53 W, at 90 feet; 100 miles northeast of Charleston in the center of the Atlantic coast area known as the Grand Strand.

Landscape: Low and swampy inland, and quite flat. Elevations are no greater than 50 feet above sea level. There are many more trees—stands of southern yellow pine, mixed with hickory, sweetgum, and other deciduous varieties—than are usually found in a beach area. The beaches are white sand, and the water is quite clean, as there are no harbors or major industries nearby. Also, no rivers or streams empty into the sea for a distance of almost 30 miles.

Cimate: Subtropical, having mild winters and warm summers. Sunny days are common. The ocean has a pronounced modifying effect on temperatures, and the Blue Ridge Mountains inland block the cold air from the interior. Some tropical storms reach the area every few years. The frost-free growing period extends from the end of March to the beginning of November.

Winter mildness: 69	**Seasonal affect:** 65
Summer mildness: 32	**Hazardousness:** 60
Score: 62.60	**Rank: 133**

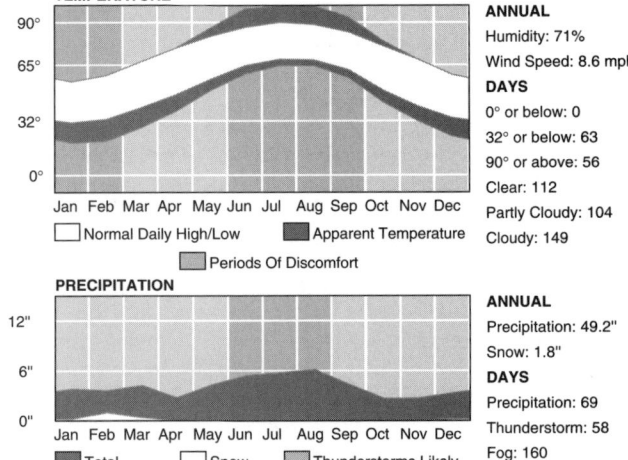

TEMPERATURE

ANNUAL
Humidity: 71%
Wind Speed: 8.6 mph
DAYS
0° or below: 0
32° or below: 63
90° or above: 56
Clear: 112
Partly Cloudy: 104
Cloudy: 149

PRECIPITATION

ANNUAL
Precipitation: 49.2"
Snow: 1.8"
DAYS
Precipitation: 69
Thunderstorm: 58
Fog: 160

★Naples, FL

Location: 26.10 N, 81.47 W, at 0 feet, on Florida's southern Gulf coast; 25 miles south of Ft. Myers.

Landscape: On a 7-mile mainland beach at the edge of the Everglades. The inland area is a waste of mangrove islands and stands of cypress, evergreen oaks, laurel, small palms, and shrubs. Much of the surrounding flat, sandy land is less than 15 feet in elevation and vulnerable to hurricane-borne tidal surges.

Cimate: Subtropical, with summer and winter temperature extremes checked by the influence of the Gulf. Mild winters have many bright, warm days. Traces of snow have occurred only a few times this century. Nights are moderately cool. Rainfall averages more than 50 inches annually, with two-thirds of this total coming daily between June and September. Most rain falls as late afternoon or early evening thunderstorms, bringing relief from the heat.

Winter mildness: 99	**Seasonal affect:** 79
Summer mildness: 21	**Hazardousness:** 84
Score: 92.06	**Rank: 29**

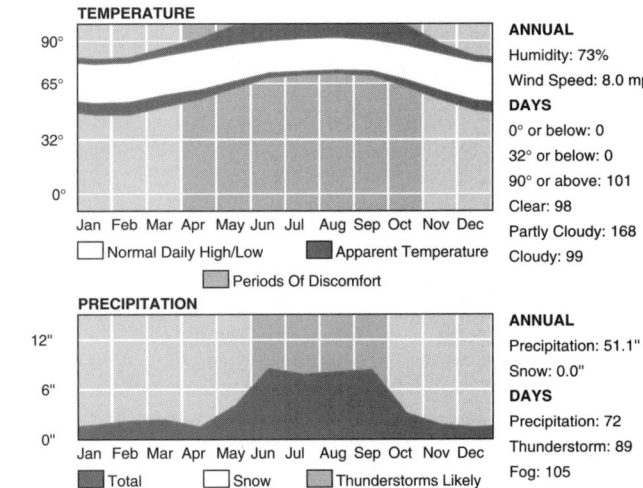

TEMPERATURE

ANNUAL
Humidity: 73%
Wind Speed: 8.0 mph
DAYS
0° or below: 0
32° or below: 0
90° or above: 101
Clear: 98
Partly Cloudy: 168
Cloudy: 99

PRECIPITATION

ANNUAL
Precipitation: 51.1"
Snow: 0.0"
DAYS
Precipitation: 72
Thunderstorm: 89
Fog: 105

Nashville, TN

Location: 36.07 N, 86.41 W, at 590 feet, on the Cumberland River in the northwestern corner of the Nashville Basin; 200 miles northeast of Memphis and 175 miles west of Knoxville.

Landscape: The escarpment of the Highland Rim rises 400 feet above the mean elevation of the basin, forming an amphitheater around the city from the southwest to the southeast.

Cimate: Temperate Continental temperatures where extremes of heat or cold are rare, yet fairly frequent changes give variety. In July, the mean temperature is 80°F. In January it averages 37°F. The humidity is moderate when compared with other locations east of the Mississippi and south of the Ohio River. The city is not in the most highly traveled path of general storm systems that cross the country. However, it is in a zone that experiences thunderstorms fairly often and snow falls each winter. The growing season is some 211 days with rainfall averaging 47 inches each year.

Winter mildness: 61	**Seasonal affect:** 25
Summer mildness: 34	**Hazardousness:** 55
Score: 42.49	**Rank: 204**

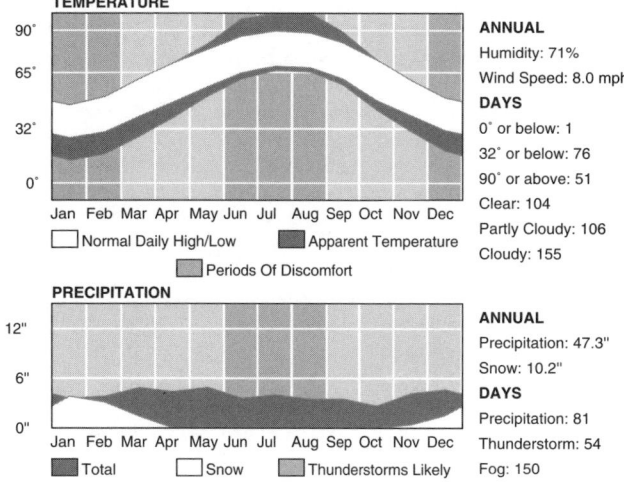

ANNUAL
Humidity: 71%
Wind Speed: 8.0 mph
DAYS
0° or below: 1
32° or below: 76
90° or above: 51
Clear: 104
Partly Cloudy: 106
Cloudy: 155

ANNUAL
Precipitation: 47.3"
Snow: 10.2"
DAYS
Precipitation: 81
Thunderstorm: 54
Fog: 150

New Haven-Meriden, CT

Location: 41.10 N, 73.08 W, at 10 feet, a port city in south central Connecticut on Long Island Sound at the mouth of the Quinnipiac River; 75 miles east of New York.

Landscape: Lying in the central lowlands of the state, where the surrounding land is wide and fertile. A narrow strip along Long Island Sound includes an indented shoreline with low, rocky headlands; smooth, sandy beaches; and broad, flat tidal marshes. Much of the landscape is urban.

Cimate: Moderate Continental climate, with four well-defined seasons and considerable diversity of weather over short time periods. Nearness to the Atlantic moderates the temperatures, often through cloud cover. The first frost comes in mid-October and the last frost comes in late April. There is a January mean temperature of 30°F, and July averages 74°F. Precipitation falls as snow in winter; thunderstorms may bring heavy rains in summer. Annual precipitation is 42 inches. Hurricanes occasionally strike along the shore during August or September.

Winter mildness: 50	**Seasonal affect:** 41
Summer mildness: 79	**Hazardousness:** 50
Score: 60.33	**Rank: 140**

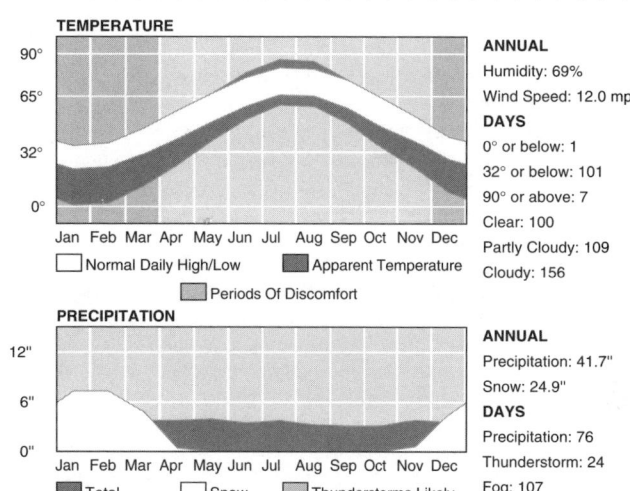

ANNUAL
Humidity: 69%
Wind Speed: 12.0 mph
DAYS
0° or below: 1
32° or below: 101
90° or above: 7
Clear: 100
Partly Cloudy: 109
Cloudy: 156

ANNUAL
Precipitation: 41.7"
Snow: 24.9"
DAYS
Precipitation: 76
Thunderstorm: 24
Fog: 107

New London-Norwich, CT-RI

Location: 41.32 N, 72.04 W, at 20 feet, in southeast Connecticut. New London is on the Thames River, near its mouth on Long Island Sound. Norwich sits just north, where the Yantic and Shetucket rivers form the Thames.

Landscape: New London is a deepwater port of entry, and the excellent harbor is used by the U.S. Navy as a principal submarine base. The United States Coast Guard Academy is located in the city. Norwich is an industrial city where the skyline includes chemical, plastic, and paper plants. These are the hilly fertile central lowlands of the state, but much of the area landscape is urban.

Cimate: Continental climate, with four well-defined seasons. Nearness to the Atlantic moderates the temperatures. Precipitation falls as snow in winter; thunderstorms may bring heavy rains in summer. Expect the first freeze around October 15; anticipate the last freeze at the end of April. Hurricanes sometimes move along the shore during August or September. January temperatures average 30°F; July averages 74°F.

Winter mildness: 37	**Seasonal affect:** 25
Summer mildness: 71	**Hazardousness:** 47
Score: 38.81	**Rank: 217**

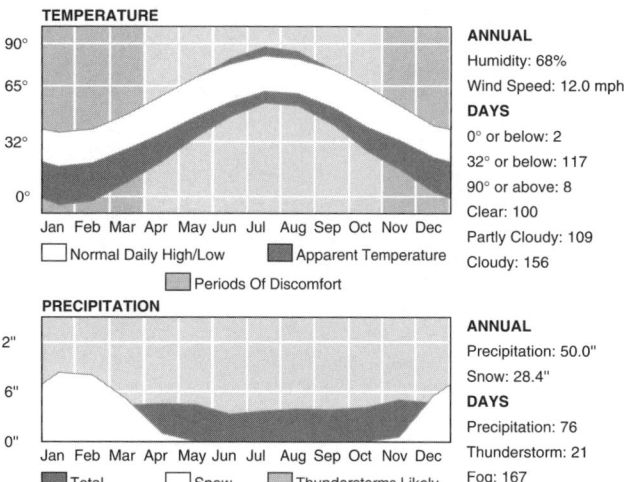

ANNUAL
Humidity: 68%
Wind Speed: 12.0 mph
DAYS
0° or below: 2
32° or below: 117
90° or above: 8
Clear: 100
Partly Cloudy: 109
Cloudy: 156

ANNUAL
Precipitation: 50.0"
Snow: 28.4"
DAYS
Precipitation: 76
Thunderstorm: 21
Fog: 167

New Orleans, LA

Location: 29.59 N, 90.15 W, at 0 feet, in southern Louisiana, mostly on the east bank of the Mississippi River.

Landscape: The metropolitan area is surrounded by water—Lake Pontchartrain, the Mississippi River, and bayous, lakes, and marshy delta land. Elevations in the city vary from a few feet above sea level to a few feet below. A massive levee system offers protection from river flooding and tidal surges.

Cimate: Humid with surrounding water modifying the temperature. Heavy and frequent rains are typical, and there are daily afternoon thunderstorms from mid-June through September. From December to March, precipitation is likely to be steady rain of two or three days' duration, instead of showers. During winter and spring, cold rain forms fogs that inhibit air and river transportation. The city has been hard hit by three hurricanes since 1900. Temperatures in January average 55°F and in July 82°F. Annual rainfall is 62 inches. The typical first freeze occurs on November 29, and the last one on February 20.

Winter mildness: 91	**Seasonal affect:** 44
Summer mildness: 26	**Hazardousness:** 75
Score: 75.92	**Rank: 86**

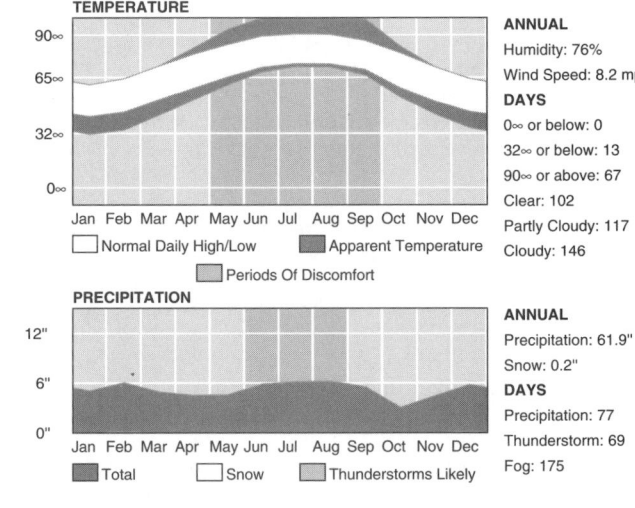

TEMPERATURE

ANNUAL
Humidity: 76%
Wind Speed: 8.2 mph
DAYS
0∞ or below: 0
32∞ or below: 13
90∞ or above: 67
Clear: 102
Partly Cloudy: 117
Cloudy: 146

Normal Daily High/Low   Apparent Temperature
Periods Of Discomfort

PRECIPITATION

ANNUAL
Precipitation: 61.9"
Snow: 0.2"
DAYS
Precipitation: 77
Thunderstorm: 69
Fog: 175

Total   Snow   Thunderstorms Likely

New York, NY

Location: 40.47 N, 73.58 W, at 130 feet, on the Atlantic Coastal Plain at the mouth of the Hudson River on the southernmost tip of New York state.

Landscape: Topography is diversified by numerous waterways. The city's physical setting is an assortment of islands and parts of islands. Only the Bronx is on the mainland. The core of the city is Manhattan, which is totally urban except for Central Park and other smaller parks.

Cimate: Close to the path of most storm and frontal systems that move across the continent. Weather affecting the city approaches from the west. New York City can thus expect higher temperatures in summer and lower ones in winter than would otherwise be expected in a coastal area. Although Continental characteristics are dominant, ocean influence is by no means absent. Sea breezes moderate summer afternoon heat and delay the advent of winter snows. The Atlantic's influence is also measured in the 200-day frost-free season, from mid-April to mid-November. Precipitation averages 44 inches annually.

Winter mildness: 58	**Seasonal affect:** 55
Summer mildness: 56	**Hazardousness:** 56
Score: 70.53	**Rank: 105**

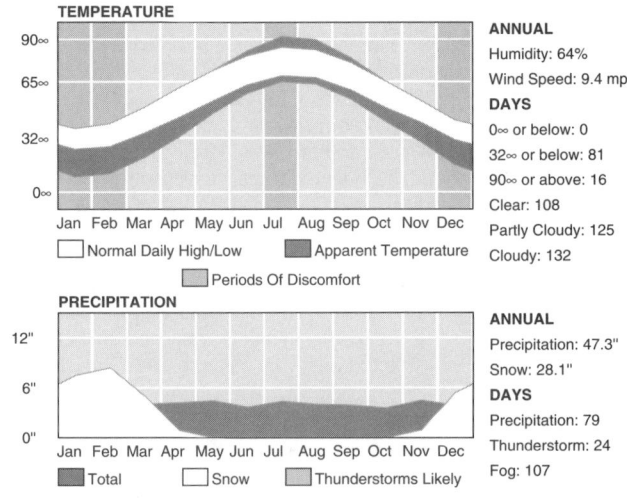

TEMPERATURE

ANNUAL
Humidity: 64%
Wind Speed: 9.4 mph
DAYS
0∞ or below: 0
32∞ or below: 81
90∞ or above: 16
Clear: 108
Partly Cloudy: 125
Cloudy: 132

Normal Daily High/Low   Apparent Temperature
Periods Of Discomfort

PRECIPITATION

ANNUAL
Precipitation: 47.3"
Snow: 28.1"
DAYS
Precipitation: 79
Thunderstorm: 24
Fog: 107

Total   Snow   Thunderstorms Likely

Norfolk-Virginia Beach-Newport News, VA-NC

Location: 36.54 N, 76.12 W, at 20 feet, on low-level land, with the Chesapeake Bay immediately to the north, Hampton Roads to the west, and the Atlantic Ocean to the east.

Landscape: Tidewater lowlands near the coast and the southern border of Virginia, the area is almost surrounded by water. Crossed by numerous rivers and waterways, arable land is flat and descends gently to sea level with no nearby hilly areas. Norfolk and its sister cities compose the Port of Hampton Roads, one of the world's finest natural harbors.

Cimate: Subtropical characteristics with mild winters and especially pleasant springs and falls. Summers, though, are warm, humid, and long. A temperature of zero has never been recorded here, although there is occasional snow. The average first freeze is November 3, and the average last freeze is April 5. The metro area is in a favorable geographic position, being north of the track of hurricanes and tropical storms and south of high latitude storm systems.

Winter mildness: 69	**Seasonal affect:** 44
Summer mildness: 49	**Hazardousness:** 57
Score: 69.40	**Rank: 109**

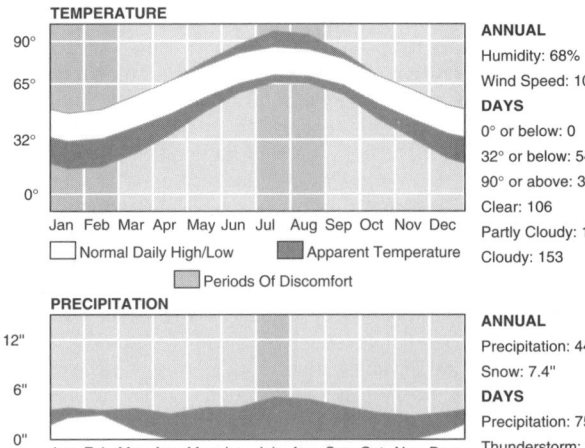

TEMPERATURE

ANNUAL
Humidity: 68%
Wind Speed: 10.6 mph
DAYS
0° or below: 0
32° or below: 54
90° or above: 30
Clear: 106
Partly Cloudy: 106
Cloudy: 153

Normal Daily High/Low   Apparent Temperature
Periods Of Discomfort

PRECIPITATION

ANNUAL
Precipitation: 44.6"
Snow: 7.4"
DAYS
Precipitation: 75
Thunderstorm: 37
Fog: 157

Total   Snow   Thunderstorms Likely

Ocala, FL

Location: 29.12 N, 82.05 W, at 80 feet, in north central Florida; 20 miles south of Gainesville and 90 miles west of Daytona Beach and the Atlantic.

Landscape: This is hilly and rural ridge country, just west of Ocala National Forest where there are local deposits of pure limestone, the geological basis for the peninsula. The terrain and climate has proved perfect for breeding horses and cattle. Artesian springs and outlets form the Silver River. Stands of sand pine, long-leaf, slash and other yellow southern pine, and cypress mix with hardwoods of the eastern deciduous forest. Old live oaks outnumber palm trees.

Cimate: Subtropical in character with summers that are hotter and more humid than coastal locations, but that are cooled by afternoon thunderstorms. Winters are mild and without snow. The annual range of temperature changes is small, but there is a subtle though definite four-season climate. Freezes do occur from December 9 until mid-February.

Winter mildness: 94	**Seasonal affect:** 48
Summer mildness: 17	**Hazardousness:** 88
Score: 83.85	**Rank: 58**

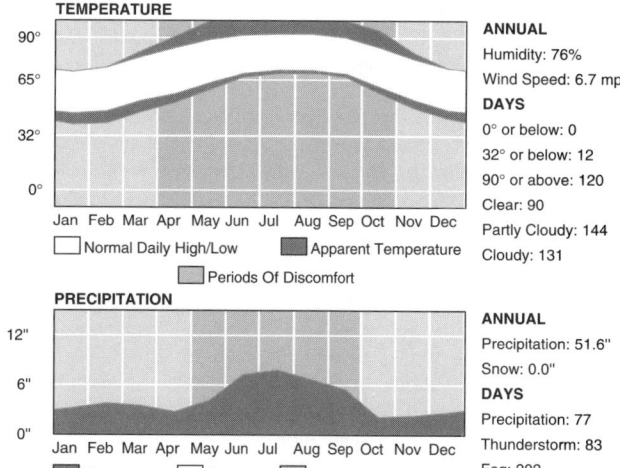

ANNUAL
Humidity: 76%
Wind Speed: 6.7 mph
DAYS
0° or below: 0
32° or below: 12
90° or above: 120
Clear: 90
Partly Cloudy: 144
Cloudy: 131

ANNUAL
Precipitation: 51.6"
Snow: 0.0"
DAYS
Precipitation: 77
Thunderstorm: 83
Fog: 202

Odessa Midland, TX

Location: 31.57 N, 102.11 W, at 2,860 feet, on the southern edge of the High Plains panhandle; 336 miles northwest of Austin.

Landscape: Grassy high plains coverage consisting mainly of short grasses; there are few trees in the area. The topography is flat tableland, with only slight and infrequent breaks. This is the petroleum rich Permian Basin. A large crater remains from a meteorite shower, and the Guadalupe Mountains are a dim blue bulk on the western horizon.

Cimate: Semiarid Desert-Steppe. Droughts occur with monotonous frequency, resulting in dust storms so severe that suspended dust remains in the air several days after the storm has passed. Though summer afternoon temperatures are frequently above 90°F, low humidity and rapid evaporation have a cooling effect. The climate is generally pleasant, with the most disagreeable weather concentrated in late winter and spring. The first freeze is the beginning of November; the last, the end of March. Most precipitation is the result of violent thunderstorms in spring and early summer.

Winter mildness: 63	**Seasonal affect:** 97
Summer mildness: 5	**Hazardousness:** 62
Score: 54.10	**Rank: 163**

TEMPERATURE

ANNUAL
Humidity: 59%
Wind Speed: 11.1 mph
DAYS
0° or below: 0
32° or below: 63
90° or above: 103
Clear: 165
Partly Cloudy: 96
Cloudy: 104

PRECIPITATION

ANNUAL
Precipitation: 15.0"
Snow: 4.3"
DAYS
Precipitation: 23
Thunderstorm: 37
Fog: 47

Oklahoma City, OK

Location: 35.24 N, 97.36 W, at 1,280 feet, along the North Canadian River near Oklahoma's geographic center, some 1,000 miles south of Canada and 500 miles north of the Gulf of Mexico.

Landscape: The surrounding countryside is a plain or gently rolling grassland. The nearest hills, or low-rise mountains, are the Arbuckles, some 80 miles south. A major oil field is beneath the city, and derricks mark the skyline.

Cimate: Although some influence is exerted by warm, moist air from the Gulf of Mexico, the city's Continental climate falls mainly under controls that are characteristic of the Great Plains. This produces pronounced daily and seasonal temperature changes and considerable variation in seasonal and annual precipitation. The typical first freeze is October 20, and the last is April 14. Summers are long and hot, broken by rain falling both as showers and thunderstorms. Occasionally there will be hail and destructive winds. Winters are comparatively mild and short. Moisture in the form of sleet arrives on frontal passages from the north.

Winter mildness: 58	**Seasonal affect:** 84
Summer mildness: 10	**Hazardousness:** 40
Score: 34.56	**Rank: 232**

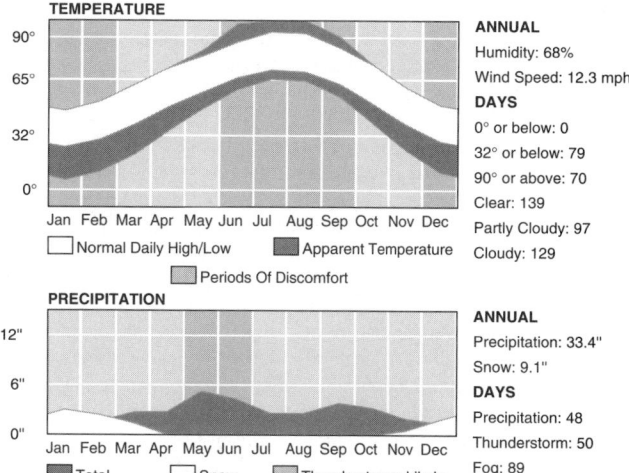

ANNUAL
Humidity: 68%
Wind Speed: 12.3 mph
DAYS
0° or below: 0
32° or below: 79
90° or above: 70
Clear: 139
Partly Cloudy: 97
Cloudy: 129

ANNUAL
Precipitation: 33.4"
Snow: 9.1"
DAYS
Precipitation: 48
Thunderstorm: 50
Fog: 89

Olympia, WA

Location: 46.58 N, 122.54 W, at 190 feet, the capital lies at the southernmost end of Puget Sound, some 60 miles south-south-west of Seattle.

Landscape: The Olympic Peninsula, with its fine remnants of Pacific Northwest rain forests, active glaciers, and alpine meadows, lies to the northwest. The city and vicinity are well protected by the Coastal Ranges from the strong south and southwest winds accompanying many Pacific storms.

Cimate: Characterized by warm, generally dry summers and wet, mild winters. Fall rains begin in October and continue with few interruptions until spring. The first freeze is November 4; the last freeze is April 10. During the rainy season there is little variation in temperature, with days in the 40s and 50s and nights in the 30s, and constant cloud cover. The summer highs are between 60°F and 80°F, with up to 20 days without rain. The summer is marked by clear skies at night and frequent morning fog.

Winter mildness: 70	**Seasonal affect:** 0
Summer mildness: 93	**Hazardousness:** 88
Score: 77.90	**Rank: 79**

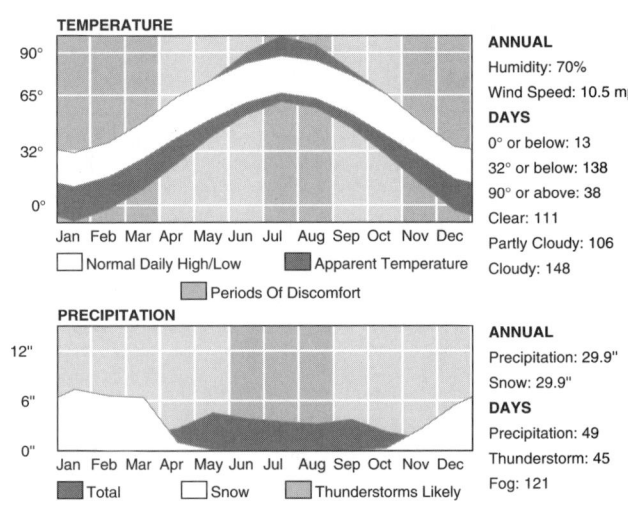

TEMPERATURE

Normal Daily High/Low — Apparent Temperature — Periods Of Discomfort

ANNUAL
Humidity: 79%
Wind Speed: 6.7 mph
DAYS
0° or below: 0
32° or below: 85
90° or above: 6
Clear: 54
Partly Cloudy: 84
Cloudy: 227

PRECIPITATION

Total — Snow — Thunderstorms Likely

ANNUAL
Precipitation: 50.6"
Snow: 17.3"
DAYS
Precipitation: 84
Thunderstorm: 4
Fog: 225

Omaha, NE-IA

Location: 41.18 N, 95.54 W, at 1,000 feet, in eastern Nebraska, on the west bank of the Missouri River opposite Council Bluffs, Iowa.

Landscape: Among rolling hills that rise 300 feet above the riverbank, this is a fertile agricultural region, part of a glacial plain with a well-developed drainage system. Soil is silt loam and sandy loam, highly suitable for growing corn, grain sorghums, and wheat.

Cimate: Typically Continental, with relatively warm summers and cold, dry winters. Situated midway between the humid East and the dry West, the region is controlled by weather conditions characteristic of both. The freeze-free growing season is from April 27 to October 8. Omaha is affected by most storms that cross the country, causing periodic and rapid changes in weather, especially during the winter. Snowfall is not significant, but the days do get cold and these cold spells may linger. Sunshine is well distributed throughout the year. Because of prolonged rainfall, Omaha experienced severe flooding in the summer of 1993.

Winter mildness: 12	**Seasonal affect:** 75
Summer mildness: 42	**Hazardousness:** 19
Score: 12.46	**Rank: 310**

TEMPERATURE

Normal Daily High/Low — Apparent Temperature — Periods Of Discomfort

ANNUAL
Humidity: 70%
Wind Speed: 10.5 mph
DAYS
0° or below: 13
32° or below: 138
90° or above: 38
Clear: 111
Partly Cloudy: 106
Cloudy: 148

PRECIPITATION

Total — Snow — Thunderstorms Likely

ANNUAL
Precipitation: 29.9"
Snow: 29.9"
DAYS
Precipitation: 49
Thunderstorm: 45
Fog: 121

Orlando, FL

Location: 28.27 N, 81.19 W, at 100 feet, in the east central ridge section of the Florida peninsula.

Landscape: The countryside is flat, almost surrounded by lakes, with no natural barriers to exterior weather systems. More than 50 lakes lie within the city limits, and Orange County's thousand lakes moderate the climate throughout the year. Sinkholes are also part of the terrain. Land is fertile, highly suitable for citrus, bulb flowers, and winter vegetable growth. Deciduous hardwoods flourish along with palms. Azaleas are a winter treat, blooming January through March.

Cimate: Typical Subtropical with high year-round relative humidity owing to surrounding water, near 90 percent at night and dipping to 50 percent in the afternoon. The rainy season extends from June through September; afternoon thundershowers occur daily. Rain is light during the winter, and snow and sleet are rare. Winter temperatures may drop to freezing at night, but days are clear and dry, with brilliant sunshine. The first freeze is December 21st; the last, February 9.

Winter mildness: 96	**Seasonal affect:** 76
Summer mildness: 20	**Hazardousness:** 83
Score: 87.53	**Rank: 45**

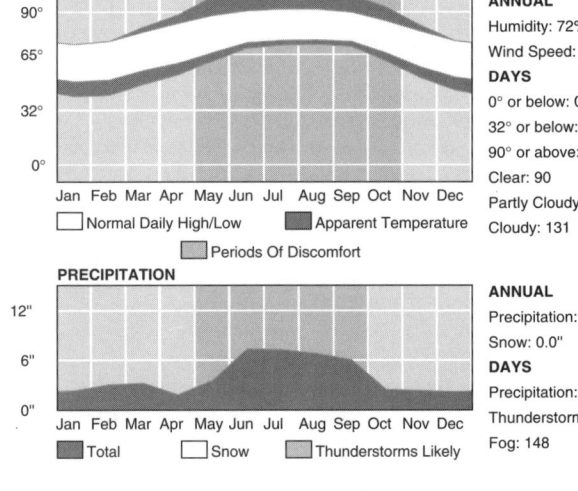

TEMPERATURE

Normal Daily High/Low — Apparent Temperature — Periods Of Discomfort

ANNUAL
Humidity: 72%
Wind Speed: 8.6 mph
DAYS
0° or below: 0
32° or below: 3
90° or above: 90
Clear: 90
Partly Cloudy: 144
Cloudy: 131

PRECIPITATION

Total — Snow — Thunderstorms Likely

ANNUAL
Precipitation: 48.1"
Snow: 0.0"
DAYS
Precipitation: 65
Thunderstorm: 80
Fog: 148

Ottawa-Hull, ON-PQ

Location: 45.19 N, 75.40 W, at 374 feet, the capital of Canada is in the southeastern part of the province at the confluence of the Ottawa, Gatineau, and Rideau rivers.

Landscape: The Ottawa River marks the provincial boundary between Ontario and Quebec, with the city of Ottawa on the Ontario side and the city of Hull on the Quebec side. South of the city there is a rise in elevation from the river valley to an area of rolling farmland. On the north side of the Ottawa River the terrain rises sharply in a wooded section of the Gatineau Hills.

Cimate: Stimulating and variable, cold and snowy in winter, warm in summer. This is Continental climate with Maritime air from both the Atlantic Ocean and the Gulf of Mexico. There are two main seasons with shorter transitional periods of spring and autumn. Good or bad periods commonly do not last for more than a few days. Temperatures average 14°F in January and 70°F in July.

Winter mildness: 7	**Seasonal affect:** 9
Summer mildness: 90	**Hazardousness:** 15
Score: 5.38	**Rank: 335**

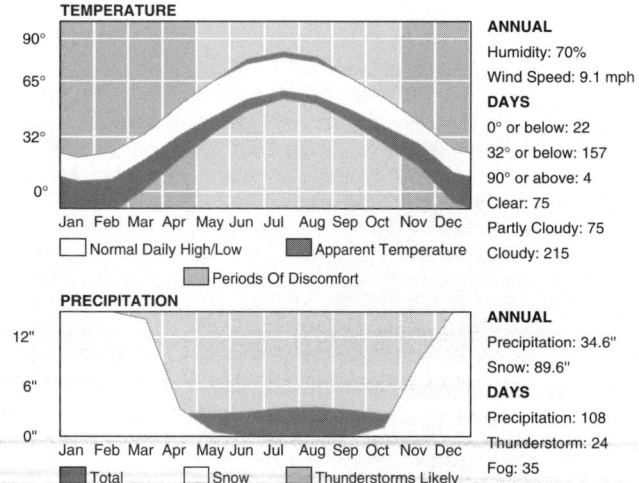

ANNUAL
Humidity: 70%
Wind Speed: 9.1 mph
DAYS
0° or below: 22
32° or below: 157
90° or above: 4
Clear: 75
Partly Cloudy: 75
Cloudy: 215

ANNUAL
Precipitation: 34.6"
Snow: 89.6"
DAYS
Precipitation: 108
Thunderstorm: 24
Fog: 35

Panama City, FL

Location: 30.13 N, 85.36 W, at 30 feet, on the Gulf of Mexico in Florida's panhandle; 120 miles west of Tallahassee, the capital.

Landscape: Landlocked, deepwater harbor on the Atlantic Intracoastal Waterway, with a port of entry on St. Andrew Bay. A sandy coastal region of shallow bays, white beaches, and dunes where elevations range from a few feet above sea level to more than 100 feet. The interior forested swamp includes evergreen oaks and members of the laurel and magnolia families. There is a lower stratum of tree ferns, shrubs, and herbaceous plants. The longleaf, loblolly, and slash pines represent second growth forest.

Cimate: Subtropical in temperature and rainfall. The panhandle of Florida is cooler in summer and still pleasant in winter. The Mediterranean climate is suitable for the growing of citrus fruits and vegetables, and for tourism. The Yucatan Current runs near here bringing its moderating influence. There are predictable freezes—the first occurring November 14 and the latest around March 9.

Winter mildness: 86	**Seasonal affect:** 73
Summer mildness: 30	**Hazardousness:** 72
Score: 84.70	**Rank: 55**

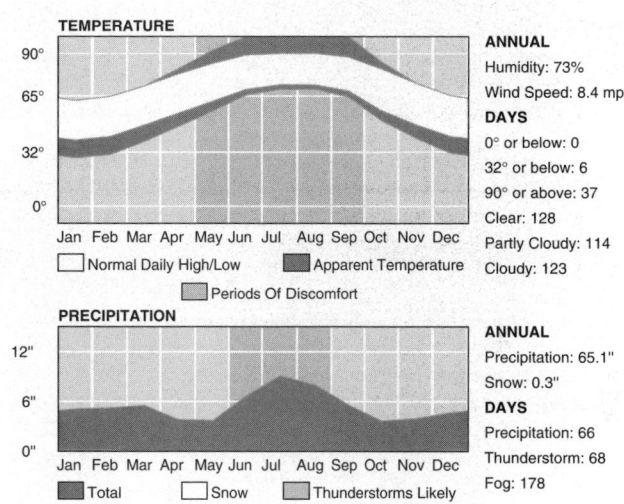

ANNUAL
Humidity: 73%
Wind Speed: 8.4 mph
DAYS
0° or below: 0
32° or below: 6
90° or above: 37
Clear: 128
Partly Cloudy: 114
Cloudy: 123

ANNUAL
Precipitation: 65.1"
Snow: 0.3"
DAYS
Precipitation: 66
Thunderstorm: 68
Fog: 178

Pensacola, FL

Location: 30.28 N, 87.12 W, at 110 feet, in the panhandle of Florida on Pensacola Bay, 6 miles from the Gulf of Mexico.

Landscape: On a somewhat hilly, sandy slope separated from the Gulf of Mexico by a long, narrow island that forms a natural breakwater for the harbor. The sand is a glistening white that is nearly pure quartz. Salt marshes are common features. Elevations are high enough so that most of the city is well above storm tides. Pensacola's deep, natural harbor has made it a shipping and commercial fishing center.

Cimate: The Gulf of Mexico, about 6 miles away, moderates the weather throughout the year, tempering the cold northers of winter, and causing cool and refreshing sea breezes during summer days. Average summer temperature is 80°F; average winter temperature is 55°F. The first freeze is November 24, the last at the beginning of March. Precipitation is well distributed throughout the year and averages 61 inches annually. Hurricanes can occur.

Winter mildness: 90	**Seasonal affect:** 69
Summer mildness: 32	**Hazardousness:** 72
Score: 85.55	**Rank: 52**

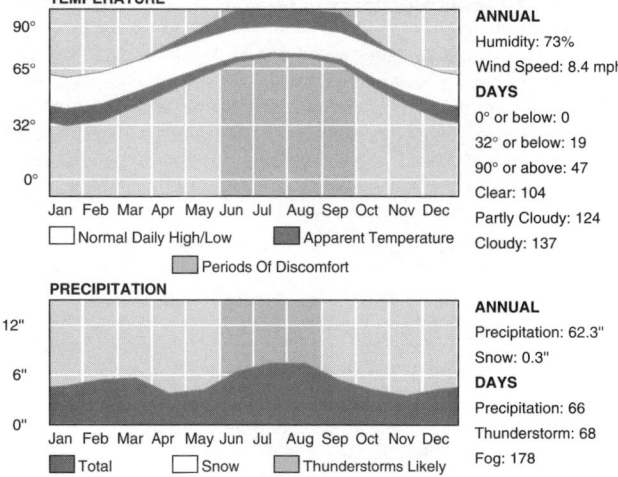

ANNUAL
Humidity: 73%
Wind Speed: 8.4 mph
DAYS
0° or below: 0
32° or below: 19
90° or above: 47
Clear: 104
Partly Cloudy: 124
Cloudy: 137

ANNUAL
Precipitation: 62.3"
Snow: 0.3"
DAYS
Precipitation: 66
Thunderstorm: 68
Fog: 178

Peoria-Pekin, IL

Location: 40.40 N, 89.41 W, at 650 feet, in north central Illinois; 150 miles southwest of Chicago.

Landscape: The Illinois River widens into Lake Peoria with gently rising topography extending to level tableland. This is the heart of Illinois's central farm country. All soil is rich and arable. Once forested with eastern deciduous oak, maple, and other hardwoods, which now serve as windbreaks for wide fields.

Cimate: Typically Continental, characterized by changeable weather and a wide range of temperatures. For example, 1936 had 17 days with temperatures of 100°F or higher in July, and 26 days within a 31-day winter period when the temperature was zero. The same year had the maximum high record of 113° set on June 13. June and September are usually the most pleasant months of the year. During October and early November, residents enjoy Indian summer, with its extended period of warm, dry weather. The average first freeze is late October; the average last freeze is late April.

Winter mildness: 18   **Seasonal affect:** 59
Summer mildness: 52   **Hazardousness:** 28
Score: 18.69   **Rank: 288**

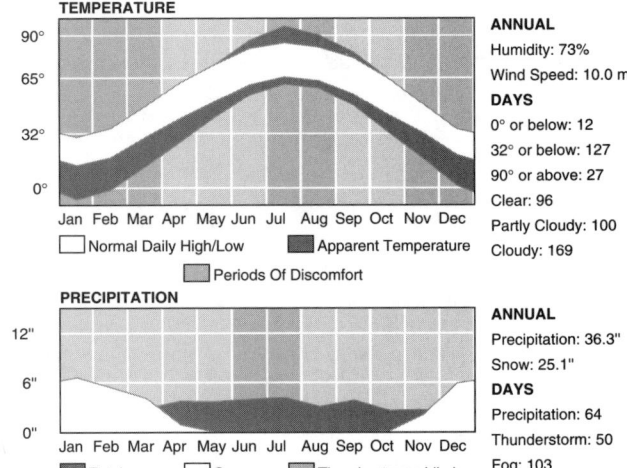

ANNUAL
Humidity: 73%
Wind Speed: 10.0 mph
DAYS
0° or below: 12
32° or below: 127
90° or above: 27
Clear: 96
Partly Cloudy: 100
Cloudy: 169

ANNUAL
Precipitation: 36.3"
Snow: 25.1"
DAYS
Precipitation: 64
Thunderstorm: 50
Fog: 103

Philadelphia, PA-NJ

Location: 39.53 N, 75.15 W, at 0 feet, on the Schuylkill and Delaware rivers on the eastern border of Pennsylvania.

Landscape: The Appalachian Mountains to the west and the Atlantic Ocean to the east have a moderating effect on the city's climate. The Schuykill flows through the city. Philadelphia Harbor ranks as one of the most important in the United States. Surrounding land is low and fertile.

Cimate: Sustained periods of either extreme highs or lows seldom last for more than three or four days. Occasionally during the summer, high humidity adds to the discomfort of warm temperatures. Precipitation is evenly distributed throughout the year. Snowfall often is considerably higher in the northern suburbs than in the city, where sometimes rain will fall instead. Winters often bring high winds, accompanying cold air after the passage of a deep low-pressure system. Average annual precipitation totals 41 inches. Daily temperature averages range from 24°F in January to 66°F in July.

Winter mildness: 52   **Seasonal affect:** 35
Summer mildness: 50   **Hazardousness:** 62
Score: 56.94   **Rank: 153**

ANNUAL
Humidity: 66%
Wind Speed: 9.6 mph
DAYS
0° or below: 0
32° or below: 94
90° or above: 23
Clear: 94
Partly Cloudy: 112
Cloudy: 159

ANNUAL
Precipitation: 41.4"
Snow: 20.8"
DAYS
Precipitation: 74
Thunderstorm: 27
Fog: 163

★Phoenix-Mesa, AZ

Location: 33.26 N, 112.01 W, at 1,110 feet, in Arizona's Salt River Valley in the south central part of the state.

Landscape: The valley is oval and flat. Mountain ranges are found to the south, west, and north and the famous Superstition Mountains, which rise to an elevation of 5,000 feet, are 35 miles to the east. Though desert, the valley supports large cotton and citrus growth. The Sonoran Desert itself blooms with saguaro, cholla, and cereus. The water supply is from reservoirs on the Salt and Verde rivers and from an underground water table.

Cimate: Typical arid Desert, with low annual rainfall and low humidity. Daytime temperatures are high throughout the summer. Many days exceed 100°F in the afternoon and remain above 85°F all night. Winters are mild, but nighttime temperatures frequently drop below freezing from the beginning of December through mid-February. The majority of days are clear and sunny, and the valley floor is generally free of wind except during the thunderstorm season in July and August.

Winter mildness: 89   **Seasonal affect:** 100
Summer mildness: 1   **Hazardousness:** 96
Score: 94.33   **Rank: 21**

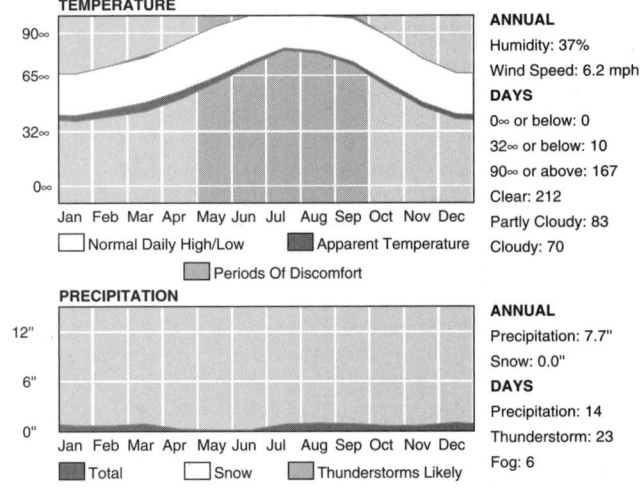

ANNUAL
Humidity: 37%
Wind Speed: 6.2 mph
DAYS
0∞ or below: 0
32∞ or below: 10
90∞ or above: 167
Clear: 212
Partly Cloudy: 83
Cloudy: 70

ANNUAL
Precipitation: 7.7"
Snow: 0.0"
DAYS
Precipitation: 14
Thunderstorm: 23
Fog: 6

Pittsburgh, PA

Location: 40.30 N, 80.13 W, at 1,140 feet, in the foothills of the Allegheny Mountains where the Allegheny and Monongahela rivers meet and form the Ohio River; about 100 miles south of Lake Erie.

Landscape: Pittsburgh was built over a rich bituminous coal seam. Its terrain has been highly dissected and is now rugged hill country. Steep slopes predominate, but some gently sloping or level plateau remnants are found. Forests are categorized as Appalachian oak.

Cimate: Humid Continental, modified only slightly by its nearness to the Atlantic Seaboard and Great Lakes. The predominant air is of polar origin from Canada and moves in by way of storm tracks, which vary in origin from the Hudson Bay to the Rockies. There are frequent inversions of air from the Gulf of Mexico during the summer, resulting in spells of warm, humid weather. Precipitation is well distributed and there is a 50 percent chance of measurable precipitation on any given day. During winter, one-fourth of it is in the form of snow.

Winter mildness: 41	**Seasonal affect:** 17
Summer mildness: 73	**Hazardousness:** 30
Score: 48.15	**Rank: 184**

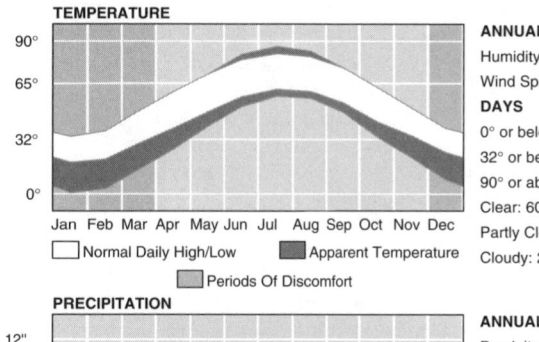

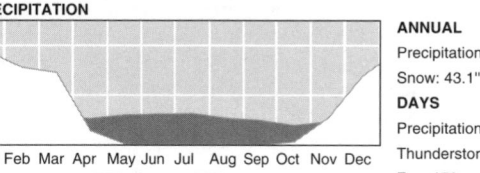

TEMPERATURE

Normal Daily High/Low — Apparent Temperature — Periods Of Discomfort

ANNUAL
Humidity: 68%
Wind Speed: 9.1 mph
DAYS
0° or below: 5
32° or below: 124
90° or above: 7
Clear: 60
Partly Cloudy: 103
Cloudy: 202

PRECIPITATION

Total — Snow — Thunderstorms Likely

ANNUAL
Precipitation: 36.9"
Snow: 43.1"
DAYS
Precipitation: 71
Thunderstorm: 35
Fog: 178

Pocatello, ID

Location: 42.52 N, 112.26 W, at 4,462 feet, in the Snake River Valley at the mouth of Portneuf Canyon; about 230 miles east of Boise, the capital.

Landscape: Desert composed of sand, lava rock, and craters, extends to the west, while to the east the ground level rises steadily toward the Continental Divide.

Cimate: Varied. In winter, southwest winds bring a mildness, like the winters of the north Pacific Coast. During cold periods, precipitation falling as snow occasionally accumulates to a depth of a foot or more. In spring there is gradual warming over months that are the wettest and windiest of the year. The last freeze is mid-May. The summer season begins with a relatively sudden break in the disagreeable spring weather. During summer, precipitation usually falls as local showers, often accompanied by light to moderate thunderstorms and occasionally by hail. Long periods of extremely hot weather are uncommon. Although afternoon temperatures may run into the 90s, nights are usually cool. Exceptionally fine weather predominates during autumn.

Winter mildness: 24	**Seasonal affect:** 24
Summer mildness: 41	**Hazardousness:** 38
Score: 32.86	**Rank: 238**

TEMPERATURE

Normal Daily High/Low — Apparent Temperature — Periods Of Discomfort

ANNUAL
Humidity: 58%
Wind Speed: 10.2 mph
DAYS
0° or below: 10
32° or below: 165
90° or above: 33
Clear: 105
Partly Cloudy: 98
Cloudy: 162

PRECIPITATION

Total — Snow — Thunderstorms Likely

ANNUAL
Precipitation: 12.1"
Snow: 42.7"
DAYS
Precipitation: 95
Thunderstorm: 24
Fog: 49

Portland, ME

Location: 43.39 N, 70.19 W, at 40 feet, on a hilly section of the southern Maine's Atlantic coast, some 45 miles southeast of the White Mountains.

Landscape: The position on two peninsulas jutting into Casco Bay gives the largest city in Maine a large deepwater harbor, making it the economic center of the state. Terrain is rolling, coastal lowland, penetrated extensively by ocean inlets. The forest is primarily evergreen with oak, maple, and other hardwoods throughout.

Cimate: As a rule, the city has pleasant summers and falls, cold winters with frequent thaws, and disagreeable muddy springs. Autumn has the greatest number of sunny days. Winters are severe; they begin late but extend deep into what is normally considered springtime, and temperatures well below zero are recorded frequently. The first freeze is mid-October, the last at the end of April. Normal monthly precipitation is uniform throughout the year, but heavy snowfalls, sometimes totaling more than 100 inches per year, do occur.

Winter mildness: 14	**Seasonal affect:** 14
Summer mildness: 90	**Hazardousness:** 32
Score: 45.04	**Rank: 195**

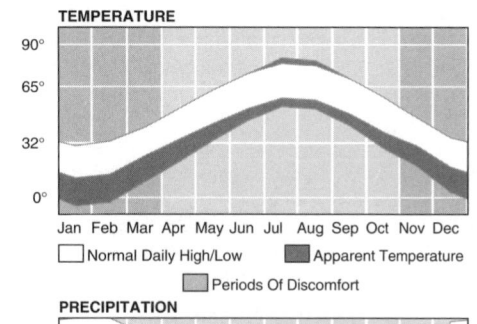

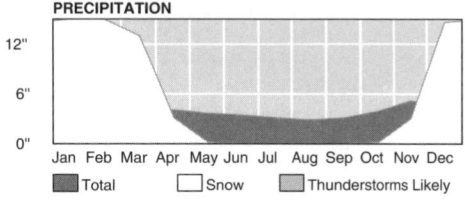

TEMPERATURE

Normal Daily High/Low — Apparent Temperature — Periods Of Discomfort

ANNUAL
Humidity: 69%
Wind Speed: 8.8 mph
DAYS
0° or below: 15
32° or below: 156
90° or above: 5
Clear: 102
Partly Cloudy: 100
Cloudy: 163

PRECIPITATION

Total — Snow — Thunderstorms Likely

ANNUAL
Precipitation: 44.3"
Snow: 70.5"
DAYS
Precipitation: 81
Thunderstorm: 16
Fog: 170

Portland-Vancouver, OR-WA

Location: 45.36 N, 122.36 W, at 20 feet, on the Columbia River, 65 miles inland from the Pacific Ocean, in northwest Oregon.

Landscape: Midway between the low Coastal Ranges on the west and the higher Cascade Range on the east, each 30 miles distant. The long growing season, with its mild temperatures and ample moisture, favors nursery and seed industries. The port is used by barges carrying grain and ores downstream through the Columbia Gorge, and by oceangoing vessels navigating the Columbia as far upstream as Portland. Mount Hood and its large national forest are nearby.

Cimate: A rainy climate in winter, marked by relatively mild temperatures and cloudy skies. Summers are pleasantly mild with northwesterly winds and little precipitation. Fall and spring are transitional in nature. The first freeze arrives at the end of October. The last occurs in mid-April. Fog occurs frequently in fall and winter. At all times, incursions of Marine air are a moderating influence. Extremes in winter and summer come from the continental interior.

Winter mildness: 75	**Seasonal affect:** 8
Summer mildness: 88	**Hazardousness:** 49
Score: 67.13	**Rank: 117**

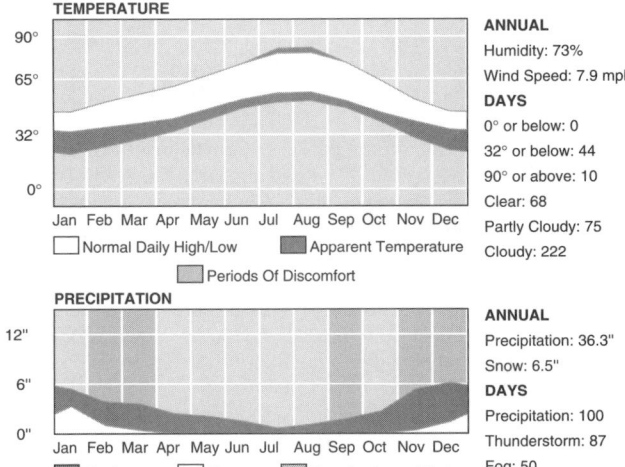

TEMPERATURE

Normal Daily High/Low · Apparent Temperature · Periods Of Discomfort

ANNUAL
Humidity: 73%
Wind Speed: 7.9 mph
DAYS
0° or below: 0
32° or below: 44
90° or above: 10
Clear: 68
Partly Cloudy: 75
Cloudy: 222

PRECIPITATION

Total · Snow · Thunderstorms Likely

ANNUAL
Precipitation: 36.3"
Snow: 6.5"
DAYS
Precipitation: 100
Thunderstorm: 87
Fog: 50

Portsmouth-Rochester, NH-ME

Location: 43.01 N, 70.50 W, at 80 feet, on the Atlantic coast of southeastern New Hampshire, at the mouth of the Piscataqua River, opposite Kittery, Maine. Rochester is on the east bank of the Cocheco River.

Landscape: New Hampshire's Eastern Slope descends gradually to the sea. Part of the state's brief seacoast consists of sandy beaches and Portsmouth Harbor. The Eastern Slope itself is covered with a moderately fertile soil produced from disintegrating slate. The Piscataqua River provides drainage.

Cimate: Definitely Continental in temperature range and precipitation. The nearness of the Atlantic moderates the weather's severity. January's average high is just over freezing and the monthly mean is 21°F. There are four zero-degree days and more than 100 freezing days each year. The high for July is 82°F, cooling at night to less than 60°F. Much of the yearly precipitation falls as snow from December through April. The first freeze is September 21, and the last is May 19.

Winter mildness: 18	**Seasonal affect:** 47
Summer mildness: 80	**Hazardousness:** 15
Score: 17.28	**Rank: 293**

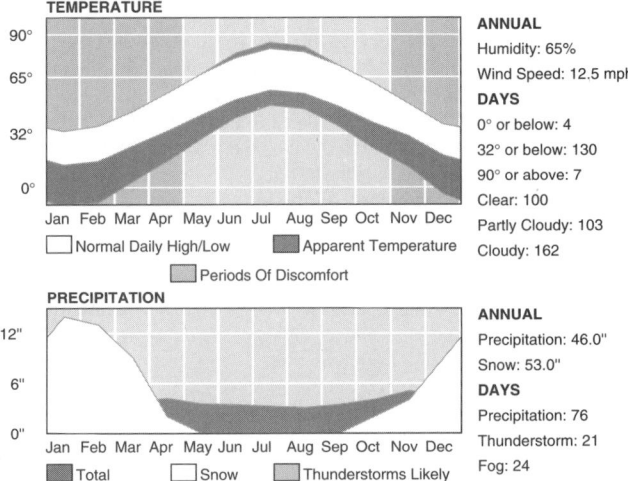

TEMPERATURE

Normal Daily High/Low · Apparent Temperature · Periods Of Discomfort

ANNUAL
Humidity: 65%
Wind Speed: 12.5 mph
DAYS
0° or below: 4
32° or below: 130
90° or above: 7
Clear: 100
Partly Cloudy: 103
Cloudy: 162

PRECIPITATION

Total · Snow · Thunderstorms Likely

ANNUAL
Precipitation: 46.0"
Snow: 53.0"
DAYS
Precipitation: 76
Thunderstorm: 21
Fog: 24

Providence-Fall River-Warwick, RI-MA

Location: 41.44 N, 71.26 W, at 50 feet, three cities located on the Providence River at the head of Narragansett Bay; 45 miles south of Boston. Providence is one of New England's largest seaports.

Landscape: Narragansett Bay reaches into the eastern end of Long Island Sound and the Atlantic Ocean. The Providence River flows through Providence and empties into the Bay. This is an area protected from severe climatic changes by both the ocean and land forms. Terrain is typical eastern lowland, gently rolling, including the bay shores and islands. Soil is sandy and gravelly.

Cimate: A moderate Marine climate. Many major snowstorms change to rain before reaching the area. Snow is not uncommon but does not remain for long periods of time. In summer, the area is cooled by refreshing breezes. Fog may be dense at times but is not frequent. Severe coastal storms in the fall can bring destructive winds. Annual rainfall is 45 inches; average snowfall is 36 inches.

Winter mildness: 42	**Seasonal affect:** 26
Summer mildness: 76	**Hazardousness:** 45
Score: 54.67	**Rank: 161**

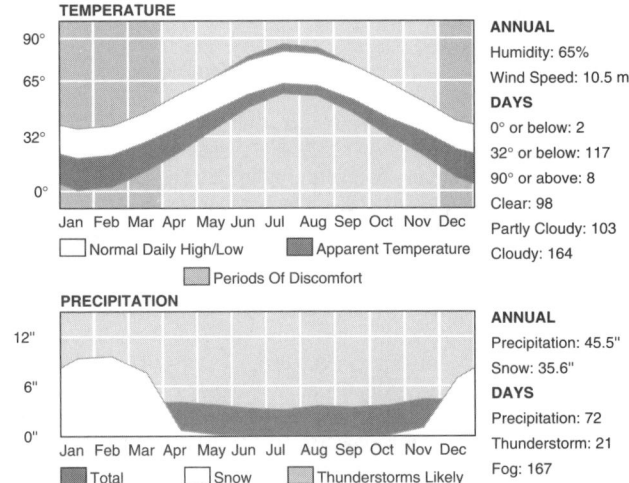

TEMPERATURE

Normal Daily High/Low · Apparent Temperature · Periods Of Discomfort

ANNUAL
Humidity: 65%
Wind Speed: 10.5 mph
DAYS
0° or below: 2
32° or below: 117
90° or above: 8
Clear: 98
Partly Cloudy: 103
Cloudy: 164

PRECIPITATION

Total · Snow · Thunderstorms Likely

ANNUAL
Precipitation: 45.5"
Snow: 35.6"
DAYS
Precipitation: 72
Thunderstorm: 21
Fog: 167

Quebec City, PQ

Location: 46.48 N, 71.23 W, at 239 feet, at the confluence of the St. Lawrence and St. Charles rivers in southeastern Quebec Province; 150 miles northeast of Montreal.

Landscape: In the vicinity of Quebec City, the relatively narrow St. Lawrence River valley is oriented in a southwest to northeast direction. It is bordered 30 miles to the northeast by the abrupt rise of the Laurentian Mountains and 25 miles to the south by the more gradual rise of the Appalachian Mountains. The area immediately surrounding the airport is generally flat and slopes south to the river.

Cimate: The snow season is long, lasting four to five months. January temperatures average 3°F. Spring arrives suddenly and sometimes not at all. The July average temperature is 67°F. Fall may be as fleeting as spring but it is almost always pleasant. Winter's first significant snowfall arrives in early November. Foul weather of any kind seldom lasts for long; most storms leave the area within two days. Annual precipitation averages 46 inches.

Winter mildness: 5	**Seasonal affect:** 8
Summer mildness: 93	**Hazardousness:** 7
Score: 0.84	**Rank: 351**

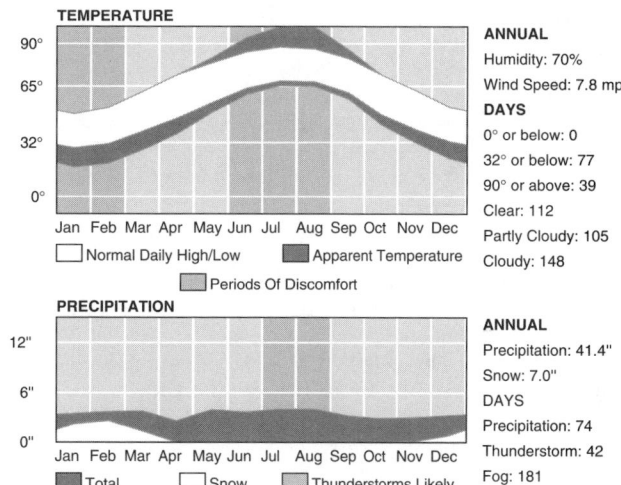

TEMPERATURE
90° 65° 32° 0°
Jan Feb Mar Apr May Jun Jul Aug Sep Oct Nov Dec
☐ Normal Daily High/Low ■ Apparent Temperature
☐ Periods Of Discomfort

PRECIPITATION
12" 6" 0"
Jan Feb Mar Apr May Jun Jul Aug Sep Oct Nov Dec
■ Total ☐ Snow ☐ Thunderstorms Likely

ANNUAL
Humidity: 73%
Wind Speed: 9.9 mph
DAYS
0° or below: 35
32° or below: 172
90° or above: 2
Clear: 69
Partly Cloudy: 70
Cloudy: 226

ANNUAL
Precipitation: 46.3"
Snow: 135.1"
DAYS
Precipitation: 117
Thunderstorm: 24
Fog: 35

Raleigh-Durham-Chapel Hill, NC

Location: 35.52 N, 78.47 W, at 420 feet, located between North Carolina's Coastal Plain and Piedmont Plateau.

Landscape: The topography is rolling, with elevations from 200 feet to 500 feet within a 10-mile radius. Broadleaf deciduous and needle-leaf evergreen trees make up the medium tall forests. Low shrubs of dogwood, viburnum, and blueberry are common.

Cimate: Located between mountains to the west and the Atlantic Coast to the east and south, the metro area enjoys a favorable climate. The western mountains form a partial barrier to cold air masses moving eastward from the nation's interior. There are few days in the heart of the winter when the temperature falls below 20°F. Tropical air is present during much of the summer, bringing warm temperatures and high humidity. In midsummer, afternoon temperatures reach 90°F or higher every fourth day. Rainfall is well distributed throughout the year. The frost-free season extends from mid-April to mid-October.

Winter mildness: 64	**Seasonal affect:** 49
Summer mildness: 42	**Hazardousness:** 70
Score: 70.82	**Rank: 104**

TEMPERATURE
90° 65° 32° 0°
Jan Feb Mar Apr May Jun Jul Aug Sep Oct Nov Dec
☐ Normal Daily High/Low ■ Apparent Temperature
☐ Periods Of Discomfort

PRECIPITATION
12" 6" 0"
Jan Feb Mar Apr May Jun Jul Aug Sep Oct Nov Dec
■ Total ☐ Snow ☐ Thunderstorms Likely

ANNUAL
Humidity: 70%
Wind Speed: 7.8 mph
DAYS
0° or below: 0
32° or below: 77
90° or above: 39
Clear: 112
Partly Cloudy: 105
Cloudy: 148

ANNUAL
Precipitation: 41.4"
Snow: 7.0"
DAYS
Precipitation: 74
Thunderstorm: 42
Fog: 181

Rapid City, SD

Location: 44.03 N, 103.04 W, at 3,160 feet, in southwest South Dakota on Rapid Creek at the eastern edge of the Black Hills, not far from the geographical center of America.

Landscape: The city is surrounded by contrasting landforms, including the forested Black Hills to the west and rolling prairie to the east. Rapid Creek rushes through the heart of town on its way east to the Missouri River, 200 miles away. To the southeast lie the eroded Badlands and the White River. Prairie soils are fertile. Coniferous forests cover the Black Hills. The area is a mining center for gold, silver, and uranium.

Cimate: Semiarid Continental, greatly affected by the Black Hills. There are large daily and seasonal temperature ranges. In the lee of the Black Hills, storms are deflected from the city making winters here among the warmest in South Dakota. Snowfall is light, averaging 40 inches annually. Spring temperatures vary widely. Summer days are warm; nights are cool.

Winter mildness: 12	**Seasonal affect:** 78
Summer mildness: 50	**Hazardousness:** 9
Score: 26.62	**Rank: 260**

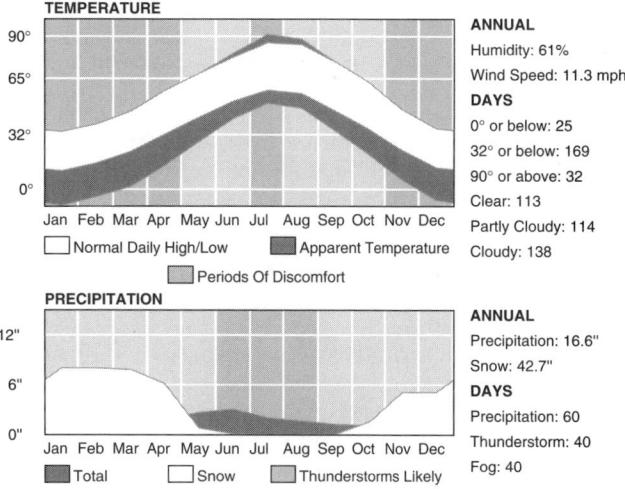

TEMPERATURE
90° 65° 32° 0°
Jan Feb Mar Apr May Jun Jul Aug Sep Oct Nov Dec
☐ Normal Daily High/Low ■ Apparent Temperature
☐ Periods Of Discomfort

PRECIPITATION
12" 6" 0"
Jan Feb Mar Apr May Jun Jul Aug Sep Oct Nov Dec
■ Total ☐ Snow ☐ Thunderstorms Likely

ANNUAL
Humidity: 61%
Wind Speed: 11.3 mph
DAYS
0° or below: 25
32° or below: 169
90° or above: 32
Clear: 113
Partly Cloudy: 114
Cloudy: 138

ANNUAL
Precipitation: 16.6"
Snow: 42.7"
DAYS
Precipitation: 60
Thunderstorm: 40
Fog: 40

★Redding, CA

Location: 40.30 N, 122.18 W, at 500 feet, in the Sacramento Valley, some 150 miles north of Sacramento and 100 miles south of the Oregon border.

Landscape: Mountains surround the city on three sides, forming a huge horseshoe. The Coastal Ranges are located 30 miles west, the Sierra Nevada system 40 miles east, and the Cascade Range about 50 miles north-northeast. The western part of the valley floor is mostly rolling hills with scrub oak trees. The Sacramento River flows in a north-south direction through the eastern portion of the valley. At Redding, the river forms Shasta Lake behind the immense Shasta Dam built in 1945 as part of the Central Valley Project.

Cimate: Precipitation is confined mostly to rain during the winter and spring months. Snowfall is infrequent and light. June through September are hot months and temperatures often exceed 100°F. Temperatures almost always drop into comfortable ranges at night. The summer and fall are nearly cloudless. The frost-free growing season extends from April 1 to November 1.

Winter mildness: 80	**Seasonal affect:** 89
Summer mildness: 2	**Hazardousness:** 91
Score: 92.63	**Rank: 27**

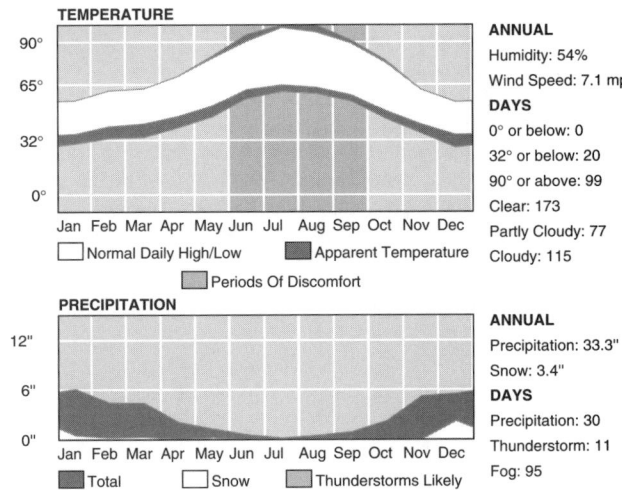

ANNUAL
Humidity: 54%
Wind Speed: 7.1 mph
DAYS
0° or below: 0
32° or below: 20
90° or above: 99
Clear: 173
Partly Cloudy: 77
Cloudy: 115

ANNUAL
Precipitation: 33.3"
Snow: 3.4"
DAYS
Precipitation: 30
Thunderstorm: 11
Fog: 95

Regina, SK

Location: 50.27 N, 104.37 W, at 1,893 feet, in southern Saskatchewan Province on the banks of Wascana Creek, which lies in a shallow basin running southeast to northwest.

Landscape: The surrounding area is a level plain. The land rises slowly to the northeast and peaks at an elevation of about 2,500 feet some 20 miles away. The Ou'Appelle River to the north meanders in an easterly direction in a deep narrow valley. Draining into the Ou'Appelle, Last Mountain Lake, 50 miles long and 2 to 3 miles wide, lies northwest. In the southwest direction is the Missouri Coteau, a broken escarpment with an average elevation of 2,400 feet. The Dirt Hills, part of the escarpment, rise over 2,700 feet to the southwest.

Cimate: Regina is Canada's sunniest provincial capital. Being far from influences of oceans or mountains, it has wide daily, and extremely large annual, ranges of temperature. High temperature, low humidity, strong winds, and clear skies cause moisture deficits in summer. Winter cold is not only severe but of extremely long duration.

Winter mildness: 1	**Seasonal affect:** 66
Summer mildness: 90	**Hazardousness:** 22
Score: 7.36	**Rank: 328**

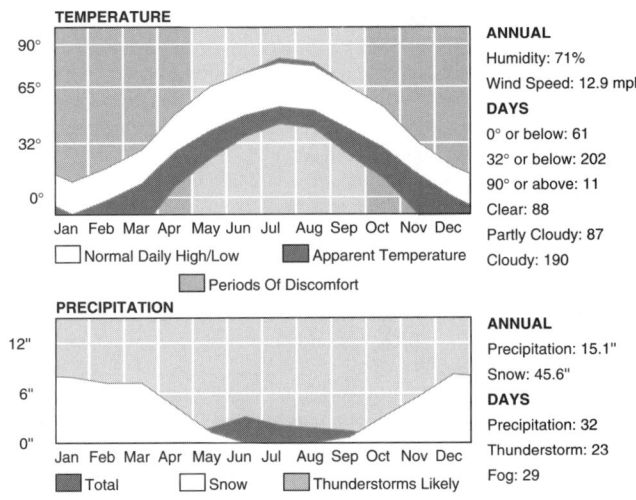

ANNUAL
Humidity: 71%
Wind Speed: 12.9 mph
DAYS
0° or below: 61
32° or below: 202
90° or above: 11
Clear: 88
Partly Cloudy: 87
Cloudy: 190

ANNUAL
Precipitation: 15.1"
Snow: 45.6"
DAYS
Precipitation: 32
Thunderstorm: 23
Fog: 29

Reno, NV

Location: 39.30 N, 119.47 W, at 4,400 feet, in western Nevada near the northern shore of Lake Tahoe, in the lee of the Sierra Nevadas.

Landscape: At the west edge of Truckee Meadows. The Sierra Nevadas rise to elevations of 9,000 to 10,000 feet. Hills to the east reach 6,000 to 7,000 feet. The Truckee River drains into Pyramid Lake to the northeast. The rivers here flow into landlocked lakes or simply evaporate in the desert.

Cimate: High Desert with sunshine abundant throughout the year. Temperatures are mild, but the daily range may exceed 45°F. Even when afternoons reach the upper 90s, a light jacket is needed shortly after sunset. Nights with a minimum temperature over 60°F are rare. Afternoon temperatures are moderate, and only about ten days a year fail to reach a level above freezing. The first noted freeze is September 22, the last around Memorial Day. Humidity is low during the summer months and moderately low during winter.

Winter mildness: 47	**Seasonal affect:** 95
Summer mildness: 18	**Hazardousness:** 81
Score: 88.10	**Rank: 43**

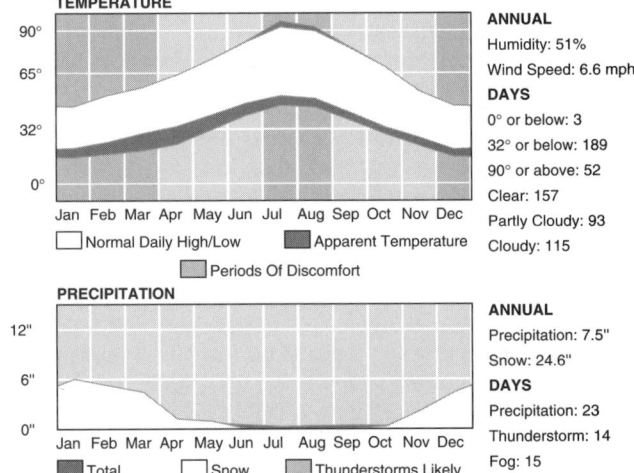

ANNUAL
Humidity: 51%
Wind Speed: 6.6 mph
DAYS
0° or below: 3
32° or below: 189
90° or above: 52
Clear: 157
Partly Cloudy: 93
Cloudy: 115

ANNUAL
Precipitation: 7.5"
Snow: 24.6"
DAYS
Precipitation: 23
Thunderstorm: 14
Fog: 15

Richmond-Petersburg, VA

Location: 37.30 N, 77.20 W, at 160 feet, in east-central Virginia at the head of navigation on the James River.

Landscape: This is a hilly region rising to the Blue Ridge Mountains about 90 miles to the west. Elevations range from a few feet above sea level along the rocky course of the James River to a little over 300 feet in parts of the western section of the city.

Cimate: Subtropical, or a water- and mountain-modified Continental, with warm, humid summers and generally mild winters. The mountains to the west act as a barrier to cold air in winter; the open waters of the Chesapeake Bay 60 miles to the east, and the Atlantic contribute to mild winters and to humid summers. Coldest weather occurs in late December and in January, with a normal temperature range from 20°F to 50°F. Precipitation is uniformly distributed throughout the year, though dry periods do occur in the autumn, when long periods of pleasant, mild weather are most common.

Winter mildness: 59　　**Seasonal affect:** 46
Summer mildness: 40　　**Hazardousness:** 60
Score: 63.45　　　　　**Rank: 130**

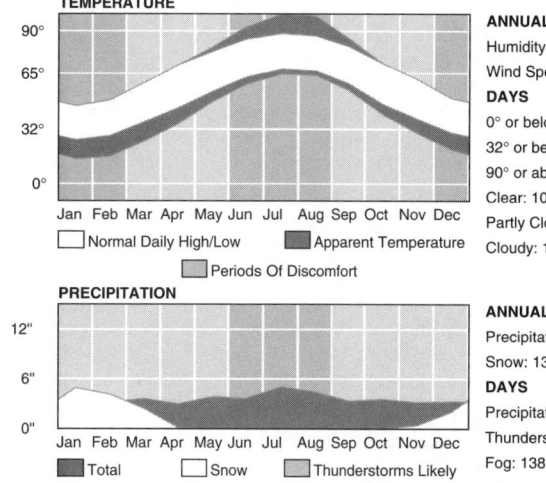

ANNUAL
Humidity: 68%
Wind Speed: 7.7 mph
DAYS
0° or below: 0
32° or below: 85
90° or above: 41
Clear: 101
Partly Cloudy: 106
Cloudy: 158

ANNUAL
Precipitation: 43.2"
Snow: 13.9"
DAYS
Precipitation: 74
Thunderstorm: 43
Fog: 138

★Riverside-San Bernardino, CA

Location: 33.57 N, 117.23 W, at 840 feet, the station at Riverside is in California's desert country, 60 miles east of Los Angeles.

Landscape: Riverside lies beside the Santa Ana River, at the edge of the dry basin Sonoran Desert, sometimes known as the upper Colorado Desert. Nearby a transition vegetation area of mountain, valley, and desert includes cactus and evergreen scrub pine. California fan palm trees also grow here. Joshua Tree National Monument is to the southeast.

Cimate: Arid high desert effects show in the warm, dry summers. Nights are always noticeably cooler. Most of the annual precipitation falls in the winter as rain. There are few cloudy days, and thunderstorms or other destructive weather events are rare. The area is the center of a large citrus fruit- and vegetable-growing region. The frost-free growing season is long, from mid-February to mid-December.

Winter mildness: 88　　**Seasonal affect:** 97
Summer mildness: 8　　**Hazardousness:** 98
Score: 97.73　　　　　**Rank: 9**

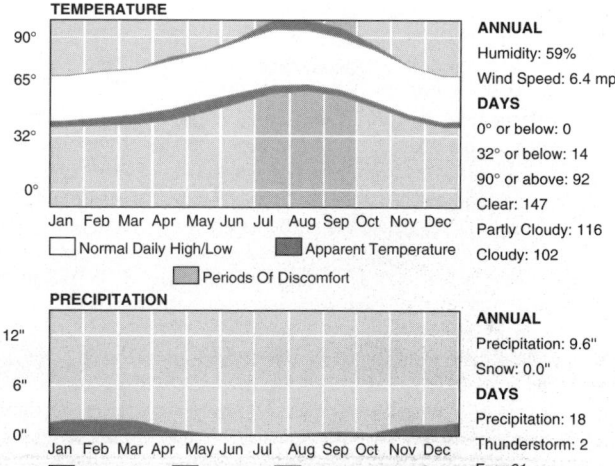

ANNUAL
Humidity: 59%
Wind Speed: 6.4 mph
DAYS
0° or below: 0
32° or below: 14
90° or above: 92
Clear: 147
Partly Cloudy: 116
Cloudy: 102

ANNUAL
Precipitation: 9.6"
Snow: 0.0"
DAYS
Precipitation: 18
Thunderstorm: 2
Fog: 61

Roanoke, VA

Location: 37.19 N, 79.58 W, at 1,150 feet, in the southern part of the Great Valley, near the headwaters of the Roanoke River; 223 miles southeast of Washington, DC.

Landscape: In a natural bowl with the Blue Ridge Mountains to the west, and the Allegheny Mountains to the north. Within the city, Mill Mountain rises detached from surrounding ranges. Numerous creeks and small streams from nearby mountains intersect the landscape and empty into the winding Roanoke River. Great Valley soils are dark and fertile while mountain soils are thin. Wooded areas are a typical southeastern forest mixing broadleaf deciduous and needleleaf evergreens.

Cimate: Mild Continental, as the mountain barrier moderates cold air from the north before it reaches the area. The elevation of the city produces cool summer nights. Rainfall is well distributed throughout the year, with an average of 23 inches in the warm season. Snow falls each winter, with extremes ranging from a trace to 60 inches. The first freeze is October 13; the last is April 26.

Winter mildness: 57　　**Seasonal affect:** 68
Summer mildness: 49　　**Hazardousness:** 59
Score: 73.37　　　　　**Rank: 95**

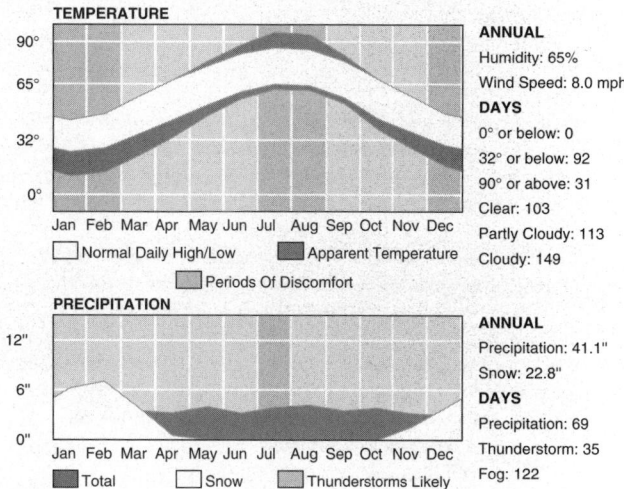

ANNUAL
Humidity: 65%
Wind Speed: 8.0 mph
DAYS
0° or below: 0
32° or below: 92
90° or above: 31
Clear: 103
Partly Cloudy: 113
Cloudy: 149

ANNUAL
Precipitation: 41.1"
Snow: 22.8"
DAYS
Precipitation: 69
Thunderstorm: 35
Fog: 122

Rochester, MN

Location: 43.55 N, 92.30 W, at 1,300 feet, in the Zumbro River valley in southeastern Minnesota.

Landscape: Farmland surrounds this city on the upland plateau. The south branch of the Zumbro River flows through the city. The country is flat glaciated terrain with little relief except for gentle rolling contours, suitable for grazing.

Cimate: Continental weather pattern with four definite seasons. Winters are cold, but summers are pleasant, with temperatures reaching as high as 90°F on only seven days in a typical season. On the average, heavy fog occurs 35 times a year, and thunderstorms occur about once every three days during the growing season. These storms are often heavy downpours with high winds bringing occasional flash flooding. Hail falls about four times each year. Tornadoes are rare but do occur. The first freeze normally occurs at the beginning of October; the last at the beginning of May.

Winter mildness: 5	**Seasonal affect:** 43
Summer mildness: 78	**Hazardousness:** 2
Score: 1.13	**Rank: 350**

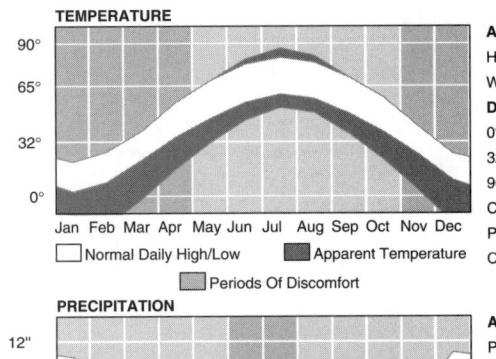

ANNUAL
Humidity: 74%
Wind Speed: 13.1 mph
DAYS
0° or below: 35
32° or below: 165
90° or above: 10
Clear: 86
Partly Cloudy: 97
Cloudy: 182

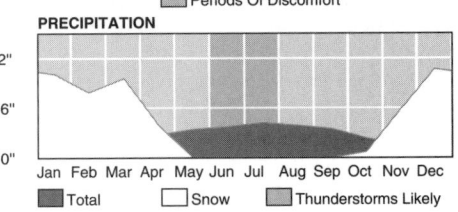

ANNUAL
Precipitation: 29.7"
Snow: 48.8"
DAYS
Precipitation: 61
Thunderstorm: 41
Fog: 120

Rochester, NY

Location: 43.08 N, 77.40 W, at 600 feet, in western New York State at the mouth of the Genesee River, the midpoint of the south shore of Lake Ontario.

Landscape: Sloping terrain with lime-rich soils. The land rises from a lakeshore elevation of 246 feet to over 1,000 feet 20 miles south. Moisture in the air from the lake enhances conditions for growing fruit and vegetables. Rochester is a major industrial city, a cultural and educational center, and a port of entry on the St. Lawrence Seaway.

Cimate: Lake Ontario plays a major moderating role in the weather. Summer temperatures rarely rise above 90°F. Winter temperatures seldom fall below -15°F. The area is prone to heavy snowstorms and blizzards. These storms are even heavier near the lake. Snow cover is continuous from December to May. The average growing season is 150 to 180 days, from mid-May to mid-October.

Winter mildness: 32	**Seasonal affect:** 19
Summer mildness: 84	**Hazardousness:** 8
Score: 34.27	**Rank: 233**

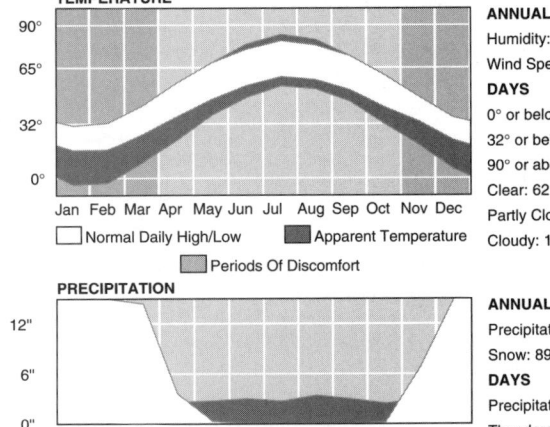

ANNUAL
Humidity: 72%
Wind Speed: 9.7 mph
DAYS
0° or below: 10
32° or below: 135
90° or above: 11
Clear: 62
Partly Cloudy: 105
Cloudy: 198

ANNUAL
Precipitation: 32.0"
Snow: 89.9"
DAYS
Precipitation: 72
Thunderstorm: 27
Fog: 123

★Sacramento, CA

Location: 38.31 N, 121.30 W, at 20 feet, California's capital is on the American and Sacramento rivers over 90 miles northeast of San Francisco.

Landscape: Connected by a deepwater ship channel, this inland port is the geographical center of one of the great interior low-lying, broad valleys between California's Coastal Ranges and the Sierra Nevada. The land is tabletop-flat and, when irrigated, perfect for growing fruits and vegetables.

Cimate: Mediterranean. Mountain ranges shelter the area from many storms and violent weather, adding to the mildness of the climate. Occasionally, northerly winds reach the valley over the Siskiyou Mountains, bringing tumultuous weather. These winds may bring heavy rains in winter or increased heat in summer. Summers are sunny and hot, but low humidity lessens the felt heat. Winters are short and mild; snow is rare, though the Sierra Nevada snow fields, 70 miles east, usually provide an adequate water supply. The first frost is at the end of November; the latest is around March 1.

Winter mildness: 84	**Seasonal affect:** 92
Summer mildness: 11	**Hazardousness:** 96
Score: 94.05	**Rank: 22**

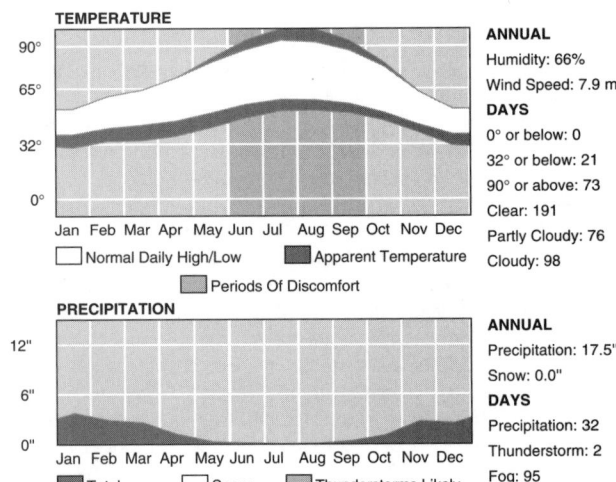

ANNUAL
Humidity: 66%
Wind Speed: 7.9 mph
DAYS
0° or below: 0
32° or below: 21
90° or above: 73
Clear: 191
Partly Cloudy: 76
Cloudy: 98

ANNUAL
Precipitation: 17.5"
Snow: 0.0"
DAYS
Precipitation: 32
Thunderstorm: 2
Fog: 95

St. John's, NF

Location: 47.37 N, 52.45 W, at 459 feet, at the eastern end of Newfoundland's rocky Avalon Peninsula.

Landscape: Rugged, with small lakes and rivers dominating the surrounding area. The Atlantic Ocean lies to the east, Conception Bay to the west, and Windsor Lake to the southwest. The land slopes east to the ocean and, to the west, the terrain plunges in sheer cliffs at Conception Bay.

Cimate: Marine climate brings changeable weather: ample precipitation in a variety of forms, high humidity, low visibility, more clouds, less sunshine, and strong winds. The open sea keeps winter air temperatures a little higher and summer temperatures slightly lower on the coast than at places inland. Spring comes rather late and is short; summer is also short and keeps its cool character. Hardly a winter goes by without three or four east coast gales. The seasons are called character building and invigorating by proud natives. Freezing rainstorms, called silver thaws, are a major winter hazard

Winter mildness: 42	**Seasonal affect:** 1
Summer mildness: 99	**Hazardousness:** 5
Score: 46.17	**Rank: 191**

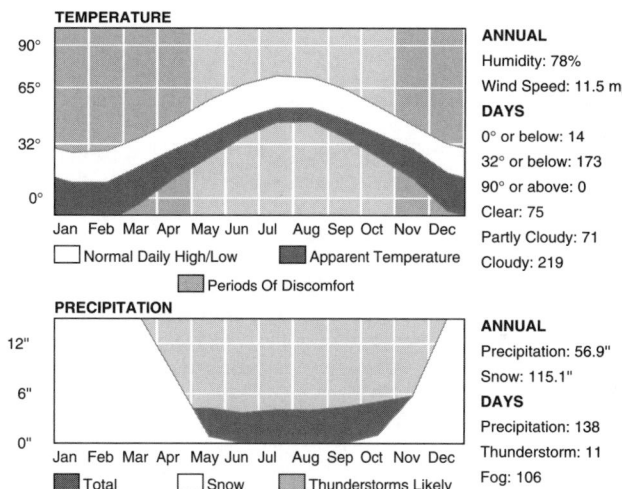

ANNUAL
Humidity: 83%
Wind Speed: 15.1 mph
DAYS
0° or below: 0
32° or below: 176
90° or above: 0
Clear: 56
Partly Cloudy: 54
Cloudy: 255

ANNUAL
Precipitation: 59.6"
Snow: 141.4"
DAYS
Precipitation: 144
Thunderstorm: 3
Fog: 124

Saint John, NB

Location: 45.19 N, 65.53 W, at 358 feet, on New Brunswick's southern coast; 90 miles east of Fredricton. The airport station is about 10 miles northeast of downtown.

Landscape: Rolling and wooded hills slope down to tidal marshes at the Bay of Fundy. The Saint John River is greatly affected by the high tides of the Bay at this deepwater port. The Reversing Falls at the mouth of the Saint John River—caused by these high tides—occur twice daily.

Cimate: Marine, with a definite Continental flavor. During the winter, cold air flows from the center of North America. Most storms originate either over the North Pacific or the Gulf of Mexico. In summer, the predominant air mass is warmed by passage over the North American landmass. Off-shore winds modify the air masses, producing mild periods during the winter and cool weather the rest of the year. Winter storms frequently bring rain to the Fundy coast. The port remains ice-free throughout the year.

Winter mildness: 10	**Seasonal affect:** 3
Summer mildness: 98	**Hazardousness:** 6
Score: 30.59	**Rank: 246**

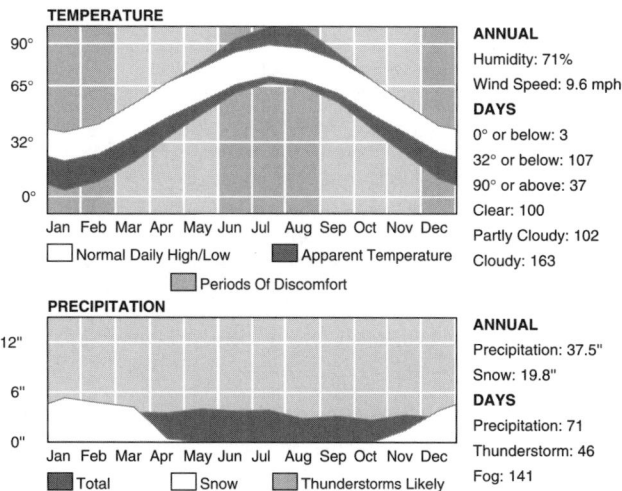

ANNUAL
Humidity: 78%
Wind Speed: 11.5 mph
DAYS
0° or below: 14
32° or below: 173
90° or above: 0
Clear: 75
Partly Cloudy: 71
Cloudy: 219

ANNUAL
Precipitation: 56.9"
Snow: 115.1"
DAYS
Precipitation: 138
Thunderstorm: 11
Fog: 106

St. Louis, MO-IL

Location: 38.45 N, 90.22 W, at 570 feet, at Missouri's central eastern edge, slightly east of the geographic center of the United States.

Landscape: On the west bank of the Mississippi River where it meets with the Missouri. The surrounding terrain is gently rolling hills and undulating plains, with occasional high limestone bluffs.

Cimate: Modified Continental. St. Louis is in the enviable position of having a changeable, four-season climate without prolonged periods of extreme cold, heat, or humidity. To the south is the warm, moist air of the Gulf of Mexico and to the north the cold polar air masses. Alternating invasions by these influences, and the conflict along the frontal zones where they meet, produce a great variety of weather conditions, but none lasting long enough to become monotonous. Winters are brisk but seldom severe. Snowfall averages less than 20 inches per season. Summers are quite warm, often uncomfortably so when coupled with high humidity. The first freeze is mid-October; the latest, mid-April.

Winter mildness: 47	**Seasonal affect:** 47
Summer mildness: 36	**Hazardousness:** 41
Score: 28.61	**Rank: 253**

TEMPERATURE
90°
65°
32°
0°
Jan Feb Mar Apr May Jun Jul Aug Sep Oct Nov Dec
Normal Daily High/Low   Apparent Temperature
Periods Of Discomfort

PRECIPITATION
12"
6"
0"
Jan Feb Mar Apr May Jun Jul Aug Sep Oct Nov Dec
Total   Snow   Thunderstorms Likely

ANNUAL
Humidity: 71%
Wind Speed: 9.6 mph
DAYS
0° or below: 3
32° or below: 107
90° or above: 37
Clear: 100
Partly Cloudy: 102
Cloudy: 163

ANNUAL
Precipitation: 37.5"
Snow: 19.8"
DAYS
Precipitation: 71
Thunderstorm: 46
Fog: 141

★Salinas, CA

Location: 36.36 N, 121.54 W, at 380 feet, on the Salinas River; about 85 miles south of San Francisco.

Landscape: Monterey Bay to the west is a great sweeping indentation on the Pacific coast. Sandy and rocky beaches verge on tidepools along the shore. High, grassy bluffs of the Diablo and Santa Lucia mountains of the Coastal Range provide added relief. Inland, the natural vegetation is a mixed evergreen forest dominated by cypress and pine groves.

Cimate: Marine, with year-round mild temperatures moving through gradual transitions. The ocean is the biggest climate factor. Under the influence of the Pacific High, cooling produces nightly low-stratus clouds, known as California stratus, and early morning fog. Both dissipate before noon leaving most afternoons clear and sunny. Most precipitation falls from December through March. Winter fog is also common. Summers are dry and thunderstorms rare. The Salinas Valley is a major supplier of lettuce, poultry, and almonds. There are no noted freezing days.

Winter mildness: 93	**Seasonal affect:** 91
Summer mildness: 99	**Hazardousness:** 92
Score: 98.01	**Rank: 8**

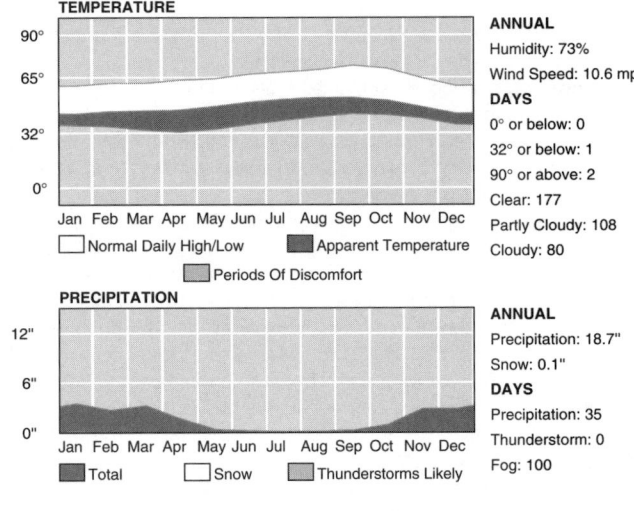

Salt Lake City-Ogden, UT

Location: 40.47 N, 111.57 W, at 4,220 feet, in north central Utah on the Jordan River, about 100 miles from borders with Idaho and Nevada to the north and west, and 70 miles southwest of Wyoming.

Landscape: A vast, high desert valley surrounded by imposing peaks. To the east, the rugged Wasatch Mountains rise from heights of 8,000 feet to 12,000 feet; to the southwest, the Oguirrh Mountains climb to 10,000 feet. Nearby, the Great Salt Lake stretches 48 miles west and 90 miles north.

Cimate: Though by no means mild, it is modified by the surrounding mountains that deflect stormy weather elsewhere. There are four well-defined seasons, including a long winter. Summers are hot, but the dry air lessens felt heat, and nights are cool. Winters are cold but not severe. Most of the precipitation is snow, with accumulations staying on the ground for most of the winter. Fall is short; spring is longer and sometimes stormy. Frosts arrive by mid-October and depart by the beginning of May.

Winter mildness: 44	**Seasonal affect:** 82
Summer mildness: 17	**Hazardousness:** 11
Score: 62.03	**Rank: 135**

San Angelo, TX

Location: 31.22 N, 100.30 W, at 1,900 feet, near the center of Texas on the edge of the Edwards Plateau.

Landscape: Prairie brushland. Slightly rolling plains and plateaus; broken hills and grassy slopes are excellent for grazing livestock. Semiarid, or Steppe, but with sufficient water from the Concho River and deep wells for extensive irrigation.

Cimate: Desert characteristics prevail between the humid climate of eastern Texas and the dry High Plains of west Texas. Summers are long and hot. Rapid temperature drops occur after sunset, desert-like, and are certainly welcome. Rainfall is typical of the Great Plains, most often occurring from thunderstorm activity. Heaviest rains are in spring and fall. Tropical disturbances moving inland from the Gulf bring the late summer rains. The prevailing south to southwest winds are brisk and modify summer heat. Occasional uncomfortable hot spells with humid air permeate the area. Winters are short and mild. Rapid temperature drops may occur when cold polar air invades the region.

Winter mildness: 68	**Seasonal affect:** 94
Summer mildness: 3	**Hazardousness:** 67
Score: 52.69	**Rank: 168**

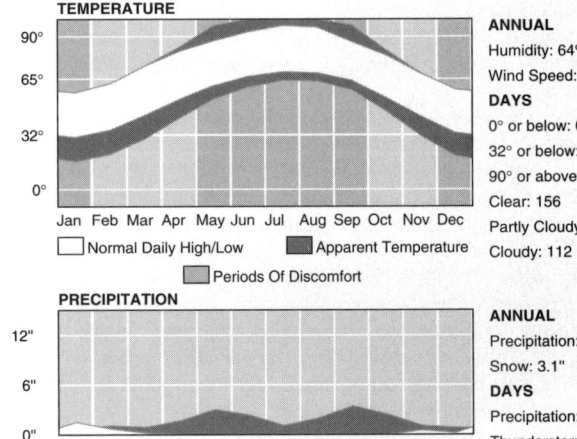

ANNUAL
Humidity: 73%
Wind Speed: 10.6 mph
DAYS
0° or below: 0
32° or below: 1
90° or above: 2
Clear: 177
Partly Cloudy: 108
Cloudy: 80

ANNUAL
Precipitation: 18.7"
Snow: 0.1"
DAYS
Precipitation: 35
Thunderstorm: 0
Fog: 100

ANNUAL
Humidity: 56%
Wind Speed: 8.8 mph
DAYS
0° or below: 3
32° or below: 134
90° or above: 58
Clear: 127
Partly Cloudy: 101
Cloudy: 137

ANNUAL
Precipitation: 16.2"
Snow: 57.9"
DAYS
Precipitation: 41
Thunderstorm: 38
Fog: 42

ANNUAL
Humidity: 64%
Wind Speed: 10.4 mph
DAYS
0° or below: 0
32° or below: 52
90° or above: 109
Clear: 156
Partly Cloudy: 97
Cloudy: 112

ANNUAL
Precipitation: 20.5"
Snow: 3.1"
DAYS
Precipitation: 33
Thunderstorm: 38
Fog: 43

San Antonio, TX

Location: 29.32 N, 98.28 W, at 790 feet, in the south central Texas Blacklands, 150 miles north of Mexico.

Landscape: This is typical prairie land. Rolling hill country yields to gently sloping open acres between the Edwards Plateau and the Gulf Coastal Plain. The headwaters of the San Antonio River, which winds through the downtown area, is here. Soils are blackland clay and silty loam. Vegetation consists of grasses and live oak trees, along with mesquite and cacti.

Cimate: Subtropical, with only two seasons. There is mild weather during normal winter months and a long, hot summer. Though 140 miles from the Gulf of Mexico, the city frequently feels the influence of its hot, moist air. Thunderstorms and rains have occurred in every month of the year. They are common during the summer, with most rain falling in May and September. The winds during the winter are from the north, and from the south in the summer. Frosts begin in late November and generally end by the beginning of March.

Winter mildness: 84   **Seasonal affect:** 80
Summer mildness: 7   **Hazardousness:** 85
Score: 65.15   **Rank: 124**

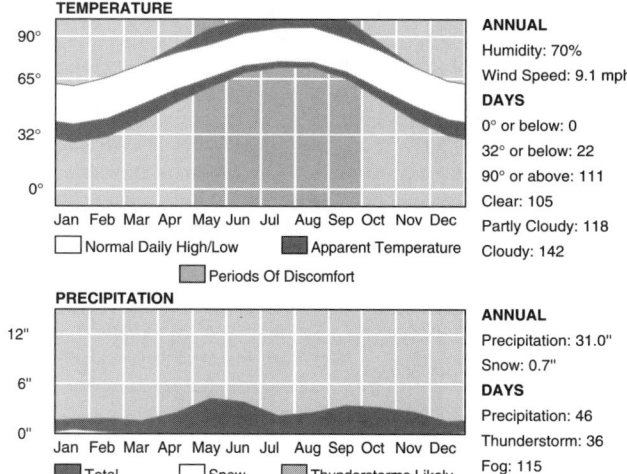

TEMPERATURE

☐ Normal Daily High/Low   ■ Apparent Temperature   ▨ Periods Of Discomfort

PRECIPITATION

■ Total   ☐ Snow   ▨ Thunderstorms Likely

ANNUAL
Humidity: 70%
Wind Speed: 9.1 mph
DAYS
0° or below: 0
32° or below: 22
90° or above: 111
Clear: 105
Partly Cloudy: 118
Cloudy: 142

ANNUAL
Precipitation: 31.0"
Snow: 0.7"
DAYS
Precipitation: 46
Thunderstorm: 36
Fog: 115

★San Diego, CA

Location: 32.44 N, 117.10 W, at 10 feet, just above the Mexican border on San Diego Bay, a deepwater harbor on the Pacific Ocean.

Landscape: Backed by coastal foothills and mountains to the east. Topographical relief is further provided by cliffs that rise from the bay. Stream valleys are narrow where they drain the hills. Evergreens with thick, hard leaves like eucalyptus are prevalent. California live oak, tan oak, and California laurel are also common.

Cimate: Typically Marine, sometimes called Mediterranean. There are no freezing days and an average of only three 90-degree days each year. Dry easterly winds sometimes blow in the vicinity for several days at a time, bringing temperatures in the 90s and even in the 100s. Summers tend to be dry and mild; springs are cooler, and there is rain from November through March. Storms are practically unknown. Sunshine is abundant though there is considerable fog along the coast, and many low clouds in early morning and evening during the summer.

Winter mildness: 96   **Seasonal affect:** 96
Summer mildness: 94   **Hazardousness:** 98
Score: 99.71   **Rank: 2**

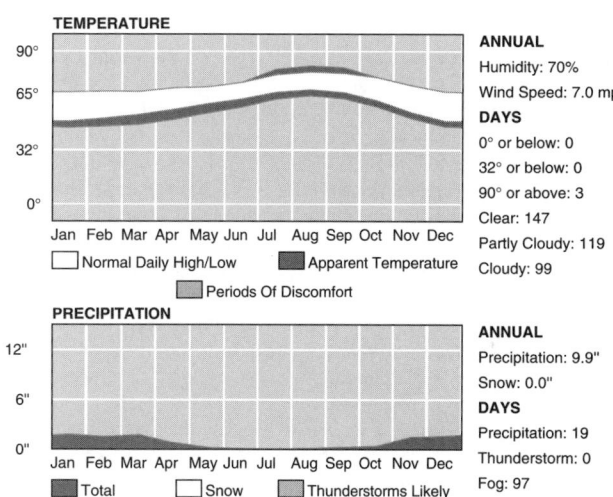

TEMPERATURE

☐ Normal Daily High/Low   ■ Apparent Temperature   ▨ Periods Of Discomfort

PRECIPITATION

■ Total   ☐ Snow   ▨ Thunderstorms Likely

ANNUAL
Humidity: 70%
Wind Speed: 7.0 mph
DAYS
0° or below: 0
32° or below: 0
90° or above: 3
Clear: 147
Partly Cloudy: 119
Cloudy: 99

ANNUAL
Precipitation: 9.9"
Snow: 0.0"
DAYS
Precipitation: 19
Thunderstorm: 0
Fog: 97

★San Francisco, CA

Location: 37.46 N, 122.26 W, at 80 feet, on a narrow peninsula of 43 hills on California's northern coast; 90 miles southwest of Sacramento.

Landscape: The peninsula's 49 square miles separate the natural harbor of San Francisco Bay from the Pacific Ocean. A range of hills with elevations of nearly 1,000 feet runs from north to south. The complex topography causes great climatic variability in patterns of fog, sun, and temperature. Now highly urbanized, the natural forest includes fir, spruce, and hemlock found in Golden Gate Park or the Presidio. Flowers bloom throughout the year, and warm clothing is needed every month.

Cimate: Two-season Mediterranean climate with a cool, pleasant summer and a mild spring. San Francisco's unique location causes it to be known as the air-conditioned city because of the seabreezes. Sea fogs and associated low stratus clouds are a striking characteristic of the city's climate. On the average, though, the sun shines during 66 percent of the daylight hours. Every month except January is frost-free.

Winter mildness: 95   **Seasonal affect:** 86
Summer mildness: 100   **Hazardousness:** 93
Score: 97.45   **Rank: 10**

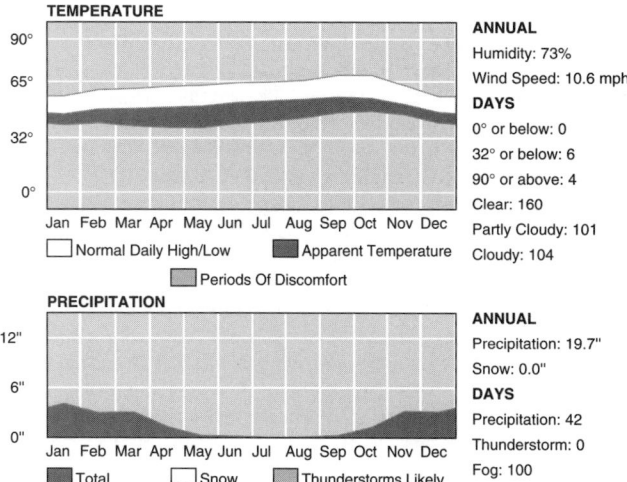

TEMPERATURE

☐ Normal Daily High/Low   ■ Apparent Temperature   ▨ Periods Of Discomfort

PRECIPITATION

■ Total   ☐ Snow   ▨ Thunderstorms Likely

ANNUAL
Humidity: 73%
Wind Speed: 10.6 mph
DAYS
0° or below: 0
32° or below: 6
90° or above: 4
Clear: 160
Partly Cloudy: 101
Cloudy: 104

ANNUAL
Precipitation: 19.7"
Snow: 0.0"
DAYS
Precipitation: 42
Thunderstorm: 0
Fog: 100

★San Luis Obispo-Atascadero-Paso Robles, CA

Location: 35.18 N, 120.40 W, at 310 feet, inland from the Pacific Ocean in the foothills of the Santa Lucia Mountains; about 90 miles northwest of Santa Barbara.

Landscape: Wooded San Luis Obispo Creek has stretches of fast falling water. The Santa Lucia Mountains rise to clifftop, ocean views. Cypress and pine groves predominate in the mixed ever-green forest. Almond trees are a fruitful cultivation. Orchards of walnuts, apples, and vineyards also grow well.

Cimate: Mediterranean with generally two seasons. The ocean is the biggest climate factor. The Coastal Ranges and higher alti-tude also serve to keep the weather mild most of the year. Only January runs the risk of freezing weather. Cool temperatures and sea breezes are common. Daily and seasonal temperature shifts are slight. Thunderstorms are rare, but fog and cloudy mornings are typical.

Winter mildness: 90	**Seasonal affect:** 94
Summer mildness: 92	**Hazardousness:** 99
Score: 98.86	**Rank: 5**

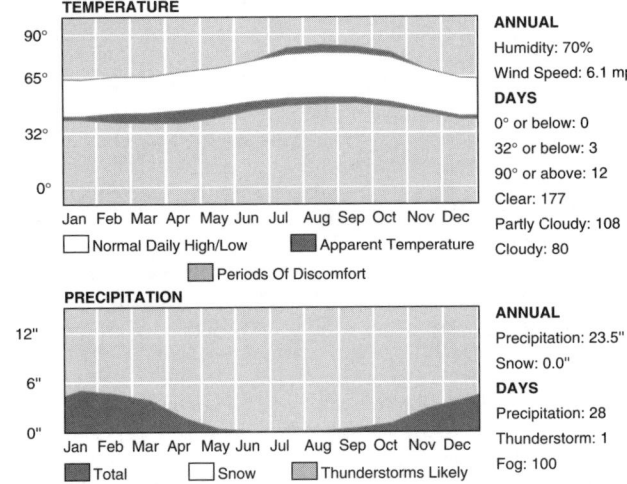

ANNUAL
Humidity: 70%
Wind Speed: 6.1 mph
DAYS
0° or below: 0
32° or below: 3
90° or above: 12
Clear: 177
Partly Cloudy: 108
Cloudy: 80

ANNUAL
Precipitation: 23.5"
Snow: 0.0"
DAYS
Precipitation: 28
Thunderstorm: 1
Fog: 100

★Santa Barbara-Santa Maria-Lompoc, CA

Location: 34.26 N, 119.50 W, at 10 feet, on the Pacific Ocean in the Santa Maria Valley; 90 miles northwest of Los Angeles.

Landscape: Bounded by the foothills of the San Rafael Moun-tains, the Solomon Hills, and the Casmalia Hills, the valley is flat and fertile. These three cities lie along the Pacific coast at the base of the Santa Ynez mountains. The Los Padres National Forest en-compasses many of the ranges in the area. Vegetation ranges from chaparral to oak woodlands, and pine groves thrive in the mixed evergreen forest. Cypress and palm trees complete the va-riety.

Cimate: Mediterranean that includes a rainy season, typical of the California coast, in winter. During the rest of the year, particu-larly from June to October, there is little or no precipitation. Clear, sunshiny afternoons prevail on most days. At night and in the morning, however, the California stratus—low stratus clouds—and fog appear. The freeze-free growing season is from the be-ginning of May to the beginning of December.

Winter mildness: 87	**Seasonal affect:** 96
Summer mildness: 97	**Hazardousness:** 99
Score: 100	**Rank: 1**

TEMPERATURE

Normal Daily High/Low — Apparent Temperature — Periods Of Discomfort

PRECIPITATION

Total — Snow — Thunderstorms Likely

ANNUAL
Humidity: 70%
Wind Speed: 6.1 mph
DAYS
0° or below: 0
32° or below: 6
90° or above: 3
Clear: 177
Partly Cloudy: 108
Cloudy: 80

ANNUAL
Precipitation: 16.3"
Snow: 0.0"
DAYS
Precipitation: 21
Thunderstorm: 0
Fog: 100

Santa Fe, NM

Location: 35.52 N, 106.19 W, at 7,360 feet, in north central New Mexico; 60 miles from Albuquerque.

Landscape: Sits in the northern Rio Grande Valley on the Santa Fe River in the rolling foothills of the Sangre de Cristo Mountains, which rise to 10,000 feet. Westward the terrain slopes down-ward to the Rio Grande River, some 20 miles away. The high moun-tains to the east protect the city from much of the winter's cold. Treeless alpine tundra covers upper slopes. Spruce, subalpine fir, and aspen cover intermediate slopes, and ponderosa pine is on lower, drier, more exposed slopes.

Cimate: Semiarid Steppe with cool and pleasant summers. Dry and invigorating. Days are in the 80s, but nights in the 50s. Long cloudy periods are unknown. Winters are crisp, clear, and sunny, with considerable daytime warming. Snowfall averages 35 inches a year in the city while a half-hour's drive east brings 250 inches for alpine skiing. First ground freeze is October 8; the last is mid-May.

Winter mildness: 37	**Seasonal affect:** 98
Summer mildness: 84	**Hazardousness:** 38
Score: 84.98	**Rank: 54**

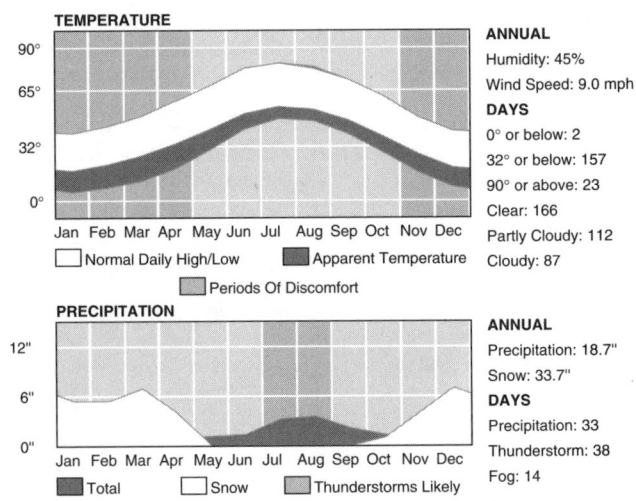

ANNUAL
Humidity: 45%
Wind Speed: 9.0 mph
DAYS
0° or below: 2
32° or below: 157
90° or above: 23
Clear: 166
Partly Cloudy: 112
Cloudy: 87

ANNUAL
Precipitation: 18.7"
Snow: 33.7"
DAYS
Precipitation: 33
Thunderstorm: 38
Fog: 14

★Santa Rosa, CA

Location: 38.27 N, 122.42 W, at 170 feet, in the Russian River Valley; 50 miles north of San Francisco.

Landscape: This valley runs parallel to the Pacific Coast, with only low hills, 300 feet to 500 feet, between it and the ocean that is 25 miles southwest. Higher hills rise 10 miles to the east leading into the foothills of the Coast Ranges. Principal trees of the conifer forest are Douglas fir, western red cedar, western hemlock, and Sitka spruce.

Cimate: The nearness of the ocean and the surrounding topography join with the prevailing westerly circulation to produce a predominantly southerly air flow year-round. However, the area is sufficiently far inland to assure it a varied climate. There is chance of freezing weather from the middle of November until the end of March. Summers are warm, winters cool, and there is a daily temperature shift. There is less fog and drizzle than at other points along the coast.

Winter mildness: 82	**Seasonal affect:** 86
Summer mildness: 65	**Hazardousness:** 92
Score: 95.18	**Rank: 18**

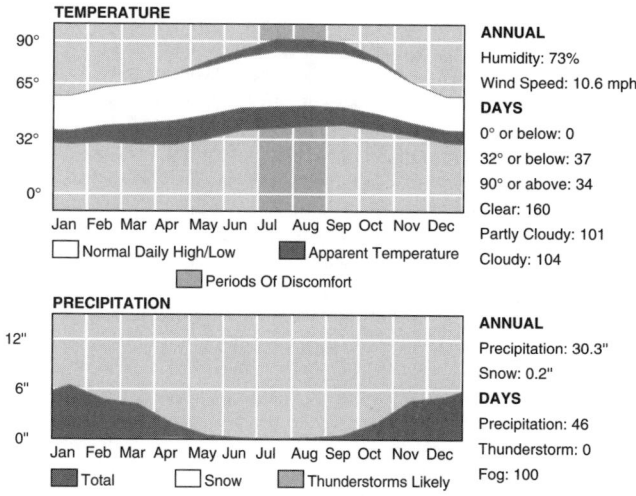

TEMPERATURE

Normal Daily High/Low — Apparent Temperature — Periods Of Discomfort

PRECIPITATION

Total — Snow — Thunderstorms Likely

ANNUAL
Humidity: 73%
Wind Speed: 10.6 mph
DAYS
0° or below: 0
32° or below: 37
90° or above: 34
Clear: 160
Partly Cloudy: 101
Cloudy: 104

ANNUAL
Precipitation: 30.3"
Snow: 0.2"
DAYS
Precipitation: 46
Thunderstorm: 0
Fog: 100

Sarasota-Bradenton, FL

Location: 27.27 N, 82.28 W, at 20 feet, on the south bank of the Manatee River near its mouth at Tampa Bay, midway on Florida's west coast; 50 miles south of Tampa.

Landscape: The area includes numerous islands, separating Sarasota Bay from the Gulf of Mexico, and miles of white-sand beaches. The southern Gulf Coastal Plains are flat and irregular. There is less than 300 feet variation in altitude over the gently rolling areas. Most of the numerous streams are sluggish; marshes, swamps, and lakes are numerous. Evergreen oaks, laurel, and magnolia are common. Trees are not tall and the leaf canopy is not dense. There is a well-developed underbrush of ferns, shrubs, and herbaceous plants.

Cimate: Subtropical. Humidity is relatively high year-round. Winters are not cold but are inclined to be rainy. Summers are hot with frequent thunderstorms. Cloudiness is also a factor. The Gulf of Mexico moderates temperature extremes of both summer and winter. August is to Sarasota what February is to New England: The time for vacation elsewhere.

Winter mildness: 97	**Seasonal affect:** 78
Summer mildness: 25	**Hazardousness:** 83
Score: 89.80	**Rank: 37**

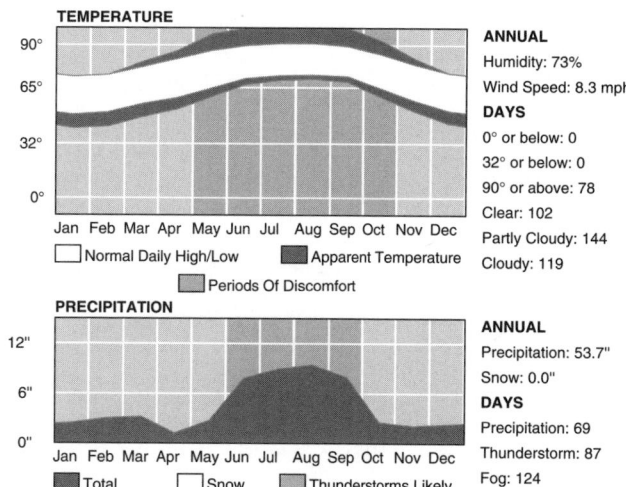

TEMPERATURE

Normal Daily High/Low — Apparent Temperature — Periods Of Discomfort

PRECIPITATION

Total — Snow — Thunderstorms Likely

ANNUAL
Humidity: 73%
Wind Speed: 8.3 mph
DAYS
0° or below: 0
32° or below: 0
90° or above: 78
Clear: 102
Partly Cloudy: 144
Cloudy: 119

ANNUAL
Precipitation: 53.7"
Snow: 0.0"
DAYS
Precipitation: 69
Thunderstorm: 87
Fog: 124

Saskatoon, SK

Location: 52.14 N, 106.37 W, at 1,644 feet, on the South Saskatchewan River in the central south region of the Province.

Landscape: Vast, without any landscape barriers to impede air mass movements, and a flat, undulating, hummocky plain, with deep, fertile soils. A mixed forest of white and black spruce, jack pine, tamarack, and birch covers the northern reaches of the Province. Prarie grasses and woodlands cover the southwest.

Cimate: The Prairies are the sunniest region in Canada, and Saskatoon is the country's sunniest major city. There are 324 days with some sunshine. July is the sunniest month; December is the dullest. In June frequent storms reduce the number of hours of sun, in spite of the 17-hour days. Though winters are long, 8 hours of sunshine are possible. The area is also dry with most precipitation concentrated during the growing season, from May to August. Blizzards are a notorious feature of Prairie winters. Snowfall during such storms may be negligible but strong winds and intense cold can be lethal.

Winter mildness: 0	**Seasonal affect:** 70
Summer mildness: 92	**Hazardousness:** 35
Score: 15.86	**Rank: 298**

TEMPERATURE

Normal Daily High/Low — Apparent Temperature — Periods Of Discomfort

PRECIPITATION

Total — Snow — Thunderstorms Likely

ANNUAL
Humidity: 69%
Wind Speed: 10.9 mph
DAYS
0° or below: 59
32° or below: 202
90° or above: 12
Clear: 94
Partly Cloudy: 92
Cloudy: 179

ANNUAL
Precipitation: 13.7"
Snow: 44.4"
DAYS
Precipitation: 24
Thunderstorm: 19
Fog: 25

Savannah, GA

Location: 32.08 N, 81.12 W, at 50 feet, on Georgia's north coast border at the mouth of the Savannah River, 18 miles from the Atlantic Ocean. The city is Georgia's major seaport, and the port dominates the economy.

Landscape: Surrounded by flat land, low and marshy to the north and east, rising to several feet above sea level to the west and south. About half the land to the west and south is clear of trees and the other half is woods, much of which lie in swamp. The outer coastal plain is a temperate rain forest that includes live oak, loblolly pine, laurel, and magnolia.

Cimate: Temperate Subtropical with summer temperatures moderated by thundershowers almost every afternoon. Sunshine is adequate in all seasons; seldom are there more than two or three days in succession without it. The long growing season—from the end of February to the beginning of December—is accompanied by abundant rain.

Winter mildness: 84	**Seasonal affect:** 61
Summer mildness: 24	**Hazardousness:** 74
Score: 81.01	**Rank: 68**

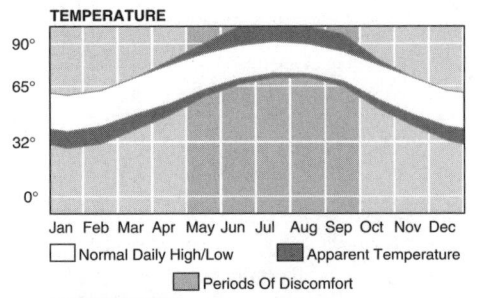

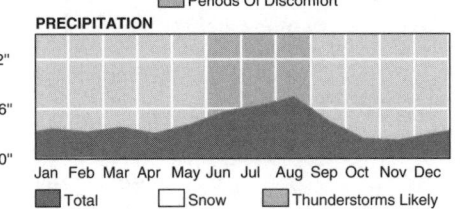

ANNUAL
Humidity: 70%
Wind Speed: 7.9 mph
DAYS
0° or below: 0
32° or below: 31
90° or above: 69
Clear: 103
Partly Cloudy: 111
Cloudy: 151

ANNUAL
Precipitation: 49.2"
Snow: 0.4"
DAYS
Precipitation: 68
Thunderstorm: 62
Fog: 172

Scranton–Wilkes-Barre–Hazleton, PA

Location: 41.20 N, 75.44 W, at 930 feet, the weather station is located at the airport, between the cities of Scranton and Wilkes-Barre in the Wyoming Valley; 100 miles northeast of Philadelphia. Hazleton, which calls itself the highest city in Pennsylvania, is located on top of Spring Mountain to the south.

Landscape: The Lackawanna River flows through Scranton, the largest city on its banks, and into the Susquehanna River. Wilkes-Barre is also on the Susquehanna, 18 miles southwest of Scranton. The surrounding Pocono Mountains protect the Wyoming Valley from high winds and adverse precipitation. The valley land is rich, fertile, and well drained. Mountains, which once yielded iron, and later coal, are covered with primitive forests. There are many lakes and streams in the area.

Cimate: Climate is cool in summer with frequent, brief showers. Winter temperatures in the valley are not severe. Though the annual snowfall is 47 inches, severe snowstorms are infrequent. Annual precipitation is 36 inches. Some tropical storm effect can be felt.

Winter mildness: 37	**Seasonal affect:** 21
Summer mildness: 78	**Hazardousness:** 20
Score: 39.94	**Rank: 213**

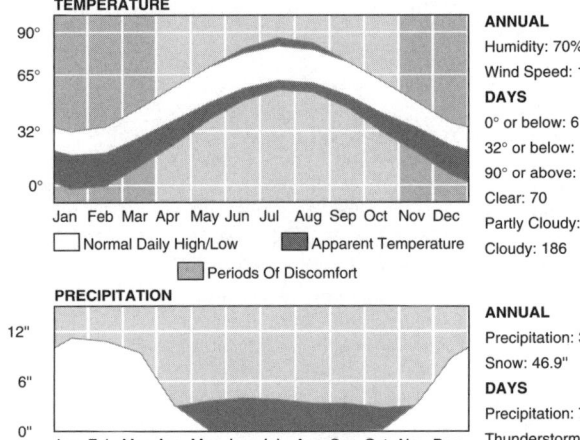

ANNUAL
Humidity: 70%
Wind Speed: 10.2 mph
DAYS
0° or below: 6
32° or below: 127
90° or above: 8
Clear: 70
Partly Cloudy: 109
Cloudy: 186

ANNUAL
Precipitation: 36.2"
Snow: 46.9"
DAYS
Precipitation: 72
Thunderstorm: 29
Fog: 143

Seattle-Bellevue-Everett, WA

Location: 47.39 N, 122.18 W, at 20 feet, on Puget Sound on Washington's northwest Pacific coast.

Landscape: Situated on a narrow, hilly isthmus between Puget Sound on the west and Lake Washington on the east. The spectacular peaks of the Cascade Range and the Olympic Mountains dominate the horizon and serve as barriers to easterly and northerly weather systems. The metro area landscape is highly urbanized, fronting the eastern shore of Puget Sound.

Cimate: Mid-latitude Coast climate, characterized by moderate temperatures, a pronounced though not sharply defined rainy season, and considerable cloudiness, particularly during the winter. Occasionally, severe winter storms come in from the north. Summers are pleasant, and winters are relatively mild, with prevailing temperatures in the 40s. Summer heat and winter cold are modified by the nearness of the ocean. There is measurable rainfall on an average of 150 days a year. The first freeze is November 15th, the last in later March.

Winter mildness: 81	**Seasonal affect:** 2
Summer mildness: 96	**Hazardousness:** 84
Score: 77.62	**Rank: 80**

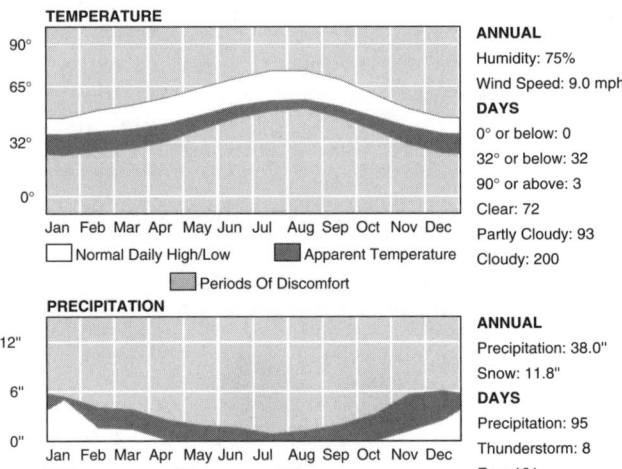

ANNUAL
Humidity: 75%
Wind Speed: 9.0 mph
DAYS
0° or below: 0
32° or below: 32
90° or above: 3
Clear: 72
Partly Cloudy: 93
Cloudy: 200

ANNUAL
Precipitation: 38.0"
Snow: 11.8"
DAYS
Precipitation: 95
Thunderstorm: 8
Fog: 161

Shreveport-Bossier City, LA

Location: 32.28 N, 93.49 W, at 250 feet, on the banks of the Red River, in northwest Louisiana, 30 miles south of Arkansas and 15 miles east of Texas.

Landscape: Part of the city is situated in the Red River bottomlands and the remainder in the gently rolling hills that begin a mile west of the river. Land area resources include petroleum, natural gas, cotton, and lumber.

Cimate: Transitional between the Subtropical climate prevalent to the south and the Continental climates of the Great Plains and Middle West to the north. Winter months are mild, with cold spells generally of short duration. The typical pattern is a drop in temperature the first day, minimum temperatures the second day, and gradual warming on the third. Summers are hot and humid, relieved only by the thunderstorms that come about eight times per month. April and May are pleasant. Fall, which lasts from late September to December, is delightful for outdoor activities. The freeze-free growing season is long, from mid-May to mid-November.

Winter mildness: 78	**Seasonal affect:** 74
Summer mildness: 12	**Hazardousness:** 65
Score: 54.39	**Rank: 162**

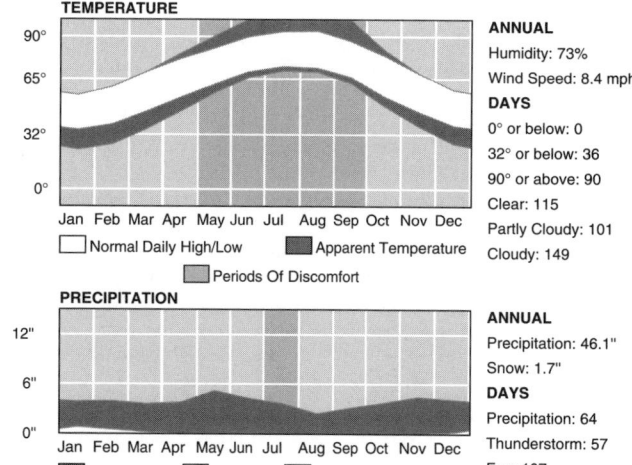

ANNUAL
Humidity: 73%
Wind Speed: 8.4 mph
DAYS
0° or below: 0
32° or below: 36
90° or above: 90
Clear: 115
Partly Cloudy: 101
Cloudy: 149

ANNUAL
Precipitation: 46.1"
Snow: 1.7"
DAYS
Precipitation: 64
Thunderstorm: 57
Fog: 107

Sioux City, IA-NE

Location: 42.24 N, 96.23 W, at 1,090 feet, along the Missouri River at a point where Iowa touches both Nebraska and South Dakota.

Landscape: The terrain is rolling, except for the river valleys and bottomlands. The Sioux City business district lies in the river valley, and the residential sections, for the most part, are spread over the hills, which range from 100 feet to 200 feet higher. Corn, small grains, and grazing grasses are products of abundant rainfall here.

Cimate: Typically Continental and largely determined by the movement and interaction of the large-scale weather systems. Under normal conditions, winters are cold and summers warm, with most rain failing between April and September. Except for an occasional dry year, rain is plentiful. As elsewhere in the Northern Plains, there is considerable fluctuation in temperature and precipitation from season to season and year to year. Average growing season is 160 days. The first freeze is in early October, the last in late April.

Winter mildness: 8	**Seasonal affect:** 73
Summer mildness: 48	**Hazardousness:** 19
Score: 11.33	**Rank: 314**

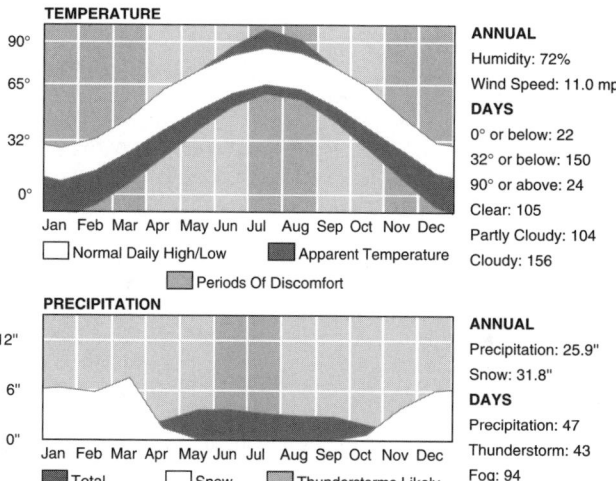

ANNUAL
Humidity: 72%
Wind Speed: 11.0 mph
DAYS
0° or below: 22
32° or below: 150
90° or above: 24
Clear: 105
Partly Cloudy: 104
Cloudy: 156

ANNUAL
Precipitation: 25.9"
Snow: 31.8"
DAYS
Precipitation: 47
Thunderstorm: 43
Fog: 94

Sioux Falls, SD

Location: 43.34 N, 96.44 W, at 1,420 feet, in the Big Sioux River valley in southeastern South Dakota.

Landscape: Surrounding terrain is gently rolling. Within a 100-mile radius of the city, the land slopes upward 300 to 400 feet in the north and northwest and downward in the southeast. There is little change in elevation in the other directions.

Cimate: Invigorating Continental. Cold air masses from the north often move in rapidly, causing strong, gusty winds for several hours. During late fall and winter, these cold fronts sometimes bring temperature drops of 20 to 30 degrees in a day. Severe cold spells rarely last more than a few days. During a cold winter, frost may penetrate the ground to a depth of 3 feet to 4 feet unless there is heavy snow cover protection. There are usually one or two heavy snowstorms each winter. Summer temperatures may climb over 100°F once or twice a year. Thunderstorms are frequent, especially during June and July.

Winter mildness: 6	**Seasonal affect:** 77
Summer mildness: 49	**Hazardousness:** 2
Score: 5.09	**Rank: 336**

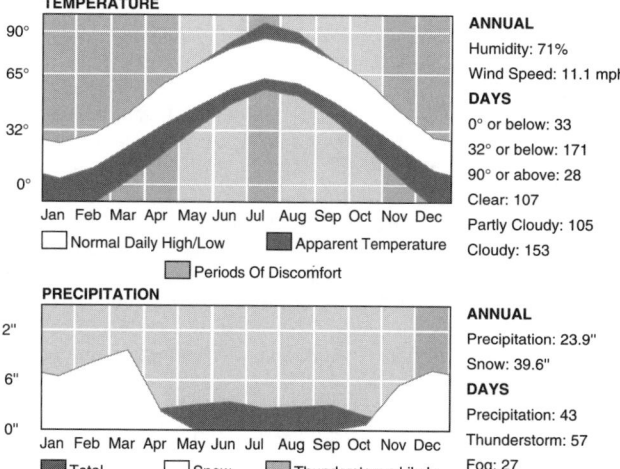

ANNUAL
Humidity: 71%
Wind Speed: 11.1 mph
DAYS
0° or below: 33
32° or below: 171
90° or above: 28
Clear: 107
Partly Cloudy: 105
Cloudy: 153

ANNUAL
Precipitation: 23.9"
Snow: 39.6"
DAYS
Precipitation: 43
Thunderstorm: 57
Fog: 27

South Bend, IN

Location: 41.42 N, 86.19 W, at 770 feet, on the Saint Joseph River in northern Indiana; about 80 miles east of Chicago.

Landscape: Mostly level to gently rolling terrain and some former marshland. Drainage for the area is through the Saint Joseph and Kankakee rivers. The nearest shore of Lake Michigan is 20 miles to the northwest.

Cimate: The lake has a moderating effect on the temperature. Temperatures of 100° or higher are rare, and cold waves are less severe than at many locations at the same latitude. This results in favorable conditions for orchard and vegetable growth. The average first freeze is October 5 and the average last freeze is May 6. Precipitation is evenly distributed throughout the year with the greatest amounts during the growing season. Winter is marked by considerable cloudiness and rather high humidity along with frequent periods of snow from November to March. Heavy snowfalls, resulting from a cold northwest wind passing over Lake Michigan are not uncommon.

Winter mildness: 30	**Seasonal affect:** 13
Summer mildness: 70	**Hazardousness:** 1
Score: 6.23	**Rank: 332**

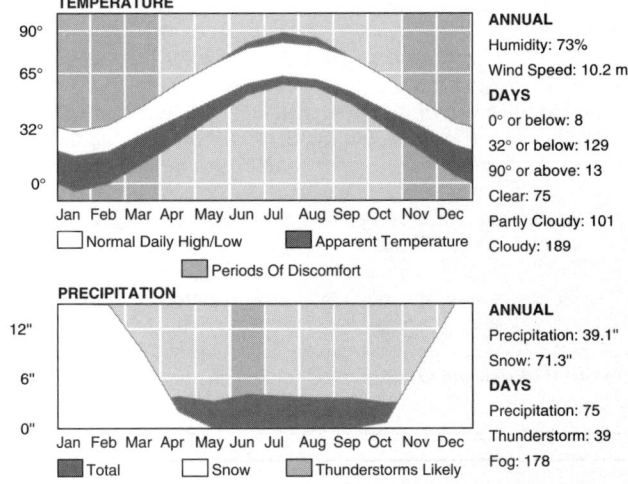

TEMPERATURE

Normal Daily High/Low — Apparent Temperature — Periods Of Discomfort

ANNUAL
Humidity: 73%
Wind Speed: 10.2 mph
DAYS
0° or below: 8
32° or below: 129
90° or above: 13
Clear: 75
Partly Cloudy: 101
Cloudy: 189

PRECIPITATION

Total — Snow — Thunderstorms Likely

ANNUAL
Precipitation: 39.1"
Snow: 71.3"
DAYS
Precipitation: 75
Thunderstorm: 39
Fog: 178

Spokane, WA

Location: 47.38 N, 117.32 W, at 2,360 feet, on the eastern edge of the broad Columbia Basin, bounded by the Cascade Range on the west and the Rocky Mountains to the east.

Landscape: The elevations in eastern Washington vary from less than 400 feet above sea level near Pasco to 5,000 feet in the extreme eastern edge of the state. Spokane is in the upper plateau area, where the long, gradual slope from the Columbia River meets the sharp rise of the Rocky Mountains.

Cimate: Combines some of the characteristics of the damp coastal climate with the arid interior climate. Air masses are brought from the west or southwest and lose most of their moisture passing over the mountains. Sometimes dry, Continental air masses from the east invade the area, bringing high temperatures with low humidity in the summer and subzero temperatures in the winter. Generally, Spokane has a mild climate during summer and a cold climate during winter. Freezes begin in early October and last until mid-May.

Winter mildness: 47	**Seasonal affect:** 43
Summer mildness: 69	**Hazardousness:** 39
Score: 67.70	**Rank: 115**

TEMPERATURE

Normal Daily High/Low — Apparent Temperature — Periods Of Discomfort

ANNUAL
Humidity: 65%
Wind Speed: 8.9 mph
DAYS
0° or below: 5
32° or below: 141
90° or above: 21
Clear: 87
Partly Cloudy: 88
Cloudy: 190

PRECIPITATION

Total — Snow — Thunderstorms Likely

ANNUAL
Precipitation: 16.5"
Snow: 50.4"
DAYS
Precipitation: 57
Thunderstorm: 11
Fog: 101

Springfield, IL

Location: 39.51 N, 89.41 W, at 590 feet, in the central part of the state on the Sangamon River.

Landscape: The surrounding country is nearly level. There are no large hills in the area, but rolling terrain is found near the Sangamon River and Spring Creek. The city is in the midst of a rich agricultural and coal region.

Cimate: Typically Continental in character, with warm to hot summers and cold winters. There are sharp seasonal changes, but no extended periods of severely cold weather. Monthly average temperatures range from the upper 20s in January to the upper 70s in July. The first freeze in fall arrives around October 18. The last in spring comes around April 22. Considerable variation takes place frequently within each season. Summer weather is sunny and often uncomfortably warm and humid. While winters are less severe than those farther to the north, prairie winds may accentuate the cold. The prevailing wind direction is southerly.

Winter mildness: 29	**Seasonal affect:** 55
Summer mildness: 46	**Hazardousness:** 24
Score: 11.89	**Rank: 312**

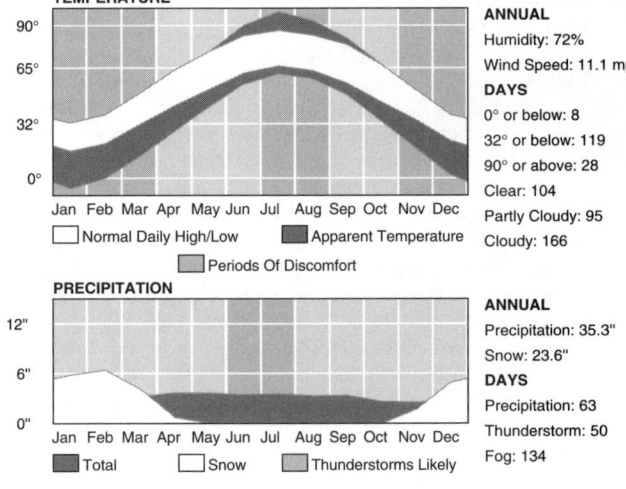

TEMPERATURE

Normal Daily High/Low — Apparent Temperature — Periods Of Discomfort

ANNUAL
Humidity: 72%
Wind Speed: 11.1 mph
DAYS
0° or below: 8
32° or below: 119
90° or above: 28
Clear: 104
Partly Cloudy: 95
Cloudy: 166

PRECIPITATION

Total — Snow — Thunderstorms Likely

ANNUAL
Precipitation: 35.3"
Snow: 23.6"
DAYS
Precipitation: 63
Thunderstorm: 50
Fog: 134

Springfield, MO

Location: 37.14 N, 93.23 W, at 1,270 feet, on the Missouri Ozark Plateau on the northern edge of the Ozark Mountains; 135 miles southwest of Jefferson City, the state capital.

Landscape: This is flat or gently rolling tableland, practically atop the crest of the Ozark Plateau. Located in the state's poultry and dairy region, the economy is based on agriculture and lumber products. Trees are in scattered wood lots and include oak, maple, cottonwood, and walnut.

Cimate: The mild and changeable climate is often associated with high places in southerly latitudes, with warmer winters and cooler summers than other parts of the state at lower elevations. As a result, the city and surrounding countryside enjoy what is described as a Plateau climate. The city sits astride two major drainage systems: the Missouri River system to the north and the White Mississippi system to the south. The freeze-free growing season lasts from mid-April to mid-October.

Winter mildness: 46	**Seasonal affect:** 69
Summer mildness: 33	**Hazardousness:** 33
Score: 27.47	**Rank: 257**

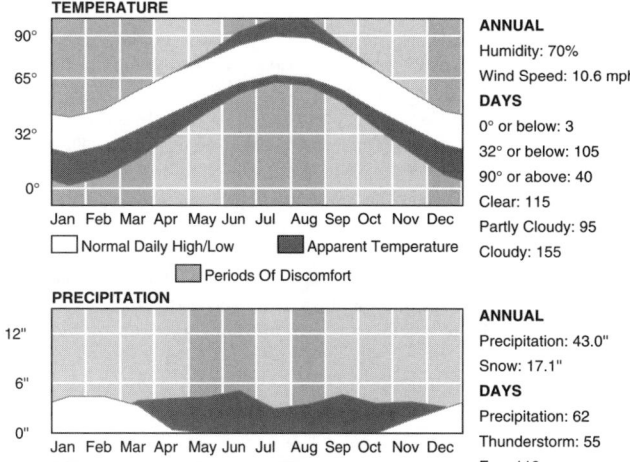

ANNUAL
Humidity: 70%
Wind Speed: 10.6 mph
DAYS
0° or below: 3
32° or below: 105
90° or above: 40
Clear: 115
Partly Cloudy: 95
Cloudy: 155

ANNUAL
Precipitation: 43.0"
Snow: 17.1"
DAYS
Precipitation: 62
Thunderstorm: 55
Fog: 119

State College, PA

Location: 40.48 N, 77.52 W, at 1,170 feet, in Centre County, the geographic center of Pennsylvania.

Landscape: The orientation of the ridges and valleys of the Appalachian Mountains is northeast to southwest. Elevations within Centre County vary from 977 to 2,400 feet. The rolling meadows of the Nittany Valley and foothills of the Allegheny Plateau rise to the west. Forests of pine, hemlock, and hardwoods of beech, maple, oak, ash, and cherry were once more common before the clear-cut harvests. The surrounding higher elevations are now covered with second-growth forests.

Cimate: The weather is moderated by the surrounding mountain elevations and protected by its eastern slope location. This translates to drier, somewhat less humid seasons. Winters are cold and relatively dry, with thick cloud cover. Summer and fall are the most pleasant seasons of the year. The first freeze in fall occurs at the beginning of October; the last freeze in spring is mid-May.

Winter mildness: 33	**Seasonal affect:** 17
Summer mildness: 77	**Hazardousness:** 17
Score: 33.99	**Rank: 234**

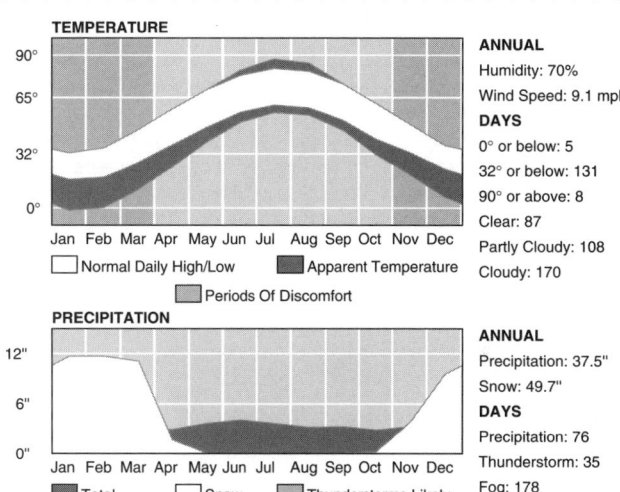

ANNUAL
Humidity: 70%
Wind Speed: 9.1 mph
DAYS
0° or below: 5
32° or below: 131
90° or above: 8
Clear: 87
Partly Cloudy: 108
Cloudy: 170

ANNUAL
Precipitation: 37.5"
Snow: 49.7"
DAYS
Precipitation: 76
Thunderstorm: 35
Fog: 178

Syracuse, NY

Location: 43.07 N, 76.07 W, at 410 feet, at approximately the geographic center of New York State; 135 miles northwest of Albany.

Landscape: Gently rolling terrain stretches northward for about 30 miles to the eastern end of Lake Ontario. Oneida Lake lies about 8 miles northeast of the city. Five miles to the south, hills rise to about 1,500 feet. Immediately to the west, the terrain is gently rolling, with elevations of 500 to 800 feet above sea level.

Cimate: Continental and comparatively humid. Nearly all cyclonic systems moving from the interior of the country and passing through the St. Lawrence Valley will affect Syracuse. Seasonal and daily changes are marked and produce an invigorating climate. Winters can be cold and severe; daytime temperatures average 35°F, nighttime, around 18°F. Summer nights generally are cool, but days can be uncomfortable because of the humidity. The first freeze is an early October 5, and the last, mid-May. The area is overcast, and the cloudiest months are December, January, and February.

Winter mildness: 22	**Seasonal affect:** 15
Summer mildness: 79	**Hazardousness:** 7
Score: 17.84	**Rank: 291**

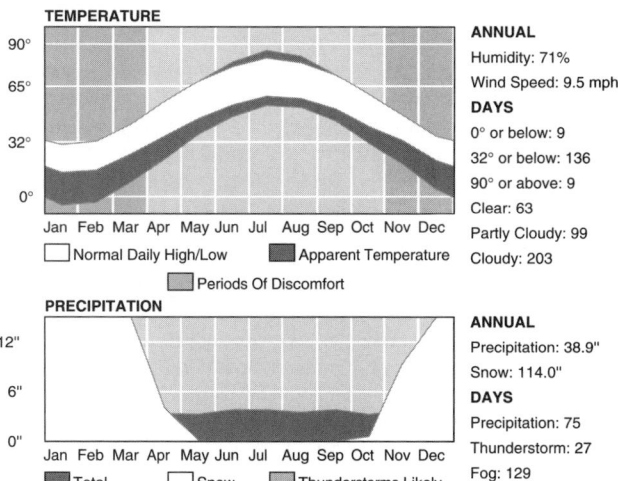

ANNUAL
Humidity: 71%
Wind Speed: 9.5 mph
DAYS
0° or below: 9
32° or below: 136
90° or above: 9
Clear: 63
Partly Cloudy: 99
Cloudy: 203

ANNUAL
Precipitation: 38.9"
Snow: 114.0"
DAYS
Precipitation: 75
Thunderstorm: 27
Fog: 129

Tallahassee, FL

Location: 30.23 N, 84.22 W, at 60 feet, midway between Pensacola and Jacksonville, 30 miles north of the Gulf of Mexico and 20 miles south of Georgia.

Landscape: Rolling red clay hills are covered with natural forests of oak and magnolia. The larger plant growth in north Florida is pine, cypress, magnolia, bays, gum, and oak—the scrubby black-jack and imposing live oak. The many artesian wells, springs, and small lakes in the area support a variety of water plants.

Cimate: Average year-round temperatures compare with those of southern portions of California, Brazil, China, and Australia. The yearly average temperature is 68°F. In contrast to the southern part of Florida, there is a more definite march of the four seasons here, with considerable winter rainfall and much less winter sunshine. The freeze-free growing season is from March 9 to November 16. Summer is the least pleasant time of the year; thunderstorms occur on the average of every other day. High humidity and high temperatures cause discomfort.

Winter mildness: 84	**Seasonal affect:** 57
Summer mildness: 22	**Hazardousness:** 89
Score: 83.56	**Rank: 59**

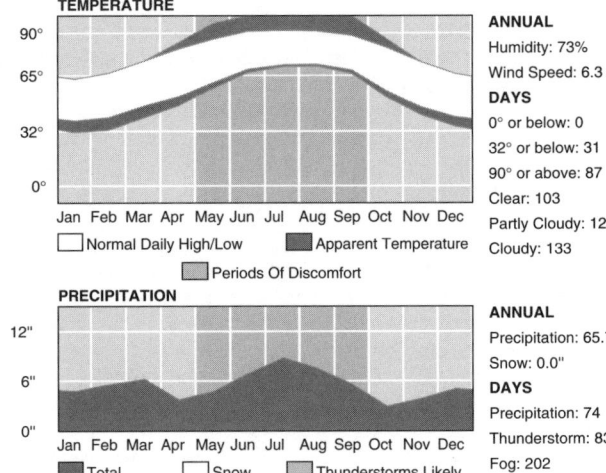

TEMPERATURE

ANNUAL
Humidity: 73%
Wind Speed: 6.3 mph
DAYS
0° or below: 0
32° or below: 31
90° or above: 87
Clear: 103
Partly Cloudy: 129
Cloudy: 133

PRECIPITATION

ANNUAL
Precipitation: 65.7"
Snow: 0.0"
DAYS
Precipitation: 74
Thunderstorm: 83
Fog: 202

★Tampa-St. Petersburg-Clearwater, FL

Location: 27.58 N, 82.32 W, at 20 feet, on Florida's central Gulf coast near the tip of Pinellas Peninsula, adjacent to Tampa Bay.

Landscape: The Hillsborough River and an estuary form a marine horseshoe around Tampa proper. This is flat country connected on the east and south by bridges. A string of sand-reef island resorts lies to the west. Outer Coastal Plain forests are evergreen southern yellow pine and laurel. Many citrus groves and other agriculture abound in the fertile, rolling country to the east. Clearwater occupies a high coastal elevation along the Pinellas Peninsula. St. Petersburg lies at the southern tip of the peninsula, 22 miles southwest and across the bay from Tampa.

Cimate: Temperature throughout the year is modified by the waters of the Gulf of Mexico and surrounding bays. Thunderstorms are frequent during late summer afternoons. The resulting temperature drop feels good. Snowfall is negligible, and freezing temperatures are rare. During the cool season, night ground fogs occur frequently because of the flat terrain.

Winter mildness: 97	**Seasonal affect:** 78
Summer mildness: 28	**Hazardousness:** 83
Score: 90.65	**Rank: 34**

TEMPERATURE

ANNUAL
Humidity: 73%
Wind Speed: 8.3 mph
DAYS
0° or below: 0
32° or below: 3
90° or above: 85
Clear: 102
Partly Cloudy: 144
Cloudy: 119

PRECIPITATION

ANNUAL
Precipitation: 43.9"
Snow: 0.0"
DAYS
Precipitation: 69
Thunderstorm: 87
Fog: 124

Thunder Bay, ON

Location: 48.22N, 89.19W, at 596 feet, on Lake Superior, where Canada's east and west meet, the geographic center of the country.

Landscape: Thunder Bay sits atop the world's largest inland waterway, at the northwestern end of the St. Lawrence-Great Lakes System, 2,000 miles from the sea. A major rail and port city, the landscape includes grain elevators, mills, and refineries. Lake Superior is important as both a commercial asset and a recreational area. Nearby Kakabeka Falls is a source of water power. Four mountain areas, with vertical drops of up to 800 feet are within a 20-minute drive of the city.

Cimate: Humid Continental. Lake Superior plays a major role in modifying the weather. Summer temperatures seldom rise above 90°F. Winter temperatures seldom fall below -20°F. Snow cover is continuous from November to April, with an average of 84 inches annually. The seaway is closed to navigation by ice from December to April. Golf season is from May until mid-October, weather permitting.

Winter mildness: 1	**Seasonal affect:** 18
Summer mildness: 95	**Hazardousness:** 17
Score: 1.98	**Rank: 347**

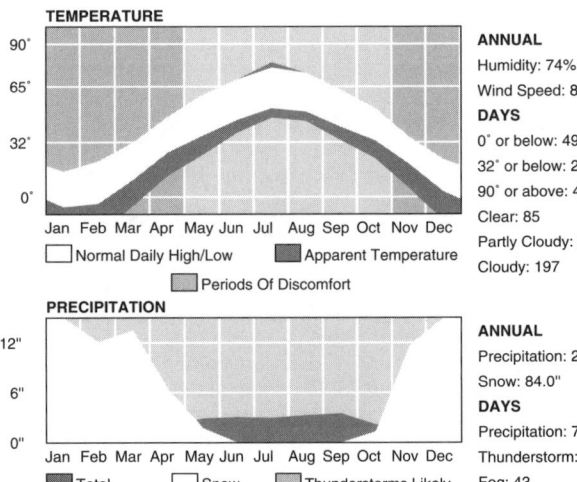

TEMPERATURE

ANNUAL
Humidity: 74%
Wind Speed: 8.3 mph
DAYS
0° or below: 49
32° or below: 204
90° or above: 4
Clear: 85
Partly Cloudy: 83
Cloudy: 197

PRECIPITATION

ANNUAL
Precipitation: 28.0"
Snow: 84.0"
DAYS
Precipitation: 76
Thunderstorm: 26
Fog: 43

Toledo, OH

Location: 41.36 N, 83.48 W, at 670 feet, on the western end of Lake Erie at the mouth of the Maumee River; 60 miles north of Detroit.

Landscape: With only a slight slope toward the river and Lake Erie, the land is generally flat. Rich agricultural land is found in the surrounding area, especially up the Maumee River toward the Indiana state line. The terrain is level and drainage rather poor, conducive to flooding.

Cimate: Lake Erie has a moderating effect on temperature, and extremes are seldom recorded. The typical first freeze comes at the end of October; the latest is mid-April. Humidity is high, and there is an excessive amount of cloudiness. In the winter months, the sun shines during only 30 percent of the daylight hours; December and January, the cloudiest months, sometimes receive as little as 16 percent of the possible amount of sunshine. Snowfall is light and distributed evenly from November to March.

Winter mildness: 25	**Seasonal affect:** 26
Summer mildness: 67	**Hazardousness:** 34
Score: 29.74	**Rank: 249**

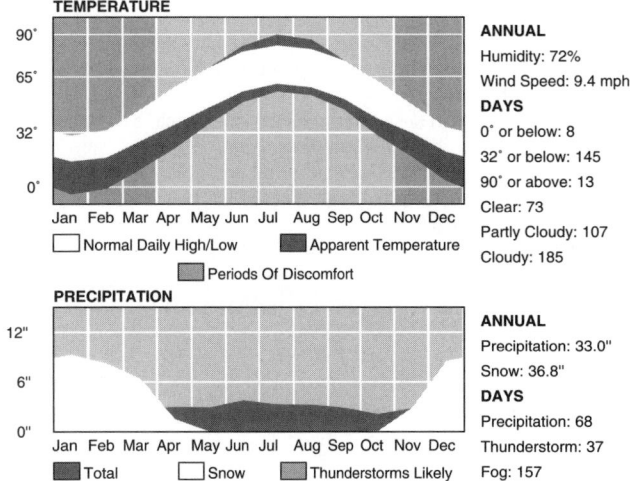

ANNUAL
Humidity: 72%
Wind Speed: 9.4 mph
DAYS
0° or below: 8
32° or below: 145
90° or above: 13
Clear: 73
Partly Cloudy: 107
Cloudy: 185

ANNUAL
Precipitation: 33.0"
Snow: 36.8"
DAYS
Precipitation: 68
Thunderstorm: 37
Fog: 157

Topeka, KS

Location: 39.04 N, 95.38 W, at 880 feet, near the geographical center of the United States, on both banks of the Kansas River, and about 60 miles above the junction with the Missouri River.

Landscape: The Kansas River valley ranges from 2 to 4 miles wide, and is bordered on both sides by rolling prairie uplands of 200 to 300 feet. Flooding is always a threat.

Cimate: Temperate with sharp Continental features from year to year. April through September brings 70 percent of the annual precipitation. These rains arrive as thunderstorms that are of short duration and occur most often at night and in the early morning hours. Oppressively warm and humid periods in summer and bitter cold spells in winter are brief. Spring and fall are transitional seasons with numerous days of fair weather interspersed with short bouts of stormy weather, or cold air invasions that gradually increase in intensity. The first frost in fall is October 18; the last in spring is April 23.

Winter mildness: 32	**Seasonal affect:** 72
Summer mildness: 36	**Hazardousness:** 35
Score: 28.32	**Rank: 254**

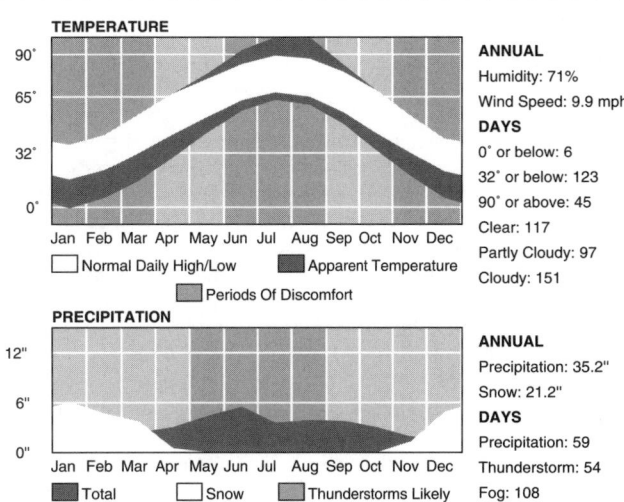

ANNUAL
Humidity: 71%
Wind Speed: 9.9 mph
DAYS
0° or below: 6
32° or below: 123
90° or above: 45
Clear: 117
Partly Cloudy: 97
Cloudy: 151

ANNUAL
Precipitation: 35.2"
Snow: 21.2"
DAYS
Precipitation: 59
Thunderstorm: 54
Fog: 108

Toronto, ON

Location: 43.40 N, 79.38 W, at 568 feet, on the northwest shore of Lake Ontario; 135 highway miles from Buffalo, NY.

Landscape: Nestled in a shallow basin with a gentle rise inland to the Niagara escarpment west to northwest. Toronto benefits from its Great Lakes location and its role as an inland port on the St. Lawrence Seaway. The city is also the focus of Canada's major railroad lines. With a highly diversified manufacturing base, Toronto is Canada's industrial hub.

Cimate: One of the most reliable precipitation regimes in the world, with markedly dry or wet spells both uncommon. The four well-marked seasons include cold-to-cool winters with periods of snow, or rain and snow, alternating with bright sunshine. There is a slow return to warmth in spring along with showery weather. Summer brings periods of heat and humidity with occasional thunderstorms. Increasing cloudiness, more frequent rains and rapidly dropping temperatures are characteristic of autumn's precipitation pattern.

Winter mildness: 15	**Seasonal affect:** 32
Summer mildness: 87	**Hazardousness:** 22
Score: 31.72	**Rank: 242**

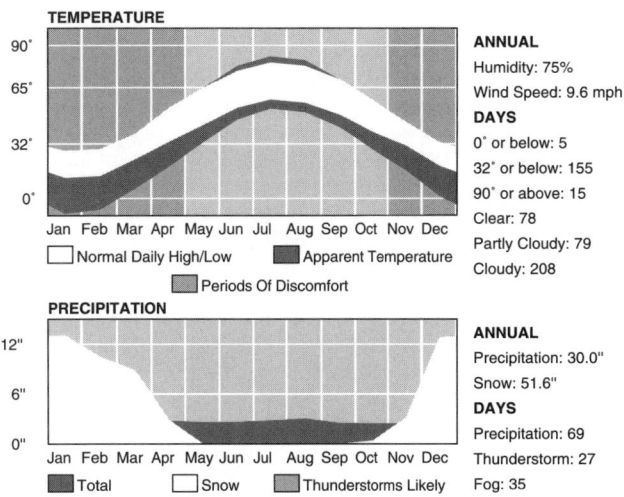

ANNUAL
Humidity: 75%
Wind Speed: 9.6 mph
DAYS
0° or below: 5
32° or below: 155
90° or above: 15
Clear: 78
Partly Cloudy: 79
Cloudy: 208

ANNUAL
Precipitation: 30.0"
Snow: 51.6"
DAYS
Precipitation: 69
Thunderstorm: 27
Fog: 35

Tucson, AZ

Location: 32.08 N, 110.56 W, at 2,580 feet, on the Santa Cruz River; 120 miles southeast of Phoenix and 60 miles above the Mexican border.

Landscape: High desert at the foot of the Catalina Mountains in a broad, flat to gently rolling valley floor rimmed by mountains. The city is in the midst of a citrus fruit, vegetable, cotton, livestock, and dairy producing area. Copper mining in the nearby mountains is also important.

Cimate: Desert. A sunny, dry climate and a unique desert-mountain location. There is a long, hot season beginning in April that ends in October. High temperatures are modified by low humidity, reducing discomfort. July and August can be unpleasant. Tucson lies in the zone receiving more sunshine than any other in the United States. Clear skies or thin, high clouds permit intense surface heating during the day and active radiational cooling at night. Temperatures below freezing are rare, as is snowfall. The freeze-free growing season lasts from mid-February to the beginning of December. Summer is the rainy season with active thunderstorms.

Winter mildness: 85	**Seasonal affect:** 100
Summer mildness: 1	**Hazardousness:** 82
Score: 87.25	**Rank: 46**

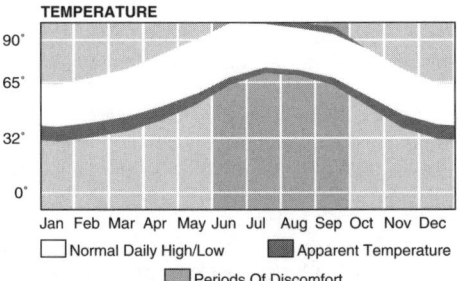

ANNUAL
Humidity: 39%
Wind Speed: 8.3 mph
DAYS
0° or below: 0
32° or below: 18
90° or above: 140
Clear: 195
Partly Cloudy: 89
Cloudy: 81

ANNUAL
Precipitation: 12.0"
Snow: 1.3"
DAYS
Precipitation: 12
Thunderstorm: 42
Fog: 3

Tulsa, OK

Location: 36.12 N, 95.54 W, at 650 feet, lies along the Arkansas River in northeast Oklahoma at an elevation of almost 700 feet above sea level.

Landscape: The surrounding terrain is gently rolling. There are no natural formations such as mountains or large water surfaces that influence its climate. This is a major oil-producing region.

Cimate: Tulsa is far enough north to escape long periods of heat in summer, yet far enough south to miss the extreme cold of winter. The influence of warm moist air from the Gulf of Mexico is often felt in the high humidity, but the climate is essentially Continental, characterized by rapid temperature changes. Generally, the winter months are mild. The last freeze in spring is April 6. Temperatures of 100°F or higher are frequently experienced from the latter part of July to early September but are accompanied by low humidity and a good southerly breeze. Fall is long, with sunny days and cool, bracing nights. The first freeze is November 1.

Winter mildness: 57	**Seasonal affect:** 81
Summer mildness: 9	**Hazardousness:** 45
Score: 36.54	**Rank: 225**

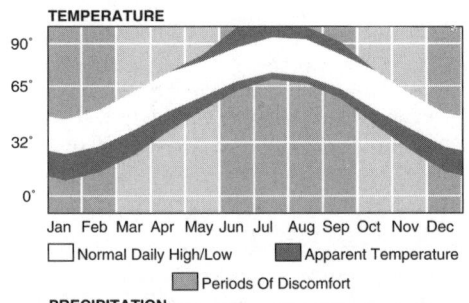

ANNUAL
Humidity: 69%
Wind Speed: 10.3 mph
DAYS
0° or below: 1
32° or below: 78
90° or above: 74
Clear: 127
Partly Cloudy: 102
Cloudy: 136

ANNUAL
Precipitation: 40.6"
Snow: 9.1"
DAYS
Precipitation: 54
Thunderstorm: 50
Fog: 92

Vancouver, BC

Location: 49.11 N, 123.10 W, at 10 feet, on a narrow peninsula between an arm of the Fraser River on the south, the Strait of Georgia on the west, and Burrard Inlet on the north. The Coastal Range mountain peaks are to the immediate west.

Landscape: Occupying one of the world's most attractive city sites, Vancouver is surrounded by water and overlooked by mountains. It is sheltered from the Pacific Ocean by the mass of Vancouver Island, but the ocean's proximity keeps climate moderate throughout the year.

Cimate: The infinite variety of Canada's climate is most striking in British Columbia. Within the Greater Vancouver area it is possible to play golf and ski on the same midwinter day. January is normally the most severe month. Spring arrives by March. July is the most pleasant month with moderate temperatures, long periods of sunshine, and only a little rain. The transition to winter occurs from mid-August through September with cooler and longer nights and more moisture in the air, making fog more prevalent. Then the rainy season returns in October.

Winter mildness: 71	**Seasonal affect:** 7
Summer mildness: 99	**Hazardousness:** 81
Score: 79.88	**Rank: 72**

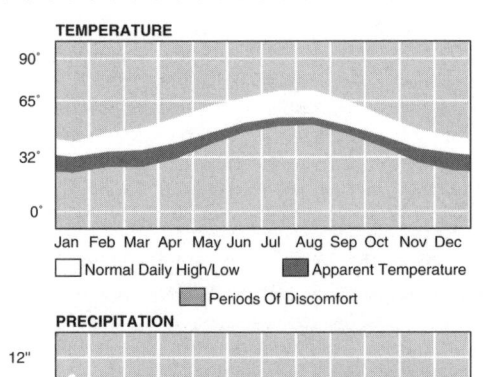
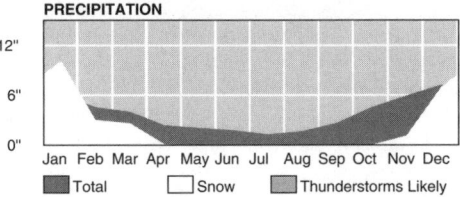

ANNUAL
Humidity: 81%
Wind Speed: 7.5 mph
DAYS
0° or below: 0
32° or below: 55
90° or above: 0
Clear: 71
Partly Cloudy: 73
Cloudy: 221

ANNUAL
Precipitation: 43.8"
Snow: 23.8"
DAYS
Precipitation: 114
Thunderstorm: 6
Fog: 45

Victoria, BC

Location: 48.39 N, 123.26 W, at 62 feet, the capital of British Columbia, Victoria is located on the southeast tip of Vancouver Island, 66 miles across the bay from the city of Vancouver, BC. Victoria is connected to mainland Canada by air and ferry services.

Landscape: Victoria is a major port with two harbors—the outer for ocean shipping, the inner for coastal shipping to the Canadian and U.S. mainlands. Surrounding countryside is rolling farmland, hedgerows, and gardens, resembling rural Great Britain.

Cimate: Climate is Marine mild, nurtured by the California Current, and protected from the open sea by mainland British Columbia on the southeast and Washington state on the southwest. The Pacific air stream allows for mild winters, mild but not hot summers, and small seasonal temperature differences. Rain is more common than snow in the winter, and there have been some winters without any snowfall. Victoria's summers are typically dry, warm, and sunny. Residents claim Victoria has the most pleasant, most kind climate in Canada.

Winter mildness: 71   **Seasonal affect:** 10
Summer mildness: 99   **Hazardousness:** 87
Score: 82.43   **Rank: 63**

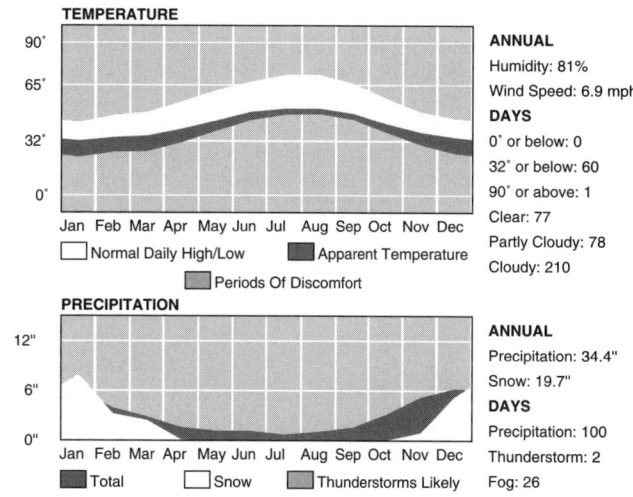

TEMPERATURE

Normal Daily High/Low   Apparent Temperature   Periods Of Discomfort

PRECIPITATION

Total   Snow   Thunderstorms Likely

ANNUAL
Humidity: 81%
Wind Speed: 6.9 mph
DAYS
0° or below: 0
32° or below: 60
90° or above: 1
Clear: 77
Partly Cloudy: 78
Cloudy: 210

ANNUAL
Precipitation: 34.4"
Snow: 19.7"
DAYS
Precipitation: 100
Thunderstorm: 2
Fog: 26

Victoria, TX

Location: 28.51 N, 96.55 W, at 100 feet, in the south central Texas Coastal Plain; 120 miles southeast of Austin, the state capital.

Landscape: Low, rolling prairie and plateau, with occasional forested areas. Areas of wide salt meadows provide for cattle grazing. The Guadalupe River runs nearby, its mile-wide valley well forested with oaks, pecans, and cypress.

Cimate: Humid Subtropical. Rain is the principal weather feature and is well distributed throughout the year. Often cloudy and stormy, thunderstorms reach a peak in August. Summer temperatures over 90°F more than 100 days are bearable due to sea breezes from the Gulf of Mexico, 30 miles or so south. Moderately humid year-round, nights can be oppressive from late June to early August. Destructive storms with tornadoes are rare. Winter weather conditions alternate between clear, cold, dry periods and cloudy, mild, drizzly days as fronts move down from the north.

Winter mildness: 92   **Seasonal affect:** 62
Summer mildness: 10   **Hazardousness:** 75
Score: 67.98   **Rank: 114**

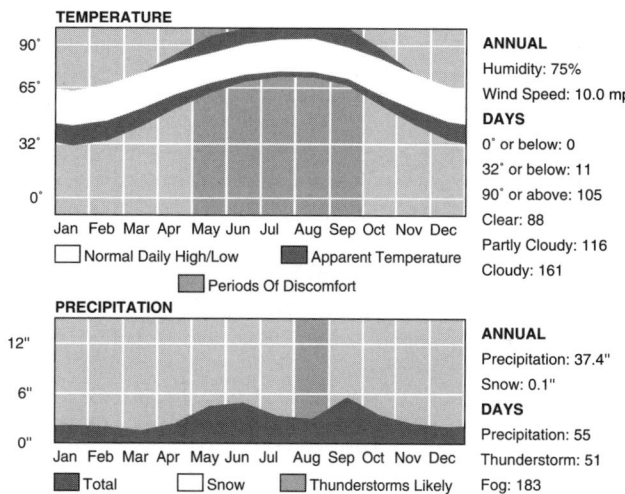

TEMPERATURE

Normal Daily High/Low   Apparent Temperature   Periods Of Discomfort

PRECIPITATION

Total   Snow   Thunderstorms Likely

ANNUAL
Humidity: 75%
Wind Speed: 10.0 mph
DAYS
0° or below: 0
32° or below: 11
90° or above: 105
Clear: 88
Partly Cloudy: 116
Cloudy: 161

ANNUAL
Precipitation: 37.4"
Snow: 0.1"
DAYS
Precipitation: 55
Thunderstorm: 51
Fog: 183

Waco, TX

Location: 31.37 N, 97.13 W, at 500 feet, on the Brazos River in north central Texas; 100 miles northeast of Austin.

Landscape: In the wide, rich valley of the Brazos River on the edge of the gently rolling Blackland Prairie, and rimmed by the low hills of the Balcones Escarpment. Soils are rich bottomland, black, waxy, loam, and sandy types, suitable for growing cotton and raising cattle. Wooded areas of pecan, elm, live oak, burr oak, cottonwood, and mesquite are common. Lake Waco, a reservoir of 7,260 surface acres, lies inside the city limits.

Cimate: Humid Subtropical though a Continental element is captured in the extreme variations of temperature. Tropical Maritime air masses predominate throughout the late spring, summer, and early fall. Summers are hot. Though winters are mild, polar air comes in as cold fronts move down from the High Plains with strong, gusty winds. The cold lasts only a few days before a rapid warming occurs. Spring and fall are pleasant.

Winter mildness: 76   **Seasonal affect:** 83
Summer mildness: 3   **Hazardousness:** 61
Score: 43.62   **Rank: 200**

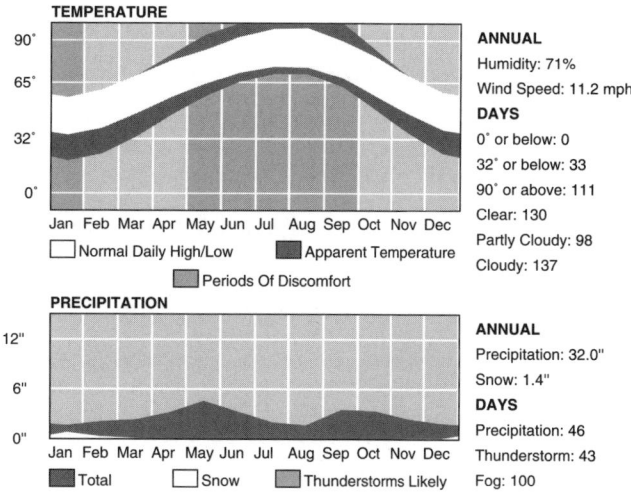

TEMPERATURE

Normal Daily High/Low   Apparent Temperature   Periods Of Discomfort

PRECIPITATION

Total   Snow   Thunderstorms Likely

ANNUAL
Humidity: 71%
Wind Speed: 11.2 mph
DAYS
0° or below: 0
32° or below: 33
90° or above: 111
Clear: 130
Partly Cloudy: 98
Cloudy: 137

ANNUAL
Precipitation: 32.0"
Snow: 1.4"
DAYS
Precipitation: 46
Thunderstorm: 43
Fog: 100

Washington, DC-MD-VA-WV

Location: 38.51 N, 77.02 W, at 10 feet, 50 miles east of the Blue Ridge Mountains and 35 miles west of Chesapeake Bay at the junction of the Potomac and Anacostia rivers.

Landscape: The national capital is surrounded on three sides by Maryland and is across the Potomac River from Virginia. The area's landscape is urban and suburban residential. The city itself is divided along a north-south axis by Rock Creek and Rock Creek Park.

Cimate: The area has a temperate mid-latitude climate. Summers are warm and humid, winters mild. The best weather prevails in the spring and autumn. The last freeze is mid-April; the first is in early October. The coldest weather occurs in late January and early February, and the warmest month is July. There are no pronounced wet and dry seasons. Thunderstorms during the summer often bring sudden heavy showers and damaging winds, hail, or lightning. In winter, snow accumulations of more than 10 inches are rare.

Winter mildness: 61	**Seasonal affect:** 19
Summer mildness: 40	**Hazardousness:** 65
Score: 56.09	**Rank: 156**

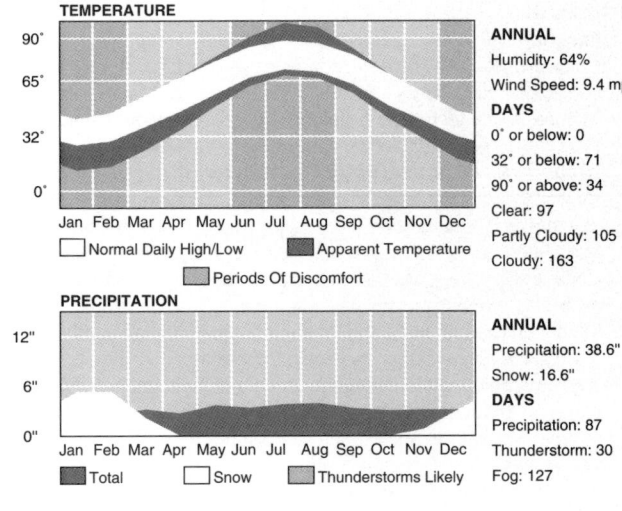

Waterloo-Cedar Falls, IA

Location: 42.33 N, 92.24 W, at 870 feet, on the banks of the Cedar River in northeast Iowa.

Landscape: This area is far removed from the moderating influences of any large body of water. The terrain is level to gently rolling and is ideally suited to agriculture. The flat, open topography has no influence on climate other than offering little resistance to winds, which in winter can greatly increase felt cold.

Cimate: Definitely Continental in character, with hot summers, cold winters, and short springs and falls. The first freeze occurs September 30, the last around May 10. The average annual rainfall is 34 inches, with two-thirds of this total falling in the April-to-September crop season. As befits its landlocked, northerly location, the temperature range is wide: January's mean temperature is 16°F, July's 73°F. In a year, there are more than 30 days of zero or below, and 15 days when the mercury hits 90°F or above including two 100-degree days.

Winter mildness: 6	**Seasonal affect:** 53
Summer mildness: 63	**Hazardousness:** 23
Score: 6.51	**Rank: 331**

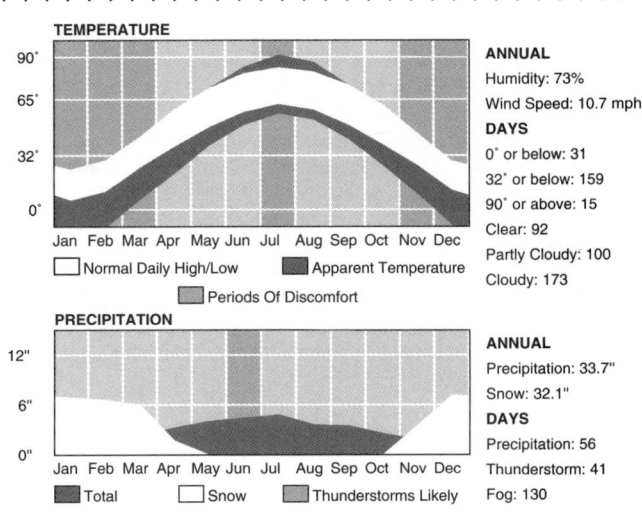

West Palm Beach-Boca Raton, FL

Location: 26.41 N, 80.07 W, at 20 feet, along the densely settled Atlantic coast in the southeastern part of the state, above Fort Lauderdale.

Landscape: Originally a barren sand key transformed by a shipwreck, when a cargo of coconuts washed ashore and took root. The Boca Raton Inlet and its lakes harbor hidden, sharp-pointed rocks. The Atlantic Ocean forms the eastern edge of the coastal ridge, and the Gulf Stream flows northward 2 miles offshore, its nearest approach to the Florida coast. The Coastal Plain growth at the eastern edge of the Everglades is primarily sawgrass and mangrove. Most of the swampland has now been drained for development.

Cimate: Because of its southerly location near the ocean, the area has an equable climate. Winters are pleasantly warm. Summer daytime temperatures are high but are tempered by the ocean breeze. Cumulus clouds often shade the land without completely obscuring the sun. The thermometer rarely climbs beyond 95°F. The moist unstable air results in frequent short rain showers.

Winter mildness: 99	**Seasonal affect:** 70
Summer mildness: 32	**Hazardousness:** 80
Score: 88.38	**Rank: 42**

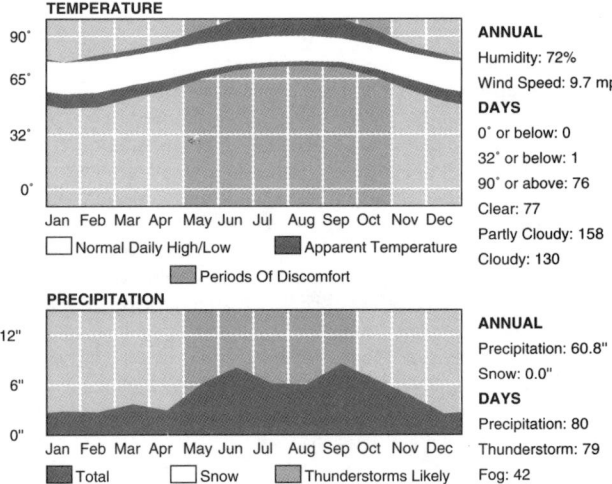

Wheeling, WV-OH

Location: 39.54 N, 80.45 W, at 620 feet, on the Ohio River in the northern part of West Virginia's western Panhandle; some 60 miles northeast of Pittsburgh.

Landscape: The dominating features are the Ohio River and the Appalachians. The topography consists of steep slopes following the irregular boundary of the river. The upland soil is shallow, clay, and acidic, favoring forest growth. Near the river, soil is blacker and more fertile. Coal mining continues to be an economic mainstay, as does harvesting hardwood. Wheeling Island in the Ohio River, part of the city, is connected to the mainland by bridges.

Cimate: Mid-latitude Continental climate, featuring cyclonic storms in winter and thunderstorms in summer. Steep narrow valleys make flash flooding a feared weather phenomenon. Precipitation averages 4 inches each month, and greater amounts occur at higher elevations. Temperatures range from an average 34°F in January to 72°F in July. The first freeze is the end of October, the latest at the end of April.

Winter mildness: 39	**Seasonal affect:** 6
Summer mildness: 54	**Hazardousness:** 30
Score: 21.24	**Rank: 279**

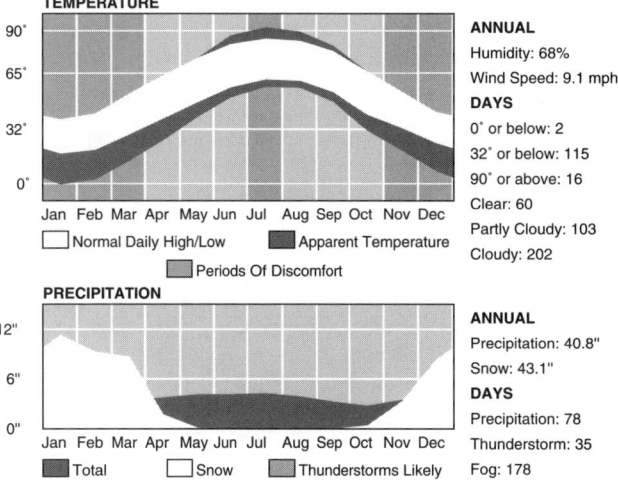

ANNUAL
Humidity: 68%
Wind Speed: 9.1 mph
DAYS
0° or below: 2
32° or below: 115
90° or above: 16
Clear: 60
Partly Cloudy: 103
Cloudy: 202

ANNUAL
Precipitation: 40.8"
Snow: 43.1"
DAYS
Precipitation: 78
Thunderstorm: 35
Fog: 178

Wichita, KS

Location: 37.39 N, 97.26 W, at 1,320 feet; 100 miles southwest of Topeka and 45 miles north of the Oklahoma border.

Landscape: Located in gentle sloping topography along the Arkansas River in the flat terrain of the Central Great Plains. There are no large bodies of water nearby to affect the city's climate. Natural tree areas occur along the river and its tributaries.

Cimate: Continental, lying in the path of alternate masses of warm, moist air moving northward from the Gulf of Mexico and cold, dry air from the polar regions. The average freeze-free growing season is from April 15 to October 24. Winds are generally from the south. Summers can be hot, with more than 60 days over 90°F during that time. Winters are mild, and snowfalls are light, averaging 16 inches a year. Thunderstorms occur mainly during the spring and early summer. They can be severe and cause damage from heavy rain, large hail, strong winds, and tornadoes.

Winter mildness: 43	**Seasonal affect:** 81
Summer mildness: 12	**Hazardousness:** 32
Score: 23.79	**Rank: 270**

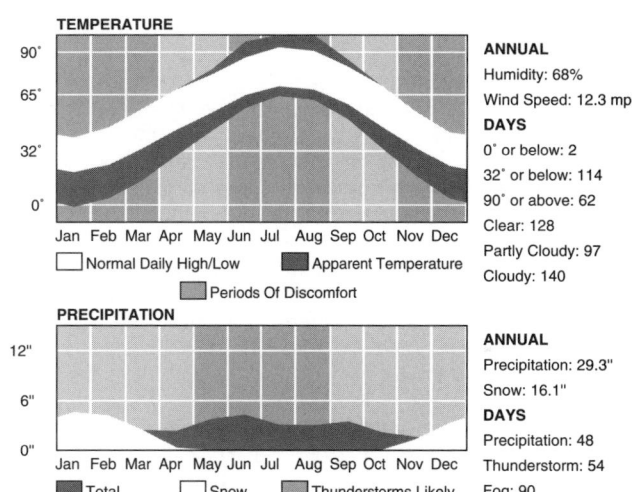

ANNUAL
Humidity: 68%
Wind Speed: 12.3 mph
DAYS
0° or below: 2
32° or below: 114
90° or above: 62
Clear: 128
Partly Cloudy: 97
Cloudy: 140

ANNUAL
Precipitation: 29.3"
Snow: 16.1"
DAYS
Precipitation: 48
Thunderstorm: 54
Fog: 90

Wichita Falls, TX

Location: 33.58 N, 98.29 W, at 990 feet, on the Wichita River in the North Central Plains, 10 miles south of the Red River and Oklahoma border; 284 miles southeast of Austin.

Landscape: Gently rolling mesquite plain and buffalo grass prairie. The big river valley with high bluffs is also an important feature. The good, rich soil has long been used for agricultural production, first through dry-land farming and later through irrigation.

Cimate: Continental with Subtropical features. Characterized by rapid changes in temperature, large daily and annual temperature extremes, and erratic rainfall. While Blue Northers may drop the temperature 20° to 30° within an hour, winters are relatively mild. Snow over an inch occurs only two days a year. The average temperature in the coldest month of January is around 40°F. Summer temperatures average in the mid-80s, but 100° days are frequent in periods of hot weather. Prolonged dry periods are common. Winds are southerly and are strong in all months. Dust storms are rare.

Winter mildness: 62	**Seasonal affect:** 89
Summer mildness: 2	**Hazardousness:** 47
Score: 38.24	**Rank: 219**

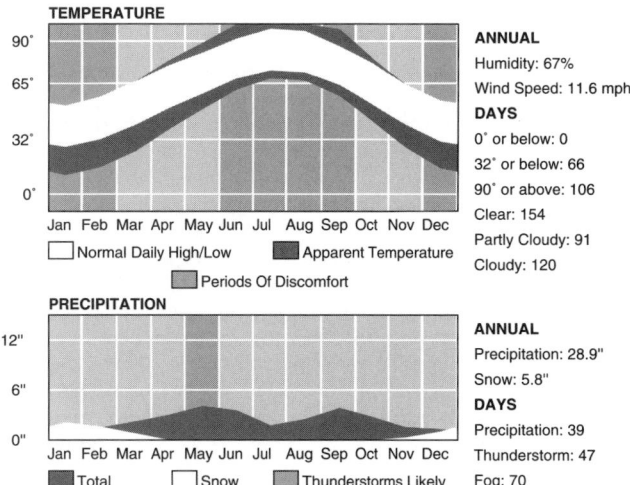

ANNUAL
Humidity: 67%
Wind Speed: 11.6 mph
DAYS
0° or below: 0
32° or below: 66
90° or above: 106
Clear: 154
Partly Cloudy: 91
Cloudy: 120

ANNUAL
Precipitation: 28.9"
Snow: 5.8"
DAYS
Precipitation: 39
Thunderstorm: 47
Fog: 70

Wilmington-Newark, DE-MD

Location: 39.40 N, 75.36 W, at 80 feet, 29 miles south of Philadelphia on the Delaware River above Delaware Bay and the Atlantic Ocean.

Landscape: Part of the Atlantic Coastal Plain, which is mainly flat lowland with many marshes. Small streams and tidal estuaries make up the drainage. Low rolling hills begin near here and extend north and west into Pennsylvania. The Delaware and Chesapeake Canal provides access for shipping into Chesapeake Bay.

Cimate: Greatly influenced by nearby large bodies of water as well as the broad bay 35 miles west. Humidity is high year-round. Fog is frequent and may occur in any month. Rain distribution is uniform throughout the year, though summer brings the greatest amounts as thunderstorms. Southeast winds may bring storms up from the South Atlantic; hurricanes may bring heavy rains, but high winds are seldom a problem. Snowfall is generally light and rarely remains long on the ground. The first fall freeze arrives October 20, and the latest comes April 19.

Winter mildness: 51	**Seasonal affect:** 36
Summer mildness: 53	**Hazardousness:** 63
Score: 59.77	**Rank:** 143

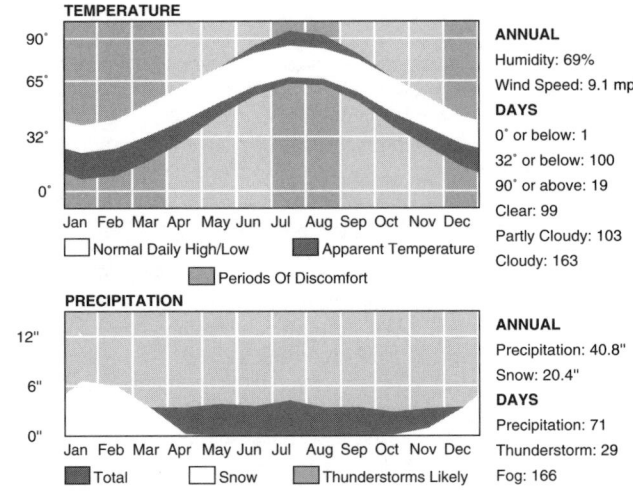

TEMPERATURE

Normal Daily High/Low · Apparent Temperature · Periods Of Discomfort

ANNUAL
Humidity: 69%
Wind Speed: 9.1 mph
DAYS
0° or below: 1
32° or below: 100
90° or above: 19
Clear: 99
Partly Cloudy: 103
Cloudy: 163

PRECIPITATION

Total · Snow · Thunderstorms Likely

ANNUAL
Precipitation: 40.8"
Snow: 20.4"
DAYS
Precipitation: 71
Thunderstorm: 29
Fog: 166

Wilmington, NC

Location: 34.16 N, 77.54 W, at 30 feet, in the Tidewater section of southeast North Carolina, on the Atlantic Ocean.

Landscape: The city proper is built adjacent to the east bank of the Cape Fear River. The surrounding terrain is level and low. There are many rivers, creeks, and lakes nearby, most with considerable swampy growth surrounding them. Large tracts of woods alternate with cultivated fields.

Cimate: A strong Maritime influence from the Atlantic Ocean moderates all four seasons. Summers are quite warm and humid, but excessive heat is rare. During winter, polar air masses reach the coastal areas, causing sharp drops in temperature. However, much of the bite of these air masses has diminished by the time they reach the Wilmington area. Snowfall is slight. Rainfall is ample and well distributed, with most occurring in summer thundershowers. In winter, rain may fall steadily for several days. Hurricanes hit with strong tides, high winds, and heavy rains. The first freeze is November 19; the last, March 20.

Winter mildness: 76	**Seasonal affect:** 33
Summer mildness: 40	**Hazardousness:** 71
Score: 68.55	**Rank:** 112

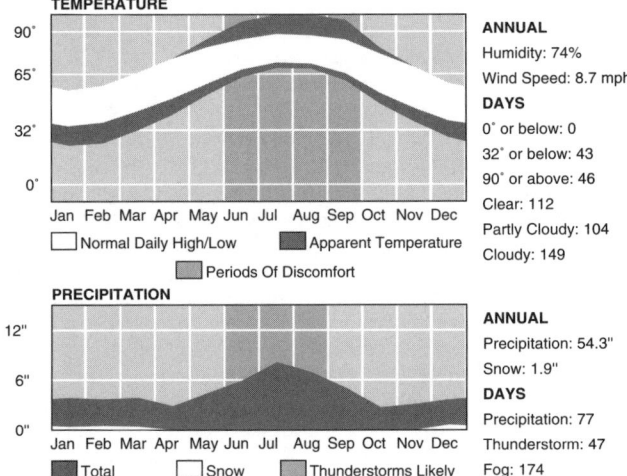

TEMPERATURE

Normal Daily High/Low · Apparent Temperature · Periods Of Discomfort

ANNUAL
Humidity: 74%
Wind Speed: 8.7 mph
DAYS
0° or below: 0
32° or below: 43
90° or above: 46
Clear: 112
Partly Cloudy: 104
Cloudy: 149

PRECIPITATION

Total · Snow · Thunderstorms Likely

ANNUAL
Precipitation: 54.3"
Snow: 1.9"
DAYS
Precipitation: 77
Thunderstorm: 47
Fog: 174

Winnipeg, MB

Location: 49.54 N, 97.14 W, at 784 feet, situated in the broad flat valley of the Red River, which flows northeast through the city.

Landscape: The east side of the valley is a nearly level plain comprised of extensive swamplands. The west side terminates with an abrupt rise known as the Manitoba escarpment, which is pierced by the broad flat Assiniboine Valley extending to the west.

Cimate: Typically Continental. The main features are precipitation of all sorts and a wide range of annual, seasonal, day-to-day, and daily temperatures. Snowfall, which has fallen in Manitoba in every month but July, is not heavy—it just seems that way. Once the snow arrives in mid-November, it normally stays until the middle of April, making winter seem long.

Winter mildness: 0	**Seasonal affect:** 61
Summer mildness: 90	**Hazardousness:** 14
Score: 3.96	**Rank:** 340

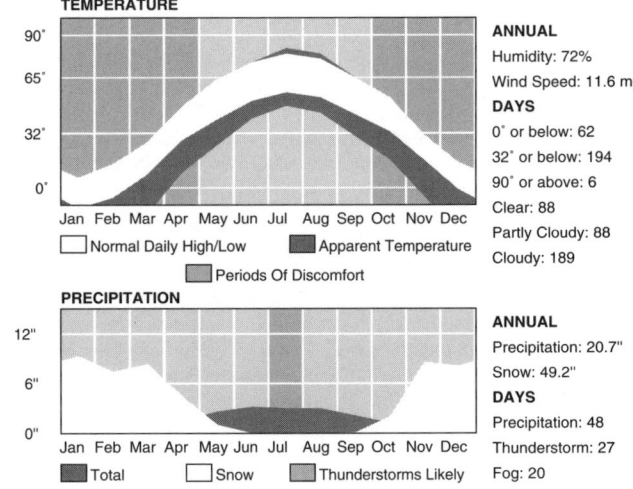

TEMPERATURE

Normal Daily High/Low · Apparent Temperature · Periods Of Discomfort

ANNUAL
Humidity: 72%
Wind Speed: 11.6 mph
DAYS
0° or below: 62
32° or below: 194
90° or above: 6
Clear: 88
Partly Cloudy: 88
Cloudy: 189

PRECIPITATION

Total · Snow · Thunderstorms Likely

ANNUAL
Precipitation: 20.7"
Snow: 49.2"
DAYS
Precipitation: 48
Thunderstorm: 27
Fog: 20

Yakima, WA

Location: 46.34 N, 120.32 W, at 1,060 feet, in a small valley 173 miles southeast of Olympia, the state capital.

Landscape: The local topography is complex, with a number of minor valleys and ridges giving a local elevation as high as 1,000 feet in this irrigated upper part of the Yakima Valley east of the Cascade Range. There are marked variations in air drainage, winds, and temperatures within short distances.

Cimate: Relatively mild and dry, with characteristics of both Maritime and Continental climates, modified by the Cascade and the Rocky Mountain ranges. Yakima lies in the rain shadow of the Cascades; precipitation is generally light. The first freeze is October 13; the last is May 1. Summers are dry and hot. There is a rapid temperature fall after sunset, making the nights pleasantly cool. Shielded from most of the cold air masses from Canada, winters are cool with only light snowfall of 20 inches to 25 inches per year. Irrigation is necessary for almost all crops.

Winter mildness: 50	**Seasonal affect:** 75
Summer mildness: 48	**Hazardousness:** 81
Score: 86.96	**Rank: 47**

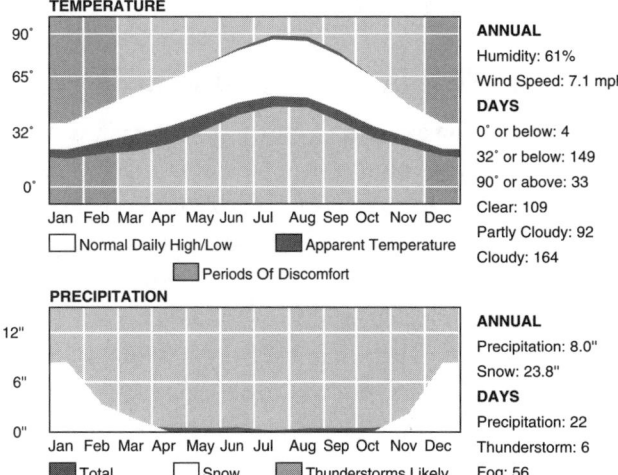

TEMPERATURE
☐ Normal Daily High/Low ■ Apparent Temperature ■ Periods Of Discomfort
PRECIPITATION
■ Total ☐ Snow ■ Thunderstorms Likely

ANNUAL
Humidity: 61%
Wind Speed: 7.1 mph
DAYS
0° or below: 4
32° or below: 149
90° or above: 33
Clear: 109
Partly Cloudy: 92
Cloudy: 164

ANNUAL
Precipitation: 8.0"
Snow: 23.8"
DAYS
Precipitation: 22
Thunderstorm: 6
Fog: 56

Youngstown-Warren, OH

Location: 41.15 N, 80.40 W, at 1,180 feet, in northeastern Ohio; 65 miles southeast of Cleveland.

Landscape: There are numerous man-made and natural bodies of water in the region, including Lake Erie, 45 miles to the north. Drainage from the area flows southward to the Beaver River at New Castle, Pennsylvania.

Cimate: Frequent outbreaks of cold Canadian air masses are modified by passage over Lake Erie. However, this route produces widespread cloudiness, especially during cooler months. Most winters, the bulk of the snow falls as flurries of 2 inches or less per occurrence, although several snowstorms will produce amounts in the 4- to l0-inch range. Flood control projects have all but eliminated the threat of serious river flooding. Temperatures seldom reach extremes. However, high humidity during most days of the year tends to accentuate the temperature. Rainfall is more than adequate and reasonably well distributed throughout the year. The first frost in the fall is October 5 and the last occurrence in spring is May 14.

Winter mildness: 32	**Seasonal affect:** 5
Summer mildness: 82	**Hazardousness:** 12
Score: 22.09	**Rank: 276**

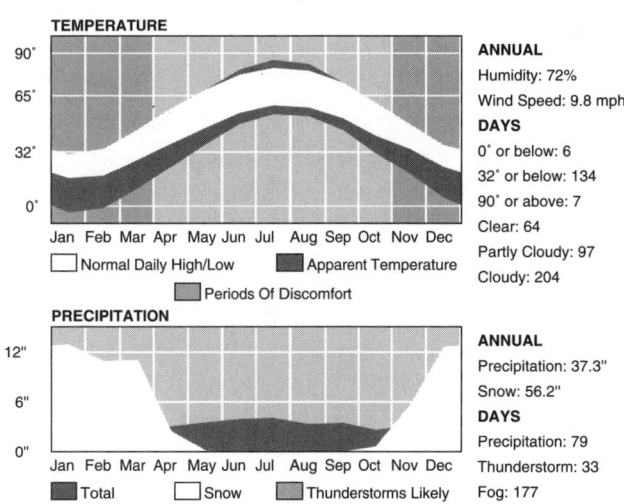

TEMPERATURE
☐ Normal Daily High/Low ■ Apparent Temperature ■ Periods Of Discomfort
PRECIPITATION
■ Total ☐ Snow ■ Thunderstorms Likely

ANNUAL
Humidity: 72%
Wind Speed: 9.8 mph
DAYS
0° or below: 6
32° or below: 134
90° or above: 7
Clear: 64
Partly Cloudy: 97
Cloudy: 204

ANNUAL
Precipitation: 37.3"
Snow: 56.2"
DAYS
Precipitation: 79
Thunderstorm: 33
Fog: 177

Yuma, AZ

Location: 32.40 N, 114.36 W, at 210 feet, in the extreme southwest corner of Arizona near the California and Mexican borders, about 6 miles west of the confluence of the Gila and Colorado rivers.

Landscape: The land is typical desert steppe, with dry, sandy, and dusty soil. There is scant vegetation. Sagebrush and prairie shortgrass are common. Craggy buttes and mountains take their characteristic texture from wind erosion rather than water erosion. Surrounding mountain ranges are the dominant geologic feature. They include the Trigo, Chocolate, Castle Dome, Mohawk, and Gila ranges.

Cimate: Definitely a Desert product. Home heating is necessary from late October to mid-April as the evenings and nights cool dramatically. The first freeze occurs at the beginning of December, the last at the beginning of February. Yuma is dry, with many places in the world receiving more rain in a year than has fallen here in the past 90 years. Yuma is officially the sunniest place in America.

Winter mildness: 93	**Seasonal affect:** 99
Summer mildness: 0	**Hazardousness:** 97
Score: 88.95	**Rank: 40**

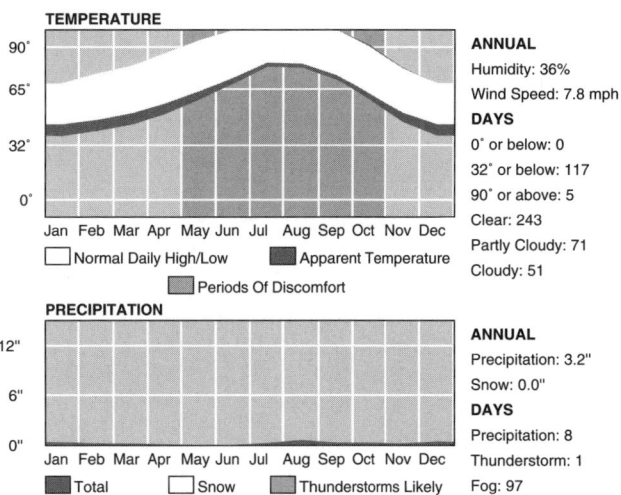

TEMPERATURE
☐ Normal Daily High/Low ■ Apparent Temperature ■ Periods Of Discomfort
PRECIPITATION
■ Total ☐ Snow ■ Thunderstorms Likely

ANNUAL
Humidity: 36%
Wind Speed: 7.8 mph
DAYS
0° or below: 0
32° or below: 117
90° or above: 5
Clear: 243
Partly Cloudy: 71
Cloudy: 51

ANNUAL
Precipitation: 3.2"
Snow: 0.0"
DAYS
Precipitation: 8
Thunderstorm: 1
Fog: 97

ET CETERA: Climate

IT'S NOT THE HEAT, IT'S THE HUMIDITY

Humidity, or the amount of moisture in the air, is a big factor in climatic comfort. It intensifies heat. Hot days that are also humid aren't comfortable when the body's natural evaporative cooling becomes overloaded.

Moreover, just as warm air is able to hold more moisture, so damp air is able to hold heat better and longer. In hot, humid climates, heat is retained in the damp air even after sundown, producing nights almost as hot as the days. In contrast, drier climates offer greater comfort not only during hot summer days but also at night, which can be cool and sometimes even chilly.

Excessive humidity can aggravate certain types of arthritis and rheumatism and, combined with low temperatures, can have a harmful effect on those suffering from pulmonary diseases. Very moist air also encourages the growth of a wide variety of bacteria and molds, thus increasing the chances of infection.

Low humidity has its own undesirable consequences. When it drops below 50 percent, most people experience dry nasal passages and perhaps a dry, tickling throat. In the American Southwest, where relative humidity can drop to 20 percent, many people suffer from nosebleeds, flaking skin, and a chronic sore throat.

Humidity affects hair, too. The range between dry and saturated air produces a 3 percent difference in hair length. In moist air, people with naturally curly hair have the frizzies as hair length increases, while others with long straight hair find it going limp. Hair is such a reliable indicator of humidity that it is the primary element of the hair hygrometer, a meteorological instrument in use from the late 1700s through the 1960s.

The table "Heat Index" shows the relationship between relative humidity and temperature. To find the apparent temperature, locate air temperature at the left and relative humidity along the bottom. The intersection of the temperature figure with the humidity figure produces the apparent temperature. For example, air temperature of 85°F feels like 88° at 50 percent humidity and 102° when the humidity is 90 percent.

WHEN THE WIND BLOWS

As long as air temperature is lower than skin temperature, when the wind blows your body loses heat more quickly than if the wind is calm. Each molecule of air that touches exposed skin carries off some body heat. The faster the wind, the more molecules of air come in contact with skin, which in turn gives up heat to each molecule by conduction.

Windchill is a centuries-old concept, but it was first experimentally measured in Antarctica during World War II when two explorers, Charles Passel and Paul Siple, exposed a plastic container of water to varying combinations of wind speed and air temperature and timed how long the water turned to ice. It is now a popular index heard on local weather reports.

The idea remains controversial. After all, sunshine and exercise warm the body even as it gives up heat from windchill. Moreover, the index assumes the skin is bare, which is unlikely if people dress properly.

The table "Windchill" gives the windchill temperature as a relationship between air temperature and the wind's speed. First locate the air temperature across the top, then the wind speed in the left column. At 0°F, for example, the windchill index in a wind of 20 miles per hour is minus 39°F. When it's 45°F outside, the temperature feels more like 20°F to the face whenever the wind gusts to 35 miles per hour.

Heat Index

APPARENT TEMPERATURE (°F)

AIR TEMPERATURE (°F)	0%	5	10	15	20	25	30	35	40	45	50	55	60	65	70	75	80	85	90	95	100
110°	99	102	105	108	112	117	123	130	137	143	150										
105	95	97	100	102	105	109	113	118	123	129	135	142	149								
100	91	93	95	97	99	101	104	107	110	115	120	126	132	138	144						
95	87	88	90	91	93	94	96	98	101	104	107	110	114	119	124	130	136				
90	83	84	85	86	87	88	90	91	93	95	96	98	100	102	106	109	113	117	122		
85	78	79	80	81	82	83	84	85	86	87	88	89	90	91	93	95	97	99	102	105	108
80	73	74	75	76	77	77	78	79	79	80	81	81	82	83	85	86	86	87	88	89	91
75	69	69	70	71	72	72	73	73	74	74	75	75	76	76	77	77	78	78	79	79	80
70	64	64	65	65	66	66	67	67	68	68	69	69	70	70	70	70	71	71	71	71	72

% RELATIVE HUMIDITY

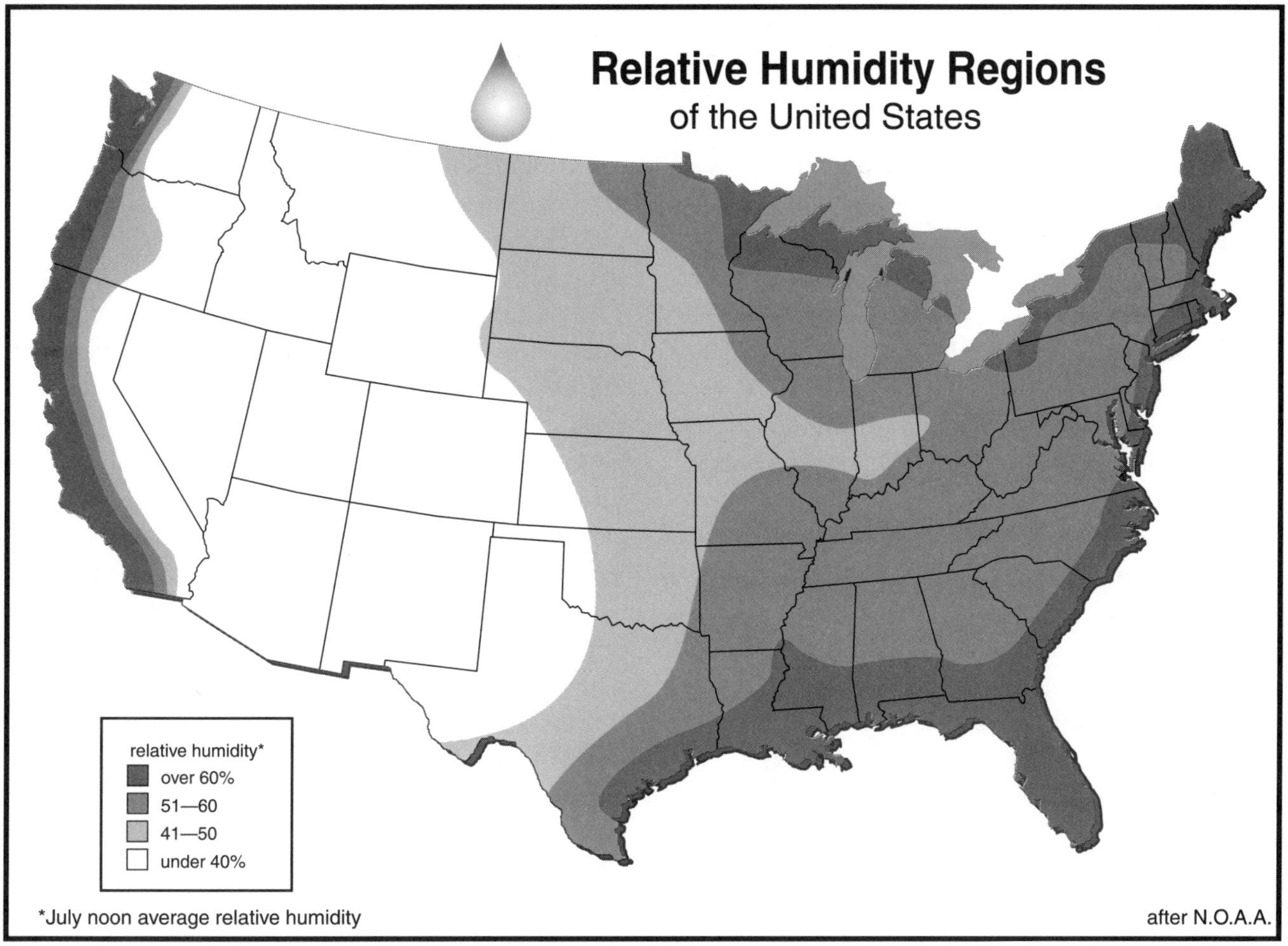

Relative Humidity Regions
of the United States

relative humidity*
- ■ over 60%
- ■ 51—60
- ■ 41—50
- □ under 40%

*July noon average relative humidity

after N.O.A.A.

Copyright © 2000 by Places Rated Partnership

Cape Ann Mapping

NATURAL HAZARDS

Perhaps no natural sight was more dramatic on live TV than the eruption of Mount St. Helens in 1980. An internal blast equal to 10 million tons of TNT blew off the topmost 1,300 feet of the mountain. Fortunately, volcanoes usually give warning. Even more fortunately, the places where volcanic activity is a potential hazard are very few.

Other violent natural events are more common and, although less cataclysmic than a volcanic eruption, can cause great damage and threaten lives. Many of these natural hazards follow definite geographic patterns in North America, and some metro areas are at much greater risk than others.

The Sun Belt Is Also a Storm Belt

Most severe storms occur in the southern half of the United States. For this reason, you might say that the Sun Belt is also a storm belt.

Thunderstorms and Lightning. Thunderstorms are common and don't usually cause death. But lightning kills 250 North Americans a year. It remains the most common and frequent natural danger. At any given moment there are about 2,000 thunderstorms in progress around the globe. In the time it takes to read this paragraph, lightning will have struck the earth 700 times.

Florida, the Sunshine State, is actually the country's stormiest state, with three times as much thunder and lightning as any other. California, along with Oregon and Washington, is one of the most storm-free states. In a typical year, coastal California towns will average between two and five thunderstorm episodes. Most American places average between 35 and 50. Fort Myers-Cape Coral, Florida, averages 128. (A thunderstorm episode represents the presence of a single storm cell; a metro area like Fort Myers-Cape Coral can register four or five episodes in a single day.)

The Place Profiles earlier in this chapter tell how many thunderstorm days each place can expect in an average year. The southeastern quadrant of the country generally receives more rain and thunderstorms than the rest, although the thunderstorms of the Great Plains are awesome spectacles.

367

Tornadoes. While they are not nearly as large or long-lived as hurricanes and they release far less total force, tornadoes have more destructive and killing power concentrated in a small area than any other storm known. For absolute ferocity and wind speed, a tornado has no rival.

The hallmark of this vicious inland storm is the violently rotating air column that sweeps and bounces along the ground. Inside, pressure drops to less than 90 percent of normal atmosphere. This vacuum wrecks buildings and sweeps up cars, trains, livestock, and trees, sucking them up hundreds of feet into a whirling vortex. Wind speeds close to 300 miles per hour have been recorded.

Although no one can tell for certain just where tornadoes might touch down, their season, origin, and direction of travel are predictable. Tornadoes peak in late spring and early summer, and most originate in the central and southern American Great Plains, in Oklahoma, Texas, Arkansas, Kansas, and Missouri.

After forming in intense heat and rising air, the storms proceed northeastward at 25 to 40 miles per hour. Most do not last very long or travel very far. Half travel less than 5 miles, although several have been tracked over 200 miles.

In season, one tornado every 5 days is reported in Canada, compared to five tornadoes every day in the United States. One-third of all tornadoes reported in North America occur in Kansas, Oklahoma, and Texas. Metro areas in Oklahoma, eastern Texas, Arkansas, northern Louisiana and Mississippi, eastern Tennessee, Kansas, Missouri, and parts of Nebraska, Iowa, and Illinois have a high potential for tornado danger. About 70 or 80 hit Canada's populated places in a typical year, mainly in Ontario. Most are too weak to cause serious damage.

Hurricanes. Giant tropical cyclonic storms starting up at sea, hurricanes are unmatched for sheer power over a very large area. They last for days, measure hundreds of miles across, and release tremendous energy in the form of high winds, torrential rains, lightning, and tidal surges. They usually occur from June through November and strike the Gulf and southern Atlantic Coast, though they will also strike locations farther north. Like thunderstorms, hurricanes are much less frequent and less severe on the Pacific Coast.

Hurricanes usually originate in the tropical waters of the Atlantic Ocean. Most occur toward summer's end because it takes that long for the water temperature and evaporation rate to rise sufficiently to begin the spiraling, counterclockwise rotation of wind around a low pressure system. When the winds are less than 39 miles per hour, the cyclone is a tropical depression; when winds speed up to between 39 and 74 miles per hour, the cyclone becomes a tropical storm. And when the winds reach 75 miles per hour, the storm becomes a hurricane.

Often the greatest danger and destruction from hurricanes aren't winds but tidal surges that sweep ashore with seas 15 or more feet higher than normal high tides. Although Florida and the southern coasts are most vulnerable to hurricanes, locations as far north as Cape Cod and Maine are not immune.

Earthquake Risks

The cause of an earthquake is the pressure building between two contiguous masses of rock—called tectonic plates—that move slowly but inexorably toward each other in slightly different directions. When the pressure becomes too great for the rock substance to hold, it shears suddenly. This shearing, along with the consequent shuddering, swaying, and even shifting of immense masses of underground rock, is experienced on the earth's surface as an earthquake.

Those conditions necessary to cause an earthquake exist only in certain areas. The entire area ringing the Pacific Ocean is earthquake prone—from western South America to Central America, to North America's Pacific states and provinces, through Alaska's Aleutian Island chain across to Japan, down through China, and ending

Windchill

AIR TEMPERATURE (°F)

WIND SPEED (M.P.H.)	45°	40	35	30	25	20	15	10	5	0	−5	−10	−15	−20	−25	−30	−35	−40	−45
5	43	37	32	27	22	16	11	6	0	−5	−10	−15	−21	−26	−31	−36	−42	−47	−52
10	34	28	22	16	10	3	−3	−9	−15	−22	−27	−34	−40	−46	−52	−58	−64	−71	−77
15	29	23	16	9	2	−5	−11	−18	−25	−31	−38	−45	−51	−58	−64	−71	−78	−85	−92
20	26	19	12	4	−3	−10	−17	−24	−31	−39	−46	−53	−60	−67	−74	−81	−88	−95	−103
25	23	26	8	1	−7	−15	−22	−29	−36	−44	−51	−59	−66	−74	−81	−88	−96	−103	−110
30	21	13	6	−2	−10	−18	−25	−33	−41	−49	−58	−64	−71	−79	−86	−93	−101	−109	−116
35	20	12	4	−4	−12	−20	−27	−35	−43	−52	−58	−64	−72	−82	−89	−97	−107	−113	−120

APPARENT TEMPERATURE (°F)

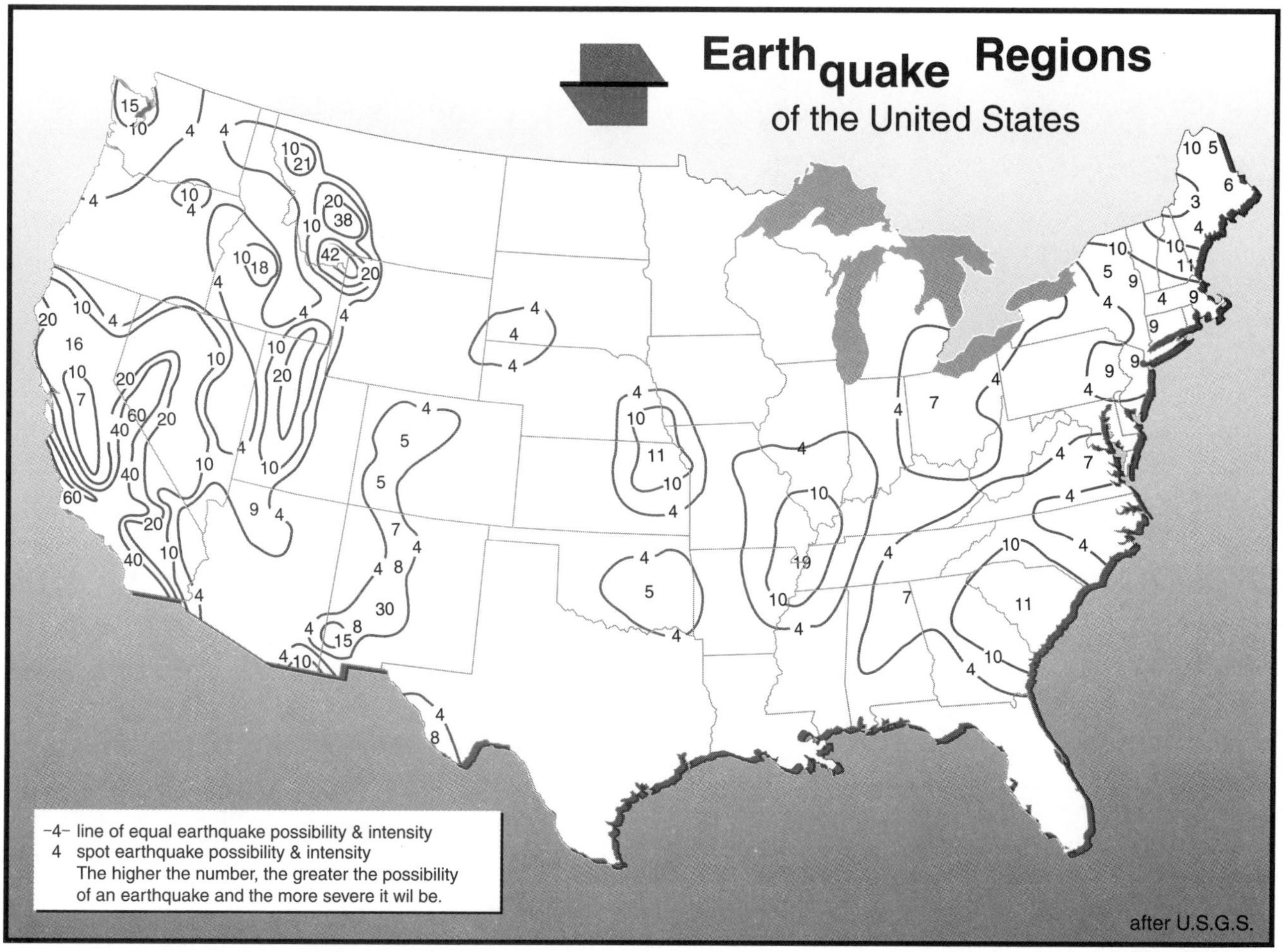

Earthquake Regions
of the United States

-4- line of equal earthquake possibility & intensity
 4 spot earthquake possibility & intensity
    The higher the number, the greater the possibility
    of an earthquake and the more severe it wil be.

after U.S.G.S.

Copyright © 2000 by Places Rated Partnership

Thomas Nast, Cartographer

Climate

in New Zealand. This last area has more earthquakes than any other place in the world.

According to the map "Earthquake Regions of the United States," although much of North America is free from the threat of earthquakes, some areas appear to be resting on powder kegs. (U.S. Geological Survey seismologists warn that the map is experimental and that its predictions cannot be guaranteed.)

Northeast. There is much disagreement among geologists concerning earthquake risk in the northeast. A number of theories about seismic trends have been advanced, and attempts have been made to relate these trends to various fault systems. The best known of these systems is the Boston-Ottawa trend, shown on the map as a continuous area from the Atlantic coast of Massachusetts to the St. Lawrence River valley, encompassing the two cities for which it is named. Most people are unaware that Boston suffered a severe earthquake in the 1700s and that it remains earthquake-prone today.

Southeast. One theory about earthquake risk is that possible earthquake epicenters (the points of origin of ground tremors) are not randomly distributed but occur in zones. In the southeast, these zones run both parallel to and across the Appalachians. Historically, the greatest shock recorded east of the Mississippi occurred in Charleston, South Carolina, in 1886. The present hazard in South Carolina and eastern Georgia is as high as in the Boston-Ottawa trend.

Midwest and Rocky Mountains. The zone of greatest hazard in the Mississippi Valley lies around the side of the cataclysmic series of quakes that occurred near New Madrid, Missouri. The biggest city in this zone is Memphis. The risk of seismic activity is greater in the Rocky Mountains region. The three biggest mountain cities—Denver, Albuquerque, and Salt Lake City—all lie within risk zones.

Pacific Northwest. The Puget Sound area near Seattle has experienced three major shocks within the past 40 years, causing considerable damage. In 1964, an earthquake in Anchorage registered 8.4 on the Richter scale (a 9-point span on a seismograph used to express the relative magnitude of an earthquake).

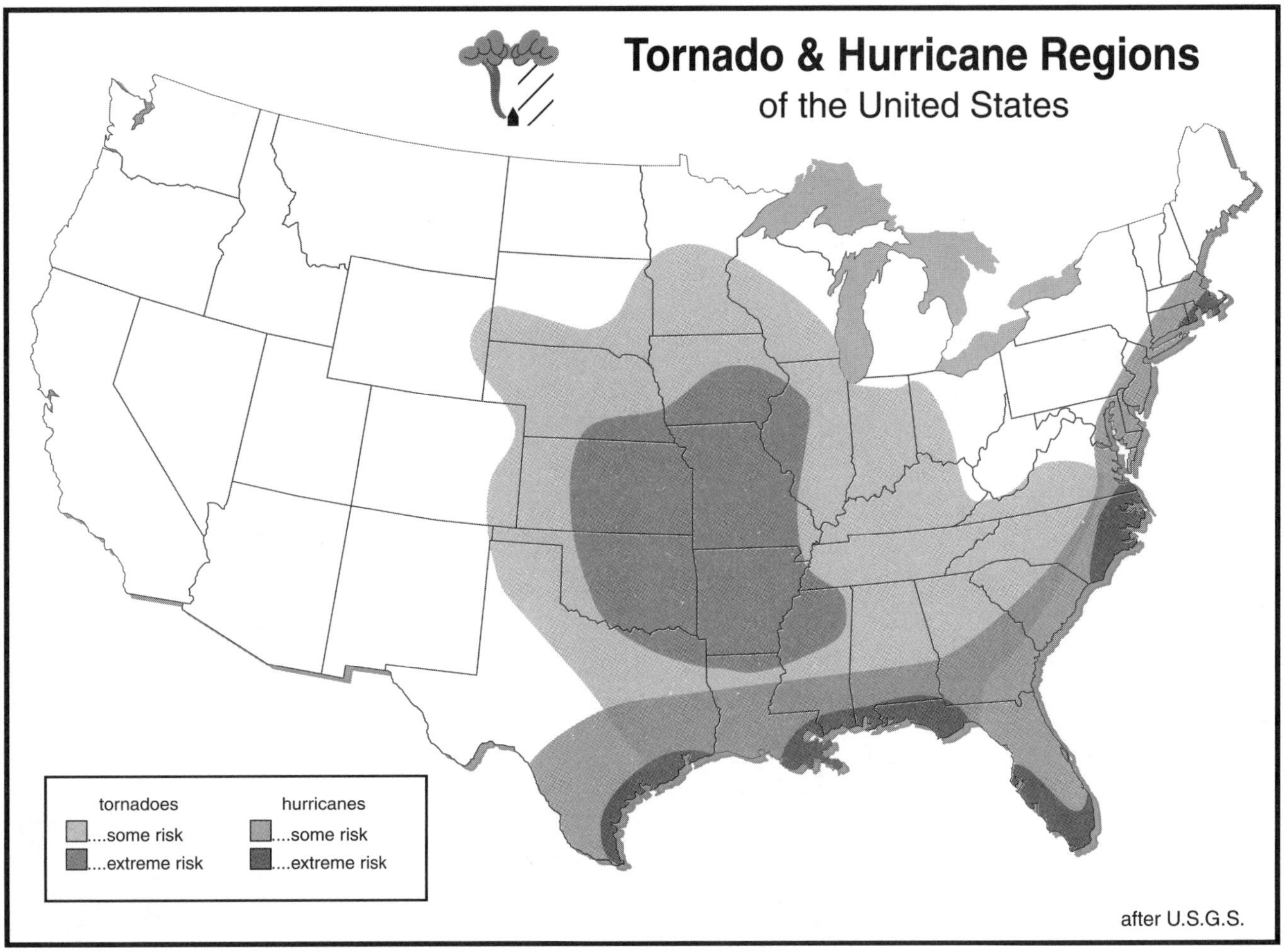

Tornado & Hurricane Regions
of the United States

tornadoes
☐ ...some risk
☐ ...extreme risk

hurricanes
☐ ...some risk
☐ ...extreme risk

after U.S.G.S.

Copyright © 2000 by Places Rated Partnership

Cape Ann Mapping

California and Nevada. Much more seismic activity (and, therefore, more research and data) is present in California and Nevada than anywhere else in North America. The greatest hazards are found in the San Andreas, Owens Valley, and Garlock fault systems, shown on the map as zones numbered as high as 60. All the metro areas in California are affected by these faults, particularly Bakersfield, Los Angeles-Long Beach, Oakland, San Francisco, San Jose, and Santa-Cruz-Watsonville. These places, most of which have mild climates and pleasant terrain, are in real danger.

NORTH AMERICAN WEATHER EXTREMES

No organization validates world records for climate. Data from Environment Canada and from the U.S. Environmental Data Service are current and reliable for North America. These agencies also recognize several world records for temperature, differing forms of precipitation, and other phenomena.

Temperature records are reported by more than 10,000 stations around the world. Theoretically, the hottest it can ever get is just under 140°F, because hot air is lighter and quickly rises above overlying, cooler layers. More than 70 years ago, the highest point a thermometer ever reached in ambient air in the shade was 136°F at El Azizia, Libya, in the northern Sahara.

The current North American heat record, 134°F, was set more than 8 decades ago at Greenland Ranch station in California's Death Valley. Canada's record high temperature, a milder 113°F, hit Midale and Yellow Grass, Saskatchewan, in 1937.

In theory, the coldest it can get on the earth's surface is around minus 130°F, in still air, at 14,000 feet in the middle of polar night. The new world record is minus 129°F, measured at 11,000 feet at Vostok, Antarctica, in 1983. The North American record is minus 81°F, measured at 2,000 feet at Snag, in Canada's Yukon Territory. An imperceptibly milder reading, minus 80°F, resulted in the United States record, at Prospect Creek Camp, Alaska, in 1971.

World *snowfall* records are entirely North American for a single reason: Among countries that keep meteorological records, Canada and the United States record snow depth while others measure snow in terms of water content. Thus, the world's greatest recorded 24-hour snowfall, 76 inches, occurred at Silver Lake, Colorado, in mid-April of 1921. The greatest annual snowfall, more than 93 feet total, fell on Rainier Paradise Ranger Station, Washington, during the 1971–72 season. The greatest depth of snow on the ground, nearly 38 feet, was measured at Tamarack, California, on March, 11, 1911. Canadian snowfall records, all set in British Columbia, are nowhere near these amounts.

The world's heaviest annual average *rainfall* has been recorded by gauges set 5,000 feet up on Mt. Waialeale, Kauai Island, Hawaii: 460 inches. The North American record outside of Hawaii, 256 inches, was established at Henderson Lake on Vancouver Island, British Columbia.

The world's heaviest 1-hour rainfall, 12 inches, hit Holt, Missouri, on June 22, 1947. Nine years later, in 1956, an identical amount fell on Kilauea Sugar Plantation, Kauai Island, Hawaii. Réunion Island, in the path of Indian Ocean tropical storms, regularly gets the world's heaviest short-term rains: 12-hour rain, 53 inches; 24-hour rain, 74 inches; 5-day rain, 152 inches.

Two locations are noteworthy for lack of rain. Nearly 9 decades ago, at Bagdad, California, weather instruments recorded not a trace of moisture for over 2 years,

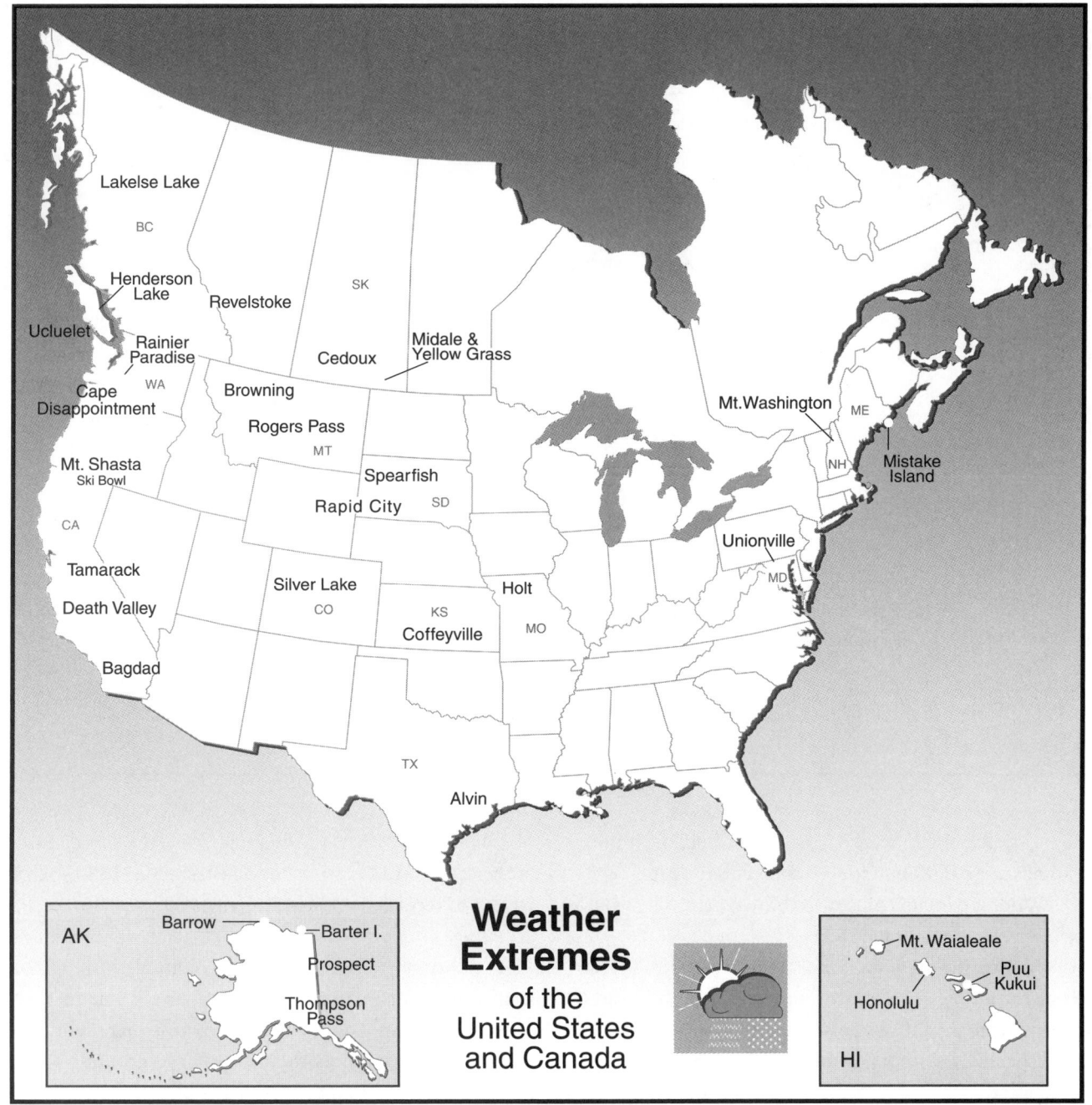

Weather Extremes of the United States and Canada

Copyright © 2000 by Places Rated Partnership

Thomas Nast, Cartographer

GOING TO EXTREMES

Air temperature decreases with increasing elevation. The usual rate of increase—called the *lapse rate*—is 3.3°F per 1,000 feet. In general, the mean temperature of a high location is 3.3° lower per 1,000 feet of elevation than that of nearby lower-altitude stations.

	Highest Place (Elevation ft.)	Lowest Place (Elevation ft.)
United States	**Mount McKinley, AK (20,320)**	**Death Valley, CA (-282)**
Alabama	Cheaha Mountain (2,407)	Gulf of Mexico (sea level)
Alaska	Mount McKinley (20,320)	Pacific Ocean (sea level)
Arizona	Humphreys Peak (12,633)	Colorado River (70)
Arkansas	Magazine Mountain (2,753)	Ouachita River (55)
California	Mount Whitney (14,494)	Death Valley (-282)
Colorado	Mount Elbert (14,433)	Arkansas River (3,350)
Connecticut	Mount Frissell (2,380)	Long Island Sound (sea level)
Delaware	On Ebright Road (442)	Atlantic Ocean (sea level)
Florida	Sec. 30, T. 6N., R. 20W (345)	Atlantic Ocean (sea level)
Georgia	Brasstown Bald (4,784)	Atlantic Ocean (sea level)
Hawaii	Mauna Kea (13,796)	Pacific Ocean (sea level)
Idaho	Borah Peak (12,662)	Snake River (710)
Illinois	Charles Mound (1,235)	Ohio River (320)
Indiana	Franklin Township (1,257)	Ohio River (320)
Iowa	Sec. 29, T. 100N, R. 41W (1,670)	Mississippi River (480)
Kansas	Mount Sunflower (4,039)	Verdigris River (680)
Kentucky	Black Mountain (4,145)	Mississippi River (257)
Louisiana	Driskill Mountain (535)	New Orleans (-5)
Maine	Mount Katahdin (5,268)	Atlantic Ocean (sea level)
Maryland	Backbone Mountain (3,360)	Atlantic Ocean (sea level)
Massachusetts	Mount Greylock (3,491)	Atlantic Ocean (sea level)
Michigan	Mount Curwood (1,980)	Lake Erie (572)
Minnesota	Eagle Mountain (2,301)	Lake Superior (602)
Mississippi	Woodall Mountain (806)	Gulf of Mexico (sea level)
Missouri	Taum Sauk Mountain (1,772)	St. Francis River (230)
Montana	Granite Peak (12,799)	Kootenai River (1,800)
Nebraska	Johnson Township (5,426)	SE corner of State (840)
Nevada	Boundary Peak (13,145)	Colorado River (470)

the North American record. At Arica, Chile, the annual readings were 0.00 mm for 14 consecutive years.

Wind is climate's most variable element. The values include peak wind, or the greatest 5-second average wind speed during the previous hour, and fastest mile, the fastest speed in miles per hour of any wind over a 24-hour observation day. Canada's highest average annual wind, 22 miles per hour, is measured at Cape Warwick, on Resolution Island, Northwest Territories. The North American record is 35 miles per hour, measured on top of New Hampshire's Mt. Washington, where the world's fastest peak wind (231 m.p.h.) and fastest mile (188 m.p.h.) were also recorded in the spring of 1934.

Fog, simply put, is a cloud that touches the ground. As a cloud, it is composed of uncountable millions of visible water droplets formed when air is cooled to the saturation point. Cooling occurs when strong nighttime surface radiation cools the air near the ground; when humid and warm air moves across colder land; and when moist air moves up and over higher terrain. Thick fog is

United States (cont.)	Highest Place (Elevation ft.)	Lowest Place (Elevation ft.)
New Hampshire	Mount Washington (6,288)	Atlantic Ocean (sea level)
New Jersey	High Point (1,803)	Atlantic Ocean (sea level)
New Mexico	Wheeler Peak (13,161)	Red Bluff Reservoir (2,817)
New York	Mount Marcy (5,344)	Atlantic Ocean (sea level)
North Carolina	Mount Mitchell (6,684)	Atlantic Ocean (sea level)
North Dakota	White Butte (3,506)	Red River (750)
Ohio	Campbell Hill (1,550)	Ohio River (433)
Oklahoma	Black Mesa (4,978)	Little River (287)
Oregon	Mount Hood (11,239)	Pacific Ocean (sea level)
Pennsylvania	Mount Davis (3,213)	Delaware River (sea level)
Rhode Island	Jerimoth Hill (812)	Atlantic Ocean (sea level)
South Carolina	Sassafras Mountain (3,560)	Atlantic Ocean (sea level)
South Dakota	Harney Peak (7,242)	Big Stone Lake (962)
Tennessee	Clingmans Dome (6,643)	Mississippi River (182)
Texas	Guadalupe Peak (8,749)	Gulf of Mexico (sea level)
Utah	Kings Peak (13,528)	Beaverdam Creek (2,000)
Vermont	Mount Mansfield (4,393)	Lake Champlain (95)
Virginia	Mount Rogers (5,729)	Atlantic Ocean (sea level)
Washington	Mount Rainier (14,410)	Pacific Ocean (sea level)
West Virginia	Spruce Knob (4,862)	Potomac River (240)
Wisconsin	Timms Hill (1,951)	Lake Michigan (581)
Wyoming	Gannett Peak (13,804)	Belle Fourche River (3,100)
Canada	**Mount Logan, Yukon (19,534)**	**sea level**
Alberta	Mount Columbia (12,293)	Slave River (557)
British Columbia	Fairweather Mountain (15,298)	Pacific Ocean (sea level)
Manitoba	Baldy Mountain (2,730)	Hudson Bay (sea level)
New Brunswick	Mount Carleton (2,690)	Gulf of St. Lawrence (sea level)
Newfoundland	Mount Caubvick (5,321)	Atlantic Ocean (sea level)
Nova Scotia	Cape Breton Highlands (1,745)	Atlantic Ocean (sea level)
Ontario	Ishpatina Ridge (2,274)	Hudson Bay (sea level)
Quebec	Mount d'Iberville (5,321)	Hudson Bay (sea level)
Saskatchewan	Cypress Hills (4,816)	Lake Athabasca (700)

Source: U.S. Geological Survey, Elevations and Distances; Canadian National Atlas Information Service.

reported when visibility is less than half a mile; a day of fog is defined as one on which thick fog occurred once during the day.

The foggiest area in Canada (indeed one of the world's foggiest) is Newfoundland's Avalon Peninsula, socked in more than half the year. The two foggiest points in the United States, at opposite ends of the country, are Cape Disappointment, at the mouth of the Columbia River in Washington, and Moose Peak Lighthouse, off Maine's northern coast.

Hail is rain collecting into ice lumps as it falls to earth from a convective cloud during a thunderstorm. In North America, the area along the eastern slope of the Rocky Mountains from New Mexico on up to Alberta gets more hail days, more hailstorms, and more and bigger hailstones than any other area on the continent. The heaviest authenticated hailstone (1.67 pounds) fell east of here at Coffeyville, Kansas in 1970. Canada's heaviest hailstone (10.23 ounces) fell near Cedoux, Saskatchewan in 1973.

Crime

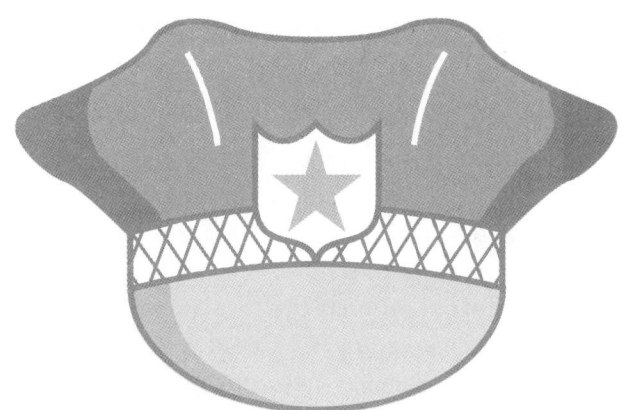

Domestic violence on the farm and pushers developing a base for their illegal pharmaceutical trade aren't uncommon items in Duluth's *News Tribune*. Down I-35 in the Twin Cities, stories of convenience store stickups and drug-related drive-by killings aren't uncommon in the Minneapolis *Star Tribune*, either. If you were passing through either metro area and heard of these crimes, you might wonder whether you were any safer on the northern prairie than you'd be in East Los Angeles or the Bronx.

In fact, neither Duluth nor Minneapolis-St. Paul has crime rates anywhere near the metro-area average. The odds of you being a crime victim in either place are much below what they would be elsewhere. Among the metro areas profiled in *Places Rated Almanac,* reporters working the police beat in some have so few violent crime stories to write up that a reader of the paper may wonder whether anything interesting goes on there at all. In other metro areas, day-to-day existence seems just plain dangerous.

If you decide to live in Johnstown, PA, for instance, the odds of your being a violent crime victim in a year's residence are 555 to 1. On the other hand, should you choose Miami the odds increase to 50 to 1. One could say that life in rapidly growing southern Florida is more than 11 times as dangerous as it is in Pennsylvania's lagging, post-industrial Conemaugh River Valley.

But quoting odds distorts the local crime picture. Violence doesn't lurk in every metro area neighborhood. Veteran cops tell you that most murders occur within the same few square miles or even blocks. Sailors going ashore in an unfamiliar port get the word from commanders on which streets to avoid because of high risk for robberies and aggravated assaults.

Moreover, if you're young, white, and female and if you earn enough money, your chances of meeting up with crime are much less than those of an older, poor male. Why, then, a chapter on crime if a combination of factors such as age, sex, race, income, and a wise selection of neighborhood can statistically remove you from danger?

The simple answer is that you are a different kind of crime victim depending on whether you have to trim back shrubbery along your home's foundation to restrict a crook's potential hiding places, or get rid of the mailbox and install a mail slot in your front door, or press down your car's door locks when driving down a darkened avenue, or keep feeling for your wallet at street festivals, or use only empty elevators, or stay indoors evenings more than you really care to. In some metro areas such tactics are advised, in others they are merely prudent, and in still others they may not be necessary at all.

CRIME RISK: SEVERAL CONNECTIONS

Why some metro areas are safer than others incites arguments among citizens, politicians, police, and social scientists. Conservatives blame the criminal, the criminal's parents, and lenient courts. Liberals indict an oppressive society as the real offender. With all the debate, experts do agree on several factors.

Population size is closely tied to crime rates. Metro areas with lower crime rates—Grand Forks, ND, or Wausau, WI, for example—have smaller populations. Metro areas with the highest rates—Los Angeles-Long Beach or New York are two extreme examples—have large, overcrowded populations. There are exceptions, to be sure. Toronto's crime rate is as low as that of Ann Arbor's. Gainesville's, Jacksonville's, and Tallahassee's crime rates resemble those of New York.

Climate, too, has a striking connection with lawbreaking. Hot weather seems to tip some people over the edge, given the increased rates for murder, rape, and assault in the summer and in hot locations. In fact, police respond to more disturbance calls on days immediately after summer temperatures are highest than on any other days of the year. Burglary and vandalism increase with ambient temperature up to 85°F.

Indeed, in the Sun Belt and in the Frost Belt, cops and criminals are busiest throughout July and August when all crimes except robbery are the likeliest to happen. Since people spend more time outdoors during these months, they are more exposed. Homes, too, are more unprotected during this time of year because they are left with open windows and unlocked doors. Robbery is the cold-weather exception. It is highest in December when shoppers and retail stores doing brisk holiday business make tempting targets.

IS IT THE WEATHER?

For Canadians, the best lesson on how bad crime can be is the United States. Yet by *Places Rated*'s standards, forty metro areas south of the border are safer than Saint John, NB, the safest one in Canada. The ten that look the most like Canadian areas by their combination of rock-bottom violence and average property crime are nearest the Canadian border.

Great Falls, MT	Fargo-Moorhead, ND-MN
Billings, MT	Manchester, NH
Burlington, VT	Bellingham, WA
Missoula, MT	Grand Forks, ND-MN
Bangor, ME	Lewiston-Auburn, ME

Time of day and the *photoperiod,* or length of the day, are two other factors. After sundown is the time most cars are stolen, most persons and businesses are robbed, most persons are assaulted, and most thefts are committed. Burglaries, purse-snatchings, and pocket-pickings, on the other hand, happen more often during daylight hours. Indeed, some police dispatchers contend that the number of daylight minutes is a predictor of the kind of 911 calls they handle.

Even local *traffic* plays a role. The ease with which a criminal can drive off down the street, escape onto an arterial road, and disappear among commuters on the Interstate is an encouragement. Neighborhoods near Houston's I-610 Beltway urged the city to turn their streets into cul-de-sacs, and in Elizabeth, NJ, cops stationed barricades at the corner of Madison Avenue and Fanny Street to stop neighboring Newark lawbreakers from fleeing into their jurisdiction.

Age and sex figure into the equation, too. Some 4 million persons in North America have arrest records for misdeeds other than traffic violations. The proportion of suspects who are male is much higher than their proportion in the general population. Half the persons picked up by police for violent and property crimes are under 20 years of age and four-fifths are male.

None of this should be taken to mean that persons hold up convenience stores, boost Chevrolet Camaros, or duke it out in disco parking lots because they are young and male, but these characteristics are associated with other factors in crime. Some criminologists warn that falling crime rates may well be short-lived once a huge group of pre-teen males grows up and takes to the streets.

The *economy* also plays a role. In most metro areas, each time the unemployment rate goes up the police make more arrests. But joblessness and loss of income won't automatically make a place unsafe. Metro areas in the Ohio Valley, in the Northern Plains, and in Atlantic Canada suffer job losses during business slumps but continue to experience low crime rates.

More affluent areas, given similar sets of circumstances, aren't nearly as safe as they seem. Rich offenders are arrested less often than poor ones, especially on suspicion. Once arrested, they are convicted with less frequency. This is especially true in juvenile cases involving thefts and break-ins.

Transience affects crime rates. A warning sign for crooks is a stable neighborhood where people know one another and look out for one another's safety and property, no matter how many cops cruise the area. High neighborhood turnover leading to more and more strangers living next to each other leads to higher crime rates. Moreover, resort areas that draw transients—Las Vegas, Miami, or Orlando for instance—also have serious crime problems. When visitors are added to the year-round residents, the higher population raises the odds that victim and crook will meet.

Police strength, too, is linked to the local crime rate. Most metro areas have between one and three sworn uniformed officers for every 1,000 residents. In Manhattan, there are 1,300 police officers per square mile. In sparsely populated parts of Alaska and the Canadian Yukon and Northwest Territories, there aren't any.

It's natural to think personal safety in a metro area rises or falls in proportion to the size of the local police force, but it just isn't so. Police enforce traffic codes, investigate accidents, find lost children, and calm down fighting spouses. They battle crime, too, but most of what they do is after the fact. They respond to complaints; they interview victims and fill out reports; they follow up on tips; and they collar suspects and book them.

Criminologists still recount the famous Kansas City experiment conducted in 1972. Three precincts of the city were selected. In one area, the number of cruisers was doubled; in the control neighborhood, the police maintained usual strength; and in the third area, the police pulled out, entering only in response to calls. All areas were carefully monitored for a year. The difference in crime rates? Practically none.

A large number of police usually means a high-crime area rather than an area where crime is being foiled. Washington, DC, has the most men and women in blue per capita and it has long experienced one of the highest crime rates in the country, too.

Other factors related to criminal activity include the practices of local prosecutors, judges, juries, and parole boards; the attitudes of the community toward crime; and the willingness of ordinary citizens to report crime.

CRIME INDEXES

Each year, the Federal Bureau of Investigation in Washington and the Canadian Centre for Justice Statistics in Ottawa report crime figures from police departments in their respective countries. Eight crimes, because of their seriousness, frequency, and likelihood of being reported to police, make up a Crime Index for measuring local wrongdoing. Four are violent crimes; the other four are property crimes.

Violent Crime

Murder is the most reported of all crimes and has the highest rate of charges being pressed. City hall press

VIOLENCE: PRISON SENTENCES VS. TIME SERVED

Average state court sentences (exclusive of life imprisonment or death) for violent crimes are made shorter by good behavior or the need to relieve overcrowding.

Offense	Average Sentence	Actual Time Served
Murder	12 years, 5 months	5 years, 11 months
Rape	9 years, 9 months	5 years, 11 months
Robbery	7 years, 11 months	3 years, 8 months
Assault	5 years, 1 month	2 years, 5 months

Source: Bureau of Justice Statistics

releases announcing dramatic drops in homicide rates are only underscoring a national trend: The rate of people killing one another is at its lowest rate since 1967. Canada's rate is less than a fourth that of its more violent southern neighbor.

Murder victims are male in three of every four instances, and most were slain in single-victim, single-killer situations. Half of all victims knew their killers, perhaps even sat across from them at the breakfast table the morning of the crime or loaned them money the week before.

Victims and killers are becoming less connected, however. One murder in eight involves a victim and a stranger, one in twenty a juvenile gang killing. Based on the number of unsolved homicides each year and an increase in slayings involving strangers, the FBI estimates at least 25 serial killers are on the loose in the United States.

Rape, too, frequently involves acquainted victims and aggressors. It is the most under-reported violent crime and has the highest proportion of "unfounded" complaints. Except in Illinois, Michigan, Minnesota, and Canada, victims are always female by current crime reporting standards.

Robbery is the violent crime most often involving more than one criminal and is the one violent crime committed less out of impulsive anger than as a way of earning a living. It is different from common theft because it requires force or threat of violence, thereby placing the victim in fear.

The robbery rate is highest in large cities, where half of the holdups take place on the street and a quarter occur in commercial establishments and banks. Except for some rural sections, the robbery rate is declining everywhere.

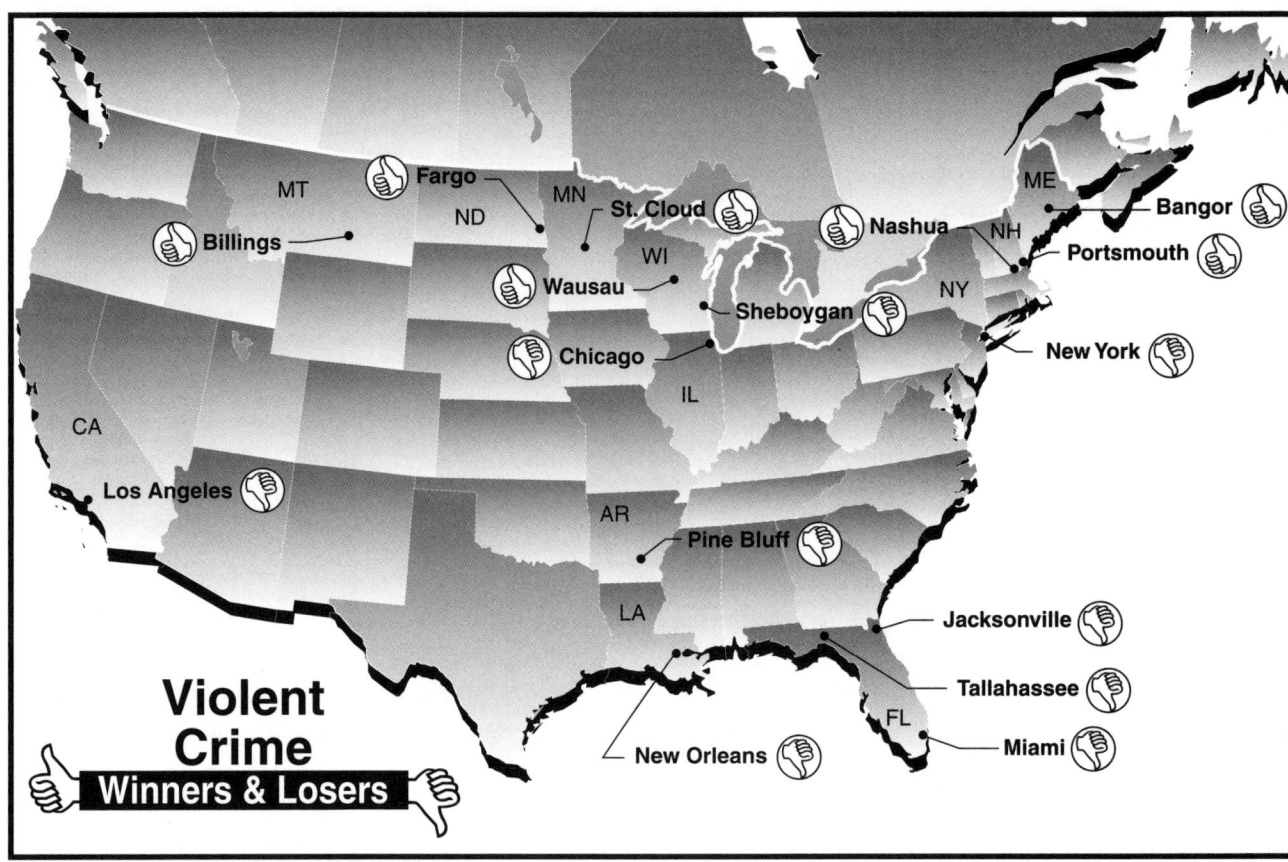

Violent Crime
Winners & Losers

MT
Billings
Fargo
ND
MN
St. Cloud
WI
Wausau
Sheboygan
Chicago
IL
Nashua
ME
NH
Bangor
Portsmouth
NY
New York
CA
Los Angeles
AR
Pine Bluff
LA
New Orleans
Jacksonville
Tallahassee
FL
Miami

Copyright © 2000 by Places Rated Partnership   Cape Ann Mapping

Property Crime
Winners & Losers

BC
Vancouver
SK
Regina
Scranton
Altoona
MA
Pittsfield
Sharon
Johnstown
PA
Hagerstown
OH
MD
Steubenville
WV
Wheeling
AZ
SC
Myrtle Beach
Tucson
Tallahassee
Gainesville
FL
West Palm Beach
Miami

Copyright © 2000 by Places Rated Partnership   Cape Ann Mapping

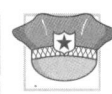

It is possible to see a crime in progress without recognizing it as such. Here are some situations that might be observed in any neighborhood. These are situations a trained police officer would investigate if he or she were making the observation.

SITUATIONS	POSSIBLE SIGNIFICANCE
Situations Involving Vehicles	
Moving vehicles, especially if moving slowly without lights, following an aimless or repetitive course	Casing for a place to rob or burglarize; drug pusher, sex offender, or vandal
Parked, occupied vehicle, especially at an unusual hour	Lookout for burglary in progress (sometimes two people masquerading as lovers)
Vehicle parked in neighbor's drive being loaded with valuables, even if the vehicle looks legitimate, i.e., moving van or commercial van	Burglary or larceny in progress
Abandoned vehicle with or without license plate	Stolen or abandoned after being used in a crime
Persons loitering around parked cars	Burglary of vehicle contents, theft of accessories, vandalism
Persons detaching accessories and mechanical parts	Theft or vandalism
Apparent business transactions from a vehicle near school, park, or quiet residential neighborhood	Drug sales
Persons being forced into vehicle	Kidnapping, rape, robbery
Objects thrown from a moving vehicle	Disposal of contraband
Situations Involving Property	
Property in homes, garages, or storage areas, especially if several items of the same kind such as TVs and bicycles	Storage of stolen property
Property in vehicles, especially meaningful at night or if property is household goods, appliances, unmounted tape decks, stereo equipment	Stolen property, burglary in progress
Property being removed from a house or building; meaningful if residents are at work, on vacation, or known to be absent	Burglary or larceny in progress
Open doors, broken doors or windows, or other signs of a forced entry	Burglary in progress or the scene of a recent burglary
Situations Involving Persons	
Door-to-door solicitors—especially significant if one goes to the back of the house and one stays in front. Can be men or women, clean-cut and well dressed	Casing for burglary, burglary in progress, soliciting violation
Waiting in front of a house	Lookout for burglary in progress
Forced entry or entry through window	Burglary, vandalism, theft
Persons shortcutting through yards	Fleeing the scene of a crime
Persons running, especially if carrying items of value	Fleeing the scene of a crime
Person carrying property, especially if property isn't boxed or wrapped	Offender leaving the scene of a burglary, robbery, or larceny
High volume of human traffic in and out of residence	Drug sales, vice activities, "fence operation"

Assault is simply an attempt, successful or not, to injure another person severely. Assault is usually accompanied by the use of a weapon. Its rate is highest in August, lowest in February, higher in Canada's west and America's west than in other parts of these countries and higher in areas with resort or military economies. With more than one million incidents, it is the most frequently reported violent crime.

Property Crime

Burglary is either forcible entry, unlawful entry where no force is used, or attempted forcible entry, all to commit a felony or theft. Most burglaries, jailed pros say, take hours to plan and minutes to pull off. Two of every three targets are a home or apartment. Nearly half of the incidents involve walking in rather than breaking in. The usual time is between 9am and 11am or between 1pm and 3pm, when you're least likely to be inside. The typical householder's dollar loss is $1,300.

Larceny-theft, after drunk driving and drug offenses, is the most common crime in North America. Skipping out of a self-serve gas station is one example. Shoplifting a Russian sable coat is another. Except for purse snatches and picked pockets, in almost all of the larceny-theft cases, the victim never sees the offender.

Auto theft, it's been said, is a victimless crime because you get over your loss with a check from the insurance company. About one in ten stolen luxury vehicles shows up in third-world showrooms, where a market for used Mercedes, Lexuses, Ford Explorers, and even Harley-Davidson motorcycles flourishes.

The North American auto-theft capitals—Miami, FL, and Vancouver, BC—are ports at opposite ends of the continent. In fact, nearly every metro area with a high auto theft rate is on either coast or near the Mexican border, where cars can be in another country before owners find it gone. Cops in Miami and in Vancouver report an increase in persons arrested who recently arrived from California and New York, where auto insurance fraud and packing ship containers with automobiles are underground arts.

In the continent's interior, though, cars are infrequently stolen for export. In areas like Omaha, Indianapolis, and Winnipeg, choice vehicles are taken to chop shops and plundered for their air bags, seats, and fenders. These high-price components end up at crooked auto repairers for resale as if they were new, legal parts.

Arson was added to the Crime Index in 1979 following a Congressional mandate. It includes any willful or malicious burning or attempt to burn, with or without the intent to defraud, a house, building, car, airplane, or the personal property of someone else. It doesn't include fires of suspicious or unknown origin.

A CAVEAT

Metro areas are rated for personal safety based on the number of crimes actually reported to local police. Yet more than 60 percent of all crime goes unreported, according to national victim surveys, and that percentage can vary from one metro area to another.

Victims in the inner city may believe it futile to file complaints on each missing garden hose, slashed tire, or domestic disturbance, while suburban victims may report every single incident. Even if a complaint is filed, the investigating officer's definition of the crime may change the numbers. Purse-snatching, for instance, is either a robbery or a larceny depending on the jurisdiction. Likewise, a slap in the face is either an aggravated or simple assault depending on motive.

In the past, too, some police departments have either padded the figures to oust a judge considered soft on crime or to persuade the city council to increase the department's budget, or they have fudged the number of crimes to create an image of effective law enforcement.

The Crime Clock

doesn't imply a regularity in crimes committed. It represents the annual ratio of crime to short periods of time.

One Murder
every 29 Minutes

One Forcible Rape
every 5 Minutes

One Robbery
every 2 seconds

One Aggravated Assault
every 31 seconds

One Crime Index Offense
every 2 seconds

One Burglary
every 13 seconds

One Violent Crime
every 19 seconds

One Larceny-Theft
every 4 seconds

One Property Crime
every 3 seconds

One Motor Vehicle Theft
every 23 seconds

Copyright © 2000 by Places Rated Partnership   Cape Ann Mapping

A Caveat

JUDGING CRIME

One problem with understanding crime statistics is the confusion between crime *incidence* and the crime *rate*. Incidence is simply how many crimes are reported in a given place. The more people living in a place, the greater the crime incidence will be. In Quebec City, police investigate some 600 aggravated assaults a year. South of Chicago, police in Kankakee handle a similar number. From these figures, you might think that Quebec's capital is as dangerous as Kankakee. But 693,000 people live in Quebec City and its environs, while just 103,000 live in Kankakee.

A truer measure of safety is the crime rate—the number of crimes per 100,000 people. Quebec City's assault rate is 91. Kankakee's rate is 554, or more than five times that of Quebec City.

Another problem to understanding crime statistics comes from lumping all crimes together. The single offense most often reported to local cops is larceny-theft: a stolen bike, a necklace missing from a jewelry retailer's display case, hubcaps gone from a used-car lot, a customer bolting from a fast-food restaurant. Yet these heists are counted as heavily as homicides to determine an area's crime rate. When it comes to comparing places, this method doesn't realistically show relative danger.

SCORING: CRIME

The realistic way to judge metro areas for personal safety is simple. For each place, *Places Rated* averages the rates for violent and property crimes for the most recent 8-year period; but since property crimes are much less serious than crimes against people, they are given one-tenth the weight of violent crimes. [Note that (1) although rape is a violent crime, figures for rape aren't included in the scoring because comparable data aren't reported for Canada or for Illinois, Michigan, and Minnesota; and (2) although arson has been considered a property crime since 1979, arson figures aren't included in the scoring because they are unavailable for many metro areas.] Each metro area earns its score by adding two factors:

1. Violent crime

   The rates for murder, robbery, and aggravated assault are added together.

2. Property crime

   The rates for burglary, larceny-theft, and motor vehicle theft are totaled, and the result is divided by 10.

The results for each metro area are then scaled into percentiles where 0 is worst, 50 is average, and 100 is best. The higher the score, the safer the metro area.

SCORING EXAMPLES

A small location in southwest Pennsylvania, a larger one in southeast Florida, and an even larger one in Canada's Quebec province are respectively the best, worst, and average metro areas by *Places Rated*'s scoring method for crime.

Best: Johnstown, PA

The one connection most people make with this metro area occurred at the South Fork Fishing and Hunting Club, in 1889, when an earthen dam burst after a week of heavy rain. The resulting flood swept through the Conemaugh River Valley toward Johnstown, 10 miles downstream. Some 2,100 lives were lost. Sixty miles east of Pittsburgh, Johnstown is now a small coal, chemicals, and concrete producing center.

The area has another distinction: Violent and property crime rates here are well below the average as they are for a handful of other post-industrial metro areas near the upper Ohio River valley. While break-ins, bar fights, and an infrequent murder are reported to cops in town and in surrounding Cambria and Somerset counties, Johnstown's score of 100 is still the best among all metro areas in North America.

Average: Montreal, PQ

Is there an area with a score of 50, exactly at the middle on the scale of 0 to 100? No, there isn't. The one coming closest to this mythical mean is Montreal.

With more than 3 million people, Metropolitan Montreal includes a major city and a group of some 80 suburban *villes* on both banks of the lower St. Lawrence River within commuting distance of the great *centre ville*. The city is a frequent site for international police conferences on money laundering and drug trafficking, and the sound of emergency vehicles remind tourists of any large American city.

As in most other Canadian metro areas, property crime here is slightly above average, but violent crime is

a shade below. When its violent crime rate is added to one-tenth its property crime rate and the sum scaled against the average for all metro areas, Greater Montreal earns a score of 50.14. You can't get much closer to 50 than that.

Worst: Miami, FL

Most metro areas in Florida rank near the bottom in personal safety. Of all the states, Florida has the highest rate for both violent crime and property crime. Miami, the state's best-known city, was the tropical backdrop for a bloody Friday-night television series in the early 1980s where undercover narcs and drug lords brandished locally made TEC 9 machine pistols at each other. The city continues to be the setting for Edna Buchanan's, Carl Hiaasen's, and Elmore Leonard's best-selling crime fiction.

Beset by rapid population growth and caught in the crosscurrents of the drug trade, Miami is truly a North American crime capital. Lawbreaking is so startlingly high in this vacation area that a standard item in hotel and rental car packets is a bulletin on guerrilla tactics for staying out of harm's way.

Metro Miami's violent crime rate is nearly four times the metro area average, and its property crime is more than twice that average. How dangerous is that? On a scale of 0 to 100 where the metro area average is 50, Miami earns a 0.

RANKINGS: CRIME

In ranking each metro area for relative safety, *Places Rated* adds two numbers: (1) its violent crime rate and (2) its property crime rate divided by 10. The result is then scaled into percentiles where 0 is worst, 50 average, and 100 best. The higher the percentile, the safer the metro area. Places that are tied get the same rank and are listed in alphabetical order.

Metro Areas from Best to Worst

RANK	SCORE
1. Johnstown, PA	100.00
2. Nashua, NH	99.72
3. Wausau, WI	99.44
4. Parkersburg-Marietta, WV-OH	99.16
5. Altoona, PA	98.87
6. State College, PA	98.59
7. Portsmouth-Rochester, NH-ME	98.31
8. St. Cloud, MN	98.02
9. Appleton-Oshkosh-Neenah, WI	97.74
10. Wheeling, WV-OH	97.46
11. Scranton–Wilkes-Barre–Hazleton, PA	97.17
12. Sharon, PA	96.89
13. Danbury, CT	96.61
14. Steubenville-Weirton, OH-WV	96.32
15. Binghamton, NY	96.04
16. Lancaster, PA	95.76
17. Eau Claire, WI	95.47
18. Bismarck, ND	95.19
19. Fargo-Moorhead, ND-MN	94.91
20. La Crosse, WI-MN	94.62
21. Bangor, ME	94.34
22. Sheboygan, WI	94.06
23. York, PA	93.77
24. Utica-Rome, NY	93.49
25. Williamsport, PA	93.21
26. Rochester, MN	92.92
27. Danville, VA	92.64
28. Grand Forks, ND-MN	92.36
29. Dubuque, IA	92.07
30. Bloomington-Normal, IL	91.79
31. Lewiston-Auburn, ME	91.51

RANK	SCORE
32. Provo-Orem, UT	91.22
33. Johnson City-Kingsport-Bristol, TN-VA	90.94
34. Fayetteville-Springdale-Rogers, AR	90.66
35. Huntington-Ashland, WV-KY-OH	90.37
36. New London-Norwich, CT-RI	90.09
37. Allentown-Bethlehem-Easton, PA	89.81
38. Hagerstown, MD	89.52
39. Owensboro, KY	89.24
40. Florence, AL	88.96
41. Saint John, NB	88.67
42. Punta Gorda, FL	88.39
43. St. John's, NF	88.11
44. Duluth-Superior, MN-WI	87.82
45. Long Island, NY	87.54
46. Middlesex-Somerset-Hunterdon, NJ	87.26
47. Jamestown, NY	86.97
48. Pittsfield, MA	86.69
49. Monmouth-Ocean, NJ	86.41
50. Fort Collins-Loveland, CO	86.12
51. Green Bay, WI	85.84
52. Decatur, AL	85.56
53. Manchester, NH	85.27
54. Cheyenne, WY	84.99
55. Chicoutimi-Jonquiere, PQ	84.71
56. Cumberland, MD-WV	84.42
57. Pittsburgh, PA	84.14
58. Brazoria, TX	83.86
59. Elmira, NY	83.57
60. Syracuse, NY	83.29
61. Oshawa, ON	83.01
62. Erie, PA	82.72

RANK	SCORE
63. Billings, MT	82.44
64. Bloomington, IN	82.16
65. Lafayette, IN	81.87
66. Olympia, WA	81.59
67. Dutchess County, NY	81.31
68. Kitchener-Waterloo, ON	81.02
69. Lynchburg, VA	80.74
70. Charlottesville, VA	80.46
71. Sioux Falls, SD	80.17
72. Stamford-Norwalk, CT	79.89
73. Harrisburg-Lebanon-Carlisle, PA	79.61
74. Newburgh, NY-PA	79.33
75. Glens Falls, NY	79.04
76. Jacksonville, NC	78.76
77. Missoula, MT	78.48
78. Kenosha, WI	78.19
79. Iowa City, IA	77.91
80. Bremerton, WA	77.63
81. Joplin, MO	77.34
82. Trois-Rivieres, PQ	77.06
83. Sherbrooke, PQ	76.78
84. Kokomo, IN	76.49
85. Bergen-Passaic, NJ	76.21
86. Portland, ME	75.93
87. Fort Walton Beach, FL	75.64
88. Janesville-Beloit, WI	75.36
89. Reading, PA	75.08
90. Madison, WI	74.79
91. St. Catharines-Niagara, ON	74.51
92. Boulder-Longmont, CO	74.23
93. Albany-Schenectady-Troy, NY	73.94
94. Quebec City, PQ	73.66
95. Roanoke, VA	73.38
96. Hickory-Morganton-Lenoir, NC	73.09
97. Charleston, WV	72.81
98. Windsor, ON	72.53
99. Burlington, VT	72.24
100. Boise City, ID	71.96
101. Grand Junction, CO	71.68
102. Rochester, NY	71.39
103. Bellingham, WA	71.11
104. Fort Wayne, IN	70.83
105. Waterloo-Cedar Falls, IA	70.54
106. Ann Arbor, MI	70.26
107. Ventura, CA	69.98
108. Springfield, MO	69.69
109. Cedar Rapids, IA	69.41
110. Pocatello, ID	69.13
111. San Luis Obispo-Atascadero-Paso Robles, CA	68.84
112. Asheville, NC	68.56
113. Fort Smith, AR-OK	68.28
114. Providence-Fall River-Warwick, RI-MA	67.99
115. Toronto, ON	67.71
116. Richland-Kennewick-Pasco, WA	67.43
117. Jonesboro, AR	67.14
118. Greeley, CO	66.86
119. Chico-Paradise, CA	66.58
120. Santa Barbara-Santa Maria-Lompoc, CA	66.29
121. Hamilton, ON	66.01
122. Santa Rosa, CA	65.73
123. Killeen-Temple, TX	65.44
124. Rapid City, SD	65.16

RANK	SCORE
125. St. Joseph, MO	64.88
126. Medford-Ashland, OR	64.59
127. Great Falls, MT	64.31
128. Sudbury, ON	64.03
129. Muncie, IN	63.74
130. Des Moines, IA	63.46
131. Worcester, MA-CT	63.18
132. Houma, LA	62.89
133. Minneapolis-St. Paul, MN-WI	62.61
134. Honolulu, HI	62.33
135. Columbia, MO	62.04
136. London, ON	61.76
137. Colorado Springs, CO	61.48
138. Ottawa-Hull, ON-PQ	61.19
139. Salem, OR	60.91
140. Lowell, MA-NH	60.63
141. San Jose, CA	60.34
142. Eugene-Springfield, OR	60.06
143. Canton-Massillon, OH	59.78
144. Waterbury, CT	59.50
145. Elkhart-Goshen, IN	59.21
146. Davenport-Moline-Rock Island, IA-IL	58.93
147. Racine, WI	58.65
148. Hartford, CT	58.36
149. Lawrence, MA-NH	58.08
150. Sherman-Denison, TX	57.80
151. Lafayette, LA	57.51
152. Casper, WY	57.23
153. Grand Rapids-Muskegon-Holland, MI	56.95
154. Orange County, CA	56.66
155. Evansville-Henderson, IN-KY	56.38
156. Cleveland-Lorain-Elyria, OH	56.10
157. Cincinnati, OH-KY-IN	55.81
158. Columbus, GA-AL	55.53
159. Redding, CA	55.25
160. Wilmington-Newark, DE-MD	54.96
161. Dothan, AL	54.68
162. South Bend, IN	54.40
163. Akron, OH	54.11
164. Salt Lake City-Ogden, UT	53.83
165. Milwaukee-Waukesha, WI	53.55
166. Dover, DE	53.26
167. Las Cruces, NM	52.98
168. Calgary, AB	52.70
169. Peoria-Pekin, IL	52.41
170. Lansing-East Lansing, MI	52.13
171. Fitchburg-Leominster, MA	51.85
172. Louisville, KY-IN	51.56
173. Trenton, NJ	51.28
174. Flagstaff, AZ-UT	51.00
175. Youngstown-Warren, OH	50.71
176. Merced, CA	50.43
177. Montreal, PQ	50.15
178. Dayton-Springfield, OH	49.86
179. Abilene, TX	49.58
180. Spokane, WA	49.30
181. San Angelo, TX	49.01
182. Bryan-College Station, TX	48.73
183. Lawrence, KS	48.45
184. Hattiesburg, MS	48.16
185. Brockton, MA	47.88

continues

Metro Areas from Best to Worst (cont.)

RANK	SCORE
186. Bridgeport, CT	47.60
187. Saskatoon, SK	47.31
188. Decatur, IL	47.03
189. Boston, MA-NH	46.75
190. Richmond-Petersburg, VA	46.46
191. Champaign-Urbana, IL	46.18
192. Barnstable-Yarmouth, MA	45.90
193. Reno, NV	45.61
194. Philadelphia, PA-NJ	45.33
195. Seattle-Bellevue-Everett, WA	45.05
196. Hamilton-Middletown, OH	44.76
197. Edmonton, AB	44.48
198. Victoria, BC	44.20
199. Augusta-Aiken, GA-SC	43.91
200. Norfolk-Virginia Beach-Newport News, VA-NC	43.63
201. Huntsville, AL	43.35
202. Salinas, CA	43.06
203. Jackson, MI	42.78
204. Denver, CO	42.50
205. Longview-Marshall, TX	42.21
206. Omaha, NE-IA	41.93
207. Macon, GA	41.65
208. Biloxi-Gulfport-Pascagoula, MS	41.36
209. Toledo, OH	41.08
210. Raleigh-Durham-Chapel Hill, NC	40.80
211. Terre Haute, IN	40.51
212. Austin-San Marcos, TX	40.23
213. Buffalo-Niagara Falls, NY	39.95
214. Santa Cruz-Watsonville, CA	39.67
215. Fort Myers-Cape Coral, FL	39.38
216. Lincoln, NE	39.10
217. Santa Fe, NM	38.82
218. Texarkana, TX-Texarkana, AR	38.53
219. Washington, DC-MD-VA-WV	38.25
220. Thunder Bay, ON	37.97
221. New Haven-Meriden, CT	37.68
222. Saginaw-Bay City-Midland, MI	37.40
223. Visalia-Tulare-Porterville, CA	37.12
224. Athens, GA	36.83
225. Yolo, CA	36.55
226. Lexington, KY	36.27
227. Rocky Mount, NC	35.98
228. McAllen-Edinburg-Mission, TX	35.70
229. Greensboro–Winston-Salem–High Point, NC	35.42
230. Brownsville-Harlingen-San Benito, TX	35.13
231. Halifax, NS	34.85
232. Mansfield, OH	34.57
233. Columbus, OH	34.28
234. Odessa-Midland, TX	34.00
235. Montgomery, AL	33.72
236. Vallejo-Fairfield-Napa, CA	33.43
237. Goldsboro, NC	33.15
238. Portland-Vancouver, OR-WA	32.87
239. Kalamazoo-Battle Creek, MI	32.58
240. Springfield, IL	32.30
241. Lubbock, TX	32.02
242. Naples, FL	31.73
243. Tulsa, OK	31.45
244. Indianapolis, IN	31.17
245. Yakima, WA	30.88
246. Lawton, OK	30.60

RANK	SCORE
247. Knoxville, TN	30.32
248. Panama City, FL	30.03
249. Fort Pierce-Port St. Lucie, FL	29.75
250. Clarksville-Hopkinsville, TN-KY	29.47
251. Tyler, TX	29.18
252. Yuma, AZ	28.90
253. Amarillo, TX	28.62
254. Wichita Falls, TX	28.33
255. Wilmington, NC	28.05
256. Winnipeg, MB	27.77
257. Sioux City, IA-NE	27.48
258. San Antonio, TX	27.20
259. Enid, OK	26.92
260. Melbourne-Titusville-Palm Bay, FL	26.63
261. Daytona Beach, FL	26.35
262. New Bedford, MA	26.07
263. Wichita, KS	25.78
264. Laredo, TX	25.50
265. San Diego, CA	25.22
266. Anchorage, AK	24.93
267. Houston, TX	24.65
268. Rockford, IL	24.37
269. Bakersfield, CA	24.08
270. Savannah, GA	23.80
271. Yuba City, CA	23.52
272. St. Louis, MO-IL	23.23
273. Anniston, AL	22.95
274. Chattanooga, TN-GA	22.67
275. Sacramento, CA	22.38
276. Beaumont-Port Arthur, TX	22.10
277. Vineland-Millville-Bridgeton, NJ	21.82
278. Jackson, MS	21.53
279. Victoria, TX	21.25
280. Lima, OH	20.97
281. Phoenix-Mesa, AZ	20.68
282. Fort Worth-Arlington, TX	20.40
283. Springfield, MA	20.12
284. Regina, SK	19.84
285. Kankakee, IL	19.55
286. Tacoma, WA	19.27
287. Sarasota-Bradenton, FL	18.99
288. Gary, IN	18.70
289. Oklahoma City, OK	18.42
290. Newark, NJ	18.14
291. San Francisco, CA	17.85
292. Galveston-Texas City, TX	17.57
293. Greenville, NC	17.29
294. Detroit, MI	17.00
295. Las Vegas, NV-AZ	16.72
296. Modesto, CA	16.44
297. Greenville-Spartanburg-Anderson, SC	16.15
298. Corpus Christi, TX	15.87
299. Albany, GA	15.59
300. Gadsden, AL	15.30
301. Charleston-North Charleston, SC	15.02
302. Waco, TX	14.74
303. Vancouver, BC	14.45
304. Birmingham, AL	14.17
305. Riverside-San Bernardino, CA	13.89
306. Benton Harbor, MI	13.60
307. Atlantic-Cape May, NJ	13.32

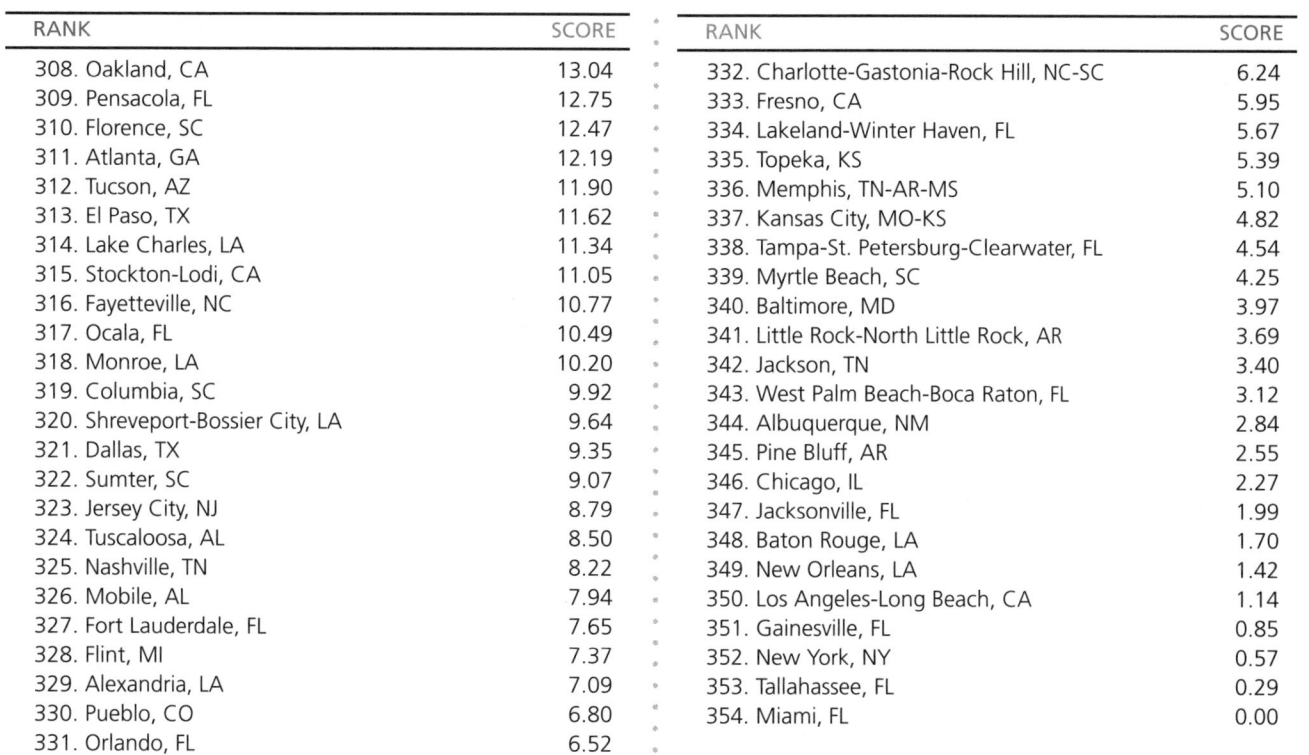

RANK	SCORE
308. Oakland, CA	13.04
309. Pensacola, FL	12.75
310. Florence, SC	12.47
311. Atlanta, GA	12.19
312. Tucson, AZ	11.90
313. El Paso, TX	11.62
314. Lake Charles, LA	11.34
315. Stockton-Lodi, CA	11.05
316. Fayetteville, NC	10.77
317. Ocala, FL	10.49
318. Monroe, LA	10.20
319. Columbia, SC	9.92
320. Shreveport-Bossier City, LA	9.64
321. Dallas, TX	9.35
322. Sumter, SC	9.07
323. Jersey City, NJ	8.79
324. Tuscaloosa, AL	8.50
325. Nashville, TN	8.22
326. Mobile, AL	7.94
327. Fort Lauderdale, FL	7.65
328. Flint, MI	7.37
329. Alexandria, LA	7.09
330. Pueblo, CO	6.80
331. Orlando, FL	6.52

RANK	SCORE
332. Charlotte-Gastonia-Rock Hill, NC-SC	6.24
333. Fresno, CA	5.95
334. Lakeland-Winter Haven, FL	5.67
335. Topeka, KS	5.39
336. Memphis, TN-AR-MS	5.10
337. Kansas City, MO-KS	4.82
338. Tampa-St. Petersburg-Clearwater, FL	4.54
339. Myrtle Beach, SC	4.25
340. Baltimore, MD	3.97
341. Little Rock-North Little Rock, AR	3.69
342. Jackson, TN	3.40
343. West Palm Beach-Boca Raton, FL	3.12
344. Albuquerque, NM	2.84
345. Pine Bluff, AR	2.55
346. Chicago, IL	2.27
347. Jacksonville, FL	1.99
348. Baton Rouge, LA	1.70
349. New Orleans, LA	1.42
350. Los Angeles-Long Beach, CA	1.14
351. Gainesville, FL	0.85
352. New York, NY	0.57
353. Tallahassee, FL	0.29
354. Miami, FL	0.00

PLACE PROFILES: CRIME

The following Place Profiles show each metro area's average annual rates for seven crimes: murder, rape, robbery, aggravated assault, burglary, larceny-theft, and motor vehicle theft for the latest 8 years for which data are available. The rates for these crimes are grouped into violent and property categories, and a total rate for each of these categories is given.

Note: Although figures for rape are shown for most metro areas, they aren't included in the scoring because comparable data are unavailable for jurisdictions in Illinois, Michigan, and Minnesota, and for all of Canada.

Figures for the United States are derived from the FBI's *Crime in the United States* for the latest 8 years for which data are available, and from the Bureau's unpublished "Crime by County" reports for each of these years. For American metro areas not included in either of the FBI's sources, figures are derived from surveying state Uniform Crime Reporting programs.

Canadian figures are derived from the Centre for Justice Statistics' unpublished "Table 3" reports for the latest 8 years for which data are available.

The next to the last column indicates the crime trend. Most metro areas are reporting falling crime, though a few are seeing rising rates. If an area's trend is statistically significant, that is, if it definitely points up or down over time, the trend is depicted by an arrow. Eleven metro areas have an arrow pointing upward (↑), meaning their *Places Rated* crime rates during this period are up. Seventy-one metro areas have an arrow pointing downward (↓), meaning their crime rates are definitely falling. A blank cell means the *Places Rated* crime score is essentially unchanged. A star (★) to the left of a metro area's name highlights it as one of the top 35 places for safety from crime.

METRO AREA	___ Violent Crime Rates ___					___ Property Crime Rates ___				SCORE	TREND	RANK
	MURDER	RAPE	ROBBERY	ASSAULT	TOTAL	BURGLARY	THEFT	AUTO THEFT	TOTAL			
Metro Area Average	6.5	42.6	155.6	383.4	546	1,160	3,358	457	4,975	50.00	↓	
Abilene, TX	6.0	66.8	120.1	456.3	582	1,164	3,040	192	4,396	49.58		179
Akron, OH	5.0	49.9	181.6	331.8	518	918	3,157	452	4,527	54.11		163
Albany, GA	14.0	61.0	333.6	413.3	761	2,279	4,338	419	7,036	15.59		299
Albany-Schenectady-Troy, NY	2.7	24.5	109.7	252.9	365	870	2,489	172	3,531	73.94		93
Albuquerque, NM	10.8	60.7	273.7	848.3	1,133	1,853	4,587	822	7,261	2.84		344
Alexandria, LA	10.9	42.2	125.6	963.9	1,100	1,414	3,841	326	5,581	7.09		329
Allentown-Bethlehem-Easton, PA	2.8	19.2	81.2	142.2	226	628	2,317	207	3,153	89.81		37
★ Altoona, PA	1.1	27.5	41.6	118.9	162	613	1,473	155	2,240	98.87		5
Amarillo, TX	9.3	47.6	132.5	445.8	588	1,372	4,937	338	6,646	28.62		253
Anchorage, AK	8.8	88.9	227.7	490.5	727	924	4,204	681	5,808	24.93	↓	266
Ann Arbor, MI	2.7	51.3	83.0	269.9	356	795	3,016	267	4,078	70.26	↓	106
Anniston, AL	9.9	43.3	153.1	719.0	882	1,356	2,993	258	4,607	22.95		273
★ Appleton-Oshkosh-Neenah, WI	1.3	11.7	11.4	71.6	84	471	2,675	102	3,247	97.74	↓	9
Asheville, NC	7.0	28.1	102.0	262.5	372	1,177	2,598	288	4,063	68.56		112
Athens, GA	8.6	46.7	180.6	362.4	551	1,411	4,324	471	6,207	36.83		224
Atlanta, GA	11.5	47.1	343.6	479.3	834	1,456	4,410	921	6,787	12.19		311
Atlantic-Cape May, NJ	6.7	55.0	280.5	429.6	717	1,460	6,004	345	7,809	13.32	↓	307
Augusta-Aiken, GA-SC	13.1	44.6	202.0	377.3	592	1,469	2,922	562	4,952	43.91		199
Austin-San Marcos, TX	6.1	51.4	176.4	299.2	482	1,437	4,575	544	6,557	40.23		212
Bakersfield, CA	11.0	36.0	187.3	596.1	794	1,510	3,204	572	5,286	24.08	↓	269
Baltimore, MD	15.7	48.0	573.6	632.7	1,222	1,275	3,779	806	5,860	3.97		340
★ Bangor, ME	3.0	22.3	30.1	54.4	87	594	3,171	137	3,901	94.34		21
Barnstable-Yarmouth, MA	1.6	27.6	31.5	689.1	722	1,121	2,135	192	3,448	45.90	↓	192
Baton Rouge, LA	16.5	44.1	313.8	855.3	1,186	1,761	5,138	860	7,759	1.70		348
Beaumont-Port Arthur, TX	9.7	74.6	246.7	501.3	758	1,611	3,713	562	5,887	22.10	↓	276
Bellingham, WA	2.8	63.8	45.3	181.0	229	1,003	3,988	238	5,229	71.11		103
Benton Harbor, MI	8.9	85.7	163.8	748.1	921	1,408	3,979	370	5,757	13.60	↓	306
Bergen-Passaic, NJ	2.8	14.7	156.4	183.5	343	656	2,194	554	3,404	76.21	↓	85
Billings, MT	4.4	21.4	54.2	47.2	106	933	3,951	318	5,202	82.44		63
Biloxi-Gulfport-Pascagoula, MS	12.7	107.5	189.2	321.4	523	1,883	3,636	434	5,953	41.36		208
★ Binghamton, NY	2.8	20.4	34.9	131.0	169	530	2,314	83	2,927	96.04		15
Birmingham, AL	19.4	49.0	297.3	625.8	942	1,337	3,335	680	5,352	14.17	↓	304
★ Bismarck, ND	2.1	23.4	10.3	104.7	117	461	2,894	178	3,532	95.19		18
Bloomington, IN	1.6	21.6	16.5	285.7	304	586	2,451	191	3,228	82.16		64
★ Bloomington-Normal, IL	4.2	n.a.	29.0	143.7	177	724	2,474	92	3,291	91.79		30
Boise City, ID	2.4	36.5	29.2	249.5	281	882	3,455	232	4,569	71.96		100
Boston, MA-NH	4.1	28.2	202.4	468.9	675	799	2,297	762	3,858	46.75	↓	189
Boulder-Longmont, CO	2.1	42.7	37.2	163.4	203	944	3,971	233	5,149	74.23		92
Brazoria, TX	4.6	35.8	41.3	244.9	291	738	2,173	268	3,179	83.86		58
Bremerton, WA	3.1	65.2	54.4	216.1	274	848	2,883	243	3,974	77.63		80
Bridgeport, CT	11.7	24.5	324.7	257.9	594	1,162	2,350	1,107	4,620	47.60		186
Brockton, MA	4.3	27.8	154.9	493.9	653	1,088	1,899	1,000	3,987	47.88		185
Brownsville-Harlingen-San Benito, TX	9.3	19.8	112.8	455.3	577	1,586	4,052	459	6,096	35.13		230
Bryan-College Station, TX	3.9	59.9	96.7	362.2	463	1,184	4,207	306	5,697	48.73		182
Buffalo-Niagara Falls, NY	6.5	37.3	284.5	404.9	696	1,108	2,726	602	4,435	39.95		213
Burlington, VT	3.1	42.5	36.1	143.4	183	1,176	4,105	257	5,537	72.24		99
Calgary, AB	2.2	n.a.	132.6	231.7	366	1,500	3,856	834	6,191	52.70		168
Canton-Massillon, OH	4.5	40.4	199.4	246.6	451	1,075	2,833	665	4,574	59.78		143
Casper, WY	3.2	34.2	34.7	321.5	359	1,274	4,263	293	5,830	57.23		152
Cedar Rapids, IA	1.2	9.4	56.6	195.2	253	963	3,936	237	5,137	69.41		109
Champaign-Urbana, IL	4.0	n.a.	137.7	371.6	513	1,286	4,017	223	5,526	46.18		191
Charleston, WV	7.0	29.2	122.2	212.8	342	892	2,677	340	3,909	72.81		97
Charleston-North Charleston, SC	8.5	57.9	199.7	673.5	882	1,298	4,007	546	5,851	15.02		301
Charlotte-Gastonia-Rock Hill, NC-SC	12.7	46.2	309.0	747.7	1,069	1,691	4,080	401	6,172	6.24		332
Charlottesville, VA	4.9	33.3	69.3	195.9	270	582	2,974	173	3,729	80.46		70
Chattanooga, TN-GA	11.5	46.8	213.2	611.1	836	1,334	3,087	657	5,078	22.67		274
Cheyenne, WY	2.5	41.9	28.0	140.7	171	469	3,678	130	4,277	84.99		54
Chicago, IL	15.7	n.a.	644.9	725.1	1,386	1,188	3,581	907	5,676	2.27		346
Chico-Paradise, CA	4.9	44.7	68.6	307.9	381	1,290	2,867	356	4,513	66.58		119
Chicoutimi-Jonquiere, PQ	0.9	n.a.	56.6	125.9	183	1,562	2,077	528	4,167	84.71		55
Cincinnati, OH-KY-IN	4.5	52.2	193.3	321.7	520	927	3,187	265	4,378	55.81		157
Clarksville-Hopkinsville, TN-KY	7.7	60.2	91.9	753.4	853	1,033	2,647	192	3,873	29.47		250
Cleveland-Lorain-Elyria, OH	10.8	62.9	305.5	246.0	562	905	2,142	825	3,872	56.10		156
Colorado Springs, CO	4.8	58.5	97.0	261.4	363	1,039	3,894	317	5,250	61.48		137
Columbia, MO	3.6	35.1	92.5	302.6	399	708	3,980	182	4,869	62.04		135
Columbia, SC	10.2	68.0	278.6	701.5	990	1,352	3,922	535	5,809	9.92		319
Columbus, GA-AL	9.7	29.3	168.4	292.5	471	1,083	3,427	370	4,881	55.53		158
Columbus, OH	8.5	65.7	309.1	288.8	606	1,430	3,790	678	5,898	34.28		233
Corpus Christi, TX	8.3	61.2	141.0	532.1	681	1,579	5,731	457	7,767	15.87		298
Cumberland, MD-WV	1.6	18.3	18.8	330.4	351	535	1,892	98	2,526	84.42		56
Dallas, TX	14.9	57.0	344.0	561.9	921	1,508	4,233	974	6,715	9.35	↓	321

METRO AREA	MURDER	RAPE	ROBBERY	ASSAULT	TOTAL	BURGLARY	THEFT	AUTO THEFT	TOTAL	SCORE	TREND	RANK
Metro Area Average	6.5	42.6	155.6	383.4	546	1,160	3,358	457	4,975	50.00	↓	
★ Danbury, CT	1.8	11.3	47.5	78.6	128	605	2,248	277	3,131	96.61	↓	13
★ Danville, VA	10.7	27.2	86.9	129.9	227	556	2,016	149	2,721	92.64	↑	27
Davenport-Moline-Rock Island, IA-IL	2.8	14.9	96.2	381.2	480	1,002	3,291	159	4,453	58.93		146
Dayton-Springfield, OH	7.5	60.8	226.2	296.4	530	1,006	3,354	559	4,920	49.86		178
Daytona Beach, FL	5.5	52.2	185.1	569.1	760	1,608	3,319	419	5,346	26.35		261
Decatur, AL	5.9	21.0	69.3	166.7	242	827	2,412	193	3,431	85.56		52
Decatur, IL	5.1	n.a.	146.2	416.6	568	1,241	3,515	149	4,905	47.03		188
Denver, CO	6.7	47.5	156.4	404.6	568	1,124	3,579	630	5,333	42.50	↓	204
Des Moines, IA	3.8	29.9	86.5	229.0	319	842	4,325	338	5,505	63.46		130
Detroit, MI	15.0	52.1	345.2	525.2	885	1,054	3,346	1,121	5,522	17.00	↓	294
Dothan, AL	8.6	30.7	99.1	465.2	573	881	2,850	188	3,919	54.68		161
Dover, DE	3.7	101.2	113.4	438.5	556	845	3,196	211	4,253	53.26		166
★ Dubuque, IA	0.7	33.3	15.7	187.0	203	616	2,224	154	2,994	92.07		29
Duluth-Superior, MN-WI	2.7	46.2	36.6	134.0	173	827	2,768	239	3,834	87.82		44
Dutchess County, NY	3.8	17.3	102.9	248.3	355	601	2,057	140	2,797	81.31		67
★ Eau Claire, WI	1.2	9.8	15.5	96.3	113	628	2,805	138	3,571	95.47		17
Edmonton, AB	3.1	n.a.	161.8	241.9	407	1,670	4,189	810	6,669	44.48		197
El Paso, TX	7.2	46.7	212.7	637.6	858	1,053	5,049	774	6,875	11.62		313
Elkhart-Goshen, IN	4.4	39.6	92.8	367.6	465	930	3,372	259	4,561	59.21		145
Elmira, NY	2.6	27.1	41.3	198.4	242	610	2,994	80	3,684	83.57		59
Enid, OK	5.9	53.6	84.3	548.0	638	1,561	4,501	338	6,400	26.92	↓	259
Erie, PA	2.7	38.7	139.6	167.0	309	688	2,212	219	3,119	82.72		62
Eugene-Springfield, OR	2.5	44.9	113.1	193.9	309	1,219	4,350	384	5,952	60.06		142
Evansville-Henderson, IN-KY	4.5	31.2	74.4	458.8	538	918	2,946	231	4,095	56.38		155
★ Fargo-Moorhead, ND-MN	1.2	31.8	16.6	67.2	85	486	3,154	215	3,855	94.91	↓	19
Fayetteville, NC	14.3	64.2	287.1	542.6	844	2,070	4,523	538	7,132	10.77	↓	316
★ Fayetteville-Springdale-Rogers, AR	4.1	29.8	22.9	148.8	176	699	2,735	196	3,630	90.66		34
Fitchburg-Leominster, MA	1.7	43.0	83.7	561.0	646	991	2,112	383	3,487	51.85		171
Flagstaff, AZ-UT	4.9	42.7	56.1	325.4	386	965	5,006	214	6,185	51.00		174
Flint, MI	12.8	65.6	286.3	741.2	1,040	1,587	3,733	809	6,130	7.37	↓	328
Florence, AL	4.8	12.9	39.9	208.1	253	594	2,221	103	2,919	88.96		40
Florence, SC	12.5	64.3	188.3	756.9	958	1,567	3,601	355	5,523	12.47	↓	310
Fort Collins-Loveland, CO	1.6	52.4	20.5	191.4	213	607	2,902	138	3,647	86.12		50
Fort Lauderdale, FL	6.9	38.0	341.4	540.7	889	1,711	4,888	967	7,567	7.65		327
Fort Myers-Cape Coral, FL	6.6	50.8	215.2	395.3	617	1,456	3,120	705	5,282	39.38		215
Fort Pierce-Port St. Lucie, FL	8.4	48.7	173.8	538.2	720	1,589	3,208	401	5,198	29.75		249
Fort Smith, AR-OK	5.8	40.2	50.1	300.8	357	906	3,142	305	4,353	68.28		113
Fort Walton Beach, FL	2.8	19.0	60.9	292.8	357	787	2,418	176	3,381	75.64		87
Fort Wayne, IN	7.0	32.6	134.7	171.3	313	762	3,163	480	4,405	70.83		104
Fort Worth-Arlington, TX	11.2	56.4	243.7	487.6	743	1,448	4,174	845	6,468	20.40	↓	282
Fresno, CA	14.2	51.0	356.8	644.5	1,015	1,682	3,636	1,757	7,075	5.95	↓	333
Gadsden, AL	10.8	42.0	164.6	758.9	934	1,288	3,583	445	5,316	15.30	↑	300
Gainesville, FL	8.0	77.7	281.2	938.4	1,228	2,309	5,750	588	8,647	0.85		351
Galveston-Texas City, TX	13.6	61.3	227.1	549.0	790	1,570	4,212	647	6,430	17.57	↓	292
Gary, IN	18.6	44.7	231.2	679.7	929	975	2,778	1,064	4,817	18.70	↑	288
Glens Falls, NY	2.2	21.6	14.8	346.2	363	600	2,206	73	2,879	79.04		75
Goldsboro, NC	12.2	30.7	184.8	507.4	704	1,471	3,237	306	5,014	33.15	↓	237
★ Grand Forks, ND-MN	1.0	24.9	14.9	96.8	113	502	3,114	256	3,872	92.36		28
Grand Junction, CO	6.0	27.9	38.0	211.4	255	954	3,668	218	4,840	71.68		101
Grand Rapids-Muskegon-Holland, MI	4.2	58.6	121.5	377.9	504	985	3,129	288	4,403	56.95	↓	153
Great Falls, MT	11.5	58.8	37.8	123.6	173	909	5,683	313	6,905	64.31		127
Greeley, CO	4.4	44.1	45.0	247.9	297	1,029	3,889	255	5,174	66.86		118
Green Bay, WI	1.6	27.8	28.7	185.3	216	505	2,980	157	3,643	85.84	↓	51
Greensboro–Winston-Salem–High Point, NC	9.2	37.7	205.7	428.1	643	1,565	3,540	331	5,436	35.42	↓	229
Greenville, NC	11.3	45.5	217.3	541.6	770	2,113	4,212	331	6,655	17.29		293
Greenville-Spartanburg-Anderson, SC	8.5	48.9	168.6	782.8	960	1,283	3,339	349	4,972	16.15		297
Hagerstown, MD	3.3	21.6	60.2	242.5	306	543	1,658	157	2,357	89.52		38
Halifax, NS	2.5	n.a.	129.6	339.4	472	1,710	4,941	516	7,167	34.85		231
Hamilton, ON	2.1	n.a.	90.7	219.2	312	1,214	3,283	808	5,306	66.01		121
Hamilton-Middletown, OH	4.6	51.0	141.0	416.7	562	1,181	3,616	313	5,110	44.76		196
Harrisburg-Lebanon-Carlisle, PA	4.7	27.7	131.2	207.8	344	582	2,249	238	3,069	79.61	↓	73
Hartford, CT	4.3	27.9	212.8	273.0	490	992	2,819	584	4,395	58.36	↓	148
Hattiesburg, MS	9.9	47.6	106.6	398.3	515	1,547	3,547	213	5,307	48.16		184
Hickory-Morganton-Lenoir, NC	8.0	26.1	80.5	267.7	356	1,095	2,477	195	3,766	73.09		96
Honolulu, HI	3.7	30.6	127.8	127.1	259	1,092	4,562	565	6,219	62.33		134
Houma, LA	7.0	30.6	99.2	426.8	533	942	2,273	204	3,419	62.89		132
Houston, TX	15.2	51.8	318.7	428.6	763	1,267	3,090	1,143	5,500	24.65		267

METRO AREA	Violent Crime Rates						Property Crime Rates					SCORE	TREND	RANK
	MURDER	RAPE	ROBBERY	ASSAULT	TOTAL		BURGLARY	THEFT	AUTO THEFT	TOTAL				
Metro Area Average	6.5	42.6	155.6	383.4	546		1,160	3,358	457	4,975		50.00	↓	
★ Huntington-Ashland, WV-KY-OH	4.7	41.2	66.4	167.3	238		763	2,091	159	3,013		90.37		35
Huntsville, AL	7.4	32.4	125.9	442.5	576		1,032	3,785	357	5,174		43.35		201
Indianapolis, IN	10.0	63.2	241.8	446.7	698		1,211	3,343	704	5,258		31.17		244
Iowa City, IA	1.0	32.9	27.1	314.4	343		669	2,476	129	3,274		77.91		79
Jackson, MI	5.0	85.1	77.2	627.5	710		745	2,909	218	3,873		42.78		203
Jackson, MS	21.9	60.7	361.5	289.4	673		2,132	3,843	985	6,960		21.53	↓	278
Jackson, TN	14.9	63.2	284.4	843.3	1,143		1,724	4,509	510	6,743		3.40		342
Jacksonville, FL	14.0	83.6	391.1	843.0	1,248		1,902	4,356	815	7,073		1.99		347
Jacksonville, NC	4.6	29.6	85.0	179.4	269		1,109	2,586	200	3,896		78.76		76
Jamestown, NY	1.7	17.9	43.3	175.9	221		728	2,597	101	3,427		86.97	↓	47
Janesville-Beloit, WI	2.2	29.0	62.6	156.5	221		815	3,716	214	4,745		75.36		88
Jersey City, NJ	7.0	25.3	547.5	499.0	1,053		1,358	2,732	1,385	5,475		8.79	↓	323
★ Johnson City-Kingsport-Bristol, TN-VA	4.1	25.0	29.9	221.7	256		664	1,933	185	2,781		90.94	↑	33
★ Johnstown, PA	2.0	17.6	27.4	149.9	179		425	962	116	1,503		100.00		1
Jonesboro, AR	6.6	38.4	99.1	249.6	355		1,254	2,938	277	4,468		67.14		117
Joplin, MO	3.8	28.2	51.4	166.5	222		1,024	3,234	265	4,523		77.34		81
Kalamazoo-Battle Creek, MI	6.2	62.3	142.0	541.1	689		1,214	3,678	309	5,202		32.58		239
Kankakee, IL	11.7	n.a.	258.3	553.8	824		1,546	3,786	448	5,780		19.55		285
Kansas City, MO-KS	14.1	62.3	409.4	705.9	1,129		1,653	3,689	980	6,322		4.82		337
Kenosha, WI	3.5	39.4	91.4	158.8	254		832	3,053	270	4,155		78.19		78
Killeen-Temple, TX	7.5	70.3	95.1	326.2	429		1,015	2,894	240	4,149		65.44		123
Kitchener-Waterloo, ON	1.4	n.a.	55.9	116.8	174		1,198	3,023	414	4,635		81.02		68
Knoxville, TN	8.7	40.2	184.1	546.8	740		1,437	2,942	592	4,972		30.32		247
Kokomo, IN	2.0	28.1	49.2	280.5	332		653	2,680	173	3,505		76.49		84
★ La Crosse, WI-MN	1.3	17.9	13.6	92.7	108		309	3,215	113	3,637		94.62		20
Lafayette, IN	1.7	28.5	30.5	199.7	232		596	3,198	183	3,977		81.87		65
Lafayette, LA	7.6	36.2	107.1	413.6	528		975	2,904	233	4,112		57.51		151
Lake Charles, LA	11.8	57.7	186.7	703.7	902		1,487	4,551	465	6,502		11.34		314
Lakeland-Winter Haven, FL	7.9	42.7	246.4	685.3	940		2,300	4,649	896	7,845		5.67		334
★ Lancaster, PA	2.7	19.3	74.7	107.5	185		569	2,042	191	2,802		95.76		16
Lansing-East Lansing, MI	3.5	77.1	104.7	410.9	519		851	3,579	324	4,754		52.13		170
Laredo, TX	11.0	15.4	121.6	500.2	633		1,394	4,579	700	6,673		25.50		264
Las Cruces, NM	7.1	53.4	81.3	380.4	469		1,501	3,308	353	5,162		52.98		167
Las Vegas, NV-AZ	13.5	61.4	385.1	442.4	841		1,517	3,664	879	6,061		16.72		295
Lawrence, KS	2.8	43.2	68.6	317.3	389		1,340	4,918	204	6,462		48.45		183
Lawrence, MA-NH	2.4	31.8	137.1	366.4	506		1,016	2,032	1,190	4,237		58.08		149
Lawton, OK	7.3	53.6	135.3	589.6	732		1,351	3,340	323	5,014		30.60		246
★ Lewiston-Auburn, ME	2.4	24.1	47.9	78.7	129		928	2,784	141	3,854		91.51		31
Lexington, KY	6.4	50.5	155.3	520.9	683		1,077	3,643	268	4,987		36.27		226
Lima, OH	6.3	56.3	180.3	762.6	949		1,214	2,901	228	4,343		20.97		280
Lincoln, NE	2.0	44.1	62.5	431.9	496		1,003	5,275	224	6,502		39.10		216
Little Rock-North Little Rock, AR	15.9	74.1	292.6	789.4	1,098		1,670	4,884	621	7,175		3.69	↓	341
London, ON	1.3	n.a.	60.7	218.4	280		1,310	4,147	597	6,054		61.76		136
Long Island, NY	2.8	7.8	113.0	127.6	243		621	2,022	513	3,156		87.54	↓	45
Longview-Marshall, TX	9.9	64.1	122.5	449.6	582		1,326	3,524	416	5,266		42.21	↓	205
Los Angeles-Long Beach, CA	18.3	38.4	627.6	859.1	1,505		1,178	2,579	1,236	4,993		1.14	↓	350
Louisville, KY-IN	6.9	31.8	190.0	385.0	582		1,016	2,725	420	4,161		51.56		172
Lowell, MA-NH	2.9	30.9	88.8	498.6	590		663	1,719	647	3,030		60.63	↓	140
Lubbock, TX	7.7	64.8	129.5	512.3	650		1,316	3,958	362	5,636		32.02		241
Lynchburg, VA	6.2	28.2	69.0	289.5	365		536	2,089	149	2,774		80.74	↓	69
Macon, GA	11.9	43.3	162.6	332.6	507		1,300	4,312	463	6,076		41.65		207
Madison, WI	1.3	28.7	92.1	183.1	276		693	3,289	262	4,243		74.79		90
Manchester, NH	2.5	22.5	95.2	47.1	145		1,054	3,024	330	4,408		85.27		53
Mansfield, OH	2.2	41.3	102.8	643.7	749		1,156	3,077	209	4,443		34.57		232
McAllen-Edinburg-Mission, TX	7.8	26.5	99.2	438.5	545		1,792	3,948	656	6,396		35.70		228
Medford-Ashland, OR	3.7	44.5	47.6	291.4	343		900	3,999	272	5,170		64.59		126
Melbourne-Titusville-Palm Bay, FL	4.5	38.8	133.2	585.9	724		1,393	3,886	362	5,640		26.63		260
Memphis, TN-AR-MS	19.8	91.9	549.3	531.0	1,100		1,915	3,214	1,413	6,542		5.10		336
Merced, CA	6.9	37.9	101.1	437.1	545		1,444	2,786	490	4,720		50.43		176
Miami, FL	16.8	57.4	864.8	1,075.1	1,957		2,362	6,294	1,878	10,534		0.00		354
Middlesex-Somerset-Hunterdon, NJ	1.6	12.9	91.9	146.4	240		634	2,215	357	3,206		87.26	↓	46
Milwaukee-Waukesha, WI	10.5	34.4	294.1	172.3	477		830	3,277	907	5,014		53.55		165
Minneapolis-St. Paul, MN-WI	4.1	45.4	167.8	224.9	397		929	3,440	458	4,827		62.61		133
Missoula, MT	3.8	42.1	25.0	132.6	161		625	4,136	265	5,026		78.48		77
Mobile, AL	15.0	46.2	330.0	691.9	1,037		1,699	3,696	551	5,946		7.94	↓	326
Modesto, CA	7.1	44.3	162.5	670.2	840		1,601	3,786	757	6,144		16.44	↓	296
Monmouth-Ocean, NJ	2.1	20.5	73.0	166.5	241		690	2,442	180	3,312		86.41	↓	49
Monroe, LA	9.9	41.1	113.0	778.9	902		1,536	4,818	328	6,682		10.20	↑	318
Montgomery, AL	14.1	44.1	216.6	456.3	687		1,478	3,206	427	5,110		33.72		235
Montreal, PQ	2.7	n.a.	264.3	177.4	444		1,763	2,953	1,039	5,755		50.15		177
Muncie, IN	9.9	26.4	142.0	341.9	494		818	2,700	206	3,724		63.74		129

METRO AREA	MURDER	RAPE	ROBBERY	ASSAULT	TOTAL	BURGLARY	THEFT	AUTO THEFT	TOTAL	SCORE	TREND	RANK
		Violent Crime Rates					**Property Crime Rates**					
Metro Area Average	6.5	42.6	155.6	383.4	546	1,160	3,358	457	4,975	50.00	↓	
Myrtle Beach, SC	10.8	62.1	207.8	732.6	951	2,113	5,823	573	8,509	4.25	↑	339
Naples, FL	8.0	69.6	150.9	544.8	704	1,551	3,198	375	5,124	31.73		242
★ Nashua, NH	2.0	36.2	18.9	46.4	67	449	2,051	212	2,712	99.72	↑	2
Nashville, TN	11.0	69.9	289.2	725.6	1,026	1,313	4,017	694	6,023	8.22		325
New Bedford, MA	2.6	39.6	176.6	705.9	885	1,306	2,053	739	4,099	26.07		262
New Haven-Meriden, CT	6.0	31.2	277.8	339.9	624	1,214	3,392	805	5,411	37.68		221
New London-Norwich, CT-RI	2.5	32.9	59.3	194.8	256	676	1,973	193	2,842	90.09		36
New Orleans, LA	32.9	54.1	564.3	663.9	1,261	1,627	4,268	1,220	7,115	1.42		349
New York, NY	19.3	32.8	909.5	706.4	1,635	1,123	2,806	1,242	5,171	0.57	↓	352
Newark, NJ	8.4	33.5	517.5	415.0	941	1,036	2,489	1,280	4,806	18.14	↓	290
Newburgh, NY-PA	3.7	21.8	85.5	268.3	357	718	2,064	151	2,934	79.33	↓	74
Norfolk-Virginia Beach- Newport News, VA-NC	11.9	45.0	277.4	270.9	560	960	3,868	451	5,279	43.63		200
Oakland, CA	11.9	41.0	368.3	533.1	913	1,244	3,784	827	5,856	13.04		308
Ocala, FL	7.5	65.7	209.8	797.6	1,015	1,654	3,527	306	5,488	10.49		317
Odessa-Midland, TX	8.4	59.4	107.9	449.2	566	1,512	4,478	333	6,324	34.00		234
Oklahoma City, OK	10.6	67.4	196.4	488.9	696	1,686	4,785	725	7,196	18.42	↓	289
Olympia, WA	2.3	61.9	42.4	159.1	204	928	3,116	260	4,304	81.59		66
Omaha, NE-IA	5.1	37.4	130.2	509.3	645	840	3,287	565	4,692	41.93		206
Orange County, CA	6.1	23.1	204.7	283.3	494	998	2,755	743	4,497	56.66	↓	154
Orlando, FL	5.3	51.2	263.1	753.1	1,021	1,795	4,166	619	6,580	6.52		331
Oshawa, ON	1.4	n.a.	59.8	171.5	233	1,008	2,359	484	3,851	83.01		61
Ottawa-Hull, ON-PQ	1.8	n.a.	135.0	149.5	286	1,516	3,715	807	6,037	61.19		138
Owensboro, KY	3.0	27.5	50.7	125.4	179	815	2,679	150	3,643	89.24		39
Panama City, FL	5.6	50.9	90.6	540.9	637	1,356	4,359	312	6,027	30.03		248
★ Parkersburg-Marietta, WV-OH	3.4	28.2	22.7	100.6	127	550	1,860	139	2,550	99.16		4
Pensacola, FL	5.6	57.9	194.1	787.1	987	1,521	3,369	306	5,196	12.75	↓	309
Peoria-Pekin, IL	4.2	n.a.	151.8	400.3	556	1,124	2,995	183	4,303	52.41		169
Philadelphia, PA-NJ	11.5	31.7	360.1	309.9	681	804	2,299	794	3,896	45.33		194
Phoenix-Mesa, AZ	10.0	36.6	201.3	490.9	702	1,643	4,000	1,185	6,828	20.68		281
Pine Bluff, AR	19.7	90.1	341.6	947.8	1,309	2,224	2,811	682	5,717	2.55	↑	345
Pittsburgh, PA	4.0	27.2	144.5	193.5	342	547	1,624	481	2,652	84.14		57
Pittsfield, MA	1.0	14.4	39.3	283.7	324	720	1,495	189	2,403	86.69	↓	48
Pocatello, ID	1.4	38.2	30.7	312.8	345	708	3,374	182	4,264	69.13		110
Portland, ME	2.0	36.5	57.9	163.9	224	1,032	3,389	240	4,661	75.93		86
Portland-Vancouver, OR-WA	4.7	52.6	200.4	436.4	641	1,110	3,772	785	5,667	32.87		238
★ Portsmouth-Rochester, NH-ME	2.8	32.2	21.7	58.6	83	548	2,449	197	3,194	98.31		7
Providence-Fall River- Warwick, RI-MA	3.7	29.6	105.1	270.2	379	1,000	2,463	682	4,145	67.99		114
★ Provo-Orem, UT	0.9	32.9	16.3	97.2	114	576	3,374	180	4,129	91.22	↑	32
Pueblo, CO	7.7	65.7	133.5	1,011.3	1,153	1,293	3,635	314	5,242	6.80	↓	330
Punta Gorda, FL	4.0	17.8	59.8	188.1	252	796	2,005	192	2,993	88.39		42
Quebec City, PQ	1.5	n.a.	135.6	91.0	228	1,633	2,707	582	4,922	73.66		94
Racine, WI	6.6	18.2	205.3	237.1	449	1,004	3,359	427	4,790	58.65		147
Raleigh-Durham-Chapel Hill, NC	9.5	33.7	213.4	346.0	569	1,561	3,610	368	5,539	40.80		210
Rapid City, SD	2.3	97.9	53.9	263.0	319	858	4,207	203	5,269	65.16		124
Reading, PA	3.7	22.6	164.8	202.7	371	764	2,244	274	3,283	75.08	↑	89
Redding, CA	5.8	60.2	86.2	423.9	516	1,248	2,846	377	4,471	55.25	↑	159
Regina, SK	2.5	n.a.	138.7	348.0	489	2,960	5,025	1,094	9,080	19.84		284
Reno, NV	7.0	68.2	194.4	308.1	510	1,121	4,069	385	5,575	45.61	↓	193
Richland-Kennewick-Pasco, WA	4.9	59.1	56.0	249.8	311	923	3,712	266	4,901	67.43		116
Richmond-Petersburg, VA	18.3	38.2	239.1	296.0	553	1,041	3,613	435	5,089	46.46		190
Riverside-San Bernardino, CA	12.3	38.7	279.8	634.7	927	1,739	2,952	1,005	5,695	13.89	↓	305
Roanoke, VA	6.1	26.5	118.1	186.3	311	710	3,234	197	4,141	73.38		95
★ Rochester, MN	1.6	34.1	34.9	117.3	154	686	2,562	178	3,426	92.92		26
Rochester, NY	6.2	25.4	165.9	144.1	316	868	3,124	346	4,338	71.39		102
Rockford, IL	6.3	n.a.	237.1	421.4	665	1,776	4,280	438	6,494	24.37		268
Rocky Mount, NC	14.1	31.6	207.1	402.2	623	1,686	3,629	278	5,593	35.98	↓	227
Sacramento, CA	8.4	40.4	276.7	450.0	735	1,512	3,383	1,207	6,102	22.38	↓	275
Saginaw-Bay City-Midland, MI	8.1	74.1	157.5	569.8	735	986	3,087	239	4,311	37.40	↓	222
St. Catharines-Niagara, ON	1.9	n.a.	51.0	160.7	214	1,469	2,991	564	5,024	74.51		91
★ St. Cloud, MN	1.8	33.7	19.4	77.1	98	482	2,410	187	3,079	98.02		8
Saint John, NB	2.0	n.a.	28.2	129.0	159	1,048	2,511	345	3,905	88.67		41
St. John's, NF	1.8	n.a.	31.8	132.6	166	971	2,618	303	3,893	88.11		43
St. Joseph, MO	3.3	24.3	44.6	316.6	364	944	3,756	235	4,935	64.88		125
St. Louis, MO-IL	14.0	52.2	298.7	523.6	836	1,123	3,205	633	4,961	23.23		272
Salem, OR	4.5	49.3	109.8	153.4	268	1,083	4,669	500	6,253	60.91		139
Salinas, CA	8.2	34.2	185.4	476.0	670	976	2,913	359	4,248	43.06		202
Salt Lake City-Ogden, UT	3.8	50.4	91.2	245.7	341	989	4,948	405	6,342	53.83		164
San Angelo, TX	5.0	52.7	41.6	481.7	528	1,056	3,791	183	5,030	49.01		181
San Antonio, TX	14.5	50.7	218.3	267.9	501	1,634	5,214	916	7,763	27.20	↓	258
San Diego, CA	8.1	33.1	259.7	538.6	806	1,120	2,745	1,118	4,983	25.22	↓	265

continues

METRO AREA	MURDER	RAPE	ROBBERY	ASSAULT	TOTAL	BURGLARY	THEFT	AUTO THEFT	TOTAL	SCORE	TREND	RANK
Metro Area Average	6.5	42.6	155.6	383.4	546	1,160	3,358	457	4,975	50.00	↓	
San Francisco, CA	8.3	32.4	480.2	412.2	901	915	3,491	849	5,256	17.85	↓	291
San Jose, CA	3.9	38.6	115.0	390.9	510	702	2,773	416	3,892	60.34		141
San Luis Obispo-Atascadero-Paso Robles, CA	2.7	38.0	41.0	408.5	452	801	2,271	164	3,236	68.84	↓	111
Santa Barbara-Santa Maria-Lompoc, CA	3.3	35.8	94.3	348.0	446	1,044	2,647	205	3,897	66.29	↓	120
Santa Cruz-Watsonville, CA	3.6	32.4	118.3	506.0	628	1,063	3,764	324	5,151	39.67	↓	214
Santa Fe, NM	4.6	38.6	70.9	804.2	880	865	1,666	210	2,741	38.82		217
Santa Rosa, CA	3.9	42.2	80.8	337.3	422	1,052	2,865	294	4,211	65.73	↓	122
Sarasota-Bradenton, FL	5.1	40.1	196.6	605.2	807	1,688	3,966	371	6,024	18.99		287
Saskatoon, SK	3.0	n.a.	124.3	295.0	422	1,949	3,747	658	6,354	47.31		187
Savannah, GA	14.0	44.4	352.1	315.9	682	1,434	4,362	617	6,413	23.80		270
★ Scranton–Wilkes-Barre–Hazleton, PA	2.4	18.6	40.4	161.2	204	448	1,504	170	2,122	97.17		11
Seattle-Bellevue-Everett, WA	4.7	62.2	182.8	274.5	462	1,092	4,333	672	6,098	45.05		195
★ Sharon, PA	1.3	17.4	40.8	173.7	216	415	1,552	154	2,120	96.89		12
★ Sheboygan, WI	0.7	17.3	19.9	91.7	112	530	3,024	116	3,670	94.06		22
Sherbrooke, PQ	1.0	n.a.	67.1	101.1	169	2,008	2,398	708	5,114	76.78		83
Sherman-Denison, TX	5.9	55.3	101.6	293.4	401	1,288	3,792	282	5,362	57.80		150
Shreveport-Bossier City, LA	19.5	47.7	242.2	622.1	884	1,612	4,813	478	6,902	9.64		320
Sioux City, IA-NE	3.5	43.0	74.8	646.6	725	1,137	4,040	293	5,469	27.48		257
Sioux Falls, SD	1.8	66.1	36.4	231.4	270	659	2,932	145	3,736	80.17		71
South Bend, IN	8.1	42.9	179.2	249.8	437	1,300	3,656	370	5,326	54.40		162
Spokane, WA	4.5	42.4	123.3	302.9	431	1,322	4,295	346	5,963	49.30		180
Springfield, IL	6.0	n.a.	188.4	486.4	681	1,523	3,553	247	5,323	32.30		240
Springfield, MA	4.0	44.8	186.6	757.6	948	1,218	2,396	872	4,486	20.12		283
Springfield, MO	2.7	31.6	62.7	217.2	283	1,050	3,528	249	4,828	69.69		108
Stamford-Norwalk, CT	3.9	11.8	136.7	129.2	270	766	2,541	460	3,766	79.89	↓	72
★ State College, PA	1.8	28.9	17.3	99.7	119	460	2,284	79	2,824	98.59		6
★ Steubenville-Weirton, OH-WV	1.7	10.8	26.1	270.7	298	440	1,058	113	1,611	96.32		14
Stockton-Lodi, CA	13.4	49.7	335.3	527.4	876	1,631	4,082	1,062	6,775	11.05	↓	315
Sudbury, ON	2.7	n.a.	68.3	213.7	285	1,878	2,942	976	5,796	64.03		128
Sumter, SC	10.6	53.0	213.4	873.1	1,097	1,652	2,959	405	5,015	9.07		322
Syracuse, NY	3.0	23.1	97.5	165.7	266	813	2,484	158	3,455	83.29		60
Tacoma, WA	8.1	74.5	225.5	557.7	791	1,315	4,159	662	6,136	19.27		286
Tallahassee, FL	7.3	77.2	339.3	996.8	1,343	2,191	5,476	736	8,404	0.29		353
Tampa-St. Petersburg-Clearwater, FL	6.7	51.2	308.9	825.7	1,141	1,602	4,119	762	6,483	4.54		338
Terre Haute, IN	10.5	49.9	79.6	484.2	574	1,211	4,036	384	5,631	40.51		211
Texarkana, TX-Texarkana, AR	10.4	53.9	159.6	456.8	627	1,214	3,814	281	5,308	38.53		218
Thunder Bay, ON	2.7	n.a.	96.0	403.6	502	1,798	4,151	667	6,616	37.97		220
Toledo, OH	6.5	66.0	267.7	258.8	533	1,241	3,914	731	5,886	41.08		209
Topeka, KS	11.1	58.6	225.1	740.3	977	2,460	4,843	308	7,611	5.39		335
Toronto, ON	2.0	n.a.	139.2	208.2	349	923	3,050	480	4,453	67.71		115
Trenton, NJ	5.0	42.3	238.4	315.1	559	926	2,571	946	4,443	51.28	↓	173
Trois-Rivieres, PQ	1.5	n.a.	79.0	126.4	207	1,481	2,572	619	4,672	77.06		82
Tucson, AZ	8.6	56.8	176.5	529.6	715	1,343	5,880	885	8,108	11.90		312
Tulsa, OK	7.3	57.3	175.4	544.2	727	1,390	2,716	818	4,924	31.45		243
Tuscaloosa, AL	7.3	49.9	207.9	637.0	852	1,363	5,909	362	7,634	8.50		324
Tyler, TX	9.9	72.3	138.3	465.2	613	1,488	4,361	459	6,308	29.18		251
★ Utica-Rome, NY	3.8	22.6	62.0	136.4	202	664	2,067	131	2,863	93.49		24
Vallejo-Fairfield-Napa, CA	6.0	40.1	205.4	508.1	720	1,081	3,205	506	4,791	33.43		236
Vancouver, BC	3.3	n.a.	244.7	249.5	497	2,443	6,012	1,248	9,702	14.45		303
Ventura, CA	4.2	26.2	128.3	300.4	433	849	2,090	372	3,310	69.98	↓	107
Victoria, BC	2.0	n.a.	131.8	237.2	371	1,479	5,131	539	7,149	44.20		198
Victoria, TX	7.4	42.6	113.9	677.2	798	1,543	3,940	311	5,794	21.25	↓	279
Vineland-Millville-Bridgeton, NJ	7.4	62.2	271.2	552.2	831	1,442	3,450	393	5,285	21.82		277
Visalia-Tulare-Porterville, CA	9.5	37.0	120.4	546.4	676	1,269	3,087	590	4,946	37.12		223
Waco, TX	12.9	72.3	221.6	582.9	817	1,666	4,214	622	6,502	14.74	↓	302
Washington, DC-MD-VA-WV	14.6	30.5	308.2	362.0	685	812	3,264	654	4,729	38.25		219
Waterbury, CT	6.2	27.5	167.3	193.9	367	1,364	3,329	804	5,496	59.50		144
Waterloo-Cedar Falls, IA	2.9	35.0	95.0	232.3	330	1,078	3,035	202	4,315	70.54		105
★ Wausau, WI	0.6	15.1	10.3	76.4	87	391	2,245	113	2,749	99.44		3
West Palm Beach-Boca Raton, FL	8.0	45.4	333.8	700.8	1,043	2,069	4,999	864	7,932	3.12		343
★ Wheeling, WV-OH	4.0	19.0	51.3	137.1	192	620	1,404	158	2,182	97.46		10
Wichita, KS	8.5	74.2	308.9	294.2	612	1,739	4,454	672	6,866	25.78		263
Wichita Falls, TX	8.0	63.7	177.2	471.1	656	1,346	4,348	348	6,042	28.33	↓	254
★ Williamsport, PA	2.0	22.7	69.7	117.8	190	664	2,208	147	3,019	93.21		25
Wilmington, NC	8.2	37.3	172.5	429.7	610	1,844	4,321	384	6,549	28.05		255
Wilmington-Newark, DE-MD	4.2	58.9	187.0	350.3	541	857	2,876	492	4,224	54.96		160
Windsor, ON	2.4	n.a.	67.2	161.6	231	1,141	3,493	386	5,020	72.53		98
Winnipeg, MB	2.8	n.a.	251.7	340.4	595	1,802	3,980	967	6,750	27.77		256
Worcester, MA-CT	2.4	30.1	120.6	428.1	551	887	1,922	392	3,201	63.18		131

METRO AREA	Violent Crime Rates					Property Crime Rates				SCORE	TREND	RANK
	MURDER	RAPE	ROBBERY	ASSAULT	TOTAL	BURGLARY	THEFT	AUTO THEFT	TOTAL			
Metro Area Average	6.5	42.6	155.6	383.4	546	1,160	3,358	457	4,975	50.00	↓	
Yakima, WA	6.2	74.5	107.1	392.5	506	1,878	4,830	497	7,204	30.88	↓	245
Yolo, CA	6.0	39.8	105.6	470.8	582	1,190	4,172	591	5,953	36.55		225
★ York, PA	3.1	22.4	80.7	97.2	181	482	2,391	147	3,019	93.77	↓	23
Youngstown-Warren, OH	13.2	32.8	236.8	428.0	678	980	1,831	548	3,359	50.71		175
Yuba City, CA	7.2	45.7	77.8	752.9	838	1,390	3,131	416	4,937	23.52		271
Yuma, AZ	5.4	39.7	81.1	546.8	633	1,166	4,541	450	6,157	28.90		252

ET CETERA: CRIME

CAPITAL PUNISHMENT

In 1972, the U.S. Supreme Court struck down, on Eighth Amendment grounds (forbidding cruel and unusual punishment), laws that permitted wide discretion in the application of the death penalty. In 1976, the court also struck down mandatory use of the death penalty for specified crimes but upheld laws that permitted executions after consideration of aggravating and mitigating circumstances. That same year, Canada abolished the death penalty entirely.

While the justice of capital punishment continues to be debated in state houses, courts, and political campaigns throughout the United States, one thing is clear: Execution doesn't follow soon after a guilty verdict. In the 38 states with death penalty laws, half of the 3,000 convicted inmates have been on Death Row more than 3 years. Several recent executions have taken place 15 years after sentencing.

Supporters of capital punishment cite the huge financial burden caused by the delays and point to the demographics of Death Row: All inmates are convicted murderers, two out of three have at least one prior felony conviction, nearly 10 percent have a prior murder conviction, and 40 percent were out on bail, probation, or parole at the time of the murder.

The most compelling arguments against capital punishment are that it is barbaric and irreversible, that mistakes have been and will be made, and that in many areas adequate legal defenses aren't provided. Moreover, a life sentence would cost a state one-third of the millions it spends seeing a typical death conviction through the extensive appeals process.

Death Penalty Differences

Twelve states, the District of Columbia, and Canada have abandoned or avoided the death penalty in the modern age. Implementation in the 38 states that have it on their statutes is far from consistent.

Twenty-six states have executed convicted murderers in the years since capital punishment was reinstated. Among some 3,000 persons sentenced, fewer than 300 have been executed. Three out of five executions have taken place in Georgia, Florida, Louisiana, and Texas. New Hampshire and South Dakota have capital punishment statutes but have never imposed the sentence.

States with Death Penalties and Their Methods of Execution

LETHAL INJECTION

Arizona	Mississippi*	Oregon
Arkansas*	Missouri*	Pennsylvania
California	Montana*	South Carolina*
Colorado	Nevada	South Dakota
Connecticut	New Hampshire*	Tennessee*
Delaware*	New Jersey	Texas
Idaho*	New Mexico	Utah*
Illinois	New York	Virginia*
Indiana	North Carolina*	Washington*
Kansas	Ohio*	Wyoming*
Louisiana	Oklahoma	

ELECTROCUTION / LETHAL GAS

ELECTROCUTION	LETHAL GAS
Alabama	Maryland*
Arkansas*	Mississippi*
Florida	Missouri*
Georgia	North Carolina*
Kentucky	Wyoming*
Nebraska	
Ohio*	
South Carolina*	
Tennessee*	
Virginia*	

FIRING SQUAD / HANGING

FIRING SQUAD	HANGING
Idaho*	Delaware*
Utah*	Montana*
	New Hampshire*
	Washington*

Source: Bureau of Justice Statistics, Punishment.
* *Authorizes two methods of execution.*

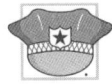

Regional Crime Rates

REGION	MURDER	RAPE	ROBBERY	ASSAULT	BURGLARY	THEFT	AUTO THEFT
United States Average	6.8	35.9	186.1	382.0	920	2,887	506
New England: Connecticut, Maine, Massachusetts, New Hampshire, Rhode Island, Vermont	2.4	26.6	97.1	315.1	659	2,080	390
Mid-Atlantic: New Jersey, New York, Pennsylvania	5.6	23.8	240.4	300.0	648	2,142	432
Great Lakes: Illinois, Indiana, Michigan, Ohio, Wisconsin	6.9	38.8	179.5	351.3	813	2,808	471
Plains: Iowa, Kansas, Minnesota, Missouri, Nebraska, North Dakota, South Dakota	4.5	35.4	103.0	265.1	784	2,800	351
South Atlantic: Delaware, DC, Florida, Georgia, Maryland, North Carolina, South Carolina, Virginia, West Virginia	8.1	39.0	222.9	484.2	1,143	3,421	531
East South Central: Alabama, Kentucky, Mississippi, Tennessee	9.3	41.8	157.4	354.7	1,015	2,633	418
West South Central: Arkansas, Louisiana, Oklahoma, Texas	8.4	41.9	159.3	418.9	1,082	3,341	509
Mountain: Arizona, Colorado, Idaho, Montana, Nevada, New Mexico, Utah, Wyoming	6.1	40.5	125.8	331.6	1,054	3,656	609
Pacific: Alaska, California, Hawaii, Oregon, Washington	7.0	35.3	219.2	447.5	960	2,806	674
Canadian Average	1.7	n.a.	98.6	186.2	1,244	2,606	591
Atlantic: New Brunswick, Newfoundland, Nova Scotia, Prince Edward Island	1.4	n.a.	27.5	107.0	843	1,872	204
East: Ontario, Quebec	1.5	n.a.	94.2	155.8	1,145	2,219	567
West: Alberta, British Columbia, Manitoba, Saskatchewan	2.2	n.a.	127.6	257.1	1,549	3,597	742

Source: FBI, Crime in the United States; Statistics Canada, Canadian Crime Statistics.

Methods of execution vary. Idaho and Utah offer the choice of receiving a lethal injection or facing a firing squad. The latter method is a relic of 19th-century Mormonism requiring murderers to atone for their crime by having their blood spilled on the ground. Lethal injections and electrocution are the most common execution methods. Four states prescribe hanging as one of two acceptable methods.

NATIONAL AND REGIONAL CRIME RATES

With one-fourth the murder rate, one-third the robbery rate, and less than half the aggravated assault rate of the United States, Canada is a much less violent country than its southern neighbor. For all that, there are more burglaries in Canada per capita and a nearly identical rate for theft.

Although criminal activity varies from place to place and from year to year, regional patterns haven't changed much in decades. The murder rate in the west south central states, where the frequency of people killing one another has traditionally been the country's highest, is nearly nine times that of Canada's Atlantic provinces. Armed robbery, a big-city crime, is highest in the Mid-Atlantic states, lowest again in the Atlantic provinces.

Criminologists recognize the geographic pattern of crime-ridden places immediately. The continent's more dangerous places are located on the East Coast south of Delaware Bay. This area is growing, and the resulting conditions of strangers living close together are strongly associated with crime.

There are other reasons for high crime in this area. Professional crooks travel to where the living is easy and the pickings bountiful; they don't stay in the industrial towns of the North but head South to warm weather and popular resorts. This is one factor behind Miami's decades-old crime image.

Finally, most of the more dangerous places are hot much of the year. Knowing what we do about climate's influence on crime, it isn't surprising that large southern cities going through a steamy summer are America's most violent. Persons bidding farewell to Cedar Rapids, Milwaukee, Pittsburgh, or Syracuse to make their new homes in Palm Beach, Orlando, Phoenix, or Las Vegas may need time not only for acclimatizing to warm weather but also for getting used to crime's share in the local evening news.

DRUNK DRIVING

In a typical year, 1.6 million people are arrested for DUI/DWI. Drunk driving, as it's otherwise called, is the most common single cause of arrest in the United States, and the penalties for the crime have gotten more severe. Most states and all provinces in Canada mandate license suspensions for first offenses and license revocations and jail terms for repeat offenses. Three other ways of controlling the drunk driver come by means of legislation.

Blood-Alcohol Exceptions: The American Medical Association (AMA) says that anyone with a blood-alcohol (BAC) level of 0.05 percent is too drunk to drive. Above that threshold, the probability of a crash rises dramatically.

Laws on Driving Under the Influence

STATE/PROVINCE	PER SE LAW/ BAC LEVEL	OPEN CONTAINER PROHIBITION	ANTI-CONSUMPTION LAWS	HAPPY HOURS PROHIBITION
Alabama	0.08			•
Alaska	0.10	•	•	•
Alberta	0.08			
Arizona	0.10		•	•
Arkansas	0.10		•	
British Columbia	0.08			
California	0.08	•	•	
Colorado	0.10			
Connecticut	0.10		•	
Delaware	0.10		•	
District of Columbia	0.10	•	•	
Florida	0.08	•		
Georgia	0.08	•		
Hawaii	0.08	•	•	•
Idaho	0.08	•	•	
Illinois	0.08	•	•	•
Indiana	0.10	•	•	•
Iowa	0.10	•	•	
Kansas	0.08	•	•	•
Kentucky	0.10		•	
Louisiana	0.10			
Maine	0.08		•	•
Manitoba	0.07			
Maryland	0.10	•	•	
Massachusetts	0.08	•	•	
Michigan	0.10	•		
Minnesota	0.10	•	•	
Mississippi	0.10			
Missouri	0.10		•	
Montana	0.10			

continues 393

Crime

Handguns

STATE/PROVINCE	PER SE LAW/ BAC LEVEL	OPEN CONTAINER PROHIBITION	ANTI- CONSUMPTION LAWS	HAPPY HOURS PROHIBITION
Nebraska	0.10		●	
Nevada	0.10	●	●	
New Brunswick	0.10			
New Hampshire	0.08	●		
New Jersey	0.10		●	●
New Mexico	0.08	●	●	
New York	0.10		●	
Newfoundland	0.08			
North Carolina	0.08	●	●	●
North Dakota	0.10	●	●	
Nova Scotia	0.08			
Ohio	0.10	●	●	●
Oklahoma	0.10	●	●	●
Ontario	0.08			
Oregon	0.08	●	●	
Pennsylvania	0.08	●	●	●
Quebec	0.08			
Rhode Island	0.10		●	●
Saskatchewan	0.08			
South Carolina	0.10			●
South Dakota	0.10	●		
Tennessee	0.10	●		
Texas	0.10		●	●
Utah	0.08	●	●	
Vermont	0.08		●	
Virginia	0.08	●	●	●
Washington	0.10	●	●	
West Virginia	0.10		●	
Wisconsin	0.10	●	●	
Wyoming	0.10			

Source: American Automobile Association, Transport Canada, U.S. Department of Transportation.

Legislation in Congress to create a uniform 0.08 standard has been introduced. Over 40 percent of all traffic fatalities are alcohol-related; nearly a quarter of these crashes involve drivers who came in under 0.10 in the Breathalyzer test. As many as 600 lives a year would be saved, supporters argue, if 0.08 were imposed nationwide.

For all that, most state law uses the 0.10 percent baseline, or twice the AMA standard. Fifteen states, including California (with the highest number of drunk-driving arrests on the continent), have lowered the illegal per se BAC level to 0.08 percent. Canadian federal law sets the threshold at 0.08 percent, but most of the provinces have gone further, lowering it to 0.05 percent.

Dram Shop Laws allow the last person and establishment to serve a drink to an intoxicated patron to be held responsible for the patron's actions immediately afterward. Victims of drunk drivers may sue not just the driver but also the bar owner, bartender, or party host who served the driver.

Happy Hour Prohibitions, a new form of server responsibility law, means that drinking establishments cannot encourage excessive or immoderate consumption. Prohibitions against bars advertising a Happy Hour, selling two drinks for the price of one, or changing their prices at any time during the day make up the law in Ontario and the following 15 states:

Arizona	Missouri	Rhode Island
Illinois	Nebraska	Tennessee
Indiana	New Jersey	Texas
Kansas	New Mexico	Utah
Massachusetts	Pennsylvania	Vermont

HANDGUNS

Handgun control isn't a subject to be lightly entered into in conversation unless you have the time and are ready for a prolonged discussion.

Canada's 1992 gun control law, C-17, passed after the mass-murder of 14 young women on a Montreal campus, requires would-be buyers of rifles and shotguns to obtain a Firearms Acquisition Certificate (FAC), wait 28 days for background checks, and then undergo mandatory training in firearms use. All handguns are restricted weapons, available only to collectors and gun-club members after rigorous background checks.

In the United States, the controversy continues. Changes in regulations occur frequently from state to state and even within municipalities.

The National Rifle Association, the fiercest defender of gun enthusiasts, attempts to keep its members informed of regulation changes with a regular publication of state-by-state gun purchase and carrying laws, but even this comes with a disclaimer warning of the constant changes. The variations in different states' restrictions can be immense, reflecting how well those who vehemently defend their weapons and those who would take them away have done their jobs in state legislatures.

In Georgia and South Carolina, for example, there are few constraints. You can walk into a store, buy a pistol, and walk out. There's not even a record of the sale. In Illinois, on the other hand, a prospective gun buyer has to apply for a permit, then wait 30 days for a check of criminal records. A gun must then be registered and the sale reported. However, carrying a handgun, either openly or concealed, is unlawful in the state. You may store it at home or business, or broken and unloaded in a car.

In Chicago, the same rules apply, but only to guns purchased before a new law went into effect that prohibits any newly purchased handgun from being brought into the city. In the suburbs of Evanston, Oak Park, and Morton Grove, there are no handguns at all; they're prohibited.

Most of the states fall somewhere between these extremes, but the penalties for not knowing the law or for violating the law can be severe. Massachusetts, for example, has a law requiring a mandatory 1-year jail term for anyone caught with an unlicensed gun.

State Restrictions on Purchase and Carrying of Handguns

| STATE | PURCHASE OF HANDGUNS | | | | PROHIBITED | | |
	INSTANT CHECK	WAITING PERIOD (DAYS)	PERMIT TO PURCHASE	OWNER ID CARD	OPEN CARRY	ASSAULT WEAPONS	CONCEALED CARRY
Alabama	●	2			●		▲
Alaska	●						▲
Arizona	●						▲
Arkansas	●				●		▲
California	●	15			●	●	▲
Colorado	●						▲
Connecticut	●	14	●		●	●	▲
Delaware	●						▲
District of Columbia	●			●	●	●	●
Florida	●	3			●		▲
Georgia	●				●		▲
Hawaii	●	14	●	●	●		▲
Idaho	●						▲
Illinois	●	3	●	●	●	*	●
Indiana	●				●		▲
Iowa	●		●		●		▲
Kansas	●	1					●
Kentucky	●						▲
Louisiana	●						▲
Maine	●						▲
Maryland	●	7			●		▲
Massachusetts	●	7	●	●	●	●	▲
Michigan	●		●				▲
Minnesota	●	7	●				▲
Mississippi	●						▲
Missouri	●	7	●				▲
Montana	●						▲
Nebraska	●		●				●
Nevada	●	1					▲
New Hampshire	●						▲

continues

State Restrictions on Purchase and Carrying of Handguns (cont.)

| STATE | PURCHASE OF HANDGUNS | | | | PROHIBITED | | |
	INSTANT CHECK	WAITING PERIOD (DAYS)	PERMIT TO PURCHASE	OWNER ID CARD	OPEN CARRY	ASSAULT WEAPONS	CONCEALED CARRY
New Jersey	●		●	●	●	●	▲
New Mexico	●						●
New York	●		●	●	●	*	▲
North Carolina	●		●				▲
North Dakota	●				●		▲
Ohio	●	1	●	●		*	●
Oklahoma	●				●		▲
Oregon	●						▲
Pennsylvania	●	2			●		▲
Rhode Island	●	7			●		▲
South Carolina	●	8			●		▲
South Dakota	●	2					▲
Tennessee	●				●		▲
Texas	●				●		▲
Utah	●				●		▲
Vermont	●				●		▲
Virginia	●	8				●	▲
Washington	●	5					▲
West Virginia	●						▲
Wisconsin	●	2					●
Wyoming	●						▲

Source: National Rifle Association, Institute for Legislative Action: www.nraila.org.

A solid blue bullet ● indicates state law. Under the prohibited concealed carry column, a solid blue bullet ● indicates extremely restrictive state laws and a solid blue triangle ▲ indicates moderately restrictive state laws.

*Many cities ban assault weapons in the absence of similar state legislation.

Note: Since state laws are subject to frequent change, this chart is not to be considered legal advice or a restatement of the law.

Handguns

The Arts

Most people would exchange any worn-out city for a serene place that's safer, cheaper, and less crowded. The escape to a smaller place is a sustaining dream for big-city residents, according to opinion polls.

You might even pack up and make your own break if the chance arrives in the form of a job transfer, a mid-life change, or retirement. You may be pleased to discover that towns with courthouse squares, angle parking, and kids riding two-wheelers on streets actually named Main still exist. You might write home that you'd finally found a sense of cohesion, of continuity and tradition, of community spirit and neighborliness that you thought had vanished. You're happier than you've been in years.

For about 4 months.

Because in your headlong rush to abandon the aggravations of big-city life, you abandoned the classic marble art museum you barely glanced at in passing twice each day in the crush of commuter traffic. You also turned your back on the local newspaper's arts section, the local public television station's earnest fund-raising auctions, and your annual subscription to the repertory theater's season.

Of all the factors that come together into "quality of life," the one called the arts inevitably gets better with the size of the city. True, the likelihood of professional sports teams, zoological gardens, and amusement parks being found anywhere improves with population size. But many of the most valuable recreation assets—lakes, hiking trails, forests, campgrounds—are found far from cities; indeed, they *must* be far from cities. The arts alone are big-city phenomena.

Places Rated's top locations for the arts are Chicago, Los Angeles, New York, Toronto, and Washington. This isn't to say that culture cannot be found in smaller metro areas. Although it is safe to assume that the larger a metro area is, the more artistic and cultural amenities it will possess, there are exceptions.

ART MUSEUMS AND GALLERIES

In ancient Greece, it wasn't just the devoutly religious who visited temples; uninvited tourists also stole in to admire the statues and paintings. In Revolutionary France, artists had their daily exclusive run of the Louvre in order to copy the great works of

WHAT ARE THE ARTS, ANYWAY?

"We know what culture is," says a Sharon, PA, newspaper editor. "We find it in our refrigerators every week." Although people can't get together on a single definition, or even on one element that all forms of culture share, it's possible to name certain things about art that seem to ring true. For example, the following two lists draw a distinction that most would recognize:

Definitely Art	Possibly Art
anything by Shakespeare	comic books
ballet	folk music, blues, jazz
Chicago Symphony Orchestra	grunge bands
Greek sculpture	John Tesh or Yanni
Monet paintings	rap music
Placido Domingo	subway graffiti
poet Dylan Thomas	tap dancing
stained glass	Woody Allen

Places Rated doesn't make choices from the right-hand list regarding what precisely constitutes art. Instead, it focuses on the categories in the list on the left, which most agree have artistic or cultural merit. Whether any of the items in the second list are art is moot; most are controversial or dubious because they haven't withstood the test of time.

the past. But on infrequent public days, the peasants, prostitutes, soldiers, and common laborers came in great numbers. To this day, going to an art museum has something of the democratic, the sacred, and the carnival to it.

To qualify for inclusion in *Places Rated*, the American Association of Museums' requirements are as solid as any: "an organized and permanent nonprofit institution, essentially educational or aesthetic in purpose, with professional staff, which owns and utilizes tangible objects, cares for them, and exhibits them to the public on some regular schedule."

The first great North American art museums were founded in Montreal in 1860 and in Boston and New York 10 years later. New York now has more art museums than any other city on the continent, and the Metropolitan Museum, with almost 5 million visitors a year, is its most popular tourist attraction.

Museums count visitors religiously. New York's Metropolitan counts each tin button it hands out, reconciles that number with an electronic eye at the museum's front door, and records the weather, too—all for comparing each day's visitors with those on the same date the previous year.

The number of visitors to art museums is impressive. Combining regular tickets sales with those from traveling special exhibitions makes art museums and nonprofit exhibit spaces more popular than professional theater and opera. "Picasso: The Early Years" packed in nearly 1 million people when it ran in Boston's Museum of Fine Arts and Washington's National Gallery. In fact, the National Gallery's recent van Gogh exhibit drew crowds bigger than all of the Redskins' home games combined.

TUNING IN TO CONCERT RADIO

While album rock, oldies, and country dominate FM radio formats, nearly 8 of every 100 hours of FM listening in New York and Toronto is classical music. Metropolitan audiences can tune in to music aired around the clock by 447 concert- or classical-format radio stations. Forty-one of these stations with the biggest share of the fine-arts audience (CFMX-FM in Toronto or WCRB-FM in Boston, for example) are commercial operations, but most belong to National Public Radio or the CBC in Canada. The cities of license for nearly all are within 232 metro areas; 50 metro areas have two stations, and 29 have three or more.

THE LIVELY ARTS CALENDAR

The cultural side of urban life might be divided into two categories: possessions and performances. Collected art on museum walls and floors and in gardens belongs in the first group. The lively arts—symphony, opera, dance, and theater—belong in the second.

Despite the competition, the audience's increasingly precious leisure time, rolling economic recessions, and the drop in government arts funding, the lively arts continue to endure. This isn't the case everywhere, however.

In recent years, the Nashville Symphony filed for bankruptcy; the Oklahoma and New Orleans symphonies closed for good; and Montreal's, Toronto's, and Vancouver's orchestras slowly emerged from life-support. Most professional theaters are operating in the red. The Joffrey Ballet, going broke in New York, moved to less expensive Chicago. Other major ballet companies have merged or formed partnerships—Cleveland's with San Jose's, Tulsa's with Knoxville's—to cut costs, ensure a strong repertory, lengthen dancers' contracts and, in the end, to survive.

For all their troubles, the lively arts still outdraw professional sports. Unlike professional football or major league baseball, however, resident symphony orchestras, opera companies, professional theater, and dance companies are urban assets that are all the more exceptional in a metro area because they are endangered.

Touring Artists Bookings

Long before the Brassissimo Vienna, Harlem Spiritual Ensemble, or Borealis Wind Quintet comes to town for a date at the local performing arts center, they are booked by a college or nonprofit community concert association.

Filling the concert halls with classical artists, once big business for agents and presenters, is getting tougher and less fun. In spite of 1990s marketing twists like rush-hour recitals, sound clips on the Internet, park concerts, tie-ins with art exhibits, celebrity narrators, and free admission for kids, younger audiences are demanding more popular entertainment.

Opera

Opera fans boast that their passion embraces the greatest of the performing arts, since it combines a love for orchestral and vocal music, theater, and dance. The first grand opera performed in this country was Rossini's *The Barber of Seville*, at New York's Park Theatre in 1825.

To this day, New York remains America's operatic capital. More than thirty companies with some kind of budget call New York home, including the grand New York City Opera and the even grander Metropolitan Opera, where superstars Placido Domingo and Luciano Pavarotti recently celebrated 30 years of association.

Outside New York, opera has been diffused throughout the continent. From some 75 professional companies in the late 1970s, opera has expanded to more than 150, reaching an audience of 8 million during the 1998–99 season.

These companies have typical annual budgets topping $500,000. Full-scale opera productions using professional orchestras and bringing the world's leading singers to the stage aren't cheap tickets, and most metro areas haven't the resources or audiences to support this singular form of the lively arts.

Ballet

New York is the center for great dance as it is a center for so much more in the performing arts. America's top companies are here, including the New York City Ballet, the American Ballet Theater, and the Dance Theater of Harlem.

THE MOST POPULAR ART MUSEUMS

Not counting special exhibitions, twenty-four North American art museums are visited by at least one-half million people each year.

National Gallery of Art Washington, DC	6,500,000
Metropolitan Museum of Art New York, NY	4,700,000
Art Institute of Chicago Chicago, IL	1,300,000
Los Angeles County Museum of Art Los Angeles, CA	1,000,000
Hirshhorn Museum & Sculpture Garden Washington, DC	908,000
New York State Museum Albany, NY	900,000
Ringling Museum of Art Sarasota-Bradenton, FL	900,000
Fine Arts Museums of San Francisco San Francisco, CA	800,000
Museum of Fine Arts Boston, MA	800,000
Carnegie Museum of Art Pittsburgh, PA	700,000
Solomon Guggenheim Museum New York, NY	700,000
Saint Louis Art Museum St. Louis, MO	650,000
Walker Art Center Minneapolis, MN	650,000
Philadelphia Museum of Art Philadelphia, PA	600,000
Arthur M. Sackler Gallery Washington, DC	500,000
Cleveland Museum of Art Cleveland, OH	500,000
High Museum of Art Atlanta, GA	500,000
The Huntington Los Angeles-Long Beach, CA	500,000
Indianapolis Museum of Art Indianapolis, IN	500,000
National Gallery of Canada Ottawa, ON	500,000
National Museum of African Art Washington, DC	500,000
National Museum of American Art Washington, DC	500,000
Oakland Museum Oakland, CA	500,000
Whitney Museum of American Art New York, NY	500,000

Source: American Art Directory; The Art Newspaper; Places Rated research.

The Arts

In the 1960s, Rudolf Nureyev heralded a boom in ballet when he jumped the fence from Russia to the West. He showed how athletic dance could be, and suddenly it was socially acceptable for teenage boys to join dance classes. The growth decade for dance was the 1970s, when touring New York dance troupes spread the gospel to new audiences. The charisma of Mikhail Baryshnikov, another Russian émigré who became artistic director of the American Ballet Theater, helped consolidate the popularity of dance.

North America has a number of well-established dance companies. The New York City Ballet and Toronto's National Ballet of Canada have been around since the end of World War II, and Seattle's Pacific Northwest Ballet is past its first quarter century. Unlikely as it may seem, the ballet company of Dayton, OH is older than all three, at well over half a century.

OPERATIC CHESTNUTS

There are more than 50,000 opera scores and librettos; for better or worse, a majority have never been produced. During 1999, there were eighteen familiar operas that, although they represented only a fraction of all *productions* in North America, accounted for one-third of all *performances*. The last, *Of Mice and Men,* is now the most popular opera by an American composer.

Opera, Composer	Productions
Madame Butterfly, Puccini	21
Don Giovanni, Mozart	16
La Bohème, Puccini	15
Rigoletto, Verdi	12
Aïda, Verdi	11
La Traviata, Verdi	11
Carmen, Bizet	9
Così Fan Tutte, Mozart	9
Die Fledermaus, Strauss	9
The Magic Flute, Mozart	9
Lucia di Lammermoor, Donizetti	8
Tosca, Puccini	7
Macbeth, Verdi	6
The Marriage of Figaro, Mozart	6
Falstaff, Verdi	5
Hansel and Gretel, Humperdinck	5
Pagliacci, Leoncavallo	5
Of Mice and Men, Floyd	5

Source: Opera America.

Symphony Orchestras

"The greatest instrument ever invented," Andre Previn once called the symphony. Of course, it is really a collection of many different instruments and musicians. The original definition—"to sound together," from the Greek—is just vague enough to embrace all the ensembles playing some type of symphonic music today in North America.

In all, there are some 1,500 groups, ranging in size and experience from youths playing before captive audi-

THE *TONYS'* OUTSTANDING REGIONAL THEATERS

It isn't just directors, lead actors, and *Death of a Salesman* revivals that get recognition. Since 1976, the American Theater Wing has given twenty-four regional theaters a Tony Award for artistic achievement. When the Denver Center Theater got its Tony, the small object was reverently passed around at a special ceremony; in the eyes of professional theater, the mountain time zone had finally arrived.

1999	Crossroads Theatre Company (New Brunswick, NJ)
1998	Denver Center Theater Company (Denver, CO)
1997	Berkeley Repertory Theater (Berkeley, CA)
1996	Alley Theater (Houston, TX)
1995	Goodspeed Opera House (Haddam, CT)
1994	McCarter Theatre (Princeton, NJ)
1993	La Jolla Playhouse (La Jolla, CA)
1992	Goodman Theatre (Chicago, IL)
1991	Yale Repertory Theatre (New Haven, CT)
1990	Seattle Repertory Theatre (Seattle, WA)
1989	Hartford Stage Company (Hartford, CT)
1988	South Coast Repertory (Costa Mesa, CA)
1987	San Francisco Mime Troupe (San Francisco, CA)
1986	American Repertory Theatre (Cambridge, MA)
1985	Steppenwolf Theatre Company (Chicago, IL)
1984	Old Globe Theatre (San Diego, CA)
1983	Oregon Shakespeare Festival (Ashland, OR)
1982	Guthrie Theater (Minneapolis, MN)
1981	Trinity Repertory Company (Providence, RI)
1980	Actors Theatre of Louisville (Louisville, KY)
1979	American Conservatory Theatre (San Francisco, CA)
1978	Long Wharf Theatre (New Haven, CT)
1977	Mark Taper Forum (Los Angeles, CA)
1976	Arena Stage (Washington, DC)

Source: American Theater Wing, Inc.

ences of parents to accomplished and well-paid professionals working under the baton of Kurt Masur at the New York Philharmonic. Orchestras are far from uncommon in metro areas: 276 metro areas claim at least one. Thirty-six of these places support four or more orchestras, and fourteen metro areas support eight or more.

Professional Theater

Long known as the "fabulous invalid," theater continues to hold its own despite perennial predictions of its demise. In *Huckleberry Finn,* Mark Twain described two scamsters who arrive in a small Arkansas town and tout a theatrical production pompously titled the "Royal Nonesuch." The performance consisted of an actor, wearing bright body paint but nothing else, streaking across the stage to the delight and outrage of the audience.

The history of American theater is a blend of the grand and comic; its many forms have encompassed Shakespeare, vaudeville, and Broadway musicals. Its first challenge came with silent movies at the century's turn, when the number of legitimate theaters fell from 1,500 to 500. In the 1920s, a resurgence took place on Broadway, which opened more than 400 new theaters in less than a decade. In the 1950s, Off-Broadway grew in response to overly commercial mainstream theater.

Broadway was once *the* center of American theater. It alone determined what was successful and sent these hits on the road to the provinces. New York still has the greatest concentration of theaters. Yet a number of regional theaters have long been recognized for their vigor and innovation, including the Arena Stage in Washington, DC, the Guthrie in Minneapolis, MN, and the Trinity Rep in Providence, RI.

On another level are the fringe theater groups across the continent, surviving on a shoestring, disappearing only to be replaced by others. Some of the productions could well make Twain's "Royal Nonesuch" seem like great theater. Yet the appeal of small theater is that you may be happily surprised by its spunk and sense of craft. Thanks to subsidies, fringe and small theaters in Canadian metro areas have a better chance of survival than those in the United States, where the free market can turn a house dark in days.

SCORING: THE ARTS

Let's admit the point that it isn't possible to rank metro areas in the arts with total fairness. But let's also point out that some seem shortchanged while others have riches, and all can be compared using arts-related data elements. *Places Rated* considers eight.

For **Art Museums and Galleries** these are: (1) number of art museums, (2) annual museum attendance, and (3) per capita museum attendance. For **The Lively Arts Calendar** they include: (4) annual ballet performances, (5) touring artist bookings, (6) opera performances, (7) professional theater performances, and (8) symphony performances.

RANKINGS: THE ARTS

Eight data elements are used to derive a metro area's score for the arts. These are grouped into two broad factors, possessions and performances. Places that are tied get the same rank and are listed in alphabetical order.

Metro Areas from Best to Worst

RANK	SCORE
1. New York, NY	100.00
2. Washington, DC-MD-VA-WV	99.72
3. Los Angeles-Long Beach, CA	99.44
4. Chicago, IL	99.16
5. Toronto, ON	98.87
6. Boston, MA-NH	98.59
7. Philadelphia, PA-NJ	98.31

RANK	SCORE
8. Minneapolis-St. Paul, MN-WI	98.02
9. Denver, CO	97.74
10. San Francisco, CA	97.46
11. Cleveland-Lorain-Elyria, OH	97.17
12. Montreal, PQ	96.89
13. Newark, NJ	96.61

continues

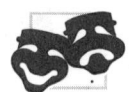

Metro Areas from Best to Worst (cont.)

RANK	SCORE
14. Oakland, CA	96.32
15. Indianapolis, IN	96.04
16. Vancouver, BC	95.76
17. Baltimore, MD	95.47
18. Detroit, MI	95.19
19. St. Louis, MO-IL	94.91
20. Atlanta, GA	94.62
21. San Jose, CA	94.34
22. Cincinnati, OH-KY-IN	94.06
23. Hartford, CT	93.77
24. Buffalo-Niagara Falls, NY	93.49
25. Dallas, TX	93.21
26. Milwaukee-Waukesha, WI	92.92
27. Columbus, OH	92.64
28. Salt Lake City-Ogden, UT	92.36
29. Riverside-San Bernardino, CA	92.07
30. Seattle-Bellevue-Everett, WA	91.79
31. Portland-Vancouver, OR-WA	91.51
32. San Diego, CA	91.22
33. Pittsburgh, PA	90.94
34. Middlesex-Somerset-Hunterdon, NJ	90.66
35. Honolulu, HI	90.37
36. Bergen-Passaic, NJ	90.09
37. Houston, TX	89.81
38. Miami, FL	89.52
39. Kansas City, MO-KS	89.24
40. Ottawa-Hull, ON-PQ	88.96
41. Stamford-Norwalk, CT	88.67
42. Charlotte-Gastonia-Rock Hill, NC-SC	88.39
43. Calgary, AB	88.11
44. Fort Lauderdale, FL	87.82
45. Dayton-Springfield, OH	87.54
46. Monmouth-Ocean, NJ	87.26
47. Orange County, CA	86.97
48. Phoenix-Mesa, AZ	86.69
49. New Haven-Meriden, CT	86.41
50. Raleigh-Durham-Chapel Hill, NC	86.12
51. Toledo, OH	85.84
52. Fort Worth-Arlington, TX	85.56
53. Birmingham, AL	85.27
54. St. Cloud, MN	84.99
55. Tacoma, WA	84.71
56. Norfolk-Virginia Beach-Newport News, VA-NC	84.42
57. Winnipeg, MB	84.14
58. New Orleans, LA	83.86
59. Fort Wayne, IN	83.57
60. Rochester, NY	83.29
61. Hamilton, ON	83.01
62. Edmonton, AB	82.72
63. Omaha, NE-IA	82.44
64. Fargo-Moorhead, ND-MN	82.16
65. Chattanooga, TN-GA	81.87
66. Akron, OH	81.59
67. Syracuse, NY	81.31
68. Olympia, WA	81.02
69. Trenton, NJ	80.74
70. Louisville, KY-IN	80.46
71. Burlington, VT	80.17
72. Saskatoon, SK	79.89
73. Albany-Schenectady-Troy, NY	79.61

RANK	SCORE
74. Bloomington, IN	79.33
75. Madison, WI	79.04
76. Orlando, FL	78.76
77. Nashville, TN	78.48
78. Jacksonville, FL	78.19
79. Bridgeport, CT	77.91
80. Providence-Fall River-Warwick, RI-MA	77.63
81. Richmond-Petersburg, VA	77.34
82. Grand Rapids-Muskegon-Holland, MI	77.06
83. St. Catharines-Niagara, ON	76.78
84. West Palm Beach-Boca Raton, FL	76.49
85. Oklahoma City, OK	76.21
86. Jamestown, NY	75.93
87. Boise-City, ID	75.64
88. Albuquerque, NM	75.36
89. Evansville-Henderson, IN-KY	75.08
90. Sacramento, CA	74.79
91. Worcester, MA-CT	74.51
92. Duluth-Superior, MN-WI	74.23
93. Regina, SK	73.94
94. Springfield, MA	73.66
95. Greensboro–Winston-Salem–High Point, NC	73.38
96. Sarasota-Bradenton, FL	73.09
97. Long Island, NY	72.81
98. Kitchener-Waterloo, ON	72.53
99. Austin-San Marcos, TX	72.24
100. London, ON	71.96
101. Quebec City, PQ	71.68
102. Spokane, WA	71.39
103. Jersey City, NJ	71.11
104. Wilmington-Newark, DE-MD	70.83
105. Memphis, TN-AR-MS	70.54
106. Hattiesburg, MS	70.26
107. Boulder-Longmont, CO	69.98
108. Victoria, BC	69.69
109. Pittsfield, MA	69.41
110. Lincoln, NE	69.13
111. New London-Norwich, CT-RI	68.84
112. Grand Forks, ND-MN	68.56
113. Lancaster, PA	68.28
114. Ann Arbor, MI	67.99
115. Scranton–Wilkes-Barre–Hazleton, PA	67.71
116. Greenville-Spartanburg-Anderson, SC	67.43
117. Bellingham, WA	67.14
118. Peoria-Pekin, IL	66.86
119. Tampa-St. Petersburg-Clearwater, FL	66.58
120. Tucson, AZ	66.29
121. Knoxville, TN	66.01
122. Halifax, NS	65.73
123. Santa Fe, NM	65.44
124. Kalamazoo-Battle Creek, MI	65.16
125. Vallejo-Fairfield-Napa, CA	64.88
126. Fayetteville-Springdale-Rogers, AR	64.59
127. Columbia, SC	64.31
128. Tallahassee, FL	64.03
129. Ventura, CA	63.74
130. Bangor, ME	63.46
131. Tulsa, OK	63.18
132. Barnstable-Yarmouth, MA	62.89
133. South Bend, IN	62.61

RANK	SCORE
134. Bloomington-Normal, IL	62.33
135. Colorado Springs, CO	62.04
136. Sheboygan, WI	61.76
137. Montgomery, AL	61.48
138. Charleston-North Charleston, SC	61.19
139. San Antonio, TX	60.91
140. Huntsville, AL	60.63
141. Des Moines, IA	60.34
142. Columbia, MO	60.06
143. Charlottesville, VA	59.78
144. Janesville-Beloit, WI	59.50
145. Davenport-Moline-Rock Island, IA-IL	59.21
146. Portland, ME	58.93
147. Gainesville, FL	58.65
148. Melbourne-Titusville-Palm Bay, FL	58.36
149. Allentown-Bethlehem-Easton, PA	58.08
150. Portsmouth-Rochester, NH-ME	57.80
151. Saginaw-Bay City-Midland, MI	57.51
152. Iowa City, IA	57.23
153. Medford-Ashland, OR	56.95
154. Santa Cruz-Watsonville, CA	56.66
155. Cedar Rapids, IA	56.38
156. Champaign-Urbana, IL	56.10
157. Lexington, KY	55.81
158. Mansfield, OH	55.53
159. St. Joseph, MO	55.25
160. Santa Rosa, CA	54.96
161. Salinas, CA	54.68
162. Provo-Orem, UT	54.40
163. El Paso, TX	54.11
164. Trois-Rivieres, PQ	53.83
165. Windsor, ON	53.55
166. Santa Barbara-Santa Maria-Lompoc, CA	53.26
167. Rochester, MN	52.98
168. Lakeland-Winter Haven, FL	52.70
169. Charleston, WV	52.41
170. Wichita, KS	52.13
171. Hamilton-Middletown, OH	51.85
172. Roanoke, VA	51.56
173. Reno, NV	51.28
174. Eugene-Springfield, OR	51.00
175. Appleton-Oshkosh-Neenah, WI	50.71
176. Augusta-Aiken, GA-SC	50.43
177. Las Vegas, NV-AZ	50.15
178. Little Rock-North Little Rock, AR	49.86
179. Jackson, MS	49.58
180. Wheeling, WV-OH	49.30
181. Lansing-East Lansing, MI	49.01
182. Topeka, KS	48.73
183. Fayetteville, NC	48.45
184. Dutchess County, NY	48.16
185. Benton Harbor, MI	47.88
186. Mobile, AL	47.60
187. Binghamton, NY	47.31
188. Columbus, GA-AL	47.03
189. Dubuque, IA	46.75
190. Lafayette, IN	46.46
191. Harrisburg-Lebanon-Carlisle, PA	46.18
192. Baton Rouge, LA	45.90
193. Sioux Falls, SD	45.61

RANK	SCORE
194. Fort Myers-Cape Coral, FL	45.33
195. Savannah, GA	45.05
196. Asheville, NC	44.76
197. Rockford, IL	44.48
198. Manchester, NH	44.20
199. Decatur, IL	43.91
200. Flint, MI	43.63
201. Lima, OH	43.35
202. Greeley, CO	43.06
203. Eau Claire, WI	42.78
204. Casper, WY	42.50
205. Johnson City-Kingsport-Bristol, TN-VA	42.21
206. La Crosse, WI-MN	41.93
207. Salem, OR	41.65
207. Thunder Bay, ON	41.65
209. Parkersburg-Marietta, WV-OH	41.08
210. Alexandria, LA	40.80
211. Waterloo-Cedar Falls, IA	40.51
212. Elkhart-Goshen, IN	40.23
213. Lowell, MA-NH	39.95
214. Fort Collins-Loveland, CO	39.67
215. Shreveport-Bossier City, LA	39.38
216. Green Bay, WI	39.10
217. Erie, PA	38.82
218. Racine, WI	38.53
219. Atlantic-Cape May, NJ	38.25
220. Bismarck, ND	37.97
221. Springfield, IL	37.68
222. Athens, GA	37.40
223. Clarksville-Hopkinsville, TN-KY	37.12
224. Stockton-Lodi, CA	36.83
225. Brockton, MA	36.55
226. Bremerton, WA	36.27
226. Sioux City, IA-NE	36.27
228. Huntington-Ashland, WV-KY-OH	35.70
229. Hagerstown, MD	35.42
230. Amarillo, TX	35.13
231. Waco, TX	34.85
232. Kenosha, WI	34.57
233. Springfield, MO	34.28
234. New Bedford, MA	34.00
235. Bryan-College Station, TX	33.72
236. Fresno, CA	33.43
237. Albany, GA	33.15
238. Pueblo, CO	32.87
239. Waterbury, CT	32.58
240. Hickory-Morganton-Lenoir, NC	32.30
241. Glens Falls, NY	32.02
242. Sumter, SC	31.73
243. Elmira, NY	31.45
244. Biloxi-Gulfport-Pascagoula, MS	31.17
245. Utica-Rome, NY	30.88
246. Gadsden, AL	30.60
247. Las Cruces, NM	30.32
248. Fort Pierce-Port St. Lucie, FL	30.03
249. San Luis Obispo-Atascadero-Paso Robles, CA	29.75
250. Anchorage, AK	29.47
251. Naples, FL	29.18
252. Oshawa, ON	28.90

The Arts

continues

Metro Areas from Best to Worst (cont.)

RANK	SCORE
253. San Angelo, TX	28.62
254. Yakima, WA	28.33
255. Terre Haute, IN	28.05
256. Reading, PA	27.77
257. Jackson, TN	27.48
258. Abilene, TX	27.20
258. St. John's, NF	27.20
260. Grand Junction, CO	26.63
261. Jackson, MI	26.35
262. Monroe, LA	26.07
263. Cheyenne, WY	25.78
264. Missoula, MT	25.50
264. State College, PA	25.50
266. Lawrence, KS	24.93
267. Beaumont-Port Arthur, TX	24.65
268. Williamsport, PA	24.37
269. Flagstaff, AZ-UT	24.08
270. Lafayette, LA	23.80
271. Nashua, NH	23.52
272. Danbury, CT	23.23
273. Galveston-Texas City, TX	22.95
274. Rocky Mount, NC	22.67
275. Modesto, CA	22.38
276. Daytona Beach, FL	22.10
277. Youngstown-Warren, OH	21.82
278. Fort Smith, AR-OK	21.53
279. Saint John, NB	21.25
280. Cumberland, MD-WV	20.97
281. Lynchburg, VA	20.68
282. Wausau, WI	20.40
283. Richland-Kennewick-Pasco, WA	20.12
284. Johnstown, PA	19.84
285. Sherman-Denison, TX	19.55
286. Yolo, CA	19.27
287. Bakersfield, CA	18.99
288. Corpus Christi, TX	18.70
289. Danville, VA	18.42
290. Wilmington, NC	18.14
291. Fitchburg-Leominster, MA	17.85
292. Pensacola, FL	17.57
293. Billings, MT	17.29
294. Myrtle Beach, SC	17.00
295. Sherbrooke, PQ	16.72
296. Visalia-Tulare-Porterville, CA	16.44
297. Lubbock, TX	16.15
298. Macon, GA	15.87
298. Odessa-Midland, TX	15.87
300. Altoona, PA	15.30
301. Great Falls, MT	15.02
302. Longview-Marshall, TX	14.74
303. Pocatello, ID	14.45

RANK	SCORE
304. Sudbury, ON	14.17
305. Brazoria, TX	13.89
306. Vineland-Millville-Bridgeton, NJ	13.60
307. Owensboro, KY	13.32
308. Tuscaloosa, AL	13.04
309. Gary, IN	12.75
310. McAllen-Edinburg-Mission, TX	12.47
311. York, PA	12.19
312. Muncie, IN	11.90
313. Lake Charles, LA	11.62
314. Enid, OK	11.34
315. Pine Bluff, AR	11.05
316. Wichita Falls, TX	10.77
317. Chico-Paradise, CA	10.49
318. Fort Walton Beach, FL	10.20
319. Lewiston-Auburn, ME	9.92
320. Panama City, FL	9.64
321. Tyler, TX	9.35
322. Rapid City, SD	9.07
323. Canton-Massillon, OH	8.79
324. Victoria, TX	8.50
325. Florence, AL	8.22
326. Ocala, FL	7.94
327. Punta Gorda, FL	7.65
328. Jonesboro, AR	7.37
329. Goldsboro, NC	7.09
330. Chicoutimi-Jonquiere, PQ	6.80
331. Merced, CA	6.52
332. Greenville, NC	6.24
333. Florence, SC	5.95
334. Redding, CA	5.67
335. Steubenville-Weirton, OH-WV	5.39
336. Dothan, AL	5.10
337. Joplin, MO	4.82
338. Anniston, AL	4.54
339. Jacksonville, NC	4.25
340. Kankakee, IL	3.97
341. Yuma, AZ	3.69
342. Brownsville-Harlingen-San Benito, TX	3.40
343. Dover, DE	3.12
344. Decatur, AL	2.84
345. Sharon, PA	2.55
346. Kokomo, IN	2.27
347. Laredo, TX	1.99
348. Killeen-Temple, TX	1.70
349. Lawton, OK	1.42
350. Texarkana, TX-Texarkana, AR	1.14
351. Lawrence, MA-NH	0.85
352. Newburgh, NY-PA	0.57
353. Yuba City, CA	0.29
354. Houma, LA	0.00

PLACE PROFILES: THE ARTS

The profiles that follow are divided into seven possible headings in alphabetical order to show cultural and artistic features in each metro area.

Under the heading **Art Museums and Galleries** are nonprofit institutions whose main function is exhibiting art to the public. Museums listed are either accredited by the American Association of Museums; are institutions with three or more curators, a publication program, and a research library; or record more than 15,000 annual visitors.

Under the heading **Concert Radio** are stations whose city of license is within the metro area. Concert radio stations are stations with all or a significant part of their programming dedicated to a classical music format. For radio stations with especially strong signals, programming may also be received in nearby metro areas. In these instances, the media market defined by A.C. Nielsen Ratings Service in the U.S. or the Bureau of Broadcast Measurement in Canada is listed for the metro area that receives fine arts broadcasting from another area.

The remaining headings detail the names of resident Ballet Companies, Opera Companies, Performance Halls, Professional Theaters, and Symphony Orchestras.

The information is derived from these sources: American Association of Museums, *Official Museum Directory*, 1999; American Symphony Orchestra League, *Symphony* magazine, January-February 1999, and *Orchestra and Business Directory*, 1999; Association of Canadian Orchestras, *Directory of Canadian Orchestras*, 1999; Brant Art Publications, *Art in America's 1999 Guide to Galleries, Museums and Artists*; Canadian Museums Association, *Official Directory of Canadian Museums*, 1999; Conseil Quebecois de Theatre, *Repertoire Theatral de Quebec*, 1996; Corporation for Public Broadcasting, *Public Broadcasting Directory*, 1999; Musical America, *International Directory of the Performing Arts*, 1999; Opera America, *Profile*, 1999; Opera Canada Publications, *Opera Canada* magazine, 1999; Professional Association of Canadian Theatres, *The Theatre Listing*, 1999; R.R. Bowker Publishing, *American Art Directory*, 1996, and *Broadcasting and Cable Yearbook*, 1999; Theatre Communications Group, *Profile 12*, 1996.

A star (★) in front of the metro area's name highlights it as one of the top thirty-five places for the arts.

The Arts

Abilene, TX
  Concert Radio
    KACU-FM
  Opera
    Abilene Opera Association
  Performance Hall
    Abilene Civic Center
  Symphony Orchestra
    Abilene Philharmonic Association
  Score: 27.20   Rank: 258

Akron, OH
  Art Museums and Galleries
    Akron Art Museum
    Kent State U Art Galleries
    U of Akron Galleries
  Ballet Company
    Ohio Ballet
  Concert Radio
    In Cleveland media market
    WKSU-FM
  Performance Hall
    Thomas Performing Arts Hall
  Symphony Orchestra
    Akron Symphony
  Score: 81.59   Rank: 66

Albany, GA
  Art Museum and Gallery
    Albany Museum of Art

  Concert Radio
    WUNV-FM
  Performance Hall
    Municipal Auditorium
  Symphony Orchestra
    Albany Symphony
  Score: 33.15   Rank: 237

Albany-Schenectady-Troy, NY
  Art Museums and Galleries
    Albany Institute of History & Art
    Canajoharie Art Gallery
    New York State Museum
  Ballet Company
    Albany Berkshire Ballet
  Concert Radio
    WAMC-FM, WCAN-FM, WMHT-FM
  Performance Halls
    Palace Theatre
    Proctor's Theater
  Professional Theatres
    Capital Repertory Theatre
    Masque Theatre
    New York State Theatre Institute
  Symphony Orchestras
    Albany Symphony
    Music Company Orchestra
    Schenectady Symphony
  Score: 79.61   Rank: 73

Albuquerque, NM
  Art Museums and Galleries
    Albuquerque Museum
    Indian Pueblo Cultural Center
    U of New Mexico Art Galleries
  Ballet Company
    New Mexico Ballet Company
  Concert Radio
    KHFM-FM, KANW-FM, KUNM-FM
  Opera
    Opera Southwest
  Performance Hall
    University Popejoy Hall
  Symphony Orchestras
    Chamber Orchestra of Albuquerque
    New Mexico Symphony
  Score: 75.36   Rank: 88

Alexandria, LA
  Art Museum and Gallery
    Alexandria Museum of Art
  Concert Radio
    KLSA-FM
  Performance Hall
    Guinn Auditorium
  Symphony Orchestra
    Rapides Symphony
  Score: 40.80   Rank: 210

Allentown-Bethlehem-Easton, PA
Art Museums and Galleries
Allentown Art Museum
Kemerer Museum of Decorative Arts
Lafayette College Williams Gallery
Ballet Company
Ballet Guild of Lehigh Valley
Concert Radio
In Philadelphia media market
WDIY-FM
Professional Theatres
Pennsylvania Stage Company
Touchstone Theatre
Symphony Orchestras
Allentown Symphony
Pennsylvania Sinfonia Orchestra
Score: 58.08   Rank: 149

Altoona, PA
Performance Hall
Roosevelt Auditorium
Symphony Orchestra
Altoona Symphony
Score: 15.30   Rank: 300

Amarillo, TX
Art Museum and Gallery
Amarillo Art Center
Ballet Company
Lone Star Ballet
Opera Company
Amarillo Opera
Performance Hall
Civic Center Auditorium
Symphony Orchestra
Amarillo Symphony
Score: 35.13   Rank: 230

Anchorage, AK
Art Museums and Galleries
Anchorage Museum of History & Art
Visual Arts Center of Alaska
Concert Radio
KLEF-FM, KNBA-FM, KSKA-FM
Opera Company
Anchorage Opera
Performance Hall
Alaska Center for Performing Arts
Symphony Orchestra
Anchorage Symphony
Score: 29.47   Rank: 250

Ann Arbor, MI
Art Museums and Galleries
U of Michigan Museum of Art
Artrain
Concert Radio
In Detroit media market
WUOM-FM, WEMU-FM
Opera Companies
Comic Opera Guild
Opera Lenawee
Performance Halls
Hill Auditorium
Michigan Theatre

Professional Theatres
The Purple Rose Theatre Company
University Productions
Symphony Orchestras
Adrian Symphony
Ann Arbor Symphony
Score: 67.99   Rank: 114

Anniston, AL
Concert Radio
WLJS-FM
Performance Hall
Anniston Auditorium
Score: 4.54   Rank: 338

Appleton-Oshkosh-Neenah, WI
Art Museums and Galleries
Bergstrom-Mahler Museum
Paine Art Center & Arboretum
Concert Radio
In Green Bay media market
WLFM-FM, WRST-FM
Performance Hall
Civic Auditorium
Symphony Orchestras
Fox Valley Symphony
Oshkosh Symphony
Score: 50.71   Rank: 175

Asheville, NC
Art Museum and Gallery
Asheville Art Museum
Concert Radio
In Greenville-Spartanburg media
market
WCQS-FM
Performance Hall
Thomas Wolfe Auditorium
Symphony Orchestra
Asheville Symphony
Score: 44.76   Rank: 196

Athens, GA
Art Museum and Gallery
Georgia Museum of Art
Concert Radio
In Atlanta media market
WUGA-FM
Professional Theatre
U of Georgia Theatre
Performance Hall
U of Georgia Performing Arts Center
Score: 37.40   Rank: 222

★Atlanta, GA
Art Museums and Galleries
Agnes Scott College Dalton Gallery
Callanwolde Fine Arts Center
Emory U Museum of Art
Georgia State U Art Gallery
High Museum of Art
Nexus Contemporary Art Center
Ballet Company
Atlanta Ballet

Concert Radio
WABE-FM, WGKA-AM, WCLK-FM,
WJSP-FM, WWGC-FM
Opera Company
Atlanta Opera
Performance Halls
Atlanta Civic Center
Fox Theatre
Rialto Center for Performing Arts
Woodruff Arts Center
Professional Theatres
Academy Theatre
Alliance Theatre–Mainstage
Alliance Theatre–Studio Theatre
Art Station Theatre
Horizon Theater Company
Jomandi Productions
The Shakespeare Tavern
Theatre Gael
Theatre in the Square
Theatrical Outfit
Symphony Orchestras
Atlanta Community Symphony
Atlanta Pops
Atlanta Symphony
Cobb Symphony
De Kalb Symphony
Orchestra Atlanta
Score: 94.62   Rank: 20

Atlantic City-Cape May, NJ
Art Museum and Gallery
Noyes Museum
Ballet Company
Atlantic Contemporary Ballet Theatre
Concert Radio
In Philadelphia media market
WNJN-FM, WRTQ-FM
Professional Theatre
South Jersey Regional Theatre
Symphony Orchestra
Ocean City Pops
Score: 38.25   Rank: 219

Augusta-Aiken, GA-SC
Art Museum and Gallery
Gertrude Herbert Institute of Art
Ballet Company
Augusta Ballet Company
Concert Radio
WACG-FM, WLJK-FM
Opera Company
Augusta Opera Company
Performance Hall
Maxwell Grover Performing Arts
Theatre
Symphony Orchestra
Augusta Symphony
Score: 50.43   Rank: 176

Austin-San Marcos, TX
Art Museums and Galleries
Elisabet Ney Museum
Laguna Gloria Art Museum
UT Huntington Art Gallery

Concert Radio
KMFA-FM, KUT-FM
Opera Company
Austin Lyric Opera
Performance Halls
Paramount Theatre for Performing Arts
U of Texas Performing Arts Center
Symphony Orchestras
Austin Civic Orchestra Society
Austin Symphony
Score: 72.24   Rank: 99

Bakersfield, CA
Art Museum and Gallery
Bakersfield Museum of Art
Concert Radio
KPRX-FM
Performance Hall
Bakersfield Convention Center
Symphony Orchestra
Bakersfield Symphony
Score: 18.99   Rank: 287

★Baltimore, MD
Art Museums and Galleries
Baltimore Museum of Art
James Lewis Museum of Art
Maryland Institute
Mitchell Art Gallery St. John's College
Museum for Contemporary Art
Walters Art Gallery
Ballet Company
Ballet Theatre of Annapolis
Concert Radio
WBJC-FM, WHFC-FM, WJHU-FM,
WEAA-FM
Opera Companies
Annapolis Opera
Baltimore Opera Company
Baltimore Opera Touring Theatre
Performance Halls
Friedberg Concert Hall
Lyric Opera House
Meyerhoff Symphony Hall
Professional Theatres
Center Stage - Head Theatre
Center Stage - Pearlstone Theatre
Symphony Orchestras
Annapolis Chamber Orchestra
Annapolis Symphony
Baltimore Chamber Orchestra
Baltimore Concert Artists
Baltimore Symphony
Hopkins Symphony
Peabody Conservatory Symphony
Score: 95.47   Rank: 17

Bangor, ME
Art Museum and Gallery
UM Museum of Art
Concert Radio
WMEH-FM
Performance Hall
Maine Center for the Arts

Professional Theatre
Penobscot Theatre Company
Symphony Orchestra
Bangor Symphony
Score: 63.46   Rank: 130

Barnstable-Yarmouth, MA
Concert Radio
In Boston media market
WFCC-FM, WCCT-FM, WKKL-FM,
WSDH-FM
Performance Hall
Cape Cod Community College
Auditorium
Symphony Orchestra
Cape Cod Symphony
Score: 62.89   Rank: 132

Baton Rouge, LA
Art Museums and Galleries
Louisiana Arts & Science Center
LSU Galleries
Ballet Company
Baton Rouge Ballet Theatre
Concert Radio
WRKF-FM, WBRH-FM
Performance Hall
Riverside Centroplex
Symphony Orchestra
Baton Rouge Symphony
Score: 45.90   Rank: 192

Beaumont-Port Arthur, TX
Art Museum and Gallery
Art Museum of Southeast Texas
Concert Radio
KVLU-FM
Performance Hall
Julie Rogers Theatre
Symphony Orchestra
Symphony of Southeast Texas
Score: 24.65   Rank: 267

Bellingham, WA
Art Museum and Gallery
Whatcom Museum of History & Art
Concert Radio
In Seattle-Tacoma media market
KZAZ-FM
Performance Hall
Mount Baker Theater
Symphony Orchestra
Whatcom Symphony
Score: 67.14   Rank: 117

Benton Harbor, MI
Art Museum and Gallery
Krasl Art Center
Concert Radio
In South Bend-Elkhart media market
WAUS-FM
Performance Hall
Mendel Center Mainstage

Symphony Orchestra
Southwest Michigan Symphony
Score: 47.88   Rank: 185

Bergen-Passaic, NJ
Art Museum and Gallery
Bergen Museum of Art & Science
Ballet Company
Irine Fokine Ballet Company
Concert Radio
In New York media market
Professional Theatre
American Stage Company
Symphony Orchestras
Ars Musica Chorale & Orchestra
Bergen Philharmonic Orchestra
New Jersey Philharmonic
Ridgewood Symphony
Wayne Chamber Orchestra
Score: 90.09   Rank: 36

Billings, MT
Art Museum and Gallery
Yellowstone Art Center
Concert Radio
KEMC-FM
Performance Hall
Alberta Bair Theatre
Symphony Orchestra
Billings Symphony & Chorale
Score: 17.29   Rank: 293

Biloxi-Gulfport-Pascagoula, MS
Concert Radio
WMAH-FM
Opera Company
Gulf Coast Opera Theatre
Performance Hall
Saenger Theater
Symphony Orchestra
Gulf Coast Symphony
Score: 31.17   Rank: 244

Binghamton, NY
Art Museum and Gallery
Roberson Museum
Concert Radio
WSKG-FM, WSQX-FM
Opera Company
Tri-Cities Opera
Performance Hall
Anderson Center
Symphony Orchestra
Binghamton Symphony & Choral
Society
Score: 47.31   Rank: 187

Birmingham, AL
Art Museum and Gallery
Birmingham Museum of Art
Ballet Company
Alabama Ballet
Concert Radio
WBHM-FM

Opera Company
Opera Birmingham
Performance Halls
Birmingham-Jefferson Convention
Complex
Stephens Performing Arts Center
Professional Theatre
Birmingham Children's Theatre
Symphony Orchestra
Alabama Symphony
Score: 85.27   Rank: 53

Bismarck, ND
Concert Radio
In Minot-Dickinson media market
KCND-FM
Performance Hall
Belle Mehus City Auditorium
Symphony Orchestra
Bismarck-Mandan Symphony
Score: 37.97   Rank: 220

Bloomington, IN
Art Museum and Gallery
IU Art Museum
Concert Radio
In Indianapolis media market
WFIU-FM
Performance Halls
Creative Arts Auditorium
Musical Arts Center
Professional Theatre
Indiana U Theatre
Symphony Orchestra
Bloomington Symphony
Score: 79.33   Rank: 74

Bloomington-Normal, IL
Art Museum and Gallery
Illinois Wesleyan Galleries
Concert Radio
In Peoria media market
WGLT-FM
Performance Hall
Braden Auditorium
Professional Theatre
ISU Theatre
Score: 62.33   Rank: 134

Boise City, ID
Art Museums and Galleries
Boise Art Museum
Rosenthal Gallery of Art
Ballet Company
Ballet Idaho
Concert Radio
KBSU-AM, KBSU-FM, KBSX-FM
Opera Company
Opera Idaho!
Performance Hall
Morrison Center
Symphony Orchestra
Boise Philharmonic
Score: 75.64   Rank: 87

★**Boston, MA-NH**
Art Museums and Galleries
Art Complex Museum
Boston College Museum of Art
Boston Athenaeum
Danforth Museum of Art
De Cordova Museum & Sculpture Park
Harvard Art Museums
Institute of Contemporary Art
Isabella Stewart Gardner Museum
Museum of Fine Arts
Rose Art Museum Brandeis
Wellesley College Museum
Ballet Companies
Boston Ballet
Boston Flamenco Ballet
Concert Radio
WBOQ-FM, WBUR-FM, WCRB-FM,
WGBH-FM, WHRB-FM, WUMB-FM
Opera Companies
Boston Festival Opera Ltd.
Boston Lyric Opera Company
Longwood Opera
Opera New England
Performance Halls
New England Conservatory Jordan Hall
Sanders Theatre at Harvard
Symphony Hall
Tsai Performance Center
Wang Center
Professional Theatres
American Repertory Theatre
Huntington Theatre Company
Jewish Theatre of New England
Lyric Stage
New Repertory Theatre
New Theatre
North Shore Music Theatre
Underground Railway Theater
Wheelock Family Theatre
Symphony Orchestras
Boston Baroque
Boston Classical Orchestra
Boston Modern Orchestra Project
Boston Philharmonic
Boston Symphony Chamber Players
Boston Symphony
Cape Ann Symphony
Civic Symphony of Boston
Concord Orchestra
French Symphony of Boston
Handel & Haydn Society
Indian Hill Symphony
Jamaica Plain Symphony
Melrose Symphony
New England Conservatory Orchestras
New England Philharmonic
New England String Ensemble
Newton Symphony
Plymouth Philharmonic Orchestra
Pro Arte Chamber Orchestra of Boston
Quincy Symphony
Symphony by the Sea

Symphony Pro Musica
Thayer Symphony
The Alloy Orchestra
Score: 98.59   Rank: 6

Boulder-Longmont, CO
Art Museums and Galleries
CU Art Galleries
Leanin' Tree Museum of Western Art
Concert Radio
In Denver media market
KGNU-FM
Performance Hall
Macky Auditorium
Symphony Orchestras
Boulder Philharmonic Orchestra
Colorado Music Festival Orchestra
Longmont Symphony
Sinfonia of Colorado
U of Colorado Symphony
Score: 69.98   Rank: 107

Brazoria, TX
Concert Radio
In Houston media market
Score: 13.89   Rank: 305

Bremerton, WA
Concert Radio
In Seattle-Tacoma media market
Performance Hall
Bremerton Performing Arts Center
Symphony Orchestra
Bremerton Symphony
Score: 36.27   Rank: 226

Bridgeport, CT
Art Museum and Gallery
Housatonic Museum of Art
Concert Radio
In Hartford-New Haven media market
WMNR-FM, WRXC-FM, WSHU-FM
Performance Hall
Klein Memorial Auditorium
Professional Theatre
Downtown Cabaret Theatre
Symphony Orchestra
Greater Bridgeport Symphony
Score: 77.91   Rank: 79

Brockton, MA
Art Museum and Gallery
Fuller Museum of Art
Concert Radio
In Boston media market
Symphony Orchestra
Brockton Symphony
Score: 36.55   Rank: 225

Brownsville-Harlingen-San Benito, TX
Art Museum and Gallery
Brownsville Art League Museum
Concert Radio
KMBH-FM
Score: 3.40   Rank: 342

Bryan-College Station, TX
Concert Radio
In Waco-Temple-Bryan media market
KAMU-FM
Performance Hall
Texas A & M Auditorium
Symphony Orchestra
Brazos Valley Symphony
Score: 33.72   Rank: 235

★Buffalo-Niagara Falls, NY
Art Museums and Galleries
Albright-Knox Art Gallery
Burchfield-Penney Art Center
Hallwall's Contemporary Art Center
Concert Radio
WBFO-FM, WNED-FM
Opera Company
Greater Buffalo Opera Company
Performance Hall
Kleinhans Music Hall
Professional Theatres
Artpark at the Church
Studio Arena Theatre
Symphony Orchestras
Amherst Symphony
Ars Nova Musicians Chamber
Orchestra
Buffalo Philharmonic Orchestra
Score: 93.49   Rank: 24

Burlington, VT
Art Museums and Galleries
Francis Colburn Gallery
Robert H. Fleming Museum
Ballet Company
Burklyn Ballet Theatre
Concert Radio
In Plattsburgh media market
WVPR-FM, WVPS-FM
Performance Halls
Burlington Memorial Auditorium
Flynn Theatre
Professional Theatres
Green Mountain Guild
Vermont Stage Company
Symphony Orchestra
Vermont Symphony
Score: 80.17   Rank: 71

Calgary, AB
Art Museums and Galleries
Alberta College of Art Gallery
Centre Eye Photography Gallery
Glenbow Museum
Mount Royal College Gallery
Muttart Gallery
Triangle Gallery of Visual Arts
Concert Radio
CBR-AM, CBR-FM
Ballet Companies
Alberta Ballet
Alberta Theatre Projects
Opera Company
Calgary Opera Association

Performance Halls
Calgary Center
Jubilee Auditorium
Professional Theatres
Alberta Theatre Projects
All Nations International Theatre
Garry Theatre
Loose Moose Theatre
Lunchbox Theatre
Maenad Theatre
One Yellow Rabbit Theatre
Pegasus
Pleiades Mystery Theatre
Pumphouse Theatres Society
Quest Theatre
Shakespeare in the Park
Sun.Ergos
Theatre Calgary
Trickster
Symphony Orchestra
Calgary Philharmonic Orchestra
Score: 88.11   Rank: 43

Canton-Massillon, OH
Art Museum and Gallery
Canton Museum of Art
Concert Radio
In Cleveland media market
WRMU-FM
Ballet Company
Canton Ballet
Performance Hall
Palace Theatre
Symphony Orchestra
Canton Symphony
Score: 8.79   Rank: 323

Casper, WY
Art Museum and Gallery
Nicolaysen Art Museum
Concert Radio
KUWC-FM
Performance Hall
Casper Events Center
Symphony Orchestra
Wyoming Symphony
Score: 42.50   Rank: 204

Cedar Rapids, IA
Art Museums and Galleries
Museum of Art
Cornell College Armstrong Gallery
Performance Hall
Paramount Theatre
Symphony Orchestra
Cedar Rapids Symphony
Score: 56.38   Rank: 155

Champaign-Urbana, IL
Art Museum and Gallery
UI Krannert Art Museum
Concert Radio
WILL-AM, WILL-FM
Performance Hall
Krannert Center

Symphony Orchestras
Champaign-Urbana Symphony
Sinfonia Da Camera
Score: 56.10   Rank: 156

Charleston, WV
Art Museum and Gallery
Sunrise Art Museum
Ballet Company
Charleston Ballet
Concert Radio
WVPN-FM
Performance Hall
Charleston Civic Center
Symphony Orchestra
West Virginia Symphony
Score: 52.41   Rank: 169

Charleston-North Charleston, SC
Art Museum and Gallery
Gibbes Museum of Art
Ballet Company
Charleston Ballet Theatre
Concert Radio
WSCI-FM
Performance Hall
Gaillard Municipal Auditorium
Symphony Orchestra
Charleston Symphony
Score: 61.19   Rank: 138

Charlotte-Gastonia-Rock Hill, NC-SC
Art Museums and Galleries
Davidson College Art Gallery
Gaston County Museum of Art &
History
Mint Museum of Art
Concert Radio
WDAV-FM, WFAE-FM, WNSC-FM,
WSGE-FM
Opera Company
Opera Carolina
Performance Halls
Blumenthal Performing Arts Center
Ovens Auditorium
Professional Theatre
Charlotte Repertory Theatre
Symphony Orchestras
Charlotte Philharmonic Orchestra
Charlotte Repertory Orchestra
Charlotte Symphony Society
Salisbury Symphony
Score: 88.39   Rank: 42

Charlottesville, VA
Art Museum and Gallery
Bayly Art Museum
Concert Radio
WMRY-FM, WTJU-FM
Opera Company
Ash Lawn-Highland Opera Company
Performance Halls
Cabell Hall Auditorium
Charlottesville Performing Arts Center
Score: 59.78   Rank: 143

Chattanooga, TN-GA
Art Museums and Galleries
Houston Museum of Decorative Arts
Hunter Museum of Art 55
Ballet Company
Ballet Tennessee
Concert Radio
WSMC-FM, WUTC-FM
Opera Company
Chattanooga Opera
Performance Hall
Tivoli Theatre
Symphony Orchestra
Chattanooga Symphony & Opera
Association
Score: 81.87   Rank: 65

Cheyenne, WY
Art Museum and Gallery
State Museum Art Gallery
Concert Radio
In Scottsbluff-Sterling media market
Performance Hall
Civic Center
Symphony Orchestra
Cheyenne Symphony
Score: 25.78   Rank: 263

★Chicago, IL
Art Museums and Galleries
Art Institute of Chicago
Block Gallery
Hyde Park Art Center
Illinois State Museum Art Gallery
Museum of Contemporary Art
Spertus Museum of Judaica
Terra Museum of American Art
U of Illinois Gallery
U of Chicago Galleries
Ballet Companies
Ballet Chicago
Joffrey Ballet of Chicago
Von Heidecke's Chicago Festival Ballet
Concert Radio
WBEZ-FM, WFMT-FM, WMWA-FM,
WNIB-FM, WNIU-FM, WNIZ-FM
Opera Companies
Chicago Opera Theater
Du Page Opera Theatre
Light Opera Works
Lyric Opera of Chicago
Opera Factory
Performance Halls
Civic Opera House
Norris Cultural Arts Center
Orchestra Hall
Paramount Arts Center
Ravinia Pavilion
Professional Theatres
Apple Tree Theatre
Bailiwick Repertory
Center Theater Ensemble
Child's Play Touring Theatre
Court Theatre

ETA Creative Arts Foundation Inc
Goodman Theatre
Goodman Theatre Studio
Illinois Theatre Center
International Performance Studio
Lifeline Theatre–Mainstage
Light Opera Works–Cahn Auditorium
New Tuners Theatre
Next Theatre
Northlight Theatre
Organic Touchstone Company
Piven Theatre Workshop
Stage Left Theatre
Steppenwolf Studio Theatre
The Chicago Theatre Company
Theatre Building
Victory Gardens Theatre
Symphony Orchestras
American Chamber Strings
American Festival Orchestra
Chicago Bar Association Symphony
Chicago Chamber Orchestra
Chicago Philharmonia
Chicago Sinfonietta
Chicago String Ensemble
Chicago Symphonic Wind Ensemble
Chicago Symphony
Civic Orchestra of Chicago
Classical Symphony & Protégé
Philharmonic
Concerts Symphoniques
Downers Grove Choral Society &
Orchestra
DuPage Symphony
Elgin Symphony
Elmhurst Symphony
Fox Valley Symphony
Grant Park Symphony & Chorus
Illinois Philharmonic Orchestra
Lake Forest Symphony
Loop Chamber Orchestra
Metropolis Symphony
New Philharmonic
Northbrook Symphony
Northwest Symphony
Sinfonia Americana
Skokie Valley Symphony
Southwest Symphony
Symphony II
Symphony of Oak Park & River Forest
The Chinese Classical Orchestra
Waukegan Symphony
Wheaton Symphony
Zion Chamber Orchestra
Score: 99.16   Rank: 4

Chico-Paradise, CA
Art Museum and Gallery
CSU Art Gallery
Concert Radio
KCHO-FM
Symphony Orchestra
Paradise Symphony
Score: 10.49   Rank: 317

Chicoutimi-Jonquiere, PQ
Art Museums and Galleries
Centre National d'Exposition
Espace Virtuel
Performance Hall
Auditoire Dufour
Professional Theatre
La Rubrique
Symphony Orchestra
Orchestre Symphonique du Saguenay–
Lac-St-Jean
Score: 6.80   Rank: 330

★Cincinnati, OH-KY-IN
Art Museums and Galleries
Cincinnati Art Museum
Cincinnati Institute of Fine Arts
Contemporary Arts Center
UC Tangeman Gallery
Ballet Company
Cincinnati Ballet
Concert Radio
WGUC-FM, WNKU-FM, WVXU-FM
Opera Company
Cincinnati Opera Association
Performance Halls
Aronoff Center for the Arts
Hamilton County Memorial Hall
Music Hall
Riverbend Music Center
Professional Theatres
Artreach
Ensemble Theatre of Cincinnati
Playhouse in the Park
Shakespeare Festival
Symphony Orchestras
Cincinnati Chamber Orchestra
Cincinnati Philharmonia & Concert
Orchestra
Cincinnati Symphony
Northern Kentucky Symphony
Score: 94.06   Rank: 22

Clarksville-Hopkinsville, TN-KY
Art Museum and Gallery
Trahern Gallery
Concert Radio
In Nashville media market
Performance Hall
Austin Peay Concert Theatre
Score: 37.12   Rank: 223

★Cleveland-Lorain-Elyria, OH
Art Museums and Galleries
Cleveland Center for Contemporary Art
Cleveland Museum of Art
CSU Art Gallery
Oberlin College Allen Art Museum
Reinberger Galleries
Ballet Companies
Cleveland San Jose Ballet
North Coast Ballet Theatre
Concert Radio
WCPN-FM, WCLV-FM

Opera Companies
Cleveland Opera
Lyric Opera Cleveland
Performance Halls
Playhouse Square
Severance Hall
Professional Theatres
Cleveland Play House
Cleveland Public Theatre
Great Lakes Theatre Festival
Karamu House
Signstage Theatre
Symphony Orchestras
Cleveland Chamber Symphony
Cleveland Orchestra
Cleveland Women's Orchestra
Lakeland Civic Orchestra
Oberlin Orchestra
Ohio Chamber Orchestra
Shaker Symphony
Suburban Symphony
Trinity Chamber Orchestra
Score: 97.17   Rank: 11

Colorado Springs, CO
Art Museums and Galleries
Colorado Springs Fine Arts Center
CU Gallery of Contemporary Art
Concert Radio
KCME-FM, KRCC-FM
Opera Company
Colorado Opera Festival
Performance Hall
Pikes Peak Center
Professional Theatre
UCCS Theatreworks
Symphony Orchestras
Colorado Springs Symphony
Pikes Peak Civic Orchestra
Score: 62.04   Rank: 135

Columbia, MO
Art Museum and Gallery
Museum of Art & Archaeology
Concert Radio
KBIA-FM, KOPN-FM
Performance Halls
Missouri Theatre
U of Missouri Jesse Auditorium
Symphony Orchestra
Missouri Symphony Society
Score: 60.06   Rank: 142

Columbia, SC
Art Museums and Galleries
Columbia Museum of Art
USC McKissick Museum
Ballet Companies
Carolina Ballet
Columbia City Ballet
Concert Radio
WLTR-FM
Performance Hall
Koger Center for the Arts

Symphony Orchestras
South Carolina Philharmonic Orchestra
U of South Carolina Orchestra
Score: 64.31   Rank: 127

Columbus, GA-AL
Art Museums and Galleries
Columbus College Gallery
Columbus Museum
Concert Radio
WTJB-FM
Performance Hall
Three Arts Theatre
Symphony Orchestra
Columbus Symphony
Score: 47.03   Rank: 188

★Columbus, OH
Art Museums and Galleries
Columbus Cultural Arts Center
Columbus Museum of Art
Denison University Gallery
OSU Wexner Center for the Arts
Schumacher Gallery
Ballet Company
BalletMet
Concert Radio
WCBE-FM, WOSU-FM
Opera Company
Columbus Light Opera
Opera/Columbus
Performance Halls
Ohio Theatre
OSU Wexner Center for the Arts
Palace Theatre
Professional Theatres
Contemporary American Theatre
    Company
Phoenix Theatre Circle
Symphony Orchestras
Central Ohio Symphony
Columbus Symphony
Land of Legend Philharmonic
Pro Musica Chamber Orchestra
Westerville Civic Symphony
Score: 92.64   Rank: 27

Corpus Christi, TX
Art Museum and Gallery
Art Museum of South Texas
Ballet Company
Corpus Christi Ballet
Concert Radio
KEDT-FM
Performance Hall
Bayfront Plaza Auditorium
Symphony Orchestra
Corpus Christi Symphony
Score: 18.70   Rank: 288

Cumberland, MD-WV
Concert Radio
In Washington media market
WFWM-FM

Performance Hall
Western Maryland Center
Symphony Orchestra
Western Maryland Symphony
Score: 20.97   Rank: 280

★Dallas, TX
Art Museums and Galleries
Dallas Museum of Art
Dallas Visual Art Center
SMU Qwens Art Center
Ballet Company
Dallas Metropolitan Ballet
Concert Radio
KERA-FM, WRR-FM
Opera Company
Dallas Opera
Performance Halls
Majestic Theatre
Meyerson Symphony Center
Music Hall at Fair Park
Professional Theatres
Dallas Children's Theater
Dallas Theatre Center
Theatre Three
Undermain Theatre
Symphony Orchestras
Dallas Bach Orchestra & Choir
Dallas Chamber Orchestra
Dallas Symphony
Garland Symphony
Irving New Philharmonic Orchestra
Irving Symphony
Las Colinas Symphony
Metrocrest Chamber Symphony
Northeast Texas Symphony
Orchestra of New Spain
Plano Chamber Orchestra
SMC Symphony
Texas Symphony
Score: 93.21   Rank: 25

Danbury, CT
Art Museum and Gallery
Aldrich Museum of Contemporary Art
Concert Radio
In Hartford-New Haven media market
Performance Hall
Ives Center for the Arts
Symphony Orchestra
Ridgefield Symphony
Score: 23.23   Rank: 272

Danville, VA
Art Museum and Gallery
Museum of Fine Arts & History
Concert Radio
In Roanoke-Lynchburg media market
Performance Hall
Danville Auditorium
Score: 18.42   Rank: 289

Davenport-Moline-Rock Island, IA-IL
Art Museums and Galleries
Augustana College Gallery of Art
Davenport Museum of Art
Concert Radio
WVIK-FM
Performance Halls
Adler Theatre
Centennial Hall
Symphony Orchestras
Augustana Symphony
Quad City Symphony
Score: 59.21   Rank: 145

Dayton-Springfield, OH
Art Museums and Galleries
Dayton Art Institute
Springfield Museum of Art
Concert Radio
WDPR-FM, WYSO-FM
Opera Companies
Dayton Opera Association
Ohio Lyric Theatre of Springfield
Performance Halls
Montgomery County Memorial Hall
Victoria Theatre Association
Professional Theatre
Human Race Theatre Company
Symphony Orchestras
Dayton Philharmonic Orchestra
Springfield Symphony
Score: 87.54   Rank: 45

Daytona Beach, FL
Art Museum and Gallery
Deland Museum of Art
Duncan Gallery
Museum of Arts & Sciences
Performance Hall
Ocean Center
Score: 22.10   Rank: 276

Decatur, AL
Art Museum and Gallery
CSCC Art Gallery
Performance Hall
Princess Theatre Center
Score: 2.84   Rank: 344

Decatur, IL
Art Museum and Gallery
Kirkland Fine Arts Center
Performance Hall
Kirkland Center Theatre
Symphony Orchestra
Millikin-Decatur Symphony
Score: 43.91   Rank: 199

★Denver, CO
Art Museums and Galleries
Denver Art Museum
Museum of Western Art
Ballet Companies
Ballet Denver
Colorado Ballet

Concert Radio
KCFR-FM, KPOF-AM, KUVO-FM,
KVOD-FM
Opera Companies
Central City Opera House
Opera Colorado
Performance Halls
Auditorium Theatre
Boettcher Concert Hall
Buell Theatre
Red Rocks Amphitheatre
Professional Theatres
Denver Center Theatre Company
Ricketson Theatre
Symphony Orchestras
Arapahoe Philharmonic
Colorado Symphony
Denver Young Artists Orchestra
Jefferson Symphony
Score: 97.74   Rank: 9

Des Moines, IA
Art Museums and Galleries
Des Moines Art Center
Salisbury House
Opera Company
Des Moines Metro Opera
Performance Halls
Civic Center
Sheslow Auditorium
Symphony Orchestras
Des Moines Community Orchestra
Des Moines Symphony
Drake Symphony
Score: 60.34   Rank: 141

★Detroit, MI
Art Museums and Galleries
Cranbrook Academy of Art Museum
Creative Arts Center
Detroit Institute of Arts
Meadow Brook Art Gallery
WSU Community Arts Gallery
Concert Radio
WDET-FM, WQRS-FM
Opera Company
Michigan Opera Theatre
Performance Halls
Detroit Opera House
Fisher Theatre
Masonic Temple Theatre
Symphony Hall
Professional Theatres
Detroit Repertory Theatre
Hilberry Repertory Theatre
Meadow Brook Theatre
Symphony Orchestras
Birmingham-Bloomfield Symphony
Dearborn Orchestral Society
Detroit Symphony Civic Orchestra
Detroit Symphony
Farmington Area Philharmonic
Grosse Pointe Symphony
Lake St. Clair Symphony

Livonia Symphony
Michigan Chamber Orchestra
National Sinfonietta
Pontiac-Oakland Symphony
Warren Symphony, The Michigan
Orchestra
Score: 95.19   Rank: 18

Dothan, AL
Art Museum and Gallery
Wiregrass Museum of Art
Concert Radio
WRWA-FM
Performance Hall
Dothan Center
Score: 5.10   Rank: 336

Dover, DE
Concert Radio
In Philadelphia media market
WAMU-FM, WETA-FM, WRTX-FM
Score: 3.12   Rank: 343

Dubuque, IA
Art Museum and Gallery
Dubuque Association of Art
Performance Hall
Five Flags Theatre
Symphony Orchestra
Dubuque Symphony
Score: 46.75   Rank: 189

Duluth-Superior, MN-WI
Art Museum and Gallery
UM Tweed Museum of Art
Ballet Company
Minnesota Ballet
Concert Radio
KUWS-FM, WHSA-FM, WIRN-FM,
WSCN-FM, WSCD-FM
Performance Halls
Marshall Center
St. Louis County Center
Symphony Orchestras
Duluth-Superior Symphony
Lake Superior Chamber Orchestra
Score: 74.23   Rank: 92

Dutchess County, NY
Art Museum and Gallery
Vassar College Art Gallery
Concert Radio
In New York media market
WRHV-FM
Performance Hall
Bardavon 1896 Opera House
Symphony Orchestra
Hudson Valley Philharmonic Society
Score: 48.16   Rank: 184

Eau Claire, WI
Concert Radio
WUEC-FM
Performance Halls
Gantner Concert Hall
Regional Arts Center

Symphony Orchestras
Chippewa Valley Symphony
U of Wisconsin/Eau Claire Symphony
Score: 42.78   Rank: 203

Edmonton, AB
Art Museums and Galleries
Latitude 53 Gallery
The Edmonton Art Gallery
U of Alberta Collections
Concert Radio
CBX-FM, CKUA-FM
Opera Company
Edmonton Opera Association
Performance Halls
Northern Alberta Jubilee Auditorium
Winspear Centre for Music
Professional Theatres
Azimuth Theatre Association
Catalyst Theatre
Chinook Theatre Society
Citadel Theatre
Concrete Theatre
Fringe Theatre Event
Leave It to Jane Theatre
Northern Light Theatre
Stage Polaris
The Phoenix Theatre
Theatre Network Society
Workshop West Theatre
Symphony Orchestra
Edmonton Symphony
Score: 82.72   Rank: 62

El Paso, TX
Art Museum and Gallery
El Paso Museum of Art
Concert Radio
KTEP-FM
Opera Company
El Paso Opera
Performance Hall
El Paso Performing Arts Theater
Symphony Orchestras
El Paso Philharmonic Strings
El Paso Symphony
Score: 54.11   Rank: 163

Elkhart-Goshen, IN
Art Museum and Gallery
Midwest Museum of American Art
Concert Radio
WGCS-FM, WVPE-FM
Performance Hall
Elco Performing Arts Center
Symphony Orchestra
Elkhart County Symphony
Score: 40.23   Rank: 212

Elmira, NY
Art Museum and Gallery
Arnot Art Museum
Performance Hall
The Clemens Center
Score: 31.45   Rank: 243

Enid, OK
Concert Radio
In Oklahoma City media market
Performance Hall
Convention Hall
Symphony Orchestra
Enid-Phillips Symphony
Score: 11.34   Rank: 314

Erie, PA
Art Museum and Gallery
Erie Art Museum
Concert Radio
WMCE-FM, WQLN-FM
Performance Hall
Civic Center Complex
Symphony Orchestra
Erie Philharmonic
Score: 38.82   Rank: 217

Eugene-Springfield, OR
Art Museum and Gallery
University Museum of Art
Ballet Company
Eugene Ballet Company
Concert Radio
KLCC-FM, KWAX-FM
Opera Company
Eugene Opera
Performance Halls
Beall Concert Hall
Hult Center
Symphony Orchestras
Eugene Symphony
Oregon Mozart Players
Score: 51.00   Rank: 174

Evansville-Henderson, IN-KY
Art Museum and Gallery
Museum of Art & Science
Concert Radio
WKPB-FM, WNIN-FM
Performance Hall
Vanderburgh Auditorium
Professional Theatre
New Harmony Theatre
Symphony Orchestra
Evansville Philharmonic Orchestra
Score: 75.08   Rank: 89

Fargo-Moorhead, ND-MN
Art Museum and Gallery
NDSU Art Gallery
Plains Art Museum
Concert Radio
KCCM-FM, KCCD-FM, KDSU-FM
Opera Company
Fargo-Moorhead Civic Opera Company
Performance Hall
NDSU Festival Concert Hall
Symphony Orchestra
Fargo-Moorhead Symphony
Score: 82.16   Rank: 64

Fayetteville, NC
Art Museum and Gallery
Fayetteville Museum of Art
Concert Radio
In Raleigh-Durham media market
WFSS-FM
Performance Hall
Reeves Auditorium
Symphony Orchestra
Fayetteville Symphony
Score: 48.45   Rank: 183

Fayetteville-Springdale-Rogers, AR
Art Museum and Gallery
Arts Center for the Ozarks
Concert Radio
In Ft. Smith media market
KUAF-FM
Performance Hall
Walton Arts Center
Symphony Orchestra
North Arkansas Symphony
Score: 64.59   Rank: 126

Fitchburg-Leominster, MA
Art Museum and Gallery
Fitchburg Art Museum
Concert Radio
In Boston media market
Score: 17.85   Rank: 291

Flagstaff, AZ-UT
Art Museum and Gallery
Museum of Northern Arizona
Concert Radio
In Phoenix media market
KGHR-FM, KNAD-FM, KNAQ-FM,
KNAU-FM
Performance Hall
Ardrey Memorial Auditorium
Symphony Orchestras
Flagstaff Festival of the Arts
Flagstaff Symphony
Score: 24.08   Rank: 269

Flint, MI
Art Museum and Gallery
Flint Institute of Arts
Concert Radio
WFBE-FM, WFUM-FM
Performance Hall
Whiting Auditorium
Symphony Orchestra
Flint Symphony
Score: 43.63   Rank: 200

Florence, AL
Concert Radio
In Huntsville-Decatur media market
WQPR-FM
Score: 8.22   Rank: 325

Florence, SC
  Art Museum and Gallery
    Florence Museum
  Symphony Orchestra
    Florence Symphony
  Score: 5.95   Rank: 333

Fort Collins-Loveland, CO
  Art Museum and Gallery
    CSU Gallery
  Concert Radio
    In Denver media market
  Opera Company
    Opera Fort Collins
  Performance Halls
    Lincoln Center Auditorium
    Lory Student Center, CSU
  Symphony Orchestra
    Fort Collins Symphony
  Score: 39.67   Rank: 214

Fort Lauderdale, FL
  Art Museums and Galleries
    Hollywood Art Museum
    Museum of Art
  Opera Company
    Gold Coast Opera
  Performance Halls
    Bailey Concert Hall
    Broward Performing Arts Center
    War Memorial Auditorium
  Professional Theatre
    Vinnette Carroll Repertory Company
  Symphony Orchestras
    Greater Palm Beach Symphony
    Symphony of the Americas
  Score: 87.82   Rank: 44

Fort Myers-Cape Coral, FL
  Art Museum and Gallery
    ECC Gallery of Fine Art
  Concert Radio
    WGCU-FM, WSFP-FM
  Performance Hall
    Barbara Mann Hall
  Professional Theatres
    Pirate Playhouse
  Symphony Orchestra
    Southwest Florida Symphony
  Score: 45.33   Rank: 194

Fort Pierce-Port St. Lucie, FL
  Concert Radio
    WQCS-FM
  Performance Hall
    St. Lucie County Civic Center
  Symphony Orchestra
    Treasure Coast Symphony
  Score: 30.03   Rank: 248

Fort Smith, AR-OK
  Art Museum and Gallery
    Fort Smith Art Center
  Performance Hall
    Fort Smith Civic Center

  Symphony Orchestra
    Fort Smith Symphony
  Score: 21.53   Rank: 278

Fort Walton Beach, FL
  Concert Radio
    In Mobile-Pensacola media market
  Performance Hall
    Civic Auditorium
  Symphony Orchestra
    Okaloosa Symphony
  Score: 10.20   Rank: 318

Fort Wayne, IN
  Art Museum and Gallery
    Fort Wayne Museum of Art
  Ballet Company
    Fort Wayne Ballet
  Concert Radio
    WBNI-FM
  Performance Hall
    Embassy Theatre
  Symphony Orchestra
    Fort Wayne Philharmonic Orchestra
  Score: 83.57   Rank: 59

Fort Worth-Arlington, TX
  Art Museums and Galleries
    Amon Carter Museum
    Kimbell Art Museum
    Modern Art Museum
  Ballet Company
    Fort Worth Dallas Ballet
  Concert Radio
    KTCU-FM
  Opera Company
    Fort Worth Opera
  Performance Halls
    Bass Performance Hall
    Fort Worth Convention Center
  Professional Theatre
    Stage West
  Symphony Orchestra
    Fort Worth Symphony & Chamber
    Orchestra
  Score: 85.56   Rank: 52

Fresno, CA
  Art Museum and Gallery
    Fresno Art Center & Museum
  Concert Radio
    KUBO-FM, KVPR-FM
  Performance Halls
    Tower Theatre for Performing Arts
    William Saroyan Theatre
  Professional Theatre
    Theatre Three Repertory Co.
  Symphony Orchestra
    Fresno Philharmonic Orchestra
  Score: 33.43   Rank: 236

Gadsden, AL
  Art Museum and Gallery
    Gadsden Museum of Fine Arts

  Concert Radio
    In Birmingham media market
    WSGN-FM
  Performance Hall
    Wallace Hall and Gadsden
    Amphitheatre
  Symphony Orchestra
    Gadsden Symphony
  Score: 30.60   Rank: 246

Gainesville, FL
  Art Museums and Galleries
    Samuel P. Harn Museum of Art
    U of Florida Gallery
  Concert Radio
    WUFT-FM
  Performance Hall
    U of Florida Performing Arts Center
  Symphony Orchestra
    Gainesville Symphony
  Score: 58.65   Rank: 147

Galveston-Texas City, TX
  Concert Radio
    In Houston media market
  Performance Hall
    1894 Grand Opera House
  Symphony Orchestra
    Galveston Symphony
  Score: 22.95   Rank: 273

Gary, IN
  Art Museum and Gallery
    Valparaiso Museum of Art
  Concert Radio
    In Chicago media market
  Symphony Orchestras
    Northwest Indiana Symphony
    Valparaiso Symphony
  Score: 12.75   Rank: 309

Glens Falls, NY
  Art Museum and Gallery
    Hyde Collection
  Concert Radio
    In Albany-Schenectady-Troy media
    market
  Opera Company
    Lake George Opera Festival
  Symphony Orchestra
    Glens Falls Symphony
  Score: 32.02   Rank: 241

Goldsboro, NC
  Concert Radio
    In Raleigh-Durham media market
  Score: 7.09   Rank: 329

Grand Forks, ND-MN
  Art Museum and Gallery
    North Dakota Museum of Art
  Concert Radio
    In Fargo-Valley City media market
    KFJM-FM, KFJM-AM, KUND-AM

Performance Hall
UND Fritz Auditorium
Symphony Orchestra
Greater Grand Forks Symphony
Score: 68.56   Rank: 112

Grand Junction, CO
Art Museum and Gallery
Western Colorado Center for the Arts
Concert Radio
KPRN-FM
Performance Hall
Grand Junction HS Auditorium
Symphony Orchestra
Grand Junction Symphony
Score: 26.63   Rank: 260

Grand Rapids-Muskegon-Holland, MI
Art Museums and Galleries
Calvin College Art Gallery
Grand Rapids Art Museum
Hope College Gallery
Muskegon Museum of Art
Ballet Company
Grand Rapids Ballet Company
Concert Radio
WBLU-FM, WBLV-FM, WGVU-AM,
WGVU-FM, WFGR-FM, WVGR-FM
Opera Company
Opera Grand Rapids
Performance Halls
Frauenthal Theatre
Grand Center
Symphony Orchestras
Grand Rapids Symphony
Holland Chamber Orchestra
West Shore Symphony
Score: 77.06   Rank: 82

Great Falls, MT
Art Museum and Gallery
C.M. Russell Museum
Concert Radio
KGPR-FM
Performance Hall
Civic Center
Symphony Orchestra
Great Falls Symphony
Score: 15.02   Rank: 301

Greeley, CO
Concert Radio
In Denver media market
KUNC-FM
Performance Hall
Union Colony Civic Auditorium
Symphony Orchestras
Greeley Philharmonic Orchestra
U of Northern Colorado Symphony
Score: 43.06   Rank: 202

Green Bay, WI
Art Museum and Gallery
Neville Public Museum
Concert Radio
WHID-FM, WPNE-FM
Opera Company
Pamiro Opera Company
Performance Hall
Weidner Center
Symphony Orchestra
Green Bay Symphony
Score: 39.10   Rank: 216

Greensboro–Winston-Salem–High Point, NC
Art Museums and Galleries
Green Hill Center for North Carolina Art
Reynolda House Museum of American Art
Scales Fine Arts Center
Southeastern Center for Contemporary Art
UNC Weatherspoon Art Gallery
Concert Radio
WFDD-FM
Opera Companies
Greensboro Opera Company
Piedmont Opera Theatre
Performance Halls
Aycock Auditorium
Carolina Theatre
Stevens Center
War Memorial Auditorium
Professional Theatres
North Carolina Black Repertory Theatre
North Carolina Shakespeare Festival
Symphony Orchestras
Winston-Salem Piedmont Triad Symphony
Eastern Philharmonic Orchestra
Greensboro Symphony
North Carolina School of Arts Symphony
Philharmonia of Greensboro
Score: 73.38   Rank: 95

Greenville, NC
Art Museums and Galleries
ECU Gray Gallery
Greenville Museum of Art
Performance Hall
Mendenhall Center
Score: 6.24   Rank: 332

Greenville-Spartanburg-Anderson, SC
Art Museums and Galleries
Anderson County Arts Center
BJU Collection of Sacred Art
Greenville County Museum of Art
Lee Gallery
Sandor Teszler Library Gallery
Performance Halls
Peace Center for Performing Arts
Twitchell Auditorium

Professional Theatre
Warehouse Theatre
Symphony Orchestras
Anderson Symphony
Converse Sinfonietta
Greater Spartanburg Philharmonic
Greenville Symphony
Score: 67.43   Rank: 116

Hagerstown, MD
Art Museum and Gallery
Washington County Museum of Fine Arts
Concert Radio
In Washington media market
WETH-FM
Performance Hall
Maryland Theatre
Symphony Orchestra
Maryland Symphony
Score: 35.42   Rank: 229

Halifax, NS
Art Museums and Galleries
Art Gallery of Nova Scotia
Dalhousie Art Gallery
Eye-Level Gallery
Mount St. Vincent Art Gallery
Saint Mary's University Art Gallery
Concert Radio
CBH-FM
Performance Hall
Cohn Auditorium, Dalhousie Arts Center
Professional Theatres
Alive Theatre Company
Eastern Front Theatre Company
Mulgrave Road Theatre
Neptune Theatre
Symphony Orchestra
Symphony Nova Scotia
Score: 65.73   Rank: 122

Hamilton, ON
Art Museums and Galleries
Art Gallery of Hamilton
Dundas Valley School of Art Gallery
Grimsby Public Art Gallery
Hamilton Place Gallery
McMaster University Art Gallery
Concert Radio
In Toronto media market
Opera Company
Opera Ontario
Performance Hall
The Great Hall, Hamilton Place
Professional Theatres
Theatre Aquarius
Theatre Erebus
Symphony Orchestras
Symphony Hamilton
Te Deum Orchestra
Score: 83.01   Rank: 61

Hamilton-Middletown, OH
Art Museum and Gallery
Miami University Art Gallery
Concert Radio
In Cincinnati media market
WMUB-FM
Opera Company
Sorg Opera Company
Symphony Orchestra
Middletown Symphony
Score: 51.85   Rank: 171

Harrisburg-Lebanon-Carlisle, PA
Concert Radio
WITF-FM, WJAZ-FM
Opera Company
Harrisburg Opera Association
Performance Hall
The Forum
Symphony Orchestra
Harrisburg Symphony
Score: 46.18   Rank: 191

★Hartford, CT
Art Museums and Galleries
Davison Art Center Wesleyan U
Ezra & Cecile Zilkha Gallery
Hill-Stead Museum
New Britain Museum of American Art
Wadsworth Atheneum
Ballet Company
Hartford Ballet
Concert Radio
WJMJ-FM, WPKT-FM
Opera Companies
Connecticut Concert Opera
Connecticut Opera Association
Goodspeed Opera House
Performance Halls
Lincoln Theater
The Bushnell
Professional Theatres
Goodspeed Opera House
Hartford Stage Company
TheaterWorks
Symphony Orchestras
Greater New Britain Symphony
Hartford Symphony
Score: 93.77   Rank: 23

Hattiesburg, MS
Concert Radio
WUSM-FM
Opera Companies
Opera at USM
Southern Arts Festival Opera
Performance Hall
Bennett Performing Arts Center
Symphony Orchestra
USM Symphony
Score: 70.26   Rank: 106

Hickory-Morganton-Lenoir, NC
Art Museum and Gallery
Hickory Museum of Art
Concert Radio
In Charlotte media market
WFHE-FM
Performance Hall
Monroe Auditorium
Symphony Orchestra
Western Piedmont Symphony
Score: 32.30   Rank: 240

★Honolulu, HI
Art Museums and Galleries
Contemporary Museum
Honolulu Academy of Arts
U of Hawaii Gallery
Ballet Company
Hawaii State Ballet
Concert Radio
KHPR-FM, KIFO-AM, KIPO-FM
Performance Hall
Blaisdell Concert Hall
Professional Theatres
Honolulu Theatre for Youth
Score: 90.37   Rank: 35

Houma, LA
Concert Radio
In New Orleans media market
KTLN-FM
Score: 0   Rank: 354

Houston, TX
Art Museums and Galleries
Contemporary Arts Museum
Museum of Fine Arts
Ballet Companies
Houston Ballet
Southwest Jazz Ballet Company
Concert Radio
KPVU-FM, KUHF-FM
Opera Company
Houston Ebony Opera Guild
Houston Grand Opera Association
Performance Halls
Jones Hall for Performing Arts
Rice University Brown Hall
Professional Theatre
A. D. Players
Symphony Orchestras
Clear Lake Symphony
Houston Symphony
Score: 89.81   Rank: 37

Huntington-Ashland, WV-KY-OH
Art Museum and Gallery
Huntington Museum of Art
Concert Radio
WOUL-FM, WVWV-FM
Performance Hall
Huntington Civic Arena
Symphony Orchestra
Huntington Chamber Orchestra
Score: 35.70   Rank: 228

Huntsville, AL
Art Museums and Galleries
Huntsville Museum of Art
UAH Gallery of Art
Concert Radio
WLRH-FM
Opera Company
Huntsville Opera Theater
Performance Hall
Von Braun Civic Center Concert Hall
Symphony Orchestra
Huntsville Symphony
Score: 60.63   Rank: 140

★Indianapolis, IN
Art Museums and Galleries
Anderson Fine Arts Center
Indianapolis Center for Contemporary Art
Indianapolis Museum of Art
Ballet Company
Ballet Internationale
Concert Radio
WBSB-FM, WFYI-FM, WICR-FM, WSYW-FM
Opera Company
Indianapolis Opera
Performance Halls
Clowes Memorial Hall
Hilbert Circle Theatre
Professional Theatre
Indiana Repertory Theatre
Symphony Orchestras
Anderson Symphony
Butler Symphony
Carmel Symphony
Indianapolis Chamber Orchestra
Indianapolis Symphony
Philharmonic Orchestra
Score: 96.04   Rank: 15

Iowa City, IA
Art Museum and Gallery
U of Iowa Museum of Art
Concert Radio
In Cedar Rapids-Waterloo-Dubuque media market
KSUI-FM
Performance Hall
Hancher Auditorium
Professional Theatre
U of Iowa Theatre
Score: 57.23   Rank: 152

Jackson, MI
Art Museum and Gallery
Ella Sharp Museum
Concert Radio
In Lansing media market
Performance Hall
Potter Center Music Hall
Symphony Orchestra
Jackson Symphony
Score: 26.35   Rank: 261

Jackson, MS
  Art Museum and Gallery
    Mississippi Museum of Art
  Ballet Company
    Ballet Mississippi
  Concert Radio
    WJSU-FM, WMPN-FM
  Opera Company
    Mississippi Opera
  Performance Hall
    Thalia Mara Hall
  Professional Theatre
    New Stage Theatre
  Symphony Orchestra
    Mississippi Symphony
  Score: 49.58   Rank: 179

Jackson, TN
  Concert Radio
    WKNP-FM
  Performance Hall
    Civic Center
  Symphony Orchestra
    Jackson Symphony
  Score: 27.48   Rank: 257

Jacksonville, FL
  Art Museums and Galleries
    Cummer Gallery of Art
    Jacksonville Art Museum
  Ballet Company
    Florida Ballet
  Concert Radio
    WFCF-FM, WJCT-FM
  Performance Hall
    Times-Union Center
  Symphony Orchestra
    Jacksonville Symphony
  Score: 78.19   Rank: 78

Jacksonville, NC
  Concert Radio
    In Greenville-New Bern-Washington
      media market
  Score: 4.25   Rank: 339

Jamestown, NY
  Concert Radio
    In Buffalo media market
    WUBJ-FM
  Opera Company
    Chautauqua Opera
  Symphony Orchestra
    Fredonia Chamber Players
  Score: 75.93   Rank: 86

Janesville-Beloit, WI
  Art Museum and Gallery
    Wright Museum of Art
  Concert Radio
    In Madison media market
  Symphony Orchestra
    Beloit Janesville Symphony
  Score: 59.50   Rank: 144

Jersey City, NJ
  Art Museums and Galleries
    JCSC Courtney Art Gallery
    Jersey City Museum
  Concert Radio
    In New York media market
  Symphony Orchestra
    Lyric Theatre Ltd.
  Score: 71.11   Rank: 103

Johnson City-Kingsport-Bristol, TN-VA
  Art Museum and Gallery
    ETSU Carroll Reece Museum
  Concert Radio
    WCSK-FM, WETS-FM
  Performance Hall
    Seeger Hall
  Professional Theatres
    Barter Theatre, Mainstage
    Barter Theatre, Second Stage
  Symphony Orchestras
    Johnson City Symphony
    Kingsport Symphony
  Score: 42.21   Rank: 205

Johnstown, PA
  Performance Hall
    Pasquerilla Performing Arts Center
  Symphony Orchestra
    Johnstown Symphony & Chamber
      Orchestra
  Score: 19.84   Rank: 284

Jonesboro, AR
  Performance Halls
    Ellis Convocation Center
    Jonesboro Forum
  Symphony Orchestra
    Northeast Arkansas Symphony
  Score: 7.37   Rank: 328

Joplin, MO
  Art Museums and Galleries
    Spiva Center for the Arts
  Concert Radio
    KXMS-FM
  Score: 4.82   Rank: 337

Kalamazoo-Battle Creek, MI
  Art Museums and Galleries
    Art Center of Battle Creek
    Kalamazoo Institute of Arts
    Western Michigan University Gallery
  Concert Radio
    WMUK-FM
  Performance Halls
    Chenery Auditorium
    Kellogg Auditorium
  Symphony Orchestras
    Battle Creek Symphony
    Kalamazoo Symphony
  Score: 65.16   Rank: 124

Kankakee, IL
  Concert Radio
    In Chicago media market
  Performance Hall
    Larsen Fine Arts Center
  Symphony Orchestra
    Kankakee Valley Symphony
  Score: 3.97   Rank: 340

Kansas City, MO-KS
  Art Museums and Galleries
    Kansas City Art Institute
    Nelson-Atkins Museum of Art
  Ballet Companies
    State Ballet of Missouri
    Unicorn Theatre
  Concert Radio
    KCUR-FM, KXTR-FM
  Opera Company
    Lyric Opera of Kansas City
  Performance Halls
    Folly Theatre
    Lyric Theatre
    Music Hall
  Professional Theatres
    Missouri Repertory Theatre
    Unicorn Theatre
  Symphony Orchestras
    Independence Symphony
    Kansas City Chamber Orchestra
    Kansas City Symphony
    Liberty Symphony
    Northland Symphony
    Philharmonia of Greater Kansas City
  Score: 89.24   Rank: 39

Kenosha, WI
  Art Museum and Gallery
    Kenosha Public Museum
  Concert Radio
    In Milwaukee media market
    WGTD-FM
  Symphony Orchestra
    Kenosha Symphony
  Score: 34.57   Rank: 232

Killeen-Temple, TX
  Concert Radio
    KNCT-FM
  Performance Hall
    Cultural Activities Center
  Symphony Orchestra
    Temple Symphony
  Score: 1.70   Rank: 348

Kitchener, ON
  Art Museums and Galleries
    Kitchener-Waterloo Art Gallery
    U of Waterloo Gallery
  Performance Hall
    Centre in the Square
  Professional Theatres
    The Waterloo Stage Theatre
    Theatre & Company

The Arts

417

Symphony Orchestras
  Kitchener-Waterloo Chamber Orchestra
  Kitchener-Waterloo Symphony
Score: 72.53   Rank: 98

Knoxville, TN
  Art Museums and Galleries
    Ewing Gallery of Art & Architecture
    Knoxville Museum of Art
    UT McClung Museum
  Ballet Company
    Appalachian Ballet Company
  Concert Radio
    WUOT-FM
  Opera Company
    Knoxville Opera Company
  Performance Hall
    Tennessee Theatre
  Professional Theatre
    Clarence Brown Theatre
  Symphony Orchestras
    Knoxville Symphony
    Oak Ridge Symphony
Score: 66.01   Rank: 121

Kokomo, IN
  Concert Radio
    In Indianapolis media market
  Performance Hall
    Havens Auditorium
  Symphony Orchestra
    Kokomo Symphony
Score: 2.27   Rank: 346

La Crosse, WI-MN
  Art Museum and Gallery
    Pump House Center for the Arts
  Concert Radio
    KXLC-FM, WLSU-FM, WHLA-FM
  Performance Hall
    Viterbo Fine Arts Center
  Symphony Orchestra
    La Crosse Symphony
Score: 41.93   Rank: 206

Lafayette, IN
  Art Museums and Galleries
    Greater Lafayette Museum of Art
    Purdue University Galleries
  Concert Radio
    WBAA-AM, WBAA-FM
  Performance Hall
    Long Center for Performing Arts
  Symphony Orchestra
    Lafayette Symphony
Score: 46.46   Rank: 190

Lafayette, LA
  Art Museum and Gallery
    University Art Museum
  Concert Radio
    KRVS-FM
  Performance Hall
    Heymann Center for Performing Arts

Symphony Orchestra
  Arcadiana Symphony
Score: 23.80   Rank: 270

Lake Charles, LA
  Art Museum and Gallery
    Imperial Calcasieu Museum
  Performance Hall
    Lake Charles Civic Centre
  Symphony Orchestra
    Lake Charles Symphony
Score: 11.62   Rank: 313

Lakeland-Winter Haven, FL
  Art Museum and Gallery
    Polk Museum of Art
  Concert Radio
    In Tampa-St. Petersburg media market
  Performance Hall
    Lakeland Center Theatre
  Symphony Orchestra
    Imperial Symphony
Score: 52.70   Rank: 168

Lancaster, PA
  Art Museums and Galleries
    Community Gallery of Lancaster
    Heritage Center of Lancaster County
  Concert Radio
    WIXQ-FM
  Opera Company
    Lancaster Opera Company
  Performance Hall
    Fulton Opera House
  Professional Theatre
    Fulton Theatre Company
  Symphony Orchestra
    Lancaster Symphony
Score: 68.28   Rank: 113

Lansing-East Lansing, MI
  Art Museums and Galleries
    Kresge Art Museum
    Lansing Art Gallery
  Concert Radio
    WKAR-AM, WKAR-FM
  Opera Company
    Opera Company of Mid Michigan
  Performance Hall
    Wharton Center
  Professional Theatre
    BoarsHead Theatre
  Symphony Orchestra
    Greater Lansing Symphony
Score: 49.01   Rank: 181

Laredo, TX
  Performance Hall
    Civic Center
  Symphony Orchestras
    Chamber Orchestra of the Two Laredos
    Laredo Philharmonic Orchestra
Score: 1.99   Rank: 347

Las Cruces, NM
  Art Museum and Gallery
    NMSU Art Gallery
  Concert Radio
    In El Paso media market
    KRWG-FM
  Performance Hall
    NMSU Performance Center
  Symphony Orchestra
    Las Cruces Symphony
Score: 30.32   Rank: 247

Las Vegas, NV-AZ
  Art Museum sand Galleries
    Las Vegas Art Museum
    UNLV Beam Fine Art Gallery
  Ballet Company
    Nevada Ballet Theatre
  Concert Radio
    KNPR-FM, KCEP-FM, KTPH-FM
  Opera Company
    Nevada Opera Theatre
  Performance Halls
    Artemus Ham Concert Hall
    Sammy Davis Jr. Festival Plaza
    Wipple Cultural Center
  Symphony Orchestras
    Las Vegas Civic Symphony
    Nevada Symphony
Score: 50.15   Rank: 177

Lawrence, KS
  Art Museum and Gallery
    KU Spencer Museum of Art
  Concert Radio
    In Kansas City media market
    KANU-FM
  Performance Hall
    Leid Centre of Kansas
  Symphony Orchestra
    U of Kansas Symphony
Score: 24.93   Rank: 266

Lawrence, MA-NH
  Art Museum and Gallery
    Addison Gallery of American Art
  Concert Radio
    In Boston media market
Score: 0.84   Rank: 351

Lawton, OK
  Concert Radio
    In Wichita Falls media market
    KCCU-FM
  Performance Hall
    McMahon Auditorium
  Symphony Orchestra
    Lawton Philharmonic Orchestra
Score: 1.42   Rank: 349

Lewiston-Auburn, ME
  Concert Radio
    In Portland media market
  Professional Theatre
    The Public Theatre
Score: 9.91   Rank: 319

Lexington, KY

Art Museums and Galleries
Berea College Museums
Headley-Whitney Museum
UK Art Museum
Ballet Company
Lexington Ballet
Concert Radio
WEKU-FM, WUKY-FM
Performance Halls
Lexington Opera House
Singletary Center for the Arts
Symphony Orchestra
Lexington Philharmonic Orchestra
Score: 55.81   Rank: 157

Lima, OH

Concert Radio
In Dayton media market
WGLE-FM
Performance Hall
Veterans Civic Center
Symphony Orchestra
Lima Symphony
Score: 43.35   Rank: 201

Lincoln, NE

Art Museums and Galleries
Nebraska Wesleyan Elder Art Gallery
U of Nebraska Sheldon Art Gallery
Concert Radio
KUCV-FM
Performance Halls
Lied Center for Performing Arts
Pershing Auditorium
Professional Theatre
Nebraska Repertory Theatre
U of Nebraska Theatre
Symphony Orchestras
Lincoln Civic Orchestra
Lincoln Symphony
Nebraska Jazz Orchestra
Score: 69.13   Rank: 110

Little Rock-North Little Rock, AR

Art Museum and Gallery
Arkansas Arts Center
Ballet Company
Ballet Arkansas
Concert Radio
KLRE-FM, KUAR-FM
Opera Company
Opera Theatre at Wildwood
Performance Halls
Robinson Center Music Hall
Wildwood Park for Performing Arts
Professional Theatre
Arkansas Repertory Theatre
Symphony Orchestra
Arkansas Symphony
Score: 49.86   Rank: 178

London, ON

Art Museums and Galleries
Art Gallery St. Thomas–Elgin
London Regional Art Gallery
McIntosh Gallery
Concert Radio
In Toronto media market
CBBL-FM, CBBL-FM
Performance Hall
Centennial Hall
Professional Theatres
Port Stanley
The Grand Theatre
Symphony Orchestras
London Community Orchestra
Orchestra London Canada
U of Western Ontario Symphony
Score: 71.96   Rank: 100

Long Island, NY

Art Museums and Galleries
Fine Arts Museum of Long Island
Guild Hall Museum
Heckscher Museum
Hofstra Museum
Institute for Contemporary Art
Parrish Art Museum
Ballet Company
Ballet Long Island
Concert Radio
In New York media market
WCWP-FM, WPBX-FM, WRHU-FM,
WUSB-FM
Performance Halls
Staller Center for the Arts
Tilles Center at CW Post
Professional Theatres
Arena Players Repertory Co.
Broadhollow Players, LTD
Theatre Three Productions
Symphony Orchestras
Forest Hills Chamber Players
Forest Hills Symphony of the Queens
Great Neck Philharmonic
Long Island Philharmonic
New Orchestra of Long Island
Queens Festival Orchestra
Sound Symphony
Stony Brook Symphony
Score: 72.81   Rank: 97

Longview-Marshall, TX

Art Museum and Gallery
Longview Museum & Arts Center
Concert Radio
In Shreveport media market
Performance Hall
Civic Center and Auditorium
Symphony Orchestra
Longview Symphony
Score: 14.74   Rank: 302

★Los Angeles-Long Beach, CA

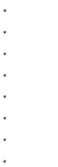

Art Museums and Galleries
Armand Hammer Museum of Art
Brand Library & Art Galleries
California Museum of Ancient Art
CSU Art Museum
Huntington Library Art Collections
J. Paul Getty Museum
Lang Galleries of Claremont Colleges
Long Beach Museum of Art
Los Angeles County Museum of Art
Loyola Marymount Laband Art Gallery
Norton Simon Museum
Otis-Parsons Art Gallery
Pacific-Asia Museum
Palos Verdes Art Center
Plaza De La Raza
Skirball Museum, Hebrew Union
  College
Southwest Museum
UCLA Wight Art Gallery
USC Fisher Gallery
Ballet Companies
Ballet Folklorico de Mexico
Los Angeles Ballet
Los Angeles Classical Ballet
Mainstage International Chamber
  Ballet
Concert Radio
KCRW-FM, KLON-FM, KPCC-FM,
  KCSN-FM, KKGO-FM, KUSC-FM
Opera Companies
California Festival Opera
Casa Italiana Opera Company
Guild Opera Company
Long Beach Opera
Los Angeles Music Center Opera
Los Angeles Opera
Opera A la Carte
Santa Cecilia Opera
Performance Halls
Carpenter Performing Arts Center
Dorothy Chandler Pavilion
Hollywood Bowl
Pasadena Civic Auditorium
Santa Monica Civic Auditorium
Wilshire-Ebell Theatre
Professional Theatres
Actors Forum Theatre
Alliance Repertory Company
Cast Theatre
Cornerstone Theatre Company
Fountain Theatre
Los Angeles Designers' Theatre
Mark Taper Forum
Odyssey Theatre Ensemble
Playwrights' Arena
Stages Theatre
The Colony Studio Theatre
The Pasadena Playhouse
Theatre Forty
Theatre West
Victory Theatre
Will Geer's Theatricum Botanicum

Symphony Orchestras
American Jazz Philharmonic
Asia America Symphony
Beverly Hills Symphony
Brentwood Westwood Symphony
Carson Dominguez Hills Symphony
Claremont Chamber Orchestra
Claremont Symphony
Culver City-Marina del Rey-
   Westchester Symphony
Glendale Symphony
Long Beach Symphony
Los Angeles Chamber Orchestra
Los Angeles Doctors Symphony
Los Angeles Mozart Orchestra
Los Angeles Performing Arts Orchestra
Los Angeles Philharmonic Orchestra
New Valley Symphony
Pasadena Symphony
Santa Monica Symphony
Torrance Symphony
U of Southern California Symphony
Score: 99.44   Rank: 3

Louisville, KY-IN
Art Museums and Galleries
Allen Hite Art Institute Gallery
J.B. Speed Art Museum
Ballet Company
Louisville Ballet
Concert Radio
WFPK-FM, WFPL-FM, WUOL-FM
Opera Company
Kentucky Opera
Performance Halls
Brown Theatre
Kentucky Center for the Arts
Professional Theatres
Actors Theatre of Louisville
Stage One, Louisville Children's Theatre
Symphony Orchestra
The Louisville Orchestra
Score: 80.46   Rank: 70

Lowell, MA-NH
Art Museum and Gallery
Whistler House Museum of Art
Concert Radio
In Boston media market
Performance Hall
U of Massachusetts Auditorium
Professional Theatre
Merrimack Repertory Theatre
Score: 39.95   Rank: 213

Lubbock, TX
Art Museum and Gallery
Municipal Garden & Art Center
Concert Radio
KOHM-FM
Performance Hall
Lubbock Memorial Civic Center
Symphony Orchestra
Lubbock Symphony
Score: 16.15   Rank: 297

Lynchburg, VA
Art Museum and Gallery
Maier Museum of Art
Symphony Orchestra
Lynchburg Symphony
Score: 20.68   Rank: 281

Macon, GA
Art Museums and Galleries
Museum of Arts & Sciences
Tubman African American Museum
Concert Radio
WDCO-FM
Score: 15.87   Rank: 298

Madison, WI
Art Museums and Galleries
Madison Art Center
UW Elvehjem Museum of Art
Concert Radio
WERN-FM, WORT-FM
Opera Company
Madison Opera
Performance Halls
Civic Center
Oscar Mayer Theatre
Professional Theatre
Madison Repertory Theatre
Symphony Orchestras
Madison Symphony
Wisconsin Chamber Orchestra
Score: 79.04   Rank: 75

Manchester, NH
Art Museums and Galleries
Chapel Art Center
Currier Gallery of Art
Concert Radio
In Boston media market
Performance Hall
Palace Theatre
Symphony Orchestras
New Hampshire Philharmonic
   Orchestra
New Hampshire Symphony
Score: 44.20   Rank: 198

Mansfield, OH
Art Museum and Gallery
Mansfield Art Center
Concert Radio
In Cleveland media market
WOSV-FM
Performance Hall
Renaissance Theatre
Symphony Orchestra
Mansfield Symphony
Score: 55.53   Rank: 158

McAllen-Edinburg-Mission, TX
Ballet Company
Rio Grande Valley Ballet
Concert Radio
KHID-FM

Performance Hall
Pan American Fine Arts Auditorium
Symphony Orchestra
Valley Symphony & Chorale
Score: 12.47   Rank: 310

Medford-Ashland, OR
Art Museums and Galleries
Rogue Gallery
Stevenson Union Gallery
Concert Radio
KSMF-FM, KSOR-FM, KSRG-FM
Opera Company
Rogue Opera
Performance Hall
Britt Pavilion
Professional Theatres
Actor's Theatre
Angus Bowmer Theater
The Black Swan Theatre
The Elizabethan Theatre
Symphony Orchestras
Britt Festival Orchestra
Rogue Valley Symphony
Score: 56.95   Rank: 153

Melbourne-Titusville-Palm Bay, FL
Art Museum and Gallery
Brevard Art Center & Museum
Concert Radio
WFIT-FM
Performance Hall
King Center for Performing Arts
Symphony Orchestras
Brevard Symphony
Space Coast Pops Inc
Score: 58.36   Rank: 148

Memphis, TN-AR-MS
Art Museums and Galleries
Dixon Gallery & Gardens
Memphis Brooks Museum of Art
MSU Art Museum
Ballet Company
Memphis Ballet
Concert Radio
WKNO-FM
Opera Company
Opera Memphis
Performance Hall
Orpheum Theatre
Professional Theatres
Playhouse on the Square
Theatre Memphis
Symphony Orchestras
Germantown Symphony
Memphis Symphony
Score: 70.54   Rank: 105

Merced, CA
Concert Radio
In Fresno-Visalia media market
Score: 6.52   Rank: 331

Miami, FL
  Art Museums and Galleries
    Bass Museum of Art
    Center For Fine Arts
    FIU Art Museum
    North Miami Center of Contemporary
      Art
    UM Lowe Art Museum
  Ballet Companies
    Ballet Spectacular
    Miami City Ballet
  Concert Radio
    WLRN-FM, WTMI-FM
  Opera Companies
    Florida Grand Opera
    North Miami Beach Opera
  Performance Halls
    Gusman Concert Hall
    Jackie Gleason Center
    Knight International Center
    Performing Arts Center of Greater
      Miami
  Professional Theatres
    Actors' Playhouse
    Coconut Grove Playhouse
    New Theatre
  Symphony Orchestras
    Miami Chamber Symphony
    New World Symphony
    North Miami Beach Symphony
    The New World Symphony
  Score: 89.52   Rank: 38

★**Middlesex-Somerset-Hunterdon, NJ**
  Art Museums and Galleries
    Hunterdon Art Center
    Jane V. Zimmerli Art Museum
  Ballet Company
    American Repertory Ballet
  Concert Radio
    In New York media market
  Performance Hall
    New Brunswick State Theater
  Professional Theatres
    Crossroads Theatre Company
    Forum Theatre Group
    George Street Playhouse
  Symphony Orchestras
    Philharmonic Orchestra of New Jersey
    Riverside Symphonia
  Score: 90.66   Rank: 34

★**Milwaukee-Waukesha, WI**
  Art Museums and Galleries
    Charles Allis Art Museum
    Haggerty Museum of Art
    Milwaukee Art Museum
    Ozaukee Art Center
    UWM Art Museum
    West Bend Gallery of Fine Arts
  Ballet Company
    Milwaukee Ballet
  Concert Radio
    WFMR-FM, WHAD-FM, WUWM-FM

  Opera Companies
    Florentine Opera Company
    Skylight Opera Theatre
  Performance Hall
    Marcus Performing Arts Center
  Professional Theatres
    Broadway Theatre
    Milwaukee Chamber Theatre
    Milwaukee Repertory Theater
    Next Act Theatre
    Skylight Opera Theatre
    Stackner Cabaret
    Stiemke Theater
    Theatre X
  Symphony Orchestras
    Milwaukee Chamber Orchestra
    Milwaukee Symphony
    Waukesha Symphony
  Score: 92.92   Rank: 26

★**Minneapolis-St. Paul, MN-WI**
  Art Museums and Galleries
    Bloomington Art Center
    Gallery 101
    Hamline University Galleries
    Minneapolis Institute of Art
    Minnesota Museum of American Art
    UM Weisman Art Museum
    Walker Art Center
  Ballet Company
    James Sewell Ballet
  Concert Radio
    KNOW-FM, KSJN-FM
  Opera Companies
    Minnesota Opera
    Nautilus Music Theatre
  Performance Halls
    Fitzgerald Theatre
    Northrup Memorial Auditorium
    Orchestra Hall
    Ordway Music Theatre
    Walker Art Center
  Professional Theatres
    Climb Theatre
    Illusion Theatre
    Mixed Blood Theatre Company
    Penumbra Theatre Company
    The Guthrie Theater
    Theatre de la Jeune Lune
  Symphony Orchestras
    Century Symphony
    Civic Orchestra of Minneapolis
    Metropolitan Symphony
    Minneapolis Pops Orchestra
    Minnesota Orchestra
    Minnetonka Symphony
    St. Paul Chamber Orchestra
  Score: 98.02   Rank: 8

Missoula, MT
  Concert Radio
    KUFM-FM
  Performance Hall
    Wilma Theatre

  Professional Theatre
    Montana Repertory Theatre
  Symphony Orchestra
    Missoula Symphony
  Score: 25.50   Rank: 264

Mobile, AL
  Art Museums and Galleries
    Eastern Shore Art Center
    Mobile Museum of Art
  Concert Radio
    WHIL-FM
  Opera Company
    Mobile Opera
  Performance Hall
    Civic Center Concert Hall
  Symphony Orchestra
    Mobile Symphony
  Score: 47.60   Rank: 186

Modesto, CA
  Art Museum and Gallery
    University Art Gallery
  Opera Company
    Townsend Opera Players
  Performance Hall
    Modesto Junior College Auditorium
  Symphony Orchestra
    Modesto Symphony
  Score: 22.38   Rank: 275

Monmouth-Ocean, NJ
  Concert Radio
    In New York media market
    WBJB-FM, WWNJ-FM
  Opera Company
    Metro Lyric Opera
  Performance Halls
    Count Basie Theatre
    Ocean County Center for the Arts
  Professional Theatres
    Creative Productions
    Two River Theatre Company
  Symphony Orchestras
    Garden State Philharmonic Symphony
    Monmouth Symphony
    Paradise Chamber Orchestra
  Score: 87.26   Rank: 46

Monroe, LA
  Art Museum and Gallery
    Masur Museum of Art
  Concert Radio
    KEDM-FM
  Performance Hall
    Monroe Civic Center Theatre
  Symphony Orchestra
    Monroe Symphony
  Score: 26.07   Rank: 262

Montgomery, AL
  Art Museum and Gallery
    Montgomery Museum of Fine Arts
  Ballet Company
    Montgomery Ballet

Concert Radio
WTSU-FM, WVAS-FM
Performance Hall
Davis Theatre
Professional Theatre
Alabama Shakespeare Festival
Symphony Orchestra
Montgomery Symphony
Score: **61.48**   Rank: **137**

★Montreal, PQ
Art Museums and Galleries
Bronfman Centre Art Gallery
Centre Canadien d'Architecture
Centre International d'Art
Contemporain
Concordia Art Gallery
Dorval Cultural Centre
Galerie l'Industrielle-Alliance
Galerie Powerhouse
Maison Louis-Hippolyte Lafontaine
Musee d'Art Contemporain
Musee de la Ville de Lachine
Musee des Arts Decoratifs
Musee des Beaux-Arts de Montreal
Musee Itinerant d'Art Byzantin
Musee Marc-Aurele Fortin
Visual Arts Centre
Ballet Companies
Les Ballets Jazz de Montreal
Les Grands Ballets Canadiens
Opera Company
L'Opera de Montreal
Performance Halls
Bronfman Center for the Arts
Peterson Hall, Concordia U
Place des Arts
Professional Theatres
Beton Blues
Black Theatre Workshop
Bronfman Performing Arts Centre
Carbone 14
Centaur Theatre Company
Clowns Gone Bad Productions
DynamO Theatre
Elysian River Theatre
Festival Theatre Des Ameriques
Geordie Productions
Groupe de la Veilee
Imago Theatre
infinitheatre
Le Carrousel
Momentum
Montreal Fringe Festival
Nouveau Theatre Experimental
Nouvelle Compagnie Theatrale
OUT Productions
Playwrights' Workshop
Productions Chocolat Show
Repercussion Theatre
Saidye Bronfman Centre for the Arts
Strange Fish Productions
Teesri Duniya Theatre
The Other Theatre

Theatre 1774
Theatre d'aujourd'hui
Theatre de Campagnie Carrousel
Theatre de La Ligue Nationale Di
Theatre de La Manufacture
Theatre de Quat'sous
Theatre du Cafe de la Place
Theatre du Nouveau Monde
Theatre du Rideau Vert
Theatre du Vieux-Terrebonne
Theatre Experimental Des Femmes
Theatre sans Fils
Theatre Ubu
Theatre Zoopsie
Tricycle Productions
Village Theatre West
Symphony Orchestras
McGill Chamber Orchestra
Montreal Chamber Orchestra
Musici de Montreal
Nouvel Ensemble Moderne
Orchestre Baroque de Montreal
Orchestre Symphonique de Montreal
Score: **96.89**   Rank: **12**

Muncie, IN
Art Museum and Gallery
Ball State University Museum of Art
Concert Radio
In Indianapolis media market
WBST-FM
Performance Hall
Emens Auditorium
Symphony Orchestra
Muncie Symphony
Score: **11.90**   Rank: **312**

Myrtle Beach, SC
Concert Radio
WHMC-FM
Performance Hall
Myrtle Beach Auditorium
Symphony Orchestras
Long Bay Symphony
Myrtle Beach Philharmonic
Score: **17.00**   Rank: **294**

Naples, FL
Art Museum and Gallery
Naples Art Gallery
Performance Hall
Philharmonic Center for the Arts
Symphony Orchestra
Naples Philharmonic
Score: **29.18**   Rank: **251**

Nashua, NH
Concert Radio
In Boston media market
Professional Theatre
American Stage Festival
Symphony Orchestra
Nashua Symphony & Choral
Score: **23.52**   Rank: **271**

Nashville, TN
Art Museums and Galleries
Botanical Gardens & Museum of Art
Fisk University Galleries
Vanderbilt Fine Arts Gallery
Ballet Company
Nashville Ballet
Concert Radio
WMOT-FM, WPLN-FM
Opera Companies
Nashville Opera
Tennessee Opera Theatre
Performance Hall
Tennessee Performing Arts Center
Professional Theatre
Tennessee Repertory Theatre
Symphony Orchestra
Nashville Symphony
Score: **78.48**   Rank: **77**

New Bedford, MA
Concert Radio
In Providence media market
Performance Hall
Zeiterion Theatre
Symphony Orchestra
New Bedford Symphony
Score: **34.00**   Rank: **234**

New Haven-Meriden, CT
Art Museums and Galleries
Yale Center for British Art
Yale University Art Gallery
Concert Radio
In Hartford media market
WGRS-FM, WPKT-FM
Performance Halls
Palace Theatre
Shubert Performing Arts Center
Sprague Memorial Hall
Professional Theatres
Long Wharf Theatre–Mainstage
Long Wharf Theatre–Second Stage
Yale Repertory Theatre
Symphony Orchestras
Connecticut Chamber Orchestra
Meriden Symphony
New Haven Symphony
Orchestra New England
Wallingford Symphony
Score: **86.41**   Rank: **49**

New London-Norwich, CT-RI
Art Museums and Galleries
Florence Griswold Museum
Lyman Allyn Art Museum
Concert Radio
In Hartford-New Haven media market
WNPR-FM
Performance Hall
Garde Arts Center
Symphony Orchestra
Eastern Connecticut Symphony
Score: **68.84**   Rank: **111**

New Orleans, LA

Art Museums and Galleries
Louisiana State Museum
New Orleans Museum of Art
Tulane University Galleries
UNO Fine Arts Gallery

Ballet Company
Delta Festival Ballet

Concert Radio
WTUL-FM, WWNO-FM

Opera Company
New Orleans Opera Association

Performance Halls
Mahalia Jackson Theatre
Orpheum Theater
Saenger Center

Professional Theatre
Contemporary Arts Center

Symphony Orchestras
Jefferson Symphony
Louisiana Philharmonic Orchestra
Score: 83.86   Rank: 58

★New York, NY

Art Museums and Galleries
American Craft Museum
Americas Society
Asia Society Galleries
Bronx Museum of the Arts
Bronx River Art Center
Brooklyn Museum
The Cloisters
Frick Collection
Hammond Museum
Hispanic Society of America
International Museum of African Art
International Center of Photography
Jamaica Arts Center
Jewish Museum
Katonah Museum of Art
Metropolitan Museum of Art
Museum of Modern Art
National Academy of Design Museum
NYU Grey Art Gallery
Pelham Art Center
Pierpont Morgan Library & Art Museum
Solomon Guggenheim Museum
Whitney Museum of American Art
Yeshiva University Museum

Ballet Companies
American Ballet Theatre
Anglo-American Ballet
Ballet Hispanico of New York
Ballet Manhattan
Ballet Tech
Brighton Ballet Theatre
Les Ballets Trockadero de Monte Carlo
New York City Ballet
New York Theatre Ballet

Concert Radio
WKCR-FM, WFUV-FM, WNYC-AM & FM, WQXR-AM & FM, WVIP-AM

Opera Companies
Amato Opera Theatre
American Chamber Opera
American International Lyric Theatre
American Opera Music Theater
American Opera Projects
Bel Canto Society
Bronx Opera Company
Center For Contemporary Opera
Dicapo Opera Theatre
Empire State Opera
Encompass Music Theatre
Juilliard Opera Center
L'Opera Francais de New York
La Gran Scena Opera Company
Liederkranz Opera Theatre
Magic Circle Opera Repertory Ensemble
Manhattan Opera Association
Marcel Achille Opera
Metropolitan Opera Association
Music Theatre Group
New Rochelle Opera
New York City Opera
New York City Opera National Company
New York Gilbert & Sullivan Players
New York Grand Opera
New York Opera Project
Opera Manhattan
Opera Northeast
Opera on the Go
Opera Orchestra of New York
Operaworks
P A L A Opera Association
Queens Opera Association
Regina Opera Company
Rockland Opera
Theatre Rococo
Village Light Opera Group

Performance Halls
Alice Tully Hall
Avery Fisher Hall
Carnegie Hall
Lincoln Center
Opera House Brooklyn Academy of Music
Town Hall

Professional Theatres

Broadway Stage
Amas Musical Theatre
American Indian Community House
American Jewish Theatre
BW Roundabout Theatre Company
Creation Production Company
Czechoslovak-American Marionette Theatre
Fanfare Theatre Ensemble
Golden Fleece, Ltd.
Helen Hayes Performing Arts Center
Home for Contemporary Theatre & Art
Interart Theatre
Irondale Ensemble Project
Jewish Repertory Theatre
Latin American Theatre Ensemble

Mabou Mines
Music-Theatre Group
Musical Theatre Works
National Actors Theatre
Negro Ensemble Company
New Dramatists
New Federal Theatre
New York Shakespeare Festival
Pan Asian Repertory Theatre
Paper Bag Players
Penguin Rep
Playwrights Horizons
Primary Stages
Repertorio Espanol
Shadow Box Theatre
Tada!
The Acting Company
The Ensemble Studio Theatre
The Pearl Theatre Company
The Wooster Group
Theatre for the New City
Vineyard Theatre

Off-Broadway Stage
American Place Theatre
Atlantic Theatre Company
Classic Stage Company
Intar
Jean Cocteau Repertory
Manhattan Theatre Club
New York Theatre Workshop
The Second Stage
Theatreworks/USA
Thirteenth Street Repertory Co
Westbeth Theatre Center
Westside Repertory Theatre
Wings Theatre Company
WPA Theatre

Symphony Orchestras
American Composers Orchestra
American Symphony
Bachanalia Festival Orchestra
Bronx Arts Ensemble Orchestra
Brooklyn Philharmonic Orchestra
Concert Royal
Concordia Orchestra
Cosmopolitan Symphony
Empire State Pops Orchestra
Eos Music
Gotham Chamber Orchestra
Hunter Symphony
International Chamber Orchestra
ISO Symphony
Julius Grossman Orchestra
Juilliard Orchestra
Lautus Chamber Orchestra
Little Orchestra Society
Manhattan Philharmonic
Mozart Festival Orchestra
New American Chamber Orchestra
New York Chamber Symphony
New York City Symphony
New York Orchestral Society
New York Philharmonic

The Arts

423

New York Pops Orchestra
New York Pro Arte Chamber Orchestra
New York Scandia Symphony
New York Sinfonia Orchestra
Opera Orchestra of New York
Orchestra of St. Luke's
Orpheus Chamber Orchestra
Philharmonia Virtuosi
Riverside Symphony
Solisti New York Orchestra
Symphony for United Nations
West End Symphony
Westchester Philharmonic
Westchester Symphony
Score: 100   Rank: 1

★Newark, NJ
  Art Museums and Galleries
    Kean College Gallery
    Montclair Art Museum
    Morris Museum
    Newark Museum
  Ballet Company
    New Jersey Ballet Company
  Concert Radio
    In New York media market
    WBGO-FM
  Opera Companies
    ARS Musica
    Community Opera of New York
    New Jersey State Opera
    Opera at Florham
  Performance Hall
    New Jersey Performing Arts Center
  Professional Theatres
    Artspower National Touring Theatre
    Centenary Stage Co.
    Paper Mill Playhouse
    Playwrights Theatre
    Pushcart Players
  Symphony Orchestras
    Livingston Symphony
    Metropolitan Orchestra
    New Jersey Symphony
    New Philharmonic of New Jersey
    New Sussex Symphony
    Plainfield Symphony
    South Orange Symphony
    Summit Symphony
    Westfield Symphony
  Score: 96.61   Rank: 13

Newburgh, NY-PA
  Concert Radio
    In New York media market
    WOSR-FM
  Score: 0.57   Rank: 352

Norfolk-Virginia Beach-Newport
News, VA-NC
  Art Museums and Galleries
    Abby Rockefeller Folk Art Center
    Charles H. Taylor Arts Center
    Chrysler Museum

Hampton University Museum
Heritage Foundation Museum
Muscarelle Museum of Art
Peninsula Fine Arts Center
Portsmouth Fine Arts Gallery
Virginia Beach Center for the Arts
  Ballet Company
    Virginia Ballet Theatre
  Concert Radio
    WFOS-FM, WHRO-FM, WHRV-FM,
    WNSB-FM
  Opera Company
    Virginia Opera
  Performance Halls
    Chrysler Hall
    Pavillion
  Professional Theatre
    Virginia Stage Company
  Symphony Orchestras
    Virginia Beach Symphony
    Virginia Symphony
    Williamsburg Symphonia
  Score: 84.42   Rank: 56

★Oakland, CA
  Art Museums and Galleries
    Bedford Gallery
    Berkeley Art Center
    Judah Magnes Memorial Museum
    Oakland Museum
    Richmond Art Center
    U of California Art Museum
  Ballet Companies
    Berkeley Ballet Theater
    Oakland Ballet
  Concert Radio
    KSMC-FM
  Opera Companies
    Berkeley Opera
    Festival Opera Association
    Oakland Lyric Opera
  Performance Halls
    Paramount Theatre
    Zellerbach Hall
  Professional Theatre
    Willows Theatre Company
  Symphony Orchestras
    Berkeley Symphony
    California Chamber Orchestra
    California Symphony
    Classical Philharmonic of Northern
      California
    Fremont Symphony
    Livermore Amador Symphony
    Oakland East Bay Symphony
    Prometheus Symphony
    San Francisco Chamber Orchestra
  Score: 96.32   Rank: 14

Ocala, FL
  Art Museum and Gallery
    Appleton Museum of Art
  Concert Radio
    In Orlando-Daytona Beach-
      Melbourne media market

Symphony Orchestra
  Central Florida Symphony
Score: 7.94   Rank: 326

Odessa-Midland, TX
  Art Museums and Galleries
    Art Institute for the Permian Basin
  Concert Radio
    KOCV-FM, KRIL-AM
  Performance Hall
    Midland Center
  Symphony Orchestra
    Midland-Odessa Symphony & Chorale
  Score: 15.87   Rank: 298

Oklahoma City, OK
  Art Museums and Galleries
    Mabee-Gerrer Museum of Art
    Oklahoma City Art Museum
    OU Jones Museum of Art
  Ballet Companies
    Ballet Oklahoma
    Oklahoma Festival Ballet
  Concert Radio
    KCSC-FM, KGOU-FM, KROU-FM
  Opera Company
    Cimarron Circuit Opera Company
  Performance Halls
    Civic Center Music Hall
    Sooner Theatre
  Professional Theatre
    Pollard Theatre
  Symphony Orchestra
    Oklahoma City Philharmonic Orchestra
  Score: 76.21   Rank: 85

Olympia, WA
  Art Museums and Galleries
    Evergreen Galleries
    Washington State Capital Museum
  Concert Radio
    In Seattle-Tacoma media market
  Performance Hall
    Washington Center for Performing Arts
  Symphony Orchestra
    Olympia Symphony
  Score: 81.02   Rank: 68

Omaha, NE-IA
  Art Museum and Gallery
    Joslyn Art Museum
  Ballet Company
    Ballet Omaha
  Concert Radio
    KIOS-FM, KIWR-FM, KVNO-FM
  Opera Company
    Opera Omaha
  Performance Halls
    Orpheum Theater
    Witherspoon Concert Hall
  Professional Theatres
    Circle Theatre
    Nebraska Theatre Caravan
    Omaha Magic Theatre
    Omaha Playhouse

Symphony Orchestras
  Nebraska Wind Symphony
  Omaha Symphony Chamber Orchestra
  Omaha Symphony
  Score: 82.44   Rank: 63

Orange County, CA
  Art Museums and Galleries
    Art Institute of Southern California
    Brea Civic & Cultural Center Gallery
    Charles W. Bowers Museum
    Irvine Fine Arts Center
    Laguna Art Museum
    Newport Harbor Art Museum
  Ballet Company
    Ballet Pacifica
  Concert Radio
    In Los Angeles media market
  Opera Companies
    Fullerton Civic Light Opera
    Opera Pacific
  Performance Halls
    Bren Events Center
    Orange County Performing Arts
      Center
    Spreckels Performing Arts Center
  Professional Theatres
    Grove Theater Center
    Laguna Playhouse
    South Coast Repertory Mainstage
    South Coast Repertory Second Stage
    U of California Theatre
  Symphony Orchestras
    Capistrano Valley Symphony
    Chapman Symphony & Chamber
      Orchestra
    Mozart Classical Orchestra
    Orchestra Sonoma
    Pacific Symphony
    Saddleback Chamber Players
  Score: 86.97   Rank: 47

Orlando, FL
  Art Museums and Galleries
    Maitland Art Center
    Morse Museum of American Art
    Orlando Museum of Art
    Rollins College Cornell Museum
  Ballet Company
    Southern Ballet Theatre
  Concert Radio
    WMFE-FM, WPRK-FM, WUCF-FM
  Opera Companies
    Central Florida Lyric Opera
    Orlando Opera Company
  Performance Hall
    Carr Performing Arts Center
  Professional Theatre
    UCF Shakespeare Festival
  Symphony Orchestra
    Orlando Philharmonic
  Score: 78.76   Rank: 76

Oshawa, ON
  Art Museums and Galleries
    Robert McLaughlin Gallery
    The Station Gallery
  Symphony Orchestra
    Oshawa-Durham Symphony
  Score: 28.90   Rank: 252

Ottawa-Hull, ON-PQ
  Art Museums and Galleries
    Algonquin College Museum
    Axe Neo-7 Art Contemporain
    Centre Culturel l'Imagier
    Galerie Montcalm
    Gallery 101
    Museum of Contemporary
      Photography
    National Gallery of Canada
    Saw Gallery
    Wildlife & Wilderness Art Museum
  Opera Company
    Opera Lyra Ottawa
  Performance Hall
    National Arts Centre
  Professional Theatres
    Company of Fools
    Great Canadian Theatre Company
    Groupe Derives Urbaines
    National Arts Centre
    Odyssey Theatre
    Passionate Balance
    Rag & Bone Puppet Theatre
    Theatre De L'ille
  Symphony Orchestra
    National Arts Centre Orchestra
  Score: 88.96   Rank: 40

Owensboro, KY
  Art Museum and Gallery
    Owensboro Museum of Fine Art
  Concert Radio
    In Evansville media market
    WKWC-FM
  Performance Hall
    Riverpark Center
  Symphony Orchestra
    Owensboro Symphony
  Score: 13.32   Rank: 307

Panama City, FL
  Art Museum and Gallery
    Visual Arts Center of Northwest Florida
  Concert Radio
    WFSW-FM, WKGC-AM, WKGC-FM
  Performance Hall
    Marina Civic Center
  Score: 9.64   Rank: 320

Parkersburg-Marietta, WV-OH
  Art Museum and Gallery
    Parkersburg Art Center
  Ballet Company
    Mid Ohio Valley Ballet Company
  Concert Radio
    WMRT-FM, WVPG-FM

Performance Hall
    College Activity Center
  Score: 41.08   Rank: 209

Pensacola, FL
  Art Museums and Galleries
    Pensacola Museum of Art
    Visual Arts Gallery Pensacola
  Concert Radio
    WUWF-FM
  Performance Hall
    Saenger Theater
  Symphony Orchestra
    Pensacola Symphony
  Score: 17.57   Rank: 292

Peoria-Pekin, IL
  Art Museum and Gallery
    Lakeview Museum of Arts & Sciences
  Concert Radio
    WCBU-FM
  Opera Company
    Opera Illinois
  Performance Hall
    Peoria Civic Center
  Symphony Orchestra
    Peoria Symphony
  Score: 66.86   Rank: 118

★Philadelphia, PA-NJ
  Art Museums and Galleries
    Brandywine River Museum
    Institute For Contemporary Art
    La Salle University Art Museum
    Paley Gallery
    Pennsylvania Academy of the Fine Arts
    Perkins Center For the Arts
    Philadelphia Museum of Art
    Philadelphia Art Alliance
    Please Touch Museum
    Stedman Art Gallery
    U of Pennsylvania Galleries
    Widner University Art Museum
    Woodmere Art Museum
  Ballet Companies
    National Ballet of New Jersey
    Peninsula Ballet
  Concert Radio
    WFLN-FM, WHYY-FM, WNJS-FM,
      WNJS-FM, WRTI-FM
  Opera Companies
    AVA Opera Theater
    Lyric Opera Theatre
    Opera Company of Philadelphia
  Performance Halls
    Academy of Music
    Annenburg Center
    Mann Center for Performing Arts
    Merriam Theatre
    Walnut Street Theatre
  Professional Theatres
    American Music Theater Festival
    Arden Theatre Company–Arcadia Stage
    Bristol Riverside Theatre

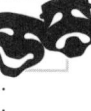

Bushfire Theatre of Performing Arts
Cheltenham Center for the Arts at the
    Berger
Foundation Theatre
Hedgerow Theatre
Philadelphia Theatre Company
Society Hill Playhouse
Temple University Theatre
The Independent Eye at Old City Stage
    Works
The People's Light and Theatre
    Company
The Wilma Theater
Venture Theatre Company
Walnut Street Theatre Company
Symphony Orchestras
    Delaware Valley Philharmonic
        Orchestra
    Haddonfield Symphony
    Kennett Symphony
    Lansdowne Symphony
    North Penn Symphony
    Orchestra of The Pennsylvania Ballet
    Orchestra Society of Philadelphia
    Pennsy Pops
    Philadelphia concerto Soloists Chamber
    Orchestra
    Philadelphia Orchestra
    Philadelphia Virtuosi Chamber
        Orchestra
    Philharmonic of Southern New Jersey
    Rose Tree Pops Orchestra
    Symphony of the Curtis Institute of
        Music
    West Jersey Chamber Symphony
Score: 98.31   **Rank: 7**

Phoenix-Mesa, AZ
Art Museums and Galleries
    Fleischer Museum
    Heard Museum
    Phoenix Art Museum
    Plotkin Judaica Museum
    Scottsdale Center for the Arts
Ballet Companies
    Ballet Arizona
    Childsplay
Concert Radio
    KBAQ-FM, KJZZ-FM
Performance Halls
    Centennial Hall
    Gammage Auditorium
    Phoenix Symphony Hall
    Scottsdale Center of the Arts
Professional Theatre
    Arizona Theatre Company
Symphony Orchestras
    Mesa Symphony
    Scottsdale Symphony
    Sun Cities Symphony
    The Phoenix Symphony
Score: 86.69   **Rank: 48**

Pine Bluff, AR
Art Museum and Gallery
    Southeast Arkansas Arts Center
Performance Hall
    Pine Bluff Auditorium
Symphony Orchestra
    Pine Bluff Symphony
Score: 11.05   **Rank: 315**

★Pittsburgh, PA
Art Museums and Galleries
    Associated Artists of Pittsburgh Gallery
    Carnegie Museum of Art
    Frick Art Museum
    Pittsburgh Center for the Arts
    Westmoreland Museum of Art
Ballet Company
    Pittsburgh Ballet Theatre
Concert Radio
    WQED-FM, WDUQ-FM, WYEP-FM
Opera Companies
    Civic Light Opera
    Opera Theater of Pittsburgh
    Pittsburgh Opera
Performance Halls
    Carnegie Music Hall
    Heinz Hall for Performing Arts
Professional Theatres
    City Theatre
    Pittsburgh Public Theater
    Saltworks Theatre Company
Symphony Orchestras
    American Wind Symphony
    Carnegie-Mellon Philharmonic
    Edgewood Symphony
    McKeesport Symphony
    Pittsburgh Symphony
    River City Brass Band
    Westmoreland Symphony
Score: 90.94   **Rank: 33**

Pittsfield, MA
Art Museums and Galleries
    Norman Rockwell Museum at
        Stockbridge
    The Berkshire Museum
Concert Radio
    In Albany-Schenectady-Troy media
        market
Opera Company
    Berkshire Opera Company
Performance Hall
    South Mountain Concert Hall
Score: 69.41   **Rank: 109**

Pocatello, ID
Performance Hall
    Goranson Hall
Symphony Orchestra
    Idaho State Civic Symphony
Score: 14.45   **Rank: 303**

Portland, ME
Art Museum and Gallery
    Portland Museum of Art
Concert Radio
    WMEA-FM, WPKM-FM
Performance Hall
    Merrill Auditorium at City Hall
Professional Theatre
    Portland Stage Company
Symphony Orchestra
    Portland Symphony
Score: 58.93   **Rank: 146**

★Portland-Vancouver, OR-WA
Art Museums and Galleries
    Portland Art Museum
    North View Gallery
Ballet Company
    Oregon Ballet Theatre
Concert Radio
    KBPS-AM, KBPS-FM, KOAC-AM,
        KOPB-FM
Opera Company
    Portland Opera Association
Performance Hall
    Schnitzer Concert Hall
Professional Theatres
    Portland Center Stage
    Portland Repertory Theatre
    Tygres Heart Shakespeare
Symphony Orchestras
    Columbia Symphony
    Mt. Hood Pops Orchestra
    Oregon Symphony
    Portland Baroque Orchestra
    Sinphonia Concertante Orchestra
    Vancouver Symphony
Score: 91.51   **Rank: 31**

Portsmouth-Rochester, NH-ME
Art Museums and Galleries
    Lamont Gallery
    UNH Art Gallery
Ballet Company
    Ballet New England
Concert Radio
    In Boston media market
Professional Theatre
    The Seacoast Repertory Theatre
Score: 57.80   **Rank: 150**

Providence-Fall River-Warwick, RI-MA
Art Museums and Galleries
    Brown University Art Galleries
    Rhode Island School of Design Gallery
Ballet Company
    State Ballet of Rhode Island
Concert Radio
    WLKW-AM
Performance Hall
    Veterans Memorial Auditorium
Professional Theatres
    Kaleidoscope Theatre
    Looking Glass Theatre

Rites and Reason
Trinity Repertory Company
Symphony Orchestras
Rhode Island Civic Chorale & Orchestra
Rhode Island College Symphony
Rhode Island Philharmonic Orchestra
U of Rhode Island Symphony
Score: 77.63   Rank: 80

Provo-Orem, UT
Art Museums and Galleries
BYU Larsen Gallery
Museum of Art
Concert Radio
In Salt Lake City media market
KBYU-FM
Performance Hall
Harris Center Concert Hall
Symphony Orchestra
Utah Valley Symphony
Score: 54.40   Rank: 162

Pueblo, CO
Art Museum and Gallery
Sangre de Cristo Arts Center
Concert Radio
In Colorado Springs media market
KCFP-FM
Performance Hall
Sangre de Cristo Arts Center
Symphony Orchestra
Pueblo Symphony
Score: 32.87   Rank: 238

Punta Gorda, FL
Concert Radio
In Ft. Myers-Naples media market
Performance Hall
Port Charlotte Auditorium
Symphony Orchestra
Charlotte Symphony
Score: 7.65   Rank: 327

Quebec City, PQ
Art Museums and Galleries
Centre d'Animation Photographie
Musee du Quebec
Musee du Seminaire de Quebec
Concert Radio
CBV-FM
Opera Company
L'Opera de Quebec
Performance Halls
Grand Theatre de Quebec
Salle Albert-Rousseau
Professional Theatres
Theatre de la Bordee
Theatre de la Commune
Theatre du Bois de Coulonge
Theatre du Gros Mecano
Theatre Niveau Parking
Theatre Repere
Symphony Orchestras
Les Violons du Roy
Orchestre Symphonique de Quebec
Score: 71.68   Rank: 101

Racine, WI
Art Museum and Gallery
Wurstum Museum of Fine Arts
Concert Radio
In Milwaukee media market
Performance Hall
Festival Hall
Symphony Orchestra
Racine Symphony
Score: 38.53   Rank: 218

Raleigh-Durham-Chapel Hill, NC
Art Museums and Galleries
City Gallery of Contemporary Art
Duke University Museum of Art
North Carolina Museum of Art
UNC Ackland Art Museum
Concert Radio
WCPE-FM, WUNC-FM
Opera Companies
National Opera Company
Triangle Opera Theater Associates
Performance Halls
Civic Center Complex Theatre
Page Auditorium
Raleigh Memorial Auditorium
Professional Theatres
North Carolina Theatre
PlayMakers Repertory Company
Symphony Orchestras
North Carolina Symphony
Raleigh Symphony
The Durham Symphony
Score: 86.12   Rank: 50

Rapid City, SD
Art Museums and Galleries
Dahl Fine Arts Center
Sioux Indian Museum
Concert Radio
KBHE-FM
Performance Hall
Rushmore Plaza Civic Center
Symphony Orchestra
Black Hills Symphony
Score: 9.07   Rank: 322

Reading, PA
Art Museum and Gallery
Freedman Gallery-Albright College
Reading Public Museum & Art Gallery
Concert Radio
In Philadelphia media market
Performance Hall
Rajah Theatre
Symphony Orchestra
Reading Symphony
Score: 27.77   Rank: 256

Redding, CA
Art Museum and Gallery
Redding Museum of Art & History
Concert Radio
KFPR-FM, KNCA-FM

Performance Hall
Redding Civic Auditorium
Symphony Orchestra
Shasta Symphony
Score: 5.67   Rank: 334

Regina, SK
Art Museums and Galleries
Dunlop Art Gallery
Legislative Building Galleries
MacKenzie Art Gallery
Rosemont Art Gallery
Performance Hall
Saskatchewan Centre of the Arts
Professional Theatre
Globe Theatre
Symphony Orchestra
Regina Symphony
Score: 73.94   Rank: 93

Reno, NV
Art Museum and Gallery
The Nevada Museum of Art
Ballet Company
Nevada Festival Ballet
Concert Radio
KUNR-FM
Opera Company
Nevada Opera Association
Performance Hall
Pioneer Center for Performing Arts
Symphony Orchestras
Reno Chamber Orchestra
Reno Philharmonic
Reno Pops Orchestra
Score: 51.28   Rank: 173

Richland-Kennewick-Pasco, WA
Concert Radio
KFAE-FM
Symphony Orchestra
Mid-Columbia Symphony
Score: 20.12   Rank: 283

Richmond-Petersburg, VA
Art Museums and Galleries
Virginia Museum of Fine Arts
VCU Anderson Gallery
Ballet Companies
Concert Ballet of Virginia
Richmond Ballet
The State Ballet of Virginia
Concert Radio
WCVE-FM
Performance Hall
Carpenter Center for Performing Arts
Professional Theatres
Theatre IV
TheatreVirginia
Symphony Orchestra
Richmond Symphony
Score: 77.34   Rank: 81

The Arts

427

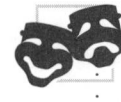

★Riverside-San Bernardino, CA
Art Museums and Galleries
Cabot's Old Indian Pueblo Museum
Edward-Dean Museum of Decorative Arts
Palm Springs Desert Museum
Riverside Art Museum
U of California Galleries
Ballet Company
California Riverside Ballet
Concert Radio
In Los Angeles media market
KCRY-FM, KPSC-FM, KVCR-FM
Opera Companies
San Bernardino Civic Light Opera
West Coast Opera Theatre
Performance Halls
California Theatre for the Arts
Riverside Municipal Auditorium
Symphony Orchestras
Redlands Symphony
Riverside County Philharmonic
San Bernardino Symphony
Victor Valley Symphony
Score: 92.07   Rank: 29

Roanoke, VA
Art Museum and Gallery
Art Museum of Western Virginia
Concert Radio
WVTF-FM
Opera Company
Opera Roanoke
Performance Hall
Civic Center
Professional Theatre
Mill Mountain Theatre
Symphony Orchestra
Roanoke Symphony
Score: 51.56   Rank: 172

Rochester, MN
Art Museum and Gallery
Rochester Art Center
Concert Radio
KZSE-FM
Performance Hall
Mayo Civic Center
Score: 52.98   Rank: 167

Rochester, NY
Art Museums and Galleries
Eastman Museum of Photography
UR Memorial Art Gallery
Concert Radio
WEOS-FM, WRUR-FM, WXXI-FM
Opera Company
Opera Rochester
Performance Hall
Eastman Theater
Professional Theatre
Geva Theatre

Symphony Orchestras
Eastman Philharmonia
Genesee Symphony
Rochester Chamber Orchestra
Rochester Philharmonic Orchestra
Score: 83.29   Rank: 60

Rockford, IL
Art Museum and Gallery
Rockford Art Museum
Concert Radio
WNIJ-FM
Performance Hall
Midway Theatre
Professional Theatre
New American Theater
Symphony Orchestra
Rockford Symphony
Score: 44.48   Rank: 197

Rocky Mount, NC
Art Museum and Gallery
Hobson Pittman Memorial Gallery
Concert Radio
In Raleigh-Durham media market
WESQ-FM, WRQM-FM
Performance Hall
Dunn Center
Symphony Orchestra
Tar River Choral & Orchestral Society
Score: 22.67   Rank: 274

Sacramento, CA
Art Museum and Gallery
Crocker Art Museum
Ballet Companies
Phares Theatre Ballet
Sacramento Ballet
Concert Radio
KXKB-FM, KXJZ-FM, KXPR-FM
Opera Company
Sacramento Opera Company
Performance Hall
Sacramento Community Center Theatre
Professional Theatre
Sacramento Theatre Company
Symphony Orchestras
Camellia Symphony
Mozart Academy Chamber Orchestra
Sacramento Symphony
Score: 74.79   Rank: 90

Saginaw-Bay City-Midland, MI
Art Museums and Galleries
Arts Midland Galleries
Saginaw Art Museum
Concert Radio
WUCX-FM
Performance Halls
Midland Center for the Arts
Saginaw Civic Center
Symphony Orchestras
Midland Symphony
Saginaw Symphony
Score: 57.51   Rank: 151

St. Catharines-Niagara, ON
Art Museum and Gallery
Rodman Hall Arts Centre
Performance Hall
Brock Centre for the Arts
Professional Theatres
Carousel Players
Shaw Festival
Theatre Beyond Words
Symphony Orchestra
Niagara Symphony
Score: 76.78   Rank: 83

St. Cloud, MN
Art Museum and Gallery
Kiehle Gallery
Concert Radio
In Minneapolis-St. Paul media market
KSJR-FM
Opera Company
Quite Light Opera Company
Performance Halls
Auditorium
Benedicta Arts Center
Symphony Orchestras
Sonare Chamber Orchestra
St. Cloud Symphony
Score: 84.99   Rank: 54

Saint John, NB
Art Museum and Gallery
New Brunswick Museum
Performance Hall
Imperial Theatre
Professional Theatre
Imperial Theatre
Symphony Orchestra
Symphony New Brunswick
Score: 21.25   Rank: 279

St. John's, NF
Art Museums and Galleries
Eastern Edge Gallery
Memorial University Art Gallery
Resource Centre for the Arts
Concert Radio
CBN-FM
Performance Hall
Arts & Culture Centre
Professional Theatres
R.C.A. Theatre
Rising Tide Theatre
Symphony Orchestra
Newfoundland Symphony
Score: 27.20   Rank: 258

St. Joseph, MO
Art Museum and Gallery
Albrecht-Kemper Museum of Art
Performance Hall
Missouri Theatre
Symphony Orchestra
St. Joseph Symphony
Score: 55.25   Rank: 159

★St. Louis, MO-IL
   Art Museums and Galleries
      Forum for Contemporary Art
      Laumeier Sculpture Park & Museum
      Saint Louis Art Museum
   Ballet Companies
      Gateway Ballet of St. Louis
      St. Louis Ballet
   Concert Radio
      KFUO-FM, KWMU-FM, KDHX-FM, WSIE-FM
   Opera Company
      Opera Theatre of Saint Louis
   Performance Halls
      Fox Theatre
      Powell Symphony Hall
   Professional Theatres
      Metro Theatre Company
      The Repertory Theatre of St. Louis
   Symphony Orchestras
      Bellville Philharmonic Society
      Gateway Festival Orchestra
      Kirkwood Symphony
      Saint Louis Symphony
      St. Louis Philharmonic Orchestra
      Town and Country Symphony
   Score: 94.91   Rank: 19

Salem, OR
   Art Museums and Galleries
      Bush Barn Art Center
      George Putnam University Center
   Concert Radio
      In Portland media market
   Performance Hall
      Smith Auditorium
   Symphony Orchestra
      Salem Chamber Orchestra
   Score: 41.65   Rank: 207

Salinas, CA
   Art Museum and Gallery
      Monterey Peninsula Museum of Art
   Concert Radio
      KBOQ-FM, KVRG-AM
   Opera Company
      Hidden Valley Opera Ensemble
   Professional Theatre
      The Western Stage
   Symphony Orchestras
      Monterey Bay Chamber Orchestra
      Monterey County Symphony
   Score: 54.68   Rank: 161

★Salt Lake City-Ogden, UT
   Art Museums and Galleries
      Eccles Community Arts Center
      Museum of Church History & Art
      Salt Lake Art Center
      University Museum of Fine Arts
   Ballet Company
      Ballet West
   Concert Radio
      KUER-FM

   Opera Companies
      Salt Lake Opera Theatre
      Utah Opera Company
   Performance Halls
      Kinsbury Hall
      Salt Lake County Performing Arts Center
   Professional Theatres
      Pioneer Theatre Company
   Symphony Orchestras
      Mormon Symphony
      Utah Symphony
      Wasatch Community Symphony
   Score: 92.36   Rank: 28

San Angelo, TX
   Art Museum and Gallery
      San Angelo Museum of Fine Arts
   Concert Radio
      KUTX-FM
   Performance Hall
      City Auditorium
   Symphony Orchestra
      San Angelo Symphony
   Score: 28.62   Rank: 253

San Antonio, TX
   Art Museums and Galleries
      McNay Art Museum
      San Antonio Museum of Art
   Ballet Company
      San Antonio Ballet Company
   Concert Radio
      KPAC-FM, KRTU-FM, KSTX-FM
   Performance Halls
      Lauri Auditorium
      Lila Cockrell Theatre
      Majestic Theater
      Municipal Auditorium
   Symphony Orchestras
      Mid-Texas Symphony
      San Antonio Symphony
   Score: 60.91   Rank: 139

★San Diego, CA
   Art Museums and Galleries
      Grossmont College Art Gallery
      Mandeville Gallery
      Mingei International World Folk Art
      Museum of Contemporary Art
      Museum of Photographic Arts
      San Diego Museum of Art
      Timken Museum of Art
   Ballet Company
      California Ballet Company
   Concert Radio
      KFSD-FM, KPBS-FM
   Opera Companies
      San Diego Civic Light Opera
      San Diego Comic Opera Company
      San Diego Opera
   Performance Halls
      Old Globe Theatre
      San Diego Concourse

   Professional Theatres
      La Jolla Playhouse
      Lamb's Players Theatre
      North Coast Repertory Theatre
      Old Globe Theatre
      San Diego Repertory
   Symphony Orchestras
      La Jolla Symphony & Chorus
      Tifereth Israel Community Orchestra
   Score: 91.22   Rank: 32

★San Francisco, CA
   Art Museums and Galleries
      Ansel Adams Photography Center
      Arts Council of San Mateo County
      Asian Art Museum of San Francisco
      California Crafts Museum
      Cartoon Art Museum
      Exploratorium
      Falkirk Cultural Center
      Fine Arts Museums of San Francisco
      San Francisco Camerawork
      San Francisco Museum of Modern Art
      San Francisco Art Institute Galleries
      Wiegand Gallery
   Ballet Companies
      LINES Contemporary Ballet
      Marin Ballet Company
      Peninsula Ballet Theatre
      San Francisco Ballet
      San Francisco's Ballet Celeste International
      Theatre Ballet of San Francisco
   Concert Radio
      KALW-FM, KCSM-FM, KQED-FM, KDFC-AM, KKHI-FM
   Opera Companies
      Opera Center Singers
      Pocket Opera
      San Francisco Conservatory Opera Theatre
      San Francisco Opera
      Western Opera Theater
   Performance Halls
      Graham Civic Auditorium
      Nob Hill Masonic Center
      War Memorial & Performing Arts Center
   Professional Theatres
      American Conservatory Theatre
      Magic Theatre
      Marin Theatre Company
      Theatre of Yugen
   Symphony Orchestras
      American Classical Players
      Marin Symphony
      New Century Chamber Orchestra
      Peninsula Symphony
      Philharmonia Baroque Orchestra
      Redwood Symphony
      San Francisco Community Music Center Orchestra
      San Francisco Symphony
      The Women's Philharmonic
   Score: 97.46   Rank: 10

★San Jose, CA
  Art Museums and Galleries
    De Saisset Museum
    Los Gatos Museum
    Palo Alto Cultural Center
    San Jose Museum of Art
    San Jose Museum of Contemporary Art
    Stanford University Galleries
    State University Art Galleries
    Triton Museum of Art
  Ballet Company
    Santa Clara Ballet Company
  Concert Radio
    KDFC-FM
  Opera Companies
    American Musical Theatre of San Jose
    Opera San Jose
    West Bay Opera
  Performance Halls
    Center for Performing Arts
    Dinkelspiel Auditorium
  Professional Theatres
    Alliance Repertory Company
    American Musical Theatre of San Jose
    Northside Theatre Company
    San Jose Repertory Theatre
    TheatreWorks
    Victory Theatre
  Symphony Orchestras
    Hewlett-Packard Symphony
    Nova Vista Symphony
    San Jose Symphony
    South Valley Symphony
    Stanford Symphony
  Score: 94.34   Rank: 21

San Luis Obispo-Atascadero-Paso Robles, CA
  Concert Radio
    In Santa Barbara-Santa Maria media market
    KCBX-FM
  Opera Company
    Pacific Repertory Opera
  Performance Hall
    Performing Arts Center
  Symphony Orchestra
    San Luis Obispo County Symphony
  Score: 29.75   Rank: 249

Santa Barbara-Santa Maria-Lompoc, CA
  Art Museums and Galleries
    Santa Barbara Museum of Art
    U of California Galleries
  Concert Radio
    KDB-FM, KFAC-FM
  Opera Companies
    Santa Barbara Civic Light Opera
    Santa Barbara Grand Opera
  Performance Halls
    Grenada Theatre
    Lobero Theatre

  Professional Theatres
    Ensemble Theatre Company
    PCPA Theaterfest
  Symphony Orchestras
    Summer Festival Orchestra
    Santa Barbara Chamber Orchestra
    Santa Barbara Symphony
    The West Coast Symphony
  Score: 53.26   Rank: 166

Santa Cruz-Watsonville, CA
  Art Museum and Gallery
    Art Museum Santa Cruz County
  Concert Radio
    In Monterey-Salinas media market
    KUSP-FM
  Symphony Orchestra
    Santa Cruz County Symphony
  Score: 56.66   Rank: 154

Santa Fe, NM
  Art Museums and Galleries
    Center for Contemporary Arts
    Fuller Lodge Art Center
    Governor's Gallery Museum
    Institute of American Indian Arts
    Museum of Fine Arts
    Museum of International Folk Art
    Wheelwright Museum of the American Indian
  Concert Radio
    In Albuquerque media market
    KSFR-FM
  Opera Company
    Santa Fe Opera
  Performance Hall
    Sweeney Center
  Symphony Orchestras
    Santa Fe Pro Musica
    Santa Fe Symphony
  Score: 65.44   Rank: 123

Santa Rosa, CA
  Concert Radio
    In San Francisco-Oakland-San Jose media market
    KRCB-FM
  Performance Hall
    Burbank Center for the Arts
  Symphony Orchestra
    Santa Rosa Symphony
  Score: 54.96   Rank: 160

Sarasota-Bradenton, FL
  Art Museum and Gallery
    Ringling Museum of Art
  Ballet Company
    Sarasota Ballet of Florida
  Concert Radio
    In Tampa–St. Petersburg media market
    WSPB-AM
  Opera Company
    Sarasota Opera Association

  Performance Halls
    Sarasota Opera House
    Van Wezel Performing Arts Hall
  Professional Theatres
    Asolo Theatre Company
    Florida Studio Theatre
  Symphony Orchestras
    Florida West Coast Symphony
    Sarasota Pops
    Venice Symphony
  Score: 73.09   Rank: 96

Saskatoon, SK
  Art Museums and Galleries
    AKA Gallery
    Diefenbaker Centre
    Gorden Snelgrove Art Gallery
    Mendel Art Gallery
    Photographers Gallery
    Saskatoon Library Art Gallery
    St. Thomas More Art Gallery
    Ukrainian Museum of Canada
  Concert Radio
    CBKS-FM
  Performance Hall
    Saskatoon Centennial Auditorium
  Professional Theatres
    Persephone Theatre
    Saskatoon Fringe Festival
    Shakespeare on the Saskatchewan
    Twenty-Fifth Street Theatre
  Symphony Orchestra
    Saskatoon Symphony
  Score: 79.89   Rank: 72

Savannah, GA
  Art Museums and Galleries
    Kiah Museum
    Telfair Academy of Arts & Sciences
  Concert Radio
    WSVH-FM
  Performance Hall
    Johnny Mercer Theatre
  Symphony Orchestra
    Savannah Symphony
  Score: 45.05   Rank: 195

Scranton–Wilkes-Barre–Hazleton, PA
  Art Museum and Gallery
    Everhart Museum
  Concert Radio
    WVIA-FM
  Performance Hall
    Cultural Center at Masonic Temple
  Professional Theatre
    Bloomsburg Theatre Ensemble
  Symphony Orchestras
    Marywood College Community Orchestra
    Northeastern Pennsylvania Philharmonic
  Score: 67.71   Rank: 115

★Seattle-Bellevue-Everett, WA
  Art Museums and Galleries
    Bellevue Art Museum
    Charles & Emma Frye Art Museum
    Edmonds Art Festival Museum
    Pacific Arts Center
    Seattle Art Museum
    University Henry Art Gallery
  Ballet Companies
    Olympic Ballet Theatre
    Pacific Northwest Ballet
  Concert Radio
    KING-FM, KUOW-FM
  Opera Companies
    Chaspen Opera Theater
    Civic Light Opera
    La Stella Foundation
    Seattle Opera Association
  Performance Halls
    Meany Hall
    Seattle Center
  Professional Theatres
    A Contemporary Theatre
    Bathhouse Theatre
    Intiman Theatre Company
    Seattle Children's Theatre
    Seattle Repertory Theatre
    The Empty Space Theatre
    The Group Theatre
  Symphony Orchestras
    Bellevue Philharmonic Orchestra
    Cascade Symphony
    Chaspen Symphony
    Everett Symphony
    Federal Way Philharmonic
    Northwest Chamber Orchestra
    Northwest Symphony
    Orchestra Seattle
    Seattle Philharmonic Orchestra
    Seattle Symphony
  Score: 91.79   Rank: 30

Sharon, PA
  Concert Radio
    In Youngstown media market
    WSAJ-AM, WSAJ-FM
  Symphony Orchestra
    Greenville Symphony
  Score: 2.55   Rank: 345

Sheboygan, WI
  Art Museum and Gallery
    John M. Kohler Arts Center
  Concert Radio
    In Milwaukee media market
  Performance Hall
    Kohler Memorial Theatre
  Symphony Orchestra
    Sheboygan Symphony
  Score: 61.76   Rank: 136

Sherbrooke, PQ
  Art Museums and Galleries
    Bishop's Champlain Art Gallery
    Universite de Sherbrooke
  Concert Radio
    CFLX-FM
  Performance Hall
    Centre Culturel de L'Universite
  Professional Theatre
    Theatre du Sang Neuf
  Symphony Orchestra
    Concerts Symphonique de Sherbrooke
  Score: 16.72   Rank: 295

Sherman-Denison, TX
  Performance Hall
    Wynne Chapel
  Symphony Orchestra
    Sherman Symphony
  Score: 19.55   Rank: 285

Shreveport-Bossier City, LA
  Art Museums and Galleries
    Centenary College Meadows Museum
    R.W. Norton Art Gallery
  Concert Radio
    KDAQ-FM
  Opera Company
    Shreveport Opera
  Performance Halls
    Shreveport Civic Center
    Strand Theatre of Shreveport
  Symphony Orchestra
    Shreveport Symphony
  Score: 39.38   Rank: 215

Sioux City, IA-NE
  Art Museum and Gallery
    Sioux City Art Center
  Concert Radio
    KWIT-FM
  Performance Hall
    Eppley Auditorium
  Symphony Orchestra
    Sioux City Symphony
  Score: 36.27   Rank: 226

Sioux Falls, SD
  Art Museum and Gallery
    Civic Fine Arts Center
  Concert Radio
    KCSD-FM, KRSD-FM
  Performance Hall
    Convention Center Grand Ballroom
  Symphony Orchestra
    South Dakota Symphony
  Score: 45.61   Rank: 193

South Bend, IN
  Art Museums and Galleries
    Notre Dame Snite Museum of Art
    South Bend Art Center
  Concert Radio
    WSND-FM

  Performance Hall
    Morris Performing Arts Center
  Symphony Orchestra
    South Bend Symphony
  Score: 62.61   Rank: 133

Spokane, WA
  Art Museums and Galleries
    Ad Art Gallery
    Cheney Cowles Museum
  Concert Radio
    KPBX-FM, KSFC-FM, KSVY-FM
  Performance Halls
    Metropolitan Performing Arts Center
    Opera House
  Professional Theatre
    Spokane Interplayers Ensemble
  Symphony Orchestra
    Spokane Symphony
  Score: 71.39   Rank: 102

Springfield, IL
  Art Museum and Gallery
    Illinois State Museum
  Ballet Company
    Springfield Ballet Company
  Concert Radio
    WUIS-FM
  Performance Hall
    Sangamon State University Auditorium
  Symphony Orchestras
    Illinois Chamber Orchestra
    Illinois Symphony
  Score: 37.68   Rank: 221

Springfield, MA
  Art Museums and Galleries
    George Smith Art Museum
    Jasper Rand Art Museum
    Mead Art Museum
    Museum of Fine Arts
    Smith College Museum of Art
  Ballet Company
    Amherst Ballet Theatre Company
  Concert Radio
    WFCR-FM
  Opera Company
    Commonwealth Opera
  Performance Halls
    Paramount Theatre
    Symphony Hall
  Professional Theatre
    StageWest
  Symphony Orchestras
    Smith College Student Orchestra
    Springfield Symphony
  Score: 73.66   Rank: 94

Springfield, MO
  Art Museum and Gallery
    Springfield Art Museum
  Ballet Company
    Springfield Ballet

Concert Radio
KSMU-FM
Opera Company
Springfield Regional Opera
Performance Hall
Hammons Hall for Performing Arts
Symphony Orchestra
Springfield Symphony
Score: 34.28   Rank: 233

Stamford-Norwalk, CT
Art Museums and Galleries
The Bruce Museum
Whitney Museum Fairfield County
Ballet Company
Connecticut Ballet Theatre
Concert Radio
In New York media market
WEDW-FM, WMMM-AM, WSLX-FM
Opera Companies
Connecticut Grand Opera & Orchestra
New England Lyric Operetta
Performance Halls
Norwalk Concert Hall
Stamford Center for the Arts
Professional Theatre
Stamford Theatre Works
Symphony Orchestras
Connecticut Philharmonic Orchestra
Fairfield Orchestra
Greenwich Symphony
Norwalk Symphony
Stamford Symphony
Symphony on the Sound
Score: 88.67   Rank: 41

State College, PA
Art Museum and Gallery
PSU Palmer Museum of Art
Concert Radio
In Johnstown-Altoona media market
WPSU-FM
Performance Hall
PSU Center for Performing Arts
Professional Theatre
University Resident Theatre Co.
Symphony Orchestras
Nittany Valley Symphony
Pennsylvania Centre Chamber Orchestra
Score: 25.50   Rank: 264

Steubenville-Weirton, OH-WV
Concert Radio
In Pittsburgh media market
Score: 5.39   Rank: 335

Stockton-Lodi, CA
Art Museum and Gallery
Haggin Museum
Concert Radio
In Sacramento-Modesto media market
KUOP-FM
Opera Company
Stockton Opera

Performance Halls
Atherton Auditorium
Faye Spanos Concert Hall
Symphony Orchestras
Stockton Symphony
University Symphony
Score: 36.83   Rank: 224

Sudbury, ON
Art Museum and Gallery
Laurentian University Museum
Performance Hall
Fraser Auditorium
Professional Theatre
Sudbury Theatre
Score: 14.17   Rank: 304

Sumter, SC
Art Museum and Gallery
Sumter Gallery of Art
Concert Radio
In Columbia media market
WRJA-FM
Score: 31.73   Rank: 242

Syracuse, NY
Art Museums and Galleries
Everson Museum of Art
Lowe Art Gallery
Concert Radio
WCNY-FM, WAER-FM, WRVO-FM
Opera Company
Syracuse Opera Company
Performance Halls
Landmark Theater
Mulroy Civic Center
Professional Theatre
Syracuse Stage
Symphony Orchestras
Auburn Chamber Orchestra
Onondaga Civic Symphony
Syracuse Symphony
Score: 81.31   Rank: 67

Tacoma, WA
Art Museum and Gallery
Tacoma Art Museum
Concert Radio
KPLU-FM
Opera Company
Tacoma Opera
Performance Hall
Broadway Center for Performing Arts
Professional Theatre
Tacoma Actors Guild
Symphony Orchestra
Tacoma Symphony
Score: 84.71   Rank: 55

Tallahassee, FL
Art Museum and Gallery
FSU Fine Arts Gallery
Ballet Company
Tallahassee Ballet Company

Concert Radio
WFSQ-FM, WFSU-FM
Performance Hall
Tallahassee-Leon County Civic Center
Symphony Orchestras
Big Bend Community Orchestra
Tallahassee Symphony
Score: 64.03   Rank: 128

Tampa-St. Petersburg-Clearwater, FL
Art Museums and Galleries
Florida Gulf Coast Art Center
Museum of Fine Arts
Ruth Eckerd Hall
Salvador Dali Museum
Tampa Museum of Art
University Scarfone Gallery
USF Contemporary Art Museum
Ballet Company
Acanthus Ballet
Concert Radio
WMNF-FM, WUSF-FM
Opera Companies
Florida Lyric Opera & Theatre
Spanish Lyric Theatre
Tampa Bay Opera
Performance Halls
Baumgardner Center for Performing
Arts
Bayfront Center, Mahaffey Theatre
Tampa Bay Performing Arts Center
Tampa Theatre
Professional Theatres
American Stage
Angel "Garden Café" Theatre
Symphony Orchestras
Tampa Bay Chamber Orchestra
The Florida Orchestra
Score: 66.58   Rank: 119

Terre Haute, IN
Art Museum and Gallery
Sheldon Swope Art Museum
Performance Hall
Tilson Music Hall
Symphony Orchestra
Terre Haute Symphony
Score: 28.05   Rank: 255

Texarkana, TX-Texarkana, AR
Concert Radio
In Shreveport media market
KTXK-FM
Score: 1.14   Rank: 350

Thunder Bay, ON
Art Museum and Gallery
Thunder Bay Art Gallery
Performance Hall
Thunder Bay Community Auditorium
Professional Theatre
Magnus Theatre Company Northwest
Symphony Orchestra
Thunder Bay Symphony
Score: 41.65   Rank: 207

Toledo, OH
  Art Museums and Galleries
    Toledo Museum of Art
    Spectrum Gallery of Toledo
  Concert Radio
    WGTE-FM
  Opera Company
    Toledo Opera
  Performance Hall
    Stranahan Theatre
  Symphony Orchestras
    Bowling Green Philharmonia
    Toledo Symphony
  Score: 85.84   Rank: 51

Topeka, KS
  Art Museum and Gallery
    Mulvane Art Museum
  Performance Hall
    Topeka Performing Arts Center
  Professional Theatre
    Topeka Civic Theatre
  Symphony Orchestra
    Topeka Symphony
  Score: 48.73   Rank: 182

★Toronto, ON
  Art Museums and Galleries
    Art Gallery at Harbourfront
    Art Gallery of Ontario
    Art Gallery of York University
    Art Metropole
    Brampton Library Art Gallery
    Centennial Gallery
    Gardiner Museum of Ceramic Art
    Glendon Gallery
    Koffler Gallery
    Mississauga Library Art Gallery
    Mississauga Springbank Centre
    Oakville Galleries
    Royal Ontario Museum
    Toronto Centre for Contemporary Art
    Toronto Sculpture Garden
    U of Toronto Gallery
  Ballet Company
    National Ballet of Canada
  Concert Radio
    CFMX-FM, CJBC-FM, CJRT-FM
  Opera Companies
    Canadian Opera Company
    Opera Atelier
    Opera in Concert
    Opera Mississauga
    Tapestry Opera Works
  Performance Halls
    Ford Center
    Hummingbird Center
    Living Arts Center
    Massey Hall
    Roy Thomson Hall
  Professional Theatres
    Autumn Leaf Performance
    Bald Ego Theatre

Bananafish Company
Best Boys Productions
Brookstone Performing Arts
Buddies In Bad Times Theatre
Cahoots Theatre Projects
Canadian Stage Company
Cascade Theatre
Children's Dance Theatre
Classical Cabaret
Comedy on Wry
Company of Sirens
Crow's Theatre
Da Da Kamera
DNA Theatre
ELA Theatre Projects
Equity Showcase Theatre
FA DO
Factory Theatre
Feast of Fools
Festival of Classics
First Draft Theatre
Friendly Spike Theatre Band
Full Fathom Productions
G. & T. Productions
Ground Zero Productions
Harbourfront Centre
Honestman Productions
Illustrated Men
Inner Stage Theatre
Jewel Productions
Joe's Theatre
Kensington Carnival
LeTHAL
M.C.U. Productions
Meta-Physical Theatre
Mime Company Limited
Mirvish Productions
Mixed Company
Mump & Smoot
Mysteriously Yours
Native Earth Performing Arts
Necessary Angel Theatre
New Globe Theatre
Nightwood Theatre
Pacun Peras The-A-Tro
Pea Green Theatre Group
Petty Rebel Theatre
Phyzikal Theatre
Platform 9 Theatre
Random Acts Theatre
Roseneath Theatre
Scarab Productions
Script Lab
Shakespeare In Action
Skylight Theatre
Smile Theatre Company
Solar Stage
Solar Stage Theatre
Soulpepper Theatre Company
Sound Image Theatre
Spend Your Rent Theatre
Stiletto Company
Straight Stitching Productions

Tapestry Musical Theatre
Tarragon Theatre
Tempest Theatre Group
The Canadian Stage Company
The Crankee Consort
The Fringe: Toronto Theatre Festival
The Other Theatre of Toronto
Theatre Boku-Maru
Theatre Centre
Theatre Columbus
Theatre Counterclockwise
Theatre Direct Canada
Theatre Francais De Toronto
Theatre Gargantua
Theatre Orangeville
Theatre Passe Muraille
Theatre Plus
Theatre Resource Centre
Theatre Smith-Gilmour
Theatre Voce
Theatre WUM
TheatreSports Toronto
Threshold Theater
Tolmec Dance Theatre
Toronto Operetta Theatre
Tribal Productions
Trinity Theatre Toronto
UNI Theatre
We Are One Theatre Productions
Wild Pig Theatre
World Miracle Theatre
Young People's Theatre
Zingaro Productions
Zisis Theatre Company
  Symphony Orchestras
    Cathedral Bluffs Symphony
    Esprit Orchestra
    Etobicoke Philharmonic Orchestra
    Hart House Orchestra
    Mississauga Symphony
    North York Symphony
    Oakville Symphony
    Orchestra Toronto
    Scarborough Philharmonic Orchestra
    Tafelmusik Baroque Orchestra
    The Toronto Symphony
    Toronto Chinese Philharmonic
    U of Toronto Symphony
  Score: 98.87   Rank: 5

Trenton, NJ
  Art Museums and Galleries
    Art Museum Princeton U
    New Jersey State Museum
  Concert Radio
    In Philadelphia media market
    WPRB-FM, WNJT-FM, WPRB-FM,
      WWFM-FM
  Opera Company
    Opera Festival of New Jersey
  Performance Hall
    War Memorial Auditorium

Place Profiles: The Arts

Professional Theatres
McCarter Theatre
Passage Theatre Company
Princeton Repertory Company
Symphony Orchestras
Greater Trenton Symphony
Princeton Chamber Symphony
Score: 80.74   Rank: 69

Trois-Rivieres, PQ
Art Museum and Gallery
Galerie d'Art du Parc
Concert Radio
CBF-FM
Performance Hall
Salle J. Antonio Thompson
Score: 53.83   Rank: 164

Tucson, AZ
Art Museums and Galleries
Aquary Museum
De Grazia Art Foundation
Tucson Museum of Art
University Museum of Art
Concert Radio
KUAT-FM, KUAZ-FM
Opera Company
Arizona Opera Company
Performance Halls
Centennial Hall
Tucson Center
Professional Theatre
Arizona Theatre Company
Symphony Orchestras
Catalina Chamber Orchestra
Civic Orchestra of Tucson
Southern Arizona Symphony
Tucson Symphony
Score: 66.29   Rank: 120

Tulsa, OK
Art Museums and Galleries
Gilcrease Institute of Art
Philbrook Museum of Art
Ballet Company
Tulsa Ballet
Concert Radio
KOAS-FM, KWGS-FM
Opera Company
Tulsa Opera
Performance Hall
Tulsa Performing Arts Center
Symphony Orchestras
Sinfonia
Tulsa Philharmonic Orchestra
U of Tulsa Symphony
Score: 63.18   Rank: 131

Tuscaloosa, AL
Art Museum and Gallery
University Moody Gallery
Concert Radio
WUAL-FM

Performance Hall
Bama Performing Arts Center
Professional Theatre
U Alabama Theatre
Symphony Orchestra
Tuscaloosa Symphony
Score: 13.04   Rank: 308

Tyler, TX
Art Museum and Gallery
Tyler Museum of Art
Performance Hall
Vaughn Auditorium
Symphony Orchestra
East Texas Symphony
Score: 9.35   Rank: 321

Utica-Rome, NY
Art Museum and Gallery
Munson-Williams-Proctor Museum
Concert Radio
WRVN-FM, WUNY-FM
Performance Hall
Stanley Performing Arts Center
Symphony Orchestras
Hamilton College Orchestra
Utica Symphony
Score: 30.88   Rank: 245

Vallejo-Fairfield-Napa, CA
Concert Radio
In Sacramento-Stockton-Modesto
media market
Symphony Orchestras
Napa Valley Symphony
Vallejo Symphony
Score: 64.88   Rank: 125

★**Vancouver, BC**
Art Museums and Galleries
Burnaby Art Gallery
Canadian Craft Museum
Cartwright Gallery
Charles H. Scott Gallery
Maple Ridge Art Gallery
Place des Arts
Richmond Art Gallery
Simon Fraser Gallery
Surrey Art Gallery
UBC Fine Arts Gallery
Vancouver Art Gallery
Concert Radio
CBU-AM
Opera Companies
Europera Productions
Modern Baroque Opera Company
Vancouver Opera
Performance Halls
Chan Centre for Performing Arts
Vancouver Civic Theatre
Professional Theatres
Arts Club Theatre
Axis Theatre Company

Bard on the Beach Shakespeare
Festival
Carousel Theatre Company
Coconut Theatre
Evergreen Theatre
Fend Players Society
Firehall Arts Centre
Gateway Theatre
Green Thumb Theatre
Grinning Dragon Theatre
Headlines Theatre
Hoarse Raven Theatre
Musical Theatre Works
Pacific Theatre
Pink Ink Theatre Productions
Playwrights Theatre Centre
Ruby slippers Productions Society
Rumble Productions
Tamahnous Theatre
Theatre la Siezieme
Theatre Terrific
Theatrespace/Vancouver Fringe
Touchstone Theatre
Vancouver Moving Theatre
Vancouver Playhouse
Vancouver TheatreSports League
Vancouver Youth Theatre Society
Western Gold Theatre Society
Symphony Orchestras
Richmond Community Orchestra
Vancouver Philharmonic Orchestra
Vancouver Symphony
Vancouver Youth Symphony
Score: 95.76   Rank: 16

Ventura, CA
Art Museum and Gallery
Carnegie Art Museum
Concert Radio
In Los Angeles media market
KCPB-FM, KCLU-FM, KCRU-FM
Symphony Orchestra
New West Symphony
Score: 63.74   Rank: 129

Victoria, BC
Art Museums and Galleries
Art Gallery of Greater Victoria
Emily Carr Gallery
Open Space Gallery
UV Maltwood Art Museum
Opera Company
Pacific Opera Victoria
Performance Hall
Royal Theatre
Professional Theatres
Asylum Theatre
Belfry Theatre
Intrepid Theatre Company
Kaleidoscope Theatre
New Bastion Theatre Company
Symphony Orchestra
Victoria Symphony
Score: 69.69   Rank: 108

Victoria, TX
Concert Radio
KVRT-FM
Performance Hall
Victoria College Auditorium
Symphony Orchestra
Victoria Symphony
Score: 8.50   Rank: 324

Vineland-Millville-Bridgeton, NJ
Concert Radio
In Philadelphia media market
WNJB-FM
Symphony Orchestra
Bay Atlantic Symphony
Score: 13.60   Rank: 306

Visalia-Tulare-Porterville, CA
Performance Hall
Visalia Convention Center and Theatres
Symphony Orchestra
Tulare County Symphony
Score: 16.44   Rank: 296

Waco, TX
Art Museum and Gallery
The Art Center
Concert Radio
KWBU-FM
Opera Company
Lyric Opera of Waco
Performance Halls
Waco Hall
Waco Hippodrome Theatre
Symphony Orchestras
Baylor University Symphony
Waco Symphony
Score: 34.85   Rank: 231

★Washington, DC-MD-VA-WV
Art Museums and Galleries
Anacostia Museum
Arlington Arts Center
Art Museum of the Americas
Arthur M. Sackler Gallery
B'nai B'rith Klutznick Museum
Corcoran Gallery of Art
Freer Gallery of Art
Georgetown University Collection
GWU Dimock Gallery
Hirshhorn Museum & Sculpture Garden
Howard University Gallery of Art
Mary Washington College
   Belmont Gallery
National Gallery of Art
National Museum American Art
National Museum of African Art
National Portrait Gallery
National Museum of Women in the Arts
Phillips Collection
Studio Gallery
U of Maryland Art Gallery

Ballet Company
Washington Ballet
Concert Radio
WETA-FM, WGMS-FM, WGTS-FM,
   WVEP-FM
Opera Companies
Capitol City Opera
National Lyric Opera Company
Opera Music Theater International
Opera Theatre of Northern Virginia
Potomac Valley Opera Company
Summer Opera Theatre Company
The Washington Opera
Washington Concert Opera
Washington Savoyards Ltd.
Wolf Trap Opera Company
Performance Halls
DAR Constitution Hall
Kennedy Center for the Performing Arts
Lisner Auditorium, George
   Washington U
Wolf Trap Performing Arts Foundation
Professional Theatres
Arena Stage
Discovery Theatre
Horizons Theatre
Metrostage
Round House Theater
Signature Theatre
Source Theatre Company
The Shakespeare Theatre
The Studio Theatre
Theatre of the First Amendment
Washington Jewish Theatre
Washington Stage Guild
Woolly Mammoth Theatre Company
Symphony Orchestras
Alexandria Symphony
Amadeus Orchestra
American Chamber Orchestra
Arlington Symphony
Columbia Orchestra
Fairfax Symphony
George Washington U. Symphony
Jewish Community Center Symphony
Kennedy Center Opera House
   Orchestra
Loudoun Symphony
Mary Washington College Community
Symphony
McLean Orchestra
McLean Symphony
Millbrook Orchestra
Mount Vernon Orchestra
National Chamber Orchestra
National Gallery Orchestra
National Symphony
Prince George's Philharmonic
Theater Chamber Players
United States Air Force Concert Band
United States Air Force Symphony
Virginia Chamber Orchestra

Washington Bach Consort
Washington Chamber Symphony
Washington Symphony
Score: 99.72   Rank: 2

Waterbury, CT
Concert Radio
In Hartford-New Haven media market
Performance Hall
Fine Arts Center
Symphony Orchestra
Waterbury Symphony
Score: 32.58   Rank: 239

Waterloo-Cedar Falls, IA
Art Museums and Galleries
Hearst Center for the Arts
UNI Gallery of Art
Waterloo Museum of Art
Concert Radio
In Cedar Rapids-Waterloo-Dubuque
   media market
KHKE-FM, KUNI-FM
Performance Hall
Kersenbrock Auditorium
Symphony Orchestra
Waterloo–Cedar Falls Symphony
Score: 40.51   Rank: 211

Wausau, WI
Art Museum and Gallery
Leigh Yawkey Woodson Art Museum
Concert Radio
WHRM-FM, WLBL-FM, WXPW-FM
Performance Hall
Grand Theatre
Symphony Orchestra
Wausau Symphony & Band
Score: 20.40   Rank: 282

West Palm Beach-Boca Raton, FL
Art Museums and Galleries
Boca Raton Museum of Art
Hibel Museum of Art
International Museum of Cartoon Art
Morikami Museum
Norton Museum of Art
Ballet Company
Ballet Florida
Concert Radio
WXEL-FM
Opera Companies
Lyric Opera Theatre of the Palm Beaches
Palm Beach Opera
Piccolo Opera Company
Performance Hall
Kravis Center for Performing Arts
Professional Theatres
Caldwell Theatre Company
Florida Stage
Symphony Orchestras
Boca Pops
Palm Beach Pops
Score: 76.49   Rank: 84

Wheeling, WV-OH
Concert Radio
WVNP-FM
Performance Hall
Capitol Music Hall
Symphony Orchestra
Wheeling Symphony
Score: 49.30   Rank: 180

Wichita, KS
Art Museums and Galleries
Coutts Memorial Museum of Art
Edwin Ulrich Museum of Art
Friends University Whittier Gallery
Wichita Art Museum
Concert Radio
KMUW-FM
Performance Hall
Century II Concert Hall
Symphony Orchestras
Newton Mid-Kansas Symphony
Wichita Symphony
Score: 52.13   Rank: 170

Wichita Falls, TX
Art Museum and Gallery
Wichita Falls Museum & Art Center
Performance Hall
Memorial Auditorium
Symphony Orchestra
Wichita Falls Symphony
Score: 10.77   Rank: 316

Williamsport, PA
Concert Radio
In Wilkes-Barre–Scranton media market
Performance Hall
Community Arts Center
Symphony Orchestra
Williamsport Symphony
Score: 24.37   Rank: 268

Wilmington, NC
Art Museum and Gallery
St. John's Museum of Art
Concert Radio
WHQR-FM
Performance Hall
Kenan Memorial Auditorium
Symphony Orchestra
Wilmington Symphony
Score: 18.14   Rank: 290

Wilmington-Newark, DE-MD
Art Museums and Galleries
Delaware Art Museum
Winterthur Museum
Concert Radio
In Philadelphia media market

Opera Company
OperaDelaware
Performance Halls
Grand Opera House
Playhouse Theatre
Professional Theatre
Delaware Theatre Company
Symphony Orchestras
Brandywine Baroque
Delaware Symphony
Score: 70.83   Rank: 104

Windsor, ON
Art Museum and Gallery
Art Gallery of Windsor
Concert Radio
CBE-AM
Performance Hall
Cleary International Centre
Professional Theatres
Capitol Theatre and Arts Centre
Such and Such Productions
Symphony Orchestra
Windsor Symphony
Score: 53.55   Rank: 165

Winnipeg, MB
Art Museums and Galleries
U of Manitoba Gallery III
Winnipeg Art Gallery
Ballet Company
Royal Winnipeg Ballet
Concert Radio
CBW-FM
Opera Company
Manitoba Opera Association
Performance Hall
Centennial Concert Hall
Professional Theatres
Le Cercle Moliere
Manitoba Theatre Center
Prairie Theatre Exchange
Primus Theatre
Shakespeare in the Ruins
Theatre Projects Manitoba
Winnipeg Jewish Theatre
Symphony Orchestras
Manitoba Chamber Orchestra
Winnipeg Symphony
Score: 84.14   Rank: 57

Worcester, MA-CT
Art Museum and Gallery
Worcester Art Museum
Concert Radio
In Boston media market
WBPR-FM, WICN-FM
Opera Company
Salisbury Lyric Opera

Performance Hall
Mechanics Hall
Professional Theatre
Worcester Foothills Theatre
Symphony Orchestra
Central Massachusetts Symphony
Score: 74.51   Rank: 91

Yakima, WA
Concert Radio
KNWY-FM
Performance Hall
Capitol Theatre
Symphony Orchestra
Yakima Symphony
Score: 28.33   Rank: 254

Yolo, CA
Art Museum and Gallery
UC Nelson Gallery
Concert Radio
In Sacramento-Stockton-Modesto
media market
Performance Hall
Freeborn Hall
Score: 19.27   Rank: 286

York, PA
Concert Radio
In Harrisburg-Lancaster-Lebanon-
York media market
Performance Hall
Strand Capitol Performing Arts Center
Symphony Orchestra
York Symphony
Score: 12.19   Rank: 311

Youngstown-Warren, OH
Art Museum and Gallery
Butler Institute of American Art
Concert Radio
WYSU-FM
Performance Hall
Stambaugh Auditorium
Symphony Orchestra
Youngstown Symphony
Score: 21.82   Rank: 277

Yuba City, CA
Concert Radio
In Sacramento-Stockton-Modesto
media market
Score: 0.29   Rank: 353

Yuma, AZ
Art Museum and Gallery
Yuma Fine Arts Association Center
Concert Radio
KAWC-AM, KAWC-FM
Score: 3.69   Rank: 341

ET CETERA: The Arts

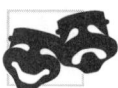

NEW YORK, NEW YORK

"New York, New York, it's a hell of a town!" says the song from *On the Town*. Certainly the Big Apple is hellish for its crime, gridlock traffic, and appalling living costs. The city's government is parodied in TV's *Spin City* as a quick-on-its feet dodger of special interest groups, but it does maintain a revolving loan fund to help performing arts groups end their "space chase," a constant quest for affordable, long-term work and performance rental property.

For many reasons, New York is beyond doubt the culture capital of North America. Consider these assets:

- **Concert Radio:** Five radio stations, together airing more than 500 hours per week, compete fiercely for a share of the limited classical-music market.

- **Dance Companies:** Among all companies in North America with annual budgets over $500,000, one in four is headquartered in metropolitan New York.

- **Professional Theaters:** When one considers not only Broadway, but also Off-Broadway and Off-Off Broadway, the actual number of theaters is unknown. *Playbill,* a publisher of theater programs, counts 138 professional theaters among its customers here. There are certainly more.

- **Symphony Orchestras:** Aside from its major symphony orchestra, the New York Philharmonic, Metropolitan New York has thirty-eight orchestras.

- **Opera Companies:** Thirty-seven companies, including two Grand Operas (The Met and the New York City Opera) make New York the opera capital of America.

THE DAVID AND GOLIATH PROPOSITION

Aside from New York, investigate other big metro areas and you'll find the best places to live for the arts: Chicago, Los Angeles, Washington, Toronto, and San Francisco. The consistent relationship between a metro area's size and its performing arts assets might make you think places such as Little Rock and Louisville, or Calgary and Peoria—all with populations under 1 million—

must resign themselves to being cultural underdogs. Think again.

Pick on Someone Your Own Size

What would happen if Calgary, Little Rock, Louisville, and Peoria (remembering the old playground cliché) were to say to New York, "Go pick on someone your own size"? By grouping metro areas into those with more than 1 million people and those with less, we are able to explore which have a large supply of cultural assets relative to their size and which might be considered cultural backwaters because they don't.

Sure, it's intuitive that big winners will be the largest metro areas. The top four in the arts are the top four in population. New York, Washington, Los Angeles, and Chicago each have critical masses to support ballet, opera, professional theater, and the symphony. They also tend to have older central cities with long-established arts facilities and a tradition of philanthropy.

What isn't intuitive are the big losers (see map on the next page). These are metro areas with populations over 1 million where people ought to enjoy a full calendar of professional, non-profit ballet, opera, theatre, and symphony—but don't. Most, like Orange County in southern California or Long Island, are suburbs to cultural meccas. Getting a performing arts fix in these places means a long evening commute to the central city. Others, like Las Vegas or Orlando, have grown so fast there's either no lively arts tradition in town, or the arts have withered in the face of tourist attractions, or both.

But small winners show where the "isolation-proximity" principle in geography is at play (see map on the next page). According to this notion, sizeable locations that are somewhat removed get more than their share of scarce amenities. Though smaller than the giants, they nevertheless are the only game for miles around.

Calgary, stuck as it is on the plains immediately in front of the Canadian Rockies, is still the largest and nearest area to the 1,600-mile emptiness between Minneapolis and the Seattle-Vancouver corridor. Little Rock is the biggest spot on the 450-mile stretch between Memphis and Dallas. Omaha is a minor culture oasis roughly midway on an 18-hour drive between Chicago and Denver.

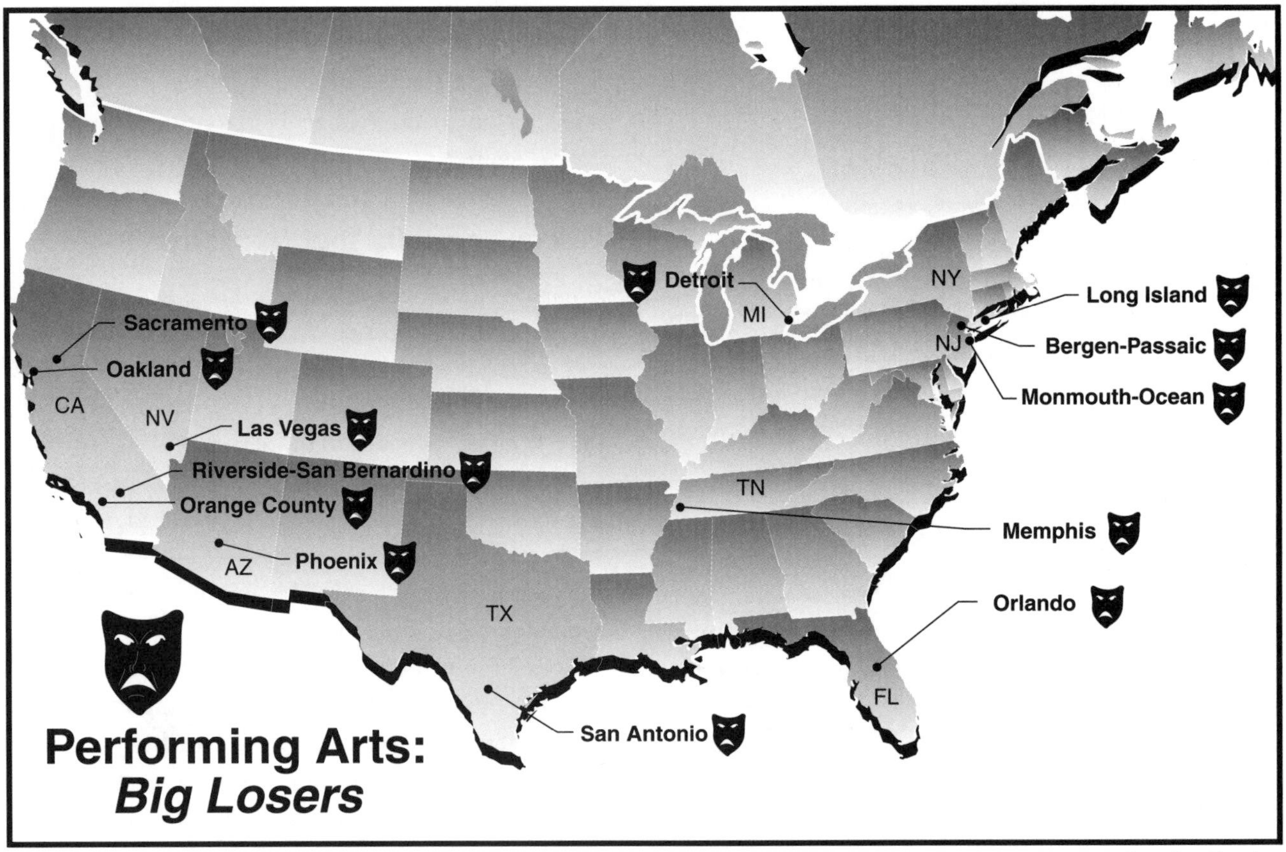
Detroit
MI
NY
Long Island
Sacramento
Oakland
CA
NV
Las Vegas
Riverside-San Bernardino
Orange County
Phoenix
AZ
TX
NJ
Bergen-Passaic
Monmouth-Ocean
TN
Memphis
Orlando
FL
San Antonio
Performing Arts:
Big Losers

Copyright © 2000 by Places Rated Partnership Cape Ann Mapping

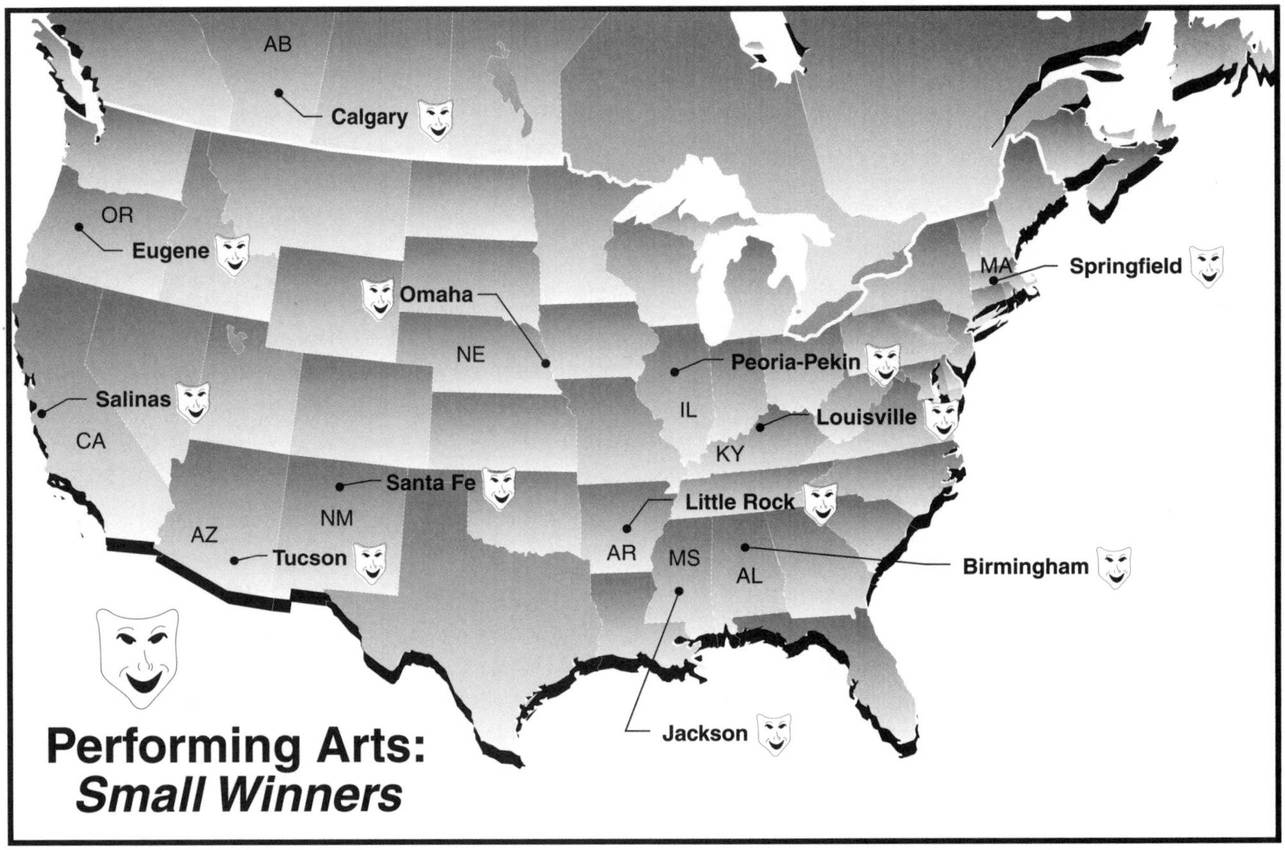
AB
Calgary
OR
Eugene
Omaha
NE
MA
Springfield
Salinas
CA
Peoria-Pekin
IL
Louisville
KY
Santa Fe
NM
AZ
Tucson
Little Rock
AR
MS
AL
Birmingham
Jackson
Performing Arts:
Small Winners

Copyright © 2000 by Places Rated Partnership Cape Ann Mapping

Health Care

America isn't the world's healthiest nation. For all of its wealth and technological superiority, this country lags behind Canada in life expectancy and in infant mortality. For its part, Canada lags behind Sweden and Japan.

Millions of Americans are uninsured and lack access to the full range of health services. Indeed, almost one-third of America's children aren't covered by any health insurance; their school's nurse is the primary provider. In spite of an abundance of physicians packing advanced training and technical support, unfair distribution of medical care remains a central problem.

WHAT THE NUMBERS SAY

Americans continue to get healthier. Judging by two universal measures of population health, infant mortality and life expectancy, the United States is healthier now than it was a generation ago. Why are life expectancy and infant mortality such commonly accepted indicators of a nation's health?

First, these data can be found in almost every developed nation in the form of birth and death certificates. Second, the quality of postpartum and infant care available in a nation, state, or metro area generally reflects the quality of other important health services. Finally, life expectancy remains a very broad but meaningful indicator of a nation's ability to provide sanitary food and drinking water, proper immunization and disease screening, and professional medical attention throughout life.

Infant mortality in America has dropped to its lowest level ever, with data showing 7.2 deaths per 1,000 live births (compared to 6.9 per 1,000 live births in Canada). At the same time, life expectancy for children born in 2000 is projected to rise to 76.4 years (79.1 in Canada). This represents an increase of nearly 4 years since 1975, and a gain of 32 years since 1900.

TWO SYSTEMS—INSURANCE, ACCESS, AND THE REST

Unfortunately, not all Americans share in these statistical gains, and the inequality contributes to the modest U.S. health ranking compared with other countries. Black/white. Rich/poor. Urban/rural. Insured/uninsured. Profit/nonprofit. Short-term/long-term care. Consumer/provider. These are the poles of a health-care system operated as a business enterprise. To get at the real essence of the system, one needs to look at the providers—the doctors and the hospitals.

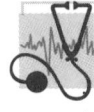

THE DOCTORS

Not every physician has a number in the yellow pages. Some are hospital administrators, medical school professors, journalists, lawyers, or researchers for pharmaceutical companies. Others work for government public-health services or Department of Defense service branches. Still others are in residency training, or are clinical fellows at teaching hospitals, or are full-time members of hospital staffs. When it comes to the number of physicians per capita, what really counts is the number of doctors who maintain offices and see patients. It's surprising how many of them don't.

AMA PHYSICIAN CATEGORIES

The American Medical Association (AMA) classifies a physician as a family practitioner, general practitioner, medical specialist, surgeon, or other specialist, chosen from among thirty-five categories in which the physician reports spending the largest number of his or her professional hours.

General/Family Practitioners

General Practice	Family Practice

Medical Specialists

Allergy	Pediatrics
Cardiovascular Diseases	Pediatric Allergy
Dermatology	Pediatric Cardiology
Gastroenterology	Pulmonary Diseases
Internal Medicine	

Surgical Specialists

General Surgery	Plastic Surgery
Neurological Surgery	Colon and Rectal
Obstetrics and Gynecology	Surgery
Ophthalmology	Thoracic Surgery
Orthopedic Surgery	Urology
Otolaryngology	

Other Specialists

Aerospace Medicine	Pathology
Anesthesiology	Physical Medicine and
Child Psychiatry	Rehabilitation
Diagnostic Radiology	Psychiatry
Forensic Pathology	Public Health
General Preventive Medicine	Radiology
Neurology	Therapeutic Radiology
Occupational Medicine	

Three Treating Doctors

Whether in the United States or in Canada, depending on how office-based or fee-for-service physicians spend their professional hours, almost all can be classified into three groups:

General and Family Practitioners are physicians who treat diseases and injuries, provide preventive care, give routine checkups, prescribe drugs, and perform some surgery. Demand for general and family practitioners is at an all-time high in the United States for one big reason: The managed care system prefers that generalists oversee a patient's total medical treatment. GPs and FPs, as they are called, use all accepted methods of medical care. They can also refer you to a specialist.

Medical Specialists focus on specific medical disciplines such as cardiology, allergy, gastroenterology, and dermatology. They are the largest of the three groups because, frankly, specializing is still where the money is. Medical specialists (and general practitioners) are likely to give attention to surgical and non-surgical approaches to treatment. If they decide that surgery is the method of treatment, they refer their patients to surgeons.

Surgical Specialists regularly operate several times a week. Of the three groups of physicians, surgeons are the highest paid. In the United States the letters F.A.C.S. (Fellow of the American College of Surgeons) after the surgeon's name indicate that he or she has passed an evaluation of surgical training and skills as well as ethical fitness.

Where Physicians Cluster—One Measure of Health Care

Where doctors end up practicing is partly determined by sentiment, their perceptions of local quality of life, or both. But mainly it's a matter of economics. The physician has invested 3 to 7 years in graduate medical education and frequently has to start out with an enormous loan to repay.

Some begin work on a hospital staff, develop a practice, and then open an office. Others buy practices from doctors who are preparing to retire. Still others are recruited into partnerships or group practices through advertisements such as the following from the *Journal of the American Medical Association:*

> GROWING INFECTIOUS DISEASE PRACTICE with two board-certified ID physicians seeking third physician. Southwestern desert recreational activities abound, with proximity to Colorado, New Mexico, Utah, and California attractions. Varied, interesting patient population (winter visitors, Native Americans,

immigrants, as well as increasingly young resident Arizonans). Fax CV to 800-838-3476.

PULMONOLOGIST NEEDED immediately to join established practice. Family-oriented, peaceful community in Oklahoma. Excellent salary and benefits with progression to partnership. Send CV to Box 1205, c/o JAMA, 515 N State St, 12th Fl, Chicago, IL 60610.

By whatever means they introduce themselves professionally, new physicians who wish to specialize are mainly concerned with a place's "covered census" (i.e., the size of its insured population).

Many physicians want to practice near a major hospital while also wanting to live in a city large enough to provide them with the amenities their incomes allow. In general, larger, more affluent places—Boston, New York, San Francisco, and Toronto, for example—have a greater proportion of health-care facilities, medical specialists, high-tech equipment, and exotic procedures.

On the other hand, small American metro areas tend to have more general and family practitioners than specialists. The common explanation is that the smaller metro areas don't have enough patients to support a large number of specialists. There's not enough business for an allergist to open an office in one out of five smaller metro areas, for example. Doctors in these areas who want to see 30 to 40 patients a day need to be generalists.

Another pattern is for expensive, complex procedures to be available only in major metro areas or in areas with medical schools and veterans' hospitals. You can't get a bone marrow transplant in most metro areas in North America. In Utica, NY, no one performs open-heart surgery. A patient has to go to Syracuse—about 50 miles away—for that. Surgeons, too, tend to cluster in metro areas with medical schools, veterans' hospitals, and ancillary medical centers.

A counter trend in physician clustering is developing, however. Some newly graduated specialists are leaving big cities where things have become so competitive that they can't find jobs and where it's simply too expensive for them to set up their own practices. They choose, instead, to go to smaller metro areas—often the towns in which they grew up—to establish a practice and to penetrate the existing referral network of doctors.

Another trend in Canada is the active and successful recruitment of physicians by American headhunters whose seminars detail the intricacies of emigration and setting up a practice in underserved areas in the United States. Some 10,000 physicians now practicing in the United States are graduates of Canadian medical schools.

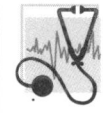

Health Care

SPECIALIST METRO AREAS

Most American doctors specialize. Their number per 100,000 people tends to rise in smaller areas with medical schools and veterans' hospitals, or where medical care is a basic industry attracting patients from outside. Below are metro areas, mainly American, with more than 100 medical specialists per 100,000 people.

Metro Area	Specialists per 100,000 people
Rochester, MN	425
Iowa City, IA	173
Charlottesville, VA	151
Columbia, MO	146
Greenville, NC	123
Boston, MA-NH	121
Gainesville, FL	121
San Francisco, CA	121
Long Island, NY	120
Lowell, MA-NH	117
London, ON	116

Still another development is the "too many doctors, not enough jobs" prediction from as long ago as 1980. One in ten new medical school graduates have difficulty finding a suitable first post, and unemployment rates among graduates of foreign medical schools is higher than ever.

THE HOSPITAL

The word health can also mean its opposite, illness. A hospital is not really a health-care institution; its business is to take care of sick people. The truly healthy need little health care except for an occasional shot or checkup; the unhealthy need a lot more.

Not all hospitals handle typical illnesses and emergencies. Many of them exclusively treat chronic diseases or alcohol and drug addiction, or they may be burn centers, psychiatric hospitals, or rehabilitation hospitals. When rating a metro area for its health care, *Places Rated* counts only general hospitals where patients stay less than 30 days.

The number of accredited acute-care hospitals and their inpatient beds varies among places. Although the total number of hospital beds isn't as valuable an indicator as it was before advances in medicine and pharmacology shortened a hospital stay, it is still a reliable gauge of relative health-care supply.

441

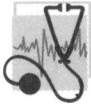

MEDICALLY GENERALIZED METRO AREAS

North of the border, the proportion of physicians who are general or family practitioners is three times greater than in the United States. Below are fourteen Canadian metro areas with more than 100 GPs and FPs per 100,000 people. The American metro area closest to this group is Boulder-Longmont, CO, with 97.

Metro Area	General Practitioners per 100,000 people
Halifax, NS	155
Vancouver, BC	147
Saskatoon, SK	143
London, ON	136
Victoria, BC	135
Ottawa-Hull, ON-PQ	119
Regina, SK	118
Sherbrooke, PQ	116
Quebec City, PQ	112
St. John's, NF	110
Toronto, ON	108
Edmonton, AB	105
Winnipeg, MB	103
Hamilton, ON	101

MDs WITH NON-UNITED STATES DEGREES

The AMA wants to restrict enrollment of foreign students in American medical schools and to limit graduates of foreign medical schools from practicing in the United States. In seven metro areas, more than half of the physicians got their degrees from abroad.

Metro Area	Physicians with Foreign Medical Degrees (%)
Jersey City, NJ	71
Laredo, TX	61
McAllen-Edinburg-Mission, TX	57
Miami, FL	55
Steubenville-Weirton, OH-WV	55
Flint, MI	54
Newburgh, NY-PA	51

Source: The lists on this page and on page 441 are derived from U.S. Department of Health and Human Services "Area Resource File" and Health and Welfare Canada "National Physician Database."

Hospital Services

Each year, the American Hospital Association (AHA) surveys its thousands of member hospitals, enumerating which of eighty-four AHA-defined services each institution provides. The number of services a hospital offers is one index of the level of care you may receive there and certainly of the level of technology and specialization in that hospital.

Though most operate as nonprofits, general hospitals are actually businesses that can't afford to go deeply into the red. They offer common services such as an emergency department, a postoperative recovery room, a blood bank, an intensive-care unit, and outpatient surgery. Some stake out market niches with additional services—a radioactive implant department, a sports medicine clinic, a histopathology laboratory, a certified trauma center, or a department with organ transplant capabilities. Of course, it really depends on one's situation; if a woman is of childbearing years, access to genetic counseling services, an obstetrics unit, a neonatal intensive-care unit, and a pediatric inpatient unit may be extremely important.

Quality Care—What's a Consumer to Do?

Many hospitals, pressured by public and private cost-containment efforts, have slashed services and staff. Consequently, hospitals remain critically short of qualified nurses. No wonder the quality of care is such a concern today. Since it's just about impossible to measure quality of care in any statistical way, how do we judge the skills of a doctor or hospital? Accreditation, with certain caveats, is one way.

Hospital Accreditation

The Joint Commission on Accreditation of Healthcare Organizations (JCAHO) is the private nonprofit body that investigates and certifies hospitals. The JCAHO certification determines which hospitals are eligible for federal funds or state licensure. Since JCAHO assessments had always been kept confidential, consumers had no way of knowing how to interpret any discrepancies between JCAHO findings and those of federal investigators. In other words, a patient could only find out whether or not a hospital was accredited.

Since 1995, however, you have been able to buy a performance report from the JCAHO on local hospitals. Hospitals are scored on a scale of 0 to 100 in twenty-eight categories, including dietary services, medication use, and staff preparation. Then each gets an overall score.

The American Hospital Association (AHA) classifies hospital services into eighty-four categories.

Adult day-care program

Alcohol/drug abuse or dependency inpatient unit

Alcohol/drug abuse or dependency outpatient services

Alzheimer's diagnostic/assessment services

Angioplasty

Arthritis treatment center

Birthing room/LDRP room

Blood bank

Burn-care unit

Cardiac catheterization laboratory

Cardiac intensive-care unit

Cardiac rehabilitation program

Chaplaincy/Pastoral care services

Chronic obstructive pulmonary disease services

Community health promotion

Comprehensive geriatric assessment

CT scanner

Diagnostic radioisotope facility

Emergency department

Emergency department social work services

Emergency response (geriatric)

Ethics committee

Extracorporeal shock wave lithotripter

Fitness center

General inpatient care for AIDS/ARC

Genetic counseling/screening services

Geriatric acute-care unit

Geriatric clinics

Health sciences library

Hemodialysis

Histopathology laboratory

HIV/AIDS unit

Home health services

Hospice

Magnetic resonance imaging

Mammography diagnostic

Mammography screening

Medical-surgical or other intensive-care unit

Megavoltage radiation therapy

Neonatal intensive-care unit

Noninvasive cardiac assessment services

Obstetrics unit

Occupational health services

Occupational therapy services

Oncology services

Open-heart surgery

Organ/tissue transplant

Organized outpatient services

Organized social work services

Orthopedic surgery

Outpatient social work services

Outpatient surgery services

Patient education

Patient representative services

Pediatric acute inpatient unit

Physical therapy services

Psychiatric child/adolescent services

Psychiatric consultation/liaison services

Psychiatric education services

Psychiatric emergency services

Psychiatric geriatric services

Psychiatric inpatient services

Psychiatric outpatient services

Psychiatric partial hospitalization program

Radioactive implants

Recreational therapy services

Rehabilitation inpatient unit

Rehabilitation outpatient services

Reproductive health services

Respiratory therapy services

Respite care

Senior membership program

Single photon emission computerized tomography (SPECT)

Skilled nursing or other long-term-care facility

Specialized outpatient program for AIDS/ARC

Speech therapy services

Sports medicine clinic/services

Therapeutic radioisotope facility

Trauma center (certified)

Ultrasound

Volunteer services department

Women's health center/services

Worksite health promotion

X-ray radiation therapy

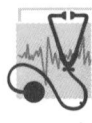

A hospital has incentives to qualify for accreditation. It makes it easier to recruit doctors and operate residency programs, and it reduces malpractice liability. Now that accreditation status is becoming a more public matter, it may also become a useful tool for attracting patients—the consumers of health care.

Teaching Hospitals

Two of every three hospitals are *nonteaching*. That is, they are staffed almost entirely by "attending physicians" who have an outside practice, are paid by the patient, and have admitting privileges at the hospital.

Teaching hospitals grant admitting privileges to attending physicians, but they also employ full-time "house staff," taking in first-year and advanced residents and a teaching faculty. The attending physician heads a team of house staff members (including the "hospitalist," a newly defined physician specialty) to make important decisions about a patient's care. The patient pays the attending physician and the hospital; the hospital pays the house staff.

SCORING: HEALTH CARE

This chapter judges health care in each metro area, not how sick the resident population is. Moreover, *Places Rated* doesn't assess the quality of health care but its supply. As for the expense of health care to the consumer, see the Costs of Living chapter.

Keeping these distinctions in mind, the reader should avoid assuming that a low score in this chapter means: (1) that the people in a given place are unhealthy and don't live very long, or (2) that basic health care—including even such complex emergency surgery as a coronary bypass—would be unavailable or inferior in that place. *Both of these conclusions are incorrect.* A low score in this chapter does indicate, however, that the emphasis in that metro area is probably on basic health care and that the latest techniques and equipment, and personnel trained to implement them, are more likely to be found elsewhere.

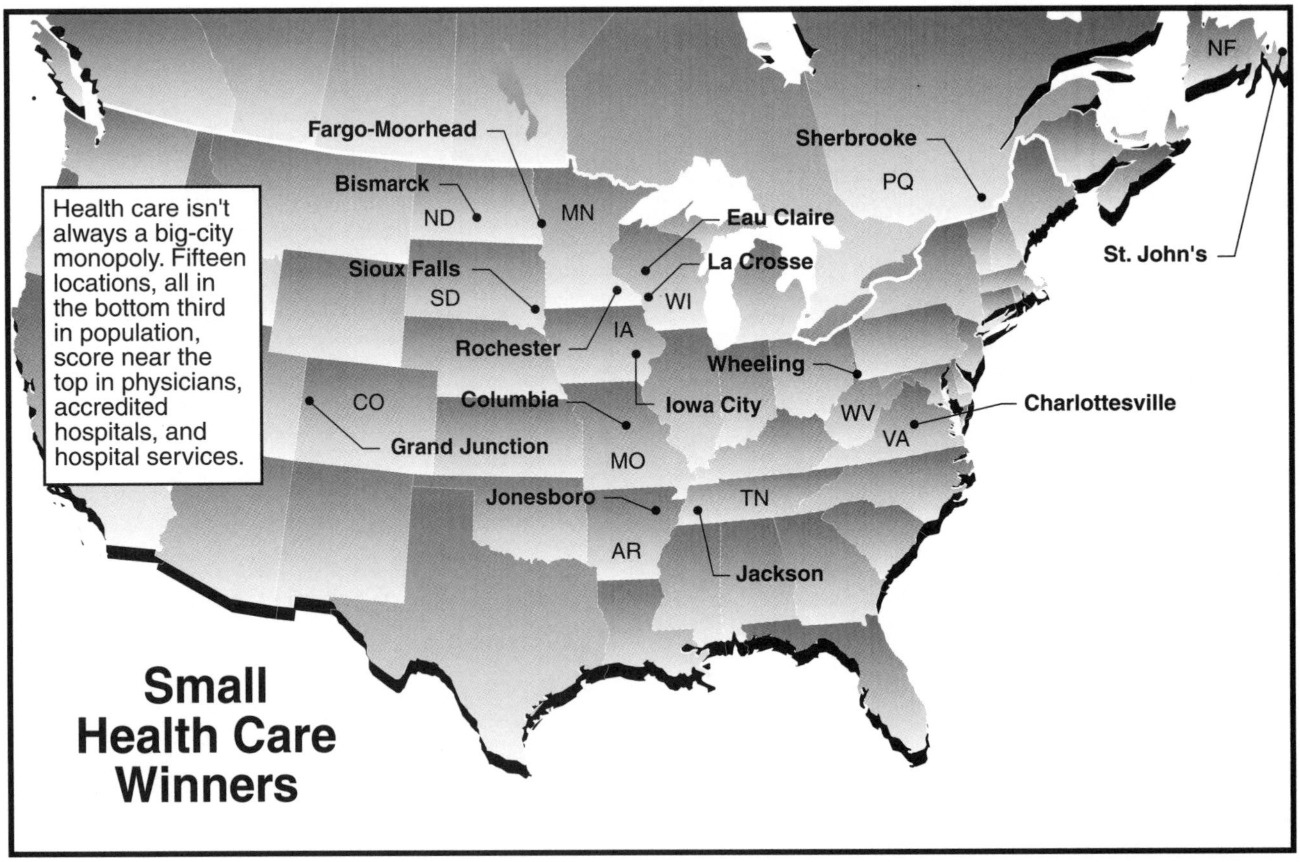

Health care isn't always a big-city monopoly. Fifteen locations, all in the bottom third in population, score near the top in physicians, accredited hospitals, and hospital services.

NF

Fargo-Moorhead

Sherbrooke
PQ

Bismarck
ND   MN

Eau Claire

Sioux Falls   La Crosse
SD   WI

St. John's

IA
Rochester

Wheeling

Columbia   Iowa City   WV   Charlottesville
CO   VA

Grand Junction
MO

Jonesboro   TN

AR

Jackson

Small Health Care Winners

Copyright © 2000 by Places Rated Partnership

Cape Ann Mapping

444

To rate metro areas for relative strength in health care, *Places Rated* considers five items:

1. *General/Family Practitioners* per 100,000: physicians who generalize because of the size of the patient base or choose to specialize in family practice.

2. *Medical Specialists* per 100,000: physicians who concentrate on specific medical disciplines such as pediatrics or cardiovascular diseases.

3. *Surgical Specialists* per 100,000: physicians who regularly operate several times a week.

As stated earlier, just as not all MDs see patients, not all hospitals handle typical illnesses and emergencies. In the Short-Term General Hospitals category, *Places Rated* counts only hospitals classified by the American Hospital Association or the Canadian Hospital Association as acute-care facilities whose patients stay fewer than 30 days.

4. *Accredited General Hospital Beds.* In U.S. metro areas, 91 percent of short-term general hospitals are accredited by the JCAHO. In Canadian metro areas, 94 percent are accredited by the CCHSA. While the lack of accreditation doesn't necessarily mean a facility is substandard, the presence of such accreditation means the hospital has passed rigorous and periodic reviews. While the number of hospital beds is dropping throughout North America because of cost-containment policies and the shift to outpatient services, it still is an indicator of health-care supply.

5. *Physician Residency Programs.* One-third of short-term general hospitals in the United States and half of Canada's general hospitals have approved physician-training programs. Hospitals with no teaching programs aren't necessarily lagging in quality, but facilities with such programs tend to be larger urban institutions where the interaction between students and faculty encourages the development and use of the latest techniques, equipment, and therapy.

Affluent, big-city metro areas generally score higher in the rankings than the smaller, poorer metro areas. This doesn't mean that a person cannot receive excellent medical care in a rural clinic or, conversely, experience medical care that is bad enough to be life-threatening in even the finest of big-city hospitals. The quality of medical and nursing care most people receive depends on a number of factors, including the patient's ability to pay, blind chance, and human error.

RANKINGS: HEALTH CARE

Five criteria are used to rate the supply of health care in a metro area: (1) office-based physicians in general and family practice; (2) office-based medical specialists; (3) office-based surgeons; (4) accredited short-term, general hospital beds; and (5) hospitals with physician-teaching programs certified by the AMA or Association of Canadian Teaching Hospitals. Places that receive tie scores get the same rank and are listed alphabetically.

Metro Areas from Best to Worst

RANK	SCORE
1. Vancouver, BC	100.00
2. Quebec City, PQ	99.71
3. Sherbrooke, PQ	99.43
4. Long Island, NY	99.15
5. Halifax, NS	98.86
6. Montreal, PQ	98.58
7. Little Rock-North Little Rock, AR	98.30
8. Lexington, KY	98.01
9. Columbia, MO	97.73
10. Birmingham, AL	97.45
11. Edmonton, AB	97.16
12. Miami, FL	96.88
13. Toronto, ON	96.60
14. Gainesville, FL	96.31

RANK	SCORE
15. St. John's, NF	96.03
16. Iowa City, IA	95.75
17. San Francisco, CA	95.46
18. Ottawa-Hull, ON-PQ	95.18
19. Boston, MA-NH	94.90
20. Omaha, NE-IA	94.61
21. Ann Arbor, MI	94.33
22. Pittsburgh, PA	94.05
23. Sioux Falls, SD	93.76
24. Raleigh-Durham-Chapel Hill, NC	93.48
25. Minneapolis-St. Paul, MN-WI	93.20
26. Winnipeg, MB	92.91
27. Jackson, MS	92.63
	continues

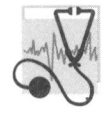

Metro Areas from Best to Worst (cont.)

RANK	SCORE
28. Little Rock-North Little Rock, AR	92.35
29. New York, NY	92.06
30. Hamilton, ON	91.78
31. New Orleans, LA	91.50
32. Lubbock, TX	91.21
33. Madison, WI	90.93
34. London, ON	90.65
35. Eau Claire, WI	90.36
36. Roanoke, VA	90.08
37. Shreveport-Bossier City, LA	89.80
38. Bergen-Passaic, NJ	89.51
39. Rochester, MN	89.23
40. Indianapolis, IN	88.95
41. Charleston-North Charleston, SC	88.66
42. Newark, NJ	88.38
43. Duluth-Superior, MN-WI	88.10
44. Louisville, KY-IN	87.81
45. Toledo, OH	87.53
46. Seattle-Bellevue-Everett, WA	87.25
47. Nashville, TN	86.96
48. Knoxville, TN	86.68
49. Baltimore, MD	86.40
50. Augusta-Aiken, GA-SC	86.11
51. Asheville, NC	85.83
52. Philadelphia, PA-NJ	85.55
53. Denver, CO	85.26
54. Milwaukee-Waukesha, WI	84.98
55. Cleveland-Lorain-Elyria, OH	84.70
56. Springfield, IL	84.41
57. Regina, SK	83.85
57. Richmond-Petersburg, VA	83.85
59. Calgary, AB	83.56
60. Charleston, WV	83.28
61. West Palm Beach-Boca Raton, FL	83.00
62. Bismarck, ND	82.71
63. Santa Rosa, CA	82.43
64. Orange County, CA	82.15
65. Evansville-Henderson, IN-KY	81.86
66. Buffalo-Niagara Falls, NY	81.58
67. Chicago, IL	81.30
68. Fargo-Moorhead, ND-MN	81.01
69. Memphis, TN-AR-MS	80.73
70. Scranton–Wilkes-Barre–Hazleton, PA	80.45
71. Spokane, WA	80.16
72. Charlottesville, VA	79.88
73. Dayton-Springfield, OH	79.60
74. Jackson, TN	79.32
75. Wheeling, WV-OH	79.03
76. Cincinnati, OH-KY-IN	78.75
77. Jonesboro, AR	78.47
78. Syracuse, NY	78.18
79. Albuquerque, NM	77.90
80. Grand Junction, CO	77.62
81. Albany-Schenectady-Troy, NY	77.33
82. Tampa-St. Petersburg-Clearwater, FL	77.05
83. Lincoln, NE	76.77
84. Wichita, KS	76.48
85. Stamford-Norwalk, CT	76.20
86. La Crosse, WI-MN	75.92
87. Trois-Rivieres, PQ	75.63

RANK	SCORE
88. Portland, ME	75.35
89. Denver, CO	75.07
90. Middlesex-Somerset-Hunterdon, NJ	74.78
91. Tucson, AZ	74.50
92. Trenton, NJ	74.22
93. Sarasota-Bradenton, FL	73.93
94. Columbia, SC	73.65
95. Rochester, NY	73.37
96. Greenville, NC	73.08
97. Saskatoon, SK	72.80
98. Victoria, TX	72.52
99. Greensboro–Winston-Salem–High Point, NC	72.23
100. Macon, GA	71.67
100. Champaign-Urbana, IL	71.67
102. Jacksonville, FL	71.38
103. Santa Barbara-Santa Maria-Lompoc, CA	71.10
104. Florence, SC	70.82
105. San Jose, CA	70.53
106. Victoria, BC	70.25
107. Worcester, MA-CT	69.97
108. Sudbury, ON	69.68
109. Harrisburg-Lebanon-Carlisle, PA	69.40
110. Hattiesburg, MS	69.12
111. Fort Lauderdale, FL	68.83
112. San Diego, CA	68.55
113. San Antonio, TX	68.27
114. Los Angeles-Long Beach, CA	67.98
115. Kansas City, MO-KS	67.70
116. Bridgeport, CT	67.42
117. Tyler, TX	67.13
118. Burlington, VT	66.85
119. St. Louis, MO-IL	66.57
120. Hartford, CT	66.28
121. Reno, NV	66.00
122. Waterloo-Cedar Falls, IA	65.72
123. Houston, TX	65.43
124. Portland-Vancouver, OR-WA	65.15
125. Austin-San Marcos, TX	64.87
126. Amarillo, TX	64.58
127. Monroe, LA	64.30
128. Altoona, PA	64.02
129. Oklahoma City, OK	63.73
130. Allentown-Bethlehem-Easton, PA	63.45
131. Huntington-Ashland, WV-KY-OH	63.17
132. Fort Lauderdale, FL	62.88
133. St. Catharines-Niagara, ON	62.60
134. Honolulu, HI	62.32
135. Alexandria, LA	62.03
136. Boulder-Longmont, CO	61.75
137. Wilmington, NC	61.47
138. Saint John, NB	61.18
139. Mobile, AL	60.90
140. Thunder Bay, ON	60.62
141. Boise City, ID	60.33
142. New Haven-Meriden, CT	60.05
143. Missoula, MT	59.77
144. Montgomery, AL	59.49
145. Sacramento, CA	59.20
146. Chattanooga, TN-GA	58.92
147. Pueblo, CO	58.64

RANK	SCORE
148. Columbus, OH	58.35
149. Springfield, MO	58.07
150. Orlando, FL	57.79
151. Baton Rouge, LA	57.50
152. Atlanta, GA	57.22
153. Oakland, CA	56.94
154. Pensacola, FL	56.65
155. Billings, MT	56.37
156. South Bend, IN	56.09
157. Galveston-Texas City, TX	55.80
158. Greenville-Spartanburg-Anderson, SC	55.52
159. Dothan, AL	55.24
160. Erie, PA	54.95
161. Rockford, IL	54.67
162. Corpus Christi, TX	54.39
163. Appleton-Oshkosh-Neenah, WI	54.10
164. Fort Smith, AR-OK	53.82
165. Eugene-Springfield, OR	53.54
166. Grand Forks, ND-MN	53.25
167. Johnstown, PA	52.69
167. Chicoutimi-Jonquiere, PQ	52.69
169. Wichita Falls, TX	52.40
170. Savannah, GA	52.12
171. Texarkana, TX-Texarkana, AR	51.84
172. Phoenix-Mesa, AZ	51.55
173. Rapid City, SD	51.27
174. Waterbury, CT	50.99
175. Fort Wayne, IN	50.70
176. Williamsport, PA	50.42
177. Charlotte-Gastonia-Rock Hill, NC-SC	50.14
178. Topeka, KS	49.85
179. Santa Fe, NM	49.57
180. Tulsa, OK	49.29
181. Detroit, MI	49.00
182. Biloxi-Gulfport-Pascagoula, MS	48.72
183. Dutchess County, NY	48.44
184. Dallas, TX	48.15
185. Terre Haute, IN	47.87
186. Kalamazoo-Battle Creek, MI	47.59
187. Providence-Fall River-Warwick, RI-MA	47.30
188. Fort Collins-Loveland, CO	47.02
189. Saginaw-Bay City-Midland, MI	46.74
190. Lake Charles, LA	46.45
191. Fayetteville-Springdale-Rogers, AR	46.17
192. San Luis Obispo-Atascadero-Paso Robles, CA	45.89
193. Chico-Paradise, CA	45.60
194. Huntsville, AL	45.32
195. Abilene, TX	45.04
196. Killeen-Temple, TX	44.75
197. Windsor, ON	44.47
198. Tallahassee, FL	44.19
199. Ventura, CA	43.90
200. Bangor, ME	43.62
201. Monmouth-Ocean, NJ	43.34
202. Redding, CA	43.05
203. Springfield, MA	42.77
204. Yolo, CA	42.49
205. Gary, IN	42.20
206. Cedar Rapids, IA	41.92
207. Bryan-College Station, TX	41.64

RANK	SCORE
208. Danbury, CT	41.35
209. Sioux City, IA-NE	41.07
210. Pocatello, ID	40.79
211. Columbus, GA-AL	40.50
212. Medford-Ashland, OR	40.22
213. Florence, AL	39.94
214. Peoria-Pekin, IL	39.66
215. Des Moines, IA	39.37
216. Pine Bluff, AR	39.09
217. Beaumont-Port Arthur, TX	38.81
218. Cumberland, MD-WV	38.52
219. Jersey City, NJ	38.24
220. Bloomington, IN	37.96
221. Santa Cruz-Watsonville, CA	37.67
222. Lowell, MA-NH	37.39
223. St. Cloud, MN	37.11
224. Glens Falls, NY	36.82
225. Lewiston-Auburn, ME	36.54
226. Sherman-Denison, TX	36.26
227. Fitchburg-Leominster, MA	35.97
228. Muncie, IN	35.69
229. Utica-Rome, NY	35.41
230. Casper, WY	35.12
231. Hickory-Morganton-Lenoir, NC	34.84
232. Kitchener-Waterloo, ON	34.56
233. Canton-Massillon, OH	34.27
234. Fort Myers-Cape Coral, FL	33.99
235. Enid, OK	33.71
236. Davenport-Moline-Rock Island, IA-IL	33.42
237. Lafayette, LA	33.14
238. Wilmington-Newark, DE-MD	32.86
239. Bellingham, WA	32.57
240. Waco, TX	32.29
241. Olympia, WA	31.72
241. Riverside-San Bernardino, CA	31.72
243. Athens, GA	31.44
244. Lancaster, PA	31.16
245. Modesto, CA	30.87
246. Great Falls, MT	30.59
247. Pittsfield, MA	30.31
248. Fresno, CA	30.02
249. Anniston, AL	29.74
250. Fort Worth-Arlington, TX	29.46
251. Wausau, WI	29.17
252. Lynchburg, VA	28.89
253. Vallejo-Fairfield-Napa, CA	28.61
254. Benton Harbor, MI	28.04
254. Decatur, IL	28.04
256. Salinas, CA	27.76
257. Flint, MI	27.47
258. Grand Rapids-Muskegon-Holland, MI	27.19
259. Lansing-East Lansing, MI	26.91
260. Reading, PA	26.62
261. Tacoma, WA	26.34
262. Daytona Beach, FL	26.06
263. Yakima, WA	25.77
264. Flagstaff, AZ-UT	25.49
265. Elmira, NY	25.21
266. Dubuque, IA	24.92

continues

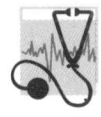

RANK	SCORE
267. Gadsden, AL	24.64
268. Las Vegas, NV-AZ	24.36
269. Akron, OH	24.07
270. Norfolk-Virginia Beach-Newport News, VA-NC	23.79
271. Melbourne-Titusville-Palm Bay, FL	23.51
272. Punta Gorda, FL	23.22
273. Binghamton, NY	22.94
274. Tuscaloosa, AL	22.66
275. Cheyenne, WY	22.37
276. Houma, LA	22.09
277. Naples, FL	21.81
278. Owensboro, KY	21.52
279. Lima, OH	21.24
280. Fort Walton Beach, FL	20.96
281. Lakeland-Winter Haven, FL	20.67
282. Youngstown-Warren, OH	20.39
283. Albany, GA	20.11
284. El Paso, TX	19.83
285. Bakersfield, CA	19.54
286. San Angelo, TX	19.26
287. Lawrence, MA-NH	18.98
288. Kokomo, IN	18.41
288. Newburgh, NY-PA	18.41
290. Green Bay, WI	18.13
291. Fayetteville, NC	17.84
292. Decatur, AL	17.56
293. Portsmouth-Rochester, NH-ME	17.28
294. Parkersburg-Marietta, WV-OH	16.99
295. Janesville-Beloit, WI	16.71
296. Lawton, OK	16.43
297. Stockton-Lodi, CA	16.14
298. Fort Pierce-Port St. Lucie, FL	15.86
299. Oshawa, ON	15.58
300. Atlantic-Cape May, NJ	15.29
301. Mansfield, OH	15.01
302. New London-Norwich, CT-RI	14.73
303. Sharon, PA	14.44
304. Barnstable-Yarmouth, MA	14.16
305. Brownsville-Harlingen-San Benito, TX	13.88
306. Bloomington-Normal, IL	13.59
307. Longview-Marshall, TX	13.31
308. Lafayette, IN	13.03
309. Manchester, NH	12.74
310. McAllen-Edinburg-Mission, TX	12.46

RANK	SCORE
311. Panama City, FL	12.18
312. Colorado Springs, CO	11.89
313. Sheboygan, WI	11.61
314. Kankakee, IL	11.33
315. Joplin, MO	11.04
316. Myrtle Beach, SC	10.76
317. Vineland-Millville-Bridgeton, NJ	10.48
318. Richland-Kennewick-Pasco, WA	10.19
319. Salem, OR	9.91
320. Rocky Mount, NC	9.63
321. St. Joseph, MO	9.34
322. Greeley, CO	9.06
323. Nashua, NH	8.78
324. Jamestown, NY	8.49
325. Merced, CA	8.21
326. Steubenville-Weirton, OH-WV	7.93
327. Racine, WI	7.64
328. Odessa-Midland, TX	7.36
329. Hagerstown, MD	7.08
330. Bremerton, WA	6.79
331. Visalia-Tulare-Porterville, CA	6.51
332. Yuba City, CA	6.23
333. York, PA	5.66
333. Hamilton-Middletown, OH	5.66
335. Lawrence, KS	5.38
336. Anchorage, AK	5.09
337. Ocala, FL	4.81
338. Danville, VA	4.53
339. Elkhart-Goshen, IN	4.24
340. Brazoria, TX	3.96
341. Provo-Orem, UT	3.68
342. Kenosha, WI	3.39
343. State College, PA	3.11
344. Goldsboro, NC	2.83
345. Clarksville-Hopkinsville, TN-KY	2.54
346. Laredo, TX	2.26
347. Jackson, MI	1.98
348. Brockton, MA	1.69
349. Sumter, SC	1.41
350. Jacksonville, NC	1.13
351. Dover, DE	0.84
352. Las Cruces, NM	0.56
353. Yuma, AZ	0.28
354. New Bedford, MA	0.00

Place Profiles: Health Care

PLACE PROFILES: HEALTH CARE

In the following pages, selected health-care assets for the 354 metro areas are detailed.

Under the heading **Office-Based Physicians** (in Canada, **Fee-for-Service Physicians**) are the number of local doctors who maintain offices and treat patients, grouped into three classes by professional activity (physicians in general practice and physicians in family practice are grouped under "Generalists").

To the right of each professional group is a style box with five columns. Cells shaded up to the center column represent a "typical" number of physicians per 100,000 people. Shaded cells to the right of the center column indicate a "higher" (or better) number of physicians per 100,000 people while shaded cells to the left indicate a "lower" (or worse) number. Each shaded cell represents 20 percent of the total support, with the leftmost box indicating 0–20 percent and the rightmost box indicating 81–100 percent. Typical support (see sample below) is indicated when the first three boxes are shaded (41–60 percent).

Generalists	■■■□□

Short-Term General Hospitals show the number of these institutions and their total number of beds. Underneath that is the number of hospitals accredited by the Joint Commission on Accreditation of Healthcare Organizations (JCAHO) or the Canadian Council on Health Services Accreditation (CCHSA).

Hospital Services provide the number of hospitals grouped by the range of American Hospital Association-defined services offered in a U.S. metro area (Canada is not included). The number of services are indicated as follows:

♦	4 services
♦ ♦	5 to 14 services
♦ ♦ ♦	15 to 24 services
♦ ♦ ♦ ♦	25 or more services

Under the heading **Teaching Hospitals** are hospitals that sponsor graduate medical education in one or more clinical departments recognized by at least one residency review committee of the American Medical Association, or, in the case of Canadian institutions, the Association of Canadian Teaching Hospitals. Names of hospitals that appear in *italics* are exclusively children's or pediatric facilities.

The information is derived from these sources: American Hospital Association, *Guide to the Health Care Field,* 1999; American Medical Association, *Graduate Medical Education Directory,* 1999; Canadian Healthcare Association, *Guide to Canadian Healthcare Facilities,* 1999; Health and Welfare Canada, Health Information Division, unpublished National Physician Database; and U.S. Department of Health and Human Services, Bureau of Health-Care Professions, unpublished "Area Resource File," 1999.

A star (★) in front of a metro area's name highlights it as one of the top thirty-five places for health care.

Abilene, TX
Office-Based Physicians

55 Generalists	■■■□□
69 Specialists	■■■□□
66 Surgeons	■■■■□

Short-Term General Hospitals: 3 (522 beds)
JCAHO Accredited: 3
Hospital Services: 1 ♦, 2 ♦♦♦♦
Score: **45.04**　　　　Rank: **195**

Akron, OH
Office-Based Physicians

240 Generalists	■■□□□
318 Specialists	■■□□□
269 Surgeons	■■□□□

Short-Term General Hospitals: 5 (1,690 beds)
JCAHO Accredited: 4
Hospital Services: 1 ♦, 4 ♦♦♦♦
Teaching Hospitals
Akron General Medical Center
Barberton Citizen's Hospital
Children's Hospital Medical Center
Summa Health Systems
Score: **24.07**　　　　Rank: **269**

Albany, GA
Office-Based Physicians

19 Generalists	■□□□□
73 Specialists	■■■■□
62 Surgeons	■■■■□

Short-Term General Hospitals: 2 (574 beds)
JCAHO Accredited: 2
Hospital Services: 1 ♦, 1 ♦♦♦♦
Teaching Hospital
Phoebe Putney Memorial Hospital
Score: **20.11**　　　　Rank: **283**

Albany-Schenectady-Troy, NY
Office-Based Physicians

323 Generalists	■■□□□
609 Specialists	■■■■□
459 Surgeons	■■■■□

Short-Term General Hospitals: 12 (3,343 beds)
JCAHO Accredited: 12
Hospital Services: 3 ♦, 9 ♦♦♦♦
Teaching Hospitals
Childs Hospital
Ellis Hospital
St. Clare's Hospital
St. Peters Hospital
Score: **77.33**　　　　Rank: **81**

Albuquerque, NM
Office-Based Physicians

361 Generalists	■■■■□
465 Specialists	■■■■□
317 Surgeons	■■■□□

Short-Term General Hospitals: 10 (1,714 beds)
JCAHO Accredited: 9
Hospital Services: 1 ♦, 1 ♦♦♦, 8 ♦♦♦♦
Teaching Hospitals
Carrie Tingley Hospital
Lovelace Health Systems
Presbyterian Hospital
St. Joseph Medical Center
University of New Mexico Hospital
Score: **77.9**　　　　Rank: **79**

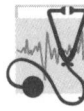

Alexandria, LA
Office-Based Physicians
41 Generalists	
78 Specialists	
75 Surgeons	

Short-Term General Hospitals: 4 (1,110 beds)
  JCAHO Accredited: 4
Hospital Services: 1 ♦♦♦, 3 ♦♦♦♦
Teaching Hospitals
  Huey P. Long Memorial Center
  Rapides Regional Medical Center
Score: 62.03   Rank: 135

Allentown-Bethlehem-Easton, PA
Office-Based Physicians
256 Generalists	
344 Specialists	
327 Surgeons	

Short-Term General Hospitals: 8 (2,152 beds)
  JCAHO Accredited: 7
Hospital Services: 1 ♦, 1 ♦♦♦, 6 ♦♦♦♦
Teaching Hospitals
  Easton Hospital
  Lehigh Valley Hospital
  Sacred Heart Hospital
  St. Luke's Hospital
Score: 63.45   Rank: 130

Altoona, PA
Office-Based Physicians
78 Generalists	
68 Specialists	
51 Surgeons	

Short-Term General Hospitals: 5 (577 beds)
  JCAHO Accredited: 5
Hospital Services: 1 ♦, 1 ♦♦♦, 3 ♦♦♦♦
Score: 64.02   Rank: 128

Amarillo, TX
Office-Based Physicians
80 Generalists	
124 Specialists	
104 Surgeons	

Short-Term General Hospitals: 6 (1,320 beds)
  JCAHO Accredited: 5
Hospital Services: 1 ♦, 5 ♦♦♦♦
Teaching Hospitals
  Baptist St. Anthony's Hospital
  Northwest Texas Hospital
Score: 64.58   Rank: 126

Anchorage, AK
Office-Based Physicians
219 Generalists	
191 Specialists	
211 Surgeons	

Short-Term General Hospitals: 3 (919 beds)
  JCAHO Accredited: 3
Hospital Services: 1 ♦♦, 2 ♦♦♦♦
Teaching Hospital
  Providence Alaska Medical Center
Score: 5.09   Rank: 336

★ **Ann Arbor, MI**
Office-Based Physicians
201 Generalists	
545 Specialists	
354 Surgeons	

Short-Term General Hospitals: 12 (2,123 beds)
  JCAHO Accredited: 11
Hospital Services: 1 ♦, 1 ♦♦, 2 ♦♦♦, 8 ♦♦♦♦
Teaching Hospitals
  Chelsea Community Hospital
  St. Joseph Mercy Hospital
  University of Michigan Health System
Score: 94.33   Rank: 21

Anniston, AL
Office-Based Physicians
50 Generalists	
53 Specialists	
46 Surgeons	

Short-Term General Hospitals: 4 (429 beds)
  JCAHO Accredited: 4
Hospital Services: 2 ♦♦♦, 2 ♦♦♦♦
Score: 29.74   Rank: 249

Appleton-Oshkosh-Neenah, WI
Office-Based Physicians
197 Generalists	
147 Specialists	
141 Surgeons	

Short-Term General Hospitals: 6 (854 beds)
  JCAHO Accredited: 6
Hospital Services: 6 ♦♦♦♦
Teaching Hospitals
  Appleton Medical Center
  Mercy Medical Center, Oskosh
  St. Elizabeth Hospital
Score: 54.1   Rank: 163

Asheville, NC
Office-Based Physicians
141 Generalists	
158 Specialists	
139 Surgeons	

Short-Term General Hospitals: 3 (1,089 beds)
  JCAHO Accredited: 3
Hospital Services: 3 ♦♦♦♦
Teaching Hospital
  Memorial Mission Hospital
Score: 85.83   Rank: 51

Athens, GA
Office-Based Physicians
54 Generalists	
72 Specialists	
80 Surgeons	

Short-Term General Hospitals: 2 (605 beds)
  JCAHO Accredited: 2
Hospital Services: 2 ♦♦♦♦
Score: 31.44   Rank: 243

Atlanta, GA

Office-Based Physicians

989 Generalists	■▢▢▢▢
2,223 Specialists	■■■■▢
1,784 Surgeons	■■■■▢

Short-Term General Hospitals: 40 (9,282 beds)
JCAHO Accredited: 39
Hospital Services: 14 ♦, 1 ♦♦, 7 ♦♦♦, 18 ♦♦♦♦
Teaching Hospitals
  Crawford Long Hospital
  Egleston Children's Hospital at Emory
  Emory University Hospital
  Georgia Baptist Medical Center
  Grady Memorial Hospital
  Piedmont Hospital
  Scottish Rite Children's Medical Center
  Southwest Hospital And Medical Center
  Wesley Woods Geriatric Hospital
  West Paces Ferry Hospital
  Wilbur & Hilda Gleen Hospital for Children
Score: 57.22   **Rank: 152**

Atlantic-Cape May, NJ

Office-Based Physicians

62 Generalists	■▢▢▢▢
152 Specialists	■■▢▢▢
140 Surgeons	■■▢▢▢

Short-Term General Hospitals: 4 (973 beds)
JCAHO Accredited: 4
Hospital Services: 2 ♦, 1 ♦♦♦, 1 ♦♦♦♦
Teaching Hospital
  Atlantic City Medical Center
Score: 15.29   **Rank: 300**

Augusta-Aiken, GA-SC

Office-Based Physicians

172 Generalists	■■▢▢▢
344 Specialists	■■■■■
266 Surgeons	■■■■■

Short-Term General Hospitals: 9 (2,636 beds)
JCAHO Accredited: 9
Hospital Services: 1 ♦, 1 ♦♦♦, 7 ♦♦♦♦
Teaching Hospitals
  Medical College of Georgia
  University Hospital
Score: 86.11   **Rank: 50**

Austin-San Marcos, TX

Office-Based Physicians

548 Generalists	■■■■▢
510 Specialists	■■■▢▢
457 Surgeons	■■■▢▢

Short-Term General Hospitals: 11 (1,713 beds)
JCAHO Accredited: 9
Hospital Services: 1 ♦♦, 4 ♦♦♦, 6 ♦♦♦♦
Teaching Hospital
  Brackenridge Hospital
Score: 64.87   **Rank: 125**

Bakersfield, CA

Office-Based Physicians

138 Generalists	■▢▢▢▢
233 Specialists	■▢▢▢▢
186 Surgeons	■▢▢▢▢

Short-Term General Hospitals: 10 (1,500 beds)
JCAHO Accredited: 9
Hospital Services: 1 ♦, 1 ♦♦, 3 ♦♦♦, 5 ♦♦♦♦
Teaching Hospital
  Kern Medical Center
Score: 19.54   **Rank: 285**

Baltimore, MD

Office-Based Physicians

701 Generalists	■▢▢▢▢
2,286 Specialists	■■■■■
1,567 Surgeons	■■■■■

Short-Term General Hospitals: 24 (8,331 beds)
JCAHO Accredited: 24
Hospital Services: 1 ♦♦♦, 23 ♦♦♦♦
Teaching Hospitals
  Children's Hospital
  Franklin Square Hospital
  Good Samaritan Hospital
  Greater Baltimore Medical Center
  Harbor Hospital Center
  James Lawrence Kernan Hospital
  John F. Kennedy Institute
  Johns Hopkins Bayview Medical Center
  Johns Hopkins Hospital
  Maryland General Hospital
  Mercy Medical Center
  Mt. Washington Pediatric Hospital
  St. Agnes Hospital
  Sinai Hospital
  Union Memorial Hospital
  University of Maryland Medical System
Score: 86.4   **Rank: 49**

Bangor, ME

Office-Based Physicians

40 Generalists	■■■▢▢
51 Specialists	■■■▢▢
45 Surgeons	■■■■▢

Short-Term General Hospitals: 2 (416 beds)
JCAHO Accredited: 2
Hospital Services: 1 ♦♦, 1 ♦♦♦♦
Teaching Hospital
  Eastern Maine Medical Center
Score: 43.62   **Rank: 200**

Barnstable-Yarmouth, MA

Office-Based Physicians

51 Generalists	■■▢▢▢
102 Specialists	■■■■▢
63 Surgeons	■■■▢▢

Short-Term General Hospitals: 1 (258 beds)
JCAHO Accredited: 1
Hospital Services: 1 ♦♦♦♦
Score: 14.16   **Rank: 304**

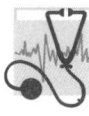

Baton Rouge, LA

Office-Based Physicians

222 Generalists	■■□□□
303 Specialists	■■■□□
262 Surgeons	■■■□□

Short-Term General Hospitals: 9 (2,425 beds)
  JCAHO Accredited: 8
Hospital Services: 4 ◆, 1 ◆◆, 1 ◆◆◆, 3 ◆◆◆◆
Teaching Hospitals
  Baton Rouge General Medical Center
  Earl K. Long Medical Center
Score: 57.5   Rank: **151**

Beaumont-Port Arthur, TX

Office-Based Physicians

151 Generalists	■■■□□
147 Specialists	■■□□□
146 Surgeons	■■□□□

Short-Term General Hospitals: 9 (1,851 beds)
  JCAHO Accredited: 7
Hospital Services: 2 ◆◆◆, 7 ◆◆◆◆
Teaching Hospital
  St. Mary Hospital, Port Arthur
Score: 38.81   Rank: **217**

Bellingham, WA

Office-Based Physicians

124 Generalists	■■■■■
62 Specialists	■■□□□
58 Surgeons	■■□□□

Short-Term General Hospitals: 1 (206 beds)
  JCAHO Accredited: 1
Hospital Services: 1 ◆◆◆◆
Score: 32.57   Rank: **239**

Benton Harbor, MI

Office-Based Physicians

78 Generalists	■■■□□
64 Specialists	■■□□□
55 Surgeons	■□□□□

Short-Term General Hospitals: 4 (662 beds)
  JCAHO Accredited: 4
Hospital Services: 2 ◆◆◆, 2 ◆◆◆◆
Score: 28.04   Rank: **254**

Bergen-Passaic, NJ

Office-Based Physicians

267 Generalists	■□□□□
1,508 Specialists	■■■■■
871 Surgeons	■■■■■

Short-Term General Hospitals: 12 (4,718 beds)
  JCAHO Accredited: 12
Hospital Services: 1 ◆, 11 ◆◆◆◆
Teaching Hospitals
  Barnert Hospital
  Bergen Pines County Hospital
  Englewood Hospital & Medical Center
  Hackensack University Medical
  St. Joseph's Hospital
Score: 89.51   Rank: **38**

Billings, MT

Office-Based Physicians

53 Generalists	■■■□□
97 Specialists	■■■■■
91 Surgeons	■■■■■

Short-Term General Hospitals: 2 (489 beds)
  JCAHO Accredited: 2
Hospital Services: 2 ◆◆◆◆
Teaching Hospital
  Deaconess Medical Center
Score: 56.37   Rank: **155**

Biloxi-Gulfport-Pascagoula, MS

Office-Based Physicians

97 Generalists	■□□□□
163 Specialists	■■□□□
162 Surgeons	■■■□□

Short-Term General Hospitals: 9 (1,922 beds)
  JCAHO Accredited: 9
Hospital Services: 1 ◆, 2 ◆◆◆, 6 ◆◆◆◆
Score: 48.72   Rank: **182**

Binghamton, NY

Office-Based Physicians

108 Generalists	■■■□□
142 Specialists	■■■□□
114 Surgeons	■■■□□

Short-Term General Hospitals: 2 (686 beds)
  JCAHO Accredited: 2
Hospital Services: 2 ◆◆◆◆
Teaching Hospital
  Wilson Regional Medical Center
Score: 22.94   Rank: **273**

★ **Birmingham, AL**

Office-Based Physicians

316 Generalists	■■□□□
793 Specialists	■■■■■
601 Surgeons	■■■■■

Short-Term General Hospitals: 16 (5,843 beds)
  JCAHO Accredited: 13
Hospital Services: 6 ◆, 2 ◆◆◆, 8 ◆◆◆◆
Teaching Hospitals
  Baptist Medical Centers
  Carraway Methodist Medical Center
  Children's Hospital of Alabama
  Cooper Green Hospital
  Eye Foundation Hospital
  Healthsouth Medical Center
  Lloyd Noland Hospital
  Medical Center East
  St. Vincent's Hospital
  University of Alabama Hospital
Score: 97.45   Rank: **10**

Bismarck, ND

Office-Based Physicians

57 Generalists	■■■■■
59 Specialists	■■■■□
60 Surgeons	■■■■■

Short-Term General Hospitals: 3 (666 beds)
  JCAHO Accredited: 2

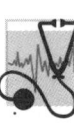

Hospital Services: 1 ◆◆◆, 2 ◆◆◆◆
Teaching Hospitals
  Medcenter One
  St. Alexius Medical Center
Score: **82.71**   Rank: **62**

Bloomington, IN
Office-Based Physicians
61 Generalists	
54 Specialists	
57 Surgeons	

Short-Term General Hospitals: 1 (617 beds)
  JCAHO Accredited: 1
Hospital Services: 1 ◆◆◆◆
Score: **37.96**   Rank: **220**

Bloomington-Normal, IL
Office-Based Physicians
54 Generalists	
69 Specialists	
54 Surgeons	

Short-Term General Hospitals: 2 (481 beds)
  JCAHO Accredited: 2
Hospital Services: 2 ◆◆◆◆
Score: **13.59**   Rank: **306**

Boise City, ID
Office-Based Physicians
221 Generalists	
150 Specialists	
191 Surgeons	

Short-Term General Hospitals: 5 (1,041 beds)
  JCAHO Accredited: 5
Hospital Services: 1 ◆, 4 ◆◆◆◆
Teaching Hospitals
  St. Alphonsus Regional Medical Center
  St. Lukes Regional Medical Center
Score: **60.33**   Rank: **141**

★ **Boston, MA-NH**
Office-Based Physicians
713 Generalists	
3,944 Specialists	
2,077 Surgeons	

Short-Term General Hospitals: 44 (9866 beds)
  JCAHO Accredited: 44
Hospital Services: 2 ◆, 7 ◆◆, 32 ◆◆◆◆
Teaching Hospitals
  Beth Israel Deaconess Medical Center
  Beverly Hospital
  Boston Medical Centers
  Braintree Hospital
  Brigham and Woman's Hospital
  Cambridge Hospital
  Carney Hospital
  Childrens Hospital
  Dana-Farber Cancer Institute
  Faulkner Hospital
  Franciscan Children's Hospital
  Malden Hospital
  Massachusetts Eye and Ear Infirmary
  Massachusetts General Hospital
  Mt. Auburn Hospital

New England Baptist Hospital
New England Medical Center Hospital
Newton-Wellesley Hospital
St. Elizabeths Hospital
Salem Hospital
Shriners Hospital for Children
Score: **94.9**   Rank: **19**

Boulder-Longmont, CO
Office-Based Physicians
250 Generalists	
150 Specialists	
107 Surgeons	

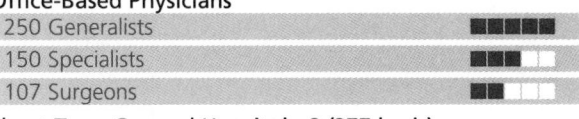

Short-Term General Hospitals: 3 (377 beds)
  JCAHO Accredited: 3
Hospital Services: 3 ◆◆◆◆
Teaching Hospitals
  Avista Adventist Hospital
  Longmont United Hospital
Score: **61.75**   Rank: **136**

Brazoria, TX
Office-Based Physicians
71 Generalists	
62 Specialists	
28 Surgeons	

Short-Term General Hospitals: 4 (328 beds)
  JCAHO Accredited: 4
Hospital Services: 1 ◆◆, 1 ◆◆◆, 2 ◆◆◆◆
Score: **3.96**   Rank: **340**

Bremerton, WA
Office-Based Physicians
121 Generalists	
79 Specialists	
66 Surgeons	

Short-Term General Hospitals: 2 (328 beds)
  JCAHO Accredited: 2
Hospital Services: 2 ◆◆◆◆
Score: **6.79**   Rank: **330**

Bridgeport, CT
Office-Based Physicians
106 Generalists	
487 Specialists	
297 Surgeons	

Short-Term General Hospitals: 4 (897 beds)
  JCAHO Accredited: 4
Hospital Services: 4 ◆◆◆◆
Teaching Hospitals
  Bridgeport Hospital
  Griffin Hospital
  St. Vincent's Medical Center
Score: **67.42**   Rank: **116**

Brockton, MA
Office-Based Physicians
49 Generalists	
122 Specialists	
72 Surgeons	

Short-Term General Hospitals: 1 (259 beds)
  JCAHO Accredited: 2

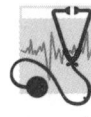

Hospital Services: 1 ♦♦♦♦
Teaching Hospitals
  Brockton Hospital
  Cardinal Cushing General Hospital
Score: 1.69   Rank: 348

Brownsville-Harlingen-San Benito, TX
Office-Based Physicians
71 Generalists	■□□□□
122 Specialists	■□□□□
89 Surgeons	■□□□□

Short-Term General Hospitals: 5 (1,007 beds)
JCAHO Accredited: 5
Hospital Services: 1 ♦♦, 1 ♦♦♦, 3 ♦♦♦♦
Score: 13.88   Rank: 305

Bryan-College Station, TX
Office-Based Physicians
90 Generalists	■■■■■
67 Specialists	■■■□□
58 Surgeons	■■■□□

Short-Term General Hospitals: 2 (301 beds)
JCAHO Accredited: 2
Hospital Services: 2 ♦♦♦♦
Teaching Hospital
  St. Joseph Regional Health Center
Score: 41.64   Rank: 207

Buffalo-Niagara Falls, NY
Office-Based Physicians
399 Generalists	■■□□□
842 Specialists	■■■■□
611 Surgeons	■■■■□

Short-Term General Hospitals: 16 (5,331 beds)
JCAHO Accredited: 14
Hospital Services: 4 ♦, 12 ♦♦♦♦
Teaching Hospitals
  Buffalo General Hospital
  Children's Hospital
  Erie County Medical Center
  Mercy Hospital
  Millard Fillmore Hospitals
  Niagara Falls Memorial Medical Center
  Sisters of Charity Hospital
Score: 81.58   Rank: 66

Burlington, VT
Office-Based Physicians
102 Generalists	■■■■■
160 Specialists	■■■■■
101 Surgeons	■■■■■

Short-Term General Hospitals: 2 (590 beds)
JCAHO Accredited: 2
Hospital Services: 2 ♦♦♦♦
Teaching Hospital
  Fletcher Allen Hospital of Vermont
Score: 66.85   Rank: 118

Calgary, AB
Office-Based Physicians
750 Generalists	■■■■■
512 Specialists	■■■■□
260 Surgeons	■□□□□

Short-Term General Hospitals: 7 (1,614 beds)
CCHFA Accredited: 7
Teaching Hospitals
  Alberta Children's Provincial Hospital
  Calgary General Hospital
  Foothills Provincial Hospital
  Grace Women's Hospital
  Holy Cross Hospital
  Peter Lougheed Centre
  Rockyview General Hospital
Score: 83.56   Rank: 59

Canton-Massillon, OH
Office-Based Physicians
157 Generalists	■■□□□
194 Specialists	■■■□□
147 Surgeons	■■□□□

Short-Term General Hospitals: 5 (1,679 beds)
JCAHO Accredited: 4
Hospital Services: 1 ♦, 4 ♦♦♦♦
Teaching Hospitals
  Aultman Hospital
  Mercy Medical Center
Score: 34.27   Rank: 233

Casper, WY
Office-Based Physicians
38 Generalists	■■■■□
31 Specialists	■■■□□
29 Surgeons	■■■□□

Short-Term General Hospitals: 1 (194 beds)
JCAHO Accredited: 1
Hospital Services: 1 ♦♦♦♦
Teaching Hospital
  Wyoming Medical Center
Score: 35.12   Rank: 230

Cedar Rapids, IA
Office-Based Physicians
110 Generalists	■■■■□
65 Specialists	■□□□□
66 Surgeons	■■□□□

Short-Term General Hospitals: 2 (812 beds)
JCAHO Accredited: 2
Hospital Services: 2 ♦♦♦♦
Teaching Hospitals
  Mercy Medical Center
  St. Luke's Hospital
Score: 41.92   Rank: 206

Champaign-Urbana, IL
Office-Based Physicians
87 Generalists	■■■■□
127 Specialists	■■■■■
84 Surgeons	■■■■□

Short-Term General Hospitals: 2 (808 beds)
JCAHO Accredited: 2
Hospital Services: 2 ♦♦♦♦
Teaching Hospitals
  Carle Foundation Hospital
  Covenant Medical Center
Score: 71.67   Rank: 100

Charleston-North Charleston, SC

Office-Based Physicians
230 Generalists	▪▪▪□□
371 Specialists	▪▪▪▪▪
318 Surgeons	▪▪▪▪▪

Short-Term General Hospitals: 10 (2,027 beds)
JCAHO Accredited: 9
Hospital Services: 2 ◆, 1 ◆◆◆, 7 ◆◆◆◆
Teaching Hospitals
Charleston Memorial Hospital
Medical University Hospital
Score: **88.66**   Rank: **41**

Charleston, WV

Office-Based Physicians
145 Generalists	▪▪▪▪□
164 Specialists	▪▪▪▪□
163 Surgeons	▪▪▪▪▪

Short-Term General Hospitals: 4 (1,216 beds)
JCAHO Accredited: 4
Hospital Services: 1 ◆◆◆, 3 ◆◆◆◆
Teaching Hospitals
Charleston Area Medical Center
Herbert J. Thomas Memorial Hospital
Score: **83.28**   Rank: **60**

Charlotte-Gastonia-Rock Hill, NC-SC

Office-Based Physicians
533 Generalists	▪▪▪□□
711 Specialists	▪▪▪□□
657 Surgeons	▪▪▪▪□

Short-Term General Hospitals: 10 (3,092 beds)
JCAHO Accredited: 10
Hospital Services: 2 ◆◆◆, 8 ◆◆◆◆
Teaching Hospitals
Carolinas Medical Center
Northeast Medical Center
Union Regional Medical Center
Score: **50.14**   Rank: **177**

Charlottesville, VA

Office-Based Physicians
96 Generalists	▪▪▪▪▪
218 Specialists	▪▪▪▪▪
133 Surgeons	▪▪▪▪▪

Short-Term General Hospitals: 2 (760 beds)
JCAHO Accredited: 2
Hospital Services: 2 ◆◆◆◆
Teaching Hospitals
University of Virginia Hospital
Score: **79.88**   Rank: **72**

Chattanooga, TN-GA

Office-Based Physicians
153 Generalists	▪▪□□□
269 Specialists	▪▪▪▪□
249 Surgeons	▪▪▪▪▪

Short-Term General Hospitals: 9 (1,691 beds)
JCAHO Accredited: 8
Hospital Services: 3 ◆, 3 ◆◆◆, 3 ◆◆◆◆

Teaching Hospitals
Erlanger Medical Center
Memorial Hospital
TC Thompson Children's Hospital Medical Center
Score: **58.92**   Rank: **146**

Cheyenne, WY

Office-Based Physicians
29 Generalists	▪▪□□□
35 Specialists	▪▪□□□
42 Surgeons	▪▪▪▪□

Short-Term General Hospitals: 3 (310 beds)
JCAHO Accredited: 2
Hospital Services: 1 ◆, 2 ◆◆◆◆
Teaching Hospital
United Medical Center
Score: **22.37**   Rank: **275**

Chicago, IL

Office-Based Physicians
2,850 Generalists	▪▪□□□
5,879 Specialists	▪▪▪▪▪
3,593 Surgeons	▪▪▪□□

Short-Term General Hospitals: 90 (25,614 beds)
JCAHO Accredited: 88
Hospital Services: 15 ◆, 5 ◆◆◆, 70 ◆◆◆◆
Teaching Hospitals
Children's Memorial Hospital
Columbia La Grange Hospital
Columbus Hospital
Cook County Hospital
Copley Memorial Hospital
Edgewater Medical Center
Evanston Hospital
Hinsdale Hospital
Illinois Masonic Medical Center
Jackson Park Hospital Foundation
Larabida Children's Hospital
Louis A Weiss Memorial Hospital
Loyola University Medical Center
Lutheran General Hospital
Mac Neal Memorial Hospital
Mercy Hospital and Medical Center
Michael Reese Hospital and Medical Center
Mt. Sinai Hospital Medical Center
Northwestern Memorial Hospital
Provident Hospital of Chicago
Ravenswood Hospital & Medical Center
Resurrection Medical Center
Rush North Shore Medical Center
Rush-Presbyterian-St. Lukes Medical Center
St. Anthony's Hospital
St. Elizabeth Hospital
St. Francis Hospital, Evanston
St. Joseph Medical Center
St. Mary of Nazareth Hospital Center
Shriners Hospital for Children
Swedish Covenant Hospital
University of Chicago Hospitals
University of Illinois Hospital
West Suburban Hospital Medical Center
Westlake Community Hospital
Wyler Children's Hospital
Score: **81.3**   Rank: **67**

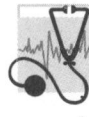

Chico-Paradise, CA
Office-Based Physicians
109 Generalists
85 Specialists
92 Surgeons
Short-Term General Hospitals: 5 (610 beds)
JCAHO Accredited: 4
Hospital Services: 1 ♦, 1 ♦♦♦, 3 ♦♦♦♦
Score: 45.6   Rank: 193

Chicoutimi-Jonquiere, PQ
Office-Based Physicians
142 Generalists
75 Specialists
Surgeons
Short-Term General Hospitals: 3 (855 beds)
CCHFA Accredited: 2
Teaching Hospitals
Hopital de Chicoutimi
Score: 52.69   Rank: 167

Cincinnati, OH-KY-IN
Office-Based Physicians
703 Generalists
1,044 Specialists
780 Surgeons
Short-Term General Hospitals: 19 (4,728 beds)
JCAHO Accredited: 18
Hospital Services: 3 ♦, 2 ♦♦, 1 ♦♦♦, 13 ♦♦♦♦
Teaching Hospitals
Bethesda Oak Hospital
Children's Hospital Medical Center
Christ Hospital
Convalescent Hospital for Children
Franciscan Hospitals
Good Samaritan Hospital
Jewish Hospital
St. Elizabeth Medical Center
University Hospital
Score: 78.75   Rank: 76

Clarksville-Hopkinsville, TN-KY
Office-Based Physicians
51 Generalists
54 Specialists
53 Surgeons
Short-Term General Hospitals: 3 (421 beds)
JCAHO Accredited: 3
Hospital Services: 3 ♦♦♦♦
Score: 2.54   Rank: 345

Cleveland-Lorain-Elyria, OH
Office-Based Physicians
614 Generalists
1,811 Specialists
1,244 Surgeons
Short-Term General Hospitals: 33 (9,212 beds)
JCAHO Accredited: 32
Hospital Services: 7 ♦, 3 ♦♦♦, 23 ♦♦♦♦
Teaching Hospitals
Cleveland Clinic Hospital
Fairview General Hospital

Health Hill Hospital for Children
Lutheran Medical Center
Meridia Huron Hospital
Metro Health Medical Center
Mt. Sinai Medical Center
Rainbow Babies and Children's Hospital
St. Luke's Medical Center
St. Vincent Charity and Health Center
University Hospitals of Cleveland
Score: 84.7   Rank: 55

Colorado Springs, CO
Office-Based Physicians
139 Generalists
167 Specialists
188 Surgeons
Short-Term General Hospitals: 4 (913 beds)
JCAHO Accredited: 4
Hospital Services: 1 ♦♦, 3 ♦♦♦♦
Teaching Hospital
Penrose St. Francis Healthcare System
Score: 11.89   Rank: 312

★ **Columbia, MO**
Office-Based Physicians
81 Generalists
184 Specialists
142 Surgeons
Short-Term General Hospitals: 4 (1,228 beds)
JCAHO Accredited: 4
Hospital Services: 4 ♦♦♦♦
Teaching Hospitals
Boone Hospital Center
University and Children's Hospital
University of Missouri Hospital & Clinics
Score: 97.73   Rank: 9

Columbia, SC
Office-Based Physicians
246 Generalists
292 Specialists
274 Surgeons
Short-Term General Hospitals: 6 (1,920 beds)
JCAHO Accredited: 6
Hospital Services: 6 ♦♦♦♦
Teaching Hospital
Palmetto Richland
Score: 73.65   Rank: 94

Columbus, GA-AL
Office-Based Physicians
126 Generalists
89 Specialists
116 Surgeons
Short-Term General Hospitals: 5 (1,299 beds)
JCAHO Accredited: 5
Hospital Services: 3 ♦, 1 ♦♦♦, 1 ♦♦♦♦
Teaching Hospitals
Hughston Sports Medicine Hospital
The Medical Center
Score: 40.5   Rank: 211

Columbus, OH
Office-Based Physicians
689 Generalists	▪▪▪
704 Specialists	▪▪▪
627 Surgeons	▪▪▪

Short-Term General Hospitals: 12 (4,052 beds)
JCAHO Accredited: 12
Hospital Services: 1 ◆, 1 ◆◆◆, 10 ◆◆◆◆
Teaching Hospitals
Arthur G. James Cancer Hospital
Children's Hospital
Grant Medical Center
Mt Carmel Health Center
Ohio State University Hospital
Park Medical Center
Riverside Methodist Hospital
Score: **58.35**   Rank: **148**

Corpus Christi, TX
Office-Based Physicians
168 Generalists	▪▪▪
222 Specialists	▪▪▪
179 Surgeons	▪▪▪

Short-Term General Hospitals: 7 (1,236 beds)
JCAHO Accredited: 7
Hospital Services: 1 ◆, 1 ◆◆◆, 5 ◆◆◆◆
Teaching Hospitals
Driscoll Children's Hospital
Memorial Medical Center
Score: **54.39**   Rank: **162**

Cumberland, MD-WV
Office-Based Physicians
41 Generalists	▪▪▪
59 Specialists	▪▪▪▪
48 Surgeons	▪▪▪

Short-Term General Hospitals: 3 (536 beds)
JCAHO Accredited: 3
Hospital Services: 1 ◆◆◆, 2 ◆◆◆◆
Score: **38.52**   Rank: **218**

Dallas, TX
Office-Based Physicians
930 Generalists	▪
1,545 Specialists	▪▪▪
1,402 Surgeons	▪▪▪

Short-Term General Hospitals: 37 (7,915 beds)
JCAHO Accredited: 35
Hospital Services: 3 ◆◆, 8 ◆◆◆, 26 ◆◆◆◆
Teaching Hospitals
Baylor Medical Center
Charlton Methodist Hospital
Children's Medical Center of Dallas
Methodist Medical Center
Parkland Memorial Hospital
Pediatric Center for Restorative Care
Presbyterian Hospital
St. Paul Medical Center
Zale Lipshy University Hospital
Score: **48.15**   Rank: **184**

Danbury, CT
Office-Based Physicians
51 Generalists	▪
200 Specialists	▪▪▪▪▪
121 Surgeons	▪▪▪▪▪

Short-Term General Hospitals: 2 (407 beds)
JCAHO Accredited: 2
Hospital Services: 1 ◆◆◆, 1 ◆◆◆◆
Teaching Hospital
Danbury Hospital
Score: **41.35**   Rank: **208**

Danville, VA
Office-Based Physicians
24 Generalists	▪
51 Specialists	▪▪
44 Surgeons	▪▪

Short-Term General Hospitals: 1 (312 beds)
JCAHO Accredited: 1
Hospital Services: 1 ◆◆◆◆
Teaching Hospital
Danville Regional Medical Center
Score: **4.53**   Rank: **338**

Davenport-Moline-Rock Island, IA-IL
Office-Based Physicians
158 Generalists	▪▪▪
132 Specialists	▪
148 Surgeons	▪▪

Short-Term General Hospitals: 6 (1,242 beds)
JCAHO Accredited: 6
Hospital Services: 1 ◆◆◆, 5 ◆◆◆◆
Teaching Hospital
Genesis Medical Center
Score: **33.42**   Rank: **236**

Dayton-Springfield, OH
Office-Based Physicians
529 Generalists	▪▪▪▪
500 Specialists	▪▪▪
380 Surgeons	▪▪

Short-Term General Hospitals: 12 (4,086 beds)
JCAHO Accredited: 11
Hospital Services: 12 ◆◆◆◆
Teaching Hospitals
Children's Medical Center
Franciscan Medical Center
Good Samaritan Hospital & Health Center
Kettering Medical Center
Miami Valley Hospital
Score: **79.6**   Rank: **73**

Daytona Beach, FL
Office-Based Physicians
185 Generalists	▪▪▪
173 Specialists	▪
168 Surgeons	▪▪

Short-Term General Hospitals: 8 (1,445 beds)
JCAHO Accredited: 6
Hospital Services: 1 ◆, 2 ◆◆◆, 5 ◆◆◆◆
Teaching Hospital
Halifax Medical Center
Score: **26.06**   Rank: **262**

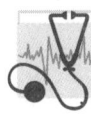

Decatur, AL
Office-Based Physicians

61 Generalists	▪▪▪□□
38 Specialists	▪□□□□
45 Surgeons	▪□□□□

Short-Term General Hospitals: 4 (530 beds)
JCAHO Accredited: 4
Hospital Services: 3 ♦, 1 ♦♦♦♦
Score: 17.56   Rank: 292

Decatur, IL
Office-Based Physicians

59 Generalists	▪▪▪▪□
45 Specialists	▪▪□□□
37 Surgeons	▪□□□□

Short-Term General Hospitals: 2 (452 beds)
JCAHO Accredited: 2
Hospital Services: 2 ♦♦♦♦
Teaching Hospitals
   Decatur Memorial Hospital
   St. Mary's Hospital
Score: 28.04   Rank: 254

Denver, CO
Office-Based Physicians

822 Generalists	▪▪▪□□
1,283 Specialists	▪▪▪▪□
954 Surgeons	▪▪▪▪□

Short-Term General Hospitals: 16 (4,075 beds)
JCAHO Accredited: 14
Hospital Services: 2 ♦, 14 ♦♦♦♦
Teaching Hospitals
   Children's Hospital
   Denver Health Medical Center
   National Jewish Medical & Research Center
   Presbyterian/St. Luke's Medical Center
   Rose Medical Center
   St. Anthony Hospitals
   St. Joseph Hospital
   Swedish Medical Center
   University Hospital
Score: 85.26   Rank: 53

Des Moines, IA
Office-Based Physicians

145 Generalists	▪▪□□□
174 Specialists	▪▪□□□
171 Surgeons	▪▪□□□

Short-Term General Hospitals: 7 (1,744 beds)
JCAHO Accredited: 6
Hospital Services: 1 ♦♦♦, 6 ♦♦♦♦
Teaching Hospitals
   Broadlawns Medical Center
   Iowa Lutheran Hospital
   Iowa Methodist Medical Center
   Mercy Hospital Medical Center
Score: 39.37   Rank: 215

Detroit, MI
Office-Based Physicians

1,034 Generalists	▪□□□□
2,688 Specialists	▪▪▪▪□
1,751 Surgeons	▪▪□□□

Short-Term General Hospitals: 47 (12,579 beds)
JCAHO Accredited: 40
Hospital Services: 5 ♦, 1 ♦♦, 1 ♦♦♦, 40 ♦♦♦♦
Teaching Hospitals
   Bon Secours Hospital
   Children's Hospital of Michigan
   Detroit Receiving Hospital & University Health Center
   Grace Hospital Northwestern Unit
   Harper Hospital
   Henry Ford Cottage Hospital
   Henry Ford Hospital
   Hutzel Hospital
   Mercy Hospital
   North Oakland Medical Centers
   Oakwood Hospital and Medical Center
   Providence Hospital
   St. John Hospital & Medical Center
   St. Joseph Mercy Hospital
   Sinai Hospital
   Wayne State University/Detroit Medical Center
   William Beaumont Hospital
Score: 49   Rank: 181

Dothan, AL
Office-Based Physicians

44 Generalists	▪▪□□□
81 Specialists	▪▪▪▪□
84 Surgeons	▪▪▪▪▪

Short-Term General Hospitals: 4 (689 beds)
JCAHO Accredited: 4
Hospital Services: 1 ♦, 1 ♦♦♦, 2 ♦♦♦♦
Score: 55.24   Rank: 159

Dover, DE
Office-Based Physicians

28 Generalists	▪□□□□
45 Specialists	▪□□□□
36 Surgeons	▪□□□□

Short-Term General Hospitals: 2 (209 beds)
JCAHO Accredited: 2
Hospital Services: 2 ♦♦♦♦
Score: 0.84   Rank: 351

Dubuque, IA
Office-Based Physicians

15 Generalists	▪□□□□
61 Specialists	▪▪▪▪□
54 Surgeons	▪▪▪▪▪

Short-Term General Hospitals: 2 (528 beds)
JCAHO Accredited: 2
Hospital Services: 2 ♦♦♦♦
Score: 24.92   Rank: 266

Duluth-Superior, MN-WI
Office-Based Physicians

196 Generalists	▪▪▪▪▪
114 Specialists	▪▪□□□
112 Surgeons	▪▪▪□□

Short-Term General Hospitals: 9 (1,343 beds)
JCAHO Accredited: 6
Hospital Services: 1 ♦, 1 ♦♦, 2 ♦♦♦, 5 ♦♦♦♦

Teaching Hospitals
St. Luke's Hospital of Duluth
St. Mary's Medical Center
Score: 88.1   Rank: 43

Dutchess County, NY
Office-Based Physicians

93 Generalists	▪▪☐☐☐
170 Specialists	▪▪▪▪☐
127 Surgeons	▪▪▪▪☐

Short-Term General Hospitals: 4 (875 beds)
JCAHO Accredited: 4
Hospital Services: 1 ♦, 3 ♦♦♦♦
Teaching Hospitals
St. Francis Hospital
Vassar Brothers Hospital
Score: 48.44   Rank: 183

★ **Eau Claire, WI**
Office-Based Physicians

119 Generalists	▪▪▪▪▪
77 Specialists	▪▪▪☐☐
82 Surgeons	▪▪▪▪▪

Short-Term General Hospitals: 5 (814 beds)
JCAHO Accredited: 5
Hospital Services: 1 ♦, 4 ♦♦♦♦
Teaching Hospitals
Luther Hospital
Sacred Heart Hospital
Score: 90.36   Rank: 35

★ **Edmonton, AB**
Office-Based Physicians

930 Generalists	▪▪▪▪▪
550 Specialists	▪▪▪▪☐
280 Surgeons	▪☐☐☐☐

Short-Term General Hospitals: 12 (3,481 beds)
CCHFA Accredited: 12
Teaching Hospitals
Alberta Hospital Edmonton
Edmonton General Hospital
Grey Nuns Hospital
Misericordia Hospital
Royal Alexandra Hospital
University of Alberta Hospital
Score: 97.16   Rank: 11

El Paso, TX
Office-Based Physicians

153 Generalists	▪☐☐☐☐
271 Specialists	▪▪☐☐☐
202 Surgeons	▪☐☐☐☐

Short-Term General Hospitals: 7 (1,834 beds)
JCAHO Accredited: 7
Hospital Services: 1 ♦, 1 ♦♦♦, 5 ♦♦♦♦
Teaching Hospitals
Texas Tech University Health Sciences Center
Thomason General Hospital
Score: 19.83   Rank: 284

Elkhart-Goshen, IN
Office-Based Physicians

91 Generalists	▪▪▪▪☐
38 Specialists	▪☐☐☐☐
44 Surgeons	▪☐☐☐☐

Short-Term General Hospitals: 2 (398 beds)
JCAHO Accredited: 2
Hospital Services: 1 ♦, 1 ♦♦♦♦
Score: 4.24   Rank: 339

Elmira, NY
Office-Based Physicians

23 Generalists	▪☐☐☐☐
68 Specialists	▪▪▪▪☐
44 Surgeons	▪▪▪☐☐

Short-Term General Hospitals: 2 (526 beds)
JCAHO Accredited: 2
Hospital Services: 2 ♦♦♦♦
Score: 25.21   Rank: 265

Enid, OK
Office-Based Physicians

26 Generalists	▪▪▪☐☐
21 Specialists	▪☐☐☐☐
27 Surgeons	▪▪▪☐☐

Short-Term General Hospitals: 2 (254 beds)
JCAHO Accredited: 2
Hospital Services: 2 ♦♦♦♦
Teaching Hospitals
Bass Baptist Health Center
St. Mary's Mercy Hospital
Score: 33.71   Rank: 235

Erie, PA
Office-Based Physicians

146 Generalists	▪▪▪▪☐
112 Specialists	▪▪☐☐☐
133 Surgeons	▪▪▪☐☐

Short-Term General Hospitals: 7 (1,222 beds)
JCAHO Accredited: 5
Hospital Services: 4 ♦♦♦, 3 ♦♦♦♦
Teaching Hospitals
Hamot Medical Center
St. Vincent Health Center
Shriners Hospital for Children
Score: 54.95   Rank: 160

Eugene-Springfield, OR
Office-Based Physicians

214 Generalists	▪▪▪▪▪
161 Specialists	▪▪▪☐☐
139 Surgeons	▪▪▪☐☐

Short-Term General Hospitals: 4 (605 beds)
JCAHO Accredited: 4
Hospital Services: 2 ♦♦♦, 2 ♦♦♦♦
Score: 53.54   Rank: 165

Evansville-Henderson, IN-KY
Office-Based Physicians

190 Generalists	▪▪▪▪▪
147 Specialists	▪▪▪☐☐
147 Surgeons	▪▪▪▪☐

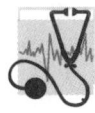

Short-Term General Hospitals: 5 (1,482 beds)
  JCAHO Accredited: 5
Hospital Services: 1 ♦, 1 ♦♦, 3 ♦♦♦♦
Teaching Hospitals
  Deaconess Hospital
  St. Mary's Medical Center of Evansville
Score: 81.86   Rank: 65

Fargo-Moorhead, ND-MN
  Office-Based Physicians

99 Generalists	▪▪▪▪▫
120 Specialists	▪▪▪▪▫
88 Surgeons	▪▪▪▪▫

Short-Term General Hospitals: 3 (667 beds)
  JCAHO Accredited: 3
Hospital Services: 3 ♦♦♦♦
Teaching Hospitals
  Dakota Heartland Health System
  Meritcare Hospital
Score: 81.01   Rank: 68

Fayetteville, NC
  Office-Based Physicians

91 Generalists	▪▪▫▫▫
101 Specialists	▪▫▫▫▫
93 Surgeons	▪▫▫▫▫

Short-Term General Hospitals: 4 (870 beds)
  JCAHO Accredited: 4
Hospital Services: 1 ♦♦♦, 3 ♦♦♦♦
Teaching Hospital
  Cape Fear Valley Medical Center
Score: 17.84   Rank: 291

Fayetteville-Springdale-Rogers, AR
  Office-Based Physicians

175 Generalists	▪▪▪▪▪
93 Specialists	▪▫▫▫▫
102 Surgeons	▪▪▫▫▫

Short-Term General Hospitals: 7 (883 beds)
  JCAHO Accredited: 3
Hospital Services: 1 ♦, 2 ♦♦♦, 4 ♦♦♦♦
Teaching Hospital
  Washington Regional Medical Center
Score: 46.17   Rank: 191

Fitchburg-Leominster, MA
  Office-Based Physicians

50 Generalists	▪▪▫▫▫
125 Specialists	▪▪▪▪▪
61 Surgeons	▪▪▪▫▫

Short-Term General Hospitals: 2 (296 beds)
  JCAHO Accredited: 2
Hospital Services: 1 ♦♦♦, 1 ♦♦♦♦
Teaching Hospital
  Health Alliance, Leominster
Score: 35.97   Rank: 227

Flagstaff, AZ-UT
  Office-Based Physicians

75 Generalists	▪▪▪▪▪
51 Specialists	▪▪▫▫▫
39 Surgeons	▪▫▫▫▫

Short-Term General Hospitals: 4 (255 beds)
  JCAHO Accredited: 3
Hospital Services: 2 ♦, 1 ♦♦, 1 ♦♦♦
Score: 25.49   Rank: 264

Flint, MI
  Office-Based Physicians

174 Generalists	▪▪▪▫▫
220 Specialists	▪▪▪▫▫
123 Surgeons	▪▫▫▫▫

Short-Term General Hospitals: 3 (1,530 beds)
  JCAHO Accredited: 3
Hospital Services: 3 ♦♦♦♦
Teaching Hospitals
  Hurley Medical Center
  Mclaren Regional Medical Center
  Regional Medical Center
Score: 27.47   Rank: 257

Florence, AL
  Office-Based Physicians

47 Generalists	▪▪▫▫▫
70 Specialists	▪▪▪▫▫
72 Surgeons	▪▪▪▪▫

Short-Term General Hospitals: 4 (892 beds)
  JCAHO Accredited: 4
Hospital Services: 2 ♦, 2 ♦♦♦♦
Score: 39.94   Rank: 213

Florence, SC
  Office-Based Physicians

80 Generalists	▪▪▪▪▪
79 Specialists	▪▪▪▪▫
72 Surgeons	▪▪▪▪▪

Short-Term General Hospitals: 3 (727 beds)
  JCAHO Accredited: 2
Hospital Services: 3 ♦♦♦♦
Teaching Hospital
  Mcleod Regional Medical Center
Score: 70.82   Rank: 104

Fort Collins-Loveland, CO
  Office-Based Physicians

193 Generalists	▪▪▪▪▪
72 Specialists	▪▫▫▫▫
107 Surgeons	▪▪▪▪▫

Short-Term General Hospitals: 3 (405 beds)
  JCAHO Accredited: 2
Hospital Services: 1 ♦♦♦, 2 ♦♦♦♦
Teaching Hospital
  Poudre Valley Hospital
Score: 47.02   Rank: 188

Fort Lauderdale, FL
  Office-Based Physicians

419 Generalists	▪▫▫▫▫
1,116 Specialists	▪▪▪▪▪
703 Surgeons	▪▪▪▪▫

Short-Term General Hospitals: 18 (5,087 beds)
  JCAHO Accredited: 17
Hospital Services: 4 ♦, 1 ♦♦♦, 13 ♦♦♦♦

Teaching Hospitals
Broward General Medical Center
Cleveland Clinic Hospital
Coral Springs Medical Center
Memorial Hospital
Score: 62.88   Rank: 132

Fort Myers-Cape Coral, FL
Office-Based Physicians
114 Generalists
210 Specialists
193 Surgeons

Short-Term General Hospitals: 5 (1,468 beds)
JCAHO Accredited: 5
Hospital Services: 2 ♦, 3 ♦♦♦♦
Score: 33.99   Rank: 234

Fort Pierce-Port St. Lucie, FL
Office-Based Physicians
95 Generalists
147 Specialists
139 Surgeons

Short-Term General Hospitals: 3 (773 beds)
JCAHO Accredited: 3
Hospital Services: 3 ♦♦♦♦
Score: 15.86   Rank: 298

Fort Smith, AR-OK
Office-Based Physicians
98 Generalists
101 Specialists
87 Surgeons

Short-Term General Hospitals: 4 (843 beds)
JCAHO Accredited: 3
Hospital Services: 2 ♦♦♦, 2 ♦♦♦♦
Teaching Hospital
Sparks Regional Medical Center
Score: 53.82   Rank: 164

Fort Walton Beach, FL
Office-Based Physicians
60 Generalists
68 Specialists
68 Surgeons

Short-Term General Hospitals: 4 (483 beds)
JCAHO Accredited: 4
Hospital Services: 1 ♦♦♦, 3 ♦♦♦♦
Score: 20.96   Rank: 280

Fort Wayne, IN
Office-Based Physicians
258 Generalists
178 Specialists
191 Surgeons

Short-Term General Hospitals: 9 (1,467 beds)
JCAHO Accredited: 8
Hospital Services: 1 ♦, 8 ♦♦♦♦
Teaching Hospitals
Lutheran Hospital
Parkview Hospital
St. Joseph Medical Center of Ft Wayne
Score: 50.7   Rank: 175

Fort Worth-Arlington, TX
Office-Based Physicians
551 Generalists
532 Specialists
528 Surgeons

Short-Term General Hospitals: 17 (3,096 beds)
JCAHO Accredited: 16
Hospital Services: 1 ♦♦, 2 ♦♦♦, 14 ♦♦♦♦
Teaching Hospitals
All Saints Episcopal Hospital
Cook Ft. Worth Children's Medical Center
Harris Methodist Fort Worth
Score: 29.46   Rank: 250

Fresno, CA
Office-Based Physicians
338 Generalists
374 Specialists
280 Surgeons

Short-Term General Hospitals: 14 (1,840 beds)
JCAHO Accredited: 11
Hospital Services: 4 ♦, 2 ♦♦, 2 ♦♦♦, 6 ♦♦♦♦
Teaching Hospitals
University Medical Center
Valley Children's Hospital
Score: 30.02   Rank: 248

Gadsden, AL
Office-Based Physicians
48 Generalists
46 Specialists
43 Surgeons

Short-Term General Hospitals: 2 (538 beds)
JCAHO Accredited: 2
Hospital Services: 2 ♦♦♦♦
Score: 24.64   Rank: 267

★ Gainesville, FL
Office-Based Physicians
165 Generalists
238 Specialists
189 Surgeons

Short-Term General Hospitals: 4 (1,495 beds)
JCAHO Accredited: 4
Hospital Services: 4 ♦♦♦♦
Teaching Hospitals
Alachua General Hospital
Shands Hospital
Score: 96.31   Rank: 14

Galveston-Texas City, TX
Office-Based Physicians
125 Generalists
155 Specialists
122 Surgeons

Short-Term General Hospitals: 2 (1,033 beds)
JCAHO Accredited: 2
Hospital Services: 2 ♦♦♦♦
Teaching Hospitals
Shriners Hospital for Children
University of Texas Medical Branch
Score: 55.8   Rank: 157

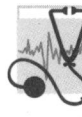

Gary, IN

Office-Based Physicians

265 Generalists	▮▮▮□□
262 Specialists	▮▮□□□
244 Surgeons	▮▮□□□

Short-Term General Hospitals: 7 (2,473 beds)
  JCAHO Accredited: 7
Hospital Services: 2 ♦, 5 ♦♦♦♦
Teaching Hospital
  Methodist Hospitals
Score: **42.2**   Rank: **205**

Glens Falls, NY

Office-Based Physicians

62 Generalists	▮▮▮▮□
66 Specialists	▮▮▮□□
56 Surgeons	▮▮▮□□

Short-Term General Hospitals: 2 (523 beds)
  JCAHO Accredited: 2
Hospital Services: 1 ♦, 1 ♦♦♦♦
Score: **36.82**   Rank: **224**

Goldsboro, NC

Office-Based Physicians

39 Generalists	▮▮□□□
34 Specialists	▮□□□□
32 Surgeons	▮□□□□

Short-Term General Hospitals: 2 (300 beds)
  JCAHO Accredited: 2
Hospital Services: 2 ♦♦♦♦
Score: **2.83**   Rank: **344**

Grand Forks, ND-MN

Office-Based Physicians

68 Generalists	▮▮▮▮▮
41 Specialists	▮▮□□□
42 Surgeons	▮▮□□□

Short-Term General Hospitals: 5 (734 beds)
  JCAHO Accredited: 2
Hospital Services: 1 ♦, 1 ♦♦♦, 3 ♦♦♦♦
Teaching Hospital
  Altru Hospital
Score: **53.25**   Rank: **166**

Grand Junction, CO

Office-Based Physicians

88 Generalists	▮▮▮▮▮
45 Specialists	▮▮□□□
46 Surgeons	▮▮▮□□

Short-Term General Hospitals: 4 (798 beds)
  JCAHO Accredited: 3
Hospital Services: 1 ♦, 1 ♦♦♦, 2 ♦♦♦♦
Teaching Hospital
  St. Mary's Hospital and Medical Center
Score: **77.62**   Rank: **80**

Grand Rapids-Muskegon-Holland, MI

Office-Based Physicians

363 Generalists	▮▮□□□
389 Specialists	▮□□□□
355 Surgeons	▮▮□□□

Short-Term General Hospitals: 11 (2,183 beds)
  JCAHO Accredited: 9
Hospital Services: 2 ♦, 1 ♦♦♦, 8 ♦♦♦♦
Teaching Hospitals
  Blodgett Memorial Medical Center
  Butterworth Hospital
  St. Marys Health Services
Score: **27.19**   Rank: **258**

Great Falls, MT

Office-Based Physicians

22 Generalists	▮□□□□
50 Specialists	▮▮▮▮□
55 Surgeons	▮▮▮▮▮

Short-Term General Hospitals: 1 (366 beds)
  JCAHO Accredited: 0
Hospital Services: 1 ♦♦♦♦
Score: **30.59**   Rank: **246**

Greeley, CO

Office-Based Physicians

88 Generalists	▮▮▮▮▮
48 Specialists	▮□□□□
51 Surgeons	▮□□□□

Short-Term General Hospitals: 1 (262 beds)
  JCAHO Accredited: 1
Hospital Services: 1 ♦♦♦♦
Teaching Hospital
  Northern Colorado Medical Center
Score: **9.06**   Rank: **322**

Green Bay, WI

Office-Based Physicians

79 Generalists	▮▮□□□
105 Specialists	▮▮▮□□
101 Surgeons	▮▮▮□□

Short-Term General Hospitals: 3 (639 beds)
  JCAHO Accredited: 3
Hospital Services: 3 ♦♦♦♦
Score: **18.13**   Rank: **290**

Greensboro–Winston-Salem–High Point, NC

Office-Based Physicians

469 Generalists	▮▮▮□□
672 Specialists	▮▮▮▮□
558 Surgeons	▮▮▮▮□

Short-Term General Hospitals: 13 (3,635 beds)
  JCAHO Accredited: 13
Hospital Services: 1 ♦♦, 4 ♦♦♦, 8 ♦♦♦♦
Teaching Hospitals
  Forsyth Memorial Hospital
  Moses H. Cone Memorial Hospital
  North Carolina Baptist Hospitals
Score: **72.23**   Rank: **99**

Greenville, NC

Office-Based Physicians

99 Generalists	▮▮▮▮▮
147 Specialists	▮▮▮▮▮
94 Surgeons	▮▮▮▮▮

Short-Term General Hospitals: 1 (680 beds)
  JCAHO Accredited: 1

Hospital Services: 1 ♦♦♦♦
Teaching Hospitals
  Pitt County Memorial Hospital
  Shriners Hospital for Children
Score: **73.08**   Rank: **96**

Greenville-Spartanburg-Anderson, SC
Office-Based Physicians

492 Generalists	▪▪▪▪▫
365 Specialists	▪▪▫▫▫
397 Surgeons	▪▪▪▫▫

Short-Term General Hospitals: 11 (2,412 beds)
  JCAHO Accredited: 9
Hospital Services: 1 ♦, 1 ♦♦, 1 ♦♦♦, 8 ♦♦♦♦
Teaching Hospitals
  Anderson Area Medical Center
  Greenville Hospital Center
  Spartanburg Regional Medical Center
Score: **55.52**   Rank: **158**

Hagerstown, MD
Office-Based Physicians

41 Generalists	▪▪▫▫▫
57 Specialists	▪▪▫▫▫
64 Surgeons	▪▪▪▪▫

Short-Term General Hospitals: 1 (333 beds)
  JCAHO Accredited: 1
Hospital Services: 1 ♦♦♦♦
Score: **7.08**   Rank: **329**

★ Halifax, NS
Office-Based Physicians

530 Generalists	▪▪▪▪▪
360 Specialists	▪▪▪▪▪
170 Surgeons	▪▪▪▪▫

Short-Term General Hospitals: 6 (1,979 beds)
  CCHFA Accredited: 6
Teaching Hospitals
  Camp Hill Medical Centre
  Izaak Walton Killam Hospital for Children
  Salvation Army Grace Maternity Hospital
  Victoria General Hospital
Score: **98.86**   Rank: **5**

★ Hamilton, ON
Office-Based Physicians

650 Generalists	▪▪▪▪▪
512 Specialists	▪▪▪▪▪
235 Surgeons	▪▪▫▫▫

Short-Term General Hospitals: 6 (2,256 beds)
  CCHFA Accredited: 5
Teaching Hospitals
  Brant Memorial Hospital
  Chedoke-McMaster Hospitals
  Hamilton General Hospital
  Henderson General Hospital
  St. Joseph's Hospital
Score: **91.78**   Rank: **30**

Hamilton-Middletown, OH
Office-Based Physicians

96 Generalists	▪▫▫▫▫
108 Specialists	▪▫▫▫▫
81 Surgeons	▪▫▫▫▫

Short-Term General Hospitals: 4 (659 beds)
  JCAHO Accredited: 4
Hospital Services: 4 ♦♦♦♦
Teaching Hospital
  Middletown Regional Hospital
Score: **5.66**   Rank: **333**

Harrisburg-Lebanon-Carlisle, PA
Office-Based Physicians

327 Generalists	▪▪▪▪▫
335 Specialists	▪▪▪▫▫
305 Surgeons	▪▪▪▪▫

Short-Term General Hospitals: 6 (2,079 beds)
  JCAHO Accredited: 6
Hospital Services: 1 ♦, 1 ♦♦♦, 4 ♦♦♦♦
Teaching Hospitals
  Good Samaritan Hospital
  Hershey Medical Center
Score: **69.4**   Rank: **109**

Hartford, CT
Office-Based Physicians

325 Generalists	▪▫▫▫▫
956 Specialists	▪▪▪▪▪
627 Surgeons	▪▪▪▪▫

Short-Term General Hospitals: 10 (2509 beds)
  JCAHO Accredited: 10
Hospital Services: 2 ♦♦♦, 8 ♦♦♦♦
Teaching Hospitals
  Connecticut Valley Hospital
  Hartford Hospital
  John Dempsey Hospital
  Middlesex Hospital
  New Britain General Hospital
  St. Francis Hospital & Medical Center
Score: **66.28**   Rank: **120**

Hattiesburg, MS
Office-Based Physicians

63 Generalists	▪▪▪▪▫
70 Specialists	▪▪▪▪▫
84 Surgeons	▪▪▪▪▪

Short-Term General Hospitals: 2 (748 beds)
  JCAHO Accredited: 2
Hospital Services: 2 ♦♦♦♦
Score: **69.12**   Rank: **110**

Hickory-Morganton-Lenoir, NC
Office-Based Physicians

187 Generalists	▪▪▪▪▫
86 Specialists	▪▫▫▫▫
124 Surgeons	▪▪▫▫▫

Short-Term General Hospitals: 6 (1,007 beds)
  JCAHO Accredited: 6
Hospital Services: 4 ♦, 2 ♦♦♦♦
Score: **34.84**   Rank: **231**

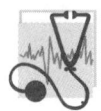

Honolulu, HI
  Office-Based Physicians
224 Generalists	▪□□□□
696 Specialists	▪▪▪▪▪
461 Surgeons	▪▪▪▪□

  Short-Term General Hospitals: 11 (2,095 beds)
    JCAHO Accredited: 11
  Hospital Services: 2 ♦, 9 ♦♦♦♦
  Teaching Hospitals
    Kaiser Foundation Hospital
    Kapiolani Medical Center
    Kapiolani Women & Children's Medical Center
    Kuakini Medical Center
    Queens Medical Center
    Shriners Hospital for Children
    St. Francis Medical Centers
    Straub Hospital
    Wahiawa General Hospital
  Score: 62.32   Rank: 134

Houma, LA
  Office-Based Physicians
60 Generalists	▪□□□□
62 Specialists	▪□□□□
80 Surgeons	▪▪▪□

  Short-Term General Hospitals: 5 (675 beds)
    JCAHO Accredited: 5
  Hospital Services: 2 ♦♦♦, 3 ♦♦♦♦
  Teaching Hospital
    Chaubert Medical Center
  Score: 22.09   Rank: 276

Houston, TX
  Office-Based Physicians
1,485 Generalists	▪▪□□□
2,215 Specialists	▪▪▪▪□
1,821 Surgeons	▪▪▪▪□

  Short-Term General Hospitals: 41 (10,993 beds)
    JCAHO Accredited: 39
  Hospital Services: 2 ♦♦, 5 ♦♦♦, 34 ♦♦♦♦
  Teaching Hospitals
    Conroe Regional Medical Center
    Harris County Hospital District
    Hermann Hospital
    Lyndon B. Johnson General Hospital
    Memorial Hospital Southwest
    Park Plaza Hospital
    St. Joseph Hospital
    St. Luke's Episcopal Hospital
    Shriners Hospital for Children
    Texas Children's Hospital
    University of Texas Anderson Cancer Center
  Score: 65.43   Rank: 123

Huntington-Ashland, WV-KY-OH
  Office-Based Physicians
163 Generalists	▪▪▪▪□
178 Specialists	▪▪▪□□
133 Surgeons	▪▪▪□

  Short-Term General Hospitals: 6 (1,627 beds)
    JCAHO Accredited: 6
  Hospital Services: 6 ♦♦♦♦

  Teaching Hospitals
    Cabell-Huntington Hospital
    St. Mary's Hospital
  Score: 63.17   Rank: 131

Huntsville, AL
  Office-Based Physicians
176 Generalists	▪▪▪▪▪
144 Specialists	▪▪□□□
147 Surgeons	▪▪▪□

  Short-Term General Hospitals: 5 (1,031 beds)
    JCAHO Accredited: 5
  Hospital Services: 1 ♦, 2 ♦♦♦, 2 ♦♦♦♦
  Teaching Hospital
    Huntsville Hospitals
  Score: 45.32   Rank: 194

Indianapolis, IN
  Office-Based Physicians
841 Generalists	▪▪▪▪□
968 Specialists	▪▪▪▪□
772 Surgeons	▪▪▪▪□

  Short-Term General Hospitals: 21 (5,420 beds)
    JCAHO Accredited: 19
  Hospital Services: 5 ♦, 1 ♦♦♦, 15 ♦♦♦♦
  Teaching Hospitals
    Clarian Health Partners
    Community Hospital
    Lifelines Children's Hospital
    Riley Hospital for Children
    St. Francis Hospital Center
    St. Vincent Health Care Center
    Wishard Memorial Hospital
  Score: 88.95   Rank: 40

★ **Iowa City, IA**
  Office-Based Physicians
75 Generalists	▪▪▪▪▪
176 Specialists	▪▪▪▪▪
149 Surgeons	▪▪▪▪▪

  Short-Term General Hospitals: 3 (1,239 beds)
    JCAHO Accredited: 3
  Hospital Services: 3 ♦♦♦♦
  Teaching Hospital
    Mercy Hospital
  Score: 95.75   Rank: 16

Jackson, MI
  Office-Based Physicians
44 Generalists	▪□□□□
51 Specialists	▪□□□□
40 Surgeons	▪□□□

  Short-Term General Hospitals: 2 (366 beds)
    JCAHO Accredited: 1
  Hospital Services: 1 ♦♦♦, 1 ♦♦♦♦
  Score: 1.98   Rank: 347

★ **Jackson, MS**
  Office-Based Physicians
188 Generalists	▪▪▪□□
293 Specialists	▪▪▪▪□
265 Surgeons	▪▪▪▪▪

Short-Term General Hospitals: 10 (3,329 beds)
   JCAHO Accredited: 9
Hospital Services: 2 ♦, 1 ♦♦, 2 ♦♦♦, 5 ♦♦♦♦
Teaching Hospitals
   Mississippi Baptist Medical Center
   St. Dominic Jackson Memorial Hospital
   University of Mississippi Medical Center
Score: 92.63   Rank: 27

Jackson, TN
Office-Based Physicians

64 Generalists	■■■■■
78 Specialists	■■■■■
87 Surgeons	■■■■■

Short-Term General Hospitals: 2 (670 beds)
   JCAHO Accredited: 2
Hospital Services: 2 ♦♦♦♦
Teaching Hospital
   Madison County General Hospital
Score: 79.32   Rank: 74

Jacksonville, FL
Office-Based Physicians

481 Generalists	■■■
614 Specialists	■■■■
458 Surgeons	■■■

Short-Term General Hospitals: 11 (3,123 beds)
   JCAHO Accredited: 11
Hospital Services: 1 ♦, 2 ♦♦♦, 8 ♦♦♦♦
Teaching Hospitals
   Baptist Medical Center
   St. Luke's Hospital
   St. Vincent's Medical Center
   University Medical Center
Score: 71.38   Rank: 102

Jacksonville, NC
Office-Based Physicians

27 Generalists	■
29 Specialists	■
40 Surgeons	■

Short-Term General Hospitals: 2 (299 beds)
   JCAHO Accredited: 2
Hospital Services: 1 ♦, 1 ♦♦♦
Score: 1.13   Rank: 350

Jamestown, NY
Office-Based Physicians

41 Generalists	■
40 Specialists	■
49 Surgeons	■■

Short-Term General Hospitals: 4 (658 beds)
   JCAHO Accredited: 2
Hospital Services: 2 ♦♦♦, 2 ♦♦♦♦
Score: 8.49   Rank: 324

Janesville-Beloit, WI
Office-Based Physicians

55 Generalists	■■
91 Specialists	■■■■■
52 Surgeons	■

Short-Term General Hospitals: 3 (454 beds)
   JCAHO Accredited: 2

Hospital Services: 3 ♦♦♦♦
Teaching Hospital
   Mercy Hospital
Score: 16.71   Rank: 295

Jersey City, NJ
Office-Based Physicians

109 Generalists	■
336 Specialists	■■■■■
187 Surgeons	■

Short-Term General Hospitals: 9 (2,382 beds)
   JCAHO Accredited: 9
Hospital Services: 2 ♦, 1 ♦♦♦, 6 ♦♦♦♦
Teaching Hospitals
   Jersey City Medical Center
   St. Mary's Hospital
Score: 38.24   Rank: 219

★ Johnson City-Kingsport-Bristol, TN-VA
Office-Based Physicians

301 Generalists	■■■■■
295 Specialists	■■■■
244 Surgeons	■■■■

Short-Term General Hospitals: 11 (2,207 beds)
   JCAHO Accredited: 9
Hospital Services: 3 ♦♦♦, 8 ♦♦♦♦
Teaching Hospitals
   Bristol Regional Medical Center
   Holston Valley Medical Center
   Johnson City Medical Center Hospital
Score: 75.07   Rank: 89

Johnstown, PA
Office-Based Physicians

130 Generalists	■■■■
99 Specialists	■■
83 Surgeons	■

Short-Term General Hospitals: 7 (1,099 beds)
   JCAHO Accredited: 7
Hospital Services: 1 ♦, 1 ♦♦, 2 ♦♦♦, 3 ♦♦♦♦
Teaching Hospital
   Conemaugh Valley Memorial Hospital
Score: 52.69   Rank: 167

Jonesboro, AR
Office-Based Physicians

62 Generalists	■■■■■
51 Specialists	■■■■
61 Surgeons	■■■■■

Short-Term General Hospitals: 2 (423 beds)
   JCAHO Accredited: 2
Hospital Services: 2 ♦♦♦♦
Teaching Hospital
   St. Bernard's Regional Medical Center
Score: 78.47   Rank: 77

Joplin, MO
Office-Based Physicians

37 Generalists	■
54 Specialists	■
63 Surgeons	■■■

Short-Term General Hospitals: 4 (743 beds)
   JCAHO Accredited: 2

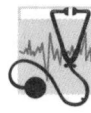

Hospital Services: 2 ♦♦♦, 2 ♦♦♦♦
Score: 11.04   Rank: 315

Kalamazoo-Battle Creek, MI
Office-Based Physicians
195 Generalists	■■■
225 Specialists	■■■
185 Surgeons	■■

Short-Term General Hospitals: 7 (1,474 beds)
JCAHO Accredited: 7
Hospital Services: 7 ♦♦♦♦
Teaching Hospitals
Borgess-Pipp Health Center
Bronson Methodist Hospital
Score: 47.59   Rank: 186

Kankakee, IL
Office-Based Physicians
27 Generalists	■
42 Specialists	■■
32 Surgeons	■

Short-Term General Hospitals: 2 (590 beds)
JCAHO Accredited: 2
Hospital Services: 2 ♦♦♦♦
Score: 11.33   Rank: 314

Kansas City, MO-KS
Office-Based Physicians
648 Generalists	■■
998 Specialists	■■■■
787 Surgeons	■■■

Short-Term General Hospitals: 35 (6,393 beds)
JCAHO Accredited: 28
Hospital Services: 1 ♦, 1 ♦♦, 2 ♦♦♦, 31 ♦♦♦♦
Teaching Hospitals
Baptist Medical Center
Bethany Medical Center
Children's Mercy Hospitals
St. Luke's Hospital of Kansas City
Trinity Lutheran Hospital
Truman Medical Center
University of Kansas Hospital
Score: 67.7   Rank: 115

Kenosha, WI
Office-Based Physicians
61 Generalists	■■■
45 Specialists	■
32 Surgeons	■

Short-Term General Hospitals: 2 (264 beds)
JCAHO Accredited: 2
Hospital Services: 2 ♦♦♦♦
Teaching Hospital
St. Catherine's Hospital
Score: 3.39   Rank: 342

Killeen-Temple, TX
Office-Based Physicians
86 Generalists	■
163 Specialists	■■■
107 Surgeons	■■

Short-Term General Hospitals: 6 (2,805 beds)
JCAHO Accredited: 6

Hospital Services: 1 ♦, 1 ♦♦, 4 ♦♦♦♦
Teaching Hospitals
Scott & White Memorial Hospital
Score: 44.75   Rank: 196

Kitchener-Waterloo, ON
Office-Based Physicians
330 Generalists	■■■■■
125 Specialists	■
92 Surgeons	■

Short-Term General Hospitals: 3 (963 beds)
CCHFA Accredited: 3
Score: 34.56   Rank: 232

Knoxville, TN
Office-Based Physicians
398 Generalists	■■■■
463 Specialists	■■■■
374 Surgeons	■■■■■

Short-Term General Hospitals: 9 (2,355 beds)
JCAHO Accredited: 9
Hospital Services: 1 ♦, 1 ♦♦♦, 7 ♦♦♦♦
Teaching Hospitals
East Tennessee Children's Hospital
St. Mary's Medical Center
University of Tennessee Memorial Hospital
Score: 86.68   Rank: 48

Kokomo, IN
Office-Based Physicians
56 Generalists	■■■■
32 Specialists	■
31 Surgeons	■

Short-Term General Hospitals: 3 (372 beds)
JCAHO Accredited: 3
Hospital Services: 3 ♦♦♦♦
Score: 18.41   Rank: 288

La Crosse, WI-MN
Office-Based Physicians
74 Generalists	■■■■
119 Specialists	■■■■■
89 Surgeons	■■■■■

Short-Term General Hospitals: 3 (608 beds)
JCAHO Accredited: 2
Hospital Services: 1 ♦, 2 ♦♦♦♦
Teaching Hospitals
Franciscan Skemp Medical Center Lacrosse
La Crosse Lutheran Hospital
Score: 75.92   Rank: 86

Lafayette, IN
Office-Based Physicians
59 Generalists	■■
80 Specialists	■■
69 Surgeons	■■

Short-Term General Hospitals: 3 (534 beds)
JCAHO Accredited: 3
Hospital Services: 3 ♦♦♦♦
Score: 13.03   Rank: 308

Lafayette, LA

Office-Based Physicians
122 Generalists	■■
153 Specialists	■■
165 Surgeons	■■■

Short-Term General Hospitals: 10 (1,408 beds)
JCAHO Accredited: 7
Hospital Services: 3 ◆, 1 ◆◆◆, 6 ◆◆◆◆
Teaching Hospital
  University Medical Center
Score: 33.14   Rank: 237

Lake Charles, LA

Office-Based Physicians
82 Generalists	■■■
82 Specialists	■■
81 Surgeons	■■

Short-Term General Hospitals: 6 (900 beds)
JCAHO Accredited: 4
Hospital Services: 2 ◆, 1 ◆◆◆, 3 ◆◆◆◆
Teaching Hospital
  Lake Charles Memorial Hospital
Score: 46.45   Rank: 190

Lakeland-Winter Haven, FL

Office-Based Physicians
124 Generalists	■
207 Specialists	■■
171 Surgeons	■■

Short-Term General Hospitals: 5 (1,487 beds)
JCAHO Accredited: 5
Hospital Services: 1 ◆◆, 1 ◆◆◆, 3 ◆◆◆◆
Score: 20.67   Rank: 281

Lancaster, PA

Office-Based Physicians
320 Generalists	■■■■■
122 Specialists	■
132 Surgeons	■

Short-Term General Hospitals: 5 (1,094 beds)
JCAHO Accredited: 4
Hospital Services: 1 ◆◆◆, 4 ◆◆◆◆
Teaching Hospital
  Lancaster General Hospital
Score: 31.16   Rank: 244

Lansing-East Lansing, MI

Office-Based Physicians
171 Generalists	■■
201 Specialists	■■
130 Surgeons	■

Short-Term General Hospitals: 6 (1,191 beds)
JCAHO Accredited: 6
Hospital Services: 3 ◆◆◆, 3 ◆◆◆◆
Teaching Hospitals
  Edward W. Sparrow Hospital
  Ingham Regional Medical Center
  St. Lawrence Hospital
Score: 26.91   Rank: 259

Laredo, TX

Office-Based Physicians
49 Generalists	■
48 Specialists	■
36 Surgeons	■

Short-Term General Hospitals: 2 (427 beds)
JCAHO Accredited: 2
Hospital Services: 2 ◆◆◆
Score: 2.26   Rank: 346

Las Cruces, NM

Office-Based Physicians
60 Generalists	■■
45 Specialists	■
41 Surgeons	■

Short-Term General Hospitals: 1 (222 beds)
JCAHO Accredited: 1
Hospital Services: 1 ◆◆◆◆
Score: 0.56   Rank: 352

Las Vegas, NV-AZ

Office-Based Physicians
355 Generalists	■
539 Specialists	■■
437 Surgeons	■■

Short-Term General Hospitals: 13 (2,596 beds)
JCAHO Accredited: 10
Hospital Services: 6 ◆, 2 ◆◆◆, 5 ◆◆◆◆
Teaching Hospitals
  Summit Hospital
  Sunrise Hospital & Medical Center
  University Medical Center of Southern Nevada
Score: 24.36   Rank: 268

Lawrence, KS

Office-Based Physicians
46 Generalists	■■■■
35 Specialists	■
29 Surgeons	■

Short-Term General Hospitals: 1 (80 beds)
JCAHO Accredited: 1
Hospital Services: 1 ◆◆◆
Score: 5.38   Rank: 335

Lawrence, MA-NH

Office-Based Physicians
115 Generalists	■
212 Specialists	■■■
154 Surgeons	■■

Short-Term General Hospitals: 4 (686 beds)
JCAHO Accredited: 4
Hospital Services: 1 ◆◆◆, 3 ◆◆◆◆
Teaching Hospital
  Lawrence General Hospital
Score: 18.98   Rank: 287

Lawton, OK

Office-Based Physicians
37 Generalists	■■
26 Specialists	■
37 Surgeons	■

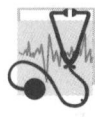

Short-Term General Hospitals: 4 (501 beds)
JCAHO Accredited: 4
Hospital Services: 2 ♦, 2 ♦♦♦♦
Score: 16.43   Rank: 296

Lewiston-Auburn, ME
Office-Based Physicians
42 Generalists	■■■□
49 Specialists	■■■□
42 Surgeons	■■■□

Short-Term General Hospitals: 2 (365 beds)
JCAHO Accredited: 2
Hospital Services: 2 ♦♦♦♦
Teaching Hospital
Central Maine Medical Center
Score: 36.54   Rank: 225

★ Lexington, KY
Office-Based Physicians
252 Generalists	■■■■□
382 Specialists	■■■■■
296 Surgeons	■■■■■

Short-Term General Hospitals: 12 (2,545 beds)
JCAHO Accredited: 11
Hospital Services: 1 ♦, 2 ♦♦♦, 9 ♦♦♦♦
Teaching Hospitals
Central Baptist Hospital
St. Joseph Hospital
Shriners Hospital for Children
University of Kentucky Hospital
Score: 98.01   Rank: 8

Lima, OH
Office-Based Physicians
90 Generalists	■■■■□
41 Specialists	■□□□□
54 Surgeons	■□□□□

Short-Term General Hospitals: 3 (604 beds)
JCAHO Accredited: 3
Hospital Services: 3 ♦♦♦♦
Score: 21.24   Rank: 279

Lincoln, NE
Office-Based Physicians
153 Generalists	■■■■■
124 Specialists	■■■□
116 Surgeons	■■■■□

Short-Term General Hospitals: 4 (762 beds)
JCAHO Accredited: 4
Hospital Services: 4 ♦♦♦♦
Teaching Hospitals
Bryan Medical Centers
Lincoln General Hospital
Score: 76.77   Rank: 83

★ Little Rock-North Little Rock, AR
Office-Based Physicians
330 Generalists	■■■■□
424 Specialists	■■■■■
367 Surgeons	■■■■■

Short-Term General Hospitals: 11 (3,341 beds)
JCAHO Accredited: 11

Hospital Services: 1 ♦♦, 2 ♦♦♦, 8 ♦♦♦♦
Teaching Hospitals
Arkansas Children's Hospital
Baptist Medical Center
St. Vincent Infirmary Medical Center
University Hospital of Arkansas
Score: 92.35   Rank: 28

★ London, ON
Office-Based Physicians
560 Generalists	■■■■■
480 Specialists	■■■■■
192 Surgeons	■■■□

Short-Term General Hospitals: 4 (1,661 beds)
CCHFA Accredited: 4
Teaching Hospitals
St. Joseph's Health Centre
University Hospital
Victoria Hospital
Score: 90.65   Rank: 34

★ Long Island, NY
Office-Based Physicians
815 Generalists	■□□□□
3,181 Specialists	■■■■■
1,892 Surgeons	■■■■■

Short-Term General Hospitals: 29 (11,322 beds)
JCAHO Accredited: 28
Hospital Services: 13 ♦, 16 ♦♦♦♦
Teaching Hospitals
Huntington Hospital
Long Island Jewish Medical Center
Mercy Medical Center
Nassau County Medical Center
North Shore University Hospitals
South Nassau Community Hospital
Southside Hospital
University Hospital
Winthrop University Hospital
Score: 99.15   Rank: 4

Longview-Marshall, TX
Office-Based Physicians
91 Generalists	■■■□
76 Specialists	■□□□□
80 Surgeons	■■□□

Short-Term General Hospitals: 4 (592 beds)
JCAHO Accredited: 3
Hospital Services: 1 ♦♦♦, 3 ♦♦♦♦
Score: 13.31   Rank: 307

Los Angeles-Long Beach, CA
Office-Based Physicians
3,248 Generalists	■■□□
6,071 Specialists	■■■■□
4,249 Surgeons	■■■□

Short-Term General Hospitals: 109 (26,867 beds)
JCAHO Accredited: 105
Hospital Services: 28 ♦, 4 ♦♦, 17 ♦♦♦, 60 ♦♦♦♦
Teaching Hospitals
California Hospital Medical Center
Cedars-Sinai Medical Center
Centinela Hospital Medical Center

Children's Hospital of Los Angeles
City of Hope National Medical Center
Glendale Adventist Medical Center
Huntington Memorial Hospital
Kaiser Foundation Hospital
LA County Harbor-UCLA Medical Center
LA County High Desert Hospital
LA County USC Medical Center
Lakewood Regional Medical Center
Long Beach Memorial Medical Center
Northridge Hospital Medical Center
Olive View Medical Center
Presbyterian Intercommunity Hospital
Rancho Los Amigos Medical Center
St. Mary Medical Center
St. Vincent Medical Center
UCLA Medical Center
USC Kenneth Norris Jr. Cancer Hospital
USC University Hospital
Valley Hospital Medical Center
White Memorial Medical Center
Score: 67.98   Rank: 114

Louisville, KY-IN
Office-Based Physicians
| 466 Generalists |
| 714 Specialists |
| 575 Surgeons |

Short-Term General Hospitals: 15 (3,911 beds)
JCAHO Accredited: 15
Hospital Services: 1 ♦, 1 ♦♦♦, 13 ♦♦♦♦
Teaching Hospitals
Jewish Hospital
Kosair Childrens Hospital
University of Louisville Hospital
Score: 87.81   Rank: 44

Lowell, MA-NH
Office-Based Physicians
| 61 Generalists |
| 339 Specialists |
| 169 Surgeons |

Short-Term General Hospitals: 2 (452 beds)
JCAHO Accredited: 2
Hospital Services: 2 ♦♦♦♦
Score: 37.39   Rank: 222

★ Lubbock, TX
Office-Based Physicians
| 118 Generalists |
| 187 Specialists |
| 159 Surgeons |

Short-Term General Hospitals: 6 (1,429 beds)
JCAHO Accredited: 5
Hospital Services: 1 ♦, 5 ♦♦♦♦
Teaching Hospitals
Methodist Children's Hospital
St. Mary of the Plains Hospital
University Medical Center
Score: 91.21   Rank: 32

Lynchburg, VA
Office-Based Physicians
| 119 Generalists |
| 72 Specialists |
| 82 Surgeons |

Short-Term General Hospitals: 3 (812 beds)
JCAHO Accredited: 3
Hospital Services: 1 ♦♦♦, 2 ♦♦♦♦♦
Score: 28.89   Rank: 252

Macon, GA
Office-Based Physicians
| 154 Generalists |
| 165 Specialists |
| 174 Surgeons |

Short-Term General Hospitals: 8 (1,209 beds)
JCAHO Accredited: 8
Hospital Services: 2 ♦, 1 ♦♦♦, 5 ♦♦♦♦
Teaching Hospital
Medical Center of Central Georgia
Score: 71.67   Rank: 100

★ Madison, WI
Office-Based Physicians
| 299 Generalists |
| 387 Specialists |
| 239 Surgeons |

Short-Term General Hospitals: 5 (1,468 beds)
JCAHO Accredited: 5
Hospital Services: 1 ♦, 4 ♦♦♦♦
Teaching Hospitals
Meriter Hospital
Parkway Hospital
St. Mary's Hospital Medical Center
University of Wisconsin Hospitals
Score: 90.93   Rank: 33

Manchester, NH
Office-Based Physicians
| 66 Generalists |
| 99 Specialists |
| 78 Surgeons |

Short-Term General Hospitals: 2 (515 beds)
JCAHO Accredited: 2
Hospital Services: 2 ♦♦♦♦
Score: 12.74   Rank: 309

Mansfield, OH
Office-Based Physicians
| 50 Generalists |
| 60 Specialists |
| 57 Surgeons |

Short-Term General Hospitals: 5 (523 beds)
JCAHO Accredited: 5
Hospital Services: 2 ♦♦♦, 3 ♦♦♦♦
Score: 15.01   Rank: 301

McAllen-Edinburg-Mission, TX
Office-Based Physicians
| 181 Generalists |
| 142 Specialists |
| 107 Surgeons |

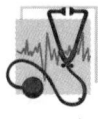

Short-Term General Hospitals: 5 (1,087 beds)
 JCAHO Accredited: 5
Hospital Services: 2 ♦♦♦, 3 ♦♦♦♦
Teaching Hospital
 McAllen Medical Center
Score: 12.46　　　　　Rank: 310

Medford-Ashland, OR
 Office-Based Physicians

90 Generalists	▪▪▪▪□
102 Specialists	▪▪▪▪□
85 Surgeons	▪▪▪▪□

Short-Term General Hospitals: 3 (426 beds)
 JCAHO Accredited: 3
Hospital Services: 1 ♦♦♦, 2 ♦♦♦♦
Score: 40.22　　　　　Rank: 212

Melbourne-Titusville-Palm Bay, FL
 Office-Based Physicians

196 Generalists	▪▪▪□□
238 Specialists	▪▪▪□□
177 Surgeons	▪▪□□□

Short-Term General Hospitals: 5 (1,116 beds)
 JCAHO Accredited: 4
Hospital Services: 5 ♦♦♦♦
Score: 23.51　　　　　Rank: 271

Memphis, TN-AR-MS
 Office-Based Physicians

365 Generalists	▪▪□□□
739 Specialists	▪▪▪▪□
583 Surgeons	▪▪▪▪□

Short-Term General Hospitals: 13 (4,874 beds)
 JCAHO Accredited: 13
Hospital Services: 3 ♦♦♦, 10 ♦♦♦♦
Teaching Hospitals
 Baptist Memorial Hospital
 Methodist Healthcare Hospitals
 Regional Medical Center
 St. Francis Hospital
 St. Joseph Hospital
 St. Jude Children's Research Hospital
 University of Tennessee Medical Center
Score: 80.73　　　　　Rank: 69

Merced, CA
 Office-Based Physicians

94 Generalists	▪▪▪□□
48 Specialists	▪□□□□
40 Surgeons	▪□□□□

Short-Term General Hospitals: 5 (345 beds)
 JCAHO Accredited: 3
Hospital Services: 2 ♦, 1 ♦♦, 1 ♦♦♦, 1 ♦♦♦♦
Teaching Hospital
 Sutter Merced Medical Center
Score: 8.21　　　　　Rank: 325

★ Miami, FL
 Office-Based Physicians

1,040 Generalists	▪▪▪▪□
1,857 Specialists	▪▪▪▪▪
1,246 Surgeons	▪▪▪▪▪

Short-Term General Hospitals: 25 (8,239 beds)
 JCAHO Accredited: 24
Hospital Services: 8 ♦, 1 ♦♦♦, 16 ♦♦♦♦
Teaching Hospitals
 Baptist Hospital of Miami
 Cedars Medical Center
 Healthsouth Doctors Hospital
 Jackson Memorial Hospital
 Miami Children's Hospital
 Mount Sinai Hospital
 University of Miami Hospital & Clinic
Score: 96.88　　　　　Rank: 12

Middlesex-Somerset-Hunterdon, NJ
 Office-Based Physicians

385 Generalists	▪▪□□□
1,012 Specialists	▪▪▪▪▪
522 Surgeons	▪▪▪▪□

Short-Term General Hospitals: 8 (2,799 beds)
 JCAHO Accredited: 7
Hospital Services: 4 ♦, 4 ♦♦♦♦
Teaching Hospitals
 Hunterdon Medical Center
 John F. Kennedy Medical Center
 Muhlenberg Regional Medical Center
 Raritan Bay Medical Center
 Robert Wood Johnson Univ Hospital
 St. Peters Medical Center
 Somerset Medical Center
Score: 74.78　　　　　Rank: 90

Milwaukee-Waukesha, WI
 Office-Based Physicians

670 Generalists	▪▪▪□□
1,061 Specialists	▪▪▪▪□
740 Surgeons	▪▪▪▪□

Short-Term General Hospitals: 19 (4,857 beds)
 JCAHO Accredited: 17
Hospital Services: 2 ♦, 1 ♦♦♦, 16 ♦♦♦♦
Teaching Hospitals
 Children's Hospital of Wisconsin
 Columbia Hospital
 Froedtert Memorial Lutheran Hospital
 St. Joseph's Hospital
 St. Mary's Hospital of Milwaukee
 St. Michael Hospital
 Sinai Samaritan Medical Center
 Waukesha Memorial Hospital
Score: 84.98　　　　　Rank: 54

★ Minneapolis-St. Paul, MN-WI
 Office-Based Physicians

1,954 Generalists	▪▪▪▪▪
1,541 Specialists	▪▪▪□□
1,114 Surgeons	▪▪□□□

Short-Term General Hospitals: 32 (6,705 beds)
 JCAHO Accredited: 27
Hospital Services: 1 ♦♦♦, 4 ♦♦♦, 27 ♦♦♦♦
Teaching Hospitals
 Abbott-Northwestern Hospital
 Children's Health Care–Minneapolis
 Children's Health Care–Saint Paul

Fairview University Medical Center
Gillette Children's Hospital
Hennepin County Medical Center
Methodist Hospital
North Memorial Medical Center
Regions Hospital
St. Johns Northeast Community Hospital
St. Joseph's Hospital
Shriners Hospital for Children
United Hospitals
Score: 93.20   Rank: 25

Missoula, MT
Office-Based Physicians

54 Generalists	▪▪▪▪□
62 Specialists	▪▪▪▪□
75 Surgeons	▪▪▪▪▪

Short-Term General Hospitals: 2 (306 beds)
JCAHO Accredited: 2
Hospital Services: 1 ♦♦♦, 1 ♦♦♦♦
Score: 59.77   Rank: 143

Mobile, AL
Office-Based Physicians

192 Generalists	▪▪□□□
293 Specialists	▪▪▪□□
279 Surgeons	▪▪▪▪□

Short-Term General Hospitals: 9 (1,953 beds)
JCAHO Accredited: 9
Hospital Services: 4 ♦, 2 ♦♦♦, 3 ♦♦♦♦
Teaching Hospitals
  University of South Alabama Medical Center
  University of South Alabama Doctors Hospital
Score: 60.9   Rank: 139

Modesto, CA
Office-Based Physicians

218 Generalists	▪▪▪▪□
167 Specialists	▪▪□□□
137 Surgeons	▪□□□□

Short-Term General Hospitals: 6 (1,251 beds)
JCAHO Accredited: 5
Hospital Services: 3 ♦, 1 ♦♦♦, 2 ♦♦♦♦
Teaching Hospital
  Doctors Medical Center
Score: 30.87   Rank: 245

Monmouth-Ocean, NJ
Office-Based Physicians

194 Generalists	▪□□□□
826 Specialists	▪▪▪▪▪
512 Surgeons	▪▪▪▪□

Short-Term General Hospitals: 9 (3,021 beds)
JCAHO Accredited: 9
Hospital Services: 1 ♦, 8 ♦♦♦♦
Teaching Hospitals
  Jersey Shore Medical Center
  Monmouth Medical Center
Score: 43.34   Rank: 201

Monroe, LA
Office-Based Physicians

74 Generalists	▪▪▪□□
79 Specialists	▪▪▪□□
71 Surgeons	▪▪▪▪□

Short-Term General Hospitals: 5 (1,034 beds)
JCAHO Accredited: 4
Hospital Services: 2 ♦, 1 ♦♦♦, 2 ♦♦♦♦
Teaching Hospital
  Conway Medical Center
Score: 64.3   Rank: 127

Montgomery, AL
Office-Based Physicians

120 Generalists	▪▪□□□
174 Specialists	▪▪▪□□
159 Surgeons	▪▪▪▪□

Short-Term General Hospitals: 9 (1,340 beds)
JCAHO Accredited: 8
Hospital Services: 4 ♦, 2 ♦♦♦, 3 ♦♦♦♦
Teaching Hospital
  Baptist Medical Center
Score: 59.49   Rank: 144

★ Montreal, PQ
Office-Based Physicians

3,100 Generalists	▪▪▪▪▪
2,600 Specialists	▪▪▪▪▪
1,200 Surgeons	▪▪□□□

Short-Term General Hospitals: 40 (12,147 beds)
CCHFA Accredited: 31
Teaching Hospitals
  Centre Hospitalier de Verdun
  Cite de la Sante de Laval
  Hopital Charles LeMoyne
  Hopital du Sacre-Coeur de Montreal
  Hopital General LaSalle
  Hopital Maisonneuve-Rosemont
  Hopital Notre-Dame
  Hopital Saint-Luc
  Hopital Sainte-Justing
  Institut de Cardiologie de Montreal
  Mount Sinai Hospital
  Queen Elizabeth Hospital
  Royal Victoria Hospital
  Shriners Hospital for Crippled Children
  Sir Mortimer Davis-Jewish General Hospital
  The Montreal Children's Hospital
  The Montreal General Hospital
Score: 98.58   Rank: 6

Muncie, IN
Office-Based Physicians

63 Generalists	▪▪▪▪□
69 Specialists	▪▪▪□□
50 Surgeons	▪▪▪□□

Short-Term General Hospitals: 1 (430 beds)
JCAHO Accredited: 1
Hospital Services: 1 ♦♦♦♦
Teaching Hospital
  Ball Memorial Hospital
Score: 35.69   Rank: 228

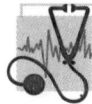

Myrtle Beach, SC
Office-Based Physicians
63 Generalists	■■□□□
65 Specialists	■■□□□
68 Surgeons	■■□□□

Short-Term General Hospitals: 3 (413 beds)
JCAHO Accredited: 3
Hospital Services: 1 ♦♦♦, 2 ♦♦♦♦
Score: 10.76　　　　　Rank: 316

Naples, FL
Office-Based Physicians
67 Generalists	■■□□□
125 Specialists	■■■■□
102 Surgeons	■■■■□

Short-Term General Hospitals: 1 (434 beds)
JCAHO Accredited: 1
Hospital Services: 1 ♦♦♦♦
Score: 21.81　　　　　Rank: 277

Nashua, NH
Office-Based Physicians
57 Generalists	■□□□□
99 Specialists	■■■□□
78 Surgeons	■■■□□

Short-Term General Hospitals: 2 (386 beds)
JCAHO Accredited: 2
Hospital Services: 2 ♦♦♦♦
Score: 8.78　　　　　Rank: 323

Nashville, TN
Office-Based Physicians
373 Generalists	■■□□□
893 Specialists	■■■■■
721 Surgeons	■■■■■

Short-Term General Hospitals: 19 (4,572 beds)
JCAHO Accredited: 17
Hospital Services: 4 ♦, 15 ♦♦♦♦
Teaching Hospitals
Baptist Hospital
George Hubbard Hospital of Meharry Medical College
Metro Nashville General Hospital
St. Thomas Hospital
Vanderbilt University Hospital
Score: 86.96　　　　　Rank: 47

New Bedford, MA
Office-Based Physicians
34 Generalists	■□□□□
71 Specialists	■■□□□
52 Surgeons	■□□□□

Score: 0　　　　　Rank: 354

New Haven-Meriden, CT
Office-Based Physicians
107 Generalists	■□□□□
579 Specialists	■■■■■
355 Surgeons	■■■■■

Short-Term General Hospitals: 2 (1289 beds)
JCAHO Accredited: 2
Hospital Services: 2 ♦♦♦♦

Teaching Hospitals
Hospital of St. Raphael
Yale-New Haven Hospital
Score: 60.05　　　　　Rank: 142

New London-Norwich, CT-RI
Office-Based Physicians
82 Generalists	■□□□□
154 Specialists	■■■□□
133 Surgeons	■■■□□

Short-Term General Hospitals: 3 (528 beds)
JCAHO Accredited: 3
Hospital Services: 3 ♦♦♦♦
Teaching Hospital
Backus Hospital
Score: 14.73　　　　　Rank: 302

★ New Orleans, LA
Office-Based Physicians
349 Generalists	■□□□□
1,113 Specialists	■■■■■
911 Surgeons	■■■■■

Short-Term General Hospitals: 26 (5,808 beds)
JCAHO Accredited: 25
Hospital Services: 7 ♦, 1 ♦♦♦, 18 ♦♦♦♦
Teaching Hospitals
Children's Hospital
East Jefferson General Hospital
Meadowcrest Hospital
Medical Center of Louisiana
Memorial Medical Center
Touro Infirmary
Tulane Hospital for Children
Tulane University Hospital
Score: 91.5　　　　　Rank: 31

★ New York, NY
Office-Based Physicians
1,468 Generalists	■□□□□
9,570 Specialists	■■■■■
4,885 Surgeons	■■■■■

Short-Term General Hospitals: 74 (35,240 beds)
JCAHO Accredited: 74
Hospital Services: 18 ♦, 1 ♦♦, 4 ♦♦♦, 51 ♦♦♦♦
Teaching Hospitals
Bayley Seton Hospital
Bellevue Hospital Center
Beth Israel Medical Center
Blythdale Children's Hospital
Bronx-Lebanon Hospital Center
Brookdale Hospital Medical Center
Brooklyn-Caledonian Hospital
Cabrini Medical Center
Catholic Medical Center, Brooklyn/Queens
Children's Medical Center of Brooklyn
Coney Island Hospital
Flushing Hospital Medical Center
Harlem Hospital Center
Hospital for Special Surgery
Interfaith Medical Center
Jacobi Medical Center
Jamaica Hospital

Kings County Hospital Center
Kingsbrook Jewish Medical Center
Lenox Hill Hospital
Lincoln Medical & Mental Health Center
Long Island College Hospital
Lutheran Medical Center
Maimonides Medical Center
Manhattan Eye Ear Throat Hospital
Memorial Hospital for Cancer
Metropolitan Hospital Center
Montefiore Medical Center
Mt. Sinai Hospital
Mt. Vernon Hospital
New York Eye and Ear Infirmary
New York Hospital
New York Hospital Medical Center of Queens
New York Infirmary Beekman
New York Methodist Hospital
North Central Bronx Hospital
North General Hospital
North Shore University Hospital, Forest Hills
NYU Medical Center-University Hospital
Our Lady of Mercy Medical Center
Queens Hospital Center
Rockefeller University Hospital
St. Agnes Hospital
St. Barnabas Hospital
St. Joseph's Hospital
St. Luke's-Roosevelt Hospital
St. Vincent's Hospital Medical Centers
Sound Shore Medical Center
Staten Island University Hospitals
University Hospital of Brooklyn
Westchester County Medical Center
Woodhull Medical Center
Wyckoff Heights Hospital
Score: 92.06   Rank: 29

Newark, NJ
Office-Based Physicians
| 392 Generalists |
| 1,834 Specialists |
| 1,127 Surgeons |

Short-Term General Hospitals: 23 (9,998 beds)
JCAHO Accredited: 22
Hospital Services: 1 1 ♦♦♦, 12 ♦♦♦♦
Teaching Hospitals
Children's Hospital of New Jersey
Children's Specialized Hospital
Elizabeth General Medical Center
Hospital Center at Orange
Morristown Memorial Hospital
Mountainside Hospital
Newark Beth Israel Medical Center
Overlook Hospital
St. Barnabas Medical Center
St. Clare's Riverside Medical Center
St. Elizabeth Hospital
St. James Hospital
St. Michael's Medical Center
University Hospital
Warren Hospital
Score: 88.38   Rank: 42

Newburgh, NY-PA
Office-Based Physicians
| 59 Generalists |
| 181 Specialists |
| 123 Surgeons |

Short-Term General Hospitals: 7 (942 beds)
JCAHO Accredited: 7
Hospital Services: 1 ♦, 3 ♦♦♦, 3 ♦♦♦♦
Teaching Hospitals
Horton Memorial Hospital
Score: 18.41   Rank: 288

Norfolk-Virginia Beach-Newport News, VA-NC
Office-Based Physicians
| 588 Generalists |
| 470 Specialists |
| 428 Surgeons |

Short-Term General Hospitals: 12 (2,774 beds)
JCAHO Accredited: 12
Hospital Services: 5 ♦, 7 ♦♦♦♦
Teaching Hospitals
Bon Secours-Depaul Medical Center
Children's Hospital King's Daughters
Leigh Hospital
Maryview Medical Center/Portsmouth General
Norfolk General Hospital
Riverside Regional Medical Center
Virginia Beach General Hospital
Score: 23.79   Rank: 270

Oakland, CA
Office-Based Physicians
| 791 Generalists |
| 1,546 Specialists |
| 939 Surgeons |

Short-Term General Hospitals: 20 (4,093 beds)
JCAHO Accredited: 19
Hospital Services: 7 ♦, 1 ♦♦, 1 ♦♦♦, 11 ♦♦♦♦
Teaching Hospitals
Alameda County Medical Center
Children's Hospital Medical Center
Kaiser Foundation Hospital
Score: 56.94   Rank: 153

Ocala, FL
Office-Based Physicians
| 80 Generalists |
| 104 Specialists |
| 88 Surgeons |

Short-Term General Hospitals: 2 (535 beds)
JCAHO Accredited: 2
Hospital Services: 2 ♦♦♦♦
Score: 4.81   Rank: 337

Odessa-Midland, TX
Office-Based Physicians
| 58 Generalists |
| 107 Specialists |
| 97 Surgeons |

Short-Term General Hospitals: 3 (683 beds)
JCAHO Accredited: 2
Hospital Services: 1 ♦♦♦, 2 ♦♦♦♦

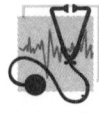

Teaching Hospital
  Medical Center Hospital
  Score: 7.36   Rank: 328

Oklahoma City, OK
Office-Based Physicians
436 Generalists	
542 Specialists	
482 Surgeons	

Short-Term General Hospitals: 19 (3,756 beds)
  JCAHO Accredited: 15
Hospital Services: 1 ♦, 1 ♦♦♦, 17 ♦♦♦♦
Teaching Hospitals
  Baptist Medical Center
  Bone and Joint Hospital
  Children's Hospital of Oklahoma
  Columbia Presbyterian Hospital
  JD McCarty Center
  St. Anthony Hospital
  University Hospital
  Score: 63.73   Rank: 129

Olympia, WA
Office-Based Physicians
122 Generalists	
87 Specialists	
82 Surgeons	

Short-Term General Hospitals: 2 (431 beds)
  JCAHO Accredited: 2
Hospital Services: 2 ♦♦♦♦
Teaching Hospitals
  Providence St. Peter Hospital
  Score: 31.72   Rank: 241

★ Omaha, NE-IA
Office-Based Physicians
408 Generalists	
429 Specialists	
373 Surgeons	

Short-Term General Hospitals: 12 (2,926 beds)
  JCAHO Accredited: 12
Hospital Services: 12 ♦♦♦♦
Teaching Hospitals
  Archbishop Bergan Mercy Medical Center
  Boys Town Institute
  Children's Memorial Hospital
  Clarkson Bishop Memorial Hospital
  Methodist Richard Young
  St. Joseph Hospital
  University of Nebraska Medical Center
  Score: 94.61   Rank: 20

Orange County, CA
Office-Based Physicians
1,376 Generalists	
1,816 Specialists	
1,338 Surgeons	

Short-Term General Hospitals: 32 (5,832 beds)
  JCAHO Accredited: 31
Hospital Services: 12 ♦♦♦, 20 ♦♦♦♦

Teaching Hospitals
  Children's Hospital at Mission
  Children's Hospital of Orange County
  Kaiser Foundation Hospital Anaheim
  St. Joseph Hospital
  Tustin Hospital and Medical Center
  University of California Irvine Medical Center
  Western Medical Center
  Score: 82.15   Rank: 64

Orlando, FL
Office-Based Physicians
592 Generalists	
748 Specialists	
647 Surgeons	

Short-Term General Hospitals: 13 (4,607 beds)
  JCAHO Accredited: 13
Hospital Services: 4 ♦, 1 ♦♦♦, 8 ♦♦♦♦
Teaching Hospitals
  Arnold Palmer Hospital for Women & Children
  Florida Hospital
  Orlando Regional Medical Center
  Score: 57.79   Rank: 150

Oshawa, ON
Office-Based Physicians
197 Generalists	
76 Specialists	
68 Surgeons	

Short-Term General Hospitals: 2 (685 beds)
  CCHFA Accredited: 2
  Score: 15.58   Rank: 299

★ Ottawa-Hull, ON-PQ
Office-Based Physicians
1,215 Generalists	
892 Specialists	
398 Surgeons	

Short-Term General Hospitals: 11 (3,240 beds)
  CCHFA Accredited: 10
Teaching Hospitals
  Centre Hospitalier de Gatineau
  Children's Hospital of Eastern Ontario
  Hopital Montfort
  Ottawa Civic Hospital
  Ottawa General Hospital
  Riverside Hospital
  Score: 95.18   Rank: 18

Owensboro, KY
Office-Based Physicians
28 Generalists	
50 Specialists	
53 Surgeons	

Short-Term General Hospitals: 1 (380 beds)
  JCAHO Accredited: 1
Hospital Services: 1 ♦♦♦♦
  Score: 21.52   Rank: 278

Panama City, FL
Office-Based Physicians

36 Generalists	
59 Specialists	
71 Surgeons	

Short-Term General Hospitals: 3 (516 beds)
JCAHO Accredited: 3
Hospital Services: 1 ◆, 2 ◆◆◆
Score: 12.18   Rank: 311

Parkersburg-Marietta, WV-OH
Office-Based Physicians

64 Generalists	
50 Specialists	
51 Surgeons	

Short-Term General Hospitals: 4 (754 beds)
JCAHO Accredited: 3
Hospital Services: 4 ◆◆◆◆
Score: 16.99   Rank: 294

Pensacola, FL
Office-Based Physicians

172 Generalists	
186 Specialists	
176 Surgeons	

Short-Term General Hospitals: 7 (1,906 beds)
JCAHO Accredited: 6
Hospital Services: 2 ◆◆◆, 5 ◆◆◆◆
Teaching Hospital
  Sacred Heart Hospital
Score: 56.65   Rank: 154

Peoria-Pekin, IL
Office-Based Physicians

152 Generalists	
185 Specialists	
133 Surgeons	

Short-Term General Hospitals: 5 (1,278 beds)
JCAHO Accredited: 4
Hospital Services: 1 ◆, 4 ◆◆◆◆
Teaching Hospitals
  Methodist Medical Center
  Saint Francis Medical Center
Score: 39.66   Rank: 214

Philadelphia, PA-NJ
Office-Based Physicians

1,590 Generalists	
4,113 Specialists	
2,607 Surgeons	

Short-Term General Hospitals: 67 (17,353 beds)
JCAHO Accredited: 57
Hospital Services: 11 ◆, 1 ◆◆, 5 ◆◆◆, 50 ◆◆◆◆
Teaching Hospitals
  Abington Memorial Hospital
  Albert Einstein Medical Center
  Allegheny University Hospitals
  Chestnut Hill Hospital
  Children's Hospital of Philadelphia
  Cooper Hospital/University Medical Center
  Crozer Chester Medical Center
  Deborah Heart & Lung Center
  Delaware County Memorial Hospital

Episcopal Hospital
Frankford Hospital
Hahnemann University Hospital
Main Line Hospitals
Memorial Hospital-Burlington County
Mercy Catholic Medical Centers
Methodist Hospital
Montgomery Hospital
Our Lady of Lourdes Medical Center
Pennsylvania Hospital
Presbyterian-University of Pennsylvania Medical Center
St. Agnes Medical Center
St. Christopher's Hospital for Children
Scheie Eye Institute
Shriners Hospital for Children
Temple University Children's Medical Center
Temple University Hospital
Thomas Jefferson University Hospital
Underwood Memorial Hospital
West Jersey Hospital
Wills Eye Hospital
Score: 85.55   Rank: 52

Phoenix-Mesa, AZ
Office-Based Physicians

1,098 Generalists	
1,337 Specialists	
1,119 Surgeons	

Short-Term General Hospitals: 31 (7,054 beds)
JCAHO Accredited: 30
Hospital Services: 7 ◆, 2 ◆◆◆, 22 ◆◆◆◆
Teaching Hospitals
  Children's Rehabilitative Services
  Good Samaritan Regional Medical Center
  Hacienda De Los Ninos
  Maricopa Medical Center
  Phoenix Baptist Hospital & Medical Center
  St. Joseph's Hospital Medical Center
Score: 51.55   Rank: 172

Pine Bluff, AR
Office-Based Physicians

45 Generalists	
39 Specialists	
37 Surgeons	

Short-Term General Hospitals: 1 (487 beds)
JCAHO Accredited: 1
Hospital Services: 1 ◆◆◆◆
Teaching Hospital
  Jefferson Regional Medical Center
Score: 39.09   Rank: 216

★ Pittsburgh, PA
Office-Based Physicians

1,030 Generalists	
1,808 Specialists	
1,297 Surgeons	

Short-Term General Hospitals: 35 (10,289 beds)
JCAHO Accredited: 34
Hospital Services: 4 ◆, 1 ◆◆, 4 ◆◆◆, 26 ◆◆◆◆
Teaching Hospitals
  Allegheny General Hospital
  Children's Hospital of Pittsburgh

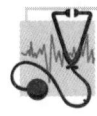

Children's Home of Pittsburgh
Forbes Regional Hospital
Latrobe Area Hospital
Magee-Womens Hospital
Medical Center, Beaver
Mercy Hospital, Pittsburgh
St. Francis Medical Center
University of Pittsburgh Medical Center
University of Pittsburgh Presbyterian Hospital
University of Pittsburgh Shadyside Hospital
University of Pittsburgh South Side Hospital
University of Pittsburgh St. Margaret Hospital
Washington Hospital
Western Pennsylvania Hospital
Westmoreland Regional Hospital
Score: 94.05   Rank: 22

Pittsfield, MA
Office-Based Physicians

23 Generalists	▨□□□□
72 Specialists	▨▨▨▨▨
45 Surgeons	▨▨▨▨□

Short-Term General Hospitals: 1 (244 beds)
   JCAHO Accredited: 1
Hospital Services: 1 ♦ ♦ ♦
Teaching Hospital
   Berkshire Medical Center
Score: 30.31   Rank: 247

Pocatello, ID
Office-Based Physicians

35 Generalists	▨▨▨□□
31 Specialists	▨▨□□□
37 Surgeons	▨▨▨▨□

Short-Term General Hospitals: 2 (328 beds)
   JCAHO Accredited: 2
Hospital Services: 2 ♦ ♦ ♦
Teaching Hospitals
   Bannock Memorial Hospital
   Pocatello Regional Medical Center
Score: 40.79   Rank: 210

Portland, ME
Office-Based Physicians

125 Generalists	▨▨▨▨□
190 Specialists	▨▨▨▨▨
143 Surgeons	▨▨▨▨▨

Short-Term General Hospitals: 3 (739 beds)
   JCAHO Accredited: 3
Hospital Services: 3 ♦ ♦ ♦
Teaching Hospitals
   Jackson Brook Institute
   Maine Medical Center
   Mercy Hospital
Score: 75.35   Rank: 88

Portland-Vancouver, OR-WA
Office-Based Physicians

688 Generalists	▨▨□□□
1,169 Specialists	▨▨▨▨□
845 Surgeons	▨▨▨▨□

Short-Term General Hospitals: 19 (4,132 beds)
   JCAHO Accredited: 18

Hospital Services: 1 ♦ , 5 ♦ ♦ ♦ , 13 ♦ ♦ ♦ ♦
Teaching Hospitals
   Emanuel Hospital & Health Center
   Good Samaritan Hospital & Medical Center
   Kaiser Foundation Hospitals
   Oregon Health Sciences University Hospital & Clinics
   Providence Portland Medical Center
   Providence St. Vincent Medical Center
   Shriners Hospital for Children
   SW Washington Medical Center
Score: 65.15   Rank: 124

Portsmouth-Rochester, NH-ME
Office-Based Physicians

86 Generalists	▨▨□□□
89 Specialists	▨□□□□
84 Surgeons	▨▨□□□

Short-Term General Hospitals: 5 (618 beds)
   JCAHO Accredited: 5
Hospital Services: 5 ♦ ♦ ♦
Score: 17.28   Rank: 293

Providence-Fall River-Warwick, RI-MA
Office-Based Physicians

263 Generalists	▨□□□□
806 Specialists	▨▨▨▨□
548 Surgeons	▨▨▨▨□

Short-Term General Hospitals: 11 (2722 beds)
   JCAHO Accredited: 11
Hospital Services: 11 ♦ ♦ ♦
Teaching Hospitals
   Butler Hospital
   Eleanor Slater Hospital
   Emma Pendleton Bradley Hospital
   Memorial Hospital, Rhode Island
   Miriam Hospital
   Rhode Island Hospital
   Roger Williams Hospital
   Women and Infants Hospital
Score: 47.3   Rank: 187

Provo-Orem, UT
Office-Based Physicians

129 Generalists	▨▨▨□□
86 Specialists	▨□□□□
109 Surgeons	▨□□□□

Short-Term General Hospitals: 4 (556 beds)
   JCAHO Accredited: 3
Hospital Services: 2 ♦ ♦ ♦ , 2 ♦ ♦ ♦ ♦
Teaching Hospital
   Utah Valley Regional Medical Center
Score: 3.68   Rank: 341

Pueblo, CO
Office-Based Physicians

89 Generalists	▨▨▨▨▨
68 Specialists	▨▨▨□□
64 Surgeons	▨▨▨▨□

Short-Term General Hospitals: 2 (520 beds)
   JCAHO Accredited: 2
Hospital Services: 1 ♦ , 1 ♦ ♦ ♦ ♦

Teaching Hospital
St. Mary Corwin Medical Center
Score: 58.64   Rank: 147

Punta Gorda, FL
Office-Based Physicians

32 Generalists	■□□□□
84 Specialists	■■■■□
56 Surgeons	■■■□□

Short-Term General Hospitals: 3 (710 beds)
JCAHO Accredited: 3
Hospital Services: 1 ◆, 2 ◆◆◆◆
Score: 23.22   Rank: 272

★ Quebec City, PQ
Office-Based Physicians

780 Generalists	■■■■■
612 Specialists	■■■■■
342 Surgeons	■■■■□

Short-Term General Hospitals: 12 (4,040 beds)
CCHFA Accredited: 11
Teaching Hospitals
Centre Hospitalier de l'Universite Laval
Hopital du Saint-Sacrement
Hopital Laval
Hopital Saint-Francois d'Assisse
Hotel Dieu de Levis
Hotel Dieu de Quebec
Score: 99.71   Rank: 2

Racine, WI
Office-Based Physicians

64 Generalists	■■□□□
69 Specialists	■□□□□
67 Surgeons	■■□□□

Short-Term General Hospitals: 3 (496 beds)
JCAHO Accredited: 3
Hospital Services: 1 ◆, 2 ◆◆◆◆
Teaching Hospitals
St. Luke's Hospital
St. Mary's Medical Center
Score: 7.64   Rank: 327

★ Raleigh-Durham-Chapel Hill, NC
Office-Based Physicians

525 Generalists	■■■■□
922 Specialists	■■■■■
641 Surgeons	■■■■■

Short-Term General Hospitals: 10 (3,745 beds)
JCAHO Accredited: 10
Hospital Services: 2 ◆, 1 ◆◆◆, 7 ◆◆◆◆
Teaching Hospitals
Dorothea Dix Hospital
Duke University Hospital
Durham Regional Hospital
University of North Carolina Hospital
Wake Medical Center
Score: 93.48   Rank: 24

Rapid City, SD
Office-Based Physicians

50 Generalists	■■■■□
57 Specialists	■■■□□
54 Surgeons	■■■■■

Short-Term General Hospitals: 2 (392 beds)
JCAHO Accredited: 2
Hospital Services: 2 ◆◆◆◆
Teaching Hospital
Rapid City Regional Hospital
Score: 51.27   Rank: 173

Reading, PA
Office-Based Physicians

182 Generalists	■■■■□
148 Specialists	■■□□□
145 Surgeons	■■□□□

Short-Term General Hospitals: 3 (885 beds)
JCAHO Accredited: 3
Hospital Services: 1 ◆, 2 ◆◆◆◆
Teaching Hospitals
Reading Hospital Medical Center
St. Joseph Medical Center
Score: 26.62   Rank: 260

Redding, CA
Office-Based Physicians

104 Generalists	■■■■■
72 Specialists	■■□□□
81 Surgeons	■■■■□

Short-Term General Hospitals: 3 (454 beds)
JCAHO Accredited: 2
Hospital Services: 1 ◆, 2 ◆◆◆◆
Teaching Hospital
Mercy Medical Center
Score: 43.05   Rank: 202

Regina, SK
Office-Based Physicians

235 Generalists	■■■■■
90 Specialists	■■□□□
78 Surgeons	■■□□□

Short-Term General Hospitals: 3 (729 beds)
CCHFA Accredited: 3
Teaching Hospitals
Plains Health Center
Regina General Hospital
Royal University Hospital
Score: 83.85   Rank: 57

Reno, NV
Office-Based Physicians

155 Generalists	■■■■□
163 Specialists	■■■□□
181 Surgeons	■■■■■

Short-Term General Hospitals: 4 (1,054 beds)
JCAHO Accredited: 4
Hospital Services: 4 ◆◆◆◆
Teaching Hospital
Washoe Medical Center
Score: 66   Rank: 121

Health Care

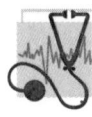

Richland-Kennewick-Pasco, WA

Office-Based Physicians

87 Generalists	
73 Specialists	
56 Surgeons	

Short-Term General Hospitals: 4 (376 beds)
 JCAHO Accredited: 3
Hospital Services: 1 ♦♦, 3 ♦♦♦♦
Score: 10.19   Rank: 318

★ Richmond-Petersburg, VA

Office-Based Physicians

494 Generalists	
673 Specialists	
482 Surgeons	

Short-Term General Hospitals: 13 (4,250 beds)
 JCAHO Accredited: 13
Hospital Services: 1 ♦, 3 ♦♦♦, 9 ♦♦♦♦
Teaching Hospitals
 Children's Hospital
 Chippenham Medical Center
 MCV Virginia Treatment Center for Children
 Medical College of Virginia Hospitals
 St. Mary's Hospital, Richmond
Score: 83.85   Rank: 57

Riverside-San Bernardino, CA

Office-Based Physicians

1,056 Generalists	
1,067 Specialists	
858 Surgeons	

Short-Term General Hospitals: 36 (6,364 beds)
 JCAHO Accredited: 34
Hospital Services: 13 ♦, 3 ♦♦♦, 20 ♦♦♦♦
Teaching Hospitals
 Kaiser Foundation Hospitals
 Loma Linda University Medical Center
 San Bernardino County Medical Center
Score: 31.72   Rank: 241

Roanoke, VA

Office-Based Physicians

129 Generalists	
163 Specialists	
163 Surgeons	

Short-Term General Hospitals: 4 (1,597 beds)
 JCAHO Accredited: 4
Hospital Services: 1 ♦, 3 ♦♦♦♦
Teaching Hospital
 Carilion Medical Center
Score: 90.08   Rank: 36

Rochester, MN

Office-Based Physicians

72 Generalists	
481 Specialists	
217 Surgeons	

Short-Term General Hospitals: 3 (1,181 beds)
 JCAHO Accredited: 3
Hospital Services: 1 ♦♦, 2 ♦♦♦♦
Teaching Hospitals
 Mayo Clinic
 Rochester Methodist Hospital
 St. Mary's Hospital
Score: 89.23   Rank: 39

Rochester, NY

Office-Based Physicians

281 Generalists	
922 Specialists	
520 Surgeons	

Short-Term General Hospitals: 17 (4,088 beds)
 JCAHO Accredited: 17
Hospital Services: 4 ♦, 2 ♦♦♦, 11 ♦♦♦♦
Teaching Hospitals
 Genesee Hospital
 Geneva General Hospital
 Highland Hospital
 Rochester General Hospital
 St. Mary's Hospital
 Strong Memorial Hospital
 Thompson Hospital
Score: 73.37   Rank: 95

Rockford, IL

Office-Based Physicians

188 Generalists	
191 Specialists	
130 Surgeons	

Short-Term General Hospitals: 6 (1,084 beds)
 JCAHO Accredited: 6
Hospital Services: 1 ♦, 1 ♦♦, 1 ♦♦♦, 3 ♦♦♦♦
Teaching Hospitals
 St. Anthony Medical Center
 Swedish American Hospital
Score: 54.67   Rank: 161

Rocky Mount, NC

Office-Based Physicians

55 Generalists	
56 Specialists	
49 Surgeons	

Short-Term General Hospitals: 3 (416 beds)
 JCAHO Accredited: 3
Hospital Services: 1 ♦, 2 ♦♦♦♦
Score: 9.63   Rank: 320

Sacramento, CA

Office-Based Physicians

672 Generalists	
826 Specialists	
667 Surgeons	

Short-Term General Hospitals: 13 (3,143 beds)
 JCAHO Accredited: 13
Hospital Services: 5 ♦, 1 ♦♦♦, 7 ♦♦♦♦
Teaching Hospitals
 Kaiser Foundation Hospitals
 Methodist Hospital
 Sutter Community Hospitals
 University of California Davis Medical Center
Score: 59.2   Rank: 145

Saginaw-Bay City-Midland, MI
Office-Based Physicians

203 Generalists	▮▮▮▯▯
156 Specialists	▮▯▯▯▯
135 Surgeons	▮▮▯▯▯

Short-Term General Hospitals: 6 (1,565 beds)
JCAHO Accredited: 6
Hospital Services: 6 ♦♦♦♦
Teaching Hospitals
　Mid-Michigan Regional Medical Center
　Saginaw General Hospital
　St. Luke's Hospital
　St. Mary's Medical Center
Score: 46.74　　　　　Rank: 189

St. Catharines-Niagara, ON
Office-Based Physicians

310 Generalists	▮▮▮▮▮
129 Specialists	▮▯▯▯▯
105 Surgeons	▮▯▯▯▯

Short-Term General Hospitals: 7 (1,334 beds)
CCHFA Accredited: 7
Score: 62.6　　　　　Rank: 133

St. Cloud, MN
Office-Based Physicians

114 Generalists	▮▮▮▮▮
66 Specialists	▮▮▯▯▯
69 Surgeons	▮▮▮▯▯

Short-Term General Hospitals: 4 (530 beds)
JCAHO Accredited: 1
Hospital Services: 1 ♦♦, 3 ♦♦♦♦
Teaching Hospital
　St. Cloud Hospital
Score: 37.11　　　　　Rank: 223

Saint John, NB
Office-Based Physicians

98 Generalists	▮▮▮▮▮
61 Specialists	▮▮▯▯▯
48 Surgeons	▮▮▯▯▯

Short-Term General Hospitals: 2 (709 beds)
CCHFA Accredited: 2
Teaching Hospital
　Saint John Regional Hospital
Score: 61.18　　　　　Rank: 138

★ St. John's, NF
Office-Based Physicians

196 Generalists	▮▮▮▮▮
156 Specialists	▮▮▮▮▮
75 Surgeons	▮▮▮▯▯

Short-Term General Hospitals: 4 (1,100 beds)
CCHFA Accredited: 4
Teaching Hospitals
　Charles Janeway Child Health Centre
　St. Clare's Mercy Hospital
　St. John's General Hospital
　Salvation Army Grace General Hospital
Score: 96.03　　　　　Rank: 15

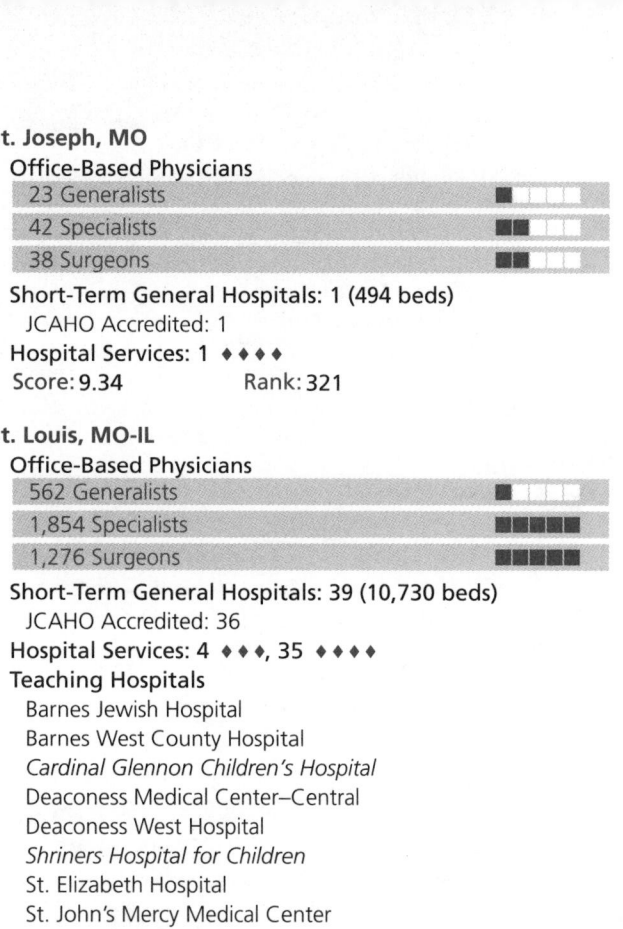

St. Joseph, MO
Office-Based Physicians

23 Generalists	▮▯▯▯▯
42 Specialists	▮▮▯▯▯
38 Surgeons	▮▮▯▯▯

Short-Term General Hospitals: 1 (494 beds)
JCAHO Accredited: 1
Hospital Services: 1 ♦♦♦♦
Score: 9.34　　　　　Rank: 321

St. Louis, MO-IL
Office-Based Physicians

562 Generalists	▮▯▯▯▯
1,854 Specialists	▮▮▮▮▮
1,276 Surgeons	▮▮▮▮▮

Short-Term General Hospitals: 39 (10,730 beds)
JCAHO Accredited: 36
Hospital Services: 4 ♦♦♦, 35 ♦♦♦♦
Teaching Hospitals
　Barnes Jewish Hospital
　Barnes West County Hospital
　Cardinal Glennon Children's Hospital
　Deaconess Medical Center–Central
　Deaconess West Hospital
　Shriners Hospital for Children
　St. Elizabeth Hospital
　St. John's Mercy Medical Center
　St. Louis Children's Hospital
　St. Louis Regional Medical Center
　St. Louis University Hospital
　St. Luke's Hospital
Score: 66.57　　　　　Rank: 119

Salem, OR
Office-Based Physicians

176 Generalists	▮▮▮▮▯
99 Specialists	▮▯▯▯▯
102 Surgeons	▮▯▯▯▯

Short-Term General Hospitals: 4 (551 beds)
JCAHO Accredited: 3
Hospital Services: 2 ♦♦♦, 2 ♦♦♦♦
Score: 9.91　　　　　Rank: 319

Salinas, CA
Office-Based Physicians

171 Generalists	▮▮▮▮▯
157 Specialists	▮▮▯▯▯
135 Surgeons	▮▮▯▯▯

Short-Term General Hospitals: 4 (574 beds)
JCAHO Accredited: 4
Hospital Services: 4 ♦♦♦♦
Teaching Hospital
　Natividad Medical Center
Score: 27.76　　　　　Rank: 256

Salt Lake City-Ogden, UT
Office-Based Physicians

445 Generalists	▮▮▯▯▯
670 Specialists	▮▮▮▯▯
603 Surgeons	▮▮▮▮▯

Short-Term General Hospitals: 14 (2,681 beds)
JCAHO Accredited: 14

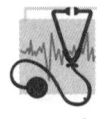

Hospital Services: 1 ♦, 2 ♦♦♦, 11 ♦♦♦♦
Teaching Hospitals
  Columbia St. Mark's Hospital
  Latter-Day Saints Hospital
  Mckay-Dee Hospital Center
  Primary Children's Medical Center
  Salt Lake Regional Medical Center
  Shriners Hospital for Children
  University of Utah Hospital
  Score: **68.83**   Rank: **111**

San Angelo, TX
  Office-Based Physicians

28 Generalists	■□□□□
54 Specialists	■■■□□
55 Surgeons	■■■■□

  Short-Term General Hospitals: 2 (472 beds)
    JCAHO Accredited: 2
  Hospital Services: 2 ♦♦♦♦
  Score: **19.26**   Rank: **286**

San Antonio, TX
  Office-Based Physicians

643 Generalists	■■■□□
798 Specialists	■■■□□
635 Surgeons	■■■□□

  Short-Term General Hospitals: 21 (6,542 beds)
    JCAHO Accredited: 16
  Hospital Services: 3 ♦, 1 ♦♦, 2 ♦♦♦, 15 ♦♦♦♦
  Teaching Hospitals
    Baptist Medical System
    Methodist Healthcare
    Nix Medical Center
    Northeastern Baptist Hospital
    San Antonio Community Hospital
    Santa Rosa Children's Hospital
    Santa Rosa Health Care Corporation
    Southwest Texas Methodist Hospital
    University Health System
  Score: **68.27**   Rank: **113**

San Diego, CA
  Office-Based Physicians

1,163 Generalists	■■■□□
1,628 Specialists	■■■■□
1,237 Surgeons	■■■□□

  Short-Term General Hospitals: 26 (6,441 beds)
    JCAHO Accredited: 26
  Hospital Services: 12 ♦, 1 ♦♦, 2 ♦♦♦, 11 ♦♦♦♦
  Teaching Hospitals
    Alvarado Hospital Medical Center
    Children's Hospital and Health Center
    Green Hospital of Scripps Clinic
    Grossmont Hospital
    Kaiser Foundation Hospital
    Mercy Hospital & Medical Center
    Sharp Chula Vista Medical Center
    Sharp Memorial Hospital
    University of California San Diego Medical Center
  Score: **68.55**   Rank: **112**

★ **San Francisco, CA**
  Office-Based Physicians

585 Generalists	■■□□□
1,998 Specialists	■■■■■
1,260 Surgeons	■■■■■

  Short-Term General Hospitals: 19 (4,882 beds)
    JCAHO Accredited: 19
  Hospital Services: 3 ♦, 1 ♦♦♦, 15 ♦♦♦♦
  Teaching Hospitals
    California Pacific Medical Center
    Davies Medical Center
    Kaiser Foundation Hospitals
    Kentfield Medical Hospital
    Mt. Zion Hospital & Medical Center
    St. Francis Memorial Hospital
    St. Mary's Hospital Medical Center
    San Francisco General Hospital
    San Mateo County General Hospital
    Seton Medical Center
    Shriners Hospital for Children
  Score: **95.46**   Rank: **17**

San Jose, CA
  Office-Based Physicians

517 Generalists	■■□□□
1,238 Specialists	■■■■■
822 Surgeons	■■■■□

  Short-Term General Hospitals: 14 (4,446 beds)
    JCAHO Accredited: 13
  Hospital Services: 7 ♦, 7 ♦♦♦♦
  Teaching Hospitals
    Kaiser Foundation Hospital
    Lucile Salter Packard Children's Hospital
    San Jose Medical Center
    Santa Clara Valley Medical Center
    Santa Teresa Community Hospital
    Stanford University Hospital
  Score: **70.53**   Rank: **105**

San Luis Obispo-Atascadero-Paso Robles, CA
  Office-Based Physicians

135 Generalists	■■■■□
114 Specialists	■■■□□
101 Surgeons	■■■□□

  Short-Term General Hospitals: 5 (406 beds)
    JCAHO Accredited: 5
  Hospital Services: 1 ♦, 3 ♦♦♦, 1 ♦♦♦♦
  Score: **45.89**   Rank: **192**

Santa Barbara-Santa Maria-Lompoc, CA
  Office-Based Physicians

197 Generalists	■■■■□
265 Specialists	■■■■□
206 Surgeons	■■■■□

  Short-Term General Hospitals: 8 (975 beds)
    JCAHO Accredited: 8
  Hospital Services: 5 ♦, 1 ♦♦♦, 2 ♦♦♦♦
  Teaching Hospital
    Santa Barbara Cottage Hospital
  Score: **71.1**   Rank: **103**

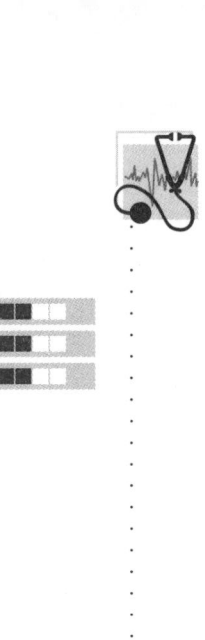

Santa Cruz-Watsonville, CA
Office-Based Physicians
179 Generalists	■■■■■
118 Specialists	■■■□□
100 Surgeons	■■■□□

Short-Term General Hospitals: 2 (414 beds)
JCAHO Accredited: 2
Hospital Services: 2 ◆◆◆
Score:37.67   Rank:221

Santa Fe, NM
Office-Based Physicians
93 Generalists	■■■■■
81 Specialists	■■■■□
72 Surgeons	■■■■□

Short-Term General Hospitals: 3 (284 beds)
JCAHO Accredited: 3
Hospital Services: 1 ◆, 2 ◆◆◆◆
Score:49.57   Rank:179

Santa Rosa, CA
Office-Based Physicians
364 Generalists	■■■■■
215 Specialists	■■■□□
204 Surgeons	■■■□□

Short-Term General Hospitals: 9 (935 beds)
JCAHO Accredited: 9
Hospital Services: 5 ◆, 2 ◆◆◆, 2 ◆◆◆◆
Teaching Hospital
  Sutter Medical Center of Santa Rosa
Score:82.43   Rank:63

Sarasota-Bradenton, FL
Office-Based Physicians
258 Generalists	■■■□□
390 Specialists	■■■■■
327 Surgeons	■■■■■

Short-Term General Hospitals: 6 (1,840 beds)
JCAHO Accredited: 6
Hospital Services: 6 ◆◆◆◆
Score:73.93   Rank:93

Saskatoon, SK
Office-Based Physicians
315 Generalists	■■■■■
185 Specialists	■■■■■
100 Surgeons	■■■□□

Short-Term General Hospitals: 2 (563 beds)
CCHFA Accredited: 2
Teaching Hospitals
  St. Paul Grey Nuns Hospital
  Saskatoon City Hospital
Score:72.8   Rank:97

Savannah, GA
Office-Based Physicians
99 Generalists	■■□□□
166 Specialists	■■■■□
167 Surgeons	■■■■■

Short-Term General Hospitals: 4 (1,159 beds)
JCAHO Accredited: 4
Hospital Services: 2 ◆, 1 ◆◆◆, 1 ◆◆◆◆

Teaching Hospital
  Memorial Medical Center
Score:52.12   Rank:170

Scranton–Wilkes-Barre–Hazleton, PA
Office-Based Physicians
311 Generalists	■■■□□
350 Specialists	■■■□□
274 Surgeons	■■■□□

Short-Term General Hospitals: 14 (3,115 beds)
JCAHO Accredited: 13
Hospital Services: 2 ◆, 2 ◆◆◆, 10 ◆◆◆◆
Teaching Hospitals
  Community Medical Center
  Mercy Hospital
  Moses Taylor Hospital
  Wilkes-Barre General Hospital
  Wyoming Valley Medical Center Hospital
Score:80.45   Rank:70

Seattle-Bellevue-Everett, WA
Office-Based Physicians
1,608 Generalists	■■■■■
1,480 Specialists	■■■■□
1,177 Surgeons	■■■■□

Short-Term General Hospitals: 24 (4,505 beds)
JCAHO Accredited: 22
Hospital Services: 5 ◆, 1 ◆◆, 3 ◆◆◆, 15 ◆◆◆◆
Teaching Hospitals
  Children's Hospital & Regional Medical Center
  Fred Hutchinson Cancer Research Center
  Group Health Eastside Hospital
  Harborview Medical Center
  Northwest Hospital
  Providence Seattle Medical Center
  Swedish Medical Center
  University of Washington Medical Center
  Valley Medical Center
  Virginia Mason Medical Center
Score:87.25   Rank:46

Sharon, PA
Office-Based Physicians
38 Generalists	■□□□□
39 Specialists	■□□□□
49 Surgeons	■■□□□

Short-Term General Hospitals: 3 (604 beds)
JCAHO Accredited: 3
Hospital Services: 1 ◆, 2 ◆◆◆◆
Score:14.44   Rank:303

Sheboygan, WI
Office-Based Physicians
53 Generalists	■■■□□
35 Specialists	■□□□□
36 Surgeons	■□□□□

Short-Term General Hospitals: 3 (314 beds)
JCAHO Accredited: 3
Hospital Services: 3 ◆◆◆◆
Teaching Hospital
  St. Luke's Medical Center
Score:11.61   Rank:313

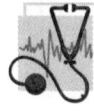

★ Sherbrooke, PQ
Office-Based Physicians

172 Generalists	■■■■■
168 Specialists	■■■■■
88 Surgeons	■■■■■

Short-Term General Hospitals: 5 (1,613 beds)
CCHFA Accredited: 5
Teaching Hospitals
Centre Hospitalier Hotel Dieu de Sherbrooke
Centre Hospitalier St. Vincent de Paul
Centre Hospitalier Universitaire de Sherbrooke
Hopital d'Youville de Sherbrooke
Pasqua Hospital
Score: 99.43   Rank: 3

Sherman-Denison, TX
Office-Based Physicians

42 Generalists	■■■□□
54 Specialists	■■■□□
49 Surgeons	■■■■□

Short-Term General Hospitals: 3 (562 beds)
JCAHO Accredited: 3
Hospital Services: 3◆◆◆◆
Score: 36.26   Rank: 226

Shreveport-Bossier City, LA
Office-Based Physicians

150 Generalists	■■■□□
270 Specialists	■■■■□
246 Surgeons	■■■■■

Short-Term General Hospitals: 12 (2,215 beds)
JCAHO Accredited: 11
Hospital Services: 6◆, 2◆◆◆, 4◆◆◆◆
Teaching Hospitals
Louisiana State University Hospital
Schumpert Medical Center
Shriners Hospital for Children
Willis Knighton Medical Center
Score: 89.8   Rank: 37

Sioux City, IA-NE
Office-Based Physicians

70 Generalists	■■■■□
47 Specialists	■□□□□
52 Surgeons	■■■□□

Short-Term General Hospitals: 2 (459 beds)
JCAHO Accredited: 2
Hospital Services: 2◆◆◆◆
Teaching Hospitals
Marian Health Center
St. Luke's Regional Medical Center
Score: 41.07   Rank: 209

★ Sioux Falls, SD
Office-Based Physicians

127 Generalists	■■■■■
126 Specialists	■■■■■
107 Surgeons	■■■■■

Short-Term General Hospitals: 5 (1,231 beds)
JCAHO Accredited: 3
Hospital Services: 1◆◆, 1◆◆◆, 3◆◆◆◆

Teaching Hospitals
Canton-Inwood Memorial Hospital
Dell Rapids Community Hospital
Mckennan Hospital
Sioux Falls Surgical Center Llp
Sioux Valley Hospital
Score: 93.76   Rank: 23

South Bend, IN
Office-Based Physicians

172 Generalists	■■■■■
105 Specialists	■■□□□
100 Surgeons	■■□□□

Short-Term General Hospitals: 4 (886 beds)
JCAHO Accredited: 3
Hospital Services: 1◆, 3◆◆◆◆
Teaching Hospitals
Memorial Hospital of South Bend
St. Joseph's Medical Center
Score: 56.09   Rank: 156

Spokane, WA
Office-Based Physicians

268 Generalists	■■■■■
222 Specialists	■■■□□
201 Surgeons	■■■■□

Short-Term General Hospitals: 7 (1,493 beds)
JCAHO Accredited: 6
Hospital Services: 5◆, 2◆◆◆◆
Teaching Hospitals
Deaconess Medical Center
Sacred Heart Medical Center
Shriners Hospital for Children
Score: 80.16   Rank: 71

Springfield, IL
Office-Based Physicians

89 Generalists	■■■□□
181 Specialists	■■■■■
143 Surgeons	■■■■■

Short-Term General Hospitals: 3 (1,185 beds)
JCAHO Accredited: 3
Hospital Services: 1◆, 2◆◆◆◆
Teaching Hospitals
Memorial Medical Center
St. John's Hospital
Score: 84.41   Rank: 56

Springfield, MA
Office-Based Physicians

145 Generalists	■□□□□
437 Specialists	■■■■■
258 Surgeons	■■■□□

Short-Term General Hospitals: 8 (1547 beds)
JCAHO Accredited: 8
Hospital Services: 1◆◆, 7◆◆◆◆
Teaching Hospital
Baystate Medical Center
Shriners Hospital for Children
Score: 42.77   Rank: 203

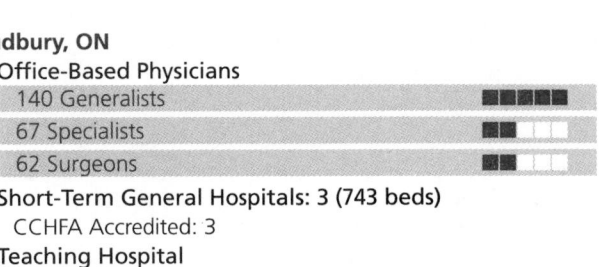

Springfield, MO
Office-Based Physicians
117 Generalists	■■■□□
182 Specialists	■■■■□
160 Surgeons	■■■■□

Short-Term General Hospitals: 3 (1,684 beds)
JCAHO Accredited: 3
Hospital Services: 3 ♦♦♦
Teaching Hospitals
  Cox Medical Center
  Cox Walnut Lawn
Score: 58.07   Rank: 149

Stamford-Norwalk, CT
Office-Based Physicians
84 Generalists	■□□□□
361 Specialists	■■■■■
220 Surgeons	■■■■■

Short-Term General Hospitals: 4 (865 beds)
JCAHO Accredited: 4
Hospital Services: 4 ♦♦♦♦
Teaching Hospitals
  Greenwich Hospital
  Norwalk Hospital
  St. Joseph Medical Center
  Stamford Hospital
Score: 76.2   Rank: 85

State College, PA
Office-Based Physicians
54 Generalists	■■■□□
53 Specialists	■■□□□
50 Surgeons	■■□□□

Short-Term General Hospitals: 1 (167 beds)
JCAHO Accredited: 1
Hospital Services: 1 ♦♦♦♦
Score: 3.11   Rank: 343

Steubenville-Weirton, OH-WV
Office-Based Physicians
31 Generalists	■□□□□
51 Specialists	■□□□□
34 Surgeons	■□□□□

Short-Term General Hospitals: 2 (773 beds)
JCAHO Accredited: 2
Hospital Services: 1 ♦, 1 ♦♦♦♦
Score: 7.93   Rank: 326

Stockton-Lodi, CA
Office-Based Physicians
186 Generalists	■■□□□
213 Specialists	■■□□□
151 Surgeons	■□□□□

Short-Term General Hospitals: 7 (1,060 beds)
JCAHO Accredited: 6
Hospital Services: 1 ♦, 1 ♦♦♦, 5 ♦♦♦♦
Teaching Hospital
  San Joaquin General Hospital
Score: 16.14   Rank: 297

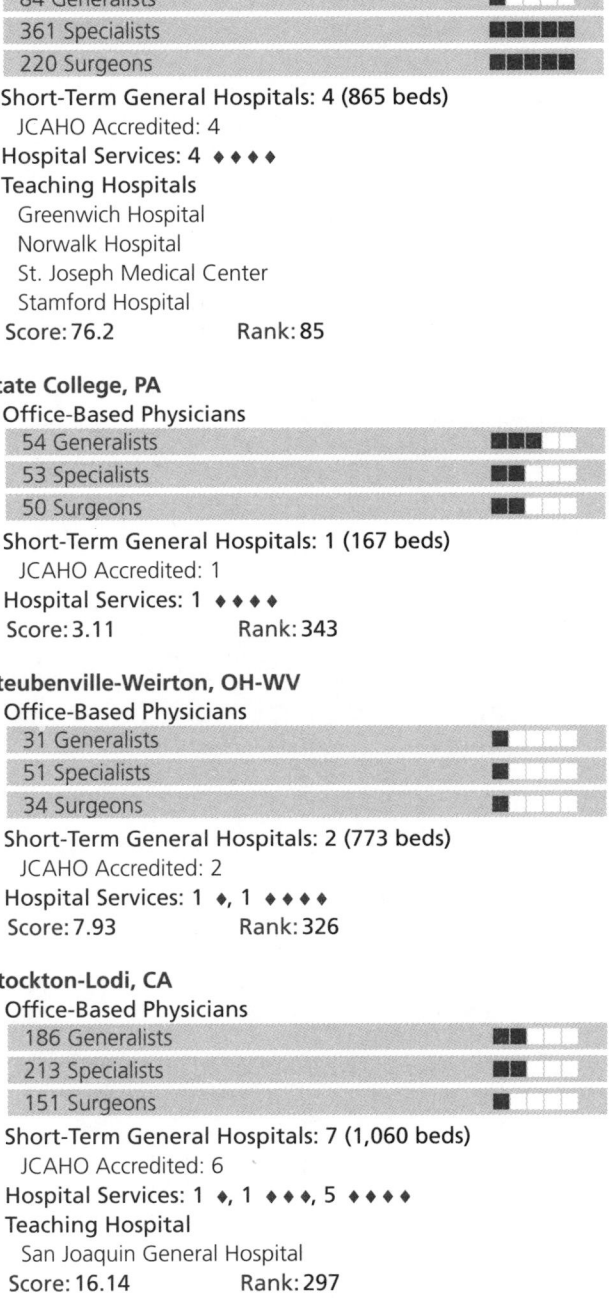

Sudbury, ON
Office-Based Physicians
140 Generalists	■■■■■
67 Specialists	■■□□□
62 Surgeons	■■□□□

Short-Term General Hospitals: 3 (743 beds)
CCHFA Accredited: 3
Teaching Hospital
  Sudbury General Hospital
Score: 69.68   Rank: 108

Sumter, SC
Office-Based Physicians
26 Generalists	■□□□□
28 Specialists	■□□□□
26 Surgeons	■□□□□

Short-Term General Hospitals: 2 (231 beds)
JCAHO Accredited: 2
Hospital Services: 1 ♦, 1 ♦♦♦♦
Score: 1.41   Rank: 349

Syracuse, NY
Office-Based Physicians
333 Generalists	■■■□□
477 Specialists	■■■■□
373 Surgeons	■■■■□

Short-Term General Hospitals: 10 (2,753 beds)
JCAHO Accredited: 10
Hospital Services: 2 ♦, 2 ♦♦♦, 6 ♦♦♦♦
Teaching Hospitals
  Community General Hospital
  Crouse-Irving Memorial Hospital
  St. Joseph's Hospital Health Center
Score: 78.18   Rank: 78

Tacoma, WA
Office-Based Physicians
303 Generalists	■■■□□
249 Specialists	■□□□□
223 Surgeons	■□□□□

Short-Term General Hospitals: 7 (1,248 beds)
JCAHO Accredited: 7
Hospital Services: 1 ♦, 1 ♦♦♦, 5 ♦♦♦♦
Teaching Hospitals
  Mary Bridge Children's Hospital
  Multicare Medical Center
  Tacoma General Allenmore Hospital
Score: 26.34   Rank: 261

Tallahassee, FL
Office-Based Physicians
168 Generalists	■■■■■
115 Specialists	■■□□□
121 Surgeons	■■■□□

Short-Term General Hospitals: 3 (818 beds)
JCAHO Accredited: 2
Hospital Services: 1 ♦, 2 ♦♦♦♦
Teaching Hospital
  Tallahassee Memorial Healthcare
Score: 44.19   Rank: 198

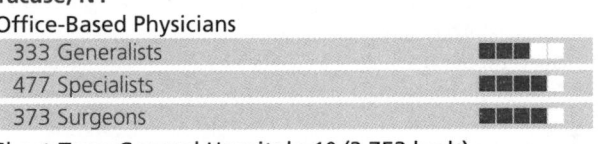

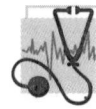

Tampa-St. Petersburg-Clearwater, FL

Office-Based Physicians

773 Generalists	
1,502 Specialists	
1,035 Surgeons	

Short-Term General Hospitals: 34 (9,415 beds)
JCAHO Accredited: 33
Hospital Services: 11 ♦, 3 ♦♦♦, 20 ♦♦♦♦
Teaching Hospitals
All Children's Hospital
Bayfront Medical Center
H. Lee Moffitt Cancer Center
Morton Plant Hospital
Tampa General Hospital
Score: 77.05   Rank: 82

Terre Haute, IN

Office-Based Physicians

82 Generalists	
63 Specialists	
64 Surgeons	

Short-Term General Hospitals: 4 (612 beds)
JCAHO Accredited: 4
Hospital Services: 2 ♦♦♦, 2 ♦♦♦♦
Teaching Hospital
Union Hospital
Score: 47.87   Rank: 185

Texarkana, TX-Texarkana, AR

Office-Based Physicians

61 Generalists	
58 Specialists	
59 Surgeons	

Short-Term General Hospitals: 4 (825 beds)
JCAHO Accredited: 4
Hospital Services: 1 ♦♦, 3 ♦♦♦♦
Score: 51.84   Rank: 171

Thunder Bay, ON

Office-Based Physicians

119 Generalists	
56 Specialists	
48 Surgeons	

Short-Term General Hospitals:
CCHFA Accredited:
Score: 60.62   Rank: 140

Toledo, OH

Office-Based Physicians

350 Generalists	
373 Specialists	
316 Surgeons	

Short-Term General Hospitals: 11 (2,664 beds)
JCAHO Accredited: 11
Hospital Services: 1 ♦♦♦, 10 ♦♦♦♦
Teaching Hospitals
Flower Hospital
Medical College of Ohio
St. Vincent's Mercy Medical Center
Toledo Hospital
Score: 87.53   Rank: 45

Topeka, KS

Office-Based Physicians

55 Generalists	
99 Specialists	
76 Surgeons	

Short-Term General Hospitals: 3 (1,058 beds)
JCAHO Accredited: 3
Hospital Services: 3 ♦♦♦♦
Teaching Hospitals
Intensiva Hospital
St. Francis Hospital & Medical Center
Stormont Vail Healthcare
Score: 49.85   Rank: 178

★ Toronto, ON

Office-Based Physicians

4,700 Generalists	
2,900 Specialists	
1,250 Surgeons	

Short-Term General Hospitals: 34 (11,557 beds)
CCHFA Accredited: 34
Teaching Hospitals
Hospital for Sick Children
Mount Sinai Hospital
North York General Hospital
The Queen Elizabeth Hospital
St. Joseph's Health Centre
St. Michael's Hospital
Scarborough General Hospital
Sunnybrook Health Science Centre
The Toronto Hospital
The Wellesley Hospital
Toronto East General Hospital
Score: 96.6   Rank: 13

Trenton, NJ

Office-Based Physicians

66 Generalists	
317 Specialists	
213 Surgeons	

Short-Term General Hospitals: 5 (1,385 beds)
JCAHO Accredited: 5
Hospital Services: 5 ♦♦♦♦
Teaching Hospitals
Helene Fuld Medical Center
Medical Center at Princeton
St. Francis Medical Center
Score: 74.22   Rank: 92

Trois-Rivieres, PQ

Office-Based Physicians

122 Generalists	
64 Specialists	
49 Surgeons	

Short-Term General Hospitals: 3 (819 beds)
CCHFA Accredited: 3
Teaching Hospital
Centre Hospitalier Sainte-Marie
Score: 75.63   Rank: 87

Tucson, AZ
Office-Based Physicians
328 Generalists	
536 Specialists	
393 Surgeons	

Short-Term General Hospitals: 11 (2,240 beds)
JCAHO Accredited: 11
Hospital Services: 2 ♦, 1 ♦♦, 1 ♦♦♦, 7 ♦♦♦♦
Teaching Hospitals
Kino Community Hospital
Tucson Medical Center
University Medical Center

Score: **74.5**   Rank: **91**

Tulsa, OK
Office-Based Physicians
303 Generalists	
390 Specialists	
302 Surgeons	

Short-Term General Hospitals: 15 (2,531 beds)
JCAHO Accredited: 11
Teaching Hospitals
Children's Medical Center
Hillcrest Medical Center
St. Francis Hospital
St. John Medical Center

Score: **49.29**   Rank: **180**

Tuscaloosa, AL
Office-Based Physicians
59 Generalists	
85 Specialists	
72 Surgeons	

Short-Term General Hospitals: 2 (608 beds)
JCAHO Accredited: 2
Hospital Services: 2 ♦♦♦♦
Teaching Hospital
DCH Regional Medical Center

Score: **22.66**   Rank: **274**

Tyler, TX
Office-Based Physicians
100 Generalists	
128 Specialists	
108 Surgeons	

Short-Term General Hospitals: 3 (654 beds)
JCAHO Accredited: 2
Hospital Services: 1 ♦♦, 2 ♦♦♦♦
Teaching Hospitals
Mother Frances Hospital
University of Texas Health Center

Score: **67.13**   Rank: **117**

Utica-Rome, NY
Office-Based Physicians
123 Generalists	
132 Specialists	
113 Surgeons	

Short-Term General Hospitals: 6 (1,258 beds)
JCAHO Accredited: 6
Hospital Services: 6 ♦♦♦♦

Teaching Hospitals
Faxton–Children's Hospital
St. Elizabeth's Hospital
Score: **35.41**   Rank: **229**

Vallejo-Fairfield-Napa, CA
Office-Based Physicians
194 Generalists	
227 Specialists	
157 Surgeons	

Short-Term General Hospitals: 8 (1,478 beds)
JCAHO Accredited: 6
Hospital Services: 3 ♦, 1 ♦♦, 1 ♦♦♦, 3 ♦♦♦♦
Score: **28.61**   Rank: **253**

★ Vancouver, BC
Office-Based Physicians
2,700 Generalists	
1,259 Specialists	
700 Surgeons	

Short-Term General Hospitals: 21 (9,551 beds)
CCHFA Accredited: 21
Teaching Hospitals
British Columbia Children's Hospital
British Columbia Women's Hospital
Pacific Health Care Society
The Royal Columbian Hospital
St. Mary's Hospital
St. Paul's Hospital
University Hospital
Vancouver Hospital and Health Sciences Centre
Score: **100**   Rank: **1**

Ventura, CA
Office-Based Physicians
395 Generalists	
330 Specialists	
272 Surgeons	

Short-Term General Hospitals: 8 (1,342 beds)
JCAHO Accredited: 8
Hospital Services: 2 ♦, 6 ♦♦♦♦
Teaching Hospital
Ventura County Medical Center
Score: **43.9**   Rank: **199**

Victoria, BC
Office-Based Physicians
421 Generalists	
189 Specialists	
124 Surgeons	

Short-Term General Hospitals:
CCHFA Accredited:
Score: **70.25**   Rank: **106**

Victoria, TX
Office-Based Physicians
58 Generalists	
48 Specialists	
46 Surgeons	

Short-Term General Hospitals: 3 (590 beds)
JCAHO Accredited: 3
Hospital Services: 3 ♦♦♦♦
Score: **72.52**   Rank: **98**

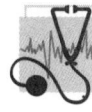

Vineland-Millville-Bridgeton, NJ
Office-Based Physicians
46 Generalists
66 Specialists
49 Surgeons
Short-Term General Hospitals: 2 (514 beds)
   JCAHO Accredited: 2
Hospital Services: 2 ♦♦♦♦
Score: 10.48   Rank: 317

Visalia-Tulare-Porterville, CA
Office-Based Physicians
122 Generalists
106 Specialists
84 Surgeons
Short-Term General Hospitals: 6 (715 beds)
   JCAHO Accredited: 4
Hospital Services: 2 ♦♦ , 2 ♦♦♦ , 2 ♦♦♦♦
Score: 6.51   Rank: 331

Waco, TX
Office-Based Physicians
120 Generalists
74 Specialists
85 Surgeons
Short-Term General Hospitals: 3 (503 beds)
   JCAHO Accredited: 2
Hospital Services: 1 ♦♦ , 2 ♦♦♦♦
Teaching Hospitals
   Hillcrest Baptist Medical Center
   Providence Health Center
Score: 32.29   Rank: 240

★ Washington, DC-MD-VA-WV
Office-Based Physicians
1,594 Generalists
4,007 Specialists
2,489 Surgeons
Short-Term General Hospitals: 44 (11,025 beds)
   JCAHO Accredited: 44
Hospital Services: 2 ♦ , 1 ♦♦ , 41 ♦♦♦♦
Teaching Hospitals
   Alexandria Hospital
   Arlington Hospital
   Children's National Medical Center
   City Hospital
   District of Columbia General Hospital
   Fairfax Hospital
   George Washington University Hospital
   Georgetown University Hospital
   Greater Southeast Hospital
   Holy Cross Hospital
   Howard University Hospital
   Mt. Vernon Hospital
   Prince Georges Hospital Center
   Providence Hospital
   Sibley Memorial Hospital
   Suburban Hospital Association
   Washington Hospital Center
Score: 98.30   Rank: 7

Waterbury, CT
Office-Based Physicians
46 Generalists
228 Specialists
139 Surgeons
Short-Term General Hospitals: 2 (480 beds)
   JCAHO Accredited: 2
Hospital Services: 2 ♦♦♦♦
Teaching Hospitals
   St. Mary's Hospital
   Waterbury Hospital Health Center
Score: 50.99   Rank: 174

Waterloo-Cedar Falls, IA
Office-Based Physicians
84 Generalists
48 Specialists
52 Surgeons
Short-Term General Hospitals: 3 (570 beds)
   JCAHO Accredited: 3
Hospital Services: 1 ♦♦♦ , 2 ♦♦♦♦
Teaching Hospitals
   Allen Memorial Hospital
   Covenant Medical Center
Score: 65.72   Rank: 122

Wausau, WI
Office-Based Physicians
88 Generalists
46 Specialists
53 Surgeons
Short-Term General Hospitals: 1 (221 beds)
   JCAHO Accredited: 1
Hospital Services: 1 ♦♦♦♦
Teaching Hospital
   Wausau Hospital
Score: 29.17   Rank: 251

West Palm Beach-Boca Raton, FL
Office-Based Physicians
318 Generalists
861 Specialists
633 Surgeons
Short-Term General Hospitals: 15 (3,483 beds)
   JCAHO Accredited: 14
Hospital Services: 3 ♦ , 3 ♦♦♦ , 9 ♦♦♦♦
Score: 83   Rank: 61

Wheeling, WV-OH
Office-Based Physicians
86 Generalists
75 Specialists
78 Surgeons
Short-Term General Hospitals: 6 (1,128 beds)
   JCAHO Accredited: 6
Hospital Services: 1 ♦♦♦ , 5 ♦♦♦♦
Teaching Hospitals
   Barnesville Hospital Association
   Ohio Valley General Hospital
   Peterson Hospital
   Wheeling Hospital
Score: 79.03   Rank: 75

Wichita, KS
Office-Based Physicians
319 Generalists	▪▪▪▪▫
248 Specialists	▪▪▪▫▫
213 Surgeons	▪▪▫▫▫

Short-Term General Hospitals: 8 (2,222 beds)
JCAHO Accredited: 6
Teaching Hospitals
Via Christi Regional Medical Center
Wesley Medical Center
Score: 76.48   Rank: 84

Wichita Falls, TX
Office-Based Physicians
81 Generalists	▪▪▪▪▫
57 Specialists	▪▪▫▫▫
58 Surgeons	▪▪▪▫▫

Short-Term General Hospitals: 4 (517 beds)
JCAHO Accredited: 3
Hospital Services: 1 ♦♦, 3 ♦♦♦♦
Teaching Hospitals
Bethania Regional Healthcare Center
Wichita General Hospital
Score: 52.4   Rank: 169

Williamsport, PA
Office-Based Physicians
83 Generalists	▪▪▪▪▪
46 Specialists	▪▫▫▫▫
46 Surgeons	▪▪▫▫▫

Short-Term General Hospitals: 2 (533 beds)
JCAHO Accredited: 2
Hospital Services: 2 ♦♦♦♦
Teaching Hospital
Williamsport Hospital
Score: 50.42   Rank: 176

Wilmington-Newark, DE-MD
Office-Based Physicians
229 Generalists	▪▪▪▫▫
292 Specialists	▪▪▪▫▫
230 Surgeons	▪▪▫▫▫

Short-Term General Hospitals: 4 (1,195 beds)
JCAHO Accredited: 4
Hospital Services: 1 ♦, 3 ♦♦♦♦
Teaching Hospitals
Dupont Hospital for Children
Eugene Dupont Memorial Division Hospital
St. Francis Hospital
Score: 32.86   Rank: 238

Wilmington, NC
Office-Based Physicians
77 Generalists	▪▪▫▫▫
153 Specialists	▪▪▪▪▪
125 Surgeons	▪▪▪▪▪

Short-Term General Hospitals: 4 (752 beds)
JCAHO Accredited: 4
Hospital Services: 1 ♦, 1 ♦♦, 2 ♦♦♦♦
Teaching Hospital
New Hanover Regional Medical Center
Score: 61.47   Rank: 137

Windsor, ON
Office-Based Physicians
219 Generalists	▪▪▪▪▪
108 Specialists	▪▫▫▫▫
100 Surgeons	▪▪▫▫▫

Short-Term General Hospitals: 2 (912 beds)
CCHFA Accredited: 2
Teaching Hospital
Hotel Dieu Grace Hospital
Score: 44.47   Rank: 197

★ Winnipeg, MB
Office-Based Physicians
701 Generalists	▪▪▪▪▪
556 Specialists	▪▪▪▪▪
259 Surgeons	▪▪▪▫▫

Short-Term General Hospitals: 7 (2,642 beds)
CCHFA Accredited: 7
Teaching Hospitals
Health Sciences Centre
St. Boniface General Hospital
Score: 92.91   Rank: 26

Worcester, MA-CT
Office-Based Physicians
176 Generalists	▪▪▫▫▫
427 Specialists	▪▪▪▪▪
209 Surgeons	▪▪▪▫▫

Short-Term General Hospitals: 7 (1437 beds)
JCAHO Accredited: 7
Hospital Services: 7 ♦♦♦♦
Teaching Hospitals
Memorial Hospital
St. Vincent Hospital
University of Massachusetts Medical Center
Worcester County Hospital
Score: 69.97   Rank: 107

Yakima, WA
Office-Based Physicians
125 Generalists	▪▪▪▪▪
76 Specialists	▪▫▫▫▫
74 Surgeons	▪▫▫▫▫

Short-Term General Hospitals: 4 (468 beds)
JCAHO Accredited: 3
Hospital Services: 1 ♦♦, 1 ♦♦♦, 2 ♦♦♦♦
Teaching Hospitals
Providence Yakima Medical Center
Yakima Valley Memorial Hospital
Score: 25.77   Rank: 263

Yolo, CA
Office-Based Physicians
117 Generalists	▪▪▪▪▪
103 Specialists	▪▪▪▪▫
60 Surgeons	▪▪▫▫▫

Short-Term General Hospitals: 2 (151 beds)
JCAHO Accredited: 2
Hospital Services: 1 ♦, 1 ♦♦♦
Teaching Hospital
Sutter Davis Hospital
Score: 42.49   Rank: 204

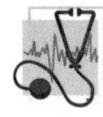

York, PA
Office-Based Physicians

177 Generalists

126 Specialists

103 Surgeons

Short-Term General Hospitals: 3 (720 beds)
JCAHO Accredited: 2
Hospital Services: 3♦♦♦
Teaching Hospital
York Hospital
Score: 5.66   Rank: 333

Youngstown-Warren, OH
Office-Based Physicians

133 Generalists

279 Specialists

204 Surgeons

Short-Term General Hospitals: 7 (1,700 beds)
JCAHO Accredited: 6
Hospital Services: 1♦♦♦, 6♦♦♦♦
Teaching Hospitals
Hillside Hospital
St. Elizabeth Health Center

Tod Children's Hospital
Western Reserve Care System
Score: 20.39   Rank: 282

Yuba City, CA
Office-Based Physicians

69 Generalists

53 Specialists

45 Surgeons

Short-Term General Hospitals: 3 (195 beds)
JCAHO Accredited: 2
Hospital Services: 3♦♦♦
Score: 6.23   Rank: 332

Yuma, AZ
Office-Based Physicians

23 Generalists

48 Specialists

38 Surgeons

Short-Term General Hospitals: 1 (238 beds)
JCAHO Accredited: 1
Hospital Services: 1♦♦♦♦
Score: 0.28   Rank: 353

ET CETERA: HEALTH CARE

HEALTH CARE IN CANADA

Canada's taxpayer-financed, comprehensive health insurance system had strong opposition when it began 3 decades ago. Because *Medicare,* as it's popularly called, was to be managed by government, business and industry predicted failure. Doctors saw it as a threat to their livelihoods and some made plans to move south. Today, most Canadian doctors rate the system as "good to excellent," and business has been brought round because the cost is spread across society on the basis of ability to pay.

How It Works

Canada's health insurance system covers all medically necessary hospital and physician services for everyone. When Canadians need medical care, they make an appointment with the doctor of their choice, pull out the health insurance card issued to them by their province, and ask for treatment. The patient fills out no forms, nor are there deductibles, co-payments, or dollar limits on coverage.

The physician's paperwork is swift and simple. He or she bills the province on a fee-for-service basis under a published schedule negotiated each year by peers in their own medical association and the provincial government.

Almost all hospitals are nonprofit institutions operated by municipalities, religious, or voluntary organizations. The hospital's board and its administrators grapple with tight budgets, but they control spending decisions as long as they don't overspend a figure they negotiate every year with the provincial ministry of health.

Canadians do have to spend their own money on dental care, eyeglasses, and some drugs. About three out of every ten dollars spent on health care comes out of pocket. There are private insurers, but they may not offer coverage that duplicates government programs, only supplemental benefits. Their customers include retired Canadians who winter in Florida, Texas, and the American Southwest.

Money Matters

Per capita health-care costs in the United States are much higher than those in Canada. American administrative costs make up the difference. Under the Canadian system, there are neither marketing expenses nor staff to estimate risk and decide who should be denied or offered coverage. Neither doctors nor hospitals have to verify coverage, complete onerous paperwork required by multiple private insurance firms, or resolve double-billing problems. Also, Canadian doctors pay relatively low premiums to the nonprofit Medical Protective Association for malpractice insurance.

Problems

For all the attention Canada's health-care system gets in the debate over reform, it isn't likely that the United States will copy the Canadian system. "America, with the world's most expensive health-care system," one expert noted, "has little to learn from a neighbor with the world's *second* most expensive system."

Canada is working out its *own* health-care crisis. As popular as it is with consumers, the system has become a monster to fund. Nearly a third of provincial budgets go to health care, with the money coming from general revenues, high sales taxes, and high employer-paid payroll taxes. Two provinces, Alberta and British Columbia, collect premiums from residents.

Critics, many of them Canadian physicians, also point to crowded hospital wards and limited availability of new medical technology. Worse, the usual wait for lifesaving surgeries is almost 2 months and begins only after a general practitioner has given the patient a referral to a specialist. The wait to see the specialist typically takes 5 weeks.

HEALTHY LIFE/LONGER LIFE

Do you subscribe to the theory of when your time is up, you go? Then you may be surprised with the current thinking. Experts now conclude that it's less likely to be a stray bullet or virus that kills you than the way you lead your life.

The most common causes of death at the turn of the century—typhoid fever, cholera, tuberculosis, smallpox, gastroenteritis, and nephritis—have been practically eliminated by scientific advances and improved sanitation. Today, more than 70 percent of the 2 million Americans who die each year are victims of heart disease, cancer, stroke, cirrhosis of the liver, bronchitis, asthma, and emphysema—the so-called lifestyle diseases that may be aggravated by such behavior as overeating, heavy drinking, smoking, and lack of exercise. To see how your daily habits measure up, take a look at the table "Risky Business." Some risk factors are more important than others, so an entirely accurate picture of your health may not emerge from practicing self-analysis. However, changing your habits so that you qualify for the low-risk ratings will almost certainly result in a longer life.

The following are some suggestions—certainly not new, but still as healthful as the first time you heard them—

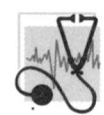

that can help you reduce your health risks. If you haven't yet paid heed to the wisdom of these suggestions, perhaps this will nudge you into a healthier style of living.

Stop smoking and drink only in moderation. Cigarette smokers run twice the risk that nonsmokers do of death from coronary disease. Smoking also contributes to stroke, lung cancer, emphysema, and bronchitis. Likewise, an excess of alcohol can be dangerous, increasing chances of developing cirrhosis of the liver (this condition is found six times as frequently among alcoholics as among nonalcoholics) and cardiovascular problems. Also, drinking combined with driving multiplies the risk of dying in an automobile accident; at least half of such accidents in the United States involve drunk drivers.

Eat a balanced diet and watch your weight. Six of the ten leading causes of death have been linked to diet: heart attack, stroke, atherosclerosis, cancer, cirrhosis of the liver, and diabetes. Reducing your intake of refined flour and sugar, salt (which in excess contributes to high blood pressure), and saturated fats (which have been implicated as factors in heart disease and stroke) while choosing from a range of meat, poultry, fish, fruits, vegetables, and fiber foods (which have been shown to prevent colon cancer) is highly recommended. A balanced diet can also help you to lose extra weight, which puts added stress on the heart and organs, aggravating disease conditions.

THE TOP KILLERS

Below are ten causes—and their death rates per 100,000 people—that account for 82 percent of all deaths. The top three non-accidental causes—heart disease, cancer, and stroke—account for 60 percent of all deaths.

Cause of Death	Rate per 100,000
Heart diseases	276.6
Malignancies	205.2
Cerebrovascular diseases	60.5
Chronic obstructive pulmonary diseases	40.0
Accidents	35.4
Pneumonia and influenza	31.1
Diabetes mellitus	23.2
Infectious and parasitic diseases	15.0
Suicide	11.6
Homicide and legal intervention	7.8

Source: U.S. National Center for Health Statistics.

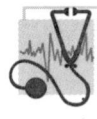

Risky Business

RISK CATEGORY	NO RISK	SLIGHT RISK	SUBSTANTIAL RISK	HEAVY RISK	DANGEROUS RISK
Alcohol	Non-drinker	Stopped drinking	6 drinks/week	More than 6 drinks/week	More than 2 drinks/day
Alcohol & driving—autos, boats, motorcycles, snowmobiles	Never drink; drive only with safety aids—seat belt, helmet, life jacket	Never drive after drinking without safety aids	Drive after 2 drinks with safety aids	Drive after 2 drinks without safety aids	Drive after more than 2 drinks with no safety aids
Blood cholesterol	Less than 180	180–220	220–280	280–320	320 and above
Blood pressure	120/80	120/80–140/90	140/90–160/100	160/100–180/105	Above 180/105
Blood sugar	Less than 120 two hours after meal of syrup and pancakes	110–130 two hours after meal; checked every 3 months	More than 150 without diet control	More than 150 without diet control or doctor's care	Diabetes without doctor's care; younger than 45 years old
Dental exams	Every 6 months	6–12 months	Infrequent or irregular visits	Only when pain or problem	Never visit dentist
Eye exam	Every 3–5 years				
Immunizations	Up-to-date	Childhood disease or immunization	Partial childhood immunizations	Partial/no childhood immunizations & compromised immune system	Compromised immune system
Motor vehicle safety	Always wear seat belt	Wear seat belt more than 50%	Wear seat belt as driver 50%	Wear seat belt as passenger 50%	Wear seat belt less than 50%
Nonprescription drugs	Use occasionally only for short periods; label warnings heeded				Continuing use; drinking or driving despite label warnings
Physical activity	Walk more than 2 miles/day or climb 20+ flights of stairs/day	Walk 1.5–2 miles/day or climb 15–20 flights of stairs/day	Walk only 0.5–1.5 miles/day or climb only 5–15 flights of stairs/day	Walk only 2–5 blocks/day or climb 2–4 flights of stairs/day	Walk less than 2 blocks a day or climb less than 2 flights of stairs/day
Physician visit	Have MD & see routinely every 1–2 years				Medical care on emergency room basis
Prescription drugs	With MD's consent; follow orders carefully	Take daily medication without side effects	Take medication when needed without side effects	Use sleeping/ nerve pills regularly without MD supervision	Take prescribed medication with other pills or alcohol without MD knowledge
Smoking	No smoking or stopped at least 10 years	Less than 10 cigarettes/day	Half a pack/day	1 pack/day	2 or more packs/day
Trimness	Lean	Slightly plump	Moderately obese	Considerably obese	Grossly obese
Water safety—swimming & boating	Qualified expert	Know how to swim & safety rules	Know how to swim & may swim after 1 drink/nerve drug	Do not know how to swim but use life jacket 50%	Do not know how to swim; never use life jacket
For Men Only Testicular exam	Monthly self exam & yearly by physician	Monthly self exam but not by physician	Self-exam 2–3 times/year; no physician exam	Only at physician visit	Never
For Women Only Breast exam	Monthly self exam & yearly by physician	Monthly self exam but not by physician	Self-exam 2–3 times/year; no physician exam	Only at physician visit	Never
Pap smear	Every year	Every 3 years	Every 4 years	Never	Never; non-menstrual bleeding

Source: Adapted from Health Hazard Appraisal System developed by Lewis C. Robbins, MD, Jack H. Hall, MD, and Pamela Hall.

ADULT EXAM SCHEDULE

Complete Physical Examination
Every 2 years for patients under 65 years of age.
Yearly for patients 65 and older

Homocysteine Level
At regularly scheduled physical

Cholesterol Level
Every 3–6 months for patients on cholesterol-lowering medication, or at regularly scheduled physical

Electrocardiogram
Every year

Pap Smear (women)
Every year

PSA (men)
Every year for men 40 and older

Stool Occult Blood
Every year

Vital Capacity Lung Test
Every year

Mammograms (women)
Every 2 years for women under 50. Yearly for women 50 and older. Occasionally every 6 months for previous abnormal mammograms

TB Skin Test
Every 2 years

Sigmoidoscopy/Colonoscopy
Every 3 years for patients 40 and older

Chest X-rays
Every 5 years. May be done if a patient has a respiratory complaint or a positive TB skin test

---

Get regular exercise. Exercise, now seen almost as a miracle drug, can help you maintain proper weight, keep your body in good operating condition, and relieve stress (which contributes to ulcers and high blood pressure). It helps prevent premature aging and degeneration of bone (osteoporosis), muscles, and joints. The use-it-or-lose-it maxim definitely applies here.

Get regular medical care. Be sure to consult your doctor regularly and have whatever checkups or tests he or she recommends, such as a Pap smear, blood pressure check, or blood cholesterol tests.

FINDING THE RIGHT DOCTOR

Not all doctors are created equal. The doctor you select and the hospital in which you're treated may be more important in determining the outcome of your illness than the disease you have. When you're selecting a surgeon, for example, you need to know how often the surgeon has done your kind of surgery (more is better) and what the outcome has been. Compare the records of several surgeons to get a sense of what a "good" track record is. Don't forget to trust your intuitions about doctors. How comfortable do you feel with the doctor? Your gut feeling could be the deciding factor.

The American Medical Association is the U.S. licensing body for physicians, but individual states vary in their licensing requirements. Highly populated states like New York and California have large staffs in their state

PAGING DR. FINDER

Learning whether cardiologists, urologists, psychiatrists, or other specialists practice in an area needn't mean a thankless session with the telephone book's Yellow Pages. Call the local hospital's public relations office for a free copy of their Physician Locator or MD Directory. Hospitals in competitive markets know they will more likely have you as a customer when you're ill if they can introduce you early on to a physician who uses their facilities.

These "Dr. Finders" aren't mere telephone contact sheets. Often they are photo galleries of physicians with capsule resumés on their education (from college through medical school to residency), their specialties, and their board certifications. You can also learn if they take walk-in patients and whether another doctor will cover for them on their day off. Some of these guides even detail their civic clubs and what they like to do on weekends.

licensing departments that can perform more thorough investigations of complaints against doctors. On the other hand, less populated states such as Idaho do not have the same investigative resources. But licensing boards alone cannot track down all the bad doctors. Medical schools (where students first enter the doctor track); licensing boards; national, state, and local professional societies; and hospitals (where most doctors have staff privileges)

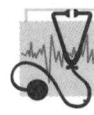

must work together in order to assure that patients are treated by competent, licensed professionals.

The Health Care Financing Administration, which reimburses doctors and hospitals that treat Medicare and Medicaid patients, also has plans to help consumers in their selection of doctors. It will soon begin a long-term project of rating doctors by how well their patients do—as indicated by mortality rates and speed of recovery.

In the meantime, consider the following suggestions. Chances are good that you'll have to choose a new physician at some point; even if you don't move, your doctor might. Finding a replacement for the person in whom you may have put a lot of trust isn't always easy. Give some thought to the kind of doctor you are most comfortable with. Do you want to place complete faith in your physician? Or do you have questions about your treatment? Do you like a cooperative arrangement in which you and your doctor work as a team? It's very important to most people that they have a doctor who will listen to their complaints, worries, and concerns, rather than one who may make patients feel that they're questioning the doctor's authority.

If you're planning to move, you might ask your present doctor if he or she knows anything about doctors in your destination. Or you may get names from the nearest hospital at the new location, from friends you make, from medical societies, and from new neighbors. Given the competition for insured patients, don't be surprised to receive mail from hospitals touting their services and the quality of physicians on their referral network.

When you have decided whom you want to contact, call that doctor's office, saying that you are a prospective patient, and ask to speak to the doctor briefly. You may have to agree to call back, but making connection with a professional voice is an important step. If you can't arrange this, if the doctor is "too busy," you probably ought to go to the next name on your list.

When you do make contact, tell the doctor enough about yourself so that he or she has a good idea of who you are and what your problems may be. If the doctor sounds "right" to you, you could ask about fees and emergencies. Or you may wish to save some of these questions for a personal visit. It is important to establish through the initial phone call or visit that you and the doctor will be at ease with each other.

Evaluate the doctor's attitude. If he or she doesn't want to bother with you now, you will probably get that don't-bother-me treatment sooner or later when dealing with specific problems. Make sure that:

- You can openly discuss your feelings and personal concerns about sexual and emotional problems.

- The doctor isn't vague, impatient, or unwilling to answer all your questions about the causes and treatment of your physical problems.

- The doctor takes a thorough history on you and asks about past physical and emotional problems,

Recommended Immunization Schedule

AGE	Diphtheria	PERTUSSIS Tetanus (DPT)	POLIO VACCINE (OPV/IPV)	VARICELLA MEASLES MUMPS RUBELLA (MMR)	HEPATITIS B (HBV)	HEMOPHILUS INFLUENZA B (Hib)	TETANUS DIPHTHERIA (Td)
Birth–2 months	✓	✓			✓	✓	
1–4 months	✓	✓			✓	✓	
6 months	✓	✓			✓	✓	
12–15 months			✓	✓		✓	
18 months	✓						
4–6 years	✓	✓	✓				
14–16 years				✓✓			✓
Adult			✓✓				Every 10 years
Adult	Pneumococcal vaccine (one time only) Influenza vaccine (annually) Hepatitis A: a series of two shots every 6 years Hepatitis B: a series of three shots						

✓✓ *if not previously vaccinated against illness, never had illness, or tested to show not immune to illness. This schedule is based on U.S. Guidelines; the Canadian schedule is similar.*

family medical history, medication you are taking, and other matters affecting your health.

- The doctor doesn't automatically prescribe drugs rather than deal with real causes of your medical problems.

- The doctor has an associate to whom you can turn should your doctor retire or die.

Talk with the doctor about the transfer of your medical records. Some doctors like to have them, especially if there is any specific medical problem or chronic condition. Other doctors prefer to develop new records.

Even if you feel fine, arrange to have a physical or at least a quick checkup. Should an emergency occur, the doctor will have basic information about you and some knowledge of your needs, and you will avoid the stress of trying to work with a doctor who has to learn about you in an emergency.

IMMUNIZATION

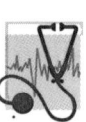

The World Health Organization characterized the United States as having the third worst immunization system in the Western Hemisphere, ahead of Bolivia and Haiti. Just two of three children are immunized by age 2. Reasons for the low immunization rate include the cost of vaccines, the lack of public awareness, and the attitudes of both parents and health-care providers.

Some vaccines induce prolonged immunity to certain diseases, and can be given just once. But others, such as pertussis (whooping cough) or diphtheria, only induce temporary immunity. These vaccines require repeat booster injections to protect against such diseases.

Your immunization record should specify the types of vaccine and be dated and signed by the doctor each time an immunization is given. Keep the record at home in a safe place, and take it on trips away from home.

Recreation

fter "Where's that?" what people ask most often about an unfamiliar place is, "Is there anything going on there?" Wherever they are, people want to make the most of leisure. Consider the billions spent each year on video rentals, insulated jogging clothes, season tickets at the ballpark, European vacations, down-filled sleeping bags, and graphite fishing rods.

Not everyone can take advantage of all the opportunities for recreation. An Aspen ski trip or a Hilton Head golf weekend costs too much for most people. Even a backpacking trip in a national park with cheap camping fees might be out of the question for the dollars and time it takes to get there and back.

Fortunately, there are many other things to do that are inexpensive and nearby. Movies, golf, and good restaurants are available almost anywhere; in fact, people living in smaller metro areas usually have better access to these than residents of bigger ones. On the other hand, zoos and professional sports enhance life in larger places. For more and more people, convenient outdoor recreation in a national forest or on a wild and scenic river is a lucky geographical circumstance; the protected outdoors is a part of the landscape just as developed urban land is. *Places Rated* looks at each of these kinds of recreation in determining the best places to play.

COMMON DENOMINATORS

For scuba diving, the coasts of Florida, California, and Hawaii are best bets. For skiing on powdery snow, British Columbia and Colorado are better than most other areas. Weather and winds turn still other areas into premier places for hang gliding. But there are certain kinds of recreation that you can find everywhere: dining out at a quality restaurant, a round of weekend golf, or moviegoing at a downtown picture palace or a multiplex cinema at a suburban mall.

Counting Diamonds: Good Restaurants

The most common service establishment in North America is the one where you walk in, sit down, and order something to eat. If you're among the one in ten who get out at least once a week for dinner, you may as well go to a worthwhile eatery instead of a portion-controlled "Casa de la Maison House," where factory-prepared frozen

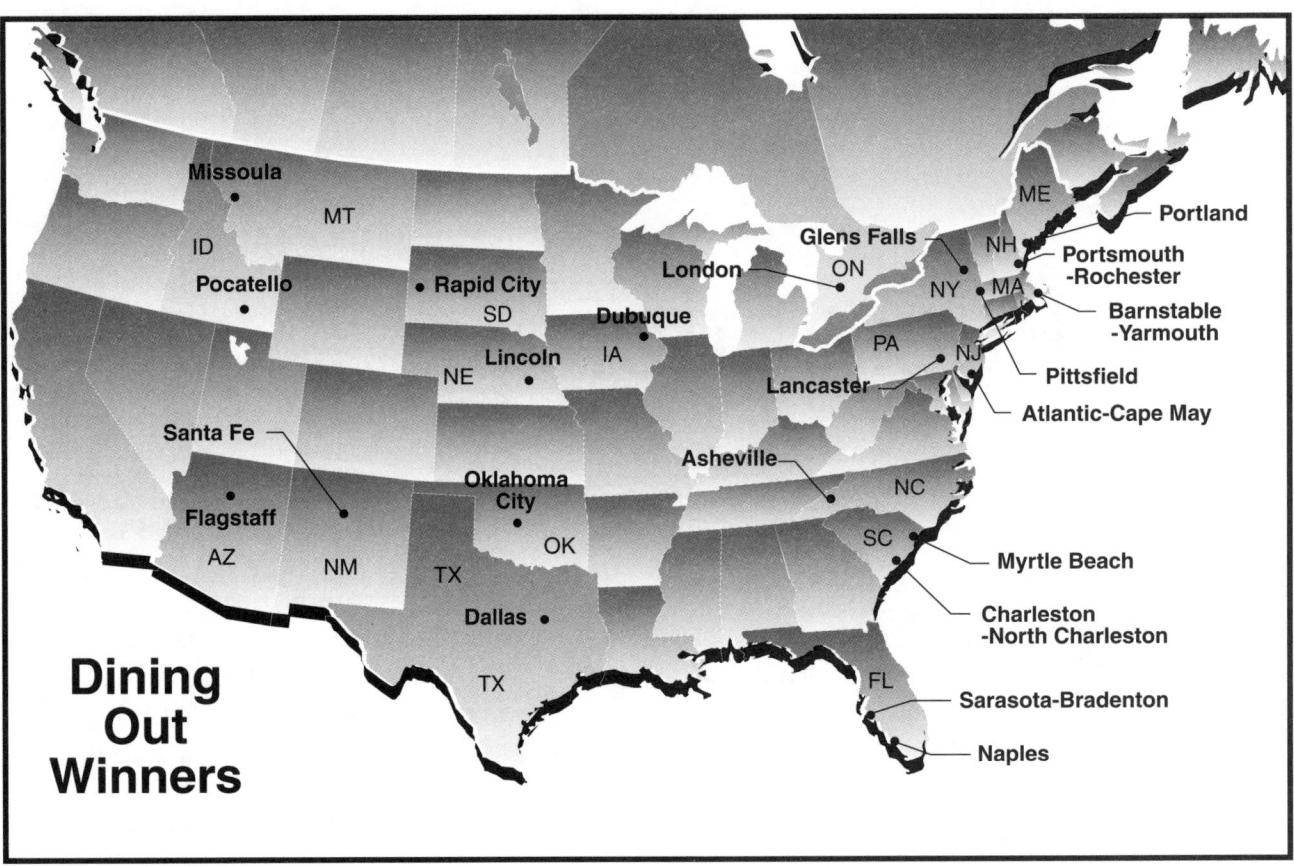

Dining Out Winners

Copyright © 2000 by Places Rated Partnership

Cape Ann Mapping

packages of beef Wellington and veal cordon bleu are microwaved, dished up, and listed at ten times what the restaurant paid for them.

To learn which places have restaurants more than just a cut or two above average, *Places Rated* consulted the American Automobile Association (AAA), which for decades has rated restaurants across the country. The AAA ratings come from two sources: customer comments and inspection reports of field representatives who dine anonymously at establishments throughout the year. Restaurants are judged by the quality of their food, service, and ambience.

A single diamond (♦) indicates a simple, family, or specialty meal in clean, pleasant, and informal surroundings. The food is basic and wholesome and the service is casual or self-serve. *Su Casa,* in downtown Chicago, fits this description with its home-style Mexican takeout and inexpensive family menu.

Cincinnati's reasonably priced *Darci's* restaurant, serving deli and pastry, is an example of a two-diamond (♦ ♦) establishment. Eateries at this level offer a more extensive menu for family or adult dining. Service is attentive but informal, and the decor presents a unified theme that is either comfortable or trendy and upbeat.

Three-diamond (♦ ♦ ♦) restaurants present upscale adult or special family dining. Reservations are suggested,

but usually required only on weekends. There is a wine list, and food is cooked to order and creatively prepared with quality ingredients. The wait staff is skilled and professional, and the ambience is inviting and trendy or formal. Indianapolis's dressy-casual *Something Different,* specializing in health-conscious American cuisine, illustrates this category.

Hidden among the garish hostelries and casino feed-your-face cafeterias in Las Vegas is a four-diamond (♦ ♦ ♦ ♦) establishment, *Monte Carlo,* in the historic Desert Inn on the strip. Here, the service is formally attired and sophisticated, the wine list is extensive, the French cuisine is complex and creatively presented, the atmosphere is elegant and quiet, and the lighting is dim.

Five diamonds (♦ ♦ ♦ ♦ ♦) mean the ultimate and most memorable adult dining experience. Chefs are typically stars in their craft. "Flawless"—in food preparation and presentation, in service, and in atmosphere—is a word restaurant critics use in their descriptions. Atlanta's *The Dining Room* at the Ritz-Carlton, in Buckhead, is a long-standing holder of this designation.

Although Myrtle Beach has 73 restaurants rated by AAA, the number pales when compared to the 845 establishments in New York. Nevertheless, Myrtle Beach restaurants collect one AAA quality diamond for every 456 residents, making it the best among metro areas.

Other areas, usually small (see map "Dining Out Winners"), have dining-out sides to them almost as good.

are blue-collar industrial locations in the Great Lakes states.

Counting Holes: Golf Courses

Certainly golf is a common denominator; it is played in every metro area but one: Jersey City, NJ. When it comes to finding a local golf course on an idle, sunny weekend, there are three options: the private equity course, typically part of a country club open only to members and guests; daily-fee operations open to all players; and city-built and operated courses, again open to everyone.

If you're a golfer who can afford to join a private country club with an 18-hole course, your dues buy one big advantage: You belong to the fortunate 14 percent of golfers who don't have to wait to tee off at a crowded municipal or daily-fee course.

On the other hand, if you're one of nearly 25 million North American golfers who've played a round at a local municipal or daily-fee course, only six out of every ten of the continent's 9,376 regulation courses are open to you. Still, access to public golf is an excellent reflection of recreation opportunities in metro areas.

Metro areas with fewer than 1,000 residents per hole of municipal or daily-fee golf are often Sun Belt resorts. But others (see map "Surprising Golf Hot Spots")

Counting Screens: The Movies

More than 50 years ago, John Huston won two academy awards—best director and best screenplay—for *The Treasure of the Sierra Madre*. His father, Walter, was named best supporting actor for his portrayal of the old prospector in the same film. Jane Wyman won an Oscar for her role in *Johnny Belinda*. *Hamlet* was named best picture, and its director and star, Lawrence Olivier, best actor.

The year was 1948, near the end of a time when moviegoing was the thing to do any evening. Popcorn was regularly swept up from the aisles between shows, the next John Wayne or Spencer Tracy film was announced on a large easel in the lobby, usherettes took you to your seat with a red-lensed flashlight, and you always got a Movietone or Warner-Pathé newsreel with the show. There were nearly 20,000 movie houses back then. Most were neighborhood establishments with a few downtown picture palaces for premieres and first-run screenings. Never again would there be so many.

Today, movie marketers count screens rather than "four wall" (as opposed to the fast-disappearing

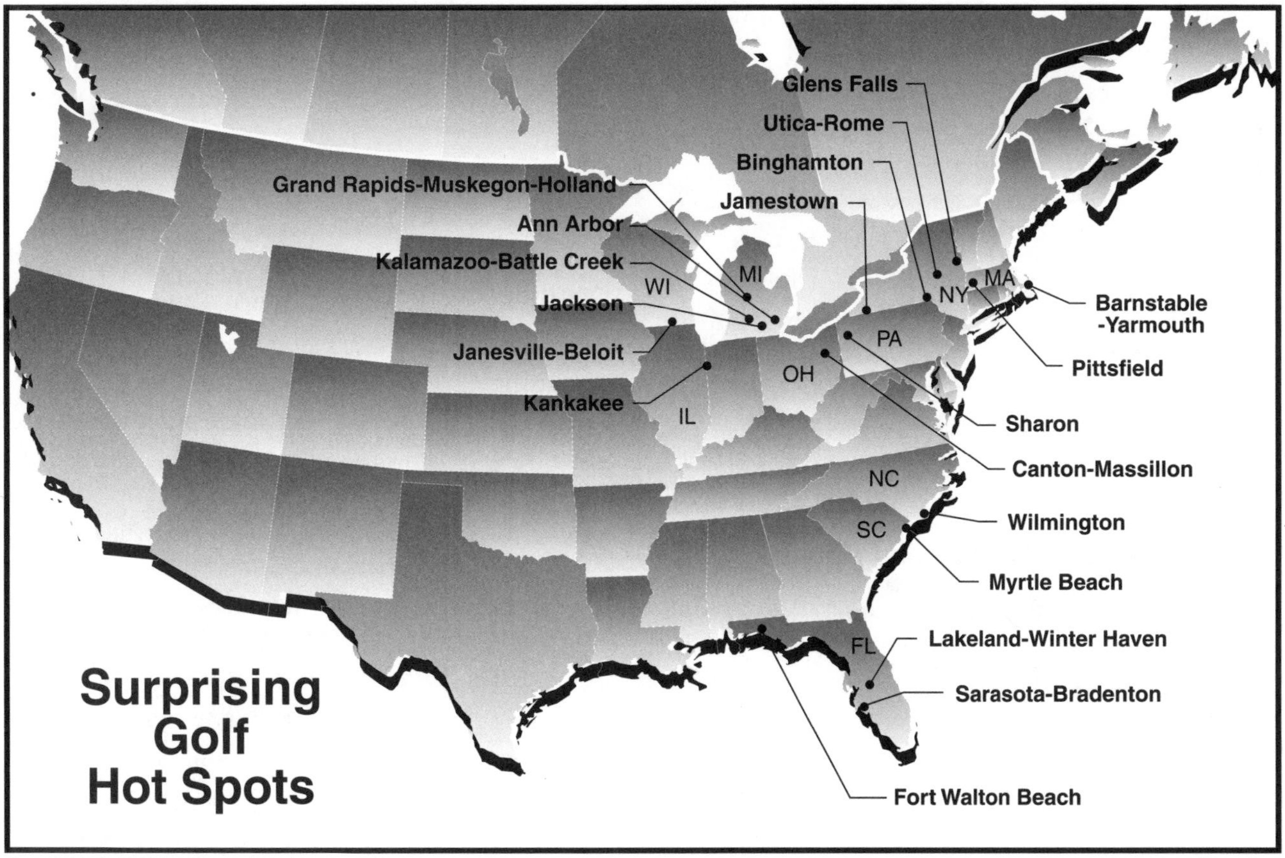

Recreation

Surprising Golf Hot Spots

Grand Rapids-Muskegon-Holland
Ann Arbor
Kalamazoo-Battle Creek
Jackson
Janesville-Beloit
Kankakee

Glens Falls
Utica-Rome
Binghamton
Jamestown

WI   MI
IL   NY   MA
OH   PA   Barnstable-Yarmouth
NC   Pittsfield
SC   Sharon
FL   Canton-Massillon
Wilmington
Myrtle Beach
Lakeland-Winter Haven
Sarasota-Bradenton
Fort Walton Beach

Copyright © 2000 by Places Rated Partnership

Cape Ann Mapping

drive-in) theaters to figure access to movies. Most screens now are in multiplex cinemas run by chain exhibitors like Famous Players, United Artists, Cinemark, or Cineplex Odeon. Still, the single-screen or twin Bijou, Roxy, or Strand variety of neighborhood theater survives in smaller metro areas and in high-density, older residential areas in larger ones.

CROWD PLEASERS

At different times of the year in Los Angeles-Long Beach, CA, you can visit the animals at the Los Angeles Zoo; join the crowds at the Universal Studios tour; wager on the horses at Hollywood Park or Santa Anita; or take in professional baseball, basketball, and hockey, as well as NCAA Division I competition.

While few metro areas have as varied a supply of crowd pleasers as Los Angeles-Long Beach, some of these opportunities are common in many larger metro areas. From Six Flags Magic Mountain in suburban Los Angeles to New York's Bronx Zoo, these attractions offer Americans interesting ways to spend their leisure time.

Amusement and Theme Parks

The person who started it all was Walter Elias Disney, and his creation was Disneyland. Because he ignored the de rigueur waterfront location and games of chance and skill, the amusement park industry viewed his 180-acre playland skeptically when it opened in Anaheim, California in 1954. Disney's plan was to adapt his cartoon characters and feature films as themes to structure a family-centered park more carefully than Ocean Park in Santa Monica or Chicago's Riverview, tawdry places with carny atmospheres avoided by families. Obviously, he succeeded. North America's tacky parks are largely gone, replaced by more than 100 that market themselves as family theme parks, draw hundreds of thousands of visitors annually, and advertise nationally and regionally as vacation attractions.

Seeing the Animals: Zoos and Aquariums

The two best metro areas for seeing the animals are Chicago and San Diego. Each has not one but two of the continent's top-ranked zoological parks. Altogether, 170 metro areas have at least one zoo. Most are accredited by the American Association of Zoological Parks and Aquariums (AAZPA) or the Canadian counterpart, CAZPA.

The idea that zoos enhance people's lives is a European transplant now flourishing in America's Midwest. Besides Chicago's two great zoos, the Cincinnati, Cleveland, Detroit, Milwaukee, and St. Louis zoological parks are among the best in the United States. It is not coincidental that the working-class citizens of these cities can trace their roots to European countries—particularly Germany—that also have great zoos.

"Postage-stamp collecting" is the name that zookeepers give to the assembling of colorful animal specimens without regard to whether the animals fit and can thrive in a zoo's limited space. This was once a sure way of drawing more patrons and carving out a reputation as an outstanding institution. Today, professionally run zoos exhibit fewer species but more specimens of each. The standard phylogenetic exhibits (grouping African lions with Bengal tigers, timber wolves with hyenas) have been replaced with ecological displays (wildlife in desert or mountain environments) and behavioral exhibits (hibernation, burrowing, nocturnalism) that group specimens more creatively and openly.

This isn't to say that zoos no longer maintain large, diverse collections, for the best zoos are those with the biggest animal populations. But today the benchmark of a zoo's quality isn't simply how many animals it can keep or breed; just as important is how creatively and naturally the animals are exhibited.

Aquariums are far less common than zoos; just 34 of the 354 metro areas have one, most of these in areas with ocean coastlines. Unlike the great zoological parks run by municipalities or by societies, some of the best aquariums, like Boston's New England Aquarium, are owned and operated for profit by private firms.

Rooting for the Home Team

A frequent topic of discussion on talk shows, in bars, and at work is where the "good" sports towns are. The question is usually argued from two perspectives: whether a town has winners or whether fans turn out to root for the teams. These two trends are often linked; over the regular seasons, the clubs with the best attendance usually have had some of the best records.

Another way to find the best sports towns is to measure the access that a metro area's fans have to regular-season games. "Game seats per capita" is an elementary measurement used most often in professional sports franchising and marketing, especially at expansion time. This figure is found by multiplying the number of home games played by all the teams in a metro

Twenty-eight North American zoos and aquariums are visited by at least 1 million people each year. Most are city- or society-owned; several are tourist destinations in their own right.

Zoo	Annual Visitors	Zoo	Annual Visitors
Lincoln Park Zoo Chicago, IL	4,000,000	**Milwaukee County Zoological Gardens** Milwaukee, WI	1,395,601
Sea World Orlando, FL	3,900,000	**Steinhart Aquarium** San Francisco, CA	1,381,000
San Diego Zoo San Diego, CA	3,412,126	**Houston Zoological Gardens** Houston, TX	1,336,336
National Zoological Park Washington, DC	3,300,000	**John G. Shedd Aquarium** Chicago, IL	1,288,966
Sea World San Diego, CA	3,000,000	**Philadelphia Zoological Garden** Philadelphia, PA	1,282,059
Busch Gardens Tampa, FL	3,000,000	**New England Aquarium** Boston, MA	1,262,772
St. Louis Zoological Park St. Louis, MO	2,600,000	**Sea World of Ohio** Aurora, OH	1,250,000
Chicago Zoological Park Chicago, IL	2,000,448	**Denver Zoological Gardens** Denver, CO	1,231,510
Bronx Zoo Bronx, NY	1,997,055	**Cincinnati Zoo & Botanical Garden** Cincinnati, OH	1,225,182
Sea World of Texas San Antonio, TX	1,800,000	**Stanley Park Zoological Gardens** Vancouver, BC	1,200,000
Los Angeles Zoo Los Angeles, CA	1,783,554	**Minnesota Zoo** Apple Valley, MN	1,166,352
Monterey Bay Aquarium Monterey, CA	1,780,721	**Biodome de Montreal** Montreal, PQ	1,100,000
Moody Gardens-Galveston Island Galveston, TX	1,500,000	**Metropolitan Toronto Zoo** Scarborough, ON	1,100,000
San Diego Wild Animal Park Escondido, CA	1,490,909	**Columbus Zoological Park** Powell, OH	1,010,531
National Aquarium Baltimore, MD	1,482,807	**Metro Washington Park Zoo** Portland, OR	1,003,413

Recreation

area (for example, 81 baseball; 41 basketball; 8 football) by the combined seating capacity of the teams' playing arenas and then dividing that number by the metro area's population.

Professional Sports. In arriving at a figure for game seats per capita at professional sporting events, *Places Rated* surveyed each of the 184 metro areas with major-league or minor-league teams in any of four sports: baseball, men's and women's basketball, football, soccer, and hockey. For example, the number of regular-season football games played by the Indianapolis Colts multiplied by the RCA Dome's capacity is 480,000. The same

calculations yield a figure of 758,500 for NBA Pacers basketball games to be played in the new Conseco Fieldhouse, and 1,080,000 for Indians Triple-A baseball games played at Victory Field. The sum of these three figures divided by Indianapolis's metro area population is less than two game seats for everyone in the nine-county metro area. Other metro areas have better averages, and in each of them the presence of a baseball team, with its large stadium and long playing season, makes a good deal of difference.

College Sports. Among the biggest crowd pleasers around are varsity teams fielded by colleges and universities. The cream of those is generally found among the

Which major-league baseball team is descended from the old Beaneaters? It's not the Boston Red Sox; in fact, it's not even an American League team. It's the Atlanta Braves.

This is just one of many odd and intriguing changes major-league baseball teams have undergone since 1876, when eight professional clubs joined forces to form the National League. Twenty-five years later, in 1901, the American League began play, also with eight teams. Since that time, many of the teams have changed names and moved from one city to another, and the leagues have expanded the number of franchises. The list below shows which of today's American League (AL) and National League (NL) teams have moved to another city and/or changed their name since their founding date.*

Anaheim Angels (AL)—*1961,* began as Los Angeles Angels; 1965, moved to Orange County and renamed California Angels; 1997, renamed Anaheim Angels.

Atlanta Braves (NL)—*1876,* began as Boston Red Caps; 1883, renamed Beaneaters; 1907, renamed Doves; 1909, renamed Pilgrims; 1936, renamed Bees; 1941, renamed Braves; 1953, moved to Milwaukee and renamed Milwaukee Braves; 1966, moved to Atlanta and renamed Atlanta Braves.

Baltimore Orioles (AL)—*1901,* began as Milwaukee Brewers; 1902, moved to St. Louis and renamed St. Louis Browns; 1954, moved to Baltimore and renamed Orioles.

Boston Red Sox (AL)—*1901,* began as Somersets; 1905, renamed Puritans; 1907, renamed Red Sox.

Chicago Cubs (NL)—*1876,* began as White Stockings; 1894, renamed Colts; 1898, renamed Orphans; 1903, renamed Cubs.

Cincinnati Reds (NL)—*1876,* began as Red Stockings; 1880, renamed Reds; 1953, renamed Red Legs; 1959, renamed Reds.

Cleveland Indians (AL)—*1901,* began as Blues; 1902, renamed Bronchos [sic]; 1903, renamed Naps; 1914, renamed Indians.

Houston Astros (NL)—*1962,* began as Houston Colt .45's; 1964, renamed Astros.

Los Angeles Dodgers (NL)—*1890,* began as Brooklyn Bridegrooms; 1898, renamed Superbas; 1914, renamed Robins; 1931, renamed Dodgers; 1958, moved to Los Angeles and renamed Los Angeles Dodgers.

Milwaukee Brewers (AL)—*1969,* began as Seattle Pilots; 1970, moved to Milwaukee and renamed Milwaukee Brewers.

Minnesota Twins (AL)—*1901,* began as Washington Senators; 1960, moved to Minneapolis–St. Paul and renamed Minnesota Twins.

New York Yankees (AL)—*1901,* began as Baltimore Orioles; 1903, moved to New York and renamed New York Highlanders; 1912, renamed Yankees.

Oakland A's (AL)—*1901,* began as Philadelphia Athletics; 1955, moved to Kansas City and renamed Kansas City Athletics; 1968, moved to Oakland and renamed Oakland Athletics; 1974, renamed A's.

Philadelphia Phillies (NL)—*1883,* began as Phillies; 1944, renamed Blue Jays; 1946, renamed Phillies.

Pittsburgh Pirates (NL)—*1887,* began as Alleghenys; 1890, renamed Innocents; 1891, renamed Pirates.

San Francisco Giants (NL)—*1879,* began as Troy (NY) Trojans; 1883, moved to New York City and renamed New York Gothams; 1886, renamed Giants; 1958, moved to San Francisco and renamed San Francisco Giants.

St. Louis Cardinals (NL)—*1892,* began as Perfectos; 1899, renamed Cardinals.

Texas Rangers (AL)—*1961,* began as Washington Senators; 1971, moved to Arlington and renamed Texas Rangers.

---

* The Chicago White Sox (AL, 1901), Detroit Tigers (AL, 1901), New York Mets (NL, 1962), Kansas City Royals (AL, 1969), Montreal Expos (NL, 1969), San Diego Padres (NL, 1969), Seattle Mariners (AL, 1977), Toronto Blue Jays (AL, 1977), Colorado Rockies (NL, 1993), Florida Marlins (NL, 1993), Arizona Diamondbacks (NL, 1997), and Tampa Bay Devil Rays (AL, 1997) have neither changed their name nor moved.

teams classified Division I (split into Divisions I-A and I-AA for football only) by the National Collegiate Athletic Association (NCAA). Eligibility for this division is based on the quality of a school's typical opponent, or "schedule strength," and game attendance figures which require big stadiums and arenas.

Nearly 35 million fans attend the 3,251 regular season games played by the 667 colleges and universities with varsity football. Although the 231 Division I-A and I-AA teams play less than one-third of these games, they draw 90 percent of the attendance.

Crowd Pleasers

Basketball is even more widely available. More than 28 million fans come out for the 11,000 or more regular season and tournament games played by the 897 schools that field men's varsity basketball teams. The 316 NCAA Division I men's teams play one-third of these games, yet they account for over 80 percent of total attendance. The 864 women's basketball teams draw another 5 million people to 7,305 season and tournament games, and 80 percent of the crowd watches the 291 NCAA Division I women's teams.

Division I and Canadian Inter-University Athletic Union (CIAU) football, men's and women's basketball, hockey, lacrosse, and soccer are on view in 282 of the 354 metro areas, from the Aces of the University of Evansville to the Zips of the University of Akron.

Using game seats per capita as the criterion, the best metro area for college football and basketball is Lawrence, KS. The number of University of Kansas Jayhawks games played at home multiplied by the seating capacities of Memorial Stadium (football) and Allen Fieldhouse (basketball) yields a figure of 465,498, an astounding seven game seats for everyone in town and in surrounding Douglas County. Fortunately, fans come from nearby Topeka and suburban Kansas City to fill the seats.

Auto Racing: Vrooming, Vrooming

America's love affair with fast cars started in Providence, RI, where the first automobile track race was sponsored in 1896. The affair isn't over, at least in the southeast. At the Atlanta Motor Speedway, true fanatics can live in a condominium above the bleachers and watch NASCAR Winston Cup stock cars race around the 1.522-mile high-banked asphalt oval as they do the dishes. Whether on a "short eight" crash track in rural Oregon or at the Molson Indy course in downtown Toronto, auto racing in all its variations draws million of fans.

Of the 1,405 auto racetracks in the United States and Canada, just 50 are sanctioned by the leading racing organizations: NASCAR, CART, IRL, and SCCA. The crowds at some of their big races are the largest to come together for any sporting event in North America. NASCAR, the National Association for Stock Car Racing, sanctions late-model and modified stock-car racing; CART, or Championship Auto Racing Team, oversees the FedEx series and Indy lights; IRL, the Indy Racing League, has jurisdiction over oval-track Indy Car racing; and SCCA, the Sports Car Club of America, sanctions sports-car events.

HOCKEY'S ODYSSEY

The National Hockey League was formed by five team owners in the Windsor Hotel, in Montreal, nearly 80 years ago.*

Calgary Flames—*1972,* began as Atlanta Flames; 1980, moved to Calgary and renamed Calgary Flames.

Carolina Hurricanes—*1992,* began as New England Whalers (Boston) of the World Hockey Association; 1977, moved to Hartford; 1979, joined NHL; 1997, moved to Greensboro, renamed Carolina Hurricanes; 1999, moved to Raleigh.

Colorado Avalanche—*1972,* began as Quebec Nordiques of the World Hockey Association; 1979, joined NHL; 1995, moved to Denver and renamed Colorado Avalanche.

Dallas Stars—*1967,* began as Minnesota North Stars; 1993, moved to Dallas and renamed Dallas Stars.

Detroit Red Wings—*1926,* began as Cougars; 1929, renamed Falcons; 1932, renamed Red Wings.

Edmonton Oilers—*1972,* began as Alberta Oilers of the World Hockey Association; 1973, renamed Edmonton Oilers; 1979, joined NHL.

New Jersey Devils—*1974,* began as Kansas City Scouts; 1976, moved to Denver and renamed Colorado Rockies; 1982, moved to East Rutherford and renamed New Jersey Devils.

Phoenix Coyotes—*1979,* began as Winnipeg Jets; 1996 moved to Phoenix and renamed Phoenix Coyotes.

Toronto Maple Leafs—*1917,* began as Arenas; 1919, changed name to St. Patricks; 1926, changed name to Maple Leafs.

* The Anaheim Mighty Ducks (1993), Boston Bruins (1924), Buffalo Sabres (1970), Chicago Black Hawks (1926), Florida Panthers (1993), Los Angeles Kings (1967), Montreal Canadiens (1917), New York Islanders (1972), New York Rangers (1926), Ottawa Senators (1992), Philadelphia Flyers (1967), Pittsburgh Penguins (1967), St. Louis Blues (1967), San Jose Sharks (1991), Tampa Bay Lightning (1992), Vancouver Canucks (1970), and Washington Capitals (1974) have neither changed their name nor moved.

Gambling

See a horse player angrily tear up his tickets and toss the confetti into the air after a bad bet at Pimlico, or watch a sad card player sit back and fold 'em at a poker parlor in southern California, and you'd question whether gambling is recreation for anybody.

After professional baseball, however, the biggest spectator sport in North America is pari-mutuel racing

501

Crowd Pleasers

The first NFL franchise in Cleveland belonged not to the Browns but to the Rams, who played such opponents as the Brooklyn Dodgers, Chicago Cardinals, and Pittsburgh Pirates back in the 1930s. Organized professional football began to take shape in 1922 with the establishment of the National Football League, although the early teams seem ragtag compared to today's juggernauts. Through a series of splits and mergers with other leagues over the years, the NFL has remained the dominant pro football organization, and presently consists of 30 teams. The list below recaps the moves and name changes of today's NFL teams since their founding date.*

Arizona Cardinals—*1913,* began as Racine Avenue (Chicago) Cardinals; 1922, renamed Chicago Cardinals; 1960, moved to St. Louis and renamed St. Louis Cardinals; 1988, moved to Phoenix and renamed Arizona Cardinals.

Baltimore Ravens—*1946,* began as Cleveland Browns of the All-America Football Conference; 1950, joined NFL; 1996, moved to Baltimore, renamed Ravens.

Detroit Lions—*1930,* began as Portsmouth (OH) Spartans; 1934, moved to Detroit and renamed Detroit Lions.

Indianapolis Colts—*1952,* defunct Dallas Texans of the All-America Football Conference moved to Baltimore, renamed Baltimore Colts, and joined the NFL; 1983, moved to Indianapolis and renamed Indianapolis Colts.

Kansas City Chiefs—*1959,* began as Dallas Texans of the American Football League; 1963, moved to Kansas City and renamed Kansas City Chiefs; 1970, joined NFL.

New England Patriots—*1959,* began as Boston Patriots of the American Football League; 1970, joined NFL; 1971, renamed New England Patriots.

New York Jets—*1959,* began as New York Titans of the American Football League; 1963, renamed New York Jets; 1970, joined NFL.

Oakland Raiders—*1959,* began as Oakland Raiders of the American Football League; 1970, joined NFL; 1982, moved to Los Angeles and renamed Los Angeles Raiders; 1995, moved to Oakland and renamed Oakland Raiders.

St. Louis Rams—*1937,* began as Cleveland Rams; 1946, moved to Los Angeles and renamed Los Angeles Rams; 1995, moved to St. Louis and renamed St. Louis Rams.

San Diego Chargers—*1959,* franchised as Los Angeles Chargers of the American Football League; 1961, moved to San Diego and renamed San Diego Chargers; 1970, joined NFL.

Tennessee Titans—*1959,* franchised as Houston Oilers of the American Football League; 1997, moved to Memphis as Tennessee Oilers; 1998, moved to Nashville; 1999, renamed Tennessee Titans.

Washington Redskins—*1932,* began as Boston Braves; 1933, renamed Boston Redskins; 1937, moved to Washington and renamed Washington Redskins.

* The Chicago Bears (1922), Green Bay Packers (1922), New York Giants (1925), Philadelphia Eagles (1933), Pittsburgh Steelers (1933), Dallas Cowboys (1960), Minnesota Vikings (1960), Atlanta Falcons (1965), New Orleans Saints (1966), Seattle Seahawks (1974), Tampa Bay Buccaneers (1974), Carolina Panthers (1994), and Jacksonville Jaguars (1994) began as NFL teams and have neither moved nor changed their team name. The Cleveland Browns (1999), a new NFL team, revived the name of the 1946-1996 home team that moved to Baltimore and was renamed the Ravens.

The San Francisco 49ers (1946) are a former All-American Football Conference team that joined the NFL in 1949. The Buffalo Bills (1959), Denver Broncos (1959), Miami Dolphins (1965), and Cincinnati Bengals (1967) are former American Football League franchises that merged with the NFL in 1970.

at the track. Based on a system in which the players who bet on the first-, second-, and third-place finishers share the total amount of money bet, pari-mutuel racing draws more than 100 million people each year.

Thoroughbred racing dominates the American racing scene, but in Delaware, upstate New York, Michigan, and the Chicago environs, harness racing (where the jockey rides behind in a small, two-wheeled cart) attracts more bettors and more money than their thoroughbred competition. In Canada, harness racing outdraws thoroughbred racing two to one.

Greyhound racing was invented more than 90 years ago in South Dakota. Of the fifty-seven tracks, ten account for half of dog racing's 28 million annual attendance. Wonderland is a 20-minute subway ride from downtown Boston. Plainfield Park, near Hartford, is Connecticut's sole pari-mutuel track. The only place where people in western Tennessee, northern Mississippi, and northeastern Arkansas can make a pari-mutuel bet is Southland Park, on the Arkansas side of the Mississippi River, near Memphis.

If they're truly obsessive about making a bet, they can go to the new casinos in Tunica, or Vicksburg, or Philadelphia in Mississippi, or upriver to the Missouri boot heel, or downriver to Louisiana. Casinos, which include table games and bingo and card parlors, are now the most common places to gamble. It's Sacramento—not Atlantic City—that has the most casinos after Las Vegas and Reno. In Boston and Miami, you can now steam 3 miles out to sea beyond the reach of state law for a night of slots and table games aboard ship.

OUTDOOR RECREATION ASSETS

To many people, recreation isn't something taking place entirely within four walls or in the middle of a crowded city. For them, it means turning to the open spaces for fishing, boating, swimming, hiking, running, picnicking, or just getting away from it all.

Just as some metro areas have more to offer in urban recreation, others undeniably are richer in access to the great outdoors. Indeed, more than one-third of the surface area in some places (see map "Outdoor Assets: The West Rules") is inland and offshore water, federal protected areas, and state parks.

Coastlines and Inland Water

Sooners boast that Oklahoma has so many impounded lakes of every size that if you were to tip the state to the south a bit, the water would flow out and flood Texas for a good while. And Maryland crabbers point out to newcomers that the true length of estuarine shore reached by the Chesapeake Bay's tide would total more than 8,000 miles if all the bends and kinks were straightened out.

You'll spot inland water in nine of ten metro areas. Aside from being a basic necessity for life, water can be a scenic and recreational amenity if there is enough to fish in, boat on, or swim in if the temperature is right. Where would Reno be without Lake Tahoe? Or Long Island without Long Island Sound?

Four of every five North Americans today live in metro areas within 100 miles of beaching and boating on the ocean or on any of the Great Lakes. Ocean or Great Lakes coastlines form part of the peripheries of 121 metro areas and 100 percent of another, Honolulu.

National Forests, Parks, and Wildlife Refuges

Some of the most popular outdoor activities—driving for pleasure, walking, picnicking, sightseeing, bird

Recreation

Outdoor Assets:
The West Rules

Copyright © 2000 by Places Rated Partnership

Cape Ann Mapping

503

watching, nature walking, and fishing—are even more enjoyable in the country's splendid system of national forests, parks, and wildlife refuges.

There are 156 national forests and 19 national grasslands on 191 million acres in the United States. The main purpose of the National Forest System is silviculture: growing wood, harvesting it carefully, and preserving naturally beautiful areas. More than 250,000 miles of roads lie within the forest system, built not only for loggers, but for everyone. They lead to a wide variety of recreation outlets: ski resorts, marinas, fishing lakes and streams, hiking trails, and campgrounds.

In contrast to the National Forest System, the National Park System is meant expressly for recreation. The founding of Yellowstone National Park in 1872 marked the beginning of the oldest and now largest national park system in the world. It comprises 354 national parks, preserves, monuments, memorials, battlefields, seashores, waterways, and trails that together cover some 80 million acres.

Whereas the National Park System acts to keep irreplaceable geographical and historical treasures in the public domain, the national wildlife refuges protect native flora and fauna from people. There are 452 of these remarkable sanctuaries throughout the country, embracing more than 89 million acres. Most of them are open to the public for a variety of wildlife activities, particularly photography and nature observation.

In certain refuges at irregular times, fishing and hunting are permitted, depending on the size of the wild populations. Although the majority of the nation's wildlife refuges are located in open, sometimes remote country, they aren't exclusively a rural amenity. Several can be found within metropolitan areas, such as the Nisqually National Wildlife Refuge in Olympia, WA, and San Pablo Bay National Wildlife Refuge in the California metro area of Santa Rosa–Petaluma.

Endless Winter: Skiing

Draw a line on a map of North America separating regions with the best conditions for skiing from those with poor conditions or none at all and you'd have a jagged northward arc. It starts in North Carolina's Great Smoky Mountains and extends upward to Atlantic Canada, west to the foothills of the Rockies, then south along the Rocky Mountain cordillera to northern New Mexico and Arizona. Next it would reappear in the California Sierra Nevada, dropping southwest to end in the San Bernardino National Forest an hour and a half out of Los Angeles.

Although ski areas exist as far south as Alabama and Georgia, the ideal conditions are found north of this imaginary curve in the rolling, rugged terrain and predictable winter weather that everyone except skiers would consider bad.

Of the 569 ski areas in North America, half are found in nine states and provinces that border the St. Lawrence River and the Great Lakes—Michigan, Minnesota, New Hampshire, New York, Ontario, Pennsylvania, Quebec, Vermont, and Wisconsin—owing to harsh, long winters and large, outdoorsy urban populations.

SCORING: RECREATION

Is there more to do in Houston than Dallas? How do the California rivals—Los Angeles and San Francisco—compare? In recreation, let's admit it may be impossible to rank metro areas with fairness. Still, some seem shortchanged while others seem rich. To compare them, *Places Rated* considers the thirteen items that are grouped into common denominators, crowd pleasers, and outdoor assets.

These items take in a lot of information. You might wonder whether there are more than really needed because many, like golf holes and movie screens, go hand in hand with population size. In other words, they are correlated.

How much can be eliminated? *Factor analysis,* a mathematical procedure, systematically reduces many pieces of information about a set of items (here, pieces of recreation information about a set of metro areas) to fewer pieces of information called "factors." Each factor embodies one or more of the original pieces of information.

For recreation, factor analysis uncovered three critical aspects. In decreasing order of importance, they are:

1. The notion of "bigness," taking into account everything from the total number of public golf holes, good restaurants, and movie theater screens to zoos, aquariums, auto racing, gambling, and professional and collegiate sports. No surprise—bigness winners start with Chicago, Los Angeles, and New York. Losers include the smaller areas of

Flagstaff and Yuma in Arizona, Rapid City, SD, and Grand Junction, CO;

2. "Recreation land," or everything from total acres of state parks and federal protected areas (national parks, forests, and wildlife refuges) as a percent of total land area, to acres of those lands per capita, to the circumference of inland lakes. Flagstaff, AZ, a loser in bigness, is a winner here, as are Bellingham, WA, Eugene-Springfield, OR, and Anchorage, AK. Losers include Louisville and Lexington in Kentucky, Columbus, OH, and North Carolina's Triad (Greensboro–Winston-Salem–High Point) and Triangle (Raleigh-Durham-Chapel Hill); and

3. A factor labeled simply "golf, movies, and good food per capita." Losers include giant New York

and Los Angeles, suggesting much time wasted in those areas queuing up for a round of golf or a new Hollywood film. Winners include Myrtle Beach, SC, and Barnstable-Yarmouth, MA, two of the country's best-known resorts.

Factor analysis produces a score for each metro area on each factor. These scores are then weighted by their relative importance—bigness at 60 percent, recreation land at 22 percent, and golf, movies, and good food per capita at 18 percent. A metro area's final score is its percentile on a scale of 0 to 100 corresponding to its rank. New Orleans's score is 100; Jackson, MI's is 50.14; and Altoona, PA's is 0.00. They are respectively the best, average, and worst North American metro areas for recreation.

RANKINGS: RECREATION

Thirteen criteria are used to rate a metro area's supply of recreation assets: (1) amusement and theme parks, (2) aquariums, (3) auto racing, (4) college sports, (5) gambling, (6) golf courses, (7) good restaurants, (8) movie theater screens, (9) professional sports, (10) protected recreation areas, (11) skiing, (12) water area, and (13) zoos. Metro areas that receive tie scores get the same rank and are listed alphabetically.

Metro Areas from Best to Worst

RANK	SCORE
1. New Orleans, LA	100.00
2. Cleveland-Lorain-Elyria, OH	99.71
3. Grand Rapids-Muskegon-Holland, MI	99.43
4. Long Island, NY	99.15
5. Milwaukee-Waukesha, WI	98.86
6. Norfolk-Virginia Beach-Newport News, VA-NC	98.58
7. Rochester, NY	98.30
8. Tampa-St. Petersburg-Clearwater, FL	98.01
9. Orlando, FL	97.73
10. Toronto, ON	97.45
11. Chicago, IL	97.16
12. Riverside-San Bernardino, CA	96.88
13. Detroit, MI	96.60
14. Salt Lake City-Ogden, UT	96.31
15. Minneapolis-St. Paul, MN-WI	96.03
16. West Palm Beach-Boca Raton, FL	95.75
17. Syracuse, NY	95.46
18. Las Vegas, NV-AZ	95.18
19. Phoenix-Mesa, AZ	94.90
20. Barnstable-Yarmouth, MA	94.61
21. Sarasota-Bradenton, FL	94.33
22. Jacksonville, FL	94.05
23. Charleston-North Charleston, SC	93.76
24. San Francisco, CA	93.48
25. Fort Myers-Cape Coral, FL	93.20
26. Honolulu, HI	92.91
27. Los Angeles-Long Beach, CA	92.63
28. New York, NY	92.35

RANK	SCORE
29. Mobile, AL	92.06
30. Daytona Beach, FL	91.78
31. Melbourne-Titusville-Palm Bay, FL	91.50
32. Atlantic-Cape May, NJ	91.21
33. Duluth-Superior, MN-WI	90.93
34. Seattle-Bellevue-Everett, WA	90.65
35. St. Louis, MO-IL	90.36
36. San Diego, CA	90.08
37. Miami, FL	89.80
38. Buffalo-Niagara Falls, NY	89.51
39. Vancouver, BC	89.23
40. Dallas, TX	88.95
41. Washington, DC-MD-VA-WV	88.66
42. Wilmington, NC	88.38
43. Edmonton, AB	88.10
44. Kalamazoo-Battle Creek, MI	87.81
45. Lakeland-Winter Haven, FL	87.53
46. Kansas City, MO-KS	87.25
47. Fort Pierce-Port St. Lucie, FL	86.96
48. Portland-Vancouver, OR-WA	86.68
49. Appleton-Oshkosh-Neenah, WI	86.40
50. Knoxville, TN	86.11
51. Greensboro–Winston-Salem–High Point, NC	85.83
52. Portland, ME	85.55
53. Houston, TX	85.26
54. Baltimore, MD	84.98
55. Monmouth-Ocean, NJ	84.70

continues **505**

Metro Areas from Best to Worst (cont.)

RANK	SCORE	RANK	SCORE
56. Tulsa, OK	84.41	116. Des Moines, IA	67.42
57. Fort Lauderdale, FL	84.13	117. Punta Gorda, FL	67.13
58. Myrtle Beach, SC	83.85	118. Fort Wayne, IN	66.85
59. Oakland, CA	83.56	119. Springfield, MA	66.57
60. Ann Arbor, MI	83.28	120. Panama City, FL	66.28
61. Houma, LA	83.00	121. Worcester, MA-CT	66.00
62. Denver, CO	82.71	122. San Antonio, TX	65.72
63. Biloxi-Gulfport-Pascagoula, MS	82.43	123. Santa Barbara-Santa Maria-Lompoc, CA	65.43
64. Indianapolis, IN	82.15	124. Lansing-East Lansing, MI	65.15
65. Columbus, OH	81.86	125. San Jose, CA	64.87
66. Nashville, TN	81.58	126. Vallejo-Fairfield-Napa, CA	64.58
67. Charlotte-Gastonia-Rock Hill, NC-SC	81.30	127. Calgary, AB	64.30
68. Orange County, CA	81.01	128. Wilmington-Newark, DE-MD	64.02
69. Burlington, VT	80.73	129. Glens Falls, NY	63.73
70. Louisville, KY-IN	80.45	130. Huntsville, AL	63.45
71. Thunder Bay, ON	80.16	131. Portsmouth-Rochester, NH-ME	63.17
72. Omaha, NE-IA	79.88	132. Madison, WI	62.88
73. Salinas, CA	79.60	133. Sheboygan, WI	62.60
74. Providence-Fall River-Warwick, RI-MA	79.32	134. Bridgeport, CT	62.32
75. Tucson, AZ	79.03	135. Brownsville-Harlingen-San Benito, TX	62.03
76. Cincinnati, OH-KY-IN	78.75	136. Chattanooga, TN-GA	61.75
77. Utica-Rome, NY	78.47	137. Harrisburg-Lebanon-Carlisle, PA	61.47
78. Pittsburgh, PA	78.18	138. Tallahassee, FL	61.18
79. Oklahoma City, OK	77.90	139. Dutchess County, NY	60.90
80. Albany-Schenectady-Troy, NY	77.62	140. New Haven-Meriden, CT	60.62
81. Akron, OH	77.33	141. Bangor, ME	60.33
82. Boston, MA-NH	77.05	142. Lexington, KY	60.05
83. Savannah, GA	76.77	143. Gainesville, FL	59.77
84. Newark, NJ	76.48	144. Shreveport-Bossier City, LA	59.49
85. Atlanta, GA	76.20	145. Santa Rosa, CA	59.20
86. Memphis, TN-AR-MS	75.92	146. St. John's, NF	58.92
87. Pensacola, FL	75.63	147. Ottawa-Hull, ON-PQ	58.64
88. Erie, PA	75.35	148. Lowell, MA-NH	58.35
89. Hartford, CT	75.07	149. Winnipeg, MB	58.07
90. Philadelphia, PA-NJ	74.78	150. Baton Rouge, LA	57.79
91. Richmond-Petersburg, VA	74.50	151. Binghamton, NY	57.50
92. Sacramento, CA	74.22	152. Chicoutimi-Jonquiere, PQ	57.22
93. Montreal, PQ	73.93	153. Dayton-Springfield, OH	56.94
94. Youngstown-Warren, OH	73.65	154. Provo-Orem, UT	56.65
95. Birmingham, AL	73.37	155. St. Cloud, MN	56.37
96. Fort Worth-Arlington, TX	73.08	156. Bergen-Passaic, NJ	56.09
97. Raleigh-Durham-Chapel Hill, NC	72.80	157. Hickory-Morganton-Lenoir, NC	55.80
98. Greenville-Spartanburg-Anderson, SC	72.52	158. Jackson, MS	55.52
99. Jamestown, NY	72.23	159. New London-Norwich, CT-RI	55.24
100. Scranton–Wilkes Barre–Hazleton, PA	71.95	160. Racine, WI	54.67
101. Benton Harbor, MI	71.67	161. Ventura, CA	54.67
102. Saint John, NB	71.38	162. Gary, IN	54.39
103. Peoria-Pekin, IL	71.10	163. Wichita, KS	54.10
104. Fort Walton Beach, FL	70.82	164. Macon, GA	53.82
105. Reno, NV	70.53	165. Augusta-Aiken, GA-SC	53.54
106. Albuquerque, NM	70.25	166. Middlesex-Somerset-Hunterdon, NJ	53.25
107. Tacoma, WA	69.97	167. Fayetteville-Springdale-Rogers, AR	52.97
108. Halifax, NS	69.68	168. Lafayette, LA	52.69
109. Columbia, SC	69.40	169. Naples, FL	52.40
110. Toledo, OH	69.12	170. Brockton, MA	52.12
111. Austin-San Marcos, TX	68.83	171. Reading, PA	51.84
112. Saginaw-Bay City-Midland, MI	68.55	172. Regina, SK	51.55
113. Little Rock-North Little Rock, AR	68.27	173. Corpus Christi, TX	51.27
114. Canton-Massillon, OH	67.98	174. Lawrence, MA-NH	50.99
115. Davenport-Moline-Rock Island, IA-IL	67.70	175. Colorado Springs, CO	50.70

RANK	SCORE
176. Newburgh, NY-PA	50.42
177. Jackson, MI	50.14
178. Manchester, NH	49.85
179. Kenosha, WI	49.57
180. Johnson City-Kingsport-Bristol, TN-VA	49.29
181. Beaumont-Port Arthur, TX	49.00
182. Huntington-Ashland, WV-KY-OH	48.72
183. Pittsfield, MA	48.44
184. Lynchburg, VA	48.15
185. Allentown-Bethlehem-Easton, PA	47.87
186. New Bedford, MA	47.59
187. Victoria, BC	47.30
188. Fargo-Moorhead, ND-MN	47.02
189. South Bend, IN	46.74
190. Boise City, ID	46.17
191. Boulder-Longmont, CO	46.17
192. Galveston-Texas City, TX	45.60
193. San Luis Obispo-Atascadero-Paso Robles, CA	45.60
194. Bloomington, IN	45.32
195. Trenton, NJ	45.04
196. Rockford, IL	44.75
197. Grand Forks, ND-MN	44.47
198. La Crosse, WI-MN	44.19
199. Iowa City, IA	43.90
200. St. Catharines-Niagara, ON	43.62
201. Bremerton, WA	43.34
202. Sudbury, ON	43.05
203. Columbus, GA-AL	42.77
204. El Paso, TX	42.49
205. Bismarck, ND	41.92
206. Green Bay, WI	41.92
207. Springfield, MO	41.64
208. Eugene-Springfield, OR	41.35
209. Saskatoon, SK	41.07
210. Lincoln, NE	40.79
211. Flint, MI	40.50
212. Florence, AL	40.22
213. Spokane, WA	39.94
214. Roanoke, VA	39.66
215. Hattiesburg, MS	39.37
216. Hamilton, ON	39.09
217. Asheville, NC	38.81
218. Cedar Rapids, IA	38.52
219. Lawrence, KS	38.24
220. Janesville-Beloit, WI	37.96
221. Jacksonville, NC	37.67
222. Lancaster, PA	37.39
223. Lafayette, IN	37.11
224. Windsor, ON	36.82
225. Columbia, MO	36.54
226. Brazoria, TX	35.97
227. State College, PA	35.97
228. Johnstown, PA	35.69
229. Eau Claire, WI	35.41
230. Charlottesville, VA	35.12
231. Quebec City, PQ	34.84
232. Stamford-Norwalk, CT	34.56
233. Sioux Falls, SD	34.27
234. Tuscaloosa, AL	33.99
235. Parkersburg-Marietta, WV-OH	33.71

RANK	SCORE
236. Montgomery, AL	33.42
237. Decatur, AL	33.14
238. Nashua, NH	32.86
239. Missoula, MT	32.57
240. Stockton-Lodi, CA	32.29
241. Athens, GA	32.01
242. Champaign-Urbana, IL	31.72
243. Fitchburg-Leominster, MA	31.44
244. Fort Smith, AR-OK	31.16
245. Bakersfield, CA	30.87
246. Amarillo, TX	30.59
247. Springfield, IL	30.31
248. Hamilton-Middletown, OH	30.02
249. Sharon, PA	29.74
250. Bloomington-Normal, IL	29.46
251. London, ON	29.17
252. Bryan-College Station, TX	28.89
253. Waco, TX	28.61
254. Richland-Kennewick-Pasco, WA	28.32
255. Waterloo-Cedar Falls, IA	28.04
256. Tyler, TX	27.76
257. Fresno, CA	27.47
258. Evansville-Henderson, IN-KY	27.19
259. Muncie, IN	26.91
260. Sherman-Denison, TX	26.62
261. Santa Cruz-Watsonville, CA	26.34
262. Fort Collins-Loveland, CO	26.06
263. Olympia, WA	25.77
264. Wausau, WI	25.49
265. Lima, OH	25.21
266. Lubbock, TX	24.92
267. Terre Haute, IN	24.64
268. Sioux City, IA-NE	24.36
269. Wichita Falls, TX	24.07
270. Sherbrooke, PQ	23.79
271. Bellingham, WA	23.51
272. Las Cruces, NM	23.22
273. McAllen-Edinburg-Mission, TX	22.94
274. Alexandria, LA	22.66
275. Hagerstown, MD	22.37
276. Topeka, KS	22.09
277. York, PA	21.81
278. Longview-Marshall, TX	21.52
279. Flagstaff, AZ-UT	21.24
280. Killeen-Temple, TX	20.96
281. Ocala, FL	20.67
282. Greeley, CO	20.39
283. Lewiston-Auburn, ME	20.11
284. Rapid City, SD	19.83
285. Dubuque, IA	19.54
286. Charleston, WV	19.26
287. Dover, DE	18.98
288. Kankakee, IL	18.69
289. Owensboro, KY	18.41
290. Yakima, WA	18.13
291. Monroe, LA	17.84
292. Wheeling, WV-OH	17.56
293. Fayetteville, NC	17.28
294. Kitchener-Waterloo, ON	16.99

continues

RANK	SCORE
295. Billings, MT	16.71
296. Lake Charles, LA	16.43
297. Jersey City, NJ	16.14
298. Redding, CA	15.86
299. Mansfield, OH	15.58
300. Danbury, CT	15.29
301. Santa Fe, NM	15.01
302. Pocatello, ID	14.73
303. Greenville, NC	14.44
304. San Angelo, TX	14.16
305. Anniston, AL	13.88
306. Salem, OR	13.59
307. Steubenville-Weirton, OH-WV	13.31
308. Medford-Ashland, OR	13.03
309. Clarksville-Hopkinsville, TN-KY	12.74
310. Kokomo, IN	12.46
311. Odessa-Midland, TX	12.18
312. Chico-Paradise, CA	11.89
313. Elmira, NY	11.61
314. Pueblo, CO	11.33
315. Casper, WY	11.04
316. Vineland-Millville-Bridgeton, NJ	10.76
317. Grand Junction, CO	10.48
318. Joplin, MO	10.19
319. Rochester, MN	9.91
320. Oshawa, ON	9.63
321. Great Falls, MT	9.34
322. Merced, CA	9.06
323. Modesto, CA	8.78
324. Yuma, AZ	8.49

RANK	SCORE
325. Gadsden, AL	8.21
326. Decatur, IL	7.93
327. Sumter, SC	7.64
328. Waterbury, CT	7.36
329. St. Joseph, MO	7.08
330. Albany, GA	6.79
331. Yolo, CA	6.51
332. Anchorage, AK	6.23
333. Cheyenne, WY	5.94
334. Jonesboro, AR	5.66
335. Yuba City, CA	5.38
336. Pine Bluff, AR	5.09
337. Visalia-Tulare-Porterville, CA	4.81
338. Jackson, TN	4.53
339. Lawton, OK	4.24
340. Texarkana, TX-Texarkana, AR	3.96
341. Elkhart-Goshen, IN	3.68
342. Victoria, TX	3.39
343. Trois-Rivieres, PQ	3.11
344. Abilene, TX	2.83
345. Cumberland, MD-WV	2.54
346. Dothan, AL	2.26
347. Florence, SC	1.98
348. Enid, OK	1.69
349. Williamsport, PA	1.41
350. Danville, VA	1.13
351. Goldsboro, NC	0.84
352. Laredo, TX	0.56
353. Rocky Mount, NC	0.28
354. Altoona, PA	0.00

PLACE PROFILES: RECREATION

The following profiles are a selective catalogue of recreation features in each metro area. A star (★) preceding a metro area's name highlights it as one of North America's top thirty-five areas for recreation assets.

American protected recreation lands include national forest, park, and wildlife refuge acres, plus state park units located within metro-area counties. Canadian protected lands include all federal parks, natural areas and wildlife areas, plus all provincial parks and natural areas located within metro-area census divisions. A number of abbreviations are used in this section:

MBS	Migratory Bird Sanctuary
NF	National Forest
NP	National Park
NRA	National Recreation Area
NS	National Seashore
NSR	National Scenic River

NWA	National Wildlife Area
NWR	National Wildlife Refuge
PNA	Provincial Natural Area
PP	Provincial Park
SF	State Forest
SNA	State Natural Area
SP	State Park
SRA	State Recreation Area

Information comes from these sources: American Association of Zoological Parks and Aquariums, *Zoological Parks and Aquariums in the Americas*, 1999; American Automobile Association, unpublished restaurant data, 1999; American Baseball League, unpublished data, 1999; American Hockey League, Media Guide, 1999; American Business Lists, unpublished movie theatre data, 1999; Association of Racing Commissioners International, unpublished data, 1999; Baseball America,

Directory, 1999; Canadian Association of Zoological Parks and Aquariums, *Zoos, Aquariums, and Game Farms,* 1998; Canadian Inter-University Athletic Union, *Directory,* 1999; Continental Basketball Association, unpublished data, 1999; Environment Canada, unpublished national conservation area data, 1997; *Film Canada Yearbook,* 1999; International Hockey League, *Media Guide,* 1999; Inter-ski Associates, *White Book of Skiing,* 1999; National Association of Professional Baseball Leagues, unpublished data, 1999; National Association of Theater Owners, *Encyclopedia of Exhibition,* 1999; National Basketball Association, unpublished data, 1999; National Collegiate Athletic Association, *National Collegiate Championships,* 1999, *NCAA Basketball,* 1999, *and NCAA Football,* 1999; National Football League, unpublished data, 1999; National Golf Foundation, unpublished data, 1996; National Hockey League, unpublished data, 1996; National League of Professional Baseball Teams, unpublished data, 1996; Quigley Publishing Company, *Motion Picture Almanac,* 1999; U.S. Department of Agriculture, Forest Service, *Land Areas of the National Forest System,* 1999; U.S. Department of Commerce: Bureau of the Census, unpublished "Coastal Counties of the United States," and unpublished area measurements, 1990; U.S. Department of the Interior, Fish and Wildlife Service, unpublished master deed listing, 1999; and National Park Service, *Index to the National Park System and Related Areas,* 1999, and unpublished master deed listing, 1999.

Abilene, TX

Golf Courses
2 Daily fee, 36 holes
2 Municipal, 27 holes
2 Private, 36 holes

Good Restaurants
4 Family ◆◆

Movie Theatres
2 Singles/Twins; 2 Multiplexes
18 Screens

Recreation Areas
State
Abilene SRA, 1,242 acres

Water Area
Lakes and rivers: 2,560 acres

Zoos
Abilene Zoo

Score: 2.83   Rank: 344

Akron, OH

Amusement & Theme Parks
Geauga Lake

Aquarium
Sea World of Ohio

College NCAA I Sports
Kent State Golden Flashes
U of Akron Zips

Golf Courses
30 Daily fee, 549 holes
4 Municipal, 72 holes
12 Private, 243 holes

Good Restaurants
3 Simple ◆
11 Family ◆◆
6 Adult ◆◆◆

Movie Theatres
4 Singles/Twins; 8 Multiplexes
80 Screens

Professional Sports
Aeros (Class AA Baseball)

Recreation Areas
Federal
Cuyahoga Valley NRA, 16,069 acres

State
Eagle Creek SNA, 441 acres
Nelson-Kennedy Ledges SP, 167 acres
Portage Lakes SP, 2,443 acres
Tinkers Creek SP, 1,143 acres
West Branch SP, 5,352 acres

Skiing
4 ski areas
Lift capacity/hour: 45,000

Water Area
Lakes and rivers: 14,080 acres

Zoos
Akron Zoological Park

Score: 77.33   Rank: 81

Albany, GA

Golf Courses
2 Daily fee, 36 holes
1 Municipal, 18 holes
4 Private, 63 holes

Good Restaurants
2 Simple ◆
1 Family ◆◆

Movie Theatres
2 Multiplexes
15 screens

Water Area
Lakes and rivers: 7,040 acres

Zoos
Chehaw Wild Animal Park

Score: 6.79   Rank: 330

Albany-Schenectady-Troy, NY

Amusement & Theme Parks
Hoffman's Playland

College NCAA I Sports
Rensselaer Engineers
Siena College Saints
Union College

Gambling
Saratoga Raceway (mixed meetings)

Golf Courses
27 Daily fee, 405 holes
6 Municipal, 126 holes
15 Private, 270 holes

Good Restaurants
6 Simple ◆
20 Family ◆◆
16 Adult ◆◆◆
1 Upscale ◆◆◆◆

Movie Theatres
7 Singles/Twins; 12 Multiplexes
125 Screens

Professional Sports
River Rats (AHL Hockey)

Recreation Areas
State
Castleton Island SP, 300 acres
Cherry Plain SP, 175 acres
Grafton Lakes SP, 2,357 acres
John B. Thatcher SP, 1,347 acres
Max V. Shaul SP, 70 acres
Mine Kill SP, 500 acres
Moreau SP, 893 acres
Peebles Island SP, 142 acres
Saratoga Lake Boat Launch SP, 4 acres
Saratoga Spa SP, 2,033 acres
Thompson's Lake Camp SP, 152 acres

Skiing
32 ski areas
Lift capacity/hour: 192,395

Water Area
Lakes and rivers: 42,880 acres

Score: 77.62   Rank: 80

Albuquerque, NM

Amusement & Theme Parks
Cliff's Amusement Park

College NCAA I Sports
U of New Mexico Lobos

Gambling
3 Casinos
The Downs (mixed meetings)

Golf Courses
7 Daily fee, 126 holes
5 Municipal, 108 holes
5 Private, 108 holes
Good Restaurants
12 Simple ♦♦
33 Family ♦♦
14 Adult ♦♦♦
Movie Theatres
3 Singles/Twins; 11 Multiplexes
95 Screens
Professional Sports
Dukes (Triple A Baseball)
Recreation Areas
Federal
Bandelier NM, 25,428 acres
Cibola NF, 137,137 acres
Petroglyph NM, 1,752 acres
Santa Fe NF, 339,094 acres
State
Fenton Lake SP, 735 acres
Senator Chavez SP, 110 acres
Skiing
5 ski areas
Lift capacity/hour: 28,100
Water Area
Lakes and rivers: 5,760 acres
Zoos
Rio Grande Zoological Park
Score: 70.25   Rank: 106

Alexandria, LA
Golf Courses
3 Daily fee, 27 holes
1 Municipal, 9 holes
2 Private, 36 holes
Good Restaurants
1 Simple ♦
2 Family ♦♦
Movie Theatres
4 Multiplexes
26 Screens
Recreation Areas
Federal
Kisatchee NF, 100,959 acres
Water Area
Lakes and rivers: 24,960 acres
Zoos
Alexandria Zoo
Score: 22.66   Rank: 274

Allentown-Bethlehem-Easton, PA
Amusement & Theme Parks
Bushkill Park
Dorney Park & Wild Water Kingdom
Auto Racing
Nazareth Speedway
College NCAA I Sports
Lafayette Leopards
Lehigh Engineers
Golf Courses
14 Daily fee, 225 holes
1 Municipal, 27 holes
8 Private, 180 holes

Good Restaurants
5 Simple ♦
7 Family ♦♦
12 Adult ♦♦♦
Movie Theatres
9 Singles/Twins; 6 Multiplexes
50 Screens
Professional Sports
Valley Dawgs (USBL Basketball)
Recreation Areas
Federal
Appalachian NT, 2,323 acres
Delaware Water Gap NRA,
1,168 acres
State
Beltzville SP, 2,972 acres
Delaware Canal SP, 70 acres
Hickory Run SP, 15,482 acres
Jacobsburg SP, 1,167 acres
Lehigh Gorge SP, 3,390 acres
Skiing
18 ski areas
Lift capacity/hour: 160,900
Water Area
Lakes and rivers: 7,680 acres
Score: 47.87   Rank: 185

Altoona, PA
Amusement & Theme Parks
Bland's Park
Golf Courses
4 Daily fee, 45 holes
3 Private, 54 holes
Good Restaurants
2 Family ♦♦
1 Adult ♦♦♦
Movie Theatres
2 Multiplexes
15 Screens
Professional Sports
Curve (Class AA Baseball)
Recreation Areas
State
Canoe Creek SP, 959 acres
Skiing
2 ski areas
Lift capacity/hour: 10,000
Water Area
Lakes and rivers: 640 acres
Score: 0.00   Rank: 354

Amarillo, TX
Amusement & Theme Parks
Wonderland
Golf Courses
5 Daily fee, 72 holes
2 Municipal, 54 holes
2 Private, 36 holes
Good Restaurants
2 Simple ♦
16 Family ♦♦
Movie Theatres
1 Single/Twin; 5 Multiplexes
30 Screens

Recreation Areas
Federal
Alibates Flint Quarries NM,
1,079 acres
Buffalo Lake NWR, 7,664 acres
Lake Meredith NRA, 23,379 acres
State
Palo Duro Canyon SP, 14,680 acres
Water Area
Lakes and rivers: 13,440 acres
Zoos
Amarillo Zoo
Storyland Zoo
Thompson Park Zoo
Score: 30.59   Rank: 246

Anchorage, AK
College NCAA I Sports
U of Alaska Seawolves
Golf Courses
3 Daily fee, 45 holes
2 Municipal, 27 holes
Good Restaurants
4 Family ♦♦
4 Adult ♦♦♦
1 Upscale ♦♦♦♦
Movie Theatres
3 Singles/Twins; 7 Multiplexes
51 Screens
Recreation Areas
Federal
Chugach NF, 274,983 acres
State
Chugach SP, 495,204 acres
Skiing
3 ski areas
Lift capacity/hour: 15,000
Water Area
Lakes and rivers: 26,240 acres
Pacific coast: 142,080 acres
Zoos
Alaska Zoo
Score: 6.23   Rank: 332

Ann Arbor, MI
Amusement & Theme Parks
Prehistoric Forest
College NCAA I Sports
Eastern Michigan Eagles
U of Michigan Wolverines
Golf Courses
35 Daily fee, 603 holes
7 Municipal, 126 holes
13 Private, 216 holes
Good Restaurants
6 Simple ♦
11 Family ♦♦
5 Adult ♦♦♦
Movie Theatres
5 Singles/Twins; 4 Multiplexes
48 Screens

Recreation Areas
State
Brighton SRA, 4,913 acres
Island Lake SRA, 3,272 acres
Lake Hudson SRA, 2,650 acres
Lakelands Trail SP, 3 acres
Pinckney SRA, 9,994 acres
W.J. Hayes SP, 632 acres
Waterloo SRA, 6,887 acres
Skiing
9 ski areas
Lift capacity/hour: 102,060
Water Area
Lakes and rivers: 26,240 acres
Zoos
University of Michigan Zoology
Museum
Score: 83.28   Rank: 60

Anniston, AL
College NCAA I Sports
Jacksonville State Gamecocks
Golf Courses
3 Daily fee, 54 holes
3 Municipal, 36 holes
1 Private, 18 holes
Good Restaurants
1 Adult ◆◆◆
Movie Theatres
1 Single/Twin; 2 Multiplexes
13 Screens
Recreation Areas
Federal
Talladega NF, 23,603 acres
Water Area
Lakes and rivers: 2,560 acres
Score: 13.88   Rank: 305

Appleton-Oshkosh-Neenah, WI
Golf Courses
19 Daily fee, 297 holes
2 Municipal, 36 holes
6 Private, 99 holes
Good Restaurants
12 Family ◆◆
3 Upscale ◆◆◆◆
Movie Theatres
2 Singles/Twins; 5 Multiplexes
45 Screens
Professional Sports
Blast (IBA Basketball)
Timber Rattlers (Class A Baseball)
Recreation Areas
State
High Cliff SP, 1,145 acres
Wiouwash State Trail, 108 acres
Skiing
8 ski areas
Lift capacity/hour: 11,400
Water Area
Lakes and rivers: 141,440 acres
Score: 86.40   Rank: 49

Asheville, NC
College NCAA I Sports
U of North Carolina Bulldogs
Golf Courses
4 Daily fee, 63 holes
2 Municipal, 36 holes
4 Private, 72 holes
Good Restaurants
2 Simple ◆
16 Family ◆◆
6 Adult ◆◆◆
2 Upscale ◆◆◆◆
Movie Theatres
5 Singles/Twins; 2 Multiplexes
33 Screens
Professional Sports
Tourists (Class A Baseball)
Recreation Areas
Federal
Appalachian NT, 250 acres
Blue Ridge Parkway, 5,673 acres
Pisgah NF, 86,161 acres
Skiing
3 ski areas
Lift capacity/hour: 6,200
Water Area
Lakes and rivers: 3,840 acres
Zoos
Western North Carolina Nature Center
Score: 38.81   Rank: 217

Athens, GA
College NCAA I Sports
U of Georgia Bulldogs
Golf Courses
4 Daily fee, 72 holes
2 Private, 45 holes
Good Restaurants
1 Simple ◆
2 Family ◆◆
Movie Theatres
1 Single/Twin; 3 Multiplexes
24 Screens
Recreation Areas
Federal
Oconee NF, 157 acres
State
Watson Mill Bridge SP, 600 acres
Water Area
Lakes and rivers: 640 acres
Zoos
Memorial Park
Score: 32.01   Rank: 241

Atlanta, GA
Amusement & Theme Parks
Six Flags Over Georgia
Sun Valley Beach
Auto Racing
Atlanta Motor Speedway
College NCAA I Sports
Georgia Tech Yellow Jackets
Georgia State Panthers

Golf Courses
60 Daily fee, 1,071 holes
15 Municipal, 252 holes
52 Private, 1,026 holes
Good Restaurants
28 Simple ◆
99 Family ◆◆
74 Adult ◆◆◆
15 Upscale ◆◆◆◆
4 Best ◆◆◆◆◆
Movie Theatres
12 Singles/Twins; 58 Multiplexes
517 Screens
Professional Sports
Braves (NL Baseball)
Falcons (NFL Football)
Hawks (NBA Basketball)
Thrashers (NHL Hockey)
Trojans (USBL Basketball)
Recreation Areas
Federal
Chattahoochee River NRA,
4,417 acres
Kennesaw Mountain NBP,
2,880 acres
State
Hard Labor Creek SP, 3,005 acres
John Tanner SP, 136 acres
Panola Mountain SP, 617 acres
Red Top Mountain SP, 1,950 acres
Sweetwater Creek SP, 1,986 acres
Water Area
Lakes and rivers: 55,040 acres
Zoos
Stone Mountain Park
Zoo Atlanta
Score: 76.20   Rank: 85

★ **Atlantic City-Cape May, NJ**
Amusement & Theme Parks
Gillian's Island Water Theme Park
Gambling
14 Casinos
Atlantic City Race Course
(thoroughbred)
Golf Courses
16 Daily fee, 252 holes
2 Municipal, 27 holes
7 Private, 144 holes
Good Restaurants
7 Simple ◆
19 Family ◆◆
17 Adult ◆◆◆
1 Upscale ◆◆◆◆
Movie Theatres
3 Singles/Twins; 20 Multiplexes
145 Screens
Professional Sports
Seagulls (USBL Basketball)
Recreation Areas
Federal
Cape May NWR, 8,099 acres
Edwin B. Forsythe NWR,
20,223 acres

State
- Cape May Point SP, 190 acres
- Cape May Wetlands SNA, 3,715 acres
- Corson's Inlet SP, 341 acres
- Great Sound SP, 217 acres
- North Brigantine SNA, 680 acres
- Strathmere SNA, 95 acres

Water Area
- Lakes and rivers: 51,200 acres
- Atlantic coast: 110,080 acres

Zoos
- Birch Grove Park Zoo

Score: 91.21   Rank: 32

Augusta-Aiken, GA-SC
Golf Courses
- 16 Daily fee, 252 holes
- 1 Municipal, 18 holes
- 9 Private, 207 holes

Good Restaurants
- 4 Simple ♦
- 9 Family ♦♦
- 3 Adult ♦♦♦

Movie Theatres
- 1 Single/Twin; 8 Multiplexes
- 63 Screens

Professional Sports
- Greenjackets (Class A Baseball)

Recreation Areas
- Federal
  - Sumter NF, 31,056 acres
- State
  - Aiken SP, 1,067 acres
  - Mistletoe SP, 1,920 acres

Water Area
- Lakes and rivers: 26,240 acres

Score: 53.54   Rank: 165

Austin-San Marcos, TX
College NCAA I Sports
- SW Texas State Bobcats
- U of Texas Longhorns

Gambling
- Manor Downs (mixed meetings)

Golf Courses
- 17 Daily fee, 297 holes
- 10 Municipal, 162 holes
- 12 Private, 279 holes

Good Restaurants
- 2 Simple ♦
- 32 Family ♦♦
- 26 Adult ♦♦♦

Movie Theatres
- 2 Singles/Twins; 19 Multiplexes
- 150 Screens

Recreation Areas
- Federal
  - Balcones Canyonlands NWR, 11,194 acres

State
- Bastrop SP, 3,504 acres
- Buescher SP, 1,017 acres
- Lake Bastrop SRA, 785 acres
- Lockhart SRA, 264 acres
- McKinney Falls SP, 641 acres

Water Area
- Lakes and rivers: 36,480 acres

Zoos
- Austin Nature Center
- Austin Zoo

Score: 68.83   Rank: 111

Bakersfield, CA
Auto Racing
- Mesa Marin Raceway

Gambling
- 7 Casinos

Golf Courses
- 7 Daily fee, 99 holes
- 6 Municipal, 108 holes
- 8 Private, 126 holes

Good Restaurants
- 5 Simple ♦
- 2 Family ♦♦
- 5 Adult ♦♦♦

Movie Theatres
- 4 Singles/Twins; 3 Multiplexes
- 22 Screens

Professional Sports
- Blaze (Class A Baseball)

Recreation Areas
- Federal
  - Bitter Creek NWR, 13,932 acres
  - Kern NWR, 10,618 acres
  - Los Padres NF, 64,803 acres
  - Sequoia NF, 312,000 acres
- State
  - Red Rock Canyon SP, 28,000 acres
  - Tule Elk SR, 946 acres

Skiing
- 10 ski areas
- Lift capacity/hour: 90,690

Water Area
- Lakes and rivers: 12,800 acres

Zoos
- California Living Museum

Score: 30.87   Rank: 245

Baltimore, MD
Aquariums
- National Aquarium

College NCAA I Sports
- Coppin State Eagles
- Johns Hopkins Blue Jays
- Loyola Greyhounds
- Morgan State Bears
- Naval Academy Midshipmen
- Towson State Tigers
- U of Maryland Retrievers

Gambling
- Pimlico (thoroughbred)
- Timonium (thoroughbred)

Golf Courses
- 22 Daily fee, 369 holes
- 12 Municipal, 216 holes
- 33 Private, 648 holes

Good Restaurants
- 4 Simple ♦
- 48 Family ♦♦
- 20 Adult ♦♦♦
- 1 Upscale ♦♦♦♦

Movie Theatres
- 9 Singles/Twins; 29 Multiplexes
- 214 Screens

Professional Sports
- Orioles (AL Baseball)
- Ravens (NFL Football)

Recreation Areas
- Federal
  - National Capital Parks, 432 acres
  - Susquehanna NWR, 4 acres
- State
  - Gunpowder Falls SP, 14,340 acres
  - Hart-Miller Island SP, 244 acres
  - Morgan Run SNA, 1,300 acres
  - Patapsco Valley SP, 13,309 acres
  - Patuxent River SP, 3,469 acres
  - Rocks SP, 855 acres
  - Sandy Point SP, 786 acres
  - Soldier's Delight SNA, 1,815 acres
  - Tuckahoe SP, 1,842 acres
  - Wye Island SNA, 2,514 acres

Skiing
- 4 ski areas
- Lift capacity/hour: 38,520

Water Area
- Lakes and rivers: 87,680 acres
- Atlantic coast: 229,120 acres

Zoos
- Baltimore Zoo

Score: 84.98   Rank: 54

Bangor, ME
College NCAA I Sports
- U of Maine Black Bears

Gambling
- Bangor Raceway (harness)

Golf Courses
- 6 Daily fee, 63 holes
- 1 Municipal, 27 holes
- 1 Private, 18 holes

Good Restaurants
- 1 Simple ♦
- 7 Family ♦♦
- 1 Adult ♦♦♦

Movie Theatres
- 1 Single/Twin; 1 Multiplex
- 11 Screens

Skiing
- 4 ski areas
- Lift capacity/hour: 7,000

Water Area
- Lakes and rivers: 11,027 acres

Score: 60.33   Rank: 141

★ Barnstable-Yarmouth, MA

Aquariums
Aquarium of Cape Cod

Golf Courses
3 Daily fee, 72 holes
4 Municipal, 54 holes
2 Private, 36 holes

Good Restaurants
10 Simple ◆
33 Family ◆ ◆
11 Adult ◆ ◆ ◆

Movie Theatres
3 Singles/Twins; 4 Multiplexes
37 Screens

Recreation Areas
State
Hawksnest SP, 218 acres
Nickerson SP, 1,995 acres
Scusset Beach State Reservation,
380 acres
South Cape Beach SP, 401 acres
Waquoit Bay Estuarine Reserve,
1,799 acres

Water Area
Lakes and rivers: 44,512 acres
Atlantic coast: 54,400 acres

Score: 94.61   Rank: 20

Baton Rouge, LA

Amusement & Theme Parks
Fun Fair Park

College NCAA I Sports
Louisiana State Tigers
Southern U Jaguars

Gambling
2 Casinos

Golf Courses
4 Daily fee, 72 holes
6 Municipal, 90 holes
9 Private, 126 holes

Good Restaurants
11 Family ◆ ◆
2 Adult ◆ ◆ ◆

Movie Theatres
5 Multiplexes
45 Screens

Professional Sports
Panthers (ECHL Hockey)

Recreation Areas
State
Tickfaw SP, 1,169 acres

Water Area
Lakes and rivers: 59,520 acres

Zoos
Greater Baton Rouge Zoo

Score: 57.79   Rank: 150

Beaumont-Port Arthur, TX

College NCAA I Sports
Lamar U Cardinals

Golf Courses
6 Daily fee, 108 holes
2 Municipal, 36 holes
6 Private, 99 holes

Good Restaurants
1 Family ◆ ◆

Movie Theatres
4 Singles/Twins; 5 Multiplexes
37 Screens

Recreation Areas
Federal
Big Thicket N Preserve, 1,636 acres
Big Thicket NP, 46,136 acres
McFaddin NWR, 47,145 acres
Texas Point NWR, 8,952 acres
State
Sea Rim SP, 15,094 acres
Village Creek SP, 942 acres

Water Area
Lakes and rivers: 72,320 acres
Gulf coast: 7680 acres

Score: 49.00   Rank: 181

Bellingham, WA

Golf Courses
13 Daily fee, 189 holes
1 Municipal, 18 holes
4 Private, 54 holes

Good Restaurants
6 Family ◆ ◆
6 Adult ◆ ◆ ◆

Movie Theatres
3 Multiplexes
15 Screens

Recreation Areas
Federal
Mt. Baker NF, 452,896 acres
North Cascades NP, 281,690 acres
Ross Lake NRA, 107,067 acres
San Juan Islands NWR, 3 acres
State
Birch Bay SP, 193 acres
Larrabee SP, 2,389 acres

Skiing
2 ski areas
Lift capacity/hour: 9,500

Water Area
Lakes and rivers: 35,200 acres
Puget Sound: 21,056 acres

Score: 23.51   Rank: 271

Benton Harbor, MI

Golf Courses
9 Daily fee, 180 holes
2 Municipal, 18 holes
6 Private, 90 holes

Good Restaurants
4 Simple ◆
5 Family ◆ ◆
1 Adult ◆ ◆ ◆

Movie Theatres
2 Singles/Twins; 1 Multiplex
8 Screens

Recreation Areas
State
Grand Mere SP, 985 acres
Warren Dunes SP, 1,950 acres
Warren Woods SP, 311 acres

Skiing
3 ski areas
Lift capacity/hour: 18,600

Water Area
Lakes and rivers: 5,760 acres
Great Lakes coast: 640,000 acres

Score: 71.67   Rank: 101

● Bergen-Passaic, NJ

Amusement & Theme Parks
Tomahawk Lake

College NCAA I Sports
Fairleigh Dickinson Knights

Gambling
Meadowlands Park (mixed meetings)

Golf Courses
6 Daily fee, 90 holes
6 Municipal, 126 holes
16 Private, 297 holes

Good Restaurants
3 Simple ◆
7 Family ◆ ◆
8 Adult ◆ ◆ ◆
1 Upscale ◆ ◆ ◆ ◆

Movie Theatres
6 Singles/Twins; 20 Multiplexes
117 Screens

Professional Sports
Giants (NFL Football)
Jets (NFL Football)
Nets (NBA Basketball)
Devils (NHL Hockey)

Recreation Areas
Federal
Appalachian NT, 26 acres
State
Greenwood Lake SP, 217 acres
Ringwood SP, 5,237 acres
Wawayanda SP, 4,454 acres

Skiing
10 ski areas
Lift capacity/hour: 54,700

Water Area
Lakes and rivers: 16,000 acres

Zoos
Bergen County Zoological Park
Van Saun Park Zoo

Score: 56.09   Rank: 156

● Billings, MT

Gambling
9 Casinos
Metra Park (mixed meetings)

Golf Courses
3 Daily fee, 45 holes
1 Municipal, 18 holes
5 Private, 90 holes

Good Restaurants
1 Simple ◆
4 Family ◆ ◆
3 Adult ◆ ◆ ◆

Movie Theatres
2 Singles/Twins; 3 Multiplexes
22 Screens

Professional Sports

Rim Rockers (IBA Basketball)

Recreation Areas

State

Lake Elmo SP, 120 acres

Skiing

2 ski areas

Lift capacity/hour: 23,200

Water Area

Lakes and rivers: 8,960 acres

Zoos

Zoo Montana

Score: **16.71**   Rank: **295**

Biloxi-Gulfport-Pascagoula, MS

Amusement & Theme Parks

Fun Time USA

Marine Life

Gambling

12 Casinos

Golf Courses

16 Daily fee, 297 holes

1 Municipal, 18 holes

4 Private, 63 holes

Good Restaurants

1 Simple ◆

4 Family ◆◆

3 Adult ◆◆◆

Movie Theatres

3 Singles/Twins; 7 Multiplexes

41 Screens

Professional Sports

Sea Wolves (ECHL Hockey)

Recreation Areas

Federal

Desoto NF, 81,476 acres

Grand Bay NWR, 5,081 acres

Gulf Islands N Seashore,

70,190 acres

Mississippi Sandhill Crane NWR,

18,033 acres

State

Buccaneer SP, 398 acres

Shepard S, 307 acres

Water Area

Lakes and rivers: 31,360 acres

Gulf coast: 47,240 acres

Score: **82.43**   Rank: **63**

Binghamton, NY

Golf Courses

17 Daily fee, 324 holes

3 Municipal, 63 holes

3 Private, 54 holes

Good Restaurants

3 Simple ◆

7 Family ◆◆

1 Adult ◆◆◆

Movie Theatres

2 Singles/Twins; 3 Multiplexes

28 Screens

Professional Sports

Mets (Class AA Baseball)

Recreation Areas

State

Chenango Valley SP, 1,071 acres

Skiing

7 ski areas

Lift capacity/hour: 43,650

Water Area

Lakes and rivers: 8,320 acres

Zoos

Ross Park Zoo

Score: **57.50**   Rank: **151**

Birmingham, AL

College NCAA I Sports

Samford Bulldogs

U of Alabama Blazers

Gambling

Birmingham Race Course (greyhound)

Golf Courses

14 Daily fee, 288 holes

5 Municipal, 90 holes

22 Private, 414 holes

Good Restaurants

2 Simple ◆

6 Family ◆◆

9 Adult ◆◆◆

Movie Theatres

3 Singles/Twins; 11 Multiplexes

127 Screens

Professional Sports

Barons (Class AA Baseball)

Bulls (ECHL Hockey)

Recreation Areas

Federal

Watercress Darter NWR, 7 acres

State

Oak Mountain SP, 9,940 acres

Rickwood Caverns SP, 380 acres

Water Area

Lakes and rivers: 32,640 acres

Zoos

Birmingham Zoo

Score: **73.37**   Rank: **95**

Bismarck, ND

Gambling

5 Casinos

Golf Courses

5 Municipal, 72 holes

1 Private, 18 holes

Good Restaurants

2 Simple ◆

3 Family ◆◆

1 Adult ◆◆◆

Movie Theatres

3 Multiplexes

17 Screens

Professional Sports

Wizards (IBA Basketball)

Recreation Areas

Federal

Canfield Lake NWR, 3 acres

Florence Lake NWR, 1,468 acres

Long Lake NWR, 10,330 acres

State

Missouri River SNA, 157 acres

Skiing

2 ski areas

Lift capacity/hour: 5,000

Water Area

Lakes and rivers: 34,560 acres

Zoos

Dakota Zoo

Score: **41.92**   Rank: **205**

Bloomington, IN

College NCAA I Sports

Indiana U Hoosiers

Golf Courses

3 Daily fee, 54 holes

1 Municipal, 18 holes

1 Private, 18 holes

Good Restaurants

1 Simple ◆

2 Family ◆◆

2 Adult ◆◆◆

Movie Theatres

1 Single/Twin; 3 Multiplexes

19 Screens

Recreation Areas

Federal

Hoosier NF, 18,994 acres

Muscatatuck NWR, 78 acres

Water Area

Lakes and rivers: 10,880 acres

Score: **45.32**   Rank: **194**

Bloomington-Normal, IL

College NCAA I Sports

Illinois State Redbirds

Golf Courses

4 Daily fee, 36 holes

5 Municipal, 90 holes

3 Private, 45 holes

Good Restaurants

2 Family ◆◆

1 Adult ◆◆◆

Movie Theatres

3 Multiplexes

20 Screens

Recreation Areas

State

Moraine View SP, 1,688 acres

Water Area

Lakes and rivers: 1,920 acres

Zoos

Miller Park Zoo

Score: **29.46**   Rank: **250**

Boise City, ID

College NCAA I Sports

Boise State Broncos

Gambling

Les Bois Park (mixed meetings)

Golf Courses

8 Daily fee, 126 holes

6 Municipal, 108 holes

5 Private, 81 holes

Good Restaurants
4 Simple ♦
7 Family ♦♦
4 Adult ♦♦♦

Movie Theatres
5 Singles/Twins; 7 Multiplexes
58 Screens

Professional Sports
Hawks (Class A Baseball)
Stampede (CBA Basketball)

Recreation Areas
Federal
Boise NF, 3,724 acres
Deer Flat NWR, 1,245 acres
State
Eagle Island SP, 545 acres
Lucky Peak SP, 240 acres
Veterans Memorial SP, 78 acres

Skiing
4 ski areas
Lift capacity/hour: 14,200

Water Area
Lakes and rivers: 12,160 acres

Zoos
Zoo Boise

Score: 46.17   Rank: 190

Boston, MA-NH

Amusement & Theme Parks
Spooky World
Star*Land Recreation Center

Aquariums
New England Aquarium

College NCAA I Sports
Boston College Eagles
Boston U Terriers
Harvard Crimson
Northeastern Huskies

Gambling
Foxboro Raceway (mixed meetings)
Seabrook Greyhound Park
Suffolk Downs (thoroughbred)
Wonderland Park (greyhound)

Golf Courses
49 Daily fee, 738 holes
22 Municipal, 306 holes
42 Private, 648 holes

Good Restaurants
20 Simple ♦
61 Family ♦♦
37 Adult ♦♦♦
5 Upscale ♦♦♦♦
1 Best ♦♦♦♦♦

Movie Theatres
22 Singles/Twins; 39 Multiplexes
322 Screens

Professional Sports
Bruins (NHL Hockey)
Celtics (NBA Basketball)
Red Sox (AL Baseball)
New England Patriots (NFL Football)
New England Revolution (MLS Soccer)

Recreation Areas
State
Ashland SP, 47 acres
Boston Harbor Islands SP, 195 acres
Bradley Palmer SP, 721 acres
Bristol Blake SP, 200 acres
Callahan SP, 819 acres
Cochituate SP, 1,126 acres
Cushing Memorial SP, 9 acres
Dighton Rock SP, 108 acres
Ellisville Harbor SP, 101 acres
Great Brook Farm SP, 934 acres
Halibut Point SP, 56 acres
Hopkinton SP, 1,450 acres
Horseneck Beach, 537 acres
Massasoit SP, 1,500 acres
Maudslay SP, 480 acres
Pearl Hill SP, 1,000 acres
Plum Island SR, 73 acres
Salisbury Beach SR, 520 acres
Sandy Point SR, 73 acres
Seabrook Fish Pier SRA, 4 acres
Squannacook River SNA, 300 acres
Walden Pond SR, 304 acres
Watson Pond SP, 10 acres
Webb Memorial SP, 37 acres
Whitehall SP, 909 acres
Wompatuck SP, 3,500 acres

Skiing
31 ski areas
Lift capacity/hour: 119,200

Water Area
Lakes and rivers: 224,486 acres
Atlantic coast: 3,840 acres

Zoos
Franklin Park Zoo
Stone Memorial Zoo

Score: 77.05   Rank: 82

Boulder-Longmont, CO

College NCAA I Sports
U of Colorado Golden Buffaloes

Golf Courses
5 Daily fee, 72 holes
5 Municipal, 81 holes
2 Private, 45 holes

Good Restaurants
1 Simple ♦
14 Family ♦♦
10 Adult ♦♦♦
1 Upscale ♦♦♦♦

Movie Theatres
7 Multiplexes
37 Screens

Recreation Areas
Federal
Rocky Mountain NP, 27,253 acres
Roosevelt NF, 137,422 acres
State
Eldorado Canyon SP, 845 acres

Skiing
3 ski areas
Lift capacity/hour: 45,250

Water Area
Lakes and rivers: 5,760 acres

Score: 46.17   Rank: 191

Brazoria, TX

Golf Courses
6 Daily fee, 72 holes
1 Municipal, 18 holes
3 Private, 54 holes

Movie Theatres
2 Singles/Twins; 2 Multiplexes
11 Screens

Recreation Areas
Federal
Brazoria NWR, 43,323 acres
San Bernard NWR, 21,807 acres
State
Christmas Bay SRA, 485 acres

Water Area
Lakes and rivers: 63,360 acres
Gulf coast: 7,168 acres

Score: 35.97   Rank: 226

Bremerton, WA

Gambling
1 Casino

Golf Courses
5 Daily fee, 81 holes
2 Municipal, 54 holes
2 Private, 36 holes

Good Restaurants
5 Family ♦♦

Movie Theatres
5 Multiplexes
29 Screens

Recreation Areas
State
Blake Island SP, 476 acres
Camp Calvinwood, 118 acres
Fay-Bainbridge SP, 17 acres
Fort Ward SP, 137 acres
Harper SP, 3 acres
Illahee SP, 75 acres
Kitsap Memorial SP, 58 acres
Manchester SP, 111 acres
Scenic Beach SP, 88 acres

Skiing
2 ski areas
Lift capacity/hour: 19,550

Water Area
Lakes and rivers: 40,320 acres
Pacific coast: 6,8480 acres

Score: 43.34   Rank: 201

Bridgeport, CT

College NCAA I Sports
Fairfield U Stags

Gambling
Milford Jai-Alai
Shoreline Star (greyhound)

Golf Courses
3 Daily fee, 36 holes
7 Municipal, 108 holes
8 Private, 126 holes

Place Profiles: Recreation

Good Restaurants
  2 Simple ◆
Movie Theatres
  3 Singles/Twins; 7 Multiplexes
  59 Screens
Professional Sports
  Skyhawks (USBL Basketball)
Recreation Areas
  State
    Indian Well SP, 153 acres
    Osbornedale SP, 700 acres
    Silver Sands SP, 223 acres
    Southford Falls SP, 120 acres
Water Area
  Lakes and rivers: 8,568 acres
Zoos
  Beardsley Zoo
Score: 62.32   Rank: 134

Brockton, MA
  Gambling
    Raynham Greyhound Park
  Golf Courses
    7 Daily fee, 108 holes
    3 Municipal, 45 holes
    3 Private, 45 holes
  Good Restaurants
    2 Family ◆◆
  Movie Theatres
    2 Singles/Twins; 3 Multiplexes
    21 Screens
  Recreation Areas
    State
      Ames Nowell SP, 607 acres
      Borderland SP, 1,772 acres
  Water Area
    Lakes and rivers: 9,097 acres
  Score: 52.12   Rank: 170

Brownsville-Harlingen-San Benito, TX
  Golf Courses
    8 Daily fee, 126 holes
    3 Municipal, 63 holes
    2 Private, 54 holes
  Good Restaurants
    2 Simple ◆
    1 Family ◆◆
  Movie Theatres
    1 Single/Twin; 6 Multiplexes
    33 Screens
  Recreation Areas
    Federal
      Laguna Atascosa NWR, 44,922 acres
      Lower Rio Grande Valley NWR,
        15,464 acres
  Water Area
    Lakes and rivers: 168,320 acres
  Zoos
    Gladys Porter Zoo
  Score: 62.03   Rank: 135

Bryan-College Station, TX
  Golf Courses
    1 Daily fee, 18 holes
    1 Municipal, 18 holes
    2 Private, 36 holes
  Good Restaurants
    1 Simple ◆
    2 Family ◆◆
  Movie Theatres
    1 Single/Twin; 5 Multiplexes
    32 Screens
  Water Area
    Lakes and rivers: 3,200 acres
  Score: 28.89   Rank: 252

Buffalo-Niagara Falls, NY
  Aquariums
    Aquarium of Niagara Falls
  College NCAA I Sports
    Canisius Golden Griffins
    Niagara Purple Eagles
    SUNY At Buffalo Bulls
  Gambling
    Buffalo Raceway (harness)
  Golf Courses
    22 Daily fee, 315 holes
    14 Municipal, 252 holes
    18 Private, 324 holes
  Good Restaurants
    6 Simple ◆
    28 Family ◆◆
    33 Adult ◆◆◆
    2 Upscale ◆◆◆◆
  Movie Theatres
    2 Singles/Twins; 13 Multiplexes
    101 Screens
  Professional Sports
    Bills (NFL Football)
    Bisons (Triple A Baseball)
    Sabres (NHL Hockey)
  Recreation Areas
    State
      Beaver Island SP, 952 acres
      Big Six Mile Creek Marina SP,
        19 acres
      Buckhorn Island SP, 895 acres
      Devil's Hole SP, 42 acres
      Earl Brydges Artpark, 197 acres
      Evangola SP, 733 acres
      Fort Niagara SP, 504 acres
      Four Mile Creek SP, 248 acres
      Golden Hill SP, 510 acres
      Joseph Davis SP, 388 acres
      Niagara Reservation SP, 435 acres
      Reservoir SP, 132 acres
      Whirlpool SP, 109 acres
      Wilson-Tuscarora SP, 390 acres
  Skiing
    6 ski areas
    Lift capacity/hour: 34,130
  Water Area
    Lakes and rivers: 12,800 acres
    Great Lakes coast: 49,560 acres

Zoos
  Buffalo Zoological Gardens
Score: 89.51   Rank: 38

Burlington, VT
  College NCAA I Sports
    U of Vermont Catamounts
  Golf Courses
    13 Daily fee, 198 holes
    1 Municipal, 9 holes
    1 Private, 18 holes
  Good Restaurants
    10 Family ◆◆
    4 Adult ◆◆◆
  Movie Theatres
    7 Multiplexes
    36 Screens
  Professional Sports
    Expos (Class A Baseball)
  Recreation Areas
    State
      Burton Island SP, 253 acres
      Grand Isle SP, 226 acres
      Woods Island SP, 125 acres
  Skiing
    14 ski areas
    Lift capacity/hour: 102,415
  Water Area
    Lakes and rivers: 159,360 acres
  Score: 80.73   Rank: 69

Calgary, AB
  Amusement & Theme Parks
    Calaway Park
  College CIAU Sports
    U of Calgary Dinosaurs
  Gambling
    3 Casinos
    Stampede Park (mixed meetings)
  Golf Courses
    9 Daily fee, 144 holes
    7 Municipal, 99 holes
    9 Private, 162 holes
  Good Restaurants
    1 Simple ◆
    22 Family ◆◆
    14 Adult ◆◆◆
    3 Upscale ◆◆◆◆
  Movie Theatres
    6 Singles/Twins; 15 Multiplexes
    105 Screens
  Professional Sports
    Cannons (Triple A Baseball)
    Flames (NHL Hockey)
    Stampeders (CFL Football)
  Recreation Areas
    Federal
      Inglewood MBS, 395 acres
    Provincial
      Brag Creek PP, 301 acres
      Emerson Creek Natural Area,
        479 acres
      Fish Creek PP, 1,804 acres

Sheep River Wildlife Sanctuary, 14,295 acres
Threepoint Creek Natural Area, 153 acres
Skiing
8 ski areas
Lift capacity/hour: 70,069
Water Area
Lakes and rivers: 21,000 acres
Zoos
Calgary Zoo
Score: **64.30**   Rank: **127**

Canton-Massillon, OH
Golf Courses
24 Daily fee, 486 holes
1 Municipal, 18 holes
8 Private, 135 holes
Good Restaurants
1 Simple ◆
7 Family ◆◆
3 Adult ◆◆◆
Movie Theatres
2 Singles/Twins; 8 Multiplexes
60 Screens
Recreation Areas
State
    Jackson Bog SNA, 6 acres
    Quail Hollow SP, 698 acres
Skiing
1 ski area
Lift capacity/hour: 16,000
Water Area
Lakes and rivers: 5,760 acres
Score: **67.98**   Rank: **114**

Casper, WY
Golf Courses
1 Daily fee, 9 holes
1 Municipal, 27 holes
2 Private, 36 holes
Good Restaurants
1 Simple ◆
2 Family ◆◆
1 Adult ◆◆◆
Movie Theatres
3 Singles/Twins; 1 Multiplex
10 Screens
Recreation Areas
Federal
    Medicine Bow NF, 5,598 acres
    Pathfinder NWR, 1,535 acres
State
    Wilkins SP, 319 acres
Skiing
3 ski areas
Lift capacity/hour: 7,100
Water Area
Lakes and rivers: 23,040 acres
Score: **11.04**   Rank: **315**

Cedar Rapids, IA
Golf Courses
6 Daily fee, 81 holes
4 Municipal, 63 holes
3 Private, 45 holes
Good Restaurants
8 Simple ◆
8 Family ◆◆
Movie Theatres
1 Single/Twin; 5 Multiplexes
27 Screens
Professional Sports
Kernels (Class A Baseball)
Recreation Areas
State
    Palisades-Kepler SP, 603 acres
Water Area
Lakes and rivers: 4,480 acres
Zoos
Beaver Park Zoo
Score: **38.52**   Rank: **218**

Champaign-Urbana, IL
College NCAA I Sports
U of Illinois Illini
Golf Courses
2 Daily fee, 54 holes
2 Municipal, 45 holes
3 Private, 54 holes
Good Restaurants
1 Simple ◆
3 Family ◆◆
1 Adult ◆◆◆
Movie Theatres
3 Singles/Twins; 4 Multiplexes
34 Screens
Score: **31.72**   Rank: **242**

Charleston, WV
Gambling
Tri-State Greyhound Park
Golf Courses
1 Daily fee, 18 holes
5 Municipal, 72 holes
4 Private, 72 holes
Good Restaurants
3 Family ◆◆
1 Upscale ◆◆◆
Movie Theatres
1 Single/Twin; 2 Multiplexes
13 Screens
Professional Sports
Alley Cats (Class A Baseball)
Water Area
Lakes and rivers: 7,680 acres
Score: **19.26**   Rank: **286**

★ **Charleston-North Charleston, SC**
College NCAA I Sports
Charleston Southern Buccaneers
College of Charleston Cougars
The Citadel Bulldogs

Golf Courses
20 Daily fee, 414 holes
2 Municipal, 36 holes
7 Private, 135 holes
Good Restaurants
44 Simple ◆
71 Family ◆◆
31 Adult ◆◆◆
4 Upscale ◆◆◆◆
3 Best ◆◆◆◆◆
Movie Theatres
2 Singles/Twins; 10 Multiplexes
73 Screens
Professional Sports
Riverdogs (Class A Baseball)
Stingrays (ECHL Hockey)
Recreation Areas
Federal
    Ace Basin NWR, 6,528 acres
    Cape Romain NWR, 34,049 acres
    Francis Marion NF, 251,622 acres
State
    Givhans Ferry SP, 888 acres
Water Area
Lakes and rivers: 160,640 acres
Atlantic coast: 20,544 acres
Zoos
Charles Towne Landing
Score: **93.76**   Rank: **23**

Charlotte-Gastonia-Rock Hill, NC-SC
Amusement & Theme Parks
Paramount's Carowinds
Auto Racing
Lowe's Motor Speedway
College NCAA I Sports
Davidson College Wildcats
U of North Carolina 49ers
Winthrop College Eagles
Golf Courses
39 Daily fee, 684 holes
6 Municipal, 99 holes
25 Private, 477 holes
Good Restaurants
3 Simple ◆
15 Family ◆◆
7 Adult ◆◆◆
2 Upscale ◆◆◆◆
Movie Theatres
5 Singles/Twins; 29 Multiplexes
229 Screens
Professional Sports
Boll Weevils (Class A Baseball)
Sting (WNBA)
Checkers (ECHL Hockey)
Hornets (NBA Basketball)
Knights (Triple A Baseball)
Carolina Panthers (NFL Football)
Recreation Areas
State
    Crowder's Mountain SP, 1,966 acres
Water Area
Lakes and rivers: 41,600 acres
Score: **81.3**   Rank: **67**

Charlottesville, VA

College NCAA I Sports
U of Virginia Cavaliers

Golf Courses
2 Daily fee, 36 holes
2 Municipal, 27 holes
6 Private, 108 holes

Good Restaurants
8 Family ♦♦
3 Adult ♦♦♦
1 Upscale ♦♦♦♦

Movie Theatres
5 Singles/Twins; 4 Multiplexes
34 Screens

Recreation Areas
Federal
Appalachian NT, 817 acres
Blue Ridge Parkway
Shenandoah NP, 30,427 acres

Skiing
1 ski area
Lift capacity/hour: 8,200

Water Area
Lakes and rivers: 3,840 acres
Score: 35.12   Rank: 230

Chattanooga, TN-GA

Amusement & Theme Parks
Lake Winnepesaukah Fun Town

Aquariums
Tennessee Aquarium

College NCAA I Sports
U of Tennessee Moccasins

Golf Courses
13 Daily fee, 171 holes
3 Municipal, 54 holes
9 Private, 153 holes

Good Restaurants
5 Simple ♦
21 Family ♦♦
4 Adult ♦♦♦

Movie Theatres
1 Single/Twin; 9 Multiplexes
63 Screens

Professional Sports
Lookouts (Class AA Baseball)

Recreation Areas
Federal
Chattahoochee NF, 18,850 acres
State
Booker T. Washington SP, 353 acres
Cloudland Canyon SP, 2,219 acres
Harrison Bay SP, 1,199 acres
South Cumberland SRA, 5,803 acres

Skiing
1 ski area
Lift capacity/hour: 800

Water Area
Lakes and rivers: 30,080 acres

Zoos
Warner Park Zoo
Score: 61.75   Rank: 136

Cheyenne, WY

Golf Courses
3 Daily fee, 45 holes
2 Municipal, 27 holes

Good Restaurants
1 Simple ♦
4 Family ♦♦
2 Adult ♦♦♦

Movie Theatres
1 Single/Twin; 2 Multiplexes
11 Screens

Recreation Areas
State
Curt Gowdy SP, 1,960 acres

Skiing
1 ski area
Lift capacity/hour: 3,000

Water Area
Lakes and rivers: 1,280 acres

Zoos
Lions Park Native Animal Display
Score: 5.94   Rank: 333

★ Chicago, IL

Amusement & Theme Parks
Kiddieland
Racing Rapids Action Waterpark
Six Flags Great America
Three Worlds of Santa's Village

Aquariums
John G. Shedd Aquarium

College NCAA I Sports
Chicago State Cougars
De Paul Blue Demons
Loyola Ramblers
NE Illinois Golden Eagles
Northern Illinois Huskies
Northwestern Wildcats
U of Illinois Flames

Gambling
4 Casinos
Arlington Racecourse (thoroughbred)
Balmoral Park (harness)
Hawthorne Race Course (mixed meetings)
Maywood Park (harness)
Sportsman's Park (mixed meetings)

Golf Courses
95 Daily fee, 1791 holes
109 Municipal, 1755 holes
91 Private, 1683 holes

Good Restaurants
19 Simple ♦
102 Family ♦♦
81 Adult ♦♦♦
36 Upscale ♦♦♦♦
8 Best ♦♦♦♦♦

Movie Theatres
37 Singles/Twins; 102 Multiplexes
823 Screens

Professional Sports
Bears (NFL Football)
Blackhawks (NHL Hockey)
Bulls (NBA Basketball)
Cubs (NL Baseball)
Fire (MLS Soccer)
Geneva Cougars (Class A Baseball)
White Sox (AL Baseball)
Wolves (IHL Hockey)

Recreation Areas
State
Braidwood/Mazonia Area 1,017 acres
Chain O' Lakes SP, 6,063 acres
Des Plaines Conservation Area, 5,012 acres
Gebhard Woods SP, 30 acres
Goose Lake Prairie SP, 2,468 acres
Illinois Beach SP, 2,978 acres
Moraine Hills SP, 1,763 acres
Shabbona Lake SP, 1,546 acres
Silver Springs SP, 1,314 acres
William G. Stratton SP, 6 acres

Skiing
16 ski areas
Lift capacity/hour: 82,885

Water Area
Lakes and rivers: 45,440 acres
Lake Michigan: 100,800 acres

Zoos
Brookfield Zoo
Cosley Children's Animal Farm
Jurica Natural History Museum
Lincoln Park Zoo
Lords Park Zoo
Phillips Park Zoo
Randall Oaks Park Zoo
Score: 97.16   Rank: 11

Chico-Paradise, CA

Gambling
6 Casinos

Golf Courses
4 Daily fee, 36 holes
1 Municipal, 18 holes
2 Private, 36 holes

Good Restaurants
2 Family ♦♦

Movie Theatres
2 Singles/Twins; 4 Multiplexes
32 Screens

Recreation Areas
Federal
Lassen NF, 51,178 acres
North Central Valley NWR, 1,732 acres
Plumas NF, 82,299 acres
Sacramento River NWR, 825 acres
State
Bidwell-Sacramento River SP, 175 acres
Clay Pit SVRA, 220 acres
Lake Oroville SRA, 31,600 acres

Skiing
2 ski areas
Lift capacity/hour: 16,366

Water Area
Lakes and rivers: 24,320 acres
Score: **11.89**   Rank: **312**

Chicoutimi-Jonquiere, PQ

Gambling
Hippodrome Saguenay (harness)
Golf Courses
2 Daily fee, 36 holes
1 Municipal, 9 holes
Good Restaurants
1 Family ◆◆
2 Adult ◆◆◆
1 Upscale ◆◆◆◆
Movie Theatres
2 Singles/Twins; 2 Multiplexes
11 Screens
Recreation Areas
Provincial
Claude-Melancon Reserve,
1,285 acres
Oscar-Villeneuve Reserve,
1,401 acres
Riviere Petit Saguenay Wildlife
Sanctuary, 494 acres
Saguenay PP, 70,078 acres
Skiing
3 ski areas
Lift capacity/hour: 61,360
Water Area
Lakes and rivers: 395,000 acres
Score: **57.22**   Rank: **152**

Cincinnati, OH-KY-IN

Amusement & Theme Parks
Paramount's Kings Island
The Beach Waterpark
College NCAA I Sports
U of Cincinnati Bearcats
Xavier Musketeers
Gambling
2 Casinos
Lebanon Raceway (harness)
River Downs (thoroughbred)
Turfway Park (thoroughbred)
Golf Courses
36 Daily fee, 567 holes
24 Municipal, 450 holes
33 Private, 585 holes
Good Restaurants
4 Simple ◆
25 Family ◆◆
22 Adult ◆◆◆
3 Upscale ◆◆◆◆
Movie Theatres
8 Singles/Twins; 17 Multiplexes
173 Screens
Professional Sports
Bengals (NFL Football)
Cyclones (IHL Hockey)
Mighty Ducks (AHL Hockey)
Reds (NL Baseball)

Recreation Areas
State
Big Bone Lick SP, 525 acres
Caesar Creek SP, 7,941 acres
East Fork SP, 8,420 acres
Kincaid Lake SP, 850 acres
Little Miami SP, 466 acres
Stonelick SP, 1,058 acres
Skiing
5 ski areas
Lift capacity/hour: 52,600
Water Area
Lakes and rivers: 33,920 acres
Zoos
Zoo of Cincinnati
Score: **78.75**   Rank: **76**

Clarksville-Hopkinsville, TN-KY

College NCAA I Sports
Austin Peay Governors
Golf Courses
3 Daily fee, 54 holes
4 Municipal, 63 holes
2 Private, 36 holes
Good Restaurants
1 Family ◆◆
Movie Theatres
5 Multiplexes
26 Screens
Recreation Areas
State
Dunbar Cave SNA, 110 acres
Pennyrile Forest Resort, 863 acres
Water Area
Lakes and rivers: 5,120 acres
Score: **12.74**   Rank: **309**

★ Cleveland-Lorain-Elyria, OH

Amusement & Theme Parks
Erieview Park
Pioneer Waterland & Dry Fun Park
Auto Racing
Burke Lakefront Airport
College NCAA I Sports
Cleveland State Vikings
Gambling
Northfield Park (harness)
Thistledown (thoroughbred)
Golf Courses
71 Daily fee, 1233 holes
21 Municipal, 414 holes
31 Private, 576 holes
Good Restaurants
7 Simple ◆
36 Family ◆◆
21 Adult ◆◆◆
5 Upscale ◆◆◆◆
Movie Theatres
12 Singles/Twins; 30 Multiplexes
236 Screens
Professional Sports
Browns (NFL Football)
Cavaliers (NBA Basketball)

Indians (AL Baseball)
Lumberjacks (IHL Hockey)
Rockers (WNBA)
Recreation Areas
Federal
Cuyahoga Valley NRA, 2,732 acres
State
Cleveland Lakefront SP, 450 acres
Findley SP, 838 acres
Geneva SP, 698 acres
Hach-Otis SNA, 81 acres
Headlands Beach SP, 125 acres
Mentor Marsh SNA, 644 acres
Punderson SP, 846 acres
Pymatuning SP, 3,500 acres
Skiing
8 ski areas
Lift capacity/hour: 76,400
Water Area
Lakes and rivers: 13,440 acres
Lake Erie: 167,800 acres
Zoos
Cleveland Metro Park Zoo
Score: **99.71**   Rank: **2**

Colorado Springs, CO

Amusement & Theme Parks
Santa's Workshop
Auto Racing
Pikes Peak International Raceway
College NCAA I Sports
Colorado College Tigers
Air Force Academy Falcons
Gambling
Rocky Mountain Park (greyhound)
Golf Courses
6 Daily fee, 99 holes
3 Municipal, 63 holes
7 Private, 189 holes
Good Restaurants
13 Family ◆◆
8 Adult ◆◆◆
3 Upscale ◆◆◆◆
Movie Theatres
11 Multiplexes
74 Screens
Professional Sports
Sky Sox (Triple A Baseball)
Recreation Areas
Federal
Pike NF, 100,597 acres
Skiing
4 ski areas
Lift capacity/hour: 14,400
Water Area
Lakes and rivers: 1,920 acres
Zoos
Cheyenne Mountain Zoological Park
Score: **50.70**   Rank: **175**

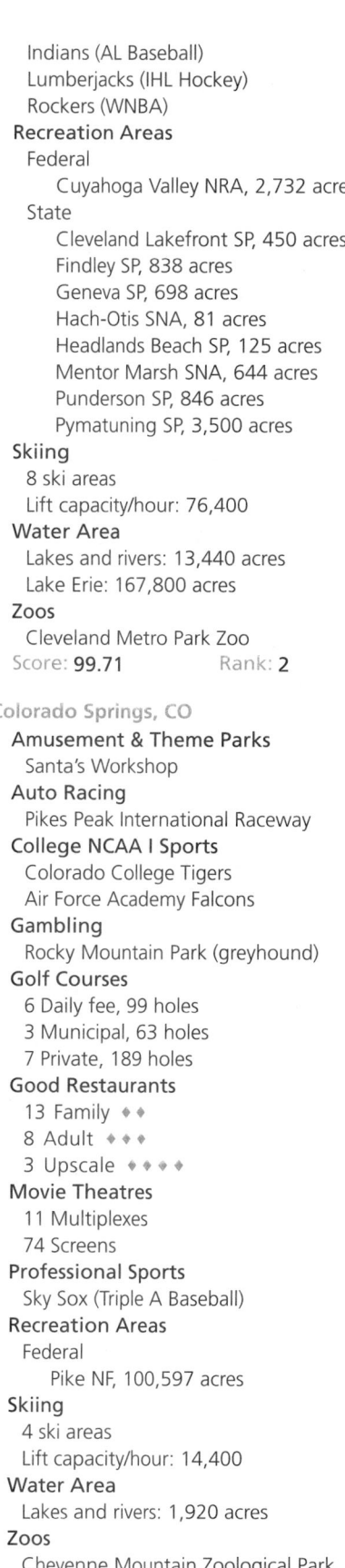

Columbia, MO
College NCAA I Sports
U of Missouri Tigers
Golf Courses
2 Daily fee, 36 holes
2 Municipal, 36 holes
4 Private, 54 holes
Good Restaurants
7 Family ◆◆
1 Adult ◆◆◆
Movie Theatres
1 Single/Twin; 3 Multiplexes
17 Screens
Recreation Areas
Federal
Mark Twain NF, 3,762 acres
State
Finger Lakes SP, 1,132 acres
Rock Bridge Memorial SP,
2,238 acres
Water Area
Lakes and rivers: 3,840 acres
Score: 36.54   Rank: 225

Columbia, SC
College NCAA I Sports
U of South Carolina Gamecocks
Golf Courses
14 Daily fee, 234 holes
1 Municipal, 18 holes
10 Private, 216 holes
Good Restaurants
2 Simple ◆
9 Family ◆◆
8 Adult ◆◆◆
Movie Theatres
1 Single/Twin; 9 Multiplexes
73 Screens
Professional Sports
Bombers (Class A Baseball)
Recreation Areas
Federal
Congaree Swamp NM, 21,100 acres
State
Sesquicentennial SP, 1,445 acres
Water Area
Lakes and rivers: 47,360 acres
Zoos
Riverbanks Zoological Park
Score: 69.40   Rank: 109

Columbus, GA-AL
Golf Courses
5 Daily fee, 126 holes
3 Municipal, 63 holes
3 Private, 72 holes
Good Restaurants
1 Simple ◆
3 Family ◆◆
1 Adult ◆◆◆
Movie Theatres
2 Singles/Twins; 5 Multiplexes
40 Screens

Professional Sports
Redstixx (Class A Baseball)
Recreation Areas
State
Roosevelt SP, 10,000 acres
Sprewell Bluff SP, 1,400 acres
Water Area
Lakes and rivers: 13,440 acres
Score: 42.77   Rank: 203

Columbus, OH
Amusement & Theme Parks
Wyandot Lake Park
College NCAA I Sports
Ohio State Buckeyes
Gambling
Beaulah Park (thoroughbred)
Beulah Park (mixed meetings)
Scioto Downs (harness)
Golf Courses
43 Daily fee, 693 holes
11 Municipal, 180 holes
31 Private, 558 holes
Good Restaurants
12 Simple ◆
68 Family ◆◆
48 Adult ◆◆◆
6 Upscale ◆◆◆◆
Movie Theatres
7 Singles/Twins; 22 Multiplexes
247 Screens
Professional Sports
Blue Jackets (NHL Hockey)
Chill (ECHL Hockey)
Clippers (Triple A Baseball)
Crew (MLS Soccer)
Recreation Areas
State
Alum Creek SP, 5,213 acres
Blackhand Gorge SNA, 955 acres
Buckeye Lake SP, 2,478 acres
Deer Creek SP, 368 acres
Delaware SP, 7,411 acres
Gahanna Woods SNA, 51 acres
Madison Lake SP, 80 acres
Marion SP, 308 acres
Morris Woods SNA, 104 acres
Shallenberger SNA, 88 acres
Stage's Pond SNA, 178 acres
Walther Tucker SNA, 55 acres
Water Area
Lakes and rivers: 17,280 acres
Zoos
Columbus Zoological Park
Score: 81.86   Rank: 65

Corpus Christi, TX
Aquariums
Texas State Aquarium
College NCAA I Sports
Texas A & M University
Gambling
Corpus Christi Track (greyhound)

Golf Courses
1 Daily fee, 18 holes
3 Municipal, 63 holes
8 Private, 126 holes
Good Restaurants
10 Simple ◆
15 Family ◆◆
3 Adult ◆◆◆
Movie Theatres
5 Multiplexes
39 Screens
Recreation Areas
State
Lake Corpus Christi SRA, 576 acres
Mustang Island SP, 3,704 acres
Water Area
Lakes and rivers: 174,720 acres
Gulf coast: 4,672 acres
Score: 51.27   Rank: 173

Cumberland, MD-WV
Golf Courses
3 Daily fee, 36 holes
2 Private, 36 holes
Good Restaurants
1 Adult ◆◆◆
Movie Theatres
2 Multiplexes
9 Screens
Recreation Areas
State
Dans Mountain SP, 481 acres
Rocky Gap SP, 2,983 acres
Skiing
3 ski areas
Lift capacity/hour: 30,740
Water Area
Lakes and rivers: 3,200 acres
Score: 2.54   Rank: 345

Dallas, TX
Amusement & Theme Parks
Sandy Lake Amusement Park
Aquariums
Dallas Aquarium
College NCAA I Sports
Southern Methodist Mustangs
U of North Texas Mean Green Eagles
Golf Courses
38 Daily fee, 621 holes
19 Municipal, 396 holes
39 Private, 774 holes
Good Restaurants
54 Simple ◆
155 Family ◆◆
188 Adult ◆◆◆
35 Upscale ◆◆◆◆
10 Best ◆◆◆◆◆
Movie Theatres
7 Singles/Twins; 60 Multiplexes
491 Screens
Professional Sports
Burn (MLS Soccer)
Cowboys (NFL Football)

Mavericks (NBA Basketball)
Stars (NHL Hockey)
Recreation Areas
State
Cedar Hill SRA, 1,811 acres
Lake Lewisville SRA, 721 acres
Lake Tawakoni SRA, 376 acres
Purtis Creek SRA, 566 acres
Ray Roberts Lake SRA, 3,026 acres
Water Area
Lakes and rivers: 195,200 acres
Zoos
Dallas Zoo
Score: **88.95**   Rank: **40**

Danbury, CT
Golf Courses
2 Daily fee, 27 holes
3 Municipal, 54 holes
10 Private, 126 holes
Good Restaurants
2 Simple ◆
10 Family ◆◆
1 Adult ◆◆◆
2 Upscale ◆◆◆◆
Movie Theatres
4 Singles/Twins; 2 Multiplexes
20 Screens
Recreation Areas
State
Collis P. Huntington SP, 878 acres
Lovers Leap SP, 281 acres
Mount Bushnell SP, 114 acres
Seth Low Pierpoint SP, 305 acres
Squantz Pond SP, 172 acres
Water Area
Lakes and rivers: 9,689 acres
Score: **15.29**   Rank: **300**

Danville, VA
Golf Courses
2 Daily fee, 36 holes
5 Private, 81 holes
Good Restaurants
1 Adult ◆◆◆
Movie Theatres
1 Single/Twin; 2 Multiplexes
9 Screens
Water Area
Lakes and rivers: 5,120 acres
Score: **1.13**   Rank: **350**

Davenport-Moline-Rock Island, IA-IL
Gambling
3 Casinos
Quad City Downs (harness)
Golf Courses
11 Daily fee, 135 holes
9 Municipal, 153 holes
9 Private, 144 holes
Good Restaurants
7 Simple ◆
10 Family ◆◆
6 Adult ◆◆◆

Movie Theatres
1 Single/Twin; 3 Multiplexes
29 Screens
Professional Sports
Mallards (CoHL Hockey)
River Bandits (Class A Baseball)
Thunder (CBA Basketball)
Recreation Areas
Federal
Upper Mississippi NWR, 398 acres
Skiing
3 ski areas
Lift capacity/hour: 17,400
Water Area
Lakes and rivers: 23,040 acres
Zoos
Fejervary Zoo
Niabi Zoo
Score: **67.7**   Rank: **115**

Dayton-Springfield, OH
College NCAA I Sports
U of Dayton Flyers
Wright State Raiders
Golf Courses
15 Daily fee, 252 holes
12 Municipal, 279 holes
16 Private, 306 holes
Good Restaurants
13 Simple ◆
46 Family ◆◆
7 Adult ◆◆◆
Movie Theatres
9 Singles/Twins; 11 Multiplexes
91 Screens
Professional Sports
Bombers (ECHL Hockey)
Recreation Areas
State
Buck Creek SP, 1,910 acres
John Bryan SP, 1,750 acres
Little Miami SP, 67 acres
Sycamore SP, 2,295 acres
Water Area
Lakes and rivers: 6,400 acres
Score: **56.94**   Rank: **153**

★ Daytona Beach, FL
Aquariums
Marineland of Florida
Auto Racing
Daytona International Speedway
College NCAA I Sports
Bethune Cookman Wildcats
Stetson Hatters
Gambling
Daytona Beach Kennel Club
(greyhound)
Golf Courses
23 Daily fee, 387 holes
4 Municipal, 90 holes
5 Private, 90 holes

Good Restaurants
4 Simple ◆
18 Family ◆◆
5 Adult ◆◆◆
Movie Theatres
1 Single/Twin; 11 Multiplexes
78 Screens
Professional Sports
Cubs (Class A Baseball)
Recreation Areas
Federal
Canaveral N Seashore, 28,169 acres
Lake Woodruff NWR, 18,225 acres
Merritt Island NWR, 872 acres
State
Blue Spring SP, 2,192 acres
Bulow Creek SP, 2,577 acres
De Leon Springs SRA, 401 acres
Flagler Beach SRA, 145 acres
Hontoon Island SP, 1,051 acres
North Peninsula SRA, 442 acres
Spruce Creek SRA, 83 acres
Tomoka SP, 1,539 acres
Water Area
Lakes and rivers: 116,480 acres
Atlantic coast: 14,784 acres
Score: **91.78**   Rank: **30**

Decatur, AL
Golf Courses
3 Daily fee, 54 holes
2 Municipal, 36 holes
2 Private, 36 holes
Good Restaurants
2 Simple ◆
Movie Theatres
3 Multiplexes
20 Screens
Recreation Areas
Federal
Bankhead NF, 90,332 acres
Wheeler NWR, 3,566 acres
State
Joe Wheeler SP, 400 acres
Water Area
Lakes and rivers: 26,880 acres
Score: **33.14**   Rank: **237**

Decatur, IL
Golf Courses
1 Daily fee, 9 holes
5 Municipal, 81 holes
2 Private, 36 holes
Good Restaurants
2 Family ◆◆
Movie Theatres
2 Multiplexes
15 Screens
Recreation Areas
State
Spitler Woods SP, 202 acres
Water Area
Lakes and rivers: 3,200 acres

Zoos
Decatur Park Zoo
Scovill Children's Zoo
Score: **7.93**   Rank: **326**

Denver, CO
Amusement & Theme Parks
Six Flags Elitch Gardens
Water World
Aquarium
Ocean Journey
College NCAA I Sports
U of Denver Pioneers
Gambling
Arapahoe Park (quarter horse)
Mile High Kennel Club (greyhound)
Golf Courses
14 Daily fee, 216 holes
26 Municipal, 558 holes
23 Private, 432 holes
Good Restaurants
8 Simple ♦
44 Family ♦♦
34 Adult ♦♦♦
6 Upscale ♦♦♦♦
Movie Theatres
2 Singles/Twins; 33 Multiplexes
263 Screens
Professional Sports
Broncos (NFL Football)
Colorado Avalanche (NHL Hockey)
Colorado Rockies (NL Baseball)
Nuggets (NBA Basketball)
Rapids (MLS Soccer)
Recreation Areas
Federal
Arapaho NF, 2,057 acres
Pike NF, 244,237 acres
Roosevelt NF, 160 acres
State
Barr Lake SP, 692 acres
Castlewood Canyon SP, 873 acres
Chatfield SRA, 3,768 acres
Cherry Creek SRA, 3,305 acres
Roxborough SP, 1,620 acres
Skiing
3 ski areas
Lift capacity/hour: 24,858
Water Area
Lakes and rivers: 12,160 acres
Zoos
Denver Zoological Gardens
Englewood Childrens Zoo
Score: **82.71**   Rank: **62**

Des Moines, IA
College NCAA I Sports
Drake Bulldogs
Gambling
1 Casino
Prairie Meadows Flats (mixed meetings)
Golf Courses
13 Daily fee, 225 holes
5 Municipal, 99 holes
11 Private, 171 holes

Good Restaurants
4 Simple ♦
15 Family ♦♦
5 Adult ♦♦♦
1 Upscale ♦♦♦♦
Movie Theatres
2 Singles/Twins; 12 Multiplexes
64 Screens
Professional Sports
Cubs (Triple A Baseball)
Dragons (IBA Basketball)
Recreation Areas
State
Big Creek SP, 1,536 acres
Lake Ahquabi SP, 770 acres
Margo Frankel Woods SP, 136 acres
Walnut Woods SP, 300 acres
Skiing
2 ski areas
Lift capacity/hour: 3,000
Water Area
Lakes and rivers: 18,560 acres
Zoos
Blank Park Zoo
Score: **67.42**   Rank: **116**

★ Detroit, MI
Auto Racing
Detroit Grand Prix
College NCAA I Sports
U of Detroit Titans
Gambling
Detroit Race Course (thoroughbred)
Hazel Park (harness)
Northville Downs (harness)
Golf Courses
114 Daily fee, 2232 holes
48 Municipal, 783 holes
46 Private, 846 holes
Good Restaurants
28 Simple ♦
67 Family ♦♦
40 Adult ♦♦♦
2 Upscale ♦♦♦♦
Movie Theatres
11 Singles/Twins; 44 Multiplexes
343 Screens
Professional Sports
Lions (NFL Football)
Pistons (NBA Basketball)
Port Huron Bordercats (CoHL Hockey)
Red Wings (NHL Hockey)
Shock (WNBA)
Tigers (AL Baseball)
Vipers (IHL Hockey)
Recreation Areas
Federal
Wyandotte NWR, 304 acres
State
Algonac SP, 1,307 acres
Bald Mountain SRA, 4,637 acres
Highland SRA, 5,524 acres
Holly SRA, 7,670 acres
Island Lake SRA, 194 acres

Lakelands Trail SP, 14 acres
Lakeport SP, 566 acres
Maybury SP, 944 acres
Metamora-Hadley SRA, 683 acres
Ortonville SRA, 4,875 acres
Pontiac Lake SRA, 3,700 acres
Proud Lake SRA, 3,614 acres
Seven Lakes SP, 1,410 acres
Sterling SP, 1,000 acres
Wetzel SP, 900 acres
Skiing
22 ski areas
Lift capacity/hour: 183,320
Water Area
Lakes and rivers: 67,840 acres
Great Lakes coast: 20,680 acres
Zoos
Belle Isle Zoo
Detroit Zoological Park
Score: **96.60**   Rank: **13**

Dothan, AL
Golf Courses
6 Daily fee, 117 holes
2 Private, 45 holes
Good Restaurants
6 Family ♦♦
Movie Theatres
1 Single/Twin; 2 Multiplexes
16 Screens
Recreation Areas
State
Chattahoochee SP, 596 acres
Water Area
Lakes and rivers: 1,920 acres
Score: **2.26**   Rank: **346**

Dover, DE
Auto Racing
Dover Downs International Speedway
College NCAA I Sports
Delaware State Hornets
Gambling
1 Casino
Dover Downs (harness)
Harrington Raceway (harness)
Golf Courses
3 Daily fee, 54 holes
3 Private, 54 holes
Good Restaurants
2 Family ♦♦
3 Adult ♦♦♦
Movie Theatres
3 Multiplexes
18 Screens
Recreation Areas
Federal
Bombay Hook NWR, 15,978 acres
State
Killens Pond SP, 1,061 acres
Murderkill River Preserve, 140 acres
Water Area
Lakes and rivers: 5,120 acres
Atlantic coast: 12,860 acres
Score: **18.98**   Rank: **287**

Dubuque, IA

Gambling
2 Casinos
Dubuque Park (greyhound)

Golf Courses
4 Daily fee, 54 holes
2 Municipal, 27 holes
2 Private, 36 holes

Good Restaurants
2 Simple ♦
9 Family ♦♦
2 Adult ♦♦♦

Movie Theatres
2 Multiplexes
14 Screens

Recreation Areas
Federal
Driftless Area NWR, 52 acres
Upper Mississippi NWR, 475 acres
State
Mines of Spain SP, 1,380 acres

Skiing
2 ski areas
Lift capacity/hour: 18,400

Water Area
Lakes and rivers: 5,120 acres

Score: **19.54**   Rank: **285**

★ Duluth-Superior, MN-WI

College NCAA I Sports
U Of Minnesota Fulldogs

Gambling
2 Casinos

Golf Courses
13 Daily fee, 162 holes
8 Municipal, 144 holes
4 Private, 54 holes

Good Restaurants
2 Simple ♦
14 Family ♦♦

Movie Theatres
3 Singles/Twins; 6 Multiplexes
35 Screens

Recreation Areas
Federal
Saint Croix SRiver, 3,128 acres
Superior NF, 692,086 acres
Voyageurs NP, 121,254 acres
State
Amnicon Falls SP, 825 acres
Bear Head Lake SP, 4,375 acres
Gandy DancerState Trail, 191 acres
McCarthy Beach SP, 2,311 acres
Pattison SP, 1,374 acres
Saunders GradeState Trail, 336 acres

Skiing
11 ski areas
Lift capacity/hour: 51,500

Water Area
Lakes and rivers: 352,000 acres
Lake Superior: 16,560 acres

Zoos
Lake Superior Zoological Gardens

Score: **90.93**   Rank: **33**

Dutchess County, NY

College NCAA I Sports
Marist College Red Foxes

Golf Courses
9 Daily fee, 126 holes
5 Municipal, 72 holes
6 Private, 72 holes

Good Restaurants
6 Family ♦♦
8 Adult ♦♦♦
2 Upscale ♦♦♦♦

Movie Theatres
3 Singles/Twins; 8 Multiplexes
57 Screens

Professional Sports
Renegades (Class A Baseball)

Recreation Areas
Federal
Appalachian NT, 4,358 acres
State
Clermont SP, 44 acres
Hudson Highlands SP, 697 acres
James Baird SP, 590 acres
Norrie SP, 330 acres
Ogden Mills SP, 637 acres
Taconic SP, 1,868 acres

Skiing
9 ski areas
Lift capacity/hour: 38,560

Water Area
Lakes and rivers: 15,360 acres

Score: **60.90**   Rank: **139**

Eau Claire, WI

Golf Courses
8 Daily fee, 108 holes
2 Municipal, 27 holes
2 Private, 36 holes

Good Restaurants
2 Simple ♦
7 Family ♦♦
2 Adult ♦♦♦

Movie Theatres
3 Singles/Twins; 3 Multiplexes
28 Screens

Recreation Areas
State
Brunet Island SP, 1,032 acres
Chippewa Moraine RA, 2,762 acres
Chippewa River Trail, 673 acres
Lake Wissota SP, 1,062 acres
Old Abe Trail, 259 acres

Skiing
3 ski areas
Lift capacity/hour: 5,400

Water Area
Lakes and rivers: 24,960 acres

Score: **35.41**   Rank: **229**

Edmonton, AB

Amusement & Theme Parks
West Edmonton Mall Park

College CIAU Sports
U of Alberta Golden Bears

Gambling
5 Casinos
Northlands Park (harness)
Northlands Park (mixed meetings)

Golf Courses
13 Daily fee, 180 holes
16 Municipal, 243 holes
5 Private, 90 holes

Good Restaurants
2 Simple ♦
7 Family ♦♦
7 Adult ♦♦♦
1 Upscale ♦♦♦♦

Movie Theatres
10 Singles/Twins; 12 Multiplexes
102 Screens

Professional Sports
Eskimos (CFL Football)
Oilers (NHL Hockey)
Trappers (Triple A Baseball)

Recreation Areas
Provincial
Alsike-Bat Lake, 321 acres
Bat Lake, 640 acres
Battle Creek, 158 acres
Buck Creek, 321 acres
Buck Lake, 272 acres
Easyford Creek, 247 acres
Easyford, 321 acres
Genesse, 161 acres
Hasse Lake PP, 170 acres
Horseshoe Creek, 801 acres
Modeste Creek, 803 acres
Modeste Creek, 964 acres
Modeste-Saskatchewan, 996 acres
Pembina River PP, 413 acres
Pembina River/Moon Lake,
264 acres
Pigeon Lake PP, 1,095 acres
Redwater, 4,480 acres
Sherwood Park, 161 acres
Strathcona Science PP, 269 acres
Thorsby, 161 acres
Tomahawk, 321 acres
Wabamum Lake PP, 521 acres
Washout Creek, 309 acres

Skiing
3 ski areas
Lift capacity/hour: 15,000

Water Area
Lakes and rivers: 83,000 acres

Zoos
Alberta Wildlife Park
Valley Zoo

Score: **88.10**   Rank: **43**

El Paso, TX

Amusement & Theme Parks
Western Playland

College NCAA I Sports
U of Texas Miners

Gambling
1 Casino

Golf Courses
1 Daily fee, 18 holes
3 Municipal, 63 holes
5 Private, 99 holes
Good Restaurants
1 Simple ♦
12 Family ♦♦
4 Adult ♦♦♦
Movie Theatres
2 Singles/Twins; 7 Multiplexes
47 Screens
Professional Sports
Diablos (Class AA Baseball)
Recreation Areas
Federal
Chamizal Memorial, 55 acres
State
Franklin Mountains SP, 23,867 acres
Skiing
1 ski area
Lift capacity/hour: 1,800
Water Area
Lakes and rivers: 1,280 acres
Zoos
El Paso Zoo
Score: 42.49   Rank: 204

Elkhart-Goshen, IN
Golf Courses
5 Daily fee, 90 holes
2 Municipal, 36 holes
5 Private, 90 holes
Good Restaurants
2 Simple ♦
9 Family ♦♦
2 Adult ♦♦♦
Movie Theatres
1 Single/Twin; 1 Multiplex
10 Screens
Skiing
1 ski area
Lift capacity/hour: 9,800
Water Area
Lakes and rivers: 2,560 acres
Score: 3.68   Rank: 341

Elmira, NY
Golf Courses
1 Daily fee, 27 holes
2 Municipal, 36 holes
1 Private, 18 holes
Good Restaurants
1 Simple ♦
1 Upscale ♦♦♦♦
Movie Theatres
4 Multiplexes
20 Screens
Recreation Areas
State
Mark Twain SP, 462 acres
Skiing
1 ski areas
Lift capacity/hour: 3,200

Water Area
Lakes and rivers: 1,920 acres
Score: 11.61   Rank: 313

Enid, OK
Golf Courses
1 Daily fee, 9 holes
1 Municipal, 18 holes
1 Private, 18 holes
Good Restaurants
1 Family ♦♦
Movie Theatres
1 Single/Twin; 1 Multiplex
7 Screens
Water Area
Lakes and rivers: 1,280 acres
Score: 1.69   Rank: 348

Erie, PA
Amusement & Theme Parks
Waldameer Park & Water World
Golf Courses
14 Daily fee, 180 holes
4 Municipal, 63 holes
5 Private, 90 holes
Good Restaurants
2 Family ♦♦
Movie Theatres
1 Single/Twin; 4 Multiplexes
37 Screens
Professional Sports
Sea Wolves (Class AA Baseball)
Recreation Areas
State
Presque Isle SP, 3,209 acres
Skiing
2 ski areas
Lift capacity/hour: 6,600
Water Area
Lakes and rivers: 5,120 acres
Lake Erie: 47,360 acres
Zoos
Erie Zoological Park
Score: 75.35   Rank: 88

Eugene-Springfield, OR
College NCAA I Sports
U of Oregon Ducks
Golf Courses
11 Daily fee, 171 holes
1 Municipal, 9 holes
4 Private, 63 holes
Good Restaurants
1 Simple ♦
6 Family ♦♦
3 Adult ♦♦♦
Movie Theatres
3 Singles/Twins; 6 Multiplexes
45 Screens
Professional Sports
Emeralds (Class A Baseball)
Recreation Areas
Federal
Oregon Islands NWR, 12 acres
Siuslaw NF, 247,282 acres

Umpqua NF, 151,248 acres
Willamette NF, 1,025,541 acres
State
AlderwoodState Wayside, 76 acres
Armitage SP, 5,776 acres
Blachly Mountain Forest Wayside,
69 acres
Carl Washburne Memorial SP,
1,089 acres
Darlingtonia Wayside, 18 acres
Devil's Elbow SP, 547 acres
Dorris SP, 92 acres
Elijah Bristow SP, 848 acres
Hendricks Bridge Wayside, 17 acres
Howard Morton Memorial SP,
24 acres
Jennie Harris Wayside, 4 acres
Jessie Honeyman Memorial SP,
522 acres
Joaquin Miller Forest Wayside,
112 acres
Muriel Ponsler Memorial, 2 acres
Neptune SP, 303 acres
Squaw Creek Wayside, 7 acres
Stonefield Beach Wayside, 19 acres
Willamette River Greenway,
925 acres
Skiing
3 ski areas
Lift capacity/hour: 33,700
Water Area
Lakes and rivers: 40,960 acres
Pacific coast: 6,656
Score: 41.35   Rank: 208

Evansville-Henderson, IN-KY
College NCAA I Sports
U of Evansville Aces
Gambling
2 Casinos
Ellis Park (thoroughbred)
Riverside Downs (mixed meetings)
Golf Courses
5 Daily fee, 90 holes
6 Municipal, 81 holes
8 Private, 126 holes
Good Restaurants
1 Simple ♦
7 Family ♦♦
1 Adult ♦♦♦
Movie Theatres
1 Multiplex
5 Screens
Recreation Areas
State
Harmonie SP, 3,465 acres
John James Audubon SP, 619 acres
Water Area
Lakes and rivers: 29,440 acres
Zoos
Mesker Park Zoo
Score: 27.19   Rank: 258

Fargo-Moorhead, ND-MN

College NCAA I Sports
U of North Dakota Sioux
Gambling
11 Casinos
Golf Courses
4 Daily fee, 36 holes
9 Municipal, 126 holes
3 Private, 63 holes
Good Restaurants
1 Simple ◆
6 Family ◆◆
3 Adult ◆◆◆
Movie Theatres
2 Singles/Twins; 4 Multiplexes
31 Screens
Professional Sports
Beez (IBA Basketball)
Recreation Areas
State
Buffalo River SP, 1,367 acres
Skiing
2 ski areas
Lift capacity/hour: 4,600
Water Area
Lakes and rivers: 5,760 acres
Score: **47.02**   Rank: **188**

Fayetteville, NC

Amusement & Theme Parks
Fantasy Lake
Golf Courses
6 Daily fee, 99 holes
5 Private, 81 holes
Good Restaurants
1 Simple ◆
1 Family ◆◆
Movie Theatres
6 Multiplexes
41 Screens
Professional Sports
Cape Fear Crocs (Class A Baseball)
Water Area
Lakes and rivers: 3,200 acres
Score: **17.28**   Rank: **293**

Fayetteville-Springdale-Rogers, AR

College NCAA I Sports
U of Arkansas Razorbacks
Gambling
1 Casino
Golf Courses
10 Daily fee, 135 holes
6 Private, 198 holes
Good Restaurants
4 Family ◆◆
2 Adult ◆◆◆
Movie Theatres
4 Singles/Twins; 6 Multiplexes
63 Screens
Recreation Areas
Federal
Logan Cave NWR, 124 acres
Ozark NF, 30,168 acres

State
Beaver Lake SP, 10,790 acres
Devil's Den SP, 1,047 acres
Water Area
Lakes and rivers: 25,600 acres
Score: **52.97**   Rank: **167**

Fitchburg-Leominster, MA

Amusement & Theme Parks
Whalom Park
Golf Courses
6 Daily fee, 90 holes
1 Municipal, 18 holes
1 Private, 18 holes
Good Restaurants
1 Simple ◆
2 Family ◆◆
Movie Theatres
2 Singles/Twins; 1 Multiplex
15 Screens
Recreation Areas
State
Dunn Pond SP, 115 acres
Lake Dennison SRA, 4,221 acres
Skiing
10 ski areas
Lift capacity/hour: 48,790
Water Area
Lakes and rivers: 5,726 acres
Score: **31.44**   Rank: **243**

Flagstaff, AZ-UT

College NCAA I Sports
Northern Arizona Lumberjacks
Gambling
1 Casino
Golf Courses
3 Daily fee, 36 holes
3 Municipal, 36 holes
2 Private, 36 holes
Good Restaurants
3 Simple ◆
17 Family ◆◆
7 Adult ◆◆◆
Movie Theatres
6 Singles/Twins; 2 Multiplexes
15 Screens
Recreation Areas
Federal
Bryce Canyon NP, 8,901 acres
Coconino NF, 1,415,700 acres
Dixie NF, 124,283 acres
Glen Canyon NRA, 492,267 acres
Grand Canyon NP, 662,038 acres
Kaibab NF, 1,528,320 acres
Lake Mead NRA, 83,116 acres
Prescott NF, 43,695 acres
Sitgreaves NF, 284,707 acres
Sunset Crater NM, 3,040 acres
Walnut Canyon NM, 2,012 acres
Wupatki NM, 35,253 acres
Zion NP, 9,391 acres

State
Coral Pink Sand Dunes SP,
3,730 acres
Slide Rock SP, 43 acres
Skiing
6 ski areas
Lift capacity/hour: 38,100
Water Area
Lakes and rivers: 101,760 acres
Score: **21.24**   Rank: **279**

Flint, MI

Gambling
Sports Creek Raceway (harness)
Golf Courses
17 Daily fee, 261 holes
4 Municipal, 72 holes
9 Private, 162 holes
Good Restaurants
1 Family ◆◆
Movie Theatres
2 Singles/Twins; 3 Multiplexes
39 Screens
Professional Sports
Generals (CoHL Hockey)
Recreation Areas
Federal
Manistee NF, 8 acres
Skiing
5 ski areas
Lift capacity/hour: 53,830
Water Area
Lakes and rivers: 6,400 acres
Score: **40.50**   Rank: **211**

Florence, AL

Golf Courses
4 Daily fee, 63 holes
3 Municipal, 45 holes
4 Private, 54 holes
Good Restaurants
3 Family ◆◆
Movie Theatres
1 Single/Twin; 2 Multiplexes
12 Screens
Recreation Areas
Federal
Natchez Trace Parkway, 4,175 acres
State
Joe Wheeler SP, 2,080 acres
Water Area
Lakes and rivers: 49,920 acres
Score: **40.22**   Rank: **212**

Florence, SC

Golf Courses
3 Daily fee, 54 holes
3 Private, 54 holes
Good Restaurants
2 Family ◆◆
1 Adult ◆◆◆
Movie Theatres
3 Multiplexes
10 Screens

Recreation Areas
State
Lynches River SP, 668 acres
Woods Bay SP, 3 acres
Water Area
Lakes and rivers: 2,560 acres
Score: 1.98   Rank: 347

Fort Collins-Loveland, CO
College NCAA I Sports
Colorado State Rams
Gambling
Cloverleaf Kennel Club (greyhound)
Golf Courses
5 Daily fee, 72 holes
7 Municipal, 99 holes
2 Private, 36 holes
Good Restaurants
4 Simple ♦
12 Family ♦♦
2 Adult ♦♦♦
Movie Theatres
5 Singles/Twins; 5 Multiplexes
42 Screens
Recreation Areas
Federal
Rocky Mountain NP, 144,374 acres
Roosevelt NF, 645,983 acres
State
Boyd Lake SRA, 197 acres
Lory SP, 2,479 acres
Picnic Rock SP, 13 acres
Skiing
4 ski areas
Lift capacity/hour: 48,250
Water Area
Lakes and rivers: 21,120 acres
Score: 26.06   Rank: 262

Fort Lauderdale, FL
Gambling
Dania Jai Alai
Gulfstream Park (thoroughbred)
Hollywood Greyhound Track
Pompano Park (harness)
Golf Courses
32 Daily fee, 738 holes
7 Municipal, 144 holes
17 Private, 369 holes
Good Restaurants
7 Simple ♦
43 Family ♦♦
22 Adult ♦♦♦
3 Upscale ♦♦♦♦
Movie Theatres
1 Single/Twin; 27 Multiplexes
253 Screens
Professional Sports
Florida Panthers (NHL Hockey)
Recreation Areas
State
Birch SRA, 180 acres
Lloyd Beach SRA, 251 acres

Water Area
Lakes and rivers: 8,320 acres
Atlantic coast: 6,272 acres
Score: 84.13   Rank: 57

★ Fort Myers-Cape Coral, FL
Amusement & Theme Parks
Cape Coral Waterpark
Gambling
Naples-Ft. Myers Park (greyhound)
Golf Courses
34 Daily fee, 612 holes
3 Municipal, 54 holes
22 Private, 459 holes
Good Restaurants
3 Simple ♦
14 Family ♦♦
2 Adult ♦♦♦
1 Upscale ♦♦♦♦
Movie Theatres
1 Single/Twin; 4 Multiplexes
46 Screens
Professional Sports
Miracle (Class A Baseball)
Recreation Areas
Federal
Caloosahatchee NWR, 40 acres
Ding Darling NWR, 5,174 acres
Matlacha Pass NWR, 512 acres
Pine Island NWR, 548 acres
State
Cayo Cosia SP, 2,241 acres
Gasparilla Island SRA, 144 acres
Lovers Key SRA, 434 acres
Water Area
Lakes and rivers: 151,040 acres
Gulf coast: 11,008 acres
Score: 93.20   Rank: 25

Fort Pierce-Port St. Lucie, FL
Gambling
Fort Pierce Jai-Alai (jai-alai)
Golf Courses
18 Daily fee, 360 holes
3 Municipal, 72 holes
26 Private, 468 holes
Good Restaurants
10 Family ♦♦
2 Adult ♦♦♦
Movie Theatres
1 Single/Twin; 7 Multiplexes
45 Screens
Recreation Areas
Federal
Hobe Sound NWR, 972 acres
State
Avalon SP, 570 acres
Dickinson SP, 11,550 acres
Fort Pierce Inlet SRA, 973 acres
St. Lucie Inlet SP, 808 acres
Water Area
Lakes and rivers: 104,960 acres
Atlantic coast: 9,536 acres
Score: 86.96   Rank: 47

Fort Smith, AR-OK
Gambling
Blue Ribbon Downs (mixed meetings)
Golf Courses
10 Daily fee, 126 holes
2 Municipal, 36 holes
2 Private, 36 holes
Good Restaurants
1 Simple ♦
5 Family ♦♦
Movie Theatres
1 Single/Twin; 3 Multiplexes
17 Screens
Recreation Areas
Federal
Ouachita NF, 18,956 acres
Ozark NF, 86,263 acres
State
Lake Fort Smith SP, 126 acres
Lake Tenkiller SP, 1,190 acres
Sallisaw SP, 90 acres
Water Area
Lakes and rivers: 38,400 acres
Score: 31.16   Rank: 244

Fort Walton Beach, FL
Amusement & Theme Parks
Florida's Silver Springs
Golf Courses
12 Daily fee, 270 holes
1 Municipal, 36 holes
4 Private, 81 holes
Good Restaurants
2 Simple ♦
3 Family ♦♦
1 Adult ♦♦♦
Movie Theatres
2 Singles/Twins; 5 Multiplexes
28 Screens
Recreation Areas
Federal
Choctawhatchee NF, 523 acres
Gulf Islands Seashore, 3,485 acres
State
Henderson Beach SRA, 209 acres
Rocky Bayou SRA, 357 acres
Water Area
Lakes and rivers: 38,400 acres
Score: 70.82   Rank: 104

Fort Wayne, IN
Golf Courses
29 Daily fee, 486 holes
3 Municipal, 54 holes
5 Private, 90 holes
Good Restaurants
1 Simple ♦
6 Family ♦♦
2 Adult ♦♦♦
Movie Theatres
5 Singles/Twins; 5 Multiplexes
41 Screens

Professional Sports
Fury (CBA Basketball)
Komets (IHL Hockey)
Wizards (Class A Baseball)
Recreation Areas
State
Ouabache SP, 1,065 acres
Water Area
Lakes and rivers: 7,680 acres
Zoos
Fort Wayne Children's Zoo
Score: **66.85**   Rank: **118**

Fort Worth-Arlington, TX
Amusement & Theme Parks
Six Flags Hurricane Harbor
Six Flags Over Texas
Auto Racing
Texas Motor Speedway
College NCAA I Sports
Texas Christian Horned Frogs
U of Texas Mavericks
Gambling
Trinity Meadows (mixed meetings)
Golf Courses
20 Daily fee, 270 holes
14 Municipal, 261 holes
17 Private, 351 holes
Good Restaurants
4 Simple ◆
20 Family ◆◆
3 Adult ◆◆◆
2 Upscale ◆◆◆◆
Movie Theatres
4 Singles/Twins; 25 Multiplexes
199 Screens
Professional Sports
Rangers (AL Baseball)
Recreation Areas
State
Cleburne SRA, 529 acres
Eagle Mountain SRA, 802 acres
Lake Mineral Wells SP, 3,008 acres
Water Area
Lakes and rivers: 39,040 acres
Zoos
Fort Worth Zoological Park
Score: **73.08**   Rank: **96**

Fresno, CA
Amusement & Theme Parks
Blackbeard's
Wild Water Adventures
College NCAA I Sports
Fresno State Bulldogs
Gambling
3 Casinos
Golf Courses
10 Daily fee, 144 holes
5 Municipal, 81 holes
8 Private, 135 holes
Good Restaurants
3 Adult ◆◆◆
1 Best ◆◆◆◆◆

Movie Theatres
2 Singles/Twins; 9 Multiplexes
71 Screens
Professional Sports
Grizzlies (Triple A Baseball)
Recreation Areas
Federal
Devils Postpile NM, 798 acres
Inyo NF, 52,296 acres
Kings Canyon NP, 354,828 acres
Sequoia NF, 130,757 acres
Sierra NF, 1,217,995 acres
Yosemite NP, 66,886 acres
State
Millerton Lake SRA, 6,551 acres
Skiing
7 ski areas
Lift capacity/hour: 160,400
Water Area
Lakes and rivers: 44,800 acres
Zoos
Chaffee Zoological Gardens
Score: **27.47**   Rank: **257**

Gadsden, AL
Golf Courses
3 Daily fee, 72 holes
3 Private, 54 holes
Movie Theatres
3 Multiplexes
15 Screens
Skiing
1 ski area
Lift capacity/hour: 800
Water Area
Lakes and rivers: 8,960 acres
Score: **8.21**   Rank: **325**

Gainesville, FL
College NCAA I Sports
U of Florida Gators
Golf Courses
4 Daily fee, 72 holes
1 Municipal, 18 holes
2 Private, 36 holes
Good Restaurants
2 Family ◆◆
2 Adult ◆◆◆
Movie Theatres
1 Single/Twin; 3 Multiplexes
29 Screens
Recreation Areas
State
O'Leno SP, 299 acres
Paynes Prairie, 20,678 acres
River Rise SNA, 1,706 acres
San Felasco Hammock SNA,
6,903 acres
Water Area
Lakes and rivers: 60,800 acres
Zoos
Santa Fe Community College Teaching
Zoo
Score: **59.77**   Rank: **143**

Galveston-Texas City, TX
Gambling
Gulf Park (greyhound)
Golf Courses
3 Daily fee, 45 holes
2 Municipal, 36 holes
4 Private, 63 holes
Good Restaurants
2 Simple ◆
1 Family ◆◆
2 Adult ◆◆◆
Movie Theatres
1 Single/Twin; 2 Multiplexes
17 Screens
Recreation Areas
State
Galveston Island SP, 1,950 acres
Water Area
Lakes and rivers: 63,360 acres
Gulf coast: 24,192 acres
Zoos
Moody Gardens-Galveston Island
Score: **45.60**   Rank: **192**

Gary, IN
College NCAA I Sports
Valparaiso Crusaders
Gambling
4 Casinos
Golf Courses
16 Daily fee, 288 holes
5 Municipal, 81 holes
8 Private, 171 holes
Good Restaurants
5 Family ◆◆
1 Adult ◆◆◆
Movie Theatres
6 Singles/Twins; 6 Multiplexes
61 Screens
Recreation Areas
Federal
Indiana Dunes Lakeshore, 9,760
acres
State
Indiana Dunes SP, 2,182 acres
Skiing
1 ski area
Lift capacity/hour: 800
Water Area
Lakes and rivers: 4,480 acres
Lake Michigan coast: 14,400 acres
Score: **54.39**   Rank: **162**

Glens Falls, NY
Amusement & Theme Parks
The Great Escape
Golf Courses
16 Daily fee, 207 holes
2 Private, 36 holes
Good Restaurants
1 Simple ◆
18 Family ◆◆
2 Adult ◆◆◆
1 Upscale ◆◆◆◆

Movie Theatres

3 Singles/Twins; 2 Multiplexes

17 Screens

Professional Sports

Adirondack Red Wings (AHL Hockey)

Recreation Areas

State

Eagle Point SRA, 16 acres

Hearthstone Point SRA, 99 acres

Lake George Beach SRA, 69 acres

Lake George Islands, 306 acres

Lake Lauderdale SP, 117 acres

Luzerne SRA, 728 acres

Prospect Mountain SRA, 2,700 acres

Rogers Rock SRA, 1,863 acres

Skiing

15 ski areas

Lift capacity/hour: 127,402

Water Area

Lakes and rivers: 46,080 acres

Score: **63.73**   Rank: **129**

Goldsboro, NC

Golf Courses

3 Daily fee, 54 holes

3 Private, 54 holes

Good Restaurants

1 Simple ♦

1 Family ♦ ♦

Movie Theatres

2 Multiplexes

8 Screens

Recreation Areas

State

Cliffs-Of-The-Neuse SP, 608 acres

Water Area

Lakes and rivers: 2,560 acres

Score: **0.84**   Rank: **351**

Grand Forks, ND-MN

Gambling

7 Casinos

Golf Courses

11 Daily fee, 117 holes

2 Municipal, 27 holes

1 Private, 18 holes

Good Restaurants

1 Simple ♦

2 Family ♦ ♦

1 Adult ♦ ♦ ♦

Movie Theatres

3 Singles/Twins; 2 Multiplexes

19 Screens

Recreation Areas

Federal

Kelly's Slough NWR, 680 acres

Rydell NWR, 2,070 acres

State

Turtle River SP, 784 acres

Water Area

Lakes and rivers: 18,560 acres

Score: **44.47**   Rank: **197**

Grand Junction, CO

Golf Courses

2 Daily fee, 36 holes

2 Municipal, 27 holes

1 Private, 18 holes

Good Restaurants

6 Family ♦ ♦

Movie Theatres

2 Singles/Twins; 2 Multiplexes

14 Screens

Recreation Areas

Federal

Colorado NM, 20,454 acres

Grand Mesa NF, 252,971 acres

Manti-La Sal NF, 4,542 acres

Uncompahgre NF, 207,256 acres

White River NF, 83,069 acres

State

Highline SRA, 580 acres

Island acres SRA, 130 acres

Vega SRA, 898 acres

Skiing

7 ski areas

Lift capacity/hour: 76,329

Water Area

Lakes and rivers: 8,320 acres

Score: **10.48**   Rank: **317**

★ **Grand Rapids-Muskegon-Holland, MI**

Amusement & Theme Parks

Michigan's Adventures

Pleasure Island Water Theme Park

Auto Racing

Western Michigan Grand Prix

Gambling

Muskegon Racecourse (mixed

meetings)

Golf Courses

64 Daily fee, 1224 holes

3 Municipal, 54 holes

17 Private, 324 holes

Good Restaurants

5 Simple ♦

19 Family ♦ ♦

6 Adult ♦ ♦ ♦

Movie Theatres

2 Singles/Twins; 9 Multiplexes

80 Screens

Professional Sports

Fury (CoHL Hockey)

Hoops (CBA Basketball)

Whitecaps (Class A Baseball)

Recreation Areas

Federal

Manistee NF, 12,514 acres

State

Duck Lake SP, 704 acres

Grand Haven SP, 48 acres

Hoffmaster SP, 1,043 acres

Holland SP, 142 acres

Muskegon SP, 1,165 acres

Saugatuck Dunes SP, 866 acres

Skiing

12 ski areas

Lift capacity/hour: 62,200

Water Area

Lakes and rivers: 39,040 acres

Lake Michigan: 190,920 acres

Zoos

John Ball Zoological Gardens

Score: **99.43**   Rank: **3**

Great Falls, MT

Gambling

1 Casino

Golf Courses

2 Daily fee, 27 holes

2 Municipal, 36 holes

1 Private, 18 holes

Good Restaurants

2 Simple ♦

2 Family ♦ ♦

Movie Theatres

2 Singles/Twins; 2 Multiplexes

18 Screens

Recreation Areas

Federal

Benton Lake NWR, 11,955 acres

Lewis & Clark NF, 178,635 acres

State

Giant Springs SP, 280 acres

Sluice Boxes SP, 1,454 acres

Skiing

2 ski areas

Lift capacity/hour: 5,300

Water Area

Lakes and rivers: 8,960 acres

Score: **9.34**   Rank: **321**

Greeley, CO

Golf Courses

2 Daily fee, 36 holes

2 Municipal, 36 holes

2 Private, 27 holes

Good Restaurants

2 Simple ♦

1 Family ♦ ♦

Movie Theatres

2 Singles/Twins; 2 Multiplexes

13 Screens

Recreation Areas

Federal

Pawnee Grasslands, 193,060 acres

State

Barbour Ponds SRA, 50 acres

Skiing

1 ski area

Lift capacity/hour: 6,150

Water Area

Lakes and rivers: 18,560 acres

Score: **20.39**   Rank: **282**

Green Bay, WI

College NCAA I Sports

U of Wisconsin Phoenix

Gambling

1 Casino

Golf Courses
11 Daily fee, 207 holes
1 Municipal, 18 holes
2 Private, 36 holes
Good Restaurants
9 Family ♦♦
3 Adult ♦♦♦
Movie Theatres
2 Singles/Twins; 5 Multiplexes
32 Screens
Professional Sports
Packers (NFL Football)
Recreation Areas
State
Lost Dauphin SP, 19 acres
Mountain-Bay Trail, 188 acres
Skiing
4 ski areas
Lift capacity/hour: 4,200
Water Area
Lakes and rivers: 5,120 acres
Lake Michigan: 50,560 acres
Zoos
Bay Beach Wildlife Sanctuary
Northeastern Wisconsin Zoo
Score: **41.92**   Rank: **206**

Greensboro–Winston-Salem–High Point, NC
College NCAA I Sports
North Carolina A & T Aggies
U of North Carolina Spartans
Wake Forest Demon Deacons
Golf Courses
53 Daily fee, 882 holes
13 Municipal, 261 holes
15 Private, 306 holes
Good Restaurants
3 Simple ♦
14 Family ♦♦
14 Adult ♦♦♦
Movie Theatres
5 Singles/Twins; 17 Multiplexes
135 Screens
Professional Sports
Bats (Class A Baseball)
Hurricanes (NHL Hockey)
Warthogs (Class A Baseball)
Recreation Areas
Federal
Uwharrie NF, 10,298 acres
State
Boone's Cave SP, 110 acres
Hanging Rock SP, 5,862 acres
Pilot Mountain SP, 298 acres
Water Area
Lakes and rivers: 25,600 acres
Zoos
Natural Science Center of Greensboro
North Carolina Zoological Park
Score: **85.83**   Rank: **51**

Greenville, NC
College NCAA I Sports
East Carolina Pirates
Golf Courses
6 Daily fee, 99 holes
3 Private, 54 holes
Good Restaurants
4 Family ♦♦
Movie Theatres
1 Single/Twin; 4 Multiplexes
16 Screens
Water Area
Lakes and rivers: 1,920 acres
Score: **14.44**   Rank: **303**

Greenville-Spartanburg-Anderson, SC
College NCAA I Sports
Clemson Tigers
Furman Paladins
Wofford Terriers
Golf Courses
33 Daily fee, 576 holes
19 Private, 351 holes
Good Restaurants
1 Simple ♦
3 Family ♦♦
6 Adult ♦♦♦
Movie Theatres
2 Singles/Twins; 12 Multiplexes
101 Screens
Professional Sports
Braves (Class AA Baseball)
Recreation Areas
State
Caesars Head SP, 7,467 acres
Croft SP, 7,054 acres
Jones Gap SP, 3,346 acres
Keowee Toxaway SP, 1,000 acres
Paris Mountain SP, 1,275 acres
Sadlers Creek SP, 395 acres
Table Rock SP, 3,083 acres
Wildcat Wayside SP, 63 acres
Skiing
2 ski areas
Lift capacity/hour: 3,600
Water Area
Lakes and rivers: 46,080 acres
Zoos
Greenville Zoo
Score: **75.52**   Rank: **98**

Hagerstown, MD
Golf Courses
3 Daily fee, 45 holes
2 Municipal, 27 holes
1 Private, 18 holes
Good Restaurants
2 Simple ♦
2 Family ♦♦
3 Adult ♦♦♦
Movie Theatres
1 Single/Twin; 3 Multiplexes
17 Screens

Professional Sports
Suns (Class A Baseball)
Recreation Areas
Federal
Appalachian NT, 527 acres
Catoctin Mountain Park, 75 acres
State
Greenbrier SP, 1,288 acres
South Mountain SP, 6,087 acres
Skiing
2 ski areas
Lift capacity/hour: 22,120
Water Area
Lakes and rivers: 5,760 acres
Score: **22.37**   Rank: **275**

Halifax, NS
Amusement & Theme Parks
Atlantic Playland
College CIAU Sports
Dalhousie Tigers
St. Mary's Huskies
Gambling
1 Casino
Golf Courses
4 Daily fee, 72 holes
4 Private, 72 holes
Good Restaurants
1 Simple ♦
10 Family ♦♦
10 Adult ♦♦♦
Movie Theatres
2 Singles/Twins; 5 Multiplexes
39 Screens
Recreation Areas
Federal
Musquodoboit Harbour Outer River
Estuary, 2,965 acres
Sable Island MBS, 5,807 acres
Provincial
Clam Harbour Beach PP, 974 acres
Crystal Cresent Beach PP, 452 acres
Eastern Shore Islands, 29,076 acres
Lawrencetown Beach PP, 588 acres
Lewis Lake PP, 371 acres
Martinique Beach Game Sanctuary,
761 acres
Martinique Beach PP, 151 acres
Oakfield PP, 133 acres
Porters Lake PP, 215 acres
Taylors Head PP, 2,014 acres
Waverley Game Sanctuary,
14,075 acres
Skiing
2 ski areas
Lift capacity/hour: 7,800
Water Area
Lakes and rivers: 39,000 acres
Atlantic coast: 55,000 acres
Zoos
Provincial Wildlife Park
Score: **69.68**   Rank: **108**

Hamilton, ON
College CIAU Sports
McMaster Marauders
Gambling
Flamboro Downs (harness)
Golf Courses
4 Daily fee, 72 holes
6 Municipal, 108 holes
5 Private, 81 holes
Good Restaurants
5 Family ♦♦
6 Adult ♦♦♦
Movie Theatres
5 Singles/Twins; 10 Multiplexes
68 Screens
Professional Sports
Bulldogs (AHL Hockey)
Tiger-Cats (CFL Football)
Skiing
5 ski areas
Lift capacity/hour: 10,366
Water Area
Lakes and rivers: 1,200 acres
Lake Ontario: 12,000 acres
Score: 39.09   Rank: 216

Hamilton-Middletown, OH
College NCAA I Sports
Miami U Redskins
Golf Courses
5 Daily fee, 81 holes
5 Municipal, 108 holes
7 Private, 117 holes
Good Restaurants
5 Simple ♦
8 Family ♦♦
3 Adult ♦♦♦
Movie Theatres
2 Singles/Twins; 4 Multiplexes
31 Screens
Recreation Areas
State
Hueston Woods SP, 990 acres
Skiing
1 ski area
Lift capacity/hour: 12,200
Water Area
Lakes and rivers: 1,920 acres
Score: 30.02   Rank: 248

Harrisburg-Lebanon-Carlisle, PA
Amusement & Theme Parks
Hersheypark
Pennsylvania Renaissance Faire
Williams Grove Park & Speedway
Golf Courses
20 Daily fee, 315 holes
4 Municipal, 63 holes
10 Private, 162 holes
Good Restaurants
4 Simple ♦
12 Family ♦♦
16 Adult ♦♦♦
2 Upscale ♦♦♦♦

Movie Theatres
11 Singles/Twins; 5 Multiplexes
60 Screens
Professional Sports
Hershey Bears (AHL Hockey)
Senators (Class AA Baseball)
Recreation Areas
Federal
Appalachian Trail, 5,465 acres
State
Big Spring SP, 45 acres
Colonel Denning SP, 273 acres
Fowlers Hollow SP, 104 acres
Kings Gap SP, 1,439 acres
Little Buffalo SP, 830 acres
Memorial Lake SP, 230 acres
Swatara SP, 1,050 acres
Skiing
6 ski areas
Lift capacity/hour: 57,120
Water Area
Lakes and rivers: 23,040 acres
Zoos
Zooamerica Wildlife Park
Score: 61.47   Rank: 137

Hartford, CT
Aquariums
Golf Courses
33 Daily fee, 549 holes
10 Municipal, 207 holes
15 Private, 298 holes
Good Restaurants
5 Simple ♦
24 Family ♦♦
11 Adult ♦♦♦
Movie Theatres
5 Singles/Twins; 10 Multiplexes
91 Screens
Professional Sports
Connecticut Pride (CBA Basketball)
Rock Cats (Class AA Baseball)
Wolf Pack (AHL Hockey)
Recreation Areas
State
Beaver Brook SP, 401 acres
Bolton Notch SP, 70 acres
Brainard Homestead SP, 25 acres
Dart Island SP, 4 acres
Day Pond SP, 180 acres
Devil's Hopyard SP, 860 acres
Dinosaur SP, 70 acres
George Seymour SP, 222 acres
Gillette Castle SP, 184 acres
Haddam Island SP, 14 acres
Haddam Meadows SP, 175 acres
Higganum Reservoir SP, 147 acres
Horseguard SP, 146 acres
Hurd SP, 884 acres
Lamentation Mountain SP, 47 acres
Mansfield Hollow SP, 2,328 acres
Millers Pond SP, 231 acres

Penwood SP, 787 acres
Platt Hill SP, 124 acres
Pomeroy SP, 104 acres
Stratton Brook SP, 148 acres
Sunset Rock SP, 15 acres
Talcott Mountain SP, 557 acres
Tri Mountain SP, 157 acres
Wadsworth Falls SP, 285 acres
Windsor Meadows SP, 128 acres
Skiing
15 ski areas
Lift capacity/hour: 79,330
Water Area
Lakes and rivers: 25,982 acres
Score: 75.07   Rank: 89

Hattiesburg, MS
College NCAA I Sports
USM Golden Eagles
Golf Courses
6 Daily fee, 99 holes
1 Private, 18 holes
Good Restaurants
4 Family ♦♦
Movie Theatres
3 Multiplexes
18 Screens
Recreation Areas
Federal
Desoto NF, 50,403 acres
State
Johnson SP, 744 acres
Water Area
Lakes and rivers: 3,840 acres
Zoos
Hattiesburg Zoo
Score: 39.37   Rank: 215

Hickory-Morganton-Lenoir, NC
Golf Courses
14 Daily fee, 261 holes
5 Private, 90 holes
Good Restaurants
6 Family ♦♦
6 Adult ♦♦♦
Movie Theatres
5 Singles/Twins; 3 Multiplexes
22 Screens
Professional Sports
Crawdads (Class A Baseball)
Recreation Areas
Federal
Blue Ridge Parkway, 978 acres
Pisgah NF, 97,337 acres
State
South Mountain SP, 5,783 acres
Skiing
7 ski areas
Lift capacity/hour: 47,650
Water Area
Lakes and rivers: 17,920 acres
Score: 55.80   Rank: 157

Honolulu, HI ★

Aquariums
Sea Life Park Hawaii
Waikiki Aquarium

College NCAA I Sports
U of Hawaii Rainbow Warriors

Golf Courses
17 Daily fee, 333 holes
5 Municipal, 81 holes
11 Private, 207 holes

Good Restaurants
6 Simple ◆
17 Family ◆◆
16 Adult ◆◆◆
5 Upscale ◆◆◆◆
2 Best ◆◆◆◆◆

Movie Theatres
10 Singles/Twins; 10 Multiplexes
98 Screens

Recreation Areas
Federal
  Hawaiian Islands NWR, 1,907 acres
State
  Diamond Head, 475 acres
  Hanauma Bay, 101 acres
  Heeia SP, 19 acres
  Kaena Point SP, 779 acres
  Kahana Valley SP, 5,229 acres
  Kakaako Waterfront, 35 acres
  Keaiwa Heiau SRA, 385 acres
  Malaekahana SRA, 110 acres
  Nuuanu Pali Wayside, 3 acres
  Puu Ualakaa Wayside, 50 acres
  Sacred Falls SP, 1,374 acres
  Sand Island SRA, 140 acres
  Waahila Ridge SRA, 50 acres
  Wahiawa Fresh SRA, 66 acres

Water Area
Lakes and rivers: 12,160 acres
Pacific coast: 96,512 acres

Zoos
Honolulu Zoo
Score: **92.91**   Rank: **26**

Houma, LA

College NCAA I Sports
Nicholls State Colonels

Golf Courses
3 Daily fee, 27 holes
3 Private, 36 holes

Good Restaurants
6 Simple ◆
4 Family ◆◆

Movie Theatres
2 Singles/Twins; 2 Multiplexes
12 Screens

Recreation Areas
Federal
  Mandalay NWR, 4,416 acres

Water Area
Lakes and rivers: 345,600 acres
Gulf coast: 43,008 acres
Score: **83.00**   Rank: **61**

Houston, TX

Amusement & Theme Parks
Six Flags Astroworld/WaterWorld
Splashtown

Aquariums
Kipp Aquarium

Auto Racing
Grand Prix of Houston

College NCAA I Sports
Prairie View A & M Panthers
Rice Owls
Texas Southern Tigers
U of Houston Cougars

Golf Courses
45 Daily fee, 810 holes
11 Municipal, 198 holes
41 Private, 972 holes

Good Restaurants
53 Simple ◆
183 Family ◆◆
97 Adult ◆◆◆
12 Upscale ◆◆◆◆
3 Best ◆◆◆◆◆

Movie Theatres
3 Singles/Twins; 48 Multiplexes
435 Screens

Professional Sports
Aeros (IHL Hockey)
Astros (NL Baseball)
Comets (WNBA)
Rockets (NBA Basketball)

Recreation Areas
Federal
  Anahuac NWR, 31,796 acres
  Big Thicket Preserve, 1,476 acres
  Sam Houston NF, 47,776 acres
  Trinity River NWR, 4,400 acres
State
  Brazos Bend SP, 4,897 acres
  Davis Hill SP, 1,735 acres
  Lake Houston SP, 4,912 acres

Water Area
Lakes and rivers: 95,360 acres
Gulf coast: 15,400 acres

Zoos
Houston Zoological Gardens
Score: **85.26**   Rank: **53**

Huntington-Ashland, WV-KY-OH

College NCAA I Sports
Marshall Thundering Herd

Golf Courses
15 Daily fee, 198 holes
5 Private, 81 holes

Good Restaurants
4 Family ◆◆
2 Adult ◆◆◆

Movie Theatres
3 Multiplexes
19 Screens

Professional Sports
Blizzard (ECHL Hockey)

Recreation Areas
Federal
  Wayne NF, 68,880 acres
State
  Beech Fork SP, 3,981 acres
  Carter Caves Resort, 1,350 acres
  Grayson Lake SP, 1,222 acres
  Greenbo Lake Resort, 3,008 acres

Water Area
Lakes and rivers: 16,640 acres
Score: **48.72**   Rank: **182**

Huntsville, AL

Amusement & Theme Parks
Southern Adventures

Golf Courses
8 Daily fee, 153 holes
2 Municipal, 36 holes
3 Private, 72 holes

Good Restaurants
3 Simple ◆
13 Family ◆◆

Movie Theatres
1 Single/Twin; 5 Multiplexes
63 Screens

Professional Sports
Stars (Class AA Baseball)

Recreation Areas
Federal
  Wheeler NWR, 5,006 acres
State
  Joe Wheeler SP, 70 acres
  Monte Sano SP, 2,140 acres

Water Area
Lakes and rivers: 30,080 acres
Score: **63.45**   Rank: **130**

Indianapolis, IN

Amusement & Theme Parks
River Fair Family Fun Park

Auto Racing
Indianapolis Motor Speedway
Indianapolis Raceway Park

College NCAA I Sports
Butler Bulldogs
U of Indianapolis Greyhounds

Golf Courses
57 Daily fee, 927 holes
14 Municipal, 225 holes
24 Private, 405 holes

Good Restaurants
14 Simple ◆
35 Family ◆◆
13 Adult ◆◆◆
1 Upscale ◆◆◆◆

Movie Theatres
11 Singles/Twins; 23 Multiplexes
169 Screens

Professional Sports
Colts (NFL Football)
Indians (Triple A Baseball)
Indiana Pacers (NBA Basketball)

Recreation

Recreation Areas
State
  Mounds SP, 259 acres
Skiing
5 ski areas
Lift capacity/hour: 24,000
Water Area
Lakes and rivers: 12,160 acres
Zoos
Indianapolis Zoo
Score: 82.15   Rank: 64

Iowa City, IA
College NCAA I Sports
U of Iowa Hawkeyes
Golf Courses
6 Daily fee, 63 holes
1 Municipal, 18 holes
1 Private, 9 holes
Good Restaurants
6 Family ♦♦
1 Adult ♦♦♦
Movie Theatres
2 Singles/Twins; 2 Multiplexes
11 Screens
Recreation Areas
State
  Lake Macbride SP, 2,180 acres
Water Area
Lakes and rivers: 5,760 acres
Score: 43.90   Rank: 199

Jackson, MI
Auto Racing
Michigan Speedway
Gambling
Jackson Raceway (harness)
Golf Courses
17 Daily fee, 288 holes
2 Municipal, 45 holes
2 Private, 45 holes
Good Restaurants
2 Simple ♦
2 Family ♦♦
Movie Theatres
1 Single/Twin; 1 Multiplex
11 Screens
Recreation Areas
State
  Lakelands Trail SP, 7 acres
  W.J. Hayes SP, 22 acres
  Waterloo SRA, 13,075 acres
Skiing
1 ski area
Lift capacity/hour: 17,200
Water Area
Lakes and rivers: 10,880 acres
Zoos
Jackson Zoological Park
Score: 50.14   Rank: 177

Jackson, MS
College NCAA I Sports
Jackson State Tigers
Golf Courses
7 Daily fee, 144 holes
4 Municipal, 54 holes
8 Private, 144 holes
Good Restaurants
8 Simple ♦
10 Family ♦♦
12 Adult ♦♦♦
Movie Theatres
4 Multiplexes
21 Screens
Professional Sports
Generals (Class AA Baseball)
Recreation Areas
Federal
  Natchez Trace NT, 0 acres
  Natchez Trace Parkway, 7,352 acres
State
  LeFleur's Bluff SP, 305 acres
Water Area
Lakes and rivers: 40,320 acres
Zoos
Jackson Zoological Park
Score: 55.52   Rank: 158

Jackson, TN
Golf Courses
4 Daily fee, 45 holes
1 Municipal, 18 holes
2 Private, 36 holes
Good Restaurants
2 Simple ♦
2 Family ♦♦
Movie Theatres
2 Multiplexes
18 Screens
Professional Sports
Diamond Jaxx (Class AA Baseball)
Recreation Areas
State
  Chickasaw SP, 400 acres
Water Area
Lakes and rivers: 1,280 acres
Score: 4.53   Rank: 338

★ Jacksonville, FL
College NCAA I Sports
Jacksonville U Dolphins
Gambling
Jacksonville Kennel Club (greyhound)
St. Johns Park (greyhound)
Golf Courses
18 Daily fee, 315 holes
5 Municipal, 99 holes
24 Private, 495 holes
Good Restaurants
15 Simple ♦
22 Family ♦♦
8 Adult ♦♦♦
1 Best ♦♦♦♦♦

Movie Theatres
16 Multiplexes
145 Screens
Professional Sports
Jaguars (NFL Football)
Lizard Kings (ECHL Hockey)
Suns (Class AA Baseball)
Recreation Areas
State
  Amelia Island SRA, 229 acres
  Anastasia SRA, 1,292 acres
  Big Talbot Island SP, 1,597 acres
  Faver-Dykes SP, 1,450 acres
  Fort Clinch SP, 1,153 acres
  Gold Head Branch SP, 2,099 acres
  Guana River SP, 2,398 acres
  Little Talbot Island SP, 2,633 acres
Water Area
Lakes and rivers: 129,280 acres
Atlantic coast: 17,344 acres
Zoos
Jacksonville Zoological Park
Score: 94.05   Rank: 22

Jacksonville, NC
Golf Courses
4 Daily fee, 81 holes
2 Private, 54 holes
Good Restaurants
1 Simple ♦
1 Family ♦♦
Movie Theatres
1 Single/Twin; 4 Multiplexes
22 Screens
Recreation Areas
State
  Hammocks Beach SP, 892 acres
Water Area
Lakes and rivers: 33,920 acres
Atlantic coast: 5,632 acres
Score: 37.67   Rank: 221

Jamestown, NY
Amusement & Theme Parks
Midway Park
Golf Courses
16 Daily fee, 243 holes
2 Private, 36 holes
Good Restaurants
4 Family ♦♦
4 Adult ♦♦♦
Movie Theatres
3 Singles/Twins; 2 Multiplexes
20 Screens
Professional Sports
Jammers (Class A Baseball)
Recreation Areas
State
  Lake Erie SP, 355 acres
  Long Point SP, 360 acres
Skiing
3 ski areas
Lift capacity/hour: 27,055

Water Area
Lakes and rivers: 14,720 acres
Lake Erie: 26,600 acres
Rank: **99**   Score: **72.23**

Janesville-Beloit, WI
Golf Courses
7 Daily fee, 126 holes
3 Municipal, 45 holes
2 Private, 36 holes
Good Restaurants
1 Adult ♦♦♦
Movie Theatres
1 Single/Twin; 4 Multiplexes
21 Screens
Professional Sports
Snappers (Class A Baseball)
Skiing
3 ski areas
Lift capacity/hour: 23,485
Water Area
Lakes and rivers: 3,840 acres
Score: **37.96**   Rank: **220**

Jersey City, NJ
Amusement & Theme Parks
Six Flags Great Adventure
College NCAA I Sports
St. Peter's College Peacocks
Good Restaurants
1 Simple ♦
3 Family ♦♦
3 Adult ♦♦♦
Movie Theatres
2 Singles/Twins; 8 Multiplexes
50 Screens
Professional Sports
Metro Stars (MLS Soccer)
Recreation Areas
Federal
Statue of Liberty, 45 acres
State
Liberty SP, 1,211 acres
Skiing
2 ski areas
Lift capacity/hour: 6,500
Water Area
Lakes and rivers: 10,240 acres
Score: **16.14**   Rank: **297**

Johnson City-Kingsport-Bristol, TN-VA
Auto Racing
Bristol Motor Speedway
College NCAA I Sports
East Tennessee State Buccaneers
Golf Courses
8 Daily fee, 126 holes
9 Municipal, 144 holes
8 Private, 135 holes
Good Restaurants
3 Simple ♦
19 Family ♦♦
3 Adult ♦♦♦

Movie Theatres
6 Singles/Twins; 4 Multiplexes
33 Screens
Recreation Areas
Federal
Appalachian NT, 988 acres
Cherokee NF, 195,254 acres
Jefferson NF, 56,879 acres
State
Natural Tunnel SP, 649 acres
Roan Mountain SP, 200 acres
Warriors Path SP, 905 acres
Skiing
3 ski areas
Lift capacity/hour: 21,000
Water Area
Lakes and rivers: 28,800 acres
Zoos
Bays Mountain Preserve Park
Score: **49.29**   Rank: **180**

Johnstown, PA
College NCAA I Sports
St. Francis College Red Flash
Golf Courses
17 Daily fee, 207 holes
1 Municipal, 9 holes
3 Private, 54 holes
Good Restaurants
9 Family ♦♦
3 Adult ♦♦♦
Movie Theatres
1 Single/Twin
1 Screen
Professional Sports
Chiefs (ECHL Hockey)
Recreation Areas
State
Kooser SP, 250 acres
Laurel Hill SP, 3,935 acres
Laurel Ridge SP, 8,814 acres
Prince Gallitzin SP, 6,249 acres
Skiing
6 ski areas
Lift capacity/hour: 52,520
Water Area
Lakes and rivers: 7,040 acres
Score: **35.69**   Rank: **228**

Jonesboro, AR
College NCAA I Sports
Arkansas State Indians
Golf Courses
5 Daily fee, 54 holes
2 Private, 36 holes
Good Restaurants
2 Simple ♦
1 Family ♦♦
1 Adult ♦♦♦
Movie Theatres
1 Single/Twin; 1 Multiplex
22 Screens
Water Area
Lakes and rivers: 1,280 acres
Score: **5.66**   Rank: **334**

Joplin, MO
Gambling
1 Casino
Golf Courses
3 Daily fee, 36 holes
3 Municipal, 54 holes
3 Private, 63 holes
Good Restaurants
6 Family ♦♦
1 Adult ♦♦♦
Movie Theatres
1 Single/Twin; 2 Multiplexes
12 Screens
Recreation Areas
Federal
Ozark Cavefish NWR, 2 acres
Water Area
Lakes and rivers: 1,280 acres
Score: **10.19**   Rank: **318**

Kalamazoo-Battle Creek, MI
College NCAA I Sports
Western Michigan Broncos
Golf Courses
30 Daily fee, 522 holes
5 Municipal, 81 holes
7 Private, 135 holes
Good Restaurants
3 Simple ♦
14 Family ♦♦
4 Adult ♦♦♦
1 Upscale ♦♦♦♦
Movie Theatres
1 Single/Twin; 7 Multiplexes
52 Screens
Professional Sports
Battle Cats (Class A Baseball)
Wings (IHL Hockey)
Recreation Areas
State
Fort Custer SRA, 3,033 acres
Kal-Haven Trail, 36 acres
Van Buren SP, 326 acres
Skiing
6 ski areas
Lift capacity/hour: 37,600
Water Area
Lakes and rivers: 25,600 acres
Lake Michigan: 29,880 acres
Zoos
Binder Park Zoo
Kalamazoo Nature Center
Score: **87.81**   Rank: **44**

Kankakee, IL
Golf Courses
7 Daily fee, 144 holes
1 Municipal, 18 holes
1 Private, 18 holes
Good Restaurants
1 Simple ♦
Movie Theatres
3 Multiplexes
18 Screens

Recreation Areas
State
Kankakee River SP, 3,932 acres
Water Area
Lakes and rivers: 2,560 acres
Score: **18.69**   Rank: **288**

Kansas City, MO-KS
Amusement & Theme Parks
World's of Fun
Auto Racing
I-70 Speedway
College NCAA I Sports
U of Missouri Kangaroos
Gambling
6 Casinos
The Woodlands (greyhound)
Woodlands Horse Racing
(mixed meetings)
Golf Courses
29 Daily fee, 504 holes
19 Municipal, 369 holes
27 Private, 441 holes
Good Restaurants
19 Simple ◆
60 Family ◆◆
62 Adult ◆◆◆
17 Upscale ◆◆◆◆
Movie Theatres
5 Singles/Twins; 37 Multiplexes
320 Screens
Professional Sports
Blades (IHL Hockey)
Chiefs (NFL Football)
Royals (AL Baseball)
Wizards (MLS Soccer)
Recreation Areas
Federal
Big Muddy NFWR, 85 acres
State
Hillsdale SP, 2,830 acres
Wallace SP, 502 acres
Watkins Mill SP, 818 acres
Weston Bend SP, 1,133 acres
Water Area
Lakes and rivers: 50,560 acres
Zoos
Fleming Park Zoo
Kansas City Zoological Gardens
Overland Park Zoo
Score: **87.25**   Rank: **46**

Kenosha, WI
Gambling
Dairyland Greyhound Park
Golf Courses
5 Daily fee, 90 holes
2 Municipal, 27 holes
1 Private, 18 holes
Good Restaurants
1 Family ◆◆
1 Adult ◆◆◆

Movie Theatres
1 Single/Twin; 3 Multiplexes
18 Screens
Recreation Areas
State
Bong SRA, 4,515 acres
Skiing
3 ski areas
Lift capacity/hour: 31,385
Water Area
Lakes and rivers: 3,840 acres
Lake Michigan: 30,400 acres
Score: **49.57**   Rank: **179**

Killeen-Temple, TX
Golf Courses
6 Daily fee, 90 holes
3 Municipal, 45 holes
3 Private, 54 holes
Good Restaurants
1 Family ◆◆
Movie Theatres
5 Multiplexes
28 Screens
Recreation Areas
State
Mother Neff SP, 259 acres
Water Area
Lakes and rivers: 21,120 acres
Score: **20.96**   Rank: **280**

Kitchener-Waterloo, ON
Amusement & Theme Parks
Africa Lion Safari
Bingeman's Recreation Center
Sports World
College CIAU Sports
U of Waterloo Warriors
Wilfrid Laurier Golden Hawks
Golf Courses
4 Daily fee, 63 holes
3 Municipal, 54 holes
3 Private, 54 holes
Good Restaurants
4 Simple ◆
6 Family ◆◆
5 Adult ◆◆◆
1 Upscale ◆◆◆◆
Movie Theatres
4 Singles/Twins; 3 Multiplexes
24 Screens
Recreation Areas
Provincial
Dumfries Crown Game Preserve,
2,471 acres
Skiing
4 ski areas
Lift capacity/hour: 8,500
Water Area
Lakes and rivers: 1,200 acres
Zoos
African Lion Safari
Score: **16.99**   Rank: **294**

Knoxville, TN
Amusement & Theme Parks
Dollywood
College NCAA I Sports
U of Tennessee Volunteers
Golf Courses
16 Daily fee, 288 holes
6 Municipal, 108 holes
8 Private, 144 holes
Good Restaurants
10 Simple ◆
46 Family ◆◆
4 Adult ◆◆◆
Movie Theatres
3 Singles/Twins; 12 Multiplexes
96 Screens
Professional Sports
Smokies (Class AA Baseball)
Recreation Areas
Federal
Appalachian NT, 640 acres
Great Smokey Mountains NP,
225,822 acres
State
Big Ridge SP, 3,642 acres
Norris Dam SP, 2,056 acres
Skiing
4 ski areas
Lift capacity/hour: 20,200
Water Area
Lakes and rivers: 50,560 acres
Zoos
Knoxville Zoological Gardens
Score: **86.11**   Rank: **50**

Kokomo, IN
Golf Courses
6 Daily fee, 108 holes
1 Municipal, 18 holes
1 Private, 18 holes
Good Restaurants
1 Simple ◆
1 Family ◆◆
Movie Theatres
1 Single/Twin; 2 Multiplexes
14 Screens
Water Area
Lakes and rivers: 640 acres
Score: **12.46**   Rank: **310**

La Crosse, WI-MN
Golf Courses
9 Daily fee, 126 holes
2 Municipal, 27 holes
1 Private, 18 holes
Good Restaurants
1 Simple ◆
1 Family ◆◆
2 Adult ◆◆◆
Movie Theatres
4 Singles/Twins; 3 Multiplexes
17 Screens

Professional Sports
Bobcats (CBA Basketball)
Recreation Areas
Federal
Upper Mississippi NWR,
24,215 acres
State
Beaver Creek Valley SP, 1,214 acres
Great River Trail, 270 acres
La Crosse River Trail, 381 acres
Skiing
3 ski areas
Lift capacity/hour: 7,800
Water Area
Lakes and rivers: 23,680 acres
Zoos
Myrick Park Zoo
Score: **44.19**   Rank: **198**

Lafayette, IN
College NCAA I Sports
Purdue Boilermakers
Golf Courses
6 Daily fee, 117 holes
1 Municipal, 18 holes
3 Private, 45 holes
Good Restaurants
1 Family ♦♦
Movie Theatres
1 Single/Twin; 2 Multiplexes
16 Screens
Water Area
Lakes and rivers: 1,920 acres
Zoos
Columbian Park Zoo
Score: **37.11**   Rank: **223**

Lafayette, LA
College NCAA I Sports
U of SW Louisiana Ragin' Cajuns
Gambling
Evangeline Downs (thoroughbred)
Golf Courses
5 Daily fee, 72 holes
2 Municipal, 36 holes
4 Private, 72 holes
Good Restaurants
4 Simple ♦
8 Family ♦♦
2 Adult ♦♦♦
Movie Theatres
1 Single/Twin; 7 Multiplexes
46 Screens
Professional Sports
IceGators (ECHL Hockey)
Recreation Areas
Federal
Atchafalaya NWR, 1,472 acres
State
Atchafalaya Wilderness Centre,
656 acres
Water Area
Lakes and rivers: 56,960 acres
Score: **52.69**   Rank: **168**

Lake Charles, LA
College NCAA I Sports
McNeese State Cowboys
Gambling
5 Casinos
Delta Downs (mixed meetings)
Golf Courses
1 Daily fee, 18 holes
2 Municipal, 36 holes
2 Private, 36 holes
Good Restaurants
2 Simple ♦
1 Family ♦♦
Movie Theatres
1 Single/Twin; 2 Multiplexes
11 Screens
Recreation Areas
State
Sam Houston Jones SP, 1,087 acres
Water Area
Lakes and rivers: 14,720 acres
Score: **16.43**   Rank: **296**

Lakeland-Winter Haven, FL
Amusement & Theme Parks
Florida Cypress Gardens
Gator Family Theme Park
Golf Courses
30 Daily fee, 540 holes
4 Municipal, 81 holes
12 Private, 207 holes
Good Restaurants
2 Simple ♦
1 Family ♦♦
3 Adult ♦♦♦
Movie Theatres
2 Singles/Twins; 6 Multiplexes
51 Screens
Professional Sports
Tigers (Class A Baseball)
Recreation Areas
Federal
Lake Wales Ridge NWR, 154 acres
State
Lake Arbuckle SP, 2,813 acres
Lake Kissimmee SP, 5,030 acres
Water Area
Lakes and rivers: 86,400 acres
Zoos
Cypress Gardens
Score: **87.53**   Rank: **45**

Lancaster, PA
Amusement & Theme Parks
Dutch Wonderland
Golf Courses
13 Daily fee, 216 holes
2 Municipal, 36 holes
4 Private, 81 holes
Good Restaurants
19 Simple ♦
16 Family ♦♦
18 Adult ♦♦♦

Movie Theatres
6 Singles/Twins; 2 Multiplexes
17 Screens
Recreation Areas
State
Susquehannock SP, 224 acres
Skiing
2 ski areas
Lift capacity/hour: 14,600
Water Area
Lakes and rivers: 22,400 acres
Score: **37.39**   Rank: **222**

Lansing-East Lansing, MI
College NCAA I Sports
Michigan State Spartans
Golf Courses
29 Daily fee, 468 holes
4 Municipal, 45 holes
3 Private, 45 holes
Good Restaurants
4 Simple ♦
4 Family ♦♦
Movie Theatres
2 Singles/Twins; 7 Multiplexes
47 Screens
Professional Sports
Lugnuts (Class A Baseball)
Recreation Areas
State
Lakelands Trail SP, 4 acres
Sleepy Hollow SP, 2,678 acres
Skiing
1 ski area
Lift capacity/hour: 17,200
Water Area
Lakes and rivers: 5,120 acres
Zoos
Potter Park Zoo
Score: **65.15**   Rank: **124**

Laredo, TX
Golf Courses
1 Municipal, 18 holes
1 Private, 18 holes
Good Restaurants
2 Family ♦♦
1 Adult ♦♦♦
Movie Theatres
3 Multiplexes
19 Screens
Recreation Areas
State
Lake Casa Blanca SRA, 742 acres
Water Area
Lakes and rivers: 12,160 acres
Score: **0.56**   Rank: **352**

Las Cruces, NM
College NCAA I Sports
New Mexico State Aggies
Gambling
Sunland Park (mixed meetings)

Golf Courses
3 Daily fee, 45 holes
4 Private, 81 holes
Good Restaurants
1 Simple ◆
3 Family ◆◆
2 Adult ◆◆◆
Movie Theatres
1 Single/Twin; 2 Multiplexes
13 Screens
Recreation Areas
Federal
    San Andres NWR, 2 acres
    White Sands NM, 52,778 acres
Skiing
1 ski area
Lift capacity/hour: 1,800
Water Area
Lakes and rivers: 4,480 acres
Score: 23.22   Rank: 272

★ **Las Vegas, NV-AZ**
Auto Racing
Las Vegas Motor Speedway
College NCAA I Sports
U of Nevada Runnin' Rebels
Gambling
187 Casinos
Golf Courses
37 Daily fee, 666 holes
7 Municipal, 144 holes
7 Private, 171 holes
Good Restaurants
2 Simple ◆
10 Family ◆◆
7 Adult ◆◆◆
1 Upscale ◆◆◆◆
Movie Theatres
8 Singles/Twins; 14 Multiplexes
132 Screens
Professional Sports
Stars (Triple A Baseball)
Thunder (IHL Hockey)
Recreation Areas
Federal
    Ashe Meadows NWR, 12,849 acres
    Death Valley NM, 107,616 acres
    Desert NWR, 828,794 acres
    Grand Canyon NP, 517,401 acres
    Havasu NWR, 9,382 acres
    Humboldt NF, 248,321 acres
    Kaibab NF, 5,487 acres
    Lake Mead NRA, 1,385,858 acres
    Moapa Valley NWR, 30 acres
    Pipe Spring NM, 40 acres
    Toiyabe NF, 1,559,868 acres
State
    Cattail Cove SP, 480 acres
    Floyd Lamb SP, 2,041 acres
    Lake Havasu SP, 10,859 acres
    Spring Mountain Ranch SP,
      17,608 acres
    Valley of Fire SP, 34,880 acres

Skiing
17 ski areas
Lift capacity/hour: 165,880
Water Area
Lakes and rivers: 224,000 acres
Zoos
Las Vegas Zoological-Botanical Park
Score: 95.18   Rank: 18

Lawrence, KS
College NCAA I Sports
U of Kansas Jayhawks
Golf Courses
4 Daily fee, 54 holes
2 Private, 36 holes
Good Restaurants
2 Family ◆◆
1 Adult ◆◆◆
Movie Theatres
1 Single/Twin; 2 Multiplexes
11 Screens
Recreation Areas
State
    Clinton SP, 1,425 acres
Water Area
Lakes and rivers: 11,520 acres
Score: 38.24   Rank: 219

Lawrence, MA-NH
Amusement & Theme Parks
Canobie Lake Park
College NCAA I Sports
Merrimack Warriors
Gambling
Rockingham Park (thoroughbred)
Golf Courses
14 Daily fee, 126 holes
6 Private, 81 holes
Good Restaurants
1 Simple ◆
4 Family ◆◆
3 Adult ◆◆◆
Movie Theatres
2 Multiplexes
13 Screens
Recreation Areas
State
    Kingston SP, 44 acres
    Pawtuckaway SP, 5,500 acres
Skiing
31 ski areas
Lift capacity/hour: 119,200
Water Area
Lakes and rivers: 9,886 acres
Atlantic coast: 18,752 acres
Score: 50.99   Rank: 174

Lawton, OK
Amusement & Theme Parks
Eagle Park
Gambling
1 Casino

Golf Courses
1 Municipal, 18 holes
3 Private, 54 holes
Good Restaurants
2 Simple ◆
1 Family ◆◆
1 Adult ◆◆◆
Movie Theatres
3 Multiplexes
19 Screens
Recreation Areas
Federal
    Wichita Mountains NWR,
      59,019 acres
Water Area
Lakes and rivers: 8,960 acres
Score: 4.24   Rank: 339

Lewiston-Auburn, ME
Golf Courses
4 Daily fee, 63 holes
1 Private, 18 holes
Good Restaurants
1 Simple ◆
3 Family ◆◆
Movie Theatres
1 Single/Twin; 1 Multiplex
12 Screens
Recreation Areas
State
    Range Ponds SP, 740 acres
Skiing
7 ski areas
Lift capacity/hour: 68,335
Water Area
Lakes and rivers: 13,241 acres
Score: 20.11   Rank: 283

Lexington, KY
College NCAA I Sports
Eastern Kentucky Colonels
U of Kentucky Wildcats
Gambling
Keeneland (thoroughbred)
The Red Mile (harness)
Golf Courses
16 Daily fee, 261 holes
5 Municipal, 90 holes
12 Private, 198 holes
Good Restaurants
12 Simple ◆
23 Family ◆◆
4 Adult ◆◆◆
2 Upscale ◆◆◆◆
Movie Theatres
5 Singles/Twins; 9 Multiplexes
80 Screens
Professional Sports
Thoroughblades (AHL Hockey)
Water Area
Lakes and rivers: 3,840 acres
Score: 60.05   Rank: 142

Lima, OH

Golf Courses
9 Daily fee, 180 holes
3 Private, 45 holes
Good Restaurants
11 Family ♦♦
Movie Theatres
1 Single/Twin; 4 Multiplexes
19 Screens
Recreation Areas
State
Grand Lake St. Marys SP, 2,802 acres
Lake Loramie SP, 113 acres
Skiing
1 ski area
Lift capacity/hour: 5,400
Water Area
Lakes and rivers: 1,280 acres
Score: **25.21**   Rank: **265**

Lincoln, NE

College NCAA I Sports
U of Nebraska Cornhuskers
Gambling
State Fair Park (thoroughbred)
Golf Courses
5 Daily fee, 81 holes
5 Municipal, 81 holes
4 Private, 72 holes
Good Restaurants
24 Family ♦♦
8 Adult ♦♦♦
2 Upscale ♦♦♦♦
Movie Theatres
3 Singles/Twins; 5 Multiplexes
20 Screens
Recreation Areas
State
Bluestem SRA, 742 acres
Branched Oak SRA, 1,180 acres
Conestoga SRA, 486 acres
Olive Creek SRA, 437 acres
Pawnee SRA, 1,804 acres
Stagecoach SRA, 412 acres
Wagon Train SRA, 747 acres
Water Area
Lakes and rivers: 5,120 acres
Zoos
Folsom Children's Zoo
Pioneer's Prairie Interpretive Museum
Score: **40.79**   Rank: **210**

Little Rock-North Little Rock, AR

College NCAA I Sports
U of Arkansas Trojans
Golf Courses
9 Daily fee, 135 holes
5 Municipal, 108 holes
15 Private, 252 holes
Good Restaurants
8 Simple ♦
12 Family ♦♦
4 Adult ♦♦♦
2 Upscale ♦♦♦♦

Movie Theatres
3 Singles/Twins; 11 Multiplexes
89 Screens
Professional Sports
Arkansas Travelers (Class AA Baseball)
Recreation Areas
Federal
Ouachita NF, 55,297 acres
State
Pinnacle Mountain SP, 1,803 acres
Wooly Hollow SP, 399 acres
Water Area
Lakes and rivers: 62,080 acres
Zoos
Little Rock Zoological Gardens
Score: **68.27**   Rank: **113**

London, ON

College CIAU Sports
U of Western Ontario Mustangs
Gambling
Western Fair Raceway (harness)
Golf Courses
5 Daily fee, 72 holes
6 Municipal, 90 holes
5 Private, 90 holes
Good Restaurants
16 Family ♦♦
29 Adult ♦♦♦
Movie Theatres
8 Singles/Twins; 11 Multiplexes
77 Screens
Skiing
3 ski areas
Lift capacity/hour: 9,000
Water Area
Lakes and rivers: 6,700 acres
Zoos
Storybook Gardens
Score: **29.17**   Rank: **251**

★ Long Island, NY

College NCAA I Sports
Hofstra Flying Dutchmen
SUNY, Stony Brook
Gambling
Belmont (thoroughbred)
Golf Courses
24 Daily fee, 378 holes
31 Municipal, 549 holes
61 Private, 1062 holes
Good Restaurants
12 Simple ♦
12 Family ♦♦
16 Adult ♦♦♦
2 Upscale ♦♦♦♦
Movie Theatres
18 Singles/Twins; 38 Multiplexes
275 Screens
Professional Sports
Islanders (NHL Hockey)

Recreation Areas
Federal
Amagansett NWR, 36 acres
Conscience Point NWR, 60 acres
Elizabeth Morton NWR, 187 acres
Fire Island Seashore, 6,235 acres
Oyster Bay NWR, 3,204 acres
Seatuck NWR, 209 acres
Target Rock NWR, 80 acres
Wertheim NWR, 2,423 acres
State
Belmont Lake SP, 459 acres
Bethpage SP, 2,950 acres
Brookhaven SP, 4,274 acres
Caleb Smith SP, 543 acres
Cannetoquot River SP, 3,473 acres
Captree SP, 298 acres
Caumsett SP, 1,500 acres
Connetquot River SP, 3,473 acres
Heckscher SP, 1,657 acres
Hempstead Lake SP, 727 acres
Hither Hills SP, 1,755 acres
Jones Beach SP, 2,413 acres
Massapequa SP, 596 acres
Montauk Downs SP, 171 acres
Montauk Point SP, 861 acres
Orient Beach SP, 363 acres
Robert Moses SP, 875 acres
Sunken Meadow SP, 1,266 acres
Valley Stream SP, 97 acres
Wildwood SP, 767 acres
Water Area
Lakes and rivers: 185,600 acres
Atlantic coast: 85,632 acres
Score: **99.15**   Rank: **4**

Longview-Marshall, TX

Golf Courses
8 Daily fee, 117 holes
6 Private, 72 holes
Good Restaurants
5 Family ♦♦
Movie Theatres
3 Singles/Twins; 2 Multiplexes
20 Screens
Recreation Areas
State
Caddo Lake SP, 7,090 acres
Water Area
Lakes and rivers: 14,720 acres
Score: **21.52**   Rank: **278**

★ Los Angeles-Long Beach, CA

Amusement & Theme Parks
Raging Waters
Six Flags Magic Mountain
Universal Studios Hollywood
Auto Racing
Grand Prix of Long Beach
College NCAA I Sports
Long Beach State Forty-Niners
Northridge State Matadors
Loyola Marymount Lions
Pepperdine Waves

537

U of California Bruins
U of Southern California Trojans

Gambling
8 Casinos
Hollywood Park Race Track
   (thoroughbred)
Santa Anita Park (thoroughbred)

Golf Courses
24 Daily fee, 360 holes
52 Municipal, 846 holes
35 Private, 621 holes

Good Restaurants
22 Simple ♦
94 Family ♦♦
57 Adult ♦♦♦
11 Upscale ♦♦♦♦
2 Best ♦♦♦♦♦

Movie Theatres
43 Singles/Twins; 105 Multiplexes
833 Screens

Professional Sports
Clippers (NBA Basketball)
Dodgers (NL Baseball)
Galaxy (MLS Soccer)
Ice Dogs (IHL Hockey)
Jethawks (Class A Baseball)
Lakers (NBA Basketball)
Kings (NHL Hockey)
Sparks (WNBA)

Recreation Areas
Federal
   Angeles NF, 643,572 acres
   Los Padres NF, 8,776 acres
   Santa Monica Mountains NRA,
      10,877 acres
State
   Antelope Valley Poppy SR,
      1,745 acres
   Castaic Lake SRA, 2,035 acres
   Dan Blocker Beach
   Dockweiler SB, 91 acres
   Hungry Valley SVRA, 19,000 acres
   Kenneth Hahn SRA, 310 acres
   Las Tunas SB, 3 acres
   Leo Carrillo SB, 2,217 acres
   Malibu Creek SP, 6,600 acres
   Malibu Lagoon SB, 76 acres
   Manhattan SB, 51 acres
   Placerita Canyon SP, 342 acres
   Point Dume SB, 63 acres
   Redondo SB, 26 acres
   Robert H. Meyer Memorial SB,
      18 acres
   Royal Palms SB, 18 acres
   Saddleback Butte SP, 2,955 acres
   Santa Monica SB, 49 acres
   Santa Susana Mountains
   Topanga SB, 31 acres
   Topanga SP, 9,181 acres
   Will Rogers SB, 82 acres

Skiing
9 ski areas
Lift capacity/hour: 85,890

Water Area
Lakes and rivers: 28,160 acres
Pacific coast: 41,472 acres

Zoos
Los Angeles Zoo
Mohave Desert Museum
Parnell Park Zoo
Score: 92.63　　　　Rank: 27

Louisville, KY-IN

Amusement & Theme Parks
River Fair Family Fun Park
Six Flags Kentucky Kingdom

Auto Racing
Louisville Motor Speedway

College NCAA I Sports
U of Louisville Cardinals

Gambling
Churchill Downs (thoroughbred)

Golf Courses
22 Daily fee, 315 holes
11 Municipal, 153 holes
24 Private, 423 holes

Good Restaurants
12 Simple ♦
13 Family ♦♦
14 Adult ♦♦♦
1 Upscale ♦♦♦♦
1 Best ♦♦♦♦♦

Movie Theatres
7 Singles/Twins; 7 Multiplexes
85 Screens

Professional Sports
Riverbats (Triple A Baseball)

Recreation Areas
State
   Charlestown SP, 1,983 acres
   Dream Lake SRA, 1,300 acres
   Sawyer SP, 377 acres
   Wyandotte Woods SRA, 2,000 acres

Water Area
Lakes and rivers: 16,640 acres

Zoos
Louisville Zoological Gardens
Score: 80.45　　　　Rank: 70

Lowell, MA-NH

College NCAA I Sports
U of Lowell Chiefs

Golf Courses
5 Daily fee, 63 holes
2 Municipal, 18 holes
2 Private, 18 holes

Good Restaurants
1 Simple ♦
1 Family ♦♦
1 Upscale ♦♦♦♦

Movie Theatres
5 Multiplexes
26 Screens

Professional Sports
Lock Monsters (AHL Hockey)
Spinners (Class A Baseball)

Skiing
31 ski areas
Lift capacity/hour: 119,200

Water Area
Lakes and rivers: 4,342 acres
Score: 58.35　　　　Rank: 148

Lubbock, TX

Amusement & Theme Parks
Joyland

College NCAA I Sports
Texas Tech Red Raiders

Golf Courses
3 Daily fee, 54 holes
3 Municipal, 54 holes
4 Private, 63 holes

Good Restaurants
2 Family ♦♦

Movie Theatres
3 Singles/Twins; 3 Multiplexes
35 Screens

Water Area
Lakes and rivers: 640 acres
Score: 24.92　　　　Rank: 266

Lynchburg, VA

College NCAA I Sports
Liberty U Flames

Golf Courses
10 Daily fee, 135 holes
4 Private, 63 holes

Good Restaurants
2 Family ♦♦
2 Adult ♦♦♦

Movie Theatres
4 Multiplexes
26 Screens

Professional Sports
Hillcats (Class A Baseball)

Recreation Areas
Federal
   Appalachian NT, 379 acres
   Blue Ridge Parkway, 8,678 acres
   George Washington NF,
      57,805 acres
   Jefferson NF, 18,810 acres
State
   Smith Mountain Lake SP,
      21,506 acres

Skiing
1 ski area
Lift capacity/hour: 8,200

Water Area
Lakes and rivers: 14,080 acres
Score: 48.15　　　　Rank: 184

Macon, GA

College NCAA I Sports
Mercer Bears

Golf Courses
8 Daily fee, 126 holes
3 Municipal, 54 holes
6 Private, 99 holes

Good Restaurants
  8 Simple ♦
  5 Family ♦♦
  2 Adult ♦♦♦
Movie Theatres
  1 Single/Twin; 5 Multiplexes
  49 Screens
Professional Sports
  Braves (Class A Baseball)
Recreation Areas
  Federal
    Bond Swamp NWR, 5,490 acres
    Ocmulgee NM, 702 acres
    Oconee NF, 16,302 acres
    Piedmont NWR, 28,552 acres
Water Area
  Lakes and rivers: 8,320 acres
Score: 53.82   **Rank: 164**

Madison, WI
  College NCAA I Sports
    U of Wisconsin Badgers
  Golf Courses
    11 Daily fee, 198 holes
    5 Municipal, 81 holes
    7 Private, 126 holes
  Good Restaurants
    3 Simple ♦
    6 Family ♦♦
    8 Adult ♦♦♦
  Movie Theatres
    10 Singles/Twins; 8 Multiplexes
    67 Screens
  Professional Sports
    Monsters (CoHL Hockey)
  Recreation Areas
    State
      Blue Mounds SP, 178 acres
      Cross Plains Ice Age SP, 129 acres
      Governor Nelson SP, 433 acres
      Lake Kegonsa SP, 343 acres
  Skiing
    4 ski areas
    Lift capacity/hour: 34,400
  Water Area
    Lakes and rivers: 23,040 acres
  Zoos
    Henry Vilas Park Zoo
  Score: 62.88   **Rank: 132**

Manchester, NH
  Golf Courses
    4 Daily fee, 63 holes
    1 Municipal, 18 holes
    1 Private, 18 holes
  Good Restaurants
    1 Simple ♦
    5 Family ♦♦
    2 Adult ♦♦♦
    1 Upscale ♦♦♦♦

Movie Theatres
  5 Multiplexes
  44 Screens
Recreation Areas
  State
    Bear Brook SP, 9,600 acres
    Clough SP, 2 acres
Skiing
  23 ski areas
  Lift capacity/hour: 119,835
Water Area
  Lakes and rivers: 5,683 acres
Score: 49.85   **Rank: 178**

Mansfield, OH
  Auto Racing
    Mid-Ohio Sports Car Course
  Golf Courses
    13 Daily fee, 207 holes
    3 Private, 54 holes
  Good Restaurants
    1 Simple ♦
    3 Family ♦♦
  Movie Theatres
    1 Single/Twin; 3 Multiplexes
    18 Screens
  Professional Sports
    Hawks (IBA Basketball)
  Recreation Areas
    State
      Fowler Woods SNA, 133 acres
  Skiing
    4 ski areas
    Lift capacity/hour: 28,100
  Water Area
    Lakes and rivers: 2,560 acres
  Score: 15.58   **Rank: 299**

McAllen-Edinburg-Mission, TX
  College NCAA I Sports
    U of Texas Broncs
  Golf Courses
    9 Daily fee, 144 holes
    3 Municipal, 63 holes
    5 Private, 63 holes
  Good Restaurants
    2 Simple ♦
    1 Family ♦♦
  Movie Theatres
    4 Multiplexes
    41 Screens
  Recreation Areas
    Federal
      Lower Rio Grande Valley NWR,
        22,180 acres
      Santa Ana NWR, 2,087 acres
    State
      Bentsen-Rio Grande Valley SP,
        588 acres
  Water Area
    Lakes and rivers: 8,960 acres
  Score: 22.94   **Rank: 273**

Medford-Ashland, OR
  Golf Courses
    7 Daily fee, 90 holes
    1 Municipal, 9 holes
    2 Private, 36 holes
  Good Restaurants
    1 Family ♦♦
    5 Adult ♦♦♦
  Movie Theatres
    6 Multiplexes
    39 Screens
  Professional Sports
    Timberjacks (Class A Baseball)
  Recreation Areas
    Federal
      Crater Lake NP, 944 acres
      Klamath NF, 26,334 acres
      Rogue River NF, 414,306 acres
      Umpqua NF, 10,628 acres
    State
      Ben Hur Lampman Wayside,
        24 acres
      Casey SP, 80 acres
      Joseph Stewart SP, 911 acres
      Prospect Wayside, 11 acres
      Tou Velle SP, 58 acres
      Tubb Springs Wayside, 39 acres
      Valley of the Rogue SP, 278 acres
  Skiing
    3 ski areas
    Lift capacity/hour: 17,700
  Water Area
    Lakes and rivers: 10,880 acres
  Score: 13.03   **Rank: 308**

★ **Melbourne-Titusville-Palm Bay, FL**
  Gambling
    Melbourne Greyhound Park
  Golf Courses
    11 Daily fee, 180 holes
    6 Municipal, 117 holes
    6 Private, 126 holes
  Good Restaurants
    3 Simple ♦
    13 Family ♦♦
    6 Adult ♦♦♦
  Movie Theatres
    2 Singles/Twins; 6 Multiplexes
    56 Screens
  Professional Sports
    Manatees (Class A Baseball)
  Recreation Areas
    Federal
      Archie Carr NWR, 25 acres
      Canaveral Seashore, 29,479 acres
      St. Johns NWR, 6,255 acres
    State
      Sebastian Inlet SRA, 168 acres
  Water Area
    Lakes and rivers: 176,640 acres
    Atlantic coast: 16,832 acres
  Zoos
    Brevard Zoo
  Score: 91.50   **Rank: 31**

Memphis, TN-AR-MS

Amusement & Theme Parks
Libertyland
Auto Racing
Memphis Motorsports Park
College NCAA I Sports
Memphis State Tigers
U of Memphis Tigers
Gambling
Southland Park (greyhound)
Golf Courses
13 Daily fee, 225 holes
9 Municipal, 144 holes
13 Private, 270 holes
Good Restaurants
5 Simple ◆
8 Family ◆◆
6 Adult ◆◆◆
1 Upscale ◆◆◆◆
Movie Theatres
3 Singles/Twins; 18 Multiplexes
175 Screens
Recreation Areas
Federal
Lower Hatchie NWR, 3,040 acres
Wapanocca NWR, 5,484 acres
State
Fuller SP, 384 acres
Meeman-Shelby Forest SP,
13,467 acres
Water Area
Lakes and rivers: 58,240 acres
Zoos
Memphis Zoo
Score: **75.92**   Rank: **86**

Merced, CA

Golf Courses
4 Daily fee, 54 holes
1 Municipal, 18 holes
1 Private, 18 holes
Good Restaurants
2 Family ◆◆
1 Adult ◆◆◆
Movie Theatres
1 Single/Twin; 2 Multiplexes
13 Screens
Recreation Areas
Federal
Grasslands WMA, 2,603 acres
Kesterson NWR, 10,621 acres
Merced NWR, 4,571 acres
San Luis NWR, 25,943 acres
State
George Hatfield SRA, 47 acres
Great Valley Grasslands, 2,826 acres
McConnell SRA, 74 acres
San Luis Reservoir SRA, 26,026 acres
Skiing
2 ski areas
Lift capacity/hour: 25,600

Water Area
Lakes and rivers: 27,520 acres
Zoos
Applegate Park Zoo
Score: **9.06**   Rank: **322**

Miami, FL

Amusement & Theme Parks
Let's Party
Miami Seaquarium
Parrot Jungle & Gardens
Aquariums
Miami Seaquarium
Auto Racing
Homestead-Miami Speedway
College NCAA I Sports
FIU Golden Panthers
U of Miami Hurricanes
Gambling
Calder Race Course (thoroughbred)
Flagler Track (greyhound)
Hialeah Park (thoroughbred)
Miami Jai-Alai
Golf Courses
11 Daily fee, 324 holes
13 Municipal, 207 holes
8 Private, 153 holes
Good Restaurants
8 Simple ◆
32 Family ◆◆
18 Adult ◆◆◆
5 Upscale ◆◆◆◆
Movie Theatres
4 Singles/Twins; 23 Multiplexes
215 Screens
Professional Sports
Dolphins (NFL Football)
Fusion (MLS Soccer)
Heat (NBA Basketball)
Florida Marlins (NL Baseball)
Recreation Areas
Federal
Big Cypress Preserve, 13,042 acres
Biscayne NP, 170,821 acres
Everglades NP, 475,032 acres
State
Cape Florida SRA, 406 acres
Oleta River SRA, 853 acres
Water Area
Lakes and rivers: 49,280 acres
Atlantic coast: 28,000 acres
Zoos
Metrozoo-Crandon Park
Score: **89.80**   Rank: **37**

Middlesex-Somerset-Hunterdon, NJ

Auto Racing
Flemington Speedway
College NCAA I Sports
Rutgers Scarlet Knights
Golf Courses
10 Daily fee, 189 holes
5 Municipal, 108 holes
19 Private, 369 holes

Good Restaurants
13 Simple ◆
7 Family ◆◆
11 Adult ◆◆◆
3 Upscale ◆◆◆◆
Movie Theatres
4 Singles/Twins; 13 Multiplexes
110 Screens
Recreation Areas
State
Cheesequake SP, 1,284 acres
Cook SNA, 52 acres
Hacklebarney SP, 19 acres
Pigeon Swamp SP, 1,078 acres
Round Valley SRA, 3,639 acres
Spruce Run SRA, 1,910 acres
Voorhees SP, 626 acres
Washington Rock SP, 51 acres
Skiing
2 ski areas
Lift capacity/hour: 3,000
Water Area
Lakes and rivers: 10,240 acres
Atlantic coast: 2,560 acres
Score: **53.25**   Rank: **166**

★Milwaukee-Waukesha, WI

Auto Racing
The Milwaukee Mile
College NCAA I Sports
Marquette Warriors
U of Wisconsin Panthers
Gambling
1 Casino
Golf Courses
35 Daily fee, 612 holes
23 Municipal, 351 holes
15 Private, 288 holes
Good Restaurants
15 Simple ◆
40 Family ◆◆
35 Adult ◆◆◆
3 Upscale ◆◆◆◆
Movie Theatres
25 Singles/Twins; 27 Multiplexes
244 Screens
Professional Sports
Admirals (IHL Hockey)
Brewers (AL Baseball)
Bucks (NBA Basketball)
Packers (NFL Football)
Recreation Areas
State
Glacial Drumlin Trail, 375 acres
Harrington Beach SP, 636 acres
Pike Lake SP, 678 acres
Skiing
24 ski areas
Lift capacity/hour: 55,885
Water Area
Lakes and rivers: 21,120 acres
Lake Michigan: 117,056 acres
Zoos
Milwaukee County Zoological Gardens
Score: **98.86**   Rank: **5**

★Minneapolis-St. Paul, MN-WI

Amusement & Theme Parks
Cedar Lake Farm
Gasoline Alley
Knott's Camp Snoopy
Valleyfair
Auto Racing
Grand Prix of Minnesota
College NCAA I Sports
U of Minnesota Gophers
Gambling
2 Casinos
Canterbury Downs (thoroughbred)
St. Croix Meadows (greyhound)
Golf Courses
98 Daily fee, 1602 holes
44 Municipal, 747 holes
32 Private, 567 holes
Good Restaurants
6 Simple ♦
26 Family ♦♦
37 Adult ♦♦♦
3 Upscale ♦♦♦♦
Movie Theatres
18 Singles/Twins; 62 Multiplexes
403 Screens
Professional Sports
Twins (AL Baseball)
Timberwolves (NBA Basketball)
Vikings (NFL Football)
Wild (NHL Hockey)
Recreation Areas
Federal
Lower Saint Croix NS River,
5,625 acres
Minnesota Valley NWR, 6,591 acres
Mississippi NS River, 62 acres
Saint Croix NS River, 1,961 acres
Sherburne NWR, 29,606 acres
State
Afton SP, 1,702 acres
Fort Snelling SP, 3,300 acres
InterState SP, 293 acres
Kinnickinnic SP, 1,242 acres
Lake Maria SP, 1,590 acres
Wild River SP, 6,803 acres
William O'Brien SP, 1,403 acres
Willow River SP, 2,950 acres
Skiing
34 ski areas
Lift capacity/hour: 326,000
Water Area
Lakes and rivers: 192,000 acres
Zoos
Minnesota Zoo
St. Paul's Como Zoo
Score: **96.03**   Rank: **15**

Missoula, MT

College NCAA I Sports
U of Montana Grizzlies
Gambling
1 Casino

Golf Courses
4 Daily fee, 36 holes
2 Municipal, 27 holes
1 Private, 18 holes
Good Restaurants
4 Simple ♦
6 Family ♦♦
Movie Theatres
2 Singles/Twins; 1 Multiplex
5 Screens
Recreation Areas
Federal
Bitterroot NF, 7,840 acres
Flathead NF, 170,285 acres
Lolo NF, 515,328 acres
State
Beavertail Hill SP, 65 acres
Frenchtown Pond SP, 41 acres
Placid Lake SP, 32 acres
Salmon Lake SP, 42 acres
Skiing
4 ski areas
Lift capacity/hour: 19,900
Water Area
Lakes and rivers: 12,800 acres
Score: **32.57**   Rank: **239**

★Mobile, AL

College NCAA I Sports
U of South Alabama Jaguars
Gambling
Mobile Park (greyhound)
Golf Courses
16 Daily fee, 369 holes
5 Municipal, 90 holes
5 Private, 99 holes
Good Restaurants
1 Simple ♦
3 Family ♦♦
2 Adult ♦♦♦
1 Upscale ♦♦♦♦
Movie Theatres
5 Singles/Twins; 5 Multiplexes
55 Screens
Professional Sports
BayBears (Class AA Baseball)
Mysticks (ECHL Hockey)
Recreation Areas
Federal
Bon Secour NWR, 5,893 acres
Grand Bay NWR, 840 acres
State
Gulf SP, 6,150 acres
Water Area
Lakes and rivers: 87,040 acres
Gulf coast: 45,120 acres
Zoos
Zooland Animal Park
Score: **92.06**   Rank: **29**

Modesto, CA

Gambling
4 Casinos
Golf Courses
4 Daily fee, 72 holes
3 Municipal, 45 holes
3 Private, 63 holes
Movie Theatres
1 Single/Twin; 2 Multiplexes
12 Screens
Professional Sports
A's (Class A Baseball)
Recreation Areas
Federal
San Joaquin River NWR, 1,638 acres
State
Henry W. Coe SP, 27,169 acres
Turlock Lake SRA, 409 acres
Skiing
2 ski areas
Lift capacity/hour: 25,600
Water Area
Lakes and rivers: 12,800 acres
Score: **8.78**   Rank: **323**

Monmouth-Ocean, NJ

Amusement & Theme Parks
Casino Pier & Waterworks
Fantasy Island Park
Six Flags Great Adventure
College NCAA I Sports
Monmouth College Hawks
Gambling
Freehold Raceway (harness)
Monmouth Park (thoroughbred)
Golf Courses
11 Daily fee, 180 holes
10 Municipal, 189 holes
22 Private, 360 holes
Good Restaurants
8 Simple ♦
11 Family ♦♦
5 Adult ♦♦♦
1 Upscale ♦♦♦♦
Movie Theatres
7 Singles/Twins; 16 Multiplexes
121 Screens
Professional Sports
Shorecats (USBL Basketball)
Recreation Areas
Federal
Edwin Forsythe NWR, 17,452 acres
Gateway NRA, 1,731 acres
State
Allaire SP, 3,062 acres
Barnegat Lighthouse SP, 32 acres
Double Trouble SP, 5,118 acres
Island Beach SP, 3,002 acres
Manasquan Canal SRA, 5 acres
Swan Point SNA, 147 acres
Swimming River SNA, 109 acres

Water Area
Lakes and rivers: 87,040 acres
Atlantic coast: 33,280 acres
Zoos
Popcorn Park Zoo
Score: **84.70**   Rank: **55**

Monroe, LA
College NCAA I Sports
Northeast Louisiana Indians
Golf Courses
2 Daily fee, 27 holes
3 Municipal, 36 holes
2 Private, 36 holes
Good Restaurants
3 Simple ♦
1 Family ♦♦
Movie Theatres
1 Multiplex
10 Screens
Recreation Areas
Federal
D'Arbonne NWR, 7,859 acres
Water Area
Lakes and rivers: 14,080 acres
Zoos
Louisiana Purchase Zoo
Score: **17.84**   Rank: **291**

Montgomery, AL
College NCAA I Sports
Alabama State Hornets
Golf Courses
7 Daily fee, 126 holes
1 Municipal, 18 holes
7 Private, 135 holes
Good Restaurants
3 Family ♦♦
Movie Theatres
1 Single/Twin; 4 Multiplexes
32 Screens
Water Area
Lakes and rivers: 34,560 acres
Zoos
Montgomery Zoo
Score: **33.42**   Rank: **236**

Montreal, PQ
Amusement & Theme Parks
La Ronde Park
Aqua Parc Saint-Felicien
Aquariums
Aquarium de Montreal
College CIAU Sports
Concordia Stingers
McGill Redmen
Gambling
1 Casino
Hippodrome de Montreal (harness)
Golf Courses
20 Daily fee, 306 holes
22 Municipal, 342 holes
25 Private, 414 holes

Good Restaurants
4 Simple ♦
23 Family ♦♦
32 Adult ♦♦♦
12 Upscale ♦♦♦♦
Movie Theatres
14 Singles/Twins; 35 Multiplexes
249 Screens
Professional Sports
Alouettes (CFL Football)
Canadiens (NHL Hockey)
Expos (NL Baseball)
Recreation Areas
Federal
Ile aux Herons MBS, 1,483 acres
Iles de Contrecoeur NWA, 561 acres
Iles de la Paix MBS, 2,718 acres
Iles de la Paix NWA, 299 acres
Ils St-Ours MBS, 741 acres
Mount St. Hilaire MBS, 2,347 acres
Senneville MBS, 741 acres
Provincial
Iles De Boucherville PP, 2,011 acres
Mount Saint Bruno PP, 1,458 acres
Oka PP, 5,856 acres
Skiing
18 ski areas
Lift capacity/hour: 42,500
Water Area
Lakes and rivers: 8,600 acres
Zoos
Biodome de Montreal
Insectarium de Montreal
Jardin Zoologique de Montreal
Score: **73.93**   Rank: **93**

Muncie, IN
College NCAA I Sports
Ball State Cardinals
Golf Courses
6 Daily fee, 108 holes
2 Private, 36 holes
Good Restaurants
1 Adult ♦♦♦
Movie Theatres
3 Multiplexes
18 Screens
Water Area
Lakes and rivers: 1,920 acres
Score: **26.91**   Rank: **259**

Myrtle Beach, SC
Amusement & Theme Parks
Fun Spot Park
Myrtle Beach Pavilion
Auto Racing
Myrtle Beach Speedway
College NCAA I Sports
Coastal Carolina Chanticleers
Golf Courses
47 Daily fee, 1,116 holes
1 Municipal, 18 holes
1 Private, 18 holes

Good Restaurants
14 Simple ♦
50 Family ♦♦
9 Adult ♦♦♦
Movie Theatres
7 Multiplexes
52 Screens
Professional Sports
Pelicans (Class A Baseball)
Recreation Areas
State
Myrtle Beach SP, 312 acres
Water Area
Lakes and rivers: 7,680 acres
Atlantic coast: 6,976 acres
Score: **83.85**   Rank: **58**

Naples, FL
Amusement & Theme Parks
Caribbean Gardens
Golf Courses
15 Daily fee, 279 holes
38 Private, 801 holes
Good Restaurants
6 Simple ♦
16 Family ♦♦
8 Adult ♦♦♦
4 Upscale ♦♦♦♦
Movie Theatres
3 Multiplexes
36 Screens
Recreation Areas
Federal
Big Cypress Addition, 102,543 acres
Big Cypress N Preserve,
396,637 acres
Everglades NP, 39,262 acres
Florida Panther NWR, 22,782 acres
State
Collier-Seminole SP, 6,423 acres
Delnor-Wiggins Pass SRA, 155 acres
Fakahatchee Strand SNA,
66,367 acres
Water Area
Lakes and rivers: 58,240 acres
Gulf coast: 12,096 acres
Score: **52.40**   Rank: **169**

Nashua, NH
Golf Courses
8 Daily fee, 135 holes
2 Private, 36 holes
Good Restaurants
2 Simple ♦
3 Family ♦♦
2 Adult ♦♦♦
Movie Theatres
2 Singles/Twins; 1 Multiplex
7 Screens
Recreation Areas
State
Bradford Pines SNA, 5 acres
Silver Lake SP, 15 acres

Skiing
23 ski areas
Lift capacity/hour: 119,835
Water Area
Lakes and rivers: 3,174 acres
Score: 32.86   Rank: 238

Nashville, TN
Auto Racing
Nashville Speedway USA
College NCAA I Sports
Belmont U Bruins
Middle Tennessee Blue Raiders
Tennessee State Tigers
Vanderbilt Commodores
Golf Courses
15 Daily fee, 261 holes
15 Municipal, 243 holes
18 Private, 288 holes
Good Restaurants
7 Simple ♦
37 Family ♦♦
9 Adult ♦♦♦
3 Upscale ♦♦♦♦
1 Best ♦♦♦♦♦
Movie Theatres
6 Singles/Twins; 24 Multiplexes
202 Screens
Professional Sports
Predators (NHL Hockey)
Sounds (Triple A Baseball)
Titans (NFL Football)
Recreation Areas
Federal
Natchez Trace Parkway, 2,687 acres
State
Bledsoe Creek SP, 164 acres
Cedars of Lebanon SP, 832 acres
Long Hunter SP, 2,315 acres
Montgomery Bell SP, 3,782 acres
Radnor Lake SNA, 1,000 acres
Water Area
Lakes and rivers: 39,680 acres
Zoos
Nashville Zoo
Score: 81.58   Rank: 66

New Bedford, MA
Golf Courses
4 Daily fee, 54 holes
1 Municipal, 18 holes
4 Private, 63 holes
Good Restaurants
2 Simple ♦
2 Family ♦♦
1 Adult ♦♦♦
Movie Theatres
1 Single/Twin; 2 Multiplexes
15 Screens
Recreation Areas
State
Demarest Lloyd SP, 222 acres
Fort Phoenix SNA, 23 acres

Skiing
6 ski areas
Lift capacity/hour: 17,800
Water Area
Lakes and rivers: 20,187 acres
Atlantic coast: 6,208 acres
Zoos
The Zoo at Buttonwood
Score: 47.59   Rank: 186

New Haven-Meriden, CT
College NCAA I Sports
Quinnipiac College Braves
Yale Elis
Golf Courses
6 Daily fee, 63 holes
6 Municipal, 99 holes
10 Private, 189 holes
Good Restaurants
4 Simple ♦
13 Family ♦♦
Movie Theatres
2 Singles/Twins; 5 Multiplexes
37 Screens
Professional Sports
Beast of New Haven (AHL Hockey)
Ravens (Class AA Baseball)
Recreation Areas
State
Chatfield Hollow SP, 356 acres
Foster Pond SP, 194 acres
Hammonasset Beach SRA, 919 acres
Qunnipiac SP, 342 acres
Sleeping Giant SP, 1,439 acres
West Peak SP, 177 acres
West Rock Ridge SP, 1,533 acres
Wharton Brook SP, 96 acres
Water Area
Lakes and rivers: 13,129 acres
Atlantic coast: 15,104 acres
Zoos
West Rock Nature Center
Score: 60.62   Rank: 140

New London-Norwich, CT-RI
Gambling
1 Casino
Plainfield Park (greyhound)
Golf Courses
11 Daily fee, 153 holes
5 Municipal, 81 holes
5 Private, 99 holes
Good Restaurants
2 Simple ♦
10 Family ♦♦
10 Adult ♦♦♦
Movie Theatres
2 Singles/Twins; 4 Multiplexes
27 Screens
Professional Sports
Navigators (Class AA Baseball)

Recreation Areas
State
Bluff Point Coastal Reserve SP,
806 acres
Haley Farm SP, 198 acres
Hopemead SP, 60 acres
Hopeville Pond SP, 554 acres
Minnie Island SP, 1 acre
Misquamicut SB, 51 acres
Stoddard Hill SP, 55 acres
Water Area
Lakes and rivers: 67,908 acres
Atlantic coast: 4,480 acres
Zoos
Mohegan Park Zoo
Score: 55.24   Rank: 159

★New Orleans, LA
College NCAA I Sports
Tulane Green Wave
U of New Orleans Privateers
Gambling
4 Casinos
Fair Grounds (mixed meetings)
Jefferson Downs (thoroughbred)
Golf Courses
15 Daily fee, 261 holes
5 Municipal, 81 holes
12 Private, 243 holes
Good Restaurants
19 Simple ♦
52 Family ♦♦
40 Adult ♦♦♦
4 Upscale ♦♦♦♦
1 Best ♦♦♦♦♦
Movie Theatres
2 Singles/Twins; 14 Multiplexes
102 Screens
Professional Sports
Brass (ECHL Hockey)
Saints (NFL Football)
Zephyrs (Triple A Baseball)
Recreation Areas
Federal
Bayou Sauvage NWR, 18,000 acres
Big Branch Marsh NWR, 9,007 acres
Bogue Chitto NWR, 27,839 acres
Breton NWR, 9,047 acres
Delta NWR, 45,907 acres
State
Bayou Segnette SP, 580 acres
Fairview-Riverside SP, 99 acres
Fontainebleau SP, 2,809 acres
Grand Isle East SP, 120 acres
Grand Isle West SP, 40 acres
Slidell SP, 71 acres
St. Bernard SP, 358 acres
Water Area
Lakes and rivers: 1,173,760 acres
Gulf coast: 135,232 acres
Zoos
Audubon Zoo
Score: 100.00   Rank: 1

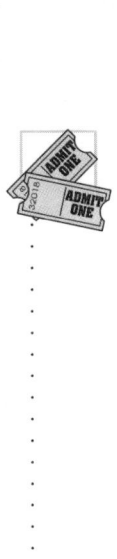

★New York, NY

Amusement & Theme Parks
Playland Park

Aquariums
Aquarium for Wildlife Conservation
New York Aquarium

College NCAA I Sports
Columbia Lions
Fordham Rams
Iona College Gaels
Long Island U Blackbirds
Manhattan College Jaspers
Manhattanville Valients
St. Francis College Terriers
St. John's Red Storm
Wagner College Seahawks

Gambling
Aqueduct (thoroughbred)
Yonkers Raceway (harness)

Golf Courses
10 Daily fee, 126 holes
23 Municipal, 441 holes
50 Private, 927 holes

Good Restaurants
53 Simple ◆
250 Family ◆◆
374 Adult ◆◆◆
138 Upscale ◆◆◆◆
30 Best ◆◆◆◆◆

Movie Theatres
60 Singles/Twins; 70 Multiplexes
525 Screens

Professional Sports
Brooklyn Kings (USBL Basketball)
Knicks (NBA Basketball)
Liberty (WNBA)
Mets (NL Baseball)
Rangers (NHL Hockey)
Yankees (AL Baseball)

Recreation Areas
Federal
Appalachian NT, 956 acres
Gateway NRA, 18,702 acres
State
Appalachian Trail SP, 544 acres
Bayswater Point SP, 12 acres
Bear Mountain/Iona SP, 2,533 acres
Blauvelt SP, 590 acres
Clarence Fahnestock SP, 6,799 acres
Clay Pit Pond SP, 258 acres
Harriman SP, 23,307 acres
Haverstraw Beach SP, 73 acres
High Tor SP, 565 acres
Hook Mountain SP, 676 acres
Hudson Highlands SP, 4,000 acres
Nyack Beach SP, 61 acres
Old Croton Trailway SP, 216 acres
Palisades Parkway SP, 1,839 acres
Riverbank SP, 28 acres
Roberto Clemente SP, 22 acres
Rockefeller Preserve SP, 743 acres
Rockland Lake SP, 1,080 acres
Rockwood Hall SP, 151 acres

Roosevelt SP, 761 acres
Tallman Mountain SP, 687 acres

Skiing
20 ski areas
Lift capacity/hour: 92,000

Water Area
Lakes and rivers: 97,920 acres
Atlantic coast: 6,976 acres

Zoos
Central Park Wildlife Center
New York Zoological Park
Staten Island Zoo
Score: **92.35**   Rank: **28**

Newark, NJ

Amusement & Theme Parks
Land of Make Believe

College NCAA I Sports
Seton Hall Pirates

Golf Courses
21 Daily fee, 306 holes
15 Municipal, 261 holes
37 Private, 666 holes

Good Restaurants
14 Simple ◆
16 Family ◆◆
18 Adult ◆◆◆
18 Upscale ◆◆◆◆
1 Best ◆◆◆◆◆

Movie Theatres
11 Singles/Twins; 24 Multiplexes
162 Screens

Professional Sports
Cardinals (Class A Baseball)

Recreation Areas
Federal
Appalachian NT, 3,948 acres
Delaware Water Gap NRA,
30,706 acres
Great Swamp NWR, 4,890 acres
Wallkill River NWR, 2,761 acres
State
Allmuchy SP, 6,966 acres
Bursch Sugar Maple SNA, 25 acres
Cranberry Lake SP, 199 acres
Farney SP, 803 acres
Finesville SP, 3 acres
Great Piece Meadow SP, 794 acres
Hacklebarney SP, 873 acres
High Point SP, 14,193 acres
Hopatcong SP, 112 acres
Johnsonburg SNA, 11 acres
Kittatinny Valley, 1,354 acres
Musconetong SP, 328 acres
Osmun Forest SNA, 10 acres
Swartswood SP, 1,356 acres
Troy Meadows SNA, 334 acres
Wawayanda SP, 8,968 acres

Skiing
20 ski areas
Lift capacity/hour: 138,200

Water Area
Lakes and rivers: 23,680 acres

Zoos
Space Farms Zoo
Turtle Back Zoo
Score: **76.48**   Rank: **84**

Newburgh, NY-PA

College NCAA I Sports
U.S.M.A. Black Knights

Golf Courses
12 Daily fee, 171 holes
3 Municipal, 54 holes
9 Private, 144 holes

Good Restaurants
2 Simple ◆
4 Family ◆◆
4 Adult ◆◆◆

Movie Theatres
5 Singles/Twins; 4 Multiplexes
33 Screens

Recreation Areas
Federal
Appalachian NT, 2,678 acres
Delaware Water Gap NRA,
17,589 acres
Upper Delaware NSRiver, 2 acres
Wallkill River NWR, 147 acres
State
Bear Mountain/Iona SP, 2,533 acres
Goose Pond Mountain SP,
1,543 acres
Harriman SP, 23,306 acres
Highland Lakes SP, 3,086 acres
Promised Land SP, 5,700 acres
Storm King SP, 1,874 acres

Skiing
24 ski areas
Lift capacity/hour: 167,510

Water Area
Lakes and rivers: 26,880 acres
Score: **50.42**   Rank: **176**

★Norfolk-Virginia Beach-Newport News, VA-NC

Amusement & Theme Parks
Busch Gardens Williamsburg

College NCAA I Sports
Hampton Pirates
Norfolk State Spartans
Old Dominion Monarchs
William & Mary Indian Tribe

Golf Courses
22 Daily fee, 486 holes
10 Municipal, 198 holes
17 Private, 306 holes

Good Restaurants
7 Simple ◆
54 Family ◆◆
40 Adult ◆◆◆
2 Upscale ◆◆◆◆
1 Best ◆◆◆◆◆

Movie Theatres
4 Singles/Twins; 25 Multiplexes
168 Screens

Professional Sports
  Admirals (ECHL Hockey)
  Tides (Triple A Baseball)
Recreation Areas
  Federal
      Back Bay NWR, 8,246 acres
      Currituck NWR, 1,820 acres
      Great Dismal Swamp NWR,
        82,197 acres
      Mackay Island NWR, 7,150 acres
      Nansemond NWR, 208 acres
      Plum Tree Island NWR, 3,291 acres
  State
      False Cape SP, 4,321 acres
      Seashore SP, 2,770 acres
      York River SP, 2,505 acres
Water Area
  Lakes and rivers: 264,320 acres
  Atlantic coast: 51,712 acres
Zoos
  Bluebird Gap Farm
  Lafayette Zoo
  Newport News Zoo
  Virginia Zoological Park
Score: 98.58   Rank: 6

Oakland, CA
College NCAA I Sports
  U of California Golden Bears
Gambling
  12 Casinos
  Golden Gate Fields (thoroughbred)
Golf Courses
  14 Daily fee, 261 holes
  12 Municipal, 243 holes
  15 Private, 315 holes
Good Restaurants
  4 Simple ♦
  4 Family ♦♦
  14 Adult ♦♦♦
  1 Upscale ♦♦♦♦
Movie Theatres
  11 Singles/Twins; 26 Multiplexes
  187 Screens
Professional Sports
  Athletics (AL Baseball)
  Golden State Warriors (NBA Basketball)
  Raiders (NFL Football)
Recreation Areas
  Federal
      Antoich Dunes NWR, 55 acres
      San Francisco Bay NWR,
        12,784 acres
  State
      Bethany Reservoir SRA, 608 acres
      Franks Tract SRA, 3,515 acres
      Lake Del Valle SRA, 3,732 acres
      Mount Diablo SP, 20,090 acres
      Robert Crown Memorial SB,
        132 acres
Water Area
  Lakes and rivers: 106,240 acres

Zoos
  Knowland Park-Oakland Zoo
  Walnut Creek Zoo
Score: 83.56   Rank: 59

Ocala, FL
Amusement & Theme Parks
  Florida's Silver Springs
Gambling
  Ocala Jai-Alai
Golf Courses
  9 Daily fee, 153 holes
  2 Municipal, 45 holes
  3 Private, 63 holes
Good Restaurants
  1 Simple ♦
  3 Family ♦♦
  2 Adult ♦♦♦
Movie Theatres
  1 Single/Twin; 4 Multiplexes
  31 Screens
Recreation Areas
  Federal
      Ocala NF, 275,503 acres
  State
      Lake Rousseau SRA, 696 acres
      Silver River SP, 5,138 acres
Water Area
  Lakes and rivers: 53,760 acres
Score: 20.67   Rank: 281

Odessa-Midland, TX
Golf Courses
  2 Daily fee, 45 holes
  1 Municipal, 27 holes
  5 Private, 99 holes
Good Restaurants
  6 Family ♦♦
Movie Theatres
  1 Single/Twin; 8 Multiplexes
  38 Screens
Professional Sports
  Rock Hounds (Class AA Baseball)
Water Area
  Lakes and rivers: 1,920 acres
Score: 12.18   Rank: 311

Oklahoma City, OK
Amusement & Theme Parks
  Frontier City
  White Water Bay
Aquariums
  Aquaticus Aquarium
College NCAA I Sports
  U of Oklahoma Sooners
Gambling
  1 Casino
  Remington Park (mixed meetings)
Golf Courses
  14 Daily fee, 261 holes
  10 Municipal, 225 holes
  12 Private, 216 holes

Good Restaurants
  16 Simple ♦
  73 Family ♦♦
  19 Adult ♦♦♦
Movie Theatres
  2 Singles/Twins; 19 Multiplexes
  138 Screens
Professional Sports
  Redhawks (Triple A Baseball)
Recreation Areas
  State
      John Miskelley SP, 160 acres
      Little River SP, 1,834 acres
      State Capitol Park SP, 58 acres
Water Area
  Lakes and rivers: 35,840 acres
Zoos
  Oklahoma City Zoo
Score: 77.90   Rank: 79

Olympia, WA
Gambling
  1 Casino
Golf Courses
  6 Daily fee, 81 holes
  1 Municipal, 18 holes
  2 Private, 36 holes
Good Restaurants
  2 Simple ♦
  8 Family ♦♦
  3 Adult ♦♦♦
Movie Theatres
  3 Multiplexes
  16 Screens
Recreation Areas
  Federal
      Nisqually NWR, 1,983 acres
      Olympic NF, 10 acres
      Snoqualmie NF, 612 acres
  State
      Elbow Lake SP, 320 acres
      Millersylvania Memorial SP,
        843 acres
      Nisqually, 140 acres
      Tolmie SP, 106 acres
Skiing
  2 ski areas
  Lift capacity/hour: 19,550
Water Area
  Lakes and rivers: 30,080 acres
  Puget Sound: 2,180 acres
Score: 25.77   Rank: 263

Omaha, NE-IA
Aquariums
  Ak-Sar-Ben Aquarium
College NCAA I Sports
  Creighton Bluejays
Gambling
  3 Casinos
  Ak-Sar-Ben (thoroughbred)
  Bluffs Run (greyhound)

Golf Courses
22 Daily fee, 342 holes
14 Municipal, 171 holes
13 Private, 225 holes

Good Restaurants
7 Simple ♦
17 Family ♦♦
15 Adult ♦♦♦
4 Upscale ♦♦♦♦

Movie Theatres
5 Singles/Twins; 13 Multiplexes
103 Screens

Professional Sports
Golden Spikes (Triple A Baseball)

Recreation Areas
Federal
    De Soto NWR, 595 acres
    DeSoto NWR, 4,324 acres
State
    Lake Manawa SP, 1,529 acres
    Louisville SRA, 142 acres
    Mahoney SP, 479 acres
    Platte River SP, 413 acres
    Schramm Park SRA, 326 acres
    Two Rivers SRA, 302 acres
    Wilson Island SRA, 577 acres

Skiing
8 ski areas
Lift capacity/hour: 26,800

Water Area
Lakes and rivers: 20,480 acres

Zoos
Henry Doorly Zoo
Score: 79.88   Rank: 72

Orange County, CA
Amusement & Theme Parks
Adventure City Theme Park
American Sports World
Disneyland
Knott's Berry Farm

College NCAA I Sports
Fullerton State Titans
U of California Anteaters

Gambling
Los Alamitos (mixed meetings)

Golf Courses
23 Daily fee, 369 holes
9 Municipal, 180 holes
20 Private, 414 holes

Good Restaurants
6 Simple ♦
39 Family ♦♦
29 Adult ♦♦♦
8 Upscale ♦♦♦♦

Movie Theatres
12 Singles/Twins; 51 Multiplexes
381 Screens

Professional Sports
Anaheim Angels (AL Baseball)
Anaheim Mighty Ducks (NHL Hockey)

Recreation Areas
Federal
    Cleveland NF, 54,343 acres
State
    Bolsa Chica SB, 78 acres
    Chino Hills SP, 3,115 acres
    Corona Del Mar SB, 30 acres
    Crystal Cove SP, 2,300 acres
    Doheny SB, 62 acres
    Huntington SB, 164 acres
    San Clemente SB, 110 acres

Skiing
9 ski areas
Lift capacity/hour: 85,890

Water Area
Lakes and rivers: 6,400 acres
Pacific coast: 9,472 acres

Zoos
Orange County Zoo
Santa Ana Zoo
Score: 81.01   Rank: 68

★Orlando, FL
Amusement & Theme Parks
Disney World
Universal Studios Florida

Aquariums
Sea World

College NCAA I Sports
Central Florida Knights

Gambling
Orlando Jai-Alai
Sanford-Orlando Kennel Club
    (greyhound)
Seminole Greyhound Park

Golf Courses
60 Daily fee, 1161 holes
4 Municipal, 54 holes
24 Private, 486 holes

Good Restaurants
18 Simple ♦
69 Family ♦♦
30 Adult ♦♦♦
9 Upscale ♦♦♦♦

Movie Theatres
9 Singles/Twins; 24 Multiplexes
237 Screens

Professional Sports
Cobras (Class A Baseball)
Magic (NBA Basketball)
Miracle (WNBA)
Rays (Class AA Baseball)
Solar Bears (IHL Hockey)

Recreation Areas
Federal
    Lake Woodruff NWR, 280 acres
    Ocala NF, 84,107 acres
State
    Hontoon Island SP, 599 acres
    Lake Griffin SRA, 255 acres
    Lake Louisa SP, 4,211 acres
    Lower Wekiva River SNA,
      12,407 acres
    Rock Springs Run Reserve,
      13,871 acres
    Tosohatchee SNA, 30,349 acres
    Wekiwa Springs SP, 7,705 acres

Water Area
Lakes and rivers: 333,440 acres
Score: 97.73   Rank: 9

Oshawa, ON
Golf Courses
2 Daily fee, 36 holes
1 Private, 18 holes

Good Restaurants
1 Simple ♦
2 Family ♦♦

Movie Theatres
2 Multiplexes
14 Screens

Recreation Areas
Provincial
    Darlington PP, 516 acres
    Scugog Island Wildlife Area,
      450 acres

Skiing
4 ski areas
Lift capacity/hour: 15,360

Water Area
Lakes and rivers: 4,500 acres
Lake Ontario: 16,500 acres
Score: 9.63   Rank: 320

Ottawa-Hull, ON-PQ
College CIAU Sports
Carleton Ravens
U of Ottawa Gees Gees

Gambling
1 Casino
Hippodrome Connaught (harness)
Rideau Carleton Raceway (harness)

Golf Courses
11 Daily fee, 180 holes
5 Municipal, 81 holes
12 Private, 198 holes

Good Restaurants
2 Simple ♦
19 Family ♦♦
13 Adult ♦♦♦
3 Upscale ♦♦♦♦

Movie Theatres
4 Singles/Twins; 14 Multiplexes
82 Screens

Professional Sports
Lynx (Triple A Baseball)
Senators (NHL Hockey)

Recreation Areas
Federal
    Beckett Creek MBS, 247 acres
    Ile Carillon MBS, 1,236 acres
Provincial
    Carillon PP, 3,501 acres
    Fitzroy PP, 457 acres
    Rideau River PP, 242 acres
    Shirley Bay Crown Game Preserve,
      4,569 acres

Skiing
15 ski areas
Lift capacity/hour: 23,000
Water Area
Lakes and rivers: 15,000 acres
Score: **58.64**   Rank: **147**

Owensboro, KY
Golf Courses
2 Daily fee, 27 holes
2 Municipal, 36 holes
2 Private, 36 holes
Good Restaurants
3 Family ♦♦
Movie Theatres
1 Single/Twin; 1 Multiplex
14 Screens
Recreation Areas
State
Hawes SP, 297 acres
Water Area
Lakes and rivers: 8,960 acres
Score: **18.41**   Rank: **289**

Panama City, FL
Amusement & Theme Parks
Coconut Creek Amusements
Miracle Strip/Shipwreck Island
Golf Courses
5 Daily fee, 108 holes
2 Municipal, 36 holes
3 Private, 45 holes
Good Restaurants
1 Simple ♦
6 Family ♦♦
Movie Theatres
3 Multiplexes
34 Screens
Recreation Areas
State
St. Andrews SRA, 1,268 acres
Water Area
Lakes and rivers: 76,160 acres
Gulf coast: 9,600 acres
Score: **66.28**   Rank: **120**

Parkersburg-Marietta, WV-OH
Golf Courses
9 Daily fee, 144 holes
2 Private, 36 holes
Good Restaurants
4 Family ♦♦
Movie Theatres
2 Singles/Twins; 2 Multiplexes
16 Screens
Recreation Areas
Federal
Ohio River Islands NWR, 45 acres
Wayne NF, 38,374 acres
State
Muskingum River Parkway SP,
40 acres
Water Area
Lakes and rivers: 9,600 acres
Score: **33.71**   Rank: **235**

Pensacola, FL
Gambling
Pensacola Greyhound Track
Golf Courses
13 Daily fee, 234 holes
1 Municipal, 18 holes
5 Private, 108 holes
Good Restaurants
11 Family ♦♦
1 Adult ♦♦♦
Movie Theatres
5 Multiplexes
36 Screens
Professional Sports
Ice Pilots (ECHL Hockey)
Recreation Areas
Federal
Choctawhatchee NF, 108 acres
Gulf Islands Seashore, 25,912 acres
State
Big Lagoon SRA, 698 acres
Blackwater River SP, 590 acres
Perdido Key SRA, 285 acres
Water Area
Lakes and rivers: 138,880 acres
Gulf coast: 9,088 acres
Score: **75.63**   Rank: **87**

Peoria-Pekin, IL
College NCAA I Sports
Bradley Braves
Gambling
1 Casino
Golf Courses
8 Daily fee, 126 holes
9 Municipal, 153 holes
7 Private, 117 holes
Good Restaurants
7 Family ♦♦
3 Adult ♦♦♦
Movie Theatres
3 Singles/Twins; 6 Multiplexes
55 Screens
Professional Sports
Chiefs (Class A Baseball)
Rivermen (ECHL Hockey)
Recreation Areas
State
Mackinaw River Wildlife Area,
1,423 acres
Powerton Lake Wildlife Area,
1,426 acres
Rock Island Trail SP, 392 acres
Spring Lake Wildlife Area,
2,032 acres
Woodford Wildlife Area, 2,901 acres
Water Area
Lakes and rivers: 22,400 acres
Zoos
Glen Oak Zoo
Wildlife Prairie Park
Score: **71.10**   Rank: **103**

Philadelphia, PA-NJ
Amusement & Theme Parks
Clementon Park & Splash World
Sesame Place
Aquariums
Thomas Kean State Aquarium
College NCAA I Sports
Drexel Dragons
La Salle Explorers
St. Joseph's Hawks
Temple Owls
U of Pennsylvania Quakers
Villanova Wildcats
Gambling
Garden State Park (mixed meetings)
Philadelphia Park (thoroughbred)
Golf Courses
62 Daily fee, 1098 holes
18 Municipal, 315 holes
77 Private, 1359 holes
Good Restaurants
15 Simple ♦
62 Family ♦♦
47 Adult ♦♦♦
13 Upscale ♦♦♦♦
2 Best ♦♦♦♦♦
Movie Theatres
27 Singles/Twins; 40 Multiplexes
380 Screens
Professional Sports
76ers (NBA Basketball)
Eagles (NFL Football)
Flyers (NHL Hockey)
Phantoms (AHL Hockey)
Phillies (NL Baseball)
Recreation Areas
Federal
Edwin Forsythe NWR, 2,552 acres
John Heinz NWR, 919 acres
Supawna Meadows NWR,
2,855 acres
State
Benjamin Rush SP, 275 acres
Delaware Canal SP, 487 acres
Evansburg SP, 3,349 acres
Fort Washington SP, 493 acres
French Creek SP, 875 acres
Hawk Island SP, 2 acres
Marsh Creek SP, 1,705 acres
Mount Laurel SP, 20 acres
Neshaminy SP, 336 acres
Nockamixon SP, 5,283 acres
Parvin SP, 1,135 acres
Ralph Stover SP, 45 acres
Rancocas SP, 1,252 acres
Ridley Creek SP, 2,607 acres
Tyler SP, 1,711 acres
Warren Grove SRA, 617 acres
White Clay Creek SP, 1,254 acres
Skiing
5 ski areas
Lift capacity/hour: 24,300

Water Area
Lakes and rivers: 51,200 acres
Atlantic coast: 1,560 acres
Zoos
Philadelphia Zoological Garden
Score: **74.78**   Rank: **90**

★Phoenix-Mesa, AZ
Amusement & Theme Parks
Enchanted Island
Golfland
Rawhide
Auto Racing
Phoenix International Raceway
College NCAA I Sports
Arizona State Sun Devils
Gambling
4 Casinos
Apache Park (greyhound)
Phoenix Park (greyhound)
Turf Paradise (mixed meetings)
Golf Courses
101 Daily fee, 1899 holes
14 Municipal, 225 holes
49 Private, 1008 holes
Good Restaurants
8 Simple ♦
29 Family ♦♦
18 Adult ♦♦♦
6 Upscale ♦♦♦♦
1 Best ♦♦♦♦♦
Movie Theatres
6 Singles/Twins; 49 Multiplexes
448 Screens
Professional Sports
Arizona Cardinals (NFL Football)
Arizona Diamondbacks (NL Baseball)
Coyotes (NHL Hockey)
Mercury (WNBA)
Suns (NBA Basketball)
Recreation Areas
Federal
Casa Grande Ruins NM, 472 acres
Coronado NF, 23,331 acres
Tonto NF, 857,519 acres
State
Lost Dutchman SP, 292 acres
Oracle SP, 4,000 acres
Pichaco Peak SP, 3,440 acres
Skiing
2 ski areas
Lift capacity/hour: 1,600
Water Area
Lakes and rivers: 16,000 acres
Zoos
Phoenix Zoo
Wildlife World Zoo
Score: **94.90**   Rank: **19**

Pine Bluff, AR
College NCAA I Sports
U of Arkansas Golden Lions
Golf Courses
1 Daily fee, 9 holes
2 Municipal, 27 holes
2 Private, 36 holes
Good Restaurants
1 Family ♦♦
Movie Theatres
3 Multiplexes
15 Screens
Water Area
Lakes and rivers: 18,560 acres
Score: **5.09**   Rank: **336**

Pittsburgh, PA
Amusement & Theme Parks
Idlewild Park
Kennywood Park
Williams Grove Park & Speedway
College NCAA I Sports
Duquesne Dukes
Robert Morris Colonials
U of Pittsburgh Panthers
Gambling
Meadows (harness)
Golf Courses
88 Daily fee, 1467 holes
5 Municipal, 90 holes
53 Private, 927 holes
Good Restaurants
33 Simple ♦
60 Family ♦♦
40 Adult ♦♦♦
1 Upscale ♦♦♦♦
Movie Theatres
17 Singles/Twins; 28 Multiplexes
203 Screens
Professional Sports
Penguins (NHL Hockey)
Pirates (NL Baseball)
Steelers (NFL Football)
Recreation Areas
Federal
Ohio River Islands NWR, 55 acres
State
Hillman SP, 3,654 acres
Jennings SP, 297 acres
Keystone SP, 1,187 acres
Laurel Mountain SP, 493 acres
Laurel Ridge SP, 5,886 acres
Laurel Summit SP, 6 acres
Linn Run SP, 613 acres
Moraine SP, 16,132 acres
Ohiopyle SP, 18,719 acres
Point SP, 36 acres
Raccoon Creek SP, 7,572 acres
Skiing
11 ski areas
Lift capacity/hour: 168,220

Water Area
Lakes and rivers: 35,840 acres
Zoos
Pittsburgh Aviary
Pittsburgh Zoo
Score: **78.18**   Rank: **78**

Pittsfield, MA
Golf Courses
8 Daily fee, 108 holes
3 Private, 54 holes
Good Restaurants
4 Family ♦♦
5 Adult ♦♦♦
2 Upscale ♦♦♦♦
Movie Theatres
1 Multiplex
10 Screens
Professional Sports
Mets (Class A Baseball)
Recreation Areas
State
Bash Bish Falls SP, 200 acres
Mt. Everett SR, 1,356 acres
Mt. Greylock SR, 12,500 acres
Taconic Trail SP, 930 acres
Wahconah Falls SP, 104 acres
Skiing
32 ski areas
Lift capacity/hour: 192,395
Water Area
Lakes and rivers: 3,670 acres
Zoos
Berkshire Museum
Score: **48.44**   Rank: **183**

Pocatello, ID
College NCAA I Sports
Idaho State Bengals
Gambling
1 Casino
Pocatello Downs (mixed meetings)
Golf Courses
1 Daily fee, 9 holes
2 Municipal, 36 holes
1 Private, 18 holes
Good Restaurants
3 Simple ♦
4 Family ♦♦
2 Adult ♦♦♦
Movie Theatres
2 Singles/Twins; 2 Multiplexes
12 Screens
Recreation Areas
Federal
Caribou NF, 118,995 acres
Skiing
1 ski area
Lift capacity/hour: 3,300
Water Area
Lakes and rivers: 21,760 acres
Zoos
Ross Park Zoological Gardens
Score: **14.73**   Rank: **302**

Portland, ME
Amusement & Theme Parks
Palace Playland
Gambling
Scarborough Downs (harness)
Golf Courses
14 Daily fee, 180 holes
3 Municipal, 54 holes
5 Private, 90 holes
Good Restaurants
4 Simple ♦
12 Family ♦♦
11 Adult ♦♦♦
Movie Theatres
3 Singles/Twins; 5 Multiplexes
39 Screens
Professional Sports
Pirates (AHL Hockey)
Sea Dogs (Class AA Baseball)
Recreation Areas
State
  Crescent Beach SP, 244 acres
  Scarboro Beach SP, 5 acres
  Sebago Lake SP, 1,342 acres
  Two Lights SP, 41 acres
  Wolfe's Neck Woods SP, 244 acres
Skiing
5 ski areas
Lift capacity/hour: 44,100
Water Area
Lakes and rivers: 125,860 acres
Atlantic coast: 12,096 acres
Score: 85.55   Rank: 52

Portland-Vancouver, OR-WA
Amusement & Theme Parks
Oaks Amusement Park
Auto Racing
Portland International Raceway
College NCAA I Sports
Portland State Vikings
U of Portland Pilots
Gambling
Multnomah Kennel Club (greyhound)
Portland Meadows (mixed meetings)
Golf Courses
41 Daily fee, 621 holes
7 Municipal, 135 holes
16 Private, 288 holes
Good Restaurants
3 Simple ♦
55 Family ♦♦
35 Adult ♦♦♦
Movie Theatres
27 Singles/Twins; 31 Multiplexes
192 Screens
Professional Sports
Rockies (Class A Baseball)
Trail Blazers (NBA Basketball)
Recreation Areas
Federal
  Gifford Pinchot NF, 1,180 acres
  Julia Butler Hansen NWR, 771 acres
  Mt. Hood NF, 615,840 acres

Ridgefield NWR, 5,218 acres
Siuslaw NF, 25,423 acres
Steigerwald Lake NWR, 923 acres
Tualatin River NWR, 776 acres
Willamette NF, 856 acres
State
  Ainsworth SP, 156 acres
  Bald Peak SP, 26 acres
  Banks-Vernonia SP, 38 acres
  Battle Ground Lake SP, 280 acres
  Benson SP, 272 acres
  Bonneville SP, 51 acres
  Bonnie Lure SP, 94 acres
  Bridal Veil Falls SP, 16 acres
  Clackamas River Scenic Waterway, 7 acres
  Columbia River, 45 acres
  Crown Point SP, 307 acres
  Dabney SP, 135 acres
  Erratic Rock SP, 4 acres
  George Joseph SP, 150 acres
  Guy Talbot SP, 378 acres
  John Yeon SP, 284 acres
  Lewis and Clark SP, 54 acres
  Mary Young SP, 133 acres
  Maud Williamson SP, 24 acres
  McLoughlin SP, 216 acres
  Milo McIver SP, 952 acres
  Molalla River SP, 567 acres
  Paradise Point SP, 92 acres
  Portland Women's Forum SP, 7 acres
  Reed Island SP, 508 acres
  Rocky Butte SP, 14 acres
  Rooster Rock SP, 873 acres
  Sandy River Scenic Waterway, 69 acres
  Shepperd's Dell SP, 519 acres
  Sunset Highway Forest Wayside, 338 acres
  Tryon Creek SP, 790 acres
  Willamette Mission SP, 624 acres
  Willamette River Greenway, 1,147 acres
  Willamette Stone SP, 3 acres
  Wilson River Highway Forest Wayside, 120 acres
  Wormald SP, 160 acres
Skiing
6 ski areas
Lift capacity/hour: 36,000
Water Area
Lakes and rivers: 68,480 acres
Zoos
Metro Washington Park Zoo
Score: 86.68   Rank: 48

Portsmouth-Rochester, NH-ME
College NCAA I Sports
U of New Hampshire Wildcats
Golf Courses
12 Daily fee, 153 holes
2 Private, 36 holes

Good Restaurants
7 Simple ♦
21 Family ♦♦
21 Adult ♦♦♦
Movie Theatres
2 Singles/Twins; 4 Multiplexes
29 Screens
Recreation Areas
State
  Hampton Beach SP, 50 acres
  Jenness Beach SB, 1 acre
  North Hampton SB, 3 acres
  Odiorne Point SP, 370 acres
  Rye Harbor SP, 63 acres
  Wallis Sands SB, 9 acres
Skiing
8 ski areas
Lift capacity/hour: 31,470
Water Area
Lakes and rivers: 36,045 acres
Atlantic coast: 4,352 acres
Score: 63.17   Rank: 131

Providence-Fall River-Warwick, RI-MA
Amusement & Theme Parks
Fantasyland
College NCAA I Sports
Brown Bears
Providence College Friars
U of Rhode Island Rams
Gambling
Lincoln Greyhound Park
Golf Courses
26 Daily fee, 342 holes
4 Municipal, 45 holes
18 Private, 297 holes
Good Restaurants
9 Simple ♦
32 Family ♦♦
12 Adult ♦♦♦
Movie Theatres
8 Singles/Twins; 17 Multiplexes
131 Screens
Professional Sports
Bruins (AHL Hockey)
Pawtucket Red Sox (Triple A Baseball)
Recreation Areas
State
  Beavertail SP, 153 acres
  Burlingame SP, 2,100 acres
  Charlestown Beachway SB, 62 acres
  Colt SP, 464 acres
  Diamond Hill SP, 373 acres
  East Beach SB, 174 acres
  Fall River Heritage SP, 9 acres
  Fishermen's Memorial SP, 91 acres
  Fort Wetherill SP, 100 acres
  Goddard Memorial SP, 489 acres
  Haines Memorial SP, 102 acres
  Lincoln Woods SP, 627 acres
  Salty Brine SB, 1 acre
  Scarborough SB, 42 acres
  Wheeler SB, 27 acres
  World War II Memorial SP, 14 acres

Skiing
6 ski areas
Lift capacity/hour: 17,800
Water Area
Lakes and rivers: 137,590 acres
Atlantic coast: 12,096 acres
Zoos
Capron Park Zoo
Roger Williams Park Zoo
Slater Memorial Park
Score: **79.32**   Rank: **74**

Provo-Orem, UT
College NCAA I Sports
Brigham Young Cougars
Golf Courses
3 Daily fee, 45 holes
5 Municipal, 99 holes
2 Private, 36 holes
Good Restaurants
2 Adult ◆ ◆ ◆
Movie Theatres
9 Singles/Twins; 5 Multiplexes
42 Screens
Recreation Areas
Federal
Ashley NF, 3,797 acres
Manti-La Sal NF, 91,293 acres
Timpanogos Cave NM, 250 acres
Uinta NF, 391,578 acres
State
Scofield SP, 77 acres
Utah Lake SP, 308 acres
Skiing
9 ski areas
Lift capacity/hour: 105,217
Water Area
Lakes and rivers: 91,520 acres
Score: **56.65**   Rank: **154**

Pueblo, CO
Gambling
Pueblo Park (greyhound)
Golf Courses
1 Daily fee, 18 holes
3 Municipal, 72 holes
1 Private, 18 holes
Good Restaurants
3 Family ◆ ◆
1 Adult ◆ ◆ ◆
Movie Theatres
1 Single/Twin; 3 Multiplexes
23 Screens
Recreation Areas
Federal
San Isabel NF, 32,761 acres
State
Pueblo SRA, 9,045 acres
Water Area
Lakes and rivers: 5,760 acres
Zoos
Pueblo Zoo
Score: **11.33**   Rank: **314**

Punta Gorda, FL
Golf Courses
13 Daily fee, 261 holes
3 Private, 54 holes
Good Restaurants
2 Family ◆ ◆
Movie Theatres
1 Multiplex
8 Screens
Professional Sports
Rangers (Class A Baseball)
Recreation Areas
Federal
Island Bay NWR, 20 acres
State
Don Pedro Island SRA, 133 acres
Port Charlotte Beach SRA, 213 acres
Water Area
Lakes and rivers: 78,080 acres
Gulf coast: 2,752 acres
Score: **67.13**   Rank: **117**

Quebec City, PQ
Aquariums
Aquarium du Quebec
Gambling
Hippodrome de Quebec (harness)
Golf Courses
10 Daily fee, 153 holes
2 Municipal, 36 holes
2 Private, 36 holes
Good Restaurants
1 Simple ◆
14 Family ◆ ◆
16 Adult ◆ ◆ ◆
2 Upscale ◆ ◆ ◆ ◆
Movie Theatres
1 Single/Twin; 7 Multiplexes
46 Screens
Recreation Areas
Federal
Cap Tourmente R. NWA, 5,510 acres
St-Vallier MBS, 988 acres
Provincial
Jacques Cartier PP, 165,705 acres
Laurentides Wildlife Sanctuary,
1,967,163 acres
Riviere Sainte-Anne Wildlife
Sanctuary, 988 acres
Skiing
21 ski areas
Lift capacity/hour: 49,000
Water Area
Lakes and rivers: 63,000 acres
Zoos
Jardin Zoologique de Quebec
Score: **34.84**   Rank: **231**

Racine, WI
Golf Courses
3 Daily fee, 45 holes
6 Municipal, 126 holes
2 Private, 36 holes

Good Restaurants
2 Simple ◆
2 Family ◆ ◆
1 Adult ◆ ◆ ◆
Movie Theatres
2 Multiplexes
13 Screens
Skiing
6 ski areas
Lift capacity/hour: 36,035
Water Area
Lakes and rivers: 4,480 acres
Lake Michigan: 28,980 acres
Zoos
Racine Zoological Garden
Score: **54.67**   Rank: **160**

Raleigh-Durham-Chapel Hill, NC
College NCAA I Sports
Duke Blue Devils
North Carolina State Wolfpack
U of North Carolina Tarheels
Golf Courses
34 Daily fee, 576 holes
16 Private, 324 holes
Good Restaurants
7 Simple ◆
22 Family ◆ ◆
18 Adult ◆ ◆ ◆
8 Upscale ◆ ◆ ◆ ◆
1 Best ◆ ◆ ◆ ◆ ◆
Movie Theatres
6 Singles/Twins; 15 Multiplexes
106 Screens
Professional Sports
Bulls (Triple A Baseball)
Cougars (USBL Basketball)
Icecaps (ECHL Hockey)
Mudcats (Class AA Baseball)
Recreation Areas
Federal
Blue Ridge Parkway
State
Eno River SP, 1,965 acres
Falls Lake SRA, 1,100 acres
Jordan Lake SRA, 1,475 acres
Umstead SP, 5,334 acres
Water Area
Lakes and rivers: 41,600 acres
Zoos
North Carolina Museum of Life &
Science
Score: **72.80**   Rank: **97**

Rapid City, SD
Golf Courses
2 Daily fee, 27 holes
4 Municipal, 54 holes
3 Private, 45 holes
Good Restaurants
10 Simple ◆
13 Family ◆ ◆
1 Adult ◆ ◆ ◆

Movie Theatres
2 Singles/Twins; 1 Multiplex
10 Screens
Professional Sports
Thillers (IBA Basketball)
Recreation Areas
Federal
Badlands NP, 94,755 acres
Black Hills NF, 394,800 acres
Buffalo Gap NGL, 199,410 acres
Mount Rushmore NM, 1,238 acres
Skiing
2 ski areas
Lift capacity/hour: 7,700
Water Area
Lakes and rivers: 5,120 acres
Zoos
Bear Country U.S.A.
Score: 19.83   Rank: 284

Reading, PA
Golf Courses
17 Daily fee, 297 holes
5 Private, 90 holes
Good Restaurants
3 Simple ♦
4 Family ♦♦
2 Adult ♦♦♦
Movie Theatres
2 Singles/Twins; 3 Multiplexes
20 Screens
Professional Sports
Phillies (Class AA Baseball)
Recreation Areas
Federal
Appalachian NT, 1,589 acres
State
French Creek SP, 6,470 acres
Nolde Forest SP, 666 acres
Skiing
2 ski areas
Lift capacity/hour: 11,400
Water Area
Lakes and rivers: 3,840 acres
Score: 51.84   Rank: 171

Redding, CA
Gambling
3 Casinos
Golf Courses
6 Daily fee, 72 holes
4 Private, 54 holes
Good Restaurants
1 Simple ♦
3 Family ♦♦
Movie Theatres
1 Single/Twin; 3 Multiplexes
23 Screens
Recreation Areas
Federal
Lassen NF, 248,007 acres
Lassen Volcanic NP, 66,862 acres
Shasta NF, 470,018 acres

Trinity NF, 30,626 acres
Whiskeytown-Shasta-Trinity NRA,
42,459 acres
State
Ahjumawi Lava Springs SP,
6,000 acres
Castle Crags SP, 4,350 acres
McArthur-Burney Falls Memorial SP,
850 acres
Skiing
4 ski areas
Lift capacity/hour: 28,871
Water Area
Lakes and rivers: 39,680 acres
Score: 15.86   Rank: 298

Regina, SK
College CIAU Sports
U of Regina Cougars
Gambling
2 Casinos
Queensbury Downs (harness)
Golf Courses
2 Daily fee, 27 holes
10 Municipal, 135 holes
1 Private, 18 holes
Good Restaurants
4 Family ♦♦
2 Adult ♦♦♦
Movie Theatres
3 Singles/Twins; 4 Multiplexes
33 Screens
Professional Sports
Roughriders (CFL Football)
Recreation Areas
Federal
Wascana Lake Bird Sanctuary,
321 acres
Provincial
Condie Nature Refuge, 719 acres
Echo Valley PP, 1,594 acres
Mclean, 131 acres
Rowan'S Ravine PP, 672 acres
Valeport, 148 acres
Valley Centre, 200 acres
Wascana Trails, 324 acres
White Butte Trails, 1,065 acres
Skiing
2 ski areas
Lift capacity/hour: 6,366
Water Area
Lakes and rivers: 32,000 acres
Score: 51.55   Rank: 172

Reno, NV
Amusement & Theme Parks
Ponderosa Branch
Wild Island
College NCAA I Sports
U of Nevada Wolf Pack
Gambling
41 Casinos

Golf Courses
6 Daily fee, 108 holes
5 Municipal, 99 holes
2 Private, 36 holes
Good Restaurants
1 Simple ♦
3 Family ♦♦
1 Adult ♦♦♦
1 Upscale ♦♦♦♦
Movie Theatres
2 Singles/Twins; 3 Multiplexes
22 Screens
Recreation Areas
Federal
Anaho Island NWR, 248 acres
Sheldon NWR, 187,240 acres
Toiyabe NF, 80,377 acres
State
Lake Tahoe SP, 10,552 acres
Washoe Lake SRA, 8,038 acres
Skiing
11 ski areas
Lift capacity/hour: 145,735
Water Area
Lakes and rivers: 133,760 acres
Score: 70.53   Rank: 105

Richland-Kennewick-Pasco, WA
Gambling
Sun Downs Race Meet (mixed meetings)
Golf Courses
3 Daily fee, 54 holes
4 Municipal, 72 holes
1 Private, 18 holes
Good Restaurants
5 Family ♦♦
Movie Theatres
1 Single/Twin; 5 Multiplexes
22 Screens
Recreation Areas
Federal
Umatilla NWR, 1,466 acres
State
Crow Butte SP, 1,312 acres
Palouse Falls SP, 83 acres
Pasco/Fish Lake Trail, 680 acres
Potholes SP, 3,737 acres
Sacajawea SP, 284 acres
Skiing
2 ski areas
Lift capacity/hour: 10,325
Water Area
Lakes and rivers: 51,200 acres
Score: 28.32   Rank: 254

Richmond-Petersburg, VA
Amusement & Theme Parks
Paramount's Kings Dominion
Auto Racing
Richmond International Raceway
College NCAA I Sports
U of Richmond Spiders
Virginia Commonwealth Rams

Golf Courses
16 Daily fee, 288 holes
1 Municipal, 18 holes
15 Private, 306 holes

Good Restaurants
10 Simple ◆
30 Family ◆◆
17 Adult ◆◆◆
3 Upscale ◆◆◆◆
1 Best ◆◆◆◆◆

Movie Theatres
6 Singles/Twins; 11 Multiplexes
92 Screens

Professional Sports
Braves (Triple A Baseball)
Renegades (ECHL Hockey)

Recreation Areas
Federal
James River NWR, 4,173 acres
Presquile NWR, 1,329 acres
Richmond NBP, 767 acres
State
Pocahontas SP, 7,778 acres

Water Area
Lakes and rivers: 52,480 acres

Zoos
Maymont

Score: **74.50**   Rank: **91**

★Riverside-San Bernardino, CA

Amusement & Theme Parks
Santa's Village

Auto Racing
California Speedway

Gambling
12 Casinos

Golf Courses
74 Daily fee, 1413 holes
14 Municipal, 243 holes
61 Private, 1251 holes

Good Restaurants
9 Simple ◆
44 Family ◆◆
28 Adult ◆◆◆
7 Upscale ◆◆◆◆

Movie Theatres
7 Singles/Twins; 44 Multiplexes
370 Screens

Professional Sports
Mavericks (Class A Baseball)
Quakes (Class A Baseball)
Stampede (Class A Baseball)
Storm (Class A Baseball)

Recreation Areas
Federal
Angeles NF, 10,656 acres
Cleveland NF, 78,293 acres
Coachella Valley NWR, 3,592 acres
Death Valley NP, 81,152 acres
Joshua Tree NM, 708,230 acres
Mojave Desert N Preserve,
1,355,637 acres
San Bernardino NF, 670,381 acres

State
Anza-Borrego Desert SP,
35,177 acres
Chino Hills SP, 7,071 acres
Lake Elsinore SRA, 2,976 acres
Lake Perris SRA, 8,800 acres
Mount San Jacinto SP, 13,522 acres
Providence Mountains SRA,
5,250 acres
Salton Sea SRA, 9,400 acres
Seccombe Lake SRA, 50 acres
Silverwood Lake SRA, 2,400 acres

Skiing
16 ski areas
Lift capacity/hour: 164,180

Water Area
Lakes and rivers: 90,240 acres

Zoos
Hi-Desert Nature Museum
Moonridge Zoo
The Living Desert

Score: **96.88**   Rank: **12**

Roanoke, VA

Golf Courses
7 Daily fee, 108 holes
1 Municipal, 9 holes
3 Private, 63 holes

Good Restaurants
2 Simple ◆
8 Family ◆◆
3 Adult ◆◆◆
2 Upscale ◆◆◆◆

Movie Theatres
2 Singles/Twins; 4 Multiplexes
24 Screens

Professional Sports
Avalanche (Class A Baseball)
Express (ECHL Hockey)

Recreation Areas
Federal
Appalachian NT, 3,981 acres
Blue Ridge Parkway, 5,683 acres
George Washington NF,
13,034 acres
Jefferson NF, 71,033 acres

Water Area
Lakes and rivers: 1,920 acres

Zoos
Mill Mountain Zoo

Score: **39.66**   Rank: **214**

Rochester, MN

Golf Courses
6 Daily fee, 90 holes
1 Municipal, 18 holes
1 Private, 18 holes

Good Restaurants
4 Family ◆◆
7 Adult ◆◆◆

Movie Theatres
4 Multiplexes
19 Screens

Professional Sports
Skeeters (IBA Basketball)

Skiing
3 ski areas
Lift capacity/hour: 19,100

Water Area
Lakes and rivers: 640 acres

Score: **9.91**   Rank: **319**

★Rochester, NY

Amusement & Theme Parks
Seabreeze Park
Six Flags Darien Lake

College NCAA I Sports
Hobart William Smith Statesmen

Gambling
Batavia Downs (harness)

Golf Courses
62 Daily fee, 1035 holes
3 Municipal, 72 holes
20 Private, 351 holes

Good Restaurants
5 Simple ◆
11 Family ◆◆
11 Adult ◆◆◆

Movie Theatres
7 Singles/Twins; 12 Multiplexes
136 Screens

Professional Sports
Americans (AHL Hockey)
Muckdogs (Class A Baseball)
Redwings (Triple A Baseball)

Recreation Areas
Federal
Iroquois NWR, 10,819 acres
State
Canandaigua Lake Boat Launch SP,
15 acres
Chimney Bluffs SP, 597 acres
Conesus Lake Boat Launch SP,
3 acres
Darien Lakes SP, 1,845 acres
Hamlin Beach SP, 1,224 acres
Harriet Spencer SP, 678 acres
Honeoye Boat Launch SP, 4 acres
Irondequoit Bay Marine Park,
35 acres
Lakeside Beach SP, 734 acres
Letchworth SP, 10,000 acres
Oak Orchard Marine Park, 81 acres
Seneca Lake SP, 80 acres

Skiing
21 ski areas
Lift capacity/hour: 71,875

Water Area
Lakes and rivers: 28,800 acres

Zoos
Seneca Park Zoo

Score: **98.30**   Rank: **7**

Rockford, IL

Golf Courses
7 Daily fee, 99 holes
8 Municipal, 135 holes
6 Private, 99 holes

Good Restaurants
3 Simple ♦
4 Family ♦♦
3 Adult ♦♦♦
1 Upscale ♦♦♦♦

Movie Theatres
6 Multiplexes
44 Screens

Professional Sports
Lightning (CBA Basketball)
Reds (Class A Baseball)

Recreation Areas
State
Castle Rock SP, 1,995 acres
Franklin Creek SP, 520 acres
Lowden SP, 207 acres
Lowden-MillerState Forest,
2,234 acres
Rock Cut SP, 3,092 acres
White Pines Forest SP, 385 acres

Skiing
3 ski areas
Lift capacity/hour: 20,085

Water Area
Lakes and rivers: 6,400 acres

Score: **44.75**   Rank: **196**

Rocky Mount, NC

Golf Courses
4 Daily fee, 54 holes
3 Private, 45 holes

Good Restaurants
2 Simple ♦
4 Family ♦♦

Movie Theatres
3 Multiplexes
10 Screens

Water Area
Lakes and rivers: 2,560 acres

Score: **0.28**   Rank: **353**

Sacramento, CA

Amusement & Theme Parks
Funderland
Waterworld USA

College NCAA I Sports
Sacramento State Hornets

Gambling
15 Casinos
Cal-Expo (mixed meetings)

Golf Courses
24 Daily fee, 333 holes
11 Municipal, 207 holes
15 Private, 234 holes

Good Restaurants
3 Simple ♦
10 Family ♦♦
11 Adult ♦♦♦
1 Upscale ♦♦♦♦

Movie Theatres
9 Singles/Twins; 16 Multiplexes
144 Screens

Professional Sports
Kings (NBA Basketball)
Monarchs (WNBA)

Recreation Areas
Federal
Eldorado NF, 545,411 acres
Tahoe NF, 275,894 acres
Toiyabe NF, 31 acres
State
Auburn SRA, 42,000 acres
Bliss SP, 1,237 acres
Brannan Island SRA, 336 acres
Burton Creek SP, 1,981 acres
Delta Meadows River Park, acres
Emerald Bay SP, 593 acres
Folsom Lake SRA, 17,718 acres
Kings Beach SRA, 8 acres
Lake Valley SRA, 150 acres
Prairie City SVRA, 836 acres
Sugar Pine Point SP, 2,011 acres
Tahoe SRA, 57 acres
Washoe Meadows SP, 620 acres

Skiing
25 ski areas
Lift capacity/hour: 432,165

Water Area
Lakes and rivers: 131,840 acres

Zoos
Folsom Zoo
Roseville City Zoo
Sacramento City Zoo

Score: **74.22**   Rank: **92**

Saginaw-Bay City-Midland, MI

Gambling
Saginaw Raceway (harness)

Golf Courses
20 Daily fee, 351 holes
2 Municipal, 54 holes
7 Private, 117 holes

Good Restaurants
9 Simple ♦
14 Family ♦♦
2 Adult ♦♦♦

Movie Theatres
1 Single/Twin; 6 Multiplexes
40 Screens

Professional Sports
Wheels (CoHL Hockey)

Recreation Areas
Federal
Shiawassee NWR, 2,053 acres
State
Bay City SP, 196 acres

Skiing
4 ski areas
Lift capacity/hour: 21,600

Water Area
Lakes and rivers: 12,800 acres
Lake Huron: 11,540 acres

Zoos
Saginaw Children's Zoo

Score: **68.55**   Rank: **112**

St. Catharines-Niagara, ON

Aquariums
Marine Land of Canada

College CIAU Sports
Brock U Badgers

Gambling
1 Casino
Fort Erie (thoroughbred)

Golf Courses
6 Daily fee, 90 holes
7 Municipal, 108 holes
3 Private, 45 holes

Good Restaurants
7 Simple ♦
12 Family ♦♦
12 Adult ♦♦♦
2 Upscale ♦♦♦♦

Movie Theatres
3 Singles/Twins; 5 Multiplexes
35 Screens

Professional Sports
Stompers (Class A Baseball)

Skiing
16 ski areas
Lift capacity/hour: 23,660

Water Area
Lakes and rivers: 890 acres
Lake Ontario: 21,000 acres

Score: **43.62**   Rank: **200**

St. Cloud, MN

College NCAA I Sports
St. Cloud State Huskies

Golf Courses
11 Daily fee, 180 holes
2 Municipal, 27 holes
2 Private, 27 holes

Good Restaurants
1 Simple ♦
9 Family ♦♦
3 Adult ♦♦♦

Movie Theatres
1 Single/Twin; 4 Multiplexes
24 Screens

Skiing
3 ski areas
Lift capacity/hour: 16,000

Water Area
Lakes and rivers: 32,000 acres

Score: **56.37**   Rank: **155**

Saint John, NB

Gambling
Exhibition Park Raceway (harness)

Golf Courses
1 Daily fee, 18 holes
1 Municipal, 9 holes
2 Private, 36 holes

Good Restaurants
3 Simple ◆
6 Family ◆◆
2 Adult ◆◆◆
Movie Theatres
3 Singles/Twins; 1 Multiplex
11 Screens
Professional Sports
Flames (AHL Hockey)
Recreation Areas
Federal
Grand Manan Bird Sanctuary,
618 acres
Provincial
Becaguimec, 27,532 acres
Herring Cove PP, 1,048 acres
Lepreau River, 60,184 acres
Minister'S Island, 499 acres
New River Beach PP, 897 acres
Oak Mountain Reserve, 247 acres
The Anchorage PP, 447 acres
Utopia Wildlife Refuge, 7,682 acres
Water Area
Lakes and rivers: 54,000 acres
Bay of Fundy: 65,000 acres
Zoos
Cherry Brook Zoo
Score: **71.38**   Rank: **102**

St. John's, NF
College CIAU Sports
Memorial U Sea Hawks
Gambling
Avalon Raceway (harness)
Golf Courses
1 Daily fee, 18 holes
1 Municipal, 18 holes
2 Private, 36 holes
Good Restaurants
2 Family ◆◆
2 Adult ◆◆◆
1 Upscale ◆◆◆◆
Movie Theatres
1 Single/Twin; 2 Multiplexes
12 Screens
Professional Sports
Maple Leafs (AHL Hockey)
Water Area
Lakes and rivers: 25,000 acres
Atlantic coast: 76,000 acres
Zoos
Pippy Park Zoo
Score: **58.92**   Rank: **146**

St. Joseph, MO
Gambling
2 Casinos
Golf Courses
1 Daily fee, 9 holes
2 Municipal, 36 holes
2 Private, 36 holes
Good Restaurants
3 Family ◆◆

Movie Theatres
3 Multiplexes
20 Screens
Recreation Areas
State
Lewis & Clark SP, 121 acres
Water Area
Lakes and rivers: 3,840 acres
Score: **7.08**   Rank: **329**

★**St. Louis, MO-IL**
Amusement & Theme Parks
Raging Waters Waterpark
Six Flags Over Mid-America
Auto Racing
Gateway International Raceway
College NCAA I Sports
Saint Louis U Billikens
Gambling
5 Casinos
Fairmount Park (mixed meetings)
Golf Courses
79 Daily fee, 1305 holes
14 Municipal, 198 holes
35 Private, 630 holes
Good Restaurants
18 Simple ◆
46 Family ◆◆
36 Adult ◆◆◆
7 Upscale ◆◆◆◆
1 Best ◆◆◆◆◆
Movie Theatres
17 Singles/Twins; 32 Multiplexes
271 Screens
Professional Sports
Blues (NHL Hockey)
Cardinals (NL Baseball)
Rams (NFL Football)
Recreation Areas
Federal
Jefferson National Expansion NM,
91 acres
Mark Twain NWR, 1,224 acres
State
Castlewood SP, 1,780 acres
Cuivre River SP, 6,351 acres
Edmund Babler Memorial SP,
2,439 acres
Eldon Hazlett SP, 3,000 acres
Frank Holton SP, 1,180 acres
Horsehoe Lake SP, 2,850 acres
Meramec SP, 4,114 acres
Mississippi River Wildlife Area,
24,386 acres
Pere Marquette SP, 7,900 acres
Robertsville SP, 1,172 acres
South Shore SP, 800 acres
Skiing
7 ski areas
Lift capacity/hour: 40,600
Water Area
Lakes and rivers: 98,560 acres
Zoos
Forest Park Zoo
Score: **90.36**   Rank: **35**

Salem, OR
Golf Courses
14 Daily fee, 189 holes
4 Private, 63 holes
Good Restaurants
4 Family ◆◆
2 Adult ◆◆◆
Movie Theatres
6 Singles/Twins; 4 Multiplexes
23 Screens
Recreation Areas
Federal
Ankeny NWR, 2,796 acres
Baskett Slough NWR, 2,492 acres
Mt. Hood NF, 66,583 acres
Siuslaw NF, 1,479 acres
Willamette NF, 135,526 acres
State
Champoeg SP, 615 acres
Detroit Lake SP, 104 acres
Holman Wayside, 10 acres
North Santiam SP, 120 acres
Sarah Helmich SP, 82 acres
Silver Falls SP, 8,546 acres
Van Duzer Forest Corridor Wayside,
463 acres
Willamette Mission SP, 1,686 acres
Willamette River Greenway,
1,109 acres
Skiing
1 ski area
Lift capacity/hour: 1,800
Water Area
Lakes and rivers: 8,320 acres
Score: **13.59**   Rank: **306**

Salinas, CA
Aquariums
Monterey Bay Aquarium
Auto Racing
Laguna Seca
Gambling
7 Casinos
Golf Courses
8 Daily fee, 171 holes
5 Municipal, 90 holes
6 Private, 126 holes
Good Restaurants
1 Simple ◆
14 Family ◆◆
15 Adult ◆◆◆
6 Upscale ◆◆◆◆
Movie Theatres
3 Singles/Twins; 6 Multiplexes
45 Screens
Recreation Areas
Federal
Los Padres NF, 305,907 acres
Pinnacles NM, 1,283 acres
Salinas River NWR, 364 acres
State
Andrew Molera SP, 4,786 acres
Asilomar Conference and SB,
106 acres

Carmel River SB, 106 acres
Fremont Peak SP, 54 acres
Garrapata SP, 2,800 acres
John Little SR, 21 acres
Julia Pfeiffer Burns SP, 3,583 acres
Marina SB, 170 acres
Monterey SB, 14 acres
Moss Landing SB, 55 acres
Pfeiffer Big Sur SP, 821 acres
Point Lobos SR, 1,325 acres
Salinas River SB, 246 acres
Zmudowski SB, 177 acres
Water Area
Lakes and rivers: 8,320 acres
Pacific coast: 27,904 acres
Score: 79.60   Rank: 73

★Salt Lake City-Ogden, UT
Amusement & Theme Parks
Lagoon Amusement Park
College NCAA I Sports
U of Utah Utes
Weber State Wildcats
Golf Courses
16 Daily fee, 225 holes
23 Municipal, 387 holes
8 Private, 135 holes
Good Restaurants
10 Family ◆◆
6 Adult ◆◆◆
1 Upscale ◆◆◆◆
Movie Theatres
13 Singles/Twins; 27 Multiplexes
194 Screens
Professional Sports
Buzz (Triple A Baseball)
Grizzlies (IHL Hockey)
Jazz (NBA Basketball)
Starzz (WNBA)
Recreation Areas
Federal
Cache NF, 67,974 acres
Wasatch NF, 133,256 acres
State
Antelope Island SP, 25,790 acres
Jordan River Parkway SP, 440 acres
Saltaire Beach SP, 3,115 acres
Skiing
20 ski areas
Lift capacity/hour: 180,067
Water Area
Lakes and rivers: 309,120 acres
Zoos
Hogle Zoological Garden
Score: 96.31   Rank: 14

San Angelo, TX
Golf Courses
2 Daily fee, 36 holes
1 Municipal, 9 holes
2 Private, 36 holes
Good Restaurants
1 Simple ◆
1 Family ◆◆

Movie Theatres
1 Single/Twin; 2 Multiplexes
10 Screens
Water Area
Lakes and rivers: 11,520 acres
Score: 14.16   Rank: 304

San Antonio, TX
Amusement & Theme Parks
Schlitterbahn Waterpark & Resort
Six Flags Fiesta Texas
Aquariums
Sea World of Texas
College NCAA I Sports
U of Texas Roadrunners
Golf Courses
20 Daily fee, 324 holes
9 Municipal, 162 holes
11 Private, 216 holes
Good Restaurants
18 Simple ◆
38 Family ◆◆
29 Adult ◆◆◆
2 Upscale ◆◆◆◆
Movie Theatres
2 Singles/Twins; 19 Multiplexes
195 Screens
Professional Sports
Spurs (NBA Basketball)
Recreation Areas
State
Guadalupe River SP, 1,000 acres
Water Area
Lakes and rivers: 17,280 acres
Zoos
San Antonio Zoological Gardens
Score: 65.72   Rank: 122

San Diego, CA
Aquariums
Sea World of San Diego
Stephen Birch Aquarium-Museum
College NCAA I Sports
San Diego State Aztecs
U of San Diego Toreros
Gambling
11 Casinos
Del Mar (thoroughbred)
Golf Courses
40 Daily fee, 783 holes
9 Municipal, 180 holes
28 Private, 504 holes
Good Restaurants
20 Simple ◆
43 Family ◆◆
38 Adult ◆◆◆
7 Upscale ◆◆◆◆
Movie Theatres
14 Singles/Twins; 38 Multiplexes
307 Screens
Professional Sports
Chargers (NFL Football)
Padres (NL Baseball)

Recreation Areas
Federal
Cabrillo NM, 137 acres
Cleveland NF, 290,095 acres
Sweetwater Marsh NWR, 316 acres
Tijuana Slough NWR, 407 acres
State
Anza-Borrego Desert SP,
522,097 acres
Border Field SP, 680 acres
Cardiff SB, 25 acres
Carlsbad SB, 14 acres
Cuyamaca Rancho SP, 24,677 acres
Leucadia SB, 11 acres
Moonlight SB, 14 acres
Ocotillo Wells SVRA, 42,000 acres
Palomar Mountain SP, 1,897 acres
San Elijo SB, 39 acres
San Onofre SB, 3,036 acres
Silver Strand SB, 428 acres
South Carlsbad SB, 135 acres
Torrey Pines SB, 41 acres
Torrey Pines SR, 1,082 acres
Water Area
Lakes and rivers: 34,560 acres
Pacific coast: 17,152 acres
Zoos
National City Zoo
San Diego Wild Animal Park
San Diego Zoo
Score: 90.08   Rank: 36

★San Francisco, CA
Aquariums
Steinhart Aquarium
College NCAA I Sports
U of San Francisco Dons
Gambling
6 Casinos
Bay Meadows (thoroughbred)
Golf Courses
9 Daily fee, 144 holes
10 Municipal, 153 holes
12 Private, 243 holes
Good Restaurants
2 Simple ◆
28 Family ◆◆
22 Adult ◆◆◆
6 Upscale ◆◆◆◆
2 Best ◆◆◆◆◆
Movie Theatres
31 Singles/Twins; 23 Multiplexes
200 Screens
Professional Sports
49ers (NFL Football)
Giants (NL Baseball)
Recreation Areas
Federal
Farallon NWR, 91 acres
Golden Gate NRA, 30,071 acres
Marin Islands NWR, 132 acres
Muir Woods NM, 523 acres
Point Reyes Seashore, 64,517 acres
San Francisco Bay NWR, 2,865 acres

State
   Angel Island SP, 740 acres
   Ano Nuevo SR, 4,000 acres
   Bean Hollow SB, 44 acres
   Big Basin Redwoods SP, 908 acres
   Burleigh Murray Ranch, 1,128 acres
   Butano SP, 3,200 acres
   Candlestick Point SRA, 252 acres
   China Camp SP, 1,512 acres
   Half Moon Bay SB, 170 acres
   Montara SB, 680 acres
   Mount Tamalpais SP, 6,300 acres
   Pacifica SB, 21 acres
   Pescadero SB, 638 acres
   Pomponio SB, 410 acres
   Portola SP, 2,800 acres
   Samuel P. Taylor SP, 2,708 acres
   San Bruno Mountain SP, 298 acres
   San Gregorio SB, 172 acres
   Thornton SB, 58 acres
   Tomales Bay SP, 2,001 acres
Water Area
   Lakes and rivers: 158,080 acres
   Pacific coast: 34,840 acres
Zoos
   San Francisco Zoological Gardens
Score: **93.48**   Rank: **24**

San Jose, CA
Amusement & Theme Parks
   Paramount's Great America
   Raging Waters
College NCAA I Sports
   San Jose State Spartans
   Santa Clara Broncos
   Stanford Cardinals
Gambling
   4 Casinos
Golf Courses
   6 Daily fee, 108 holes
   9 Municipal, 144 holes
   9 Private, 162 holes
Good Restaurants
   2 Simple ◆
   7 Family ◆◆
   16 Adult ◆◆◆
   2 Upscale ◆◆◆◆
Movie Theatres
   14 Singles/Twins; 22 Multiplexes
   216 Screens
Professional Sports
   Clash (MLS Soccer)
   Giants (Class A Baseball)
   Sharks (NHL Hockey)
Recreation Areas
   Federal
      San Francisco Bay NWR, 3,566 acres
   State
      Castle Rock SP, 50 acres
      Henry W. Coe SP, 41,038 acres
Water Area
   Lakes and rivers: 8,320 acres

Zoos
   Happy Hollow Zoo
   Palo Alto Junior Museum
   San Jose Baby Zoo
Score: **64.87**   Rank: **125**

San Luis Obispo-Atascadero-Paso Robles, CA
College NCAA I Sports
   California State Polytechnic Mustangs
Gambling
   3 Casinos
Golf Courses
   6 Daily fee, 108 holes
   5 Municipal, 72 holes
   2 Private, 27 holes
Good Restaurants
   9 Simple ◆
   24 Family ◆◆
   12 Adult ◆◆◆
Movie Theatres
   6 Singles/Twins; 3 Multiplexes
   28 Screens
Recreation Areas
   Federal
      Los Padres NF, 188,944 acres
   State
      Cayuccos SB, 16 acres
      Los Osos Oaks SR, 85 acres
      Montana De Oro SP, 8,400 acres
      Morro Bay SP, 2,749 acres
      Morro Strand SB, 117 acres
      Pismo Dunes SVRA, 2,500 acres
      Pismo SB, 1,051 acres
      San Simeon SP, 541 acres
      William Randolph Hearst SB, 8 acres
Water Area
   Lakes and rivers: 12,160 acres
   Pacific coast: 34,840 acres
Zoos
   Charles Paddock Zoo
Score: **45.6**   Rank: **193**

Santa Barbara-Santa Maria-Lompoc, CA
Amusement & Theme Parks
   Neverland Valley Ranch
College NCAA I Sports
   U of California Gauchos
Gambling
   2 Casinos
Golf Courses
   11 Daily fee, 153 holes
   1 Municipal, 18 holes
   8 Private, 144 holes
Good Restaurants
   5 Simple ◆
   17 Family ◆◆
   10 Adult ◆◆◆
   1 Upscale ◆◆◆◆
Movie Theatres
   8 Singles/Twins; 6 Multiplexes
   44 Screens

Recreation Areas
   Federal
      Channel Islands NP, 69,816 acres
      Los Padres NF, 629,118 acres
   State
      Carpinteria SB, 84 acres
      El Capitan SB, 133 acres
      Gaviota SP, 2,790 acres
      Point Sal SB, 84 acres
      Refugio SB, 155 acres
Water Area
   Lakes and rivers: 8,320 acres
   Pacific coast: 66,496 acres
Zoos
   Santa Barbara Zoological Gardens
Score: **65.43**   Rank: **123**

Santa Cruz-Watsonville, CA
Amusement & Theme Parks
   Santa Cruz Beach Boardwalk
Gambling
   9 Casinos
Golf Courses
   8 Daily fee, 117 holes
   1 Municipal, 18 holes
Good Restaurants
   6 Family ◆◆
   2 Adult ◆◆◆
Movie Theatres
   7 Singles/Twins; 3 Multiplexes
   27 Screens
Recreation Areas
   Federal
      Ellicott Slough NWR, 133 acres
   State
      Big Basin Redwoods SP, 17,092 acres
      Castle Rock SP, 3,650 acres
      Forest of Nisene Marks SP,
         10,121 acres
      Henry Cowell Redwoods SP,
         4,300 acres
      Lighthouse Field SB, 38 acres
      Manresa SB, 83 acres
      Natural Bridges SB, 65 acres
      New Brighton SB, 94 acres
      Seacliff SB, 85 acres
      Sunset SB, 324 acres
      Twin Lakes SB, 110 acres
      Wilder Ranch SP, 4,505 acres
Water Area
   Lakes and rivers: 640 acres
   Pacific coast: 53,120 acres
Score: **26.34**   Rank: **261**

Santa Fe, NM
Gambling
   3 Casinos
   Downs at Santa Fe (thoroughbred)
Golf Courses
   1 Daily fee, 18 holes
   2 Municipal, 36 holes
   2 Private, 27 holes

Good Restaurants
5 Simple ◆
8 Family ◆ ◆
8 Adult ◆ ◆ ◆
Movie Theatres
1 Single/Twin; 3 Multiplexes
20 Screens
Recreation Areas
Federal
Bandelier NM, 7,309 acres
Santa Fe NF, 275,838 acres
State
Hyde Memorial SP, 350 acres
Santa Fe River SP, 5 acres
Skiing
4 ski areas
Lift capacity/hour: 25,600
Water Area
Lakes and rivers: 1,280 acres
Score: 15.01   Rank: 301

Santa Rosa, CA
Amusement & Theme Parks
Windsor Waterworks & Slide
Auto Racing
Sears Point Raceway
Gambling
2 Casinos
Golf Courses
12 Daily fee, 189 holes
4 Municipal, 81 holes
2 Private, 27 holes
Good Restaurants
1 Simple ◆
5 Family ◆ ◆
3 Adult ◆ ◆ ◆
Movie Theatres
2 Singles/Twins; 7 Multiplexes
39 Screens
Recreation Areas
Federal
San Pablo Bay NWR, 249 acres
State
Annadel SP, 5,000 acres
Armstrong Redwoods SR, 752 acres
Austin Creek SRA, 4,236 acres
Bothe-Napa Valley SP, 203 acres
Kruse Rhododendron SR, 317 acres
Robert Louis Stevenson SP, 1,538 acres
Salt Point SP, 5,970 acres
Sonoma Coast SB, 5,000 acres
Sugarloaf Ridge SP, 2,514 acres
Water Area
Lakes and rivers: 18,560 acres
Pacific coast: 10,432 acres
Score: 59.20   Rank: 145

★Sarasota-Bradenton, FL
Gambling
Sarasota Kennel Club (greyhound)
Golf Courses
39 Daily fee, 747 holes
5 Municipal, 126 holes
18 Private, 459 holes

Good Restaurants
5 Simple ◆
38 Family ◆ ◆
19 Adult ◆ ◆ ◆
1 Upscale ◆ ◆ ◆ ◆
Movie Theatres
1 Single/Twin; 10 Multiplexes
90 Screens
Professional Sports
Red Sox (Class A Baseball)
Sundogs (USBL Basketball)
Recreation Areas
Federal
Passage Key NWR, 36 acres
State
Lake Manatee SRA, 556 acres
Myakka River SP, 28,875 acres
Oscar Scherer SRA, 1,377 acres
Water Area
Lakes and rivers: 56,960 acres
Gulf coast: 13,824 acres
Score: 94.33   Rank: 21

Saskatoon, SK
College CIAU Sports
U of Saskatchewan Huskies
Gambling
1 Casino
Marquis Downs (mixed meetings)
Golf Courses
2 Daily fee, 36 holes
8 Municipal, 108 holes
2 Private, 36 holes
Good Restaurants
3 Family ◆ ◆
Movie Theatres
4 Singles/Twins; 4 Multiplexes
29 Screens
Recreation Areas
Federal
Bradwell NWA, 304 acres
Last Mountain Lake Bird Sanctuary,
11,713 acres
Last Mountain Lake NWA,
38,553 acres
Prairie NWA, 7,448 acres
Stalwart NWA, 3,608 acres
Sutherland Bird Sanctuary, 321 acres
Provincial
Blackstrap PP, 1,300 acres
Coldwell Park, 259 acres
Elbow Harbou, 482 acres
Etter's Beach, 363 acres
Otapasoo Trails, 321 acres
Pike Lake PP, 1,236 acres
Skiing
2 ski areas
Lift capacity/hour: 4,400
Water Area
Lakes and rivers: 47,000 acres
Zoos
Forestry Farm Zoo
Score: 41.07   Rank: 209

Savannah, GA
Amusement & Theme Parks
Tybee Island Park
Gambling
2 Casinos
Golf Courses
8 Daily fee, 135 holes
2 Municipal, 45 holes
3 Private, 135 holes
Good Restaurants
5 Simple ◆
14 Family ◆ ◆
4 Adult ◆ ◆ ◆
Movie Theatres
3 Multiplexes
25 Screens
Professional Sports
Sand Gnats (Class A Baseball)
Recreation Areas
Federal
Fort Pulaski NM, 5,365 acres
Savannah Coastal NWR,
12,011 acres
Wassaw NWR, 10,050 acres
State
Skidaway Island SP, 533 acres
Water Area
Lakes and rivers: 44,800 acres
Atlantic coast: 13,440 acres
Zoos
Oatland Island Education Center
Score: 76.77   Rank: 83

Scranton–Wilkes-Barre–Hazleton, PA
Gambling
Pocono Downs (harness)
Golf Courses
27 Daily fee, 378 holes
2 Municipal, 27 holes
13 Private, 225 holes
Good Restaurants
10 Simple ◆
16 Family ◆ ◆
12 Adult ◆ ◆ ◆
1 Upscale ◆ ◆ ◆ ◆
Movie Theatres
6 Singles/Twins; 9 Multiplexes
63 Screens
Professional Sports
Red Barons (Triple A Baseball)
Recreation Areas
State
Archbald Pothole SP, 153 acres
Frances Slocum SP, 1,035 acres
Lackawanna SP, 1,411 acres
Lehigh Gorge SP, 271 acres
Nescopeck SP, 2,981 acres
Ricketts Glen SP, 11,258 acres
Skiing
21 ski areas
Lift capacity/hour: 166,400
Water Area
Lakes and rivers: 21,760 acres
Score: 71.95   Rank: 100

★**Seattle-Bellevue-Everett, WA**
Amusement & Theme Parks
  Enchanted Village/Wild Waves
Aquariums
  Seattle Aquarium
Auto Racing
  Evergreen Speedway
College NCAA I Sports
  U of Washington Huskies
Gambling
  20 Casinos
  Longacres Park (mixed meetings)
Golf Courses
  31 Daily fee, 495 holes
  17 Municipal, 288 holes
  23 Private, 369 holes
Good Restaurants
  6 Simple ♦
  53 Family ♦♦
  57 Adult ♦♦♦
  3 Upscale ♦♦♦♦
Movie Theatres
  21 Singles/Twins; 34 Multiplexes
  270 Screens
Professional Sports
  Everett Aquasox (Class A Baseball)
  Mariners (AL Baseball)
  Seahawks (NFL Football)
  Supersonics (NBA Basketball)
Recreation Areas
  Federal
    Ebey's Landing NHR, 1,646 acres
    Mt. Baker NF, 463,381 acres
    San Juan Islands NWR, 65 acres
    Snoqualmie NF, 506,062 acres
  State
    Black Diamond SP, 163 acres
    Bridle Trails SP, 480 acres
    Cama Beach, 224 acres
    Camano Island SP, 134 acres
    Dash Point SP, 230 acres
    Deception Pass SP, 2,515 acres
    Ebey's Landing SP, 46 acres
    Everett Jetty SP, 160 acres
    Federation Forest SP, 619 acres
    Flaming Geyser SP, 667 acres
    Fort Casey SP, 421 acres
    Fort Ebey SP, 644 acres
    Hanging Gardens SP, 369 acres
    Iron Horse West SP, 613 acres
    Jellum SP, 367 acres
    Joseph Whidbey SP, 112 acres
    Kanaskat-Palmer SP, 391 acres
    Lake Sammamish SP, 510 acres
    Lord Hill, 1,769 acres
    Lower Green River SP, 74 acres
    Mahler SP, 30 acres
    Mercer Slough SP, 85 acres
    Mount Pilchuck SP, 1,893 acres
    Mukilteo SP, 18 acres
    Nolte SP, 117 acres
    Olallie SP, 539 acres
    Saltwater SP, 88 acres

    Skykomish River SP, 39 acres
    South Whidbey SP, 349 acres
    Squak Mountain SP, 1,008 acres
    Useless Bay, 1 acre
    Wallace Falls SP, 1,403 acres
    Wenberg SP, 46 acres
    West Hylebos SP, 58 acres
Skiing
  7 ski areas
  Lift capacity/hour: 88,405
Water Area
  Lakes and rivers: 71,040 acres
  Puget Sound coast: 39,120 acres
Zoos
  Washington Zoological Park
  Woodland Park Zoological Gardens
Score: 90.65   **Rank: 34**

Sharon, PA
Golf Courses
  10 Daily fee, 162 holes
  4 Private, 72 holes
Good Restaurants
  1 Simple ♦
  3 Family ♦♦
  1 Upscale ♦♦♦♦
Movie Theatres
  1 Multiplex
  8 Screens
Recreation Areas
  State
    Goddard SP, 2,857 acres
Skiing
  1 ski area
  Lift capacity/hour: 2,400
Water Area
  Lakes and rivers: 7,040 acres
Score: 29.74   **Rank: 249**

Sheboygan, WI
Auto Racing
  Road America
Golf Courses
  8 Daily fee, 153 holes
  1 Private, 18 holes
Good Restaurants
  1 Simple ♦
  1 Family ♦♦
  6 Adult ♦♦♦
  2 Upscale ♦♦♦♦
Movie Theatres
  1 Multiplex
  10 Screens
Recreation Areas
  State
    Kohler-Andrae S, 962 acres
Skiing
  5 ski areas
  Lift capacity/hour: 6,900
Water Area
  Lakes and rivers: 2,560 acres
  Lakes Michigan coast: 48,192 acres
Score: 62.60   **Rank: 133**

Sherbrooke, PQ
College CIAU Sports
  Bishop's U Gaiters
Golf Courses
  3 Daily fee, 45 holes
  2 Municipal, 27 holes
Good Restaurants
  1 Simple ♦
  2 Family ♦♦
  2 Adult ♦♦♦
  2 Upscale ♦♦♦♦
Movie Theatres
  3 Multiplexes
  19 Screens
Recreation Areas
  Provincial
    Mount-Orford PP, 14,423 acres
    Tantare Reserve, 3,684 acres
Skiing
  12 ski areas
  Lift capacity/hour: 31,606
Water Area
  Lakes and rivers: 45,000 acres
Score: 23.79   **Rank: 270**

Sherman-Denison, TX
Golf Courses
  3 Daily fee, 54 holes
  1 Private, 18 holes
Movie Theatres
  2 Multiplexes
  12 Screens
Recreation Areas
  State
    Eisenhower SRA, 457 acres
Water Area
  Lakes and rivers: 29,440 acres
Score: 26.62   **Rank: 260**

Shreveport-Bossier City, LA
Amusement & Theme Parks
  Hamel's Park
College NCAA I Sports
  Centenary College Gentlemen
Gambling
  4 Casinos
  Louisiana Downs (thoroughbred)
Golf Courses
  6 Daily fee, 81 holes
  3 Municipal, 45 holes
  9 Private, 126 holes
Good Restaurants
  3 Simple ♦
  9 Family ♦♦
  1 Adult ♦♦♦
  2 Upscale ♦♦♦♦
Movie Theatres
  5 Multiplexes
  33 Screens
Professional Sports
  Captains (Class AA Baseball)
Recreation Areas
  Federal
    Kisatchee NF, 12,456 acres

State
    Bickham Dickson SP, 585 acres
    Lake Bistineau SP, 750 acres
Water Area
    Lakes and rivers: 65,920 acres
Score: **59.49**   Rank: **144**

Sioux City, IA-NE
Gambling
    3 Casinos
    Atokad Park (thoroughbred)
Golf Courses
    10 Daily fee, 126 holes
    2 Municipal, 36 holes
    2 Private, 27 holes
Good Restaurants
    4 Simple ♦
    2 Family ♦♦
Movie Theatres
    2 Singles/Twins; 1 Multiplex
    16 Screens
Skiing
    1 ski area
    Lift capacity/hour: 2,270
Water Area
    Lakes and rivers: 5,120 acres
Score: **24.36**   Rank: **268**

Sioux Falls, SD
Amusement & Theme Parks
    Wild Water West Waterpark
Golf Courses
    5 Daily fee, 63 holes
    4 Municipal, 72 holes
    3 Private, 54 holes
Good Restaurants
    5 Simple ♦
    6 Family ♦♦
    4 Adult ♦♦♦
Movie Theatres
    1 Single/Twin; 3 Multiplexes
    21 Screens
Professional Sports
    Sky Force (CBA Basketball)
Recreation Areas
    State
        Beaver Creek SNA, 160 acres
        Big Sioux SRA, 430 acres
        Newton Hills SP, 948 acres
        Palisades SP, 157 acres
Water Area
    Lakes and rivers: 3,200 acres
Zoos
    Great Plains Zoo
Score: **34.27**   Rank: **233**

South Bend, IN
College NCAA I Sports
    Notre Dame Fighting Irish
Golf Courses
    5 Daily fee, 63 holes
    5 Municipal, 81 holes
    4 Private, 81 holes

Good Restaurants
    1 Adult ♦♦♦
    2 Upscale ♦♦♦♦
Movie Theatres
    6 Multiplexes
    48 Screens
Professional Sports
    Silver Hawks (Class A Baseball)
Recreation Areas
    State
        Potato Creek SP, 3,815 acres
Skiing
    2 ski areas
    Lift capacity/hour: 10,600
Water Area
    Lakes and rivers: 2,560 acres
Zoos
    Potawatomi Zoo
Score: **46.74**   Rank: **189**

Spokane, WA
College NCAA I Sports
    Eastern Washington Eagles
    Gonzaga Zags
Gambling
    Playfair Race Course (mixed meetings)
Golf Courses
    6 Daily fee, 81 holes
    7 Municipal, 126 holes
    2 Private, 36 holes
Good Restaurants
    3 Simple ♦
    5 Family ♦♦
    6 Adult ♦♦♦
Movie Theatres
    2 Singles/Twins; 7 Multiplexes
    38 Screens
Professional Sports
    Indians (Class A Baseball)
Recreation Areas
    Federal
        Turnbull NWR, 15,468 acres
    State
        Centennial Trail SP, 374 acres
        Mount Spokane SP, 13,821 acres
        Pasco/Fish Lake Trail, 255 acres
        Riverside SP, 7,188 acres
        Spokane River Cent Trail, 376 acres
Skiing
    3 ski areas
    Lift capacity/hour: 16,200
Water Area
    Lakes and rivers: 10,880 acres
Zoos
    Inland Northwest Zoo
Score: **39.94**   Rank: **213**

Springfield, IL
Golf Courses
    8 Daily fee, 117 holes
    4 Municipal, 54 holes
    2 Private, 36 holes

Good Restaurants
    1 Simple ♦
    3 Family ♦♦
    1 Adult ♦♦♦
    1 Upscale ♦♦♦♦
Movie Theatres
    2 Singles/Twins; 4 Multiplexes
    28 Screens
Water Area
    Lakes and rivers: 6,400 acres
Zoos
    Henson Robinson Zoo
Score: **30.31**   Rank: **247**

Springfield, MA
Amusement & Theme Parks
    Riverside Park
College NCAA I Sports
    U of Massachusetts Minutemen
Golf Courses
    17 Daily fee, 261 holes
    5 Municipal, 81 holes
    7 Private, 126 holes
Good Restaurants
    1 Simple ♦
    7 Family ♦♦
    4 Adult ♦♦♦
Movie Theatres
    10 Singles/Twins; 4 Multiplexes
    56 Screens
Professional Sports
    Falcons (AHL Hockey)
Recreation Areas
    State
        Chicopee Memorial SP, 574 acres
        Deer Hill SP, 259 acres
        Elwell SP, 1 acre
        Gardner SP, 29 acres
        Hampton Ponds SP, 42 acres
        Holyoke Range SP, 2,936 acres
        Lake Lorraine SP, 2 acres
        Mt. Tom SR, 1,800 acres
        Red Bridge SP, 42 acres
        Robinson SP, 811 acres
        Skinner SP, 390 acres
Skiing
    23 ski areas
    Lift capacity/hour: 132,380
Water Area
    Lakes and rivers: 15,768 acres
Zoos
    Forest Park Children's Zoo
    Museum of Zoology
Score: **66.57**   Rank: **119**

Springfield, MO
College NCAA I Sports
    Southwest Missouri State Bears
Golf Courses
    7 Daily fee, 117 holes
    4 Municipal, 63 holes
    5 Private, 90 holes

Good Restaurants
4 Simple ◆
3 Family ◆◆
2 Adult ◆◆◆
Movie Theatres
8 Multiplexes
57 Screens
Recreation Areas
Federal
    Mark Twain NF, 51,692 acres
Skiing
1 ski area
Lift capacity/hour: 3,500
Water Area
Lakes and rivers: 2,560 acres
Zoos
Dickerson Park Zoo
Score: **41.64**   Rank: **207**

Stamford-Norwalk, CT
Golf Courses
1 Daily fee, 18 holes
7 Municipal, 126 holes
18 Private, 324 holes
Good Restaurants
1 Simple ◆
3 Family ◆◆
7 Adult ◆◆◆
1 Upscale ◆◆◆◆
Movie Theatres
9 Singles/Twins; 4 Multiplexes
44 Screens
Recreation Areas
State
    Mianus SP, 335 acres
    Sherwood Island SP, 234 acres
Water Area
Lakes and rivers: 46,620 acres
Atlantic coast: 11,520 acres
Score: **34.56**   Rank: **232**

State College, PA
College NCAA I Sports
Penn State Nittany Lions
Golf Courses
5 Daily fee, 90 holes
1 Private, 9 holes
Good Restaurants
2 Simple ◆
3 Family ◆◆
2 Adult ◆◆◆
Movie Theatres
4 Singles/Twins; 2 Multiplexes
17 Screens
Recreation Areas
State
    Bald Eagle SP, 5,900 acres
    Black Moshannon SP, 3,394 acres
    McCall Dam SP, 8 acres
    Penn Roosevelt SP, 41 acres
    Poe Paddy SP, 23 acres
    Poe Valley SP, 620 acres

Skiing
2 ski areas
Lift capacity/hour: 10,000
Water Area
Lakes and rivers: 2,560 acres
Score: **35.97**   Rank: **227**

Steubenville-Weirton, OH-WV
Gambling
Mountaineer Park (thoroughbred)
Golf Courses
9 Daily fee, 135 holes
2 Municipal, 27 holes
4 Private, 63 holes
Movie Theatres
1 Single/Twin; 1 Multiplex
8 Screens
Recreation Areas
State
    Jefferson Lake SP, 906 acres
    Tomlinson Run SP, 1,398 acres
Skiing
4 ski areas
Lift capacity/hour: 52,800
Water Area
Lakes and rivers: 5,760 acres
Score: **13.31**   Rank: **307**

Stockton-Lodi, CA
College NCAA I Sports
U of the Pacific Tigers
Gambling
4 Casinos
Golf Courses
5 Daily fee, 72 holes
3 Municipal, 54 holes
8 Private, 135 holes
Good Restaurants
1 Simple ◆
2 Family ◆◆
1 Adult ◆◆◆
Movie Theatres
1 Single/Twin; 6 Multiplexes
40 Screens
Professional Sports
Ports (Class A Baseball)
Recreation Areas
State
    Caswell Memorial SP, 258 acres
    Durham Ferry SRA, 183 acres
Water Area
Lakes and rivers: 17,280 acres
Zoos
Micke Grove Zoo
Score: **32.29**   Rank: **240**

Sudbury, ON
College CIAU Sports
Laurentian Voyageurs
Gambling
1 Casino
Golf Courses
1 Daily fee, 18 holes
3 Municipal, 45 holes
1 Private, 18 holes

Good Restaurants
2 Simple ◆
3 Family ◆◆
1 Adult ◆◆◆
Movie Theatres
1 Single/Twin; 2 Multiplexes
8 Screens
Skiing
5 ski areas
Lift capacity/hour: 8,700
Water Area
Lakes and rivers: 186,000 acres
Score: **43.05**   Rank: **202**

Sumter, SC
Golf Courses
3 Daily fee, 54 holes
1 Municipal, 9 holes
2 Private, 36 holes
Good Restaurants
1 Family ◆◆
Movie Theatres
2 Singles/Twins; 1 Multiplex
7 Screens
Recreation Areas
State
    Poinsett SP, 1,000 acres
    Woods Bay SP, 924 acres
Water Area
Lakes and rivers: 10,880 acres
Score: **7.64**   Rank: **327**

★Syracuse, NY
College NCAA I Sports
Colgate Red Raiders
Syracuse Orangemen
Gambling
Syracuse Mile (harness)
Golf Courses
54 Daily fee, 855 holes
4 Municipal, 54 holes
17 Private, 279 holes
Good Restaurants
3 Simple ◆
20 Family ◆◆
11 Adult ◆◆◆
2 Upscale ◆◆◆◆
Movie Theatres
4 Singles/Twins; 10 Multiplexes
91 Screens
Professional Sports
Crunch (AHL Hockey)
Doubledays (Class A Baseball)
Sky Chiefs (Triple A Baseball)
Recreation Areas
State
    Battle Island SP, 235 acres
    Chittenango Falls SP, 193 acres
    Clark Reservation, 326 acres
    Fair Haven Beach SP, 739 acres
    Fillmore Glen SP, 941 acres
    Green Lakes SP, 1,400 acres
    Long Point SP, 229 acres
    Mexico Point Boat Launch SP,
        20 acres

Otisco Lake Boat Launch SP, 4 acres
Owasco Lake Marine Park, 1 acre
Selkirk Shores SP, 980 acres
South Shore Boat Launch SP,
12 acres
Skiing
25 ski areas
Lift capacity/hour: 119,625
Water Area
Lakes and rivers: 88,960 acres
Lake Ontario coast: 21,568 acres
Zoos
Burnet Park Zoo
Score: 95.46   **Rank: 17**

Tacoma, WA
Gambling
9 Casinos
Golf Courses
12 Daily fee, 189 holes
4 Municipal, 72 holes
8 Private, 135 holes
Good Restaurants
5 Simple ♦
13 Family ♦♦
6 Adult ♦♦♦
Movie Theatres
5 Singles/Twins; 8 Multiplexes
58 Screens
Professional Sports
Tacoma Raniers (Triple A Baseball)
Recreation Areas
Federal
Mount Ranier NP, 206,441 acres
Nisqually NWR, 808 acres
Snoqualmie NF, 124,579 acres
State
Dash Point SP, 168 acres
Eagle Island SP, 10 acres
Haley Property, 178 acres
Joemma Beach, 122 acres
Kopachuck SP, 113 acres
Nisqually, 441 acres
Pensrose Point SP, 152 acres
Puyallup 40 SP, 40 acres
Steilacom Lake Tidelands SP, 1 acre
Skiing
3 ski areas
Lift capacity/hour: 51,125
Water Area
Lakes and rivers: 73,600 acres
Puget Sound coast: 1,024 acres
Zoos
Port Defiance Zoo
Score: 69.97   **Rank: 107**

Tallahassee, FL
College NCAA I Sports
Florida A & M Rattlers
Florida State Seminoles
Gambling
Golden Crown (jai-alai)

Golf Courses
4 Daily fee, 63 holes
3 Municipal, 36 holes
4 Private, 72 holes
Good Restaurants
2 Simple ♦
6 Family ♦♦
1 Adult ♦♦♦
Movie Theatres
1 Single/Twin; 6 Multiplexes
59 Screens
Professional Sports
Tallahassee Tiger Sharks (ECHL Hockey)
Recreation Areas
Federal
Appalachicola NF, 104,568 acres
State
Lake Talquin SRA, 607 acres
Water Area
Lakes and rivers: 30,080 acres
Zoos
Tallahassee Junior Museum
Score: 61.18   **Rank: 138**

★Tampa-St. Petersburg-Clearwater, FL
Amusement & Theme Parks
Adventure Island
Busch Gardens Tampa Bay
Aquariums
C.M.S.C. Aquarium
College NCAA I Sports
U of South Florida Bulls
Gambling
2 Casinos
St. Petersburg Kennel Club (greyhound)
Tampa Bay Downs (thoroughbred)
Tampa Greyhound Track
Golf Courses
66 Daily fee, 1269 holes
12 Municipal, 216 holes
38 Private, 927 holes
Good Restaurants
19 Simple ♦
76 Family ♦♦
25 Adult ♦♦♦
3 Upscale ♦♦♦♦
Movie Theatres
8 Singles/Twins; 34 Multiplexes
287 Screens
Professional Sports
Buccaneers (NFL Football)
Clearwater Phillies (Class A Baseball)
Dunedin Blue Jays (Class A Baseball)
Lightning (NHL Hockey)
Mutiny (MLS Soccer)
St. Petersburg Devil Rays (Class A
Baseball)
Tampa Bay Devil Rays (AL Baseball)
Tampa Yankees (Class A Baseball)
Windjammers (USBL Basketball)
Recreation Areas
Federal
Chassahowitzka NWR, 7,113 acres
Egmont Key NWR, 328 acres
Pinellas NWR, 17 acres

State
Anclote Key SNA, 287 acres
Caladesi Island SP, 631 acres
Egmont Key SP, 381 acres
Hillsborough River SP, 3,738 acres
Honeymoon Island SRA, 2,400 acres
Little Manatee River SRA, 2,010 acres
Water Area
Lakes and rivers: 97,280 acres
Gulf coast: 40,000 acres
Zoos
Busch Gardens
Lowry Park Zoological Garden
Score: 98.01   **Rank: 8**

Terre Haute, IN
College NCAA I Sports
Indiana State Sycamores
Golf Courses
6 Daily fee, 90 holes
5 Municipal, 72 holes
2 Private, 27 holes
Good Restaurants
6 Family ♦♦
1 Adult ♦♦♦
Movie Theatres
2 Multiplexes
11 Screens
Recreation Areas
State
Shakamak SP, 942 acres
Water Area
Lakes and rivers: 8,320 acres
Score: 24.64   **Rank: 267**

Texarkana, TX-Texarkana, AR
Golf Courses
2 Daily fee, 27 holes
3 Private, 45 holes
Good Restaurants
1 Simple ♦
1 Family ♦♦
Movie Theatres
1 Multiplex
12 Screens
Water Area
Lakes and rivers: 30,720 acres
Score: 3.96   **Rank: 340**

Thunder Bay, ON
College CIAU Sports
Lakehead Nor'westers
Gambling
1 Casino
Golf Courses
1 Daily fee, 18 holes
4 Municipal, 54 holes
2 Private, 18 holes
Good Restaurants
2 Family ♦♦
3 Adult ♦♦♦
Movie Theatres
2 Singles/Twins; 2 Multiplexes
17 Screens

Professional Sports
Senators (CoHL Hockey)
Recreation Areas
Federal
Pukaskwa National Park,
464,004 acres
Provincial
Albert Lake Mesa PP, 321 acres
Arrow Lake PP, 1,063 acres
Arrowhead Peninsula, 2,014 acres
Bat Cove Wilderness Area, 178 acres
Castle Creek, 2,656 acres
Cavern Lake, 467 acres
Clearwater Lake, 1,035 acres
Craigs Pit, 1,310 acres
Devon Road Mesa, 148 acres
Divide Ridge, 581 acres
Edward Island, 1,483 acres
Fraleigh Lake, 2,039 acres
Geikie Island Crown Game Preserve,
13,657 acres
Gravel River, 1,310 acres
Kabitotikwia River, 4,856 acres
Kaiashk Reserve, 568 acres
Kakabeka Falls PP, 1,038 acres
Kashabowie PP, 5,078 acres
Klotz Lake PP, 294 acres
Lake Nipigon PP, 3,603 acres
Le Pate Nature Reserve PP, 618 acres
Little Greenwater Lake, 603 acres
Livingstone Point, 4,448 acres
Mac Leod PP, 183 acres
Matawin River, 6,462 acres
Michipicoten Island PP, 90,785 acres
Middle Falls PP, 2,241 acres
Neys PP, 8,513 acres
Ouimet Canyon Reserve, 1,920 acres
Outer Barn Island Wilderness Area,
161 acres
Pantagruel Creek Reserve,
5,436 acres
Pigeon River Clay Plain, 7,092 acres
Porphyry Island, 264 acres
Prairie River Mouth, 939 acres
Rainbow Falls PP, 1,421 acres
Red Sucker Point PP, 890 acres
Sedgman Lake PP, 14,109 acres
Shesheeb Bay PP, 680 acres
Sibley PP, 60,379 acres
Silver Falls PP, 8,058 acres
Sleeping Giant Wilderness Area,
633 acres
Thompson Island, 358 acres
Wabakimi Wilderness PP,
383,005 acres
West Bay Reserve PP, 2,768 acres
White Lake PP, 4,265 acres
Windigo Bay, 20,509 acres
Water Area
Lakes and rivers: 250,000 acres
Lake Superior coast: 55,000 acres
Zoos
Chippewa Park Zoo
Score: **80.16**   Rank: **71**

562

Toledo, OH
College NCAA I Sports
Bowling Green State Falcons
U of Toledo Rockets
Gambling
Raceway Park (harness)
Golf Courses
15 Daily fee, 252 holes
5 Municipal, 72 holes
8 Private, 153 holes
Good Restaurants
4 Simple ◇
7 Family ◇◇
Movie Theatres
3 Singles/Twins; 8 Multiplexes
61 Screens
Professional Sports
Mud Hens (Triple A Baseball)
Storm (ECHL Hockey)
Recreation Areas
Federal
Cedar Point NWR, 2,445 acres
Ottawa NWR, 2,078 acres
West Sister Island NWR, 77 acres
State
Crane Creek SP, 852 acres
Goll Woods SNA, 321 acres
Harrison Lake SP, 142 acres
Irwin Prairie SNA, 187 acres
Mary Jane Thurston SP, 104 acres
Maumee Bay SP, 1,736 acres
Water Area
Lakes and rivers: 8,960 acres
Lake Ontario coast: 13,400 acres
Zoos
Toledo Zoological Gardens
Score: **69.12**   Rank: **110**

Topeka, KS
Auto Racing
Heartland Park Topeka
Golf Courses
3 Daily fee, 45 holes
3 Municipal, 45 holes
3 Private, 54 holes
Good Restaurants
1 Simple ◇
5 Family ◇◇
Movie Theatres
3 Multiplexes
18 Screens
Water Area
Lakes and rivers: 3,840 acres
Zoos
Gage Park Zoo
Topeka Zoological Park
Score: **22.09**   Rank: **276**

★Toronto, ON
Amusement & Theme Parks
Centreville Park
Ontario Place
Auto Racing
Molson Indy Toronto

College CIAU Sports
Ryerson Polytechnical Institute Rams
U of Toronto Varsity Blues
York Yeomen
Gambling
Greenwood Race Course (mixed
meetings)
Orangeville Raceway (harness)
Golf Courses
33 Daily fee, 531 holes
16 Municipal, 252 holes
35 Private, 587 holes
Good Restaurants
14 Simple ◇
63 Family ◇◇
65 Adult ◇◇◇
13 Upscale ◇◇◇◇
1 Best ◇◇◇◇◇
Movie Theatres
27 Singles/Twins; 46 Multiplexes
331 Screens
Professional Sports
Argonauts (CFL Football)
Blue Jays (AL Baseball)
Maple Leafs (NHL Hockey)
Raptors (NBA Basketball)
Recreation Areas
Federal
Fielding MBS, 3,212 acres
Wye Marsh NWA, 116 acres
Provincial
Awenda PP, 7,208 acres
Bronte Creek PP, 1,581 acres
Earl Rowe PP, 771 acres
Fairbank PP, 259 acres
Holland Marsh Wildlife Area,
1,416 acres
Matchedash Bay Wildlife Area,
556 acres
Mc Rae Point PP, 341 acres
Noisy River Reserve, 964 acres
Springwater PP, 116 acres
Tiny Marsh Wildlife Area,
1,401 acres
Wasaga Beach PP, 3,818 acres
Wye Marsh Wildlife Area,
2,271 acres
Skiing
18 ski areas
Lift capacity/hour: 36,699
Water Area
Lakes and rivers: 82,000 acres
Lake Ontario coast: 134,400 acres
Zoos
Metropolitan Toronto Zoo
Score: **97.45**   Rank: **10**

Trenton, NJ
College NCAA I Sports
Princeton Tigers
Rider College Broncs
Golf Courses
3 Daily fee, 54 holes
3 Municipal, 54 holes
7 Private, 117 holes

Good Restaurants
7 Simple ♦
3 Family ♦♦
9 Adult ♦♦♦
Movie Theatres
6 Multiplexes
42 Screens
Professional Sports
Thunder (Class AA Baseball)
Skiing
1 ski area
Lift capacity/hour: 1,500
Water Area
Lakes and rivers: 1,920 acres
Score: **45.04**   Rank: **195**

Trois-Rivieres, PQ
Auto Racing
Circuit Trois Rivieres
Gambling
Hippodrome Trois-Rivieres (harness)
Golf Courses
1 Municipal, 18 holes
4 Private, 63 holes
Good Restaurants
2 Family ♦♦
3 Adult ♦♦♦
1 Upscale ♦♦♦♦
Movie Theatres
1 Single/Twin; 3 Multiplexes
21 Screens
Skiing
11 ski areas
Lift capacity/hour: 19,366
Water Area
Lakes and rivers: 32,000 acres
Score: **3.11**   Rank: **343**

Tucson, AZ
Amusement & Theme Parks
Old Tucson Studios
College NCAA I Sports
U of Arizona Wildcats
Gambling
3 Casinos
Tucson Park (greyhound)
Golf Courses
19 Daily fee, 369 holes
5 Municipal, 108 holes
12 Private, 225 holes
Good Restaurants
4 Simple ♦
12 Family ♦♦
10 Adult ♦♦♦
5 Upscale ♦♦♦♦
1 Best ♦♦♦♦♦
Movie Theatres
2 Singles/Twins; 11 Multiplexes
83 Screens
Professional Sports
Sidewinders (Triple A Baseball)
Recreation Areas
Federal
Buenos Aires NWR, 113,642 acres
Cabeza Prieta NWR, 416,242 acres

Coronado NF, 390,326 acres
Grand Canyon NP, 1,424 acres
Organ Pipe Cactus NM,
329,316 acres
Saguaro NM, 85,686 acres
State
Catalina SP, 5,511 acres
Skiing
1 ski area
Lift capacity/hour: 800
Water Area
Lakes and rivers: 1,280 acres
Zoos
Arizona-Sonora Desert Museum
Reid Park Zoo
Score: **79.03**   Rank: **75**

Tulsa, OK
College NCAA I Sports
Oral Roberts Golden Eagles
U of Tulsa Golden Hurricane
Gambling
1 Casino
Fair Meadows (mixed meetings)
Will Rogers Downs (thoroughbred)
Golf Courses
14 Daily fee, 189 holes
8 Municipal, 198 holes
9 Private, 171 holes
Good Restaurants
9 Simple ♦
24 Family ♦♦
30 Adult ♦♦♦
6 Upscale ♦♦♦♦
Movie Theatres
1 Single/Twin; 12 Multiplexes
108 Screens
Professional Sports
Drillers (Class AA Baseball)
Recreation Areas
State
Heyburn SP, 438 acres
Lake Keystone SP, 715 acres
Osage Hills SP, 1,199 acres
Sequoyah Bay SP, 303 acres
Wah-Sha-She SP, 807 acres
Walnut Creek SP, 1,429 acres
Water Area
Lakes and rivers: 94,720 acres
Zoos
Tulsa Zoological Park
Score: **84.41**   Rank: **56**

Tuscaloosa, AL
College NCAA I Sports
U of Alabama Crimson Tide
Golf Courses
4 Daily fee, 72 holes
4 Private, 72 holes
Good Restaurants
2 Family ♦♦
Movie Theatres
2 Multiplexes
18 Screens

Recreation Areas
Federal
Talladega NF, 10,645 acres
State
Lake Lurleen SP, 1,625 acres
Water Area
Lakes and rivers: 17,280 acres
Score: **33.99**   Rank: **234**

Tyler, TX
Golf Courses
4 Daily fee, 108 holes
4 Private, 81 holes
Good Restaurants
1 Simple ♦
2 Family ♦♦
Movie Theatres
4 Multiplexes
19 Screens
Recreation Areas
State
Tyler SP, 986 acres
Water Area
Lakes and rivers: 13,440 acres
Zoos
Caldwell Zoo
Score: **27.76**   Rank: **256**

Utica-Rome, NY
Amusement & Theme Parks
Sylvan Beach Amusement Park
Gambling
Vernon Downs (harness)
Golf Courses
30 Daily fee, 414 holes
2 Municipal, 27 holes
8 Private, 108 holes
Good Restaurants
5 Simple ♦
16 Family ♦♦
1 Adult ♦♦♦
Movie Theatres
3 Singles/Twins; 1 Multiplex
10 Screens
Professional Sports
Blizzard (CoHL Hockey)
Blue Sox (Class A Baseball)
Recreation Areas
State
Alger Island SRA, 45 acres
Delta Lake SP, 400 acres
Fourth Lake SRA , 11 acres
Hinckley Reservoir SRA, 2,782 acres
Nicks Lake SRA, 320 acres
Pixley Falls SP, 375 acres
Verona Beach SP, 1,735 acres
Skiing
10 ski areas
Lift capacity/hour: 40,000
Water Area
Lakes and rivers: 58,240 acres
Zoos
Utica Zoo
Score: **78.47**   Rank: **77**

Vallejo-Fairfield-Napa, CA

Amusement & Theme Parks
Marine World Africa USA

Gambling
3 Casinos

Golf Courses
6 Daily fee, 99 holes
6 Municipal, 108 holes
7 Private, 126 holes

Good Restaurants
1 Simple ♦
6 Family ♦♦
6 Adult ♦♦♦
1 Upscale ♦♦♦♦

Movie Theatres
1 Single/Twin; 8 Multiplexes
58 Screens

Recreation Areas
Federal
San Pablo Bay NWR, 1,713 acres
State
Benicia SRA, 467 acres
Bothe-Napa Valley SP, 1,780 acres
Robert Louis Stevenson SP,
1,921 acres
Sugarloaf Ridge SP, 139 acres

Water Area
Lakes and rivers: 72,320 acres
Score: 64.58   Rank: 126

Vancouver, BC

Amusement & Theme Parks
Playland

Aquariums
Vancouver Public Aquarium

Auto Racing
Molson Indy Vancouver

College CIAU Sports
U of British Columbia Thunderbirds

Gambling
8 Casinos
Cloverdale Raceway (harness)
Hastings Park (thoroughbred)

Golf Courses
10 Daily fee, 162 holes
21 Municipal, 333 holes
11 Private, 198 holes

Good Restaurants
8 Simple ♦
47 Family ♦♦
36 Adult ♦♦♦
2 Upscale ♦♦♦♦
1 Best ♦♦♦♦♦

Movie Theatres
14 Singles/Twins; 23 Multiplexes
144 Screens

Professional Sports
BC Lions (CFL Football)
Canadians (Triple A Baseball)
Canuck (NHL Hockey)
Grizzlies (NBA Basketball)

Recreation Areas
Federal
Alaksen NWA, 741 acres
George Reifel MBS, 1,601 acres
Widgeon Valley NWA, 309 acres
Provincial
Bowen Island Reserve, 981 acres
Cypress PP, 7,443 acres
Davis Lake PP, 474 acres
Golden Ears PP (100%),
137,378 acres
Golden Ears PP (6.9%), 9,466 acres
Golden Ears PP (93.1%),
127,911 acres
Mount Judge Howay PP,
15,271 acres
Mount Seymour PP, 8,668 acres
Pitt Polder Reserve, 217 acres
Pitt-Addington Marsh, 10,027 acres
Rolley Lake PP, 284 acres

Skiing
5 ski areas
Lift capacity/hour: 67,336

Water Area
Lakes and rivers: 76,000 acres
Strait of Georgia coast: 35,000 acres

Zoos
Stanley Park Zoological Gardens
Score: 89.23   Rank: 39

Ventura, CA

Gambling
2 Casinos

Golf Courses
8 Daily fee, 126 holes
7 Municipal, 108 holes
8 Private, 153 holes

Good Restaurants
2 Simple ♦
9 Family ♦♦
4 Adult ♦♦♦

Movie Theatres
3 Singles/Twins; 14 Multiplexes
105 Screens

Recreation Areas
Federal
Angeles NF, 1,474 acres
Bitter Creek NWR, 122 acres
Channel Islands NP, 702 acres
Hopper Mountain NWR, 2,471 acres
Los Padres NF, 557,232 acres
Santa Monica Mountains NRA,
7,854 acres
State
Emma Wood SB, 116 acres
Hungry Valley SVRA, acres
Leo Carrillo SB, 45 acres
Mandalay SB, 92 acres
McGrath SB, 295 acres
Oxnard SB, 62 acres
Point Mugu SP, 14,980 acres
San Buenaventura SB, 116 acres

Skiing
3 ski areas
Lift capacity/hour: 11,100

Water Area
Lakes and rivers: 7,680 acres
Score: 54.67   Rank: 161

Victoria, BC

Aquariums
Sealand of the Pacific

College CIAU Sports
U of Victoria Vikes

Gambling
2 Casinos
Sandown Park (harness)

Golf Courses
5 Daily fee, 72 holes
5 Municipal, 72 holes
2 Private, 36 holes

Good Restaurants
6 Simple ♦
15 Family ♦♦
8 Adult ♦♦♦
1 Upscale ♦♦♦♦

Movie Theatres
3 Singles/Twins; 3 Multiplexes
20 Screens

Recreation Areas
Federal
Esquimalt Lagoon MBS, 321 acres
Shoal Harbour MBS, 371 acres
Victoria Harbour MBS, 4,201 acres
Provincial
Beaumont Marine PP, 143 acres
Botanical Beach PP, 867 acres
China Beach PP, 151 acres
D'Arcy Island PP, 208 acres
Dionisio Point PP, 351 acres
Discovery Island Marine PP, 151 acres
French Beach PP, 146 acres
Goldstream PP, 813 acres
John Dean PP, 430 acres
Matheson Lake PP , 400 acres
Montague Harbour PP, 240 acres
Mount Maxwell Reserve, 161 acres
Mount Maxwell PP, 492 acres
Mount Tuam Reserve, 628 acres
Oak Bay Islands Reserve, 507 acres
Princess Margaret Marine PP,
1,320 acres
Race Rocks Reserve, 544 acres
Ruckle PP, 1,201 acres
San Juan Ridge Reserve, 242 acres
Satellite Channel Reserve, 848 acres
Saturna Island Reserve, 324 acres
Sidney Spit Marine PP, 986 acres
Wallace Island Marine PP, 178 acres
Winter Cove PP, 225 acres

Water Area
Lakes and rivers: 8,500 acres
Juan de Fuca Strait coast: 30,000 acres

Zoos
Crystal Garden
Score: 47.30   Rank: 187

Victoria, TX

Golf Courses
1 Municipal, 27 holes
2 Private, 36 holes

Movie Theatres
3 Multiplexes
14 Screens

Water Area
Lakes and rivers: 3,840 acres

Zoos
The Texas Zoo

Score: 3.39   Rank: 342

Vineland-Millville-Bridgeton, NJ

Golf Courses
3 Daily fee, 54 holes

Movie Theatres
2 Multiplexes
9 Screens

Recreation Areas
State
     Bear Swamp East SNA, 1,415 acres

Water Area
Lakes and rivers: 9,600 acres
Atlantic coast: 11,080 acres

Zoos
Cohanzick Zoo

Score: 10.76   Rank: 316

Visalia-Tulare-Porterville, CA

Gambling
5 Casinos

Golf Courses
5 Daily fee, 63 holes
3 Municipal, 45 holes
2 Private, 36 holes

Good Restaurants
3 Simple ◆
5 Family ◆◆
4 Adult ◆◆◆

Movie Theatres
5 Singles/Twins; 3 Multiplexes
27 Screens

Professional Sports
Visalia Oaks (Class A Baseball)

Recreation Areas
Federal
     Blue Ridge NWR, 897 acres
     Inyo NF, 190,798 acres
     Kings Canyon NP, 107,018 acres
     Pixley NWR, 6,385 acres
     Sequoia NF, 698,977 acres
     Sequoia NP, 402,314 acres

Skiing
1 ski area
Lift capacity/hour: 4,800

Water Area
Lakes and rivers: 9,600 acres

Score: 4.81   Rank: 337

Waco, TX

College NCAA I Sports
Baylor Bears

Golf Courses
4 Daily fee, 63 holes
2 Municipal, 36 holes
2 Private, 54 holes

Movie Theatres
1 Single/Twin; 3 Multiplexes
19 Screens

Water Area
Lakes and rivers: 11,520 acres

Zoos
Cameron Park Zoo

Score: 28.61   Rank: 253

Washington, DC-MD-VA-WV

Amusement & Theme Parks
Adventure World Family Theme Park

Aquariums
National Aquarium

College NCAA I Sports
American U Eagles
George Mason Patriots
George Washington Colonials
Georgetown Hoyas
Howard Bison
Mt. St. Mary's Mountaineers
U of Maryland Terps

Gambling
Charles Town Races (thoroughbred)
Laurel Race Course (thoroughbred)
Rosecroft Raceway (harness)

Golf Courses
53 Daily fee, 909 holes
32 Municipal, 558 holes
54 Private, 1044 holes

Good Restaurants
29 Simple ◆
156 Family ◆◆
103 Adult ◆◆◆
12 Upscale ◆◆◆◆

Movie Theatres
27 Singles/Twins; 65 Multiplexes
506 Screens

Professional Sports
Bowie BaySox (Class AA Baseball)
Bowie Washington Capitals
     (NHL Hockey)
Chesapeake Icebreakers (ECHL
Congressionals (USBL Basketball)
DC United (MLS Soccer)
Frederick Keys (Class A Baseball)
Mystics (WNBA)
Redskins (NFL Football)
Wizards (NBA Basketball)
Woodbridge Cannons (Class A Baseball)

Recreation Areas
Federal
     Appalachian Trail, 7,630 acres
     Blue Ridge Parkway
     Catoctin Mountain Park, 5,695 acres
     Constitution Gardens, 52 acres
     Featherstone NWR, 326 acres

     Fort Washington Park, 341 acres
     George Washington NF, 6,270 acres
     George Washington Parkway,
       7,088 acres
     Greenbelt Park, 1,175 acres
     Manassas NBP, 4,356 acres
     Marumsco NWR, 63 acres
     Mason Neck NWR, 1,487 acres
     National Capital Parks, 6,044 acres
     National Mall, 146 acres
     Piscataway Park, 4,334 acres
     Potomac Heritage Trail
     Prince William Forest Park,
       17,410 acres
     Rock Creek Park, 1,754 acres
     Shenandoah NP, 13,690 acres
     Theodore Roosevelt Island, 88 acres
     Wolf Trap Farm Park, 130 acres
State
     Caledon NA, 2,579 acres
     Calvert Cliffs SP, 1,313 acres
     Cunningham Falls SP, 4,946 acres
     Gambrill SP, 1,137 acres
     Lake Anna SP, 2,000 acres
     Leesylvania SP, 500 acres
     Mason Neck SP, 3,608 acres
     Merkle Wildlife Sanctuary,
       1,670 acres
     Patuxent River SP, 3,177 acres
     Seneca Creek SP, 6,109 acres
     Sky Meadows SP, 1,618 acres
     South Mountain SP, 2,356 acres

Skiing
3 ski areas
Lift capacity/hour: 24,620

Water Area
Lakes and rivers: 95,360 acres
Chesapeake coast: 167,040 acres

Zoos
Catoctin Mountain Zoological Park
National Zoological Park

Score: 88.66   Rank: 41

Waterbury, CT

Amusement & Theme Parks
Quassy Park

Golf Courses
2 Daily fee, 18 holes
8 Municipal, 117 holes
5 Private, 90 holes

Good Restaurants
2 Simple ◆
5 Family ◆◆
3 Adult ◆◆◆

Movie Theatres
1 Multiplex
10 Screens

Recreation Areas
State
     Black Rock SP, 443 acres
     George Waldo SP, 150 acres
     Kettletown SP, 492 acres
     Whittemore Glen SP, 242 acres

Water Area
Lakes and rivers: 2,662 acres
Score: 7.36   Rank: 328

Waterloo-Cedar Falls, IA
College NCAA I Sports
U of Northern Iowa Panthers
Gambling
1 Casino
Golf Courses
3 Daily fee, 36 holes
5 Municipal, 81 holes
2 Private, 36 holes
Good Restaurants
3 Simple ♦
6 Family ♦♦
Movie Theatres
1 Single/Twin; 2 Multiplexes
15 Screens
Water Area
Lakes and rivers: 3,200 acres
Score: 28.04   Rank: 255

Wausau, WI
Golf Courses
7 Daily fee, 99 holes
1 Private, 18 holes
Good Restaurants
2 Family ♦♦
1 Adult ♦♦♦
Movie Theatres
1 Single/Twin; 3 Multiplexes
15 Screens
Recreation Areas
State
Mountain-Bay State Trail, 232 acres
Rib Mountain SP, 1,051 acres
Skiing
6 ski areas
Lift capacity/hour: 11,025
Water Area
Lakes and rivers: 19,840 acres
Score: 25.49   Rank: 264

★West Palm Beach-Boca Raton, FL
Aquariums
South Florida Aquarium
College NCAA I Sports
Florida Atlantic Owls
Gambling
Palm Beach Jai-Alai
Palm Beach Kennel Club (greyhound)
Golf Courses
27 Daily fee, 522 holes
14 Municipal, 261 holes
75 Private, 1944 holes
Good Restaurants
3 Simple ♦
18 Family ♦♦
13 Adult ♦♦♦
4 Upscale ♦♦♦♦
1 Best ♦♦♦♦♦
Movie Theatres
2 Singles/Twins; 19 Multiplexes
182 Screens

Professional Sports
Jupiter Hammerheads (Class A Baseball)
Recreation Areas
Federal
Loxahatchee NWR, 2,550 acres
State
Macarthur Beach SP, 225 acres
Water Area
Lakes and rivers: 163,840 acres
Atlantic coast: 6,208 acres
Zoos
Dreher Park Zoo
Score: 95.75   Rank: 16

Wheeling, WV-OH
Gambling
Wheeling Downs (greyhound)
Golf Courses
4 Daily fee, 45 holes
4 Municipal, 99 holes
3 Private, 54 holes
Good Restaurants
1 Simple ♦
2 Family ♦♦
2 Adult ♦♦♦
Movie Theatres
1 Multiplex
9 Screens
Professional Sports
Nailers (ECHL Hockey)
Recreation Areas
Federal
Ohio River Islands NWR, 18 acres
State
Barkcamp SP, 1,115 acres
Skiing
5 ski areas
Lift capacity/hour: 54,600
Water Area
Lakes and rivers: 7,680 acres
Zoos
Oglebay Good Children's Zoo
Score: 17.56   Rank: 292

Wichita, KS
Amusement & Theme Parks
Joyland
College NCAA I Sports
Wichita State Shockers
Gambling
Wichita Park (greyhound)
Golf Courses
8 Daily fee, 99 holes
8 Municipal, 117 holes
11 Private, 198 holes
Good Restaurants
2 Simple ♦
6 Family ♦♦
5 Adult ♦♦♦
1 Upscale ♦♦♦♦
Movie Theatres
6 Singles/Twins; 7 Multiplexes
49 Screens
Professional Sports
Wranglers (Class AA Baseball)

Recreation Areas
State
Cheney SP, 203 acres
El Dorado SP, 3,800 acres
Water Area
Lakes and rivers: 17,920 acres
Zoos
Sedgwick County Zoo
Score: 54.10   Rank: 163

Wichita Falls, TX
Golf Courses
2 Daily fee, 36 holes
4 Municipal, 54 holes
1 Private, 18 holes
Good Restaurants
2 Simple ♦
2 Family ♦♦
Movie Theatres
3 Multiplexes
18 Screens
Water Area
Lakes and rivers: 13,440 acres
Score: 24.07   Rank: 269

Williamsport, PA
Golf Courses
1 Municipal, 45 holes
1 Private, 18 holes
Good Restaurants
1 Simple ♦
3 Family ♦♦
4 Adult ♦♦♦
Movie Theatres
2 Singles/Twins; 2 Multiplexes
13 Screens
Professional Sports
Crosscutters (Class A Baseball)
Recreation Areas
State
Little Pine SP, 2,158 acres
Susquehanna SP, 20 acres
Upper Pine Bottom SP, 5 acres
Skiing
3 ski areas
Lift capacity/hour: 8,100
Water Area
Lakes and rivers: 5,760 acres
Score: 1.41   Rank: 349

Wilmington, NC
Amusement & Theme Parks
Jungle Rapids
Aquariums
North Carolina Aquarium
College NCAA I Sports
U of North Carolina Seahawks
Golf Courses
31 Daily fee, 657 holes
1 Municipal, 18 holes
3 Private, 72 holes
Good Restaurants
8 Family ♦♦

Movie Theatres
  6 Multiplexes
  34 Screens
Recreation Areas
  State
    Carolina Beach SP, 1,773 acres
Water Area
  Lakes and rivers: 37,760 acres
  Atlantic coast: 16,960 acres
Score: 88.38   **Rank: 42**

Wilmington-Newark, DE-MD
College NCAA I Sports
  U of Delaware Blue Hens
Gambling
  1 Casino
  Delaware Park (thoroughbred)
Golf Courses
  7 Daily fee, 117 holes
  2 Municipal, 36 holes
  8 Private, 207 holes
Good Restaurants
  1 Simple ♦
  12 Family ♦♦
  5 Adult ♦♦♦
  3 Upscale ♦♦♦♦
Movie Theatres
  2 Singles/Twins; 6 Multiplexes
  55 Screens
Professional Sports
  Blue Rocks (Class A Baseball)
Recreation Areas
  State
    Brandywine Creek SP, 873 acres
    Carpenter SP, 1,164 acres
    Elk Neck SP, 2,188 acres
    Fail Hill SNA, 5,613 acres
    Flint Woods Nature Preserve,
      138 acres
    Fort DuPont SP, 323 acres
    Fox Point SP, 171 acres
    Lums Pond SP, 1,777 acres
    White Clay Creek Preserve,
      593 acres
    White Clay Creek SP, 1,009 acres
Skiing
  1 ski area
  Lift capacity/hour: 9,200
Water Area
  Lakes and rivers: 34,560 acres
  Atlantic coast: 5,376 acres
Zoos
  Brandywine Zoo
Score: 64.02   **Rank: 128**

Windsor, ON
College CIAU Sports
  U of Windsor Lancers
Gambling
  1 Casino
  Windsor Raceway (harness)
Golf Courses
  5 Daily fee, 81 holes
  5 Municipal, 72 holes
  3 Private, 54 holes

Good Restaurants
  6 Family ♦♦
  4 Adult ♦♦♦
Movie Theatres
  5 Multiplexes
  27 Screens
Skiing
  8 ski areas
  Lift capacity/hour: 9,200
Water Area
  Lakes and rivers: 1,500 acres
  Lake St. Claire coast: 17,000 acres
Score: 36.82   **Rank: 224**

Winnipeg, MB
College CIAU Sports
  U of Manitoba Bisons
  U of Winnipeg Wesmen
Gambling
  3 Casinos
  Assiniboia Downs (mixed meetings)
Golf Courses
  7 Daily fee, 108 holes
  3 Municipal, 54 holes
  8 Private, 126 holes
Good Restaurants
  2 Simple ♦
  9 Family ♦♦
  4 Adult ♦♦♦
Movie Theatres
  4 Singles/Twins; 9 Multiplexes
  56 Screens
Professional Sports
  Blue Bombers (CFL Football)
  Cyclone (IBA Basketball)
Recreation Areas
  Provincial
    Beaudry PP, 2,170 acres
    Birds Hill PP, 8,700 acres
    Libau Bog Reserve, 460 acres
    Patricia Beach PP, 153 acres
Skiing
  2 ski areas
  Lift capacity/hour: 10,366
Water Area
  Lakes and rivers: 85,000 acres
Zoos
  Assiniboine Park Zoo
Score: 58.07   **Rank: 149**

Worcester, MA-CT
College NCAA I Sports
  Holy Cross Crusaders
Golf Courses
  14 Daily fee, 189 holes
  3 Municipal, 36 holes
  7 Private, 108 holes
Good Restaurants
  2 Simple ♦
  6 Family ♦♦
  5 Adult ♦♦♦
Movie Theatres
  7 Singles/Twins; 3 Multiplexes
  31 Screens

Professional Sports
  IceCats (AHL Hockey)
Recreation Areas
  State
    Buffumville SRA, 400 acres
    Campbell's Falls SP, 5 acres
    Holland Pond SRA, 35 acres
    Moore SP, 595 acres
    Purgatory Chasm SP, 533 acres
    Quaddick SP, 116 acres
    Quinsigamond SP, 51 acres
    Rutland SP, 396 acres
    Streeter Point SRA, 10 acres
    Wachusett Mountain SR,
      2,849 acres
    Wells SP, 1,470 acres
Skiing
  10 ski areas
  Lift capacity/hour: 48,790
Water Area
  Lakes and rivers: 23,316 acres
Zoos
  Greenhill Farm Nature Center
  New England Science Center
Score: 66.00   **Rank: 121**

Yakima, WA
Gambling
  Yakima Meadows Race Track
    (thoroughbred)
Golf Courses
  5 Daily fee, 81 holes
  1 Municipal, 9 holes
  2 Private, 36 holes
Good Restaurants
  1 Simple ♦
  2 Family ♦♦
Movie Theatres
  1 Single/Twin; 4 Multiplexes
  24 Screens
Professional Sports
  Bears (Class A Baseball)
  Sun Kings (CBA Basketball)
Recreation Areas
  Federal
    Gifford Pinchot NF, 37,089 acres
    Snoqualmie NF, 466,543 acres
    Toppenish NWR, 1,979 acres
  State
    Yakima Sportsmans SP, 246 acres
Skiing
  3 ski areas
  Lift capacity/hour: 51,125
Water Area
  Lakes and rivers: 10,240 acres
Score: 18.13   **Rank: 290**

Yolo, CA
Gambling
  1 Casino
Golf Courses
  2 Daily fee, 27 holes
  1 Municipal, 18 holes
  2 Private, 36 holes

Movie Theatres
1 Single/Twin; 3 Multiplexes
16 Screens
Water Area
Lakes and rivers: 6,400 acres
Score: **6.51**   Rank: **331**

York, PA
Golf Courses
15 Daily fee, 288 holes
4 Private, 63 holes
Good Restaurants
3 Simple ♦
1 Family ♦♦
6 Adult ♦♦♦
Movie Theatres
4 Singles/Twins; 3 Multiplexes
30 Screens
Recreation Areas
State
Codorus SP, 3,290 acres
Gifford Pinchot SP, 2,338 acres
Samuel Lewis SP, 71 acres
Skiing
2 ski areas
Lift capacity/hour: 20,120
Water Area
Lakes and rivers: 3,840 acres
Score: **21.81**   Rank: **277**

Youngstown-Warren, OH
College NCAA I Sports
Youngstown State Penguins
Golf Courses
44 Daily fee, 603 holes
3 Municipal, 81 holes
7 Private, 117 holes

Good Restaurants
3 Simple ♦
7 Family ♦♦
3 Adult ♦♦♦
Movie Theatres
5 Singles/Twins; 7 Multiplexes
73 Screens
Professional Sports
Scrappers (Class A Baseball)
Recreation Areas
State
Beaver Creek SP, 3,038 acres
Guilford Lake SP, 92 acres
Kyle Woods SNA, 82 acres
Mosquito Creek SP, 3,961 acres
Skiing
2 ski areas
Lift capacity/hour: 8,900
Water Area
Lakes and rivers: 18,560 acres
Score: **73.65**   Rank: **94**

Yuba City, CA
Gambling
1 Casino
Golf Courses
3 Daily fee, 36 holes
2 Municipal, 36 holes
1 Private, 18 holes
Good Restaurants
1 Family ♦♦
Movie Theatres
1 Single/Twin; 1 Multiplex
9 Screens

Recreation Areas
Federal
Butte Sink WMA, 733 acres
Plumas NF, 24,086 acres
Sutter NWR, 2,590 acres
Tahoe NF, 20,334 acres
Skiing
14 ski areas
Lift capacity/hour: 202,870
Water Area
Lakes and rivers: 12,160 acres
Score: **5.38**   Rank: **335**

Yuma, AZ
Gambling
1 Casino
Golf Courses
5 Daily fee, 81 holes
3 Municipal, 54 holes
1 Private, 18 holes
Good Restaurants
2 Simple ♦
1 Family ♦♦
1 Adult ♦♦♦
Movie Theatres
1 Multiplex
5 Screens
Recreation Areas
Federal
Cabeza Prieta NWR, 443,800 acres
Kofa NWR, 528,481 acres
Skiing
1 ski area
Lift capacity/hour: 800
Water Area
Lakes and rivers: 3,200 acres
Score: **8.49**   Rank: **324**

ET CETERA: Recreation

LOOKING FOR THE BEST SKIING?

By definition, a ski area is more than a snow-covered hill or mountain. It also has developed trails and lift machinery. Usually, too, there is a lodge for meals and overnight stays. If the area is large and popular, it also has *après-ski*—nighttime entertainment from music to movies to disco—which is as critical as fresh snow and challenging runs to many skiers.

But if you're a skier with time and money, skiing Hanley's Happy Hill in Pennsylvania, Little Switzerland in Wisconsin, or even Vermont's Killington or Stowe isn't quite the same as skiing "destination" areas in the West such as Aspen, Park City, Jackson Hole, or Whistler/Blackcomb. Ski areas are where you find them, but the best *skiing* is in the highest part of the continent: the Rocky Mountain West and the Sierra Nevada near Lake Tahoe.

This Statement isn't purely a matter of opinion. According to ski-industry surveys, most of North America's ten to twelve million skiers are of intermediate ability, tending toward advanced. If they could ski anywhere, they would choose areas that enhance their ability, that is, places with high mountains, great vertical rises, long runs, and heavy powder snowfalls that begin early in winter and last into spring. You'll find more of these qualities within short drives of Calgary, Denver, Boulder, Reno, Salt Lake City, Seattle, Tacoma, Spokane, and Vancouver than anywhere else.

WHERE ARE THE BEST SPORTS TOWNS?

Ask 100 sports fans to describe the ideal sports town and you'll probably get 100 different answers. Being able to attend a game easily is not the only thing a fan wants.

Vertical Rise . . .

The perpendicular distance from the base to the highest skiable point on a hill or mountain is a ski area's "vertical." Although vertical rise has little to do with the quality of trails, it is a good indication of the length of the runs and the mountain's challenge.

Blackcomb Mountain, BC	5,280 feet
Whistler Mountain, BC	5,000
Panorama Resort, BC	4,300
Jackson Hole, WY	4,139
Snowmass, CO	3,721
Aspen Highlands, CO	3,635
Steamboat, CO	3,600
Heavenly Valley, CA	3,600
Telluride, CO	3,522
Sunshine Village, AB	3,514

. . . Longest Runs, . . .

The longest run is the longest continuous trail on the mountain, from the top to the runout at the base lodge's parking lot. The average is 7,000 feet. At fifteen resorts, it's more than three times that length.

Killington, VT	53,856 feet
Jackson Hole, WY	36,960
Blackcomb Mountain, BC	36,960

Whistler Mountain, BC	35,000
Heavenly Valley, CA	29,040
Taos Ski Valley, NM	27,456
Lake Louise, AB	26,400
Mission Ridge, WA	26,400
Sunshine Village, AB	26,400
Sun Peaks Resort, BC	26,000

. . . and Lift Capacities

A ski area's lift capacity is the number of people its lifts can move up the mountain in 1 hour. The total lift capacity is a good indication of how developed the ski area is, and often of how fast the lift lines move. Ten North American ski areas have lift capacities of at least 30,000 skiers per hour.

Mammoth Mountain, CA	53,000/hour
Squaw Valley, CA	49,000
Vail, CO	45,370
Killington, VT	35,327
Mount Snow, VT	34,490
Winter Park, CO	33,700
Steamboat, CO	31,588
Heavenly Valley, CA	31,000
Sunday River, ME	31,000
Alpental-Ski Acres-Snoqualmie, WA	30,000

Source: Inter-Ski Services, The White Book of Ski Areas.

Recreation

Rooting for the home team is fun, but rooting for a winning home team is ecstasy. In the lists that follow, *Places Rated* looks at the metro areas with the winningest teams.

Major-League Title Towns

For a baseball fan in the mid-1970s, the place to be was Oakland as the A's hauled in three straight World Series championships. In the 1960s, football fans found a warm welcome in frosty Green Bay, where the Packers took five NFL Championships over a seven-year span. No baseball team can really be called a dominant World Series champ for the 1980s. Neither has any football team topped the Packers' record for the 1960s, but the Pittsburgh Steelers, with four Super Bowl wins, the San Francisco 49ers, with three, and the Washington Redskins, with two, have inspired devotion among fans in the late 1970s and throughout the 1980s. The Dallas Cowboys dominated the early 1990s, while the late 1990s belong to the Denver Broncos.

Basketball lovers from the 1960s through the 1980s, on the other hand, wouldn't have been far wrong if they backed the Boston Celtics, winners of more titles than any other team in NBA history. With all their tradition and mystique—and the renowned parquet floor of the Boston Garden where they played—they have left many opponents bewitched, bothered, and bewildered. Still, in the 1980s the Los Angeles Lakers didn't do too badly either, with more championships in that decade than any other team. In the 1990s, the Chicago Bulls and the Houston Rockets have been the teams to watch.

Our survey of metro areas with major professional championships (in the list on the next page) looks at the winners in four team sports: baseball, football, basketball, and ice hockey. In the cases of baseball and ice hockey, we include the winners of the World Series (since 1903) and Stanley Cup (since 1894). For football and basketball, we include the NFL Super Bowl, the CFL Grey Cup, and NBA Championship winners. Going back a little

569

more toward the roots, we also list the winning teams from the leagues that preceded the modern NFL (the National Football League, 1933–1969, and American Football League, 1960–1969) and the NBA (the Basketball Association of America, 1947–1949). The NFL and AFL champions of 1966, 1967, and 1968 met in the Super Bowls of 1967, 1968, and 1969, before the formation of the modern NFL; for those years, we name the winners of both the individual league championships and the Super Bowl.

If a team has changed names or towns, we list it with the name it used and the town it played in at the time it won the championship.

Professional Championships

Anaheim-Santa Ana, CA
NFL Championship: Los Angeles Rams, 1951

Atlanta, GA
World Series: Braves, 1995

Baltimore, MD
World Series: Orioles, 1966, 1970, 1983
Super Bowl: Colts, 1971; *CFL Grey Cup:* Stallions, 1995
NFL Championship: Colts 1958, 1959, 1968
BAA Championship: Bullets, 1948

Bergen-Passaic, NJ
Super Bowl: New York Giants, 1987, 1991
NHL Stanley Cup: New Jersey Devils, 1995

Boston, MA
World Series: Somersets, 1903; Red Sox, 1912, 1914, 1915, 1916, 1918
NBA Championship: Celtics, 1957, 1959, 1960, 1961, 1962, 1963, 1964, 1965, 1966, 1968, 1969, 1974, 1976, 1981, 1984, 1986
NHL Stanley Cup: Bruins, 1929, 1939, 1941, 1970, 1972

Buffalo, NY
AFL Championship: Bills, 1964, 1965

Calgary, AB
CFL Grey Cup: Stampeders, 1948, 1971, 1992, 1995
NHL Stanley Cup: Flames, 1989

Chicago, IL
World Series: White Sox, 1906, 1917; Cubs, 1907, 1908
Super Bowl: Bears, 1986
NFL Championship: Bears, 1933, 1940, 1941, 1943, 1946; Cardinals, 1947; Bears, 1963
NBA Championship: Bulls, 1991, 1992, 1993, 1996, 1997, 1998
NHL Stanley Cup: Black Hawks, 1934, 1938, 1961

Cincinnati, OH-KY-IN
World Series: Reds, 1919, 1940, 1975, 1976, 1990

Cleveland, OH
World Series: Indians, 1920, 1948
NFL Championship: Rams, 1945; Browns, 1950, 1954, 1955, 1964

Dallas, TX
Super Bowl: Cowboys, 1972, 1978, 1993, 1994, 1996
AFL Championship: Texans, 1962
NHL Stanley Cup: Stars, 1999

Denver, CO
Super Bowl: Broncos, 1998, 1999
NHL Stanley Cup: Colorado Avalanche, 1996

Detroit, MI
World Series: Tigers, 1935, 1945, 1968, 1984
NFL Championship: Lions, 1935, 1952, 1953, 1957
NBA Championship: Pistons, 1989, 1990
NHL Stanley Cup: Red Wings, 1936, 1937, 1943, 1950, 1952, 1954, 1955, 1997, 1998

Edmonton, AB
CFL Grey Cup: Eskimos, 1954, 1955, 1956, 1975, 1978, 1979, 1980, 1981, 1982, 1987, 1993
NHL Stanley Cup: Oilers, 1984, 1985, 1987, 1988, 1990

Green Bay, WI
Super Bowl: Packers, 1967, 1968, 1997
NFL Championship: Packers, 1936, 1937, 1939, 1944, 1961, 1962, 1965, 1966, 1967

Hamilton, ON
CFL Grey Cup: Alerts, 1912; Tigers, 1913, 1915, 1925, 1929, 1932; Flying Wildcats, 1943; Tiger-Cats, 1953, 1957, 1963, 1965, 1967, 1972, 1986

Houston, TX
AFL Championship: Oilers, 1960, 1961
NBA Championship: Rockets, 1994, 1995

Kansas City, MO
World Series: Royals, 1985
Super Bowl: Chiefs, 1970
AFL Championship: Chiefs, 1966, 1969

Long Island, NY
NHL Stanley Cup: New York Islanders, 1980, 1981, 1982, 1983

Los Angeles-Long Beach, CA
World Series: Dodgers, 1959, 1963, 1965, 1981, 1988
Super Bowl: Raiders, 1984
NFL Championship: Rams, 1951
NBA Championship: Lakers, 1972, 1980, 1982, 1985, 1987, 1988

Miami, FL
World Series: Florida Marlins, 1997
Super Bowl: Dolphins, 1973, 1974

Milwaukee, WI
World Series: Braves, 1957
NBA Championship: Bucks, 1971

Minneapolis-St. Paul, MN
World Series: Minnesota Twins, 1987, 1991
NFL Championship: Minnesota Vikings, 1969
BAA Championship: Minneapolis Lakers, 1949; *NBA Championship:* Lakers, 1950, 1952, 1953, 1954

Montreal, PQ

CFL Grey Cup: M.A.A.A., 1931; HMCS St. Hyacinthe-Connacona, 1944; Alouettes, 1949, 1970, 1974, 1977

NHL Stanley Cup: M.A.A., 1893, 1894; Victorias, 1895, 1896, 1897, 1898, 1899; Shamrocks, 1899, 1900; M.A.A., 1902, 1903; Wanderers, 1906, 1907, 1908, 1910; Canadiens, 1916, 1924; Maroons, 1926; Canadiens, 1930, 1931; Maroons, 1935; Canadiens, 1944, 1946, 1953, 1956, 1957, 1958, 1959, 1960, 1965, 1966, 1968, 1969, 1971, 1973, 1976, 1977, 1978, 1979, 1986, 1993

New York, NY

World Series: Giants, 1905, 1921, 1922, 1933, 1954; Yankees, 1923, 1927, 1928, 1932, 1936, 1937, 1938, 1939, 1941, 1943, 1947, 1949, 1950, 1951, 1952, 1953, 1956, 1958, 1961, 1962, 1977, 1978, 1996, 1998; Brooklyn Dodgers, 1955; Mets, 1969, 1986

Super Bowl: Jets, 1969

AFL Championship: Jets, 1968

NFL Championship: Giants, 1934, 1938, 1944, 1956

NBA Championship: Knickerbockers, 1970, 1973

NHL Stanley Cup: Rangers, 1928, 1933, 1940, 1994

Oakland, CA

World Series: Athletics, 1972, 1973; A's, 1974, 1989

Super Bowl: Raiders, 1977, 1981

AFL Championship: Raiders, 1967

NBA Championship: Golden State Warriors, 1975

Ottawa-Hull, ON-PQ

CFL Grey Cup: Senators, 1925, 1926; Rough Riders, 1940, 1951, 1960, 1968, 1969, 1973, 1976

NHL Stanley Cup: Silver Seven, 1903, 1904, 1905, 1906; Senators, 1909, 1911, 1920, 1921, 1923, 1927

Philadelphia, PA

World Series: Athletics, 1910, 1911, 1913, 1929, 1930; Phillies, 1980

NFL Championship: Eagles, 1948, 1949, 1960

BAA Championship: Warriors, 1947; *NBA Championship:* Warriors, 1956; 76ers, 1967, 1983

NHL Stanley Cup: Flyers, 1974, 1975

Pittsburgh, PA

World Series: Pirates, 1909, 1925, 1960, 1971, 1979

Super Bowl: Steelers, 1975, 1976, 1979, 1980

NHL Stanley Cup: Penguins, 1991, 1992

Portland, OR

NBA Championship: Trail Blazers, 1977

Quebec City, PQ

NHL Stanley Cup: Bulldogs, 1912, 1913

Regina, SK

CFL Grey Cup: Roughriders, 1966, 1989

Rochester, NY

NBA Championship: Royals, 1951

San Antonio, TX

NBA Championship: Spurs, 1999

St. Louis, MO-IL

World Series: Cardinals, 1926, 1931, 1934, 1942, 1944, 1946, 1964, 1967, 1982

NBA Championship: Hawks, 1958

San Diego, CA

AFL Championship: Chargers, 1963

San Francisco, CA

Super Bowl: 49ers, 1982, 1985, 1989, 1990, 1995

Seattle, WA

NBA Championship: Supersonics, 1979

NHL Stanley Cup: Metropolitans, 1917

Syracuse, NY

NBA Championship: Nationals, 1955

Toronto, ON

CFL Grey Cup: Argonauts, 1914, 1921, 1933, 1937, 1938, 1945,1946, 1947, 1950, 1952, 1983, 1991, 1996, 1997; Balmy Beach, 1927, 1930; University of Toronto, 1909, 1910, 1911, 1920; RCAF Hurricanes, 1942

NHL Stanley Cup: Blueshirts, 1914; Arenas, 1918; St. Patricks, 1922; Maple Leafs, 1932, 1942, 1945, 1947, 1948, 1949, 1951, 1962, 1963, 1964, 1967

World Series: Blue Jays, 1992, 1993

Vancouver, BC

CFL Grey Cup: Lions, 1964, 1985, 1994

NHL Stanley Cup: Millionaires, 1915

Victoria, BC

NHL Stanley Cup: Cougars, 1925

Washington, DC-MO-VA

World Series: Senators, 1924

Super Bowl: Redskins, 1983, 1988, 1992

NFL Championship: Redskins, 1937, 1942

NBA Championship: Bullets, 1978

Winnipeg, MB

CFL Grey Cup: Winnipegs, 1935; Blue Bombers, 1939, 1941, 1958, 1959, 1961, 1962, 1984, 1988, 1990

NHL Stanley Cup: Victorias, 1901, 1902

Collegiate Title Towns

The 1999–2000 academic year marks the 116th season of American college athletic championships, which began when Harvard University's J. S. Clark captured the first singles title in college tennis in 1883. Founded in 1906, the National Collegiate Athletic Association (NCAA) began sponsoring college athletic championships in 1921, beginning with its first outdoor track meet. It was not until 1981 that the association initiated women's championships. Over the years, some 600 colleges and universities have been named national champions in each of the NCAA's three divisions. What follows is a list covering the past two decades showing Division I champions within metropolitan areas.

Many NCAA sports, such as basketball and volleyball, have both men's and women's championships. An M or W after the sport in the list below indicates whether the title was in men's or women's competition. Sports

such as baseball, football, ice hockey, and wrestling are played at the championship level by men only, whereas field hockey and softball championships are for women only; accordingly, no M or W designation is given for those sports. Ski teams are coed.

In Division I–A Football, the NCAA recognizes as unofficial national champion the team selected each year by the Associated Press poll of sportswriters and the United Press International poll of coaches.

NCAA Division I Championships

Albany-Schenectady-Troy, NY
Rensselaer Polytechnic Institute: Ice Hockey, 1985

Ann Arbor, MI
University of Michigan: Basketball (M), 1989; Football (Division I–A), 1997; Gymnastics (M), 1999; Ice Hockey, 1996, 1998; Swimming and Diving (M), 1995

Athens, GA
University of Georgia: Baseball, 1990; Football (Division I–A), 1980; Golf (M), 1999; Gymnastics (W), 1987, 1989, 1993, 1998, 1999; Swimming and Diving (W), 1999; Tennis (M), 1985, 1987, 1999; Tennis (W), 1994

Atlanta, GA
Georgia Institute of Technology: Football (Division I–A), 1990

Austin, TX
University of Texas: Baseball, 1983; Basketball (W), 1986; Cross Country (W), 1986; Gymnastics (W), 1987; Indoor Track (W), 1986, 1988, 1990, 1998, 1999; Outdoor Track (W), 1986, 1998, 1999; Swimming and Diving (M), 1981, 1988, 1989, 1990, 1991, 1996; Swimming and Diving (W), 1984, 1985, 1986, 1987, 1988, 1990, 1991; Tennis (W), 1993, 1995; Volleyball (W), 1988

Baltimore, MD
Johns Hopkins University: Lacrosse (M), 1980, 1984, 1985, 1987

Bangor, ME
University of Maine, Orono: Ice Hockey, 1993, 1999

Baton Rouge, LA
Louisiana State University: Baseball, 1991, 1993, 1996, 1997; Indoor Track (W), 1987, 1989, 1991, 1993, 1994, 1995, 1996, 1997; Outdoor Track (M), 1989, 1990; Outdoor Track (W), 1987, 1988, 1989, 1990, 1991, 1992, 1993, 1994, 1995, 1997

Bloomington, IN
Indiana University: Basketball (M), 1981, 1987; Soccer (M), 1982, 1983, 1988

Boise City, ID
Boise State University: Football (Division I–AA), 1980

Boston, MA
Harvard University: Ice Hockey, 1989
Boston University: Ice Hockey, 1995

Boulder–Longmont, CO
University of Colorado: Football (Division I–A), 1990; Skiing, 1982, 1991, 1995, 1998, 1999

Bryan-College Station, TX
Texas A & M University: Softball, 1983, 1987

Burlington, VT
University of Vermont: Skiing, 1980, 1989, 1990, 1992, 1994

Charlottesville, VA
University of Virginia: Cross Country (W), 1981, 1982; Lacrosse (M), 1999; Lacrosse (W), 1993; Soccer (M), 1989, 1991, 1992, 1993, 1994

Columbus, OH
Ohio State University: Gymnastics (M), 1985

Dallas, TX
Southern Methodist University: Indoor Track (M), 1983; Outdoor Track (M), 1983, 1986

Denver, CO
University of Denver: Gymnastics (W), 1983

El Paso, TX
University of Texas, El Paso: Cross Country (M), 1980, 1981, 1983; Indoor Track (M), 1980, 1981, 1982; Outdoor Track (M), 1980, 1981, 1982

Eugene-Springfield, OR
University of Oregon: Cross Country (W), 1983, 1987; Outdoor Track (M), 1984; Outdoor Track (W), 1985

Fayetteville, AR
University of Arkansas: Basketball (M), 1994; Cross Country (M), 1986, 1987, 1991, 1992, 1993, 1995, 1998; Indoor Track (M), 1984, 1985, 1986, 1987, 1988, 1989, 1990, 1991, 1992, 1993, 1995, 1995, 1996, 1997, 1998, 1999; Outdoor Track (M), 1988, 1992, 1993, 1994, 1995, 1996, 1997, 1998, 1999

Fort Worth-Arlington, TX
Texas Christian University: Golf (W), 1983

Fresno, CA
California State University: Softball, 1998

Gainesville, FL
University of Florida: Football (Division I–A), 1996; Golf (W), 1985, 1986, 1993; Indoor Track(W), 1992; Swimming and Diving (M), 1983, 1984; Swimming and Diving (W), 1982; Tennis (W), 1992

Grand Forks, ND
University of North Dakota: Ice Hockey, 1980, 1982, 1987, 1997

Greensboro–Winston-Salem–High Point, NC
Wake Forest University: Golf (M), 1986

Greenville-Spartanburg, SC
Clemson University: Football (Division I–A), 1981; Soccer, 1984, 1987
Furman University: Football (Division I–AA), 1988

Honolulu, HI

University of Hawaii: Volleyball (W), 1982, 1983, 1987

Houston, TX

University of Houston: Golf (M), 1982, 1984, 1985

Huntington-Ashland, WV-OH

Marshall University: Football (Division I-AA), 1996

Iowa City, IA

University of Iowa: Field Hockey, 1986; Wrestling, 1980, 1981, 1982, 1983, 1984, 1985, 1986, 1991, 1992, 1993, 1995, 1996, 1997, 1998, 1999

Knoxville, TN

University of Tennessee: Basketball (W), 1987, 1989, 1991, 1996; Football, 1998; Outdoor Track (M), 1991

Lansing-East Lansing, MI

Michigan State University: Ice Hockey, 1986

Las Vegas, NV

University of Nevada: Basketball (M), 1990; Golf (M), 1998

Lawrence, KS

Kansas University: Basketball (M), 1988

Lexington-Fayette, KY

University of Kentucky: Cross Country (W), 1988; Basketball (M), 1996, 1998

Lincoln, NE

University of Nebraska: Football (Division I-A), 1994, 1995, 1997; Gymnastics (M), 1980, 1981, 1982, 1983, 1988, 1994; Indoor Track (W), 1983, 1984

Los Angeles-Long Beach, CA

California State University, Long Beach: Volleyball (M), 1991; Volleyball (W), 1989, 1993, 1998

California State University, Northridge: Gymnastics (W), 1982

Pepperdine University: Baseball, 1992; Golf (M), 1997; Volleyball (M), 1985, 1986, 1992; Water Polo, 1997

University of California, Los Angeles: Basketball (M), 1995; Golf (M), 1988; Golf (W), 1991; Gymnastics (M), 1984, 1987; Outdoor Track (M), 1987, 1988; Outdoor Track (W), 1982, 1983; Soccer (M), 1985, 1990, 1997; Softball, 1982, 1984, 1985, 1988, 1989, 1990, 1992, 1995; Swimming and Diving (M), 1982; Swimming and Diving (W), 1997; Tennis (M), 1982, 1984; Volleyball (M), 1981, 1982, 1983, 1984, 1987, 1989, 1993, 1995, 1996, 1998; Volleyball (W), 1984, 1990, 1991, 1993, 1995; Water Polo, 1995

University of Southern California: Baseball, 1998; Basketball (W), 1983, 1984; Outdoor Track (W), 1982, 1983; Tennis (M), 1991, 1993, 1994; Tennis (W), 1983, 1985; Volleyball (W), 1981; Volleyball (M), 1980, 1988, 1990; Water Polo, 1998

Louisville, KY-IN

University of Louisville: Basketball (M), 1980, 1986

Madison, WI

University of Wisconsin: Cross Country (M), 1984; Cross Country (W), 1984, 1985; Ice Hockey, 1981, 1983, 1990; Soccer (M), 1995

Miami, FL

University of Miami: Baseball, 1982, 1985; Football (Division I-A), 1983, 1987, 1989; Golf (W), 1984

Monroe, LA

Northeast Louisiana University: Football (Division I-AA), 1987

New York, NY

Columbia University: Fencing, 1992, 1993

Norfolk-Virginia Beach-Newport News, VA

Old Dominion University: Field Hockey, 1982, 1983, 1984, 1988, 1990, 1991, 1992, 1998; Basketball (W), 1985

Oakland, CA

University of California, Berkeley: Gymnastics (M), 1997, 1998; Swimming and Diving (M), 1980; Water Polo, 1991, 1992

Oklahoma City, OK

University of Oklahoma: Baseball, 1994; Football (Division I-A), 1985; Golf (M), 1989

Orange County, CA

California State University, Fullerton: Baseball, 1984, 1995; Softball, 1986

University of California, Irvine: Water Polo, 1982

Philadelphia, PA

Temple University: Lacrosse (W), 1984

Villanova University: Basketball (M), 1985; Cross Country (W), 1989, 1990, 1991, 1992, 1993, 1994, 1998

Phoenix, AZ

Arizona State University: Baseball, 1981; Golf (M), 1990, 1996; Golf (W),1990, 1993, 1994, 1995, 1997, 1998; Gymnastics (M), 1986; Wrestling, 1988

Providence-Fall River-Warwick, RI-MA

Providence College: Cross Country (W), 1995

Provo-Orem, UT

Brigham Young University: Cross Country (W), 1997; Football Division I-A), 1984; Golf (M), 1981; Volleyball (M), 1999

Raleigh-Durham-Chapel Hill, NC

Duke University: Basketball, 1991, 1992; Golf (W), 1999; Soccer, 1986

North Carolina State University: Basketball (M), 1983

University of North Carolina: Basketball (M), 1982, 1993; Basketball (W), 1994; Field Hockey, 1989, 1995, 1996, 1997; Lacrosse (M), 1981, 1982, 1986, 1991; Soccer (W), 1982, 1983, 1984, 1986, 1987, 1988, 1990, 1991, 1992, 1993, 1994, 1996, 1997, 1998

Richmond-Petersburg, VA

University of Richmond: Soccer (M), 1998

Salt Lake City-Ogden, UT

University of Utah: Gymnastics (W), 1982, 1983, 1984, 1985, 1986, 1990, 1992, 1994, 1995; Skiing, 1981, 1983, 1984, 1986, 1987, 1988, 1993, 1996, 1997

San Francisco, CA
University of San Francisco: Soccer (M), 1980

San Jose, CA
San Jose State University: Golf (W), 1987, 1989, 1991, 1992
Stanford University: Baseball, 1987, 1988; Basketball (W), 1990, 1992; Cross Country (M), 1996, 1997; Cross Country (W), 1996; Golf (M), 1994; Gymnastics, 1992, 1993, 1995; Swimming and Diving (M), 1985, 1986, 1987, 1992, 1993, 1994, 1998; Swimming and Diving (W), 1983, 1989, 1992, 1993, 1994, 1995, 1996, 1998; Tennis (M), 1980, 1981, 1983, 1986, 1988, 1989, 1990, 1992, 1995, 1996, 1997, 1998; Tennis (W), 1982, 1984, 1986, 1987, 1988, 1989, 1990, 1991, 1997, 1998; Volleyball (M), 1997; Volleyball (W), 1992, 1994, 1996, 1997; Water Polo (M), 1980, 1981, 1993, 1994
University of Santa Clara: Soccer (M), 1989

Seattle, WA
University of Washington: Football (Division I–A), 1992

South Bend-Mishawaka, IN
University of Notre Dame: Fencing, 1994; Football (Division I–A), 1988; Soccer (W), 1995

Springfield, MA
University of Massachusetts: Football (Division I–AA), 1998

State College, PA
Pennsylvania State University: Fencing, 1990, 1991, 1995, 1996, 1997, 1998; Football (Division I–A), 1982, 1986; Volleyball (M), 1994

Stockton, CA
University of the Pacific: Volleyball (W), 1985, 1986

Syracuse, NY
Syracuse University: Lacrosse (M), 1983, 1988, 1989, 1990, 1993, 1995

Tallahassee, FL
Florida State University: Football (Division I–A), 1993; Indoor Track (W), 1985; Outdoor Track (W), 1984

Toledo, OH
Bowling Green University: Ice Hockey, 1984

Trenton, NJ
Princeton University: Lacrosse (M), 1992, 1994, 1996, 1997, 1998; Lacrosse (W), 1994

Tucson, AZ
University of Arizona: Baseball, 1980, 1986; Basketball, 1997; Golf (M), 1992; Golf (W), 1996; Softball, 1991, 1993, 1994, 1996, 1997

Tulsa, OK
University of Tulsa: Golf (W), 1982, 1988

Tuscaloosa, AL
University of Alabama: Football (Division I–A), 1992; Gymnastics (W), 1988, 1991

Washington, DC-MD-VA-WV
George Mason University: Soccer (W), 1985
Georgetown University: Basketball (M), 1984
University of Maryland: Field Hockey, 1987, 1993; Lacrosse (W), 1992, 1995, 1996, 1997, 1998, 1999

Wichita, KS
Wichita State University: Baseball, 1989

Wilmington, DE-NJ-MD
University of Delaware: Lacrosse (W), 1983

Youngstown, OH
Youngstown State University: Football (Division I–AA), 1991, 1993, 1994, 1997

Source: *National Collegiate Athletic Association, College Champions, 1993.*

CIAU Championships

Canadian college athletes get only 3 years to play in inter-university competition. Because there are no athletic scholarships, many football and hockey stars are playing at American universities. Still, rivalry among institutions here goes back to the mid–19th century. Canadian football predates American football by several years. Ice hockey, the national sport, was invented here.

Calgary, ON
University of Calgary: Football, 1983, 1985, 1988, 1995

Edmonton, AB
University of Alberta: Basketball, 1994, 1994; Ice Hockey, 1992, 1998

Kitchener, ON
Wilfred Laurier University: Football, 1991

London, ON
University of Western Ontario: Football, 1989, 1994; Basketball, 1991

Montreal, PQ
Concordia University: Basketball, 1990; Women's Ice Hockey, 1998, 1999
McGill University: Football, 1987

St. Catharines-Niagara, ON
Brock University: Basketball, 1992

Saskatoon, SK
University of Saskatchewan: Ice Hockey, 1983, 1999; Football, 1990, 1997

Sherbrooke, PQ
Bishop's University: Basketball (M), 1998

Toronto, ON
University of Toronto: Ice Hockey, 1984; Football, 1993
York University: Ice Hockey, 1985, 1988, 1989

Trois-Rivieres, PQ
University de Quebec: Ice Hockey, 1987, 1991

Vancouver, BC
University of British Columbia: Football, 1986, 1998

Victoria, BC
University of Victoria: Basketball (M), 1983, 1984, 1985, 1986, 1997; Basketball (W), 1998

Winnipeg, MB
University of Manitoba: Basketball (W), 1996, 1997
University of Winnipeg: Basketball (W), 1994, 1995

Putting It All Together

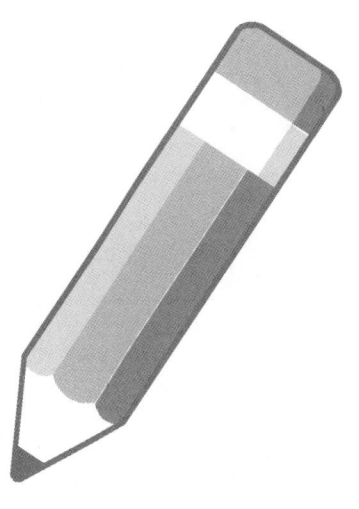

Questions: Where will you find rock-bottom living costs and weather that's bright and shirt-sleeve mild all year? Where are the great hospitals? In which metropolitan area is the crime rate so low that no one remembers how a police siren sounds? How about a short commute, easy parking, excellent schools, top universities, a beach *and* alpine skiing, a generous helping of the arts, and a rosy job outlook? Where will you find men and women who are good-looking and children who are above-average?

Answer: The best place to live. But if you think about the odds of finding these qualities in one place, it all sounds too good to be true. Does such a place exist?

To meet all the requirements, this ideal place would resemble San Francisco or Oakland, where the weather is moderated by the warm Pacific Ocean and the temperature seldom varies much from a mild 65°F. The place's overall costs of living might resemble that of Texarkana, a small metro area astride the Arkansas and Texas border.

This ideal place must be large enough to match Boston's variety of higher education options, New York's array of arts attractions, Toronto's public transit system, Chicago's ease of travel to other parts of the continent, and Philadelphia's supply of physicians and hospitals.

Yet this place would also need to be small if it were to have a crime rate as low as Johnstown, PA. For quality and variety of man-made and natural recreation amenities, the standard set by Miami would have to be met. Finally, our ideal location would have to present individuals with employment prospects as bright as those of Phoenix.

Obviously, this ideal spot is fictional. You can explore the geography long and hard, but you will never find the one metro area that combines all of the "bests" in each of *Places Rated*'s nine categories. Moreover, because one person's long-sought heaven can be another's purgatory, one can argue that there really *is* no such thing as the ideal metro area.

If you could move anywhere you wish, choosing your destination would still not be easy. The best strategy is to focus on your own preferences and needs. (The section "Decisions, Decisions" at the beginning of the book can help you identify what these preferences and needs might be.) Having said as much, we can still try to discover which of North America's 354 metro areas come closest to the ideal.

575

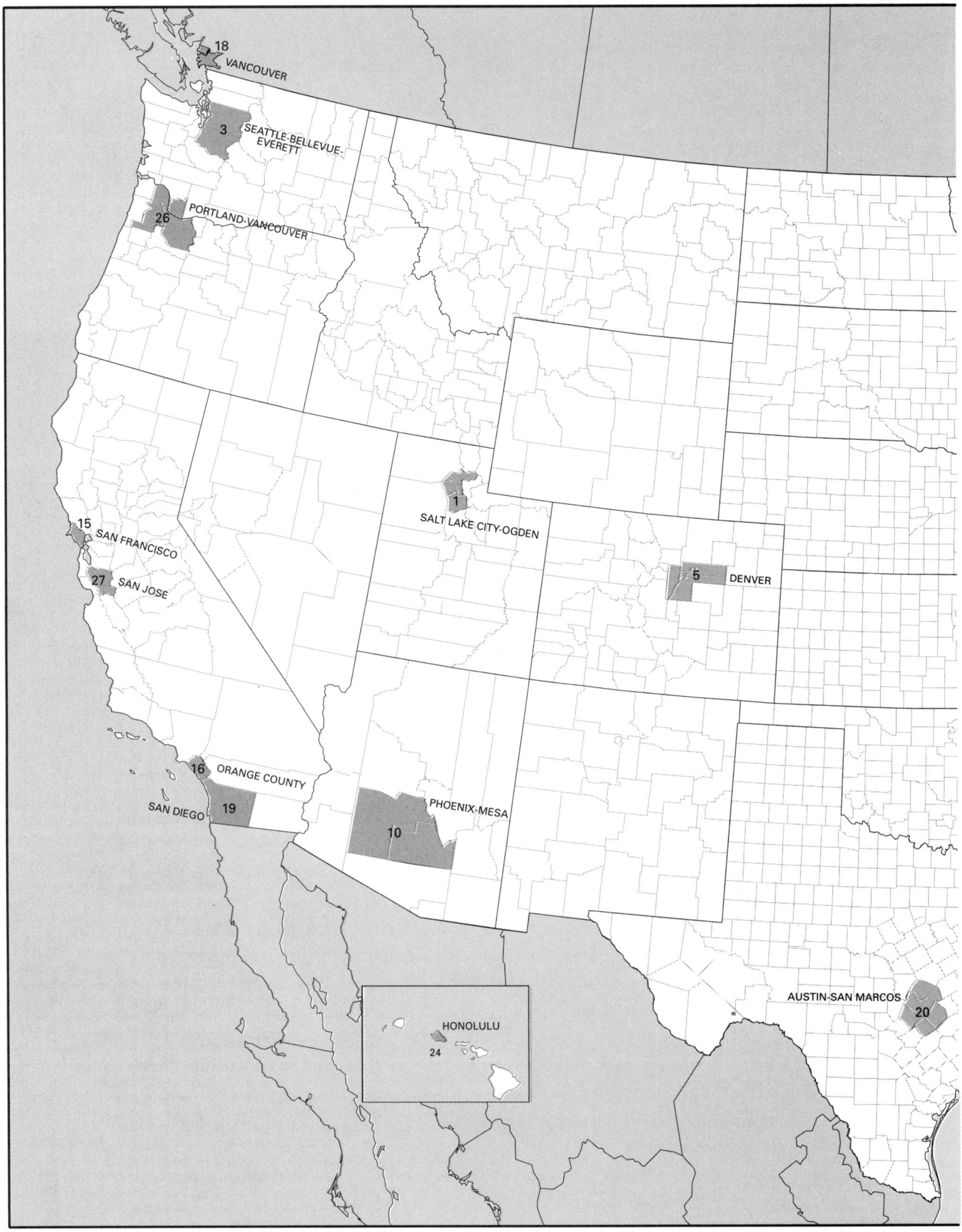

18
VANCOUVER

3
SEATTLE-BELLEVUE-
EVERETT

26
PORTLAND-VANCOUVER

1
SALT LAKE CITY-OGDEN

5
DENVER

15
SAN FRANCISCO

27
SAN JOSE

16
ORANGE COUNTY

19
SAN DIEGO

10
PHOENIX-MESA

HONOLULU
24

AUSTIN-SAN MARCOS
20

Copyright © 2000 by Places Rated Partnership

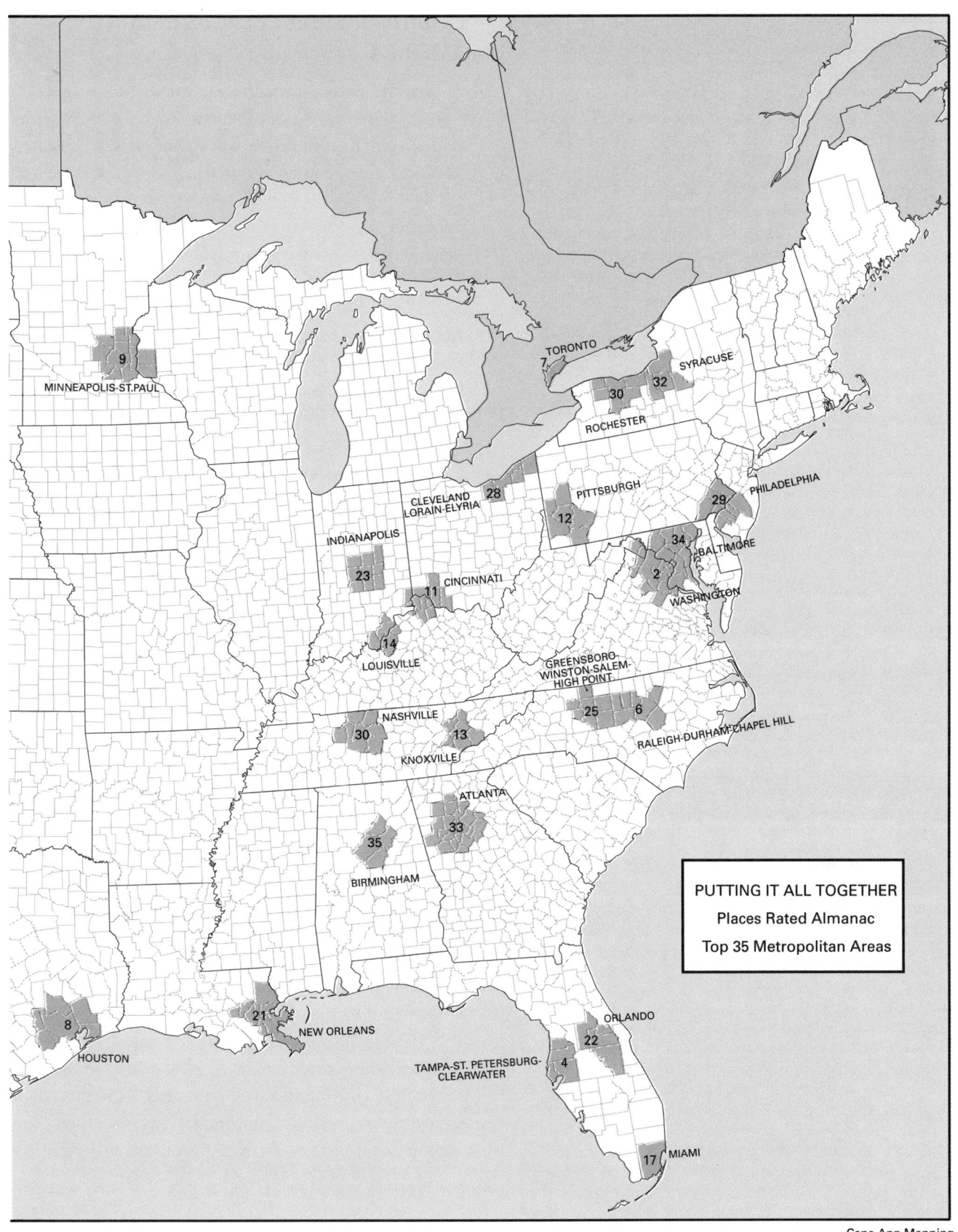

PUTTING IT ALL TOGETHER
Places Rated Almanac
Top 35 Metropolitan Areas

Cape Ann Mapping

Readers who've skipped ahead to see how it all comes out may be surprised by many of the results shown in the table on the following pages. If you are curious about how a metro area is scored in a particular category, see the explanation of the scoring system in the appropriate chapter.

Places Rated's categories include five relating to facilities (health care, education, recreation, transportation, and the arts) and four relating to indicators (climate, crime, costs of living, and jobs). Smaller metro areas do better on the indicators (these places typically have lower crime rates and lower costs of living), while larger places score higher on facilities. Climate favors neither large places nor small ones. Because of *Places Rated*'s emphasis on facilities, larger metro areas have an edge.

When you review the rankings in each of the chapters, be sure to note the close groupings of scores. With such close results, ranking metro areas from 1 to 354 may give the impression of greater differences among them than actually exist. Remember, too, that throughout this almanac the unit of comparison is not the incorporated city but the officially defined metropolitan area, typically made up of cities, towns, and other minor political divisions in New England and Canada, and one or more counties in the rest of the United States.

THE MOST NORMAL METRO AREAS

Here are five areas whose scores across all nine of *Places Rated*'s categories differ the least from the average. In other words, these are the most normal metro areas among all 354 in North America.

"Normal" is one adjective. But the five can also be regarded as "cool." Each turns up on trendy magazine lists for the best places to retire, telecommute, downshift, raise a family, protect the environment, or join the New Age.

Metro Area	Average Percentile Difference from Normal
Eugene-Springfield, OR	9.9
Asheville, NC	12.2
Savannah, GA	12.5
Missoula, MT	12.9
Athens, GA	13.5

FINDING THE BEST PLACES IN NORTH AMERICA

A quarter century ago, the Environmental Protection Agency rated 243 American metro areas for livability by such diverse factors as unemployment rates, crime rates, and per capita contributions to charity. Their method for determining the best all-around city (it was Minneapolis, by the way) was very simple: The scores for each place in each of the factors were averaged for a final score.

Places Rated's method is no different. Atlanta, for example, has a score of 39.38 in costs of living, 98.30 in transportation, 99.15 in job outlook, 82.71 in education options, 69.12 in climate mildness, 12.19 in crime, 94.62 in the arts, 57.22 in health care, and 76.20 in recreation. If you think of these scores as percentages (which they actually are), Atlanta's job outlook elevates it above 99 out of 100 metro areas in North America, its climate beats almost 7 out of 10 areas, but some 88 out of 100 areas are better than the Georgia capital when it comes to crime.

Because the system is based on scores, the higher the average (or overall) score, the better the metro area is judged to be all-around. (Atlanta places 33rd overall among the metro areas.) The map on the preceding pages locates the thirty-five metro areas that rise to the top as the best places to live in North America.

These leading metro areas closely resemble those in *Places Rated*'s previous (1997) edition. Although their rankings have changed somewhat, twenty-five were in the top thirty-five before. Of the ten newcomers to the list, five were among the previous top fifty.

By no means are these top-rated places untarnished. Seventeen score near the bottom in costs of living, eleven are among the worst in crime, and four have low scores in climate. More importantly, not one metro area scores in the upper half in all of *Places Rated*'s nine categories.

Back to the point: There isn't an ideal haven in North America. In spite of a blot or two, many come close through a combination of strengths. Whether their strengths are vital or unimportant, or whether their blots are knockout factors or trivial, is for you to decide.

RANKINGS: PUTTING IT ALL TOGETHER

The following table recaps each metro area's score in *Places Rated*'s nine categories. Scores range from 0 to 100 and are normalized such that the 50th percentile point is the average for all metro areas. Scores that are among the top thirty-five in each category are highlighted.

The mean of these nine scores is also shown, as is the overall rank. Abilene's mean score, 42.18 (the sum of its scores in each category divided by nine), ranks it 232nd overall among the 354 metro areas. Akron's mean score of 59.42 ranks it 102nd. Albuquerque's mean score is 66.16, ranking it 56th. Lower mean scores indicate worse metro areas and higher mean scores indicate better metro areas. The highest possible score would be 100, meaning a perfect score in all nine categories.

METRO AREA	COSTS OF LIVING	TRANSPOR-TATION	JOBS	EDUCATION	CLIMATE	CRIME	ARTS	HEALTH CARE	RECREATION	MEAN SCORE	OVERALL RANK
Abilene, TX	96.32	36.54	17.28	49.29	55.52	49.58	27.20	45.04	2.83	42.18	231
Akron, OH	47.31	69.68	86.11	71.95	22.66	54.11	81.59	24.07	77.33	59.42	105
Albany, GA	86.12	28.04	32.01	26.62	75.63	15.59	33.15	20.11	6.79	36.01	291
Albany-Schenectady-Troy, NY	25.22	82.71	52.97	99.43	8.78	73.94	79.61	77.33	77.62	64.18	78
Albuquerque, NM	44.48	84.13	90.65	71.67	78.18	2.84	75.36	77.90	70.25	66.16	57
Alexandria, LA	92.36	42.49	19.26	11.61	66.00	7.09	40.80	62.03	22.66	40.48	253
Allentown-Bethlehem-Easton, PA	33.72	66.57	29.46	63.45	47.30	89.81	58.08	63.45	47.87	55.52	131
Altoona, PA	61.76	26.91	12.18	1.69	54.95	98.87	15.30	64.02	0.00	37.30	277
Amarillo, TX	96.89	60.05	28.32	54.10	39.66	28.62	35.13	64.58	30.59	48.66	184
Anchorage, AK	15.87	84.41	76.48	41.35	71.10	24.93	29.47	5.09	6.23	39.44	262
Ann Arbor, MI	7.37	15.86	77.33	83.00	32.57	70.26	67.99	94.33	83.28	59.11	108
Anniston, AL	93.21	7.08	7.64	21.81	62.32	22.95	4.54	29.74	13.88	29.24	332
Appleton-Oshkosh-Neenah, WI	54.40	70.82	79.32	47.30	4.24	97.74	50.71	54.10	86.40	60.56	98
Asheville, NC	54.11	54.67	54.10	59.77	66.57	68.56	44.76	85.83	38.81	58.58	113
Athens, GA	62.04	29.46	47.30	45.32	69.12	36.83	37.40	31.44	32.01	43.44	223
★Atlanta, GA	39.38	98.30	99.15	82.71	69.97	12.19	94.62	57.22	76.20	69.97	33
Atlantic-Cape May, NJ	30.03	66.85	62.03	20.39	65.43	13.32	38.25	15.29	91.21	44.76	212
Augusta-Aiken, GA-SC	77.91	35.41	63.45	46.45	72.52	43.91	50.43	86.11	53.54	58.86	111
★Austin-San Marcos, TX	50.43	78.75	98.01	98.30	71.67	40.23	72.24	64.87	68.83	71.48	20
Bakersfield, CA	24.65	50.70	85.55	18.69	96.88	24.08	18.99	19.54	30.87	41.11	242
★Baltimore, MD	22.38	94.90	75.92	94.05	69.68	3.97	95.47	86.40	84.98	69.75	34
Bangor, ME	34.57	66.28	3.11	90.36	27.19	94.34	63.46	43.62	60.33	53.70	142
Barnstable-Yarmouth, MA	6.24	38.24	26.34	10.19	75.35	45.90	62.89	14.16	94.61	41.55	237
Baton Rouge, LA	68.28	57.22	82.43	39.09	75.07	1.70	45.90	57.50	57.79	53.89	140
Beaumont-Port Arthur, TX	93.49	41.92	36.26	30.02	64.87	22.10	24.65	38.81	49.00	44.57	213
Bellingham, WA	27.77	48.15	71.95	38.52	79.32	71.11	67.14	32.57	23.51	51.12	168
Benton Harbor, MI	45.61	45.60	7.08	25.49	10.76	13.60	47.88	28.04	71.67	32.86	311
Bergen-Passaic, NJ	2.55	14.44	26.06	69.97	44.19	76.21	90.09	89.51	56.09	52.12	158
Billings, MT	70.83	74.22	28.89	11.89	28.89	82.44	17.29	56.37	16.71	43.06	225
Biloxi-Gulfport-Pascagoula, MS	74.79	36.82	77.90	1.13	82.71	41.36	31.17	48.72	82.43	53.00	147
Binghamton, NY	28.90	67.13	14.73	37.11	24.36	96.04	47.31	22.94	57.50	44.00	217
★Birmingham, AL	51.28	79.88	77.33	80.73	66.85	14.17	85.27	97.45	73.37	69.59	35
Bismarck, ND	83.86	33.42	35.12	37.39	13.03	95.19	37.97	82.71	41.92	51.18	165
Bloomington-Normal, IL	57.80	72.23	40.79	64.87	21.52	91.79	62.33	13.59	29.46	50.49	174
Boise City, ID	54.96	67.42	91.78	61.75	85.26	71.96	75.64	60.33	46.17	68.36	46
Boston, MA-NH	1.14	94.61	49.00	99.71	59.20	46.75	98.59	94.90	77.05	68.99	41
Boulder-Longmont, CO	15.02	12.74	75.35	45.04	61.47	74.23	69.98	61.75	46.17	51.31	164
Brazoria, TX	88.39	0.28	47.59	9.34	81.30	83.86	13.89	3.96	35.97	40.51	252
Bremerton, WA	37.40	20.11	50.70	6.79	78.75	77.63	36.27	6.79	43.34	39.75	259
Bridgeport, CT	13.89	34.84	9.34	57.79	60.33	47.60	77.91	67.42	62.32	47.94	188
Brockton, MA	12.19	3.68	18.98	35.69	48.72	47.88	36.55	1.69	52.12	28.61	336
Brownsville-Harlingen-San Benito, TX	98.31	27.47	69.97	18.98	88.66	35.13	3.40	13.88	62.03	46.43	198
Bryan-College Station, TX	91.51	31.72	50.42	32.29	73.65	48.73	33.72	41.64	28.89	48.06	185
Buffalo-Niagara Falls, NY	41.36	86.11	50.99	92.63	19.26	39.95	93.49	81.58	89.51	66.10	59
Burlington, VT	20.12	66.00	30.87	77.90	9.06	72.24	80.17	66.85	80.73	55.99	129
Calgary, AB	26.07	90.36	83.56	57.22	48.44	52.70	88.11	83.56	64.30	66.04	62
Canton-Massillon, OH	58.65	65.43	56.37	47.87	22.66	59.78	8.79	34.27	67.98	46.87	195

continues

METRO AREA	COSTS OF LIVING	TRANSPOR-TATION	JOBS	EDUCATION	CLIMATE	CRIME	ARTS	HEALTH CARE	RECREATION	MEAN SCORE	OVERALL RANK
Casper, WY	90.66	38.81	12.74	9.06	8.21	57.23	42.50	35.12	11.04	33.93	306
Cedar Rapids, IA	52.41	64.02	34.27	56.09	5.94	69.41	56.38	41.92	38.52	46.55	197
Champaign-Urbana, IL	66.29	73.93	35.97	60.33	28.04	46.18	56.10	71.67	31.72	52.25	156
Charleston, WV	64.59	73.37	33.14	62.60	51.27	72.81	52.41	83.28	19.26	56.97	124
Charleston-North Charleston, SC	47.60	58.64	81.86	68.83	83.28	15.02	61.19	88.66	93.76	66.54	54
Charlotte-Gastonia-Rock Hill, NC-SC	27.20	94.05	94.05	83.56	72.80	6.24	88.39	50.14	81.30	66.41	55
Charlottesville, VA	20.40	53.25	40.50	72.23	71.38	80.46	59.78	79.88	35.12	57.00	123
Chattanooga, TN-GA	94.91	56.94	65.15	56.94	64.58	22.67	81.87	58.92	61.75	62.64	87
Cheyenne, WY	85.84	37.96	11.33	12.46	40.22	84.99	25.78	22.37	5.94	36.32	288
Chicago, IL	9.35	100.00	86.96	98.86	16.14	2.27	99.16	81.30	97.16	65.69	67
Chico-Paradise, CA	36.55	30.31	51.27	21.24	94.61	66.58	10.49	45.60	11.89	40.95	245
Chicoutimi-Jonquiere, PQ	24.08	46.45	4.53	33.42	0.28	84.71	6.80	52.69	57.22	34.46	302
★ Cincinnati, OH-KY-IN	34.85	99.15	82.71	96.60	39.37	55.81	94.06	78.75	78.75	73.34	11
Clarksville-Hopkinsville, TN-KY	100.00	13.03	57.22	27.76	31.16	29.47	37.12	2.54	12.74	34.56	300
★ Cleveland-Lorain-Elyria, OH	21.25	96.31	75.07	88.95	16.43	56.10	97.17	84.70	99.71	70.63	28
Colorado Springs, CO	41.65	76.77	90.08	80.45	58.64	61.48	62.04	11.89	50.70	59.30	106
Columbia, MO	68.56	34.27	73.08	64.58	25.77	62.04	60.06	97.73	36.54	58.07	116
Columbia, SC	64.03	63.73	88.95	92.35	68.27	9.92	64.31	73.65	69.40	66.07	60
Columbus, GA-AL	80.17	45.04	39.37	38.24	76.77	55.53	47.03	40.50	42.77	51.71	160
Columbus, OH	28.62	91.21	86.40	95.18	44.75	34.28	92.64	58.35	81.86	68.14	47
Corpus Christi, TX	94.62	49.29	58.92	16.71	84.13	15.87	18.70	54.39	51.27	49.32	179
Cumberland, MD-WV	60.06	28.61	5.38	51.55	24.64	84.42	20.97	38.52	2.54	35.19	297
Dallas, TX	49.30	95.46	95.18	90.08	47.59	9.35	93.21	48.15	88.95	68.59	44
Danbury, CT	2.84	3.39	3.96	17.28	37.67	96.61	23.23	41.35	15.29	26.85	342
Danville, VA	83.01	7.93	4.24	22.66	56.65	92.64	18.42	4.53	1.13	32.36	315
Davenport-Moline-Rock Island, IA-IL	72.81	80.16	34.84	78.47	20.11	58.93	59.21	33.42	67.70	56.18	128
Dayton-Springfield, OH	48.45	88.38	63.73	96.88	20.96	49.86	87.54	79.60	56.94	65.82	64
Daytona Beach, FL	94.06	41.35	69.40	66.85	86.40	26.35	22.10	26.06	91.78	58.26	115
Decatur, AL	90.94	2.26	10.19	20.96	45.60	85.56	2.84	17.56	33.14	34.34	303
Decatur, IL	69.69	36.26	0.28	16.99	13.31	47.03	43.91	28.04	7.93	29.27	331
★ Denver, CO	22.10	98.58	95.46	92.06	50.42	42.50	97.74	85.26	82.71	74.09	5
Des Moines, IA	50.15	78.18	68.83	96.31	8.49	63.46	60.34	39.37	67.42	59.17	107
Detroit, MI	14.74	98.86	80.73	70.53	30.02	17.00	95.19	49.00	96.60	61.41	94
Dothan, AL	89.81	29.74	32.86	25.77	85.83	54.68	5.10	55.24	2.26	42.37	229
Dover, DE	32.87	10.19	27.76	31.44	59.49	53.26	3.12	0.84	18.98	26.44	343
Dubuque, IA	63.46	54.39	8.78	80.16	3.11	92.07	46.75	24.92	19.54	43.69	218
Duluth-Superior, MN-WI	45.33	52.40	19.83	85.83	1.41	87.82	74.23	88.10	90.93	60.65	97
Dutchess County, NY	4.25	23.22	30.59	65.43	43.05	81.31	48.16	48.44	60.90	45.04	209
Eau Claire, WI	44.20	45.32	66.57	49.00	3.39	95.47	42.78	90.36	35.41	52.50	153
Edmonton, AB	43.63	91.78	67.70	72.52	36.26	44.48	82.72	97.16	88.10	69.37	37
El Paso, TX	95.47	70.25	86.68	30.59	82.15	11.62	54.11	19.83	42.49	54.80	137
Elkhart-Goshen, IN	84.71	16.14	43.05	23.51	2.83	59.21	40.23	4.24	3.68	30.84	322
Elmira, NY	31.45	63.45	1.41	17.56	29.17	83.57	31.45	25.21	11.61	32.76	312
Enid, OK	90.37	26.06	2.26	3.96	30.87	26.92	11.34	33.71	1.69	25.24	348
Erie, PA	56.66	60.90	20.11	70.25	24.07	82.72	38.82	54.95	75.35	53.76	141
Eugene-Springfield, OR	42.21	59.77	57.79	61.18	79.60	60.06	51.00	53.54	41.35	56.28	127
Evansville-Henderson, IN-KY	85.56	65.15	27.47	57.50	39.09	56.38	75.08	81.86	27.19	57.25	122
Fargo-Moorhead, ND-MN	87.54	41.64	67.42	59.20	10.19	94.91	82.16	81.01	47.02	63.45	81
Fayetteville, NC	78.19	42.77	60.62	29.74	64.02	10.77	48.45	17.84	17.28	41.08	243
Fayetteville-Springdale-Rogers, AR	72.53	50.14	91.21	39.37	49.29	90.66	64.59	46.17	52.97	61.88	91
Fitchburg-Leominster, MA	14.17	4.53	2.83	34.27	41.07	51.85	17.85	35.97	31.44	26.00	345
Flagstaff, AZ-UT	29.75	25.21	63.17	28.89	74.50	51.00	24.08	25.49	21.24	38.15	269
Flint, MI	24.93	58.92	19.54	43.34	27.76	7.37	43.63	27.47	40.50	32.61	314
Florence, AL	84.42	17.56	21.81	37.96	45.60	88.96	8.22	39.94	40.22	42.74	227
Florence, SC	78.76	33.14	47.87	24.92	81.58	12.47	5.95	70.82	1.98	39.72	260
Fort Collins-Loveland, CO	32.30	13.31	79.88	34.56	46.74	86.12	39.67	47.02	26.06	45.07	208
Fort Lauderdale, FL	33.43	81.58	93.48	48.44	90.93	7.65	87.82	62.88	84.13	65.59	69
Fort Myers-Cape Coral, FL	86.97	75.35	85.26	2.83	92.91	39.38	45.33	33.99	93.20	61.69	92
Fort Pierce-Port St. Lucie, FL	69.98	0.84	60.90	7.08	91.50	29.75	30.03	15.86	86.96	43.66	219
Fort Smith, AR-OK	81.59	40.22	64.30	7.36	43.34	68.28	21.53	53.82	31.16	45.73	201
Fort Walton Beach, FL	53.26	43.05	55.52	5.09	76.48	75.64	10.20	20.96	70.82	45.67	203
Fort Wayne, IN	83.57	65.72	56.09	79.88	13.88	70.83	83.57	50.70	66.85	63.45	81

METRO AREA	COSTS OF LIVING	TRANSPOR-TATION	JOBS	EDUCATION	CLIMATE	CRIME	ARTS	HEALTH CARE	RECREATION	MEAN SCORE	OVERALL RANK
Fort Worth-Arlington, TX	74.23	92.63	98.58	66.57	47.59	20.40	85.56	29.46	73.08	65.34	71
Fresno, CA	40.23	69.12	87.25	51.84	93.76	5.95	33.43	30.02	27.47	48.79	182
Gadsden, AL	91.22	4.24	3.11	8.49	60.90	15.30	30.60	24.64	8.21	27.41	338
Gainesville, FL	67.99	55.52	69.68	50.14	84.41	0.85	58.65	96.31	59.77	60.37	99
Galveston-Texas City, TX	73.94	1.98	59.49	43.62	83.00	17.57	22.95	55.80	45.60	44.88	211
Gary, IN	46.18	19.26	37.11	63.17	7.08	18.70	12.75	42.20	54.39	33.43	309
Glens Falls, NY	22.95	6.23	1.98	15.01	3.68	79.04	32.02	36.82	63.73	29.05	333
Goldsboro, NC	75.64	6.51	11.04	8.21	61.18	33.15	7.09	2.83	0.84	22.94	351
Grand Forks, ND-MN	71.68	37.67	21.24	56.37	11.61	92.36	68.56	53.25	44.47	50.80	172
Grand Junction, CO	41.93	51.55	32.29	18.13	74.22	71.68	26.63	77.62	10.48	44.95	210
Grand Rapids-Muskegon-Holland, MI	52.70	77.33	90.36	79.32	6.79	56.95	77.06	27.19	99.43	63.01	85
Great Falls, MT	76.49	58.35	2.54	2.54	16.71	64.31	15.02	30.59	9.34	30.65	324
Greeley, CO	58.36	11.61	36.26	34.84	33.14	66.86	43.06	9.06	20.39	34.84	298
Green Bay, WI	39.95	60.33	68.55	62.88	10.48	85.84	39.10	18.13	41.92	47.46	190
★Greensboro–Winston-Salem–High Point, NC	32.58	85.83	84.41	88.10	80.73	35.42	73.38	72.23	85.83	70.95	25
Greenville, NC	58.93	26.62	70.25	41.92	58.35	17.29	6.24	73.08	14.44	40.79	249
Greenville-Spartanburg-Anderson, SC	58.08	75.92	85.83	74.50	74.78	16.15	67.43	55.52	72.52	64.53	75
Hagerstown, MD	76.78	31.44	17.56	11.04	41.64	89.52	35.42	7.08	22.37	36.98	280
Halifax, NS	17.57	85.26	39.66	90.93	50.99	34.85	65.73	98.86	69.68	61.50	93
Hamilton, ON	16.44	39.37	59.77	39.66	25.49	66.01	83.01	91.78	39.09	51.18	165
Hamilton-Middletown, OH	39.10	6.79	68.27	60.90	29.46	44.76	51.85	5.66	30.02	37.42	276
Harrisburg-Lebanon-Carlisle, PA	48.73	77.62	81.30	73.93	56.37	79.61	46.18	69.40	61.47	66.07	60
Hartford, CT	11.90	87.81	35.41	91.21	41.35	58.36	93.77	66.28	75.07	62.35	89
Hattiesburg, MS	81.87	20.39	22.94	52.40	55.24	48.16	70.26	69.12	39.37	51.08	169
Hickory-Morganton-Lenoir, NC	60.63	24.64	56.37	32.57	70.25	73.09	32.30	34.84	55.80	48.94	180
★Honolulu, HI	0.57	78.47	66.28	86.96	98.58	62.33	90.37	62.32	92.91	70.98	24
Houma, LA	84.99	20.39	22.94	5.94	79.03	62.89	0.00	22.09	83.00	40.10	257
★Houston, TX	59.50	94.33	94.90	71.10	80.45	24.65	89.81	65.43	85.26	73.94	8
Huntington-Ashland, WV-KY-OH	74.51	41.07	30.31	67.13	57.22	90.37	35.70	63.17	48.72	56.47	126
Huntsville, AL	67.71	51.84	67.98	89.51	53.25	43.35	60.63	45.32	63.45	60.34	100
★Indianapolis, IN	55.53	93.20	84.70	83.85	23.51	31.17	96.04	88.95	82.15	71.01	23
Iowa City, IA	43.91	22.66	47.02	42.20	7.64	77.91	57.23	95.75	43.90	48.69	183
Jackson, MI	57.23	8.78	16.14	10.48	21.81	42.78	26.35	1.98	50.14	26.19	344
Jackson, MS	86.41	67.98	77.05	69.68	49.85	21.53	49.58	92.63	55.52	63.36	83
Jackson, TN	99.16	30.59	49.85	52.69	35.12	3.40	27.48	79.32	4.53	42.46	228
Jacksonville, FL	71.39	81.86	91.50	44.75	86.11	1.99	78.19	71.38	94.05	69.02	40
Jacksonville, NC	82.72	30.87	22.37	0.84	66.28	78.76	4.25	1.13	37.67	36.10	289
Jamestown, NY	38.25	27.19	0.84	53.54	14.44	86.97	75.93	8.49	72.23	41.99	233
Janesville-Beloit, WI	53.83	17.28	29.17	37.67	9.63	75.36	59.50	16.71	37.96	37.46	275
Jersey City, NJ	5.39	9.91	16.43	40.22	76.20	8.79	71.11	38.24	16.14	31.38	318
Johnson City-Kingsport-Bristol, TN-VA	97.46	49.57	49.57	67.42	64.30	90.94	42.21	75.07	49.29	65.09	73
Johnstown, PA	56.95	37.39	21.52	33.99	20.39	100.00	19.84	52.69	35.69	42.05	232
Jonesboro, AR	73.66	25.49	24.92	22.94	18.41	67.14	7.37	78.47	5.66	36.01	291
Joplin, MO	87.82	32.86	60.33	35.41	31.44	77.34	4.82	11.04	10.19	39.03	265
Kalamazoo-Battle Creek, MI	56.38	61.47	60.05	75.35	14.73	32.58	65.16	47.59	87.81	55.68	130
Kankakee, IL	45.05	5.94	33.42	26.34	18.98	19.55	3.97	11.33	18.69	20.36	354
Kansas City, MO-KS	47.03	93.76	87.81	96.03	26.91	4.82	89.24	67.70	87.25	66.73	54
Kenosha, WI	41.08	9.63	27.19	55.24	30.31	78.19	34.57	3.39	49.57	36.57	285
Killeen-Temple, TX	96.61	31.16	44.47	41.64	52.40	65.44	1.70	44.75	20.96	44.35	214
Kitchener-Waterloo, ON	17.29	68.55	53.25	46.74	35.69	81.02	72.53	34.56	16.99	47.40	192
★Knoxville, TN	88.11	69.97	88.38	81.58	57.50	30.32	66.01	86.68	86.11	72.74	13
Kokomo, IN	77.34	11.89	3.11	40.50	15.58	76.49	52.70	18.41	12.46	34.28	304
La Crosse, WI-MN	49.86	52.97	31.72	82.15	20.67	94.62	41.93	75.92	44.19	54.89	136
Lafayette, IN	69.41	49.85	45.32	49.85	23.22	81.87	46.46	13.03	37.11	46.24	199
Lafayette, LA	90.09	44.47	68.83	31.72	72.23	57.51	23.80	33.14	52.69	52.72	151
Lake Charles, LA	84.14	35.12	34.56	10.76	68.83	11.34	11.62	46.45	16.43	35.47	295
Lakeland-Winter Haven, FL	73.09	8.49	53.54	53.25	86.68	5.67	2.27	20.67	87.53	43.47	221
Lancaster, PA	36.83	40.50	57.50	39.94	50.70	95.76	68.28	31.16	37.39	50.90	171

continues

Rankings: Putting It All Together

METRO AREA	COSTS OF LIVING	TRANSPOR-TATION	JOBS	EDUCATION	CLIMATE	CRIME	ARTS	HEALTH CARE	RECREATION	MEAN SCORE	OVERALL RANK
Lansing-East Lansing, MI	45.90	70.53	61.18	64.30	11.04	52.13	49.01	26.91	65.15	49.57	178
Laredo, TX	99.72	46.74	72.80	8.78	91.78	25.50	1.99	2.26	0.56	38.90	267
Las Cruces, NM	69.13	32.01	45.04	31.16	58.92	52.98	30.32	0.56	23.22	38.15	269
Las Vegas, NV-AZ	38.53	87.53	99.71	16.43	87.81	16.72	50.15	24.36	95.18	57.38	121
Lawrence, KS	75.36	11.33	22.66	71.38	26.06	48.45	24.93	5.38	38.24	35.98	293
Lawrence, MA-NH	11.34	5.38	39.09	33.71	40.50	58.08	0.85	18.98	50.99	28.77	335
Lawton, OK	89.24	24.92	17.56	13.31	34.84	30.60	1.42	16.43	4.24	25.84	346
Lewiston-Auburn, ME	26.63	15.01	8.49	44.19	33.42	91.51	9.92	36.54	20.11	31.76	317
Lexington, KY	59.21	73.08	82.15	93.48	44.47	36.27	55.81	98.01	60.05	66.95	50
Lima, OH	78.48	18.13	7.93	35.12	19.83	20.97	49.86	21.24	25.21	30.75	323
Lincoln, NE	64.31	68.27	70.53	88.38	14.16	39.10	69.13	76.77	40.79	59.05	110
Little Rock-North Little Rock, AR	63.18	76.20	79.03	77.33	49.00	3.69	43.35	92.35	68.27	61.38	95
London, ON	19.84	59.20	41.64	78.75	9.34	61.76	71.96	90.65	29.17	51.37	163
Long Island, NY	2.27	63.17	67.13	52.97	81.86	87.54	72.81	99.15	99.15	69.56	36
Longview-Marshall, TX	96.04	23.51	56.94	45.60	53.54	42.21	14.74	13.31	21.52	40.82	248
Los Angeles-Long Beach, CA	5.67	93.48	48.15	77.05	99.15	1.14	99.44	67.98	92.63	64.97	74
★Louisville, KY-IN	51.00	90.08	80.16	85.55	47.02	51.56	80.46	87.81	80.45	72.68	14
Lowell, MA-NH	14.45	2.83	13.31	12.18	37.96	60.63	56.95	37.39	58.35	32.67	313
Lubbock, TX	88.96	62.88	38.52	54.95	45.32	32.02	16.15	91.21	24.92	50.55	173
Lynchburg, VA	75.08	43.90	25.77	76.20	77.33	80.74	20.68	28.89	48.15	52.97	149
Macon, GA	71.11	29.17	35.69	76.48	58.07	41.65	15.87	71.67	53.82	50.39	176
Madison, WI	18.14	73.65	79.60	92.91	4.81	74.79	79.04	90.93	62.88	64.08	79
Manchester, NH	23.23	47.59	26.91	79.03	2.54	85.27	44.20	12.74	49.85	41.26	239
Mansfield, OH	59.78	16.71	38.24	16.14	9.91	34.57	55.53	15.01	15.58	29.05	333
McAllen-Edinburg-Mission, TX	98.59	32.29	88.10	3.68	78.47	35.70	12.47	12.46	22.94	42.74	226
Medford-Ashland, OR	42.78	47.87	62.60	7.64	89.23	64.59	39.95	40.22	13.03	45.32	206
Melbourne-Titusville-Palm Bay, FL	83.29	23.79	58.92	61.47	92.35	26.63	58.36	23.51	91.50	57.76	119
Memphis, TN-AR-MS	77.06	92.91	92.35	67.70	40.79	5.10	70.54	80.73	75.92	67.01	49
Merced, CA	31.73	22.94	31.16	0.00	94.90	50.43	6.52	8.21	9.06	28.33	337
★Miami, FL	35.13	90.65	83.85	73.65	91.21	0.00	89.52	96.88	89.80	72.30	17
Middlesex-Somerset-Hunterdon, NJ	5.10	18.98	64.58	73.37	50.14	87.26	90.66	74.78	53.25	57.57	120
Milwaukee-Waukesha, WI	16.72	96.60	65.72	95.75	15.29	53.55	92.92	84.98	98.86	68.93	42
★Minneapolis-St. Paul, MN-WI	21.53	97.45	94.61	95.46	4.53	62.61	98.02	93.20	96.03	73.72	9
Missoula, MT	51.85	57.50	42.20	33.14	51.55	78.48	25.50	59.77	32.57	48.06	185
Mobile, AL	64.88	51.27	74.22	60.62	67.42	7.94	47.60	60.90	92.06	58.55	114
Modesto, CA	29.47	21.24	43.90	4.53	95.75	16.44	22.38	30.87	8.78	30.37	325
Monmouth-Ocean, NJ	11.62	12.18	54.95	59.49	71.95	86.41	87.26	43.34	84.70	56.88	125
Monroe, LA	87.26	56.37	45.60	24.07	43.90	10.20	26.07	64.30	17.84	41.73	236
Montgomery, AL	60.34	50.42	44.19	74.22	73.08	33.72	61.48	59.49	33.42	54.48	139
Montreal, PQ	11.05	95.18	78.47	83.28	2.26	50.15	96.89	98.58	73.93	65.53	70
Muncie, IN	62.89	18.69	18.41	54.39	37.39	63.74	11.90	35.69	26.91	36.67	282
Myrtle Beach, SC	42.50	60.62	76.77	12.74	62.60	4.25	17.00	10.76	83.85	41.23	240
Naples, FL	20.68	35.69	76.20	13.88	92.06	31.73	29.18	21.81	52.40	41.51	238
Nashua, NH	13.04	1.13	15.29	47.59	1.69	99.72	23.52	8.78	32.86	27.07	339
★Nashville, TN	67.14	88.95	93.76	84.13	42.49	8.22	78.48	86.96	81.58	70.19	30
New Bedford, MA	20.97	32.57	9.06	6.51	65.72	26.07	34.00	0.00	47.59	26.94	341
New Haven-Meriden, CT	13.60	42.20	11.61	90.65	60.33	37.68	86.41	60.05	60.62	51.46	162
New London-Norwich, CT-RI	8.79	20.67	18.13	53.82	38.81	90.09	68.84	14.73	55.24	41.01	244
★New Orleans, LA	54.68	84.98	74.78	75.07	75.92	1.42	83.86	91.50	100.00	71.36	21
New York, NY	0.00	99.43	41.92	94.61	70.53	0.57	100.00	92.06	92.35	65.72	65
Newark, NJ	3.97	96.03	32.57	93.76	60.05	18.14	96.61	88.38	76.48	62.89	86
Newburgh, NY-PA	6.80	48.72	46.74	29.46	49.57	79.33	0.57	18.41	50.42	36.67	282
Norfolk-Virginia Beach-Newport News, VA-NC	44.76	81.30	83.00	86.68	69.40	43.63	84.42	23.79	98.58	68.40	45
Oakland, CA	3.69	72.80	87.53	84.41	97.16	13.04	96.32	56.94	83.56	66.16	57
Ocala, FL	97.74	1.69	43.62	0.56	83.85	10.49	7.94	4.81	20.67	30.15	326
Odessa-Midland, TX	95.19	53.82	18.69	19.83	54.10	34.00	15.87	7.36	12.18	34.56	300
Oklahoma City, OK	82.44	74.78	72.23	93.20	34.56	18.42	76.21	63.73	77.90	65.94	63
Olympia, WA	36.27	13.88	73.93	29.17	77.90	81.59	88.96	31.72	25.77	51.02	170
Omaha, NE-IA	51.56	85.55	84.13	87.81	12.46	41.93	82.44	94.61	79.88	68.93	42
★Orange County, CA	0.85	72.52	95.75	77.62	98.30	56.66	86.97	82.15	81.01	72.43	16
★Orlando, FL	70.54	87.25	97.45	55.80	87.53	6.52	78.76	57.79	97.73	71.04	22
Oshawa, ON	17.85	21.52	45.89	6.23	52.12	83.01	28.90	15.58	9.63	31.19	320
Ottawa-Hull, ON-PQ	12.47	89.80	83.28	75.63	5.38	61.19	81.02	95.18	58.64	62.51	88
Owensboro, KY	79.04	30.02	15.58	26.06	41.92	89.24	13.32	21.52	18.41	37.23	278

METRO AREA	COSTS OF LIVING	TRANSPOR- TATION	JOBS	EDUCATION	CLIMATE	CRIME	ARTS	HEALTH CARE	RECREATION	MEAN SCORE	OVERALL RANK
Panama City, FL	65.44	43.34	44.75	11.33	84.70	30.03	9.64	12.18	66.28	40.85	247
Parkersburg- Marietta, WV-OH	81.31	34.56	13.88	49.57	55.80	99.16	41.08	16.99	33.71	47.34	193
Pensacola, FL	80.46	64.30	74.50	9.63	85.55	12.75	17.57	56.65	75.63	53.00	147
Peoria-Pekin, IL	71.96	57.79	55.24	58.92	18.69	52.41	66.86	39.66	71.10	54.74	138
★Philadelphia, PA-NJ	10.20	95.75	78.18	89.80	56.94	45.33	98.31	85.55	74.78	70.54	29
★Phoenix-Mesa, AZ	37.68	89.51	100.00	84.98	94.33	20.68	86.69	51.55	94.90	73.37	10
Pine Bluff, AR	81.02	8.21	7.36	7.93	52.97	2.55	11.05	39.09	5.09	23.92	350
★Pittsburgh, PA	38.82	99.71	62.88	60.05	48.15	84.14	90.94	94.05	78.18	72.99	12
Pittsfield, MA	22.67	19.54	0.56	4.81	22.37	86.69	69.41	30.31	48.44	33.87	307
Pocatello, ID	65.16	40.79	33.71	30.87	32.86	69.13	14.45	40.79	14.73	38.05	271
Portland, ME	49.01	71.95	36.82	89.23	45.04	75.93	58.93	75.35	85.55	65.31	72
★Portland- Vancouver, OR-WA	10.77	88.10	98.86	96.88	67.13	32.87	91.51	65.15	86.68	70.88	26
Portsmouth- Rochester, NH-ME	15.59	2.54	48.44	70.82	17.28	98.31	57.80	17.28	63.17	43.47	221
Providence-Fall River- Warwick, RI-MA	18.70	83.00	23.51	88.66	54.67	67.99	77.63	47.30	79.32	60.09	101
Provo-Orem, UT	48.16	11.04	89.51	50.99	57.79	91.22	54.40	3.68	56.65	51.49	161
Pueblo, CO	75.93	28.89	26.62	17.84	38.52	6.80	32.87	58.64	11.33	33.05	310
Punta Gorda, FL	61.19	3.11	58.07	0.28	90.08	88.39	7.65	23.22	67.13	44.35	215
Quebec City, PQ	16.15	81.01	46.45	74.78	0.84	73.66	71.68	99.71	34.84	55.46	132
Racine, WI	24.37	9.06	13.03	5.38	12.18	58.65	38.53	7.64	54.67	24.83	349
★Raleigh-Durham- Chapel Hill, NC	13.32	92.06	96.88	100.00	70.82	40.80	86.12	93.48	72.80	74.03	6
Rapid City, SD	86.69	54.95	29.74	22.37	26.62	65.16	9.07	51.27	19.83	40.63	250
Reading, PA	27.48	48.44	30.02	46.17	32.29	75.08	27.77	26.62	51.84	40.63	250
Redding, CA	46.75	43.62	49.29	18.41	92.63	55.25	5.67	43.05	15.86	41.17	241
Regina, SK	47.88	90.93	12.46	84.70	7.36	19.84	73.94	83.85	51.55	52.50	153
Reno, NV	28.33	86.40	61.75	48.72	88.10	45.61	51.28	66.00	70.53	60.75	96
Richland-Kennewick- Pasco, WA	72.24	61.18	55.80	1.98	89.51	67.43	20.12	10.19	28.32	45.20	207
Richmond- Petersburg, VA	32.02	80.45	84.98	58.07	63.45	46.46	77.34	83.85	74.50	66.79	51
Riverside- San Bernardino, CA	23.52	79.60	99.43	56.65	97.73	13.89	92.07	31.72	96.88	65.72	65
Roanoke, VA	62.33	67.70	43.34	68.27	73.37	73.38	51.56	90.08	39.66	63.30	84
Rochester, MN	35.70	47.30	23.51	36.82	1.13	92.92	52.98	89.23	9.91	43.28	224
★Rochester, NY	28.05	82.15	62.32	98.58	34.27	71.39	83.29	73.37	98.30	70.19	30
Rockford, IL	56.10	52.12	33.99	15.29	12.74	24.37	44.48	54.67	44.75	37.61	272
Rocky Mount, NC	65.73	22.09	24.07	22.09	63.17	35.98	22.67	9.63	0.28	29.52	329
Sacramento, CA	25.50	79.03	96.03	55.52	94.05	22.38	74.79	59.20	74.22	64.52	76
Saginaw-Bay City- Midland, MI	66.58	54.10	37.96	65.72	17.56	37.40	57.51	46.74	68.55	50.24	177
St. Catharines- Niagara, ON	18.42	20.96	25.49	14.44	24.92	74.51	76.78	62.60	43.62	40.19	255
St. Cloud, MN	40.80	50.99	52.40	41.07	18.13	98.02	84.99	37.11	56.37	53.32	145
Saint John, NB	35.42	59.49	4.81	3.11	30.59	88.67	21.25	61.18	71.38	41.77	235
St. John's, NF	12.75	76.48	9.63	14.73	46.17	88.11	27.20	96.03	58.92	47.78	189
St. Joseph, MO	82.16	16.43	1.69	38.81	13.59	64.88	55.25	9.34	7.08	32.14	316
St. Louis, MO-IL	50.71	97.73	71.38	99.15	28.61	23.23	94.91	66.57	90.36	69.18	38
Salem, OR	35.98	14.73	73.65	62.03	80.16	60.91	41.65	9.91	13.59	43.62	220
Salinas, CA	9.07	56.09	53.82	51.27	98.01	43.06	54.68	27.76	79.60	52.60	152
★Salt Lake City- Ogden, UT	30.32	96.88	98.30	81.30	62.03	53.83	92.36	68.83	96.31	75.57	1
San Angelo, TX	92.92	26.34	10.48	24.36	52.69	49.01	28.62	19.26	14.16	35.32	296
San Antonio, TX	91.79	80.73	96.31	66.00	65.15	27.20	60.91	68.27	65.72	69.12	39
★San Diego, CA	3.12	89.23	97.73	79.60	99.71	25.22	91.22	68.55	90.08	71.61	19
★San Francisco, CA	0.29	86.68	66.85	98.01	97.45	17.85	97.46	95.46	93.48	72.61	15
★San Jose, CA	1.70	79.32	81.58	87.25	96.31	60.34	94.34	70.53	64.87	70.69	27

San Luis Obispo-
  Atascadero-
  Paso Robles, CA
	7.09	39.66	58.35	26.91	98.86	68.84	29.75	45.89	45.60	46.77	196

Santa Barbara-
  Santa Maria-
  Lompoc, CA
	1.99	64.87	66.00	69.12	100.00	66.29	53.26	71.10	65.43	62.01	90

Santa Cruz- Watsonville, CA	3.40	7.64	52.12	36.26	96.60	39.67	56.66	37.67	26.34	50.45	261
Santa Fe, NM	9.92	33.71	75.63	81.01	84.98	38.82	65.44	49.57	15.01	50.45	175
Santa Rosa, CA	6.52	22.37	80.45	27.47	95.18	65.73	54.96	82.43	59.20	54.92	135
Sarasota-Bradenton, FL	60.91	69.40	92.06	25.21	89.80	18.99	73.09	73.93	94.33	66.41	55
Saskatoon, SK	26.35	83.28	14.44	97.45	15.86	47.31	79.89	72.80	41.07	53.16	146
Savannah, GA	57.51	55.24	48.72	42.49	81.01	23.80	45.05	52.12	76.77	53.63	143

continues

METRO AREA	COSTS OF LIVING	TRANSPOR- TATION	JOBS	EDUCATION	CLIMATE	CRIME	ARTS	HEALTH CARE	RECREATION	MEAN SCORE	OVERALL RANK
Scranton–Wilkes- Barre–Hazleton, PA	52.13	62.32	20.96	81.86	39.94	97.17	67.71	80.45	71.95	63.83	80
★ Seattle-Bellevue- Everett, WA	8.50	86.96	97.16	86.11	77.62	45.05	91.79	87.25	90.65	74.57	3
Sharon, PA	55.25	12.46	22.09	15.86	32.01	96.89	2.55	14.44	29.74	31.25	319
Sheboygan, WI	49.58	21.81	16.99	14.16	35.41	94.06	61.76	11.61	62.60	40.89	246
Sherbrooke, PQ	19.55	25.77	6.23	68.55	25.21	76.78	16.72	99.43	23.79	40.23	254
Sherman-Denison, TX	97.17	0.56	15.86	20.67	46.45	57.80	19.55	36.26	26.62	35.66	294
Shreveport- Bossier City, LA	92.07	64.58	39.94	27.19	54.39	9.64	39.38	89.80	59.49	52.94	150
Sioux City, IA-NE	55.81	46.17	51.55	43.90	11.33	27.48	36.27	41.07	24.36	37.55	274
Sioux Falls, SD	93.77	61.75	70.82	52.12	5.09	80.17	45.61	93.76	34.27	59.71	104
South Bend, IN	85.27	71.67	61.47	87.53	6.23	54.40	62.61	56.09	46.74	59.11	108
Spokane, WA	66.01	77.05	73.37	75.92	67.70	49.30	71.39	80.16	39.94	66.76	52
Springfield, IL	79.33	62.60	24.64	64.02	11.89	32.30	37.68	84.41	30.31	47.46	191
Springfield, MA	34.00	92.35	10.76	91.50	7.93	20.12	73.66	42.77	66.57	48.85	181
Springfield, MO	88.67	55.80	71.67	91.78	27.47	69.69	34.28	58.07	41.64	59.90	103
Stamford-Norwalk, CT	1.42	9.34	5.94	13.03	35.97	79.89	88.67	76.20	34.56	38.34	268
State College, PA	30.60	53.54	52.40	43.05	33.99	98.59	25.50	3.11	35.97	41.86	234
Steubenville- Weirton, OH-WV	68.84	7.36	0.00	28.61	26.34	96.32	31.73	7.93	13.31	31.16	321
Stockton-Lodi, CA	23.80	1.41	64.87	24.64	95.46	11.05	36.83	16.14	32.29	34.05	305
Sudbury, ON	25.78	56.65	9.91	19.26	0.00	64.03	14.17	69.68	43.05	33.61	308
Sumter, SC	79.61	13.59	20.67	32.01	73.93	9.07	5.39	1.41	7.64	27.04	340
★ Syracuse, NY	37.97	88.66	54.39	94.33	17.84	83.29	81.31	78.18	95.46	70.16	32
Tacoma, WA	34.28	82.43	89.80	44.47	77.05	19.27	84.71	26.34	69.97	58.70	112
Tallahassee, FL	62.61	62.03	81.01	63.73	83.56	0.29	64.03	44.19	61.18	58.07	116
★ Tampa-St. Petersburg- Clearwater, FL	79.89	91.50	94.33	67.98	90.65	4.54	66.58	77.05	98.01	74.50	4
Terre Haute, IN	76.21	27.76	6.79	69.40	33.71	40.51	28.05	47.87	24.64	39.44	262
Texarkana, TX- Texarkana, AR	94.34	24.07	16.71	30.31	63.73	38.53	1.14	51.84	3.96	36.07	290
Thunder Bay, ON	30.88	68.83	6.51	32.86	1.98	37.97	41.65	60.62	80.16	40.16	256
Toledo, OH	46.46	75.07	58.64	85.26	29.74	41.08	85.84	87.53	69.12	64.30	77
Topeka, KS	92.64	44.75	15.01	23.22	28.32	5.39	48.73	49.85	22.09	36.67	282
★ Toronto, ON	5.95	98.01	96.60	73.08	31.72	67.71	98.87	96.60	97.45	74.00	7
Trenton, NJ	9.64	44.19	41.35	94.90	53.82	51.28	80.74	74.22	45.04	55.02	134
Trois-Rivieres, PQ	26.92	10.48	5.66	58.35	0.56	77.06	53.83	75.63	3.11	34.62	299
Tucson, AZ	53.55	71.10	92.63	54.67	87.25	11.90	66.29	74.50	79.03	65.66	68
Tulsa, OK	80.74	71.38	72.52	50.42	36.54	31.45	63.18	49.29	84.41	59.99	102
Tuscaloosa, AL	77.63	15.58	38.81	65.15	62.88	8.50	13.04	22.66	33.99	37.58	273
Tyler, TX	95.76	28.32	42.49	45.89	51.84	29.18	9.35	67.13	27.76	44.19	216
Utica-Rome, NY	17.00	39.09	24.36	78.18	15.01	93.49	30.88	35.41	78.47	45.77	200
Vallejo-Fairfield- Napa, CA	7.94	5.66	89.23	23.79	93.20	33.43	64.88	28.61	64.58	45.70	202
★ Vancouver, BC	4.82	84.70	93.20	86.40	79.88	14.45	95.76	100.00	89.23	72.05	18
Ventura, CA	8.22	5.09	88.66	36.54	99.43	69.98	63.74	43.90	54.67	52.25	156
Victoria, BC	7.65	83.85	28.61	47.02	82.43	44.20	69.69	70.25	47.30	53.44	144
Victoria, TX	99.44	16.99	20.39	20.11	67.98	21.25	8.50	72.52	3.39	36.73	281
Vineland-Millville- Bridgeton, NJ	18.99	15.29	8.21	5.66	61.75	21.82	34.85	10.48	10.76	20.87	353
Visalia-Tulare- Porterville, CA	37.12	24.36	41.07	1.41	96.03	37.12	16.44	6.51	4.81	29.43	330
Waco, TX	98.02	33.99	42.77	50.70	43.62	14.74	13.60	32.29	28.61	39.82	258
★ Washington, DC- MD-VA-WV	4.54	97.16	92.91	97.73	56.09	38.25	99.72	98.30	88.66	74.82	2
Waterbury, CT	19.27	3.96	5.09	15.58	37.11	59.50	32.58	50.99	7.36	25.72	347
Waterloo- Cedar Falls, IA	89.52	52.69	11.89	42.77	6.51	70.54	40.51	65.72	28.04	45.35	205
Wausau, WI	52.98	58.07	40.22	19.54	5.66	99.44	20.40	29.17	25.49	39.00	266
West Palm Beach- Boca Raton, FL	39.67	77.90	90.93	48.15	88.38	3.12	76.49	83.00	95.75	67.04	48
Wheeling, WV-OH	67.43	14.16	13.59	62.32	21.24	97.46	49.30	79.03	17.56	46.90	194
Wichita, KS	66.86	74.50	50.14	72.80	23.79	25.78	52.13	76.48	54.10	55.18	133
Wichita Falls, TX	98.87	35.97	25.21	13.59	38.24	28.33	10.77	52.40	24.07	36.38	287
Williamsport, PA	61.48	38.52	1.13	21.52	42.77	93.21	24.37	50.42	1.41	37.20	279
Wilmington, NC	40.51	45.89	78.75	40.79	68.55	28.05	18.14	61.47	88.38	52.28	167
Wilmington- Newark, DE-MD	29.18	18.41	64.02	66.28	59.77	54.96	70.83	32.86	64.02	51.15	155
Windsor, ON	21.82	75.63	31.16	28.04	16.99	72.53	53.55	44.47	36.82	42.33	230
Winnipeg, MB	43.06	83.56	51.84	76.77	3.96	27.77	84.14	92.91	58.07	58.01	118
Worcester, MA-CT	15.30	39.94	14.16	82.43	42.20	63.18	74.51	69.97	66.00	51.97	159
Yakima, WA	73.38	47.02	37.67	4.24	86.96	30.88	28.33	25.77	18.13	39.15	264
Yolo, CA	10.49	19.83	71.10	28.32	93.48	36.55	19.27	42.49	6.51	36.45	286
York, PA	31.17	10.76	45.89	9.91	36.82	93.77	12.19	5.66	21.81	29.78	327

METRO AREA	COSTS OF LIVING	TRANSPOR-TATION	JOBS	EDUCATION	CLIMATE	CRIME	ARTS	HEALTH CARE	RECREATION	MEAN SCORE	OVERALL RANK
Youngstown-Warren, OH	70.26	49.00	65.43	58.64	22.09	50.71	21.82	20.39	73.65	48.00	187
Yuba City, CA	33.15	4.81	37.39	3.39	90.36	23.52	9.35	6.23	5.38	23.73	352
Yuma, AZ	43.35	37.11	54.67	2.26	88.95	28.90	3.69	0.28	8.49	29.74	328

ET CETERA: PUTTING IT ALL TOGETHER

FINDING *YOUR* BEST PLACE TO LIVE

Using *Places Rated*, you can put together a custom-made list of possibilities. Just add up the scores in the categories you think are important and eliminate the others, thereby ferreting out the ones best suited to your own preferences. The "Decisions, Decisions" chapter at the beginning of the book may help.

One way to start is to consult the **Rankings** section in the chapters most important to you and consider only the places that rank in the first 50 or 100. You may want to add a certain category's score twice if it is a critical need for you.

If you're a recent graduate, unmarried and just entering the job market, you might be interested mainly in the prospects for employment and having a good time. For you, the best areas could be those that have the best scores for recreation and job outlook. Here are five that have the highest average scores in those categories.

METRO AREA	AVERAGE SCORE
Riverside-San Bernardino, CA	98.2
Orlando, FL	97.6
Las Vegas, NV-AZ	97.4
Phoenix-Mesa, AZ	97.4
Salt Lake City-Ogden, UT	97.3

If you're looking for a place to retire, your main considerations might be a mild climate, low costs of living, adequate health-care facilities, and a low crime rate. Here are five metro areas that have the highest average scores in those four categories.

METRO AREA	AVERAGE SCORE
Johnson City-Kingsport-Bristol, TN-VA	81.9
Roanoke, VA	74.8
Huntington-Ashland, WV-KY-OH	71.3
Augusta-Aiken, GA-SC	70.1
Asheville, NC	68.8

Finding the ideal spot is a matter of personal choice. *Places Rated* doesn't pretend to be the final arbiter of the best and worst metro areas; rather, it is designed as an instrument you can fine-tune and adjust to help you find the kind of place where *you* want to live.

A BIG POND OR A SMALL ONE?

Places Rated's top thirty-five metro areas include just three with populations under one million. Yet there are many persons who would prefer not to live in a large city or even a medium-sized one if they could help it.

In 1974, the National Science Foundation (NSF) published *City Size and Quality of Life*. The study pointed out that large metro areas offer desirable social opportunities for many people: economic diversity, cultural events, anonymity, free expression of diverse life-styles, and the chance for personal achievement.

NORTH AMERICA'S 20 BEST SMALL METRO AREAS (POPULATION UNDER 250,000)

Metro Area	Average Score
Portland, ME	65.31
Fargo-Moorhead, ND-MN	63.45
Roanoke, VA	63.30
Duluth-Superior, MN-WI	60.65
Gainesville, FL	60.37
Sioux Falls, SD	59.71
Lincoln, NE	59.05
Asheville, NC	58.58
Columbia, MO	58.07
Charlottesville, VA	57.00
Bismarck, ND	55.36
La Crosse, WI-MN	54.89
Bangor, ME	53.70
St. Cloud, MN	53.32
Saskatoon, SK	53.16
Lynchburg, VA	52.97
Eau Claire, WI	52.50
Regina, SK	52.50
Wilmington, NC	52.28
Champaign-Urbana, IL	52.24

585

On the other hand, rates of violent crime increase as places get larger; air and water pollution increases; there is less discretionary time; larger places tend to diminish an individual's sense of relative significance; and access to the natural environment shrinks. Ominously, the NSF predicted larger cities would grow "to a point where they yield diminishing returns to scale."

Most important, perhaps, the study found that although the trend was toward growth of big metro areas, most people didn't want to live in big cities. They preferred small towns or suburbs but were being forced by economics to leave the smaller places for the bigger ones. By the year 2000, the study predicted, 63 percent of Americans—as compared with 38 percent in 1960—would live in the forty-four largest metropolitan areas, each of which would have a population greater than one million.

The NSF's forecast, it turns out 25 years later, was wrong. Just half of us live in metro areas with more than 1 million people; yet there are now sixty-one such areas in America, not forty-four.

During this century, a general worldwide trend has been "smaller pieces into bigger ones." Large corporations buy up smaller ones and grow even larger; people flock from the countryside or small towns into ever-swelling cities and their surrounding suburbs.

However, we may have reached a population watershed during the last 2 decades. The latest mobility data indicate that people are moving out of the cities and into the less populous places.

Could the early years of the 21st century usher in the era of "bigger pieces into smaller ones"? Certainly, the advent of the latest electronics technology—especially in the communications field—has robbed the biggest metro areas of the advantage in one of the most significant factors in their development: swift and effective communication between all branches of business, industry, and commerce.

For those readers who have already decided that they would prefer a smaller metro area, a careful consideration of population size may be the fairest way to compare *Places Rated* rankings.

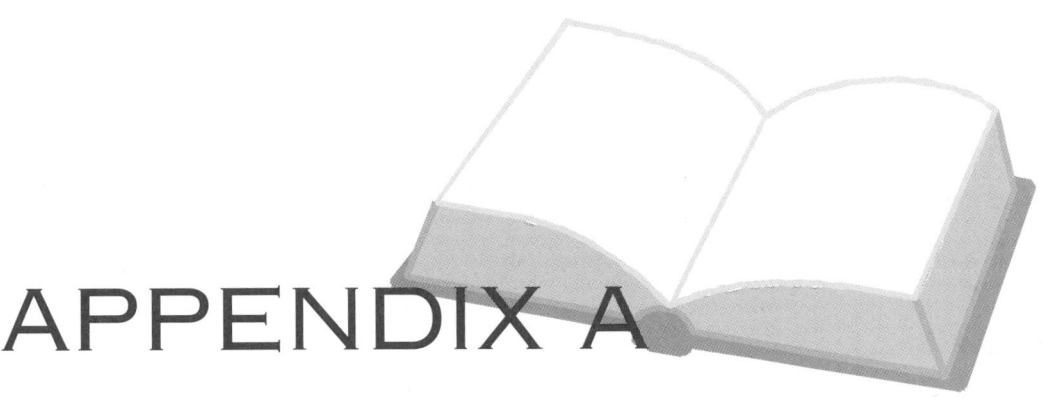

APPENDIX A

METROPOLITAN AREAS BY STATE AND PROVINCE

Every state and every Canadian province except Prince Edward Island has at least one officially defined metro area. New Jersey is the only state whose entire land area is covered by these combinations of urban and suburban counties, though Connecticut isn't far behind.

One of every five metro areas are found in Texas, which has twenty-seven; California, which has twenty-five; and Florida with twenty. Alaska, Hawaii, Manitoba, New Brunswick, Newfoundland, and Vermont have just one. Below is a list of metro areas, grouped by state and province. Many metro areas include parts of two or more states. These are listed under every state in which they have a component county. Ottawa-Hull is the only Canadian metro area located in more than one province.

Alabama
  Anniston
  Birmingham
  Columbus (GA-AL)
  Decatur
  Dothan
  Florence
  Gadsden
  Huntsville
  Mobile
  Montgomery
  Tuscaloosa

Alaska
  Anchorage

Alberta
  Calgary
  Edmonton

Arizona
  Flagstaff (AZ-UT)
  Las Vegas (NV-AZ)
  Phoenix-Mesa
  Tucson
  Yuma

Arkansas
  Fayetteville-Springdale-Rogers
  Fort Smith (AR-OK)
  Jonesboro
  Little Rock-North Little Rock
  Memphis (TN-AR-MS)
  Pine Bluff
  Texarkana (TX) Texarkana (AR)

British Columbia
  Vancouver
  Victoria

California
  Bakersfield
  Chico-Paradise
  Fresno
  Los Angeles-Long Beach
  Merced
  Modesto
  Oakland
  Orange County
  Redding
  Riverside-San Bernardino
  Sacramento
  Salinas

Metropolitan Areas by State and Province

California (cont.)
San Diego
San Francisco
San Jose
San Luis Obispo-Atascadero-Paso
  Robles
Santa Barbara-Santa Maria-Lompoc
Santa Cruz-Watsonville
Santa Rosa
Stockton-Lodi
Vallejo-Fairfield-Napa
Ventura
Visalia-Tulare-Porterville
Yolo
Yuba City

Colorado
Boulder-Longmont
Colorado Springs
Denver
Fort Collins-Loveland
Grand Junction
Greeley
Pueblo

Connecticut
Bridgeport
Danbury
Hartford
New Haven-Meriden
New London-Norwich (CT-RI)
Stamford-Norwalk
Waterbury
Worcester (MA-CT)

Delaware
Dover
Wilmington-Newark (DE-MD)

District of Columbia
Washington (DC-MD-VA-WV)

Florida
Daytona Beach
Fort Lauderdale
Fort Myers-Cape Coral
Fort Pierce-Port St. Lucie
Fort Walton Beach
Gainesville
Jacksonville
Lakeland-Winter Haven
Melbourne-Titusville-Palm Bay
Miami
Naples
Ocala
Orlando
Panama City
Pensacola
Punta Gorda
Sarasota-Bradenton
Tallahassee
Tampa-St. Petersburg-Clearwater
West Palm Beach-Boca Raton

Georgia
Albany
Athens
Atlanta
Augusta-Aiken (GA-SC)
Chattanooga (TN-GA)
Columbus (GA-AL)
Macon
Savannah

Hawaii
Honolulu

Idaho
Boise City
Pocatello

Illinois
Bloomington-Normal
Champaign-Urbana
Chicago
Davenport-Moline-Rock Island (IA-IL)
Decatur
Kankakee
Peoria-Pekin
Rockford
St. Louis (MO-IL)
Springfield

Indiana
Bloomington
Cincinnati (OH-KY-IN)
Elkhart-Goshen
Evansville-Henderson (IN-KY)
Fort Wayne
Gary
Indianapolis
Kokomo
Lafayette
Louisville (KY-IN)
Muncie
South Bend
Terre Haute (IN)

Iowa
Cedar Rapids
Davenport-Moline-Rock Island (IA-IL)
Des Moines
Dubuque
Iowa City
Omaha (NE-IA)
Sioux City (IA-NE)
Waterloo-Cedar Falls

Kansas
Kansas City (MO-KS)
Lawrence
Topeka
Wichita

Kentucky
Cincinnati (OH-KY-IN)
Clarksville-Hopkinsville (TN-KY)
Evansville-Henderson (IN-KY)

Huntington-Ashland (WV-KY-OH)
Lexington
Louisville (KY-IN)
Owensboro

Louisiana
Alexandria
Baton Rouge
Houma
Lafayette
Lake Charles
Monroe
New Orleans
Shreveport-Bossier City

Maine
Bangor
Lewiston-Auburn
Portland
Portsmouth-Rochester (NH-ME)

Manitoba
Winnipeg

Maryland
Baltimore
Cumberland (MD-WV)
Hagerstown
Washington (DC-MD-VA-WV)
Wilmington-Newark (DE-MD)

Massachusetts
Barnstable-Yarmouth
Boston
Brockton
Fitchburg-Leominster
Lawrence (MA-NH)
Lowell (MA-NH)
New Bedford
Pittsfield
Providence-Fall River-Warwick
  (RI-MA)
Springfield
Worcester (MA-CT)

Michigan
Ann Arbor
Benton Harbor
Detroit
Flint
Grand Rapids-Muskegon-Holland
Jackson
Kalamazoo-Battle Creek
Lansing-East Lansing
Saginaw-Bay City-Midland

Minnesota
Duluth-Superior (MN-WI)
Fargo-Moorhead (ND-MN)
Grand Forks (ND-MN)
La Crosse (WI-MN)
Minneapolis-St. Paul (MN-WI)
Rochester
St. Cloud

Mississippi
  Biloxi-Gulfport-Pascagoula
  Hattiesburg
  Jackson
  Memphis (TN-AR-MS)

Missouri
  Columbia
  Joplin
  Kansas City (MO-KS)
  St. Joseph
  St. Louis (MO-IL)
  Springfield

Montana
  Billings
  Great Falls
  Missoula

Nebraska
  Lincoln
  Omaha (NE-IA)
  Sioux City (IA-NE)

Nevada
  Las Vegas (NV-AZ)
  Reno

New Brunswick
  Saint John

New Hampshire
  Boston (MA-NH)
  Lawrence (MA-NH)
  Lowell (MA-NH)
  Manchester
  Nashua
  Portsmouth-Rochester (NH-ME)

New Jersey
  Atlantic City-Cape May
  Bergen-Passaic
  Jersey City
  Middlesex-Somerset-Hunterdon
  Monmouth-Ocean
  Newark
  Philadelphia (PA-NJ)
  Trenton
  Vineland-Millville-Bridgeton

New Mexico
  Albuquerque
  Las Cruces
  Santa Fe

New York
  Albany-Schenectady-Troy
  Binghamton
  Buffalo-Niagara Falls
  Dutchess County
  Elmira
  Glens Falls
  Jamestown
  Long Island
  New York

  Newburgh (NY-PA)
  Rochester
  Syracuse
  Utica-Rome

Newfoundland
  St. John's

North Carolina
  Asheville
  Charlotte-Gastonia-Rock Hill (NC-SC)
  Fayetteville
  Goldsboro
  Greensboro–Winston-Salem–High Point
  Greenville
  Hickory-Morganton-Lenoir
  Jacksonville
  Norfolk-Virginia Beach-Newport News (VA-NC)
  Raleigh-Durham-Chapel Hill
  Rocky Mount
  Wilmington, NC

North Dakota
  Bismarck
  Fargo-Moorhead (ND-MN)
  Grand Forks (ND-MN)

Nova Scotia
  Halifax

Ohio
  Akron
  Canton-Massillon
  Cincinnati (OH-KY-IN)
  Cleveland-Lorain-Elyria
  Columbus
  Dayton-Springfield
  Hamilton-Middletown
  Huntington-Ashland (WV-KY-OH)
  Lima
  Mansfield
  Parkersburg-Marietta (WV-OH)
  Steubenville-Weirton (OH-WV)
  Toledo
  Wheeling (WV-OH)
  Youngstown-Warren

Oklahoma
  Enid
  Fort Smith (AR-OK)
  Lawton
  Oklahoma City
  Tulsa

Ontario
  Hamilton
  Kitchener
  London
  Oshawa
  Ottawa-Hull (ON-PQ)
  St. Catharines-Niagara
  Sudbury

  Thunder Bay
  Toronto
  Windsor

Oregon
  Eugene-Springfield
  Medford-Ashland
  Portland-Vancouver (OR-WA)
  Salem

Pennsylvania
  Allentown-Bethlehem-Easton
  Altoona
  Erie
  Harrisburg-Lebanon-Carlisle
  Johnstown
  Lancaster
  Newburgh (NY-PA)
  Philadelphia (PA-NJ)
  Pittsburgh
  Reading
  Scranton–Wilkes-Barre–Hazleton
  Sharon
  State College
  Williamsport
  York

Quebec
  Chicoutimi-Jonquiere
  Montreal
  Ottawa-Hull (ON-PQ)
  Quebec City
  Sherbrooke
  Trois-Rivieres

Rhode Island
  New London-Norwich (CT-RI)
  Providence-Fall River-Warwick (RI-MA)

Saskatchewan
  Regina
  Saskatoon

South Carolina
  Augusta-Aiken (GA-SC)
  Charleston-North Charleston
  Charlotte-Gastonia-Rock Hill (NC-SC)
  Columbia
  Florence
  Greenville-Spartanburg-Anderson
  Myrtle Beach
  Sumter

South Dakota
  Rapid City
  Sioux Falls

Tennessee
  Chattanooga (TN-GA)
  Clarksville-Hopkinsville (TN-KY)
  Jackson
  Johnson City-Kingsport-Bristol (TN-VA)

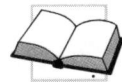

Metropolitan Areas by State and Province

Tennessee (cont.)
- Knoxville
- Memphis (TN-AR-MS)
- Nashville

Texas
- Abilene
- Amarillo
- Austin-San Marcos
- Beaumont-Port Arthur
- Brazoria
- Brownsville-Harlingen-San Benito
- Bryan-College Station
- Corpus Christi
- Dallas
- El Paso
- Fort Worth-Arlington
- Galveston-Texas City
- Houston
- Killeen-Temple
- Laredo
- Longview-Marshall
- Lubbock
- McAllen-Edinburg-Mission
- Odessa-Midland
- San Angelo
- San Antonio
- Sherman-Denison
- Texarkana (TX) Texarkana (AR)
- Tyler
- Victoria
- Waco
- Wichita Falls

Utah
- Flagstaff (AZ-UT)
- Provo-Orem
- Salt Lake City-Ogden

Vermont
- Burlington

Virginia
- Charlottesville
- Danville
- Johnson City-Kingsport-Bristol (TN-VA)
- Lynchburg
- Norfolk-Virginia Beach-Newport News (VA-NC)
- Richmond-Petersburg
- Roanoke
- Washington (DC-MD-VA-WV)

Washington
- Bellingham
- Bremerton
- Olympia
- Portland-Vancouver (OR-WA)
- Richland-Kennewick-Pasco
- Seattle-Bellevue-Everett
- Spokane
- Tacoma
- Yakima

West Virginia
- Charleston
- Cumberland (MD-WV)
- Huntington-Ashland (WV-KY-OH)
- Parkersburg-Marietta (WV-OH)
- Steubenville-Weirton (OH-WV)
- Washington (DC-MD-VA-WV)
- Wheeling (WV-OH)

Wisconsin
- Appleton-Oshkosh-Neenah
- Duluth-Superior (MN-WI)
- Eau Claire
- Green Bay
- Janesville-Beloit
- Kenosha
- La Crosse (WI-MN)
- Madison
- Milwaukee-Waukesha
- Minneapolis-St. Paul (MN-WI)
- Racine
- Sheboygan
- Wausau

Wyoming
- Casper
- Cheyenne

APPENDIX B

PEOPLE

The following tables show figures for population diversity, age, and income in each metro area. Additionally, political data are given for American metro areas. Because of differences in definition, Canadian figures aren't comparable with those of the United States and are presented in a separate table.

DIVERSITY

A typical metro area in the United States is 70 percent White, 13 percent Black, 12.6 percent Latino, 4.2 percent Asian and Pacific Islander, and 0.5 percent Native American.

   While no metro areas have Black majorities, eight have Latino populations greater than 50 percent. Honolulu has an Asian and Pacific Islander majority. The metro area with the highest portion of Native Americans—28 percent—is Flagstaff, Arizona.

   Which metro areas are the most diverse? Via the "chi-square test," a statistical technique used to compare observed data with expected data, metro areas are scored from 100 (most diverse) to 0 (least diverse) by how closely they match national diversity. Dallas and nearby Fort Worth-Arlington are most like metropolitan America. Other metro areas close behind are Orlando, Las Vegas, and Chicago. At the other extreme, Wheeling, WV, with a population that is 97 percent White, and Laredo, TX, that has a 95 percent Latino population, are among the least diverse.

MEDIAN AGE

Iowa City, IA; Lawrence, KS; Bloomington, IN; and Provo-Orem, UT, certainly are college towns. Their residents' 20-something median age—a point where half is younger and the other half older—makes them the youngest metro areas. Since 1970, this point has advanced from 27.5 to 35.3 across North America. The oldest metro area, at almost 53, is Punta Gorda on Florida's gulf coast.

PER CAPITA INCOME

While most money counted as per capita income comes from earnings, some of it can also come from interest, rent, and welfare. It has rocketed from $4,000 in 1970 to

$27,000 today. It's no surprise that price inflation has taken a similar trajectory. The richest metro areas are found among New York suburbs and the San Francisco Bay area. The poorest are smaller metro areas along the Rio Grande and in the inner South.

POLITICS

If all the votes in metro areas were totaled over the last three elections for metro area congressional representatives, Republicans have a paper-thin majority of 0.6 percent echoing the thin majority in the House. In the table, an R indicates Republican and a D indicates Democrat and is followed by the vote margin. Burlington, VT, is the only metro area represented by an Independent. A heavy Democratic win doesn't necessarily mean the metro area is more liberal, nor does a big Republican margin always mean the metro area is more conservative. One hundred percent majorities mean the winner was unopposed.

	% WHITE	% BLACK	% LATINO	% ASIAN	% NATIVE AMERICAN	DIVERSITY SCORE	MEDIAN AGE	PER CAPITA INCOME	POLITICS
U.S.Metro Area Average	69.9	12.9	12.6	4.2	0.5	50	35.3	$26,700	R 50.6
Abilene, TX	73.8	6.3	18.1	1.6	0.3	88	33.2	$23,600	R 53.2
Akron, OH	87.0	10.8	0.7	1.2	0.2	19	36.4	$29,300	D 57.3
Albany, GA	49.6	48.1	1.4	0.6	0.2	30	32.7	$22,400	D 55.2
Albany-Schenectady-Troy, NY	91.1	4.9	2.2	1.7	0.2	53	36.5	$28,500	D 59.3
Albuquerque, NM	52.3	2.3	38.9	1.6	5.0	50	34.9	$25,500	R 60.0
Alexandria, LA	67.3	30.1	1.4	0.9	0.4	38	34.6	$22,700	R 60.3
Allentown-Bethlehem-Easton, PA	90.3	2.1	6.0	1.5	0.1	53	38.2	$28,800	R 50.4
Altoona, PA	98.1	1.0	0.4	0.4	0.1	4	39.4	$23,200	R 100
Amarillo, TX	75.2	5.6	16.4	2.2	0.6	89	34.6	$24,400	R 78.7
Anchorage, AK	76.8	6.0	4.9	5.8	6.4	79	33.2	$33,200	R 63.2
Ann Arbor, MI	86.3	7.1	2.9	3.3	0.4	72	33.5	$33,800	D 51.9
Anniston, AL	78.2	19.2	1.6	0.8	0.2	47	36.4	$20,600	D 50.5
Appleton-Oshkosh-Neenah, WI	96.1	0.3	1.0	1.7	1.0	2	35.2	$28,300	R 74.6
Asheville, NC	90.2	7.7	1.2	0.6	0.3	33	39.3	$26,000	R 55.9
Athens, GA	71.9	23.0	2.4	2.6	0.1	66	30.3	$23,500	R 55.6
Atlanta, GA	68.4	25.6	3.2	2.6	0.2	73	33.9	$31,600	R 54.3
Atlantic-Cape May, NJ	75.1	14.7	7.5	2.5	0.2	95	37.2	$33,100	R 64.9
Augusta-Aiken, GA-SC	62.7	32.8	2.3	2.0	0.2	60	34.2	$23,300	R 65.1
Austin-San Marcos, TX	62.8	9.1	25.1	2.8	0.3	91	31.2	$27,300	D 55.3
Bakersfield, CA	55.6	5.6	34.5	3.4	1.0	78	30.8	$20,900	R 72.3
Baltimore, MD	68.4	27.2	1.8	2.4	0.3	53	36.3	$31,600	D 53.7
Bangor, ME	97.5	0.4	0.6	0.8	0.8	2	36.9	$22,400	D 76.2
Barnstable-Yarmouth, MA	95.2	1.8	1.6	0.8	0.6	25	42.1	$33,200	D 65.7
Baton Rouge, LA	65.8	31.0	1.7	1.3	0.2	48	32.3	$25,000	R 53.0
Beaumont-Port Arthur, TX	68.0	24.3	5.4	2.0	0.2	86	37.0	$23,500	D 59.8
Bellingham, WA	89.9	0.5	4.2	2.4	3.0	12	35.7	$25,000	R 52.8
Benton Harbor, MI	80.3	16.1	2.0	1.2	0.4	57	36.8	$25,600	R 74.7
Bergen-Passaic, NJ	68.8	8.4	15.1	7.5	0.1	96	38.3	$40,900	R 53.5
Billings, MT	92.9	0.5	3.1	0.5	3.0	6	37.7	$25,600	R 54.7
Biloxi-Gulfport-Pascagoula, MS	75.6	19.9	1.9	2.3	0.3	59	34.1	$21,400	D 66.3
Binghamton, NY	94.4	1.9	1.4	2.1	0.2	26	36.4	$24,800	D 53.8
Birmingham, AL	69.7	28.9	0.7	0.5	0.2	17	36.3	$28,100	R 58.7
Bismarck, ND	96.1	0.1	0.7	0.5	2.6	0	36.7	$24,600	R 50.1
Bloomington, IN	92.1	2.8	1.8	3.1	0.2	39	28.2	$22,400	R 50.8
Bloomington-Normal, IL	91.8	4.7	1.8	1.6	0.1	47	31.5	$29,100	R 64.9
Boise City, ID	89.7	0.4	7.9	1.4	0.6	6	33.5	$27,800	R 57.1
Boston, MA-NH	82.4	6.9	6.1	4.4	0.2	88	36.4	$37,700	D 73.7
Boulder-Longmont, CO	87.8	0.9	7.9	2.9	0.5	24	35.0	$34,700	D 61.9
Brazoria, TX	68.8	8.2	21.3	1.3	0.4	89	33.4	$23,600	R 66.7
Bremerton, WA	85.9	2.8	4.5	5.3	1.6	60	34.4	$24,600	D 57.6

	% WHITE	% BLACK	% LATINO	% ASIAN	% NATIVE AMERICAN	DIVERSITY SCORE	MEDIAN AGE	PER CAPITA INCOME	POLITICS
U.S.Metro Area Average	69.9	12.9	12.6	4.2	0.5	50	35.3	$26,700	R 50.6
Bridgeport, CT	77.2	10.1	9.8	2.7	0.1	97	37.8	$48,700	D 51.2
Brockton, MA	91.7	4.0	2.9	1.3	0.2	58	36.6	$29,900	D 84.9
Brownsville-Harlingen-San Benito, TX	14.5	0.2	85.0	0.3	0.1	1	29.1	$14,600	D 66.1
Bryan-College Station, TX	66.4	11.5	17.3	4.6	0.2	98	23.9	$19,400	R 84.3
Buffalo-Niagara Falls, NY	84.1	11.3	2.6	1.3	0.7	67	37.2	$27,400	R 53.3
Burlington, VT	96.4	0.8	1.1	1.4	0.3	10	33.7	$29,800	I 63.0
Canton-Massillon, OH	91.3	7.0	0.9	0.5	0.3	22	38.0	$26,300	R 68.1
Casper, WY	94.3	0.7	3.8	0.6	0.6	13	37.5	$29,600	R 52.3
Cedar Rapids, IA	95.1	2.1	1.5	1.1	0.2	27	36.3	$29,000	R 53.2
Champaign-Urbana, IL	81.1	10.6	2.3	5.8	0.2	66	29.3	$24,800	R 55.9
Charleston-North Charleston, SC	65.4	30.8	2.0	1.5	0.3	53	32.5	$22,600	R 73.2
Charleston, WV	93.3	5.5	0.5	0.6	0.1	8	39.6	$27,100	D 70.7
Charlotte-Gastonia-Rock Hill, NC-SC	76.1	20.3	1.7	1.5	0.4	51	35.2	$29,200	R 57.2
Charlottesville, VA	80.2	15.8	1.4	2.5	0.1	48	33.9	$30,400	R 52.0
Chattanooga, TN-GA	83.5	14.5	0.9	0.9	0.2	27	37.4	$26,100	R 60.1
Cheyenne, WY	84.8	2.5	10.6	1.3	0.7	64	36.1	$25,300	R 52.0
Chicago, IL	62.8	18.9	14.1	4.1	0.1	97	34.3	$34,600	D 54.2
Chico-Paradise, CA	83.8	1.3	9.8	3.5	1.6	38	36.5	$22,200	R 62.5
Cincinnati, OH-KY-IN	85.4	12.8	0.7	1.0	0.1	17	35.1	$29,600	R 66.3
Clarksville-Hopkinsville, TN-KY	72.5	20.4	4.6	2.1	0.4	85	30.1	$19,600	R 62.2
Cleveland-Lorain-Elyria, OH	77.6	18.2	2.8	1.3	0.2	68	37.3	$31,400	D 57.2
Colorado Springs, CO	79.0	7.1	10.4	2.9	0.6	94	33.1	$25,900	R 79.8
Columbia, MO	86.0	8.6	1.4	3.6	0.3	46	29.1	$25,900	R 60.1
Columbia, SC	66.7	29.8	1.8	1.4	0.2	52	34.7	$26,000	R 72.2
Columbus, GA-AL	54.1	39.4	4.5	1.7	0.3	70	33.1	$22,900	R 59.7
Columbus, OH	83.8	13.1	1.0	1.9	0.2	31	34.0	$28,600	R 68.9
Corpus Christi, TX	37.6	3.6	57.7	0.8	0.2	41	32.7	$21,800	D 59.8
Cumberland, MD-WV	96.3	2.6	0.6	0.5	0.1	10	40.6	$21,500	R 50.4
Dallas, TX	64.8	15.0	16.4	3.4	0.4	99	32.8	$32,900	R 66.6
Danbury, CT	79.7	8.5	9.0	2.7	0.1	95	38.2	$50,300	R 61.8
Danville, VA	64.9	34.0	0.6	0.4	0.1	12	39.6	$21,500	D 58.8
Davenport-Moline-Rock Island, IA-IL	87.7	5.8	5.3	0.9	0.2	74	36.8	$26,500	R 52.4
Dayton-Springfield, OH	83.2	14.4	0.9	1.3	0.2	28	36.5	$28,100	R 52.3
Daytona Beach, FL	82.7	10.5	5.4	1.1	0.3	84	41.5	$22,600	R 59.2
Decatur, AL	85.3	12.1	0.9	0.4	1.4	19	36.4	$23,900	D 57.2
Decatur, IL	85.5	13.2	0.6	0.6	0.1	15	37.7	$27,200	D 61.2
Denver, CO	76.7	5.7	14.4	2.7	0.6	91	36.3	$33,800	R 54.6
Des Moines, IA	91.0	4.0	2.7	2.1	0.2	58	35.5	$29,900	R 53.1
Detroit, MI	73.2	22.3	2.4	1.8	0.3	64	36.0	$32,000	D 59.0
Dothan, AL	74.4	22.3	1.9	1.0	0.3	53	34.3	$22,200	R 71.8
Dover, DE	74.1	20.3	3.2	1.8	0.6	74	34.4	$23,200	R 74.1
Dubuque, IA	98.1	0.4	0.8	0.7	0.1	3	36.5	$25,800	D 50.3
Duluth-Superior, MN-WI	95.9	0.7	0.7	0.8	1.9	4	39.1	$24,600	D 75.6
Dutchess County, NY	83.5	8.4	4.7	3.2	0.1	85	35.7	$30,900	R 62.4
Eau Claire, WI	96.4	0.2	0.6	2.4	0.5	1	35.0	$23,800	D 58.2
El Paso, TX	21.2	3.0	74.4	1.2	0.2	18	29.7	$16,400	D 72.7
Elkhart-Goshen, IN	91.3	5.0	2.6	0.8	0.3	54	34.7	$27,400	R 56.6
Elmira, NY	91.3	5.8	1.8	1.0	0.2	47	36.7	$23,900	R 85.0
Enid, OK	90.8	3.6	2.6	1.1	1.9	52	37.2	$24,000	R 74.7
Erie, PA	91.5	6.0	1.7	0.7	0.2	41	35.7	$24,900	R 56.7
Eugene-Springfield, OR	92.1	0.8	3.7	2.4	1.1	17	36.9	$25,000	D 75.6
Evansville-Henderson, IN-KY	92.4	6.2	0.7	0.6	0.2	14	36.9	$27,000	D 50.1
Fargo-Moorhead, ND-MN	95.5	0.4	1.8	1.3	1.1	3	33.1	$25,400	D 58.8

continues

	% WHITE	% BLACK	% LATINO	% ASIAN	% NATIVE AMERICAN	DIVERSITY SCORE	MEDIAN AGE	PER CAPITA INCOME	POLITICS
U.S.Metro Area Average	69.9	12.9	12.6	4.2	0.5	50	35.3	$26,700	R 50.6
Fayetteville, NC	56.3	30.8	8.2	3.0	1.6	86	28.8	$22,700	D 65.1
Fayetteville-Springdale-Rogers, AR	94.0	1.0	2.9	0.9	1.2	18	35.3	$24,100	R 72.7
Fitchburg-Leominster, MA	89.4	2.2	5.8	2.4	0.2	57	36.0	$29,000	D 72.0
Flagstaff, AZ-UT	58.3	1.4	11.6	1.0	27.6	32	29.0	$20,600	D 50.7
Flint, MI	75.4	20.6	2.5	0.9	0.7	59	35.0	$27,200	D 70.4
Florence, AL	85.9	13.1	0.6	0.3	0.2	10	38.6	$22,400	D 61.4
Florence, SC	59.6	39.4	0.6	0.3	0.1	10	35.8	$23,000	R 51.7
Fort Collins-Loveland, CO	89.5	0.6	7.7	1.8	0.4	12	34.5	$27,200	R 59.2
Fort Lauderdale, FL	69.6	16.9	11.5	1.8	0.2	97	39.3	$31,900	D 59.1
Fort Myers-Cape Coral, FL	85.1	7.6	6.3	0.8	0.2	77	43.2	$29,300	R 74.6
Fort Pierce-Port St. Lucie, FL	78.9	14.1	6.0	0.9	0.2	83	41.7	$29,300	R 63.4
Fort Smith, AR-OK	86.0	4.2	2.4	2.6	4.8	55	35.5	$21,800	R 70.4
Fort Walton Beach, FL	81.2	10.3	4.4	3.5	0.6	86	33.4	$24,700	R 80.0
Fort Wayne, IN	89.4	7.2	2.3	0.8	0.3	55	34.9	$28,000	R 59.4
Fort Worth-Arlington, TX	72.2	10.6	13.7	3.0	0.4	100	33.2	$27,700	R 63.4
Fresno, CA	44.6	4.3	42.0	8.4	0.7	60	30.6	$21,500	R 64.9
Gadsden, AL	84.3	14.6	0.5	0.4	0.2	9	39.2	$20,600	D 64.0
Gainesville, FL	69.4	22.1	4.9	3.4	0.2	87	29.5	$24,700	D 73.4
Galveston-Texas City, TX	62.5	17.7	17.4	2.1	0.3	96	35.8	$25,600	R 50.6
Gary, IN	69.1	19.8	10.2	0.8	0.1	86	35.8	$26,300	D 64.9
Glens Falls, NY	95.6	1.5	2.1	0.5	0.2	21	36.5	$22,800	R 63.2
Goldsboro, NC	63.1	33.1	2.3	1.2	0.3	58	34.3	$20,200	R 57.2
Grand Forks, ND-MN	92.3	1.5	3.1	1.3	1.7	34	31.9	$22,400	D 63.8
Grand Junction, CO	88.8	0.4	9.5	0.7	0.6	6	39.1	$22,900	R 76.9
Grand Rapids-Muskegon-Holland, MI	87.5	7.0	3.8	1.2	0.5	73	33.6	$28,300	R 73.1
Great Falls, MT	91.3	1.5	2.0	1.1	4.1	24	37.0	$24,600	D 51.7
Greeley, CO	74.1	0.4	24.1	1.0	0.5	6	33.5	$22,100	R 64.3
Green Bay, WI	94.7	0.5	1.1	1.8	1.9	5	34.5	$28,800	R 51.3
Greensboro–Winston-Salem–High Point, NC	77.8	19.5	1.4	1.0	0.4	40	36.8	$28,500	R 71.9
Greenville, NC	63.2	34.0	1.6	1.0	0.2	41	31.9	$24,100	R 56.7
Greenville-Spartanburg-Anderson, SC	80.1	17.9	1.1	0.8	0.1	28	37.2	$24,600	R 69.1
Hagerstown, MD	90.5	7.3	1.1	0.8	0.2	27	37.5	$23,600	R 59.5
Hamilton-Middletown, OH	93.0	5.0	0.6	1.2	0.1	14	34.4	$26,100	R 78.4
Harrisburg-Lebanon-Carlisle, PA	88.8	7.4	2.3	1.4	0.1	57	37.6	$29,100	R 96.2
Hartford, CT	81.5	8.0	8.1	2.2	0.2	92	36.9	$34,900	D 53.9
Hattiesburg, MS	72.2	26.0	1.0	0.8	0.1	23	31.3	$19,700	D 60.2
Hickory-Morganton-Lenoir, NC	90.1	7.5	1.2	0.9	0.2	30	37.4	$24,300	R 75.4
Honolulu, HI	27.6	3.4	7.4	61.3	0.4	26	35.7	$31,200	D 60.6
Houma, LA	77.7	16.0	1.8	0.9	3.6	50	32.0	$20,500	R 100
Houston, TX	52.1	17.8	24.9	5.0	0.2	89	32.6	$31,300	R 62.8
Huntington-Ashland, WV-KY-OH	96.8	2.2	0.5	0.3	0.1	6	38.9	$21,000	D 61.1
Huntsville, AL	76.3	19.8	1.7	1.7	0.5	51	34.5	$26,100	D 59.1
Indianapolis, IN	84.1	13.5	1.2	1.0	0.2	32	35.2	$29,700	R 64.7
Iowa City, IA	90.1	2.2	2.4	5.2	0.2	39	28.6	$27,400	D 51.3
Jackson, MI	88.9	8.2	1.9	0.6	0.4	46	36.5	$24,100	R 62.3
Jackson, MS	55.6	43.2	0.6	0.6	0.1	11	33.2	$25,000	R 51.7
Jackson, TN	69.4	29.4	0.7	0.4	0.1	11	35.4	$24,800	D 64.8
Jacksonville, FL	71.8	22.2	3.5	2.2	0.3	75	34.3	$27,500	R 54.8
Jacksonville, NC	69.2	18.6	8.8	2.8	0.6	97	25.3	$18,400	R 60.1
Jamestown, NY	93.3	2.0	3.8	0.5	0.4	36	36.7	$21,800	R 75.9
Janesville-Beloit, WI	91.1	6.0	1.7	0.9	0.3	44	36.4	$26,500	D 52.6
Jersey City, NJ	39.5	12.3	39.3	8.7	0.2	66	35.2	$28,000	D 77.8

	% WHITE	% BLACK	% LATINO	% ASIAN	% NATIVE AMERICAN	DIVERSITY SCORE	MEDIAN AGE	PER CAPITA INCOME	POLITICS
U.S.Metro Area Average	69.9	12.9	12.6	4.2	0.5	50	35.3	$26,700	R 50.6
Johnson City-Kingsport-Bristol, TN-VA	96.5	2.3	0.6	0.4	0.2	9	39.5	$22,700	R 62.5
Johnstown, PA	96.8	2.2	0.7	0.3	0.1	9	39.8	$22,100	D 72.0
Jonesboro, AR	91.7	6.1	1.2	0.7	0.2	28	33.9	$21,500	R 56.8
Joplin, MO	95.4	1.2	1.1	0.7	1.7	11	37.1	$23,300	R 70.6
Kalamazoo-Battle Creek, MI	86.1	9.6	2.5	1.4	0.5	62	35.3	$26,600	R 65.0
Kankakee, IL	80.1	16.2	2.7	0.8	0.1	61	35.3	$24,700	R 63.6
Kansas City, MO-KS	81.4	13.1	3.7	1.4	0.4	76	35.5	$30,100	D 58.5
Kenosha, WI	88.0	4.9	5.9	0.7	0.4	68	35.6	$25,100	D 50.4
Killeen-Temple, TX	61.5	18.7	15.6	3.7	0.5	98	28.6	$19,200	D 63.2
Knoxville, TN	91.4	6.4	0.9	1.1	0.3	20	37.4	$25,800	R 79.9
Kokomo, IN	92.3	5.1	1.7	0.7	0.2	38	37.8	$28,700	R 67.7
La Crosse, WI-MN	95.3	0.5	0.8	3.1	0.4	4	34.8	$25,900	D 56.6
Lafayette, LA	68.6	29.0	1.5	0.8	0.2	37	32.5	$21,700	D 100
Lafayette, IN	92.1	1.8	2.1	3.8	0.2	31	30.5	$24,000	R 67.1
Lake Charles, LA	73.3	24.7	1.3	0.5	0.2	29	34.7	$23,100	D 100
Lakeland-Winter Haven, FL	77.8	15.4	5.7	0.8	0.3	79	38.5	$23,100	R 62.4
Lancaster, PA	91.1	2.4	4.9	1.5	0.1	52	35.5	$27,900	R 80.9
Lansing-East Lansing, MI	84.8	7.4	4.7	2.5	0.6	83	32.5	$26,500	D 50.4
Laredo, TX	4.5	0.1	95.1	0.4	0.0	0	27.0	$13,900	D 56.0
Las Cruces, NM	38.9	1.4	58.0	1.0	0.7	22	29.5	$16,600	R 54.7
Las Vegas, NV-AZ	71.7	8.3	15.1	3.9	1.0	99	36.3	$28,700	R 59.8
Lawrence, KS	86.3	4.2	3.6	3.8	2.2	64	27.2	$21,700	D 53.4
Lawrence, MA-NH	90.0	1.5	6.6	1.8	0.1	39	36.8	$34,000	D 52.5
Lawton, OK	67.1	17.3	8.5	3.1	4.0	96	29.9	$20,000	R 57.7
Lewiston-Auburn, ME	97.6	0.5	1.0	0.6	0.2	5	37.0	$23,700	D 77.3
Lexington, KY	87.4	10.0	1.0	1.4	0.1	25	34.3	$27,200	D 51.8
Lima, OH	89.3	8.8	1.2	0.6	0.1	28	35.8	$23,900	R 77.2
Lincoln, NE	91.6	2.3	3.2	2.4	0.6	46	33.2	$27,100	R 64.6
Little Rock-North Little Rock, AR	76.5	20.8	1.7	0.8	0.3	43	34.2	$26,300	D 55.2
Long Island, NY	80.9	7.7	7.9	3.4	0.2	94	37.4	$39,700	R 55.9
Longview-Marshall, TX	73.9	21.5	3.7	0.5	0.4	56	36.6	$23,400	D 57.6
Los Angeles-Long Beach, CA	34.2	9.8	43.7	12.0	0.3	53	32.1	$28,900	D 59.5
Louisville, KY-IN	85.3	12.9	0.8	0.8	0.2	18	37.0	$29,000	R 50.5
Lowell, MA-NH	87.5	3.1	4.2	5.1	0.1	60	36.7	$40,400	D 67.7
Lubbock, TX	62.8	7.7	27.7	1.6	0.3	87	31.1	$24,600	R 82.4
Lynchburg, VA	79.0	19.4	0.8	0.6	0.2	18	38.0	$24,300	R 59.7
Macon, GA	58.7	38.4	1.7	1.0	0.2	39	34.6	$24,100	R 54.5
Madison, WI	91.0	3.4	2.1	3.1	0.3	46	33.6	$32,400	R 53.7
Manchester, NH	95.6	0.8	2.1	1.4	0.2	13	35.7	$32,300	R 60.8
Mansfield, OH	91.7	6.8	0.8	0.5	0.2	15	37.5	$24,000	R 73.7
McAllen-Edinburg-Mission, TX	11.7	0.1	87.8	0.3	0.1	0	27.4	$13,200	D 65.0
Medford-Ashland, OR	91.5	0.2	6.0	1.2	1.2	2	39.6	$24,800	R 59.2
Melbourne-Titusville-Palm Bay, FL	84.2	9.2	4.4	1.9	0.4	81	38.5	$25,300	R 55.3
Memphis, TN-AR-MS	55.7	41.9	1.2	1.1	0.2	25	33.5	$29,300	R 50.9
Merced, CA	46.9	4.1	39.0	9.4	0.6	58	28.4	$19,100	D 75.9
Miami, FL	24.1	18.6	55.7	1.5	0.1	28	36.2	$25,800	R 62.9
Middlesex-Somerset-Hunterdon, NJ	75.9	6.9	9.0	8.1	0.1	92	36.3	$39,300	R 50.9
Milwaukee-Waukesha, WI	78.4	14.9	4.5	1.7	0.5	85	35.7	$32,000	R 50.6
Minneapolis-St. Paul, MN-WI	89.2	4.4	2.1	3.5	0.9	48	34.6	$34,100	D 50.9
Missoula, MT	94.9	0.2	1.4	1.1	2.4	1	34.8	$24,500	D 58.4
Mobile, AL	69.5	27.9	1.3	0.8	0.4	29	35.6	$22,400	R 75.2
Modesto, CA	63.9	1.7	27.4	6.1	0.9	43	31.6	$21,600	D 77.6
Monmouth-Ocean, NJ	85.7	6.3	4.9	2.9	0.1	81	38.9	$33,400	R 61.2

	% WHITE	% BLACK	% LATINO	% ASIAN	% NATIVE AMERICAN	DIVERSITY SCORE	MEDIAN AGE	PER CAPITA INCOME	POLITICS
U.S.Metro Area Average	69.9	12.9	12.6	4.2	0.5	50	35.3	$26,700	R 50.6
Monroe, LA	65.3	32.9	1.0	0.6	0.2	21	32.8	$23,000	R 62.1
Montgomery, AL	61.5	36.5	1.1	0.7	0.2	24	34.4	$25,300	R 61.4
Muncie, IN	91.5	6.6	1.0	0.7	0.2	21	34.7	$24,900	R 51.8
Myrtle Beach, SC	79.8	17.7	1.3	1.0	0.2	29	37.5	$23,500	R 86.5
Naples, FL	77.0	4.3	18.0	0.5	0.3	58	41.6	$40,500	R 75.7
Nashua, NH	95.2	0.8	2.4	1.5	0.2	12	35.6	$32,000	R 61.3
Nashville, TN	81.6	15.6	1.2	1.4	0.2	29	34.8	$30,500	D 61.7
New Bedford, MA	93.0	2.1	3.4	1.3	0.2	39	37.1	$27,000	D 81.6
New Haven-Meriden, CT	80.0	10.3	7.6	1.9	0.2	93	36.9	$34,200	D 64.0
New London-Norwich, CT-RI	89.5	4.2	4.0	1.8	0.5	61	35.6	$31,200	D 62.5
New Orleans, LA	58.3	34.5	4.9	2.0	0.3	72	34.6	$26,000	D 100
New York, NY	43.3	23.2	25.0	8.3	0.2	73	35.8	$37,300	D 73.1
Newark, NJ	62.2	21.3	12.3	4.0	0.2	98	36.8	$39,200	R 52.5
Newburgh, NY-PA	83.5	6.6	8.1	1.5	0.2	88	34.3	$26,000	R 66.4
Norfolk-Virginia Beach-Newport News, VA-NC	64.0	29.6	3.0	3.1	0.3	67	32.6	$24,600	D 59.5
Oakland, CA	53.2	14.3	16.6	15.4	0.5	88	35.6	$34,800	D 66.3
Ocala, FL	80.1	14.7	4.2	0.7	0.4	71	41.6	$22,000	R 71,8
Odessa-Midland, TX	61.3	6.1	31.3	0.9	0.4	73	32.6	$25,600	R 81.8
Oklahoma City, OK	78.3	10.6	4.8	2.0	4.3	85	34.1	$24,300	R 67.7
Olympia, WA	87.7	1.9	4.2	4.7	1.4	46	36.6	$28,200	D 56.8
Omaha, NE-IA	85.2	8.2	4.6	1.5	0.5	81	34.2	$29,000	R 59.4
Orange County, CA	57.3	1.5	28.5	12.3	0.3	38	32.8	$34,000	R 68.2
Orlando, FL	72.9	13.4	11.1	2.3	0.3	100	35.3	$26,000	R 70.5
Owensboro, KY	94.7	4.3	0.5	0.3	0.1	6	36.4	$23,200	R 55.7
Panama City, FL	81.5	12.7	2.6	2.5	0.8	69	35.4	$22,200	R 52.8
Parkersburg-Marietta, WV-OH	97.9	1.2	0.4	0.4	0.2	2	39.1	$24,000	D 68.3
Pensacola, FL	76.3	17.8	2.5	2.3	1.1	68	34.5	$22,400	R 74.0
Peoria-Pekin, IL	89.2	8.0	1.5	1.1	0.2	39	36.9	$27,600	R 68.6
Philadelphia, PA-NJ	73.3	19.2	4.4	2.9	0.2	86	36.3	$32,900	D 52.6
Phoenix-Mesa, AZ	72.5	3.5	20.2	1.9	1.8	75	35.1	$26,800	R 61.6
Pine Bluff, AR	52.5	45.7	1.0	0.5	0.3	20	33.6	$20,100	R 53.1
Pittsburgh, PA	89.9	8.3	0.8	1.0	0.1	17	39.6	$29,700	D 63.1
Pittsfield, MA	95.2	2.2	1.4	1.0	0.2	23	39.2	$30,100	D 75.6
Pocatello, ID	90.1	0.7	5.9	1.1	2.1	15	30.6	$20,900	R 55.8
Portland, ME	97.3	0.7	0.8	1.0	0.2	4	37.4	$30,200	D 62.9
Portland-Vancouver, OR-WA	87.3	2.7	5.0	4.2	0.8	58	36.3	$30,700	D 60.9
Portsmouth-Rochester, NH-ME	96.8	0.6	1.2	1.1	0.2	5	35.4	$29,100	R 55.8
Providence-Fall River-Warwick, RI-MA	87.9	3.6	6.2	2.0	0.3	72	36.8	$27,500	D 76.0
Provo-Orem, UT	93.1	0.1	4.3	1.9	0.6	1	23.1	$18,800	R 64.8
Pueblo, CO	57.6	1.8	39.6	0.6	0.5	31	38.9	$22,200	R 59.2
Punta Gorda, FL	91.2	4.0	3.6	1.0	0.2	55	52.7	$25,000	R 64.7
Racine, WI	80.2	11.9	6.9	0.8	0.3	82	35.7	$28,500	R 53.7
Raleigh-Durham-Chapel Hill, NC	71.0	23.9	2.3	2.5	0.3	59	33.7	$30,300	D 56.0
Rapid City, SD	86.1	2.1	3.0	1.4	7.3	36	32.5	$23,778	R 65.1
Reading, PA	89.2	3.1	6.7	1.0	0.1	58	38.1	$29,400	D 54.5
Redding, CA	89.1	0.8	5.3	2.4	2.5	14	37.6	$23,500	R 70.4
Reno, NV	78.1	2.2	12.9	4.9	1.8	58	35.8	$33,700	R 72.3
Richland-Kennewick-Pasco, WA	77.3	1.7	17.8	2.6	0.7	46	33.4	$24,100	R 60.7
Richmond-Petersburg, VA	66.8	29.6	1.5	1.8	0.3	40	36.1	$31,500	R 63.9
Riverside-San Bernardino, CA	55.9	6.3	32.8	4.4	0.7	80	31.4	$22,200	R 60.2
Roanoke, VA	84.7	13.3	0.9	0.9	0.1	18	39.6	$30,000	R 83.2
Rochester, MN	93.1	1.0	1.3	4.4	0.3	12	34.9	$30,300	R 59.4
Rochester, NY	84.5	9.5	3.8	1.9	0.4	78	35.3	$29,500	D 51.4

	% WHITE	% BLACK	% LATINO	% ASIAN	% NATIVE AMERICAN	DIVERSITY SCORE	MEDIAN AGE	PER CAPITA INCOME	POLITICS
U.S.Metro Area Average	69.9	12.9	12.6	4.2	0.5	50	35.3	$26,700	R 50.6
Rockford, IL	86.2	7.6	4.7	1.3	0.2	77	36.1	$26,800	R 72.8
Rocky Mount, NC	57.3	41.0	1.1	0.3	0.2	15	35.9	$22,100	D 55.7
Sacramento, CA	69.2	6.9	13.7	9.2	0.9	93	34.9	$28,400	D 52.0
Saginaw-Bay City-Midland, MI	83.6	10.0	5.2	0.8	0.4	79	36.2	$27,500	D 54.9
St. Cloud, MN	97.7	0.4	0.7	0.9	0.3	1	30.8	$22,500	D 59.8
St. Joseph, MO	93.9	3.1	2.4	0.4	0.3	29	37.0	$23,500	D 78.6
St. Louis, MO-IL	79.7	17.5	1.4	1.2	0.2	35	35.6	$30,600	D 53.0
Salem, OR	85.1	0.8	10.9	2.0	1.2	14	36.2	$23,700	D 50.6
Salinas, CA	44.9	5.6	40.4	8.6	0.5	65	31.4	$28,900	D 55.8
Salt Lake City-Ogden, UT	87.7	1.0	7.7	2.9	0.7	20	28.7	$24,900	R 57.6
San Angelo, TX	63.7	4.0	30.8	1.3	0.3	70	34.1	$23,300	R 71.9
San Antonio, TX	39.2	6.0	53.2	1.4	0.2	48	32.9	$24,800	R 52.8
San Diego, CA	58.9	5.7	25.6	9.3	0.6	80	33.0	$28,400	R 61.1
San Francisco, CA	51.0	7.0	17.6	24.1	0.3	73	38.3	$46,100	D 75.4
San Jose, CA	50.6	3.3	25.4	20.3	0.4	58	33.6	$39,800	D 58.1
San Luis Obispo-Atascadero-Paso Robles, CA	77.0	2.0	16.9	3.3	0.8	56	35.4	$24,800	R 51.3
Santa Barbara-Santa Maria-Lompoc, CA	59.1	2.5	32.8	5.1	0.6	57	33.4	$31,600	D 55.1
Santa Cruz-Watsonville, CA	68.6	1.0	25.6	4.2	0.5	23	34.8	$32,500	D 63.3
Santa Fe, NM	50.7	0.5	45.9	0.9	2.1	6	38.4	$29,400	D 70.6
Santa Rosa, CA	80.4	1.4	13.9	3.5	0.9	37	37.0	$32,000	D 62.4
Sarasota-Bradenton, FL	87.8	6.8	4.4	0.8	0.2	68	47.1	$37,500	R 64.6
Savannah, GA	59.7	36.8	1.9	1.4	0.2	46	34.4	$26,000	R 75.5
Scranton–Wilkes-Barre–Hazleton, PA	97.5	1.0	0.8	0.7	0.1	5	40.4	$25,000	D 58.6
Seattle-Bellevue-Everett, WA	82.1	4.4	3.9	8.4	1.1	66	36.0	$37,400	D 55.3
Sharon, PA	93.2	5.7	0.6	0.4	0.1	5	39.5	$23,000	R 51.3
Sheboygan, WI	94.1	0.6	2.3	2.7	0.4	7	36.9	$27,400	R 83.8
Sherman-Denison, TX	87.3	7.2	3.8	0.6	1.1	56	39.2	$23,500	D 66.2
Shreveport-Bossier City, LA	61.4	36.2	1.5	0.7	0.2	28	35.6	$24,200	R 82.3
Sioux City, IA-NE	89.7	1.7	5.1	1.9	1.6	38	35.4	$26,000	R 66.6
Sioux Falls, SD	96.1	0.8	0.8	0.7	1.6	4	35.0	$29,200	R 54.9
South Bend, IN	85.0	10.6	2.8	1.3	0.3	61	35.5	$26,800	D 63.9
Spokane, WA	91.9	1.6	2.8	2.3	1.5	26	36.1	$25,400	R 53.6
Springfield, IL	89.6	8.3	1.0	1.0	0.2	17	37.0	$27,400	R 63.2
Springfield, MO	96.0	1.6	1.0	0.8	0.5	9	35.4	$25,000	R 62.6
Springfield, MA	81.3	6.6	10.0	1.9	0.2	83	35.6	$27,500	D 86.5
Stamford-Norwalk, CT	76.5	9.9	10.4	3.0	0.1	100	38.2	$53,400	R 61.6
State College, PA	91.6	2.5	1.5	4.3	0.1	19	29.0	$23,300	R 100
Steubenville-Weirton, OH-WV	94.6	4.3	0.6	0.4	0.1	5	40.8	$21,700	D 65.7
Stockton-Lodi, CA	51.9	5.0	28.4	14.1	0.7	61	32.1	$21,900	R 61.9
Sumter, SC	53.1	44.0	1.6	1.1	0.2	23	32.2	$18,900	D 57.3
Syracuse, NY	90.2	6.1	1.7	1.5	0.6	32	34.6	$25,900	R 64.5
Tacoma, WA	80.0	7.6	4.9	6.2	1.3	72	33.9	$26,000	D 55.8
Tallahassee, FL	61.3	33.7	3.1	1.6	0.2	57	30.6	$24,400	D 72.9
Tampa-St. Petersburg-Clearwater, FL	79.0	10.1	9.1	1.5	0.3	91	40.5	$27,900	R 56.6
Terre Haute, IN	93.6	4.2	0.9	1.0	0.2	9	36.8	$22,300	R 55.4
Texarkana, TX-Texarkana, AR	73.7	23.4	2.0	0.4	0.4	31	36.8	$21,800	D 54.7
Toledo, OH	82.4	12.1	4.0	1.3	0.2	67	34.6	$27,900	D 72.7
Topeka, KS	83.0	8.4	6.7	0.9	1.0	70	36.6	$27,500	R 54.0
Trenton, NJ	68.0	19.6	7.8	4.5	0.2	96	36.3	$40,000	R 57.4
Tucson, AZ	63.7	3.0	28.7	2.0	2.5	64	35.8	$23,800	R 59.4
Tulsa, OK	81.3	8.4	2.8	1.1	6.4	59	35.6	$26,600	R 64.1
Tuscaloosa, AL	70.1	27.9	0.9	0.9	0.1	11	33.3	$22,800	R 52.5

continues

People

	% WHITE	% BLACK	% LATINO	% ASIAN	% NATIVE AMERICAN	DIVERSITY SCORE	MEDIAN AGE	PER CAPITA INCOME	POLITICS
U.S.Metro Area Average	69.9	12.9	12.6	4.2	0.5	50	35.3	$26,700	R 50.6
Tyler, TX	69.9	21.8	7.4	0.6	0.3	68	36.8	$26,200	D 58.4
Utica-Rome, NY	91.6	4.7	2.5	1.0	0.2	45	36.6	$23,600	R 78.4
Vallejo-Fairfield-Napa, CA	60.0	9.9	17.1	12.4	0.7	91	34.2	$27,100	D 57.6
Ventura, CA	58.6	2.1	32.5	6.2	0.5	45	33.5	$30,500	R 63.7
Victoria, TX	53.3	6.2	39.9	0.4	0.2	52	33.9	$25,800	R 52.9
Vineland-Millville-Bridgeton, NJ	63.5	17.5	16.7	1.2	1.0	90	35.4	$24,300	R 64.4
Visalia-Tulare-Porterville, CA	47.2	1.3	45.8	4.8	0.9	21	29.9	$19,100	R 70.3
Waco, TX	67.5	15.9	15.4	0.9	0.3	83	34.3	$22,600	D 66.4
Washington, DC-MD-VA-WV	61.7	24.8	7.0	6.2	0.3	88	35.1	$37,600	R 52.2
Waterbury, CT	82.7	8.8	6.6	1.7	0.2	87	37.2	$34,300	D 58.6
Waterloo-Cedar Falls, IA	90.2	7.4	1.2	1.1	0.2	26	36.5	$24,400	D 51.2
Wausau, WI	96.0	0.1	0.6	2.9	0.4	0	36.1	$25,700	R 50.2
West Palm Beach-Boca Raton, FL	74.4	13.7	10.3	1.4	0.1	92	41.2	$42,400	D 52.6
Wheeling, WV-OH	97.0	2.1	0.4	0.4	0.1	0	40.8	$22,600	D 62.7
Wichita, KS	83.4	7.7	5.6	2.3	0.9	90	34.7	$27,100	R 53.6
Wichita Falls, TX	77.0	8.8	11.6	1.9	0.7	100	34.8	$24,400	R 63.2
Williamsport, PA	95.9	2.6	0.8	0.6	0.2	0	37.9	$23,000	R 65.7
Wilmington-Newark, DE-MD	78.0	16.5	3.4	2.0	0.2	100	35.6	$33,200	R 69.6
Wilmington, NC	77.8	19.7	1.4	0.6	0.5	14	37.6	$24,500	D 61.5
Worcester, MA-CT	89.5	2.2	5.9	2.3	0.2	83	36.0	$28,700	D 74.2
Yakima, WA	63.6	1.0	30.5	1.1	3.8	0	32.9	$21,900	R 55.2
Yolo, CA	61.6	2.0	25.6	9.8	1.0	75	30.6	$26,200	D 64.0
York, PA	93.4	3.6	2.0	0.9	0.1	33	37.5	$27,600	R 83.9
Youngstown-Warren, OH	87.7	10.1	1.6	0.5	0.2	0	38.8	$24,800	D 82.2
Yuba City, CA	66.5	2.6	18.2	10.9	1.8	100	32.8	$20,600	R 64.8
Yuma, AZ	48.9	2.4	45.8	1.4	1.6	100	33.5	$17,500	R 55.5
Canada Metro Area average	92.2	1.5	5.1	0.7	0.5	50	35.6	$21,900	
Calgary, AB	86.2	1.2	10.9	0.9	0.7	56	34.2	$24,600	
Chicoutimi -Jonquiere, PQ	99.6	0.1	0.2	0.0	0.0	32	36.4	$18,800	
Edmonton, AB	87.5	1.3	9.6	0.9	0.7	4	34.2	$21,500	
Halifax, NS	93.7	3.5	1.9	0.9	0.1	34	34.6	$21,700	
Hamilton,ON	92.8	1.5	4.3	0.7	0.6	50	36.2	$23,400	
Kitchener-Waterloo, ON	92.9	1.4	3.9	0.7	1.1	100	34.0	$22,400	
London, ON	93.0	1.4	3.4	1.3	0.9	85	34.9	$22,900	
Montreal, PQ	88.3	3.6	4.5	2.2	1.4	57	36.5	$21,100	
Oshawa, ON	94.8	2.1	2.7	0.3	0.2	66	34.2	$23,800	
Ottawa-Hull, ON-PQ	89.1	3.0	5.0	2.3	0.6	35	35.3	$25,500	
Quebec City, PQ	98.6	0.4	0.5	0.3	0.2	50	37.2	$21,100	
Regina, SK	95.0	0.9	3.7	0.1	0.3	26	34.4	$21,800	
Saint John, NB	90.0	2.6	5.5	0.8	1.1	42	35.3	$21,300	
Saskatoon, SK	99.0	0.1	0.8	0.1	0.0	46	33.8	$19,800	
Sherbrooke, PQ	98.3	0.9	0.6	0.1	0.1	66	36.4	$19,700	
St. Catharines-Niagara, ON	97.2	0.4	2.1	0.2	0.2	54	37.5	$19,500	
St. John's, NF	98.3	0.4	0.5	0.3	0.5	80	34.2	$18,800	
Sudbury, ON	98.4	0.6	0.8	0.1	0.1	100	35.6	$23,000	
Thunder Bay, ON	98.0	0.3	1.4	0.1	0.2	87	35.7	$22,900	
Toronto,ON	71.5	6.2	19.3	1.6	1.4	14	35.1	$26,000	
Trois-Rivieres, PQ	99.2	0.4	0.3	0.1	0.0	33	38.6	$19,100	
Vancouver,BC	71.0	0.9	26.4	1.0	0.7	0	35.9	$22,600	
Victoria, BC	92.9	0.7	5.9	0.2	0.3	25	39.3	$23,400	
Windsor,ON	90.8	2.2	4.3	2.2	0.5	33	35.1	$22,800	
Winnipeg, MB	89.6	1.5	8.1	0.2	0.6	50	35.4	$20,700	

Sources: U.S. figures for race and Latino origin, median age in years, and per capita income dollars are forecasts from Woods & Poole Economics. The dominant political party's average plurality from the three latest congressional elections come from Election Data Services. Canadian per capita income dollars come from Strategic Projections. Canadian figures for Black, Asian, Arab, and Latino populations are derived from "visible minorities" tables from Statistics Canada.

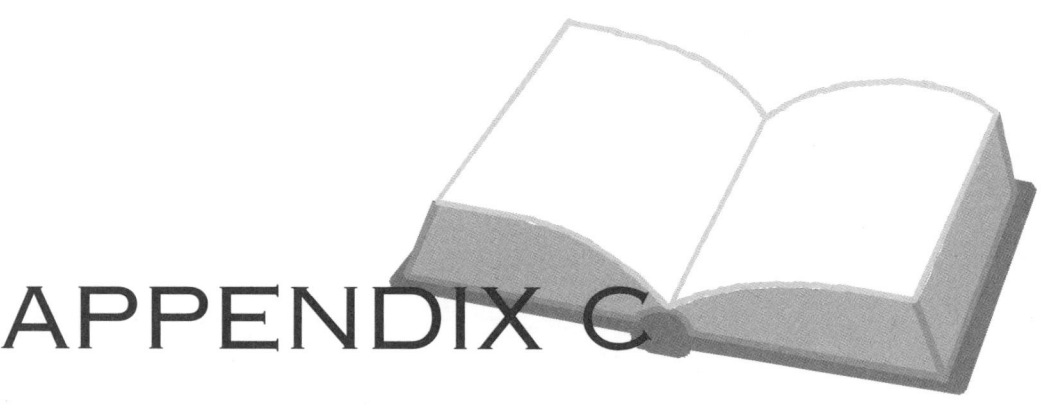

APPENDIX C

METROPOLITAN AREA CONTACTS AND PLACE FINDER

Each metropolitan area's listing includes the telephone number and address for its largest daily newspaper, its Convention and Visitors Bureau (CVB), and its Chamber of Commerce (C/C). Internet addresses are included wherever possible. Underneath is a listing of cities, towns, and unincorporated places with more than 2,500 people within metro area boundaries. In instances where there is only one place over 2,500, the largest places are listed. Whenever metro areas cross state or provincial lines, the postal abbreviation for each state or province follows the place name.

ABILENE, TX

Abilene Reporter-News
P.O. Box 30
Abilene 79604
(915) 673-4271
www.texnews.com

Abilene CVB
1101 N. First St.
Abilene 79601
(800) 727-7704
www.abilene.com/visitors

Abilene C/C
325 Hickory
Abilene 79604
(915) 677-7241
www.abilene.com/chamber
Abilene, 108,476
Merkel, 2,462
Tye, 1,137

AKRON, OH

Akron Beacon Journal
44 E. Exchange St.
Akron 44328
(330) 996-3000
www.ohio.com

Akron/Summit CVB
77 E. Mill St.
Akron 44308
(800) 245-4254
www.visitakron-summit.org

Akron Regional Development Board
One Cascade Plaza
Akron 44308
(216) 376-5550
Akron, 216,882
Aurora, 11,584
Barberton, 27,249
Cuyahoga Falls, 49,278

Fairlawn, 6,049
Green, 21,653
Kent, 27,072
Lakemore, 2,579
Macedonia, 8,685
Mogadore, 4,015
Munroe Falls, 5,485
Northfield, 3,545
Norton, 11,541
Portage Lakes, 13,373
Ravenna, 11,829
Richfield, 3,598
Silver Lake, 2,686
Stow, 30,864
Streetsboro, 10,905
Tallmadge, 15,767
Twinsburg, 14,093
Windham, 2,841

ALBANY, GA

Albany Herald
P.O. Box 48
Albany 31703
(912) 888-9316

Albany-Dougherty C/C & CVB
225 W. Broad Ave.
Albany 31701
(912) 434-8700
www.albanyga.com
Albany, 78,591
Leesburg, 1,831

ALBANY-SCHENECTADY-TROY, NY

Albany Times Union
Box 15000
Albany 12212
(518) 454-5694
www.timesunion.com

Daily Gazette
2345 Maxon Rd.
Schnectady 12301
(518) 374-4141
www.dailygazette.com

Albany County CVB
52 S. Pearl St.
Albany 12207
(800) 258-3582
www.albany.org

Albany-Colonie Regional C/C
540 Broadway
Albany 12207
(518) 431-1400
www.ac-chamber.org

Rensselaer County Regional C/C
31 Second St.
Troy 12180
(518) 274-7020

Schenectady County C/C
306 State St.
Schenectady 12305
(518) 372-3217
www.schenectadychamber.org
Albany, 103,564
Amsterdam, 19,843
Ballston Spa, 5,512
Cobleskill, 4,997
Cohoes, 15,215
Colonie, 7,996
Corinth, 2,793
Delmar, 8,360
East Glenville, 6,518
Hoosick Falls, 3,339
Latham, 10,131
Loudonville, 10,822
Mechanicville, 5,212
Menands, 4,570
Ravena, 3,543
Rensselaer, 7,986
Roessleville, 10,753
Rotterdam, 21,228
Saratoga Springs, 25,118
Schenectady, 62,893
Scotia, 7,505
South Glens Falls, 3,535
Troy, 52,518
Voorheesville, 3,048
Watervliet, 9,837
Westmere, 6,750

ALBUQUERQUE, NM

Albuquerque Journal/Tribune
7777 Jefferson NE
Albuquerque 87109
(505) 823-3393
www.abqjournal.com

Albuquerque CVB
121 Tijeras NE
Albuquerque 87102
(800) 733-9918
www.abqcvb.org

Greater Albuquerque C/C
401 Second St. NW
Albuquerque 87125
(505) 764-3700
www.gacc.org
Albuquerque, 419,681
Belen, 7,838
Bernalillo, 7,450
Bosque Farms, 5,234
Corrales, 5,845

Los Lunas, 7,218
Los Ranchos de Albuquerque, 5,163
North Valley, 12,507
Paradise Hills, 5,513
Sandia, 6,742
South Valley, 35,701

ALEXANDRIA, LA

Alexandria Daily Town Talk
1201 3rd St.
Alexandria 71306
(318) 487-6397
www.thetowntalk.com

Alexandria-Pineville Area CVB
3437 Masonic Dr.
Alexandria 71301
(800) 742-7049
www.apacvb.org

Central Louisiana C/C
802 3rd St.
Alexandria 71309
(318) 442-6671
Alexandria, 46,051
Ball, 3,222
Pineville, 14,315

ALLENTOWN-BETHLEHEM-EASTON, PA

Morning Call
101 N. 6th St.
Allentown 18101
(610) 820-6500
www.mcall.com

Allentown-Lehigh County C/C
462 Walnut St.
Allentown 18102
(610) 437-9661
www.allentownchamber.org

Bethlehem Area C/C
509 Main St.
Bethlehem 18017
(610) 867-3788

Easton C/C
One S. Third St.
Easton 18042
(610) 253-4211
Allentown, 102,211
Bangor, 5,201
Bethlehem, 70,245
Catasauqua, 6,447
Coopersburg, 2,521
Coplay, 3,298

Easton, 25,782
Emmaus, 11,544
Fountain Hill, 4,459
Fullerton, 13,127
Hellertown, 5,566
Jim Thorpe, 5,121
Lansford, 4,438
Lehighton, 5,784
Macungie, 2,951
Middletown, 6,866
Nazareth, 5,529
Nesquehoning, 3,359
North Catasauqua, 2,815
Northampton, 9,025
Palmerton, 5,289
Pen Argyl, 3,395
Slatington, 4,599
Summit Hill, 3,267
Weatherly, 2,645
Wilson, 7,679
Wind Gap, 2,765

ALTOONA, PA

Altoona Mirror
301 Cayuga Ave.
Altoona 16602
(814) 946-7411

Altoona-Blair County C/C
1212 Twelfth Ave.
Altoona 16601
(814) 943-8151
www.altoona-blairchamber.com
Altoona, 50,101
Hollidaysburg, 5,443
Roaring Spring, 2,505
Tyrone, 5,688

AMARILLO, TX

Amarillo Globe-Times/Daily News
900 S. Harrison St.
Amarillo 79166
(806) 376-4488
www.amarillonet.com

Amarillo CVB
1000 Polk St.
Amarillo 79101
(800) 692-1338
www.amarillo-cvb.org

Amarillo C/C
1000 S. Polk St.
Amarillo 79101
(806) 373-7800
www.amarillo-chamber.org
Amarillo, 169,588
Canyon, 13,031

ANCHORAGE, AK

Anchorage Daily News
1001 Northway Dr.
Anchorage 99508
(907) 257-4200
www.adn.com

Anchorage CVB
524 W. Fourth Ave.
Anchorage 99501
(907) 276-4118

Anchorage C/C
441 W. Fifth Ave.
Anchorage 99501
(907) 272-2401
www.anchoragechamber.org
Anchorage, 250,505

ANN ARBOR, MI

Ann Arbor News
340 E. Huron St.
Ann Arbor 48104
(734) 994-6989
aa.mlive.com

Ann Arbor CVB
120 W. Huron St.
Ann Arbor 48104
(800) 888-9487
www.annarbor.org

Ann Arbor Area C/C
425 S. Main St.
Ann Arbor 48104
(734) 665-4433
www.annarborchamber.org
Adrian, 22,262
Ann Arbor, 108,758
Blissfield, 3,252
Brighton, 6,418
Chelsea, 4,080
Clinton, 2,516
Fowlerville, 3,255
Howell, 9,348
Hudson, 2,587
Milan, 4,243
Saline, 7,193
Tecumseh, 8,032
Ypsilanti, 23,045

ANNISTON, AL

Anniston Star
P.O. Box 189
Anniston 36202
(256) 236-1551
www.annistonstar.com

Anniston CVB
1330 Quintard Ave.
Anniston 36202
(256) 237-3536

Calhoun County C/C
P.O. Box 1087
Anniston 36202
(256) 237-3536
www.calhounchamber.org
Anniston, 25,774
Jacksonville, 9,526
Oxford, 10,408
Piedmont, 5,214
Saks, 11,138
Weaver, 2,707

APPLETON-OSHKOSH-NEENAH, WI

Post-Crescent
306 W. Washington St.
Appleton 54911
(920) 739-9437
www.wisinfo.com/postcrescent

The Northwestern
224 State St.
Oshkosh 54901
(920) 235-7700
www.wisinfo.com/northwestern

Fox Cities CVB
110 Fox River Dr.
Appleton 54915
(920) 734-3355

Fox Cities C/C & Industry
227 S. Walnut St.
Appleton 54911
(920) 734-7101

Neenah C/C
325 N. Commercial St.
Neenah 54956
(920) 722-7758

Oshkosh Association
120 Jackson St.
Oshkosh 54901
(414) 424-7700
www.oshkoshchamber.com
Appleton, 65,862
Brillion, 3,074
Chilton, 3,414
Kaukauna, 12,182
Kimberly, 5,766
Little Chute, 10,049
Menasha, 15,567

Neenah, 23,936
New Holstein, 3,444
Omro, 3,210
Oshkosh, 57,957
Seymour, 2,897

ASHEVILLE, NC

Asheville Citizen-Times
14 O'Henry Ave.
Asheville 28801
(828) 252-5611
www.carolinamountains.com/
citizen-times

Asheville Area C/C & CVB
151 Haywood St.
Asheville 28802
(800) 257-1300
www.ashevillechamber.org
Asheville, 64,067
Black Mountain, 7,572
Weaverville, 2,539
Woodfin, 3,121

ATHENS, GA

Athens Banner Herald/News
One Press Place
Athens 30601
(706) 549-0123
www.onlineathens.com

Athens Area C/C
220 College Ave.
Athens 30601
(706) 549-6800
Athens, 45,734
Gaines School, 11,354
Watkinsville, 2,016

ATLANTA, GA

Atlanta Journal-Constitution
72 Marietta St. NW
Atlanta 30302
(404) 526-5151
www.accessatlanta.com/ajc

Atlanta CVB
233 Peachtree St.
Atlanta 30303
(404) 521-6600
www.acvb.com/atlanta2.html

Metro Atlanta C/C
235 International Blvd. NW
Atlanta 30303
(404) 880-9000
www.metroatlantachamber.com
Acworth, 6,927
Alpharetta, 20,477
Atlanta, 401,907
Auburn, 5,108
Austell, 4,853
Belvedere Park, 18,089
Buford, 9,880
Candler-McAfee, 29,491
Canton, 7,880
Carrollton, 16,538
Cartersville, 12,988
Chamblee, 7,693
Clarkston, 5,859
College Park, 20,300
Conley, 5,528
Conyers, 7,551
Covington, 9,906
Cumming, 4,197
Dacula, 3,515
Dallas, 2,786
Decatur, 17,805
Doraville, 8,299
Douglasville, 14,564
Druid Hills, 12,174
Duluth, 15,015
Dunwoody, 26,302
East Point, 34,155
Fair Oaks, 6,996
Fairburn, 4,043
Fayetteville, 8,531
Forest Park, 17,060
Gresham Park, 9,000
Griffin, 21,506
Hampton, 4,311
Hapeville, 5,354
Holly Springs, 3,009
Jonesboro, 3,608
Kennesaw, 12,818
Lake City, 2,777
Lawrenceville, 19,232
Lilburn, 11,134
Lithia Springs, 11,403
Locust Grove, 2,750
Loganville, 4,607
Mableton, 25,725
Marietta, 50,937
McDonough, 3,773
Monroe, 13,982
Morrow, 5,162
Mountain Park, 11,025
Newnan, 13,355
Norcross, 6,360
North Atlanta, 27,812
North Decatur, 13,936
North Druid Hills, 14,170
Palmetto, 2,704
Panthersville, 9,874
Peachtree City, 28,156

Powder Springs, 10,092
Redan, 24,376
Riverdale, 10,020
Roswell, 55,462
Sandy Springs, 67,842
Scottdale, 8,636
Smyrna, 34,855
Snellville, 15,418
Social Circle, 2,848
Stockbridge, 5,251
Stone Mountain, 7,053
Sugar Hill, 7,783
Suwanee, 4,672
Tucker, 25,781
Tyrone, 3,573
Union City, 10,358
Villa Rica, 6,921
Vinings, 7,417
Winder, 8,441
Woodstock, 5,730

ATLANTIC-CAPE MAY, NJ

The Press of Atlantic City
11 Devins Ln.
Atlantic City 08232
(609) 645-1234

Greater Atlantic City CVB
2314 Pacific Ave.
Atlantic City 08401
(888) 222-3683
www.atlanticcitynj.com

Cape May County C/C
P.O. Box 74
Cape May Court House 08204
(609) 884-5508
www.beachcomber.com/Capemay

Greater Atlantic City C/C
1301 Atlantic Ave.
Atlantic City 08401
(609) 345-5600
www.vitinc.com/mall/ac
Absecon, 7,709
Atlantic City, 38,361
Brigantine, 11,556
Buena, 4,607
Cape May, 4,490
Egg Harbor City, 4,545
Hammonton, 12,433
Linwood, 7,083
Margate City, 8,554
North Wildwood, 4,988
Northfield, 7,430
Ocean City, 15,661
Pleasantville, 16,591
Sea Isle City, 2,801
Somers Point, 11,217
Ventnor City, 10,954

Villas, 8,136
Wildwood, 4,442
Wildwood Crest, 3,597
Woodbine, 2,615

AUGUSTA-AIKEN, GA-SC

Augusta Chronicle
725 Broad St.
Augusta 30903
(706) 724-0851
www.augustachronicle.com

Aiken Standard
326 Rutland Dr.
Aiken 29801
(803) 648-2311
www.aiken.net/nie

Augusta-Richmond County CVB
1450 Greene St.
Augusta 30903
(800) 726-0243
www.augustaga.org

Greater Aiken C/C
400 Laurens St. NW
Aiken 29802
(800) 542-4536
chamber.aiken.net

Metro Augusta C/C
600 Broad St. Plaza
Augusta 30903
(706) 821-1300
www.metroaugusta.com
Aiken, SC, 22,834
Augusta, GA, 41,783
Belvedere, SC, 6,133
Edgefield, SC, 2,549
Evans, GA, 13,713
Fort Gordon, GA, 9,140
Grovetown, GA, 4,637
Hephzibah, GA, 3,285
Johnston, SC, 2,644
Martinez, GA, 24,738
New Ellenton, 2,599
North Augusta, SC, 16,397
South Augusta, GA, 55,998
Thomson, GA, 6,723
West Augusta, GA, 27,637

AUSTIN-SAN MARCOS, TX

Austin American-Statesman
305 S. Congress St.
Austin 78704
(512) 445-3500
www.austin360.com/news

San Marcos CVB
202 N. C.M. Allen Pkwy.
San Marcos 78667
(888) 200-5620
www.sanmarcostexas.com

Austin CVB
201 E. Second St.
Austin 78701
(800) 926-2282
www.austin360.com/aCVB

San Marcos C/C
P.O. Box 2310
San Marcos 78667
(512) 393-5900
host.pc.centuryinter.net/smchamber

Greater Austin C/C
111 Congress Ave.
Austin 78767
(512) 322-5635
www.austin-chamber.org
Anderson Mill, 9,299
Austin, 541,278
Bastrop, 4,972
Brushy Creek, 5,833
Cedar Park, 10,727
Elgin, 5,813
Georgetown, 22,393
Jollyville, 14,094
Kyle, 2,943
Lago Vista, 2,607
Lakeway, 5,355
Leander, 6,456
Lockhart, 10,657
Luling, 5,151
Pflugerville, 8,168
Round Rock, 52,479
San Marcos, 34,994
Smithville, 3,830
Taylor, 14,336
Wells Branch, 7,094
West Lake Hills, 3,229

BAKERSFIELD, CA

Bakersfield Californian
P.O. Box BIN 440
Bakersfield 93302
(805) 395-7500
www.bakersfield.com

Greater Bakersfield CVB
1325 P St.
Bakersfield 93301
(805) 325-5051
www.visitbfield.com

Greater Bakersfield C/C
1033 Truxtun Ave.
Bakersfield 93303
(805) 327-4421
www.bbol.org
Arvin, 10,726
Bakersfield, 205,508
California City, 9,275
Delano, 32,098
Golden Hills, 5,423
Greenacres, 7,379
Lamont, 11,517
McFarland, 7,133
Oildale, 26,553
Ridgecrest, 30,627
Rosamond, 7,430
Shafter, 10,770
Taft, 6,455
Tehachapi, 6,602
Wasco, 18,307

BALTIMORE, MD

Baltimore Sun
501 N. Calvert St.
Baltimore 21278
(410) 332-6000
www.sunspot.net

Baltimore Area CVB
100 Light St.
Baltimore 21202
(800) 343-3468
www.baltconvstr.com

Baltimore C/C
204 E. Lombard St.
Baltimore 21202
(410) 837-7100
Aberdeen, 13,090
Annapolis, 33,234
Arbutus, 19,750
Arnold, 20,261
Baltimore, 675,401
Bel Air, 9,439
Bel Air North, 14,880
Bel Air South, 26,421
Bowleys Quarters, 5,595
Brooklyn Park, 10,987
Cape St. Claire, 7,878
Carney, 25,578
Catonsville, 35,233
Cockeysville, 18,668
Columbia, 75,883
Crofton, 12,781
Dundalk, 65,800
Edgemere, 9,226
Edgewood, 23,903
Eldersburg, 9,720
Elkridge, 12,953
Ellicott City, 41,396

Essex, 40,872
Fallston, 5,730
Ferndale, 16,355
Fort Meade, 12,509
Garrison, 5,045
Glen Burnie, 37,305
Green Haven, 14,416
Hampstead, 3,003
Havre de Grace, 10,092
Jessup, 5,324
Joppae, 11,084
Lake Shore, 13,269
Lansdowne, 15,509
Linthicum, 7,547
Lochearn, 25,240
Londone, 6,992
Lutherville-Timonium, 16,442
Manchester, 3,252
Maryland City, 6,813
Mays Chapel, 10,132
Middle River, 24,616
Milford Mill, 22,547
Mount Airy, 5,085
Naval Academy, 5,420
North Laurel, 15,008
Odenton, 12,833
Overlea, 12,137
Owings Mills, 9,474
Parkville, 31,617
Parole, 10,054
Pasadena, 10,012
Perry Hall, 22,723
Pikesville, 24,815
Pumphrey, 5,483
Randallstown, 26,277
Reisterstown, 19,314
Riviera Beach, 11,376
Rosedale 18,703
Rossville, 9,492
Savage-Guilford, 9,669
Severn, 24,499
Severna Park, 25,879
South Gate, 27,564
Sykesville, 2,665
Taneytown, 4,269
Towson, 49,445
Westminster, 15,073
White Marsh, 8,183
Woodlawn, 32,907

BANGOR, ME

Bangor Daily News
491 Main St.
Bangor 04401
(207) 990-8000
www.bangornews.com

Greater Bangor C/C
519 Main St.
Bangor 04402
(207) 947-0307
www.bangorregion.com
Bangor, 31,649
Brewer, 8,684
Glenburn, 3,503
Hampden, 6,128
Hermon, 4,035
Holden, 3,015
Milford, 2,823
Old Town, 8,003
Orono, 9,119
Orrington, 3,335
Winterport, 3,743

BARNSTABLE-YARMOUTH, MA

Cape Cod Times
319 Main St.
Hyannis 02601
(508) 775-1200
www.capecodonline.com

Cape Cod C/C
US 6 & Rte. 132
Hyannis 02601
(508) 362-3225
capecodchamber.org
Barnstable, 45,132
Brewster, 9,261
Chatham, 6,930
Dennis, 14,423
Eastham, 4,855
Harwich, 11,328
Mashpee, 8,935
Orleans, 6,185
Sandwich, 17,916
Yarmouth, 22,335

BATON ROUGE, LA

The Advocate
525 Lafayette St.
Baton Rouge 70802
(225) 383-1111
www.theadvocate.com

Baton Rouge CVB
730 North Blvd.
Baton Rouge 70821
(800) 527-6843
www.bracvb.com

Greater Baton Rouge C/C
564 Laurel St.
Baton Rouge 70821
(225) 381-7125
www.brchamber.org

Baker, 13,223
Baton Rouge, 215,882
Brownfields, 5,229
Denham Springs, 9,106
Donaldsonville, 9,060
Gardere, 7,209
Gonzales, 8,294
Merrydale, 10,395
Oak Hills Place, 5,479
Port Allen, 6,180
Shenandoah, 13,429
Village St. George, 6,242
Walker, 4,402
Zachary, 10,189

BEAUMONT-PORT ARTHUR, TX

Beaumont Enterprise
380 Main St.
Beaumont 77701
(409) 833-3311
www.beaumontenterprise.com

Port Arthur CVB
3401 Cultural Center Dr.
Port Arthur 77642
(800) 235-7822
www.portarthurtexas.com/pavb

Beaumont CVB
801 Main St.
Beaumont 77704
(800) 392-4401
www.tourtexas.com/beaumont

Greater Port Arthur C/C
4747 Twin City Hwy.
Port Arthur 77642
(409) 963-1107
www.portarthurtexas.com

Beaumont C/C
450 Bowie St.
Beaumont 77704
(409) 838-6581
www.bmtcoc.org
Beaumont, 111,224
Bridge City, 8,229
Groves, 16,728
Lumberton, 7,919
Nederland, 16,867
Orange, 18,953
Pinehurst, 2,670
Port Arthur, 57,701
Port Neches, 13,321
Silsbee, 6,785
Vidor, 11,021
West Orange, 4,174

BELLINGHAM, WA

Bellingham Herald
1155 N. State St.
Bellingham 98225
(360) 676-2600
www.bellinghamherald.com

Bellingham/Whatcom CVB
904 Potter St.
Bellingham 98226
(800) 487-2032
www.bellingham.org/cvb.html

Bellingham/Whatcom C/C
1435 Railroad Ave.
Bellingham 98225
(360) 734-1330
www.bellingham.com
Bellingham, 61,043
Blaine, 3,267
Ferndale, 7,102
Lynden, 7,943

BENTON HARBOR, MI

Herald-Palladium
3450 Hollywood Rd.
St. Joseph 49085
(616) 429-2400

Southwestern Michigan Tourism
2300 Pipestone Rd.
Benton Harbor 49022
(616) 925-6301
www.swmichigan.org

Cornerstone Alliance
185 E. Main St.
Benton Harbor 49202
(616) 925-6100
Benton Harbor, 11,824
Benton Heights, 5,465
Buchanan, 4,731
Fair Plain, 8,051
Niles, 11,813
St. Joseph, 8,766

BERGEN-PASSAIC, NJ

The Record
150 River St.
Hackensack 07601
(201) 646-4000
Allendale, 6,397
Bergenfield, 24,625
Bloomingdale, 7,565
Bogota, 7,925
Carlstadt, 5,599

Cliffside Park, 20,917
Clifton, 71,305
Closter, 8,366
Cresskill, 7,795
Demarest, 4,922
Dumont, 17,504
East Rutherford, 8,045
Edgewater, 5,218
Elmwood Park, 18,128
Emerson, 7,082
Englewood, 25,148
Englewood Cliffs, 5,776
Fair Lawn, 30,876
Fairview, 11,138
Fort Lee, 33,118
Franklin Lakes, 10,270
Garfield, 27,054
Glen Rock, 11,060
Hackensack, 37,467
Haledon, 6,893
Harrington Park, 4,864
Hasbrouck Heights, 11,618
Haworth, 3,428
Hawthorne, 17,082
Hillsdale, 10,024
Ho-Ho-Kus, 3,995
Leonia, 8,449
Little Falls, 11,294
Little Ferry, 10,108
Lodi, 22,736
Lyndhurst, 18,262
Maywood, 9,634
Midland Park, 7,144
Montvale, 7,092
Moonachie, 2,874
New Milford, 16,293
North Arlington, 14,002
North Haledon, 7,985
Northvale, 4,660
Norwood, 5,691
Oakland, 12,253
Old Tappan, 5,006
Oradell, 8,115
Palisades Park, 14,810
Paramus, 25,552
Park Ridge, 8,314
Passaic, 57,039
Paterson, 150,270
Pompton Lakes, 10,450
Prospect Park, 4,945
Ramsey, 14,343
Ridgefield, 10,114
Ridgefield Park, 12,554
Ridgewood, 24,432
Ringwood, 12,578
River Edge, 10,764
River Vale, 9,410
Rochelle Park, 5,587
Rutherford, 18,000
Saddle Brook, 13,296
Saddle River, 3,078
Teaneck 37,825
Tenafly, 13,480
Totowa, 10,247

Upper Saddle River, 7,526
Waldwick, 10,023
Wallington, 11,025
Wanaque, 9,772
Washington Township, 9,245
Wayne, 47,025
West Milford, 25,430
West Paterson, 10,929
Westwood, 10,644
Woodcliff Lake, 5,676
Wood-Ridge, 7,607
Wyckoff, 15,372

BILLINGS, MT

Billings Gazette
401 N. Broadway
Billings 59101
(406) 657-1200
www.billingsgazette.com

Billings CVB
815 S. 27th St.
Billings 59101
(800) 711-2630
billingscvb.visitmt.com/visit.htm

Billings Area C/C
815 S. 27th St.
Billings 59101
(406) 245-4111
www.wtp.net/bacc
Billings, 91,195
Laurel, 6,125

BILOXI-GULFPORT-PASCAGOULA, MS

The Sun Herald
205 DeBuys Rd.
Gulfport 39507
(800) 346-2472
www.sunherald.com

Jackson County Area C/C
825 Denny Ave.
Pascagoula 39567
(601) 762-3391

Mississippi Gulf Coast C/C
1401 Twentieth Ave.
Gulfport 39502
(601) 863-2933
Bay St. Louis, 9,433
Biloxi, 48,414
D'Iberville, 7,868
Gautier, 11,030
Gulf Hills, 5,004
Gulfport, 64,829

Long Beach, 16,756
Moss Point, 18,356
Ocean Springs, 16,439
Orange Grove, 15,676
Pascagoula, 27,026
Pass Christian, 5,957
St. Martin, 6,349
Waveland, 6,571

BINGHAMTON, NY

Press & Sun-Bulletin
Vestal Pkwy. E
Binghamton 13902
(607) 798-1234
www.binghamtonpress.com

Broome County C/C
49 Court St.
Binghamton 13902
(800) 836-6740
www.spectra.net/bcc
Binghamton, 48,294
Endicott, 12,399
Endwell, 12,602
Johnson City, 15,389
Owego, 4,203
Waverly, 4,576

BIRMINGHAM, AL

Birmingham News/Post-Herald
2200 Fourth Ave. N
Birmingham 35203
(205) 325-2444
www.al.com/birmingham

Birmingham CVB
2200 Ninth Ave. N
Birmingham 35203
(205) 252-9825

Birmingham Area C/C
2027 First Ave. N
Birmingham 35202
(205) 323-5461
www.birmingham.org/thechamber
Adamsville, 5,065
Alabaster, 20,211
Bessemer, 31,234
Birmingham, 258,543
Brighton, 4,339
Center Point 22,658
Columbiana, 3,175
Fairfield, 11,490
Forestdale, 10,395
Fultondale, 6,538
Gardendale, 9,568

Helena, 8,410
Homewood, 23,156
Hoover, 55,464
Hueytown, 15,122
Irondale, 9,214
Leeds, 10,480
Lipscomb, 2,893
Midfield, 5,301
Montevallo, 4,416
Moody, 6,285
Mountain Brook, 18,992
Oneonta, 5,168
Pelham, 13,082
Pell City, 9,491
Pinson-Clay-Chalkville, 10,987
Pleasant Grove, 8,905
Trussville, 10,796
Vestavia Hills, 20,384
Warrior, 3,361

BISMARCK, ND

Bismarck Tribune
P.O. Box 1498
Bismarck 58502
(701) 223-2500
www.ndonline.com

Bismark-Mandan CVB
107 W. Main
Bismarck 58502
(800) 767-3555
bismarck-mandancvb.org/main.html

Bismarck-Mandan C/C
P.O. Box 1675
Bismarck 58502
(701) 223-5660
chmbr.org
Bismarck, 53,514
Lincoln, 1,615
Mandan, 15,648

BLOOMINGTON, IN

Herald-Times
1900 S. Walnut St.
Bloomington 47401
(812) 332-4401
www.heraldt.com

Bloomington/Monroe County CVB
2855 N. Walnut St.
Bloomington 47404
(800) 800-0037
www.visitbloomington.com

Greater Bloomington C/C
400 W. Seventh St.
Bloomington 47402
(812) 336-6381
www.chamber.bloomington.in.us
Bloomington, 66,479
Ellettsville, 4,096

BLOOMINGTON-NORMAL, IL

The Pantagraph
301 W. Washington
Bloomington 61701
(309) 829-9411
www.pantagraph.com

Bloomington-Normal Area
  C/C & CVB
210 S. East St.
Bloomington 61701
(800) 433-8226
Bloomington, 57,365
Le Roy, 3,018
Normal, 42,655

BOISE CITY, ID

Idaho Statesman
1200 N. Curtis Rd.
Boise 83707
(208) 377-6200
www.idahostatesman.com

Boise CVB
2739 Airport Way
Boise 83702
(800) 635-5240
www.boise.org

Boise Area C/C
300 N. Sixth St.
Boise 83702
(208) 344-5515
www.boise.org
Boise City, 152,737
Caldwell, 21,089
Eagle, 6,577
Garden City, 8,714
Kuna, 2,815
Meridian, 20,627
Nampa, 37,558

BOSTON, MA-NH

Boston Globe
135 Morrissey Blvd.
Boston 02107
(617) 929-2935
www.boston.com/globe

Boston Herald
300 Harrison Ave.
Boston 02106
(617) 426-3000
www.bostonherald.com

Greater Boston CVB
Prudential Plaza
Boston 02199
(617) 536-4100
www.bostonusa.com

Greater Boston C/C
One Beacon St.
Boston 02108
(617) 557-7330
www.gbcc.org

Acton, 18,851
Amesbury, 15,784
Arlington, 43,656
Ashland, 12,940
Ayer, 7,378
Bedford, 13,676
Bellingham, 15,544
Belmont, 24,044
Berkley, 5,236
Beverly, 38,596
Blackstone, 8,270
Bolton, 3,279
Boston, 558,394
Boxborough, 3,979
Braintree, 34,708
Brookline, 54,137
Burlington, 23,493
Cambridge, 93,707
Canton 20,314
Carlisle, 4,599
Carver, 11,289
Chelsea, 27,608
Cohasset, 7,070
Concord, 17,792
Danvers, 24,467
Dedham, 23,741
Dighton, 5,871
Dover, 5,383
Duxbury, 15,007
Essex, 3,368
Everett, 35,006
Foxborough, 16,011
Framingham, 64,536
Gloucester, 29,267
Hamilton, 7,487

Hanover, 12,891
Harvard, 11,590
Hingham, 20,265
Holbrook, 11,092
Holliston, 13,381
Hopedale, 5,621
Hopkinton, 10,805
Hudson, 17,695
Hull, 10,472
Ipswich, 12,352
Kingston, 10,447
Lancaster, 6,542
Lexington, 29,484
Lincoln, 7,899
Littleton, 7,695
Lynn, 80,563
Lynnfield, 11,232
Malden, 52,749
Manchester by the Sea, 5,357
Mansfield, 18,806
Marblehead, 19,973
Marlborough, 32,974
Marshfield, 22,911
Maynard, 10,412
Medfield, 11,467
Medford, 56,190
Medway, 11,391
Melrose, 27,426
Mendon, 4,399
Middleton, 5,624
Milford, 25,194
Millis, 7,965
Milton, 25,794
Nahant, 3,782
Natick, 31,310
Needham, 27,828
Newbury, 5,985
Newburyport, 16,558
Newton, 80,238
Norfolk, 10,389
North Reading, 12,919
Norton, 15,659
Norwell, 9,652
Norwood, 28,899
Peabody, 48,365
Pembroke, 16,010
Plainville, 7,238
Plymouth, 48,329
Quincy, 85,532
Randolph, 30,554
Reading, 22,956
Revere, 41,761
Rockland, 17,236
Rockport, 7,580
Rowley, 5,196
Salem, 38,008
Salisbury, 7,093
Saugus, 26,223
Scituate, 17,242
Seabrook, NH, 6,749
Sharon, 16,684
Sherborn, 4,107

Shirley, 7,463
Somerville, 74,356
Southborough, 7,388
Stoneham, 22,131
Stoughton, 27,481
Stow, 5,731
Sudbury, 15,130
Swampscott, 13,676
Taunton, 51,937
Topsfield, 6,098
Townsend, 8,997
Upton, 5,339
Wakefield, 24,756
Walpole, 22,251
Waltham, 57,214
Wareham, 19,545
Wayland, 12,041
Wellesley, 26,809
Wenham, 4,423
Weston, 10,448
Westwood, 12,935
Weymouth, 54,847
Wilmington, 19,874
Winchester, 20,318
Winthrop, 17,305
Woburn, 36,628
Wrentham, 10,049

BOULDER-LONGMONT, CO

Daily Camera
1048 Pearl St.
Boulder 80302
(303) 442-1202
www.bouldernews.com

Boulder CVB
2440 Pearl St.
Boulder 80302
(303) 442-2911
visitor.boulder.net

Longmont Area C/C
528 N. Main St.
Longmont 80501
(303) 776-5295

Boulder C/C
2440 Pearl St.
Boulder 80302
(303) 442-1044
chamber.boulder.net

Boulder, 90,928
Broomfield, 31,743
Gunbarrel, 9,388
Lafayette, 18,784
Longmont, 58,318
Louisville, 17,780
Superior, 3,377

BRAZORIA, TX

The Brazosport Facts
720 S. Main
Clute 77531
(409) 265-7411
www.thefacts.com

Brazoria C/C
908 S. Brooks
Brazoria 77422
(409) 798-6100
Alvin, 20,579
Angleton, 20,200
Brazoria, 2,918
Clute, 9,770
Freeport, 11,680
Lake Jackson, 25,774
Manvel, 4,240
Pearland, 26,854
Richwood, 2,848
Sweeny, 3,549
West Columbia, 4,534

BREMERTON, WA

The Sun
545 Fifth St.
Bremerton 98337
(360) 377-3711
www.thesunlink.com

Bremerton-Kitsap County CVB
2 Ranier
Port Gamble 98364
(800) 416-5615
www.bremertonwa.com

Bremerton Area C/C
301 Pacific Ave.
Bremerton 98337
(360) 479-3579
www.bremertonchamber.org
Bremerton, 41,580
East Port Orchard, 5,409
Parkwood, 6,853
Port Orchard, 6,266
Poulsbo, 5,986
Silverdale, 7,660

BRIDGEPORT, CT

Connecticut Post
410 State St.
Bridgeport 06604
(203) 333-0161
www.connpost.com

Bridgeport C/C
10 Middle St.
Bridgeport 06601
(203) 335-3800
Ansonia, 17,865
Beacon Falls, 5,150
Bridgeport, 137,990
Derby, 11,960
Easton, 6,577
Fairfield, 53,522
Milford, 49,773
Monroe, 17,993
Oxford, 9,047
Seymour, 14,193
Shelton, 37,180
Stratford, 49,096
Trumbull, 33,291

BROCKTON, MA

Brockton Enterprise
60 Main St.
Brockton 02303
(508) 676-8211

Metro South C/C
60 School St.
Brockton 02401
(508) 586-0500
Abington, 14,683
Avon, 4,611
Bridgewater, 23,692
Brockton, 92,324
East Bridgewater, 12,133
Easton, 20,970
Halifax, 6,844
Hanson, 9,512
Lakeville, 8,596
Middleborough, 19,200
Plympton, 2,614
Raynham, 10,513
West Bridgewater, 6,647
Whitman, 13,743

BROWNSVILLE-HARLINGEN-SAN BENITO, TX

Brownsville Herald
P.O. Box 351
Brownsville 78522
(956) 542-4301
www.brownsvilleherald.com

Valley Morning Star
1310 S. Commerce
Harlingen 78550
(956) 423-6200
www.valleystar.com

Brownsville CVB
650 FM 802
Brownsville 78520
(800) 626-2639
brownsville.org/bcvb.html

Brownsville C/C
1600 E. Elizabeth St.
Brownsville 78520
(956) 542-4341
www.brownsvillechamber.com

Harlingen C/C
311 E. Tyler
Harlingen 78550
(800) 531-7346
www.harlingen.com

San Benito Area C/C
210 E. Heywood St.
San Benito 78586
(956) 399-5321
Brownsville, 132,091
Combes, 2,513
Harlingen, 56,893
La Feria, 4,986
Los Fresnos, 3,266
Port Isabel, 5,062
San Benito, 23,047
Santa Rosa, 2,572

BRYAN-COLLEGE STATION, TX

Bryan College Station Eagle
1729 Briarcrest Dr.
Bryan 77802
(409) 776-4444
www.bcseagle.com

Bryan/College Station CVB
715 University Dr. E
College Station 77840
(800) 777-8292
www.rtis.com/reg/bcs/org/CVB

Bryan-College Station C/C
715 University Dr. E
College Station 77840
(409) 260-5200
www.b-cs.com
Bryan, 58,247
College Station, 58,757

BUFFALO-NIAGARA FALLS, NY

The Buffalo News
One News Plaza
Buffalo 14203
(716) 849-3434
www.buffnews.com

Niagara Gazette
310 Niagara St.
Niagara Falls 14302
(716) 282-2311
www.cnhi.com/niagara

Niagara Falls CVB
310 Fourth St.
Niagara Falls 14303
(800) 421-5223
www.nfcvb.com

Greater Buffalo CVB
617 Main St.
Buffalo 14202
(800) 283-3256
www.buffalocvb.org

Greater Buffalo Partnership
350 Main St.
Buffalo 14202
(716) 852-7100
www.gbpartnership.org

Niagara Falls Area C/C
345 Third St.
Niagara Falls 14303
(716) 285-9141
Akron, 2,892
Alden, 2,547
Blasdell, 2,750
Buffalo, 310,548
Cheektowaga, 84,387
Depew, 17,164
East Aurora, 6,429
Hamburg, 10,026
Kenmore, 16,450
Lackawanna, 19,780
Lancaster, 11,406
Lewiston, 2,902
Lockport, 23,300
Niagara Falls, 58,357
North Tonawanda, 33,773
Orchard Park, 3,245
Sloan, 3,634
South Lockport, 7,112
Springville, 4,304
Tonawanda, 16,410
West Seneca, 47,866
Williamsville, 5,311

BURLINGTON, VT

Burlington Free Press
191 College St.
Burlington 05401
(802) 860-3441
www.burlingtonfreepress.com

Lake Champlain Regional C/C
60 Main St.
Burlington 05401
(802) 863-3489
www.vermont.org/chamber
Burlington, 39,004
Charlotte, 3,492
Colchester, 16,092
Essex, 17,531
Essex Junction, 8,546
Fairfax, 3,019
Georgia, 4,161
Hinesburg, 4,160
Jericho, 4,904
Milton, 9,493
Richmond, 4,038
Shelburne, 6,700
South Burlington, 13,860
St. Albans, 5,376
Swanton, 2,559
Williston, 6,602
Winooski, 6,651

CALGARY, AB

Calgary Herald
215 16th St. SE
Calgary T2P 0W8
(403) 235-7433
www.calgaryherald.com

Calgary Sun
2615 12th St. NE
algary T2E 7W9
(403) 250-4200
www.canoe.ca/CalgarySun

Calgary TCB
#200-237 8th Ave. SE
Calgary T2G 0K8
(800) 661-1678
www.visitor.calgary.ab.ca

Calgary C/C
517 Centre St. S
Calgary T2G 2C4
(403) 750-0400
Airdrie, 15,946
Calgary, 768,082
Chestermere, 1,911
Cochrane, 7,424
Crossfield, 1,899

CANTON-MASSILLON, OH

The Independent
50 North Ave.
Massillon 44647
(330) 833-2631

Repository
500 Market Ave. S
Canton 44702
(330) 454-5611
cantonrep.com

Canton C/C
229 Wells Ave. NW
Canton 44703
(330) 456-7253
www.cantonchamber.org

Canton/Stark County CVB
229 Wells Ave. NW
Canton 44703
(800) 533-4302
www.visitcantonohio.com

Massillon Area C/C
137 Lincoln Way E
Massillon 44646
(330) 833-3146
Alliance, 22,846
Canal Fulton, 4,346
Canton, 81,079
Carrollton, 3,298
Louisville, 8,240
Massillon, 30,671
Minerva, 4,366
North Canton, 15,736
Perry Heights, 9,055

CASPER, WY

Casper Star Tribune
170 Star Ln.
Casper 82604
(307) 266-0500
www.trib.com

Casper Area CVB
P.O. Box 399
Casper 82602
(800) 852-1889
www.trib.com/ADS/CASPER

Casper Area C/C
500 N. Center St.
Casper 82601
(307) 234-5311
www.casperets.com

Appendix C

Casper, 48,800
Evansville, 1,541
Mills, 1,648

CEDAR RAPIDS, IA

Cedar Rapids Gazette
500 3rd Ave. SE
Cedar Rapids 52401
(319) 398-8211
www.gazetteonline.com

Cedar Rapids Area CVB
119 First Ave. SE
Cedar Rapids 52301
(800) 735-5557
www.icvba.org/cedar_rapids.htm

Cedar Rapids Area C/C
424 First Ave. NE
edar Rapids 52407
(319) 398-5317
www.cedarrapids.org/iowa/chamber

Cedar Rapids, 113,482
Hiawatha, 5,843
Marion, 22,896
Mount Vernon, 3,783

CHAMPAIGN-URBANA, IL

News Gazette
15 Main St.
Champaign 61820
(217) 351-5252
www.news-gazette.com

Champaign Urbana CVB
40 E. University Ave.
Champaign 61820
(800) 369-6151
www.prairienet.org

Champaign County C/C
1817 S. Neil St.
Champaign 61820
(217) 359-1791
www.ccchamber.org

Champaign, 64,002
Mahomet, 3,480
Rantoul, 13,728
Savoy, 2,907
Tolono, 2,541
Urbana, 33,179

CHARLESTON-NORTH CHARLESTON, SC

Charleston Post & Courier
134 Columbus St.
Charleston 29403
(843) 577-7111
www.charleston.net

Charleston Trident CVB
375 Meeting St.
Charleston 29402
(843) 724-7174
www.charlestoncvb.com

Charleston Metro C/C
81 Mary St.
Charleston 29403
(843) 723-1773
chamber.charleston.net

Charleston, 71,052
Goose Creek, 25,943
Hanahan, 12,973
Isle of Palms, 3,908
Ladson, 10,494
Moncks Corner, 5,815
Mount Pleasant, 34,262
North Charleston, 59,923
Summerville, 24,395

CHARLESTON, WV

Charleston Gazette/Mail
1001 E. Virginia St.
Charleston 25331
(304) 348-5140
dailymail.com

Charleston CVB
200 Civic Center Dr.
Charleston 25301
(800) 733-5469
charlestontours.com/services.html

Charleston Regional C/C
106 Capitol St.
Charleston 25301
(304) 345-0770
www.charleywestchamber.org

Charleston, 56,098
Cross Lanes, 10,878
Dunbar, 8,525
Hurricane, 5,320
Nitro, 6,737
South Charleston, 13,409
St. Albans, 12,055
Teays Valley, 8,436

CHARLOTTE-GASTONIA-ROCK HILL, NC-SC

Charlotte Observer
600 S. Tryon St.
Charlotte 28202
(704) 358-5040
www.charlotte.com

The Herald
132 W. Main St.
Rock Hill 11707
(803) 582-4511
www.heraldonline.com

Charlotte CVB
122 E. Stonewall St.
Charlotte 28202
(800) 722-1994
www.charlottecvb.org

Charlotte C/C
330 S. Tryon St.
Charlotte 28202
(704) 378-1300
www.charlottechamber.org

Gastonia C/C
601 W. Franklin Ave.
Gastonia 28053
(704) 864-2621

Rock Hill Area C/C
115 Dave Lyle Blvd.
Rock Hill 29731
(803) 324-7500

Belmont, NC, 8,503
Bessemer City, NC, 4,408
Charlotte, NC, 441,297
Cherryville, NC, 4,917
China Grove, NC, 3,731
Clover, SC, 3,541
Concord, NC, 32,944
Cornelius, NC, 3,310
Dallas, NC, 2,822
Davidson, NC, 4,482
Fort Mill, NC, 5,428
Gastonia, NC, 56,575
Huntersville, NC, 3,360
Kannapolis, NC, 35,631
Lincolnton, NC, 9,748
Lowell, NC, 2,541
Marshville, NC, 2,680
Matthews, NC, 14,710
Mint Hill, NC, 12,202
Monroe, NC, 19,827
Mount Holly, NC, 7,300
Pineville, NC, 2,860

Rock Hill, SC, 44,061
Salisbury, NC, 23,181
South Gastonia, NC, 5,487
Spencer, NC, 3,093
Stallings, NC, 2,756
Stanley, NC, 2,813
Tega Cay, SC, 3,336
Weddington, NC, 4,827
Wingate, NC, 3,148
York, SC, 6,563

CHARLOTTESVILLE, VA

Daily Progress
685 W. Rio Rd.
Charlottesville 22901
(804) 978-7200
www.dailyprogress.com

Charlottesville-Albemarle Co. C/C
P.O. Box 1564
Charlottesville 22902
(804) 295-3141
Charlottesville, 40,767
Commonwealth, 5,538
Rio, 5,133
University Heights, 6,900

CHATTANOOGA, TN-GA

Chattanooga Free Press
400 E. 11th St.
Chattanooga 37401
(423) 756-6900
www.chatfreepress.com

Chattanooga Times
400 E. 10th St.
Chattanooga 37401
(423) 756-1234
www.chattimes.com

Chattanooga Area CVB
2 Broad St.
Chattanooga 37402
(800) 322-3344
www.chattanooga.net/CVB

Chattanooga Area C/C
1001 Market St.
Chattanooga 37402
(423) 756-2121
www.chattanooga.net
Chattanooga, TN, 150,425
Collegedale, TN, 5,730
East Brainerd, TN, 11,594
East Ridge, TN, 20,482
Fairview, GA, 6,444

Fort Oglethorpe, GA, 6,260
Harrison, TN, 7,191
Jasper, TN, 2,814
La Fayette, GA, 6,707
Middle Valley, TN, 12,255
Red Bank, TN, 11,842
Rossville, TN, 3,523
Signal Mountain, TN, 7,013
Soddy-Daisy, TN, 8,884
South Pittsburg, TN, 3,080

CHEYENNE, WY

Wyoming Tribune-Eagle
702 W. Lincolnway
Cheyenne 82001
(307) 634-3361
www.wyomingnews.com

Cheyenne CVB
309 W. Lincolnway
Cheyenne 82003
(800) 426-5009
www.cheyenne.org

Greater Cheyenne C/C
301 W. Sixteenth St.
Cheyenne 82001
(307) 638-3388
Cheyenne, 53,729
Pine Bluffs, 1,132

CHICAGO, IL

Chicago Tribune
435 N. Michigan Ave.
Chicago 60611
(312) 222-3232
www.chicagotribune.com

Chicago Sun Times
401 N. Wabash Ave.
Chicago 60611
(312) 321-3000
www.suntimes.com

Chicago CVB
2301 S. Lakeshore Pl.
Chicago 60616
(312) 567-8500
www.chicago.il.org

Chicagoland C/C
One IBM Plaza
Chicago 60611
(312) 494-6700
www.chicagolandchamber.org

Heritage Corridor VB
81 N. Chicago St.
Joliet 60431
(800) 926-2262
Addison, 33,580
Algonquin, 18,019
Alsip, 19,171
Antioch, 7,398
Arlington Heights, 76,740
Aurora, 116,405
Barrington, 9,885
Barrington Hills, 4,456
Bartlett, 32,943
Batavia, 21,591
Beach Park, 10,167
Bellwood, 20,122
Bensenville, 18,023
Berkeley, 5,034
Berwyn, 43,735
Bloomingdale, 19,363
Blue Island, 20,661
Bolingbrook, 51,312
Boulder Hill, 8,894
Braidwood, 4,562
Bridgeview, 15,194
Broadview, 8,362
Brookfield, 18,396
Buffalo Grove, 41,169
Burbank, 27,714
Burnham, 4,102
Burr Ridge, 9,159
Calumet City, 37,242
Calumet Park, 8,455
Carol Stream, 36,779
Carpentersville, 24,629
Cary, 13,813
Channahon, 6,340
Chicago, 2,721,547
Chicago Heights, 31,899
Chicago Ridge, 14,018
Cicero, 70,915
Clarendon Hills, 7,206
Coal City, 4,436
Country Club Hills, 16,120
Countryside, 6,049
Crest Hill, 12,190
Crestwood, 11,519
Crete, 7,765
Crystal Lake, 32,180
Darien, 23,037
Deer Park, 3,194
Deerfield, 18,294
DeKalb, 35,554
Des Plaines, 54,836
Dixmoor, 3,781
Dolton, 24,102
Downers Grove, 50,089
East Dundee, 3,126
Elgin, 86,034
Elk Grove Village, 34,470
Elmhurst, 43,290
Elmwood Park, 22,760
Evanston, 71,593

Evergreen Park, 20,584
Flossmoor, 9,045
Ford Heights, 4,169
Forest Park, 14,483
Fox Lake, 8,287
Fox River Grove, 4,419
Frankfort, 9,607
Frankfort Square, 6,227
Franklin Park, 18,125
Gages Lake, 8,349
Geneva, 16,943
Genoa, 3,115
Glen Ellyn, 25,759
Glencoe, 8,435
Glendale Heights, 30,321
Glenview, 39,159
Glenwood, 9,151
Goodings Grove, 14,054
Grayslake, 14,370
Gurnee, 22,489
Hanover Park, 35,599
Harvard, 6,857
Harvey, 29,097
Harwood Heights, 7,955
Hawthorn Woods, 5,498
Hazel Crest, 13,715
Hickory Hills, 14,053
Highland Park, 30,998
Highwood, 5,094
Hillside, 7,595
Hinsdale, 16,353
Hoffman Estates, 48,708
Hometown, 4,679
Homewood, 19,279
Huntley, 3,029
Indian Head Park, 3,590
Inverness, 6,739
Island Lake, 7,464
Itasca, 8,144
Joliet, 86,749
Justice, 11,439
Kildeer, 2,821
La Grange, 15,104
La Grange Park, 12,597
Lake Barrington, 4,440
Lake Bluff, 5,589
Lake Forest, 18,296
Lake in the Hills, 16,889
Lake Villa, 3,260
Lake Zurich, 16,786
Lansing, 28,664
Lemont, 9,571
Libertyville, 19,772
Lincolnshire, 5,914
Lincolnwood, 11,342
Lindenhurst, 9,225
Lisle, 20,524
Lockport, 12,173
Lombard, 41,806
Long Grove, 6,058
Lynwood, 7,518
Lyons, 9,788
Manhattan, 2,797
Marengo, 5,299

Markham, 13,025
Matteson, 12,071
Maywood, 26,185
McHenry, 19,144
Melrose Park, 20,597
Midlothian, 14,961
Minooka, 3,546
Mokena, 12,011
Montgomery, 5,173
Morris, 11,172
Morton Grove, 22,258
Mount Prospect, 54,040
Mundelein, 27,034
Naperville, 107,001
New Lenox, 13,088
Niles, 29,081
Norridge, 14,444
North Aurora, 7,925
North Chicago, 31,665
North Riverside, 6,106
Northbrook, 32,943
Northfield, 5,271
Northlake, 11,953
Oak Brook, 9,346
Oak Forest, 27,461
Oak Lawn, 57,696
Oak Park, 51,585
Olympia Fields, 4,727
Orland Hills, 6,232
Orland Park, 45,657
Oswego, 8,297
Palatine, 44,460
Palos Heights, 12,194
Palos Hills, 18,654
Palos Park, 4,548
Park City, 5,408
Park Forest, 24,513
Park Ridge, 37,039
Peotone, 3,195
Plainfield, 7,340
Plano, 5,563
Posen, 4,365
Prospect Heights, 15,280
Richton Park, 11,323
River Forest, 11,444
River Grove, 9,767
Riverdale, 13,375
Riverside, 8,438
Riverwoods, 3,516
Robbins, 7,291
Rolling Meadows, 22,560
Romeoville, 15,496
Roselle, 23,044
Rosemont, 3,954
Round Lake, 4,472
Round Lake, Park 4,788
Round Lake Beach, 22,211
Sandwich, 5,995
Sauk Village, 9,918
Schaumburg, 74,294
Schiller Park 11,043
Shorewood, 7,451
Skokie, 58,635
Sleepy Hollow, 3,569

South Barrington, 3,630
South Chicago Heights, 3,824
South Elgin, 12,635
South Holland, 21,747
Spring Grove, 2,840
St. Charles, 25,696
Steger, 9,642
Stickney, 5,676
Stone Park, 4,359
Streamwood, 34,258
Sugar Grove, 2,917
Summit, 9,733
Sycamore, 10,938
Thornton, 2,737
Tinley Park, 43,310
University Park, 6,340
Vernon Hills, 17,792
Villa Park, 22,563
Warrenville, 12,276
Wauconda, 8,461
Waukegan, 74,166
West Chicago, 16,892
West Dundee, 4,494
Westchester, 17,596
Western Springs, 11,844
Westmont, 22,366
Wheaton, 54,173
Wheeling, 30,216
Willow Springs, 4,758
Willowbrook, 9,134
Wilmette, 26,036
Wilmington, 5,270
Winfield, 8,107
Winnetka, 11,940
Winthrop Harbor, 7,005
Wonder Lake, 6,664
Wood Dale, 13,371
Woodridge, 28,854
Woodstock, 16,883
Worth, 11,220
Yorkville, 5,265
Zion, 22,111

CHICO-PARADISE, CA

Chico Enterprise-Record
400 E. Park Ave.
Chico 95928
(916) 891-1234
www.chicoer.com

Greater Chico C/C
300 Salem St.
Chico 95928
(916) 891-5556
www.chicochamber.com

Paradise C/C
5587 Scottwood Rd.
Paradise 95969
(530) 877-9356

Chico, 45,965
Gridley, 4,491
Magalia, 8,987
Oroville, 12,124
Oroville East, 8,462
Palermo, 5,260
Paradise, 25,630
South Oroville, 7,463
Thermalito, 5,646

CHICOUTIMI-JONQUIERE, PQ

Le Quotidien/Progres
1051 boul. Talbot
Chicoutimi G7H 5C1
(418) 545-4474
saglac.qc.ca/~progres

Chicoutimi Tourism
2525 boul. Talbot
Chicoutimi G7H 5C1
(418) 698-3167

Chicoutimi C/C
31, rue Racine
Chicoutimi G7J 1E4
(418) 543-5941

Jonquiere Tourism Office
2665 boul. du Royaume est
Jonquiere G7Z 1N6
(418) 548-4004
Chicoutimi, 63,061
Jonquière, 56,503
La Baie, 21,057
Lac-Kénogami, 1,517
Larouche, 1,049
Laterrière, 4,815
Saint-Fulgence, 2,078
Saint-Honoré, 3,851
Shipshaw, 2,858
Tremblay, 3,665

CINCINNATI, OH-KY-IN

Cincinnati Enquirer
312 Elm St.
Cincinnati 45202
(513) 721-2700
enquirer.com/today

Greater Cincinnati CVB
300 W. Sixth St.
Cincinnati 45202
(800) 344-3445
www.cincyusa.com

Greater Cincinnati C/C
441 Vine St.
Cincinnati 45202
(513) 579-3100
www.gccc.com

Northern Kentucky CVB
605 Philadelphia St.
Covington 41011
(606) 261-4677
Alexandria, KY, 7,158
Amberley, OH, 2,948
Aurora, IN, 3,806
Bellevue, KY, 6,338
Bethel, OH, 2,655
Blue Ash, OH, 12,568
Bridge North, OH, 11,748
Burlington, KY, 6,070
Carlisle, OH, 5,058
Cheviot, OH, 9,137
Cincinnati, OH, 345,818
Cold Spring, KY, 3,445
Covedale, OH, 6,669
Covington, KY, 40,971
Crescent Springs, KY, 3,636
Crestview Hills, KY, 2,526
Dayton, KY, 5,954
Deer Park, OH, 5,835
Dent, OH, 6,416
Dry Run, OH, 5,389
Edgewood, KY, 8,502
Elmwood Place, OH, 2,723
Elsmere, KY, 7,737
Erlanger, KY, 16,717
Evendale, OH, 3,267
Falmouth, KY, 2,642
Finneytown, OH, 13,096
Florence, KY, 19,726
Forest Park, OH, 19,775
Forestville, OH, 9,185
Fort Mitchell, KY, 7,156
Fort Thomas, KY, 15,300
Fort Wright, KY, 6,670
Franklin, OH, 11,158
Georgetown, OH, 3,963
Golf Manor, OH, 3,938
Greendale, IN, 3,866
Greenhills, OH, 4,131
Groesbeck, OH, 6,684
Harrison, OH, 7,404
Highland Heights, KY, 6,208
Independence, KY, 12,567
Kenwood, OH, 7,469
Lakeside Park, KY, 3,091
Landen, OH, 9,263
Lawrenceburg, IN, 4,324
Lebanon, OH, 12,515
Lincoln Heights, OH, 4,575
Lockland, OH, 4,067
Loveland, OH, 11,776
Ludlow, KY, 4,227

Mack South, OH, 5,767
Madeira, OH, 8,915
Mariemont, OH, 2,917
Mason, OH, 15,174
Milford, OH, 5,839
Montgomery, OH, 9,723
Mount Healthy, OH, 7,205
New Richmond, OH, 2,728
Newport, KY, 16,957
North College Hill, OH, 10,597
Northbrook, OH, 11,471
Northgate, OH, 7,864
Norwood, OH, 22,197
Park Hills, KY, 3,108
Reading, OH, 11,727
Sharonville, OH, 13,953
Silverton, OH, 5,646
South Lebanon, OH, 2,781
Southgate, KY, 3,736
Springboro, OH, 9,731
Springdale, OH, 10,411
St. Bernard, OH, 4,980
Taylor Mill, KY, 6,942
Villa Hills, KY, 7,432
Village of Indian Hill, OH, 5,567
White Oak, OH, 12,430
Williamsburg, OH, 2,571
Williamstown, KY, 3,480
Woodlawn, OH, 2,642
Wyoming, OH, 7,648

CLARKSVILLE-HOPKINSVILLE, TN-KY

Leaf-Chronicle
200 Commerce St.
Clarksville 37040
(931) 552-1808

Clarksville Tourist Commission
312 Madison St.
Clarksville 37041
(800) 530-2487
www.clarksville.tn.us

Clarksville Area C/C
312 Madison St.
Clarksville 37041
(931) 647-2331

Hopkinsville-Christian County C/C
1209 S. Virginia St.
Hopkinsville 42240
(270) 885-9096
www.ci.hopkinsville.ky.us
Clarksville, TN, 94,879
Fort Campbell North, KY, 18,861
Hopkinsville, KY, 28,317
Oak Grove, KY, 4,526

CLEVELAND-LORAIN-ELYRIA, OH

Cleveland Plain Dealer
1801 Superior Ave. E
Cleveland 44702
(216) 999-6000
www.cleveland.com

Morning Journal
1657 Broadway
Lorain 44052
(216) 245-6901
www.morningjournal.com

Cleveland CVB
3100 Terminal Tower
Cleveland 44113
(800) 321-1001
www.travelcleveland.com

Cleveland C/C
291 E. 222nd St.
Cleveland 44123
(216) 731-9322

Lorain County C/C
381 Broad St.
Elyria 44035
(216) 322-5438

Amherst, 11,311
Ashtabula, 21,315
Avon, 8,896
Avon Lake, 16,794
Bay Village, 16,401
Beachwood, 11,291
Bedford, 14,138
Bedford Heights, 11,790
Berea, 18,909
Brecksville, 12,654
Broadview Heights, 13,923
Brook Park, 22,646
Brooklyn, 11,251
Brunswick, 31,641
Chagrin Falls, 3,993
Chardon, 4,655
Cleveland, 498,246
Cleveland Heights, 54,293
Conneaut, 12,967
East Cleveland, 31,141
Eastlake, 20,756
Edgewood, 5,189
Elyria, 56,729
Euclid, 52,472
Fairport Harbor, 2,799
Fairview Park, 17,311
Garfield Heights, 30,207
Geneva, 6,470
Grafton, 4,754
Highland Heights, 7,329
Independence, 6,728

Jefferson, 3,459
Kirtland, 6,500
Lakewood, 55,731
Lodi, 2,981
Lorain, 69,800
Lyndhurst, 15,288
Madison, 2,700
Maple Heights, 25,971
Mayfield, 3,424
Mayfield Heights, 19,149
Medina, 22,019
Mentor, 50,251
Mentor-on-the-Lake, 7,917
Middleburg Heights, 14,744
Moreland Hills, 3,337
North Kingsville, 2,795
North Madison, 8,699
North Olmsted, 34,562
North Ridgeville, 23,070
North Royalton, 27,272
Oakwood, 3,426
Oberlin, 7,931
Olmsted Falls, 7,013
Orange, 3,075
Painesville, 15,660
Parma, 85,006
Parma Heights, 20,865
Pepper Pike, 6,171
Richmond Heights, 9,691
Rocky River, 19,799
Seven Hills, 12,256
Shaker Heights, 29,206
Sheffield Lake, 9,922
Solon, 20,171
South Euclid, 22,781
South Russell, 3,643
Strongsville, 41,260
University Heights, 13,946
Vermilion, 11,434
Wadsworth, 16,642
Warrensville Heights, 15,218
Wellington, 4,138
Westlake, 30,037
Wickliffe, 14,112
Willoughby, 21,734
Willoughby Hills, 8,816
Willowick, 14,697

COLORADO SPRINGS, CO

Colorado Springs Gazette Telegraph
30 S. Prospect St.
Colorado Springs 80903
(719) 636-0266
www.gazette.com

Colorado Springs CVB
104 S. Cascade
Colorado Springs 80903
(800) 888-4748
coloradosprings-travel.com

Colorado Springs C/C
2 N. Cascade Ave.
Colorado Springs 80903
(719) 635-1551
www2.cscc.org

Air Force Academy, 9,062
Black Forest, 8,143
Cimarron Hills, 11,160
Colorado Springs, 345,127
Fort Carson, 11,309
Fountain, 11,823
Manitou Springs, 4,835
Security-Widefield, 23,822
Stratmoor, 5,854

COLUMBIA, MO

Columbia Daily Tribune
101 N. Fourth St.
Columbia 65205
(573) 815-1500
www.showmenews.com

Columbia CVB
300 S. Providence Rd.
Columbia 65205
(573) 875-1231

Columbia C/C
300 S. Providence Rd.
Columbia 65205
(573) 874-1132
chamber.columbia.mo.us

Ashland, 1,243
Centralia, 3,242
Columbia, 76,756

COLUMBIA, SC

The State
1401 Shop Rd.
Columbia 29201
(803) 771-6161
www.thestate.com

Greater Columbia CVB
1012 Gervais St.
Columbia 29201
(800) 264-4884
www.columbiasc.net

Greater Columbia C/C
930 Richland St.
Columbia 29202
(803) 733-1110
www.gcbn.com

Cayce, 11,900
Columbia, 112,773
Dentsville, 11,839

Forest Acres, 7,124
Irmo, 11,063
Lexington, 6,180
Oak Grove, 7,173
Red Bank, 5,950
Seven Oaks, 15,722
South Congaree, 2,642
Springdale, 3,319
St. Andrews, 25,692
West Columbia, 10,994
Woodfield, 8,862

COLUMBUS, GA-AL

Columbus Ledger-Enquirer
P.O. Box 711
Columbus 31994
(706) 324-5526
www.l-e-o.com

Columbus CVB
1000 Bay Ave.
Columbus 31902
(800) 999-1613
www.columbusga.com/cCVB

Columbus C/C
901 Front Ave.
Columbus 31902
(706) 569-7287
www.columbusga.com/chamber
Columbus, GA, 182,828
Fort Benning South, GA, 14,617
Pheonix City, AL, 28,000

COLUMBUS, OH

Columbus Dispatch
34 S. 3rd St.
Columbus 43215
(614) 461-5000
www.cd.columbus.oh.us

Greater Columbus CVB
90 N. High St.
Columbus 43215
(800) 354-2657
www.columbuscvb.org

Greater Columbus C/C
37 N. High St.
Columbus 43215
(614) 221-1321
www.columbus-chamber.org
Ashville, 2,505
Baltimore, 3,039
Bexley, 12,691
Blacklick Estates, 10,080
Buckeye Lake, 3,215

Circleville, 12,088
Columbus, 657,053
Delaware, 20,267
Dublin, 23,891
Gahanna, 31,338
Grandview Heights, 6,637
Granville, 4,099
Grove City, 23,902
Groveport, 2,813
Heath, 7,633
Hilliard, 18,324
Huber Ridge, 5,255
Jefferson, 4,502
Johnstown, 3,319
Lancaster, 35,442
Lincoln Village, 9,958
London, 8,122
New Albany, 2,507
Newark, 48,856
Obetz, 3,124
Pataskala, 3,352
Pickerington, 8,696
Plain City, 2,563
Powell, 3,744
Reynoldsburg, 29,081
Upper Arlington, 32,854
Westerville, 33,701
Whitehall, 19,875
Worthington, 14,540

CORPUS CHRISTI, TX

Corpus Christi Caller-Times
820 N. Lower Broadway
Corpus Christi 78469
(361) 884-2011
www.caller.com/frontpag

Corpus Christi Area CVB
1201 N. Shoreline Blvd.
Corpus Christi 78401
(800) 678-6232
www.corpuschristi-tx-cvb.org

Corpus Christi C/C
1201 N. Shoreline Blvd.
Corpus Christi 78403
(361) 887-7408
Aransas Pass, 7,893
Bishop, 3,516
Corpus Christi, 280,260
Gregory, 2,641
Ingleside, 8,982
Mathis, 5,795
Odem, 2,590
Portland, 13,584
Robstown, 13,349
Sinton, 6,827
Taft, 3,392

CUMBERLAND, MD-WV

Cumberland Times-News
19 Baltimore St.
Cumberland 21502
(301) 722-4600
www.times-news.com/
timesnew.html

Allegany County C/C
Bell Tower Bldg.
Cumberland 21502
(301) 722-2820
Cumberland, WV, 22,341
Frostburg, MD, 7,777
Keyser, MD, 5,545

DALLAS, TX

The Dallas Morning News
508 Young St.
Dallas 75265
(214) 977-8222
www.dallasnews.com

Dallas CVB
1201 Elm St.
Dallas 75270
(800) 222-5527
www.dallascvb.com

Greater Dallas C/C
1201 Elm St.
Dallas 75270
(214) 746-6600
www.gdc.org
Addison, 11,288
Allen, 31,177
Athens, 11,588
Balch Springs, 18,392
Carrollton, 96,757
Cedar Hill, 25,555
Cockrell Hill, 3,773
Commerce, 7,071
Coppell, 26,545
Corinth, 5,934
Crandall, 2,580
Dallas, 1,053,292
Denton, 73,483
DeSoto, 34,993
Duncanville, 36,008
Ennis, 15,375
Farmers Branch, 25,382
Farmersville, 2,780
Flower Mound, 36,340
Forney, 5,260
Frisco, 17,412
Garland, 190,055
Glenn Heights, 5,140
Grand Prairie, 109,231
Greenville, 23,882

Gun Barrel City, 4,005
Heath, 3,383
Highland Park, 8,971
Highland Village, 11,326
Hutchins, 2,911
Irving, 176,993
Kaufman, 6,306
Lake Dallas, 4,791
Lancaster, 23,352
Lewisville, 61,517
Lucas, 2,687
McKinney, 32,462
Mesquite, 111,947
Midlothian, 6,429
Ovilla, 2,905
Pilot Point, 2,985
Plano, 192,280
Princeton, 2,678
Red Oak, 3,736
Richardson, 81,133
Rockwall, 13,783
Rowlett, 35,746
Royse City, 2,738
Sachse, 7,074
Sanger, 4,087
Seagoville, 9,863
Terrell, 14,060
The Colony, 25,453
Trophy Club, 4,809
University Park, 22,568
Waxahachie, 20,324
Wilmer, 2,629
Wylie, 10,894

DANBURY, CT

News-Times
333 Main St.
Danbury 06810
(203) 744-5100
www.newstimes.com

Housatonic Valley District
30 Main St.
Danbury 06813
(800) 841-4488
www.housatonic.org

Greater Danbury C/C
72 West St.
Danbury 06810
(203) 743-5565

Bethel, 17,767
Brookfield, 14,482
Danbury, 65,506
Newtown, 22,516
New Fairfield, 13,381
New Milford, 25,236
Redding, 8,068
Ridgefield, 21,679
Sherman, 2,946
Washington, 4,030

DANVILLE, VA

Danville Register & Bee
P.O. Box 331
Danville 24543
(804) 793-2311
www.registerbee.com

Danville Area C/C
635 Main St.
Danville 24541
(804) 793-5422
www.danvillechamber.com

Chatham, 1,295
Danville, 53,472
Gretna, 1,400

DAVENPORT-MOLINE-ROCK ISLAND, IA-IL

Quad-City Times
500 E. 3rd St.
Davenport 52801
(319) 383-2200
www.qctimes.com

Dispatch/Rock Island Argus
1720 5th Ave.
Moline 61265
(309) 764-4344
www.qconline.com

Quad Cities CVB
2021 River Dr.
Moline 52801
(800) 747-7800
www.quadcities.com/CVB

Davenport C/C
102 S. Harrison St.
Davenport 52801
(319) 322-1706

Illinois Quad City C/C
1819 Third Ave.
Rock Island 61201
(309) 788-6311
www.qconline.com/chamber

Bettendorf, IA, 31,015
Coal Valley, IL, 3,896
Davenport, IA, 97,010
East Moline, IL, 20,214
Eldridge, IA, 3,696
Galva, IL, 2,671
Geneseo, IL, 6,258
Green Rock, IL, 2,638
Kewanee, IL, 12,684
Le Claire, IA, 2,693
Milan, IL, 5,794

Moline, IL, 42,757
Rock Island, IL, 39,679
Silvis, IL, 6,867

DAYTON-SPRINGFIELD, OH

Dayton Daily News
45 S. Ludlow St.
Dayton 45402
(937) 225-2321
www.activedayton.com/ddn

Dayton/Montgomery County CVB
One Chamber Plaza
Dayton 45402
(800) 221-8235
www.daytoncvb.com

Springfield Area C/C
333 N. Limestone St.
Springfield 45503
(937) 325-7621

Dayton Area C/C
One Chamber Plaza
Dayton 45402
(937) 226-1444

Beavercreek, 31,054
Bellbrook, 7,750
Brookville, 4,789
Cedarville, 3,627
Centerville, 22,456
Covington, 2,653
Dayton, 172,947
Drexel, 5,143
Enon, 2,565
Fairborn, 30,529
Fort McKinley, 9,740
Germantown, 4,644
Huber Heights, 38,939
Inglewood, 11,752
Kettering, 58,204
Miamisburg, 18,308
Moraine, 6,758
New Carlisle, 5,733
New Lebanon, 4,269
Northridge, 9,448
Northview, 10,337
Oakwood, 8,387
Overlook-Page Manor, 13,242
Piqua, 20,049
Shiloh, 11,607
Springfield, 67,460
Tipp City, 6,365
Trotwood, 8,619
Troy, 21,080
Union, 5,430
Vandalia, 14,155
West Milton, 4,282

Woodbourne-Hyde Park, 7,837
Xenia, 23,456
Yellow Springs, 4,720

DAYTONA BEACH, FL

News-Journal
901 6th St.
Daytona Beach 32117
(904) 252-1511
www.n-jcenter.com

Daytona Beach Area CVB
126 E. Orange Ave.
Daytona Beach 32114
(800) 854-1234

Daytona Beach-Halifax Area C/C
126 E. Orange Ave.
Daytona Beach 32115
(904) 255-7311
www.daytonachamber.com
Daytona Beach, 65,203
Daytona Beach Shores, 3,046
De Bary, 7,176
De Land, 18,607
Deltona, 50,828
Edgewater, 17,445
Flagler Beach, 4,514
Holly Hill, 11,512
Lake Helen, 2,508
New Smyrna Beach, 17,995
Orange City, 5,967
Ormond Beach, 32,266
Ormond-By-The-Sea, 8,157
Palm Coast, 14,287
Pierson, 3,084
Port Orange, 41,387
South Daytona, 13,231

DECATUR, AL

Decatur Daily
201 First Ave. SE
Decatur 35609
(888) 353-4612
www.decaturdaily.com

Decatur CVB
719 Sixth Ave. SE
Decatur 35602
(256) 350-2028

Decatur C/C
515 Sixth Ave. NE
Decatur 35602
(256) 353-5312
www.dcc.org
Decatur, 53,797
Hartselle, 12,001

Moulton 3,256

DECATUR, IL

Herald-Review
601 E. William St.
Decatur 62525
(217) 429-5151
www.herald-review.com

Decatur Area CVB
202 E. North St.
Decatur 62523
(800) 331-4479
www.decaturcvb.com

Metro Decatur C/C
100 Merchant St.
Decatur 62523
(217) 422-2200
www.midwest.net/decatur
Decatur, 81,369
Maroa, 1,654
Mount Zion, 4,596

DENVER, CO

Denver Post
1560 Broadway
Denver 80202
(303) 820-1010
www.denverpost.com

Rocky Mountain News
400 W. Colfax Ave.
Denver 80204
(303) 892-5000
www.insidedenver.com

Denver Metro CVB
225 W. Colfax Ave.
Denver 80202
(800) 645-3446

Greater Denver C/C
1445 Market St.
Denver 80202
(303) 534-8500
www.denverchamber.org
Applewood, 11,069
Arvada, 96,340
Aurora, 252,341
Brighton, 16,116
Castle Rock, 12,868
Castlewood, 24,392
Cherry Hills Village, 6,332
Columbine, 22,397
Commerce City, 17,540
Denver, 497,840

Derby, 6,043
Edgewater, 4,598
Englewood, 31,575
Evergreen, 7,582
Federal Heights, 10,572
Gateway, 7,510
Glendale, 2,989
Golden, 15,021
Greenwood Village, 12,749
Highlands Ranch, 10,181
Ken Caryl, 24,391
Lakewood, 134,999
Littleton, 39,504
Northglenn, 29,214
Parker, 11,802
Sheridan, 5,492
Sherrelwood, 16,636
Southglenn, 43,087
Thornton, 67,217
Welby, 10,218
Westminster, 93,115
Westminster East, 5,197
Wheat Ridge, 29,922

DES MOINES, IA

Des Moines Register
P.O. Box 957
Des Moines 50304
(515) 284-8201
www.dmregister.com

Greater Des Moines CVB
601 Locust St.
Des Moines 50309
(800) 451-2625
www.icvba.org/desmoines.htm

Greater Des Moines C/C
601 Locust St.
Des Moines 50309
(515) 286-4950
www.dmchamber.com
Adel, 3,698
Altoona, 8,864
Ankeny, 23,484
Carlisle, 3,589
Clive, 10,419
Des Moines, 193,422
Grimes, 3,562
Indianola, 12,574
Johnston, 6,196
Norwalk, 6,592
Perry, 7,269
Pleasant Hill, 4,586
Urbandale, 26,902
Waukee, 3,721
West Des Moines, 40,380
Windsor Heights, 5,036

DETROIT, MI

Detroit Free Press/News
321 W. Lafayette Blvd.
Detroit 48226
(313) 222-6400
www.freep.com

Metro Detroit CVB
211 W. Fort St.
Detroit 49829
(800) 338-7648
www.visitdetroit.com

Detroit Regional C/C
600 W. Lafayette Blvd.
Detroit 48226
(313) 596-0327
www.detroitchamber.com

Algonac, 4,745
Allen Park, 31,423
Almont, 2,691
Auburn Hills, 19,315
Belleville, 3,746
Berkley, 16,766
Beverly Hills, 10,452
Birmingham, 19,794
Bloomfield Hills, 4,357
Bloomfield Township, 42,137
Canton, 57,047
Carleton, 3,428
Center Line, 8,456
Clawson, 13,759
Clinton, 85,866
Dearborn, 91,418
Dearborn Heights, 61,504
Detroit, 1,000,272
Dundee, 2,737
Ecorse, 12,272
Farmington, 10,071
Farmington Hills, 79,918
Ferndale, 24,485
Flat Rock, 7,697
Franklin, 2,683
Fraser, 14,471
Garden City, 32,336
Gibraltar, 4,368
Grosse Ile, 9,781
Grosse Pointe, 5,695
Grosse Pointe Farms, 10,183
Grosse Pointe Park, 12,869
Grosse Pointe Shores, 2,971
Grosse Pointe Woods, 17,828
Hamtramck, 18,262
Harper Woods, 14,955
Harrison, 24,685
Hazel Park, 19,734
Highland Park, 19,788
Holly, 6,024
Huntington Woods, 6,305

Imlay City, 2,916
Inkster, 30,992
Keego Harbor, 2,935
Lake Orion, 2,978
Lambertville, 7,860
Lapeer, 8,122
Lathrup Village, 4,302
Lincoln Park, 42,167
Livonia, 105,099
Madison Heights, 32,566
Marine City, 4,585
Marysville, 9,476
Melvindale, 11,246
Milford, 6,344
Monroe, 22,563
Mount Clemens, 17,170
New Baltimore, 5,901
New Haven, 2,998
Northville, 6,497
Novi, 43,634
Oak Park, 29,972
Oxford, 3,178
Pleasant Ridge, 2,692
Plymouth, 9,670
Plymouth Township, 23,646
Pontiac, 70,471
Port Huron, 32,873
Redford, 54,387
Richmond, 4,450
River Rouge, 11,091
Riverview, 14,250
Rochester, 7,452
Rochester Hills, 67,408
Rockwood, 3,265
Romeo, 3,688
Romulus, 23,636
Roseville, 51,275
Royal Oak, 64,942
St. Clair, 5,492
St. Clair Shores, 64,065
Shelby, 48,655
South Lyon, 8,057
South Monroe, 5,266
Southfield, 76,184
Southgate, 31,438
Sterling Heights, 118,698
Taylor, 71,939
Temperance, 6,542
Trenton, 21,474
Troy, 79,120
Utica, 4,773
Walled Lake, 6,672
Warren, 138,078
Waterford, 66,692
Wayne, 20,661
West Bloomfield Township, 54,843
Westland, 90,798
Wixom, 10,498
Wolverine Lake, 4,780
Woodhaven, 12,828
Wyandotte, 31,803

DOTHAN, AL

Dothan Eagle
227 N. Oates
Dothan 36303
(334) 792-3141

Dothan Area CVB
3311 Ross Clark Circle
Dothan 36304
(334) 794-6622

Dothan Area C/C
440 Honeysuckle Rd.
Dothan 36302
(334) 792-5138
www.dothan.com

Daleville, 5,352
Dothan, 55,944
Fort Rucker, 7,593
Ozark, 12,745

DOVER, DE

Delaware State News
P.O. Box 737
Dover 19903
(302) 674-3600
www.newszap.com

Central Delaware C/C
3 The Plaza
Dover 19901
(302) 736-1800

Dover, 30,414
Milford, 2,614
Smyrna, 5,502

DUBUQUE, IA

Dubuque Telegraph Herald
801 Bluff St.
Dubuque 52004
(319) 588-5611
www.thonline.com

Dubuque Area C/C
770 Town Clock Plaza
Dubuque 52004
(319) 557-9200
www.dubuque.org/chamber

Asbury, 2,241
Dubuque, 57,312
Dyersville, 3,856

DULUTH-SUPERIOR, MN-WI

Duluth News-Tribune
424 W. First St.
Duluth 55802
(218) 723-5313
www.duluthnews.com

Duluth CVB
100 Lake Place Dr.
Duluth 55802
(800) 438-5884

Superior-Douglas County CVB
305 Harbor View Pkwy.
Superior 54880
(800) 942-5313

Duluth Area C/C
118 E. Superior St.
Duluth 55802
(218) 722-5501
chamber.duluth.mn.us

Superior-Douglas County C/C
305 E. 2nd St.
Superior 54880
(800) 942-5313
www.superiorwi.com
Chisholm, MN, 5,058
Duluth, MN, 83,699
Ely, MN, 3,803
Eveleth, MN, 3,869
Hermantown, MN, 7,679
Hibbing, MN, 17,600
Mountain Iron, MN, 3,301
Proctor, MN, 2,935
Superior, WI, 27,396
Virginia, MN, 8,988

DUTCHESS COUNTY, NY

Poughkeepsie Journal
85 Civic Center Plaza
Poughkeepsie 12601
(914) 454-2000
www.pojonews.com

Poughkeepsie Area C/C
110 Main St.
Poughkeepsie 12601
(914) 454-1700
www.pokchamb.org
Arlington, 11,948
Beacon, 13,275
Myers Corner, 5,599
Poughkeepsie, 27,808
Rhinebeck, 2,645
Wappingers Falls, 4,482

EAU CLAIRE, WI

Leader-Telegram
P.O. Box 570
Eau Claire 54701
(715) 833-9200
www.leadertelegram.com

Eau Claire Area C/C & CVB
3625 Gateway Dr.
Eau Claire 54701
(800) 344-3866
Altoona, 6,583
Bloomer, 3,290
Chippewa Falls, 12,784
Eau Claire, 58,872

EDMONTON, AB

Edmonton Sun
4990 92nd Ave.
Edmonton T6B 3A1
(780) 468-0100
www.canoe.com/EdmontonSun

Edmonton Journal
P.O. Box 2421
Edmonton T5J 0S1
(780) 429-5200
www.edmontonjournal.com

Edmonton Tourism
104-9797 Jasper Ave.
Edmonton T5J 1N9
(800) 463-4667

Edmonton C/C
600-10123 99th St.
Edmonton T5J 3G9
(780) 426-4620
www.chamber.edmonton.ab.ca
Beaumont, 5,810
Bon Accord, 1,493
Bruderheim, 1,198
Calmar, 1,797
Devon, 4,496
Edmonton, 616,306
Fort Saskatchewan, 12,408
Gibbons, 2,748
Leduc, 14,305
Legal, 1,095
Morinville, 6,226
Redwater, 2,053
St. Albert, 46,888
Spruce Grove, 14,271
Stony Plain, 8,274

EL PASO, TX

El Paso Times
Times Plaza
El Paso 79901
(915) 546-6104
www.elpasotimes.com

El Paso CVB
One Civic Center Plaza
El Paso 79901
(800) 351-6024
www.elpasocvb.com

Greater El Paso C/C
10 Civic Center Plaza
El Paso 79901
(915) 534-0500
Anthony, 3,573
El Paso, 599,865
Fabens, 5,599
Fort Bliss, 13,915
Horizon City, 3,666
Socorro, 25,409

ELKHART-GOSHEN, IN

Elkhart Truth
421 S. 2nd St.
Elkhart 46516
(219) 294-1661
www.elktruth.com

Elkhart County CVB
219 Caravan Dr.
Elkhart 46514
(219) 262-8161
www.amishcountry.org

Elkhart County C/C
416 S. Main St.
Elkhart 46515
(219) 293-1531
www.elkhart.org

C/C of Goshen, Inc.
232 S. Main St.
Goshen 46526
(219) 533-2102
Dunlap, 5,705
Elkhart, 44,224
Goshen, 24,930
Nappanee, 5,812

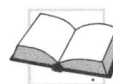
ELMIRA, NY

Star-Gazette
201 Baldwin St.
Elmira 14902
(607) 734-5151
www.star-gazette.com

Chemung County C/C
215 E. Church St.
Elmira 14901
(800) 627-5892
www.chemungchamber.org
Elmira, 32,009
Elmira Heights, 4,187
Horseheads, 6,695
Southport, 7,753
West Elmira, 5,218

ENID, OK

Enid News & Eagle
227 W. Broadway
Enid 73701
(580) 233-6600
www.enidnews.com

Greater Enid C/C
210 Kenwood Blvd.
Enid 73701
(580) 237-2494
Enid, 45,724
Waukomis, 1,325

ERIE, PA

Erie Morning News/Daily Times
205 W. 12th St.
Erie 16534
(814) 870-1600
www.goerie.com

Erie Area C/C & CVB
1006 State St.
Erie 16501
(814) 454-7191
www.eriepa.com
Albion, 2,798
Corry, 7,012
Edinboro, 6,983
Erie, 105,270
Girard, 3,101
Lake City, 2,728
North East, 4,447
Northwest Harborcreek, 6,662
Union City, 3,495
Wesleyville, 3,602

EUGENE-SPRINGFIELD, OR

Register-Guard
975 High St.
Eugene 97440
(541) 485-1234
www.registerguard.com

Springfield Area C/C
101 S. A St.
Springfield 97477
(541) 746-1651

Eugene Area C/C
1401 Willamette St.
Eugene 97440
(541) 484-1314
www.eugene-commerce.com
Cottage Grove, 7,607
Creswell, 2,721
Eugene, 123,718
Florence, 6,214
Junction City, 4,072
North Springfield, 5,451
Oakridge, 3,121
River Road, 9,443
Santa Clara, 12,834
Springfield, 49,430
Veneta, 2,763

EVANSVILLE-HENDERSON, IN-KY

Evansville Courier/Press
300 E. Walnut St.
Evansville 47713
(812) 424-7711
courierpress.evansville.net

Evansville CVB
401 SE Riverside Dr.
Evansville 47713
(800) 433-3025
www.tourism@evansvillecvb.org

Metro Evansville C/C
100 NW 2nd St.
Evansville 47708
(812) 425-8147

Henderson Tourist Comm.
2961 U.S. 41 N
Henderson 42420
(279) 826-3128
Boonville, IN, 6,605
Chandler, IN, 3,113
Evansville, IN, 123,456

Henderson, KY, 26,456
Mount Vernon, IN, 6,765
Newburgh, IN, 2,917

FARGO-MOORHEAD, ND-MN

The Forum
101 N. 5th St.
Fargo 58102
(701) 235-7311
www.in-forum.com

Fargo-Moorhead CVB
2001 44th St. SW
Fargo 58107
(800) 235-7654
www.wwb.com/company/
c010118.htm

Fargo C/C
321 N. Fourth St.
Fargo 58108
(701) 237-5678

Moorhead Area C/C
725 Center Ave.
Moorhead 56560
(218) 236-6200
Dilworth, MN, 2,925
Fargo, ND, 83,778
Moorhead, MN, 33,343
West Fargo, ND, 13,566

FAYETTEVILLE, NC

Fayetteville Observer-Times
458 Whitfield St.
Fayetteville 28306
(910) 323-4848
www.fayettevillenc.com

Fayetteville Area CVB
245 Person St.
Fayetteville 28301
(800) 255-8217
www.fayettevillenc.com

Fayetteville C/C
519 Ramsey St.
Fayetteville 28302
(910) 483-8133
www.foto.com/chamber
Fayetteville, 79,631
Fort Bragg, 34,744
Hope Mills, 9,273
Spring Lake, 7,760

FAYETTEVILLE-SPRINGDALE-ROGERS, AR

Northwest Arkansas Times
P.O. Box 1607
Fayetteville 72702
(501) 442-6242
www.mornews.com

Springdale C/C
700 W. Emma Ave.
Springdale 72764
(501) 751-4694

Fayetteville C/C
123 W. Mountain St.
Fayetteville 72702
(800) 766-4626
www.fayettevillear.com
Bella Vista, 9,083
Bentonville, 16,984
Fayetteville, 52,360
Lowell, 3,652
Rogers, 35,355
Siloam Springs, 10,055
Springdale, 38,572

FITCHBURG-LEOMINSTER, MA

Sentinel & Enterprise
808 Main St.
Fitchburg 01420
(978) 343-6911
www.newschoice.com/newspapers/
midstates/sentinel

North Central Massachusetts C/C
110 Erdman Way
Leominster 01453
(978) 840-4300
www.nc.massweb.org
Ashburnham, 5,471
Ashby, 2,934
Fitchburg, 39,843
Gardner, 20,155
Leominster, 39,263
Lunenburg, 9,285
Templeton, 6,991
Westminster, 6,562
Winchendon, 8,931

FLAGSTAFF, AZ-UT

Arizona Daily Sun
417 W. Santa Fe Ave.
Flagstaff 86001
(520) 774-4545

Flagstaff Visitor Center
211 W. Aspen Ave.
Flagstaff 86001
(520) 779-7611
www.flagstaff.az.us/visguide

Flagstaff C/C
101 E. Route 66
Flagstaff 86001
(800) 842-7293
www.flagstaff.az.us/chamber
Flagstaff, 55,094
Kanab, 3,616
Page, 7,653
Tuba City, 7,323
Williams, 2,706

FLINT, MI

Flint Journal
200 E. First St.
Flint 48502
(810) 766-6100
fl.mlive.com/index.html

Flint Area CVB
519 S. Saginaw St.
Flint 48502
(800) 253-5468
www.flint.org

Flint Area C/C
316 W. Water St.
Flint 48503
(810) 232-7101
Beecher, 14,465
Burton, 27,357
Clio, 2,531
Davison, 5,615
Fenton, 9,705
Flint, 134,881
Flushing, 8,422
Grand Blanc, 8,160
Linden, 2,627
Mount Morris, 3,227
Swartz Creek, 4,827

FLORENCE, AL

Times Daily
219 W. Tennessee St.
Florence 35631
(256) 766-3434
www.timesdaily.com/tdnewspa.htl

Florence C/C
612 S. Court St.
Florence 35630
(256) 764-4661
www.shoalscc.org
Florence, 38,999
Muscle Shoals, 10,487
Sheffield, 10,216
Tuscumbia, 8,253

FLORENCE, SC

Florence Morning News
310 S. Dargan St.
Florence 29501
(803) 317-6397
morningnewsonline.com

Greater Florence C/C
610 W. Palmetto St.
Florence 29501
(803) 665-0515
www.florencesc.com
Florence, 30,168
Lake City, 7,096
Timmonsville, 2,175

FORT COLLINS-LOVELAND, CO

Fort Collins Coloradoan
P.O. Box 1577
Fort Collins 80522
(970) 224-7730
www.coloradoan.com

Fort Collins CVB
420 S. Howes St.
Fort Collins 80522
(800) 274-3678
www.ftcollins.org

Loveland C/C
5400 Stone Creek Circle
Loveland 80537
(970) 667-6311
www.loveland.org

Fort Collins Area C/C
225 S. Meldrum St.
Fort Collins 80522
(970) 482-3746
www.fcchamber.org
Berthoud, 3,904
Estes Park, 3,989
Fort Collins, 104,196
Loveland, 44,923

FORT LAUDERDALE, FL

Sun-Sentinel
200 E. Las Olas Blvd.
Fort Lauderdale 33301
(954) 356-4000
www.sun-sentinel.com

Greater Ft. Lauderdale CVB
1850 Eller Dr.
Fort Lauderdale 33316
(954) 765-4466
www.sunny.org

Greater Fort Lauderdale C/C
512 NE Third Ave.
Fort Lauderdale 33301
(954) 462-6000
ftlchamber.com

Broadview Park, 6,109
Broadview-Pompano Park, 5,230
Browardale, 6,257
Coconut Creek, 34,041
Collier Manor, 7,322
Cooper City, 28,637
Coral Springs, 105,275
Dania, 14,456
Davie, 58,501
Deerfield Beach, 49,493
Fort Lauderdale, 151,805
Hallandale, 31,163
Hollywood, 127,894
Lauderdale Lakes, 28,143
Lauderdale-by-the-Sea, 2,891
Lauderhill, 50,522
Lighthouse Point, 10,639
Margate, 50,575
Melrose Park, 6,477
Miami Gardens, 7,448
Miramar, 50,956
North Andrews Gardens, 9,002
North Lauderdale, 28,277
Oakland Park, 28,135
Parkland, 10,799
Pembroke Park, 4,962
Pembroke Pines, 100,662
Pine Island Ridge, 5,244
Plantation, 78,674
Pompano Beach, 74,583
Pompano Beach Highlands, 17,915
Riverland, 5,376
Sunrise, 77,592
Tamarac, 51,081
Washington Park, 6,930
Wilton Manors, 12,091

FORT MYERS-CAPE CORAL, FL

News-Press
Martin Luther King, Jr. Blvd.
Fort Myers 33901
(941) 335-0200
www.southwestfloridaonline.com

Lee County CVB
2180 W. First St.
Fort Myers 33901
(941) 338-3500

Greater Fort Myers C/C
2310 Edwards Dr.
Fort Myers 33901
(800) 366-3622

C/C of Cape Coral
2051 Cape Coral Pkwy. E
Cape Coral 33910
(800) 226-9609
www.capecoralfl.com

Bonita Springs, 13,600
Cape Coral, 88,053
Cypress Lake, 10,491
Forest Island Park, 5,988
Fort Myers, 45,917
Fort Myers Beach, 9,284
Fort Myers Shores, 5,460
Iona, 9,565
Lehigh Acres, 13,611
McGregor, 6,504
North Fort Myers, 30,027
Page Park-Pine Manor, 5,116
San Carlos Park, 11,785
Sanibel, 5,584
Villas, 9,898
Whiskey Creek, 5,061

FORT PIERCE-PORT ST. LUCIE, FL

The Tribune
600 Edwards Rd.
Fort Pierce 34954
(561) 461-2050
www.stluciecounty.com

Greater Port St. Lucie C/C
1626 SE Port St. Lucie Blvd.
Port Saint Lucie 34985
(561) 595-9999
www.co.st-lucie.fl.us

Fort Pierce-Saint Lucie County C/C
2200 Virginia Ave.
Fort Pierce 34982
(561) 595-9999

Fort Pierce, 36,876
Fort Pierce North, 5,833
Fort Pierce South, 5,320
Hobe Sound, 11,507
Jensen Beach, 9,884
Lakewood Park, 7,211
Port Salerno, 7,786
Stuart, 12,537

FORT SMITH, AR-OK

Southwest Times Record
920 Rogers Ave.
Fort Smith 72901
(501) 785-7700
www.swtimes.com

Fort Smith CVB
North B & Clayton Expwy.
Fort Smith 72901
(800) 637-1477
www.fortsmith.org

Fort Smith C/C
612 Garrison Ave.
Fort Smith 72902
(501) 783-6118
www.fschamber.com

Alma, AR, 3,505
Barling, AR, 4,347
Fort Smith, AR, 75,776
Greenwood, AR, 5,654
Muldrow, OK, 3,133
Roland, OK, 2,620
Sallisaw, OK, 7,673
Van Buren, AR, 18,601

FORT WALTON BEACH, FL

Northwest Florida Daily News
200 Racetrack Rd. NW
Fort Walton Beach 32548
(850) 863-1111
www.nwfdailynews.com

Greater Fort Walton Beach C/C
P.O. Drawer 640
Fort Walton Beach 32548
(850) 244-8191

Crestview, 11,649
Destin, 10,555
Fort Walton Beach, 21,933
Lake Lorraine, 6,779
Mary Esther, 4,394
Niceville, 11,955
Ocean City, 5,422
Valparaiso, 6,646
Wright, 18,945

FORT WAYNE, IN

Journal-Gazette/News-Sentinel
600 W. Main St.
Fort Wayne 46802
(219) 461-8444
www.fortwayne.com/jg

Fort Wayne/Allen County CVB
1021 S. Calhoun St.
Fort Wayne 46802
(800) 767-7752
www.fwcvb.org

Greater Fort Wayne C/C
826 Ewing St.
Fort Wayne 46802
(219) 424-1435
www.fwchamber.org
Auburn, 10,533
Berne, 3,736
Bluffton, 9,423
Butler, 2,585
Columbia City, 6,408
Decatur, 8,965
Fort Wayne, 184,783
Garrett, 5,220
Huntington, 15,820
New Haven, 10,148

FORT WORTH-ARLINGTON, TX

Fort Worth Star-Telegram
400 W. 7th St.
Fort Worth 76102
(817) 390-7400
www.star-telegram.com

Arlington News
1000 Ave. H East
Arlington 76011
(817) 685-0560

Ft. Worth CVB
415 Throckmorton St.
Fort Worth 76102
(800) 433-5747
www.fortworth.com

Fort Worth C/C
777 Taylor St.
Fort Worth 76102
(817) 336-2491
www.fortworthcoc.org

Arlington CVB
1905 E. Randol Mill Rd.
Arlington 76011
(800) 342-4305
www.tourtexas.com/arlington

Arlington C/C
316 W. Main
Arlington 76010
(817) 275-2613
www.chamber.arlingtontx.com
Alvarado, 3,173
Arlington, 294,816
Azle, 9,991
Bedford, 49,431
Benbrook, 21,139
Burleson, 19,336
Cleburne, 23,904
Colleyville, 18,704
Crowley, 7,422
Eagle Mountain, 5,847
Edgecliff, 2,831
Euless, 41,627
Everman, 5,866
Forest Hill, 11,873
Fort Worth, 479,716
Granbury, 5,152
Grapevine, 37,500
Haltom City, 35,541
Hurst, 36,506
Joshua, 4,567
Keene, 4,652
Keller, 20,231
Kennedale, 4,792
Lake Worth, 4,824
Mansfield, 20,804
North Richland Hills, 53,214
Rendon, 7,658
Reno, 2,706
Richland Hills, 8,367
River Oaks, 6,776
Saginaw, 10,321
Sansom Park, 4,066
Southlake, 13,541
Watauga, 22,639
Weatherford, 17,382
White Settlement, 15,924
Willow Park, 2,855

FRESNO, CA

Fresno Bee
3425 N. First St.
Fresno 93726
(209) 441-6111
www.fresnobee.com

Fresno CVB
808 M St.
Fresno 93721
(800) 788-0836
fresno-online.com/CVB

Fresno C/C
2331 Fresno St.
Fresno 93721
(209) 495-4800
www.fresnochamber.com

Bonadelle Ranchos, 5,705
Chowchilla, 6,740
Clovis, 63,246
Coalinga, 9,542
Firebaugh, 5,589
Fowler, 3,784
Fresno, 396,011
Huron, 5,604
Kerman, 6,810
Kingsburg, 8,422
Madera, 35,648
Madera Acres, 5,245
Mendota, 7,317
Orange Cove, 7,177
Parlier, 9,887
Reedley, 18,451
San Joaquin, 2,863
Sanger, 18,248
Selma, 17,083

GADSDEN, AL

Gadsden Times
401 Locust
Gadsden 35901
(256) 549-2000
www.gadsdentimes.com

Gadsden Area C/C
One Commerce Sq.
Gadsden 35902
(256) 543-3472
Attalla, 6,865
Gadsden, 41,155
Glencoe, 5,024
Hokes Bluff, 4,416
Rainbow City, 8,492
Southside, 6,622

GAINESVILLE, FL

Gainesville Sun
2700 SW 13th St.
Gainesville 32614
(352) 378-1411
sunone.com

Alachua County VCB
30 E. University Ave.
Gainesville 32601
(352) 374-5231
www.co.alachua.fl.us/~acvacb

Gainesville Area C/C
300 E. University Ave.
Gainesville 32601
(352) 334-7100
www.gainesvillechamber.com
Alachua, 5,274
Gainesville, 87,295
High Springs, 3,237

GALVESTON-TEXAS CITY, TX

Galveston County Daily News
8522 Teichman
Galveston 77553
(409) 744-3611
www.galvnews.com

Galveston CVB
2106 Seawall Blvd.
Galveston 77550
(888) 425-4753
www.galvestontourism.com

Galveston C/C
621 Moody Ave.
Galveston 77550
(409) 763-5326
www.galvestoncc.com

Texas City-La Marque C/C
8419 Emmett F. Lowry Expwy.
Texas City 77591
(409) 935-1408
Bacliff, 5,549
Dickinson, 12,594
Friendswood, 28,218
Galveston, 60,048
Hitchcock, 6,235
La Marque, 14,631
League City, 40,631
Santa Fe, 9,487
Texas City, 42,368

GARY, IN

Post-Tribune
1065 Broadway
Gary 46402
(219) 881-3000
www.post-trib.com

Greater Gary C/C
504 Broadway
Gary 46402
(219) 885-7407
Cedar Lake, 9,088
Chesterton, 9,962
Crown Point, 19,007
Dyer, 12,675
East Chicago, 31,761
Gary, 110,975
Griffith, 18,085
Hammond, 80,081
Hebron, 3,446
Highland, 23,569
Hobart, 24,463
Lake Station, 13,983
Lowell, 7,162
Merrillville, 30,577

Munster, 20,438
Portage, 32,419
Porter, 4,138
Schererville, 23,322
South Haven, 6,112
St. John, 7,682
Valparaiso, 25,804
Whiting, 4,784

GLENS FALLS, NY

Post-Star
Lawrence & Cooper Sts.
Glens Falls 12801
(518) 792-3131
www.poststar.com

Adirondack Regional C/C
136 Warren St.
Glens Falls 12801
(518) 798-1761
Fort Edward, 3,477
Glens Falls, 14,772
Glens Falls North, 7,978
Granville, 2,650
Hudson Falls, 7,457
West Glens Falls, 5,964
Whitehall, 2,932

GOLDSBORO, NC

News-Argus
310 N. Berkeley Blvd.
Goldsboro 27532
(252) 778-2211
www.newsargus.com

Goldsboro C/C
308 N. William St.
Goldsboro 27533
(252) 734-2241
Fremont, 1,646
Goldsboro, 40,801
Mount Olive, 5,370

GRAND FORKS, ND-MN

Grand Forks Herald
303 N. 2nd Ave.
Grand Forks 58206
(701) 780-1100
vh1431.infi.net

Greater Grand Forks CVB
4251 Gateway Dr.
Grand Forks 58203
(800) 866-4566
www.grandforkscvb.org

Grand Forks C/C
202 N. Third St.
Grand Forks 58206
(701) 772-7271
Crookston, MN, 7,943
East Grand Forks, MN, 8,827
Grand Forks, ND, 50,675

GRAND JUNCTION, CO

Daily Sentinel
734 S. Seventh St.
Grand Junction 81502
(970) 242-5050
gjsentinel.com

Grand Junction Area C/C
360 Grand Ave.
Grand Junction 81501
(970) 242-3214
www.gjchamber.org
Clifton, 12,671
Fruita, 4,285
Fruitvale, 5,222
Grand Junction, 34,540
Orchard Mesa, 5,977
Redlands, 9,355

GRAND RAPIDS-MUSKEGON-HOLLAND, MI

Grand Rapids Press
155 Michigan St. NW
Grand Rapids 49503
(616) 459-1400
gr.mlive.com

Muskegon Chronicle
P.O. Box 59
Muskegon 49443
(616) 846-5750
mu.mlive.com

Grand Rapids Area CVB
140 Monroe Center NW
Grand Rapids 49503
(800) 678-9859
www.grcvb.org

Holland Area CVB
100 E. Eight St.
Holland 49423
(800) 506-1299
www.holland.org

Muskegon Area CVB
610 Western Ave.
Muskegon 49440
(616) 722-3751
www.muskegon.org

Grand Rapids Area C/C
111 Pearl St. NW
Grand Rapids 49503
(616) 771-0300

Holland Area C/C
272 E. Eighth St.
Holland 49422
(616) 392-2389
www.holland-chamber.org/
Allegan, 4,401
Allendale, 6,950
Cedar Springs, 2,669
Comstock Park, 6,530
Coopersville, 3,806
Cutlerville, 11,228
East Grand Rapids, 10,564
Ferrysburg, 3,097
Forest Hills, 16,690
Grand Haven, 12,142
Grand Rapids, 188,242
Grandville, 16,473
Holland, 33,247
Hudsonville, 6,757
Jenison, 17,882
Kentwood, 41,816
Lowell, 3,980
Muskegon, 39,518
Muskegon Heights, 12,564
North Muskegon, 3,919
Northview, 13,712
Norton Shores, 22,710
Otsego, 3,973
Plainwell, 4,112
Rockford, 3,899
Roosevelt Park, 4,078
Sparta, 4,058
Spring Lake, 2,508
Walker, 18,971
Wayland, 3,343
Whitehall, 3,298
Wyoming, 66,571
Zeeland, 5,816

GREAT FALLS, MT

Great Falls Tribune
P.O. Box 5468
Great Falls 59403
(406) 791-1444

Great Falls Area C/C
710 First Ave. N
Great Falls 59401
(406) 761-4434
Cascade, 750
Great Falls, 57,758

GREELEY, CO

Greeley Daily Tribune
501 Eighth Ave.
Greeley 80632
(970) 352-0211
www.greeleytrib.com

Greeley CVB
902 7th Ave.
Greeley 80631
(800) 449-3866
www.greeleycvb.com

Greeley-Weld C/C
902 7th Ave.
Greeley 80631
(970) 352-3566
www.greeleychamber.com
Dacono, 2,572
Evans, 7,160
Fort Lupton, 5,697
Greeley, 68,593
Windsor, 6,818

GREEN BAY, WI

Green Bay Press-Gazette
435 E. Walnut St.
Green Bay 54301
(920) 435-4411
www.greenbaypressgazette.com

Green Bay Area CVB
1901 S. Oneida St.
Green Bay 54307
(888) 867-3342
www.greenbaywi.com

Green Bay Area C/C
400 S. Washington St.
Green Bay 54301
(920) 437-8704
www.titletown.org
Ashwaubenon, 17,529
Bellevue Town, 7,541
De Pere, 19,116
Green Bay, 102,076
Howard, 12,907

GREENSBORO–WINSTON-SALEM–HIGH POINT, NC

Greensboro News & Record
200 E. Market St.
Greensboro 27401
(336) 274-5476
greensboro.com/nronline/index.htm

Winston-Salem Journal
P.O. Box 3159
Winston Salem 27102
(336) 727-7211
www.w-s-journal.com

Winston-Salem CVB
601 W. Fourth St.
Winston-Salem 27102
(800) 331-7018
www.wscvb.com

Greensboro Area CVB
317 S. Greene St.
Greensboro 27401
(800) 344-2282
www.greensboronc.org

High Point CVB
300 S. Main St.
High Point 27261
(800) 720-5255
www.highpoint.org

Greater Winston-Salem C/C
601 W. Fourth St.
Winston-Salem 27102
(336) 777-3787
www.winstonsalem.com

Greensboro Area C/C
342 N. Elm St.
Greensboro 27402
(336) 275-8675
www.webcom.com/greens

High Point C/C
1101 N. Main St.
High Point 27262
(336) 889-8151
Archdale, 7,007
Asheboro, 16,897
Burlington, 40,402
Clemmons, 6,681
Elon College, 4,644
Gibsonville, 3,971
Graham, 11,337
Greensboro, 195,426
High Point, 74,417

Jamestown, 2,678
Kernersville, 13,362
King, 4,907
Lewisville, 7,188
Lexington, 16,239
Mebane, 5,674
Mocksville, 3,234
Stokesdale, 2,617
Thomasville, 17,483
Trinity, 5,469
Winston-Salem, 153,541
Yadkinville, 2,743

GREENVILLE, NC

Greenville Daily Reflector-Morning
P.O. Box 1967
Greenville 27835
(252) 752-6166
www.reflector.com

Pitt-Greenville C/C
302 S. Greene St.
Greenville 27834
(252) 752-4101
Ayden, 4,970
Farmville, 4,149
Greenville, 54,602
Winterville, 3,058

GREENVILLE-SPARTANBURG-ANDERSON, SC

Spartanburg Herald Journal
P.O. Box 1657
Spartanburg 29304
(864) 582-4511
www.shj.com

Greenville News
P.O. Box 1688
Greenville 29601
(864) 298-4100
www.greenvilleonline.com

Greater Greenville CVB
206 S. Main St.
Greenville 29603
(800) 717-0023
www.greatergreenville.com

Anderson Area C/C
706 E. Greenville St.
Anderson 29622
(864) 226-3454

Greater Greenville C/C
24 Cleveland St.
Greenville 29601
(864) 242-1050

Greater Spartanburg Area C/C
105 N. Pine St.
Spartanburg 29304
(864) 594-5000
www.spartanburgsc.org
Anderson, 26,429
Belton, 5,498
Berea, 13,535
Clemson, 12,174
Easley, 16,880
Fountain Inn, 4,829
Gaffney, 13,275
Gantt, 13,891
Greenville, 57,064
Greer, 11,464
Homeland Park, 6,569
Honea Path, 3,732
Liberty, 3,456
Mauldin, 13,682
Parker, 11,072
Pendleton, 3,403
Pickens, 4,230
Sans Souci, 7,612
Simpsonville, 11,647
Spartanburg, 42,136
Taylors, 19,619
Travelers Rest, 3,403
Wade Hampton, 20,014
Welcome, 6,560
Wellford, 2,725
Williamston, 3,769
Woodruff, 4,296

HAGERSTOWN, MD

Hagerstown Herald-Mail
100 Summit Ave.
Hagerstown 21742
(301) 733-5131
www.herald-mail.com

Hagerstown-Washington
County C/C
111 W. Washington St.
Hagerstown 21740
(301) 739-2015
www.hagerstown.org
Boonsboro, 2,516
Hagerstown, 34,633
Halfway, 8,873
Long Meadow, 5,594

HALIFAX, NS

Halifax Herald
1650 Argyle St.
Halifax B3J 2T2
(902) 426-1187
newspapers.com/click.cgi?nid=727

Tourism Halifax
Duke & Barrington Sts.
Halifax B3J 1P3
(902) 421-8736

Metropolitan Halifax C/C
1800 Argyle St.
Halifax B3J 3N8
(902) 468-7111
www.halifaxchamber.com
Bedford, 13,638
Dartmouth, 65,629
Halifax, 113,910

HAMILTON, ON

Hamilton Spectator
44 Frid St.
Hamilton L8N 3G3
(905) 526-3333
www.southam.com/
hamiltonspectator

Greater Hamilton Tourist Centre
127 King St. E
Hamilton L8N 1B1
(800) 263-8590

Hamilton & District C/C
555 Bay St.
Hamilton L8L 1H1
(905) 522-1151
www.hamilton-cofc.on.ca
Ancaster, 23,403
Burlington, 136,976
Dundas, 23,125
Flamborough, 34,037
Glanbrook, 10,564
Grimsby, 19,585
Hamilton, 322,352
Stoney Creek, 54,318

HAMILTON-MIDDLETOWN, OH

Journal News
228 Court St.
Hamilton 45011
(513) 863-8200
www.journal-news.com/home.cfm

Middletown Journal
52 S. Broad St.
Middletown 45044
(513) 422-3611
www.journalink.com/home.cfm

Hamilton CVB
One Riverfront Plaza
Hamilton 45011
(800) 311-5353
www.hamilton-cvb.com

Hamilton C/C
201 Dayton St.
Hamilton 45011
(513) 844-1500

Middletown Area C/C
36 City Centre Plaza
Middletown 45042
(513) 422-4551
Fairfield, 42,163
Hamilton, 61,833
Middletown, 48,023
Monroe, 5,079
New Miami, 2,555
Oxford, 18,700
Trenton, 7,054

HARRISBURG-LEBANON-CARLISLE, PA

Patriot/Evening News
812 Market St.
Harrisburg 17105
(717) 255-8100

Daily News
718 Poplar St.
Lebanon 17042
(717) 272-5611
www.leba.net/lebnews

Harrisburg-Hershey-Carlisle CVB
25 N. Front St.
Harrisburg 17101
(800) 995-0969
www.visithhc.com

Capital Region C/C
3211 N. Front St.
Harrisburg 17110
(717) 232-4099
www.hbgchamber.com

Lebanon Valley C/C
252 N. Eighth St.
Lebanon 17042
(717) 273-3727
www.leba.net/chamber

Greater Carlisle Area C/C
212 N. Hanover St.
Carlisle 17013
(717) 243-4515
www.carlislechamber.org
Camp Hill, 7,554
Carlisle, 18,039
Colonial Park, 13,777
Cornwall, 3,300
Enola, 5,961
Harrisburg, 50,886
Hershey CDP, 11,860
Highspire, 2,651
Hummelstown, 3,977
Lebanon, 23,791
Lemoyne, 3,873
Linglestown, 5,862
Lower Allen, 6,329
Mechanicsburg, 9,238
Middletown, 9,141
Millersburg, 2,724
Myerstown, 3,080
New Cumberland, 7,434
Palmyra, 6,572
Penbrook, 2,759
Progress, 9,654
Shippensburg, 6,199
Steelton, 4,975
Wormleysburg, 2,738

HARTFORD, CT

Hartford Courant
285 Broad St.
Hartford 06115
(860) 241-6200
www.courant.com

Greater Hartford CVB
One Civic Center Plaza
Hartford 06103
(800) 446-7811
www.grhartfordcvb.com

Connecticut Valley TVC
393 Main St.
Middletown 06457
(860) 347-0028
www.cttourism.org

Greater Hartford C/C
250 Constitution Plaza
Hartford 06103
(860) 525-4451
www.metrohartford.com
Andover, 2,725
Ashford, 3,903
Avon, 13,833
Barkhamsted, 3,499
Berlin, 17,197
Bloomfield, 19,155
Bolton, 4,669
Bristol, 59,619
Burlington, 7,686
Canton, 8,104
Colchester, 12,620
Columbia, 4,765
Coventry, 10,845
Cromwell, 12,447
Durham, 6,346
East Granby, 4,386
East Haddam, 7,304
East Hampton, 10,930
East Hartford, 48,083
East Windsor, 9,969
Ellington, 11,521
Enfield, 43,479
Farmington, 20,942
Glastonbury, 28,500
Granby, 9,476
Haddam, 7,111
Hartford, 133,086
Harwinton, 5,331
Hebron, 7,744
Lebanon, 6,337
Manchester, 51,666
Mansfield, 18,958
Marlborough, 5,667
Middletown, 43,243
Middlefield, 4,051
New Britain, 71,512
New Hartford, 6,059
Newington, 28,379
Plainville, 16,910
Plymouth, 12,017
Portland, 8,772
Rocky Hill, 16,509
Simsbury, 21,782
Somers, 9,358
South Windsor, 22,500
Southington, 38,391
Stafford, 11,497
Suffield, 11,216
Tolland, 11,994
Vernon 29,414
West Hartford, 56,795
Wethersfield, 25,179
Willington, 6,117
Winchester, 11,440
Windham, 21,598
Windsor, 27,663
Windsor Locks, 12,076

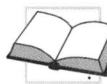

HATTIESBURG, MS

Hattiesburg American
825 N. Main St.
Hattiesburg 39401
(601) 582-4321

Hattiesburg CVB
P.O. Box 16122
Hattiesburg 39404
(800) 638-6877
www.hattiesburg.org

Hattiesburg Area C/C
607 Adeline St.
Hattiesburg 39403
(800) 238-4288
Hattiesburg, 47,803
Petal, 8,684
West Hattiesburg, 5,450

HICKORY-MORGANTON-LENOIR, NC

Hickory Daily Record
1100 Park Pl.
Hickory 28603
(828) 322-4510

Greater Hickory CVB
1055 Southgate Corporate Park SW
Hickory 28603
(800) 849-5093
www.hickorymetro.com

Hickory C/C
470 Hwy. 70 SW
Hickory 28602
(828) 328-6111

Morganton C/C
110 E. Meeting St.
Morganton 28655
(828) 437-3021
Cajah's Mountain, 2,544
Conover, 5,995
Gamewell, 3,622
Granite Falls, 3,163
Hickory, 30,523
Hudson, 2,903
Lenoir, 16,373
Long View, 3,295
Morganton, 14,927
Newton, 10,886
Sawmills, 4,517
St. Stephens, 8,734
Valdese, 3,829

HONOLULU, HI

Honolulu Advertiser
605 Kapiolani Blvd.
Honolulu 96802
(808) 525-8090
www.thehonoluluadvertiser.com

Honolulu Star-Bulletin
P.O. Box 3080
Honolulu 96802
(808) 525-8640
starbulletin.com

Hawaii VB
2270 Kalakaua Ave.
Honolulu 96815
(808) 923-1811

Honolulu C/C
42 N. King St.
Honolulu 96817
(808) 533-3181
Ahuimanu, 8,387
Aiea, 8,906
Aliamanu, 8,835
Ewa Beach, 14,315
Halawa, 13,408
Heeia, 5,010
Hickam Housing, 6,553
Honolulu, 423,475
Kailua, 36,818
Kaneohe, 35,448
Kaneohe Station, 11,662
Laie, 5,577
Maili, 6,059
Makaha, 7,990
Makakilo City, 9,828
Mililani Town, 29,359
Nanakuli, 9,575
Pearl City, 30,993
Schofield Barracks, 19,597
Village Park, 7,407
Wahiawa, 17,386
Waianae, 8,758
Waimalu, 29,967
Waipahu, 31,435
Waipio, 11,812
Waipio Acres, 5,304

HOUMA, LA

The Courier
3030 Barrow St.
Houma 70361
(504) 850-1100

Houma-Terrebonne C/C
1700 S. St. Charles
Houma 70360
(504) 876-5600
Bayou Cane, 15,876
Cut Off, 5,325
Houma, 30,148
Larose, 5,772
Raceland, 5,564
Thibodaux, 14,015

HOUSTON, TX

Houston Post
4747 Southwest Frwy.
Houston 77056
(713) 840-5000

Houston Chronicle
801 Texas Ave.
Houston 77002
(713) 220-7171
www.chron.com

Greater Houston CVB
801 Congress Ave.
Houston 77002
(713) 227-3100
www.houston-guide.com

Greater Houston Partnership
1200 South St.
Houston 77002
(713) 844-3600
Aldine, 11,133
Baytown, 68,156
Bellaire, 14,988
Brookshire, 3,253
Bunker Hill Village, 3,677
Channelview, 25,564
Cleveland, 7,437
Cloverleaf, 18,230
Conroe, 33,748
Dayton, 6,197
Deer Park, 30,220
El Lago, 3,491
First Colony, 18,327
Galena Park, 10,457
Hedwig Village, 2,757
Hempstead, 4,133
Highlands, 6,632
Houston, 1,744,058
Humble, 13,152
Hunters Creek Village, 4,242
Jacinto City, 9,761
Jersey Village, 5,535
Katy, 9,955
Kingwood, 37,350
La Porte, 31,949
Liberty, 8,196
Meadows, 6,141
Mission Bend, 14,195
Missouri City, 55,958
Nassau Bay, 4,616
Needville, 2,954

Oak Ridge North, 3,128
Pasadena, 131,620
Pecan Grove, 9,502
Piney Point Village, 3,549
Prairie View, 4,052
Richmond, 13,231
Rosenberg, 26,442
Seabrook, 8,648
South Houston, 15,064
Spring, 33,111
Spring Valley, 3,830
Stafford, 12,543
Sugar Land, 47,810
Taylor Lake Village, 3,947
The Woodlands, 29,205
Tomball, 7,237
Town West, 6,166
Webster, 5,040
West University Place, 13,810
Willis, 3,352

HUNTINGTON-ASHLAND, WV-KY-OH

Huntington Herald-Dispatch
946 Fifth Ave.
Huntington 25720
(304) 526-4000
www.hdonline.com

Cabell-Huntington CVB
P.O. Box 347
Huntington 25708
(800) 635-6329
www.wvvisit.org

Huntington Regional C/C
720 Fourth Ave.
Huntington 25701
(304) 525-5131
www.tristate-online.com/chamber

C/C of Boyd & Greenup Counties
207 Fifteenth St.
Ashland 41105
(606) 324-5111
Ashland, KY, 22,918
Barboursville, WV, 2,780
Flatwoods, KY, 7,964
Grayson, KY, 4,014
Huntington, WV, 53,941
Ironton, OH, 12,871
Kenova, WV, 3,686
Pea Ridge, WV, 6,535
Russell, KY, 4,025
South Point, OH, 4,170
Westwood, KY, 5,300

HUNTSVILLE, AL

Huntsville Times/News
P.O. Box 1487
Hunstville 35801
(256) 532-4000
www.al.com/huntsville

Huntsville-Madison County CVB
700 Monroe St.
Huntsville 35801
(800) 772-2348
www.huntsville.org

Huntsville and Madison County C/C
226 Church St. NW
Huntsville 35801
(256) 535-2000
www.hsvchamber.org
Athens, 19,112
Huntsville, 170,424
Madison, 23,620
New Hope, 2,838

INDIANAPOLIS, IN

Indianapolis Star/News
307 N. Pennsylvania St.
Indianapolis 46204
(317) 633-1240
www.starnews.com

Indianapolis CVB
One RCA Dome
Indianapolis 46225
(800) 958-4639
www.indy.org

Indianapolis C/C
320 N. Meridian St.
Indianapolis 46204
(317) 464-2200
www.indychamber.com
Alexandria, 5,769
Anderson, 59,131
Beech Grove, 13,239
Brownsburg, 9,960
Carmel, 36,837
Chesterfield, 2,772
Cicero, 4,201
Cumberland, 5,012
Danville, 4,982
Edinburgh, 4,605
Elwood, 9,119
Fishers, 20,665
Fortville, 3,075
Franklin, 16,356
Greenfield, 13,003
Greenwood, 30,600
Indianapolis, 731,327

Lawrence, 32,642
Lebanon, 13,200
Martinsville, 12,155
Mooresville, 7,553
New Whiteland, 4,708
Noblesville, 23,960
Pendleton, 2,729
Plainfield, 17,235
Shelbyville, 16,429
Speedway, 12,582
Westfield, 7,426
Whiteland, 3,452
Zionsville, 6,257

IOWA CITY, IA

Iowa City Press-Citizen
1725 N. Dodge St.
Iowa City 52245
(319) 337-3181
www.uiowa.edu/~dlyiowan

Iowa City/Coralville CVB
408 E. 1st Ave.
Coralville 52240
(800) 283-6592
www.icccvb.org

Iowa City Area C/C
325 E. Washington St.
Iowa City 52244
(319) 337-9637
www.icarea.com
Coralville, 11,789
Iowa City, 60,923
North Liberty, 4,039

JACKSON, MI

Jackson Citizen Patriot
214 S. Jackson St.
Jackson 49201
(517) 781-2300
ja.mlive.com/index.html

Jackson CTB
6007 Ann Arbor Rd.
Jackson 49201
(800) 245-5282
www.jackson-mich.org

Greater Jackson C/C
209 E. Washington Ave.
Jackson 49201
(517) 782-8221
Brooklyn, 1,000
Grass Lake, 1,012
Jackson, 35,899

JACKSON, MS

Clarion-Ledger
311 E. Pearl St.
Jackson 39205
(601) 961-7000
www.clarionledger.com

Metro Jackson CVB
921 N. President St.
Jackson 39215
(800) 354-7695
www.visitjackson.com

Metro Jackson C/C
201 S. President St.
Jackson 39225
(601) 948-7575
www.metrochamber.com
Brandon, 13,444
Canton, 10,328
Clinton, 21,992
Flowood, 4,038
Jackson, 192,923
Madison, 11,703
Pearl, 21,175
Richland, 5,383
Ridgeland, 15,579

JACKSON, TN

Jackson Sun
245 W. Lafayette St.
Jackson 38301
(901) 427-3333

The Jackson Chamber
197 Auditorium St.
Jackson 38302
(901) 423-2200
www.jacksontn.com
Henderson, 5,363
Jackson, 50,406

JACKSONVILLE, FL

Florida Times-Union
One Riverside Ave.
Jacksonville 32202
(904) 359-4111
jacksonville.com

Jacksonville & the Beaches CVB
3 Independent Dr.
Jacksonville 32202
(800) 733-2668

Jacksonville C/C
1817 N. Myrtle Ave.
Jacksonville 32202
(904) 366-6600
www.jacksonvillechamber.org
Atlantic Beach, 12,821
Bellair-Meadowbrook Terrace,
15,606
Fernandina Beach, 9,941
Fruit Cove, 5,904
Green Cove Springs, 5,156
Jacksonville Beach, 19,906
Lakeside, 29,137
Middleburg, 6,223
Neptune Beach, 7,086
Orange Park, 9,861
Palm Valley, 9,960
St. Augustine, 12,167
St. Augustine Beach, 4,232
Yulee, 6,915

JACKSONVILLE, NC

Jacksonville Daily News
724 Bell Fork Rd.
Jacksonville 28540
(910) 353-1171
www.jacksonvilledailynews.com

Greater Jacksonville/Onslow C/C
One Marine Blvd. N
Jacksonville 28541
(910) 347-3141
Camp Lejeune Central, 36,716
Half Moon, 6,306
Jacksonville, 69,889
New River Station, 9,732
Piney Green, 8,999

JAMESTOWN, NY

The Post-Journal
15 W. 2nd St.
Jamestown 14701
(716) 487-1111

Jamestown Area C/C
101 W. Fifth St.
Jamestown 14701
(716) 484-1101
Dunkirk, 13,354
Falconer, 2,591
Fredonia, 10,222
Jamestown, 33,154
Lakewood, 3,412
Silver Creek, 2,850
Westfield, 3,402

JANESVILLE-BELOIT, WI

Janesville Gazette
One S. Parker Dr.
Janesville 53547
(608) 754-3311
www.gazettextra.com

Beloit CVB
1003 Plesant St.
Beloit 53512
(608) 365-4838

Forward Janesville
20 S. Main St.
Janesville 53545
(800) 486-2757

Greater Beloit C/C
136 W. Grand Ave.
Beloit 53511
(608) 365-9170
Beloit, 35,836
Edgerton, 4,475
Evansville, 3,527
Janesville, 58,960
Milton, 4,850

JERSEY CITY, NJ

The Jersey Journal
30 Journal Sq.
Jersey City 07306
(201) 217-2455
www.nj.com

Hudson County C/C
574 Summit Ave.
Jersey City 07306
(201) 653-7400
Bayonne, 60,499
Guttenberg, 8,266
Harrison, 13,248
Hoboken, 33,136
Jersey City, 229,039
Kearny, 35,112
North Bergen, 48,414
Secaucus, 13,823
Union City, 57,126
Weehawken, 12,385
West New York, 37,695

JOHNSON CITY-KINGSPORT-BRISTOL, TN-VA

Johnson City Press
204 W. Main St.
Johnson City 37604
(615) 929-3111

Kingsport Times-News
701 Lynn Garden Dr.
Kingsport 37662
(615) 246-8121
www.timesnews.net

Bristol Herald Courier
320 Morrison Blvd.
Bristol 24201
(540) 669-2181
www.bristolnews.com

Johnson City/Jonesborough/
Washington County C/C
603 E. Market St.
Johnson City 37601
(423) 461-8000

Kingsport CVB
151 E. Main St.
Kingsport 37660
(800) 743-5282
kingsport.tricon.net/bureau.htm

Bristol C/C & VCC
20 Volunteer Pkwy.
Bristol 24203
(423) 989-4850
www.bristoltn.org

Kingsport Area C/C
151 E. Main St.
Kingsport 37662
(423) 392-8800
www.kingsportchamber.org
Abingdon, VA 7,687
Bloomingdale, TN, 10,953
Bristol, TN, 23,275
Bristol, VA, 17,957
Church Hill, TN, 5,901
Colonial Heights, TN, 6,716
Elizabethton, TN, 13,289
Erwin, TN, 5,061
Johnson City, TN, 55,542
Jonesborough, TN, 3,472
Kingsport, TN, 41,335
Mount , TN, 4,554
Rogersville, TN, 4,535

JOHNSTOWN, PA

Tribune Democrat
425 Locust St.
Johnstown 15907
(814) 532-5199

Greater Johnstown C/C
111 Market St.
Johnstown 15901
(814) 539-3838
www.citipage.com/chamber
Ebensburg, 3,708
Geistown, 2,646
Johnstown, 26,149
Nanty-Glo, 3,024
Portage, 2,936
Somerset, 6,337
Westmont, 5,519
Windber, 4,519

JONESBORO, AR

Jonesboro Sun
P.O. Box 1249
Jonesboro 72403
(870) 935-5525
www.jonesborosun.com

Greater Jonesboro C/C
593 S. Madison
Jonesboro 72403
(870) 932-6691
Bay, 1,772
Jonesboro, 52,656
Lake City, 1,896

JOPLIN, MO

Joplin Globe
117 E. Fourth St.
Joplin 64801
(417) 623-3480
www.joplinglobe.com

Joplin CVB
211 S. Main St.
Joplin 64801
(417) 625-4791

Joplin Area C/C
320 E. Fourth St.
Joplin 64801
(417) 624-4150
www.joplincc.com
Carl Junction, 5,080
Carthage, 11,381
Joplin, 43,698
Neosho, 9,399
Webb City, 8,488

KALAMAZOO-
BATTLE CREEK, MI

Kalamazoo Gazette
401 S. Burdick St.
Kalamazoo 49007
(616) 345-3511
kz.mlive.com/index.html

Kalamazoo County CVB
128 N. Kalamazoo Mall
Kalamazoo 49005
(800) 530-9192
www.kalamazoomi.com/conv.htm

Kalamazoo C/C
128 N. Kalamazoo Mall
Kalamazoo 49007
(616) 381-4000
www.kazoobiz.com

Battle Creek Area C/C
34 W. Jackson
Battle Creek 49017
(616) 962-4076
www.battlecreek.org
Albion, 9,884
Battle Creek, 53,430
Eastwood, 6,340
Kalamazoo, 77,460
Marshall, 7,251
Mattawan, 2,858
Paw Paw, 3,279
Portage, 43,317
South Haven, 5,429
Springfield, 5,654
Westwood, 8,957

KANKAKEE, IL

Daily Journal
8 Dearborn Sq.
Kankakee 60901
(815) 937-3300
www.daily-journal.com

Kankakee Area C/C
4 Dearborn Sq.
Kankakee 60901
(815) 933-7721
Bourbonnais, 15,262
Bradley, 12,368
Kankakee, 27,217
Manteno, 4,757
Momence, 2,856

KANSAS CITY, MO-KS

Kansas City Star
1729 Grand Blvd.
Kansas City 64108
(816) 234-4280
www.kcstar.com

Greater Kansas City CVB
1100 Main St.
Kansas City 64105
(800) 767-7700
www.visitkc.com

Greater Kansas City C/C
11040 Holmes St.
Kansas City 64131
(816) 942-4333
www.kcity.com

Belton, MO, 20,862
Blue Springs, MO, 44,667
Bonner Springs, KS, 6,541
Buckner, MO, 2,777
Cameron, MO, 7,672
De Soto, KS, 2,977
Edwardsville, KS, 4,097
Excelsior Springs, MO, 11,293
Fairway, KS, 4,178
Gardner, KS, 5,601
Gladstone, MO, 27,819
Grain Valley, MO, 3,248
Grandview, MO, 24,040
Harrisonville, MO, 8,450
Higginsville, MO, 4,503
Independence, MO, 110,303
Kansas City, KS, 142,654
Kansas City, MO, 441,259
Kearney, MO, 4,025
Lansing, KS, 7,996
Leavenworth, KS, 39,431
Leawood, KS, 24,786
Lee's Summit, MO, 61,861
Lenexa, KS, 37,462
Lexington, MO, 4,540
Liberty, MO, 24,270
Merriam, KS, 12,160
Mission, KS, 9,535
Mission Hills, KS, 3,440
North Kansas City, MO, 4,225
Oak Grove, MO, 4,842
Odessa, MO, 3,987
Olathe, KS, 78,666
Osawatomie, KS, 4,514
Overland Park, KS, 131,053
Paola, KS, 4,751
Parkville, MO, 3,250
Platte City, MO, 3,317
Pleasant Hill, MO, 4,644
Pleasant Valley, MO, 3,173
Prairie Village, KS, 23,545
Raymore, MO, 8,257
Raytown, MO, 29,429
Richmond, MO, 5,766
Riverside, MO, 3,318
Roeland Park, KS, 7,703
Shawnee, KS, 43,006
Smithville, MO, 3,609
Sugar Creek, MO, 3,798
Tonganoxie, KS, 2,764

KENOSHA, WI

Kenosha News
715 58th St.
Kenosha 53141
(262) 657-1000
www.kenoshanews.com

Kenosha Area C/C
7360 57th Ave.
Kenosha 53142
(262) 697-1234

Kenosha, 86,888
Paddock Lake, 2,916
Pleasant Prairie, 13,787
Twin Lakes, 4,679

KILLEEN-TEMPLE, TX

Killeen Daily Herald
1809 Florence St.
Killeen 76541
(254) 634-2125
www.kdhnews.com

Temple Daily Telegram
P.O. Box 6114
Temple 76503
(254) 778-4444
www.temple-telegram.com

Temple C/C
2 N. 5th St.
Temple 76503
(254) 773-2105
www.temple-tx.org

Greater Killeen C/C
One Santa Fe Plaza
Killeen 76540
(254) 526-9551
www.gkcc.com

Belton, 14,800
Copperas Cove, 30,311
Fort Hood, 18,559
Gatesville, 12,130
Harker Heights, 17,131
Killeen, 78,022
Temple, 51,394

KITCHENER-WATERLOO, ON

Kitchener-Waterloo Record
225 FairWay Rd. S
Kitchener N2G 4E5
(519) 894-2231
southam.com/
kitchenerwaterloorecord

C/C of Kitchener and Waterloo
80 Queen St. N
Kitchener N2H 6L4
(519) 576-5000
kitwatchamber.on.ca/advocate.htm

Cambridge, 101,429
Kitchener, 178,420
North Dumfries, 7,817
Waterloo, 77,949
Woolwich, 17,325

KNOXVILLE, TN

Knoxville News-Sentinel
208 W. Church Ave.
Knoxville 37902
(423) 523-3131
www.knoxnews.com

Knoxville Area CVB
601 W. Summit Hill Dr.
Knoxville 37902
(800) 727-8045
www.knoxville.org

Greater Knoxville C/C
301 E. Church Ave.
Knoxville 37915
(423) 637-4550
www.knoxchamber.org

Alcoa, 7,137
Clinton, 9,320
Eagleton Village, 5,169
Farragut, 16,223
Gatlinburg, 4,323
Halls, 6,450
Knoxville, 167,535
Lenoir City, 8,890
Loudon, 4,544
Maryville, 23,042
Oak Ridge, 27,742
Oliver Springs, 3,470
Pigeon Forge, 3,951
Powell, 7,534
Sevierville, 9,742
Seymour, 5,104

KOKOMO, IN

Kokomo Tribune
300 N. Union St.
Kokomo 46901
(765) 456-3821
www.ktonline.com

Howard County CVB
1504 N. Reed Rd.
Kokomo 46901
(800) 837-0971
www.iquest.net/kokomoin

Kokomo/Howard County C/C
106 N. Washington St.
Kokomo 46901
(765) 457-5301
www.kokomochamber.com
Greentown, 2,301
Kokomo, 45,785
Tipton, 4,725

LA CROSSE, WI-MN

La Crosse Tribune
401 N. 3rd St.
La Crosse 54601
(608) 782-9701
www.lacrossetribune.com

La Crosse Area CVB
410 E. Veterans Memorial Dr.
La Crosse 54602
(800) 658-9424

La Crosse Area C/C
712 Main St.
La Crosse 54602
(608) 784-4880
www.wi.centuryinter.net/lacrosse
Caledonia, MN, 2,953
Holmen, WI, 4,481
La Crescent, MN, 4,598
La Crosse, WI, 50,212
Onalaska, WI, 13,546
West Salem, WI, 4,012

LAFAYETTE, LA

Advertiser
P.O. Box 3268
Lafayette 70502
(318) 289-6300
www.acadiananow.com
    advrtsr2.html

Lafayette Parish CVB
1400 NW Evangeline Thrwy.
Lafayette 70505
(800) 346-1958
www.travelfile.com/get?lcvc

Greater Lafayette C/C
804 E. St. Mary Blvd.
Lafayette 70503
(318) 233-2705
www.lafchamber.org
Breaux Bridge, 6,837
Broussard, 3,685
Carencro, 5,921
Church Point, 4,804
Crowley, 13,809
Eunice, 11,182
Lafayette, 104,899
Opelousas, 19,117
Rayne, 8,561
Scott, 5,484
St. Martinville, 7,323

LAFAYETTE, IN

Journal & Courier
217 N. 6th St.
Lafayette 47901
(765) 423-5511
www.jconline.com

Greater Lafayette CVB
301 Frontage Rd.
Lafayette 47903
(800) 872-6648
www.wwb.com/company/
    c006428.html

Greater Lafayette C/C
122 N. Third St.
Lafayette 47902
(765) 742-4041
www.lafayettechamber.com
Frankfort, 15,231
Lafayette, 44,344
West Lafayette, 27,177

LAKE CHARLES, LA

Lake Charles American Press
P.O. Box 2893
Lake Charles 70602
(318) 433-3000
www.americanpress.com

Southwest Louisiana CVB
1211 N. Lakeshore Dr.
Lake Charles 70601
(800) 456-7952
www.travelfile.com/get?swllcCVB

The Chamber of Southwest
    Louisiana
120 Pujo St.
Lake Charles 70602
(318) 433-3632
De Quincy, 3,742
Iowa, 2,748
Lake Charles, 71,445
Moss Bluff, 8,039
Prien, 6,448
Sulphur, 20,883
Vinton, 3,194
Westlake, 5,039

LAKELAND-WINTER HAVEN, FL

The Ledger
33815 W. Lime St.
Lakeland 33802
(941) 802-7000
www.theledger.com

Lakeland C/C
35 Lake Morton Dr.
Lakeland 33802
(941) 688-8551
lakeland.tsolv.com/~chamber

Winter Haven Area C/C
401 Avenue B NW
Winter Haven 33881
(941) 293-2138
www.winterhavenfl.com/chamber
Auburndale, 9,466
Bartow, 15,003
Combee Settlement, 5,463
Crystal Lake, 5,300
Cypress Gardens, 9,188
Dundee, 2,518
Fort Meade, 5,246
Frostproof, 2,913
Gibsonia, 5,168
Haines City, 12,352
Inwood, 6,824
Jan Phyl Village, 5,308
Lake Alfred, 3,711
Lake Wales, 9,930
Lakeland, 73,157
Lakeland Highlands, 9,972
Mulberry, 3,040
Winston, 9,118
Winter Haven, 25,484

LANCASTER, PA

Lancaster New Era/Intelligencer Journal
8 W. King St.
Lancaster 17603
(717) 291-8733
www.lancnews.com/lancaster

Pennsylvania Dutch Lancaster
County CVB
Greenfield Rd.
Lancaster 17603
(800) 723-8824
www.800padutch.com/pdcvb.html

Lancaster C/C and Industry
100 S. Queen St.
Lancaster 17608
(717) 397-3531
www.lcci.com
Akron, 4,061
Columbia, 10,587
Denver, 3,138
East Petersburg, 4,472
Elizabethtown, 10,677
Ephrata, 12,954
Lancaster, 53,597
Leacock-Leola-Bareville, 5,685
Lititz, 8,533
Manheim, 4,903
Marietta, 2,683
Millersville, 7,958
Mount Joy, 6,517
New Holland, 4,783
Strasburg, 2,633
Willow Street, 5,817

LANSING-EAST LANSING, MI

Lansing State Journal
120 E. Lenawee
Lansing 48919
(517) 377-1000
www.lansingstatejournal.com

Greater Lansing CVB
119 Pere Marquette
Lansing 48901
(800) 968-8474
www.lansing.org

Lansing Regional C/C
300 E. Michigan Ave.
Lansing 48901
(517) 487-6340
www.lansingchamber.org
Charlotte, 8,002
De Witt, 4,419

East Lansing, 48,192
Eaton Rapids, 4,733
Grand Ledge, 7,770
Haslett, 10,230
Holt, 11,744
Lansing, 125,736
Mason, 7,374
Okemos, 20,216
St. Johns, 7,555
Waverly, 15,614
Williamston, 2,960

LAREDO, TX

Laredo Morning Times
111 Esperanza Dr.
Laredo 78041
(210) 728-2500
lmtonline.com

City of Laredo CVB
501 San Agustin
Laredo 78040
(800) 361-3360
www.visitlaredo.com

Laredo-Webb County C/C
2310 San Bernardo Ave.
Laredo 78040
(210) 722-9895
El Cenizo, 1,534
Laredo, 164,899
Rio Bravo, 3,450

LAS CRUCES, NM

Sun-News
256 W. Las Cruces Ave.
Las Cruces 88005
(505) 523-4581

Las Cruces CVB
311 N. Downtown Mall
Las Cruces 88001
(800) 343-7827

Las Cruces C/C
760 W. Picacho Ave.
Las Cruces 88005
(505) 524-1968
www.lascruces.org/chamber
Anthony, 5,160
Las Cruces, 74,779
Sunland Park, 9,265

LAS VEGAS, NV-AZ

Las Vegas Review-Journal
1111 W. Bonanza
Las Vegas 89106
(702) 383-0211
www.lvrj.com

Las Vegas CVB
3150 Paradise Rd.
Las Vegas 89109
(800) 332-5333
www.lasvegas24hours.com

Las Vegas C/C
711 E. Desert Inn Rd.
Las Vegas 89109
(702) 735-1616
www.lvchamber.com
Boulder City, AZ, 14,249
Colorado City, AZ, 3,509
East Las Vegas, NV, 11,087
Enterprise, NV, 6,412
Henderson, NV, 122,339
Kingman, AZ, 17,270
Lake Havasu City, AZ, 39,503
Las Vegas, NV, 376,906
Mesquite, NV, 6,200
Mohave Valley, AZ, 6,962
New Kingman-Butler, AZ, 11,627
North Las Vegas, NV, 78,659
Pahrump, NV, 7,424
Paradise, NV, 124,682
Spring Valley, NV, 51,726
Sunrise Manor, NV, 95,362
Winchester, NV, 23,365

LAWRENCE, KS

Lawrence Journal-World
P.O. Box 888
Lawrence 66044
(913) 843-1000
www.ljworld.com

Lawrence CVB
North 2nd St. & Locust St.
Lawrence 66044
(888) 529-5267
www.visitlawrence.com

Lawrence C/C
734 Vermont St. #101
Lawrence 66044
(913) 865-4411
www.lawrencekansas.org
Baldwin City, 2,789
Eudora, 3,713
Lawrence, 71,887

LAWRENCE, MA-NH

Eagle Tribune
P.O. Box 100
Lawrence 01842
(978) 685-1000
www.eagletribune.com

Haverhill Gazette
447 W. Lowell Ave.
Haverhill 02601
(800) 836-7800
www.hgazette.com

Merrimack Valley C/C
264 Essex St.
Lawrence 01840
(978) 686-0900
www.merrimackvalleychamber.com
Andover, MA, 30,891
Atkinson, NH, 6,275
Boxford, MA, 8,550
Chester, NH, 3,168
Danville, NH, 3,068
Derry, NH, 31,452
Fremont, NH, 3,102
Georgetown, MA, 7,054
Groveland, MA, 5,610
Hampstead, NH, 7,486
Haverhill, MA, 53,952
Kingston, NH, 5,893
Lawrence, MA, 68,807
Merrimac, MA, 5,670
Newton, NH, 3,663
North Andover, MA, 24,283
Plaistow, NH, 7,685
Raymond, NH, 9,537
Salem, NH, 27,195
Sandown, NH, 4,739
West Newbury, MA, 3,871
Windham, NH, 9,713

LAWTON, OK

Lawton Constitution
P.O. Box 2068
Lawton 73502
(580) 585-5070
www.lawton-constitution.com

Lawton C/C & Ind.
607 SW C Ave.
Lawton 73501
(580) 355-3541
www.lcci.org
Cache, 2,375
Fort Sill, 12,107
Lawton, 82,582

LEWISTON-AUBURN, ME

Sun-Journal
104 Park St.
Lewiston 04243
(207) 784-5411
www.sun-journal.com

Androscoggin County C/C
179 Lisbon St.
Lewiston 04240
(207) 783-2249
Auburn, 22,997
Greene, 3,757
Lewiston, 36,830
Lisbon, 9,342
Mechanic Falls, 2,873
Poland, 4,550
Sabattus, 3,683
Turner, 4,484

LEXINGTON, KY

Lexington Herald-Leader
100 Midland Ave.
Lexington 40508
(606) 231-3100
kentuckyconnect.com/heraldleader

Greater Lexington CVB
430 W. Vine St.
Lexington 40507
(606) 233-1221

Greater Lexington C/C
330 E. Main St.
Lexington 40507
(606) 254-4447
www.lexchamber.com
Berea, 10,007
Georgetown, 13,614
Lexington, 239,942
Nicholasville, 16,603
Paris, 8,788
Richmond, 26,227
Versailles, 6,882
Wilmore, 4,493
Winchester, 16,021

LIMA, OH

Lima News
3515 Elida Rd.
Lima 45802
(419) 223-1010
www.limanews.com

Lima/Allen County C/C
147 N. Main St.
Lima 45801
(419) 222-6045
www.chamber.lima.oh.us
Bluffton, 3,558
Delphos, 6,908
Fort Shawnee, 4,146
Lima, 42,913
Minster, 2,893
New Bremen, 2,801
St. Marys, 8,592
Wapakoneta, 9,414

LINCOLN, NE

Lincoln Journal-Star
926 P St.
Lincoln 68508
(402) 475-4200
www.journalstar.com

Lincoln CVB
1135 M St.
Lincoln 68508
(800) 423-8212
www.lincoln.org/CVB

Lincoln C/C
1221 N St.
Lincoln 68508
(402) 436-2350
www.lcoc.com
Hickman, 1,150
Lincoln, 209,192
Waverly, 1,960

LITTLE ROCK-NORTH LITTLE ROCK, AR

Arkansas Democrat-Gazette
Capitol Ave. & Scott St.
Little Rock 72203
(501) 378-3400
www.ardemgaz.com

Little Rock CVB
P.O. Box 3232
Little Rock 72203
(800) 844-4781
www.wwb.com/brochure/
b050888.html

Greater Little Rock C/C
One Spring St.
Little Rock 72201
(501) 374-4871
www.littlerockchamber.com

Benton, 22,036
Bryant, 8,286
Cabot, 12,956
Conway, 35,827
England, 3,679
Greenbrier, 2,965
Jacksonville, 29,191
Little Rock, 175,752
Lonoke, 4,452
Maumelle, 7,962
North Little Rock, 60,468
Sherwood, 20,902

LONDON, ON

The London Free Press
369 York St.
London N6A 4G1
(519) 679-1111
www.lfpress.com

London VCB
300 York St.
London N6A 4G1
(800) 265-2602

London C/C
244 Pall Mall St.
London N6A 5P6
(519) 432-7551
www.chamber.london.on.ca

Belmont, 1,632
Delaware, 2,436
Lobo, 5,553
London, 325,646
North Dorchester, 8,665
Port Stanley, 2,499
St. Thomas, 32,275
Southwold, 4,282
West Nissouri, 3,484
Yarmouth, 7,148

LONG ISLAND, NY

Newsday
235 Pinelawn Rd.
Melville 11747
(516) 843-2020
www.newsday.com

Long Island Assn.
80 Hauppauge Rd.
Commack 11725
(516) 499-4400
www.longislandassociation.org

Albertson, 5,166
Amityville, 9,143
Babylon, 12,056
Baldwin, 22,719
Baldwin Harbor, 7,899

Bay Shore, 21,279
Bayport, 7,702
Bayville, 7,287
Baywood, 7,351
Bellmore, 16,438
Bellport, 2,533
Bethpage, 15,761
Bohemia, 9,556
Brentwood, 45,218
Brightwaters, 3,194
Brookville, 3,859
Carle Place, 5,107
Cedarhurst, 5,715
Center Moriches, 5,987
Centereach, 26,720
Centerport, 5,333
Central Islip, 26,028
Commack, 36,124
Copiague, 20,769
Coram, 30,111
Deer Park, 28,840
Dix Hills, 25,849
East Hills, 6,781
East Islip, 14,325
East Massapequa, 19,550
East Meadow, 36,909
East Northport, 20,411
East Patchogue, 20,195
East Rockaway, 10,214
East Shoreham, 5,461
East Williston, 2,517
Elmont, 28,612
Elwood, 10,916
Farmingdale, 8,113
Farmingville, 14,842
Floral Park, 15,966
Flower Hill, 4,528
Fort Salonga, 9,176
Franklin Square, 28,205
Freeport, 40,164
Garden City, 21,721
Garden City Park, 7,437
Glen Cove, 24,716
Great Neck, 8,845
Great Neck Estates, 2,798
Great Neck Plaza, 5,921
Greenlawn, 13,208
Hampton Bays, 7,893
Hauppauge, 19,750
Hempstead, 46,609
Hewlett, 6,620
Hicksville, 40,174
Holbrook, 25,273
Holtsville, 14,972
Huntington, 18,243
Huntington Station, 28,247
Inwood, 7,767
Island Park, 4,882
Islandia, 2,856
Islip, 18,924
Islip Terrace, 5,530
Jericho, 13,141
Kings Park, 17,773

Kings Point, 4,890
Lake Grove, 9,680
Lake Ronkonkoma, 18,997
Lakeview, 5,476
Lawrence, 6,542
Levittown, 53,286
Lindenhurst, 26,499
Lloyd Harbor, 3,392
Long Beach, 34,335
Lynbrook, 19,443
Malverne, 9,076
Manhasset, 7,718
Manorhaven, 5,768
Manorville, 6,198
Massapequa, 22,018
Massapequa Park, 18,177
Mastic, 13,778
Mastic Beach, 10,293
Medford, 21,274
Melville, 12,586
Merrick, 23,042
Middle Island, 7,848
Miller Place, 9,315
Mineola, 19,054
Mount Sinai, 8,023
Munsey Park, 2,701
Muttontown, 3,161
Nesconset, 10,712
New Cassel, 10,257
New Hyde Park, 9,817
North Amityville, 13,849
North Babylon, 18,081
North Bay Shore, 12,799
North Bellmore, 19,707
North Bellport, 8,182
North Hills, 3,837
North Lindenhurst, 10,563
North Massapequa, 19,365
North Merrick, 12,113
North New Hyde Park, 14,359
North Patchogue, 7,374
North Valley Stream, 14,574
North Wantagh, 12,276
Northport, 7,447
Oakdale, 7,875
Oceanside, 32,423
Old Bethpage, 5,610
Old Westbury, 3,992
Oyster Bay, 6,687
Patchogue, 11,008
Plainedge, 8,739
Plainview, 26,207
Port Jefferson, 7,569
Port Jefferson Station, 7,232
Port Washington, 15,387
Port Washington North, 2,766
Ridge, 11,734
Riverhead, 8,814
Rockville Centre, 24,787
Rocky Point, 8,596
Ronkonkoma, 20,391
Roosevelt, 15,030
Roslyn Heights, 6,405

Salisbury, 12,226
Sands Point, 2,536
Sayville, 16,550
Sea Cliff, 5,053
Seaford, 15,597
Searingtown, 5,020
Selden, 20,608
Setauket, 13,634
Shirley, 22,936
Smithtown, 25,638
Sound Beach, 9,102
South Farmingdale, 15,377
South Huntington, 9,624
South Valley Stream, 5,328
Southampton, 4,051
Southold, 5,192
St. James, 12,703
Stony Brook, 13,726
Syosset, 18,967
Terryville, 10,275
Thomaston, 2,633
Uniondale, 20,328
Valley Stream, 34,091
Wading River, 5,317
Wantagh, 18,567
West Babylon, 42,410
West Hempstead, 17,689
West Hills, 5,849
West Islip, 28,419
Westbury, 13,176
Wheatley Heights, 5,027
Williston Park, 7,513
Woodbury, 8,008
Woodmere, 15,578
Wyandanch, 8,950

LONGVIEW-MARSHALL, TX

Longview News Journal
320 Methvin St.
Longview 75601
(903) 757-3311
www.news-journal.com

Marshall News Messenger
309 E. Austin St.
Marshall 75670
(903) 935-7914
www.coxnews.com/marshall.htm

Longview CVB
410 N. Center St.
Longview 78840
(903) 753-3281
www.longviewtx.com

Longview C/C
306 S. Mobberly Ave.
Longview 75602
(903) 236-0417

Greater Marshall C/C & CVB
213 W. Austin St.
Marshall 75670
(903) 935-7868
Gilmer, 5,509
Gladewater, 6,487
Hallsville, 2,570
Kilgore, 11,472
Longview, 74,572
Marshall, 24,147
White Oak, 5,741

LOS ANGELES-LONG BEACH, CA

Los Angeles Times
Times Mirror Sq.
Los Angeles 90012
(213) 237-5000
www.latimes.com

Los Angeles CVB
633 W. Fifth St.
Los Angeles 90024
(800) 689-8822
www.wwb.com/company/
    c006849.html

Long Beach Area CVB
One World Trade Center
Long Beach 90831
(800) 452-7829
www.ci.long-beach.ca.us

Los Angeles Area C/C
404 S. Bixel St.
Los Angeles 90051
(213) 629-0602
www.lachamber.org
Agoura Hills, 20,718
Alhambra, 83,644
Alondra Park, 12,215
Altadena, 42,658
Arcadia, 50,483
Artesia, 15,758
Avalon, 3,091
Avocado Heights, 14,232
Azusa, 42,124
Baldwin Park, 71,414
Bell, 35,077
Bell Gardens, 44,101
Bellflower, 63,220
Beverly Hills, 32,367
Burbank, 96,579
Carson, 86,516
Cerritos, 53,645
Charter Oak, 8,858
Citrus, 9,481
Claremont, 33,507
Commerce, 12,574
Compton, 91,700

Covina, 44,290
Cudahy, 23,355
Culver City, 39,292
Del Aire, 8,040
Diamond Bar, 54,138
Downey, 93,073
Duarte, 21,318
East Compton, 7,967
East La Mirada, 9,367
East Los Angeles, 126,379
East Pasadena, 5,910
East San Gabriel, 12,736
El Monte, 110,026
El Segundo, 15,607
Florence-Graham, 57,147
Gardena, 53,104
Glendale, 184,321
Glendora, 51,500
Hacienda Heights, 52,354
Hawaiian Gardens, 13,621
Hawthorne, 72,942
Hermosa Beach, 18,522
Huntington Park, 57,251
Inglewood, 111,040
La Canada Flintridge, 19,738
La Crescenta-Montrose, 16,968
La Habra Heights, 6,429
La Mirada, 43,871
La Puente, 38,462
La Verne, 31,996
Ladera Heights, 6,316
Lake Los Angeles, 7,977
Lakewood, 75,462
Lancaster, 115,675
Lawndale, 28,527
Lennox, 22,757
Lomita, 19,803
Long Beach, 421,904
Los Angeles, 3,553,638
Lynwood, 62,916
Manhattan Beach, 33,234
Marina Del Rey, 7,431
Maywood, 28,200
Monrovia, 37,265
Montebello, 60,281
Monterey Park, 61,912
Norwalk, 100,209
Palmdale, 106,540
Palos Verdes Estates, 13,721
Paramount, 50,793
Pasadena, 134,116
Pico Rivera, 59,968
Pomona, 134,706
Quartz Hill, 9,626
Rancho Palos Verdes, 42,340
Redondo Beach, 62,367
Rolling Hills Estates, 7,955
Rosemead, 52,700
Rowland Heights, 42,647
San Dimas, 33,691
San Fernando, 22,904
San Gabriel, 37,697
San Marino, 12,949
Santa Clarita, 125,153

Santa Fe Springs, 15,238
Santa Monica, 88,471
Sierra Madre, 10,877
Signal Hill, 8,671
South El Monte, 21,142
South Gate, 88,125
South Pasadena, 24,091
South San Gabriel, 7,700
South San Jose Hills, 17,814
South Whittier, 49,514
Temple City, 31,721
Torrance, 136,183
Valinda, 18,735
View Park, 11,769
Vincent, 13,713
Walnut, 30,848
Walnut Park, 14,722
West Athens, 8,859
West Carson, 20,143
West Compton, 5,451
West Covina, 101,526
West Hollywood, 36,501
West Puente Valley, 20,254
West Whittier, 24,164
Westlake Village, 7,780
Westmont, 31,044
Whittier, 78,740
Willowbrook, 32,772

LOUISVILLE, KY-IN

Courier-Journal
525 W. Broadway St.
Louisville 40202
(502) 582-4011
www.courier-journal.com

Louisville CVB
400 S. First St.
Louisville 40202
(800) 626-5646
www.louisville-visitors.com

Louisville Area C/C
600 W. Main St.
Louisville 40202
(502) 625-0000
www.lacc.org
Austin, IN, 4,371
Buechel, KY, 7,081
Charlestown, IN, 6,022
Clarksville, IN, 19,749
Corydon, IN, 2,652
Douglass Hills, KY, 5,195
Fairdale, KY, 6,563
Fern Creek, KY, 16,406
Graymoor, KY, 3,074
Highview, KY, 14,814
Hillview, KY, 5,815
Hurstbourne, KY, 4,698
Jeffersontown, KY, 25,596

Jeffersonville, IN, 25,787
La Grange, KY, 5,040
Louisville, KY, 260,689
Lyndon, KY, 7,675
Middletown, KY, 5,298
Mount Washington, KY, 7,051
New Albany, IN, 38,224
Newburg, KY, 21,647
Oak Park, IN, 5,630
Okolona, KY, 18,902
Pleasure Ridge Park, KY, 25,131
Prospect, KY, 2,963
St. Dennis, KY, 10,326
St. Matthews, KY, 16,562
Scottsburg, IN, 5,708
Sellersburg, IN, 6,028
Shepherdsville, IN, 4,667
Shively, KY, 14,899
Valley Station, KY, 22,840

LOWELL, MA-NH

Lowell Sun
15 Kearney Sq.
Lowell 01853
(978) 458-7100
www.newschoice.com/newspapers/
lowell/sun

Lowell C/C
77 Merrimack St.
Lowell 01852
(978) 459-8154
Billerica, MA, 38,861
Chelmsford, MA, 33,484
Dracut, MA, 27,769
Dunstable, MA, 2,585
Groton, MA, 8,789
Lowell, MA, 100,973
Pelham, NH, 10,600
Pepperell, MA, 10,606
Tewksbury, MA, 28,644
Tyngsborough, MA, 9,800
Westford, MA, 18,642

LUBBOCK, TX

Lubbock Avalanche-Journal
710 Avenue J
Lubbock 79401
(806) 762-8844
www.lubbockonline.com

Lubbock C/C
1301 Broadway
Lubbock 79408
(806) 761-7000
www.lubbock.org
Lubbock, 193,565
Slaton, 6,156
Wolffoth, 2,219

LYNCHBURG, VA

News & Daily Advance
101 Wyndale Dr.
Lynchburg 24501
(804) 385-5450
www.newsadvance.com

Greater Lynchburg C/C
2015 Memorial Ave.
Lynchburg 24501
(804) 845-5966
Altavista, 3,570
Bedford, 6,530
Forest, 5,624
Lynchburg, 67,250
Madison Heights, 11,700
Timberlake, 10,314

MACON, GA

Macon Telegraph
120 Broadway
Macon 31201
(912) 744-4200
www.macontelegraph.com

Macon-Bibb County CVB
200 Cherry St.
Macon 31208
(800) 768-3401
www.maconga.org

Greater Macon C/C
305 Coliseum Dr.
Macon 31217
(912) 741-8000
Byron, 2,755
Centerville, 3,642
Fort Valley, 8,191
Macon, 113,352
Perry, 9,657
Warner Robins, 45,559

MADISON, WI

*Wisconsin State Journal/
Capital Times*
1901 Fish Hatchery Rd.
Madison 53713
(608) 252-6100
www.madison.com

Greater Madison C/C & CVB
615 E. Washington Ave.
Madison 53703
(800) 373-6376
www.visitmadison.com
Cross Plains, 3,058
De Forest, 6,262

Fitchburg, 17,954
Madison, 197,630
Marshall, 2,743
McFarland, 5,724
Middleton, 14,369
Monona, 8,329
Mount Horeb, 4,699
Oregon, 6,220
Stoughton, 10,621
Sun Prairie, 17,825
Verona, 5,993
Waunakee, 7,717

MANCHESTER, NH

Union Leader
100 William Loeb Dr.
Manchester 03109
(603) 668-4321
www.theunionleader.com

Greater Manchester C/C
889 Elm St.
Manchester 03101
(603) 666-6600
www.manchester-chamber.org
Allenstown, 4,785
Auburn, 4,469
Bedford, 14,593
Candia, 3,733
Goffstown, 15,548
Hooksett, 9,511
Londonderry, 21,567
Manchester, 100,967
Weare, 7,000

MANSFIELD, OH

News Journal
70 W. 4th St.
Mansfield 44903
(419) 522-3311

Mansfield/Richland County CVB
52 Park Ave. W
Mansfield 44902
(800) 642-8282
www.mansfieldtourism.org

Mansfield-Richland Area C/C
55 N. Mulberry St.
Mansfield 44902
(419) 522-3211
Bucyrus, 13,134
Crestline, 4,917
Galion, 11,533
Lexington, 4,242
Mansfield, 50,906
Ontario, 3,880
Shelby, 9,416

MCALLEN-EDINBURG-MISSION, TX

McAllen Monitor
P.O. Box 760
McAllen 78501
(956) 686-4343
www.themonitor.com

McAllen C/C
10 N. Broadway
McAllen 78501
(956) 682-2871
www.mcallen.org

Edinburg C/C
521 S. 12th
Edinburg 78540
(956) 383-4974
www.vt.com/chamber

Mission C/C
220 E. 9th St.
Mission 78572
(956) 585-2727
Alamo, 10,486
Alton, 3,708
Donna, 14,832
Edcouch, 3,292
Edinburg, 37,742
Elsa, 6,250
Hidalgo, 5,424
La Joya, 2,797
McAllen, 103,352
Mercedes, 14,393
Mission, 37,777
Pharr, 40,425
Progreso, 4,568
San Juan, 16,454
Weslaco, 26,975

MEDFORD-ASHLAND, OR

Mail Tribune
111 N. Fir St.
Medford 97501
(541) 776-4422
www.mailtribune.com

Greater Medford CVB
101 E. 8th Ave.
Medford 97501
(800) 469-6307
www.visitmedford.org

Ashland C/C
110 E. Main St.
Ashland 97520
(541) 482-3486

C/C of Medford/Jackson County
101 W. Eighth
Medford 97501
(541) 779-4847
www.medfordchamber.com
Ashland, 17,678
Central Point, 9,740
Eagle Point, 3,588
Medford, 56,067
Phoenix, 3,703
Talent, 3,929
White City, 5,891

MELBOURNE-TITUSVILLE-PALM BAY, FL

Florida Today
Gannett Plaza
Melbourne 32941
(407) 242-3500
www.flatoday.com

Florida's Space Coast
Office of Tourism
1005 E. Strawbridge Ave.
Melbourne 32940
(800) 771-9922

Melbourne-Palm Bay Area C/C
1005 E. Strawbridge Ave.
Melbourne 32901
(407) 724-5400
www.melpb-chamber.org

Titusville Area C/C
2000 S. Washington Ave.
Titusville 32780
(407) 267-3036
Cape Canaveral, 8,377
Cocoa 18,279
Cocoa Beach, 12,635
Cocoa West, 6,160
Indialantic, 2,930
Indian Harbour Beach, 7,530
Melbourne, 67,631
Melbourne Beach, 3,172
Merritt Island, 32,886
Micco, 8,757
Mims, 9,412
Palm Bay, 74,982
Port St. John, 8,933
Rockledge, 18,899
Satellite Beach, 10,093
South Patrick Shores, 10,249
Titusville, 41,543
West Melbourne, 9,144

MEMPHIS, TN-AR-MS

Commercial Appeal
495 Union Ave.
Memphis 38103
(901) 529-2322
www.gomemphis.com

Memphis CVB
47 Union Ave.
Memphis 38103
(901) 543-5300
www.memphistravel.com

Memphis Area C/C
22 N. Front St.
Memphis 38103
(901) 543-3500
www.memphischamber.com

Bartlett, TN, 35,735
Collierville, TN, 24,665
Covington, TN, 8,090
Earle, AR, 3,342
Germantown,TN, 31,772
Hernando, MS, 3,891
Horn Lake, MS, 13,042
Marion, AR, 5,703
Memphis, TN, 596,725
Millington, TN, 18,142
Munford, TN, 3,941
Olive Branch, MS, 8,474
Southaven, MS, 20,778
West Memphis, AR, 26,894

MERCED, CA

Merced Sun-Star
3033 North G St.
Merced 95342
(209) 722-1511
www.mercedsun-star.com

Merced C/C and CVB
690 W. Sixteenth St.
Merced 95340
(800) 446-5353
www.yosemite-gateway.org

Atwater, 23,638
Dos Palos, 4,222
Gustine, 3,914
Livingston, 10,015
Los Banos, 19,009
Merced, 58,099
Winton, 7,559

MIAMI, FL

Miami Herald
One Herald Plaza
Miami 33132
(305) 376-3800
www.herald.com

Greater Miami CVB
701 Brickell Ave.
Miami 33131
(800) 753-8448
www.miamiandbeaches.com

Greater Miami C/C
1601 Biscayne Blvd.
Miami 33132
(305) 350-7700

Andover, 6,251
Aventura, 14,914
Bal Harbour, 3,164
Bay Harbor Islands, 4,673
Biscayne Park, 2,956
Brownsville, 15,607
Carol City, 53,331
Coral Gables, 39,916
Coral Terrace, 23,255
Cutler, 16,201
Cutler Ridge, 21,268
Florida City, 6,820
Gladeview, 15,637
Glenvar Heights, 14,823
Golden Glades, 25,474
Goulds, 7,284
Hammocks, 10,897
Hialeah, 204,684
Hialeah Gardens, 14,301
Homestead, 23,005
Ives Estates, 13,531
Kendale Lakes, 48,524
Kendall, 87,271
Kendall Lakes West, 6,038
Key Biscayne, 9,896
Lake Lucerne, 9,478
Lakes by the Bay, 5,615
Leisure City, 19,379
Lindgren Acres, 22,290
Miami, 365,127
Miami Beach, 94,540
Miami Lakes, 12,750
Miami Shores, 9,835
Miami Springs, 13,149
Naranja, 5,790
Norland, 22,109
North Bay Village, 5,333
North Miami, 50,757
North Miami Beach, 34,841
Ojus, 15,519
Olympia Heights, 37,792
Opa-locka, 15,081
Opa-locka North, 6,568
Palm Springs North, 5,300

Palmetto Estates, 12,293
Perrine, 15,576
Pinewood, 15,518
Princeton, 7,073
Richmond Heights, 8,583
Scott Lake, 14,588
South Miami, 10,454
South Miami Heights, 30,030
Sunny Isles, 11,772
Sunset, 15,810
Surfside, 3,971
Sweetwater, 13,925
Tamiami, 33,845
West Little River, 33,575
West Miami, 5,621
Westchester, 29,883
Westview, 9,668
Westwood Lakes, 11,522

MIDDLESEX-SOMERSET-HUNTERDON, NJ

Middlesex County C/C
218 N. Center Dr.
North Brunswick 08902
(908) 821-1700

Somerset County C/C
64 W. End Ave.
Somerville 08876
(908) 725-1552
www.somersetcountychamber.org

Hunterdon County C/C
2200 Rte. 31
Lebanon 08833
(908) 735-5955

Avenel, 15,504
Bernardsville, 6,928
Bound Brook, 9,617
Carteret, 19,086
Colonia, 18,238
Dunellen, 6,594
East Brunswick, 43,548
Edison, 88,680
Flemington, 4,094
Fords, 14,392
High Bridge, 3,968
Highland Park, 13,287
Iselin, 16,141
Jamesburg, 5,605
Kendall Park, 7,127
Lambertville, 4,161
Laurence Harbor, 6,361
Madison Park, 7,490
Manville, 10,754
Metuchen, 12,901
Middlesex, 13,181
Milltown, 7,032
New Brunswick, 41,534
North Brunswick Twnshp., 31,287

North Plainfield, 18,947
Old Bridge, 22,151
Perth Amboy, 42,262
Raritan, 6,115
Sayreville, 37,352
Somerset, 22,070
Somerville, 11,705
South Amboy, 7,860
South Bound Brook, 4,228
South Plainfield, 20,682
South River, 13,921
Spotswood, 8,174
Watchung, 5,280
Woodbridge, 17,434

MILWAUKEE-WAUKESHA, WI

Milwaukee Journal/Sentinel
333 W. State St.
Milwaukee 53203
(414) 224-2000
www.packerplus.com

Greater Milwaukee CVB
510 W. Kilbourn Ave.
Milwaukee 53203
(414) 273-3950

Metro Milwaukee Assn. of Comm.
756 N. Milwaukee St.
Milwaukee 53202
(414) 287-4100

Bayside, 4,614
Brookfield, 37,729
Brown Deer, 12,177
Cedarburg, 10,392
Cudahy, 18,123
Delafield, 6,026
Elm Grove, 5,964
Fox Point, 6,846
Franklin, 25,867
Germantown, 16,907
Glendale, 13,646
Grafton, 9,660
Greendale, 14,828
Greenfield, 34,409
Hales Corners, 7,428
Hartford, 9,020
Hartland, 7,845
Jackson, 3,861
Kewaskum, 3,026
Menomonee Falls, 30,395
Mequon, 21,988
Milwaukee, 590,503
Mukwonago, 5,859
Muskego, 20,634
New Berlin, 36,215
Oak Creek, 25,203
Oconomowoc, 11,484
Pewaukee, 6,823
Port Washington, 10,613
St. Francis, 9,094

Saukville, 4,116
Shorewood, 12,997
Slinger, 3,420
South Milwaukee, 20,609
Sussex, 8,137
Thiensville, 3,282
Wales, 2,655
Waukesha, 60,197
Wauwatosa, 46,759
West Allis, 60,550
West Bend, 28,218
West Milwaukee, 3,812
Whitefish Bay, 13,253

MINNEAPOLIS-ST. PAUL, MN-WI

Star Tribune
425 Portland Ave.
Minneapolis 55488
(612) 673-4000
www.startribune.com

St. Paul Pioneer Press
345 Cedar St.
St. Paul 55101
(651) 222-5011
www.pioneerplanet.com

Greater Minneapolis CVB
33 S. Sixth St.
Minneapolis 55402
(612) 348-4313
www.minneapolis.org

Saint Paul CVB
55 E. 5th St.
St. Paul 55101
(651) 297-6985

Greater Minneapolis C/C
81 S. Ninth St.
Minneapolis 55402
(612) 370-9132

St. Paul Area C/C
332 Minnesota
St. Paul 55101
(651) 223-5000
www.saintpaulchamber.com

Afton, MN, 2,711
Andover, MN, 22,387
Anoka, MN, 17,780
Apple Valley, MN, 42,949
Arden Hills, MN, 9,482
Bayport, MN, 3,282
Belle Plaine, MN, 3,231
Big Lake, MN, 3,931
Blaine, MN, 43,241
Bloomington, MN, 86,664

Branch, MN, 3,484
Brooklyn Center, MN, 28,132
Brooklyn Park, MN, 61,335
Buffalo, MN, 8,584
Burnsville, MN, 57,087
Cambridge, MN, 5,386
Champlin, MN, 20,654
Chanhassen, MN, 17,045
Chaska, MN, 14,700
Circle Pines, MN, 5,021
Columbia Heights, MN, 18,368
Coon Rapids, MN, 62,790
Corcoran, MN, 5,766
Cottage Grove, MN, 29,486
Crystal, MN, 23,292
Dayton, MN, 5,027
Deephaven, MN, 3,651
Delano, MN, 3,187
Eagan, MN, 57,294
East Bethel, MN, 9,626
Eden Prairie, MN, 47,630
Edina, MN, 46,336
Elk River, MN, 14,892
Ellsworth, WI, 2,759
Falcon Heights, MN, 5,284
Farmington, MN, 8,571
Forest Lake, MN, 6,435
Fridley, MN, 27,886
Golden Valley, MN, 20,560
Ham Lake, MN, 10,955
Hastings, MN, 16,823
Hopkins, MN, 16,262
Hudson, WI, 7,392
Hugo, MN, 5,562
Independence, MN, 3,066
Inver Grove Heights, MN, 26,962
Jordan, MN, 3,167
Lake Elmo, MN, 6,444
Lakeville, MN, 36,843
Lauderdale, MN, 2,690
Lindstrom, MN, 2,823
Lino Lakes, MN, 13,493
Little Canada, MN, 9,424
Mahtomedi, MN, 6,806
Maple Grove, MN, 45,142
Maplewood, MN, 33,983
Medina, MN, 3,645
Mendota Heights, MN, 11,193
Minneapolis, MN, 358,785
Minnetonka, MN, 50,219
Minnetrista, MN, 3,873
Monticello, MN, 6,422
Mound, MN, 9,684
Mounds View, MN, 12,769
New Brighton, MN, 22,664
New Hope, MN, 21,439
New Prague, MN, 4,035
New Richmond, WI, 5,724
Newport, MN, 3,747
North Branch, MN, 2,658
North Hudson, WI, 3,378
North Oaks, MN, 3,743
Oak Park Heights, MN, 3,867
Oakdale, MN, 25,184

Orono, MN, 7,447
Osseo, MN, 2,652
Plymouth, MN, 60,103
Prescott, WI, 3,629
Prior Lake, MN, 13,714
Ramsey, MN, 16,738
Richfield, MN, 34,387
River Falls, WI, 11,535
Robbinsdale, MN, 14,167
Rockford, MN, 3,200
Rosemount, MN, 12,242
Roseville, MN, 34,183
St. Anthony, MN, 7,831
St. Francis, MN, 3,112
St. Louis Park, MN, 42,828
St. Michael, MN, 3,477
St. Paul, MN, 259,606
St. Paul Park, MN, 5,076
Savage, MN, 15,373
Shakopee, MN, 14,537
Shoreview, MN, 25,981
Shorewood, MN, 6,926
Spring Lake Park, MN, 6,860
Stillwater, MN, 15,585
Vadnais Heights, MN, 12,926
Victoria, MN, 3,592
Waconia, MN, 4,688
Water, MN, 2,691
Wayzata, MN, 3,908
White Bear Lake, MN, 25,613
Woodbury, MN, 35,783
Wyoming, MN, 2,759

MISSOULA, MT

Missoulian
P.O. Box 8029
Missoula 59807
(406) 523-5200
www.missoulian.com

Missoula C/C
Box 7577
Missoula 59807
(406) 543-6623
Missoula, 51,204
Orchard Homes, 10,317

MOBILE, AL

Mobile Register
304 Government St.
Mobile 36630
(334) 433-1551
www.al.com/mobile

Mobile CVB
One S. Water St.
Mobile 36601
(800) 566-2453

Mobile Area C/C
451 Government St.
Mobile 36652
(334) 433-6951
www.mobcham.org
Bay Minette, 7,804
Chickasaw, 6,433
Citronelle, 3,920
Daphne, 14,972
Fairhope, 12,045
Foley, 6,433
Gulf Shores, 4,029
Mobile, 202,581
Orange Beach, 3,327
Prichard, 32,887
Robertsdale, 3,126
Saraland, 12,714
Satsuma, 5,934
Spanish Fort, 4,031
Theodore, 6,509
Tillmans Corner, 17,988

MODESTO, CA

Modesto Bee
1325 H St.
Modesto 95340
(209) 578-2351
www.modbee.com

Modesto CVB
1114 J St.
Modesto 95353
(209) 571-6480
www.modchamber.org

Modesto C/C
1114 J St.
Modesto 95353
(209) 577-5757
www.ainet.com/chamber
Ceres, 31,146
Hughson, 3,489
Modesto, 178,559
Newman, 5,691
Oakdale, 14,646
Patterson, 9,593
Riverbank, 13,629
Turlock, 48,994
Waterford, 6,703

MONMOUTH-OCEAN, NJ

Asbury Park Press
3601 Hwy. 66
Neptune 07754
(732) 922-6000
www.injersey.com/app

Toms River-Ocean County C/C
1200 Hooper Ave.
Toms River 08753
(732) 349-0220
www.oc-chamber.com
Asbury Park, 17,125
Atlantic Highlands, 4,819
Beachwood, 9,923
Belmar, 5,916
Bradley Beach, 4,542
Brick Township, 66,473
Brielle, 4,596
Crestwood Village, 8,030
Eatontown, 13,976
Fair Haven, 5,456
Freehold, 10,869
Gilford Park, 8,668
Highlands, 4,903
Holiday City South, 5,452
Holiday City-Berkeley, 14,293
Keansburg, 11,195
Keyport, 7,716
Lakehurst, 3,177
Lakewood, 26,095
Leisure Village West, 10,139
Lincroft, 6,193
Little Silver, 6,047
Long Branch, 28,918
Manasquan, 5,503
Matawan, 9,446
Monmouth Beach, 3,405
Mystic Island, 7,400
Neptune City, 5,062
Ocean Acres, 5,587
Oceanport, 6,207
Pleasant Beach, 5,302
Point Pleasant, 19,050
Point Spring Lake, 3,593
Red Bank, 10,777
Robertsville, 9,841
Rumson, 6,821
Shrewsbury, 3,210
Silverton, 9,175
South Toms River, 3,962
Spring Lake Heights, 5,414
Strathmore, 7,060
Tinton Falls, 15,079
Toms River, 7,524
Tuckerton, 3,241
Union Beach, 6,405
West Freehold, 11,166
West Long Branch, 7,949
Yorketown, 6,313

MONROE, LA

News Star
411 N. 4th St.
Monroe 71201
(318) 322-5161

Monroe-West Monroe CVB
1333 State Farm Dr.
Monroe 71211
(800) 843-1872
www.bayou.com/~web/visitors

Monroe C/C
300 Washington St.
Monroe 71201
(318) 323-3461
www.monroe.org
Brownsville-Bawcomville, 7,397
Claiborne, 8,300
Monroe, 54,588
West Monroe, 14,073

MONTGOMERY, AL

Montgomery Advertiser
200 Washington Ave.
Montgomery 36101
(334) 262-1611
www.accessmontgomery.com

Montgomery Area CVB
401 Madison Ave.
Montgomery 36101
(334) 240-9455

Montgomery Area C/C
41 Commerce St.
Montgomery 36104
(334) 834-5200
www.montgomery.al.us/chamber
Millbrook, 8,925
Montgomery, 196,363
Prattville, 24,269
Tallassee, 5,272
Wetumpka, 5,868

MONTREAL, PQ

Gazette
250 rue St. Antoine Ouest
Montreal H2Y 3R7
(514) 987-2222
www.montrealgazette.com

Le Devoir
2050 Bleury St.
Montreal H3A 3M9
(514) 985-3333
www.journaldemontreal.com

Le Journal de Montreal
4545 rue Frontenac
Montreal H2H 2R7
(514) 521-4545
www.journaldemontreal.com

La Presse
7 rue St. Jacques
Montreal H2Y 1K9
(514) 285-7272
www.ledevoir.com

Greater Montreal CTB
1001 Square Dorchester
Montreal H3B 1G2
(800) 363-7777
www.tourism-montreal.org

C/C of Metropolitan Montreal
5 Place Ville-Marie
Montreal H3B 4Y2
(514) 871-4000
www.ccmm.qc.ca
Anjou, 37,308
Baie-d'Urfé, 3,774
Beaconsfield, 19,414
Beauharnois, 6,435
Bellefeuille, 12,803
Beloeil, 19,294
Blainville, 29,603
Boisbriand, 25,227
Bois-des-Filion, 7,124
Boucherville, 34,989
Brossard, 65,927
Candiac, 11,805
Carignan, 5,614
Chambly, 19,716
Charlemagne, 5,739
Châteauguay, 41,423
Côte-Saint-Luc, 29,705
Delson, 6,703
Deux-Montagnes, 15,953
Dollard-des-Ormeaux, 47,826
Dorval, 17,572
Gore, 1,133
Greenfield Park, 17,337
Hampstead, 6,986
Hudson, 4,796
Kirkland, 18,678
La Plaine, 14,413
La Prairie, 17,128
Lachenaie, 18,489
Lachine, 35,171
Lafontaine, 9,008
LaSalle, 72,029
L'Assomption, 11,366
Laval, 330,393
Lavaltrie, 5,821
Le Gardeur, 16,853
LeMoyne, 5,052
Léry, 2,410
Les Cèdres, 4,641
L'Île-Bizard, 13,038
L'Île-Perrot, 9,178
Longueuil, 127,977
Lorraine, 8,876

Maple Grove, 2,606
Mascouche, 28,097
McMasterville, 3,813
Melocheville, 2,486
Mercier, 9,059
Mirabel, 22,689
Montréal, 1,016,376
Montréal-Est, 3,523
Montréal-Nord, 81,581
Montréal-Ouest, 5,254
Mont-Royal, 18,282
Mont-Saint-Hilaire, 13,064
Notre-Dame-de-Bon-Secours, 1,516
Notre-Dame-de-l'île-Perrot, 7,059
Oka, 1,498
Otterburn Park, 7,320
Outremont, 22,571
Pierrefonds, 52,986
Pincourt, 10,023
Pointe-Calumet, 5,443
Pointe-Claire, 28,435
Repentigny, 53,824
Richelieu, 3,195
Rosemère, 12,025
Roxboro, 5,950
Saint-Amable, 7,105
Saint-Antoine, 10,806
Saint-Antoine-de-Lavaltrie, 4,385
Saint-Basile-le-Grand, 11,771
Saint-Bruno-de-Montarville, 23,714
Saint-Colomban, 5,569
Saint-Constant, 21,933
Sainte-Anne-de-Bellevue, 4,700
Sainte-Anne-des-Plaines, 12,908
Sainte-Catherine, 13,724
Sainte-Geneviève, 3,339
Sainte-Julie, 24,030
Sainte-Marthe-sur-le-Lac, 8,295
Sainte-Thérèse, 23,477
Saint-Eustache, 39,848
Saint-Gérard-Majella, 4,207
Saint-Hubert, 77,042
Saint-Isidore, 2,401
Saint-Jérôme, 23,916
Saint-Joseph-du-Lac, 4,930
Saint-Lambert, 20,971
Saint-Laurent, 74,240
Saint-Lazare, 11,193
Saint-Léonard, 71,327
Saint-Mathias-sur-Richelieu, 4,014
Saint-Mathieu, 1,925
Saint-Mathieu-de-Beloeil, 2,143
Saint-Philippe, 3,656
Saint-Pierre, 4,739
Saint-Placide, 1,479
Saint-Sulpice, 3,307
Terrasse-Vaudreuil, 1,977
Terrebonne, 42,214
Varennes, 18,842
Vaudreuil-Dorion, 18,466
Verdun, 59,714
Westmount, 20,420

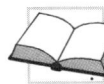

MUNCIE, IN

Muncie Star/Press
P.O. Box 2408
Muncie 47307
(765) 747-5700
web.thestarpress.com/starpress

Muncie-Delaware County C/C
401 S. High St.
Muncie 47302
(765) 288-6681
www.muncie.com
Albany, 2,073
Muncie, 69,058
Yorktown, 4,536

MYRTLE BEACH, SC

Sun News
914 Frontage Rd. E
Myrtle Beach 29577
(843) 626-8555
www.statesmanjournal.com

Myrtle Beach Area C/C & CVB
1200 N. Oak St.
Myrtle Beach 29578
(800) 356-3016
www.myrtlebeachlive.com
www.mbchamber.com
Conway, 10,115
Garden City, 6,305
Loris, 3,074
Myrtle Beach, 25,456
North Myrtle Beach, 9,216
Red Hill, 6,112
Socastee, 10,426
Surfside Beach, 4,118

NAPLES, FL

Naples Daily News
1075 Central Ave.
Naples 34102
(941) 263-4470
www.naplesnews.com

Naples Area Tourism Bureau
1400 Gulf Shore Blvd. N
Naples 33941
(800) 605-7878
www.naples-online.com

Naples Area C/C
3620 9th St. N
Naples 34103
(941) 262-6376
www.naples-online.com

East Naples, 22,951
Golden Gate, 14,148
Immokalee, 14,120
Marco, 9,493
Naples, 19,777
Naples Park, 8,002
North Naples, 13,422

NASHUA, NH

The Telegraph
17 Executive Dr.
Hudson 03061
(603) 882-2741

Greater Nashua C/C
146 Main St.
Nashua 03060
(603) 881-8333
www.nashuachamber.com
Amherst, 9,773
Brookline, 3,208
Hollis, 6,550
Hudson, 21,344
Litchfield, 6,666
Merrimack, 23,547
Milford, 12,549
Nashua, 81,094
New Ipswich, 4,746
Wilton, 3,258

NASHVILLE, TN

Tennessean
1100 Broadway St.
Nashville 37203
(615) 259-8000
www.tennessean.com

Nashville CVB
161 Fourth Ave. N
Nashville 37219
(615) 259-4730
www.nashvillecvb.com

Nashville Area C/C
161 Fourth Ave. N
Nashville 37219
(615) 259-4700
www.nashvillechamber.com
Ashland City, 3,003
Belle Meade, 2,848
Brentwood, 22,076
Dickson, 11,506
Fairview, 5,377
Forest Hills, 4,573
Franklin, 25,648
Gallatin, 21,413
Goodlettsville, 12,770
Green Hill, 6,763

Greenbrier, 3,735
Hendersonville, 37,261
La Vergne, 13,562
Lebanon, 16,375
Millersville, 3,125
Mount Juliet, 7,430
Murfreesboro, 53,966
Nashville, 511,263
Oak Hill, 4,407
Portland, 6,743
Smyrna, 20,708
Springfield, 12,486
White House, 5,002

NEW BEDFORD, MA

Standard-Times
25 Elm St.
New Bedford 02740
(508) 997-7411
www.s-t.com

New Bedford Area C/C
794 Purchase St.
New Bedford 02742
(508) 999-5231
www.nbchamber.com
Acushnet, 9,843
Dartmouth, 28,100
Fairhaven, 15,975
Freetown, 8,733
Marion, 4,953
Mattapoisett, 6,190
New Bedford, 96,903
Rochester, 4,393

NEW HAVEN-MERIDEN, CT

New Haven Register
40 Sargent Dr.
New Haven 06511
(203) 789-5200
www.ctcentral.com

Greater New Haven CVB
59 Elm St.
New Haven 06510
(800) 332-7829
www.newhavencvb.org

Greater Meriden C/C
21 Church St.
Meriden 06450
(203) 235-7901

Greater New Haven C/C
195 Church St.
New Haven 06510
(203) 786-2624
www.newhavenchamber.com

Bethany, 4,745
Branford, 27,323
Cheshire, 26,067
Clinton, 13,022
East Haven, 26,646
Guilford, 19,986
Hamden, 53,332
Killingworth, 5,418
Madison, 16,007
Meriden, 57,189
New Haven, 124,665
North Branford, 13,757
North Haven, 22,088
Orange, 12,477
Wallingford, 40,798
West Haven, 52,153
Woodbridge, 8,051

NEW LONDON-NORWICH, CT-RI

The Day
47 Eugene O'Neill Dr.
New London 06320
(860) 442-2200

C/C of Southeastern Connecticut
105 Huntington St.
New London 06320
(860) 443-8332

Eastern Connecticut C/C
One Thames Plaza
Norwich 06360
(203) 887-1647
www.ecchamber.org
Canterbury, CT, 4,614
East Lyme, CT, 16,026
Griswold, CT, 10,581
Groton, CT, 9,657
Hopkinton, RI, 7,620
Ledyard, CT, 14,708
Lisbon, CT, 3,879
Montville, CT, 16,990
New London, CT, 25,038
North Stonington, CT, 4,944
Norwich, CT, 35,869
Old Lyme, CT, 6,513
Old Saybrook, CT, 9,673
Plainfield, CT, 14,482
Preston, CT, 5,070
Salem, CT, 3,528
Sprague, CT, 2,955
Stonington, CT, 16,806
Waterford, CT, 17,971
Westerly, RI, 22,773

NEW ORLEANS, LA

Times-Picayune
3800 Howard Ave.
New Orleans 70125
(504) 826-3279
www.nolalive.com

Greater New Orleans CVB
1520 Sugar Bowl Dr.
New Orleans 70112
(800) 672-6124
www.neworleanscvb.com

New Orleans & River C/C
601 Poydras St.
New Orleans 70130
(504) 527-6900
www.gnofn.org/chamber
Arabi, 8,787
Avondale, 5,813
Belle Chasse, 8,512
Bridge City, 8,327
Chalmette, 31,860
Covington, 8,576
Destrehan, 8,031
Estelle, 14,091
Gretna, 16,862
Harahan, 9,941
Harvey, 21,222
Jefferson, 14,521
Kenner, 72,345
Lacombe, 6,523
Laplace, 24,194
Lutcher, 4,074
Mandeville, 8,677
Marrero, 36,671
Meraux, 8,849
Metairie, 149,428
New Orleans, 476,625
Reserve, 8,847
River Ridge, 14,800
Slidell, 25,846
St. Rose, 6,259
Terrytown, 23,787
Timberlane, 12,614
Violet, 8,574
Waggaman, 9,405
Westwego, 11,172

NEW YORK, NY

New York Times
229 W. 43rd St.
New York 10036
(212) 556-1234
www.nytimes.com

New York Post
1211 6th Ave.
New York 10036
(212) 930-8000
www.nypostonline.com

Daily News
450 W. 33rd St.
New York 10001
(212) 210-2100
www.mostnewyork.com

New York CVB
2 Columbus Circle
New York 10019
(800) 692-8474
www.nycvisit.com

Bronx C/C
2885 Schley Ave.
Bronx 10465
(718) 829-4111
www.bronxmall.com

Brooklyn C/C
7 Metro Tech Center
Brooklyn 11201
(718) 875-1000
www.brooklynchamber.com

C/C of the Borough of Queens
29-15 Queens Plaza N
Long Island City 11370
(718) 898-8500
www.queenschamber.org

Manhattan C/C
1555 Third Ave.
New York 10128
(212) 479-7772
www.manhattancc.org

New York C/C & Ind.
One World Trade Center
New York 10048
(212) 775-1370

Staten Island C/C
130 Bay St.
Staten Island 10301
(718) 727-1900
Airmont, 7,835
Ardsley, 4,341
Briarcliff Manor, 7,371
Bronxville, 5,993
Chestnut Ridge, 7,919
Congers, 8,003
Croton-on-Hudson, 7,134
Dobbs Ferry, 10,074

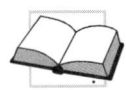

Eastchester, 18,537
Elmsford, 4,520
Greenville, 9,528
Harrison, 23,658
Hartsdale, 9,587
Hastings-on-Hudson, 8,021
Haverstraw, 9,390
Hillcrest, 6,447
Irvington, 6,426
Jefferson Valley-Yorktown, 14,118
Lake Carmel, 8,489
Larchmont, 6,159
Mahopac, 7,755
Mamaroneck, 17,436
Monsey, 13,986
Montebello, 3,109
Mount Ivy, 6,013
Mount Kisco, 9,182
Mount Vernon, 67,112
Nanuet, 14,065
New City, 33,673
New Hempstead, 4,532
New Rochelle, 67,369
New Square, 3,348
New York, 7,380,906
North Tarrytown, 8,146
Nyack, 6,688
Ossining, 22,788
Pearl River, 15,314
Peekskill, 20,805
Pelham, 6,375
Pelham Manor, 5,428
Pleasantville, 6,761
Pomona, 2,869
Port Chester, 24,859
Rye, 15,189
Rye Brook, 8,453
Scarsdale, 16,936
Sloatsburg, 3,109
South Nyack, 3,307
Spring Valley, 22,291
Stony Point, 10,587
Suffern, 11,059
Tappan, 6,867
Tarrytown, 10,756
Thiells,5,204
Thornwood,7,025
Tuckahoe,6,424
Valley Cottage,9,007
Wesley Hills,4,653
West Haverstraw,10,045
White Plains,49,653
Yonkers,190,316
York Heights,7,690

NEWARK, NJ

Star Ledger
One Star Ledger Plaza
Newark 07101
(201) 877-4141
www.nj.com

Metro Newark C/C
One Newark Center
Newark 07102
(201) 242-6237

Alpha, 2,560
Belleville, 34,213
Belvidere, 2,761
Berkeley Heights, 11,980
Bloomfield, 45,061
Boonton, 8,502
Budd Lake, 7,272
Butler, 7,721
Caldwell, 7,549
Cedar Grove, 12,053
Chatham, 7,953
Clark, 14,629
Cranford, 22,624
Dover, 15,312
East Hanover, 9,926
East Orange, 70,534
Elizabeth, 110,149
Fairfield, 7,615
Fanwood, 7,108
Florham Park, 8,986
Franklin, 5,262
Garwood, 4,216
Glen Ridge, 7,076
Hackettstown, 8,586
Hamburg, 2,842
Hanover Township, 11,538
Hillside, 21,044
Hopatcong, 16,275
Irvington, 59,774
Kenilworth, 7,613
Kinnelon, 8,944
Lake Mohawk, 8,930
Lincoln Park, 11,201
Linden, 36,857
Livingston, 26,609
Madison, 15,727
Maplewood, 21,756
Mendham, 4,935
Millburn, 18,630
Montclair, 37,729
Morristown, 16,357
Morris Plains, 5,279
Mount Arlington, 4,677
Mountain Lakes, 4,071
Mountainside, 6,655
Netcong, 3,359
New Providence, 11,793
Newark, 268,510
Newton, 7,917
North Caldwell, 6,706
Nutley, 27,099
Ogdensburg, 2,858
Orange, 29,925
Parsippany, 48,478
Pequannock Township, 12,844
Phillipsburg, 15,707
Plainfield, 46,254
Rahway, 25,228
Rockaway, 6,435

Roseland, 5,220
Roselle, 20,205
Roselle Park, 12,731
Scotch Plains, 21,160
South Orange, 16,390
Springfield, 13,420
Stanhope, 3,607
Succasunna-Kenvil, 11,781
Summit, 19,612
Union, 50,024
Verona, 13,597
Washington, 6,499
West Caldwell, 10,422
West Orange, 39,103
Westfield, 29,125
Wharton, 5,518
White Meadow Lake, 8,002

NEWBURGH, NY-PA

Times Herald-Record
40 Mulberry St.
Middletown 10940
(914) 343-1100
www.th-record.com

Eastern Orange County C/C
47 Grand St.
Newburgh 12550
(914) 562-5100

Chester, 3,377
Cornwall on Hudson, 3,092
Florida, 2,589
Goshen, 5,250
Greenwood Lake, 3,214
Highland Falls, 3,900
Kiryas Joel, 8,717
Maybrook, 2,907
Middletown, 24,192
Monroe, 7,664
Montgomery, 3,024
New Windsor, 8,898
Newburgh, 26,248
Orange Lake, 5,196
Port Jervis, 8,935
Scotchtown, 8,765
Walden, 6,247
Warwick, 6,083
Washingtonville, 5,618
West Point, 8,024

NORFOLK-VIRGINIA BEACH-NEWPORT NEWS, VA-NC

Virginian-Pilot/Ledger-Star
150 W. Brambleton Ave.
Norfolk 23510
(757) 446-2000
www.pilotonline.com

Daily Press
7505 Warwick Blvd.
Newport News 23607
(757) 928-1111
www.dailypress.com

Norfolk CVB
236 E. Plume St.
Norfolk 23510
(800) 368-3097
www.norfolk.va.us

Virginia Beach Visitor Center
2101 Parks Ave.
Virginia Beach 23451
(800) 822-3224
www.travelfile.com/get?vabch

Williamsburg Area CVB
201 Penniman Rd.
Williamsburg 23187
(800) 368-6511
www.visitwilliamsburg.com

Hampton Roads C/C
420 Bank St.
Norfolk 23501
(757) 622-2312
www.hrccva.com
Chesapeake, 192,342
Gloucester Point, 8,509
Hampton, 138,757
Newport News, 176,122
Norfolk, 233,430
Poquoson, 11,922
Portsmouth, 101,308
Smithfield, 5,522
Suffolk, 58,901
Virginia Beach, 430,385
Williamsburg, 12,922

OAKLAND, CA

The Tribune
116 W. Wenton Ave.
Oakland 94544
(510) 229-3290
www.newschoice.com/newspapers/
   alameda/tribune

Oakland CVB
250 Frank Ogawa Plaza
Oakland 94612
(510) 238-2935
www.ocva.com

Oakland C/C
475 Fourteenth St.
Oakland 94612
(510) 874-4800
Alameda, 76,042
Alamo, 12,277
Albany, 16,390
Antioch, 76,293
Ashland, 16,590
Berkeley, 103,243
Blackhawk, 6,199
Brentwood, 13,212
Castro Valley, 48,619
Cherryland, 11,088
Clayton, 8,169
Concord, 114,850
Danville, 38,395
Discovery Bay, 5,351
Dublin, 25,231
El Cerrito, 23,567
El Sobrante, 9,852
Emeryville, 6,356
Fairview, 9,045
Fremont, 187,800
Hayward, 121,631
Hercules, 19,366
Lafayette, 26,073
Livermore, 64,647
Martinez, 33,459
Moraga Town, 17,693
Newark, 39,940
Oakland, 367,230
Oakley, 18,374
Orinda, 18,578
Piedmont, 10,536
Pinole, 18,900
Pittsburg, 50,813
Pleasant Hill, 32,141
Pleasanton, 57,275
Richmond, 91,018
Rodeo, 7,589
San Leandro, 69,976
San Lorenzo, 19,987
San Pablo, 26,128
San Ramon, 39,868
Union City, 58,294
Walnut Creek, 62,786
West Pittsburg, 17,453

OCALA, FL

Ocala Star Banner
2121 SW 19th Ave.
Ocala 34478
(352) 867-4010
www.starbanner.com

Ocala-Marion County C/C
110 E. Silver Springs Blvd.
Ocala 34470
(352) 629-8051
www.ocalacc.com

Belleview, 2,852
Ocala, 44,975
Silver Springs Shores, 6,421

ODESSA-MIDLAND, TX

Midland Reporter-Telegram
201 E. Illinois
Midland 79701
(915) 682-5311
www.mrt.com

Odessa American
222 E. 4th St.
Odessa 79761
(915) 337-4661
www.oaoa.com

Odesssa CVB
700 N. Grant Ave.
Odessa 79761
(800) 780-4678
www.tourtexas.com/odessa

Midland C/C
109 N. Main St.
Midland 79701
(800) 624-6435

Odessa C/C
700 N. Grant Ave.
Odessa 79760
(915) 332-9111
www.odessachamber.com
Midland, 97,162
Odessa, 90,883
West Odessa, 16,568

OKLAHOMA CITY, OK

Daily Oklahoman
9000 N. Broadway
Oklahoma City 73114
(405) 475-3311
www.oklahoman.com

Oklahoma City CVB
189 W. Sheridan
Oklahoma City 73102
(800) 225-5652
www.okccvb.org

Oklahoma City C/C
123 Park Ave.
Oklahoma City 73102
(405) 297-8900
www.okcchamber.com

Bethany, 20,400
Bethel Acres, 2,710
Choctaw, 9,589
Del City, 23,990
Edmond, 63,475
El Reno, 16,025
Guthrie, 10,538
Harrah, 4,465
McLoud, 2,821
Midwest City, 54,252
Moore, 44,472
Mustang, 12,036
Newcastle, 5,134
Nichols Hills, 4,050
Noble, 5,055
Norman, 90,228
Oklahoma City, 469,852
Piedmont, 3,179
Purcell, 5,111
Shawnee, 26,833
Spencer, 4,041
Tecumseh, 5,914
The Village, 10,463
Warr Acres, 9,429
Yukon, 22,921

OLYMPIA, WA

The Olympian
1268 E. 4th Ave.
Olympia 98506
(360) 754-5400
www.theolympian.com/index.htm

Olympia/Thurston County C/C
521 Legion Way SE
Olympia 98501
(360) 357-3362
www.olympus.net/olympia/vcb
Lacey, 27,381
Olympia, 39,006
Tanglewilde-Thompson Place, 6,061
Tumwater, 11,520

OMAHA, NE-IA

Omaha World-Herald
1334 Dodge St.
Omaha 68102
(402) 444-1000
www.omaha.com

Greater Omaha CVB
6800 Mercy Rd.
Omaha 68106
(800) 332-1819
www.visitomaho.com

Greater Omaha C/C
1301 Harney St.
Omaha 68102
(402) 346-5000
www.accessomaha.com/Chamber
Bellevue, NE, 42,807
Blair, NE, 7,558
Carter Lake, IA, 3,331
Chalco, NE, 7,337
Council Bluffs, IA, 55,569
Elkhorn, NE, 2,573
Gretna, NE, 2,769
La Vista , NE, 11,596
Omaha, NE, 364,253
Papillion, NE, 14,516
Plattsmouth, NE, 6,863
Ralston, NE, 6,251

ORANGE COUNTY, CA

Orange County Register
625 N. Grand Ave.
Santa Ana 92701
(714) 835-1234
www.ocregister.com

Anaheim Area CVB
800 W. Katella Ave.
Anaheim 92802
(888) 598-3200

Anaheim C/C
100 S. Anaheim Blvd.
Anaheim 92805
(714) 758-0222
www.anaheimchamber.org

Garden Grove C/C
11277 Garden Grove Blvd.
Garden Grove 92843
(714) 638-7950

Santa Ana C/C
1505 E. 17th St.
Santa Ana 92705
(714) 547-2646
Aliso Viejo, 7,612
Anaheim, 288,945
Brea, 34,790
Buena Park, 71,999
Costa Mesa, 100,938
Cypress, 47,032
Dana Point, 33,875
El Toro, 62,685
El Toro Station, 6,869
Fountain Valley, 55,790
Fullerton, 120,188
Garden Grove, 149,208
Huntington Beach, 190,751

Irvine, 127,873
La Habra, 53,704
La Palma, 16,092
Laguna Beach, 24,641
Laguna Hills, 46,731
Laguna Niguel, 51,701
Los Alamitos, 12,492
Mission Viejo, 84,689
Newport Beach, 69,658
Orange, 119,890
Placentia, 44,811
Rancho Santa Margarita, 11,390
Rossmoor, 9,893
San Clemente, 45,415
San Juan Capistrano, 29,029
Santa Ana, 302,419
Seal Beach, 25,828
Stanton, 32,614
Tustin, 62,222
Tustin Foothills, 24,358
Villa Park, 6,646
Westminster, 82,425
Yorba Linda, 58,124

ORLANDO, FL

Orlando Sentinel
633 N. Orange Ave.
Orlando 32801
(407) 420-5000
www.orlandosentinel.com

Orlando/Orange County CVB
6700 Forum Dr.
Orlando 32821
(800) 551-0181
www.go2orlando.com

Greater Orlando C/C
75 E. Ivanhoe Blvd.
Orlando 32802
(407) 418-4517
www.orlando.org
Altamonte Springs, 38,379
Apopka, 18,380
Azalea Park, 8,926
Bay Hill, 5,346
Belle Isle, 4,974
Buena Ventura Lakes, 14,148
Casselberry, 24,487
Clermont, 7,073
Conway, 13,159
Doctor Phillips, 7,963
Eustis, 14,422
Fairview Shores, 13,192
Fern Park, 8,294
Forest City, 10,638
Fruitland Park, 2,988
Goldenrod, 6,602
Kissimmee, 36,510

Lady Lake, 12,315
Lake Mary, 7,988
Leesburg, 16,416
Lockhart, 11,636
Longwood, 13,707
Maitland, 8,834
Mount Dora, 8,766
Oak Ridge, 15,388
Ocoee, 18,942
Orlando, 173,902
Orlovista, 5,990
Oviedo, 20,073
Pine Castle, 8,276
Pine Hills, 35,322
St. Cloud, 14,489
Sanford, 35,559
Sky Lake, 6,202
South Apopka, 6,360
Tavares, 8,261
Umatilla, 2,517
Union Park, 6,890
Wekiva Springs, 23,026
Winter Garden, 11,312
Winter Park, 23,247
Winter Springs, 26,820

OSHAWA, ON

Oshawa Times
44 Richmond St. W
Oshawa L1G 1C8
(905) 723-3474

Oshawa C/C
5250 Richmond St. E
Oshawa L1G 7C7
(905) 728-1683
Clarington, 60,615
Oshawa, 134,364
Whitby, 73,794

OTTAWA-HULL, ON-PQ

Ottawa Sun
380 Hunt Club Rd.
Ottawa K1G 5H7
(613) 739-7000
www.canoe.ca/OttawaSun

Ottawa Citizen
1101 Baxter Rd.
Ottawa K2C 3M4
(613) 829-9100
www.ottawacitizen.com

Ottawa TCA
130 Albert St.
Ottawa K1P 5G4
(800) 363-4465
www.tourottawa.org

Ottawa-Carleton Board of Trade
350 Albert St.
Ottawa K1R 1A4
(613) 236-3631
www.board-of-trade.org
Aylmer, PQ, 34,901
Buckingham, PQ, 11,678
Cambridge, ON, 6,403
Cantley, PQ, 5,425
Casselman, ON, 2,877
Chelsea, PQ, 5,925
Clarence, ON, 10,563
Cumberland, ON, 47,367
Gatineau, PQ, 100,702
Gloucester, ON, 104,022
Goulbourn, ON, 19,267
Hull, PQ, 62,339
Kanata, ON, 47,909
La Pêche, PQ, 6,160
Masson-Angers, PQ, 7,989
Nepean, ON, 115,100
Osgoode, ON, 15,904
Ottawa, ON, 323,340
Pontiac, PQ, 4,722
Rideau, ON, 12,444
Rockcliffe Park, ON, 1,995
Rockland, ON, 8,070
Russell, ON, 11,877
South Gower, ON, 2,500
Val-des-Monts, PQ, 7,231
Vanier, ON, 17,247
West Carleton, ON, 16,541

OWENSBORO, KY

Messenger-Inquirer
1401 Frederica St.
Owensboro 42301
(270) 926-0123
www.messenger-inquirer.com

Owensboro-Daviess County
Tourist Comm.
326 St. Elizabeth
Owensboro 42301
(800) 489-1131

Owensboro-Daviess County C/C
335 Frederica St.
Owensboro 42302
(270) 926-1860

Owensboro, 54,350
Whitesville, 674

PANAMA CITY, FL

News Herald
501 W. 11th St.
Panama City 32402
(850) 763-7621
www.newsherald.com

Panama City Beach CVB
12015 Front Beach Rd.
Panama City Beach 32417
(850) 233-5070

Bay County C/C
235 W. Fifth St.
Panama City 32402
(850) 785-5206
Callaway, 13,060
Lynn Haven, 11,722
Panama City, 35,986
Panama City Beach, 5,214
Parker, 4,880
Springfield, 9,312
Upper Grand Lagoon, 7,855

PARKERSBURG-MARIETTA, WV-OH

Parkersburg News
P.O. Box 1787
Parkersburg 26102
(304) 485-1891
wvweb.com/news/
Parkersburg_news.html

Parkersburg CVB
350 7th St.
Parkersburg 26101
(800) 752-4982
www.parkersburgcvb.org

Greater Parkersburg Area C/C
214 E. Eighth St.
Parkersburg 26101
(304) 422-3588

Marietta Area C/C
316 Third St.
Marietta 45750
(740) 373-5176
Belpre, OH, 6,998
Marietta, OH, 15,092
Parkersburg, WV, 32,766
Vienna, WV, 11,248
Williamstown, WV, 2,771

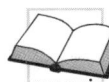

PENSACOLA, FL

Pensacola News Journal
One News Journal Pl.
Pensacola 3257432
(850) 435-8500
www.gulfcoastgateway.com

Pensacola CVB
1401 E. Gregory St.
Pensacola 32501
(800) 874-1234

Pensacola Area C/C
117 W. Garden St.
Pensacola 32593
(850) 438-4081
www.chamber.pensacola.fl.us
Bellview, 19,386
Brent, 21,624
Ensley, 16,362
Ferry Pass, 26,301
Gonzalez, 7,669
Gulf Breeze, 5,894
Milton, 7,635
Myrtle Grove, 17,402
Pace, 6,277
Pensacola, 59,162
Warrington, 16,040
West Pensacola, 22,107

PEORIA-PEKIN, IL

Pekin Daily Times
20 S. 4th St.
Pekin 61554
(309) 346-1111
www.pekin.net/times/index.html

Peoria Journal Star
One News Plaza
Peoria 61643
(309) 686-3000
www.pjstar.com

Peoria CVB
403 NE Jefferson St.
Peoria 61603
(800) 747-0302
www.peoria.org

Peoria Area C/C
124 SW Adams St.
Peoria 61602
(309) 676-0755

Pekin C/C
402 Court St.
Pekin 61555
(309) 346-2106
Bartonville, 6,487
Chillicothe, 6,084
Creve Coeur, 5,920
East Peoria, 22,201
Eureka, 4,603
Marquette Heights, 3,088
Metamora, 2,676
Morton, 14,894
Pekin, 32,433
Peoria, 112,306
Peoria Heights, 6,732
Washington, 10,635
West Peoria, 5,314

PHILADELPHIA, PA-NJ

Philadelphia Inquirer/Daily News
400 N. Broad St.
Philadelphia 19130
(215) 854-2000
www.phillynews.com

Philadelphia CVB
1515 Market St.
Philadelphia 19102
(800) 321-9563
www.libertynet.org/phila-visitor

Greater Philadelphia C/C
200 S. Broad St.
Philadelphia 19102
(215) 972-6999
www.gpcc.com
Aldan, PA, 4,560
Ambler, PA, 6,514
Ardmore, PA, 7,325
Audubon, NJ, 8,995
Barrington, NJ, 7,277
Bellmawr, NJ, 12,399
Berlin, NJ, 5,943
Beverly, NJ, 2,929
Blackwood, NJ, 5,120
Blue Bell, PA, 6,091
Boothwyn, PA, 5,069
Bordentown, NJ, 4,236
Bridgeport, PA, 4,197
Bristol, PA, 10,198
Brookhaven, PA, 8,422
Broomall, PA, 10,930
Brown Mills, NJ, 11,429
Burlington, NJ, 9,639
Camden, NJ, 84,844
Carneys Point, NJ, 7,686
Chalfont, PA, 4,006
Cherry Hill, NJ, 69,319
Chester, PA, 40,660
Chester Heights, PA, 2,565

Chester Township, PA, 5,399
Cinnaminson, NJ, 14,583
Clayton, NJ, 6,827
Clementon, NJ, 5,477
Clifton Heights, PA, 6,946
Coatesville, PA, 10,827
Collegeville, PA, 5,030
Collingdale, PA, 8,933
Collingswood, NJ, 14,820
Colwyn, PA, 2,540
Conshohocken, PA, 8,195
Croydon, PA, 9,967
Darby, PA, 10,870
Darby Township, PA, 10,955
Devon-Berwyn, PA, 5,019
Downingtown, PA, 7,841
Doylestown, PA, 8,431
Drexel Hill, PA, 29,744
East Greenville, PA, 3,103
East Lansdowne, PA, 2,614
East Norriton, PA, 13,324
Edgewater Park, NJ, 8,388
Fairless Hills, PA, 9,026
Feasterville, PA, 6,696
Florence, NJ, 8,564
Folcroft, PA, 7,412
Folsom, PA, 8,173
Fort Dix, NJ, 10,205
Glassboro, NJ, 17,463
Glendora, NJ, 5,201
Glenolden, PA, 7,203
Glenside, PA, 8,704
Gloucester City, NJ, 12,302
Haddon Heights, NJ, 7,640
Haddonfield, NJ, 11,332
Harleysville, PA, 7,405
Hatboro, PA, 7,326
Hatfield, PA, 2,615
Horsham, PA, 15,051
Jenkintown, PA, 4,479
Kennett Square, PA, 5,199
King of Prussia, PA, 18,406
Kulpsville, PA, 5,183
Lansdale, PA, 16,015
Lansdowne, PA, 11,408
Lawnside, NJ, 2,866
Levittown, PA, 55,362
Lindenwold, NJ, 18,328
Lionville, PA, 6,468
Magnolia, NJ, 4,825
Malvern, PA, 3,111
Maple Glen, PA, 5,881
Maple Shade, NJ, 19,211
Marlton, NJ, 10,228
Medford Lakes, NJ, 4,342
Media, PA, 5,832
Merchantville, NJ, 3,964
Montgomeryville, PA, 9,114
Moorestown, NJ, 13,242
Morrisville, PA, 9,530
Morton, PA, 2,818
Mount Ephraim, NJ, 4,465
Mount Holly, NJ, 10,639
Narberth, PA, 4,183

National Park, NJ, 3,382
Nether Providence, PA, 13,229
Newtown, PA, 2,509
Norristown, PA, 30,037
North Wales, PA, 3,820
Norwood, PA, 6,157
Oaklyn, NJ, 4,341
Oreland, PA, 5,695
Oxford, PA, 3,779
Palmyra, NJ, 6,950
Paoli, PA, 5,603
Parkesburg, PA, 3,060
Paulsboro, NJ, 6,407
Penn Wynne, PA, 5,807
Penndel, PA, 2,699
Penns Grove, NJ, 5,164
Pennsauken, NJ, 34,733
Pennsburg, PA, 2,559
Pennsville, NJ, 12,218
Perkasie, PA, 8,072
Philadelphia, PA, 1,478,002
Phoenixville, PA, 15,327
Pine Hill, NJ, 10,472
Pitman, NJ, 9,170
Plymouth Meeting, PA, 6,241
Pottstown, PA, 21,614
Prospect Park, PA, 6,674
Quakertown, PA, 8,975
Radnor, PA, 28,705
Ramblewood, NJ, 6,181
Richboro, PA, 5,332
Ridley Park, PA, 7,456
Riverside, NJ, 7,974
Riverton, NJ, 2,690
Rockledge, PA, 2,621
Royersford, PA, 4,452
Runnemede, NJ, 8,930
Salem, NJ, 6,847
Sanatoga, PA, 5,534
Sellersville, PA, 4,703
Sharon Hill, PA, 5,658
Somerdale, NJ, 5,510
Souderton, PA, 6,258
Spring City, PA, 3,395
Springfield, PA, 24,160
Stratford, NJ, 7,476
Swarthmore, PA, 6,053
Telford, PA, 4,432
Trooper, PA, 5,137
Upland, PA, 3,277
Upper Providence, PA, 9,727
Village Green, PA, 9,026
West Chester, PA, 17,958
West Goshen, PA, 8,948
West Norriton, PA, 15,209
Westville, NJ, 4,455
Williamstown, NJ, 10,891
Willingboro, NJ, 36,291
Willow Grove, PA, 16,325
Woodbury, NJ, 10,610
Woodbury Heights, NJ, 3,300
Woodlyn, NJ, 10,151
Woodstown, NJ, 3,163

Wrightstown, NJ, 3,742
Wyndmoor, PA, 5,682
Yeadon, PA, 11,692

PHOENIX-MESA, AZ

Arizona Republic/Phoenix Gazette
200 E. Van Buren St.
Phoenix 85004
(602) 271-8632
www.azcentral.com

Mesa Tribune
120 W. First Ave.
Mesa 85210
(480) 898-6500
www.tribaz.com

Phoenix & Valley CVB
400 E. Van Buren
Phoenix 85004
(602) 254-6500
www.arizonaguide.com/cities/
   phoenix

Mesa CVB
120 N. Center
Mesa 85201
(800) 283-6372
www.arizonaguide.com/cities/mesa

Phoenix C/C
201 N. Central Ave.
Phoenix 85073
(602) 495-2195
www.phoenixchamber.com

Mesa C/C
120 N. Center St.
Mesa 85201
(480) 969-1307
www.mesachamber.org
Apache Junction, 19,338
Avondale, 24,157
Buckeye, 5,151
Casa Grande, 21,314
Cave Creek, 3,164
Chandler, 142,918
Coolidge, 7,166
El Mirage, 5,712
Eloy, 7,642
Florence, 12,939
Fountain Hills, 15,414
Gilbert, 64,326
Glendale, 182,219
Goodyear, 10,614
Guadalupe, 5,344
Litchfield Park, 3,746
Mesa, 344,764

Paradise Valley, 14,077
Peoria, 76,045
Phoenix, 1,159,014
Queen Creek, 3,312
Scottsdale, 179,012
Sun City, 38,126
Sun City West, 15,997
Sun Lakes, 6,578
Superior, 3,516
Surprise, 10,340
Tempe, 162,701
Tolleson, 4,824
Wickenburg, 5,312
Youngtown, 2,665

PINE BLUFF, AR

Pine Bluff Commercial
300 Beech St.
Pine Bluff 71601
(870) 534-3400
www.pbcommercial.com

Greater Pine Bluff C/C
121 W. Sixth Ave.
Pine Bluff 71611
(870) 535-0110
Pine Bluff 54,165
Redfield 1,117
White Hall 4,525

PITTSBURGH, PA

Pittsburgh Post-Gazette
P.O. Box 957
Pittsburgh 15230
(412) 263-1100
www.post-gazette.com

Greater Pittsburgh CVB
Four Gateway Center
Pittsburgh 15222
(800) 359-0758
www.pittsburgh-cvb.org

Greater Pittsburgh C/C
425 Sixth Ave.
Pittsburgh 15222
(412) 392-4500
www.chamber.pgh.com
Aliquippa, 12,769
Ambridge, 7,787
Arnold, 5,855
Aspinwall, 2,714
Avalon, 5,450
Baden, 4,937
Baldwin, 21,004
Beaver, 4,886
Beaver Falls, 10,223
Bellevue, 8,589

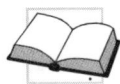

Bentleyville, 2,592
Bethel Park, 33,661
Brackenridge, 3,570
Braddock, 4,262
Brentwood, 10,236
Bridgeville, 5,278
Brownsville, 3,129
Butler, 15,179
California, 5,368
Canonsburg, 8,822
Carnegie, 8,769
Carnot-Moon, 10,187
Castle Shannon, 8,722
Centerville, 3,725
Charleroi, 4,734
Churchill, 3,683
Clairton, 9,055
Connellsville, 8,795
Coraopolis, 6,411
Crafton, 6,761
Derry, 2,907
Donora, 5,648
Dormont, 9,151
Duquesne, 7,907
Economy, 9,774
Edgewood, 3,387
Emsworth, 2,731
Etna, 3,940
Fernway, 9,072
Forest Hills, 7,023
Fox Chapel, 5,406
Franklin Park, 11,213
Glassport, 5,263
Green Tree, 4,717
Greensburg, 15,941
Hampton, 15,568
Harrison, 11,763
Homeacre, 7,511
Homestead, 3,918
Ingram, 3,673
Irwin, 4,474
Jeannette, 10,716
Jefferson, 9,740
Kennedy, 7,152
Latrobe, 9,299
Liberty, 2,591
Lower Burrell, 12,370
Manor, 2,869
Masontown, 3,754
McCandless, 28,781
McKees Rocks, 7,235
McKeesport, 23,343
Midland, 3,190
Millvale, 4,090
Monaca, 6,580
Monessen, 9,362
Monongahela, 4,674
Monroeville, 28,591
Mount Lebanon, 33,362
Mount Oliver, 3,887

Mount Pleasant, 4,750
Munhall, 12,401
Murrysville, 19,098
New Brighton, 6,581
New Kensington, 15,233
North Braddock, 6,711
North Versailles, 12,302
Oakmont, 6,760
O'Hara Township, 9,096
Ohioville, 3,907
Penn Hills, 51,430
Pitcairn, 3,844
Pittsburgh, 350,363
Pleasant Hills, 8,485
Plum, 26,530
Port Vue, 4,387
Robinson, 10,830
Rochester, 3,961
Ross, 33,482
Scott, 17,118
Scottdale, 4,989
Sewickley, 3,892
Shaler, 30,533
Sharpsburg, 3,548
Slippery Rock, 3,156
South Park, 14,292
Springdale, 3,742
Stowe, 7,681
Swissvale, 10,018
Tarentum, 5,323
Trafford, 3,287
Turtle Creek, 6,226
Union, 11,438
Upper St. Clair, 19,692
Vandergrift, 5,618
Verona, 3,072
Washington, 15,184
West Mifflin, 22,679
West Newton, 3,034
West View, 7,362
White Oak, 8,410
Whitehall, 13,968
Wilkins, 7,487
Wilkinsburg, 19,719
Youngwood, 3,280
Zelienople, 4,279

PITTSFIELD, MA

Berkshire Eagle
P.O. Box 1171
Pittsfield 01201
(413) 447-7311
www.newschoice.com/newspapers/
    newengland/eagle

Berkshire Visitors Bureau
Berkshire Common
Pittsfield 01201
(800) 237-5747

Central Berkshire C/C
66 West St.
Pittsfield 01201
(413) 499-4000
www.cbcc.bcwan.net
Adams 8,945
Cheshire 3,445
Dalton 6,965
Lanesborough 3,053
Lee 5,743
Lenox 5,022
Pittsfield 46,315

POCATELLO, ID

Idaho State Journal
305 S. Arthur
Pocatello 83204
(208) 232-4161
www.journalnet.com

Pocatello C/C
343 W. Center St.
Pocatello 83204
(208) 233-1525
Chubbuck 8,876
Pocatello 51,344

PORTLAND, ME

Portland Press Herald
390 Congress St.
Portland 04101
(207) 780-9000
www.portland.com

Greater Portland CVB
305 Commercial St.
Portland 04101
(207) 772-5800
www.visitportland.com

Greater Portland Reg. C/C
145 Middle St.
Portland 04101
(207) 772-2811
www.portlandregion.com
Buxton 7,039
Cape Elizabeth 8,994
Casco 3,190
Cumberland 6,384
Falmouth 8,280
Freeport 7,303
Gorham 12,906
Gray 6,466
Hollis 3,855
Limington 3,080
North Yarmouth 2,877

Old Orchard Beach 7,712
Portland 63,123
Raymond 3,544
Scarborough 14,075
South Portland 22,985
Standish 8,397
Westbrook 16,459
Windham 13,975
Yarmouth 8,080

PORTLAND-VANCOUVER, OR-WA

The Oregonian
1320 SW Broadway
Portland 97201
(503) 221-8327
www.oregonlive.com

Portland Visitors Association
26 SW Salmon St.
Portland 97204
(503) 678-5263
www.pova.com

Portland Metro C/C
221 NW Second Ave.
Portland 97209
(503) 228-9411
www.pdxchamber.org

Greater Vancouver C/C
404 E. Fifteenth St.
Vancouver 98663
(360) 694-2588
www.vancouverusa.com

Aloha, OR 34,284
Battle Ground, WA 5,048
Beaverton, OR 63,224
Camas, WA 9,381
Canby, OR 11,278
Cascade Park East, WA 6,996
Cascade Park West, WA 6,656
Cedar Hills, OR 9,294
Cedar Mill, OR 9,697
Cornelius, OR 7,421
Dundee, OR 2,511
Ellsworth North, WA 5,796
Evergreen, WA 11,249
Five Corners, WA 6,776
Forest Grove, OR 14,685
Garden Home, OR 6,652
Gladstone, OR 11,715
Gresham, OR 81,583
Happy Valley, OR 2,771
Hazel Dell North, WA 6,924
Hazel Dell South, WA 5,796
Hazelwood, OR 11,480
Hillsboro, OR 52,479
Jennings Lodge, OR 6,530

Lake Oswego, OR 34,661
Lake Shore, WA 6,268
McMinnville, OR 23,136
Milwaukie, OR 20,024
Minnehaha, WA 9,661
Molalla, OR 3,981
Newberg, OR 15,785
Oak Grove, OR 12,576
Oak Hills, OR 6,450
Oatfield, OR 15,348
Orchards North, WA 6,479
Orchards South, WA 12,956
Oregon City, OR 18,822
Portland, OR 480,824
Powellhurst, OR 28,756
Raleigh Hills, OR 6,066
Rockcreek, OR 8,282
St. Helens, OR 8,429
Salmon Creek, WA 11,989
Sandy, OR 4,933
Scappoose, OR 4,208
Sheridan, OR 4,017
Sherwood, OR 5,945
Tigard, OR 35,651
Troutdale, OR 12,318
Tualatin, OR 20,063
Vancouver, WA 59,982
Vancouver Mall, WA 6,938
Washougal, WA 5,599
West Haven, OR 6,009
West Linn, OR 20,141
West Slope, OR 7,959
Wilsonville, OR 11,644
Wood Village, OR 3,168

PORTSMOUTH-ROCHESTER, NH-ME

Foster's Daily Democrat
333 Central Ave.
Dover 03820
(603) 742-4455
www.fosters.com

Greater Rochester C/C
18 S. Main St.
Rochester 03867
(603) 332-5080
www.rochesternh.org

Greater Portsmouth C/C
500 Market St.
Portsmouth 03802
(603) 436-3988
www.portcity.org

Barrington, NH 6,811
Berwick, ME 6,226
Brentwood, NH 2,933
Dover, NH 25,766
Durham, NH 10,844

Eliot, ME 5,518
Epping, NH 5,656
Exeter, NH 13,213
Farmington, NH 5,876
Greenland, NH 3,007
Hampton, NH 12,781
Kittery, ME 9,156
Lee, NH 4,050
Milton NH 4,027
Newmarket, NH 7,400
North Hampton, NH 3,955
Portsmouth, NH 25,034
Rochester, NH 27,704
Rollinsford, NH 2,740
Rye, NH 4,745
Somersworth, NH 11,515
South Berwick, ME 6,112
Stratham, NH 5,648
York, ME 10,162

PROVIDENCE-FALL RIVER-WARWICK, RI-MA

Providence Journal-Bulletin
75 Fountain St.
Providence 02902
(401) 277-7008
www.projo.com

Herald News
207 Pocasset St.
Fall River 02722
(508) 343-6911
www.heraldnews.com

Greater Providence CVB
One W. Exchange St.
Providence 02903
(800) 233-1636
www.providencecvb.com

Warwick Tourism Office
3275 Post Rd.
Warwick 02886
(800) 492-7425
www.warwickri.com

Fall River Area C/C & Ind.
200 Pocasset St.
Fall River 02721
(508) 676-8226
www.frchamber.com

Greater Providence C/C
30 Exchange Terrace
Providence 02903
(401) 521-5000
www.provchamber.com

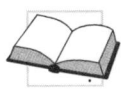

Warwick C/C
3288 Post Rd.
Warwick 02887
(401) 732-1100
Attleboro, MA 39,070
Barrington, RI 15,841
Bristol, RI 21,958
Burrillville, RI 16,102
Central Falls, RI 16,620
Charlestown, RI 6,995
Coventry, RI 32,221
Cranston, RI 74,324
Cumberland, RI 29,274
East Greenwich, RI 12,135
East Providence, RI 48,389
Exeter, RI 6,052
Fall River, MA 90,865
Foster, RI 4,407
Glocester, RI 9,277
Jamestown, RI 5,011
Johnston, RI 26,551
Lincoln, RI 18,760
Little Compton, RI 3,339
Narragansett, RI 15,706
North Attleborough, MA 25,550
North Kingstown, RI 25,594
North Providence, RI 31,194
North Smithfield , RI 10,619
Pawtucket, RI 69,068
Providence, RI 152,558
Rehoboth, MA 9,354
Richmond, RI 6,484
Scituate, RI 10,000
Seekonk, MA 13,269
Smithfield, RI 18,946
Somerset, MA 17,719
South Kingstown, RI 26,014
Swansea, MA 15,533
Tiverton, RI 14,192
Warren, RI 11,414
Warwick, RI 84,514
West Greenwich, RI 4,195
West Warwick, RI 29,120
Westport, MA 13,993
Woonsocket, RI 41,817

PROVO-OREM, UT

Daily Herald
1555 North 200 W
Provo 84604
(801) 373-5050
www.daily-herald.com

Provo/Orem C/C
56 N. State St.
Provo 84603
(801) 379-2555
www.thechamber.org
Alpine 5,161
American Fork 19,451
Highland 5,939

Lehi 13,810
Lindon 5,941
Mapleton 4,781
Orem 79,736
Payson 11,139
Pleasant Grove 19,357
Provo 99,606
Salem 3,240
Santaquin 2,685
Spanish Fork 14,854
Springville 15,855

PUEBLO, CO

Pueblo Chieftain
P.O. Box 4040
Pueblo 81003
(719) 544-3520
www.chieftain.com

Pueblo C/C
302 N. Santa Fe Dr.
Pueblo 81003
(719) 542-1704
www.pueblo.org
Boone 438
Pueblo 99,406

PUNTA GORDA, FL

Charlotte Sun Herald
23170 Harbor View Rd.
Charlotte Harbor 33980
(941) 629-2855
www.charlotte-florida.com/
newsandfeatures

Charlotte County C/C
326 W. Marion Ave.
Punta Gorda 33950
(941) 639-2222
Port Charlotte 41,535
Punta Gorda 12,552

QUEBEC CITY, PQ

Le Soleil
P.O. Box 1547
Quebec City G1K 7J6
(418) 847-3233
www.lesoleil.com

Le Journal de Quebec
450 rue Bechard
Vanier G1M 2E9
(418) 683-1573

City Region TCB
835, ave. Wilfrid-Laurier
Quebec G1R 2L3
(418) 649-2608
www.quebecregion.com

C/C du Quebec Metro
17, rue St-Louis
Quebec G1R 3Y8
(418) 692-3853
www.cciqm.megatoon.com
Beauport 72,920
Bernières-Saint-Nicolas 15,594
Boischatel 4,152
Cap-Rouge 14,163
Charlesbourg 70,942
Charny 10,661
Château-Richer 3,579
L'Ancienne-Lorette 15,895
L'Ange-Gardien 2,841
Lac-Beauport 5,008
Lac-Saint-Charles 8,540
Lévis 40,407
Loretteville 14,168
Pintendre 6,035
Québec 167,264
Saint-Émile 9,889
Saint-Étienne-de-Lauzon 8,207
Saint-Gabriel-de-Valcartier 2,204
Saint-Jean-Chrysostome 16,161
Saint-Lambert-de-Lauzon 4,590
Saint-Rédempteur 6,358
Saint-Romuald 10,604
Sainte-Brigitte-de-Laval 3,214
Sainte-Foy 72,330
Sainte-Hélène-de-Breakeyville 3,423
Shannon 3,751
Sillery 12,003
Stoneham-et-Tewkesbury 4,842
Val-Bélair 20,176
Vanier 11,174

RACINE WI

Journal Times
212 Fourth St.
Racine 53403
(262) 634-3322
www.jtracine.com

Racine County CVB
345 Main St.
Racine 53403
(800) 272-2463

Racine Area Mfg. & Comm.
300 Fifth St.
Racine 53403
(262) 634-1931
Burlington 9,623
Racine 82,572

Sturtevant 4,968
Union Grove 3,980
Waterford 3,045

RALEIGH-DURHAM-CHAPEL HILL, NC

News & Observer
215 S. McDowell St.
Raleigh 27602
(919) 829-4500
www.news-observer.com

Herald-Sun
2828 Pickett Rd.
Durham 27705
(919) 419-6500
www.herald-sun.com

Chapel Hill-Orange County CVB
P.O. Box 600
Chapel Hill 27514
(919) 968-2060

Greater Raleigh CVB
421 Fayetteville St. Mall
Raleigh 27602
(800) 849-8499
www.raleighcvb.org

Durham CVB
101 E. Morgan St.
Durham 27701
(800) 446-8604
dcvb.durham.nc.us

Chapel Hill-Carrboro C/C
104 S. Estes Dr.
Chapel Hill 27514
(919) 967-7075
www.herald-sun.com/cchamber

Greater Raleigh C/C
800 S. Salisbury St.
Raleigh 27602
(919) 664-7000
www.raleighchamber.org

Greater Durham C/C
300 W. Morgan St.
Durham 27702
(919) 682-2133
www.herald-sun
Apex 7,340
Benson 3,276
Carrboro 13,832
Cary 75,676

Chapel Hill 44,244
Clayton 5,918
Durham 149,799
Fuquay-Varina 6,525
Garner 17,004
Hillsborough 6,468
Holly Springs 3,945
Knightdale 2,624
Louisburg 3,013
New Hope 5,694
Raleigh 243,835
Selma 5,939
Siler City 4,992
Smithfield 7,947
Wake Forest 7,909
Wendell 3,030
Zebulon 4,277

RAPID CITY, SD

Rapid City Journal
507 Main St.
Rapid City 57701
(605) 394-8300

Rapid City Area C/C & CVB
444 Mt. Rushmore Rd. N
Rapid City 57709
(800) 487-3223
www.rapidcitycvb.com
Box Elder 2,917
Rapid City 57,642
Rapid Valley 5,968

READING, PA

Reading Eagle & Times
P.O. Box 582
Reading 19603
(610) 371-5000
www.readingeagle.com

Reading/Berks County CVB
633 Court St.
Reading 19601
(610) 478-6341
www.berkscounty.com

Berks County C/C
645 Penn St.
Reading 19603
(610) 376-6766
www.berkschamber.org
Birdsboro 4,625
Boyertown 3,626
Fleetwood 3,775
Hamburg 3,906
Kenhorst 2,822

Kutztown 4,681
Laureldale 3,672
Mohnton 2,744
Mount Penn 2,775
Reading 75,723
Shillington 4,912
West Reading 4,023
Womelsdorf 2,791
Wyomissing 7,590

REDDING, CA

Record Searchlight
1101 Twin View Blvd.
Redding 96003
(530) 243-2424
www.redding.com

Redding CVB
777 Auditorium Dr.
Redding 96001
(530) 225-4100
www.ci.redding.ca.us/cnvb/
tourinfo.htm

Greater Redding C/C
747 Auditorium Dr.
Redding 96099
(530) 225-4433
Anderson 8,748
Redding 76,616
Shasta Lake 9,364

REGINA, SK

The Leader-Post
1964 Park St.
Regina S4P 3G4
(306) 565-8211
www.leader-post.sk.ca

Regina CVB
500-1900 Albert St.
Regina S4P 4L9
(800) 661-5099
www.tourismregina.com

Regina C/C
2145 Albert St.
Regina S7K 1M6
(306) 757-4668
www.wcw.net/sk/regina.chamber
Balgonie 1,132
Lumsden 1,530
Pilot Butte 1,469
Regina 180,400

Appendix C

RENO, NV

Reno Gazette-Journal
P.O. Box 22000
Reno 89520
(775) 788-6397
www.nevadanet.com/renogazette

Reno-Sparks CVB
4590 S. Virginia St.
Reno 89502
(888) 448-7366
www.playreno.com

Greater Reno-Sparks C/C
405 Marsh Ave.
Reno 89505
(775) 686-3030
www.reno-sparkschamber.org

Incline Village-Crystal Bay 7,119
Reno 155,499
Sparks 59,496
Sun Valley 11,391

RICHLAND-KENNEWICK-PASCO, WA

Tri-City Herald
107 N. Cascade St.
Kennewick 99336
(509) 582-1500
www.tri-cityherald.com

Richland C/C
515 Lee Blvd.
Richland 99352
(509) 946-1651

Kennewick C/C
3180 W. Clearwater
Kennewick 99336
(509) 736-0510

Greater Pasco Area C/C
1600 N. 20th Ave.
Pasco 99301
(509) 547-9755

Connell 2,951
Kennewick 51,184
Pasco 23,910
Prosser 4,954
Richland 37,445
West Pasco 7,312
West Richland 6,170

RICHMOND-PETERSBURG, VA

Richmond Times-Dispatch
333 E. Grace St.
Richmond 23293
(804) 649-6000
www.gatewayva.com

Metro Richmond CVB
550 E. Marshall
Richmond 23219
88874246663
www.richmondva.org

Metropolitan Richmond C/C
201 E. Franklin St.
Richmond 23241
(804) 648-1234
www.grcc.com

Petersburg C/C
325 E. Washington St.
Petersburg 23804
(804) 733-8131

Ashland 5,843
Bellwood 6,178
Bensley 5,093
Bon Air 16,413
Chester 14,986
Colonial Heights 17,154
Dumbarton 8,526
East Highland Park 11,850
Ettrick 5,290
Fort Lee 6,895
Glen Allen 9,010
Highland Springs 13,823
Hopewell 22,566
Lakeside 12,081
Laurel 13,011
Mechanicsville 22,027
Montrose 6,405
Petersburg 38,234
Richmond 198,267
Tuckahoe 42,629

RIVERSIDE-SAN BERNARDINO, CA

San Bernardino County Sun
399 North D St.
San Bernardino 92401
(909) 889-9666
www.sbcsun.com

Press-Enterprise
3512 14th St.
Riverside 92502
(909) 684-1200
www.press-enterprise.com/services

Riverside CVB
3737 Sixth St.
Riverside 92501
(909) 222-4700
www.riversidecb.com

San Bernardino Area C/C
255 North D St.
San Bernardino 92401
(909) 888-2188

Greater Riverside C/C
3985 University Ave.
Riverside 92501
(909) 683-7100
www.riverside-chamber.com

Adelanto 14,554
Apple Valley 54,865
Banning 25,543
Barstow 23,196
Beaumont 10,610
Big Bear Lake 5,757
Bloomington 15,116
Blythe 12,982
Calimesa 8,188
Canyon Lake 7,938
Cathedral City 36,327
Cherry Valley 5,945
Chino 64,723
Chino Hills 42,071
Coachella 21,767
Colton 43,309
Corona 100,208
Crestline 8,594
Desert Hot Springs 14,819
East Hemet 17,611
Fontana 104,124
Glen Avon 12,663
Grand Terrace 12,132
Hemet 51,350
Hesperia 60,635
Highland 40,477
Home Gardens 7,780
Indian Wells 3,065
Indio 43,741
La Quinta 17,987
Lake Arrowhead 6,539
Lake Elsinore 25,950
Lakeland Village 5,159
Loma Linda 22,318
Los Serranos 7,099
Mentone 5,675
Mira Loma 15,786
Montclair 30,044
Moreno Valley 140,932
Murrieta 23,033
Muscoy 7,541
Needles 6,431
Norco 25,576
Ontario 144,854
Palm Desert 27,916
Palm Desert Country 5,626

Palm Springs 43,347
Pedley 8,869
Perris 31,515
Rancho Cucamonga 116,613
Rancho Mirage 10,894
Redlands 66,693
Rialto 82,320
Riverside 255,069
Rubidoux 24,367
San Bernardino 183,474
San Jacinto 23,683
Sun City 14,930
Temecula 39,315
Twentynine Palms 14,157
Twentynine Palms Base 10,606
Upland 67,095
Valle Vista 8,751
Victorville 67,089
Wildomar 10,411
Woodcrest 7,796
Yucaipa 36,074
Yucca Valley 18,723

ROANOKE, VA

Roanoke Times & World News
201 W. Campbell Ave.
Roanoke 24011
(540) 981-3353
www.roanoke.com/roatimes

Roanoke Valley CVB
114 Market St.
Roanoke 24011
(800) 635-5535
www.visitroanokeva.com

Roanoke Regional C/C
212 S. Jefferson St.
Roanoke 24011
(540) 983-0700
www.rrcc.org
Cave Spring 24,053
Hollins 13,180
Roanoke 95,548
Salem 24,159
Vinton 7,210

ROCHESTER, MN

Rochester Post-Bulletin
18 First Ave. SE
Rochester 55903
(507) 285-7600
www.postbulletin.com

Rochester CVB
150 S. Broadway
Rochester 55904
(800) 288-9144

Rochester Area C/C
220 S. Broadway
Rochester 55904
(507) 288-1122
Byron 2,576
Rochester 75,638
Stewartville 4,368

ROCHESTER, NY

Democrat & Chronicle/Times Union
55 Exchange Blvd.
Rochester 14614
(716) 232-7100
www.rochesterdandc.com

Greater Rochester Visitors Assn.
126 Andrews St.
Rochester 14604
(716) 546-3070
www.visitrochester.com

Rochester Area C/C
55 St. Paul St.
Rochester 14604
(716) 454-2220
www.rnychamber.com
Albion 6,935
Avon 2,981
Batavia 16,095
Brighton 34,455
Brockport 8,209
Canandaigua 10,736
Dansville 4,967
East Rochester 6,681
Fairport 5,824
Gates-North Gates 14,995
Geneseo 7,323
Geneva 13,890
Greece 15,632
Hilton 5,575
Irondequoit 52,322
Le Roy 4,818
Lyons 4,231
Medina 6,810
Mount Morris 3,072
Newark 9,822
Palmyra 3,558
Rochester 221,594
Spencerport 3,569
Webster 5,340

ROCKFORD, IL

Rockford Register Star
99 E. State St.
Rockford 61104
(815) 987-1302
www.rrstar.com

Rockford Area CVB
211 N. Main St.
Rockford 61101
(800) 521-0849
www.gorockford.com

Rockford Area C/C
515 N. Court St.
Rockford 61110
(815) 987-8100
Belvidere 18,712
Byron 2,542
Loves Park 17,341
Machesney Park 19,014
Mount Morris 2,973
Oregon 3,945
Rochelle 9,364
Rockford 143,531
Rockton 3,258
South Beloit 3,955

ROCKY MOUNT, NC

Rocky Mount Telegram
150 Howard St.
Rocky Mount 27804
(252) 446-5161

Rocky Mount Area C/C
2501 Sunset Ave.
Rocky Mount 27802
(800) 849-6825
www.rockymountchamber.org
Nashville 3,842
Rocky Mount 52,635
Tarboro 10,469

SACRAMENTO, CA

Sacramento Bee
2100 Q St.
Sacramento 95852
(916) 321-1000
www.sacbee.com

Sacramento CVB
1303 J St.
Sacramento 95814
(916) 264-7777
www.sacramentocvb.org

Sacramento Metro C/C
917 Seventh St.
Sacramento 95814
(916) 552-6800
www.metrochamber.org
Arden-Arcade 92,040
Auburn 12,129
Cameron Park 11,897

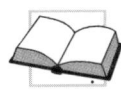

Carmichael 48,702
Citrus Heights 107,439
El Dorado Hills 6,395
Elk Grove 17,483
Fair Oaks 26,867
Florin 24,330
Folsom 41,103
Foothill Farms 17,135
Galt 15,647
La Riviera 10,986
Laguna 9,828
Lincoln 8,788
Loomis 6,348
North Auburn 10,301
North Highlands 42,105
Orangevale 26,266
Parkway-South Sacramento 31,903
Placerville 9,349
Rancho Cordova 48,731
Rio Linda 9,481
Rocklin 27,214
Rosemont 22,851
Roseville 62,649
Sacramento 376,243
South Lake Tahoe 23,301

SAGINAW-BAY CITY-MIDLAND, MI

Saginaw News
203 S. Washington Ave.
Saginaw 48607
(517) 752-7171
www.sa.mlive.com/index.html

Bay Area C/C & CVB
901 Saginaw St.
Bay City 48708
(888) 229-8696
www.baycityarea.com

Saginaw County CVB
One Tuscola St.
Saginaw 48607
(800) 444-9979
www.saginawcvb.org

Midland County CVB
300 Rodd St.
Midland 48640
(888) 464-3526
www.midlandcvb.org

Saginaw County C/C
901 Swanson Rd.
Saginaw 48609
(517) 752-7161
www.rrpc.com/chamber/

Midland Area C/C
300 Rodd St.
Midland 48640
(517) 839-9901
www.macc.org
Bay City 36,548
Bridgeport 8,569
Buena Vista 8,196
Carrollton 6,521
Chesaning 2,524
Essexville 3,918
Frankenmuth 4,591
Midland 39,849
Saginaw 65,014
Saginaw Township North 23,018
Saginaw Township South 13,987
Shields 6,634

ST. CATHARINES-NIAGARA, ON

The Standard
17 Queen St.
St. Catharines L2R 5G5
(905) 684-7251

Niagara Falls VCB
5515 Stanley Ave.
Niagara Falls L2G 3X4
(905) 356-6061
www.tourismniagara.com/nfcvcb

St. Catharines & District C/C
11 King St.
St. Catharines L2R 3H2
(905) 684-2361
www.niagara.com/stc-chamber

Niagara Falls C/C
4458 Queen St.
Niagara Falls L2E 2L3
(905) 374-3666
www.nflschamber.com
Fort Erie 27,183
Lincoln 18,801
Niagara Falls 76,917
Niagara-on-the-Lake 13,238
Pelham 14,343
Port Colborne 18,451
St. Catharines 130,926
Thorold 17,883
Wainfleet 6,253
Welland 48,411

ST. CLOUD, MN

St. Cloud Times
3000 N. 7th St.
St. Cloud 56302
(320) 255-8700
www.sctimes.com

St. Cloud Area CVB
30 Sixth Ave. S
St. Cloud 56302
(800) 264-2940
www.stcloudcvb.com

Saint Cloud Area C/C
30 Sixth Ave. S
St. Cloud 56302
(320) 251-2940
Cold Spring 2,756
Melrose 2,647
St. Cloud 50,801
St. Joseph 4,073
Sartell 7,398
Sauk Centre 3,704
Sauk Rapids 9,236
Waite Park 5,791

ST. JOHN'S, NF

Telegram
Columbus Dr.
St. John's A1C 5X7
(709) 368-5000
www.thetelegram.com

St. John's Tourist Commission
City Hall, New Gower St.
St. John's A1C 1J1
(709) 729-8106
Bay Bulls 1,063
Conception Bay South 19,265
Flatrock 1,087
Mount Pearl 25,519
Paradise 7,960
Portugal Cove-St. Philip's 5,773
Pouch Cove 1,885
St. John's 101,936
Torbay 5,230
Witless Bay 1,118

SAINT JOHN, NB

Telegraph-Journal/Times-Globe
210 Crown St.
Saint John E2L 3V8
(506) 632-8888
www.nbpub.nb.ca

Saint John CVB
P.O. Box 1971
Saint John E3L 2W9
(506) 658-2990

Saint John Board of Trade
Brunswick Sq.
Saint John E2L 4R5
(506) 634-8111

Fairvale 4,951
Gondola Point 4,324
Grand Bay 3,713
Hampton 4,081
Kingston 2,873
Quispamsis 8,839
Rothesay 2,979
Saint John 72,494
Simonds 3,823
Westfield 2,275

ST. JOSEPH, MO

News-Press
825 Edmond St.
St. Joseph 64502
(816) 271-8500
www.stjoenews-press.com

St. Joseph CVB
109 S. 4th St.
St. Joseph 64502
(800) 785-0360
www.stjomo.com

St. Joseph Area C/C
3003 Frederick Ave.
St. Joseph 64506
(816) 232-4461
www.saintjoseph.com/about/
chamber

Country Club 1,838
St. Joseph 70,208
Savannah 4,471

ST. LOUIS, MO-IL

St. Louis Post-Dispatch
900 N. Tucker Blvd.
St. Louis 63101
(314) 340-8000
www.postnet.com/postnet/
index.nsf/todayspd

St. Louis C/C & CVC
One Metropolitan Sq.
St. Louis 63102
(800) 916-0092
www.st-louis-cvc.com

Affton, MO 21,106
Alorton, IL 2,871
Alton, IL 31,562
Arnold, MO 20,473
Ballwin, MO 20,853
Bel-Ridge, MO 3,232
Bellefontaine Neighbors, MO 10,352
Belleville, IL 41,608
Berkeley, MO 10,636
Bethalto, IL 9,750
Black Jack, MO 6,295
Breckenridge Hills, MO 4,875
Breese, IL 3,804
Brentwood, MO 7,704
Bridgeton, MO 16,502
Cahokia, IL 16,803
Carlyle, IL 3,550
Caseyville, IL 4,376
Centreville, IL 7,272
Chesterfield, MO 45,490
Clarkson Valley, MO 2,693
Clayton, MO 13,513
Collinsville, IL 23,057
Columbia, IL 6,429
Concord, MO 19,859
Crestwood, MO 12,114
Creve Coeur, MO 12,093
Crystal City, MO 3,973
De Soto, MO 6,009
Dellwood, MO 4,943
Des Peres, MO 8,011
Dupo, IL 3,088
East Alton, IL 6,779
East St. Louis, IL 38,595
Edwardsville, IL 16,403
Ellisville, MO 7,841
Eureka, MO 5,250
Fairview Heights, IL 14,701
Fenton , MO 3,454
Ferguson, MO 21,126
Festus, MO 8,353
Florissant, MO 50,491
Freeburg, IL 3,368
Frontenac, MO 3,348
Glasgow Village, MO 5,199
Glen Carbon, IL 9,555
Glendale, MO 5,629
Godfrey, IL 5,436
Granite City, IL 31,449
Hazelwood, MO 14,754
Highland, IL 8,021
Jennings, MO 15,162
Jerseyville, IL 7,539
Kinloch, MO 2,541
Kirkwood, MO 27,465
Ladue, MO 8,400
Lebanon, IL 3,654
Lemay, MO 18,005
Madison, IL 4,376
Manchester, MO 6,929
Maplewood, MO 9,334
Maryland Heights, MO 24,094
Maryville, IL 3,150

Mascoutah, IL 5,672
Mehlville, MO 27,557
Millstadt, IL 2,598
Moline Acres,MO 2,557
Murphy, MO 9,342
New Baden, IL 2,891
Normandy, MO 4,785
Northwoods, MO 4,813
O'Fallon, IL 18,600
O'Fallon, MO 29,564
Oakville, MO 31,750
Olivette, MO 7,168
Overland, MO 16,936
Pacific, MO 4,783
Pagedale, MO 3,903
Pevely, MO 2,914
Pine Lawn, MO 4,729
Pontoon Beach, IL 4,418
Richmond Heights, MO 9,803
Riverview, MO 3,042
Rock Hill, MO 4,962
St. Ann, MO 13,714
St. Charles, MO 56,525
St. Clair, MO 4,341
St. John, MO 7,045
St. Louis, MO 351,565
St. Peters, MO 48,493
Sappington, MO 10,917
Shiloh, IL 3,661
Shrewsbury, MO 6,288
Spanish Lake, MO 20,322
Sullivan, MO 6,153
Sunset Hills, MO 5,314
Swansea, IL 8,936
Town and Country, MO 10,921
Trenton, IL 2,580
Troy, IL 4,963
Union, MO 6,222
University City, MO 38,086
Valley Park, MO 5,797
Venice, IL 3,630
Warrenton, MO 4,547
Washington, MO 12,210
Washington Park, IL 7,063
Waterloo, IL 5,911
Webster Groves, MO 21,890
Wellston, MO 3,378
Wentzville, MO 5,063
Wood River, IL 11,097
Woodson Terrace, MO 4,103

SALEM, OR

Statesman Journal
P.O. Box 13009
Salem 97309
(971) 399-6611
www.statesmanjournal.com

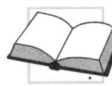

Salem Area C/C
1110 Commercial St. NE
Salem 97301
(971) 581-1466
Dallas 11,573
Four Corners 12,156
Hayesville 14,318
Independence 5,095
Keizer 27,642
Monmouth 7,371
Mount Angel 2,933
Salem 122,566
Silverton 6,473
Stayton 6,037
Woodburn 15,780

SALINAS, CA

The Californian
123 W. Alisal St.
Salinas 93901
(831) 754-4260

Salinas Area C/C
119 E. Alisal St.
Salinas 93901
(831) 424-7611

Monterey Peninsula CVB
380 Alvarado St.
Monterey 93942
(831) 649-1770
www.monterey.com

Seaside-Sand City C/C
505 Broadway
Seaside 93955
(831) 394-6501
www.seaside-sandcity.com
Carmel-by-the-Sea 4,084
Castroville 5,272
Del Monte Forest 5,069
Gonzales 5,451
Greenfield 9,313
King City 8,547
Marina 23,645
Monterey 27,722
Pacific Grove 15,339
Prunedale 7,393
Salinas 111,757
Seaside 31,406
Soledad 9,550

SALT LAKE CITY-OGDEN, UT

Salt Lake Tribune/Deseret News
143 S. Main St.
Salt Lake City 84111
(801) 237-2900
www.sltrib.com

Salt Lake CVB
90 SW Temple St.
Salt Lake City 84101
(801) 521-2822
www.visitsaltlake.com

Ogden CVB
2501 Wall Ave.
Ogden 84401
(800) 255-8824
www.ogdencvb.org

Salt Lake Area C/C
175 E. 400 South
Salt Lake City 84111
(801) 364-3631
www.slachamber.com
Bluffdale 3,373
Bountiful 39,595
Canyon Rim 10,527
Centerville 14,382
Clearfield 22,153
Clinton 9,386
Cottonwood Heights 28,766
Cottonwood West 17,476
Draper 12,478
East Millcreek 21,184
Farmington 10,462
Farr West 2,525
Fruit Heights 4,771
Harrisville 3,464
Holladay-Cottonwood 14,095
Kaysville 17,781
Kearns 28,374
Layton 50,906
Little Cottonwood Creek
  Valley 5,042
Magna 17,829
Midvale 11,867
Millcreek 32,230
Mount Olympus 7,413
Murray 33,089
North Ogden 13,731
North Salt Lake 7,396
Ogden 65,720
Oquirrh 7,593
Plain City 3,163
Pleasant View 4,631
Riverdale 6,868
Riverton 17,924
Roy 28,517
Salt Lake City 172,575
South Jordan 23,518
South Ogden 14,272
South Salt Lake 10,166
South Weber 3,539
Sunset 5,067
Syracuse 5,706
Taylorsville-Bennion 52,351
Union 13,684

Washington Terrace 8,701
West Bountiful 4,773
West Jordan 57,600
West Point 5,481
White City 6,506
Woods Cross 5,577

SAN ANGELO, TX

Standard-Times
P.O. Box 5111
San Angelo 76903
(915) 653-1221
www.texaswest.com/standard-
    times/STmenu.htm

San Angelo CVB
500 Rio Concho Dr.
San Angelo 76903
(800) 375-1206

San Angelo C/C
500 Rio Concho Dr.
San Angelo 76903
(915) 655-4136
www.sanangelo-tx.com
San Angelo 88,098

SAN ANTONIO, TX

San Antonio Express-News
P.O. Box 2171
San Antonio 78297
(210) 225-7411
www.expressnews.com

San Antonio CVB
121 Alamo Plaza
San Antonio 78298
(800) 447-3372
www.tourtexas.com/sanantonio

Greater San Antonio C/C
602 E. Commerce St.
San Antonio 78296
(210) 229-2100
www.sachamber.org
Alamo Heights 6,882
Balcones Heights 3,210
Canyon Lake 9,975
Castle Hills 4,494
Converse 10,911
Fair Oaks Ranch 3,826
Floresville 6,560
Hollywood Park 3,100
Kirby 8,851
Leon Valley 10,296

Live Oak 10,864
New Braunfels 33,906
San Antonio 1,067,816
Schertz 13,696
Seguin 20,863
Terrell Hills 4,936
Universal City 14,965
Windcrest 5,684

SAN DIEGO, CA

San Diego Union Tribune
350 Camino De La Renta
San Diego 92108
(619) 293-1211
www.uniontrib.com

San Diego CVB
401 B St.
San Diego 92101
(619) 232-3101
www.sandiego.org

Greater San Diego C/C
402 W. Broadway
San Diego 92101
(619) 544-1344
www.sdchamber.org

Alpine 9,695
Bonita 12,542
Bostonia 13,670
Camp Pendleton North 10,373
Camp Pendleton South 11,299
Carlsbad 69,069
Casa de Oro 30,727
Chula Vista 151,963
Coronado 25,701
Del Mar 5,270
El Cajon 92,057
Encinitas 57,873
Escondido 116,184
Fallbrook 22,095
Imperial Beach 28,045
La Mesa 54,844
Lakeside 39,412
Lemon Grove 25,297
National City 51,071
Oceanside 145,941
Poway 47,274
Ramona 13,040
Rancho San Diego 6,977
San Diego 1,171,121
San Diego Country Estates 6,874
San Marcos 47,265
Santee 55,934
Solana Beach 13,399
Spring Valley 55,331
Vista 78,494

SAN FRANCISCO, CA

San Francisco Examiner
110 Fifth St.
San Francisco 94103
(415) 777-2424
www.sfgate.com

San Francisco Chronicle
901 Mission St.
San Francisco 94103
(415) 777-1111
www.sfgate.com/chronicle

San Francisco CVB
201 Third St.
San Francisco 94101
(415) 974-6900
www.sfvisitor.com

San Francisco C/C
230 California St.
San Francisco 94104
(415) 392-4511

Atherton 7,577
Belmont 25,562
Brisbane 3,133
Burlingame 27,716
Corte Madera 8,195
Daly City 97,649
East Palo Alto 24,523
Fairfax 6,824
Foster City 29,698
Half Moon Bay 10,389
Hillsborough 11,307
Kentfield 6,030
Larkspur 11,330
Lucas Valley 5,982
Menlo Park 29,497
Mill Valley 12,928
Millbrae 21,241
North Fair Oaks 13,912
Novato 48,117
Pacifica 40,023
Portola Valley 4,440
Redwood City 71,140
San Anselmo 11,525
San Bruno 40,274
San Carlos 27,675
San Francisco 735,315
San Mateo 90,161
San Rafael 50,439
Sausalito 7,036
South San Francisco 57,357
Tamalpais-Homestead Valley 9,601
Tiburon 8,005
Woodside 5,417

SAN JOSE, CA

San Jose Mercury News
750 Ridder Park Dr.
San Jose 95190
(408) 920-5000
www.mercurycenter.com

Santa Clara CVB
1850 Warburton Ave.
Santa Clara 95054
(800) 272-6822
www.santaclara.org

San Jose CVB
333 W. San Carlos St.
San Jose 95110
(408) 295-9600

San Jose Metro C/C
310 S. 1st St.
San Jose 95113
(408) 291-5250
www.sjchamber.com

Cupertino 42,831
East Foothills 14,898
Gilroy 34,396
Los Altos 27,710
Los Altos Hills 7,985
Los Gatos 28,859
Milpitas 58,626
Monte Sereno 3,523
Morgan Hill 28,752
Mountain View 70,619
Palo Alto 58,304
San Jose 838,744
Santa Clara 98,726
Saratoga 29,471
Stanford 18,097
Sunnyvale 125,156

SAN LUIS OBISPO-ATASCADERO-PASO ROBLES, CA

San Luis Obispo County Telegram-Tribune
3825 S. Higuera St.
San Luis Obispo 93406
(805) 781-7902

San Luis Obispo County VCB
1037 Mill St.
San Luis Obispo 93401
(800) 634-1414
www.sanluisobispocounty.com

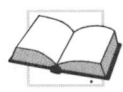

San Luis Obispo C/C
1039 Chorro St.
San Luis Obispo 93401
(805) 781-2675
www.slochamber.org
Arroyo Grande 14,914
Atascadero 24,263
Baywood-Los Osos 14,377
Cambria 5,382
El Paso de Robles 20,187
Morro Bay 9,955
Nipomo 7,109
Oceano 6,169
Pismo Beach 8,127
San Luis Obispo 42,433

SANTA BARBARA-SANTA MARIA-LOMPOC, CA

Santa Barbara News Press
715 Anacapa St.
Santa Barbara 93102
(805) 564-5200
www.sbcoast.com

Santa Barbara County C/C
504 State St.
Santa Barbara 93101
(805) 965-3023
www.santa-barbara.ca.us/chamber

Santa Maria Valley CVB & C/C
614 S. Broadway
Santa Maria 93454
(800) 331-3779
www.santamaria.com
Buellton 3,547
Carpinteria 14,103
Guadalupe 5,714
Isla Vista 20,395
Lompoc 40,925
Santa Barbara 86,154
Santa Maria 67,012
Solvang 4,933
Vandenberg Village 5,971

SANTA CRUZ-WATSONVILLE, CA

Santa Cruz County Sentinel
P.O. Box 638
Santa Cruz 95061
(408) 423-4242

Santa Cruz County CVC
701 Front St.
Santa Cruz 95060
(800) 833-3494
www.santacruz-ca.com

Santa Cruz Area C/C
725 Front St.
Santa Cruz 95060
(408) 423-1111
www.infopoint.com/orgs/sccc
Aptos 9,061
Ben Lomond 7,884
Boulder Creek 6,725
Capitola 10,377
Felton 5,350
Freedom 8,361
Interlaken 6,404
Live Oak 15,212
Opal Cliffs 5,940
Rio del Mar 8,919
Santa Cruz 51,155
Scotts Valley 9,456
Soquel 9,188
Twin Lakes 5,379
Watsonville 32,752

SANTA FE, NM

The New Mexican
202 E. Marcy St.
Santa Fe 87501
(505) 983-3303
www.sfnewmexican.com

Santa Fe CVB
P.O. Box 909
Santa Fe 87501
(800) 777-2489
www.santafe.org

Santa Fe C/C
510 N. Guadalupe St.
Santa Fe 87504
(505) 988-3279
www.santafechamber.com
Los Alamos 11,455
Santa Fe 66,522
White Rock 6,192

SANTA ROSA, CA

Press Democrat
P.O. Box 910
Santa Rosa 95402
(707) 526-8585
www.pressdemo.com/index.html

Sonoma County CVB
9 Fourth St.
Santa Rosa 95401
(800) 404-7673
www.visitsantarosa.com

Santa Rosa C/C
637 First St.
Santa Rosa 95404
(707) 545-1414
www.chamber.santarosa.com
Boyes Hot Springs 5,973
Cloverdale 5,505
Cotati 6,251
Healdsburg 9,674
Larkfield-Wikiup 6,779
Petaluma 48,455
Rohnert Park 39,477
Roseland 8,779
Santa Rosa 121,879
Sebastopol 7,331
Sonoma 8,737
Windsor 13,228

SARASOTA-BRADENTON, FL

Sarasota Herald Tribune
801 S. Tamiami Trail
Sarasota 34236
(941) 953-7755
www.newscoast.com

Bradenton Herald
102 Manatee Ave.
Bradenton 34206
(941) 748-0411
www.bhip.com

Sarasota CVB
655 N. Tamiami Trail
Sarasota 34236
(800) 522-9799

Bradenton Area CVB
1111 Third Ave. W
Bradenton 34206
(800) 822-2017

Sarasota C/C
1819 Main St.
Sarasota 34236
(941) 955-8187
www.sarasotachamber.org

Manatee C/C
222 Tenth St. W
Bradenton 34205
(941) 748-3411
Bayshore Gardens 17,062
Bee Ridge 6,406
Bradenton 47,219
Englewood 10,079
Fruitville 9,808
Gulf Gate Estates 11,622
Holmes Beach 4,871
Laurel 8,245

Longboat Key 6,251
Memphis 6,760
North Port 15,233
North Sarasota 6,702
Palmetto 10,052
Sarasota 50,891
Sarasota Springs 16,088
Siesta Key 7,772
South Bradenton 20,398
South Gate Ridge 5,924
South Sarasota 5,298
South Venice 11,951
Southgate 7,324
Venice 17,707
Venice Gardens 7,701

SASKATOON, SK

Star-Phoenix
204 5th Ave. N
Saskatoon S7K 2P1
(306) 664-8320
www.saskstar.sk.ca

Tourism Saskatoon
102-310 Idylwyld Dr. N
Saskatoon S7L 0Z1
(306) 242-1206

Saskatoon Board of Trade
345 3rd Ave. S
Saskatoon S4P 2V1
(306) 244-2151
Dalmeny 1,470
Langham 1,104
Martensville 3,477
Saskatoon 193,647
Warman 2,839

SAVANNAH, GA

Savannah Morning News/
 Evening Press
P.O. Box 1088
Savannah 31402
(912) 236-9511
www.savannahnow.com

Savannah Area CVB
101 E. Bay St.
Savannah 31401
(800) 444-2427
www.savcvb.com

Savannah Area C/C
222 W. Oglethorpe Ave.
Savannah 31401
(912) 944-0444
www.savga.com/business/chamber/
 chamber

Garden City 7,591
Georgetown 5,554
Pooler 5,174
Port Wentworth 3,971
Richmond Hill 5,858
Rincon 3,512
Savannah 136,262
Thunderbolt 2,859
Tybee Island 2,949
Wilmington Island 11,230

SCRANTON–WILKES-BARRE–HAZLETON, PA

Scranton Times-Tribune
149 Penn Ave.
Scranton 18503
(570) 348-9100
www.scrantontimes.com

Wilkes-Barre Citizens Voice
75 N. Washington St.
Wilkes Barre 18711
(570) 821-2000
www.citizensvoice.com

Times Leader
15 N. Main St.
Wilkes Barre 18701
(570) 829-7100
www.leader.net

Standard Speaker
P.O. Box 578
Hazleton 18201
(570) 455-3636
www.standardspeaker.com

Greater Hazleton C/C
One S. Church St.
Hazleton 18201
(570) 455-1508
www.hazletonchamber.org

Greater Wilkes-Barre C/C
67-69 Public Sq.
Wilkes-Barre 18710
(570) 823-2101
www.wilkes-barre.org

Greater Scranton C/C
222 Mulberry St.
Scranton 18501
(570) 342-7711
www.scrantonchamber.com
Archbald 6,417
Ashley 3,124
Avoca 2,715
Berwick 10,626

Blakely 6,877
Bloomsburg 12,349
Carbondale 9,953
Clarks Summit 5,247
Dallas 2,587
Dickson City 5,964
Dunmore 14,647
Dupont 2,889
Duryea 4,932
Edwardsville 5,099
Exeter 6,043
Forty Fort 4,705
Freeland 3,651
Harveys Lake 2,703
Hazleton 23,293
Jessup 4,550
Kingston 13,574
Larksville 4,623
Luzerne 3,238
Moosic 5,380
Nanticoke 11,505
Old Forge 8,788
Olyphant 4,972
Pittston 8,949
Plymouth 6,665
Scranton 77,189
Swoyersville 5,394
Taylor 6,699
Throop 3,905
West Hazleton 3,915
West Pittston 5,297
West Wyoming 3,070
Wilkes-Barre 44,407
Wyoming 3,081

SEATTLE-BELLEVUE-EVERETT, WA

Seattle Times/Post-Intelligencer
101 Elliott Ave. W
Seattle 98119
(206) 448-8000
www.seattle-pi.com

The Herald
1213 Grand & California Sts.
Everett 98206
(425) 339-3000
www.heraldnet.com

Eastside Journal
1705 132nd Ave. NE
Bellevue 98005
(425) 453-4240
www.eastsidejournal.com/

Seattle-King County CVB
520 Pike St.
Seattle 98101
(206) 461-5800
www.seeseattle.org

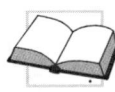

Greater Seattle C/C
1301 Fifth Ave.
Seattle 98101
(206) 389-7200
www.seattlechamber.com

Bellevue C/C
10500 NE Eighth St.
Bellevue 98004
(425) 454-2464
www.bellevuechamber.org

Alderwood Manor 22,945
Arlington 5,672
Auburn 36,393
Bellevue 92,267
Bothell 14,922
Brier 6,358
Bryn Mawr-Skyway 12,514
Burien 25,089
Cascade-Fairwood 30,107
Clyde Hill 2,939
Covington-Sawyer 24,321
Des Moines 17,811
Duvall 3,782
East Hill-Meridian 42,696
East Renton Highlands 13,218
Edmonds 32,001
Enumclaw 9,500
Esperance 11,236
Everett 81,028
Federal Way 67,554
Harbour Pointe 9,107
Inglewood-Finn Hill 29,132
Issaquah 9,664
Kenmore 8,917
Kent 42,700
Kingsgate 14,259
Kirkland 43,778
Lake Forest North 8,002
Lake Forest Park 3,632
Lake Serene-North
    Lynnwood 14,290
Lake Stevens 5,101
Lakeland North 14,402
Lakeland South 9,027
Lea Hill 6,876
Lynnwood 31,342
Martha Lake 10,155
Marysville 16,740
Medina 2,911
Mercer Island 21,277
Mill Creek 8,686
Monroe 6,548
Mountlake Terrace 20,119
Mukilteo 13,501
Newport Hills 14,736
Normandy Park 6,846
North Bend 3,215
North City-Ridgecrest 13,832
North Creek-Canyon Park 23,236
North Hill 5,706

North Marysville 18,711
Oak Harbor 19,356
Pacific 5,843
Paine Field-Lake Stickney 18,670
Pine Lake 13,940
Redmond 42,127
Renton 45,155
Richmond Beach-Innis Arden 7,242
Richmond Highlands 26,037
Riverton-Boulevard Park 15,337
Sahalee 13,951
Seatac 22,723
Seattle 524,704
Sheridan Beach 6,518
Silver Lake-Fircrest 24,474
Snohomish 8,337
Stanwood 2,887
Sultan 2,839
Tukwila 14,556
West Lake Sammamish 6,087
West Lake Stevens 12,453
White Center-Shorewood 20,531
Woodinville 23,654
Woodmont Beach 7,493

SHARON, PA

Sharon Herald
P.O. Box 51
Sharon 16146
(724) 981-6100
www.sharon-herald.com/#top

Shenango Valley C/C
41 Chestnut St.
Sharon 16146
(724) 981-5880
www.infonline.net/~merlink/
commerce/svcc

Farrell 6,585
Greenville 6,395
Grove City 8,195
Hermitage 16,119
Sharon 16,766
Sharpsville 4,549

SHEBOYGAN, WI

Sheboygan Press
632 Center Ave.
Sheboygan 53081
(920) 457-7711
www.wisinfo.com/sheboyganpress/
index.html

Sheboygan Area CVB
712 Riverfront Dr.
Sheboygan 53081
(920) 457-9495

Sheboygan C/C
712 Riverfront Dr.
Sheboygan 53081
(920) 457-9491
www.sheboygan.org

Howards Grove 2,695
Plymouth 7,441
Sheboygan 49,987
Sheboygan Falls 6,194

SHERBROOKE, PQ

La Tribune
1950 rue Roy
Sherbrooke J1K 2X8
(819) 564-5450

Sherbrook Tourism
48 rue de Pot
Sherbrook J1H 1R4
(819) 564-8331

C/C de la Region Sherbrookoise
1308 boul. Portland
Sherbrook J1H 1R4
(819) 822-6151

Ascot 8,663
Ascot Corner 2,280
Brompton 2,157
Bromptonville 3,426
Deauville 2,599
Fleurimont 16,262
Lennoxville 4,036
Rock Forest 16,604
Saint-Denis-de-Brompton 2,289
Saint-Élie-d'Orford 6,148
Sherbrooke 76,786
Stoke 2,409
Waterville 1,332

SHERMAN-DENISON, TX

Herald Democrat
603 S. Sam Rayburn Frwy. S
Sherman 75090
(903) 893-8181
www.herald-democrat.com

Sherman C/C & CVB
307 W. Washington St.
Sherman 75090
(888)893-1188
www.shermantexas.com

Denison Area C/C
313 W. Woodard
Denison 75020
(903) 465-1551

Denison 22,136
Sherman 33,155
Whitesboro 3,470

SHREVEPORT-BOSSIER CITY, LA

The Times
222 Lake St.
Shreveport 71101
(318) 459-3200
www.nwlouisiana.com

Shreveport-Bossier CVB
629 Spring St.
Shreveport 71101
(800) 551-8682
www.shreveport-bossier.org

Bossier C/C
710 Bossier Rd.
Bossier City 71111
(318) 746-0252
www.usachamber.com/bossier

Shreveport C/C
400 Edwards St.
Shreveport 71120
(318) 677-2500
www.shreveportchamber.org
Bossier City 55,686
Minden 13,480
Red Chute 5,431
Shreveport 191,558
Springhill 5,590
Vivian 4,215

SIOUX CITY, IA-NE

Sioux City Journal
515 Pavonia St.
Sioux City 51102
(712) 279-5026
www.siouxcityjournal.com

Sioux City Tourism Bureau
801 Fourth St.
Sioux City 51102
(800) 593-2228
www.siouxlan.com/ccat

Sioux City C/C
101 Pierce St.
Sioux City 51101
(712) 255-7903
www.siouxlan.com/chamber
Sergeant Bluff 3,079
Sioux City 83,791
South Sioux City 11,166

SIOUX FALLS, SD

Argus Leader
P.O. Box 5034
Sioux Falls 57117
(605) 331-2200
www.argusleader.com

Sioux Falls C/C & CVB
200 N. Phillips Ave.
Sioux Falls 57102
(605) 336-1620
www.siouxfalls.org
Canton 2,907
Dell Rapids 2,779
Sioux Falls 113,223

SOUTH BEND, IN

South Bend Tribune
225 W. Colfax Ave.
South Bend 46626
(219) 235-6474
www.southbendtribune.com

South Bend/Mishawaka CVB
401 E. Colfax St.
South Bend 46634
(800) 462-5258
www.cdiquide.com/in/219/b_com/
southben.html

C/C of St. Joseph County
Commerce Center
South Bend 46634
(219) 234-0051
Granger 20,241
Mishawaka 45,045
South Bend 102,100

SPOKANE, WA

Spokesman-Review
999 W. Riverside Ave.
Spokane 99210
(509) 459-5000
www.spokane.net

Spokane CVB
801 W. Riverside Ave.
Spokane 99201
(509) 624-1341
www.spokane-areacvb.org

Spokane Area C/C
8817 E. Mission Ave.
Spokane 99212
(509) 924-4994
www.spokane.org

Airway Heights 3,125
Cheney 8,015
Country Homes 5,126
Deer Park 2,948
Dishman 9,671
Fairwood 5,807
Medical Lake 3,750
Opportunity 22,326
Otis Orchards-East Farms 5,811
Spokane 186,562
Veradale 7,836

SPRINGFIELD, IL

State-Journal Register
One Copley Plaza
Springfield 62701
(217) 788-1300
www.sj-r.com

Greater Springfield C/C
3 S. Old State Capitol Plaza
Springfield 62701
(217) 525-1173
www.gscc.org
Auburn 4,186
Chatham 7,611
Riverton 3,011
Rochester 2,838
Springfield 112,921

SPRINGFIELD, MO

News-Leader
651 Booneville Ave.
Springfield 65806
(417) 836-1100
www.ozarksgateway.com

Springfield CVB
3315 E. Battlefield Rd.
Springfield 65804
(800) 678-8767
www.springfieldmo.org

Springfield Area C/C
202 S. Hammons Pkwy.
Springfield 65801
(417) 862-5567
www.spfld-mo-chamber.com
Marshfield 5,219
Nixa 9,483
Ozark 6,962
Republic 6,651
Springfield 143,407

SPRINGFIELD, MA

Union-News/Sunday Republican
1860 Main St.
Springfield 01101
(413) 788-1000
www.masslive.com/index.html

Greater Springfield CVB
34 Boland Way
Springfield 01103
(800) 723-1548

Greater Springfield C/C
1350 Main St.
Springfield 01103
(413) 787-1555
www.gschamber.org

Amherst 35,468
Belchertown 11,756
Chicopee 54,532
East Longmeadow 13,890
Easthampton 15,744
Granby 5,850
Hadley 4,367
Hampden 4,742
Hatfield 3,243
Holyoke 41,461
Longmeadow 14,864
Ludlow 18,786
Monson 7,949
Northampton 28,838
Palmer 11,907
South Hadley 17,047
Southampton 4,853
Southwick 8,005
Springfield 149,948
Sunderland 3,519
Ware 9,817
West Springfield 26,192
Westfield 37,539
Wilbraham 12,425
Williamsburg 2,593

STAMFORD-NORWALK, CT

The Advocate
75 Tresser Blvd.
Stamford 06901
(203) 964-2200

Stamford C/C
733 Summer St.
Stamford 06901
(203) 359-4761

Greater Norwalk C/C
101 East Ave.
Norwalk 06852
(203) 866-2521
www.chamber.norwalk.ct.us

Darien 18,135
Greenwich 58,374
New Canaan 17,931
Norwalk 77,977
Stamford 110,056
Weston 8,780
Westport 24,185
Wilton 16,329

STATE COLLEGE, PA

Centre Daily Times
3400 E. College Ave.
State College 16801
(814) 238-5000
www.centredaily.com

Centre County Lion Country CVB
1402 S. Atherton St.
State College 16801
(800) 358-5466
www.visitpennstate.org

State College Area C/C
131 S. Fraser St.
State College 16801
(814) 237-7644

Bellefonte 6,231
Park Forest Village 6,703
Philipsburg 2,966
State College 39,400

STEUBENVILLE-WEIRTON, OH-WV

Herald-Star
401 Herald Sq.
Steubenville 43952
(740) 283-4711

Weirton Area C/C
3200 Main St.
Weirton 26062
(304) 748-7212

Steubenville C/C
630 Market St.
Steubenville 43952
(800) 859-5333

Chester, WV 2,723
Follansbee, WV 3,364
Mingo Junction, OH 4,101

Steubenville, OH 20,966
Toronto, OH 5,871
Weirton, WV 21,731
Wellsburg, WV 2,612
Wintersville, OH 3,907

STOCKTON-LODI, CA

The Record
530 E. Market St.
Stockton 95202
(209) 948-1702

Stockton-San Joaquin County CVB
46 W. Fremont St.
Stockton 95202
(800) 350-1987
www.ssjcvb.org

Greater Stockton C/C
445 W. Weber Ave.
Stockton 95203
(209) 547-2770
www.stocktonchamber.org

Lodi Dist. C/C
1330 S. Ham Ln.
Lodi 95241
(209) 367-7840

August 6,376
Country Club 9,325
Escalon 5,280
Garden Acres 8,547
Lathrop 8,616
Lodi 54,585
Manteca 45,500
Ripon 8,736
Stockton 232,660
Tracy 44,776

SUDBURY, ON

The Star
33 MacKenzie St.
Sudbury P3C 4Y1
(705) 674-5271
www.thesudburystar.com

Sudbury & District C/C
100 Elm St.
Sudbury P3C 1T4
(705) 673-7133

Nickel Centre 13,017
Onaping Falls 5,277
Rayside-Balfour 16,050
Sudbury 92,059
Valley East 23,537
Walden 10,292

SUMTER, SC

The Item
20 N. Magnolia St.
Sumter 29150
(803) 775-6331
www.theitem.com

Greater Sumter C/C
32 E. Calhoun St.
Sumter 29150
(803) 775-1231
www.sumter.net
Mayesville 754
Pinewood 580
Sumter 38,565

SYRACUSE, NY

Post-Standard/Herald-Journal
One Clinton Sq.
Syracuse 13221
(315) 470-0011
www.syracuse.com

Syracuse CVB
572 S. Salina St.
Syracuse 13202
(800) 234-4797
www.syracusecvb.org

Greater Syracuse C/C
572 S. Salina St.
Syracuse 13202
(315) 470-1800
www.chamber.cny.com
Auburn 29,774
Baldwinsville 6,651
Canastota 4,703
Cazenovia 3,018
Chittenango 5,141
De Witt 8,244
East Syracuse 3,190
Fairmount 12,266
Fayetteville 4,085
Fulton 12,536
Hamilton 3,835
Liverpool 2,590
Manlius 4,924
Mattydale 6,418
Minoa 3,611
North Syracuse 7,134
Oneida 10,958
Oswego 18,522
Skaneateles 2,619
Solvay 6,455
Syracuse 155,865
Westvale 5,952

TACOMA, WA

The News Tribune
P.O. Box 11000
Tacoma 98411
(253) 597-8742
www.tribnet.com

Tacoma-Pierce County VCB
1001 Pacific Ave.
Tacoma 98401
(800) 272-2662
www.tpctourism.org

Tacoma-Pierce County C/C
950 Pacific Ave.
Tacoma 98401
(253) 627-2175
www.tpchamber.org/chamber
Artondale 7,141
Bonney Lake 9,308
Buckley 3,829
Edgewood-North Hill 9,120
Elk Plain 12,197
Fife 3,790
Fircrest 5,311
Fort Lewis 22,224
Gig Harbor 3,729
Lakewood 58,412
Midland 5,587
Milton 5,632
Orting 2,763
Parkland 20,882
Prairie Ridge 8,278
Puyallup 28,303
South Hill 12,963
Spanaway 15,001
Steilacoom 6,079
Summit 6,312
Sumner 7,908
Tacoma 179,114
University Place 27,701
Waller 6,415

TALLAHASSEE, FL

Tallahassee Democrat
277 N. Magnolia Dr.
Tallahassee 32301
(850) 599-2100
www.tdo.com

Tallahassee Area CVB
200 W. College Ave.
Tallahassee 32301
(800) 628-2866

Tallahassee C/C
100 N. Duval St.
Tallahassee 32302
(850) 224-8116
www.talchamber.com
Chattahoochee 4,239
Quincy 7,698
Tallahassee 136,812

TAMPA-ST. PETERSBURG-CLEARWATER, FL

Tampa Tribune
202 S. Parker St.
Tampa 33606
(813) 259-7711
www.tampatrib.com

St. Petersburg Times
490 First Ave. S
St. Petersburg 33701
(813) 893-8111
www.sptimes.com

St. Petersburg/Clearwater Area CVB
14450 46th St. N
St. Petersburg 33762
(800) 345-6710
www.stpete-clearwater.com

Tampa/Hillsborough CVA
11 E. Madison St.
Tampa 33601
(800) 826-8358

Greater Tampa C/C
401 E Jackson St.
Tampa 33601
(813) 228-7777
www.tampachamber.com

St. Petersburg Area C/C
100 Second Ave. NE
St. Petersburg 33701
(727) 821-4069
www.stpete.com

Greater Clearwater C/C
100 Coronado Dr.
Clearwater 34615
(727) 447-7600
Apollo Beach 6,025
Bayonet Point 21,860
Beacon Square 6,265
Belleair 3,983
Bloomingdale 13,912
Brandon 57,985
Brooksville 8,072

Carrollwood 7,195
Carrollwood Village 15,051
Clearwater 100,132
Dade City 5,867
Del Rio 8,248
Dunedin 34,797
East Lake-Orient Park 6,171
Egypt Lake 14,580
Elfers 12,356
Gibsonton 7,706
Greater Northdale 16,318
Gulfport 11,539
Highpoint 13,818
Holiday 19,360
Hudson 7,344
Indian Rocks Beach 4,146
Jasmine Estates 17,136
Kenneth City 4,245
Lake Magdalene 15,973
Land O' Lakes 7,892
Largo 65,793
Lealman 21,748
Lutz 10,552
Madeira Beach 4,383
Mango 8,700
New Port Richey 14,797
New Port Richey East 9,683
Oldsmar 8,884
Palm Harbor 50,256
Palm River-Clair Mel 13,691
Pinellas Park 43,980
Plant City 25,919
Port Richey 2,634
Riverview 6,478
Ruskin 6,046
St. Petersburg 235,988
Safety Harbor 15,924
Seffner 5,371
Seminole 9,715
South Pasadena 5,576
Spring Hill 31,117
Sun City Center 8,326
Tampa 285,206
Tarpon Springs 18,660
Temple Terrace 17,796
Town 'n' Country 60,946
Treasure Island 7,061
University West 23,760
West Park 10,347
Zephyrhills 8,991

TERRE HAUTE, IN

Tribune-Star
P.O. Box 149
Terre Haute 47808
(812) 231-4200
www.tribstar.com

Terre Haute CVB
643 Wabash Ave.
Terre Haute 47807
(800) 366-3043
www.terrehaute.com/thcvb/
thcvb.html

Greater Terre Haute C/C
643 Wabash Ave.
Terre Haute 47808
(812) 232-2391
mama.indstate.edu/users/commerce
Brazil 8,034
Clinton 4,625
Terre Haute 54,585
West Terre Haute 2,656

TEXARKANA, TX-TEXARKANA, AR

Texarkana Gazette
315 Pine St.
Texarkana 75501
(903) 794-3311
www.txargaz.com

Texarkana C/C
819 State Line Ave.
Texarkana 75501
(903) 792-7191
www.texarkana.org
Hooks, TX 2,819
New Boston, TX 5,349
Texarkana, AR 22,918
Texarkana, TX 32,462
Wake Village, TX 5,393

THUNDER BAY, ON

Times-News/Chronicle-Journal
75 S. Cumberland St.
Thunder Bay P7B 1A3
(807) 343-6200
www.nolalive.com

Tourism Thunder Bay
520 Leith St.
Thunder Bay P7C 1M9
(800) 667-8386

Thunder Bay C/C
1531 E. Donald
Thunder Bay P7C 5W3
(807) 623-2299
www.tb-chamber.on.ca
Neebing 1,021
Oliver 2,711
Paipoonge 3,196

Shuniah 2,346
Thunder Bay 113,662

TOLEDO, OH

Blade
541 N. Superior St.
Toledo 43660
(419) 245-6000
www.toledoblade.com

Greater Toledo CVB
401 W. Jefferson Ave.
Toledo 43604
(800) 243-4667
www.toledocvb.com

Toledo C/C
300 Madison Ave.
Toledo 43604
(419) 243-8191
www.toledochamber.com
Archbold 3,966
Bowling Green 28,307
Delta 3,124
Maumee 15,157
North Baltimore 2,958
Northwood 5,918
Oregon 18,677
Ottawa Hills 4,283
Perrysburg 13,234
Rossford 5,537
Swanton 3,635
Sylvania 16,568
Toledo 317,606
Walbridge 2,883
Waterville 4,861
Wauseon 6,712
Whitehouse 2,737

TOPEKA, KS

Topeka Capital-Journal
616 SE Jefferson St.
Topeka 66607
(913) 295-1111
www.cjonline.com/index.shtml

Topeka CVB
1275 SW Topeka Blvd.
Topeka 66603
(800) 235-1030
www.topekacvb.org

Greater Topeka C/C
120 SE Sixth Ave.
Topeka 66603
(913) 234-2644
www.topekachamber.org

Auburn 1,032
Rossville 1,074
Topeka 119,658
Silver Lake 1,384

TORONTO, ON

The Globe and Mail
444 Front St. W
Toronto M5V 2S9
(416) 585-5000
www.globeandmail.ca

Toronto Star
One Yonge St.
Toronto M5E 1E6
(416) 367-2000
www.thestar.com

The Toronto Sun
333 King St.
Toronto M5A 3X5
(416) 947-2222
www.canoe.com/TorontoSun

Metro Toronto CVA
207 Queen's Quay West
Toronto M5J 1A7
(800) 363-1990
www.tourism-toronto.com

Metro Toronto Board of Trade
One First Canadian Pl.
Toronto M5X 1C1
(416) 862-4530
www.bot.com
Ajax 64,430
Aurora 34,857
Bradford West Gwillimbury 20,213
Brampton 268,251
Caledon 39,893
East Gwillimbury 19,770
East York 107,822
Etobicoke 328,718
Georgina 34,777
Halton Hills 42,390
King 18,223
Markham 173,383
Milton 32,104
Mississauga 544,382
Mono 6,552
New Tecumseth 22,902
Newmarket 57,125
North York 589,653
Oakville 128,405
Orangeville 21,498
Pickering 78,989
Richmond Hill 101,725
Scarborough 558,960
Toronto 653,734

Uxbridge 15,882
Vaughan 132,549
Whitchurch-Stouffville 19,835
York 146,534

TRENTON, NJ

The Times
500 Perry St.
Trenton 08605
(609) 989-5454
www.nj.com/times

Trenton CVB
Lafayette & Barrack Sts.
Trenton 08608
(609) 777-1770
www.prodworks.com/trenton/
visitors.htm

Mercer County C/C
214 W. State St.
Trenton 08608
(609) 393-4043
Ewing 34,185
Hightstown 4,974
Lawrenceville 6,446
Mercerville-Hamilton Square 26,873
Princeton 11,869
Trenton 85,437
Twin Rivers 7,715
White Horse 9,397
Yardville-Groveville 9,248

TROIS-RIVIERES, PQ

Le Nouvelliste
1920 rue Bellefeuille
Trois Rivieres G9A 3Y2
(819) 376-2501

Trois Rivieres Tourism & Congress
1563 Notre Dame St.
Trois Rivieres G9A 4X7
(819) 375-1122

Trois Rivieres & District C/C
168 Bonaventure
Trois Rivieres G9A 2A9
(819) 375-9628
Becancour 11,489
Cap-de-la-Madeleine 33,438
Champlain 1,608
Pointe-du-Lac 6,197
Saint-Louis-de-France 7,327
Saint-Maurice 2,295
Sainte-Marthe-du-Cap 6,150
Trois-Rivieres 48,419
Trois-Rivieres-Ouest 22,886

TUCSON, AZ

Arizona Daily Star/Tucson Citizen
4850 S. Park Ave.
Tucson 85714
(520) 573-4220
www.azstarnet.com

Metropolitan Tucson CVB
130 S. Scott Ave.
Tucson 85701
(800) 638-8350
www.arizonaguide.com/cities/tucson

Tucson Metropolitan C/C
465 W. St. Mary's Rd.
Tucson 85702
(520) 792-1212
www.hcstucson.com/tc
Flowing Wells 14,013
Green Valley 13,231
Marana 5,711
Oro Valley 17,379
South Tucson 5,924
Tucson 449,002

TULSA, OK

Tulsa World
315 S. Boulder Ave.
Tulsa 74103
(918) 581-8300
www.tulsaworld.com

Tulsa CVB
616 S. Boston Ave.
Tulsa 74119
(800) 558-3311
www.tourism.tulsachamber.com

Metro Tulsa C/C
616 S. Boston Ave.
Tulsa 74119
(918) 585-1201
www.tulsachamber.com
Bixby 10,770
Bristow 4,165
Broken Arrow 69,175
Catoosa 3,617
Claremore 17,982
Collinsville 3,796
Coweta 6,514
Drumright 2,880
Glenpool 7,533
Jenks 8,654
Owasso 13,430
Pawhuska 3,651
Sand Springs 16,770
Sapulpa 19,357
Skiatook 5,197

Tulsa 378,491
Wagoner 7,309

TUSCALOOSA, AL

Tuscaloosa News
2001 6th St.
Tuscaloosa 35401
(205) 345-0505

Tuscaloosa CVB
P.O. Box 032167
Tuscaloosa 35403
(205) 341-9200
www.tcvb.org

C/C of West Alabama
2200 University Blvd.
Tuscaloosa 35401
(800) 330-2025
Northport 20,024
Tuscaloosa 82,379

TYLER, TX

Tyler Morning Telegraph
410 W. Erwin
Tyler 75702
(903) 597-8111

Tyler Area CVB
407 N. Broadway
Tyler 75710
(800) 235-5712
www.tylertexas.com

Tyler Area C/C
315 N. Broadway Ave.
Tyler 75710
(800) 235-5712
www.tylertexas.com
Lindale 2,742
Tyler 82,185
Whitehouse 4,956

UTICA-ROME, NY

Daily Sentinel
223 W. Dominick St.
Rome 13442
(315) 337-4000
www.rny.com

Observer-Dispatch
221 Oriskany Plaza
Utica 13501
(315) 792-5000

Utica Area C/C
258 Genesee St.
Utica 13502
(315) 724-3151
www.utica.org

Rome Area C/C
139 Liberty Plaza
Rome 13440
(315) 337-1700
www.romechamber.com
Frankfort 2,597
Herkimer 7,622
Ilion 8,467
Little Falls 5,536
Mohawk 2,843
New York Mills 3,246
Rome 40,979
Sherrill 3,093
Utica 61,368
Whitesboro 3,762
Yorkville 2,689

VALLEJO-FAIRFIELD-NAPA, CA

Napa Valley Register
1615 2nd St.
Napa 94559
(707) 226-3711
www.napanews.com

Daily Republic
1250 Texas St.
Fairfield 94533
(707) 425-4646
www.dailyrepublic.com

Vallejo Times-Herald
440 Curtola Pkwy.
Vallejo 94590
(707) 644-1141
www.timesheraldonline.com

Vallejo CVB
495 Mare Island Way
Vallejo 94590
80048255356
www.visitvallejo.com

Napa Valley CVB
1310 Town Center Mall
Napa 94559
(707) 226-7459
www.napavalley.com/cvb/
    nvcvb.html

Vallejo C/C
2 Florida St.
Vallejo 94590
(707) 644-5551

Fairfield-Suisun C/C
1111 Webster St.
Fairfield 94533
(707) 425-4625
www.ffsc-chamber.com

Napa C/C
1556 First St.
Napa 94559
(707) 226-7455
American Canyon **7,880**
Benicia 25,800
Calistoga 4,680
Dixon 13,047
Fairfield 85,610
Napa 65,030
Rio Vista 3,503
St. Helena 5,414
Suisun City 26,402
Vacaville 81,355
Vallejo 109,593
Yountville 3,375

VANCOUVER, BC

The Province
220 Granville St.
Vancouver V6C 3N3
(604) 605-2000
www.vancouverprovince.com

Vancouver Sun
2250 Granville St.
Vancouver V6C 3N3
(604) 605-2222
www.vancouversun.com

Tourism Vancouver
200 Burrard St.
Vancouver V6C 3L6
(604) 683-2000
www.tourism-vancouver.org

Vancouver Board of Trade
400-999 Canada Pl.
Vancouver V6C 3C1
(604) 681-2111
www.bcchamber.org
Burnaby 179,209
Coquitlam 101,820
Delta 95,411
Langley 2,523
Langley 80,179
Lions Bay 1,347
Maple Ridge 56,173

New Westminster 49,350
North Vancouver 80,418
Pitt Meadows 13,436
Port Coquitlam 46,682
Port Moody 20,847
Richmond 148,867
Surrey 304,477
Vancouver 514,008
West Vancouver 40,882
White Rock 17,210

VENTURA, CA

Ventura County Star
5250 Ralson St.
Ventura 93003
(805) 650-2900
www.staronline.com

Ventura VCB
89 S. California St.
Ventura 93001
(800) 333-2989
www.ventura-usa.com

Greater Ventura C/C
785 S. Seaward Ave.
Ventura 93001
(805) 648-2875
Camarillo 57,090
El Rio 6,419
Fillmore 12,808
Mira Monte 7,744
Moorpark 28,843
Ojai 7,872
Oxnard 151,009
Port Hueneme 20,193
San Buenaventura (Ventura) 97,205
Santa Paula 26,469
Simi Valley 106,974
Thousand Oaks 113,368

VICTORIA, BC

Times-Colonist
2621 Douglas St.
Victoria V8W 2N4
(250) 380-5211
www.islandnet.com/~tc

Tourism Victoria
812 Wharf St.
Victoria V8W 1T2
(250) 953-2033
www.victoriabc.com

Victoria C/C
525 Fort St.
Victoria V8W !E8
(250) 383-7191
www.gvcc.org
Central Saanich 14,611
Colwood 13,848
Esquimalt 16,151
Highlands 1,423
Langford 17,484
Metchosin 4,709
North Saanich 10,411
Oak Bay 17,865
Saanich 101,388
Sidney 10,701
Victoria 73,504
View Royal 6,441

VICTORIA, TX

Victoria Advocate
311 E. Constitution
Victoria 77901
(361) 575-1451
www.victoriaadvocate.com

Victoria CVB
700 Main Center
Victoria 77902
(800) 926-5774
www.txcoastalbendtourism.org/
    victoria.htm

Greater Victoria C/C
700 Main Center
Victoria 77902
(361) 573-5277
www.victexchamber.org
Victoria 61,059

VINELAND-MILLVILLE-BRIDGETON, NJ

Daily Journal
891 E. Oak Rd.
Vineland 08360
(609) 691-5000

Bridgeton Evening News
100 E. Commerce St.
Bridgeton 08302
(609) 451-1000

Greater Vineland C/C
City Hall
Vineland 08360
(609) 691-7400

Millville C/C
415 N. High St.
Millville 08332
(609) 825-7000

Bridgeton C/C
Commerce & Laurel Sts.
Bridgeton 08302
(609) 455-1312
Bridgeton 18,493
Millville 26,366
Vineland 55,906

VISALIA-TULARE-PORTERVILLE, CA

Visalia Times-Delta
330 N. West St.
Visalia 93291
(209) 734-5821

Tulare C/C
260 N. L St.
Tulare 93275
(209) 686-1547

Porterville C/C
36 W. Cleveland Ave.
Porterville 93257
(209) 784-7502

Visalia C/C
720 W. Mineral King
Visalia 93291
(800) 524-0303
Dinuba 14,562
Earlimart 5,881
East Porterville 5,790
Exeter 8,282
Farmersville 7,381
Lindsay 8,740
Orosi 5,486
Porterville 34,518
Tulare 39,927
Visalia 87,787
Woodlake 6,587

WACO, TX

Waco Tribune Herald
900 Franklin Ave.
Waco 76701
(254) 757-5757
www.accesswaco.com/news/
    index.html

Waco CVB
100 Washington Ave.
Waco 76702
(800) 321-9226
www.tourtexas.com/waco

Greater Waco C/C
P.O. Box 1220
Waco 76703
(254) 752-6551
www.waco-chamber.com
Bellmead 8,953
Hewitt 10,557
Lacy-Lakeview 3,882
McGregor 4,940
Robinson 7,903
Waco 108,412
West 2,685
Woodway 9,844

WASHINGTON, DC-MD-VA-WV

Washington Times
3600 New York Ave. NE
ashington 20002
(202) 636-3000
www.washtimes.com

Washington Post
1150 15th St. NW
Washington 20071
(202) 334-6160
www.washingtonpost.com

Washington D.C. CVB
1212 New York Ave. NW
Washington 20005
(202) 789-7000

Alexandria CVB
221 King St.
Alexandria 22314
(800) 388-9119
www.wwb.com/brochure/
b069030.html

Fairfax City Visitor Center
8300 Boone Blvd.
Tysons Corner 22182
80073247329
www.visitfairfax.org

District of Columbia C/C
1301 Pennsylvania Ave. NW
Washington 20014
(202) 347-7201
www.dcchamber.org

Adelphi, MD 13,524
Alexandria, VA 117,586
Annandale, VA 50,975
Aquia Harbour, VA 6,308
Arlington, VA 170,936
Aspen Hill, MD 45,494
Bailey's Crossroads, VA 19,507
Ballenger Creek, MD 5,546
Belle Haven, VA 6,427
Beltsville, MD 14,476
Berryville, VA 3,183
Berwyn Heights, MD 3,143
Bethesda, MD 62,936
Bladensburg, MD 8,577
Bowie, MD 40,181
Brentwood, MD 3,160
Brunswick, MD 6,071
Bull Run, VA 5,525
Burke, VA 57,734
Burtonsville, MD 5,853
Cabin John, VA 5,341
Calverton, MD 7,585
Camp Springs, MD 16,392
Capitol Heights, MD 3,852
Centreville, VA 26,585
Chantilly, VA 29,337
Charles Town, WV 3,012
Chesapeake Beach, MD 3,118
Chesapeake Ranch
  Estates, MD 5,423
Cheverly, MD 6,393
Chevy Chase, MD 8,559
Chillum, MD 31,309
Clinton, MD 19,987
Cloverly, MD 7,904
Colesville, MD 18,819
College Park, MD 24,987
Coral Hills, MD 11,032
Countryside, VA 8,349
Culpeper, VA 8,627
Dale City, VA 47,170
Damascus, MD 9,817
District Heights, MD 7,153
Dumfries, VA 4,659
Dunn Loring, VA 6,509
East Riverdale, MD 14,187
Fairfax, VA 20,990
Fairland, MD 19,828
Falls Church, VA 9,781
Forest Heights, MD 3,062
Forestville, VA 16,731
Fort Belvoir, VA 8,590
Fort Washington, MD 24,032
Franconia, VA 19,882
Frederick, MD 46,227
Fredericksburg, VA 22,586
Friendly, MD 9,028
Front Royal, VA 13,094
Gaithersburg, MD 45,361
Germantown, MD 41,145
Glenarden, MD 5,361
Glenn Dale, MD 9,689
Great Falls, VA 6,945

Greater Upper Marlboro, MD 11,528
Green Valley, MD 9,424
Greenbelt, MD 21,840
Groveton, VA 19,997
Herndon, VA 19,156
Hillandale, MD 8,151
Hillcrest Heights, MD 17,136
Huntington, VA 7,489
Hyattsville, MD 14,674
Hybla Valley, VA 15,491
Idylwood, VA 14,710
Indian Head, MD 3,863
Jefferson, VA 25,782
Kentland, MD 7,967
Kettering, MD 9,901
La Plata, MD 6,504
Lake Barcroft, VA 8,686
Lake Ridge, VA 23,862
Landover, MD 5,052
Langley Park, MD 14,345
Lanham-Seabrook, MD 16,792
Largo, MD 9,475
Laurel, MD 18,718
Leesburg, VA 21,270
Lincolnia, VA 13,041
Lorton, VA 15,385
Manassas, VA 33,200
Manassas Park, VA 7,541
Mantua, VA 6,804
Marlow Heights, MD 5,885
Marlton, MD 5,523
Martinsburg, WV 14,541
McLean, VA 38,168
Merrifield, VA 8,399
Mitchellville, MD 12,593
Montclair, VA 11,399
Montgomery Village, MD 32,315
Mount Rainier, MD 8,408
Mount Vernon, VA 27,485
New Carrollton, MD 12,811
New Market, MD 3,444
Newington, VA 17,965
North Bethesda, MD 29,656
North Kensington, MD 8,607
North Potomac, MD 18,456
North Springfield, VA 8,996
Oakton, VA 24,610
Olney, MD 23,019
Oxon Hill-Glassmanor, MD 35,794
Palmer Park, MD 7,019
Pimmit Hills, VA 6,019
Poolesville, MD 4,100
Potomac, MD 45,634
Quantico Station, VA 7,425
Redland, MD 16,145
Reston, VA 48,556
Riverdale, MD 5,120
Rockville, MD 46,019
Rosaryville, MD 8,976
Rose Hill, VA 12,675
Rossmoor, MD 6,182
St. Charles, MD 28,717
Seat Pleasant, MD 5,694

Seven Corners, VA 7,280
Silver Spring, MD 76,046
South Kensington, MD 8,777
South Laurel, MD 18,591
Springfield, VA 23,706
Sterling, VA 20,512
Sudley, VA 7,321
Sugarland Run, VA 9,357
Suitland-Silver Hill, MD 35,111
Takoma Park, MD 17,792
Temple Hills, MD 6,865
Thurmont, MD 3,228
Tysons Corner, VA 13,124
Vienna, VA 14,612
Waldorf, MD 15,058
Walker Mill, MD 10,920
Walkersville, MD 5,019
Warrenton, VA 5,405
Washington, DC 543,213
West Gate, VA 6,565
West Springfield, VA 28,126
Wheaton-Glenmont, MD 53,720
White Oak, MD 18,671
Wolf Trap, VA 13,133
Woodbridge, VA 26,401
Woodlawn, MD 5,329
Yorkshire, VA 5,699

WATERBURY, CT

Waterbury Republican-American
389 Meadow St.
Waterbury 06722
(203) 574-3636
www.rep-am.com

Waterbury Region CVB
21 Church St.
Waterbury 06702
(203) 597-9527
www.state.ct.us/MUNIC/
    WATERBURY

Greater Waterbury C/C
83 Bank St.
Waterbury 06716
(203) 757-0701
www.waterburychamber.org
Bethlehem 3,243
Middlebury 6,017
Naugatuck 30,319
Prospect 8,137
Southbury 16,370
Thomaston 7,273
Watertown 21,470
Waterbury 106,412
Wolcott 14,145
Woodbury 8,508

WATERLOO-CEDAR FALLS, IA

Waterloo Courier
501 Commercial St.
Waterloo 50701
(319) 291-1400
www.wcfcourier.com

Waterloo CVB
215 E. Fourth St.
Waterloo 50704
(800) 728-8431
www.waterloo.cvb.org

Cedar Falls Tourism Association
10 Main St.
Cedar Falls 50613
(800) 845-1955
www.cedarnet.org/cf.tourism

Waterloo C/C
215 E. Fourth St.
Waterloo 50704
(319) 233-8431

Cedar Falls C/C
10 Main St.
Cedar Falls 50613
(319) 266-3593
www.cedarnet.org/chamber
Cedar Falls 34,884
Evansdale 4,597
Waterloo 65,022

WAUSAU, WI

Wausau Daily Herald
800 Scott St.
Wausau 54401
(715) 842-2101

Wausau Area C/C & CVB
300 Third St.
Wausau 54402
(800) 236-9728
www.wausauchamber.com
Mosinee 3,918
Rothschild 4,128
Wausau 36,809
Weston 9,714

WEST PALM BEACH-BOCA RATON, FL

Palm Beach Post
2751 S. Dixie Hwy.
West Palm Beach 33405
(561) 820-1233
www.pbpost.com

Palm Beach County CVB
1555 Palm Beach Lakes Blvd.
West Palm Beach 33401
(800) 833-5733

C/C of the Palm Beaches
401 N. Flagler Dr.
West Palm Beach 33401
(561) 833-3711
www.palmbeaches.com

Greater Boca Raton C/C
1800 N. Dixie Hwy.
Boca Raton 33432
(561) 395-4433
www.bocaratonchamber.com
Belle Glade 16,656
Boca Del Mar 17,754
Boca Raton 68,507
Boynton Beach 50,742
Century Village 8,363
Delray Beach 50,720
Hamptons at Boca Raton 11,686
Highland Beach 3,193
Jupiter 27,586
Kings Point 12,422
Lake Clarke Shores 3,560
Lake Park 6,735
Lake Worth 28,491
Lantana 8,470
North Palm Beach 11,748
Pahokee 6,993
Palm Beach 9,637
Palm Beach Gardens 32,425
Palm Springs 9,761
Riviera Beach 28,627
Royal Palm Beach 17,896
Sandalfoot Cove 14,214
South Bay 5,043
Tequesta 4,656
Villages of Oriole 5,698
Wellington 20,670
West Palm Beach 79,305
Westgate-Belvedere Homes 6,880

WHEELING, WV-OH

*Morning Intelligencer/
    News-Register*
1500 Main St.
Wheeling 26003
(304) 233-0100
www.oweb.com/intelligencer

Wheeling CVB
1401 Main St.
Wheeling 26003
(800) 828-3097
www.wheelingcvb.com

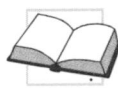

Wheeling Area C/C
1310 Market St.
Wheeling 26003
(304) 233-2575
Barnesville, OH 4,310
Bellaire, OH 5,751
Bethlehem, WV 2,754
Martins Ferry, OH 7,643
Moundsville, WV 10,161
Shadyside, OH 3,887
St. Clairsville, OH 5,262
Wheeling, WV 33,311

WICHITA, KS

Wichita Eagle
P.O. Box 820
Wichita 67201
(316) 268-6000
www.wichitaeagle.com

Wichita CVB
100 S. Main St.
Wichita 67202
(800) 288-9424

Wichita Area C/C
350 W. Douglas Ave.
Wichita 67202
(316) 265-7771
www.wacc.org
Andover 5,203
Augusta 8,641
Bel Aire 5,019
Derby 17,496
El Dorado 12,809
Haysville 8,683
Hesston 2,888
Mulvane 4,997
Newton 16,604
Park City 5,426
Rose Hill 3,144
Valley Center 4,007
Wichita 320,395

WICHITA FALLS, TX

Times Record News
1301 Lamar
Wichita Falls 76301
(940) 767-8341
www.trnonline.com

Wichita Falls CVB
P.O. Box 123
Wichita Falls 76301
(940) 322-1212
www.wichitafalls.org

Wichita Falls Board of Commerce
P.O. Box 1860
Wichita Falls 76307
(940) 723-2741
Burkburnett 10,740
Electra 3,080
Iowa Park 6,339
Wichita Falls 100,138

WILLIAMSPORT, PA

Williamsport Sun-Gazette
252 W. Fourth St.
Williamsport 17701
(570) 326-1551
www.pacentral.com/html/
SUN-GAZETTE.html

Williamsport-Lycoming C/C
454 Pine St.
Williamsport 17701
(570) 326-1971
www.williamsport.org
Jersey Shore 4,149
Montoursville 4,784
Muncy 2,622
South Williamsport 6,338
Williamsport 30,537

WILMINGTON-NEWARK, DE-MD

News Journal
950 W. Basin Rd.
New Castle 19720
(302) 324-2700
www.delawareonline.com

Greater Wilmington CVB
100 W. 10th St.
Wilmington 19801
(800) 422-1181
www.wilmcvb.org

Wilmington C/C
P.O. Box 11247
Wilmington 19850
(302) 737-4343
www.ncccc.com
Brookside, DE 15,307
Claymont, DE 9,800
Edgemoor, DE 5,853
Elkton, MD 10,308
Elsmere, DE 5,787
Middletown, DE 4,291
New Castle, DE 4,912
Newark, DE 27,870

Perryville, MD 2,717
Pike Creek , DE 10,163
Stanton, DE 5,028
Talleyville, DE 6,346
Wilmington, DE 69,490
Wilmington Manor, DE 8,568

WILMINGTON, NC

Wilmington Morning Star
P.O. Box 840
Wilmington 28401
(910) 343-2000
www.starnews.wilmington.net

Greater Wilmington C/C
One Estelle Pl.
Wilmington 28401
(910) 762-2611
www.wilmington.net/chamber
Carolina Beach 4,227
Long Beach 5,450
Masonboro 7,010
Seagate 5,444
Smith Creek 7,461
Southport 2,581
Wilmington 62,192
Wrightsville Beach 2,685

WINDSOR, ON

Windsor Star
167 Ferry St.
Windsor N9A 4M5
(519) 255-5711
www.southam.com/windsorstar

Windsor CVB
333 Riverside Dr. W
Windsor N9A 5K4
(800) 265-3633

Windsor & District C/C
500 Riverside Dr. W
Windsor N9A 6T8
(519) 256-2641
Anderdon 5,730
Belle River 4,531
Colchester North 4,000
Essex 6,785
LaSalle 20,566
Maidstone 11,770
Rochester 4,458
Sandwich South 6,618
St. Clair Beach 3,705
Tecumseh 12,828
Windsor 197,694

WINNIPEG, MB

Winnipeg Sun
1700 Church Ave.
Winnipeg P2X 3A2
(204) 694-2022

Free Press
1355 Mountain Ave.
Winnipeg P2X 3A2
(204) 697-7000
www.freepress.mb.ca/freepress

Tourism Winnipeg
279 Portage Ave.
Winnipeg R3B 2B4
(800) 665-0204
www.tourism.winnipeg.mb.ca

Winnipeg C/C
167 Lombard Ave.
Winnipeg R3B 3E5
(204) 944-8484
www.winnipegchmbr.mb.ca
East St. Paul 6,437
Headingley 1,587
Ritchot 5,364
Rosser 1,349
St. Clements 8,516
Springfield 12,162
Taché 8,273
West St. Paul 3,720
Winnipeg 618,477

WORCESTER, MA-CT

Telegram & Gazette
20 Franklin St.
Worcester 01615
(508) 793-9100
www.telegram.com

Worcester County CVB
33 Waldo St.
Worcester 01608
(508) 753-2920

Worcester Area C/C
33 Waldo St.
Worcester 01608
(508) 753-2924
www.chamber.worcester.ma.us
Auburn, MA 15,002
Barre, MA 4,805
Boylston, MA 3,791
Brookfield, MA 2,915
Charlton, MA 10,073
Clinton, MA 13,071
Douglas, MA 6,145

Dudley, MA 9,676
Grafton, MA 13,286
Holden, MA 14,960
Leicester, MA 10,327
Millbury, MA 12,329
Northborough, MA 12,801
North Brookfield, MA 4,817
Northbridge, MA 13,693
Oxford, MA 13,034
Paxton, MA 4,121
Princeton, MA 3,331
Rutland, MA 5,186
Shrewsbury, MA 26,771
Southbridge, MA 17,447
Spencer, MA 12,091
Sterling, MA 6,858
Sturbridge, MA 7,911
Sutton, MA 7,340
Thompson, CT 8,975
Uxbridge, MA 11,027
Webster, MA 16,089
Westborough, MA 15,005
West Boylston, MA 6,625
West Brookfield, MA 3,619
Worcester, MA 166,350

YAKIMA, WA

Yakima Herald-Republic
114 N. Ninth St.
Yakima 98909
(509) 248-1251
www.yakima-herald.com

Greater Yakima C/C
10 N. Ninth St.
Yakima 98901
(509) 248-2021
Grandview 8,131
Selah 6,200
Sunnyside 12,434
Toppenish 8,019
Union Gap 3,506
Wapato 4,063
West Valley 6,594
Yakima 65,110

YOLO, CA

Davis Enterprise
303 G St.
Davis 95616
(530) 756-0800
www.davisenterprise.com

Davis Area C/C
228 B St.
Davis 95616
(530) 756-5160

Davis 52,321
West Sacramento 29,704
Winters 5,146
Woodland 42,229

YORK, PA

York Dispatch/Record/News
122 S. George St.
York 17405
(717) 771-2000
www.newschoice.com/newspapers/
york/dispatch

York County CVB
One Market Way E
York 17401
(800) 673-2429
www.yorkpa.org

York County C/C
One Market Way E
York 17405
(717) 848-4000
www.york-chamber.com
Dallastown 3,901
East York 8,487
Hanover 14,355
New Freedom 3,285
Parkville 6,014
Red Lion 8,070
Shiloh 8,245
Shrewsbury 3,115
Weigelstown 8,665
West York 4,116
York 40,779

YOUNGSTOWN-WARREN, OH

Vindicator
Vindicator Sq.
Youngstown 44501
(216) 747-1471
www.vindi.com

Tribune Chronicle
240 Franklin St. SE
Warren 44482
(216) 841-1600
www.tribune-chronicle.com

Youngstown Warren Regional C/C
1200 Stambaugh Bldg.
Youngstown 44503
(330) 744-2131
www.regionalchamber.com
Austintown 32,371
Boardman 38,596
Campbell 9,594

Canfield 5,576
Columbiana 5,315
Cortland 5,698
East Liverpool 13,449
East Palestine 5,191
Girard 11,085
Howland Center 6,732
Hubbard 7,914
Lisbon 3,033
Lordstown 3,545
McDonald 3,501
Newton Falls 4,692
Niles 21,110
Poland 2,830
Salem 12,188
Sebring 4,741
Struthers 11,611
Warren 48,347
Wellsville 4,611
Youngstown 87,405

YUBA CITY, CA

Appeal-Democrat
1530 Ellis Lake Dr.
Marysville 95901
(530) 741-2345
www.appeal-democrat.com

Yuba-Sutter C/C
429 Tenth St.
Marysville 95901
(530) 743-6501

Linda 13,033
Live Oak 5,119
Marysville 12,141
Olivehurst 9,738
South Yuba City 8,816
Yuba City 32,433

YUMA, AZ

Yuma Daily Sun
2055 Arizona Ave.
Yuma 85364
(520) 783-3333
www.yumasun.com

Yuma CVB
377 S. Main St.
Yuma 85366
(800) 293-0071
www.visityuma.com

Yuma County C/C
377 S. Main St.
Yuma 85364
(520) 782-2567
www.yumachamber.org

Fortuna Foothills 7,737
San Luis 9,539
Somerton 6,271
Yuma 60,519

Notes

Notes

Notes

Notes

Notes

Notes

Notes

683

Notes